W9-CGY-389

PROGRAMMING LANGUAGES:

A GRAND TOUR

No Longer Property of
Phillips Memorial Library

PHILLIPS MEMORIAL
LIBRARY
PROVIDENCE COLLEGE

COMPUTER SOFTWARE ENGINEERING SERIES

ELLIS HOROWITZ, EDITOR
University of Southern California

WAYNE AMSBURY
Structured BASIC and Beyond

JEAN-LOUP BAER
Computer Systems Architecture

PETER CALINGAERT
Assemblers, Compilers, and Program Translation

M. S. CARBERRY, H. M. KHALIL, J. F. LEATHRUM, J. S. LEVY
Foundations of Computer Science

SHIMON EVEN
Graph Algorithms

W. FINDLAY and D. A. WATT
Pascal: An Introduction to Methodical Programming, Second Edition

ELLIS HOROWITZ and SARTAJ SAHNI
Fundamentals of Computer Algorithms

ELLIS HOROWITZ and SARTAJ SAHNI
Fundamentals of Data Structures

ELLIS HOROWITZ
Fundamentals of Programming Languages

ELLIS HOROWITZ
Programming Languages: A Grand Tour

TOM LOGSDON
Computers and Social Controversy

IRA POHL and ALAN SHAW
The Nature of Computation: An Introduction to Computer Science

ARTO SALOMMA
Jewels of Formal Language Theory

DONALD D. SPENCER
Computers in Number Theory

JEFFREY D. ULLMAN
Principles of Database Systems, Second Edition

PROGRAMMING LANGUAGES:

A GRAND TOUR

ELLIS HOROWITZ
University of Southern California

COMPUTER SCIENCE PRESS

PHILLIPS MEMORIAL
LIBRARY
PROVIDENCE COLLEGE

OVERSIZE

QA
76.7
P78
1983

Copyright © 1983 Computer Science Press, Inc.

Printed in the United States of America.

All rights reserved. No part of this book may be reproduced in any form, including photostat, microfilm, and xerography, and not in information storage and retrieval systems, without permission in writing from the publisher, except by a reviewer who may quote brief passages in a review or as provided in the Copyright Act of 1976.

Computer Science Press
11 Taft Court
Rockville, MD 20850 U.S.A.

1 2 3 4 5 6   88 87 86 85 84 83

Library of Congress Cataloging in Publication Data
Main entry under title:

Programming languages, a grand tour.

Includes index.
1. Programming languages (Electronic computers)
I. Horowitz, Ellis.
QA76.7.P78   001.64'24   82-7370
ISBN 0-914894-67-6   AACR2

FOREWORD

Even on "A Grand Tour" one cannot afford to visit all of the interesting spots. So too with an anthology on programming languages, I could not afford to include all of the interesting articles. The arena of programming languages is a marvelously rich and diverse field. The objective of this work is to present an organized collection of readable articles *and* language reference materials for the student of programming languages. My original purpose in creating this book was to use it for a university course on programming languages. Since then I've discovered that professional computer scientists will also find it useful and entertaining.

The book begins with a section on the history of programming languages. But the articles do more than just chronicle the dates of appearance of each new language. They emphasize the difficulty of successful language design, cite specific contributions of different languages, and at the same time they throw darts at many existing languages. This sort of reading can be fun, especially when the articles are written by talented people such as the ones represented here. Section 2 is devoted to the ALGOL family of languages including ALGOL60, ALGOL-W, ALGOL68 and Pascal. This group has had a major influence on the development of programming languages over the last twenty years and no student of computer science should miss reading these works. Section 3 is an exposure for most people to a very different world of computing. If we judge applicative languages by the number of people who write programs using them, then we would have to delete these articles entirely. But instead we must marvel at how these languages have survived, without the support of any major computer manufacturer and how they continue to please groups of people who make exceptionally strong demands on their computing languages. Thus for any individual to be really knowledgeable in this field, he must have an understanding of the so-called "applicative programming languages." The classic paper in this section is the one by John McCarthy in which he first introduced the notions of LISP. Secondly I decided to reprint the first (and major) section of the LISP 1.5 Manual as it is not usually found in bookstores and yet it still represents the clearest and simplest introduction to the language. The articles by Falkoff-Iverson and Backus give a cogent presentation of APL and FFP, two other relevant languages in this category.

Then in Section 4 we see a relatively new trend in programming languages, the abstract data type. The languages CLU and Euclid were designed (in part) to incorporate this concept of good software design into a programming language. Both languages are implemented and are actively being used. Another major trend in programming languages today is the notion of concurrent execution which is the subject of Section 5. Advances in hardware have made this concept a reality. Now we are beginning to see how programming languages are adapting to the need to express concurrency. Concurrent-Pascal is one such language which takes Pascal as its base. MODULA is another attempt to add concurrency to a Pascal-like language, in this instance a language developed by the original designer of Pascal, Niklaus Wirth. Finally the article entitled *Communicating Sequential Processes* by C.A.R. Hoare represents an important intellectual step forward in the quest to find the appropriate language primitives for concurrency. This paper will continue to have a major influence on such developments in this decade.

In the 1980s, no anthology would be complete without some material on Ada, the new language developed by the U.S. Department of Defense. Ada is well represented here, including an excellent survey paper by Barnes followed by the entire Ada manual. But at the same time, FORTRAN continues on the scene. The new FORTRAN 77 standard has corrected mistakes and added new features making FORTRAN all the more pleasant to use. Though language designers may scoff at attempts to keep FORTRAN up-to-date, we cannot ignore the fact that FORTRAN will continue to survive and any attempt to improve it must be seriously considered. The article included here is a carefully done presentation which criticizes an early draft of the new FORTRAN standard. The FORTRAN77 language manual is itself too long and costly to reprint. However, the article by Feldman points out many issues of interest which can be used to guide someone as he approaches the new standard. But to see how they were resolved one will have to look at the ANSI-FORTRAN77 manual. Also in this section is a pair of articles which deal with the systems programming language called C. The rising use of UNIX[1], especially on 16-bit microprocessors, has

---

[1]UNIX is a trademark of Bell Telephone Laboratories.

given a great impetus to the number of C users, making these articles more important than ever.

One way to view this anthology is as a collection of language reference manuals. The anthology includes the complete reference manual for these languages:

- ☐ Ada
- ☐ ALGOL60
- ☐ ALGOL-W
- ☐ LISP 1.5
- ☐ MODULA
- ☐ C

Viewed from this perspective alone I believe that this anthology is a valuable resource for everyone's bookshelf. To balance the language reference manuals I have included some classic research papers, some historical analyses, some tutorials, and some papers which offer new concepts which I judge will be important in the future. My hope is that I have provided a sufficiently broad spectrum of articles, which are clearly focused on the topic of programming languages, so that this book is suitable both for comparative programming languages courses and as a reference work.

Nevertheless, because of cost and space limitations and in some cases because of the lack of reprint permission, I have not been able to cover all areas of interest, nor to necessarily balance the various subject areas with an appropriate number of papers. In particular the lack of any paper on SNOBOL, BASIC, or COBOL is not meant to imply that these languages are uninteresting objects of study. Rather the more practical matters previously mentioned prevented such inclusions. In the case of SNOBOL the interested reader is advised to look at the excellently written language reference manual by Griswold, Poage, and Polonsky, *The SNOBOL 4 Programming Language*, (Prentice-Hall). For a book containing a historical analysis of BASIC, COBOL and several other contemporary programming languages the reader should consult *History of Programming Languages*, edited by R. L. Wexelblat (Academic Press).

In looking over my choices I realize that no anthology could possibly cover all of this diverse field. Hopefully the papers included here will be sufficient to form the basis for readings in programming languages courses, will prolong the life of several seminal papers, and will provide the language reference manuals for some often used languages.

A Guide to Reading These Articles

A guide is someone who points out important details and provides the context in which an event took place. For some of these articles little or no guidance is necessary as the article itself provides this information. But for many articles guidance is required. In particular the language reference manuals are difficult to read, as they are not written as prose, but primarily for reference.

ACKNOWLEDGMENTS

No anthology can be a success without the help and cooperation of many people and organizations. I would especially like to thank all of the authors, professional societies and publishers who gave me permission to reprint these articles. The following list gives the full citation for all of the articles contained here plus an acknowledgment to the organization for allowing me to reproduce their copyrighted material.

1. **Programming Languages: History and Good Design**
"Programming Languages—the First 25 Years" by P. Wegner, *IEEE Transactions on Computers*, Dec. 1976, 1207–1225, copyright 1976, reprinted by permission.
"On the Design of Programming Languages" by N. Wirth, *Proc. IFIP Congress 74*, 386–393, North-Holland, Amsterdam, copyright 1974, North-Holland Publishing Company, reprinted by permission.
"Hints on Programming Language Design" by C. A. R. Hoare, *Sigact/Sigplan Symposium on Principles of Programming Languages*, October 1973, no copyright.

2. **The ALGOL Family**
"Revised Report on the Algorithmic Language ALGOL60" by P. Naur et al., *Comm ACM*, 6, 1, 1963, 1–17, copyright 1963, Association for Computing Machinery Inc., reprinted by permission.
"The Remaining Troublespots in ALGOL60" by D. E. Knuth, *Comm ACM* 10, 10, 1967, 611–617, copyright 1967, Association for Computing Machinery Inc., reprinted by permission.
"A Contribution to the Development of ALGOL" by C. A. R. Hoare & N. Wirth, *Comm ACM* 9, 6, June 1966, 413–431, copyright 1966, Association for Computing Machinery Inc., reprinted by permission.
"A Tutorial on ALGOL68, by A. S. Tanenbaum, *Computing Surveys*, 8, 2, June 1976, copyright 1976, Association for Computing Machinery Inc., reprinted by permission.
"Ambiguities and Insecurities in Pascal" by J. Welsh, W. J. Sneeringer, and C. A. R. Hoare, *Software Practice and Experience*, 7, 1977, 685–

696, copyright 1977, reprinted by permission.
"An Assessment of the Programming Language Pascal" by N. Wirth, *IEEE Transactions on Software Engineering*, June 1975, 192–198, copyright 1975, reprinted by permission.

3. **Applicative Languages**
"Can Programming be Liberated From the von Neumann Style? A Functional Style and its Algebra of Programs" by J. Backus, *Comm ACM* 21, 8, August 1978, 613–641, copyright 1978, Association for Computing Machinery Inc., reprinted by permission.
"Recursive Functions of Symbolic Expressions" by J. McCarthy, *Comm ACM*, 3, 4, April 1960, 184–195, copyright 1960, Association for Computing Machinery Inc., reprinted by permission.
"LISP 1.5 Programmers Manual" by J. McCarthy and M. Levin, MIT Press, Cambridge, Mass. 1965, reprinted by permission of the MIT Press and John McCarthy.
"The Design of APL" by A. D. Falkoff and K. E. Iverson, *IBM Journal of Research and Development*, July 1973, 324–334. copyright 1973, IBM Corp., reprinted by permission.

4. **Programming Languages and Data Abstraction**
"Abstraction Mechanisms in CLU" by B. Liskov, A. Snyder, R. Atkinson, and C. Schaffert, *Comm ACM*, 20, 8, August 1977, 564–576, copyright 1977, Association for Computing Machinery Inc., reprinted by permission.
"Exception Handling in CLU" by B. Liskov and A Snyder, *IEEE Transactions on Software Engineering*, Nov. 1979, 546–558, reprinted by permission.
"Notes on the Design of Euclid" by G. J. Popek, J. J. Horning, B. W. Lampson, J. G. Mitchell, R. L. London, *ACM Sigplan Notices*, 12, 3, 1977, 11–19. copyright 1977, Association for Computing Machinery Inc., reprinted by permission.

5. **Programming Languages and Concurrency**
"The Programming Language Concurrent-Pascal" by P. Brinch-Hansen, *IEEE Transac-*

tions on Software Engineering, June 1975, 199–207 reprinted by permission.

"MODULA: a Language for Modular Multiprogramming" by N. Wirth, *Software Practice and Experience*, 7, 1977, 3–35, copyright 1977, reprinted by permission.

"Communicating Sequential Processes" by C. A. R. Hoare, *Comm ACM*, 21, 8, August 1978, 666–677. copyright 1978, Association for Computing Machinery Inc., reprinted by permission.

6. More Languages for the 1980s

"An Overview of Ada" J. G. P. Barnes, *Software Practice and Experience* vol. 10, 851–887, 1980, copyright 1980, reprinted by permission.

"A FORTRANner's Lament: Comments on the Draft Proposed ANS Fortran Standard" by S. I. Feldman, *ACM Sigplan Notices*, Dec. 1976, 25–34, no copyright.

"The C Programming Language" by D. M. Ritchie, S. C. Johnson, M. E. Lesk, B. W. Kernighan, *Bell System Technical Journal*, July-August 1978, 179–219, copyright 1978, American Telephone and Telegraph Company, reprinted by permission.

"The C Reference Manual" by D. M. Ritchie, appearing in *The C Programming Language*, by B. Kernighan and D. M. Ritchie, Prentice Hall, 1978, 1991–2019, copyright 1978, Bell Telephone Laboratories, reprinted by permission.

"Ada Programming Language" U.S. Department of Defense, MIL-STD-1815, Washington, D.C. April, 1982, no copyright.

TABLE OF CONTENTS

SECTION 1

PROGRAMMING LANGUAGES: HISTORY AND GOOD DESIGN

PROGRAMMING LANGUAGES—THE FIRST
25 YEARS BY P. WEGNER

ON THE DESIGN OF PROGRAMMING
LANGUAGES BY N. WIRTH

HINTS ON PROGRAMMING LANGUAGE
DESIGN BY C. A. R. HOARE

INTRODUCTION

PROGRAMMING LANGUAGES: HISTORY AND GOOD DESIGN

The first paper, which is by P. Wegner, is a retrospection on computer languages which surveys the developments which have been made over the past 25 years. It presents and evaluates the major trends both in programming language features and in programming language theory. For those people who are new to computer science this article is an excellent starting place.

One of the nice aspects of Wegner's paper is that he divides the past twenty-five years into thirty milestones. Each milestone represents a significant contribution to the field of programming languages. To help the reader see his organization the milestones are listed here.

M1: EDVAC Report

M2: Book by Wilkes, Wheeler, Gill

M3: Development of assemblers

M4: Macro Assemblers '55-'65

M5: FORTRAN '54-'58

M6: ALGOL60 '57-'60

M7: COBOL61 '59-'61

M8: PL/1 '64-'69

M9: ALGOL68 '63-'69

M10: SIMULA 67

M11: IPL V '54-'58

M12: LISP '59-'60

M13: SNOBOL '62-'67

M14: Language Theory

M15: Compiler Technology

M16: Compiler-Compilers

M17: Models of Implementation

M18: Language Definition

M19: Program Correctness

M20: Verification and Testing

M21: Verification and Synthesis

M22: Semantic Models

M23: Abstraction

M24: Pascal

M25: APL

M26: Structured Programming

M27: Structured Model Building

M28: Life-Cycle Concepts

M29: Modularity

M30: Data-Oriented Languages

From this list one observes that 11 programming languages are listed as milestones: FORTRAN, ALGOL60, COBOL, LISP, SNOBOL, APL, PL/1, ALGOL68, Pascal, SIMULA, and IPL V. All of these languages are around today except IPL V. FORTRAN and COBOL remain as two of the most widely used languages. Thus we see again the inability of the programming community to get rid of outmoded tools and replace them by better ones. As you read this paper, make note of why Wegner feels that these events were milestones.

The next two papers in this section all have at least one thing in common, the word *design* in their title. The subject of these papers is the design of programming languages, a difficult and challenging task for which only very few have been successful. The first author, Niklaus Wirth is best known as the designer of the popular language Pascal. However he is also the designer of several other languages including Euler, ALGOL-W, PL/360 and MODULA. The author of the second paper, C.A.R. Hoare is also a programming language

designer, but is probably better known for his contribution to programming language theory (Hoare axiomatics), or for his sorting algorithm called QUICKSORT.

The second paper in this section is fascinating as it gives us a glimpse into the intellectual development of Niklaus Wirth as a programming language designer. We also see why simplicity has become a major design goal for him and for others. In his case it was the desire to see the language used as a tool to tame the baroque and complex technology that he encountered as a student. I observe in passing that not all programming language designers have pursued simplicity as a major goal, and the Ada programming language in section 6 attests to this.

Many of the issues that Wirth discusses in his paper have been reconciled in Pascal. It will be useful to keep Pascal in mind as you read his discussion of simplicity versus generality, or the use of abstraction. His criticism of the pointer data type will be echoed in several papers in this anthology, but the concept is too important to eliminate it entirely. It must be tamed. The issue of aliasing is considered harmful by Wirth, but Pascal allows it. Many of the issues concerning how to provide for the extension of data types in a programming language are no longer considered issues at all. The

solutions offered by Wirth are now normally included in new language designs. I am thinking in particular of enumerated data types, records, sets and files.

The third paper in this section, by C.A.R. Hoare is primarily a lambasting of many of our existing languages. Surely every anthology on programming languages should have at least one such article. But in reading this paper you should not overlook the main outline that the author has used to guide his criticism. Topics such as program design, program debugging, simplicity, readability, fast translation, efficient object code, comment convention, syntax, arithmetic expressions, program structures, variables, block structure, types, procedures and parameters are the overall criteria under which his discussion is guided.

After you have read all of these papers you may wish to go back over them and list all the *advice to language designers* that they have offered. As Wirth has pointed out, many of these criteria will be contradictory. The challenge of the language designer is to concentrate on a few of these goals and use them to create a robust language. Though most of us will never design our own language, it is very helpful to know and understand the criteria by which a language is judged.

PROGRAMMING LANGUAGES—THE FIRST 25 YEARS*

P. WEGNER

Abstract—The programming language field is certainly one of the most important subfields of computer science. It is rich in concepts, theories, and practical developments. The present paper attempts to trace the 25 year development of programming languages by means of a sequence of 30 milestones (languages and concepts) listed in more or less historical order. The first 13 milestones (M1–M13) are largely concerned with specific programming languages of the 1950's and 1960's such as Fortran, Algol 60, Cobol, Lisp, and Snobol 4. The next ten milestones (M14–M23) relate to concepts and theories in the programming language field such as formal language theory, language definition, program verification, semantics and abstraction. The remaining milestones (M24–M30) relate to the software engineering methodology of the 1970's and include a discussion of structured programming and the life cycle concept. This discussion of programming language development is far from complete and there are both practical developments such as special purpose languages and theoretical topics such as the lambda calculus which are not adequately covered. However, it is hoped that the discussion covers the principal concepts and languages in a reasonably nontrivial way and that it captures the sense of excitement and the enormous variety of activity that was characteristic of the programming language field during its first 25 years.

Index Terms—Abstraction, assemblers, Algol, axioms, Cobol, compilers, Fortran, Lisp, modularity, programming languages, semantics, structures programming, syntax, verification.

I. THREE PHASES OF PROGRAMMING LANGUAGE DEVELOPMENT

THE 25 year development of programming languages may be characterized by three phases corresponding roughly to the 1950's, 1960's, and 1970's. The 1950's were concerned primarily with the *discovery* and *description* of programming language concepts. The 1960's were concerned primarily with the *elaboration* and *analysis* of concepts developed in the 1950's. The 1970's were concerned with the development of an effective software *technology*. As pointed out in [96], the 1950's emphasized the *empirical* approach to the study of programming language concepts, the 1960's emphasized a *mathematical* approach in its attempts to develop theories and generalizations of concepts developed in the 1950's, and the 1970's emphasized an *engineering* approach in its attempt to harness concepts and theories for the development of software technology.

*Reprinted from *IEEE Transactions on Computers*, Dec. 1976, 1207–1225.

The author is with the Division of Applied Mathematics, Brown University, Providence, RI 02912.

Manuscript received September 3, 1976; revised August 23, 1976. This work was supported in part by the AFOST, the ARO, and the ONR under Contract N00014-76-C-0160.

1950–1960 Discovery and Description

A remarkably large number of the basic concepts of programming languages had been discovered and implemented by 1960. This period includes the development of symbolic assembly languages, macro-assembly languages, Fortran, Algol 60, Cobol, IPL V, Lisp, and Comit [72]. It includes the discovery of many of the basic implementation techniques such as symbol table construction and look-up techniques for assemblers and macro-assemblers, the stack algorithm for evaluating arithmetic expressions, the activation record stack with display technique for keeping track of accessible identifiers during execution of block structure languages, and marking algorithms for garbage collection in languages such as IPL V and Lisp.

This period was one of discovery and description of programming languages and implementation techniques. Programming languages were regarded solely as tools for facilitating the specification of programs rather than as interesting objects of study in their own right. The development of models, abstractions, and theories concerning programming languages was largely a phenomenon of the 1960's.

1961–1969 Elaboration and Analysis

The 1960's were a period of elaboration of programming languages developed in the 1950's and of analysis for the purpose of constructing models and theories of programming languages.

The languages developed in the 1960's include Jovial, PL/I, Simula 67, Algol 68, and Snobol 4. These languages are, each in a different way, elaborations of languages developed in the 1950's. For example, PL/I is an attempt to combine the "good" features of Fortran, Algol, Cobol, and Lisp into a single language. Algol 68 is an attempt to generalize, as systematically and clearly as possible, the language features of Algol 60. Both the attempt to achieve greater richness by synthesis of existing features and the attempt to achieve greater richness by generalization have led to excessively elaborate languages. We have learned that in order to achieve flexibility and power of expression in programming languages we must pay the price of greater complexity. In the 1970's there is a tendency to retrench towards simpler languages like Pascal, even at the price of restricting flexibility and power of expression.

Theoretical work in the 1960's includes many of the basic results of formal languages and automata theory with

applications to parsing and compiling [1]. It includes the development of theories of operational and mathematical semantics, of language definition techniques, and of several frameworks for modeling the compilation and execution process [26]. It includes the development of the basic ideas of program correctness and program verification [54].

Although much of the theoretical work started in the 1960's continued into the 1970's, the emphasis on theoretical research as an end in itself is essentially a phenomenon of the 1960's. In the 1970's theoretical research in areas such as program verification is increasingly motivated by practical technological considerations rather than by the "pure research" objective of advancing our understanding independently of any practical payoff.

In the programming language field the pure research of the 1960's tended to emphasize the study of abstract structures such as the lambda calculus or complex structures such as Algol 68. In the 1970's this emphasis on abstraction and elaboration is gradually being replaced by an emphasis on methodologies aimed at improving the technology of programming.

1970–? Technology

During the 1970's emphasis shifted away from "pure research" towards practical management of the environment, not only in computer science but also in other scientific areas. Decreasing hardware costs and increasingly complex software projects created a "complexity barrier" in software development which caused the management of software-hardware complexity to become the primary practical problem in computer science. Research was directed away from the development of powerful new programming languages and general theories of programming language structure towards the development of tools and methodologies for controlling the complexity, cost, and reliability of large programs.

Research emphasized methodologies such as structured programming, module design and specification, and program verification [41]. Attempts to design verifiable languages which support structured programming and modularity are currently being made. Pascal, Clu, Alphard, Modula, and Euclid are examples of such "methodology-oriented languages."

The technological, methodology-oriented approach to language design results in a very different view of what is important in programming language research. Whereas work in the 1960's was aimed at increasing expressive power, work in the 1970's is aimed at constraining expressive power so as to allow better management of the process of constructing large programs from their components. It remains to be seen whether the management of software complexity can be substantially improved by imposing structure, modularity, and verifiability constraints on program construction.

II. MILESTONES, LANGUAGES, AND CONCEPTS

The body of this paper outlines in greater detail some of the principal milestones of programming language development. The milestones include the development of specific programming languages, and the development of implementation techniques, concepts and theories.

The four most important milestones are probably the following ones.

Fortran, which provided an existence proof for higher level languages, and is still one of the most widely used programming languages.

Algol 60, whose clean design and specification served as an inspiration for the development of a discipline of programming languages.

Cobol, which pioneered the development of data description facilities, was adopted as a required language on department of defense computers and has become the most widely used language of the 1970's.

Lisp, whose unique blend of simplicity and power have caused it to become both the most widely used language in artificial intelligence and the starting point for the development of a mathematical theory of computation.

We shall consider about 30 milestones, and use this section as a vehicle for presenting a brief history of the programming language field. The milestones can be split into three groups. Milestones M1–M13 are concerned largely with specific programming languages developed during the 1950's and 1960's. Milestones M14–M23 consider certain conceptual and theoretical programming language notions. Milestones M24–M30 are concerned with programming languages and methodology of the 1970's.

M1—The EDVAC report, 1944 [81]: This report, written by Von Neumann in September 1944, contains the first description of the stored program computers, subsequently called Von Neumann machines. It develops a (one address) machine language for such computers and some examples of programs in this machine language.

M2—Book by Wilkes, Wheeler, and Gill, 1951 [83]: This is the first book on both application software and system software. It discusses subroutines and subroutine linkage, and develops subroutines for a number of applications. It contains a set of "initial orders" which act like a sophisticated loader, performing decimal to binary conversion for operation codes and addresses, and having relative addressing facilities. Thus, the basic idea of using the computer to translate user specified instructions into a considerably different internal representation was already firmly established by 1951.

M3—The development of assemblers, 1950–1960: The term "assembler" was introduced by Wilkes, Wheeler, and Gill [83] to denote a program which assembles a master program with several subroutines into a single run-time program. The meaning of the term was subsequently narrowed to denote a program which translates from symbolic machine language (with symbolic instruction codes and addresses) into an internal machine representation. Early assemblers include Soap, developed for the IBM 650 in the mid 1950's and Sap developed for the IBM 704 in the late 1950's.

The principal phases of the assembly process are as follows:
1) scanning of input text;
2) construction of symbolic address symbol table;

3) transliteration of symbolic instruction and address codes;

4) code generation.

The first assemblers were among the most complex and ingeneous programs of their day. However, during the 1960's the writing of assemblers was transformed from an art into a science, so that an assembler may now be regarded as a "simple" program. The development of an implementation technology for assemblers was an essential prerequisite to the development of an implementation technology for compilers.

M4—Macro assemblers, 1955–1965: Macro-assemblers allow the user to define "macro-instructions" by means of macro-definitions and to call them by means of macro-calls. A macro-facility is effectively a language extension mechanism which allows the user to introduce new language forms (macro-calls) and to define the "meaning" of each new language form by a macro-definition.

A macro-assembler may be implemented by generalizing phases 2 and 3 of the previously discussed assembly process. Phase 2 is generalized by construction of an additional symbol table for macro-definitions. Phase 3 is generalized by requiring table look-up not only for symbolic instruction and address codes but also for macro-calls. The table look-up process for macro-calls is no longer simple transliteration, since the determination of a macro-value may involve parameter substitution and nested macro-calls. However, the implementation technology for macro-assemblers may be regarded as an extension and generalization of the implementation technology for assemblers. The seminal paper on macro-assemblers is the paper by McIlroy [54]. A discussion of implementation technology for macro-assemblers is given in [84].

Macro-systems may be generalized by relaxing restrictions on the form of the text generated as a result of a macro-call. Macro-systems which allow the "value" of a macro-call to be an arbitrary string (as opposed to a sequence of machine language instructions) are called macro-generators. Trac [55] is an interesting example of a macro-generator.

Macro-systems may be generalized even further by generalizing the permitted syntax of macro-calls. Waite's Limp system [85] and Leavenworth's syntax macros [52] are early examples of such generalized macro-systems. Macro-systems of this kind are useful for implementing language preprocessors which translate statement forms and abbreviations of an "extended language" into a "strict language" which generally has a smaller vocabulary but is more verbose.

Generalized macro-systems may be implemented by macro-definition tables which are constructed and used in precisely the same way as for macro-assemblers. Generalized macro "values" require more general macro-body specifications in the macro-definition table while more general syntax for macro-calls requires a more sophisticated scanner for recognizing macro-calls in the source language text.

Assembly and macro-languages have been discussed in some detail because they illustrate how a simple language idea (the idea of transliteration) backed up by a simple implementation mechanism (the symbol table) leads to a class of simple languages (symbolic assembly languages) and how progressive generalization of the language idea together with a corresponding generalization of the implementation technology leads to progressively more complex classes of languages. This example is useful also because it illustrates how the language and implementation mechanism for assemblers are related to the language and implementation mechanisms for compilers.

M5—Fortran, 1954–1958 [27]: Fortran is perhaps the single most important milestone in the development of programming languages. It was developed at a time of considerable scepticism concerning the compile-time and run-time efficiency of higher level languages, and its successful implementation provided an existence proof for both the feasibility and the viability of higher level languages. Important language concepts introduced by Fortran include:

variables, expressions and statements (arithmetic and Boolean);

arrays whose maximum size is known at compile-time;

iterative and conditional branching control structures;

independently compiled (nonrecursive) subroutines;

COMMON and EQUIVALENCE statements for data sharing;

FORMAT directed input-output.

Advances of implementation technology developed in connection with Fortran include the stack model of arithmetic expression evaluation.

Fortran was designed around a model of implementation in which run-time storage requirements for programs, data and working storage was known at compile-time so that relative addresses of entities in all subroutines and COMMON data blocks could be assigned at compile-time and converted to absolute addresses at load time.

This model of implementation required the exclusion from the language of arrays with dynamic bounds and recursive subroutines. Thus, Fortran illustrates the principle that the model of implementation in the mind of the language designers may strongly affect the design of the language. Although Fortran is machine independent in the sense that it is independent of the assembly level instruction set of a specific computer, it is machine dependent in the sense that its design is dependent on a virtual machine that constitutes the model of implementation in the mind of the programming language designer.

M6—Algol 60, 1957–1960: Whereas Fortran is the most important practical milestone in programming language development, Algol 60 is perhaps the most important conceptual milestone. Its defining document, known as the Algol report [62], presents a method of language definition which is an enormous advance over previous definition techniques and allows us for the first time to think of a language as an object of study rather than as a tool in problem solution. Language syntax is defined by a variant of the notation of context-free grammars known as Backus–Naur Form (BNF). The semantics of each syntactic

language construct is characterized by an English language description of the execution time effect of the construct.

The Algol report generated a great deal of sometimes heated debate concerning obscurities, ambiguities and trouble spots in the language specification. The revised report [63] corrected many of the less controversial anomalies of the original report. Knuth's 1967 paper on "The remaining trouble spots of Algol 60" [44] illustrates the nature of this great programming language debate. The participants in the debate were at first called Algol lawyers and later called Algol theologians.

Important language constructs introduced by Algol 60 include:

block structure;

explicit type declaration for variables;

scope rules for local variables;

dynamic as opposed to static lifetimes for variables;

nested if-then-else expressions and statements;

call by value and call by name for procedure parameters;

recursive subroutines;

arrays with dynamic bounds.

Algol 60 is carefully designed around a model of implementation in which storage allocation for expression evaluation, block entry and exit and procedure entry and exit can be performed in a single run-time stack. Dijkstra developed an implementation of Algol 60 as early as the fall of 1960 based on this simple model of implementation [23]. However, this semantic model of implementation was implicit rather than explicit in the Algol report. Failure to understand the model led to a widespread view that Algol 60 required a high price in run-time overhead, and to an exaggerated view of the difficulty of implementing Algol 60. An explicit account of the model of implementation is given in [69].

Algol 60 is a good example of a language which becomes semantically very simple if we have the right model of implementation but appears to be semantically complex if we have the wrong model of implementation. The model of implementation is more permissive than Fortran with regard to run-time storage allocation, and can handle arrays with dynamic bounds and recursive procedures. However, it cannot handle certain other language features such as assignment of pointers to pointer valued variables and procedures which return procedures as their result. These language features are accordingly excluded from Algol 60, illustrating again the influence of the model of implementation on the source language.

The Algol 60 notion of block structure quickly became the accepted canonical programming language design folklore and, in spite of its merits, excercised an inhibiting influence on programming language designers during the 1960's. Viewed from the vantage point of the 1970's it appears that nested scope rules for accessibility of identifiers and nested lifetime rules for existence of data structures may be too restrictive a basis for specifying modules and module interconnections in programming languages of the future. Alternatives to block structures are discussed in the sections on Simula 67, Snobol 4, and APL.

M7—Cobol 61, 1959–1961 [12]: Cobol represents the culmination and synthesis of several different projects for the development of business data processing languages, the first of which (flowmatic) was started in the early 1950's by Hopper. See [72] for an account of this development. Important language constructs introduced by Cobol include:

explicit distinction between identification division, environment division, data division, and procedure division;

natural language style of programming;

record data structures;

file description and manipulation facilities.

The two principal contributions of Cobol are its natural language programming style and its greater emphasis on data description. Natural language programming style makes programs more readable (by executives) but does not enhance writability or the ability to find errors. It constitutes a cosmetic change of syntax, sometimes referred to as "syntactic sugaring." It has not been widely adopted in subsequent programming languages but may possibly come into its own if and when the use of computers becomes commonplace in the home and in other nontechnical environments.

The contribution of Cobol to programming language development is probably greater in the area of data description than in the area of natural language programming. By introducing an explicit data division for data description to parallel a procedure division for procedure description Cobol factors out the data description problem as being of equal importance and visibility as the procedure description problem.

The significance of Cobol was greatly enhanced when it was chosen as a required language on DOD computers. Cobol was one of the earliest languages to be standardized, and has provided valuable experience (both positive and negative) concerning the creation and maintenance of programming language standards. It is currently used by more programmers than any other programming language.

Why is it that Cobol, in spite of certain defects in its procedure division, has become the most widely used language among commercial, industrial and government programmers? One reason is perhaps that standardization carries with it advantages that make the use of an imperfect standard more desirable than a more perfect but possibly more volatile alternative. Another perhaps more important reason may be that the advantages of Cobol's powerful facilities in its data division outweigh its imperfections in the procedure division, making it more suitable than languages like Fortran in the large number of medium and large scale data processing applications in business, industry and government. Cobol was behind the state of the art in its procedure division facilities but ahead of the state of the art in its data division facilities. The attractiveness of a language for data processing problems does not appear to depend as critically on its procedure description facilities as on its data description facilities.

M8—PL/I, 1964–1969 [67]: Fortran, Algol 60, and Cobol 61 may be regarded as the three principal first generation higher level languages, while PL/I and Algol 68 may be

regarded as the two principal second generation higher level languages. PL/I was developed as a synthesis of Fortran, Algol 60, and Cobol, taking over its expression and statement syntax from Fortran, block structure and type declaration from Algol 60, and data description facilities from Cobol. Additional language features include the following:

programmer defined exception conditions (the ON statement);

based variables (pointers and list processing);

static, automatic and controlled storage;

external (independently compiled) procedures;

multitasking.

PL/I illustrates both the advantages and the problems of developing a rich general purpose language by synthesis of features of existing languages. One of the lessons learned was that greater richness and power of expression led to greater complexity both in language definition and in language use. PL/I is a language in which programming is relatively easy once the language has been mastered, but in which verifiability and subsequent readability of programs may present a problem. Any language definition of PL/I is so complex that its use for the informal or formal verification of correctness for specific programs is intractable.

M9—Algol 68, 1963–1969 [82]: Whereas PL/I was developed by synthesis of the features of a number of existing languages, Algol 68 was developed by systematic generalization of the features of a single language, namely Algol 60. The language contains a relatively small number of "orthogonal" language concepts. The power of the language is obtained by minimizing the restrictions on how features of the language may be combined. Interesting language features of Algol 68 include:

a powerful mechanism for building up composite modes from the five primitive modes *int, real, bool, char, format*;

identity declarations;

pointer values, structures, etc;

carefully designed coercion from one mode to another;

a parallel programming facility.

The generality of the language can be illustrated by considering the mode (type) mechanism. Composite modes can be built up from modes m,n by the mode construction operators [ ] m (multiples), *struct* (m,n) (structures), *proc* $(m)n$ (procedures), *ref m* (references) and *union* (m,n) (unions). Any mode constructed in this way may itself be the "operand" of a further mode construction operator as in *struct* ([ ] *ref m, proc* (*ref ref m*) *ref n*). Thus, an infinite number of different modes can be constructed from the primitive ones. Each definable mode has a set of values which must be manipulatable by the assignment operator and other applicable operators. Procedures may have any definable mode as a parameter, so that there must be provision for passing of parameters in any definable mode. The above discussion illustrates how generality in Algol 68 is obtained by starting from a small set of orthogonal concepts (the primitive modes and mode construction operators) and generating a very rich class of objects (modes and mode values) by simply removing all restrictions on the manner of composition.

The defining document for Algol 68 (Algol 68 report) [80], is an important example of a high quality language definition, using a powerful syntactic notation for expressing syntax and semiformal English for expressing semantics. However, the report introduces its own syntactic and semantic terminology and can be read only after a considerable investment of time and effort. The reader must become familiar with syntactic terms such as "notion," "metanotion," and "protonotion," and with semantic terms such as "elaboration," "unit," "closed clause," and "identity declaration."

Algol 68 has not been widely accepted by the programming language community in part because of the lack of adequate implementation and user manuals. However, an ultimately more important reason appears to be that the language constructs of Algol 68 are too general and flexible to be readily assimilated and used by the applications programmer.

M10—Simula 67 1965–1967 [17]: Simula 67 is a milestone in the development of programming languages because it contains an important generalization of the notion of a block, which is called a *class*. A Simula class, just like an Algol block, consists of a set of procedure and data declarations followed by a sequence of executable statements enclosed in begin-end parentheses. However, Simula has a "class" data type and allows the assignment of instances of classes to class-valued variables. Whereas local procedures and data structures of a block are created on entry to the block and disappear on exit from a block, local objects of a class (declared in its outer block) remain in existence independently of whether the class body is being executed as long as the variable to which the instance of the class has been assigned as a value remains in existence.

Classes may function as *coroutines* with interleaved execution of executable instructions of two or more class bodies. Execution of a command "resume C_2" in class C_1 causes the current state of execution of C_1 to be saved followed by transfer of control to the current point of execution of C_2.

The separation between class creation and class execution allows data structures in a class to endure between instances of execution and makes the class more useful than the block as a modeling tool for inventory control systems, operating system modules, data types and other entities which may be characterized by a data structure representing the "current state" and a set of operations for querying and updating the current state.

The usefulness of classes in modeling is enhanced even further by Simula conventions concerning the accessibility of local procedure and data declarations in a class.

If an instance of the class C has been assigned to the variable X, then the local identifier I of this instance of the class C can be accessed as $X \cdot I$. The ability to access local identifiers of a class in this way has both advantages (direct access to class attributes) and disadvantages (not enough control over restricting communication between system modules).

The *subclass* mechanism of Simula 67 allows the procedure and data declarations of a class C to become part of the environment of the class B by means of the declaration "C *class* B." If we think of the procedure and data declarations of a class as its set of attributes, then "C *class* B" causes B to have all the attributes of C plus any additional attributes local to B. B is called a subclass of C since it is the subset of C which has the attributes of B in addition to those of C.

The subclass mechanism is a very effective language extension mechanism. It has been used by the Simula 67 designers to design hierarchies of environments for Simula 67 users. Perhaps the best known of these environments is the simulation environment, which is created by first creating a list processing class containing a set of useful list processing procedures, and then defining a subclass simulation which uses list processing procedures to implement simulation primitives. Thus, Simula is not inherently a simulation language but merely a language which may easily be adapted to simulation by language extension.

A Simula class is a better primitive module for modeling objects or concepts than the Algol procedure because of its ability to remember its data state between instances of execution. It has been used as a starting point for the development of a notion of modularity appropriate to modular programming languages of the 1970's.

M11—IPL V, 1954–1958 [65]: IPL V is a list processing language developed specifically for the solutions of problems in artificial intelligence. It was widely used in the 1950's and 1960's for the programming artificial intelligence applications in areas such as chess, automatic theorem proving and general problem solving.

IPL V has primitive instructions for creating and manipulating list data structures. It is an assembly level list processing language with a $1 + 1$ address code (the first address names an operand and the second address names the next instruction). Both programs and data are represented by lists. There are a number of system cells with reserved names, such as a communication cell for communicating system parameters, a subroutine call stack and a free storage list cell. A large number (over 100) of system defined subroutines (processes) are available to aid the user. The semantics of IPL V instructions is specified by defining an instruction interpreter for IPL V instructions.

IPL V was an important milestone both because it was widely used for a period of over ten years by an important segment of the artificial intelligence community and because it pioneered many of the basic concepts of list processing. For example, the notion of a free storage list serving as a source for storage allocation and as a sink to which cells no longer needed are returned was pioneered in IPL V. IPL V may well have been the first language to define its instructions by a software specified instruction execution cycle (virtual machine).

M12—Lisp, 1959–1960 [56]: Lisp, like IPL V, was developed for the solution of problems in artificial intelligence. However, Lisp may be thought of as a higher level (as opposed to machine level) programming language.

Lisp has two primitive data types referred to as lists and atoms. It has the following simple but powerful set of primitive operations.

A *constructor cons*$[x;y]$ for constructing a composite list from components x and y.

Two *selectors car*$[x]$, *cdr*$[x]$ for, respectively, selecting the first component and remainder of the list.

Two predicates atom$[x]$, eq$[x;y]$ which, respectively, test whether x is an atom and whether two atoms x and y are identical.

A compound conditional of the form $[p_1 \rightarrow a_1; p_2 \rightarrow a_2; \cdots ; p_n \rightarrow a_n]$ which may be read as "*if* p_1 *then* a_1 *else if* p_2 *then* $a_2 \cdots$ *else if* p_n *then* a_n" and results in execution of the action a_i corresponding to the first true predicate p_i. Binding operators *lambda*$[x;f]$ and *label*$[x;f]$ which bind free instances of x in f so that they, respectively, denote function arguments and recursive function calls.

The set of primitive Lisp operations have been enumerated explicitly because they exhibit in the simplest terms the essential operators in a nonnumerical processing language. Every nonnumerical processing language must contain constructors for constructing composite structures from their components, selectors for selecting components of composite structures and predicates which permit conditional branching determined by the "value" of the arguments. The compound conditional is a very attractive control structure which was first developed for Lisp and later incorporated into Algol 60. The Lisp binding operators (lambda and label) provide a mechanism for handling functions which have functions as arguments as in the lambda calculus.

Lisp is sufficiently simple to permit the development of a relatively tractable mathematical model. McCarthy used this model as a starting point for the development of a mathematical theory of computation [57]. He considered many of the basic theoretical programming language issues such as mathematical semantics, proofs of program correctness (including compiler correctness) and proofs of program equivalence (by recursion induction) several years before they were considered by anyone else.

McCarthy also developed a definition of Lisp by means of a Lisp interpreter (the APPLY function) which, given an arbitrary Lisp program P with its data D executes the program P with data D. The Lisp APPLY function demonstrated as early as 1960 the technique of defining a programming language L by an interpreter written either in L or in some language definition language. It became the starting point for the subsequent development of theories of operational semantics [95], and for the development of interpreter based language definition languages such as VDL [49].

Lisp contributed a great deal to our understanding of programming language theory. It is also the most influential and widely used artificial intelligence language, its popularity being due in no small measure to its unique blend of simplicity and power. Lisp is certainly among the most important milestones in the development of programming languages.

M13—Snobol 4 1962–1967 [32]: During the 1950's it was felt that mechanical translation and other glamorous

language understanding tasks could be greatly facilitated by the development of string manipulation languages with special purpose linguistic transformation aids. The Comit language [99] was developed for this purpose during the period 1957–1961. Comit was a good linguists language with many special purpose linguistic transformation features, but is not a clean programming language because it does not have string-valued variables to which strings may be assigned as values. The deficiencies of Comit led to the development of Snobol 4 during 1962–1967.

Snobol 4 has data values of the type—integer, real, string and pattern, as well as programmer defined data types. However, Snobol 4 has no block structure or declarations. A given variable, say X, may take on string values, numerical values or pattern values at different points of execution. The data type is carried along as part of the Snobol 4 data value and is checked dynamically at execution time to determine whether it is compatible with the operation that is to be applied to it. Dynamic type checking runs counter to the philosophy of static type checking in conventional block structure languages. It introduces additional run-time overhead and increases the proportion of programming errors that will not be discovered until execution time. However, introduction of block structure and explicit type declarations into Snobol 4 would totally change its character, and it is not clear that such a change would be for the better.

The most important programming language contribution of Snobol 4 is the pattern data type. A pattern is an ordered (finite or infinite) set of strings (and string attributes). Snobol 4 has pattern construction operators for constructing composite patterns from their constituents, pattern valued functions, and pattern matching operations which determine if a string S is an instance of the pattern P. The pattern matching process may be extremely complex involving the matching of a sequence of subpatterns, back-tracking if a partial match of subpatterns cannot be completed into a complete match, and possible side effects during pattern matching caused by assignments triggered by subpattern matching. The development of Snobol 4 has considerably advanced both our theoretical understanding of the nature of one dimensional (string) patterns and our ability to manipulate such patterns. A good theoretical discussion of Snobol 4 patterns is given by Gimpel [33].

Another nice feature of Snobol 4 is its programmer defined data types facility which allows selector names for each field of a structured data type to be easily defined. The mechanisms for defining, creating and manipulating data types are greatly simplified because no explicit type information need be specified in the program.

The use of the Snobol 4 data definition mechanism in defining and using Lisp data structures will be briefly illustrated. The data type definition "DATA('CONS-(CAR,CDR)')" defines a new data type called CONS with two subfields called CAR and CDR. The assignment statement "X = CONS('A', 'NIL')" constructs an initialized instance of this data structure and assigns it to X. The expression "CAR(X)" selects the first subfield "A" of the data structure assigned to X. The naturalness of Snobol 4 for specifying nested construction and selection for programmer defined

data structures is illustrated by the assignment statement "Y = CONS('B', CONS('A', 'NIL'))" and the expression "CAR(CDR(Y))" which retrieves the CAR subfield of the CDR subfield of Y (which happens again to be the element "A").

Although Snobol 4 is a relatively rich and complex language its implementation appears to be an order of magnitude simpler than PL/I or Algol 68. In order to increase portability of the language, it has been defined in terms of a relatively machine-independent macro-language, and can be implemented on a new machine simply by implementing the macro-language. An efficient compiler—the Spitbol compiler [18]—makes Snobol 4 competitive for a wide range of nonnumerical programming problems.

M14—Language theory, 1948–1962: Whereas milestones M1–M13 were concerned largely with the development of programming languages, milestones M14–M23 will be concerned with concepts and theories in the programming language field. The topics to be considered include language theory, models of implementation, language definition, program verification, semantics and abstraction. The starting point both historically and conceptually, is the development of language theory.

Both natural languages and programming languages are mechanisms for the communication of messages from a "sender" or "generator" to a "receiver" or "recognizer."

This model of communication was used by Shannon in the late 1940's in developing a mathematical theory of communication [73]. It was used in the late 1950's by linguists and psychologists, such as Chomsky and Miller [16], in the development of a theory of natural languages. In the field of computer science, the great success of the generative (context-free grammar) definition of Algol 60 [63] led to the generative specification of language syntax for all subsequent programming languages, and to the systematic use of recognizers (finite automata and pushdown automata) in implementing translators and interpreters.

The study of natural languages concerns itself with the study of *mental* mechanisms that allow *human* senders and receivers to generate and comprehend a potentially infinite class of sentences after having encountered and learned only a small finite subset of the set of all possible sentences in a language. The study of computer languages is similarly concerned with finite structures that allow languages with an infinite number of sentences to be defined. However, in the case of computer languages, we are not restricted to the study of preexisting human mental mechanisms, but can create language generating and recognition mechanisms with nice mathematical and computational properties. The language generating mechanisms are called *grammars* while the language recognition mechanisms are called *automata*.

One of the most important results in language theory is due to Chomsky, who defined a hierarchy of grammars (type 0, 1, 2, 3 grammars) and a hierarchy of automata (Turing machines, linear bounded automata, pushdown automata, finite automata) and proved the following re-

markable four-part result concerning the equivalence of language generating power of grammars and language recognition power of automata.

1) A language L can be generated by a type 0 (unrestricted) grammar iff it can be recognized by a Turing machine.

2) A language L can be generated by a type 1 (context-sensitive) grammar if it can be recognized by a linear bounded automaton.

3) A language L can be generated by a type 2 (context-free) grammar iff it can be recognized by a pushdown automaton.

4) A language L can be generated by a type 3 (finite-state) grammar iff it can be recognized by a finite automaton.

Proof of the above result provides a number of interesting insights concerning the relation between the processes of language generation and language recognition. Moreover, the four part hierarchy allows us to distinguish between type 0 and type 1 grammars and automata, which are primarily of theoretical interest, and type 2 and type 3 grammars and automata, which are occasionally useful in compiler construction. Much of the practical work in language theory is concerned with the characterization and study of subclasses of type 2 and type 3 grammars and automata.

M15—Compiler technology and theory 1960–1970: The notion of a compiler was developed in the early and mid 1950's by Hopper, the developers of Fortran and many others. By the early 1960's the notion that compiling was a three phase process consisting of lexical analysis, parsing and code generation had been firmly established. During the 1960's there was a great deal of both practical and theoretical work on the mechanization of lexical analysis and parsing [28]. Lexical analysis was modeled by finite automata while parsing was modeled by various subclasses of context-free grammars, such as precedence grammars, $LR(k)$ grammars and $LL(k)$ grammars. The mechanization of code generation proved to be more difficult because it was target language dependent but there was some progress in this area also. The cost of building compilers of given complexity decreased considerably in the 1960's as our understanding of compiler structure increased. In the late 1960's and 1970's there was considerable work on program optimization using techniques such as interval analysis for analyzing the flowchart of a program. The state of the art in compiler technology and theory is ably summarized in [1].

M16—Compiler Compilers: Since there is a lot of similarity between compilers for different languages, the notion was developed of a program which, when primed with the syntatic and semantic specification of a given programming language L, would create a compiler for the programming language L. This concept led to interesting work on specifying the compiler-oriented semantics of programming languages by rules for translating source language constituents into the target language. However, the creation of a working compiler compiler which could

actually be used in the production of compilers for new languages or new target machines proved to be too ambitious, because the complexity and diversity of languages and machines is simply too great to permit automation. The purely syntactic task of creating an efficient automatic parser from a BNF syntax specification of a language is possible for certain restricted classes of grammars such as precedence grammars, but becomes unmanageable for more ambitious classes of grammars such as $LR(k)$ grammars because of the difficulty of automatically constructing the tables required for automatic parsing. The automation of compiler semantics is even more difficult than the automation of parsing. The best documented example of a compiler compiler (compiler generator) is probably [58].

M17—Models of implementation, interpreters, 1965–1971: Programming languages such as Fortran and Algol 60 have a lot of "surface complexity" but derive their "integrity" from a simple underlying model of implementation, which specifies how programs are to be executed. A model of implementation is a programming language interpreter rather than a compiler. In the early 1960's compiler models of programming languages were emphasized because compiler construction was a pressing technological problem. By the late 1960's it was realized that interpreter models captured the important characteristics of programming languages much more directly than compiler models, so that serious students of programming language structure discarded compiler models in favor of interpreter models.

Fortran is based on a model in which subroutines and COMMON storage areas occupy fixed size blocks, each object is characterized by a relative address relative to the beginning of its block, and no storage allocation is performed during execution. This model gives rise to language restrictions against arrays with dynamic bounds and recursive subroutines.

Algol 60 is based on an activation record stack model of implementation [84] which can handle recursive procedures and arrays with dynamic bounds but cannot handle pointer-valued variables or procedures which return procedures as their values. Algol 68 can be clearly modeled by a run-time environment with two stacks and one heap [86]. Simula 67 requires each created instance of a class to be modeled by a stack. PL/I has no clean model of implementation, and its lack of integrity may be due precisely to the fact that the language designers were more concerned with the synthesis of source language features than with the development of an underlying model of implementation.

The notion of a model of implementation is important because it pinpoints the simple starting point from which the apparent complexity of a programming language is derived. Man is inherently incapable of handling or manipulating great complexity so it stands to reason that there is some simple internalized model that is used as a starting point for designing complex structures such as programming languages. It is argued here that the simple starting

point for developing a complex programming language may well be a model of implementation in the mind of the designer.

The 1971 conference on data structures in programming languages [26] contained several papers on models of implementation including a paper on the contour model by Johnston [42], a paper on the B 6700 by Organick and Cleary [66], and a paper on data structure models in programming languages by Wegner [87].

Wegner [86] proposed a class of models called information structure models for characterizing models of implementation by their execution time states and state transitions. An information structure model is a triple $M = (I, I^0, F)$ where I is a set of states $I^0 \subseteq I$ is a set of initial states and F is a state transition function which specifies how a state S can be transformed into a new state S' by the execution of an instruction. A computation in an information structure model is a sequence $S_0 \rightarrow S_1 \rightarrow S_2 \rightarrow \cdots$ where $S_0 \in I^0$ and S_{i+1} is otained from S_i by the execution of an instruction (state transition).

The Lisp APPLY function and the Vienna definition language, discussed in the next section, can be characterized very naturally by information structure models.

Specific assumptions about the structure of the state I and the state transition function F give rise to specific models of implementation. For example states of a Turing machine may be described in terms of three components (t, q, i) where t is the current tape content, q is the current state, and i is the position of the input head. Finite automata are distinguished from Turing machines by the fact that the state transition function F cannot modify the tape component. Pushdown automata have an additional state component called a pushdown tape with characteristic transformation properties.

Programming languages have more complex states and state transitions than automata but may generally be characterized by states with three components (P, C, D) where P is a program component, C is a control component, and D is a data component. Programming languages may be classified in terms of attributes of the P, C, D, components associated with models of implementation. For example the model of implementation of Algol 60 assumes an invariant (reentrant) program component P, a control component C consisting of an instruction pointer ip and an environment pointer ep, and a data component D which is an activation record stack. Fortran does not require P to be reentrant, but requires the size of P, C, and D to be fixed prior to execution.

Information structure models provide a very natural framework for describing programming languages and systems operationally in terms of a specific, possibly abstract, model of implementation. This approach goes against the conventional view that higher level languages should be defined in an implementation-independent way. However, implementation-dependent models reflect the fact that programming-language designers and system programmers think in implementation-dependent ways about programming languages. Implementation-dependent models are therefore valid and important for language designers and system programmers, while implementation independent models are important in other contexts such as program verification.

M18—Language definition, 1960–1970: It is convenient to distinguish between interpreter-oriented language definitions which define the meaning of programs and program constituents in terms of their execution-time effect and compiler-oriented language definitions which define the meaning of source programs in terms of compiled target programs of a target language.

The Algol report is an example of an early (1960) interpreter-oriented language definition with verbal definitions of the meaning of source program constituents. The Lisp APPLY function is an interpreter-oriented language definition in which the execution time effect of source language constructs is rigorously specified by a program.

During the 1960's the interest in compiler technology gave rise to a number of compiler-oriented definitions such as the definition of Euler [89]. Feldman and Gries [28] includes a good review of compiler-oriented language definitions. Knuth [43] proposed an interesting compiler-oriented method of defining the semantics of context-free grammars by associating inherited and synthesized attributes with each vertex of the parse tree of language strings.

During the late 1960's interpreter-oriented definitions of programming languages came back into fashion. The Algol 68 report [80] uses a powerful syntactic notation (VWF notation) to define syntax and semiformal English to define interpreter-oriented semantics. The Vienna definition language [48], [86] is an extension of the Lisp APPLY function definition technique which allows complex languages like PL/I to be defined in terms of an execution-time interpreter.

The Vienna definition language is probably the most practical of the above-mentioned language definition mechanisms. However, it requires approximately 400 pages of "programs" to define PL/I and about 50 pages to define Algol 60. The work on language definition suggests that languages like PL/I are inherently complex in the sense that there simply is no simple way of defining them.

Programming language definitions are intended to serve at least the following two purposes.

1) As a specification of "correctness" for the language implementer.

2) As a specification of "correctness" for the user who wishes to determine whether a program performs its intended task.

The language definition of Algol 60 served as an important frame of reference for a spirited discussion of ambiguities and trouble spots [44]. It was sufficiently precise to serve as an informal tool in checking implementation correctness and program correctness, but was of little help in developing formal methods of program verification. Tools for specifying formal (axiomatic) models of programming languages were developed in the late 1960's and led to an intensive effort in the 1970's to develop

tractable formal language definition models [37], [71].

It is important that programming languages of the future have tractable formal language definitions so that program correctness can be formally determined. One of the objectives of programming language design in the 1970's is "simplicity" where simplicity is increasingly defined in terms of ease of developing a formal definition.

M19—Program correctness, 1963–1969: A program is said to be correct if it correctly performs a designated task (computes a designated function). A program may be thought of as a "how" specification and the designated task or function as an associated "what" specification. A correctness demonstration is a demonstration that the how specification determined by the program is a realization (implementation) of the independently given what specification.

Program correctness was considered by McCarthy (1962) [57], Naur (1965) [64], Dijkstra (1966) [19], Floyd (1967) [29] and Hoare (1969) [36]. Floyd developed the axiomatic approach to program correctness which specifies axioms for primitive program statements and a rule of inference for statement composition. Input-output relations of composite programs may be derived as theorems from input-output relations for primitive statements using the rule of inference for statement composition.

Hoare [36] developed a linear notation for the Floyd formalism. Both axioms and theorems have the form $\{P\}S\{Q\}$ where S is a program statement, P is a precondition, and Q is a post condition. Hoare stated axioms for assignment statements, if-then-else statements and while statements, thus producing a formal system sufficient to prove theorems for programs written in a strict structured programming style. Subsequently, Hoare, together with Wirth, developed a formal definition of Pascal [37] which has been widely used as a starting point for correctness proofs by research workers in program verification.

The axiomatic approach has been widely used for proving the correctness of "small" programs [50], but there are some unresolved problems which prevent its being used as a standard tool for program verification in a production environment. One of the principal limitations of correctness proof techniques is that such techniques are applicable only when the what specification of a program can be given in a simple functional form. The majority of large problems have intractable what specifications (requirements specifications) which may be several hundred pages long, and constantly changing. Thus, it may turn out that formal correctness proofs are simply not applicable to "real" problems, being applicable only to "toy" problems with simple functional what specifications.

M20—Verification, testing and symbolic execution: Program verification may be regarded as an ambitious attempt to prove the correctness of program execution for *all* elements of an infinite input domain and may be contrasted with program testing which is concerned with establishing correctness for individual elements of the input domain. Program correctness for subsets of the input domain may be established by a technique called symbolic execution which is intermediate in generality between program verification and program testing.

The concept of symbolic execution arrived on the scene relatively late and was first publicly presented in 1975 at the international conference on reliable software [41] in papers by King [47] and Boyer, Elspas, and Levitt [6]. It involves the tracing of execution paths of a program with symbolic values of program variables. The set of all execution paths of a program may be thought of as a (possibly infinite) execution tree. Terminal nodes of the tree represent completed execution paths. When a terminal node is reached during symbolic execution then symbolic relations between input and output values for that terminal node are available and program correctness (or incorrectness) can be determined for the subset of values of the input domain which cause the particular execution path to be executed.

Symbolic execution is marginally easier than complete program verification because it is unnecessary to determine loop invariants of program loops. However, other problems which arise in program verification such as the algebraic simplification of algebraic expressions along an execution path are, if anything, more acute because "unfolding" of loops in symbolic execution requires longer sequences of algebraic transformations to be handled. The problem of keeping track of the input domain associated with an execution path is also very difficult. The difficulty of this problem is illustrated by the fact that the "emptyness problem" for execution paths is undecidable. That is, we cannot in general determine whether the input domain associated with a given execution path is empty.

Program testing for a particular value of the input domain is clearly easier than symbolic execution or complete verification since it only involves running the program for the particular input value. However, the key problem in testing is to determine "good" test cases by means of a test data selection criterion.

We may think of a "good" test case as a representative of an equivalence class of "similar" data values with the property that correct execution of the test case increases our confidence in the correctness of the program for all data elements in the equivalence class. If we can partition the input domain into a finite, relatively small, number of such equivalence classes then testing of the program for one element of each equivalence class should increase our level of confidence in the correctness of the complete program.

A number of alternative criteria may be used for determining such equivalence classes. For example the set of all data values associated with a given control path is an example of such an equivalence class. Alternatively, we may directly partition the input domain into input equivalence classes (such as large, medium, and small). Equivalence classes based on the internal program structure which systematically select test cases to exercise all control paths are on the whole more effective than arbitrary equivalence classes imposed on the input domain.

Test data selection criteria can be developed by *program*

structure analysis (control path analysis) *operational profile analysis* (classification of inputs by expected frequency of use) and *error analysis* (testing for specific kinds of errors). The papers by Goodenough and Gerhardt [35], Brown and Lipow [7], and Schneiderwind [74], all presented at the International Conference on Reliable Software [41], illustrate these three approaches to test data selection.

M21—Program verification, program synthesis and semantic definition [98]: Program verification is the process of verifying that a given program Prog correctly performs the task specified by a predicate *P*. If we are given axioms of the form {*Q*}*S*{*P*} for a set of primitive statement types and an axiom for statement composition then verification that a program Prog correctly performs the task *P* requires us to prove the theorem {*true*}Prog{*P*}. That is, the postcondition *P* for the program Prog implies the precondition *true*.

In the case of program synthesis, we are given a specification of a task *P* and are required to find a program Prog that correctly performs the task. Program synthesis clearly involves program verification of the synthesized program *P* as a subtask. However, verification need be performed only for the class of programs which can be synthesized and not for all possible programs of a programming language. Systematic (or automatic) program synthesis avoids unnecessary complexity resulting from bad programming and might actually turn out to be easier than the development of a general purpose verifier for both good and bad programs.

The object of program synthesis is to convert a static description *P* of what is to be computed into a dynamic description Prog of how it is computed. This can be done in a structured way by the stepwise introduction of dynamic features into the static description. At each step one or more statically defined components is expanded into a structure composed of dynamically defined components which may have inner statically defined components as parameters. A structured development of a program Prog from a specification *P* consists of a sequence $P_0, P_1, \cdots, P_n$ of successively more dynamic descriptions of *P* where P_0 = *P*, P_n = Prog and P_{i+1} is obtained from P_i by "expanding" a component of P_i into a more dynamic form. A formal system such as Hoare [36] may be used to prove that P_{i+1} realizes *P* if P_i realizes *P*. Examples of this approach are given by Manna [59], Wirth [90] and Mills [60].

A semantic definition of a programming language *L* is a mechanism which, given an arbitrary program Prog $\in$ *L*, defines the "meaning" of the program. If the task specification *P* for a program Prog is taken to be the meaning of Prog, then the semantic definition supplies *P* given Prog and may be regarded as an inverse process to program synthesis (which supplies Prog given *P*).

It is very reasonable to think of the input-output predicate *P* as the meaning of program Prog whenever Prog determines a well defined input-output relation. Unfortunately, there are programs (with an undecidable halting problem) which have no associated input-output predicate

P and therefore would have no "meaning" using this notion semantics. Since a semantic definition of a programming language *L* should associate a meaning with *all* programs of the programming language, this method of assigning meaning is not altogether satisfactory. The set of meanings expressible by input-output predicates *P* is restricted to the set of recursive functions while the set of meanings expressible by programs is the richer set of recursively enumerable functions.

Floyd [29] called his seminal paper or program verification "Assigning Meaning to Programs," implying that a formal system for program verification also provides a framework for program semantics. It is often convenient for practical purposes to think of the meaning of a program Prog as its input-output predicate. However, input-output semantics determined by axiomatic models is incomplete because the domain of meanings is not sufficiently rich to express the meaning of all programs. In order to achieve completeness, mathematically more sophisticated semantic theories such as those of Scott [71], [80] must be used which map programs into partial recursive functions rather than total recursive functions.

M22—Semantic models: In order to clarify the notion of semantics, it is convenient to introduce the notion of a semantic model as a triple $M = (E, D, \phi)$ where *E* is a syntactic domain (of programs) *D* is a semantic domain of denotations and ϕ is a semantic mapping function which maps elements $e \in E$ of the syntactic domain into their denotations $\phi(e) \in D$.

Semantic models for programming languages may be classified in terms of the nature of the domain *D* of denotations. In particular it is convenient to distinguish between compiler models in which the semantic domain *D* is a set of programs in a target language, interpreter models in which the meaning of a program is defined in terms of the computations to which it gives rise, and mathematical models in which the meaning of a program is defined in terms of the mathematical function it denotes. Mathematical models may in turn be subdivided into axiomatic models which restrict the semantic domain to total functions and specify functions by a relation between a precondition (inputs) and a post condition (outputs), and functional models (such as those of Scott [71]) in which the meaning of a program is given by an abstract (partial recursive) function. The relation among these models is given by the following figure:

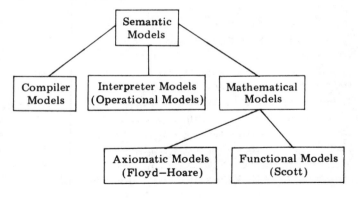

The above discussion makes it clear that the semantics (meaning) of a program is not an absolute (platonic) notion but rather a relative notion which depends on the context of discourse. When we are concerned with compiling, it is natural to think in terms of a compiler oriented semantics for programs. When we are concerned with the process of execution, it is natural to make use of an interpreter oriented semantics. When we are concerned with program verification, then axiomatic semantics is appropriate. When programs are regarded as abstract mathematical objects then the functional semantics of Scott is appropriate.

Each group of semantic models has given rise to a subculture of computer science with its own group of researchers. The subcultures associated with compiler models, interpreter models and axiomatic models have already been discussed (in the sections on compiler methodology, models of implementation and program verification). The Scott approach is the most abstract and Scott's notion of "meaning" has perhaps a greater claim than any other to be considered *the* (platonic) meaning of a program. However, one difficulty with Scott's notion of meaning is that the difference between the how specification of a program and the what specification as an abstract function is so great that the mapping from programs to functions cannot be effectively performed. If it could be effectively performed, then we could decide whether two programs realize the same function by mapping them onto their abstract functions and checking for identity. However, we know that the problem of determining whether two programs realize the same function is undecidable (not even partially decidable) and therefore conclude that the semantic mapping function from programs to abstract functions cannot be constructive.

M23—Abstraction [91]: An abstraction of an object (program) is a characterization of the object by a subset of its attributes. The attribute subset determines an equivalence class objects containing the original object as an element. The objects in the equivalence class are called refinements, realizations or implementations of the abstraction. If the attribute subset captures the "essential" attributes of the object then the user need not be concerned with the object itself but only with the abstract attributes. Moreover, if the attribute subset defining the abstraction is substantially simpler than its realizations then use of the abstraction in place of a realization simplifies the problem addressed by the user.

The input-output relation realized by a program is an example of a program abstraction. It determines an equivalence class of programs (the set of all programs realizing the given input-output relation). Any program in the equivalence class is a realization (refinement) of the abstraction. The input-output relation captures the essential behavior of the program. When the input-output behavior is a simple or well known mathematical function then use of the abstraction in place of a realization serves a useful purpose.

The input-output relation determined by a program may be thought of as a *what* specification (of what the program does) while the program itself is a *how* specification (of how the program is realized). We may, in general, think of an abstraction as a what specification and of its realizations as associated how specifications. The process of abstraction is useful if the what specification characterizing the essential attributes of an object is substantially simpler than the how specification.

Unfortunately, the what specification for programs is not always simpler than the how specification. A program is a relatively compact specification of a functional correspondence between arbitrarily large input and output domains and there is no reason why an explicit description of the input-output relation in a mathematical notation should be simpler than the implicit description by the program. In fact, programs are a more powerful notation for describing functional correspondences than input-output relations because programs can describe recursively enumerable functions (including functions with an undecidable halting problem) while input-output relations can describe only recursive functions (for which the halting problem is decidable).

The equivalence class of all programs (algorithms) associated with a given functional abstraction is studied in the analysis of algorithms. Such equivalence classes can be extraordinarily rich. For example, Knuth in [45] develops an enormous number of different programs for the problem of sorting. It can be shown that the problem of determining whether two programs realize the same abstraction is undecidable (not even partially decidable). The study of the structure of equivalences of how specifications realizing a given what specification is of interest both for programs and other kinds of abstraction.

The notion of abstraction is important in the study of program modularity. All forms of modular programming are concerned with breaking a complex task into modular components where each component has a what specification (abstraction) specifying what the module accomplishes and a how specification (refinement) which specifies how the what specification is realized. If the how specification is specified in terms of a collection of modules which are what specifications to lower level how specifications, then we are led to stepwise abstraction and stepwise refinement. The process of stepwise refinement is illustrated in [88].

The notion of abstraction arises in many different disciplines and may always be characterized in terms of a relation between an equivalence class specification and elements of the equivalence class. The problem of specifying abstractions (equivalence classes) as well as the problem of characterizing the structure of the space of realization (elements) is of interest in many domains of discourse. However, the tools for studying the specification problem and the equivalence problem is determined by the nature of the elements in the domain of discourse. We have already discussed the nature of the specification and equivalence problems when our elements are programs. In the section on "modularity" we will consider the spec-

ification and equivalence problems for a class of modules called *data abstractions* which cannot be completely specified by an input-output relation because they have an internal state.

M24—Pascal [92]: Although Pascal was developed in the late 1960's, its structure and design objectives make it a language of the 1970's. Its designer, Wirth, participated in the early stages of design of Algol 68 as a member of the IFIP working group 2.1, but felt that the generality and attendant complexity of the emerging language was a step in the wrong direction. Pascal, like Algol 68, was designed as a successor to Algol 60. However, whereas Algol 68 aimed at generality, Pascal was concerned with simplicity at the conceptual level, the user level and the implementation level. Conceptual simplicity allows simple axiomatization which facilitates verifiability. User simplicity gives the programmer a better understanding of what he is doing and results in more readable, better structured programs with fewer errors. Simplicity of implementation enhances efficiency and portability and ensures simplicity of the associated operational semantic model.

Pascal provides richer data structures than Algol 60, including records, files, sets and programmer defined type specifications but is otherwise as simple as possible. For example, it excludes arrays with dynamic bounds so as to enhance compile time type checking, and excludes pointers and parameters called by name in the interests of conceptual and user simplicity. The notion of compile time checkable data types is central to the structure of Pascal and provides a degree of program redundancy that enhances program reliability. Control structures are designed so as to encourage good programming style such as that advocated in structured programming.

Because Pascal is conceptually simple, it has been possible to develop a fairly complete formal definition for the language [37]. The existence of this formal definition has in turn led to the widespread use of Pascal as a base language for program verification research [50]. The availability of an axiomatized language has removed one of the obstacles to the development of automatic program verification systems, thus allowing researchers to focus more explicitly on other more formidable obstacles such as the handling of tasks with complex or intractable what specifications.

Pascal and Algol 68 represent two very different approaches to the development of a successor to Algol 60. Although the verdict is not yet in, it may turn out that the Pascal approach will turn out to be more relevant to the development of future programming languages than the Algol 68 approach. However, the discussion of "the APL phenomenon" below indicates that the demands of interactive programming may require us to discard notions such as block structure and explicit type declarations which are fundamental to both Pascal and Algol 68.

M25—The APL phenomenon: The idea of time sharing caught the imagination of the computing community as early as 1960, and led to the development of a number of on-line languages in the early 1960's. Quiktran [60] was developed in 1961–1963 by IBM as an on-line dialect of Fortran but never caught on, perhaps because it could not be adequately supported by existing technology. Joss [75] was developed in 1963–1964 by Shaw and others at the Rand Corporation. Basic (beginners all purpose symbolic instruction code) [48] was developed in 1965–1966 at Dartmouth and has had great success in high schools, two year colleges, and other environments concerned with teaching elementary programming.

APL was developed by Iverson in the early 1960's [40], was implemented as an interactive language in 1967 [30], and has proved to be enormously popular in the 1970's among engineers and mathematicians who need a versatile "desk calculator" to aid them in their work.

APL has a richer set of operators than conventional languages like PL/I or Pascal, including ingeneous extensions of scalar operations to vector and matrix operations which allow loop control structures of conventional programming languages to be implicitly specified in APL. Its emphasis on expressive power at the level of expressions is appropriate to on-line languages, since use of on-line languages in the desk calculator mode is largely concerned with the evaluation of expressions. The richness of APL operators and expressions permits a far greater number of essentially different ways of accomplishing a given computation than in conventional languages. The greater scope for programmer ingenuity leads to greater programmer satisfaction but may lead to programs that are more difficult to read, debug, or maintain.

APL has an explicit mechanism for specifying scopes of identifiers, but has a mechanism for specifying local variables of subroutines. Workspaces are a very effective APL mechanism for defining "modules" containing named subroutines and data sets. There are APL extensions such as APL*PLUS and APL SV [34] specifically designed to allow use of APL for large data processing applications.

APL has no explicitly typed variables or block structure and has the *go to* statement as its only form of transfer control. There is not even an "if-then-else" statement, and conditional branching is performed by an implementation trick (branch to a label 0 is interpreted as exit from a subroutine and branch to an ill-formed label is interpreted as a "continue" statement with no effect). In these respects the structure of APL differs markedly from the current conventional wisdom of the software engineering community. However, it nevertheless strikes a strong responsive chord among practical programmers, indicating that explicit type declarations, block structure and control structure might possibly be discarded in future on-line languages, perhaps because the potential gains in program efficiency and reliability are insufficient to offset the extra program complexity resulting from redundant constituents and additional interrelations among program-constituents.

Arguments *against* block structure, explicit types and explicit control structures may be formulated as follows.

Argument against block structure: One of the original reasons for block structure was the savings in storage re-

sulting from overlays of variables in disjoint blocks. The price paid for this rather trivial saving is an inflexible set of interrelations among program identifiers which adds greatly to the program complexity. APL has scoping mechanisms at the subroutine and workspace level, but none at the block structure level. This looser scoping mechanism appears to be very appealing to practical programmers. Prior to 1970, we might have dismissed the tendency towards looser scoping as being due to a lack of education. However, now that we have become complexity conscious, we can see that block structure imposes additional complexity on a program and that the desire to ruthlessly prune such complexity by eliminating block structure may be justified by the canons of software engineering.

Argument against explicit type declarations: APL is designed so that types of variables may be determined implicitly by context, and there are in fact many syntactic checks on type compatibility between operators and operands in an APL system. Implicit type definitions may well correspond much more closely to the programmers intuitive thought processes than explicit type definitions. Moreover, explicit type declarations greatly increase the number of interactions among program constituents, and therefore increase the complexity of the program. If the programmer needs explicit information about types, APL has query facilities for providing such information to the programmer.

Argument against explicit control structures: The rich operator structure of APL often allows explicit loops and other explicit control specifications to be avoided. Since control structures are probably the single most significant cause of program complexity, languages which allow control structures to be specified implicitly rather than explicitly clearly give rise to textually simpler programs.

Since language usage in the future is likely to become increasingly interactive, and APL is probably the most widely used interactive language, language designers should analyze very carefully the reasons for the popularity of APL. It is not at present clear how much the popularity of APL is due to the quality of its programming system and how much it is due to the quality of the language design. However, it may well turn out that programming languages of the future will be more APL-like than Pascal-like.

M26—Structured programming: The term "structured programming" was introduced by Dijkstra in 1969 in a seminal paper entitled "Notes on structured programming" [24]. These notes are the culmination of several years of personal development, documented by his 1965 paper entitled "Programming Considered as a Human Activity" [20] which emphasizes the importance of programming style and program verification and contains the observation that "the quality of programmers is inversely proportional to the density of go-to statements in their programs," and by his 1968 letter entitled "Go-to Statement Considered Harmful" [21] which sparked a debate concerning the role of the go-to statements in programming that is ably summarized by Knuth [46]. Dijkstra's

recent book entitled *A Discipline of Programming* [22] reflects his current thinking on the subject.

Structured programming in its purest (narrow) form is concerned with the development of programs from assignment statements, conditional branching (if-then-else) statements and iteration (while-do) statements by statement composition. These statement forms can be nicely axiomatized [36] and correspond to "natural" forms of mathematical reasoning (the if-then-else statement corresponds to enumerative (case analysis) reasoning and the while-do statement corresponds to inductive reasoning). It was shown by Bohm and Jacopini [4] that these statement forms are sufficient for expressing any computable function. Moreover, it turns out that these statement forms are appropriate for many practical problems although they must be supplemented by other statement forms in certain cases such as unusual exit from a loop.

Structured programming in its more general meaning is concerned with the better organization of the program development process to achieve objectives such as simplicity, understandability, verifiability, modifiability, maintainability, etc. In order to achieve these objectives it is important to develop a methodology for the modular decomposition of programs into components suitable both for bottom-up and top-down program development. In this connection, it is convenient to distinguish between "programming in the small" concerned with modularity and program structuring at the primitive statement level and "programming in the large" concerned with modularity at a higher (subprogram and data structure) level. The if-then-else and while-do constructs are appropriate module building constructs for programming in the small. The Algol procedure, Simula class and APL workspace are examples of module building constructs for programming in the large. Current research on modularity will be discussed in a separate section.

Structured programming has affected programming language usage in placing greater emphasis on if-then-else and while-do constructs and deemphasizing the go-to statement. It is likely to affect the design of future programming languages by introducing new kinds of program modules for programming in the large, and by placing greater emphasis on verifiability as a programming language design objective. The availability of appropriate concepts of modularity should help the user in systematic modular program development for complex problems. However, there are important areas of program development, such as choice of an appropriate modular data structure where available tools are of little help to the programmer. The influence of the choice of data structure on program structure is discussed in a paper on "top-down program development" by Wirth [90]. The duality between program structure and data structure is discussed in a provocative way by Hoare [38], [39].

The techniques of structured programming have had an impact not only on academic computer science but also on production programming [8]. The chief programmer team approach developed by Mills and Baker [61] is an example

of a management structure which makes use of structured programming. The New York Times project [9] is perhaps the most widely advertised success story for the chief programmer team approach, claiming a productivity of 10 000 instructions per man year with only one error per man year. However, the reported success of this project was subsequently challenged, on the basis that maintenance and modifiability of the completed program was unsatisfactory. It appears that the chief programmer team approach is designed to optimize program development but pays insufficient attention to the operations and maintenance part of the life cycle (see the section on life cycle).

M27—Structured model building: Specifications of programming languages are effectively complex programs in some specification language. The notions of abstraction structuring, and stepwise refinement are just as applicable to the construction of semantic models (definitions) of programming languages as they are to the construction of applications programs. Thus, the abstract notion of a semantic model (for a specific language) can be realized by a compiler model, interpreter model, axiomatic model, or functional model (see M22). Once the desired class of models has been chosen, there is enormous scope for "structuring" the language definition by first making "high-level" decisions concerning the overall structure of the model and then filling in lower level details by a process of stepwise refinement. The term "partial model" may be used to describe an intermediate partial language specification in this process of stepwise refinement.

The above structured model building approach will be briefly illustrated by showing how stepwise refinement may be used to build an information structure model (interpreter model) of Algol 60 [97]. In the case of information structure models $(I,I°,F)$ the partial models of the stepwise refinement process will have partial (successively more complete) specifications of the state components $I,I°$, and the state transition function F. The initial model M_0 would be an arbitrary model with no restriction on $I,I°,F$. A "first-order" model M, might require states I to be of the form (P,C,D) where P is an invariant (read only) program component, C has the form (ip,ep) where ip is an instruction pointer into P and ep is an environment pointer into D, and D is a stack of activation records. A "second-order" model M_2 might then be introduced which defines the state transitions (instructions) for block entry and exit and procedure call and return. Eventually, a final model M_n would completely define the state structure I and state transitions F for every Algol statement.

The partial models which arise in the above stepwise refinement process specify partial (operational) semantics for partial syntax specifications and may be thought of as defining language classes which are abstractions of the language that is being defined. For example, the abstraction "Algol-like languages" may in principle be defined by a partial information structure model which fixes those semantic and syntactic features that are essential if the language is to be Algol-like and leaves open optional language features of Algol-like languages.

The use of structured techniques of model specification is likely to lead to more understandable definitions of a number of existing programming languages. However, an even more potent way of developing programming languages with simple specifications is to use simplicity of specification as one of the criteria of programming language design, as was done in the case of the programming language Pascal.

M28—The life cycle concept: The software life cycle as formalized by department of defense agencies consists of a *concept formulation* and *requirements specification* stage, a *software development* stage, and an *operations and maintenance* stage. These stages may in turn be refined so that the software development stage might consist of a requirements analysis stage, a program design stage, an implementation and debugging stage and a testing and evaluation stage. In analyzing three large military software projects, it was estimated that such systems typically have a life cycle of 16 years, consisting of a concept formulation and requirements stage of 6 years, a software development stage of 2 years, and an operations and maintenance stage of 8 years [70]. Thus, the software development stage comprises only one eighth of the total life cycle of a typical large military software project.

The life cycle concept provides a basis for a more complete analysis of software systems than was previously possible. In the 1960's and early 1970's programming projects were organized to minimize software development costs rather than total life cycle costs. This led to a disproportionate emphasis on program design and implementation and a comparative neglect of both the initial determination of what it is that we really want to accomplish and the long years of program usage in an environment which may involve frequent program modification.

Emphasis on the life cycle as opposed to the software development phase affects both programming language design and programming language usage. For example emphasis on software development requires programming languages to be designed for rapid and correct program development while emphasis on the life cycle requires programs to be readable and modifiable during the long operations and maintenance period, providing a strong argument for simplicity of language design. Language usage should be modular, so that modifications of one part of the program do not have unexpected side effects in another part of the program. Clever tricks which make the program less readable should be avoided like the plague.

The life cycle approach allows the systematic study of cost and effort in all stages of existence of a software system [69]. Bottlenecks can be uncovered in the manner of critical path analysis and tools and techniques may be developed for eliminating such bottlenecks. Studies of software systems have in fact uncovered some quite unexpected facts about system behavior such as the fact that 64 percent of errors are system design errors while only 36 percent are system implementation errors. This suggests that design, rather than implementation, is the

bottleneck in software system development and has implications concerning the allocation of funds for research in software engineering.

M29—Modularity: The subroutine mechanism for realizing program modularity was developed as early as 1951 [83]. It was a fundamental feature of Fortran, whose design provided an enormous impetus towards modular programming. Algol 60 was in some ways a backward step from the viewpoint of modularity because its nested module structure discouraged independent module development and because procedure modules could not adequately handle data which remained in existence between instances of execution of a procedure.

The Simula class is a very flexible generalization of the Algol 60 procedure module. It separates creation and deletion of instances of a class from entry and exit for purposes of execution. Coroutine control allows the program and data state at arbitrary points of execution to be preserved and subsequently restored. Access to objects declared in the outermost block of a class provides a more flexible (too flexible) mechanism for module intercommunication. The subclass facility is an ingenious syntactic mechanism for providing the advantages of hierarchical (nested) modular environments while avoiding the need for physical textual nesting of the associated modules. The class concept has served as an inspiration to designers of modular programming languages but is probably too rich in properties to serve as a prototype for modular design.

The collection of declarations in the outer block of a module may be regarded as a set of attributes or resources. One of the purposes of a module is to erect a "fence" around this set of attributes which allows systematic *information hiding* [68] of internal (hidden) attributes of a module and selective specification of a subset of externally known (*exportable*) attributes. Recent research on Clu [51] and Alphard [94] has been concerned with mechanisms for hiding and exporting module attributes.

The experimental language Clu [51] requires its program modules to consist of a collection of exportable procedures operating on a hidden (internal) data structure, and refers to such modules as *clusters*. Clusters are convenient for defining data types (such as stacks) by means of operations (such as push, pop, top, create, testempty) independently of the internal data structure (linear list or array) used to realize the cluster. The user sees an abstraction (the stack abstraction) which is defined by hiding the internal data structure and exporting only the operations. Such an abstraction is called a *data abstraction* because it abstracts from a specific data representation. The effect of the operators is defined by axioms such as "top(push(x,stack)) = x" which defines the effect of the "top" operation in terms of previously executed "push" operations without making any commitment to data representation. Any data structure which causes the defining axioms for the operations to be satisfied is an adequate realization of the data abstraction. Of course, the development of complete and sound sets of axioms for characterizing the set of cluster operations in a data independent way may, in general, be

difficult. However, in most practical cases, we can characterize the behavior of "output" operations of a data abstraction reasonably simply in terms of the effect of previous input operations, and a complete set of axioms can be developed by systematically using our knowledge of what the operations are supposed to accomplish.

The experimental modular programming language Alphard [94] calls its modules *forms*. Recent research on Alphard has emphasized verifiability as an objective of the language. Forms have a *representation* component which defines the representation of hidden data structures, an *implementation* component which defines the implementation of external attributes (operators) of the form and a *specification* component which specifies the "abstract" properties of attributes so that the correctness of their implementation can be verified.

Other work on modular programming languages includes Brinch Hansen's development of *monitors* in concurrent Pascal [9] and Wirth's introduction of *modules* in a Pascal-like language for modular multiprogramming called Modula [97]. Both monitors and modules are motivated by the need to provide the user with machine independent abstractions of machine resources such as disks, user consoles, synchronization primitives, etc. In [9] the relation between the implementation and user abstraction for monitors is described by considering how monitors are implemented. In [97] the relation between abstraction and implementation of modules is described at the language level by introducing notions such as *define list* of objects defined in the module for use outside the module and a *use list* of objects declared outside the module and used inside the module.

Among the problems which must be addressed in any modular programming language are the problems of module interface definition and module interconnection. These problems had already been identified in the 1950's in connection with the development of Fortran (the transfer vector mechanism). One recent example of work in this area is the thesis by Thomas [79] who develops a module interconnection language (MIL) for specifying module interfaces in terms of inherited attributes (use lists), synthesized attributes (define lists), and locally generated attributes using a model similar to Knuth's attribute grammars [43].

Although recent research on modularity and abstraction has greatly increased our understanding of how modules may be designed, it is not yet clear how effectively these notions can be incorporated in future programming languages. The explicit support of clusters or Simula classes introduces extra complexity into a language both at the level of verifiability and at the level of implementation, determining complete and consistent specifications for clusters to serve as a starting point for formal verification. Simula 67 has not become a widely used application language in spite of its superior modularity facilities. The modular programming facilities of a language are clearly among its most important design features, and it is quite likely that future programming languages will contain new

kinds of primitives for defining both program and data abstractions. But the precise nature of these primitives has not yet been determined.

M30—Data oriented programming languages: We may distinguish between the program-centered and data-centered views of programming. The program-centered view emphasizes program development and considers data only piecemeal as and when it becomes the object of program transformation. This view is appropriate to numerical problems involving complex functional transformations on simple data structures. The data-centered point of view considers the data structure (data base) as the central part of a problem specification and views programs as "bugs" which crawl around the data base and occasionally query, update or augment the portion of the data base at which they currently reside. This view is appropriate for airline reservation systems, management information systems, information retrieval systems or any other systems whose state description requires a complex data structure and whose operations (transactions) are local queries or perturbations of that data structure.

Bachman in his Turing lecture [11] compares the shift from the program-centered to the data-centered point of view with the shift from an earth-centered to a sun-centered model of the universe brought about by the Copernican revolution. There is no doubt that the increasing importance of the data-centered view of programming will affect the design of future programming languages.

Since programming was initially motivated by numerical problems early programming languages and programming methodology emphasized the programming centered point of view. Algol 60 blocks and procedures are examples of program-centered constructs since internal data structures are forced to disappear between instances of execution. Simula classes generalize block structure so that it becomes appropriate for data-centered programming.

Cobol is an example of an early programming language which allows program and data to be handled in a symmetrical fashion. Programming systems for data-centered programming developed during the 1960's include IDS (integrated data store) [5], and IMS (information management system) [25]. The data-centered view of programming led in the 1970's to the development of data-base languages and systems [14], [25].

Data-base systems may be classified [25] into *network systems* which require the user to view the data base as a network (spagghetti bowl); *hierarchical systems* which require the data base to be tree structured, and relational data-base systems which permit the user to view the data base as a set of abstract relations. Network and hierarchical systems give rise to "low level" data base languages since they require the user to be explicitly aware of the data structure implementation. Relational systems give rise to high level data base languages which allow programs to specify transactions independently of the internal data structure representation, but lead to formidable implementation problems.

Network systems are a direct outgrowth of the work of the Codasyl data-base task group (DBTG) [14] and were heavily influenced by Bachman's work on IDS [5]. Hierarchical systems are the simplest class of data-base management systems, and most of the practical systems of the 1960's such as IMS were hierarchical. The relational approach to data-base management systems was pioneered by Codd in 1970 [13]. A good recent survey of the state of the art may be found in [77].

There is a great deal of current work on the design and implementation of data-base language. Recently developed relational data-base languages include Sequel [14], Quel [2], and query by example [100].

CONCLUSIONS

The above collection of concepts and milestones is by no means complete, but illustrates the great variety of programming language concepts and products developed during the last 25 years. One of the more interesting facts that emerges from a study of programming language development is the remarkable stability of early programming languages like Fortran and Cobol, and the comparative lack of success of subsequently developed languages like PL/I, Algol 68, Simula 67, and Pascal in capturing significant numbers of adherents in a nonuniversity environment. The exception is perhaps APL which has captured the hearts of a new class of user (the desk calculator user).

All the programming languages described in this paper were developed and implemented in the 1950's and 1960's. Although there have been a number of proposals for general purpose languages in the 1970's such as CS 4 [15] and the Tinman requirements specification for a new DOD-sponsored common higher order language [31], no new general purpose languages comparable to PL/I, Algol 68, or Pascal have been launched during this period. The 1970's have been a period of retrenchment in the development of general purpose languages. A number of new insights have been developed such as the importance of simplicity, readability, verifiability, and maintainability in program design and language design. A better appreciation of the concept of modularity has been developed and we have made some gains in our understanding of program verification. But these insights have led to changes in the mode of use of existing programming languages rather than in the design of a new class of programming languages which are so clearly superior that they are automatically accepted as a replacement for existing programming languages.

The demonstrated reluctance of the programming community to accept a new language is due partly to the costs of a changeover, and partly to the natural resistance to changes in technology. It is due partly to the fact that programming language designers have not been able to come up with an acceptable compromise between simplicity and versatility that is a substantial improvement over Fortran or Cobol. However, a further reason may be that programmer productivity is not as sensitive to lan-

guage changes as programming language professionals would like to think. Fortran-like languages provided a significant increment of productivity over assembly language but it may well be that further language refinements cause only marginal or even negative increments in programmer productivity. Programming style, structured programming and other methodologies are largely language independent and are probably far more important in increasing programmer productivity than the development of new languages. Ultimately, it is the quality of programming rather than the programming language that determines the cost and reliability of production programs.

The field of programming languages was central to the development of computer science in the 1950's and 1960's, leading to important practical products and to important theoretical advances in our understanding of the nature of computer sciences. It may well be that programming language professionals did their work so well in the 1950's and 1960's that most of the important concepts have already been developed. The programming language field may play a less central (though still important) role in computer science in the 1970's and 1980's than it did in the 1950's and 1960's.

REFERENCES

Note: OSIPL refers to [25]. ICRS refers to [40].

[1] A. V. Aho and J. R. Ullman, *The Theory of Parsing, Translation and Compiling.* Englewood Cliffs, NJ: Prentice-Hall, vol. I, 1972; vol. II, 1973.
[2] E. Allman, M. Stonebraker, and G. Held, "Embedding a relational sublanguage in a general purpose programming language'" *SIGPLAN Notices,* Mar. 1976.
[3] M. M. Astrahan and D. Chamberlin, "Implementation of a structured English query language," *Commun. Ass. Comput. Mach.,* Oct. 1975.
[4] C. Bohm and G. Jacopini, "Flow diagrams, turing machines, and languages with only two formation rules," *Commun. Ass. Comput. Mach.,* May 1966.
[5] C. W. Bachman, "A general purpose system for random access, memories," in *FJCC Proc.,* 1964.
[6] R. S. Boyer, B. Elspas, and K. N. Levitt, "A formal system for testing and debugging programs by symbolic execution," *ICRS,* Apr. 1975.
[7] J. R. Brown and M. Lipow, "Testing for software reliability," *ICRS,* Apr. 1975.
[8] F. T. Baker, "Structured programming in a production programming environment," *ICRS,* Apr. 1975.
[9] P. Brinch Hansen, "The purpose of concurrent PASCAL," *ICRS,* Apr. 1975.
[10] F. T. Baker and H. D. Mills, "Chief programmer teams," *Datamation,* 1973.
[11] C. W. Bachman, "The programmer as navigator," (1973 Turing lecture), *Commun. Ass. Comput. Mach.,* Nov. 1973.
[12] *COBOL 1961: Revised Specifications for a Common Business Oriented Programming Language,* U. S. Govt. Printing Office, 1961.
[13] E. F. Codd, "A relational submodel for large shared data banks," *Commun. Ass. Comput. Mach.,* June 1970.
[14] "CODASYL," Data Base Task Group Rep., Apr. 1971.
[15] *CS-4 Language Reference Manual and Operating System Interface,* Intermetrics Publ., Oct. 1975.
[16] N. Chomsky and G. A. Miller, *Introduction to the Formal Analysis of Natural Languages, Handbook of Mathematical Psychology,* vol. II. New York: Wiley, 1963.
[17] D. Dahl and C. A. R. Hoare, *Hierarchical Program Structures, in Dahl, Dijkstra and Hoare, Structured Programming.* New York: Academic, 1972.
[18] R. Dewar, "SPITBOL 2.0," Illinois Inst. Technol. Rep., 1971.
[19] E. W. Dijkstra, "A constructive approach to the problem of program correctness, *BIT,* Aug. 1968.
[20] ——, "Programming as a human activity," *Proc. IFIP Congress,* 1965.
[21] ——, "Go to statement considered harmful," *Commun. Ass. Comput. Mach.* (Lett.), Mar. 1968.
[22] ——, *A Discipline of Programming.* Englewood Cliffs, NJ: Prentice-Hall, 1976.
[23] ——, "Making a translator for ALGOL 60," *APIC Bull.,* vol. 7, 1961.
[24] ——, *Notes on Structured Programming, in Dahl, Dijkstra and Hoare, Structured Programming.* New York: Academic, 1972.
[25] C. J. Date, *An Introduction to Data Base Systems.* New York: Addison-Wesley, 1975.
[26] *Data Structures in Programming Languages, Proc. of Symp.,* SIGPLAN Notices, Feb. 1971.
[27] "FORTRAN vs. basic FORTRAN," *Commun. Ass. Comput. Mach.,* Oct. 1964.
[28] J. Feldman and D. Gries, "Translator writing systems," *Commun. Ass. Comput. Mach.,* Nov. 1968.
[29] R. W. Floyd, *Assigning Meanings to Programs, Proc. Symp. App. Math.* vol XIX, AMS, 1967.
[30] A. D. Falkoff and K. E. Iverson, *The APL Terminal System, in Klerer and Reinfelds, Interactive Systems for Experimental Applied Mathematics.* New York: Academic, 1968.
[31] D. A. Fischer, "A common programming language for the department of defense, background and technical requirements," IDA Sci. Technol. Division, paper P-1191, June 1976.
[32] R. Griswold, J. Poage, and I. Polonsky, *The SNOBOL 4 Programming Language.* Englewood Cliffs, NJ: Prentice-Hall, 1971.
[33] J. Gimpel, "A theory of discrete patterns and their implementation in SNOBOL 4," *Commun. Ass. Comput. Mach.,* Feb. 1973.
[34] L. Gilman and A. J. Rose, *APL, an Interactive Approach,* 2nd Ed. New York: Wiley, 1974.
[35] J. B. Goodenough and S. L. Gerhard, "Towards a theory of test data selection," *ICRS,* Apr. 1975.
[36] C. A. R. Hoare, "An axiomatic basis for computer programming," *Commun. Ass. Comput. Mach.,* Oct. 1969.
[37] C. A. R. Hoare and N. Wirth, "An axiomatic definition of the programming language PASCAL," *Acta Inform.,* vol. 2, no. 4, 1973.
[38] ——, *Notes on Data Structuring, In Dahl, Dijkstra and Hoare, Structured Programming.* New York: Academic, 1972.
[39] ——, "Data reliability," *ICRS,* Apr. 1975.
[40] K. E. Iverson, *A Programming Language.* New York: Wiley, 1962.
[41] *Proc. Int. Conf. Reliable Software,* Apr. 1975; also *SIGPLAN Notices,* June 1975.
[42] J. Johnston, "The contour model of block structured processes," *DSIPL,* Feb. 1971.
[43] D. E. Knuth, "The Semantics of Context Free Languages," in *Mathematical Systems Theory,* vol. II, no. 2, 1968.
[44] ——, "The remaining trouble spots in ALGOL 60," *Commun. Ass. Comput. Mach.,* Oct. 1967.
[45] ——, *The Art of Computer Programming Volume III, Sorting and Searching,* 1973.
[46] ——, "Structured programming with go to statements," *Comput. Surveys,* Dec. 1974.
[47] J. C. King, "Symbolic execution and program testing," *Commun. Ass. Comput. Mach.,* July 1976.
[48] J. G. Kemeny and T. E. Kurtz, *Basic Programming.* New York: Wiley, 1967.
[49] P. Lucas and K. Walk, "On the formal description of PL/I," *Annu. Rev. Automatic Programming,* vol. 6, pt 3. New York: Pergamon, 1969.
[50] R. L. London, "A view of program verification," *ICRS,* Apr. 1975.
[51] B. H. Liskov, "A note on CLU," Computation Structures Group Memo 112, Nov. 1974.
[52] B. M. Leavenworth, "Syntax macros and extended translation," *Commun. Ass. Comput. Mach.,* Nov. 1966.
[53] B. H. Liskov and S. N. Zillies, "Specification techniques for data abstractions," *ICRS,* Apr. 1975.
[54] M. D. McIlroy, "Macro instruction extensions to compiler languages," *Commun. Ass. Comput. Mach.,* Apr. 1960.
[55] C. N. Mooers, "TRAC-A procedure-describing language for a reactive typewriter," *Commun. Ass. Comput. Mach.,* Mar. 1976.

[56] J. McCarthy et al., *LISP 1.5 Programmers Manual*. Cambridge, MA: MIT Press, 1965.

[57] J. McCarthy, "Towards a mathematical science of computation," in *Proc. IFIP Congr.*, 1962.

[58] W. M. McKeeman, J. H. Horning, and D. B. Wortman, *A Compiler Generator*. Englewood Cliffs, NJ: Prentice-Hall, 1970.

[59] Z. Manna, *Mathematical Theory of Computation*. New York: McGraw-Hill, 1974.

[60] H. D. Mills, "Mathematical foundations for structured programming," IBM Corp., Gaithersburg, MD, FSC 72-6012, 1972.

[61] J. H. Morissey, "The QUIKTRAN system," *Datamation*, Feb. 1964.

[62] P. Naur, Ed., "Report on the algorithmic language ALGOL 60," *Commun. Ass. Comput. Mach.*, May 1960.

[63] ——, "Revised report on the algorithmic language ALGOL 60," *Commun. Ass. Comput. Mach.*, Jan. 1963.

[64] ——, Proofs of Algorithms by General Snapshots, BIT 6, 1966.

[65] Newell et al., *Information Processing Language V Manual*, 2nd Ed. Englewood Cliffs, NJ: Prentice-Hall, 1965.

[66] E. I. Organick and J. G. Cleary, "A data structure model of the B6500 computer system," *DSIPL*, Feb. 1971.

[67] *PL/I, Current IBM System 360 Reference Manual*, (or Bates and Douglas), 2nd Ed. Englewood Cliffs, NJ: Prentice-Hall, 1975.

[68] D. I. Parnas, "A technique for software module specification with examples," *Commun. Ass. Comput. Mach.*, May 1972.

[69] B. Randell and L. J. Russell, *ALGOL 60 Implementation*. New York: Academic, 1964.

[70] D. J. Reifer, "Automated aids for reliable software," *ICRS*, Apr. 1975.

[71] D. Scott and S. Strachey, "Towards a mathematical semantics for computer languages," PRG 6, Oxford Univ. Comput. Lab., 1971.

[72] J. Sammet, *Programming Languages, History and Fundamentals*. Englewood Cliffs, NJ: Prentice-Hall, 1969.

[73] C. E. Shannon and W. Weaver, *The Mathematical Theory of Communications*. Urbana, IL: Univ. Illinois Press, 1962.

[74] N. F. Schneiderwind, "Analysis of error processes in computer software," *ICRS*, 1975.

[75] C. J. Shaw, "JOSS, a designers view of an experimental on-line system," in *Proc. FJCC*, 1964.

[76] ——, "A specification of JOVIAL," *Commun. Ass. Comput. Mach.*, Dec. 1963.

[77] E. H. Sibley, Ed., "Special issue: Data base management systems," *Comput. Surveys*, Mar. 1976.

[78] A. M. Turing, "On computable numbers with an application to the entscheidungsproblem," in *Proc. London Math. Soc.*, 1936.

[79] J. Thomas, "Module interconnection in programming systems supporting abstractions," Ph.D. dissertation, Brown Univ., Providence, RI, May 1976.

[80] R. D. Tennent, "The denotational semantics of programming languages," *Commun. Ass. Comput. Mach.*, Aug. 1976.

[81] J. Von Neumann, "The EDVAC report," in *Computer from PASCAL to Von Neumann*, H. Goldstein, Ed. Princeton, NJ: Princeton Univ. Press, 1972, Ch. 7, discussion.

[82] V. Wingaarden et al., "Report on the algorithmic language ALGOL 68," *Numer. Math.*, Feb. 1969; also revised report, *Numer. Math.*, Feb. 1975.

[83] M. V. Wilkes, D. J. Wheeler, and S. Gill, *The Preparation of Programs for a Digital Computer*. New York: Addison-Wesley, 1951 (revised Ed., 1957).

[84] P. Wegner, *Programming Languages, Information Structures and Machine Organization*. New York: McGraw-Hill, 1968.

[85] W. Waite, "A language independent macro processor," *Commun. Ass. Comput. Mach.*, July 1967.

[86] P. Wegner, "Three computer cultures, computer technology, computer mathematics and computer science," in *Advances in Computers*, vol. 10. New York: Academic, 1972.

[87] ——, "Data structure models in programming languages," *DSIPL*, Feb. 1971.

[88] ——, "The Vienna definition language," *Comput. Surveys*, Mar. 1972.

[89] N. Wirth and H. Weber, "Euler—A generalization of ALGOL and its formal definition," *Commun. Ass. Comput. Mach.*, Jan. and Feb. 1966.

[90] N. Wirth, "Program development by stepwise refinement," *Commun. Ass. Comput. Mach.*, Apr. 1971.

[91] P. Wegner, "Abstraction—A tool in the management of complexity," in *Proc. 4th Texas Symp. Comput.*, Nov. 1975.

[92] N. Wirth, "The programming language PASCAL," *Acta Inform.*, 1971.

[93] P. Wegner, "Structured model building," Brown Univ., Providence, RI, Rep., 1974.

[94] W. Wulf, R. L. London, and M. Shaw, "Abstraction and verification in ALPHARD, introduction to language and methodology," Carnegie-Mellon Univ., Dep. Comput. Sci. Rep., June 1976.

[95] P. Wegner, "Operational semantics of programming languages," in *Proc. Symp. Proving Assertions about Programs*, Jan. 1972.

[96] ——, "Research paradigms in computer science," in *Proc. 2nd Int. Conf. Reliable Software*, Nov. 1976.

[97] N. Wirth, "Modula: A language for modular multiprogramming," ETH Institute for Informatics, TR18, Mar. 1976.

[98] P. Wegner, "Structured programming, program synthesis and semantic definition," Brown Univ. Rep., Providence, RI, 1972.

[99] V. Yngve, "COMIT as an IR language," *Commun. Ass. Comput. Mach.*, Jan. 1962.

[100] M. Zloof, "Query by example," in *Proc. Nat. Comput. Conf.*, 1975.

Peter Wegner received the B.Sc. degree in mathematics from the Imperial College, London, England, the Diploma in numerical analysis and automatic computing from Cambridge University, Cambridge, England, the M.A. degree in economics from Penn State University, and the Ph.D. degree in computer science from London University, London, England.

He has taught at the London School of Economics, Penn State, Cornell University, and Brown University and has been on the staff of the Computation Center at the Massachusetts Institute of Technology, and Harvard University. He is currently with the Division of Applied Mathematics, Brown University, Providence, RI. His publications are primarily in the programming language area but include papers in operations research and statistics.

Dr. Wegner has been consultant to the ACM Curriculum Committee (1965–1968), SIGPLAN Chairman (1969–1971) and is presently a member of the ACM Council.

ON THE DESIGN OF PROGRAMMING LANGUAGES*

N. WIRTH

This paper reports on some past experiments in the design of programming languages. It presents the view that a language should be simple, and that simplicity must be achieved by transparence and clarity of its features and by a regular structure, rather than by utmost conciseness and unwanted generality. The paper contains an overview of the language designer's problems and dilemmas, and ends with some hints drawn from past experience.

In order to prevent misunderstanding or even disappointment, I should like to warn the reader not to interpret this title as an announcement of a general critique of commonly used languages. Although this might be a very entertaining subject, probably all that can be said about it has been said and heard by those willing to listen. There is no reason to repeat it now. Neither do I intend to present an objective assessment of the general situation in the development of programming languages, the technical trends, the commercial influences, and the psychology of their users. The activities in this field were enormous over the past years, and it would be presumptuous to believe that a single person could present a comprehensive, objective picture. Moreover, many aspects have been aptly reviewed and commented elsewhere (1-3).

Instead, I should like to convey a view of the development of design attitudes, of the shift of emphasis in design goals over the past decade. Also, I will try to provide some insight into the multitude of problems aspects, and demands that the designer of a language is facing, and to woo gently for recognition of the difficulties of this profession. Let me start by recalling some of my own reminiscences of incidents that caused me to end up in this role of language designer.

AN EXCURSION INTO "HISTORY"

My interest in computers had been awakened when I was an engineering student in the late 1950s; I was fascinated on the one hand by simplicity and inherent reliability of the basic building blocks, the digital circuits, and on the other hand by the astounding variety of effects that could be obtained by combining many of them in different ways. Moreover, these combinations could be varied not by extensive and cumbersome use of the soldering iron, but by merely composing ingenious sequences of hexadecimal digits placed on a magnetic drum. As the general task of an engineer is the improvement of his technical gadgets, I perceived that computers were an ideal ground for

*Reprinted from *Proc. IFIP Congress 74*, 386-393, North-Holland, Amsterdam, North-Holland Publishing Company.

The author is with the Institut für Informatik, Eidg. Technische Hochschule, Zurich, Switzerland.

engineering activities, and felt that there was ample room for further improvement. This assessment turned out to be correct up to the present day. But how was progress to be achieved? One way was by enhancing the <u>reliability</u> and <u>effectiveness</u> of their electronic components. The other — hazily defined path — seemed to be to make computers more <u>conveniently usable</u>, to make them less of an exclusive domain of the highly trained specialist.

This was the situation when I entered graduate school at Berkeley: In one room there stood a huge prototype of a computer with a bewildering number of wires and tubes. In a much smaller room nearby there were a few such specialists, talking about a "language" and a "translator". Luckily for me, a student helping to bring the big monster of a computer into operation didn't report too enthusiastically about that project, and I perceived the feeling that the future of computer hardware design did not lie in a university department anyway. Hence, I decided to explore the other alley, although that group was surrounded by skepticism, as word passed that some of these people did neither know Ohm's law nor Maxwell's equations.

The new and fascinating project under the direction of H.D. Huskey consisted in adding facilities to the programming language NELIAC by extending the translator program. This program was, remarkably, coded in the very language that it was compiling and, in retrospect, quite advanced for its time (4). Indeed, the fascination of the project originated much more from the sense of adventurousness than from the satisfaction of achieved perfection. For, although programming in NELIAC proved to be considerably more convenient than exercises in the cryptology of hexadecimal codes, the room for still further improvements continued to appear unlimited. Looking at it from the distance, that compiler was a horror; the excitement came precisely from having insight into a machinery that nobody understood fully. There was the distinct air of sorcery.

Then Algol 60 appeared in the literature and — after the difficulties of learning the new syntactic formalism were mastered — began to provide some relief from the oppressive feeling that there was no way to bring order into large languages and compilers. Yet even then, the task of constructing an Algol

compiler generating acceptably good code appeared enormous. The more the Algol compiler project neared completion, the more vanished order and clarity of purpose. It was then that I clearly felt the distinct yearning for <u>simplicity</u> for the first time. I became convinced that we should learn to master simpler tasks before tackling big ones, and that we need to be equipped with much better linguistic and mental tools. But apparently "useful" languages had to be big.

SIMPLICITY IN GENERALITY

In this situation, A. van Wijngaarden appeared like a prophet with his idea of Generalised Algol (5). His point was that languages were not only too complex, but due to this very complexity also too restrictive. "In order that a language be powerful and elegant it should not contain many concepts and it should not be defined with many words." The new trend was to discover the fundamental concepts of algorithms, to extract them from their various incarnations in different language features, and to present them in a pure, distilled form, free from arbitrary and restrictive rules of applicability.

The following short example may illustrate the principle. In Algol 60, the concept of a subprogram appears in two features: as declared procedure, and as name parameter to procedures. The passing of a parameter is realised as an assignment of an object (the actual parameter) to a variable (the formal parameter). A simplification and concurrent increase in power and flexibility of Algol can therefore be obtained by unifying the notions of procedure and parameter, by letting them become objects that can be assigned to variables like numbers or logical values. Let such an object be denoted by the program text enclosed by quote marks; the correspondence between constructs of Algol 60 and the generalised notation are shown by the following table:

Algol 60	Generalisation
<u>procedure</u> P; <statement>	P := `<statement>`
Q(<expression>)	Q(`<expression>`)

The gain in simplicity of language is obvious and the resulting gain in flexibility is striking. For example, it is now possible to assign different subroutines to a variable at different times, or even to replace a function subroutine by a constant! We are suddenly offered the power so far reserved to the assembly language coder letting his program modify some of its own instructions.

Implementation of such far reaching generalisations were on open challenge. I decided to investigate, whether these concepts could be condensed into a minimal language and compiler, as a language without compiler seemed to be of marginal value to me. This effort resulted in my first programming language, called Euler (5). It was a success in several ways, certainly if measured by the number of subsequent implementations on a wide variety of computers. The language was accepted as an intellectual challenge, a flexible and powerful vehicle. Its simplicity and compactness made it an ideal implementation exercise for many prospective compiler engineers. Its greatest value, however, lay in revealing how simplicity should <u>not</u> be understood and achieved.

The premise that a language should not be burdened by (syntactical) rules that define meaningful texts (5) led to a language where it was difficult and almost impossible to detect a flaw in the logic of a program. It led to what I like to call a high-level Turing machine. Making mistakes is human (particularly in programming), and we need all the help possible to avoid committing them. But how can one expect a language to aid in avoiding mistakes, if it is even incapable of assisting in their detection.

The lesson is, then, that if we try to achieve simplicity through generality of language we may end up with programs that through their very conciseness and lack of redundancy elude our limited intellectual grasp. It is a mistake to consider the prime characteristic of high-level languages to be that they allow to express programs merely in their shortest possible form and in terms of letters, words, and mathematical symbols instead of coded numbers. Instead, the language is to provide a framework of abstractions and structures that are appropriately adapted to our mental habits, capabilities, and limitations. The "distance" of these abstractions from the actual realisation in terms of a computer is an established measure for the "height" of a language's level.

The key, then, lies not so much in minimising the number of basic features of a language, but rather in keeping the included facilities simple to understand in all their consequences of usage and free from unexpected interactions when they are combined. A form must be found for these facilities which is convenient to remember and intuitively clear to a programmer, and which acts as a natural guidance in the formulation of his ideas. The language should not be <u>burdened</u> with syntactical rules, it must be <u>supported</u> by them. They must therefore be purposeful, and prohibit the construction of ambiguities. It is a good idea to employ adequate, concise key words, and to forbid that they can be used in any other way. Prolixity is to be avoided, as it introduces a wrong kind of redundancy.

LEVELS OF ABSTRACTIONS

One of the most crucial steps in the design of a language is the choice of the abstraction upon which programs are to base. They can be selected only if the designer has a clear picture of the purpose of his language, of the area of its intended application. But all too often that purpose is not neatly specified and includes so many diverse aspects that a designer is given only inadequate guidance from prospective users. But at least he should restrict his selection to <u>abstractions from the same level</u> which are in some sense compatible with each other. I should like to offer three examples to this topic.

Algol 60 has chosen a well-defined set of abstract objects of computation: numbers and logical values, replacing bits and words as used on a lower level. The operations that are applicable to them are governed by mathematical laws and axioms which can be understood without referring to the number's representation in terms of bits and words. In the realm of control structures, the language introduces the operations of selective execution and repetition in the form of neatly structured statements. But their form was not sufficiently flexible - e.g. repetition is intimately coupled with a variable progressing through an arithmetic series of values, and selection is only provided among two alternatives. To provide the user with a facility for cases not covered by these control structures, the designers of Algol resorted to borrowing the universally applicable jump order from the lower level of machine coding. The goto statement is but a polished form of the jump.

This may not seem too serious in itself. But consider that now the programmer is able to use these facilities combined. The following example - which an honest Algol programmer will refrain from using, or otherwise will at least get a bad conscience - shows the point.

        for i := 1 step 1 until 100 do
              begin S; if p then goto L end

The whole purpose of the for clause is to proclamate to the reader: "the qualified statement is going to be executed once for every i = 1,2,3,....,100". The jump, however, may sneakily cause this promise to be broken! Whereas jumping out of a substructure may be considered to be a matter of morale only, jumping back into a structure even raises technical problems. They require the establishment of protective rules and restrictions which are afflicted by the stigma of improvisation and afterthought. They complicate the language by burdening its definition, its comprehension, and its compiler.

The second example concerns the notion of pointers or references in high-level languages. When programming in assembly code, probably the most powerful pitfall is the possibility to compute the address of a storage cell that is to be changed. The effective address may range over the entire store (and even be that of the instruction itself). A very essential feature of high-level languages is that they permit a conceptual dissection of the store into disjoint parts by declaring distinct variables. The programmer may then rely on the assertion that every assignment affects only that variable which explicitly appears to the left of the assignment operator in his program. He may then focus his attention to the change of that single variable, whereas in machine coding he always has - in principle - to consider the entire store as the state of the computation. The necessary prerequisite for being able to think in terms of safely independent variables is of course the condition that no part of the store may assume more than a single name. Whereas this highly desirable property is sacrificed in Fortran by the use of the "equivalence" statement,

Algol loses it through its generality of parameter mechanism and rule of scope. Even if the sensible rule is observed that a procedure's parameters must denote disjoint variables, one and the same variable may be referred to under more than one name, as shown by the following example.

        begin integer a;
            procedure S(x); integer x;
            begin a := a+1; x := x ↑2
            end;
            a := 1; S(a); write(a)
        end

This design partly stems from the failure to separate the roles of textual abbreviation and of parametric program decomposition, both projected onto the same facility of the procedure. For mere textual abbreviations, one might be more willing to refrain from the use of parameters; in the case of program decomposition, communication with the environment might advantageously be restricted to explicit parameters. Hence, the notion of simplicity and frugality was rather counterproductive when viewed from the point of programming security.

We note that a parameter substitution represents an assignment of the storage address of the actual variable (a) to the formal parameter (x). In the spirit of generalisation it appeared as highly logical to admit the address into the society of computable objects. The address of a variable a - now called a reference - was thus introduced in the language Euler and denoted by @ a . It can be assigned to any other variable, say x . The variable a is then openly available under two names, a and x., and there is no limit to the number of further names that can be given to a . This experiment of reopening Pandora's box of storage addresses in Euler provided a clear warning of their undesirability, but didn't prevent the introduction of references into Algol 68 in their fullest flexibility.

The concept of data type provides added security insofar as a compiler may check against inadvertant use of incompatible variables in, for instance, assignments. This is, in itself, introducing another restriction unknown at the level of machine code, where every cell can be loaded with a copy of every other cell's content. The idea of simplicity through generality again led to the elimination of restrictive type rules, and of the data type in general. It was adopted by a family of languages designed to fill the apparent gap between high-level languages and assembly code, which are now known as machine oriented higher order languages (Mohols). They permit the construction of expressions with "untyped" operands and the application of both arithmetic and logical operations on the same variables. The result of programs written in such languages can only be understood through knowledge of the particular storage representation of data in terms of bits and words. Although effects may be produced that turn out to be the desired ones, they force the programmer to leave the realm of abstraction that a language is pretending to offer him.

So much for the third example of transgression of levels of abstraction in languages.

THE THREE EXAMPLES REVISITED

I do not deny that there are situations in programming which call for facilities not present in Algol-like languages. But they should not be met by compromising on the level of abstraction. The sneaky reintroduction of patently pernicious facilities from the era of machine coding is not an acceptable solution. In order to establish remedies, we must discover the true reasons for the programmers wish of such facilities. The language designer must not ask "what do you want?", but rather "how does your problem arise?" For, the answer to the first question will inevitably be "jumps, type-less operands, and addresses".

To convey an idea of the spirit in which a designer ought to approach such problems, I will sketch possible solutions to the three mentioned cases. The presented features do not provide the full flexibility inherent in jumps, type-less operands, and free address manipulation. But this is precisely their virtue; they still impose certain sensible restrictions of usage, and help maintain a programming discipline. In particular, they do not compromise the language's high level of abstraction; they do not introduce notions which can be explained only in terms of an underlying machine.

In the case of the for statement, what the programmer really needs is not necessarily a jump order, but merely a more flexible way to express termination of a repetition. The solution consists in providing a simpler form of repetitive statement whose termination does not necessarily depend on a variable moving through an arithmetic progression. Widely accepted forms are the while- and repeat statements, for example

$$\text{while } B \text{ do } S$$
$$\text{repeat } S \text{ until } B$$

The important point is that now the total effect of the composite statement can be deduced solely from the properties of the repeated component. The pertinent deduction rule can be formally expressed, for instance in Hoare's formalism (7). If P and Q denote any assertions on the state of the computation, then $P\{S\}Q$ means: if P holds before the execution of S, and this execution terminates, then Q holds after termination. The two deduction rules governing the above statement forms are (8):

$$\frac{P \wedge B \ \{S\} \ P}{P \ \{\text{while } B \text{ do } S\} \ P \wedge \neg B}$$

$$\frac{P \ \{S\} \ Q \ , \ \neg B \wedge Q \ \{S\} \ Q}{P \ \{\text{repeat } S \text{ until } B\} \ Q \wedge B}$$

Another situation requiring the use of a jump in Algol arises when one statement has to be selected among many. A feature invented by Hoare in exactly the same spirit, that not only replaces a jump and a switch declaration, but expresses the selection of one case among many in a structured, orderly way, is the case statement (9).

As for the second example, one may ask why addresses or pointers are needed anyway. I do not intend to pursue this argument here, but claim that if one consents to their necessity, they should be admitted only in a considerably tamed form. Security in pointer handling can be improved drastically by the following measures:

1. Every pointer variable is allowed to point to objects of a single type only (or to none); it is said to be bound to that type. This rule allows to maintain a compiler's capability of full type checking.

2. Pointers may only refer to variables that have no explicit name declared in the program, that is, they point exclusively to anonymous variables allocated when needed during execution. This rule protects the programmer from the dangers arising when variables are accessible under different names.

3. The programmer must explicitly specify whether he refers to a pointer itself or to the object to which the pointer refers (no automatic "coercion"). This rule helps to avoid ambiguous constructs and complicated default conventions liable to misunderstanding.

The reasons why programmers sometimes wish to deal with type-less variables are more difficult to pinpoint. The most frequent one is probably the necessity to pack different kinds of data densely into a single word, which the available language always regards as an indivisible entity. For instance, we might have to pack a triple r - say a file descriptor - consisting of a name x of 6 characters, a 5-bit status information s, and a 2-digit length count n. (The 5 status bits may, for example, indicate a tape's loadpoint, end of tape, and end of record positions, its density mode and parity check status.) A pictorial representation might be

	x	s	n
r	A B C D E F	10001	89
	36	5	7

and a common way to denote the value of such a triple is as an octal (or hexadecimal) number, because the word is available in the language under the misnomer "integer". In order to determine this number, the programmer must forget his original abstractions and perform the binary encoding "by hand". If he is lucky, he obtains

$r = 010203040506 4331_8$ or $r = 0420C41468C9_{16}$

Part of the true information is arithmetic in its nature (n), another is logical (s), and a third alphabetic (x). Hence, all kinds

of orders must be applicable. But this is only possible, if the operand is not restricted by its characterisation through an associated type. What the programmer really needs in this case is a data structuring facility relieving him from the tedious and errorprone labor of data encoding and packing.

As an illustration, in the programming language Pascal the triple r can be directly declared as a structured variable, yielding the dense packing indicated by the picture above (10). The first component of r is declared to be an array of 6 characters, the second to be a set of status indicators, and the third a number in the range of 0 to 99.

```
type string = packed array[0..5] of char;
     indicator = (loadpoint,eof,eor,pchk,
                  highdensity);
var r: packed record
          x: string;
          s: set of indicator;
          n: 0 .. 99
       end
```

Assignments, instead of involving obscure arithmetic operations expressing shifts etc., are simply written as

```
    r.x := 'ABCDEF';
    r.s := [loadpoint,highdensity];
    r.n := 89
```

Each of the three components has a distinct name and a distinct type. Its proper usage can be completely checked by compiler and program reader alike. Naturally, such a structuring facility complicates a compiler considerably, much depending on the quality of the underlying hardware architecture. It even increases the "volume" of a language; but significantly, it does not reduce its conceptual simplicity.

The proposed solutions to the three mentioned problem areas lie in introducing restrictive rules, and are contrary to the spirit of "power through simplicity" and "simplicity through generality". But they have already proven to be wisely chosen precautions and have aided tremendously in practical programming. The additional burden of type checking by the compiler has been much more than compensated by the amount of confidence gained in the final programs. And this is what good language design should mainly aim for.

COMBINING FEATURES INTO A LANGUAGE

A characteristic of a well-designed feature is that is does not imply any unexpected, hidden inefficiencies of implementation. The packed record structure shown above displays this property: a compiler has full knowledge of the address of each such variable and of the position of the components within a word. It can therefore generate appropriate and efficient instructions for access, packing and unpacking. The whole advantage of this scheme, however, immediately vanishes, if, for example, we introduce so-called dynamic arrays, that is, if we allow information about the actual dimensions of an array to

be withheld from the compiler. The textual scan of the program does not reveal the amount of storage needed; as a consequence dynamic allocation must be used involving indirect addressing. This not only impairs the efficiency of the code, but — more importantly — destroys the whole scheme of storage economy.

This is but one example for many that could be listed to show how the combination of two seemingly harmless and well-understood features may suddenly have disastrous effects. A capable language designer must not only be able to select appropriate features, but must also be able to foresee all effects of their being used in combination.

Naturally, one might suggest that a compiler be designed that generates efficient and dense code when the component sizes are known, and less effective code otherwise. But this attitude leads to the optimising monster compilers so well known for their bulkiness and unreliability. Even more significant is the consideration that a good language should not only aid the programmer in avoiding mistakes, but that it must also give him an idea of the complexity and effectiveness of the features it offers. However, if the use of the same feature under only slightly different circumstances yields widely different factors of economy, then the language clearly lacks this highly desirable property. It is very important that the basic method of implementation of each feature can be explained independently from all other features in a manner sufficiently precise to give the programmer a good estimate of the computational effort involved. Some modern languages fail miserably when measured on this criterion.

Transparence is particularly vital with respect to storage allocation and access technique, since storage access is such a frequent operation that any unanticipated, hidden complexity can have disastrous effects of the performance on a whole program. In fact, I found that a large number of programs perform poorly because of the language's tendency to hide "what is going on" with the misguided intention of "not bothering the programmer with details". Transparence of access mechanism can be achieved by neatly categorising data structuring facilities with respect to applicable access technique. This rule was taken as a guiding principle in the design of the language Pascal, which offers the following structuring facilities:

1. Arrays. Components are selected by computable index. Their offset calculation must in general be deferred until execution time (using index registers if available).

2. Records. Components are selected by a fixed selector name. Their address can therefore be evaluated entirely at compile time. As the compiler may retain their offsets individually in a table, the components are not restricted to be of the same size and type, as in the case of arrays.

3. Sets. Components are not individually
selectable at all. Instead, the membership operator <u>in</u> allows to test for their
presence or absence. If the size of sets
is sufficiently small, they can be represented by their characteristic function
fitting into a single word.

4. Files (sequences). Since the length of a
sequence may vary during program execution,
a dynamic allocation mechanism is required.
But it is considerably simplified, because
only sequential access is permitted through
a "window" displaying the component at the
current position.

Variables of these fundamental structures can
either be declared explicitly, or they may be
invoked dynamically. In the first case they
are known by their identifier, in the latter
they must be accessed via pointer.

Knowledge of these access characteristics is
vital for the programmer, as it is indispensible for the selection of data representation
suitable for the algorithm. Regrettably, the
current trend in language design seems to
move in the opposite direction, namely to
obscure these differences. The common excuse
is that through the development of more
suitable and more efficient hardware these
differences would gradually disappear. The
fact remains, however, that supposedly more
suitable hardware becomes phenomenally
complex. It is no longer economical to realise
it directly in terms of electronic circuitry,
and a new technique has therefore been
invented — microprogramming. The essence of
this development is that complicated
features become the standard with their weird
complexity well disguised, and that the programmer is denied the possibility to solve
his tasks by simpler means. He doesn't even
have a possibility to measure the built-in
inefficiencies through quantitative
comparisons!

LANGUAGE DESIGN IS DECISION MAKING

From the foregoing it may appear that the
secret of good language design lies in a few
rules and a sound attitude. In pracitce, of
course, the designer is confronted with a
bewildering variety of demands from various
agents ranging from theoreticians to practitioners, from novices to experts, from
revolutionaries crying for innovations to
conservatives emphasising compatibility. Let
me list a few of the most frequently encountered demands.

- The language must be easy to learn and
  easy to use.

- It must be safe from misinterpretation and
  misuse.

- It must be extensible without change of
  existing features.

- There must be a rigorous, mathematical
  definition, based on axioms and withstanding
  the scrutiny of logicians.

- The notation must be convenient and compatible with widely used (and sometimes not
  so logical) standards.

- The definition must be machine independent,

that is without reference to a particular
mechanism.

- The language must allow to make efficient
  use of the facilities of the available
  computer.

- The compiler must be able to generate
  efficient code and economise storage.

- The compiler must be fast and compact; it
  should be void of complex optimisation
  routines that are rarely used.

- The definition must be self-contained and
  complete. A reader must easily be able to
  identify the facilities needed for his
  purpose.

- The implementation must provide ready
  access to other facilities available on the
  system, such as program libraries and
  (therefore) subprograms written in different
  languages.

- The language and its compiler must be easily
  adaptable to different environments with
  different character sets and different
  operating system facilities.

- The compiler must be easily portable to
  other computers. Almost all of it should be
  conceived without specific reliance on a
  given order code and storage organisation.

- Time and cost for developing compiler and
  documentation must be minimal.

It is plain that several of these points are
contradictory, but certainly not all of them.
The designer must decide where he wishes to
place emphasis. It is his task to find a
carefully balanced compromise. In fact, the
reconciliation of conflicting demands by well
chosen compromises is an essential part of
every engineering profession; language
design should therefore be regarded as a
typical engineering discipline. It can be
mastered only by experience, and experience
is usually gained only after a few failures!
The designer's task is even aggravated by the
fact that the conflicting demands come from
different people whom he is supposed to serve.
Whatever he decides, he should never expect
unanimous approval.

However, I do not wish to convey the impression that sytisfying one criterion must
necessarily mean sacrificing another. True
progress appears through the invention of
facilities that cater to several seemingly
contradictory aims. The three examples
mentioned before demonstrate that such
progress is indeed feasible.

LANGUAGE DESIGN IS COMPILER CONSTRUCTION

In practice, a programming language is as
good as its compiler(s). The believe that it
should first be designed entirely in the
abstract realm of, say, a set of axioms or
an official document, is equally mistaken as
the opinion that it must grow out of a
practical experiment of implementation before
being neatly documented. A successful
language must grow out of clear ideas of
design goals and of <u>simultaneous</u> attempts to
define it in terms of abstract structures,
and to implement it on a computer, or
preferrably even on several computers. It

follows that experience in compiler construction is a prerequisite to successful language design. Compiler design courses have indeed appeared in the curricula of many computer science department, and seem to be regarded as the epitome of the software craft. Unfortunately they are often strongly biased toward the aspect of syntax analysis, since much theoretical work has been done in this subject. However, the deep penetration of this branch of theory has been of rather small benefit to language design and sometimes was even detrimental. I am afraid that it has misled many language designers to believe that the complexity of a language's syntax was of no concern, since an appropriate parsing algorithm, if not already available, could readily be found for any construction introduced. But it is evident that a language that is simple to parse for the compiler, is also simple to parse for the human programmer, and that can only be an asset. Moreover, the real challenge in compiling is not the detection of correct sentential forms, but coping with ill-formed, erroneous programs, in diagnosing the mistakes and in being able to proceed in a sensible way.

The really essential prerequisite for successful compiler construction is experience in the development of large, complex programs. This includes mastery of techniques in structuring programs and data in general, and in selecting methods for various tasks in particular, such as for scanning of text, construction and search of symbol tables, and composition of code sequences.

One is inclined to wonder where the training of so many compiler and language designers will lead, and whether it is justified. Here I should like to point out that a general appreciation of compiler principles will help the understanding of computer operations and promote the state of the art of programming at large. But there is no reason to believe that the growth rate of the population of programming languages is thereby going to decrease. The emphasis in new developments, however, is gradually shifting from general purpose toward application oriented languages. It is precisely toward this trend that design courses should be directed: exposition of features and presentation of techniques that are common to most areas amenable to algorithmic solution. Such features are, for instance, the fundamental control concepts of sequencing, conditioning, selection, repetition, and recursion. They form a well established basis from which a designer can proceed to fill the given framework with specific facilities oriented toward his particular task and area of application (11).

CONCLUSIONS

I have tried to convey a picture of the problems, challenges, and ordeals facing a language designer, and to draw some lessons from experience gained in the design of a series of languages and compilers. To conclude, let me summarise these lessons learned.

- If you wish to develop a language, you must have a clear idea of how it is intended to be used.

- Keep in mind that a programming language is of no use without an efficient, reliable compiler and a clear, readable documentation. This should provide sufficient incentive to keep the language as simple as ever possible.

- Do not equate simplicity with lack of structure or limitless generality, but rather with transparence, clarity of purpose, and integrity of concepts.

- Adhere to a syntactic structure that can be analysed by simple techniques such as recursive descent with one-symbol lookahead. This not only aids a compiler, but also the programmer, and is vital for successful diagnosis of errors.

- Identify the basic abstractions on which the language is to be based. Try to define the language in terms of a mathematical formalism. This may help to detect hidden inconsistencies and to eliminate notions that cannot be understood in terms of the given abstractions.

- Do not consider the establishment of a formal definition as an end in itself. In particular, the formal definition cannot be a substitute for an informal presentation and for tutorial material. It is mostly an aid to the designer but not a user's document, in which mathematical rigor will contribute to volume but seldom serves the programmer's needs.

- Choose the basic features from the same level of abstraction. Obtain a clear idea on how to represent them in terms of a computer's order code and store. Be aware of the consequences arising from the coexistence of all the various features. They can sometimes be surprising and disastrous.

- Do not hesitate to exclude certain features that prove to be incompatible and too costly in terms of implementation. The fact that other languages include them is no guarantee for their indispensability.

- Obtain a sketch of the complete language before starting work on the compiler. Refrain from adopting highly controversial features; language changes are usually costly in time and effort even during development, and are virtually impossible after a compiler's release, if the language is successful.

- Design the language such that most checking operations can be performed at compile time and need not be deferred until execution. The concept of static data types of variables is essential in this respect, and enhances both programming security and system efficiency.

- Keep the responsability for the design of the language (and possible changes) confined to a single person. If implementation work is delegated, keep closely in touch with it, and make sure to obtain adequate feedback. Beware of programmers who will quietly find solutions no matter what they cost.

And finally, when the project is at its end, carefully reassess it, recognise that many aspects could be improved, and do it all over again.

REFERENCES

[1] T.E. Cheatham, Jr., The recent evolution of programming languages, _Information Processing 71_ (ed. C.V. Freimann), North-Holland Publ. Co., Amsterdam, 1972, 298-313.

[2] J. Sammet, Programming languages: history and fundamentals, Prentice-Hall, Englewood-Cliffs, 1969.

[3] P. Naur, Programming languages - Status and trends, _Proc. NordDATA 72_, Helsinki 1972, 36-38.

[4] H.D. Huskey, R. Love, N. Wirth, A syntactic description of BC NELIAC, _Comm. ACM_ vol. _6_, no. 7, 367-375 (July 1963).

[5] A. van Wijngaarden, Generalised ALGOL, Ann. Rev. in _Autom. Programming 3_, (1963) 17-26.

[6] N. Wirth, H. Weber, EULER, A generalization of ALGOL, and its formal description, _Comm. ACM_ vol. _9_, no. 1 and 2, 13-23, 89-99, and no. 12, 878 (Jan., Feb., Dec. 1966).

[7] C.A.R. Hoare, An axiomatic basis for computer programming, _Comm. ACM_ vol. _12_, no. 10, (Oct. 1969) 576-581.

[8] C.A.R. Hoare, N. Wirth, An axiomatic definition of the programming language Pascal, _Acta Informatica_ vol. _2_, (1973) 335-355.

[9] C.A.R. Hoare, Hints on programming language design, SIGACT/SIGPLAN Symposium on priciples of programming languages, Boston, Oct. 1973.

[10] N. Wirth, The programming language Pascal, _Acta Informatica_ vol. _1_, (1971) 35-63.

[11] M.V. Wilkes, The outer and inner syntax of a programming language, _Comp. J._ vol. _11_, no. 3, (Nov. 1968) 260-263.

HINTS ON PROGRAMMING LANGUAGE DESIGN*†

C. A. R. HOARE

Introduction

I would like in this paper to present a philosophy of the design and evaluation of programming languages which I have adopted and developed over a number of years, namely that the primary purpose of a programming language is to help the programmer in the practice of his art. I do not wish to deny that there are many other desirable properties of a programming language—for example, machine independence, stability of specification, use of familiar notations, a large and useful library, existing popularity, or sponsorship by a rich and powerful organization. These aspects are often dominant in the choice of a programming language by its users, but I wish to argue that they ought not to be. I shall therefore express myself strongly. I fear that each reader will find some of my points wildly controversial; I expect he will find other points that are obvious and even boring; I hope that he will find a few points which are new and worth pursuing.

My approach is first to isolate the most difficult aspects of the programmer's task, and state in general terms how a programming language design can assist in meeting these difficulties. I discuss a number of goals which have been followed in the past by language designers, and which I regard as comparatively irrelevant or even illusory. I then turn to particular aspects of familiar high-level programming languages and explain why they are in some respects much better than machine code programming, and in certain cases worse. Finally, I draw a distinction between language feature design and the design of complete languages. The appendix contains an annotated reading list; I recommend it as a general educational background for language designers of the future.

Principles

If a programming language is regarded as a tool to aid the programmer, it should give him the greatest assistance in the most difficult aspects of his art, namely program design, documentation, and debugging.

†Reprinted from *Sigact/Sigplan Symposium on Principles of Programming Languages*, October 1973.

The author is with the Oxford University Computing Laboratory.
*First published as Stanford University Computer Science Department Technical Report No. CS-73-403, Dec. 1973.
EH0164-4/80/0000-0043$00.75 © 1980 IEEE

Program design. The first and very difficult aspect of design is deciding what the program is to do, and formulating this as a clear, precise, and acceptable specification. Often just as difficult is deciding how to do it—how to divide a complex task into simpler subtasks, specify the purpose of each part, and define clear, precise, and efficient interfaces between them. A good programming language should give assistance in expressing not only how the program is to run, but what it is intended to accomplish; and it should enable this to be expressed at various levels, from the overall strategy to the details of coding and data representation. It should assist in establishing and enforcing the programming conventions and disciplines which will ensure harmonious cooperation of the parts of a large program when they are developed separately and finally assembled together.

Programming documentation. The purpose of program documentation is to explain to a human reader the way in which a program works, so that it can be successfully adapted after it goes into service, either to meet the changing requirements of its users, to improve it in the light of increased knowledge, or just to remove latent errors and oversights. The view that documentation is something that is added to a program after it has been commissioned seems to be wrong in principle and counterproductive in practice. Instead, documentation must be regarded as an integral part of the process of design and coding. A good programming language will encourage and assist the programmer to write clear self-documenting code, and even perhaps to develop and display a pleasant style of writing. The readability of programs is immeasurably more important than their writeability.

Program debugging. Program debugging can often be the most tiresome, expensive, and unpredictable phase of program development, particularly at the stage of assembling subprograms written by many programmers over a long period. The best way to reduce these problems is by successful initial design of the program and by careful documentation during the construction of code. But even the best designed and documented programs will contain errors and inadequacies which the computer itself can help to eliminate. A good programming language will give maximum assistance in this. First, the notations should be designed to

reduce as far as possible the scope for coding error; or at least to guarantee that such errors can be detected by a compiler, before the program even begins to run. Certain programming errors cannot always be detected in this way, and must be cheaply detectable at run time; in no case can they be allowed to give rise to machine or implementation dependent effects, which are inexplicable in terms of the language itself. This is a criterion to which I give the name "security." Of course, the compiler itself must be utterly reliable, so that its user has complete confidence that any unexpected effect was obtained by his own program. And the compiler must be compact and fast, so that there is no appreciable delay or cost involved in correcting a program in source code and resubmitting for another run; and the object code too should be fast and efficient, so that extra instructions can be inserted even in large and time-consuming programs in order to help detect their errors or inefficiencies.

A necessary condition for the achievement of any of these objectives is the utmost simplicity in the design of the language. Without simplicity, even the language designer himself cannot evaluate the consequences of his design decisions. Without simplicity, the compiler writer cannot achieve even reliability, and certainly cannot construct compact, fast, and efficient compilers. But the main beneficiary of simplicity is the user of the language. In all spheres of human intellectual and practical activity, from carpentry to golf, from sculpture to space travel, the true craftsman is the one who thoroughly understands his tools. And this applies to programmers too. A programmer who fully understands his language can tackle more complex tasks, and complete them more quickly and more satisfactorily than if he did not. In fact, a programmer's need for an understanding of his language is so great that it is almost impossible to persuade him to change to a new one. No matter what the deficiencies of his current language, he has learned to live with them; he has learned how to mitigate their effects by discipline and documentation, and even to take advantage of them in ways which would be impossible in a new and cleaner language which avoided the deficiency.

It therefore seems especially necessary in the design of a new programming language, intended to attract programmers away from their current high-level language, to pursue the goal of simplicity to an extreme, so that a programmer can readily learn and remember all its features, can select the best facility for each of his purposes, can fully understand the effects and consequences of each decision, and can then concentrate the major part of his intellectual effort on understanding his problem and his programs rather than his tool.

A high standard of simplicity is set by the machine or assembly code programming for a small computer. Such a machine has an extremely uniform structure—for example, a main store consisting of 2^m words numbered consecutively from zero up, a few registers, and a simple synchronous standard interface for communication and control of peripheral equipment. There is a small range of instructions, each of which has a uniform format; and the effect of each instruction is simple, affecting at most one register and one location of store or one peripheral. Even more important, this effect can be described and understood quite independently of every other instruction in the repertoire. And finally, the programmer has an immediate feedback on the compactness and efficiency of his code. Enthusiasts for high-level languages are often surprised at the complexity of the problems which have been tackled with such simple tools.

On larger modern computers, with complex instruction repertoires and even more complex operating systems, it is especially desirable that a high-level language design should aim at the simplicity and clear modular description of the best hardware designs. But the only widely used languages which approach this ideal are Fortran, LISP, and Algol 60, and a few languages developed from them. I fear that most more modern programming languages are getting even more complicated; and it is particularly irritating when their proponents claim that future hardware designs should be oriented toward the implementation of this complexity.

Discussion

The previous two sections have argued that the objective criteria for good language design may be summarized in five catch phrases: simplicity, security, fast translation, efficient object code, and readability. However desirable these may seem, many language designers have adopted alternative principles which belittle the importance of some or all of these criteria, perhaps those which their own languages have failed to achieve.

Simplicity. Some language designers have replaced the objective of simplicity by that of modularity, by which they mean that a programmer who cannot understand the whole of his language can get by with a limited understanding of only part of it. For programs that work as the programmer intended this may be feasible; but if his program does not work, and accidentally invokes some feature of the language which he does not know, he will get into serious trouble. If he is lucky, the implementation will detect his mistake, but he will not be able to understand the diagnostic message. Otherwise, he is even more helpless. If to the complexity of his language is added the complexity of its implementation, the complexity of its operating environment, and even the complexity of institutional standards for the use of the language, it is not surprising that when faced with a complex programming task, so many programmers are overwhelmed.

Another replacement of simplicity as an objective has been orthogonality of design. An example of orthogonality is the provision of complex integers, on the argument that we need reals and integers and complex reals, so why not complex integers? In the early days of hardware design, some very ingenious but arbitrary features turned up in order codes as a result of orthogonal combinations of the function bits of an instruction, on the grounds that some clever programmer would find a use for them—and some clever programmer always did. Hardware designers have now learned more sense; but language designers are clever programmers and have not.

The principles of modularity, or orthogonality, insofar as they contribute to overall simplicity, are an excellent means to an end; but as a substitute for simplicity they are very questionable. Since in practice they have proved to be a technically more difficult achievement than simplicity, it is foolish to adopt them as primary objectives.

Security. The objective of security has also been widely ignored; it is believed instead that coding errors should be removed by the programmer with the assistance of a so-

called "checkout" compiler. But this approach has several practical disadvantages. For example, the debugging compiler and the standard compiler are often not equally reliable. Even if they are, it is impossible to guarantee that they will give the same results, especially on a subtly incorrect program; and when they do not, there is nothing to help the programmer find the mistake. For a large and complex program, the extra inefficiency of the debugging runs may be serious; and even on small programs, the cost of loading a large debugging system can be high. You should always pity the fate of the programmer whose task is so difficult that his program will not fit into the computer together with your sophisticated debugging package. Finally, it is absurd to make elaborate security checks on debugging runs, when no trust is put in the results, and then remove them in production runs, when an erroneous result could be expensive or disastrous. What would we think of a sailing enthusiast who wears his lifejacket when training on dry land, but takes it off as soon as he goes to sea? Fortunately, with a secure language the security is equally tight for production and for debugging.

Fast translation. In the early days of high-level languages, it was openly stated that speed of compilation was of minor importance, because programs would be compiled only once and then executed many times. After a while it was realized that the reverse was often true, that a program would be compiled frequently while it was being debugged. But instead of constructing a fast translator, language designers turned to independent compilation, which permits a programmer to avoid recompiling parts of his program which he has not changed since the last time. But this is a poor substitute for fast compilation, and has many practical disadvantages. Often it encourages or even forces a programmer to split a large program into modules which are too small to express properly the structure of his problem. It entails the use of wide interfaces and cumbersome and expensive parameter lists at inappropriate places. And even worse, it prevents the compiler from adequately checking the validity of these interfaces. It requires additional file space to store bulky intermediate code, in addition to source code which must, of course, never be thrown away. It discourages the programmer from making changes in his data structure or representation, since this would involve a heavy burden of recompilation. And, finally, the linkage editor is often cumbersome to invoke and expensive to execute. And it is all so unnecessary, if the compiler for a good language can work faster than the linkage editor anyway.

If you want to make a fast compiler even faster still, I can suggest three techniques which have all the benefits of independent compilation and none of the disadvantages.

(1) Prescan. The slowest part of a modern fast compiler is the lexical scan which inputs individual characters, assembles them into words or numbers, identifies basic symbols, removes spaces and separates the comments. If the source text of the program can be stored in a compact form in which this character handling does not have to be repeated, compilation time may be halved, with the added advantage that the original source program may still be listed (with suitably elegant indentation); and so the amount of file storage is reduced by a factor considerably greater than two. A similar technique was used by the PACT I assembler for the IBM 701.

(2) Precompile. This is a directive which can be given to the compiler after submitting *any* initial segment of a large program. It causes the compiler to make a complete dump of its workspace, including dictionary and object code, in a specified user file. When the user wishes to add to his program and run it, he directs the compiler to recover the dump and proceed. When his additions are adequately tested, a further precompile instruction can be given. If the programmer needs to modify a precompiled procedure, he can just redeclare it in the block containing his main program, and normal Algol-like scope rules will do the rest. An occasional complete recompilation will consolidate the changes after they have been fully tested. The technique of precompilation is effective only on single-pass compilers; it was successfully incorporated in the Elliott Algol programming system.

(3) Dump. This is an instruction which can be called by the user program during execution, and causes a complete binary dump of its code and workspace into a named user file. The dump can be restored and restarted at the instruction following the dump by an instruction to the operating system. If all necessary data input and initialization is carried out before the dump, the time spent on this as well as recompilation time can be saved. This provides a simple and effective way of achieving the Fortran effect of block data, and was successfully incorporated in the implementation of Elliott Algol.

The one remaining use of independent compilation is to link a high-level language with machine code. But even here independent compilation is the wrong technique, involving all the inefficiency of procedure call and all the complexity of parameter access at just the point where it hurts most. A far better solution is to allow machine code instructions to be inserted in-line within a high-level language program, as was done in Elliott Algol; or better, provide a macro facility for machine code, as in PL/360.

Independent compilation is a solution to yesterday's problems; today it has grown into a problem in its own right. The wise designer will prefer to avoid rather than solve such problems.

Efficient object code. There is another argument which is all too prevalent among enthusiastic language designers—that efficiency of object code is no longer important, that the speed and capacity of computers is increasing and their price is coming down, and the programming language designer might as well take advantage of this. This is an argument that would be quite acceptable if used to justify an efficiency loss of 10 or 20 percent, or even 30 and 40 percent. But all too frequently it is used to justify an efficiency loss of a factor of two, or 10, or even more; and worse, the overhead is not only in time taken but in space occupied by the running program. In no other engineering discipline would such avoidable overhead be tolerated, and it should not be in programming language design, for the following reasons:

- The magnitude of the tasks we wish computers to perform is growing faster than the cost-effectiveness of the hardware.
- However cheap and fast a computer is, it will be cheaper and faster to use it more efficiently.
- In the future we must hope that hardware designers will pay increasing attention to reliability rather than to speed and cost.
- The speed, cost, and reliability of peripheral equipment is not improving at the same rate as those of processors.

• If anyone is to be allowed to introduce inefficiency, it should be the user programmer, not the language designer. The user programmer can take advantage of this freedom to write better structured and clearer programs, and should not have to expend extra effort to obscure the structure and write less clear programs just to regain the efficiency which has been so arrogantly preempted by the language designer.

There is a widespread myth that a language designer can afford to ignore machine efficiency, because it can be regained, when required, by the use of a sophisticated optimizing compiler. This is false; there is nothing that the good engineer can afford to ignore. The only language which has been optimized with general success is Fortran, which was very specifically designed for that very purpose. But even in Fortran, optimization has grave disadvantages:

• An optimizing compiler is usually large, slow, unreliable, and late.
• Even with a reliable compiler, there is no guarantee that an optimized program will have the same results as a normally compiled one.
• A small change in an optimized program may switch off optimization with an unpredictable and unacceptable loss of efficiency.
• The most subtle danger is that optimization tends to remove from the programmer his fundamental control over and responsibility for the quality of his programs.

The solution to these problems is to produce a language for which a simple straightforward "non-pessimising" compiler will produce straightforward object programs of acceptable compactness and efficiency—similar to those produced by a resolutely non-clever (but also non-stupid) machine code programmer. Make sure that the language is sufficiently expressive that most other optimizations can be made in the language itself; and, finally, make the language so simple, clear, regular, and free from side effects that a general machine-independent optimizer can simply translate an inefficient program into a more efficient one with guaranteed identical effects, expressed in the same source language. The fact that the user can inspect the results of optimization in his own language mitigates many of the defects listed above.

Readability. The objective of readability by human beings has sometimes been denied in favor of readability by a machine; and sometimes it has even been denied in favor of abbreviation of writing, achieved by a wealth of default conventions and implicit assumptions. It is, of course, possible for a compiler or service program to expand the abbreviations, fill in the defaults, and make explicit the assumptions. But in practice, experience shows that it is very unlikely that the output of a computer will ever be more readable than its input, except in such trivial but important aspects as improved indentation. Since, in principle, programs should be read by others, or reread by their authors, *before* being submitted to the computer, it would be wise for the programming language designer to concentrate on the easier task of designing a readable language to begin with.

Comment conventions

If the purpose of a programming language is to assist in the documentation of programs, the design of a superb comment convention is obviously our most important concern. In low-level programming, the greater part of the space on each line is devoted to comment. A comment is always terminated by an end of line, and starts either in a fixed column, or with a special symbol allocated for this purpose:

LDA X [THIS IS A COMMENT

The introduction of free format into high-level languages prevents the use of the former method; but it is surprising that few languages have adopted the latter.

Algol 60 has two comment conventions. One is to enclose the text of a comment between the basic word *comment* and a semicolon:

comment this is a comment;

This has several disadvantages over the low-level comment convention:

(1) The basic word *comment* is too long. It occupies space which would be better occupied by the text of the comment and is particularly discouraging to short comments.

(2) The comment can appear only after a *begin* or a semicolon, although it would sometimes be more relevant elsewhere.

(3) If the semicolon at the end is accidentally omitted, the compiler will without warning ignore the next following statement.

(4) One cannot put program text within a comment, since a comment must not contain a semicolon.

The second comment convention of Algol 60 permits a comment between an *end* and the next following semicolon, *end* or *else*. This has proved most unfortunate, since omission of a semicolon has frequently led to ignoring the next following statement:

. . . *end* this is a mistake A[i] : = x;

The Fortran comment convention defines as comment the whole of a line containing a C in the first column:

C   THIS IS A COMMENT

Its main disadvantages are that it does not permit comments on the same line as the code to which they refer, and that it discourages the use of short comments. An unfortunate consequence is that a well-annotated Fortran program occupies many pages, even though the greater part of each page is blank. This in itself makes the program unnecessarily difficult to read and understand.

The comment convention of Cobol suffers from the same disadvantages as Fortran, since it insists that commentary should be a separate paragraph.

More recently designed languages have introduced special bracketing symbols (e.g., /* and */) to enclose comments, which can therefore be placed anywhere in the program text where they are relevant:

/*THIS IS A COMMENT */ .

But there still remains the awkward problem of omitting or mispunching one of the comment brackets. In some languages, this will cause omission of statements between two comments; in others it may cause the whole of the rest of the program to be ignored. Neither of these disasters are likely to occur in low-level programs, where the end of line terminates a comment.

Syntax

Another aspect of programming language design which is often considered trivial or arbitrary is its syntax. But this is also a mistake; the designer should select and observe the best possible syntactic framework for his language, for two important practical reasons:

(1) In a modern fast compiler, a significant time can be taken in assembling characters into meaningful symbols —identifiers, numbers, and basic words—and in checking the context-free structure of the program.

(2) When a program contains a syntactic error, it is important that the compiler should be able to pinpoint the error accurately, to diagnose its cause, recover from it, and continue checking the rest of the program. Recall the first American space probe to Venus, reportedly lost because Fortran cannot recognize a missing comma in a DO statement. In Fortran the statement

$$DO\ 17\ I = 1\ 10$$

looks to the compiler like an assignment to a (probably undeclared) variable DO17I:

$$DO17I = 110$$

In low-level programming, the use of fixed field format neatly solves both problems. The position and length of each meaningful symbol is known, and it can be copied and compared as a whole without even examining the individual characters; and if one field contains an error, it can be immediately pinpointed, and checking can be resumed at the very next field.

Fortunately, free format techniques have been discovered which solve the problems nearly as neatly as fixed format. The use of a finite state machine to define the assembly of characters into symbols, and one of the more restrictive forms of context-free grammars (e.g., precedence or top-down or both) to define the structure of a program—these must be recommended to every language designer. It is certainly possible for a machine to analyze more complex grammars, but there is every indication that the human programmer will find greater difficulty, particularly if an error is present or even only suspected. If a compiler cannot diagnose the syntax of an individual statement until it reaches the end of the program, what hope has a poor human?

As an example of what happens when a language departs from the best known technology, that of context-free syntax, consider the case of the labeled END. This is a convention in PL/I whereby any identifier between an END and its semicolon automatically signals the end of the procedure with that name, and of any enclosed program structure, even if it has no END of its own. At first sight this is a harmless notational convenience which Peter Landin might call "syntactic sugar"; but in practice the consequences are disastrous. If the programmer accidentally omits an END anywhere in his program, it will automatically and without warning be inserted just before the next following labeled END, which is very unlikely to be where it was wanted. Landin's phrase for this would be "syntactic rat poison." Wise programmers have therefore learned to avoid the labeled END, which is a great pity, since if the labeled END was used merely to *check* the correctness of the nesting of statements, it would have been very useful, and permitted earlier and cleaner error recovery, as well as remaining within the disciplines of context-free languages. Here is a classic example of a language feature which combines danger to the programmer with difficulty for the implementor. It is all too easy to reconcile criteria of demerit.

Arithmetic expressions

A major feature of Fortran, which gives it the name FORmula TRANslator, is the introduction of the arithmetic expression. Algol 60 extends this idea by the introduction of a conditional expression. Why is this such an advance over assembly code? The traditional answer is that it appeals to the programmer's familiarity with mathematical notation. But this only leads to the more fundamental question, why is the notation of arithmetic expressions of such benefit to the mathematician? The reason seems to be quite subtle and fundamental. It embodies the principles of structuring, which underlie all our attempts to master a complex problem or control a complex situation by analyzing it into simpler subproblems with clean and narrow interfaces between them.

Consider an arithmetic expression of the form

$$E + F,$$

where E and F may themselves be simple or complex arithmetic expressions. (1) The meaning of this whole expression can be understood wholly in terms of an understanding of the meanings of E and F; (2) the purpose of each part consists solely in its contribution to the purpose of the whole; (3) the meaning of the two parts can be understood wholly independently of each other; (4) if E or F is itself an arithmetic expression, the same structuring principle can be applied to the analysis of the parts as is applied to the understanding of the whole; (5) the interface between the parts is clear, narrow, and well controlled—in this case just a single number. And, finally, (6) the separation of the parts and their relation to the whole is clearly apparent from their written form.

These seem to be six fundamental principles of structuring—transparency of meaning and purpose, independence of parts, recursive application, narrow interfaces, and manifestness of structure. In the case of arithmetic expressions, these six principles are reconciled and achieved together with very high efficiency of implementation. But the applicability of the arithmetic expression is seriously limited by the extreme narrowness of the interface. Often the programmer wishes to deal with much larger data structures—for example, vectors or matrices or lists; and languages such as APL and LISP have permitted the use of expressions with these structures as operands and results. This seems to be an excellent direction of advance in programming language design, particularly for special-purpose languages. But the advance is not purchased without some penalty in efficiency and programmer control. The very reason why arithmetic expressions can be evaluated with such efficiency is that the operands and results of each subexpression are sufficiently small to be held in a high-speed register, or stored and recovered from a mainstore location in a single instruction. When the operands are too large, and especially when they may be partially or wholly stored on backing store, it becomes much more efficient to use updating operations, since then the space occupied by one of the operands can be used to hold the result. It would therefore seem advisable to introduce special notations into

a language to denote such operations as adding one matrix to another, appending one list to another, or making a new entry in a file. For example,

$A . + B$ instead of $A := A + B$ if A and B are matrices

Ll.append(L2)   if L1 and L2 are lists.

Another efficiency problem which arises from the attempt of a language to provide large data structures and built-in operations on them is that the implementation must select a particular machine representation for the data, and use it uniformly, even in cases where other representations might be considerably more efficient. For example, the APL representation is fine for small matrices, but is very inappropriate or even impossible for large and sparse ones. The LISP representation of lists is very efficient for data held wholly in main store, but becomes inefficient when the lists are so long that they must be held on backing store, particularly disks and tapes. Often the efficiency of a representation depends on the relative frequency of various forms of operation, and therefore should be different in different programs, or even be changed from one phase of a program to another.

A solution to this problem is to design a general-purpose language which provides the programmer with the tools to design and implement his own representation for data and code the operations upon it. This is the main justification for the design of "extensible" languages, which so many designers have aimed at, with rather great lack of success. In order to succeed, it will be necessary to recognize the following:

(1) The need for an exceptionally efficient base language in order to define the extensions.

(2) The avoidance of any form of syntactic extension to the language. All that is needed is to extend the meaning of the existing operators of the language, an idea which was called "overloading" by McCarthy.

(3) The complete avoidance of any form of automatic type transfer, coercion, or default convention, other than those implemented as an extension by the programmer himself.

I fear that most designers of extensible languages have spurned the technical simplifications which make them feasible.

Program structures

However far the use of expressions and functional notations may be extended, a programmer will eventually require the capability of updating his environment. Sometimes this will be because he wants to perform input and output, sometimes because it is more efficient to store the results of a computation so that the stored value can be used rather than recomputed at a later time, and sometimes because it is a natural way of representing his problem—for example, in the case of discrete event simulation or the monitoring and control of some real world process.

Thus it is necessary to depart from the welcome simplicity of the mathematical expression, but to attempt to preserve as far as possible the structuring principles which it embodies. Fortunately, Algol 60 (in its compound, conditional, for, and procedure statements) has shown the way in which this can be done. The advantages of the use of these program structures is becoming apparent even to programmers using languages which do not provide the notations to express them.

The introduction of program structures into a language not only helps the programmer, but does not injure the efficiency of an implementation. Indeed, the avoidance of wild jumping will be of positive benefit on machines with slave stores or paging hardware; and if a compiler makes any attempt at optimization, the clear indication of the control structure of a program can only simplify this task.

There is one case where Algol 60 does not provide an appropriate structure, and that is when a selection must be made from more than two alternatives in accordance with some integer value. In this case, the programmer must declare a switch, specifying a list of labels, and then jump to the ith label in this list.

$switch$ SS = L1, L2, L3;

    . . .

    $go\ to$ SS[i];

    L1: Q_1; $go\ to$ L;

    L2: Q_2; $go\ to$ L;

    L3: Q_3;

    L:

Unfortunately, introduction of the switch as a nameable entity is not only an extra complexity in the language and implementation, but gives plenty of scope for tricky programming and even trickier errors, particularly when jumping to some common continuation point on completion of the alternative action.

The first language designers to deal with the problem of the switch proposed to generalize it by providing the concept of the label array, into which the programmer could store label values. This has some peculiarly unpleasant consequences in addition to the disadvantages of the switch. First, it obscures the program, so that its control structure is not apparent from the form of the program, but can be determined only by a run-time trace. And second, the programmer is given the power to jump back into the middle of a block he has already exited, with unpredictable consequences unless a run-time check is inserted. In Algol 60 the scope rules make this error detectable at compile time.

The way to avoid all these problems is a very simple extension to the Algol 60 conditional notation, a construction which I have called the case construction. In this notation, the example of the switch shown above would take the form

    $case$ i of

    {Q_1,

     Q_2,

     Q_3};

This was my first programming language invention, of which I am still most proud, since it appears to bear no trace of compensating disadvantage.

Variables

One of the most powerful and most dangerous aspects of machine code programming is that each individual instruction of the code can change the content of any register, any location of store, and alter the condition of any peripheral; it can even change its neighboring instructions or itself. Worse still, the identity of the location changed is not always apparent from the written form of the instruction; it cannot be

determined until run time, when the values of base registers, index registers, and indirect addresses are known. This does not matter if the program is correct, but if there is the slightest error, even only in a single bit, there is no limit to the damage which may be done, and no limit to the difficulty of tracing the cause of the damage. In summary, the interface between every two consecutive instructions in a machine code program consists of the state of the entire machine—registers, mainstore, backing stores and all peripheral equipment.

In a high-level language, the programmer is deprived of the dangerous power to update his own program while it is running. Even more valuable, he has the power to split his machine into a number of separate variables, arrays, files, etc. When he wishes to update any of these, he must quote its name explicitly on the left of the assignment so that the identity of the part of the machine subject to change is immediately apparent. And, finally, a high-level language can guarantee that all variables are disjoint, and that updating any one of them cannot possibly have any effect on any other.

Unfortunately, many of these advantages are not maintained in the design of procedures and parameters in Algol 60 and other languages. But instead of mending these minor faults, many language designers have preferred to extend them throughout the whole language by introducing the concept of reference, pointer, or indirect address into the language as an assignable item of data. This immediately gives rise in a high-level language to one of the most notorious confusions of machine code, namely that between an address and its contents. Some languages attempt to solve this by even more confusing automatic coercion rules. Worse still, an indirect assignment through a pointer, just as in machine code, can update any store location whatsoever, and the damage is no longer confined to the variable explicitly named as the target of assignment. For example, in Algol 68, the assignment

$$x: = y;$$

always changes x, but the assignment

$$x: = y + 1;$$

if x is a reference variable, may change any other variable (of appropriate type) in the whole machine. One variable it can *never* change is $x!$. Unlike all other values (integers, strings, arrays, files, etc.) references have no meaning independent of a particular run of a program. They cannot be input as data, and they cannot be output as results. If either data or references to data have to be stored on files or backing stores, the problems are immense. And on many machines they have a surprising overhead on performance; for example, they will clog up instruction pipelines, data lookahead, slave stores, and even paging systems. References are like jumps, leading wildly from one part of a data structure to another. Their introduction into high-level languages has been a step backward from which we may never recover.

Block structure

In addition to the advantages of disjoint named variables, high-level languages provide the programmer with a powerful tool for achieving even greater security, namely the scope and locality associated with block structure. In Fortran or

Algol 60, if the programmer needs a variable for the purposes of a particular part of his program, he can declare it locally to that part of the program. This enables the programmer to make manifest in the structure of his program the close association between the variable and the code which uses it; and he can be absolutely confident that no other part of the program, whether written by himself or another, can ever interfere with, or even look at, the variable without his written permission, i.e., unless he passes it as a parameter to a particular named procedure. The use of locality also greatly reduces the width of the interfaces between parts of the program; the fact that programmers no longer need to tell each other the names of their working variables is only one of the beneficial consequences.

Like all the best programming language features, the locality and scope rules of Algol 60 are not only of great assistance to the programmer in the decomposition of his task and the implementation of its subtasks; they also permit economy in the use of machine resources, for example main store. The fact that a group of variables is required for purposes local only to part of a program means that their values will usually be relevant only while that part of the program is being executed. It is therefore possible to reallocate to other purposes the storage assigned to these variables as soon as they are no longer required. Since the blocks of a program in Algol 60 are always completed in the exact reverse of the order in which they were entered, the dynamic reallocation of storage can be accomplished by stack techniques, with small overhead of time and space, or none at all in the case of blocks which are not procedure bodies, for which the administration can be done at compile time. Finally, the programmer is encouraged to declare at the same time those variables which will be used together, and these will be allocated in contiguous locations, which will increase the efficiency of slave storage and paging techniques.

It is worthy of note that the economy of dynamic reallocation is achieved without any risk that the programmer will accidentally refer to a variable that has been reallocated, and this is guaranteed by a compile-time and not a run-time check. All these advantages are achieved in Algol 60 by the close correspondence between the statically visible scope of a variable in a source program and the dynamic lifetime of its storage when the program is run. A language designer should therefore be extremely reluctant to break this correspondence, which can easily be done, for example, by the introduction of references which may point to variables of an exited block. The rules of Algol 68, designed to detect, such so-called "dangling references" at compile time, are both complicated and ineffective; and PL/I does not bother at all.

Procedures and parameters

According to current theories of structured programming, every large-scale programming project involves the design, use, and implementation of a special-purpose programming language, with its own data concepts and primitive operations, specifically oriented to that particular project. The procedure and parameter are the major tool provided for this purpose by high-level languages since Fortran. In itself, this affords all the major advantages claimed for extensible languages. Furthermore, in its implementation as a closed subroutine, the procedure can achieve very great economies of storage at run time. For these reasons, the

language designer should give the greatest attention to this feature of his language. Procedure calls and parameter passing should produce very compact code. Lengthy preludes and postludes must be avoided. The effect of the procedure on its parameters should be clearly manifest from its syntactic form, and should be simple to understand and resistant to error. And, finally, since the procedure interface is so often the interface between major parts of a program, the correctness of its use should be subjected to the most rigorous compile-time check.

The chief defects of the Fortran parameter mechanism are:

(1) It fails to give a notational distinction at the call side between parameters that convey values into a procedure, that convey values out of a procedure, and that do both. This negates many of the advantages which the assignment statement has over machine code programming.

(2) The shibboleth of independent compilation prohibits compile-time checks on parameter passing, just where interface errors are most likely and most disastrous and most difficult to debug.

(3) The ability to define side effects of function calls negates many of the advantages of arithmetic expressions.

At least Fortran permits efficient implementation, unless a misguided but all too frequent attempt is made to permit a mixture of languages across the procedure interface. A subroutine that does not know whether it is being called from Algol or from Fortran has a hard life.

Algol 60 perpetuates all these disadvantages, but not the advantage. The difficulty of compile-time parameter checking is due to the absence of parameter specifications. Even if an implementation insists on full specification (and most do), the programmer has no way of specifying the parameters of a formal procedure parameter. This is one of the excuses for the inefficiency of many Algol implementations. The one great advance of Algol 60 is the value parameter, which is immeasurably superior to the dummy parameter of Fortran and PL/I. What a shame that the name parameter is the default!

But perhaps the most subtle defect of the Algol 60 parameter is that the user is permitted to pass the same variable twice as an actual parameter corresponding to two distinct formal parameters. This immediately violates the principle of disjointness and can lead to many curious, unexpected effects. For example, if a procedure

$$\text{matrix multiply } (A,B,C)$$

is intended to have the effect

$$A := B \times C,$$

it would seem reasonable to square A by

$$\text{matrix multiply } (A,A,A).$$

This error is prohibited in standard Fortran, but few programmers realize it, and it is rarely enforced by compile-time or run-time check. No wonder the procedure interface is the one on which run-time debugging aids have to concentrate.

Types

Among the most trivial but tiresome errors of low-level programming are type errors—for example, using a fixed-point operation to add floating-point numbers, using an address as an integer or vice versa, or forgetting the position of a field in a data structure. The effects of such errors, although fully explicable in terms of bit patterns and machine operations, are so totally unrelated to the concepts in terms of which the programmer is thinking that the detection and correction of such errors can be exceptionally tedious. The trouble is that the hardware of the computer is far too tolerant and forgiving. It is willing to accept almost any sequence of instructions and make sense of them at its own level. That is the secret of the power, flexibility, simplicity, and even reliability of computer hardware, and should therefore be cherished.

But it is also one of the main reasons why we turn to high-level languages, which can eliminate the risk of such error by a compile-time check. The programmer declares the type of each variable, and the compiler can work out the type of each result; it therefore always knows what type of machine code instruction to generate. In cases where there is no meaningful operation (for example, the addition of an integer and a Boolean), the compiler can inform the programmer of his mistake, which is far better than having to chase its curious consequences after the program has run.

However, not all language designers would agree. Some languages, by complex rules of automatic type transfers and coercions, prefer the dangerous tolerance of machine code, but with the following added disadvantages:

(1) The result will often be "nearly" right, so that the programmer has less warning of his error.
(2) The inefficiency of the conversion is often a shock.
(3) The language is much complicated by the rules.
(4) The introduction of genuine language extensibility is made much more difficult.

Apart from the elimination of risk of error, the concept of type is of vital assistance in the design and documentation phases of program development. The design of abstract and concrete data structures is one of the first tools for refining our understanding of problems, and for defining the common interfaces between the parts of a large program. The declaration of the name and structure or range of values of each variable is a most important aspect of clear programming, and the formal description of the relationship of each variable to other program variables is a most important part of its annotation. Finally, an informal description of the purpose of each variable and its manner of use is a most important part of program documentation. In fact, I believe a language should enable the programmer to declare the units in which his numbers are expressed, so that a compiler can check that he is not confusing radians and degrees, adding heights to weights, or comparing meters with yards.

Again not all language designers would agree. Many languages do not require the programmer to declare his variables at all. Instead they define complex default rules which the compiler must apply to undeclared variables. But this can only encourage sloppy program design and documentation, and nullify many of the advantages of block structure and type checking; the default rules soon get so complex that they are very likely to give results not expected by the programmer, and as ludicrously or subtly inappropriate to his intentions as a machine code program which contains a type error.

Of course, wise programmers have learned that it is worthwhile to expend the effort to avoid these dangers. They eagerly scan the compiler listings to ensure that every variable has been declared, and that all the characteristics

assigned to it by default are acceptable. What a pity that the designers of these languages take such trouble to give such trouble to their users and themselves.

Language feature design

This paper has given many practical hints on how *not* to design a programming language. It has even suggested that many recent languages have followed these hints. But there are very few positive hints on what to put into your next language design. Nearly everything I have ever published is full of positive and practical suggestions for programming language features, notations, and implementation methods; furthermore, for the last 10 years, I have tried to pursue the same objectives in language design that I have expounded here, and I have tried to make my proposals as convincing as I could. And yet I have never designed a programming language—only programming language features. It is my belief that these two design activities should be more clearly separated in the future.

(1) The designer of a new feature should concentrate on one feature at a time. If necessary, he should design it in the context of some well known programming language which he likes. He should make sure that his feature mitigates some disadvantage or remedies some incompleteness of the language, without compromising any of its existing merits. He should show how the feature can be simply and efficiently implemented. He should write a section of a user manual, explaining clearly with examples how the feature is intended to be used. He should check carefully that there are not traps lurking for the unwary user, which cannot be checked at compile time. He should write a number of example programs, evaluating all the consequences of using the feature, in comparison with its many alternatives. And, finally, if a simple proof rule can be given for the feature, this would be the final accolade.

(2) The language designer should be familiar with many alternative features designed by others, and should have excellent judgment in choosing the best and rejecting any that are mutually inconsistent. He must be capable of reconciling, by good engineering design, any remaining minor inconsistencies or overlaps between separately designed features. He must have a clear idea of the scope and purpose and range of application of his new language, and how far it should go in size and complexity. He should have the resources to implement the language on one or more machines, to write user manuals, introductory texts, advanced texts; he should construct auxiliary programming aids and library programs and procedures; and, finally, he should have the political will and resources to sell and distribute the language to its intended range of customers. One thing he should not do is to include untried ideas of his own. His task is consolidation, not innovation.

Conclusion

A final hint: listen carefully to what language users *say* they want, until you have an understanding of what they *really* want. Then find some way of achieving the latter at a small fraction of the cost of the former. This is the test of success in language design, and of progress in programming methodology. Perhaps these two are the same subject anyway. ■

Appendix: Annotated reading list

"Report on the Algorithmic Language ALGOL 60," ed. P. Naur, *Comm. ACM*, Vol. 3, 1960, pp. 299-314. The more I ponder the principles of language design and the techniques which put them into practice, the more is my amazement and admiration of Algol 60. Here is a language so far ahead of its time, that it was not only an improvement on its predecessors, but also on nearly all its successors.

Of particular interest are its introduction of all the main program structuring concepts, the simplicity and clarity of its description, rarely equalled and never surpassed. Consider especially the avoidance of abbreviation in the syntax names and equations, and the inclusion of examples in every section.

D. E. Knuth, "The Remaining Troublespots in ALGOL 60," *Comm. ACM*, Vol. 10, No. 10, Oct. 1967, pp. 611-618. Most of these troublespots have been eliminated in the widely used subsets of the language. When you can design a language with so few troublespots, you can be proud. The real remaining troublespot is the declining quality of implementations.

N. Wirth and C. A. R. Hoare, "A Contribution to the Development of ALGOL," *Comm. ACM*, Vol. 9, No. 6, June 1966, pp. 413-432. This language is widely known as Algol W. It remedies many of the defects of Algol 60 and includes many of the good features of Fortran IV and LISP. Its introduction of references avoids most of the defects described above under "Block structure." It has been extremely well implemented on the IBM 360 and has a small and scattered band of devoted followers.

N. Wirth, "PL/360," *J. ACM*, Vol. 15, No. 1, Jan. 1968. This introduces the benefits of program structures to low-level programming for the IBM/360. It was hastily designed and implemented as a tool for implementing Algol W; it excited more interest than Algol W and has been widely imitated on other machines.

N. Wirth, "The Programming Language PASCAL," *Acta Informatica*, Vol. 1, No. 1, 1971, pp. 35-63. Designed to combine the machine-independence of Algol W with the efficiency and control of PL/360. New features are the simple but powerful and efficient type-definition capabilities, including sets and a very clean treatment of files. When used to write its own translator, it achieves a remarkable combination of clarity of structure and detail together with high efficiency in producing good object code.

O-J. Dahl, E. W. Dijkstra, and C. A. R. Hoare, *Structured Programming*, Academic Press, New York, 1972. Expounds a systematic approach to the design and development and documentation of computer programs. The last section is an excellent introduction to SIMULA 67 and the ideas which underlie it.

J. McCarthy, "Recursive Functions of Symbolic Expressions and Their Computation by Machine, Part 1," *Comm. ACM*, Vol. 3, No. 4, Apr. 1960. Describes a beautifully simple and powerful, fully functional language for symbol manipulation. Introduces the scan-mark garbage collection technique, which makes such languages feasible. LISP has some good interactive implementations, widely used in artificial intelligence projects. It has also been extended in many ways, some good and some bad, some local and some short-lived.

"ASA Standard FORTRAN," *Comm. ACM*, Vol. 7, No. 10, Oct. 1964. This language had the right objectives. It introduces the array, the arithmetic expression, and the procedure. The parameter mechanism is very efficient and potentially secure. It has some very efficient implementations for numerical applications. When used outside this field, it is little more helpful or machine-independent than assembly code, and can be remarkably inefficient. Its input/output is cumbersome, prone to error, and surprisingly inefficient. The standardizers have maintained the horrors of early implementations (the equivalence algorithm, second-level definition), and have resolutely set their face against the advance of language design technology, thereby saving it from many later horrors.

"ASA Standard COBOL," *Codasyl COBOL J. Development*, 1968 (National Bureau of Standards Handbook 106). Describes a language suitable for simple applications in business data processing. It contains good data structuring capability, but poor facilities for abstraction. It aimed at readability, but unfortunately achieved only prolixity; it aimed to provide a complete programming tool, in a way few languages have since. It is poor for variable format processing. The primacy of the character data item makes it rather inefficient on modern machines; and the methods provided to regain efficiency (e.g., SYNCHRONIZED) often introduce machine-dependency and insecurity.

Acknowledgments

The form of this paper owes much to the kind suggestions of Don Knuth.

The work on this paper was supported in part by the National Science Foundation under grant number GJ 36473X and by ARPA Research Contract DAHC 15-73-C-0435.

SECTION 2

THE ALGOL FAMILY

REPORT ON THE ALGORITHMIC
LANGUAGE ALGOL 60 BY P. NAUR ET AL.

THE REMAINING TROUBLESPOTS IN
ALGOL 60 BY D. E. KNUTH

A CONTRIBUTION TO THE DEVELOPMENT
OF ALGOL BY C. A. R. HOARE AND
N. WIRTH

A TUTORIAL ON ALGOL 68 BY
A. S. TANENBAUM

AMBIGUITIES AND INSECURITIES IN
PASCAL BY J. WELSH, W. SNEERINGER &
C. A. R. HOARE

AN ASSESSMENT OF THE PROGRAMMING
LANGUAGE PASCAL BY N. WIRTH

INTRODUCTION

THE ALGOL FAMILY

The first paper in this chapter is a *classic* paper in the field of programming languages and it should be read by all computer professionals who regard programming languages as their field of specialization. Why, you ask, is it so important if ALGOL60 hardly ever got used by the computing community? First of all, this statement is not true as ALGOL60 was used extensively throughout western Europe. But it is also important for many other reasons. First of all, this paper has become a model for the way a programming language should be presented. Secondly, it was the paper which introduced Backus-Naur Form (BNF) to the world. Also, ALGOL60 introduced many concepts in programming languages for the first time. And many of those concepts are still in use today. For example if one reads the *Rationale for the Design of Ada*, (ACM Sigplan Notices, July 1979), one sees credit given to ALGOL60 for several of its major features.

As you read the ALGOL60 report take note of the difference between the reference language and the publication language. Note the description of the BNF formalism as it appears for the first time. As one reads the report it is useful to keep in mind a language similar to ALGOL60 which you know well, such as Pascal. Think about what data types are included and which ones are missing. Note the introduction of the **if-then-else** and the statements for loop control such as the **for**-statement. Notice the complete definition of the **for**-statement and compare it to definitions of the same construct in other languages.

On the other hand, notice those things in ALGOL60 which are no longer included in modern programming languages such as **own** variables and switches. Why are they no longer there? Also remember that ALGOL60 included recursive procedures. Can you find where that is mentioned in the report? After reading this article we can still marvel at the step forward that this committee made in language development so early in the history of computers.

But no language definition is entirely free of errors. The second paper in this chapter, by Donald E. Knuth, was written to help identify the *last* remaining trouble spots in ALGOL60. One major problem was the question of side-effects in the order of evaluation of expressions. Knuth points out that if side-effects are to be disallowed then several areas of expression evaluation must be made more precise. Later language definitions have eliminated side-effects in expressions, in part to avoid this need for excessive definition and for the resulting clarity in the semantics of the language. Another area worth studying is the call-by-name parameter mechanism which was introduced for the first time in ALGOL60. Knuth points out a simple program which cannot be implemented because this mechanism is used. Call-by-name has not continued to be incorporated in modern programming languages and so we must conclude that the criticisms of this method are sufficient to outweigh its advantages. And finally, as so many subsequent language designs followed the ALGOL60 tradition, i.e. they were called ALGOL-like, they had to answer the ambiguities which Knuth points out. Thus it is good to keep them in mind as you read the reports of other languages in this section.

The third article in this chapter, by Hoare and Wirth presents the language ALGOL-W. This language was developed in the mid-60s as a direct descendent of ALGOL60. Improving upon the ALGOL60 report, this paper not only includes the definition of the language, but an explanation of many of the features of the language. This explanation constitutes Part I of the paper.

It is necessary to read this paper *after* having read the ALGOL60 report. Many changes (or improvements) have been added, while other features have been removed. Here I will remark upon only a few. For example the call-by-name rule was adopted, as Wirth says, to retain compatibility with ALGOL60. On the other hand an alternative parameter passing method was introduced, called call-by-value-result. The concept of a label was simplified so that labels could no longer be assigned to variables and used in switches. The **case** statement was introduced for the first time. But the major new feature which was introduced in ALGOL-W was the record (though COBOL did have a form of it called a *structure*). Records are collections of heterogeneous data which are dynamically created objects whose lifetime is governed by garbage collection. References to

records is included and the notation for accessing fields of a record is functional in form.

The last major improvement introduced by ALGOL-W which should be studied as you read this paper is the definition of the input/output facilities. ALGOL60 did not define such facilities, feeling that they are necessarily machine dependent. Part III of the report gives a framework in which these facilities are defined. Note how they are given as procedures. The development of a framework in which input/output can be defined has continued to be a serious problem, but languages which choose to avoid the issue are taking the easy way out.

The next paper in this chapter is entitled "A Tutorial on ALGOL68." ALGOL68 is the *official* successor language to ALGOL60. After its introduction it quickly acquired a reputation as being obscure and unintelligible. This was largely due to the fact that the developers introduced a great deal of new terminology. Their purpose was to avoid terms which had vague or conflicting meanings and instead to introduce new terms which were clearly defined. Unfortunately this well-meaning objective subverted their attempt to get the rest of us to read and admire the product of their creation. Nevertheless the language developed a set of adherents and in 1975 a Revised Report was published. This was followed by more readable introductions to the language. The paper included here discusses ALGOL68 as it is defined in its revised version. More importantly it makes a special effort to avoid the use of the new terminology wherever it can be avoided. But before beginning to read this paper one must make a commitment to oneself to remain dedicated to the task at hand. I personally have found that several casual readings have helped, culminated by a complete reading later on.

ALGOL68 has introduced many new and interesting features. Moreover it gives us a chance to see where the design goals of generality and orthogonality can lead. There are some features which ALGOL68 has in common with its predecessors. It is block structured and uses static scoping. The procedure is the major form of abstraction. Its built-in data types, called modes, include the usual integer, real, boolean and char. But there is also included string, complex, bits, bytes, semaphores, formats and files. In fact, ALGOL68 does a lot with modes which even Pascal does not do.

In reading through the paper notice the way arrays can be handled and the form of the control and conditional statements. Coercions or the conversion of one type into another is another area where ALGOL68 has a carefully worked out solution. Another is the determination of type equivalence (it is done structurally). It has been pointed out that the Pascal report did not specify the method for determining type equivalence, but left it to the compiler writers. Finally one should note that the language has provided for concurrent execution of processes and provides a mechanism for their synchronization. In conclusion, ALGOL68 remains an interesting and worthwhile object of study.

The final two papers in this chapter are concerned with Pascal. For those readers who are unfamiliar with Pascal there are many primers which are more than adequate for learning the language. The first paper was written by three people who are strong advocates of Pascal. But in part because of their fondness for the language they have been motivated, like Knuth for ALGOL60, to write about the language's weaknesses. Though several other papers critical of Pascal have appeared, this one provides a balanced and reasonable presentation. One major point in their discussion is the lack of definition of type equivalence. The authors give two possible solutions, termed *name* and *structural equivalence*. Other points include the difficulty of one pass compilation and problems with variant records and procedure parameters. Many of these objections have been cleared up in the new ISO standard version of Pascal, and the paper appearing here was an inspiration to the members of that committee. The second paper on Pascal deserves to be included here as it is by the language's designer, Niklaus Wirth. Here he surveys from his own point of view the strengths and weaknesses, the strong points and the mistakes of the language as he sees them. The two points he raises are the inappropriate definition of files and the trap-door to strong typing using variant records. In the case of file structures, Wirth provides a revised definition. Perhaps the author of the language has not covered the major deficiencies? Dynamic allocation of arrays, separate compilation, a case-statement with an **else** clause have all been proposed as needed improvements.

REPORT ON THE ALGORITHMIC LANGUAGE ALGOL 60*

P. NAUER, EDITOR

Dedicated to the Memory of WILLIAM TURANSKI

SUMMARY

The report gives a complete defining description of the international algorithmic language ALGOL 60. This is a language suitable for expressing a large class of numerical processes in a form sufficiently concise for direct automatic translation into the language of programmed automatic computers.

The introduction contains an account of the preparatory work leading up to the final conference, where the language was defined. In addition, the notions, reference language, publication language and hardware representations are explained.

In the first chapter, a survey of the basic constituents and features of the language is given, and the formal notation, by which the syntactic structure is defined, is explained.

The second chapter lists all the basic symbols, and the syntactic units known as identifiers, numbers and strings are defined. Further, some important notions such as quantity and value are defined.

The third chapter explains the rules for forming expressions and the meaning of these expressions. Three different types of expressions exist: arithmetic, Boolean (logical) and designational.

The fourth chapter describes the operational units of the language, known as statements. The basic statements are: assignment statements (evaluation of a formula), go to statements (explicit break of the sequence of execution of statements), dummy statements, and procedure statements (call for execution of a closed process, defined by a procedure declaration). The formation of more complex structures, having statement character, is explained. These include: conditional statements, for statements, compound statements, and blocks.

In the fifth chapter, the units known as declarations, serving for defining permanent properties of the units entering into a process described in the language, are defined.

The report ends with two detailed examples of the use of the language and an alphabetic index of definitions.

CONTENTS

*Reprinted from *Comm ACM*, 6, 1, 1963, 1–17, copyright 1963.

INTRODUCTION

Background

After the publication of a preliminary report on the algorithmic language ALGOL,[1,2] as prepared at a conference in Zürich in 1958, much interest in the ALGOL language developed.

As a result of an informal meeting held at Mainz in November 1958, about forty interested persons from several European countries held an ALGOL implementation conference in Copenhagen in February 1959. A "hardware group" was formed for working cooperatively right down to the level of the paper tape code. This conference also led to the publication by Regnecentralen, Copenhagen, of an *ALGOL Bulletin*, edited by Peter Naur, which served as a forum for further discussion. During the June 1959 ICIP Conference in Paris several meetings, both formal and informal ones, were held. These meetings revealed some misunderstandings as to the intent of the group which was primarily responsible for the formulation of the language, but at the same time made it clear that there exists a wide appreciation of the effort involved. As a result of the discussions it was decided to hold an international meeting in January 1960 for improving the ALGOL language and preparing a final report. At a European ALGOL Conference in Paris in November 1959 which was attended by about fifty people, seven European representatives were selected to attend the January 1960 Conference, and they represent the following organizations: Association Française de Calcul, British Computer Society, Gesellschaft für Angewandte Mathematik und Mechanik, and Nederlands Rekenmachine Genootschap. The seven representatives held a final preparatory meeting at Mainz in December 1959.

Meanwhile, in the United States, anyone who wished to suggest changes or corrections to ALGOL was requested to send his comments to the *Communications of the ACM*, where they were published. These comments then became the basis of consideration for changes in the ALGOL language. Both the SHARE and USE organizations established ALGOL working groups, and both organizations were represented on the ACM Committee on Programming Languages. The ACM Committee met in Washington in November 1959 and considered all comments on ALGOL that had been sent to the ACM *Communications*. Also, seven representatives were selected to attend the January 1960 international conference. These seven representatives held a final preparatory meeting in Boston in December 1959.

January 1960 Conference

The thirteen representatives,[3] from Denmark, England, France, Germany, Holland, Switzerland, and the United States, conferred in Paris from January 11 to 16, 1960.

Prior to this meeting a completely new draft report was worked out from the preliminary report and the recommendations of the preparatory meetings by Peter Naur and the conference adopted this new form as the basis for its report. The Conference then proceeded to work for agreement on each item of the report. The present report represents the union of the Committee's concepts and the intersection of its agreements.

April 1962 Conference [Edited by M. Woodger]

A meeting of some of the authors of ALGOL 60 was held on April 2–3, 1962 in Rome, Italy, through the facilities and courtesy of the International Computation Centre. The following were present:

Authors	Advisers	Observer
F. L. Bauer	M. Paul	W. L. van der Poel
J. Green	R. Franciotti	(Chairman, IFIP
C. Katz	P. Z. Ingerman	TC 2.1 Working
R. Kogon		Group ALGOL)
(representing J. W. Backus)		
P. Naur		
K. Samelson	G. Seegmüller	
J. H. Wegstein	R. E. Utman	
A. van Wijngaarden		
M. Woodger	P. Landin	

The purpose of the meeting was to correct known errors in, attempt to eliminate apparent ambiguities in, and otherwise clarify the ALGOL 60 Report. Extensions to the language were not considered at the meeting. Various proposals for correction and clarification that were submitted by interested parties in response to the Questionnaire in *ALGOL Bulletin* No. 14 were used as a guide.

This report* constitutes a supplement to the ALGOL 60 Report which should resolve a number of difficulties therein. Not all of the questions raised concerning the original report could be resolved. Rather than risk hastily drawn conclusions on a number of subtle points, which might create new ambiguities, the committee decided to report only those points which they unanimously felt could be stated in clear and unambiguous fashion.

Questions concerned with the following areas are left for further consideration by Working Group 2.1 of IFIP, in the expectation that current work on advanced pro-

---

* [EDITOR'S NOTE. The present edition follows the text which was approved by the Council of IFIP. Although it is not clear from the Introduction, the present version is the original report of the January 1960 conference modified according to the agreements reached during the April 1962 conference. Thus the report mentioned here is incorporated in the present version. The modifications touch the original report in the following sections: Changes of text: 1 with footnote; 2.1 footnote; 2.3; 2.7; 3.3.3; 3.3.4.2; 4.1.3; 4.2.3; 4.2.4; 4.3.4; 4.7.3; 4.7.3.1; 4.7.3.3; 4.7.5.1; 4.7.5.4; 4.7.6; 5; 5.3.3; 5.3.5; 5.4.3; 5.4.4; 5.4.5.   Changes of syntax: 3.4.1; 4.1.1; 4.2.1; 4.5.1.]

[1] Preliminary report—International Algebraic Language. *Comm. ACM 1*, 12 (1958), 8.

[2] Report on the Algorithmic Language ALGOL by the ACM Committee on Programming Languages and the GAMM Committee on Programming, edited by A. J. Perlis and K. Samelson. *Num. Math. 1* (1959), 41–60.

[3] William Turanski of the American group was killed by an automobile just prior to the January 1960 Conference.

gramming languages will lead to better resolution:
1. Side effects of functions
2. The call by name concept
3. **own:** static or dynamic
4. For statement: static or dynamic
5. Conflict between specification and declaration

The authors of the ALGOL 60 Report present at the Rome Conference, being aware of the formation of a Working Group on ALGOL by IFIP, accepted that any collective responsibility which they might have with respect to the development, specification and refinement of the ALGOL language will from now on be transferred to that body.

This report has been reviewed by IFIP TC 2 on Programming Languages in August 1962 and has been approved by the Council of the International Federation for Information Processing.

As with the preliminary ALGOL report, three different levels of language are recognized, namely a Reference Language, a Publication Language and several Hardware Representations.

REFERENCE LANGUAGE

1. It is the working language of the committee.
2. It is the defining language.
3. The characters are determined by ease of mutual understanding and not by any computer limitations, coders notation, or pure mathematical notation.
4. It is the basic reference and guide for compiler builders.
5. It is the guide for all hardware representations.
6. It is the guide for transliterating from publication language to any locally appropriate hardware representations.

7. The main publications of the ALGOL language itself will use the reference representation.

PUBLICATION LANGUAGE

1. The publication language admits variations of the reference language according to usage of printing and handwriting (e.g., subscripts, spaces, exponents, Greek letters).
2. It is used for stating and communicating processes.
3. The characters to be used may be different in different countries, but univocal correspondence with reference representation must be secured.

HARDWARE REPRESENTATIONS

1. Each one of these is a condensation of the reference language enforced by the limited number of characters on standard input equipment.
2. Each one of these uses the character set of a particular computer and is the language accepted by a translator for that computer.
3. Each one of these must be accompanied by a special set of rules for transliterating from Publication or Reference language.

For transliteration between the reference language and a language suitable for publications, among others, the following rules are recommended.

Reference Language	Publication Language
Subscript bracket [ ]	Lowering of the line between the brackets and removal of the brackets
Exponentiation ↑	Raising of the exponent
Parentheses ( )	Any form of parentheses, brackets, braces
Basis of ten 10	Raising of the ten and of the following integral number, inserting of the intended multiplication sign

DESCRIPTION OF THE REFERENCE LANGUAGE

> Was sich überhaupt sagen lässt, lässt
> sich klar sagen; und wovon man nicht
> reden kann, darüber muss man schweigen.
> LUDWIG WITTGENSTEIN.

1. Structure of the Language

As stated in the introduction, the algorithmic language has three different kinds of representations—reference, hardware, and publication—and the development described in the sequel is in terms of the reference representation. This means that all objects defined within the language are represented by a given set of symbols—and it is only in the choice of symbols that the other two representations may differ. Structure and content must be the same for all representations.

The purpose of the algorithmic language is to describe computational processes. The basic concept used for the description of calculating rules is the well-known arithmetic expression containing as constituents numbers, variables, and functions. From such expressions are compounded, by applying rules of arithmetic composition, self-contained units of the language—explicit formulae —called assignment statements.

To show the flow of computational processes, certain nonarithmetic statements and statement clauses are added which may describe, e.g., alternatives, or iterative repetitions of computing statements. Since it is necessary for the function of these statements that one statement refer to another, statements may be provided with labels. A sequence of statements may be enclosed between the statement brackets **begin** and **end** to form a compound statement.

Statements are supported by declarations which are not themselves computing instructions but inform the translator of the existence and certain properties of objects appearing in statements, such as the class of numbers taken on as values by a variable, the dimension of an

array of numbers, or even the set of rules defining a function. A sequence of declarations followed by a sequence of statements and enclosed between **begin** and **end** constitutes a block. Every declaration appears in a block in this way and is valid only for that block.

A program is a block or compound statement which is not contained within another statement and which makes no use of other statements not contained within it.

In the sequel the syntax and semantics of the language will be given.[4]

1.1. FORMALISM FOR SYNTACTIC DESCRIPTION

The syntax will be described with the aid of metalinguistic formulae.[5] Their interpretation is best explained by an example

$$\langle ab\rangle ::= (\mid [\mid \langle ab\rangle (\mid \langle ab\rangle \langle d\rangle$$

Sequences of characters enclosed in the brackets ⟨ ⟩ represent metalinguistic variables whose values are sequences of symbols. The marks ::= and | (the latter with the meaning of **or**) are metalinguistic connectives. Any mark in a formula, which is not a variable or a connective, denotes itself (or the class of marks which are similar to it). Juxtaposition of marks and/or variables in a formula signifies juxtaposition of the sequences denoted. Thus the formula above gives a recursive rule for the formation of values of the variable ⟨ab⟩. It indicates that ⟨ab⟩ may have the value (or [or that given some legitimate value of ⟨ab⟩, another may be formed by following it with the character (or by following it with some value of the variable ⟨d⟩. If the values of ⟨d⟩ are the decimal digits, some values of ⟨ab⟩ are:

$$[(((1(37($$
$$(12345($$
$$((($$
$$[86$$

In order to facilitate the study, the symbols used for distinguishing the metalinguistic variables (i.e. the sequences of characters appearing within the brackets ⟨ ⟩ as ab in the above example) have been chosen to be words describing approximately the nature of the corresponding variable. Where words which have appeared in this manner are used elsewhere in the text they will refer to the corresponding syntactic definition. In addition some formulae have been given in more than one place.

Definition:

$$\langle empty\rangle ::=$$
(i.e. the null string of symbols).

_____

[4] Whenever the precision of arithmetic is stated as being in general not specified, or the outcome of a certain process is left undefined or said to be undefined, this is to be interpreted in the sense that a program only fully defines a computational process if the accompanying information specifies the precision assumed, the kind of arithmetic assumed, and the course of action to be taken in all such cases as may occur during the execution of the computation.

[5] Cf. J. W. Backus, The syntax and semantics of the proposed international algebraic language of the Zürich ACM–GAMM conference. Proc. Internat. Conf. Inf. Proc., UNESCO, Paris, June 1959.

2. Basic Symbols, Identifiers, Numbers, and Strings. Basic Concepts.

The reference language is built up from the following basic symbols:

⟨basic symbol⟩ ::= ⟨letter⟩|⟨digit⟩|⟨logical value⟩|⟨delimiter⟩

2.1. LETTERS

⟨letter⟩ ::= a|b|c|d|e|f|g|h|i|j|k|l|m|n|o|p|q|r|s|t|u|v|w|x|y|z| A|B|C|D|E|F|G|H|I|J|K|L|M|N|O|P|Q|R|S|T|U|V|W|X|Y|Z

This alphabet may arbitrarily be restricted, or extended with any other distinctive character (i.e. character not coinciding with any digit, logical value or delimiter).

Letters do not have individual meaning. They are used for forming identifiers and strings[6] (cf. sections 2.4. Identifiers, 2.6. Strings).

2.2.1. DIGITS

⟨digit⟩ ::= 0|1|2|3|4|5|6|7|8|9

Digits are used for forming numbers, identifiers, and strings.

2.2.2. LOGICAL VALUES

⟨logical value⟩ ::= **true**|**false**

The logical values have a fixed obvious meaning.

2.3. DELIMITERS

⟨delimiter⟩ ::= ⟨operator⟩|⟨separator⟩|⟨bracket⟩|⟨declarator⟩| ⟨specificator⟩
⟨operator⟩ ::= ⟨arithmetic operator⟩|⟨relational operator⟩| ⟨logical operator⟩|⟨sequential operator⟩
⟨arithmetic operator⟩ ::= +|−|×|/|÷|↑
⟨relational operator⟩ ::= <|≤|=|≥|>|≠
⟨logical operator⟩ ::= ≡|⊃|∨|∧|¬
⟨sequential operator⟩ ::= **go to**|**if**|**then**|**else**|**for**|**do**[7]
⟨separator⟩ ::= ,|.|₁₀|:|;|:=|⊔|**step**|**until**|**while**|**comment**
⟨bracket⟩ ::= (|)|[|]|'|'|**begin**|**end**
⟨declarator⟩ ::= **own**|**Boolean**|**integer**|**real**|**array**|**switch**| **procedure**
⟨specificator⟩ ::= **string**|**label**|**value**

Delimiters have a fixed meaning which for the most part is obvious or else will be given at the appropriate place in the sequel.

Typographical features such as blank space or change to a new line have no significance in the reference language. They may, however, be used freely for facilitating reading.

For the purpose of including text among the symbols of

_____

[6] It should be particularly noted that throughout the reference language underlining [in typewritten copy; boldface type in printed copy—Ed.] is used for defining independent basic symbols (see sections 2.2.2 and 2.3). These are understood to have no relation to the individual letters of which they are composed. Within the present report [not including headings—Ed.], boldface will be used for no other purpose.

[7] **do** is used in **for** statements. It has no relation whatsoever to the *do* of the preliminary report, which is not included in ALGOL 60.

a program the following "comment" conventions hold:

The sequence of basic symbols:	is equivalent to
; comment ⟨any sequence not containing ;⟩;	;
begin comment ⟨any sequence not containing ;⟩;	begin
end ⟨any sequence not containing end or ; or else⟩	end

By equivalence is here meant that any of the three structures shown in the left-hand column may be replaced, in any occurrence outside of strings, by the symbol shown on the same line in the right-hand column without any effect on the action of the program. It is further understood that the comment structure encountered first in the text when reading from left to right has precedence in being replaced over later structures contained in the sequence.

2.4. IDENTIFIERS
2.4.1. Syntax

⟨identifier⟩ ::= ⟨letter⟩|⟨identifier⟩⟨letter⟩|⟨identifier⟩⟨digit⟩

2.4.2. Examples

$$q$$
$$Soup$$
$$V17a$$
$$a34kTMNs$$
$$MARILYN$$

2.4.3. Semantics
Identifiers have no inherent meaning, but serve for the identification of simple variables, arrays, labels, switches, and procedures. They may be chosen freely (cf., however, section 3.2.4. Standard Functions).

The same identifier cannot be used to denote two different quantities except when these quantities have disjoint scopes as defined by the declarations of the program (cf. section 2.7. Quantities, Kinds and Scopes, and section 5. Declarations).

2.5. NUMBERS
2.5.1. Syntax

⟨unsigned integer⟩ ::= ⟨digit⟩|⟨unsigned integer⟩⟨digit⟩
⟨integer⟩ ::= ⟨unsigned integer⟩|+⟨unsigned integer⟩|
    −⟨unsigned integer⟩
⟨decimal fraction⟩ ::= .⟨unsigned integer⟩
⟨exponent part⟩ ::= ₁₀⟨integer⟩
⟨decimal number⟩ ::= ⟨unsigned integer⟩|⟨decimal fraction⟩|
    ⟨unsigned integer⟩⟨decimal fraction⟩
⟨unsigned number⟩ ::= ⟨decimal number⟩|⟨exponent part⟩|
    ⟨decimal number⟩⟨exponent part⟩
⟨number⟩ ::= ⟨unsigned number⟩|+⟨unsigned number⟩|
    −⟨unsigned number⟩

2.5.2. Examples

0	−200.084	−.083₁₀−02
177	+07.43₁₀8	−₁₀7
.5384	9.34₁₀+10	₁₀−4
+0.7300	2−₁₀4	+₁₀+5

2.5.3. Semantics
Decimal numbers have their conventional meaning. The exponent part is a scale factor expressed as an integral power of 10.

2.5.4. Types
Integers are of type **integer**. All other numbers are of type **real** (cf. section 5.1. Type Declarations).

2.6. STRINGS
2.6.1. Syntax

⟨proper string⟩ ::= ⟨any sequence of basic symbols not containing ' or '⟩|⟨empty⟩
⟨open string⟩ ::= ⟨proper string⟩|'⟨open string⟩',
    ⟨open string⟩⟨open string⟩
⟨string⟩ ::= '⟨open string⟩'

2.6.2. Examples

'5k,,−'[[['∧=/:'Tt''
'.. This ⊔ is ⊔ a ⊔ 'string''

2.6.3. Semantics
In order to enable the language to handle arbitrary sequences of basic symbols the string quotes ' and ' are introduced. The symbol ⊔ denotes a space. It has no significance outside strings.

Strings are used as actual parameters of procedures (cf. sections 3.2. Function Designators and 4.7. Procedure Statements).

2.7. QUANTITIES, KINDS AND SCOPES
The following kinds of quantities are distinguished: simple variables, arrays, labels, switches, and procedures.

The scope of a quantity is the set of statements and expressions in which the declaration of the identifier associated with that quantity is valid. For labels see section 4.1.3.

2.8. VALUES AND TYPES
A value is an ordered set of numbers (special case: a single number), an ordered set of logical values (special case: a single logical value), or a label.

Certain of the syntactic units are said to possess values. These values will in general change during the execution of the program. The values of expressions and their constituents are defined in section 3. The value of an array identifier is the ordered set of values of the corresponding array of subscripted variables (cf. section 3.1.4.1).

The various "types" (**integer, real, Boolean**) basically denote properties of values. The types associated with syntactic units refer to the values of these units.

3. Expressions

In the language the primary constituents of the programs describing algorithmic processes are arithmetic, Boolean, and designational expressions. Constituents of these expressions, except for certain delimiters, are logical values, numbers, variables, function designators, and elementary arithmetic, relational, logical, and sequential operators. Since the syntactic definition of both variables and function designators contains expressions, the definition of expressions, and their constituents, is necessarily recursive.

⟨expression⟩ ::= ⟨arithmetic expression⟩|⟨Boolean expression⟩|
    ⟨designational expression⟩

3.1. Variables
3.1.1. Syntax

⟨variable identifier⟩ ::= ⟨identifier⟩
⟨simple variable⟩ ::= ⟨variable identifier⟩
⟨subscript expression⟩ ::= ⟨arithmetic expression⟩
⟨subscript list⟩ ::= ⟨subscript expression⟩|⟨subscript list⟩,
  ⟨subscript expression⟩
⟨array identifier⟩ ::= ⟨identifier⟩
⟨subscripted variable⟩ ::= ⟨array identifier⟩[⟨subscript list⟩]
⟨variable⟩ ::= ⟨simple variable⟩|⟨subscripted variable⟩

3.1.2. Examples

epsilon
detA
a17
$Q[7,2]$
$x[sin(n \times pi/2),Q[3,n,4]]$

3.1.3. Semantics

A variable is a designation given to a single value. This value may be used in expressions for forming other values and may be changed at will by means of assignment statements (section 4.2). The type of the value of a particular variable is defined in the declaration for the variable itself (cf. section 5.1. Type Declarations) or for the corresponding array identifier (cf. section 5.2. Array Declarations).

3.1.4. Subscripts

3.1.4.1. Subscripted variables designate values which are components of multidimensional arrays (cf. section 5.2. Array Declarations). Each arithmetic expression of the subscript list occupies one subscript position of the subscripted variable, and is called a subscript. The complete list of subscripts is enclosed in the subscript brackets [ ]. The array component referred to by a subscripted variable is specified by the actual numerical value of its subscripts (cf. section 3.3. Arithmetic Expressions).

3.1.4.2. Each subscript position acts like a variable of type **integer** and the evaluation of the subscript is understood to be equivalent to an assignment to this fictitious variable (cf. section 4.2.4). The value of the subscripted variable is defined only if the value of the subscript expression is within the subscript bounds of the array (cf. section 5.2. Array Declarations).

3.2. Function Designators
3.2.1. Syntax

⟨procedure identifier⟩ ::= ⟨identifier⟩
⟨actual parameter⟩ ::= ⟨string⟩|⟨expression⟩|⟨array identifier⟩|
  ⟨switch identifier⟩|⟨procedure identifier⟩
⟨letter string⟩ ::= ⟨letter⟩|⟨letter string⟩⟨letter⟩
⟨parameter delimiter⟩ ::= ,|)⟨letter string⟩:(
⟨actual parameter list⟩ ::= ⟨actual parameter⟩|
  ⟨actual parameter list⟩⟨parameter delimiter⟩
  ⟨actual parameter⟩
⟨actual parameter part⟩ ::= ⟨empty⟩|(⟨actual parameter list⟩)
⟨function designator⟩ ::= ⟨procedure identifier⟩
  ⟨actual parameter part⟩

3.2.2. Examples

$sin(a-b)$
$J(v+s,n)$
R
$S(s-5)$Temperature:(T)Pressure:(P)
Compile(' := ')Stack:(Q)

3.2.3. Semantics

Function designators define single numerical or logical values, which result through the application of given **sets** of rules defined by a procedure declaration (cf. section 5.4. Procedure Declarations) to fixed sets of actual parameters. The rules governing specification of actual parameters are given in section 4.7. Procedure Statements. Not every procedure declaration defines the value of a function designator.

3.2.4. Standard functions

Certain identifiers should be reserved for the standard functions of analysis, which will be expressed as procedures. It is recommended that this reserved list should contain:

abs(E)   for the modulus (absolute value) of the value of the expression E
sign(E)   for the sign of the value of E($+1$ for E>0, 0 for E$=0$, -1 for E<0)
sqrt(E)   for the square root of the value of E
sin(E)   for the sine of the value of E
cos(E)   for the cosine of the value of E
arctan(E)   for the principal value of the arctangent of the value of E
ln(E)   for the natural logarithm of the value of E
exp(E)   for the exponential function of the value of E (e^E).

These functions are all understood to operate indifferently on arguments both of type **real** and **integer**. They will all yield values of type **real**, except for *sign*(E) which will have values of type **integer**. In a particular representation these functions may be available without explicit declarations (cf. section 5. Declarations).

3.2.5. Transfer functions

It is understood that transfer functions between any pair of quantities and expressions may be defined. Among the standard functions it is recommended that there be one, namely,

$$entier(E),$$

which "transfers" an expression of real type to one of integer type, and assigns to it the value which is the largest integer not greater than the value of E.

3.3. Arithmetic Expressions
3.3.1. Syntax

⟨adding operator⟩ ::= +|−
⟨multiplying operator⟩ ::= ×|/|÷
⟨primary⟩ ::= ⟨unsigned number⟩|⟨variable⟩|
  ⟨function designator⟩|(⟨arithmetic expression⟩)
⟨factor⟩ ::= ⟨primary⟩|⟨factor⟩↑⟨primary⟩
⟨term⟩ ::= ⟨factor⟩|⟨term⟩⟨multiplying operator⟩⟨factor⟩
⟨simple arithmetic expression⟩ ::= ⟨term⟩|
  ⟨adding operator⟩⟨term⟩|⟨simple arithmetic expression⟩
  ⟨adding operator⟩⟨term⟩
⟨if clause⟩ ::= **if** ⟨Boolean expression⟩**then**
⟨arithmetic expression⟩ ::= ⟨simple arithmetic expression⟩|
  ⟨if clause⟩⟨simple arithmetic expression⟩**else**
  ⟨arithmetic expression⟩

3.3.2. Examples

Primaries:

$$7.394_{10}-8$$
$$sum$$
$$w[i+2,8]$$
$$cos(y+z\times 3)$$
$$(a-3/y+vu\uparrow 8)$$

Factors:

$$omega$$
$$sum\uparrow cos(y+z\times 3)$$
$$7.394_{10}-8\uparrow w[i+2,8]\uparrow(a-3/y+vu\uparrow 8)$$

Terms:

$$U$$
$$omega\times sum\uparrow cos(y+z\times 3)/7.394_{10}-8\uparrow w[i+2,8]\uparrow$$
$$(a-3/y+vu\uparrow 8)$$

Simple arithmetic expression:

$$U-Yu+omega\times sum\uparrow cos(y+z\times 3)/7.394_{10}-8\uparrow w[i+2,8]\uparrow$$
$$(a-3/y+vu\uparrow 8)$$

Arithmetic expressions:

$$w\times u-Q(S+Cu)\uparrow 2$$
if $q>0$ **then** $S+3\times Q/A$ **else** $2\times S+3\times q$
if $a<0$ **then** $U+V$ **else if** $a\times b>17$ **then** U/V **else if**
    $k\neq y$ **then** V/U **else** 0
$$a\times sin(omega\times t)$$
$$0.57_{10}12\times a[N\times(N-1)/2, 0]$$
$$(A\times arctan(y)+Z)\uparrow(7+Q)$$
if q **then** $n-1$ **else** n
if $a<0$ **then** A/B **else if** $b=0$ **then** B/A **else** z

3.3.3. Semantics

An arithmetic expression is a rule for computing a numerical value. In case of simple arithmetic expressions this value is obtained by executing the indicated arithmetic operations on the actual numerical values of the primaries of the expression, as explained in detail in section 3.3.4 below. The actual numerical value of a primary is obvious in the case of numbers. For variables it is the current value (assigned last in the dynamic sense), and for function designators it is the value arising from the computing rules defining the procedure (cf. section 5.4.4. Values of Function Designators) when applied to the current values of the procedure parameters given in the expression. Finally, for arithmetic expressions enclosed in parentheses the value must through a recursive analysis be expressed in terms of the values of primaries of the other three kinds.

In the more general arithmetic expressions, which include if clauses, one out of several simple arithmetic expressions is selected on the basis of the actual values of the Boolean expressions (cf. section 3.4. Boolean Expressions). This selection is made as follows: The Boolean expressions of the if clauses are evaluated one by one in sequence from left to right until one having the value **true** is found. The value of the arithmetic expression is then the value of the first arithmetic expression following this Boolean (the largest arithmetic expression found in this position

is understood). The construction:

else ⟨simple arithmetic expression⟩

is equivalent to the construction:

else if true then ⟨simple arithmetic expression⟩

3.3.4. Operators and types

Apart from the Boolean expressions of if clauses, the constituents of simple arithmetic expressions must be of types **real** or **integer** (cf. section 5.1. Type Declarations). The meaning of the basic operators and the types of the expressions to which they lead are given by the following rules:

3.3.4.1. The operators $+$, $-$, and $\times$ have the conventional meaning (addition, subtraction, and multiplication). The type of the expression will be **integer** if both of the operands are of **integer** type, otherwise **real**.

3.3.4.2. The operations ⟨term⟩/⟨factor⟩ and ⟨term⟩ $\div$ ⟨factor⟩ both denote division, to be understood as a multiplication of the term by the reciprocal of the factor with due regard to the rules of precedence (cf. section 3.3.5). Thus for example

$$a/b\times 7/(p-q)\times v/s$$

means

$$((((a\times(b^{-1}))\times 7)\times((p-q)^{-1}))\times v)\times(s^{-1})$$

The operator / is defined for all four combinations of types **real** and **integer** and will yield results of **real** type in any case. The operator $\div$ is defined only for two operands both of type **integer** and will yield a result of type **integer**, mathematically defined as follows:

$$a\div b= sign\ (a/b)\times entier(abs(a/b))$$

(cf. sections 3.2.4 and 3.2.5).

3.3.4.3. The operation ⟨factor⟩↑⟨primary⟩ denotes exponentiation, where the factor is the base and the primary is the exponent. Thus, for example,

$$2\uparrow n\uparrow k \qquad \text{means} \qquad (2^n)^k$$

while

$$2\uparrow(n\uparrow m) \qquad \text{means} \qquad 2^{(n^m)}$$

Writing i for a number of **integer** type, r for a number of **real** type, and a for a number of either **integer** or **real** type, the result is given by the following rules:

$a\uparrow i$ If $i>0$, $a\times a\times \ldots \times a$ (i times), of the same type as a.
    If $i=0$, if $a\neq 0$, 1, of the same type as a.
        if $a=0$, undefined.
    If $i<0$, if $a\neq 0$, $1/(a\times a\times \ldots \times a)$ (the denominator has $-i$ factors), of type **real**.
        if $a=0$, undefined.

$a\uparrow r$ If $a>0$, $exp(r\times ln(a))$, of type **real**.
    If $a=0$, if $r>0$, 0.0, of type **real**.
        if $r\leq 0$, undefined.
    If $a<0$, always undefined.

3.3.5. Precedence of operators

The sequence of operations within one expression is

generally from left to right, with the following additional rules:

3.3.5.1. According to the syntax given in section 3.3.1 the following rules of precedence hold:

$$\text{first:} \quad \uparrow$$
$$\text{second:} \times / \div$$
$$\text{third:} \quad + -$$

3.3.5.2. The expression between a left parenthesis and the matching right parenthesis is evaluated by itself and this value is used in subsequent calculations. Consequently the desired order of execution of operations within an expression can always be arranged by appropriate positioning of parentheses.

3.3.6. Arithmetics of real quantities

Numbers and variables of type **real** must be interpreted in the sense of numerical analysis, i.e. as entities defined inherently with only a finite accuracy. Similarly, the possibility of the occurrence of a finite deviation from the mathematically defined result in any arithmetic expression is explicitly understood. No exact arithmetic will be specified, however, and it is indeed understood that different hardware representations may evaluate arithmetic expressions differently. The control of the possible consequences of such differences must be carried out by the methods of numerical analysis. This control must be considered a part of the process to be described, and will therefore be expressed in terms of the language itself.

3.4. BOOLEAN EXPRESSIONS
3.4.1. Syntax

⟨relational operator⟩ ::= $<|\leq|=|\geq|>|\neq$
⟨relation⟩ ::= ⟨simple arithmetic expression⟩
⟨relational operator⟩⟨simple arithmetic expression⟩
⟨Boolean primary⟩ ::= ⟨logical value⟩|⟨variable⟩|
⟨function designator⟩|⟨relation⟩|(⟨Boolean expression⟩)
⟨Boolean secondary⟩ ::= ⟨Boolean primary⟩|¬⟨Boolean primary⟩
⟨Boolean factor⟩ ::= ⟨Boolean secondary⟩|
⟨Boolean factor⟩∧⟨Boolean secondary⟩
⟨Boolean term⟩ ::= ⟨Boolean factor⟩|⟨Boolean term⟩
∨⟨Boolean factor⟩
⟨implication⟩ ::= ⟨Boolean term⟩|⟨implication⟩⊃⟨Boolean term⟩
⟨simple Boolean⟩ ::= ⟨implication⟩|
⟨simple Boolean⟩≡⟨implication⟩
⟨Boolean expression⟩ ::= ⟨simple Boolean⟩|
⟨if clause⟩⟨simple Boolean⟩ **else** ⟨Boolean expression⟩

3.4.2. Examples

$$x = -2$$
$$Y > V \lor z < q$$
$$a + b > -5 \land z - d > q \uparrow 2$$
$$p \land q \lor x \neq y$$
$$g \equiv \neg a \land b \land \neg c \lor d \lor e \supset \neg f$$
if $k < 1$ **then** $s > w$ **else** $h \leq c$
if if if a **then** b **else** c **then** d **else** f **then** g **else** $h < k$

3.4.3. Semantics

A Boolean expression is a rule for computing a logical value. The principles of evaluation are entirely analogous to those given for arithmetic expressions in section 3.3.3.

3.4.4. Types

Variables and function designators entered as Boolean

primaries must be declared **Boolean** (cf. section 5.1. Type Declarations and section 5.4.4. Values of Function Designators).

3.4.5. The operators

Relations take on the value **true** whenever the corresponding relation is satisfied for the expressions involved, otherwise **false**.

The meaning of the logical operators ¬ (not), ∧ (and), ∨ (or), ⊃ (implies), and ≡ (equivalent), is given by the following function table.

b1	false	false	true	true
b2	false	true	false	true
¬b1	true	true	false	false
b1∧b2	false	false	false	true
b1∨b2	false	true	true	true
b1⊃b2	true	true	false	true
b1≡b2	true	false	false	true

3.4.6. Precedence of operators

The sequence of operations within one expression is generally from left to right, with the following additional rules:

3.4.6.1. According to the syntax given in section 3.4.1 the following rules of precedence hold:

first: arithmetic expressions according to section 3.3.5.
second: $< \leq = \geq > \neq$
third: ¬
fourth: ∧
fifth: ∨
sixth: ⊃
seventh: ≡

3.4.6.2. The use of parentheses will be interpreted in the sense given in section 3.3.5.2.

3.5. DESIGNATIONAL EXPRESSIONS
3.5.1. Syntax

⟨label⟩ ::= ⟨identifier⟩|⟨unsigned integer⟩
⟨switch identifier⟩ ::= ⟨identifier⟩
⟨switch designator⟩ ::= ⟨switch identifier⟩[⟨subscript expression⟩]
⟨simple designational expression⟩ ::= ⟨label⟩|⟨switch designator⟩|
(⟨designational expression⟩)
⟨designational expression⟩ ::= ⟨simple designational expression⟩|
⟨if clause⟩⟨simple designational expression⟩ **else**
⟨designational expression⟩

3.5.2. Examples

17
$p9$
$Choose[n-1]$
$Town[$**if** $y < 0$ **then** N **else** $N+1]$
if $Ab < c$ **then** 17 **else** $q[$**if** $w \leq 0$ **then** 2 **else** $n]$

3.5.3. Semantics

A designational expression is a rule for obtaining a label of a statement (cf. section 4. Statements). Again the principle of the evaluation is entirely analogous to that of arithmetic expressions (section 3.3.3). In the general case the Boolean expressions of the if clauses will select a simple designational expression. If this is a label the desired result is already found. A switch designator refers to the corresponding switch declaration (cf. section 5.3.

Switch Declarations) and by the actual numerical value of its subscript expression selects one of the designational expressions listed in the switch declaration by counting these from left to right. Since the designational expression thus selected may again be a switch designator this evaluation is obviously a recursive process.

3.5.4. The subscript expression

The evaluation of the subscript expression is analogous to that of subscripted variables (cf. section 3.1.4.2). The value of a switch designator is defined only if the subscript expression assumes one of the positive values $1, 2, 3, \ldots, n$, where n is the number of entries in the switch list.

3.5.5. Unsigned integers as labels

Unsigned integers used as labels have the property that leading zeros do not affect their meaning, e.g. 00217 denotes the same label as 217.

4. Statements

The units of operation within the language are called statements. They will normally be executed consecutively as written. However, this sequence of operations may be broken by go to statements, which define their successor explicitly, and shortened by conditional statements, which may cause certain statements to be skipped.

In order to make it possible to define a specific dynamic succession, statements may be provided with labels.

Since sequences of statements may be grouped together into compound statements and blocks the definition of statement must necessarily be recursive. Also since declarations, described in section 5, enter fundamentally into the syntactic structure, the syntactic definition of statements must suppose declarations to be already defined.

4.1. Compound Statements and Blocks
4.1.1. Syntax

⟨unlabelled basic statement⟩ ::= ⟨assignment statement⟩|
   ⟨go to statement⟩|⟨dummy statement⟩|⟨procedure statement⟩
⟨basic statement⟩ ::= ⟨unlabelled basic statement⟩|⟨label⟩:
   ⟨basic statement⟩
⟨unconditional statement⟩ ::= ⟨basic statement⟩|
   ⟨compound statement⟩|⟨block⟩
⟨statement⟩ ::= ⟨unconditional statement⟩|
   ⟨conditional statement⟩|⟨for statement⟩
⟨compound tail⟩ ::= ⟨statement⟩ end |⟨statement⟩ ;
   ⟨compound tail⟩
⟨block head⟩ ::= begin ⟨declaration⟩|⟨block head⟩ ;
   ⟨declaration⟩
⟨unlabelled compound⟩ ::= begin ⟨compound tail⟩
⟨unlabelled block⟩ ::= ⟨block head⟩ ; ⟨compound tail⟩
⟨compound statement⟩ ::= ⟨unlabelled compound⟩|
   ⟨label⟩:⟨compound statement⟩
⟨block⟩ ::= ⟨unlabelled block⟩|⟨label⟩:⟨block⟩
⟨program⟩ ::= ⟨block⟩|⟨compound statement⟩

This syntax may be illustrated as follows: Denoting arbitrary statements, declarations, and labels, by the letters S, D, and L, respectively, the basic syntactic units take the forms:

Compound statement:

L: L: ... begin S ; S ; ... S ; S end

Block:

L: L: ... begin D ; D ; .. D ; S ; S ; ...S ;
   S end

It should be kept in mind that each of the statements S may again be a complete compound statement or block.

4.1.2. Examples

Basic statements:

   $a := p+q$
   go to *Naples*
   START: *CONTINUE*: $W := 7.993$

Compound statement:

   begin $x := 0$; for $y := 1$ step 1 until n do
      $x := x+A[y]$;
      if $x>q$ then go to *STOP* else if $x>w-2$ then
         go to *S* ;
   Aw: *St*: $W := x+bob$ end

Block:

   Q: begin integer i, k ; real w ;
      for $i := 1$ step 1 until m do
      for $k := i+1$ step 1 until m do
      begin $w := A[i, k]$;
         $A[i, k] := A[k, i]$;
         $A[k, i] := w$ end for i and k
   end block Q

4.1.3. Semantics

Every block automatically introduces a new level of nomenclature. This is realized as follows: Any identifier occurring within the block may through a suitable declaration (cf. section 5. Declarations) be specified to be local to the block in question. This means (a) that the entity represented by this identifier inside the block has no existence outside it, and (b) that any entity represented by this identifier outside the block is completely inaccessible inside the block.

Identifiers (except those representing labels) occurring within a block and not being declared to this block will be nonlocal to it, i.e. will represent the same entity inside the block and in the level immediately outside it. A label separated by a colon from a statement, i.e. labelling that statement, behaves as though declared in the head of the smallest embracing block, i.e. the smallest block whose brackets begin and end enclose that statement. In this context a procedure body must be considered as if it were enclosed by begin and end and treated as a block.

Since a statement of a block may again itself be a block the concepts local and nonlocal to a block must be understood recursively. Thus an identifier, which is nonlocal to a block A, may or may not be nonlocal to the block B in which A is one statement.

4.2. Assignment Statements
4.2.1. Syntax

⟨left part⟩ ::= ⟨variable⟩ := |⟨procedure identifier⟩ :=
⟨left part list⟩ ::= ⟨left part⟩|⟨left part list⟩⟨left part⟩
⟨assignment statement⟩ ::= ⟨left part list⟩⟨arithmetic expression⟩|
   ⟨left part list⟩⟨Boolean expression⟩

4.2.2. Examples

$$s := p[0] := n := n+1+s$$
$$n := n+1$$
$$A := B/C-v-q \times S$$
$$S[v,k+2] := 3-arctan(s \times zeta)$$
$$V := Q > Y \wedge Z$$

4.2.3. Semantics

Assignment statements serve for assigning the value of an expression to one or several variables or procedure identifiers. Assignment to a procedure identifier may only occur within the body of a procedure defining the value of a function designator (cf. section 5.4.4). The process will in the general case be understood to take place in three steps as follows:

4.2.3.1. Any subscript expressions occurring in the left part variables are evaluated in sequence from left to right.

4.2.3.2. The expression of the statement is evaluated.

4.2.3.3. The value of the expression is assigned to all the left part variables, with any subscript expressions having values as evaluated in step 4.2.3.1.

4.2.4. Types

The type associated with all variables and procedure identifiers of a left part list must be the same. If this type is **Boolean,** the expression must likewise be **Boolean.** If the type is **real** or **integer,** the expression must be arithmetic. If the type of the arithmetic expression differs from that associated with the variables and procedure identifiers, appropriate transfer functions are understood to be automatically invoked. For transfer from **real** to **integer** type, the transfer function is understood to yield a result equivalent to

$$entier(E+0.5)$$

where E is the value of the expression. The type associated with a procedure identifier is given by the declarator which appears as the first symbol of the corresponding procedure declaration (cf. section 5.4.4).

4.3. Go To Statements

4.3.1. Syntax

⟨go to statement⟩ ::= **go to** ⟨designational expression⟩

4.3.2. Examples

```
go to 8
go to exit [n+1]
go to Town[if y<0 then N else N+1]
go to if Ab<c then 17 else q[if w<0 then 2 else n]
```

4.3.3. Semantics

A go to statement interrupts the normal sequence of operations, defined by the write-up of statements, by defining its successor explicitly by the value of a designational expression. Thus the next statement to be executed will be the one having this value as its label.

4.3.4. Restriction

Since labels are inherently local, no go to statement can lead from outside into a block. A go to statement may, however, lead from outside into a compound statement.

4.3.5. Go to an undefined switch designator

A go to statement is equivalent to a dummy statement if the designational expression is a switch designator whose value is undefined.

4.4. Dummy Statements

4.4.1. Syntax

⟨dummy statement⟩ ::= ⟨empty⟩

4.4.2. Examples

```
L:
begin ...  ;  John: end
```

4.4.3. Semantics

A dummy statement executes no operation. It may serve to place a label.

4.5. Conditional Statements

4.5.1. Syntax

⟨if clause⟩ ::= **if** ⟨Boolean expression⟩ **then**
⟨unconditional statement⟩ ::= ⟨basic statement⟩|
    ⟨compound statement⟩|⟨block⟩
⟨if statement⟩ ::= ⟨if clause⟩ ⟨unconditional statement⟩
⟨conditional statement⟩ ::= ⟨if statement⟩|⟨if statement⟩ **else**
    ⟨statement⟩|⟨if clause⟩⟨for statement⟩|
    ⟨label⟩ : ⟨conditional statement⟩

4.5.2. Examples

```
if x>0 then n := n+1
if v>u then V: q:= n+m else go to R
if s<0∨P≤Q then AA: begin if q<v then a := v/s
            else y := 2×a end
        else if v>s then a := v-q else if v>s-1
        then go to S
```

4.5.3. Semantics

Conditional statements cause certain statements to be executed or skipped depending on the running values of specified Boolean expressions.

4.5.3.1. If statement. The unconditional statement of an if statement will be executed if the Boolean expression of the if clause is true. Otherwise it will be skipped and the operation will be continued with the next statement.

4.5.3.2. Conditional statement. According to the syntax two different forms of conditional statements are possible. These may be illustrated as follows:

if B1 **then** S1 **else if** B2 **then** S2 **else** S3 ; S4

and

if B1 **then** S1 **else if** B2 **then** S2 **else if** B3 **then** S3 ; S4

Here B1 to B3 are Boolean expressions, while S1 to S3 are unconditional statements. S4 is the statement following the complete conditional statement.

The execution of a conditional statement may be described as follows: The Boolean expression of the if clauses are evaluated one after the other in sequence from left to right until one yielding the value **true** is found. Then the unconditional statement following this Boolean is executed. Unless this statement defines its successor explicitly the next statement to be executed will be S4, i.e. the state-

ment following the complete conditional statement. Thus the effect of the delimiter **else** may be described by saying that it defines the successor of the statement it follows to be the statement following the complete conditional statement.

The construction

else ⟨unconditional statement⟩

is equivalent to

else if true then ⟨unconditional statement⟩

If none of the Boolean expressions of the if clauses is true, the effect of the whole conditional statement will be equivalent to that of a dummy statement.

For further explanation the following picture may be useful:

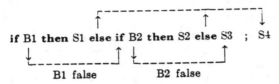

if B1 then S1 else if B2 then S2 else S3 ; S4

B1 false   B2 false

4.5.4. Go to into a conditional statement

The effect of a go to statement leading into a conditional statement follows directly from the above explanation of the effect of **else**.

4.6. FOR STATEMENTS

4.6.1. Syntax

⟨for list element⟩ ::= ⟨arithmetic expression⟩|
⟨arithmetic expression⟩ **step** ⟨arithmetic expression⟩ **until**
⟨arithmetic expression⟩|⟨arithmetic expression⟩ **while**
⟨Boolean expression⟩
⟨for list⟩ ::= ⟨for list element⟩|⟨for list⟩ , ⟨for list element⟩
⟨for clause⟩ ::= **for** ⟨variable⟩ := ⟨for list⟩ **do**
⟨for statement⟩ ::= ⟨for clause⟩⟨statement⟩|
⟨label⟩: ⟨for statement⟩

4.6.2. Examples

for q := 1 **step** s **until** n **do** $A[q]$:= $B[q]$
for k := 1, $V1 \times 2$ **while** $V1 < N$ **do**
    for j := $I+G$, L, 1 **step** 1 **until** N, $C+D$ **do**
        $A[k,j]$:= $B[k,j]$

4.6.3. Semantics

A for clause causes the statement S which it precedes to be repeatedly executed zero or more times. In addition it performs a sequence of assignments to its controlled variable. The process may be visualized by means of the following picture:

Initialize ; test ; statement S ; advance ; successor

for list exhausted

In this picture the word initialize means: perform the first assignment of the for clause. Advance means: perform the next assignment of the for clause. Test determines if the last assignment has been done. If so, the execution con-

tinues with the successor of the for statement. If not, the statement following the for clause is executed.

4.6.4. The for list elements

The for list gives a rule for obtaining the values which are consecutively assigned to the controlled variable. This sequence of values is obtained from the for list elements by taking these one by one in the order in which they are written. The sequence of values generated by each of the three species of for list elements and the corresponding execution of the statement S are given by the following rules:

4.6.4.1. Arithmetic expression. This element gives rise to one value, namely the value of the given arithmetic expression as calculated immediately before the corresponding execution of the statement S.

4.6.4.2. Step-until-element. An element of the form A **step** B **until** C, where A, B, and C, are arithmetic expressions, gives rise to an execution which may be described most concisely in terms of additional ALGOL statements as follows:

V := A ;
L1: **if** $(V-C) \times sign(B) > 0$ **then go to** *element exhausted*;
    statement S ;
    V := V+B ;
    go to L1 ;

where V is the controlled variable of the for clause and *element exhausted* points to the evaluation according to the next element in the for list, or if the step-until-element is the last of the list, to the next statement in the program.

4.6.4.3. While-element. The execution governed by a for list element of the form E **while** F, where E is an arithmetic and F a Boolean expression, is most concisely described in terms of additional ALGOL statements as follows:

L3: V := E ;
    if $-F$ **then go to** *element exhausted* ;
    Statement S ;
    go to L3 ;

where the notation is the same as in 4.6.4.2 above.

4.6.5. The value of the controlled variable upon exit

Upon exit out of the statement S (supposed to be compound) through a go to statement the value of the controlled variable will be the same as it was immediately preceding the execution of the go to statement.

If the exit is due to exhaustion of the for list, on the other hand, the value of the controlled variable is undefined after the exit.

4.6.6. Go to leading into a for statement

The effect of a go to statement, outside a for statement, which refers to a label within the for statement, is undefined.

4.7. PROCEDURE STATEMENTS

4.7.1. Syntax

⟨actual parameter⟩ ::= ⟨string⟩|⟨expression⟩|⟨array identifier⟩|
⟨switch identifier⟩|⟨procedure identifier⟩
⟨letter string⟩ ::= ⟨letter⟩|⟨letter string⟩⟨letter⟩

⟨parameter delimiter⟩ ::= ,|)⟨letter string⟩:(
⟨actual parameter list⟩ ::= ⟨actual parameter⟩|
   ⟨actual parameter list⟩⟨parameter delimiter⟩
   ⟨actual parameter⟩
⟨actual parameter part⟩ ::= ⟨empty⟩|
   (⟨actual parameter list⟩)
⟨procedure statement⟩ ::= ⟨procedure identifier⟩
   ⟨actual parameter part⟩

4.7.2. Examples

Spur (A)Order: (7)Result to: (V)
Transpose ($W,v+1$)
Absmax(A,N,M,Yy,I,K)
Innerproduct($A[t,P,u],B[P],10,P,Y$)

These examples correspond to examples given in section 5.4.2.

4.7.3. Semantics

A procedure statement serves to invoke (call for) the execution of a procedure body (cf. section 5.4. Procedure Declarations). Where the procedure body is a statement written in ALGOL the effect of this execution will be equivalent to the effect of performing the following operations on the program at the time of execution of the procedure statement:

4.7.3.1. Value assignment (call by value)

All formal parameters quoted in the value part of the procedure declaration heading are assigned the values (cf. section 2.8. Values and Types) of the corresponding actual parameters, these assignments being considered as being performed explicitly before entering the procedure body. The effect is as though an additional block embracing the procedure body were created in which these assignments were made to variables local to this fictitious block with types as given in the corresponding specifications (cf. section 5.4.5). As a consequence, variables called by value are to be considered as nonlocal to the body of the procedure, but local to the fictitious block (cf. section 5.4.3).

4.7.3.2. Name replacement (call by name)

Any formal parameter not quoted in the value list is replaced, throughout the procedure body, by the corresponding actual parameter, after enclosing this latter in parentheses wherever syntactically possible. Possible conflicts between identifiers inserted through this process and other identifiers already present within the procedure body will be avoided by suitable systematic changes of the formal or local identifiers involved.

4.7.3.3. Body replacement and execution

Finally the procedure body, modified as above, is inserted in place of the procedure statement and executed. If the procedure is called from a place outside the scope of any nonlocal quantity of the procedure body the conflicts between the identifiers inserted through this process of body replacement and the identifiers whose declarations are valid at the place of the procedure statement or function designator will be avoided through suitable systematic changes of the latter identifiers.

4.7.4. Actual-formal correspondence

The correspondence between the actual parameters of the procedure statement and the formal parameters of the procedure heading is established as follows: The actual parameter list of the procedure statement must have the same number of entries as the formal parameter list of the procedure declaration heading. The correspondence is obtained by taking the entries of these two lists in the same order.

4.7.5. Restrictions

For a procedure statement to be defined it is evidently necessary that the operations on the procedure body defined in sections 4.7.3.1 and 4.7.3.2 lead to a correct ALGOL statement.

This imposes the restriction on any procedure statement that the kind and type of each actual parameter be compatible with the kind and type of the corresponding formal parameter. Some important particular cases of this general rule are the following:

4.7.5.1.
If a string is supplied as an actual parameter in a procedure statement or function designator, whose defining procedure body is an ALGOL 60 statement (as opposed to non-ALGOL code, cf. section 4.7.8), then this string can only be used within the procedure body as an actual parameter in further procedure calls. Ultimately it can only be used by a procedure body expressed in non-ALGOL code.

4.7.5.2.
A formal parameter which occurs as a left part variable in an assignment statement within the procedure body and which is not called by value can only correspond to an actual parameter which is a variable (special case of expression).

4.7.5.3.
A formal parameter which is used within the procedure body as an array identifier can only correspond to an actual parameter which is an array identifier of an array of the same dimensions. In addition if the formal parameter is called by value the local array created during the call will have the same subscript bounds as the actual array.

4.7.5.4.
A formal parameter which is called by value cannot in general correspond to a switch identifier or a procedure identifier or a string, because these latter do not possess values (the exception is the procedure identifier of a procedure declaration which has an empty formal parameter part (cf. section 5.4.1) and which defines the value of a function designator (cf. section 5.4.4). This procedure identifier is in itself a complete expression).

4.7.5.5.
Any formal parameter may have restrictions on the type of the corresponding actual parameter associated with it (these restrictions may, or may not, be given through specifications in the procedure heading). In the procedure statement such restrictions must evidently be observed.

4.7.6. Deleted.

4.7.7. Parameter delimiters

All parameter delimiters are understood to be equivalent. No correspondence between the parameter delimiters used in a procedure statement and those used in the procedure heading is expected beyond their number being the

same. Thus the information conveyed by using the elaborate ones is entirely optional.

4.7.8. Procedure body expressed in code

The restrictions imposed on a procedure statement calling a procedure having its body expressed in non-ALGOL code evidently can only be derived from the characteristics of the code used and the intent of the user and thus fall outside the scope of the reference language.

5. Declarations

Declarations serve to define certain properties of the quantities used in the program, and to associate them with identifiers. A declaration of an identifier is valid for one block. Outside this block the particular identifier may be used for other purposes (cf. section 4.1.3).

Dynamically this implies the following: at the time of an entry into a block (through the **begin**, since the labels inside are local and therefore inaccessible from outside) all identifiers declared for the block assume the significance implied by the nature of the declarations given. If these identifiers had already been defined by other declarations outside they are for the time being given a new significance. Identifiers which are not declared for the block, on the other hand, retain their old meaning.

At the time of an exit from a block (through **end**, or by a go to statement) all identifiers which are declared for the block lose their local significance.

A declaration may be marked with the additional declarator **own**. This has the following effect: upon a re-entry into the block, the values of own quantities will be unchanged from their values at the last exit, while the values of declared variables which are not marked as own are undefined. Apart from labels and formal parameters of procedure declarations and with the possible exception of those for standard functions (cf. sections 3.2.4 and 3.2.5), all identifiers of a program must be declared. No identifier may be declared more than once in any one block head.

Syntax.

⟨declaration⟩ ::= ⟨type declaration⟩|⟨array declaration⟩|
    ⟨switch declaration⟩|⟨procedure declaration⟩

5.1. TYPE DECLARATIONS
5.1.1. Syntax

⟨type list⟩ ::= ⟨simple variable⟩|
    ⟨simple variable⟩ , ⟨type list⟩
⟨type⟩ ::= **real** | **integer** | **Boolean**
⟨local or own type⟩ ::= ⟨type⟩|**own** ⟨type⟩
⟨type declaration⟩ ::= ⟨local or own type⟩⟨type list⟩

5.1.2. Examples

    integer p,q,s
    own Boolean $Acryl,n$

5.1.3. Semantics

Type declarations serve to declare certain identifiers to represent simple variables of a given type. Real declared variables may only assume positive or negative values

including zero. Integer declared variables may only assume positive and negative integral values including zero. Boolean declared variables may only assume the values **true** and **false**.

In arithmetic expressions any position which can be occupied by a real declared variable may be occupied by an integer declared variable.

For the semantics of **own**, see the fourth paragraph of section 5 above.

5.2. ARRAY DECLARATIONS
5.2.1. Syntax

⟨lower bound⟩ ::= ⟨arithmetic expression⟩
⟨upper bound⟩ ::= ⟨arithmetic expression⟩
⟨bound pair⟩ ::= ⟨lower bound⟩:⟨upper bound⟩
⟨bound pair list⟩ ::= ⟨bound pair⟩|⟨bound pair list⟩,⟨bound pair⟩
⟨array segment⟩ ::= ⟨array identifier⟩[⟨bound pair list⟩]|
    ⟨array identifier⟩,⟨array segment⟩
⟨array list⟩ ::= ⟨array segment⟩|⟨array list⟩,⟨array segment⟩
⟨array declaration⟩ ::= **array** ⟨array list⟩|⟨local or own type⟩
    array ⟨array list⟩

5.2.2. Examples

    array a, b, $c[7:n,2:m]$, $s[-2:10]$
    own integer array $A[$**if** $c<0$ **then** 2 **else** $1:20]$
    real array $q[-7:-1]$

5.2.3. Semantics

An array declaration declares one or several identifiers to represent multidimensional arrays of subscripted variables and gives the dimensions of the arrays, the bounds of the subscripts and the types of the variables.

5.2.3.1. Subscript bounds. The subscript bounds for any array are given in the first subscript bracket following the identifier of this array in the form of a bound pair list. Each item of this list gives the lower and upper bound of a subscript in the form of two arithmetic expressions separated by the delimiter : The bound pair list gives the bounds of all subscripts taken in order from left to right.

5.2.3.2. Dimensions. The dimensions are given as the number of entries in the bound pair lists.

5.2.3.3. Types. All arrays declared in one declaration are of the same quoted type. If no type declarator is given the type **real** is understood.

5.2.4. Lower upper bound expressions

5.2.4.1 The expressions will be evaluated in the same way as subscript expressions (cf. section 3.1.4.2).

5.2.4.2. The expressions can only depend on variables and procedures which are nonlocal to the block for which the array declaration is valid. Consequently in the outermost block of a program only array declarations with constant bounds may be declared.

5.2.4.3. An array is defined only when the values of all upper subscript bounds are not smaller than those of the corresponding lower bounds.

5.2.4.4. The expressions will be evaluated once at each entrance into the block.

5.2.5. The identity of subscripted variables

The identity of a subscripted variable is not related to the subscript bounds given in the array declaration. How-

ever, even if an array is declared **own** the values of the corresponding subscripted variables will, at any time, be defined only for those of these variables which have subscripts within the most recently calculated subscript bounds.

5.3. Switch Declarations
5.3.1. Syntax

⟨switch list⟩ ::= ⟨designational expression⟩|
  ⟨switch list⟩,⟨designational expression⟩
⟨switch declaration⟩ ::= **switch** ⟨switch identifier⟩:= ⟨switch list⟩

5.3.2. Examples

switch S := $S1,S2,Q[m]$, **if** $v>-5$ **then** $S3$ **else** $S4$
switch Q := $p1,w$

5.3.3. Semantics

A switch declaration defines the set of values of the corresponding switch designators. These values are given one by one as the values of the designational expressions entered in the switch list. With each of these designational expressions there is associated a positive integer, 1, 2, ... , obtained by counting the items in the list from left to right. The value of the switch designator corresponding to a given value of the subscript expression (cf. section 3.5. Designational Expressions) is the value of the designational expression in the switch list having this given value as its associated integer.

5.3.4. Evaluation of expressions in the switch list

An expression in the switch list will be evaluated every time the item of the list in which the expression occurs is referred to, using the current values of all variables involved.

5.3.5. Influence of scopes

If a switch designator occurs outside the scope of a quantity entering into a designational expression in the switch list, and an evaluation of this switch designator selects this designational expression, then the conflicts between the identifiers for the quantities in this expression and the identifiers whose declarations are valid at the place of the switch designator will be avoided through suitable systematic changes of the latter identifiers.

5.4. Procedure Declarations
5.4.1. Syntax

⟨formal parameter⟩ ::= ⟨identifier⟩
⟨formal parameter list⟩ ::= ⟨formal parameter⟩|
  ⟨formal parameter list⟩⟨parameter delimiter⟩
  ⟨formal parameter⟩
⟨formal parameter part⟩ ::= ⟨empty⟩|(⟨formal parameter list⟩)
⟨identifier list⟩ ::= ⟨identifier⟩|⟨identifier list⟩,⟨identifier⟩
⟨value part⟩ ::= **value**⟨identifier list⟩ ; |⟨empty⟩
⟨specifier⟩ ::= **string**|⟨type⟩|**array**|⟨type⟩**array**|**label**|**switch**|
  procedure|⟨type⟩**procedure**
⟨specification part⟩ ::= ⟨empty⟩|⟨specifier⟩⟨identifier list⟩ ; |
  ⟨specification part⟩⟨specifier⟩⟨identifier list⟩ ;
⟨procedure heading⟩ ::= ⟨procedure identifier⟩
  ⟨formal parameter part⟩ ; ⟨value part⟩⟨specification part⟩
⟨procedure body⟩ ::= ⟨statement⟩|⟨code⟩
⟨procedure declaration⟩ ::=
  procedure ⟨procedure heading⟩⟨procedure body⟩|
  ⟨type⟩ **procedure** ⟨procedure heading⟩⟨procedure body⟩

5.4.2. Examples (see also the examples at the end of the report)

procedure $Spur(a)$Order:(n)Result:(s) ; **value** n ;
array a ; **integer** n ; **real** s ;
begin integer k ;
s := 0 ;
for k := 1 **step** 1 **until** n **do** s := $s+a[k,k]$
end

procedure $Transpose(a)$Order:(n) ; **value** n ;
array a ; **integer** n ;
begin real w ; **integer** i, k ;
for i := 1 **step** 1 **until** n **do**
  for k := $1+i$ **step** 1 **until** n **do**
  begin w := $a[i,k]$;
    $a[i,k]$:= $a[k,i]$;
    $a[k,i]$:= w
  end
end $Transpose$

integer procedure $Step$ (u) ; **real** u ;
$Step$:= **if** $0\leq u\wedge u\leq 1$ **then** 1 **else** 0

procedure $Absmax(a)$size:(n,m)Result:(y)Subscripts:(i,k);
comment The absolute greatest element of the matrix a, of size n by m is transferred to y, and the subscripts of this element to i and k ;
array a ; **integer** n, m, i, k ; **real** y ;
begin integer p, q ;
y := 0 ;
for p := 1 **step** 1 **until** n **do for** q := 1 **step** 1 **until** m **do**
if $abs(a[p,q])>y$ **then begin** y := $abs(a[p,q])$; i := p ;
  k := q
end end $Absmax$

procedure $Innerproduct(a,b)$Order:(k,p)Result:(y) ; **value** k ;
integer k,p ; **real** y,a,b ;
begin real s ;
s := 0 ;
for p := 1 **step** 1 **until** k **do** s := $s+a\times b$;
y := s
end $Innerproduct$

5.4.3. Semantics

A procedure declaration serves to define the procedure associated with a procedure identifier. The principal constituent of a procedure declaration is a statement or a piece of code, the procedure body, which through the use of procedure statements and/or function designators may be activated from other parts of the block in the head of which the procedure declaration appears. Associated with the body is a heading, which specifies certain identifiers occurring within the body to represent formal parameters. Formal parameters in the procedure body will, whenever the procedure is activated (cf. section 3.2. Function Designators and section 4.7. Procedure Statements) be assigned the values of or replaced by actual parameters. Identifiers in the procedure body which are not formal will be either local or nonlocal to the body depending on whether they are declared within the body or not. Those of them which are nonlocal to the body may well be local to the block in the head of which the procedure declaration appears. The procedure body always acts like a

block, whether it has the form of one or not. Consequently the scope of any label labelling a statement within the body or the body itself can never extend beyond the procedure body. In addition, if the identifier of a formal parameter is declared anew within the procedure body (including the case of its use as a label as in section 4.1.3), it is thereby given a local significance and actual parameters which correspond to it are inaccessible throughout the scope of this inner local quantity.

5.4.4. Values of function designators

For a procedure declaration to define the value of a function designator there must, within the procedure body, occur one or more explicit assignment statements with the procedure identifier in a left part; at least one of these must be executed, and the type associated with the procedure identifier must be declared through the appearance of a type declarator as the very first symbol of the procedure declaration. The last value so assigned is used to continue the evaluation of the expression in which the function designator occurs. Any occurrence of the procedure identifier within the body of the procedure other than in a left part in an assignment statement denotes activation of the procedure.

5.4.5. Specifications

In the heading a specification part, giving information about the kinds and types of the formal parameters by means of an obvious notation, may be included. In this part no formal parameter may occur more than once. Specifications of formal parameters called by value (cf. section 4.7.3.1) must be supplied and specifications of formal parameters called by name (cf. section 4.7.3.2) may be omitted.

5.4.6. Code as procedure body

It is understood that the procedure body may be expressed in non-ALGOL language. Since it is intended that the use of this feature should be entirely a question of hardware representation, no further rules concerning this code language can be given within the reference language

Examples of Procedure Declarations:

EXAMPLE 1.

```
procedure euler (fct, sum, eps, tim)  ;  value eps, tim  ;
integer tim  ;  real procedure fct  ;  real sum, eps  ;
comment euler computes the sum of fct(i) for i from zero up to
infinity by means of a suitabley refined euler transformation. The
summation is stopped as soon as tim times in succession the abso-
lute value of the terms of the transformed series are found to be
less than eps. Hence, one should provide a function fct with one
integer argument, an upper bound eps, and an integer tim. The
output is the sum sum. euler is particularly efficient in the case
of a slowly convergent or divergent alternating series  ;
begin integer i, k, n, t  ;  array m[0:15]  ;  real mn, mp, ds  ;
i := n := t := 0  ;  m[0] := fct(0)  ;  sum := m[0]/2  ;
nextterm: i := i+1  ;  mn := fct(i)  :
    for k := 0 step 1 until n do
        begin mp := (mn+m[k])/2  ;  m[k] := mn  ;
        mn := mp end means  ;
```

```
    if (abs(mn)<abs(m[n]))∧(n<15) then
        begin ds := mn/2  ;  n := n+1  ;  m[n] :=
        mn end accept
    else ds := mn  ;
    sum := sum + ds  ;
    if abs(ds)<eps then t := t+1 else t := 0  ;
    if t<tim then go to nextterm
end euler
```

EXAMPLE 2.[8]

```
procedure RK(x,y,n,FKT,eps,eta,xE,yE,fi)  ;  value x,y  ;
integer n  ;  Boolean fi  ;  real x,eps,eta,xE  ;  array
y,yE  ;  procedure FKT  ;
comment: RK integrates the system $y_k' = f_k(x,y_1,y_2,\ldots,y_n)$
```
$(k=1,2,\ldots,n)$ of differential equations with the method of Runge-Kutta with automatic search for appropriate length of integration step. Parameters are: The initial values x and $y[k]$ for x and the unknown functions $y_k(x)$. The order n of the system. The procedure $FKT(x,y,n,z)$ which represents the system to be integrated, i.e. the set of functions f_k. The tolerance values eps and eta which govern the accuracy of the numerical integration. The end of the integration interval xE. The output parameter yE which represents the solution at $x=xE$. The Boolean variable fi, which must always be given the value **true** for an isolated or first entry into RK. If however the functions y must be available at several meshpoints $x_0, x_1, \ldots, x_n$, then the procedure must be called repeatedly (with $x=x_k$, $xE=x_{k+1}$, for $k=0, 1, \ldots, n-1$) and then the later calls may occur with $fi=$ **false** which saves computing time. The input parameters of FKT must be x,y,n, the output parameter z represents the set of derivatives $z[k]=f_k(x,y[1], y[2], \ldots, y[n])$ for x and the actual y's. A procedure $comp$ enters as a nonlocal identifier ;
```
begin
    array z,y1,y2,y3[1:n]  ;  real x1,x2,x3,H  ;  Boolean out  ;
    integer k,j  ;  own real s,Hs  ;
    procedure RK1ST(x,y,h,xe,ye)  ;  real x,h,xe  ;  array
        y,ye  ;
        comment: RK1ST integrates one single RUNGE-KUTTA
            with initial values x,y[k] which yields the output
            parameters xe=x+h and ye[k], the latter being the
            solution at xe. Important: the parameters n, FKT, z
            enter RK1ST as nonlocal entities  ;
    begin
        array w[1:n], a[1:5]  ;  integer k,j  ;
        a[1] := a[2] := a[5] := h/2  ;  a[3] := a[4] := h  :
        xe := x  ;
        for k := 1 step 1 until n do ye[k] := w[k] := y[k]  ;
        for j := 1 step 1 until 4 do
        begin
            FKT(xe,w,n,z)  ;
            xe := x+a[j]  ;
            for k := 1 step 1 until n do
            begin
                w[k] := y[k]+a[j]×z[k]  ;
                ye[k] := ye[k] + a[j+1]×z[k]/3
```

[8] This RK-program contains some new ideas which are related to ideas of S. GILL, A process for the step-by-step integration of differential equations in an automatic computing machine, [*Proc. Camb. Phil. Soc.* 47 (1951), 96]; and E. FRÖBERG, On the solution of ordinary differential equations with digital computing machines, [*Fysiograf. Sällsk. Lund, Förhd. 20*, 11 (1950), 136–152]. It must be clear, however, that with respect to computing time and round-off errors it may not be optimal, nor has it actually been tested on a computer.

```
            end k
          end j
        end RK1ST ;
    Begin of program:
        if fi then begin H := xE−x ; s := 0 end else H := Hs ;
        out := false ;
AA: if (x+2.01×H−xE>0)≡(H>0) then
        begin Hs := H ; out := true ; H := (xE−x)/2
        end if ;
        RK1ST (x,y,2×H,x1,y1) ;
BB: RK1ST (x,y,H,x2,y2) ; RK1ST (x2,y2,H,x3,y3) ;
        for k := 1 step 1 until n do
            if comp(y1[k],y3[k],eta)>eps then go to CC ;
```

```
    comment: comp(a,bc,) is a function designator, the value
        of which is the absolute value of the difference of the
        mantissae of a and b, after the exponents of these quan-
        tities have been made equal to the largest of the exponents
        of the originally given parameters a,b,c :
        x := x3 ; if out then go to DD ;
        for k := 1 step 1 until n do y[k] := y3[k] ;
        if s=5 then begin s := 0 ; H := 2×H end if ;
        s := s+1 ; go to AA ;
CC: H := 0.5×H ; out := false ; x1 := x2 ;
        for k := 1 step 1 until n do y1[k] := y2[k] ;
        go to BB ;
DD: for k := 1 step 1 until n do yE[k] := y3[k]
    end RK
```

ALPHABETIC INDEX OF DEFINITIONS OF CONCEPTS AND SYNTACTIC UNITS

All references are given through section numbers. The references are given in three groups:

def   Following the abbreviation "def", reference to the syntactic definition (if any) is given.

synt   Following the abbreviation "synt", references to the occurrences in metalinguistic formulae are given. References already quoted in the def-group are not repeated.

text   Following the word "text", the references to definitions given in the text are given.

The basic symbols represented by signs other than underlined words [in typewritten copy; boldface in printed copy—Ed.] have been collected at the beginning.

The examples have been ignored in compiling the index.

⟨factor⟩, def 3.3.1
false, synt 2.2.2
for, synt 2.3, 4.6.1
⟨for clause⟩, def 4.6.1 text 4.6.3
⟨for list⟩, def 4.6.1 text 4.6.4
⟨for list element⟩, def 4.6.1 text 4.6.4.1, 4.6.4.2, 4.6.4.3
⟨formal parameter⟩, def 5.4.1 text 5.4.3
⟨formal parameter list⟩, def 5.4.1
⟨formal parameter part⟩, def 5.4.1
⟨for statement⟩, def 4.6.1 synt 4.1.1, 4.5.1 text 4.6 (complete section)
⟨function designator⟩, def 3.2.1 synt 3.3.1, 3.4.1 text 3.2.3, 5.4.4

go to, synt 2.3, 4.3.1
⟨go to statement⟩, def 4.3.1 synt 4.1.1 text 4.3.3

⟨identifier⟩, def 2.4.1 synt 3.1.1, 3.2.1, 3.5.1, 5.4.1 text 2.4.3
⟨identifier list⟩, def 5.4.1
if, synt 2.3, 3.3.1, 4.5.1
⟨if clause⟩, def 3.3.1, 4.5.1 synt 3.4.1, 3.5.1 text 3.3.3, 4.5.3.2
⟨if statement⟩, def 4.5.1 text 4.5.3.1
⟨implication⟩, def 3.4.1
integer, synt 2.3, 5.1.1 text 5.1.3
⟨integer⟩, def 2.5.1 text 2.5.4

label, synt 2.3, 5.4.1
⟨label⟩, def 3.5.1 synt 4.1.1, 4.5.1, 4.6.1 text 1, 4.1.3
⟨left part⟩, def 4.2.1
⟨left part list⟩, def 4.2.1
⟨letter⟩, def 2.1 synt 2, 2.4.1, 3.2.1, 4.7.1
⟨letter string⟩, def 3.2.1, 4.7.1
local, text 4.1.3
⟨local or own type⟩, def 5.1.1 synt 5.2.1
⟨logical operator⟩, def 2.3 synt 3.4.1 text 3.4.5
⟨logical value⟩, def 2.2.2 synt 2, 3.4.1
⟨lower bound⟩, def 5.2.1 text 5.2.4

minus −, synt 2.3, 2.5.1, 3.3.1 text 3.3.4.1
multiply ×, synt 2.3, 3.3.1 text 3.3.4.1
⟨multiplying operator⟩, def 3.3.1

nonlocal, text 4.1.3
⟨number⟩, def 2.5.1 text 2.5.3, 2.5.4

⟨open string⟩, def 2.6.1
⟨operator⟩, def 2.3
own, synt 2.3, 5.1.1 text 5, 5.2.5

⟨parameter delimiter⟩, def 3.2.1, 4.7.1 synt 5.4.1 text 4.7.7
parentheses ( ), synt 2.3, 3.2.1, 3.3.1, 3.4.1, 3.5.1, 4.7.1, 5.4.1 text 3.3.5.2
plus +, synt 2.3, 2.5.1, 3.3.1 text 3.3.4.1
⟨primary⟩, def 3.3.1
procedure, synt 2.3, 5.4.1
⟨procedure body⟩, def 5.4.1
⟨procedure declaration⟩, def 5.4.1 synt 5 text 5.4.3
⟨procedure heading⟩, def 5.4.1 text 5.4.3
⟨procedure identifier⟩ def 3.2.1 synt 3.2.1, 4.7.1, 5.4.1 text 4.7.5.4
⟨procedure statement⟩, def 4.7.1 synt 4.1.1 text 4.7.3
⟨program⟩, def 4.1.1 text 1
⟨proper string⟩, def 2.6.1

quantity, text 2.7

real, synt 2.3, 5.1.1 text 5.1.3
⟨relation⟩, def 3.4.1 text 3.4.5
⟨relational operator⟩, def 2.3, 3.4.1

scope, text 2.7
semicolon ;, synt 2.3, 4.1.1, 5.4.1
⟨separator⟩, def 2.3
⟨sequential operator⟩, def 2.3
⟨simple arithmetic expression⟩, def 3.3.1 text 3.3.3
⟨simple Boolean⟩, def 3.4.1
⟨simple designational expression⟩, def 3.5.1
⟨simple variable⟩, def 3.1.1 synt 5.1.1 text 2.4.3
space ⊔, synt 2.3 text 2.3, 2.6.3
⟨specification part⟩, def 5.4.1 text 5.4.5
⟨specificator⟩, def 2.3
⟨specifier⟩, def 5.4.1
standard function, text 3.2.4, 3.2.5
⟨statement⟩, def 4.1.1, synt 4.5.1, 4.6.1, 5.4.1 text 4 (complete section)
statement bracket, see: begin end
step, synt 2.3, 4.6.1 text 4.6.4.2
string, synt 2.3, 5.4.1
⟨string⟩, def 2.6.1 synt 3.2.1, 4.7.1 text 2.6.3
string quotes ' ', synt 2.3, 2.6.1, text 2.6.3
subscript, text 3.1.4.1
subscript bound, text 5.2.3.1
subscript brackets [ ], synt 2.3, 3.1.1, 3.5.1, 5.2.1
⟨subscripted variable⟩, def 3.1.1 text 3.1.4.1
⟨subscript expression⟩, def 3.1.1 synt 3.5.1
⟨subscript list⟩, def 3.1.1
successor, text 4
switch, synt 2.3, 5.3.1, 5.4.1
⟨switch declaration⟩, def 5.3.1 synt 5 text 5.3.3
⟨switch designator⟩, def 3.5.1 text 3.5.3
⟨switch identifier⟩, def 3.5.1 synt 3.2.1, 4.7.1, 5.3.1
⟨switch list⟩, def 5.3.1

⟨term⟩, def 3.3.1
ten ₁₀, synt 2.3, 2.5.1
then, synt 2.3, 3.3.1, 4.5.1
transfer function, text 3.2.5
true, synt 2.2.2
⟨type⟩, def 5.1.1 synt 5.4.1 text 2.8
⟨type declaration⟩, def 5.1.1 synt 5 text 5.1.3
⟨type list⟩, def 5.1.1

⟨unconditional statement⟩, def 4.1.1, 4.5.1
⟨unlabelled basic statement⟩, def 4.1.1
⟨unlabelled block⟩, def 4.1.1
⟨unlabelled compound⟩, def 4.1.1
⟨unsigned integer⟩, def 2.5.1, 3.5.1
⟨unsigned number⟩, def 2.5.1 synt 3.3.1
until, synt 2.3, 4.6.1 text 4.6.4.2
⟨upper bound⟩, def 5.2.1 text 5.2.4

value, synt 2.3, 5.4.1
value, text 2.8, 3.3.3
⟨value part⟩, def 5.4.1 text 4.7.3.1
⟨variable⟩, def 3.1.1 synt 3.3.1, 3.4.1, 4.2.1, 4.6.1 text 3.1.3
⟨variable identifier⟩, def 3.1.1

while, synt 2.3, 4.6.1 text 4.6.4.3

END OF THE REPORT

THE REMAINING TROUBLESPOTS IN ALGOL 60*

D. E. KNUTH

This paper lists the ambiguities remaining in the language ALGOL 60, which have been noticed since the publication of the Revised ALGOL 60 Report in 1963.

There is little doubt that the programming language ALGOL 60 has had a great impact on many areas of computer science, and it seems fair to state that this language has been more carefully studied than any other programming language.

When ALGOL 60 was first published in 1960 [1], many new features were introduced into programming languages, primarily with respect to the generality of "procedures." It was quite difficult at first for anyone to grasp the full significance of each of the linguistic features with respect to other aspects of the language, and therefore people commonly would discover ALGOL 60 constructions they had never before realized were possible, each time they reread the Report. Such constructions often provided counterexamples to many of the usual techniques of compiler implementation, and in many cases it was possible to construct programs that could be interpreted in more than one way.

The most notable feature of the first ALGOL 60 Report was the new standard it set for language definition, based on an almost completely systematic use of syntactic rules that prescribed the structure of programs; this innovation made it possible to know exactly what the language ALGOL 60 was, to a much greater degree than had ever been achieved previously. Of course it was inevitable that a complex document such as the ALGOL 60 Report (roughly 75 typewritten pages, prepared by an international committee) would contain some ambiguities and contradictions, since it involves a very large number of highly interdependent elements. As time passed, and especially as ALGOL 60 translators were written, these problems were noticed by many people, and in 1962 a meeting of the international committee was called to help resolve these issues. The result was the Revised ALGOL 60 Report [2], which cleaned up many of the unclear points.

Now that several more years have gone by, it is reasonable to expect that ALGOL 60 is pretty well understood. A few points of ambiguity and contradiction still remain in the Revised ALGOL 60 Report, some of which were left unresolved at the 1962 meeting (primarily because of high feelings between people who had already implemented conflicting interpretations of ambiguous aspects), and some of which have come to light more recently.

In view of the widespread interest in ALGOL 60 it seems appropriate to have a list of all its remaining problem areas, or at least of those which are now known. This list will be useful as a guide to users of ALGOL 60, who may find it illuminating to explore some of the comparatively obscure parts of this language and who will want to know what ambiguous constructions should be avoided; and useful also to designers of programming languages, who will want to avoid making similar mistakes.

The following sections of this paper therefore enumerate the blemishes which remain. A preliminary list of all the known trouble spots was compiled by the author for use by the ALGOL subcommittee of the ACM Programming Languages committee in November 1963; and after receiving extensive assistance from the committee members, the author prepared a revised document which appeared in mimeographed form in *ALGOL Bulletin 19, AB19.3.7* (Mathematisch Centrum, Amsterdam, January 1965). The present paper is a fairly extensive modification of the *ALGOL Bulletin* article; it has been prepared at the request of several people who do not have ready access to the *ALGOL Bulletin* and who have pointed out the desirability of wider circulation.

The following list is actually more remarkable for its shortness than its length. A complete critique which goes to the same level of detail would be almost out of the question for other languages comparable to ALGOL 60, since the list would probably be a full order of magnitude longer.

This paper is divided into two parts, one which lists *ambiguities* and one which lists *corrections* which seem to be necessary to the Revised Report. The word "ambiguous" is itself quite ambiguous, and it is used here in the following sense: An aspect of ALGOL 60 is said to be ambiguous if, on the basis of the Revised ALGOL 60 Report, it is

*Reprinted from *Comm ACM* 10, 10, 1967, 611–617.

The preparation of this paper has been supported in part by the National Science Foundation and in part by the Burroughs Corporation.

possible to write an ALGOL 60 program for which this feature can be interpreted in two ways leading to different computations in the program, and if it is impossible to prove conclusively from the Revised Report that either of these conflicting interpretations is incorrect. So-called "syntactic ambiguities" are not necessarily ambiguities of the language in this sense, although the original ALGOL 60 Report contained some syntactic ambiguities that did lead to discrepancies. (See [3] and [4] for a discussion of the former ambiguities; and see correction 7 below and the discussion at the end of Section 3 in [5] for comments on syntactic ambiguities remaining in the Revised Report.)

The distinction between an "ambiguity" in ALGOL 60 and a "correction" that is necessary to the Report is not clear cut; for when the Report contains an error or contradictory statement, this might lead to ambiguous interpretations, and conversely any ambiguity might be considered an error in the Report. The difference is mainly a matter of degree; the true meanings of the points that merely need to be corrected are almost universally agreed upon by people who have studied the Report carefully, because of the overall spirit of the language in spite of the fact that some of the rules are incorrectly stated.

Frequent references are made in the discussions below to the numbered sections of the Revised Report [2], and the reader is advised to have this document available for comparison if he is going to understand the significance of the comments which follow.

People who have studied the ALGOL Report carefully have often been called "ALGOL theologians," because of the analogy between the Bible and the Revised Report (which is the ultimate source of wisdom about ALGOL 60). Using the same analogy, it is possible to view the following sections as a more or less objective discussion of the conflicting doctrines that have been based on these Scriptures.

1. Ambiguities

AMBIGUITY 1: SIDE EFFECTS

A "side effect" is conventionally regarded as a change (invoked by a function designator) in the state of some quantities which are **own** variables or which are not local to the function designator. In other words, when a procedure is being called in the midst of some expression, it has side effects if in addition to computing a value it does input or output or changes the value of some variable that is not internal to the procedure.

For example, let us consider the following program:

begin integer a;
  integer procedure $f(x,y)$; **value** y,x; **integer** y,x;
    $a := f := x + 1$;
  integer procedure $g(x)$; **integer** x; $x := g := a + 2$;
    $a := 0$; *outreal* $(1, a + f(a, g(a))/g(a))$ **end**.

Here both f and g have as a side effect the alteration of an external variable.

It is clear that the value output by this program depends heavily upon the order of computation. Many compilers find more efficient object programs are obtained if the denominator of a complicated fraction is evaluated before the numerator; if we first compute $g(a)$, then $f(a, g(a))$, then $a + f(a, g(a))/g(a)$, and if the evaluation of the **value** parameters in $f(a, g(a))$ is done in the order a, $g(a)$, then we get the answer $4\frac{1}{2}$. Other possible answers are $\frac{1}{3}$, $\frac{3}{5}$, $\frac{3}{2}$, $\frac{5}{2}$, $\frac{4}{4}$, $3\frac{3}{5}$, $3\frac{1}{3}$, $5\frac{3}{5}$, $3\frac{1}{2}$, and $7\frac{1}{2}$.

The major point left unresolved in the Revised Report was the ambiguity about side effects: Are they allowed in ALGOL 60 programs, and if so what do the programs mean? If side effects are allowable, then the order of computation must be specified in the following places: evaluating the primaries of an expression; evaluating the subscripts of a variable; evaluating bound pairs in a block head; evaluating **value** parameters; and (perhaps) the step-until element of a for clause. Note, for example, that **value** parameters (which are to be evaluated just after entry to a procedure, Section 4.7.3.1.) might conceivably be evaluated in the order of their appearance in the parameter list or in the value part.

An argument may actually be made for the opinion that side effects are implicitly outlawed by the fifth paragraph in Section 4.5.3.2; or at least that paragraph says that all side effects occurring during the evaluation of an if clause of a conditional statement must be cancelled if the Boolean expression comes out false! A similar situation occurs in Section 4.3.5 where side effects, occurring during the evaluation of a designational expression which is ultimately undefined, must presumably be nullified. (On the other hand, the wording of these sections is probably just an oversight, and the implication about side effects was probably not intended.)

How close does the Report come to prescribing the order of computation? Section 3.3.5 says "the sequence of operations within one expression is generally from left to right," but the context here refers to the order of carrying out arithmetic operations; and it does not say whether the value of the first term "a" in the above example should be calculated before or after the second term "$f(a, g(a))/g(a)$" since no "operation" in the sense of the Report is involved here. Section 4.2.3.1 says subscript expressions in the left part variables of an assignment statement are evaluated "in sequence from left to right." (So in the assignment statement

$$A[a + B[f(a)] + g(a)] := C[a] := 0$$

we are perhaps to evaluate "$a + B[f(a)] + g(a)$" first, then "$f(a)$" again, then "a"?)

Section 1, footnote 4, says "Whenever ... the outcome of a certain process is left undefined ... a program only fully defines a computational process if accompanying information specifies ... the course of action to be taken in all such cases as may occur during the execution of the computation." In Section 3.3.6 we read, "It is indeed understood that different hardware representations may evaluate arithmetic expressions differently." The latter remark was made with reference to arithmetic on **real** quantities (i.e., floating-point arithmetic), but it is remarkable when viewed also from the standpoint of side effects! Footnote 4 says essentially that ALGOL 60 is not

intended to be free of ambiguity, and much can be said for the desirability of incompletely specified formalisms; indeed, this incompleteness is the basis of the axiomatic method in mathematics and it is also the basis of many good jokes. But it is doubtful whether the ambiguity of side effects is a desirable one; for further remarks in this vein see Ambiguity 9.

In view of the ambiguities of side effects, which many people do not realize because they know only the interpretations given by the ALGOL compiler they use, the author has founded SPASEPA, the Society for the Prevention of the Appearance of Side Effects in Published Algorithms. Members and/or donations are earnestly solicited.

It may be of value to digress for a moment here and to ask whether side effects are desirable or not; should ALGOL or comparable languages allow side effects? Do side effects serve any useful purpose or are they just peculiar constructions for programmers who like to be tricky? Objections to side effects have often been voiced, and the most succinct formulation is perhaps that due to Samelson and Bauer in *ALGOL Bulletin 12*, pp. 7–8. The principal points raised are that (i) an explanation of the "use" of side effects tends to waste inordinate amounts of classroom time when explaining ALGOL, giving an erroneous impression of the spirit of the language; (ii) familiar identities such as $f(x) + x = x + f(x)$ are no longer valid, and this is an unnatural deviation from mathematical conventions; (iii) many "applications" of side effects are merely programming tricks making puzzles of programs; other uses can almost always be reprogrammed easily by changing a function designator to a procedure call statement. Essentially the same objections have been voiced with respect to the concept of parameters "called by name," which was the chief new feature of ALGOL 60.

Another objection to side effects is that they may cause apparently needless computation. For example, consider

"**if** $g(a) = 2 \lor g(a) = 3$ **then** 1 **else** 0"

in connection with the procedure $g(x)$ above; according to the rules of the Revised Report it is necessary to evaluate $g(a)$ twice, thereby increasing a by 4 even if the first relation involving $g(a)$ is found to be true.

We might also mention the fact that ALGOL's call-by-name feature is deficient in the following respect: It is impossible to write an ALGOL 60 procedure "*increment* (x)" which increases the value of the variable x by unity. In particular the procedure statement "*increment* $(A[i])$" should increase the current value of $A[i]$ by unity, where i is a function designator which may produce different values when it is invoked twice.

On the other hand, consider the following procedure:

real procedure $SIGMA$ (i, l, u, x); **value** l, u; **integer** i, l, u;
   real x;
  begin real s; $s := 0$; **for** $i := l$ **step** 1 **until** u **do** $s := s + x$;
   $SIGMA := s$ **end**.

This procedure computes $\sum_{i=l}^{u} x$ and has the additional side effect of changing variable i. It is quite natural to be able to write

$$SIGMA \; (i, 1, m, SIGMA \; (j, 1, n, A[i, j])) \quad \text{for} \quad \sum_{i=1}^{m} \sum_{j=1}^{n} A_{ij}$$

without adding special summation conventions to the language itself; this is a tame and unambiguous use of side effects which also is the principal example that has been put forward to point out the usefulness of parameters called by name. (See [6] for further discussion.)

If we alter the above procedure by inserting "**integer** $i0$; $i0 := i$;" after "**real** s;" and "; $i := i0$" before "**end**", we would find that no side effect is introduced as a consequence of the total execution of the function $SIGMA$ (i, l, u, x), provided the actual parameter x does not involve side effects. So the above example does not constitute an inherent use of side effects; in fact, a study of this particular case indicates that it might be better to have some sort of facility for defining dummy variables (like i and j) which have existence only during the evaluation of a function but which may appear within the arguments to that function.

We should remark also that the principal objection to allowing parameters called by name, even in natural situations like the above example, is that the machine language implementation of these constructions is necessarily much slower than we would expect a simple summation operation to be; the inner loop (incrementation of i, testing against u, adding x to s) involves a great deal of more or less irrelevant bookkeeping because i and x are called by name, even on machines like the Burroughs B5500 [12] whose hardware was specifically designed to facilitate ALGOL's call by name. The use of "macro" definition facilities to extend languages, instead of relying solely on procedures for this purpose, results in a more satisfactory running program.

Other situations for which function designators with side effects can be useful are not uncommon, e.g., in connection with a procedure for input or for random number generation. Side effects also arise naturally in connection with the manipulation of data structures, when a function changes the structure while it computes a value; for example, it is often useful to have a function "$pop(S)$" which deletes the top value from a "stack" S and which retains the deleted value as its result. See also [7] for examples of Boolean function designators with side effects that are specifically intended for use in constructions like $p \lor q$, where q is *never* to be evaluated when p is true and where p is to be evaluated first in any case.

The objection above that $x + f(x)$ should be equal to $f(x) + x$, because of age old mathematical conventions, is not very strong; there are simple and natural rules for sequencing operations of an expression so that a programmer knows what he is doing when he is using side effects. The people who complain about "$x + f(x)$" are generally compiler writers who don't want to generate extra code to save x in temporary storage before computing $f(x)$, since this is almost always unnecessary. Such inefficiency is the real reason for the objections to side effects. These same people would *not* like to see "$x = 0 \lor f(x) = 0$" be treated

the same as "$f(x) = 0 \lor x = 0$" since the former relation can be used to suppress the computation of "$f(x) = 0$" when it is known that "$x = 0$"; in fact one naturally likes to write "$x = 0 \lor f(x) = 0$" in situations where $f(0)$ is undefined.

AMBIGUITY 2: INCOMPLETE FUNCTIONS

The question of exit from a function designator via a **go to** statement is another lively issue. This might be regarded as a special case of point 1, since such an exit is a "side effect," and indeed the discussion under point 1 does apply here. Some further points are relevant to this case, however.

Some people feel this is an important feature because of "error exits." However, the same effect can be achieved by using a procedure call statement and adding an output parameter.

Two rather convincing arguments can be put forward to contend that this type of exit is not really allowed by ALGOL, so the matter is not really an ambiguity at all.

(a) In Section 3.2.3 we read, "Function designators define single numerical or logical values." An incomplete function would not. Or, if it would, there would be mysterious, ambiguous consequences such as this:

begin real x, y;   **real procedure** F;   **begin** $F := 1$;
   go to L **end**;
   $x := F + 1$; $y := 1$; L: **end**.

We question whether x is replaced by 2, and if so, whether y is replaced by 1 (thus incorporating simultaneity into the language?). After all, F rigorously defines the value 1 and "the value so assigned is used to continue the evaluation of the expression in which the function designator occurs." (Cf. Section 5.4.4.)

(b) The discussion of the control of the program in Section 5.4.3.2 is based entirely on the values of the Boolean expressions, and the language used there implicitly excludes such a possibility. In many places the Report speaks of expressions as if they have a value, and no mention is ever made of expressions that are left unevaluated due to exits from function designators.

A further point about incomplete functions (though not really part of the ambiguity) concerns the implementation problems caused when such an exit occurs during the evaluation of the bound expressions while array declarations are being processed. Since the control words for a storage allocation scheme are not entirely set up at this time, such exits have caused bugs in more than one ALGOL compiler!

AMBIGUITY 3: STEP-UNTIL

The exact sequence occurring during the evaluation of the "step-until" element of a for clause has been the subject of much (rather heated) debate. The construction

for $V := A$ **step** B **until** C **do** S

(where V is a variable, A, B, C are expressions, and S is a procedure) can be replaced by a procedure call

for (V, A, B, C, S)

with suitable procedure called "*for*." The debate centers, more or less, on which of these parameters are to be thought of as called by value, and which as called by name.

Conservative ALGOL theologians follow the sequence given in Section 4.6.4.2 very literally, so that if statement S is executed n times, the value of A is computed once, B is computed $2 \times n + 1$ times, C is computed $n + 1$ times, and (if V is subscripted) the subscripts of V are evaluated $3 \times n + 2$ times. Liberal theologians take the expansion more figuratively, evaluating these things just once. There are many points of view between these two "extremist" positions. As a result, the following program will probably give at least four or five different output values when run on different present-day ALGOL implementations:

begin array $V, A, C[1:1]$;   **integer** k;
   integer procedure i;   **begin** $i := 1$; $k := k + 1$ **end**;
   $k := 0$; $A[1] := 1$; $C[1] := 3$;
   for $V[i] := A[i]$ **step** $A[i]$ **until** $C[i]$ **do**;
   outreal $(1, k)$ **end**;

The liberal interpretation gives an output of 4, the conservative interpretation gives something like 23, and intermediate interpretations give intermediate values; for example the compromise suggested in [9] gives the value 16.

The conservative argument is, "Read Section 4.6.4.2." The liberal arguments are: (a) "If Section 4.6.4.2 is to be taken literally, it gives a perfectly well defined value for the controlled variable upon exit. Since Section 4.6.5 says the value is undefined, however, it must mean Section 4.6.4.2 is not to be taken literally." (b) "The repeated phase '*the* controlled variable' is always used in the singular, implying that the subscript(s) of the variable need be evaluated only once during the entire for clause. Other interpretations make Section 4.6.5 meaningless."

Examination of published algorithms shows that in well over 99% of the uses of for statements, the value of the "step" B is $+1$, and in the vast majority of the exceptions the step is a constant. It is clear that programmers seldom feel the need to make use of any ambiguous cases. The liberal interpretation is clearly more efficient and it would be recommended for future programming languages; a programmer who really feels the need for some of the woollier uses of a for statement can be told to write the statements out by adding a tiny bit of program instead of using a for statement. Even though uses can be contrived for examples like

for $x := .1$ **step** x **until** 10^6

or

for $y := 1$ **step** 1 **until** $y + 1$

these are rewritten easily using the "while" element.

AMBIGUITY 4: SPECIFICATIONS

The wording of Section 5.4.5 can be interpreted as saying that parameters called by value must be specified only if the specification part is given at all! Furthermore, it is not stated to what extent, *if any*, the actual parameters must agree with a given specification, and to what extent

the specifications which do appear will affect the meaning of the program. For example, is the following program legitimate?

```
begin integer array A, B, C[0:10];  array D[0:10];
  procedure P(A, B, C);  array A, B, C;
    begin integer i;
      for i := 0 step 1 until 10 do
        C[i] := A[i]/B[i]
    end;
  integer i;
  for i := 0 step 1 until 10 do
    begin A[i] := 1;  B[i] := 2 end;
  P(A, B, C);  P(A, B, D)
end.
```

If so, the assignment statement inside the procedure will have to *round* the result or not depending on the actual parameter used. Consider also the same procedure with the formal parameters specified to be *integer* arrays. For further discussion see [9].

AMBIGUITY 5: REPEATED PARAMETERS

Several published algorithms have a procedure heading like

procedure *invert* (A) order: (n) output: (A)

where two of the formal parameters have the same name. The Report does not specifically exclude this, and it does not say what interpretation is to be taken.

AMBIGUITY 6: VALUE LABELS

It has not been clear whether or not a designational expression can be called by value, and if so, whether its value may be "undefined" as used in Section 4.3.5. This may or may not be allowed by the language of Section 4.7.3.1 (which talks about "assignment" of values to the formal parameters in a "fictitious block"). Cf. Section 4.7.5.4; if a designational expression could be called by value, a switch identifier with a single component could be also, in the same way as an array identifier can be called by value. The first paragraph of Section 2.8 is relevant here also.

AMBIGUITY 7: OWN

This has so many interpretations it will take too much space to repeat the arguments here. See [8, 9] for a discussion of the two principal interpretations, "dynamic" and "static," each of which can be useful. The additional complications of own arrays with dynamically varying subscript bounds combined with recursion, adds further ambiguities; for one apparently reasonable way to define this, see [11].

AMBIGUITY 8: NUMERIC LABELS AND "QUANTITIES"

Most ALGOL compilers exclude implementation of numeric labels, primarily because a correct implementation requires an unsigned integer constant parameter to be denoted, in machine language, both as a number and a label. Consider for example

procedure P1(q, r); if q < 5 then go to r;
procedure P2(q, r); if r < 5 then go to q;
procedure W(Z); procedure Z; Z(2, 2);
··· W(P1); x := 0; W(P2); 2: ···

There is no ambiguity here in the sense we are considering, just a difficulty of implementation in view of the double meaning of a parameter "2."

The author has shown the following procedure to several authoritative people, however, and a 50 % split developed between those saying it was or was not valid ALGOL:

procedure P(q); if q < 5 then go to q;

The idea of course is that we might later call P(2) where 2 is a numeric label. Actually this seems to be specifically outlawed by Section 2.4.3 (the identifier q cannot refer to two different quantities). But consider

procedure P(q); if B(q) then G(q);
procedure G(q); go to q;
Boolean procedure B(q); B := q < 5;

Is this now valid?

Consider also

begin integer I; array A[0:0];
procedure P1(X); array X; X[0] := 0;
procedure P2(X); integer X; X := 0;
procedure call (X, Y); X(Y);
call (P1, A); call (P2, I) end

The identifier Y is used to denote two different quantities (an array and a simple variable) which have the same scope, yet this program seems to be valid in spite of the wording of Section 2.4.3.

The latter procedure is believed to be admissible because the expansion of procedure bodies should be considered from a dynamic (not static) point of view. For example consider

integer procedure *factorial* (n); integer n;
factorial := if n > 0 then n × *factorial* (n − 1) else 1;

In this procedure body the call of *factorial* (n − 1) should not be expanded unless n > 0, or else the expansion will never terminate. From the dynamic viewpoint the identifier Y in *call* (X, Y) never does in fact denote two different quantities at the same time.

Another strong argument can be put forward that even our earlier example "if q < 5 then go to q" is allowable. Notice that Section 2.4.3 does *not* say that an identifier may denote a string; but in fact a formal parameter *may* denote a string. Therefore we conclude that Section 2.4.3 does not apply specifically to formal parameters; this is consistent with the entire spirit of the Report, which does not speak of formal parameters except where it tells how they are to be replaced by actual parameters. The syntax equations in particular reflect this philosophy. Consider for example

procedure P(Q, S); procedure Q; string S; Q(S);

there is no way to use the syntax of ALGOL to show that "Q(S)" is a procedure statement and at the same time to reflect the fact that S is a string. We show S is an ⟨identifier⟩, but to show it is an ⟨actual parameter⟩ we must show it is either an ⟨expression⟩, an ⟨array identifier⟩, a ⟨switch identifier⟩, or a ⟨procedure identifier⟩, and it really is not any of these. So the only way to account for

this is to first replace Q and S by their actual parameters, in any invocation of P, and *then* to apply the syntax equations to the result.

The distinction between what is valid and what is not according to Section 3.4.3 is unclear.

AMBIGUITY 9:   REAL ARITHMETIC

The precision of arithmetic on **real** quantities has intentionally been left ambiguous (see Section 3.3.6). In an interesting discussion van Wijngaarden [13] gives arguments to show among other things that because of this ambiguity it is not necessarily true that the relation "3.14 = 3.14" is the same as "**true**" in all implementations of ALGOL. As we have mentioned above, ambiguities as such are not necessarily undesirable; but is clear that ambiguities 1–8 are of a different nature than this one, since it can be quite useful to describe fixed ALGOL programs with varying arithmetic substituted.

So a language need not be unambiguous, but of course when intentionally ambiguous elements are introduced it is far better to state specifically what the ambiguities are, not merely to leave them undefined, lest too many people think they are writing unambiguous programs when they are not.

2.   Corrections

CORRECTION 1:   OMITTED else

In Section 3.3.3 it is stated that "the construction

else ⟨simple arithmetic expression⟩

is equivalent to the construction

else if true then ⟨simple arithmetic expression⟩

But the latter construction is erroneous since if fails to meet the syntax; we cannot write $A := $ **if** B **then** C **else if true then** D. The original incorrect sentence adds nothing to the Report and means little or nothing to non-LISP programmers.

CORRECTION 2:   CONDITIONAL STATEMENT SEQUENCE

In Section 4.5.3.2, the paragraph "If none . . . dummy statement" should be deleted or at least accompanied by a qualification that it applies only to the second form of a conditional statement. This well-known error and also Correction 11 would have been fixed in the Revised Report except for the fact that these proposals were tied to other ones involving side effects; in the heated discussion which took place, the less controversial issues were overlooked.

The Revised Report changed the syntax of conditional statements and this makes Section 4.5.3.2. even more erroneous. And the explanation is incorrect in yet another respect, since control of the program should not pass to the statement called "$S4$" when the conditional statement is a procedure body or is preceded by a for clause.

Therefore Section 4.5.3.2 should be completely rewritten, perhaps as follows:

4.5.3.2.   Conditional statement. According to the syntax, three forms of unlabelled conditional statements are possible. These may be illustrated as follows (with Section 4.5.4 eliminated):

$$\textbf{if } B \textbf{ then } S_u$$
$$\textbf{if } B \textbf{ then } S_u \textbf{ else } S$$
$$\textbf{if } B \textbf{ then } S_{for}$$

Here B is a Boolean expression, S_u is an unconditional statement, S is a statement, and S_{for} is a for statement.

The execution of a conditional statement may be described as follows: The Boolean expression B is evaluated. If its value is **true**, the statement S_u or S_{for} following "**then**" is executed. If its value is **false** and if the conditional statement has the second form, the statement S following "**else**" is executed. (This statement S may of course be another conditional statement, which is to be interpreted according to the same rule.)

If a go to statement refers to a label within S_u or S_{for}, the effect is the same as if the remainder of the conditional statement (namely "**if** B **then**," and in the second case also "**else** S") were not present.

CORRECTION 3:   FOR EXAMPLE

The second example in Section 4.6.2 is not very good since (precluding side effects) it nearly always gets into an unending loop. Therefore, change "$V1$" to "k" in both places.

CORRECTION 4:   FUNCTION VALUES

Two sentences of Section 5.4.4 should say " . . . as a left part . . . " rather than " . . . in a left part . . . " since a function designator may appear in a subscript. A clarification, stating that the value is lost if a **real**, **integer**, or **Boolean** procedure is called in a procedure statement, might also be added here.

Change sentence 2, Section 4.2.3 " . . . a function designator of the same name . . . ". This makes an implied rule explicit. Or else, consider

real procedure A; $A := B := 0$;
integer procedure $B(k)$;   **if** $k > 0$ **then** A **else** $B := 2$;

which appears to conform to all of the present rules.

CORRECTION 5:   EXPRESSIONS

In the second sentence of Section 3, insert "labels, switch designators," after "function designators." This describes the constituents of expressions much more accurately.

CORRECTION 6:   DIVISION BY ZERO

Insert after the second sentence of 3.3.4.2: "The operation is undefined if the factor has the value zero. In other cases," The present wording of this section seems to imply $1/0$ is defined somehow.

CORRECTION 7:   STRING SYNTAX

The advent of syntax-oriented compilers and the fact that the syntax of ALGOL is (in large measure) formally unambiguous, make it desirable to change the most flagrantly ambiguous syntax rule in the Report. Therefore it is suggested that in Section 2.6.1 the definition of open string be replaced by

⟨open string⟩:: = ⟨proper string⟩ |

⟨open string⟩ ⟨string⟩ ⟨proper string⟩

CORRECTION 8: LIBRARY PROCEDURES

Section 2.4.3 says "[Identifiers] may be chosen freely (cf. however, Section 3.2.4, Standard Functions)." Section 3.2.4 says "Certain identifiers should be reserved for the standard functions of analysis, which will be expressed as procedures." If the quotation from 2.4.3 is not self-contradictory it seems to be saying that an identifier like "*abs*" may not be used by a programmer. But this would be disastrous since the list of reserved identifiers is not defined. A programmer using the name "*gamma*" for a variable may find out next year that this identifier is reserved for the gamma function. It should be made clear that any identifier may be redeclared (although this can of course lead to some difficulties when a procedure is copied from the literature into the middle of a program).

Moreover, the fourth paragraph of Section 5 specifically disallows the use of any procedures assumed to exist without declaration, except function designators denoting "standard functions of analysis." Thus, procedures such as "*inreal*," etc. for accomplishing input would have to be declared in any program which uses them! A suggested change (which I think most people would say was no change from the original intention) would be to drop the sentence "Apart from labels . . . must be declared" from the paragraph mentioned, and to add the following paragraph to Section 5:

"It is understood that certain identifiers may have meaning without explicit declaration, as if they were declared in a block external to the entire program (cf. Section 3.2.4). Such identifiers might include, for example, names of standard input and output procedures. Apart from labels, formal parameters of procedure declarations, and these standard identifiers, each identifier appearing in a program must be declared."

This paragraph makes available other types of identifiers if there is a need for them, e.g., an identifier denoting a real-time clock, or a label denoting a particular part of a control program, etc.

CORRECTION 9: OUTER BOUNDS

The statement of Section 5.2.4.2: "Consequently in the outermost block of a program only array declarations with constant bounds may be declared," should be amended to allow for the possibility of calls on standard functions (or other standard identifiers as noted in correction 8). The declaration

$$\textbf{array } A[0: abs(-2)]$$

is allowable in the outermost block, or the word "consequently" does not apply.

CORRECTION 10: LABELLED PROGRAMS

The syntax for ⟨program⟩ allows a program to be labelled but the remainder of the Report always talks about labels being local to some block. To rectify this, insert three words into Section 4.1.3:

" ... a procedure body or a program must be considered ... "

This is in fact the way a compiler should probably do the implementation (see [10]). As an example, consider the following:

$$A: \quad \textbf{begin array } B[1: read]; \quad outarray \ (B); \quad \textbf{go to } A \textbf{ end};$$

CORRECTION 11: UNDEFINED **go to**

The use of the word "undefined" in Section 4.3.5 is highly ambiguous, and under some interpretations it leads to undecidable questions which would make ALGOL 60 truly impossible to implement. Under what conditions is a switch designator "undefined"? For example we could say it is undefined if its evaluation procedure makes use of real arithmetic, or if its evaluation procedure never terminates. By a suitable construction, the latter condition can be made equivalent to the problem of deciding whether or not a Turing Machine will ever stop.

The following procedure is an amusing (although unambiguous) example of the application of an undefined go to statement, which points out how difficult it can be for an optimizing ALGOL 60 translator to detect the fact that a procedure is being called recursively:

```
begin integer nn;
  switch A := B[1], B[2];
  switch B := A[G], A[2];
  integer procedure F(n, S);  value n;  integer n;  switch S;
    begin nn := n;  go to S[1];  F := nn end F;
  integer procedure G;
    begin integer n;
    n := nn; G := 0;
    nn := if n ≤ 1 then n else F(n−1, A) + F(n−2, A)
    end S;
  outreal (1, F(20, A)) end.
```

The output of this program should be 6765 (the twentieth Fibonacci number).

CORRECTION 12: CALL BY NAME

Instead of "Some important particular cases of this general rule" at the end of Section 4.7.5, it should be e.g., "Some important particular cases of this general rule, and some additional restrictions." The restrictions of Subsection 4.7.5.2 are not always special cases of the general rule, as shown in the following amusing example:

```
begin procedure S(x);  x := 0;
  real procedure r;  S(r);
  real x;  x := 1;
  S (if x = 1 then r else x);  outreal (1, x) end.
```

This program seems to have a historical claim of being the last "surprise" noticed by ALGOL punsters; it contains two unexpected twists, the first of which was suggested by P. Ingerman:

(a) Procedure r uses $S(r)$ to set the value of r to zero.

(b) The expansion of the procedure statement on the last line, according to the rules of "call by name," leads to a valid ALGOL program which has a completely different structure than the body of S:

$$\textbf{if } x = 1 \textbf{ then } r \textbf{ else } x := 0$$

Here an unconditional statement plus a conditional expression has become a conditional statement.

Fortunately both of these situations have been ruled out by Section 4.7.5.2.

Conclusion

For centuries astronomers have given the name ALGOL to a star which is also called Medusa's head. The author has tried to indicate every known blemish in [2]; and he hopes that nobody will ever scrutinize any of his own writings as meticulously as he and others have examined the ALGOL Report.

RECEIVED JANUARY 1967; REVISED JULY 1967

REFERENCES

1. NAUR, P. (Ed.) Report on the algorithmic language ALGOL 60. *Comm. ACM 3* (1960), 299–314.
2. NAUR, P., AND WOODGER, M. (Eds.) Revised report on the algorithmic language ALGOL 60. *Comm. ACM 6* (1963), 1–20.
3. ABRAHAMS, P. W. A final solution to the dangling **else** of ALGOL 60 and related languages. *Comm. ACM 9* (1966), 679–682.
4. MERNER, J. N. Discussion question. *Comm. ACM 5* (1964), 71.
5. KNUTH, D. E. On the translation of languages from left to right. *Inf. Contr. 8* (1965), 607–639.
6. DIJKSTRA, E. W. Letter to the editor. *Comm. ACM 4* (1961), 502–503.
7. LEAVENWORTH, B. M. FORTRAN IV as a syntax language. *Comm. ACM 7* (1964), 72–80.
8. KNUTH, D. E., AND MERNER, J. N. ALGOL 60 confidential. *Comm. ACM 4* (1961), 268–272.
9. INGERMAN P. Z., AND MERNER, J. N. Suggestions on ALGOL 60 (Rome) issues. *Comm. ACM 6* (1963), 20–23.
10. RANDELL, B., AND RUSSELL, L. J. *ALGOL 60 Implementation.* Academic Press, London, 1964.
11. NAUR, P. Questionnaire. *ALGOL Bulletin 14*, Regnecentralen, Copenhagen, Denmark, 1962.
12. B5500 Information processing systems reference manual. Burroughs Corp., 1964.
13. VAN WIJNGAARDEN, A. Switching and programming. In H. Aiken and W. F. Main (EDS.), *Switching Theory in Space Technology*, Stanford U. Press, Stanford, 1963, pp. 275–283.

A CONTRIBUTION TO THE DEVELOPMENT OF ALGOL*

C. A. R. HOARE

A programming language similar in many respects to ALGOL 60, but incorporating a large number of improvements based on six years' experience with that language, is described in detail. Part I consists of an introduction to the new language and a summary of the changes made to ALGOL 60, together with a discussion of the motives behind the revisions. Part II is a rigorous definition of the proposed language. Part III describes a set of proposed standard procedures to be used with the language, including facilities for input/output.

PART I. GENERAL INTRODUCTION

1. Historical Background

A preliminary version of this report was originally drafted by the first author on an invitation made by IFIP Working Group 2.1 at its meeting in May, 1965 at Princeton. It incorporated a number of opinions and suggestions made at that meeting and in its subcommittees, and it was distributed to members of the Working Group as "Proposal for a Report on a Successor of ALGOL 60" (MR75, Mathematical Centre, Amsterdam, August 1965).

However, at the following meeting of the Group at Grenoble in October, 1965 it was felt that the report did not represent a sufficient advance on ALGOL 60, either in its manner of language definition or in the content of the language itself. The draft therefore no longer had the status of an official Working Document of the Group and by kind permission of the Chairman it was released for wider publication.

At that time the authors agreed to collaborate on revising and supplementing the draft. The main changes were:

(1) verbal improvements and clarifications, many of which were kindly suggested by recipients of the original draft;

(2) additional or altered language features, in particular the replacement of tree structures by records as proposed by the second author;

(3) changes which appeared desirable in the course

*Reprinted from *Comm ACM* 9, 6, June 1966, 413–431.

This work was supported by the National Science Foundation (GP 4053 and GP 4298), and it is also published with due acknowledgment to Elliott-Automation Computers Ltd.

* Computer Science Department.

of designing a simple and efficient implementation of the language;

(4) addition of introductory and explanatory material, and further suggestions for standard procedures, in particular on input/output;

(5) use of a convenient notational facility to abbreviate the description of syntax, as suggested by van Wijngaarden in "Orthogonal Design and Description of a Formal Language" (MR76, Mathematical Centre, Amsterdam, Oct. 1965).

The incorporation of the revisions is not intended to reinstate the report as a candidate for consideration as a successor to ALGOL 60. However, it is believed that its publication will serve three purposes:

(1) To present to a wider public a view of the general direction in which the development of ALGOL is proceeding;

(2) To provide an opportunity for experimental implementation and use of the language, which may be of value in future discussions of language development;

(3) To describe some of the problems encountered in the attempt to extend the language further.

2. Aims of the Language

The design of the language is intended to reflect the outlook and intentions of IFIP Working Group 2.1, and in particular their belief in the value of a common programming language suitable for use by many people in many countries. It also recognizes that such a language should satisfy as far as possible the following criteria:

(1) The language must provide a suitable technique for the programming of digital computers. It must there-

fore be closely oriented toward the capabilities of these machines, and must take into account their inherent limitations. As a result it should be possible to construct a fast, well-structured and reliable translator, translating programs into machine code which makes economic use of the power and capacity of a computer. In addition, the design of the language should act as an encouragement to the programmer to conceive the solution of his problems in terms which will produce effective programs on the computers he is likely to have at his disposal.

(2) The language must serve as a medium of communication between those engaged in problems capable of algorithmic solution. The notational structure of programs expressed in the language should correspond closely with the dynamic structure of the processes they describe. The programmer should be obliged to express himself explicitly clearly and fully, without confusing abbreviations or implicit presuppositions. The perspicuity of programs is believed to be a property of equal benefit to their readers and ultimately to their writers.

(3) The language must present a conceptual framework for teaching, reasoning and research in both theoretical and practical aspects of the science of computation. It must therefore be based on rigourous selection and abstraction of the most fundamental concepts of computational techniques. Its power and flexibility should derive from unifying simplicity, rather than from proliferation of poorly integrated features and facilities. As a consequence, for each purpose there will be exactly one obviously appropriate facility, so that there is minimal scope for erroneous choice and misapplication of facilities, whether due to misunderstanding, inadvertence or inexperience.

(4) The value of a language is increased in proportion to the range of applications in which it may effectively and conveniently be used. It is hoped that the language will find use throughout the field of algebraic and numeric applications, and that its use will begin to spread to non-numeric data processing in areas hitherto the preserve of special purpose languages, for example, the fields of simulation studies, design automation, information retrieval, graph theory, symbol manipulation and linguistic research.

To meet any of these four requirements, it is necessary that the language itself be defined with utmost clarity and rigor. The Report on ALGOL 60 has set a high standard in this respect, and in style and notation its example has been gratefully followed.

3. Summary of New Features

A large part of the language is, of course, taken directly from ALGOL 60. However, in some respects the language has been simplified, and in others extended. The following paragraphs summarize the major changes to ALGOL 60, and relate them to the declared aims of the language.

3.1. DATA TYPES

The range of primitive data types has been extended from three in ALGOL 60 to seven, or rather nine, if the long variants are included. In compensation, certain aspects of the concept of type have been simplified. In particular, the **own** concept has been abandoned as insufficiently useful to justify its position, and as leading to semantic ambiguities in many circumstances.

3.1.1. Numeric Data Types

The type **complex** has been introduced into the language to simplify the specification of algorithms involving complex numbers.

For the types **real** and **complex,** a long variant is provided to deal with calculations or sections of calculations in which the normal precision for floating-point number representation is not sufficient. It is expected that the significance of the representation will be approximately doubled.

No provision is made for specifying the exact required significance of floating-point representation in terms of the number of binary or decimal digits. It is considered most important that the values of primitive types should occupy a small integral number of computer words, so that their processing can be carried out with the maximum efficiency of the equipment available.

3.1.2. Sequences

The concept of a *sequence* occupies a position intermediate between that of an array and of other simple data types. Like single-dimensional arrays, they consist of ordered sequences of elements; however, unlike arrays, the most frequent operations performed on them are not the extraction or insertion of single elements, but rather the processing of whole sequences, or possibly subsequences of them.

Sequences are represented in the language by two new types, **bits** (sequence of binary digits), and **string** (sequence of characters). Operations defined for bit sequences include the logical operations $\neg$, $\wedge$ and $\vee$, and those of shifting left and right.

The most important feature of a bit sequence is that its elements are sufficiently small to occupy only a fraction of a "computer word," i.e. a unit of information which is in some sense natural to the computer. This means that space can be saved by "packing," and efficiency can be gained by operating on such natural units of information. In order that use of such natural units can be made by an implementation, the maximum number of elements in a sequence must be specified, when a variable of that type is declared. Operations defined for string sequences include the catenation operator **cat**.

3.1.3. Type Determination at Compile Time

The language has been designed in such a way that the type and length of the result of evaluating every expression and subexpression can be uniquely determined by a textual scan of the program, so that no type testing is required at run time, except possibly on procedure entry.

3.1.4. Type Conversions

The increase in the number of data types has caused an even greater number of possibilities for type conversion; some of these are intended to be inserted automatically by

the translator, and others have to be specified by the programmer by use of standard transfer functions provided for the purpose.

Automatic insertion of type conversion has been confined to cases where there could be no possible confusion about which conversion is intended: from **integer** to **real,** and **real** to **complex,** but not vice versa. Automatic conversions are also performed from shorter to longer variants of the data types; and in the case of numbers, from long to short as well.

For all other conversions explicit standard procedures must be used. This ensures that the complexity and possible inefficiency of the conversion process is not hidden from the programmer; furthermore, the existence of additional parameters of the procedure, or a choice of procedures, will draw his attention to the fact that there is more than one way of performing the conversion, and he is thereby encouraged to select the alternative which corresponds to his real requirements, rather than rely on a built-in "default" conversion, about which he may have only vague or even mistaken ideas.

3.2. CONTROL OF SEQUENCING

The only changes made to facilities associated with control of sequencing have been made in the direction of simplification and clarification, rather than extension.

3.2.1. Switches and the Case Construction

The switch declaration and the switch designator have been abolished. Their place has been taken by the case construction, applying to both expressions and statements. This construction permits the selection and execution (or evaluation) of one from a list of statements (or expressions); the selection is made in accordance with the value of an integer expression.

The case construction extends the facilities of the ALGOL conditional to circumstances where the choice is made from more than two alternatives. Like the conditional, it mirrors the dynamic structure of a program more clearly than go to statements and switches, and it eliminates the need for introducing a large number of labels in the program.

3.2.2. Labels

The concept of a label has been simplified so that it merely serves as a link between a goto statement and its destination; it has been stripped of all features suggesting that it is a manipulable object. In particular, designational expressions have been abolished, and labels can no longer be passed as parameters of procedures.

A further simplification is represented by the rule that a goto statement cannot lead from outside into a conditional statement or case statement, as well as iterative statement.

The ALGOL 60 integer labels have been eliminated.

3.2.3. Iterative Statements

The purpose of iterative statements is to enable the programmer to specify iterations in a simple and perspicuous manner, and to protect himself from the unexpected effects of some subtle or careless error. They also signalize to the translator that this is a special case, susceptible of simple optimization.

It is notorious that the ALGOL 60 for statement fails to satisfy any of these requirements, and therefore a drastic simplification has been made. The use of iterative statements has been confined to the really simple and common cases, rather than extended to cover more complex requirements, which can be more flexibly and perspicuously dealt with by explicit program instructions using labels.

The most general and powerful iterative statement, capable of covering all requirements, is that which indicates that a statement is to be executed repeatedly while a given condition remains true. The only alternative type of iterative statement allows a formal counter to take successive values in a finite arithmetic progression on each execution of the statement. No explicit assignments can be made to this counter, which is implicitly declared as local to the iterative statement.

3.3. PROCEDURES AND PARAMETERS

A few minor changes have been made to the procedure concept of ALGOL 60, mainly in the interests of clarification and efficiency of implementation.

3.3.1. Value and Result Parameters

As in ALGOL 60, the meaning of parameters is explained in terms of the "copy rule," which prescribes the literal replacement of the formal parameter by the actual parameter. As a counterpart to the "value parameter," which is a convenient abbreviation for the frequent case where the formal parameter can be considered as a variable local to the procedure and initialized to the value of the actual parameter, a "result parameter" has been introduced. Again, the formal parameter is considered as a local variable, whose value is assigned to the corresponding actual parameter (which therefore always must be a variable) upon termination of the procedure.

The facility of calling an array parameter by value has been removed. It contributes no additional power to the language, and it contravenes the general policy that operations on entire arrays should be specified by means of explicit iterations, rather than concealed by an implicit notation.

3.3.2. Statement Parameters

A facility has been provided for writing a statement as an actual parameter corresponding to a formal specified as **procedure.** The statement can be considered as a proper procedure body without parameters. This represents a considerable notational convenience, since it enables the procedure to be specified actually in the place where it is to be used, rather than disjointly in the head of some embracing block.

The label parameter has been abolished; its function may be taken over by placing a goto statement in the corresponding actual parameter position.

3.3.3. Specifications

The specification of all formal parameters, and the correct matching of actuals to formals, has been made

obligatory. The purpose of specifications is to inform the user of the procedure of the correct conditions of its use, and to ensure that the translator can check that these conditions have been met.

One of the most important facts about a procedure which operates on array parameters is the dimensionality of the arrays it will accept as actual parameters. A means has therefore been provided for indicating this in the specification of the parameter.

To compensate for the obligatory nature of specifications, their notation has been simplified by including them in the formal parameter list, rather than placing them in a separate specification part, as in ALGOL 60.

3.4 DATA STRUCTURES

The concept of an array has been taken from ALGOL 60 virtually unchanged, with the exception of a slight notational simplification.

To supplement the array concept, the language has been extended by the addition of a new type of structure (the *record*) consisting, like the array, of one or more elements (or *fields*). With each record there is associated a unique value of type **reference** which is said to refer to that record. This reference may be assigned as the value of a suitable field in another record, with which the given record has some meaningful relationship. In this way, groups of records may be linked in structural networks of any desired complexity.

The concept of records has been pioneered in the AED–I language by D. T. Ross.

3.4.1. Records and Fields

Like the array, a record is intended to occupy a given fixed number of locations in the store of a computer. It differs from the array in that the types of the fields are not required to be identical, so that in general each field of a record may occupy a different amount of storage. This, of course, makes it unattractive to select an element from a record by means of a computed ordinal number, or index; instead, each field position is given a unique invented name (identifier), which is written in the program whenever that field is referred to.

A record may be used to represent inside the computer some discrete physical or conceptual object to be examined or manipulated by the program, for example, a person, a town, a geometric figure, a node of a graph, etc. The fields of the record then represent properties of that object, for example, the name of a person, the distance of a town from some starting point, the length of a line, the time of joining a queue, etc. Normally, the name of the field suggests the property represented by that field.

In contrast to arrays, records are not created by declarations; rather, they are created dynamically by statements of the program. Thus their lifetimes do not have to be nested, and stack methods of storage control must be supplemented by more sophisticated techniques. It is intended that automatic "garbage collection" will be applicable to records, so that records which have become

inaccessible may be detected, and the space they occupy released for other purposes.

3.4.2. References

The normal data types (**string, real, integer,** etc.) are sufficient to represent the properties of the objects represented by records; but a new type of data is required to represent relationships holding between these objects. Provided that the relationship is a functional relationship (i.e. many-one or one-one), it can be represented by placing as a field of one record a reference to the other record to which it is related. For example, if a record which represents a person has a field named *father*, then this is likely to be used to contain a reference to the record which represents that person's father. A similar treatment is possible to deal with the relationship between a town and the next town visited on some journey, between a customer and the person following him in some queue, between a directed line and its starting point, etc.

References are also used to provide the means by which the program gains access to records; for this purpose, variables of type **reference** should be declared in the head of the block which uses them. Such variables will at any given time refer to some subset of the currently existing records. Fields of records can be referred to directly by associating the name of the field with the value of the variable holding a reference to the relevant record. If that record itself has fields containing references to yet further records outside the initial subset, then fields of these other records may be accessed indirectly by further associating their names with the construction which identified the reference to the relevant record. By assignment of references, records previously accessible only indirectly can be made directly accessible, and records previously directly accessible can lose this status, or even become totally inaccessible, in which case they are considered as deleted.

Thus, for example, if B is a variable of type **reference** declared in the head of some enclosing block, and if *age* and *father* are field identifiers and if B contains a reference to a certain person, then

$$age\,(B)$$

(called a field designator) gives that person's age;

$$father(B)$$

is a reference to that person's father, and

$$age\,(father(B))$$

gives his father's age.

3.4.3. Record Classes

Two records may be defined as similar if they have the same number of fields, and if corresponding fields in the two records have the same names and the same types. Similarity in this sense is an equivalence relationship and may be used to split all records into mutually exclusive and exhaustive equivalence classes, called *record classes*. These classes tend to correspond to the natural classification of objects under some generic term, for example:

person, *town* or *quadrilateral*. Each record class must be introduced in a program by means of a record class declaration, which associates a name with the class and specifies the names and types of the fields which characterize the members of the class.

One of the major pitfalls in the use of references is the mistaken assumption that the value of a reference variable, –field or –parameter refers to a record of some given class, whereas on execution of the program it turns out that the reference value is associated with some record of quite a different class. If the programmer attempts to access a field inappropriate to the actual class referred to, he will get a meaningless result; but if he attempts to make an assignment to such a field, the consequences could be disastrous to the whole scheme of storage control. To avoid this pitfall, it is specified that the programmer can associate with the definition of every reference variable, –field or –parameter the name of the record class to which any record referred to by it will belong. The *translator* is then able to verify that the mistake described can never occur.

3.4.4. Efficiency of Implementation

Many applications for which record handling will be found useful are severely limited by the speed and capacity of the computers available. It has therefore been a major aim in the design of the record-handling facilities that in implementation the accessing of records and fields should be accomplished with the utmost efficiency, and that the layout of storage be subjected only to a minimum administrative overhead.

4. Possibilities for Language Extension

In the design of the language a number of inviting possibilities for extensions were considered. In many cases the investigation of these extensions seemed to reveal inconsistencies, indecisions and difficulties which could not readily be solved. In other cases it seemed undesirable to make the extension into a standard feature of the language, in view of the extra complexity involved.

In this section, suggested extensions are outlined for the consideration of implementors, users and other language designers.

4.1. Further String Operations

For some applications it seems desirable to provide facilities for referring to subsequences of bits and strings. The position of the subsequence could be indicated by a notation similar to subscript bounds, viz.

$S[i:j]$ the subsequence of S consisting of the ith to jth elements inclusive.

This notation is more compact than the use of a standard procedure, and it represents the fact that extraction is more likely to be performed by an open subroutine than a closed one. However, the notational similarity suggests that the construction might also appear in the left part of an assignment, in which case it denotes insertion rather than extraction, i.e. assignment to a part of the quantity.

Apart from the undesirability of the same construction denoting two different operations, this would require that strings be classified as structured values along with arrays.

4.2. Further Data Types

Suggestions have been made for facilities to specify the precision of numbers in a more "flexible" way, e.g. by indicating the number of required decimal places. This solution has been rejected because it ignores the fundamental distinction between the number itself and one of its possible denotations, and as a consequence is utterly inappropriate for calculators not using the decimal number representation. As an alternative, the notion of a precision hierarchy could be introduced by prefixing declarations with a sequence of symbols **long**, where the number of **long**s determines the precision class. For reasons of simplicity, and in order that an implementation may closely reflect the properties of a real machine (single vs. double precision real arithmetic), allowing for only one **long** was considered as appropriate. Whether an implementation actually distinguishes between **real** and **long real** can be determined by an environment enquiry (cf. Part III, 2).

4.3. Initial Values and Local Constants

It is a minor notational convenience to be able to assign an initial value to a variable as part of the declaration which introduces that variable. A more important advantage is that the notation enables the programmer to express a very important feature of his calculations, namely, that this is an unique initial assignment made once only on the first entry to the block; furthermore it completely rules out the possibility of the elementary but all too common error of failing to make an assignment before the use of a variable.

However, such a facility rests on the notions of "compile time" and "run time" action, which, if at all, should be introduced at a conceptually much more fundamental level.

In some cases it is known that a variable only ever takes one value throughout its lifetime, and a means may be provided to make these cases notationally distinct from those of initial assignment. This means that the intention of the programmer can be made explicit for the benefit of the reader, and the translator is capable of checking that the assumption of constancy is in fact justified. Furthermore, the translator can sometimes take advantage of the declaration of constancy to optimize a program.

4.4. Array Constructors

To provide the same technique for the initialization of arrays as for other variables, some method should be provided for enumerating the values of an array as a sequence of expressions. This would require the definition of a reference denotation for array values, which, if available, would consequently suggest the introduction of operations on values of type array. The reasons for not extending the language in this direction have already been explained.

4.5. Record Class Discrimination

In general, the rule that the values of a particular reference variable or field must be confined to a single record class will be found to present little hardship; however, there are circumstances in which it is useful to relax this rule, and to permit the values of a reference variable to range over more than one record class. A facility is then desirable to determine the record class to which a referred record actually belongs.

Two possibilities for record class discriminations are outlined as follows.

1. A record union declaration is introduced with the form

union ⟨record union identifier⟩ (⟨record class identifier list⟩)

The record class identifier accompanying a reference variable declaration could then be replaced by a record union identifier, indicating that the values of that reference variable may range over all record classes included in that union. An integer primary of the form

⟨record union identifier⟩ (⟨reference expression⟩)

would then yield the ordinal number of the record class in that union to which the record referred to by the reference expression belongs.

2. Record class specifications in reference variable declarations are omitted, and a logical primary of the form

⟨reference primary⟩ **is** ⟨record class identifier⟩

could be introduced with the value **true**, if and only if the reference primary refers to a record of the specified record class.

While the introduction of a new kind of declaration (1) may seem undesirable, solution (2) reintroduces the dangerous pitfalls described in 3.4.3.

4.6. Procedure Parameters

It has been realized that in most implementations an actual parameter being an expression constitutes a function procedure declaration, and that one being a statement constitutes a proper procedure declaration. These quasi-procedure declarations, however, are confined to being parameterless. Samelson has suggested a notation for functionals which essentially does nothing more than remove this restriction: an actual parameter may include in its heading formal parameter specifications (cf. *ALGOL Bulletin 20.3.3.*). In a paper by Wirth and Weber, the notational distinction between procedure declarations and actual parameters has been entirely removed [cf. *Comm. ACM 9*, 2 (Feb. 1966), 89 ff.]. This was done along with the introduction of a new kind of actual parameters similar in nature to the references introduced here in connection with records.

However, neither ad hoc solutions nor a radical change from the parameter mechanism and notation of ALGOL 60 seemed desirable.

PART II. DEFINITION OF THE LANGUAGE

CONTENTS

1. Terminology, Notation and Basic Definitions

The Reference Language is a phrase structure language, defined by a formal system. This formal system makes use of the notation and the definitions explained below. The structure of the language ALGOL is determined by the three quantities:

(1) $\mathcal{V}$, the set of basic constituents of the language,

(2) $\mathcal{U}$, the set of syntactic entities, and

(3) $\mathcal{P}$, the set of syntactic rules, or productions.

1.1 Notation

A syntactic entity is denoted by its name (a sequence of letters) enclosed in the brackets ⟨ and ⟩. A syntactic rule has the form

$$\langle A \rangle ::= x$$

where ⟨A⟩ is a member of $\mathcal{U}$, x is any possible sequence of basic constituents and syntactic entities, simply to be called a "sequence". The form

$$\langle A \rangle ::= x \mid y \mid \cdots \mid z$$

is used as an abbreviation for the set of syntactic rules

$$\langle A \rangle ::= x$$
$$\langle A \rangle ::= y$$
$$\cdots\cdots\cdots$$
$$\langle A \rangle ::= z$$

1.2 Definitions

1. A sequence x is said to *directly produce* a sequence y if and only if there exist (possibly empty) sequences u and w, so that either (*i*) for some $\langle A \rangle$ in $\mathfrak{U}$, $x = u \langle A \rangle w$, $y = uvw$, and $\langle A \rangle :: = v$ is a rule in $\mathscr{P}$; or (*ii*) $x = uw$, $y = uvw$ and v is a "comment" (see below).

2. A sequence x is said to *produce* a sequence y if and only if there exists an ordered set of sequences $s[0]$, $s[1]$, $\cdots$, $s[n]$, so that $x = s[0]$, $s[n] = y$, and $s[i-1]$ directly produces $s[i]$ for all $i = 1, \cdots, n$.

3. A sequence x is said to be an ALGOL program if and only if its constituents are members of the set $\mathfrak{V}$, and x can be produced from the syntactic entity $\langle$program$\rangle$.

The sets $\mathfrak{V}$ and $\mathfrak{U}$ are defined through enumeration of their members in Section 2 of this Report (cf. also 4.4). The members of the set of syntactic rules are given throughout the sequel of the Report. To provide explanations for the meaning of ALGOL programs, the letter sequences denoting syntactic entities have been chosen to be English words describing approximately the nature of that syntactic entity or construct. Where words which have appeared in this manner are used elsewhere in the text, they refer to the corresponding syntactic definition. Along with these letter sequences the symbol ℑ may occur. It is understood that this symbol must be replaced by any one of a finite set of English words (or word pairs). Unless otherwise specified in the particular section, all occurrences of the symbol ℑ within one syntactic rule must be replaced consistently, and the replacing words are

integer	logical
real	bit
long real	string
complex	reference
long complex	

It is recognized that typographical entities of lower order than basic symbols (cf. 2.1), called characters, exist. Some basic symbols may be identical with characters; others, so-called word-delimiters, are generally represented as a sequence of two or more characters. Neither the set of available characters nor the decomposition of basic symbols into them is defined here. It is understood that basic symbols are not the same as characters and that there may exist characters which are neither basic symbols nor constituents of them; these characters may, however, enter the program as constitutents of strings, i.e. character sequences delimited by so-called string quotes.

The symbol **comment** followed by any sequence of characters not containing semicolons, followed by a semicolon (;), is called a comment. A comment has no effect on the meaning of a program, and is ignored during execution of the program. An identifier immediately following the basic symbol **end** is also regarded as a comment.

The basic constituents of the language are the basic symbols (cf. 2.1), strings (cf. 4.4), and comments.

All quantities referred to in a program must be defined. Their definition is achieved either within the ALGOL program by so-called declarations and label definitions, or is thought to be done in a text, possibly written in another language, in which the ALGOL program is embedded. A program containing references to quantities defined in the latter way can only be executed in an environment where these quantities are known, and this environment is considered to be a block containing that program.

The execution of a program can be considered as a sequence of units of action. The sequence of these units of action is defined as the evaluation of expressions and the execution of statements as denoted by the program. In the definition of the language the evaluation or execution of certain constructions is (1) either not precisely defined, e.g. real arithmetic, or (2) is left undefined, e.g. the order of evaluation of primaries in expressions, or (3) is even said to be undefined or not valid. This is to be interpreted in the sense that a program which uses constructions of the first two categories fully defines a computational process only if accompanying information specifies what is not given in the definition of the language. If in case (2) this information is not supplied, then a unique result of such a process is defined only if all possible alternatives lead to the same result. No meaning can be attributed to a program using constructions of the third category.

2. Sets of Basic Symbols and Syntactic Entities

2.1. Basic Symbols

$a \mid b \mid c \mid d \mid e \mid f \mid g \mid h \mid i \mid j \mid k \mid l \mid m \mid n \mid o \mid p \mid q \mid r \mid s \mid t \mid$
$u \mid v \mid w \mid x \mid y \mid z \mid$
$A \mid B \mid C \mid D \mid E \mid F \mid G \mid H \mid I \mid J \mid K \mid L \mid M \mid N \mid O \mid P \mid Q \mid$
$R \mid S \mid T \mid U \mid V \mid W \mid X \mid Y \mid Z \mid$
$0 \mid 1 \mid 2 \mid 3 \mid 4 \mid 5 \mid 6 \mid 7 \mid 8 \mid 9 \mid$
i $\mid$ **b** $\mid$ **true** $\mid$ **false** $\mid$ **"** $\mid$ **null** $\mid$
integer $\mid$ **real** $\mid$ **complex** $\mid$ **logical** $\mid$ **bits** $\mid$ **string** $\mid$ **reference** $\mid$
long $\mid$ **array** $\mid$ **procedure** $\mid$ **record** $\mid$
$, \mid ; \mid : \mid . \mid (\mid) \mid [\mid] \mid$ **begin** $\mid$ **end** $\mid$ **if** $\mid$ **then** $\mid$ **else** $\mid$ **case** $\mid$ **of** $\mid$
$+ \mid - \mid \times \mid / \mid$ **div** $\mid$ **rem** $\mid \uparrow \mid$ **abs** $\mid \vee \mid \wedge \mid \neg \mid \downarrow \mid$ **cat** $\mid = \mid \neq \mid$
$< \mid \leq \mid \geq \mid > \mid$
$:= \mid$ **goto** $\mid$ **for** $\mid$ **step** $\mid$ **until** $\mid$ **do** $\mid$ **while** $\mid$ **comment** $\mid$ **value** $\mid$
result

2.2. Syntactic Entities
(with corresponding section numbers)

$\langle$actual parameter list$\rangle$	7.3	$\langle$declaration$\rangle$	5
$\langle$actual parameter$\rangle$	7.3	$\langle$digit$\rangle$	3.1
$\langle$array declaration$\rangle$	5.2	$\langle$equality operator$\rangle$	6.4
$\langle$bit factor$\rangle$	6.5	$\langle$expression list$\rangle$	6.7
$\langle$bit primary$\rangle$	6.5	$\langle$field list$\rangle$	5.4
$\langle$bit secondary$\rangle$	6.5	$\langle$for clause$\rangle$	7.7
$\langle$bit sequence$\rangle$	4.3	$\langle$formal parameter list$\rangle$	5.3
$\langle$bit term$\rangle$	6.5	$\langle$formal parameter	
$\langle$bit$\rangle$	4.3	segment$\rangle$	5.3
$\langle$block body$\rangle$	7.1	$\langle$formal type$\rangle$	5.3
$\langle$block head$\rangle$	7.1	$\langle$go to statement$\rangle$	7.4
$\langle$block$\rangle$	7.1	$\langle$identifier list$\rangle$	3.1
$\langle$bound pair list$\rangle$	5.2	$\langle$identifier$\rangle$	3.1
$\langle$bound pair$\rangle$	5.2	$\langle$if clause$\rangle$	6
$\langle$case clause$\rangle$	6	$\langle$if statement$\rangle$	7.5
$\langle$case statement$\rangle$	7.6	$\langle$imaginary part$\rangle$	4.1
$\langle$control identifier$\rangle$	3.1	$\langle$increment$\rangle$	7.7

3. Identifiers

3.1. SYNTAX

⟨identifier⟩ ::= ⟨letter⟩ | ⟨identifier⟩ ⟨letter⟩ | ⟨identifier⟩ ⟨digit⟩
⟨ℑ variable identifier⟩ ::= ⟨identifier⟩
⟨ℑ array identifier⟩ ::= ⟨identifier⟩
⟨procedure identifier⟩ ::= ⟨identifier⟩
⟨ℑ function identifier⟩ ::= ⟨identifier⟩
⟨record class identifier⟩ ::= ⟨identifier⟩
⟨ℑ field identifier⟩ ::= ⟨identifier⟩
⟨label identifier⟩ ::= ⟨identifier⟩
⟨control identifier⟩ ::= ⟨identifier⟩
⟨letter⟩ ::= a | b | c | d | e | f | g | h | i | j | k | l | m | n | o | p |
q | r | s | t | u | v | w | x | y | z |
A | B | C | D | E | F | G | H | I | J | K | L | M | N | O | P | Q |
R | S | T | U | V | W | X | Y | Z
⟨digit⟩ ::= 0 | 1 | 2 | 3 | 4 | 5 | 6 | 7 | 8 | 9
⟨identifier list⟩ ::= ⟨identifier⟩ | ⟨identifier list⟩, ⟨identifier⟩

3.2. SEMANTICS

Variables, arrays, procedures, record classes and record fields are said to be *quantities*. Identifiers serve to identify quantities, or they stand as labels, formal parameters or control identifiers. Identifiers have no inherent meaning, and can be chosen freely.

Every identifier used in a program must be defined. This is achieved through

(a) a declaration (cf. Section 5), if the identifier identifies a quantity. It is then said to denote that quantity and to be a ℑ variable–, ℑ array–, procedure–, ℑ

function–, record class–, or ℑ field identifier, where the symbol ℑ stands for the appropriate word reflecting the type of the declared quantity;

(b) a label definition (cf. 7.1), if the identifier stands as a label. It is then said to be a label identifier;

(c) its occurrence in a formal parameter list (cf. 5.3). It is then said to be a formal parameter;

(d) its occurrence in a for clause following the symbol **for** (cf. 7.7). It is then said to be a control identifier.

The identification of the definition of a given identifier is determined by the following rules:

Step 1. If the identifier is defined within the smallest block embracing the given occurrence of that identifier by a declaration of a quantity or by its standing as a label, then it denotes that quantity or that label. A statement following a procedure heading or a for clause is considered to be a block.

Step 2. Otherwise, if that block is a procedure body and if the given identifier is identical with a formal parameter in the associated procedure heading, then it stands as that formal parameter.

Step 3. Otherwise, if that block is preceded by a for clause and the identifier is identical to the control identifier of that for clause, then it stands as that control identifier.

Otherwise, these rules are applied considering the smallest block embracing the block which has previously been considered.

If either step 1 or step 2 could lead to more than one definition, then the identification is undefined.

The scope of a quantity, a label, a formal parameter, or a control identifier is the set of statements in which occurrences of an identifier may refer by the above rules to the definition of that quantity, label, formal parameter or control identifier.

3.3. EXAMPLES

i
Person
elder sibling
*x*15

4. Values and Types

Constants and variables are said to possess a *value*. The value of a constant is determined by the denotation of the constant. In the language, every constant (except references) has a reference denotation (cf. 4.1–4.4). The value of a variable is the one most recently assigned to that variable. A value is (recursively) defined as either being a simple value, or a structured value, i.e. an ordered set of one or more values. Every value is said to be of a certain *type*. The following types of simple values are distinguished:

integer: the value is an integer,
real or **long real**: the value is a real number,
complex or **long complex**: the value is a complex number,
logical: the value is a logical value,
bits: the value is a linear sequence of bits,

string: the value is a linear sequence of characters.

reference: the value is a reference to a record.

The following types of structured values are distinguished:

    array: the value is an ordered set of values, all of identical type and subscript bounds,

    record: the value is a set of simple values.

A procedure may yield a value, in which case it is said to be a function procedure, or it may not yield a value, in which case it is called a proper procedure. The value of a function procedure is defined as the value which results from the execution of the procedure body (cf. 6.2.2).

Subsequently, the reference denotation of constants is defined. The reference denotation of any constant consists of a sequence of characters. This, however, does not imply that the value of the denoted constant is a sequence of characters, nor that it has the properties of a sequence of characters, except, of course, in the case of strings.

4.1. NUMBERS
4.1.1 Syntax

In the first rule below, every occurrence of the symbol ℑ must be systematically replaced by one of the following words (or word pairs):

        integer
        real
        long real
        complex
        long complex

⟨ℑ number⟩ ::= ⟨unsigned ℑ number⟩ | ⟨sign⟩⟨unsigned ℑ number⟩
⟨unsigned long complex number⟩ ::=
  long ⟨unsigned complex number⟩
⟨unsigned complex number⟩ ::= ⟨real part⟩i⟨imaginary part⟩
⟨real part⟩ ::= ⟨unsigned real number⟩ | ⟨unsigned integer number⟩
⟨imaginary part⟩ ::= ⟨real number⟩ | ⟨integer number⟩
⟨unsigned long real number⟩ ::= *long* ⟨unsigned real number⟩ |
  long ⟨unsigned integer number⟩
⟨unsigned real number⟩ ::= ⟨unscaled real⟩ | ⟨unscaled real⟩
  ⟨scale factor⟩ | ⟨unsigned integer number⟩⟨scale factor⟩
⟨unscaled real⟩ ::= ⟨unsigned integer number⟩.
  ⟨unsigned integer number⟩ | .⟨unsigned integer number⟩
⟨scale factor⟩ ::= ₁₀⟨integer number⟩
⟨unsigned integer number⟩ ::= ⟨digit⟩ |
  ⟨unsigned integer number⟩ ⟨digit⟩
⟨sign⟩:: = + | −

4.1.2. Semantics

Numbers are interpreted according to the conventional decimal notation. A scale factor denotes an integral power of 10 which is multiplied by the unscaled real or integer number preceding it. Each number has a uniquely defined type.

4.1.3 Examples

1	.5	1i−1
−0100	1₁₀3	−0.33i0.67
3.1416	6.02486₁₀+23	**long** 0i1
+**long** 2.7182818284590452353602877		

Note that −0.33i0.67 denotes −(0.33i0.67).

4.2 LOGICAL VALUES
4.2.1 Syntax

⟨logical value⟩:: = **true** | **false**

4.3. BIT SEQUENCES
4.3.1. Syntax

⟨bit sequence⟩ ::= **b**⟨bit⟩ | ⟨bit sequence⟩⟨bit⟩
⟨bit⟩ ::= 0 | 1

4.3.2. Semantics

The number of bits in a bit sequence is said to be the length of the bit sequence.

4.3.3. Examples

    b10011
    b001

4.4. STRINGS
4.4.1. Syntax

⟨string⟩ ::= "⟨sequence of characters⟩"

4.4.2. Semantics

Strings consist of any sequence of characters enclosed by but not containing the character ", called string quote. They are considered to be basic constituents of the language (cf. Section 1). The number of characters in a string excluding the quotes is said to be the length of the string.

4.5. REFERENCES
4.5.1. Syntax

⟨null reference⟩ ::= **null**

4.5.2. Semantics

The reference value **null** fails to designate a record; if a reference expression occurring in a field designator has this value, then the field designator is undefined.

5. Declarations

Declarations serve to associate identifiers with the quantities used in the program, to attribute certain permanent properties to these quantities (e.g. type, structure), and to determine their scope. The quantities declared by declarations are simple variables, arrays, procedures and record classes.

Upon exit from a block, all quantities declared within that block lose their value and significance (cf. 7.1.2 and 7.4.2).

Syntax:

⟨declaration⟩ ::= ⟨simple variable declaration⟩ |
  ⟨array declaration⟩ | ⟨procedure declaration⟩ |
  ⟨record class declaration⟩

5.1. SIMPLE VARIABLE DECLARATIONS
5.1.1. Syntax

⟨simple variable declaration⟩ ::= ⟨simple type⟩ ⟨identifier list⟩
⟨simple type⟩ ::= **integer** | **real** | **long real** | **complex** |
  long complex | **logical** | **bits** (⟨unsigned integer number⟩) |
  bits | **string** | **reference** (⟨record class identifier⟩)

5.1.2. Semantics

Each identifier of the identifier list is associated with a

variable which is declared to be of the indicated type. A variable is called a simple variable, if its value is simple (cf. Section 4). If a variable is declared to be of a certain type, then this implies that only values which are assignment compatible with this type (cf. 7.2.2) can be assigned to it.

It is understood that the value of a variable of type **integer** is only equal to the value of the expression most recently assigned to it, if this value lies within certain unspecified limits. It is also understood that the value of a variable of type **real** is available only with a possible, unspecified deviation from the value of the expression most recently assigned to it. If in a declaration the symbol **real** is preceded by the symbol **long**, then this deviation is expected to be not greater than when the symbol **long** is missing. In the case of a variable of type **long complex** this holds separately for the real and imaginary parts of the complex number.

In the case of a variable of type **bits** the integer enclosed in parentheses indicates the actual length of the sequence which constitutes the value of this variable. If this specification is missing, then the length is assumed to be equal to the value of the environment enquiry function *bits in word* (cf. III.2).

In the case of a variable of type **reference**, the record class identifier enclosed within parentheses indicates the record class to whose records that reference variable may refer.

5.1.3. Examples

> **integer** i, j, k, m, n
> **real** x, y, z
> **long complex** c
> **logical** p, q
> **bits** g, h
> **string** r, s, t
> **reference** (*Person*) *Jack, Jill*

5.2. ARRAY DECLARATIONS

5.2.1. Syntax

⟨array declaration⟩ ::= ⟨simple type⟩ **array** ⟨bound pair list⟩ (identifier list)
⟨bound pair list⟩ ::= ⟨bound pair⟩ | ⟨bound pair⟩⟨bound pair list⟩
⟨bound pair⟩ ::= [⟨lower bound⟩:⟨upper bound⟩]
⟨lower bound⟩ ::= ⟨integer expression⟩
⟨upper bound⟩ ::= ⟨integer expression⟩

5.2.2. Semantics

Each identifier of the identifier list of an array declaration is associated with a variable which is declared to be of type **array**. A variable of type **array** is an ordered set of variables. Their number is determined by the leftmost element of the bound pair list. If the bound pair list consists of one element only, then their type is the simple type preceding the symbol **array**. Otherwise their type is **array**, and the number of elements and the type of these arrays are in turn defined by the given rules when applied to the remaining bound pair list.

Every element of an array is identified by an index. The indices are the integers between and including the values of the lower bound and the upper bound. Every expression in the bound pair list is evaluated exactly once upon entry to the block in which the declaration occurs. In order to be valid, for every bound pair, the value of the upper bound must not be less than the value of the lower bound.

5.2.3. Examples

> **integer array** [1:100] H
> **real array** [1:m] [1:n] A,B
> **string array** [j:k+1] *street, town, city*

5.3. PROCEDURE DECLARATIONS

5.3.1. Syntax

⟨procedure declaration⟩ ::= ⟨proper procedure declaration⟩ | ⟨ℑ function procedure declaration⟩
⟨proper procedure declaration⟩ ::= **procedure** ⟨procedure heading⟩;   ⟨proper procedure body⟩
⟨ℑ function procedure declaration⟩ ::= ⟨simple type⟩ **procedure** ⟨procedure heading⟩;   ⟨ℑ function procedure body⟩
⟨proper procedure body⟩ ::= ⟨statement⟩
⟨ℑ function procedure body⟩ ::= ⟨ℑ expression⟩ | ⟨block body⟩⟨ℑ expression⟩ **end**
⟨procedure heading⟩ ::= ⟨identifier⟩ | ⟨identifier⟩ (⟨formal parameter list⟩)
⟨formal parameter list⟩ ::= ⟨formal parameter segment⟩ | ⟨formal parameter list⟩;   ⟨formal parameter segment⟩
⟨formal parameter segment⟩ ::= ⟨formal type⟩ ⟨identifier list⟩
⟨formal type⟩ ::= ⟨type⟩ | ⟨simple type⟩ **value** | ⟨simple type⟩ **result** | ⟨simple type⟩ **value result** | ⟨simple type⟩ **procedure** | **procedure** | **reference**
⟨type⟩ ::= ⟨simple type⟩ | ⟨type⟩ **array**

5.3.2. Semantics

A procedure declaration associates the procedure body with the identifier immediately following the symbol **procedure**. The principal part of the procedure declaration is the procedure body. Other parts of the block in whose heading the procedure is declared can then cause this procedure body to be executed or evaluated. A proper procedure is activated by a procedure statement (cf. 7.3), a function procedure by a function designator (cf. 6.2). Associated with the procedure body is a heading, containing the procedure identifier and possibly a list of formal parameters.

5.3.2.1. Specifications of formal parameters. All formal parameters of a formal parameter segment are of the same indicated type. It must be such that the substitution of the formal by an actual parameter of this specified type leads to correct ALGOL expressions and statements (cf. 7.3.2). The word **array** should be repeated as many times as appropriate.

5.3.2.2. The effect of the symbols **value** and **result** appearing in a formal type is explained by the following rewriting rule which is applied to the procedure body before the procedure is invoked:

(1) The procedure body is enclosed by the symbols **begin** and **end** if it is not already enclosed by these symbols;

(2) For every formal parameter whose formal type contains the symbol **value** or **result** (or both),

(a) a declaration followed by a semicolon is inserted in the heading of the procedure body, with a simple type as indicated in the formal type, and with an identifier different from any identifier valid at the place of the declaration.

(b) throughout the procedure body, every occurrence of the formal parameter identifier is replaced by the identifier defined in step 2a;

(c) if the formal type contains the symbol **value**, an assignment statement followed by a semicolon is inserted after the declarations of the procedure body. Its left part contains the identifier defined in step 2a, and its expression consists of the formal parameter identifier. The symbol **value** is then deleted;

(d) if the formal type contains the symbol **result**, an assignment statement preceeded by a semicolon is inserted before the symbol **end** which terminates a proper procedure body. In the case of a function procedure, an assignment statement followed by a semicolon is inserted before the final expression of the function procedure body. Its left part contains the formal parameter identifier, and its expression consists of the identifier defined in step 2a. The symbol **result** is then deleted.

5.3.3. Examples

procedure *Increment*; $x := x+1$

real procedure *max* (**real value** x, y); **if** $x < y$ **then** y **else** x

procedure *Copy* (**real array** *array* U, V;   **integer value** a, b);
  for $i := 1$ **step** 1 **until** a **do**
  for $j := 1$ **step** 1 **until** b **do** $U[i][j] := V[i][j]$

real procedure *Horner* (**real array** a;   **integer value** n;
  real value x);
begin real s; $s := 0$;
  for $i := 0$ **step** 1 **until** n **do** $s := s \times x + a[i]$; s
end

long real procedure *sum* (**integer** k, n;   **long real** x);
begin long real y; $y := 0$; $k := n$;
  while $k \geq 1$ **do begin** $y := y + x$; $k := k - 1$
  end; y
end

reference (*Person*) **procedure** *youngest uncle*
  (**reference** (*Person*) R);
begin reference (*Person*) p, m;
  $p := $ *youngest offspring* (*father*(*father*(R)));
  while $(p \neq $ **null**$) \wedge (\neg male(p)) \vee (p = father(R))$ **do**
    $p := $ *elder sibling* (p);
  $m := $ *youngest offspring* (*mother*(*mother*(R)));
  while $(m \neq $ **null**$) \wedge (\neg \, male(m))$ **do** $m := $ *elder sibling* (m);
  if $p = $ **null then** m **else**
  if $m = $ **null then** p **else**
  if *age* (p) $<$ *age* (m) **then** p **else** m
end

5.4. RECORD CLASS DECLARATIONS

5.4.1. Syntax

⟨record class declaration⟩ ::= **record** ⟨record class identifier⟩
  (⟨field list⟩)
⟨field list⟩ ::= ⟨simple variable declaration⟩ |
  ⟨field list⟩; ⟨simple variable declaration⟩

5.4.2. Semantics

A record class declaration serves to define the structural properties of records belonging to the class. The principal constituent of a record class declaration is a sequence of simple variable declarations which define the fields and their types of the records of this class and associate identifiers with the individual fields. A record class identifier can be used in a record designator to construct a new record of the given class.

5.4.3. Examples

record *Node* (**reference** (*Node*) *left, right*)

record *Person* (**string** *name*;   **integer** *age*;   **logical** *male*;
  reference (*Person*) *father, mother, youngest offspring,
  elder sibling*)

6. Expressions

Expressions are rules which specify how new values are computed from existing ones. These new values are obtained by performing the operations indicated by the operators on the values of the operands. According to the type of their value, several types of expressions are distinguished. Their structure is defined by the following rules, in which the symbol ℑ has to be replaced consistently as described in Section 1, and where the triplets $\mathfrak{I}_0$, $\mathfrak{I}_1$, $\mathfrak{I}_2$ have to be either consistently replaced by the words

logical
bit
string
reference

or by any combination of words as indicated by the following table, which yields $\mathfrak{I}_0$ given $\mathfrak{I}_1$ and $\mathfrak{I}_2$:

$\mathfrak{I}_1$ \ $\mathfrak{I}_2$	integer	real	complex
integer	integer	real	complex
real	real	real	complex
complex	complex	complex	complex

$\mathfrak{I}_0$ has the quality "long" if either both $\mathfrak{I}_1$ and $\mathfrak{I}_2$ have that quality, or if one has the quality and the other is "integer".

Syntax:

⟨ℑ expression⟩ ::= ⟨simple ℑ expression⟩ |
  ⟨case clause⟩ (⟨ℑ expression list⟩)
⟨$\mathfrak{I}_0$ expression⟩ ::= ⟨if clause⟩⟨simple $\mathfrak{I}_1$ expression⟩ **else**
  ⟨$\mathfrak{I}_2$ expression⟩
⟨ℑ expression list⟩ ::= ⟨ℑ expression⟩
⟨$\mathfrak{I}_0$ expression list⟩ ::= ⟨$\mathfrak{I}_1$ expression list⟩, ⟨$\mathfrak{I}_2$ expression⟩
⟨if clause⟩ ::= **if** ⟨logical expression⟩ **then**
⟨case clause⟩ ::= **case** ⟨integer expression⟩ **of**

The operands are either constants, variables or function designators or other expressions between parentheses. The evaluation of the latter three may involve smaller units of action such as the evaluation of other expressions or the execution of statements. The value of an expression between parentheses is obtained by evaluating that expression. If an operator operates on two operands, then these operands may be evaluated in any order, or even in

parallel, with the exception of the case mentioned in 6.4.2.2. The construction

⟨if clause⟩⟨simple ℑ₁ expression⟩ **else** ⟨ℑ₂ expression⟩

causes the selection and evaluation of an expression on the basis of the current value of the logical expression contained in the if clause. If this value is **true**, the simple expression following the if clause is selected, if the value is **false**, the expression following **else** is selected. The construction

⟨case clause⟩ (⟨ℑ expression list⟩)

causes the selection of the expression whose ordinal number in the expression list is equal to the current value of the integer expression contained in the case clause. In order that the case expression is defined, the current value of this expression must be the ordinal number of some expression in the expression list.

6.1. Variables

6.1.1. Syntax

⟨ℑ variable⟩ ::= ⟨ℑ variable identifier⟩|⟨ℑ field designator⟩|
  ⟨ℑ array designator⟩ ⟨subscript⟩
⟨ℑ field designator⟩ ::= ⟨ℑ field identifier⟩ (⟨reference expression⟩)
⟨ℑ array designator⟩ ::= ⟨ℑ array identifier⟩|
  ⟨ℑ array designator⟩⟨subscript⟩
⟨subscript⟩ ::= [⟨integer expression⟩]

6.1.2. Semantics

A subscripted array designator denotes the variable whose index, in the ordered set of variables denoted by the array designator, is the current value of the expression in the subscript. This value must lie within the declared bounds.

The value of a variable may be used in expressions for forming other values, and may be changed by assignments to that variable.

A field designator designates a field in the record referred to by its reference expression. The type of the field designator is defined by the declaration of that field identifier in the record class designated by the reference expression of the field designator (cf. 5.4).

6.1.3. Examples

x
$A[i]$
$M[i+j][i-j]$
$father(Jack)$
$mother(father(Jill))$

6.2. Function Designators

6.2.1. Syntax

⟨ℑ function designator⟩ ::= ⟨ℑ function identifier⟩|
  ⟨ℑ function identifier⟩ (⟨actual parameter list⟩)

6.2.2. Semantics

A function designator defines a value which can be obtained by a process performed in the following steps:

Step 1. A copy is taken of the body of the function procedure whose procedure identifier is given by the function designator and of the actual parameters of the latter.

Steps 2, 3, 4.   As specified in 7.3.2.

Step 5. The copy of the function procedure body, modified as indicated in steps 2–4, is executed. The value of the function designator is the value of the expression which constitutes or is part of the modified function procedure body. The type of the function designator is the type preceding **procedure** preceding the heading of the corresponding function procedure declaration.

6.2.3. Examples

$max\ (x \uparrow 2,\ y \times 2)$
$sum\ (i,\ 100,\ H[i])$
$sum\ (i,\ m,\ sum(j,\ n,\ A[i][j]))$
$youngest\ uncle\ (Jill)$
$sum\ (i,\ 10,\ X[i] \times Y[i])$
$Horner\ (X,\ 10,\ 2.7)$

6.3. Arithmetic Expressions

6.3.1. Syntax

In any of the following rules, every occurrence of the symbol ℑ must be systematically replaced by one of the following words (or word pairs):

integer
real
long real
complex
long complex

The rules governing the replacement of the symbols ℑ₀ ℑ₁ and ℑ₂ are given in 6.3.2.

⟨simple ℑ expression⟩ ::= ⟨ℑ term⟩| + ⟨ℑ term⟩| − ⟨ℑ term⟩
⟨simple ℑ₀ expression⟩ ::= ⟨simple ℑ₁ expression⟩ + ⟨ℑ₂ term⟩|
  ⟨simple ℑ₁ expression⟩ − ⟨ℑ₂ term⟩
⟨ℑ term⟩ ::= ⟨ℑ factor⟩
⟨ℑ₀ term⟩ ::= ⟨ℑ₁ term⟩ × ⟨ℑ₂ factor⟩
⟨ℑ₀ term⟩ ::= ⟨ℑ₁ term⟩/⟨ℑ₂ factor⟩
⟨integer term⟩ ::= ⟨integer term⟩ **div** ⟨integer factor⟩|
  ⟨integer term⟩ **rem** ⟨integer factor⟩
⟨ℑ₁ factor⟩ ::= ⟨ℑ₀ secondary⟩|⟨ℑ₁ factor⟩ ↑ ⟨integer secondary⟩
⟨ℑ₀ secondary⟩ ::= ⟨ℑ primary⟩|⟨unsigned ℑ number⟩
⟨ℑ₀ secondary⟩ ::= **abs** ⟨ℑ₁ primary⟩|**abs** ⟨unsigned ℑ₁ number⟩
⟨long ℑ₀ primary⟩ ::= **long** ⟨ℑ₁ primary⟩
⟨ℑ primary⟩ ::= ⟨ℑ variable⟩|⟨ℑ function designator⟩|
  (⟨ℑ expression⟩)

6.3.2. Semantics

An arithmetic expression is a rule for computing a number.

According to its type it is either called an integer–, real–, long real–, complex–, or long complex expression.
6.3.2.1. The operators $+$, $-$, $\times$ and $/$ have the conventional meaning of addition, subtraction, multiplication and division. In the relevant syntactic rules of 6.3.1 the symbols ℑ₀ , ℑ₁ and ℑ₂ have to be replaced by any combination of words according to the following table which indicates ℑ₀ for any combination of given ℑ₁ and ℑ₂ .

Operators +|− ℑ₁ \ ℑ₂	integer	real	complex
integer	integer	real	complex
real	real	real	complex
complex	complex	complex	complex

$\mathfrak{I}_0$ has the quality "long" if both $\mathfrak{I}_1$ and $\mathfrak{I}_2$ have the quality "long", or if one has the quality "long" and the other is "integer".

Operator $\times$ $\mathfrak{I}_1$ \ $\mathfrak{I}_2$	integer	real	complex
integer	integer	long real	long complex
real	long real	long real	long complex
complex	long complex	long complex	long complex

$\mathfrak{I}_1$ or $\mathfrak{I}_2$ having the quality "long" does not affect the type of the result.

Operator / $\mathfrak{I}_1$ \ $\mathfrak{I}_2$	integer	real	complex
integer	real	real	complex
real	real	real	complex
complex	complex	complex	complex

The specifications for the quality "long" are those given for $+$ and $-$.

6.3.2.2. The operator $-$ standing as the first symbol of a simple expression denotes the monadic operation of sign inversion. The type of the result is the type of the operand. The operator $+$ standing as the first symbol of a simple expression denotes the monadic operation of identity.

6.3.2.3. The operator **div** is mathematically defined as

$$a \text{ div } b = sgn(a \times b) \times d(\text{abs } a, \text{abs } b)$$

where the function procedures sgn and d are declared as

    integer procedure sgn(**integer value** a);
      if $a < 0$ **then** -1 **else** 1;
    integer procedure d(**integer value** a, b);
      if $a < b$ **then** 0 **else** $d(a-b, b) + 1$

6.3.2.4. The operator **rem** (remainder) is mathematically defined as

$$a \text{ rem } b = a - (a \text{ div } b) \times b$$

6.3.2.5. The operator $\uparrow$ denotes exponentiation of the first operand to the power of the second operand. In the relevant syntactic rule of 6.3.1 the symbols $\mathfrak{I}_0$ and $\mathfrak{I}_1$ have to be replaced by any of the following combinations of words:

$\mathfrak{I}_0$	$\mathfrak{I}_1$
real	integer
real	real
complex	complex

$\mathfrak{I}_0$ has the quality "long" if and only if $\mathfrak{I}_1$ does.

6.3.2.6. The monadic operator **abs** yields the absolute value of the operand. In the relevant syntactic rule of 6.3.1 the symbols $\mathfrak{I}_0$ and $\mathfrak{I}_1$ have to be replaced by any of the following combinations of words:

$\mathfrak{I}_0$	$\mathfrak{I}_1$
integer	integer
real	real
real	complex

If $\mathfrak{I}_1$ has the quality "long", then so does $\mathfrak{I}_0$.

6.3.2.7. Precedence of operators. The syntax of 6.3.1 implies the following hierarchy of operator precedences:

long
abs
$\uparrow$
$\times$ / **div rem**
$+$ $-$

Sequences of operations of equal precedence shall be executed in order from left to right.

6.3.2.8. Precision of arithmetic. If the result of an arithmetic operation is of type **real** or **complex**, then it is the mathematically understood result of the operation performed on operands which may deviate from the actual operands. In case of the operands being of a type with the quality "long", this deviation, as described in 5.1.2, is intended to be smaller, and is expected to be not greater than if that quality is missing.

In the relevant syntactic rule of 6.3.1 the symbols $\mathfrak{I}_0$ and $\mathfrak{I}_1$ must be replaced by any of the following combinations of words (or word pairs):

Operator **long**	$\mathfrak{I}_0$	$\mathfrak{I}_1$
	long real	real
	long real	integer
	long complex	complex

6.3.3. Examples

    $x + c/H[j-1]$
    $c + A[i] \times B[i]$
    $exp\ (-x/(2 \times sigma))/sqrt\ (2 \times sigma)$

6.4. LOGICAL EXPRESSIONS

6.4.1. Syntax

In the following rules for ⟨relation⟩ the symbols $\mathfrak{I}_0$ and $\mathfrak{I}_1$ must either be identically replaced by any one of the following words:

    bit
    string
    reference

or by any of the words from:

    complex
    long complex
    real
    long real
    integer

and the symbols $\mathfrak{I}_2$ and $\mathfrak{I}_3$ must be replaced by any of the last three: real, long real, integer.

⟨simple logical expression⟩ ::= ⟨logical term⟩|⟨relation⟩
⟨logical term⟩ ::= ⟨logical factor⟩|⟨logical term⟩ $\vee$ ⟨logical factor⟩
⟨logical factor⟩ ::= ⟨logical secondary⟩|
  ⟨logical factor⟩ $\wedge$ ⟨logical secondary⟩
⟨logical secondary⟩ ::= ⟨logical primary⟩|¬⟨logical primary⟩
⟨logical primary⟩ ::= ⟨logical value⟩|⟨logical variable⟩|
  ⟨logical function designator⟩|(⟨logical expression⟩)
⟨relation⟩ ::=
  ⟨simple $\mathfrak{I}_0$ expression⟩⟨equality operator⟩⟨simple $\mathfrak{I}_1$ expression⟩|
  ⟨logical term⟩⟨equality operator⟩⟨logical term⟩|
  ⟨simple $\mathfrak{I}_2$ expression⟩⟨relational operator⟩⟨simple $\mathfrak{I}_3$ expression⟩
⟨relational operator⟩ ::= $<|\leq|\geq|>$
⟨equality operator⟩ ::= $=|\neq$

6.4.2. Semantics

A logical expression is a rule for computing a logical value.

6.4.2.1. The relational operators have their conventional meanings, and yield the logical value **true** if the relation is satisfied for the values of the two operands; **false**, otherwise. Two references are equal if and only if they are both **null** or both refer to the same record. Two strings are equal if and only if they have the same length and the same ordered sequence of characters.

A comparison of two bit sequences of different lengths is preceded by insertion of an appropriate number of 0's after the symbol **b** of the shorter operand.

6.4.2.2. The operators $\neg$ (not), $\wedge$ (and), and $\vee$ (or), operating on logical values, are defined by the following equivalences:

$$\neg x \quad \textbf{if } x \textbf{ then false else true}$$
$$x \wedge y \quad \textbf{if } x \textbf{ then } y \textbf{ else false}$$
$$x \vee y \quad \textbf{if } x \textbf{ then true else } y$$

6.4.2.3. Precedence of operators. The syntax of 6.4.1 implies the following hierarchy of operator precedences:

$$\neg$$
$$\wedge$$
$$\vee$$
$$< \leq = \neq \geq >$$

6.4.3. Examples

$$p \vee \neg q$$
$$(x < y) \wedge (y < z)$$
$$(i = j) = (m = n)$$
$$youngest\ offspring\ (Jack) \neq \textbf{null}$$

6.5. Bit Expressions

6.5.1. Syntax

⟨simple bit expression⟩ ::= ⟨bit term⟩|
  ⟨simple bit expression⟩ $\vee$ ⟨bit term⟩
⟨bit term⟩ ::= ⟨bit factor⟩|⟨bit term⟩ $\wedge$ ⟨bit factor⟩
⟨bit factor⟩ ::= ⟨bit secondary⟩|$\neg$⟨bit secondary⟩
⟨bit secondary⟩ ::= ⟨bit primary⟩|
  ⟨bit secondary⟩ $\uparrow$ ⟨integer secondary⟩|
  ⟨bit secondary⟩ $\downarrow$ ⟨integer secondary⟩
⟨bit primary⟩ ::= ⟨bit sequence⟩|⟨bit variable⟩|
  ⟨bit function designator⟩|(⟨bit expression⟩)

6.5.2. Semantics

A bit expression is a rule for computing a bit sequence. The operators $\vee$, $\wedge$ and $\neg$ produce a result of type **bits**, every bit being dependent on the corresponding bit(s) in the operand(s) as follows:

x	y	$\neg x$	$x \wedge y$	$x \vee y$
0	0	1	0	0
0	1	1	0	1
1	0	0	0	1
1	1	0	1	1

The operators $\uparrow$ and $\downarrow$ denote the shifting operation to the left and to the right respectively by the number of bit positions indicated by the absolute value of the inte-

ger secondary. Vacated bit positions to the right or left respectively are assigned the bit sequence value **b0**. If in the case of the $\wedge$ and $\vee$ operators the two operands are not of equal length, then the shorter operand is extended by insertion of an appropriate number of 0's after the symbol **b**. The length of the result of a bit operator is equal to the length of the operand(s).

6.5.3. Examples

$$g \wedge h \vee \textbf{b111000}$$
$$g \wedge \neg (h \vee g) \downarrow 8$$

6.6. String Expressions

6.6.1. Syntax

⟨simple string expression⟩ ::= ⟨string primary⟩|
  ⟨simple string expression⟩ **cat** ⟨string primary⟩
⟨string primary⟩ ::= ⟨string⟩|⟨string variable⟩|
  ⟨string function designator⟩|(⟨string expression⟩)

6.6.2. Semantics

A string expression is a rule for computing a string (sequence of characters).

6.6.2.1. The operator **cat** (catenate) yields the string consisting of the sequence of characters resulting from evaluation of the first operand, immediately followed by the sequence of characters resulting from evaluation of the second operand, mathematically defined as

''⟨sequence-1⟩'' **cat** ''⟨sequence-2⟩'' = ''⟨sequence-1⟩⟨sequence-2⟩''

The length of the result is the sum of the lengths of the operands.

6.6.3. Example

$$s \textbf{ cat } ''\sqcup + \sqcup'' \textbf{ cat } t$$

6.7. Reference Expressions

6.7.1. Syntax

⟨simple reference expression⟩ ::= ⟨null reference⟩|
  ⟨reference variable⟩|⟨reference function designator⟩|
  ⟨record designator⟩ |(⟨reference expression⟩)
⟨record designator⟩ ::= ⟨record class identifier⟩|
  ⟨record class identifier⟩ (⟨expression list⟩)
⟨expression list⟩ ::= ⟨ℑ expression⟩|
  ⟨expression list⟩, ⟨ℑ expression⟩

6.7.2. Semantics

A reference expression is a rule for computing a reference to a record. All simple reference expressions in a reference expression must be of the same record class.

The value of a record designator is the reference to a newly created record belonging to the designated record class. If the record designator contains an expression list, then the values of the expressions are assigned to the fields of the new record. The entries in the expression list are taken in the same order as the fields in the record class declaration, and the types of the fields must be assignment compatible with the types of the expressions (cf. 7.2.2).

6.7.3. Example

Person (''Carol'', 0, **false**, *Jack*, *Jill*, **null**,
  youngest offspring(Jack))

7. Statements

A statement is said to denote a unit of action. By the execution of a statement is meant the performance of this unit of action which may consist of smaller units of action such as the evaluation of expressions or the execution of other statements.

A statement containing no symbols denotes no action.

Syntax:

⟨program⟩ ::= ⟨block⟩
⟨statement⟩ ::= ⟨simple statement⟩|⟨iterative statement⟩|
  ⟨if statement⟩|⟨case statement⟩
⟨simple statement⟩ ::= ⟨block⟩|⟨$\mathfrak{I}$ assignment statement⟩| |
  ⟨procedure statement⟩|⟨goto statement⟩

7.1. Blocks

7.1.1. Syntax

⟨block⟩ ::= ⟨block body⟩ ⟨statement⟩ **end**
⟨block body⟩ ::= ⟨block head⟩|⟨block body⟩⟨statement⟩; |
  ⟨block body⟩⟨label definition⟩
⟨block head⟩ ::= **begin**|⟨block head⟩⟨declaration⟩;
⟨label definition⟩ ::= ⟨identifier⟩:

7.1.2. Semantics

Every block introduces a new level of nomenclature. This is realized by execution of the block in the following steps:

Step 1. If an identifier defined in the block head or in a label definition of the block body is already defined at the place from where the block is entered, then every occurrence of that identifier within the block is systematically replaced by another identifier, which is defined neither within the block nor at the place from where the block is entered.

Step 2. If the declarations of the block contain array bound expressions, then these expressions are evaluated.

Step 3. Execution of the statements contained in the block body begins with the execution of the first statement following the block head.

After execution of the last statement of the block body (unless it is a goto statement) a block exit occurs, and the statement following the entire block is executed.

7.1.3. Example

```
begin real u;
  u := x;  x := y;  y := z;  z := u
end
```

7.2. Assignment Statements

7.2.1. Syntax

In the following rules the symbols $\mathfrak{I}_0$ and $\mathfrak{I}_1$ must be replaced by words as indicated in Section 1, subject to the restriction that the type $\mathfrak{I}_0$ is assignment compatible with the type $\mathfrak{I}_1$ as defined in 7.2.2.

⟨$\mathfrak{I}_0$ assignment statement⟩ ::= ⟨$\mathfrak{I}_0$ left part⟩⟨$\mathfrak{I}_1$ expression⟩|
  ⟨$\mathfrak{I}_0$ left part⟩⟨$\mathfrak{I}_1$ assignment statement⟩
⟨$\mathfrak{I}$ left part⟩ ::= ⟨$\mathfrak{I}$ variable⟩ :=

7.2.2. Semantics

The execution of assignment statements causes the assignment of the value of the expression to one or several variables. The assignment is performed after the evaluation of the expression. The types of all left part variables must be assignment compatible with the type of the expression.

A type $\mathfrak{I}_0$ is said to be assignment compatible with a type $\mathfrak{I}_1$, if either

(1) the two types are identical (except possibly for length specifications), or

(2) $\mathfrak{I}_0$ is **real** or **long real**, and $\mathfrak{I}_1$ is **integer, real,** or **long real,** or

(3) $\mathfrak{I}_0$ is **complex** or **long complex**, and $\mathfrak{I}_1$ is **integer, real, long real, complex** or **long complex.**

In the case of the type **bits**, the length specified for $\mathfrak{I}_0$ must be not less than the length specified for $\mathfrak{I}_1$.

If the length of a bit sequence to be assigned is smaller than the length specified for $\mathfrak{I}_0$, then a suitable number of 0's are inserted after the symbol **b.**

In the case of a reference, the reference to be assigned must refer to a record of the class specified by the record class identifier associated with the reference variable in its declaration.

7.2.3. Examples

$$z := age\,(Jack) := 28$$
$$x := y + \textbf{abs}\ z$$
$$c := i + x + c$$
$$p := x \neq y$$

7.3. Procedure Statements

7.3.1. Syntax

⟨procedure statement⟩ ::= ⟨procedure identifier⟩|
  ⟨procedure identifier⟩ (⟨actual parameter list⟩)
⟨actual parameter list⟩ ::= ⟨actual parameter⟩|
  ⟨actual parameter list⟩, ⟨actual parameter⟩
⟨actual parameter⟩ ::= ⟨expression⟩|⟨statement⟩|
  ⟨$\mathfrak{I}$ array designator⟩|⟨procedure identifier⟩|⟨$\mathfrak{I}$ function identifier⟩

7.3.2. Semantics

The execution of a procedure statement is equivalent to a process performed in the following steps:

Step 1. A copy is taken of the body of the proper procedure whose procedure identifier is given by the procedure statement, and of the actual parameters of the latter.

Step 2. If the procedure body is a block, then a systematic change of identifiers in its copy is performed as specified by step 1 of 7.1.2.

Step 3. The copies of the actual parameters are treated in an undefined order as follows: If the copy is an expression different from a variable, then it is enclosed by a pair of parentheses, or if it is a statement it is enclosed by the symbols **begin** and **end.**

Step 4. In the copy of the procedure body every occurrence of an identifier identifying a formal parameter is replaced by the copy of the corresponding actual parameter (cf. 7.3.2.1). In order for the process to be defined, these replacements must lead to correct ALGOL expressions and statements.

Step 5. The copy of the procedure body, modified as indicated in steps 2–4, is executed.

7.3.2.1. Actual formal correspondence

The correspondence between the actual parameters and the formal parameters is established as follows: The actual parameter list of the procedure statement (or of the function designator) must have the same number of entries as the formal parameter list of the procedure declaration heading. The correspondence is obtained by taking the entries of these two lists in the same order.

7.3.2.2. Formal specifications

If a formal parameter is specified by **value,** then the formal type must be assignment compatible with the type of the actual parameter. If it is specified as **result,** then the type of the actual variable must be assignment compatible with the formal type. In all other cases, the types must be identical. If an actual parameter is a statement, then the specification of its corresponding formal parameter must be **procedure.**

7.3.3. Examples

> *Increment*
> *Copy* (A, B, m, n)

7.4. Goto Statements

7.4.1. Syntax

⟨goto statement⟩ ::= **goto** ⟨label identifier⟩

7.4.2. Semantics

An identifier is called a label identifier if it stands as a label.

A goto statement determines that execution of the text be continued after the label definition of the label identifier. The identification of that label definition is accomplished in the following steps:

Step 1. If some label definition within the most recently activated but not yet terminated block contains the label identifier, then this is the designated label definition. Otherwise,

Step 2. The execution of that block is considered as terminated and Step 1 is taken as specified above.

7.5. If Statements

7.5.1. Syntax

⟨if statement⟩ ::= ⟨if clause⟩⟨statement⟩|
　⟨if clause⟩⟨simple statement⟩ **else** ⟨statement⟩
⟨if clause⟩ ::= **if** ⟨logical expression⟩ **then**

7.5.2. Semantics

The execution of if statements causes certain statements to be executed or skipped depending on the values of specified logical expressions. An if statement of the form

> ⟨if clause⟩⟨statement⟩

is executed in the following steps:

Step 1. The logical expression in the if clause is evaluated.

Step 2. If the result of Step 1 is **true**, then the statement following the if clause is executed. Otherwise step 2 causes no action to be taken at all.

An if statement of the form

> ⟨if clause⟩⟨simple statement⟩ **else** ⟨statement⟩

is executed in the following steps:

Step 1. The logical expression in the if clause is evaluated.

Step 2. If the result of Step 1 is **true**, then the simple statement following the if clause is executed. Otherwise the statement following **else** is executed.

7.5.3. Examples

if $x = y$ **then goto** L
if $x < y$ **then** $u := x$ **else if** $y < z$ **then** $u := y$ **else** $v := z$

7.6. Case Statements

7.6.1. Syntax

⟨case statement⟩ ::= ⟨case clause⟩ **begin** ⟨statement list⟩ **end**
⟨statement list⟩ ::= ⟨statement⟩|⟨statement list⟩;　⟨statement⟩
⟨case clause⟩ ::= **case** ⟨integer expression⟩ **of**

7.6.2. Semantics

The execution of a case statement proceeds in the following steps:

Step 1. The expression of the case clause is evaluated.

Step 2. The statement whose ordinal number in the statement list is equal to the value obtained in Step 1 is executed. In order that the case statement is defined, the current value of the expression in the case clause must be the ordinal number of some statement of the statement list.

7.6.3. Examples

case i **of**
begin $x := x + y$;
　$y := y + z$;
　$z := z + x$
end

case j **of**
begin $H[i] := -H[i]$;
　begin $H[i-1] := H[i-1] + H[i]$;　$i := i - 1$ **end**;
　begin $H[i-1] := H[i-1] \times H[i]$;　$i := i - 1$ **end**;
　begin $H[H[i-1]] := H[i]$;　$i := i - 2$ **end**
end

7.7. Iterative Statements

7.7.1. Syntax

⟨iterative statement⟩ ::= ⟨for clause⟩⟨statement⟩|
　⟨while clause⟩⟨statement⟩
⟨for clause⟩ ::= **for** ⟨control identifier⟩ :=
　⟨initial value⟩ **step** ⟨increment⟩ **until** ⟨limit⟩ **do**
⟨initial value⟩ ::= ⟨integer expression⟩
⟨increment⟩ ::= ⟨integer expression⟩
⟨limit⟩ ::= ⟨integer expression⟩
⟨while clause⟩ ::= **while** ⟨logical expression⟩ **do**

7.7.2. Semantics

The iterative statement serves to express that a statement be executed repeatedly depending on certain conditions specified by a for clause or a while clause. The state-

ment following the for clause or the while clause always acts as a block, whether it has the form of a block or not.

(a) An iterative statement of the form

for ⟨control identifier⟩ := $e1$ **step** $e2$ **until** $e3$ **do** ⟨statement⟩

is exactly equivalent to the block

begin ⟨statement–0⟩; ⟨statement–1⟩; ...; ⟨statement–i⟩; ∴; ⟨statement–n⟩ **end**

when in the ith statement every occurrence of the control identifier is replaced by the reference denotation of the value of the expression $e1 + i \times e2$, enclosed in parentheses.

The index n of the last statement is determined by $n \leq (e3-e1)/e2 < n + 1$. If $n < 0$, then it is understood that the sequence is empty. The expressions $e1$, $e2$, and $e3$ are evaluated exactly once, namely before execution of ⟨statement–0⟩.

(b) An iterative statement of the form

while e **do** ⟨statement⟩

is exactly equivalent to

if e **then**
begin ⟨statement⟩;
  while e **do** ⟨statement⟩
end

7.7.3. Examples

for $v := 1$ **step** 1 **until** $n - 1$ **do** $s := s + A[v][v]$
for $k := m$ **step** $- 1$ **until** 1 **do**
  if $H[k-1] > H[k]$ **then**
  begin $m := H[k-1]$; $H[k-1] := H[k]$; $H[k] := m$ **end**
while $(j>0) \wedge (city\,[j] \neq s)$ **do** $j := j - 1$

PART III. PROPOSED SET OF STANDARD PROCEDURES

The principal language features described in previous sections should be supplemented by additional facilities supplied in the form of procedures, which are assumed to be declared in the environment in which an ALGOL program is executed. It is recommended that some or all of the procedures listed in this section be so treated. They are classified into the following groups:

(1) Input/output procedures
(2) Environment enquiries
(3) Functions of analysis
(4) Transfer functions

1. Standard Input/Output Procedures

1.1. INTRODUCTION

This proposal is based on suggestions of Jan V. Garwick [*ALGOL Bull. 19*, 39–40].

1.2. DESIGN CRITERIA

1.2.1. The input/output proposal is essentially simple, and the various facilities provided are relatively independent of one another. No attempt is made to provide discrimination, looping and sequencing facilities within the input/output proposal, since this merely duplicates features which are already provided in the general purpose language which the proposal supplements.

1.2.2. It is plainly recognized that different input/output media have radically different properties, and no attempt is made to introduce an artificial similarity into their use, nor to mislead a programmer by such an apparent similarity.

1.2.3. Advantage is taken of the essential differences between input and output, in particular of the fact that input of numbers does not require the same variety of format specifications as output.

1.2.4. Facilities are provided such that the specification of all matters associated with input and output can be written explicitly in a single sequence of instructions; errors due to incorrect mating of a format string and the sequence of input/output data which it is intended to control therefore cannot occur.

1.2.5. The number of digits of a number to be output can be specified by means of an integer expression, which can readily be calculated by the program itself.

1.2.6. The proposal is not intended to satisfy every requirement, but only to provide facilities adequate for most circumstances and capable of being used to build more complex input/output algorithms for more unusual requirements. Furthermore, there is no embargo on the provision of yet further standard procedures to perform additional, more complex functions.

1.3. SUMMARY

Input and output channels of a computer are classified into three essentially different categories:

(1) *Legible input channels*, on which the information is presented in a form closely mapping its legible transcription. The main representatives of this class are card readers and paper tape readers.

(2) *Legible output channels*, in which the form of the information output either is, or closely maps, its legible transcription. The main representatives of this class are line printers, card punches, paper tape punches, and CRT character displays.

(3) *Input/output channels*, in which the information is stored in a form not suitable for human inspection, and can be read only by a computer. Input/output channels are divided into two classes, those with random access (e.g., drums, disks, or bulk core memories) and those with which access is essentially serial (e.g., magnetic tapes).

Legible output is achieved in two stages; first an "output line" of characters is assembled, and then it is transmitted on a specified channel. Since these operations are clearly distinct, they are performed by distinct procedures.

Facilities provided for legible input are the simplest, since in general no specifications of format are required.

Operations on (nonlegible) input/output channels are defined only for arrays, which are transferred in their entirety to and from the input/output medium.

On serial input/output channels, the positioning of the information is determined by the current position of the medium. On random access channels, the output instruction provides the programmer with an integer position identification, which he may use for specifying reinput of the same information.

1.4. LEGIBLE OUTPUT CHANNELS

procedure *scaled* (**string value result** *line*; **integer value** *position, length*; **long real value** *expression*);
comment This procedure is used when the order of magnitude of a number is unknown. The value of *expression* is converted to decimal form, and placed in the *length* character positions of the string *line* starting at position *position*. The character position *position* is occupied by a minus sign if the number is negative or a space otherwise. The next position is occupied by a digit, the following position by a decimal point. The fourth last character position is occupied by $_{10}$, the next position by a plus or minus sign, and the remaining two positions by digits.

Examples: $1.234_{10}+01$
              $-1.234_{10}-70$
              $1.234_{10}+00$
              $0.000_{10}+00$;

procedure *aligned* (**string value result** *line*; **integer value** *position, length, decimals*; **long real value** *expression*);
comment This procedure is used when the order of magnitude of a number is known. The value of *expression* is converted to decimal form, and placed in the *length* character positions of the string *line*, starting at position *position*.

The last *decimals* character positions of the field are occupied by digits and preceded by a decimal point, which itself is preceded by digits. Leading zeros are suppressed, up to but not including the last position before the point, and a minus sign (if any) precedes the leftmost digit.

Examples: 1.234
              -123.456
               -0.123
                0.000

If the absolute value of the number is too great for it to be expressed in this way, the result is undefined;

procedure *decimal* (**string value result** *line*; **integer value** *position, length, expression*);
comment The value of *expression* is converted to decimal form, and placed in the *length* character positions of the string *line*, beginning at position *position*.

Leading zeros are suppressed up to, but not including the last digit. The first digit is preceded by either a space or a minus sign.

Examples: -12
             1234
               0
              123

If the absolute value of the number is too great for it to be expressed in this way, the result is undefined;

procedure *insert* (**string value result** *line*; **integer value** *position*; **string value** *message*);
comment The string *message* is inserted in the string *line*, beginning at position *position*;

string procedure *substring* (**string value** *line*; **integer value** *position, length*);
comment The substring consists of the *length* characters beginning at position *position* of the string *line*;

procedure *output* (**integer value** *channel, n*; **string value** *line*);
comment The first *n* characters of the string *line* are output on the specified legible output channel. If the channel has a natural unit of information and is incapable of accommodating in this unit (e.g. print line) the number of characters transmitted, the result is undefined. If it can accommodate more characters, then the remaining character positions are filled with spaces;

integer procedure *lastcol* (**integer value** *channel*);
comment This is an environment enquiry, and enables the programmer to find the number of characters in the natural unit of information on the specified legible channel, if there is such a unit. This procedure also applies to legible input channels;

1.5. LEGIBLE INPUT CHANNELS

procedure *inreal* (**integer value** *channel*; **real result** *x*);
comment The next real or integer number (defined in accordance with II. 4.1.1) is read in from the specified channel, and its value is assigned to the variable *x*.

In each case, the characters read consist of an initial sequence of nonnumeric characters, followed by a sequence of numeric characters, terminated by, but not including, a nonnumeric character. The decimal digits and the delimiters . $_{10}$ + and − are numeric characters, and all other characters (including space, tab, and change to a new line) are nonnumeric. If the sequence of numeric characters does not conform to the definition of a real or integer number, the consequences are undefined;

procedure *ininteger* (**integer value** *channel*; **integer result** *i*);
comment This procedure is identical to *inreal*, except that the numeric sequence must conform to the definition of an integer number, and the result is assigned to the integer variable *i*;

procedure *input* (**integer value** *channel, n*; **string result** *line*);
comment *n* characters are read on the specified legible input channel and assigned to the string variable *line*. If the channel has a natural unit of information (e.g., card record) and the number of characters in that unit is greater than *n*, then the remaining characters are ignored, and if it is smaller than *n* then the result is undefined;

1.6. SERIAL INPUT/OUTPUT CHANNELS

procedure *outserial* (**integer value** *channel*; **array** *information*);
comment The channel is a serial input/output channel. The entire array is output to the next available position of the medium in such a way that it can be read in by *inserial*. If there is insufficient room on the medium to write the information, the result is undefined. This procedure may be used for arrays of any type, order, or size;

procedure *rewind* (**integer value** *channel*);
comment On a serial channel, the medium is rewound to the position of the first information output;

procedure *inserial* (**integer value** *channel*; **array** *information*);
comment On a serial channel, the next array stored on the medium is input. This array must be of the same type and order, and have identical subscript bounds to the array output in this position; otherwise the result is undefined. Furthermore, output

instructions must be separated by a rewind from any input instruction. An attempt to read information which has not been written leads to undefined results. The procedure may be used for arrays of any type, order or size;

1.7. RANDOM INPUT/OUTPUT CHANNELS

procedure *outrandom* (**integer value** *channel*; **integer result** *identification*; **array** *information*);

comment The entire array is output on the specified random access channel, and the variable corresponding to the formal parameter *identification* is assigned a value which identifies the position of the information on the channel. If there is insufficient room on the medium, the result is undefined;

procedure *inrandom* (**integer value** *channel*, *identification*; **array** *information*);

comment The array which was output with the identification specified is reinput. The type, order and dimensions of the array must be the same as that which was output;

procedure *overwrite* (**integer value** *channel*, *identification*; **array** *information*);

comment The array is output to the specified random access channel, overwriting the information which originally was given the identification specified by the second parameter. The type, order and dimensions of the array must be the same as those which were originally written;

procedure *resetrandom* (**integer value** *channel*, *identification*);

comment All information on the channel written at the position specified by the identification is deleted, and the space which it occupied becomes free for further use;

1.8. OPERATING PROCEDURES

procedure *open input* (**integer result** *channel*; **string value** *device*);

comment The variable *channel* is assigned the number of the legible input channel identified by the string parameter;

procedure *open output* (**integer result** *channel*; **string value** *device*);

comment The variable *channel* is assigned the number of the legible output channel identified by the string parameter;

procedure *open serial input* (**integer result** *channel*; **string value** *file label*);

comment Similar to *open input*, for a serial input/output channel;

procedure *open serial output* (**integer result** *channel*; **string value** *file label*);

comment The variable *channel* is assigned the number of some available serial input/output channel, and that channel is made unavailable. The implementation ensures that if the output medium is later removed, it has the identification specified by the string parameter;

procedure *open random input* (**integer result** *channel*; **string value** *file label*);

comment Similar to *open input*, for a random input/output channel;

procedure *open random output* (**integer result** *channel*; **string value** *file label*);

comment Similar to *open output*, for a random input/output channel;

procedure *open serial* (**integer result** *channel*);

comment The variable *channel* is assigned the number of some available serial input/output channel, and that channel is made nonavailable. This procedure is recommended for claiming "scratch" tapes;

procedure *open random* (**integer result** *channel*);

comment The variable *channel* is assigned the number of some available random input/output channel, and that channel is made unavailable. This procedure is recommended for claiming "scratch" files;

procedure *close* (**integer value** *channel*);

comment The specified channel is made available for reuse;

2. Standard Environment Enquiries

2.1 INTRODUCTION

It is recognized that different implementations of the language must adopt different techniques for dealing with certain language features. The programmer may wish to obtain information on these points, so that he may adapt his algorithmic methods accordingly, or even indicate that the algorithm is inappropriate.

The concept of an environment enquiry was originated by Peter Naur [*ALGOL Bull. 18.3.9.1*].

2.2 FUNCTIONS PROVIDED

real procedure *epsilon*;

comment The smallest possible number such that both $1 + epsilon \neq 1$ and $1 - epsilon \neq 1$;

long real procedure *epsilon squared*;

integer procedure *intmax*;

comment The largest positive integer provided by the implementation;

real procedure *realmax*;

comment The largest positive real number provided by the implementation;

integer procedure *bits in word*;

comment The number of elements of a bit sequence which is accommodated in a single word;

integer procedure *lowerbound* (**array** *A*);

comment The value of the lower subscript bound of the array *A*, which may be of any type or order;

integer procedure *upperbound* (**array** *A*);

comment The value of the upper subscript bound of the array *A*, which may be of any type or order;

integer procedure *string length* (**string** *s*);

comment The number of characters in the string *s*;

3. Standard Functions of Analysis

real procedure *sin* (**real value** *x*);

real procedure *cos* (**real value** *x*);

real procedure *arctan* (**real value** *x*);
comment $-\pi/2 < arctan(x) < \pi/2$;

real procedure *ln* (**real value** *x*);

real procedure *exp* (**real value** *x*);

real procedure *sqrt* (**real value** *x*);

real procedure *arcsin* (**real value** *x*);
comment $-\pi/2 \leq arcsin(x) \leq \pi/2$;

real procedure *arccos* (**real value** *x*);
comment $-\pi/2 \leq arccos(x) \leq \pi/2$;

real procedure *tan* (**real value** *x*);

real procedure *pi*;
comment π with the accuracy available for real numbers;

It is understood that also long variants of these procedures exist, e.g.,

long real procedure *longsin* (**long real value** *x*);

4. Standard Transfer Functions

integer procedure *round* (**real value** *x*);

integer procedure *truncate* (**real value** *x*);

integer procedure *entier* (**real value** *x*);

real procedure *realpart* (**complex value** *x*);

real procedure *imagpart* (**complex value** *x*);

long real procedure *longrealpart* (**long complex value** *x*);

long real procedure *longimagpart* (**long complex value** *x*);

complex procedure *complex* (**real value** *x, y*);

long complex procedure *longcomplex* (**long real value** *x, y*);

logical procedure *odd* (**integer value** *x*);

bits procedure *bitstring* (**integer value** *i*);

integer procedure *number* (**bits value** *b*);
comment the number with binary representation *b*;

integer procedure *decode* (**string value** *char*);
comment The numeric code of the character in the single-element string *char*;

string procedure *code* (**integer value** *n*);

Acknowledgment. The authors wish to thank the referee for his most exacting and valuable suggestions.

RECEIVED JANUARY, 1966; REVISED FEBRUARY, 1966

A TUTORIAL ON ALGOL 68*

A. S. TANENBAUM

This paper is an introduction to the main features of ALGOL 68, emphasizing the novel features not found in many other programming languages. The topics, data types (modes), type conversion (coercion), generalized expressions (units), procedures, operators, the standard prelude, and input/output, form the basis of the paper. The approach is informal, relying heavily on many short examples. The paper applies to the Revised Report, published in 1975, rather than to the original report, published in 1969.

Keywords and Phrases: ALGOL 68, ALGorithmic Language, expression languages, general programming languages, high-level languages, problem-oriented languages.

CR Categories: 4.20, 4.22.

INTRODUCTION

This paper is an introduction to ALGOL 68—in plain English—for the nonspecialist. In its short lifetime, ALGOL 68 has acquired something of an international reputation for being obscure. An early description of the language [8] was entitled "ALGOL 68 with Fewer Tears." The feeling has persisted. One recent author [11] has written, "The ALGOL 68 Report is one of the most unreadable documents which has ever been printed." It is our intention to demonstrate that ALGOL 68 is neither inscrutable nor difficult, but rather is an extremely powerful programming language which is easily learned and which is applicable to a wide variety of problems.

One reason ALGOL 68 has been slow to be accepted is not hard to discover. The defining report used a completely new kind of grammar to define the language, instead of the now familiar and comfortable Backus-Naur grammar (BNF). This new grammar, often called a vW-grammar (in honor of its inventor, A. van Wijngaarden), is context sensitive rather than context free. Like many new ideas, it takes some getting used to, just as BNF grammars did. The new grammar was introduced for some very good reasons. In particular, it allows not only the syntax, but also that part of the semantics having to do with declarations to be defined by the grammar. For example, the nonterminal <program> simply does not generate any program in which variables are undefined, multiply defined, or defined inconsistently with their usage. No English prose is needed to say that variables must not be defined twice, etc. Consequently, W-grammars provide a more complete and accurate definition than do BNF grammars.

During several years of experience with the language, several trouble spots came to light, particularly features of the language

Copyright © 1976, Association for Computing Machinery, Inc. General permission to republish, but not for profit, all or part of this material is granted provided that ACM's copyright notice is given and that reference is made to the publication, to its date of issue, and to the fact that reprinting privileges were granted by permission of the Association for Computing Machinery.

*Reprinted from *Computing Surveys*, 8, 2, June 1976.

CONTENTS

that were tricky to implement efficiently. A Revised Report [13] was published in 1975, describing a slightly modified language that does not have these problems. Furthermore, the original report itself was completely rewritten, in order to make it easier to understand. It is the revised language and the Revised Report that are described in this article. References to sections in the Revised Report are indicated by the letters RR preceding the section number.

Rather than attempting to explore every nook and cranny of ALGOL 68, we concentrate on the major features, illustrating them with many examples. Readers wishing a book length introduction to ALGOL 68 are referred to the books listed in Section 11, Where To From Here?

The ALGOL 68 Report introduced a veritable cornucopia of new terminology to the computing community, all of which are precisely defined in the Revised Report (RR 2.1). This was done to force the reader to rely on the Report's definitions, rather than to rely on his previous experience with similar concepts that nonetheless may differ from the Report's definitions in subtle, but crucial, ways.

Nevertheless, to avoid inundating the reader, we try to shun when possible the bus tokens (RR 1.3.3e) invisible production trees (RR 1.1.3.2h), primal environs (RR 2.2.2a), incestuous unions (RR 4.7), notions (RR 1.1.3.1c), protonotions (RR 1.1.3.1b), metanotions (RR 1.1.3.1d), hypernotions (RR 1.1.3.1e), paranotions (RR 1.1.4.2), and their ilk, for more familiar nomenclature. As a starter, we refrain from using "assignation" when "assignment" does just as nicely, and we use "integer" rather than "integral" as an adjective.

Before plunging into the description of the language itself, it is perhaps worthwhile to say something about the principles of its design. One of the key ideas is that of orthogonality. An orthogonal language has a small number of basic constructions, and rules for combining them in regular and systematic ways. A very deliberate attempt is made to eliminate arbitrary restrictions.

The concept of orthogonal design may be made clearer by an example of nonortho-

gonal design. Many programming languages (for example, FORTRAN, ALGOL 60, and PL/I) have a concept of data types that includes arrays. They also have a concept of functions as rules for mapping parameters onto results. Logically one might expect to be able to combine the "orthogonal" (that is, independent) concepts of data types and functions to construct functions that take an array as parameter and yield an array as the result. An arbitrary restriction that allows arrays to be used as parameters but prohibits them to be used as results is an example of nonorthogonal design. A fundamental principle of ALGOL 68 is that arbitrary rules like this restriction are only used to resolve situations which might otherwise be syntactically or semantically ambiguous.

Another principle, related to that of orthogonality, is the principle of extensibility. ALGOL 68 provides a small number of primitive data types, or modes, as well as mechanisms for the user to extend these in a systematic way. For example, the programmer may create his own data types and his own operators to manipulate them. This philosophy may be contrasted with, say APL, which provides a very large number of standard operators, rather than a very small number and the machinery for programmers to define new ones. Together, orthogonality and extensibility tend to produce a "compact" yet powerful language.

1. BIRD'S-EYE VIEW OF ALGOL 68

In the following subsections we briefly mention some basic features of ALGOL 68 that are common to many programming languages in order to be able to use them in subsequent examples.

1.1 Program Structure

An ALGOL 68 program consists of a sequence of symbols enclosed by **begin** and **end**, or by parentheses. Some symbols are written in boldface type to distinguish them as keywords. Other symbols are variable identifiers (written in the same general font that is used in programs) and special characters such as < >, =, ( ), +, −, etc.

Spaces and carriage returns (change to a new card) may be used freely to improve readability. Spaces are explicitly allowed "inside" identifiers. Thus *the three little pigs* and *thethreelittlepigs* are the same identifier. Identifiers (for example, variable names) may be arbitrarily long.

Comments are enclosed between comment symbols, of which four representations are allowed: ¢, #, **co**, and **comment**. The comment must begin and end with the same comment symbol. A comment may be inserted between any two symbols.

ALGOL 68 is a block structured language, like PL/I and ALGOL 60. Blocks and procedures may be nested arbitrarily deep. Declarations may appear in any block. Semicolons are used to separate statements, similar to ALGOL 60 (and in contrast to PL/I, which uses them to terminate statements).

1.2 Data and Declarations

One of the most basic features of a programming language is the kind of data that it can manipulate. ALGOL 68 provides a rich collection of data types (described in Section 2, Modes). The ALGOL 68 Report uses the term **mode** instead of type, and we do too. Four of the simplest modes are integer, real (floating point), Boolean, and character. As one might expect, there are integer, real, Boolean, and character variables. All variables must be declared. Any variable used but not declared will be flagged by the compiler as an error. The declaration of a variable consists of a mode, followed by one or more identifiers. The following program illustrates variable declarations. An ALGOL 68 program must contain at least one statement; **skip** is a dummy statement that can be used to turn a collection of declarations into a syntactically valid program.

```
begin
real e,x,y,z; ¢ 4 real variables ¢
bool maybe; ¢ 1 boolean variable ¢
char first initial, middle initial,
    grade desired; ¢ 3 character variables ¢
int i,j,girlfriends; ¢ 3 integer variables ¢
skip ¢ dummy statement ¢
end
```

Note that the declarations are separated by semicolons. The symbols **int, real, bool,** and **char** are not abbreviations; **integer, boolean,** and **character** are not allowed (although one can explicitly define them as modes if so desired).

1.3 Statements

ALGOL 68 is an expression language. This means that every construction in the language yields a value and in principle can appear on the right-hand side of an assignment. Nevertheless, certain constructions can also be used as statements. Among these constructions are assignment statements, **if** statements, procedure calls, **for** statements, **while** statements, **case** statements, and **goto** statements. Since these are all quite familiar from other programming languages, a few examples, shown in the next column, should suffice.

A few explanatory notes may be in order. Observe that **if** statements are closed by **fi** (**if** backwards). This solves the dangling else problem. Suppose **fi** were not used. Then the statement

```
if i<0 then if j<0
then print ("hello") else print ("goodbye")
```

would be ambiguous, possibly meaning

```
if i<0
   then if j<0 then print ("hello") fi
   else print ("goodbye")
fi
```

or perhaps meaning

```
if i<0
   then if j<0 then print ("hello")
                else print ("goodbye")
        fi
fi
```

With the **fi** there is no ambiguity. Furthermore, since both **then** and **else** parts must be explicitly closed, either may contain an arbitrary number of statements without the need for **begin end** as delimiters.

```
begin
¢ mentally insert the above declarations here ¢

¢ assignment statements ¢
 girlfriends := girlfriends-1;
 middle initial := "x";
 e := 2.78;

¢ if statements ¢
 if maybe
    then grade desired := "d"
    else grade desired := "f"
 fi; ¢ fi delimits if—see note below ¢
 if x<0 then x := −x fi;
 if i = j+2
    then x := pi;
         y := 2∗e;
         z := 3∗e
 fi;

¢ procedure calls ¢
 ¢ sum & initialize must be defined elsewhere ¢
 initialize; ¢ no parameters ¢
 sum(x,y,z);
 print(grade desired);

¢ for − while statements ¢
¢ the following 5 statements are all equivalent ¢
 for k from 1 by 1 to j+3 while true
    do print (new line) od;

 for k from 1 by 1 to j+3
    do print (new line) od;

 for k from 1 to j+3
    do print (new line) od;

 for k to j+3
    do print (new line) od;

 to j+3
    do print (new line) od;

 while i<j ∨ i<0
    do i := i+1;
       j := j+2;
       print ((i,j))
    od;

¢ case statements ¢
 case i+4 in
    j := 0, j := 3, i := i−5, print(i)
 esac;
 case i in
    j := j+3,
    if j = 0 then j := i fi,
    print (i)
 out j := 4
 esac;

¢ goto statement ¢
bed: goto bed

end
```

To simplify nested **if** statements, **else if** may be contracted to **elif**, providing the **fi** matching the contracted **if** is deleted. For example,

```
if word = "oui"
   then print ("french")
   else if word = "yes"
           then print ("english")
           else if word = "ja"
                   then print ("dutch")
                   else print ("minor language")
                fi
        fi
fi
```

can be written as

```
if word = "oui"
   then print ("french")
   elif word = "yes"
      then print ("english")
      elif word = "ja"
         then print ("dutch")
         else print ("minor language")
fi
```

Even with **elif, begin** and **end** are never needed as delimiters.

The **for** and **while** statements shown on page 158 are all special cases of a general **for** statement including both counting parts (**from . . . by . . . to**) and **while** parts. The **from, by,** and **to** parts are each optional, with default values of 1, 1, and infinity, respectively. Each part may occur only once. The "controled variable" following **for** is automatically an integer; it can neither be declared nor assigned. If the same identifier occurs outside the statement, it is a different variable. This makes the controled variable inaccessible outside the loop (to give the compiler writer more freedom, and to make correctness proofs easier). Furthermore, the **from, by,** and **to** parts are evaluated once and for all before the loop begins. Subsequent changes to any of their variables have no effect on the step size or loop termination condition.

The **case** statement has an integer expression which selects the first, second, third, etc., clause if the expression is 1,2,3, etc., respectively. A clause is a statement (or a group of statements separated by semicolons and enclosed by **begin end** or parentheses). The clauses are separated by commas. If an **out** clause is present, it will be selected when the expression exceeds the number of clauses or is less than 1. If the **out** clause is omitted and the expression is out of range, the **case** statement is skipped. **esac** is **case** backwards.

Input/output in ALGOL 68 is performed by calling certain input/output procedures, rather than by executing special statements. Procedures are provided for unformatted, formatted, and binary input/output. Files and input/output devices can be handled in a consistent and machine-independent way. We examine these input/output procedures in a later section; for now, $read(x)$ is used for input and $print(x)$ is used for output. Each of these procedures may be passed a parenthesized list of variables as parameter, for example, $read((x,y,z))$ and $print((i,j,x+z))$. (The reason for the extra parentheses is explained later on.) The calls $print(new\ line)$ and $print(new\ page)$ cause subsequent output to begin at the beginning of the next line or next page, respectively.

A sample ALGOL 68 program is shown on page 160.

2. MODES

One of the most powerful features of ALGOL 68 is its rich collection of data types (modes), and the facilities it provides programmers to define their own modes. Programmer-defined modes are constructed from primitive modes, using a few simple rules for creating new modes from old modes. In the following subsections we examine primitive modes, methods for constructing new modes, and finally the mode definition facility in its full glory.

An object is an entity stored in memory during the execution of a program. Integers and reals are typical objects. Each object has a unique mode, for example, **int, real, bool,** or **char.** Each object also has a value. It is objects that are assigned to variables. For example, an integer with value 3 (some bit pattern in memory) can be assigned to an integer variable. A variable should be

```
begin
¢This program reads two numbers: the price of
an item, and the amount the customer gave to
the cashier. It then calculates how much change
he should get, and prints out the correct number
of quarters, dimes, nickels, and pennies, mini-
mizing the number of coins returned. The pro-
gram only handles change up to 99 cents. ¢

begin
int price, amount paid, change, quarters, dimes,
      nickels, pennies;
read ((price, amount paid)); ¢ read input data ¢
change := amount paid − price;
if change > 99 ∨ change < 0
    then print ("input data incorrect")
    else
    if change = 0 ¢ was the payment exact?¢
        then print ("no change")
        else ¢ compute how many of each coin ¢
        quarters := 0;
        dimes := 0;
        nickels := 0;
        while change ≥ 25
          do quarters := quarters + 1;
             change := change − 25
          od;
        while change ≥ 10
          do dimes := dimes + 1;
             change := change − 10
          od;
        while change ≥ 5
          do nickels := nickels + 1;
             change := change − 5
          od;
        pennies := change
        ¢ print results ¢
        print ((new page, "the change is",
                new line, quarters, " quarters",
                new line, dimes, " dimes",
                new line, nickels, " nickels",
                new line, pennies, " pennies",
                new line
                   ))
    fi ¢ this matches if change = 0 . . . ¢
    fi ¢ this matches if change > 99 . . . ¢
end
```

thought of as a container (memory location) into which a certain class of objects can be put. Be aware that the container and the containee are distinct kinds of entities.

2.1 Primitive Modes

We have already seen how to declare **int, real, bool,** and **char** variables. These are not the only possibilities, however. A list of the predefined modes with a brief description of each follows:

int	integer;
real	real number;
char	character;
bool	boolean;
string	string of characters;
compl	complex number (2 reals);
bits	machine word full of bits;
bytes	machine word full of characters;
sema	Dijkstra semaphore [4];
format	mode used with formatted I/O;
file	mode used for input/output.

For some applications, the number of bits in an integer or real is insufficient. To accommodate these situations, ALGOL 68 allows primitive modes of **long int, long long int,** etc., and **long real, long long real, long long long real,** etc. Furthermore, to accommodate applications where very many integers or reals are needed, but where fewer than the standard number of bits will suffice, there are modes of **short int, short short int** and **short real, short short real,** etc.

The number of different lengths and the number of bits in each is up to each ALGOL 68 compiler writer. However, the number of available lengths and the size of each is available to programs at run time to facilitate transfer of programs from one machine to another. For a computer with an 8-bit byte and a 32-bit word, a typical implementation might have: **short short int** (8 bits), **short int** (16 bits), **int** (32 bits), **long int** (64 bits), **long long int** (96 bits), and **long long long int** (128 bits).

The mode **string** defines a string of zero or more characters. Strings may be arbitrarily long, and strings of any length may be assigned to any string variable. In PL/I terms, all strings are of maximum length equal to infinity and VARYING. The following is a valid ALGOL 68 program:

```
begin
string s;
s := " "; ¢ an empty string ¢
s := "little"; ¢ a 6 character string ¢
s := "hello there, mommies and daddies"
end
```

The modes **bits** and **bytes** are intended to give the programmer the ability to pack information into machine words to save space. The number of bits in an object of mode **bits** is not determined by the programmer, but by the ALGOL 68 compiler writer. It is to be expected that in most implementations an object of mode **bits** will occupy a full machine word. Operations are provided, among others, to insert, extract, and test the individual bits. The mode **bytes** is similar, providing a way to pack characters into machine words to save storage. How many characters to pack into a machine word is a decision left to the implementer. Like **int** and **real, bits** and **bytes** have **long** and **short** versions.

The modes **sema, format,** and **file** have specialized uses and are covered later on.

ALGOL 68 allows more complex modes to be constructed from simpler modes in a variety of ways. Roughly speaking, these ways involve arrays, structures, procedures, sets, and pointers. We examine each of these in turn.

2.2 Array Modes

Many problems involve data which are organized into vectors or matrices. A vector is a one-dimensional sequence of objects, all of which have the same mode. A matrix is a two-dimensional ordering of objects of the same mode. Likewise, three, four, and higher dimensional arrays also consist of collections of objects of the same mode. The elements of an array may be of a primitive mode, such as **int,** or they may be of a constructed mode.

The official ALGOL 68 term for array is multiple value (RR 2.1.3.4); however, we continue to use the more familiar word "array." An array is a run-time object and therefore has a value and a mode. Array variables exist and may be declared and assigned values, just as variables of any other mode are. A one-dimensional array of inte-

gers has mode [ ] **int**, pronounced "row of integer"; a two-dimensional array of reals has mode [,] **real**, pronounced "row row of real"; a three-dimensional array of characters has mode [,,] **char**, pronounced "row row row of character." In general, the mode of an n-dimensional array is an opening square bracket followed by $n-1$ commas, a closing square bracket, and then the mode of the elements. Objects of different dimensions have different modes.

When array variables are declared, the bounds must be specified in order to allow sufficient space to be reserved. To declare a one-dimensional integer array variable named "month" which is to contain an array whose elements are numbered 1 to 12, one writes

[1:12] **int** *month*

The lower and upper bounds are integer expressions; they are separated by a colon. Much as you would expect,

[0:$n-1$,0:$n-1$] **real** *physicist, chemist*

declares *physicist* and *chemist* to be $n \times n$ real matrices. Note that *physicist* is a [,] **real** variable; the bounds are not part of the mode (unlike PASCAL). Thus if

[1:100,3: 9] **real** *geologist*

declares a nonsquare matrix, *physicist* and *geologist* have the same mode, albeit different sizes. The following program declares several variables:

```
begin int n,m;
read((m,n)); ¢ read 2 integers ¢
¢ unlabeled statements may be followed by
    more declarations, i.e., it is not necessary to
    put all declarations first ¢
[−n:n] int hamlet; ¢ size depends on n ¢
[1:m,1:n] real macbeth;
[1:10,1:10,1:10] bool othello;
[−100:−80] char richard 3;
[0:9*m + 6*m*n] string henry 8;

¢ array elements may themselves be arrays ¢
[1:10] [1:5,1:5] int king lear;

skip ¢ dummy statement ¢
end
```

Elements of arrays may be extracted by subscripting and trimming (see Section 3.4, Slices).

In the preceding program, *king lear* is a 10-element vector, each of whose elements is a 5×5 square matrix. A vector whose elements are matrices might be a more natural representation for, say, the successive digitized frames of television broadcasting, than a three-dimensional array. Note that *king lear*[n] can be used anywhere an object of mode [,] **int** is needed, for example, as an actual parameter. It can also be subscripted, as in *king lear*[n] [2,3], but not as in *king lear*[n,2,3].

An array variable may be declared to be flexible, in which case arrays of different sizes may be successively assigned to it, provided they are of the proper mode. A string variable is actually a flexible one-dimensional character array variable.

2.3 Structured Modes

Arrays are used to group together objects of the same mode. Structures (RR 2.1.3.3) are used to group together objects whose modes need not be identical. A structure is composed of one or more fields, each having a name, or more properly, a field selector (RR 4.8.1f). Structures themselves are objects and have modes. The mode of a structure depends upon the modes of its fields, their order, and the field selectors. Two structured modes are the same if and only if the corresponding fields have the same modes and field selectors. Structured variables exist, and may be assigned to one field at a time or "all at once." Structures are called "records" in some programming languages. An example of a structured variable declaration is:

struct (**string** *species*,
        int *number of feet*,
        bool *makes good pet*) *beastie*

This declares *beastie* to be a variable with three fields whose field selectors are: *species*, *number of feet*, and *makes good pet*. To use any of the fields of *beastie*, one writes the field selector, followed by the word **of**, followed

by the name of the structured variable, for example:

species **of** *beastie* := "brontosaurus";
number of feet **of** *beastie* := 4;
makes good pet **of** *beastie* := **false**

The extraction of one field of a structure is called selecting. Alternatively, it is possible to assign all three fields at once by using a structure display (RR 3.3.1h) on the right-hand side of the assignment statement, for example:

beastie := ("guinea pig", 4, **true**)

Some examples of structured variables follow:

```
begin int n; read(n);
struct (real value, string color,
        bool leaks, has fireplace) house;
struct ([1:3] char aircraft type,
        int wheels, max speed) plane;
struct ([1:3] char area code,
        [1:7] char phone number) telephone;
¢ farm has 3 fields: crop, farmer and dairy ¢
struct ([1:n] struct (string variety,
                real acres) crop,
        string farmer, bool dairy) farm;
skip
end
```

2.4 Procedure Modes

In contrast to most programming languages, ALGOL 68 considers procedures to be objects, complete with values and modes. Furthermore, there are procedure variables, to which procedures can be assigned. The mode of a procedure is uniquely determined by the mode of its parameters (if there are any) and the mode of the value it returns. A procedure that takes an integer as a parameter and returns a real as a value has mode **proc (int) real.** A procedure that takes a character and a Boolean matrix as parameters and returns a real vector as a value has mode **proc (char, [,] bool) [ ] real.**

A procedure that is not used as a function, that is, does not return any explicit value, is said to return **void.** For example, a procedure that accepts an **int** as parameter and cancels the corresponding flight (in an airline reservation system) has mode **proc (int) void.** A procedure which has no parameters, but which returns a **real**, such as random, has mode **proc real.** A procedure which has no parameters and which delivers no explicit value has mode **proc void.**

Both parameters and results may have any mode. Unlike FORTRAN, ALGOL 60, and PL/I, in ALGOL 68, procedures may yield strings, arrays, structures, pointers, or any other mode. Furthermore, there is no reason procedure modes cannot be used as parameters or results. For example, a procedure used to perform a numerical integration of a real function (that is, a **proc (real) real**) between two real limits might have mode

proc (proc (real) real, real, real) real.

The order of the parameters is significant; **proc (real, int) void** and **proc (int, real) void** are different modes. Because there are an infinite number of combinations of parameters and results, there are an infinite number of procedure modes, just as there are an infinite number of procedure modes.

As mentioned earlier, procedure variables exist, and can be assigned values. The following program illustrates this feature:

```
begin real x;
¢ f is a proc (real) real variable ¢
proc (real) real f;
x := 3.14;
¢ sin, cos, and tan are standard ¢
f := sin; ¢ assign sin to f ¢
print (f(x)); ¢ print sin(3.14) ¢
f := cos; ¢ now assign cos to f ¢
print (f(x)); ¢ print cos(3.14) ¢
f := tan; ¢ now assign tan to f ¢
print (f(x)) ¢ three guesses ¢
end
```

When an integer variable acquires a new value, as in $i := 3$, the bit pattern for the integer 3 is put into location i. Obviously, assigning *sin* to f is not going to cause a copy of the procedure's machine code to be stuffed into the variable f. The ALGOL 68 compiler writer must determine how to implement this, but presumably he will assign pointers to the procedure's code and environment (or the equivalent) to f. Some examples of procedure variable declarations follow:

```
begin
proc (real) real cotangent;
proc (int, int) int integer divide;
proc (int, int) bool coprime;
proc (char, char) bool char compare;
proc ([,] real, [,] real) [,] real matrix add;
proc (string, string) string concatenate;
proc (int) void page eject;
proc (int) struct (string name, int age) find;
proc (int) proc (int) int pick function;
proc (proc (real) real, real, real) real simpson;
skip ¢ dummy statement ¢
end
```

2.5 United Modes

As we discuss later on, actual parameters in procedure calls must be of the mode expected, for example, a **proc (int) real** requires an **int** as a parameter and will not accept a **real**. Sometimes it is convenient to have a procedure with a formal parameter that can be any one of several modes. For example, we might want to write a procedure that accepts a vector parameter of mode [ ] **int**, [ ] **real**, or [ ] **compl** and checks to see if any elements are zero.

To permit this sort of flexibility, ALGOL 68 permits programmers to create a special kind of mode called a united mode. A variable united from **int** and **real** can be assigned either an **int** value or a **real** value. Similarly, a variable united from [ ] **int**, [ ] **real**, and [ ] **compl** can accept a vector of integers, reals, or complex numbers as a value (but not a vector of Booleans). United mode variables are declared as indicated here:

```
begin
union (int, real) ir;
union ([ ] int, [ ] real, [ ] compl) irc;
union (proc (int) real, proc (real) real) u;
skip ¢ dummy statement ¢
end
```

It is possible at run time to determine the mode of the value currently occupying a variable of united mode. This is done by using a variation on the **case** statement (RR 3.4.1h) with clauses for the various possible modes. Each clause is headed by a mode and (optionally) by an identifier, fol-

lowed by a colon. The clause corresponding to the current mode of the united variable is executed. Unlike the normal **case** statement, the order of the clauses is irrelevant.

```
begin
union (int, real, bool, char, bits,
       bytes, [ ] int, [ ] real) kitchen sink;
¢ here are 4 valid assignments ¢
kitchen sink := 3;
kitchen sink := 3.14;
kitchen sink := true;
kitchen sink := "a";
¢ random is a standard proc real ¢
if random < .5
    then kitchen sink := 1
    else kitchen sink := 2.78
fi;
¢ now figure out whether random was < .5 ¢
case kitchen sink in
    (int i): print ((("integer", i)),
    (real r): print ((("real", r))
esac
end
```

In this example we determined the mode of the union by using the case clause, and used the value in *kitchen sink* once its mode was known. Observe the (**int** i) and (**real** r) in the case clause. To compute with the value in *kitchen sink* in the **int** part (first clause) we can use the identifier i, now known to be an **int**. The value of i is the value of *kitchen sink*. Likewise the identifier r can be used in the second clause in any context where a real number is allowed. If j had been declared as an integer variable in the preceding program, j := *kitchen sink* would have been forbidden (by the grammar) and would have been flagged by the compiler. The rea-

son is obvious: At the time of the assignment the compiler cannot guarantee that *kitchen sink* contains an integer, and we would be in trouble if it contained a [ ] **real**. However, inside the first case clause it is guaranteed that *kitchen sink* contains an integer. To make life easier for the compiler writer, the new name *i* is introduced; there is no doubt about the mode of *i*. Although *j*:= *kitchen sink* would be forbidden, even inside the first clause, the assignment *j* := *i* would be allowed (only) in the first clause.

You may be wondering how unions are implemented. Presumably the compiler will have to reserve enough space in a united variable for the largest of the alternatives (or if that is too painful, perhaps only a pointer will be stored). Also, there must be some information stored that tells which mode is the "current" one. Note that there are no objects or values of united modes, just variables.

2.6 Reference-to Modes

Most programming languages are somewhat lax about making a distinction between the address of a variable and the contents of that variable. The nature of the difficulty can be most easily seen by means of an example from FORTRAN:

```
SUBROUTINE SUM(I,J,K)
INTEGER I, J, K
I = J+K
RETURN
END
```

Now consider the result of the following call:

```
CALL SUM(1,2,3)
```

Although the subroutine declaration is grammatically correct, and the call is also grammatically correct, something is obviously wrong.

The problem is not that the actual parameters are of the wrong type. *I* is declared an integer, and the number 1 is certainly an integer. The trouble occurs because the left-hand side of an integer assignment must evaluate to the address of a variable, not to an integer value. Few compilers will even give a precise error message at run time, let alone at compile time. Typically an address pointing into the run-time constant table is passed as a parameter, and the value of the constant 1 is changed to 5 so that subsequent $N = 1+1$ statements set N equal to 10 (decimal, not binary). In ALGOL 68 integer variables and integer values have different modes; so the error we are considering will be detected at compile time as a parameter mismatch.

An integer variable in ALGOL 68 has mode **ref int**, (**ref** is a shortened form of reference to); a real variable has mode **ref real**, etc. Consider the ALGOL 68 program

begin int *i; i* := 3 **end**

In this program, *i* is an integer variable and has mode **ref int**. The constant 3, on the other hand, has mode **int**. A **ref int** corresponds to the address of a memory location into which an integer can be put, whereas an **int** is a value, not an address.

This distinction is very important and bears repeating. An integer constant and an integer variable are different kinds of objects and have different modes. The mode of the former is **int** and the mode of the latter is **ref int**. The value of an integer variable is its memory address. Of course, given an integer variable one can ask about both its value and the value of the integer it contains, but these are clearly different objects.

The ALGOL 68 rule for an integer assignment is that the left-hand side must be, or be convertible to, an object of mode **ref int**, while the right-hand side must be, or be convertible to, an object of mode **int**. Precisely the same considerations hold for other modes, of course. Although procedure definitions are discussed later, the ALGOL 68 version of SUM is presented here for contrast with the FORTRAN version.

proc *sum* = (**ref int** *i*, **int** *j,k*) **void:** *i* := *j+k*

Here *i* is clearly a different mode from *j* and *k*. Furthermore, the call *sum*(1,2,3) is invalid because the modes of the actual parameters (**int, int, int**) do not match the modes of the formal parameters (**ref int, int, int**). If *i* had been specified as mode **int** instead of

ref int, then the assignment $i := j+k$ would have been detected as an error because the left-hand side of an integer assignment must evaluate to something of mode **ref int**. Either way the error would have been detected by the compiler, which is obviously better than its subsequent appearance as an obscure program bug.

We have consistently said that the right-hand side must be, or be convertible to, to an object of mode **int**, rather than having said that the right-hand side must be an object of mode **int**. This choice of words was deliberate.

Consider the following program:

    begin int i,j; i := 3; j := i end

In this program, i and j are both of mode **ref int**. In the first assignment the right-hand side has mode **int** as it should, but in the second assignment the right-hand side has mode **ref int**. Thus it would appear that $j := i$ is forbidden. Fortunately, there exists an automatic conversion between mode **ref int** and **int**, which is called **dereferencing**. Conversions between data types are familiar from other programming languages; for example, nearly all programming languages allow an integer to be written in a position where a real number is required, with automatic conversion implied.

In exactly the same way, ALGOL 68 often allows an object of mode **ref m** to be written when an object of mode **m** (some arbitrary mode) is expected, with automatic conversion implied. Such automatic mode conversions are called **coercions**. There are six kinds, of which dereferencing is one. Integer to real coercion, called **widening,** is another. Chapter 6 of the Revised Report gives the exact rules about which coercions are allowed in what situations.

It should be pointed out that although widening from **int** to **real** is typically an actual operation performed on integers at run time, dereferencing need not be performed at run time. If the computer has an instruction to move the contents of location i to location j, the compiler writer is obviously allowed to use it. No one is going to compel him to first put the address of i in a register and then explicitly dereference it using in-

direct addressing before storing the contents of i in j.

Dereferencing is more than simply a syntactic trick to allow variables on the right-hand side of assignments. Since **ref int** is a valid mode, the curious reader may wonder if reference-to-integer variables exist. The answer is yes. Just as an integer variable is a location in memory intended to hold an integer, a reference-to-integer variable is a location in memory intended to hold an object of mode **ref int**, that is, the address of an integer variable. In other words, a reference-to-integer variable can contain a pointer to an integer variable. It cannot contain a pointer to a real variable or to any other kind of variable, however. Likewise, a reference-to-complex variable may contain only a pointer to a complex variable.

Consider the following program:

    begin
    ref int pt;
    int i,j;
    i := 0; j := 4;
    if random < 0.5
      then pt := i
      else pt := j
    fi
    end

If pt is dereferenced once, it yields either the address of i or the address of j. If it is dereferenced twice, it yields either 0 or 4. Barring some unusual hardware, dereferencing a pointer twice is going to involve some run-time action. Note that pt itself has mode **ref ref int**.

Finally we get back to the subject of mode construction. The rule for creating pointer modes is simple. If **m** is some arbitrary mode, then **ref m** is also a mode of pointers to **m**. Applied repeatedly we discover that, **m ref m**, **ref ref m**, **ref ref ref m**, etc., are all distinct modes. The program at the top of page 167 shows how to declare some modes involving pointers:

Variables involving **ref** "something" are typically used in list processing applications. The distinction between the mode of a variable and the mode of the objects that can be assigned to it is crucial, but often initially confusing to people accustomed to other programming languages. Variables have

```
begin
[ ] ref int a; ¢ a row of pointers ¢
ref [ ] real b; ¢ a pointer to a vector ¢
ref [ ] ref char c; ¢ a pointer to a pointer vector ¢
struct (ref int p, ref real q) d; ¢ 2 pointers ¢
proc ref bool e; ¢ proc yielding a pointer ¢
ref proc bool f; ¢ pointer to a proc bool ¢
union (ref int, ref bool) g; ¢ either of 2 pointers ¢
skip ¢ dummy statement ¢
end
```

mode ref "something," and can contain objects of mode "something." In addition, a variable is itself an object, with a mode and a value. The mode of an integer variable is **ref int**, and its value is the address where its integer is stored. Thus an integer variable can be regarded as an object of mode **ref int**, and it can be assigned to a pointer variable whose mode is **ref ref int**.

In some programming languages (for example, PL/I), a pointer can point to an object of any mode. This is a frequent source of errors. Often a pointer somehow ends up pointing to a variable of the wrong mode, or worse yet, points into the program itself or to unused memory. By strictly categorizing pointers according to what they may point to, ALGOL 68 greatly reduces the opportunities for making errors.

2.7 Mode Declarations

We have now seen how ALGOL 68 programmers can construct new modes from primitive modes through the use of arrays, structures, procedures, unions, and references. ALGOL 68 provides a mechanism for programmers to give names to newly created modes, so they can be used in the same way that built-in modes are used. New modes are declared by means of a mode declaration (RR 4.2) as illustrated in the next column.

Mode declarations are used to create new data types. It is possible for user-defined modes to be used to create still more complex modes, as in **family**, which uses **person**. ALGOL 68 provides the ability for the programmer to build up an entire library of

mode definitions tailored to his particular application.

```
begin int n, size; read ((n, size));
mode vector = [1:n] real;
mode matrix = [1:n, 1 :n] real;
mode rational = struct (int num, denom);
mode functionset = [1:n] proc (real) real;
mode book = struct (string title, author,
    publisher, int pages, year,
    bool paperback);
mode magazine = struct (string title,
    int subscribers, publ frequency);
    publisher,
mode library = [1: size] union (book,
    magazine);
mode person = struct (string initials,
    ref person ma, pa,
    int age,
    bool too fat);
mode family = struct (person mommy, daddy,
    [1:2] person child);
mode bridgehand = [1:13] struct (char rank,
    suit);
mode word = [0:15] bool;
mode memory = [0:4095] words;
mode instruction1 = struct (int opcode,
    address1,address2,address3);
mode instruction2 = [1:4] int;
mode flight = struct (string plane, pilot,
    movie, bool nonstop, [1:size] struct
    (string name, [1:10] char phone)
    passenger);
mode multireal = union (real, long real,
    long long real);
mode tree = struct (int value,
    ref tree right, left);
mode integer = int;
mode interger = int; ¢ for bad spellors ¢
skip ¢ dummy statement ¢
end
```

A few comments about mode declarations may be helpful. The modes **instruction1** and **instruction2** each consist of four integers. If *add* is declared to be **instruction1** and *sub* is declared to be **instruction2**, then the fields of *add* are accessed via the field selections:

opcode **of** *add*, address1 **of** *add*,
address2 **of** *add*, address3 **of** *add*,

whereas the components of *sub* are accessed by subscripting:

sub[1], *sub*[2], *sub*[3], *sub*[4].

Which choice is made depends upon the application.

The mode **tree** is interesting. It has three fields, an integer and two pointers. In terms of allocating space for **tree** variables, it hardly matters that the pointers point to objects of mode **tree**. Binary trees and graphs are widely used in computer science, so modes like this are valuable. A mode that is defined in terms of itself, like **tree**, is called a recursive mode. Note that although the nonrecursive mode declarations are used merely for convenience, the recursive modes really require the mode definition facility (try declaring a variable with the same mode as **tree** just using a **struct** (**ref** . . .)).

One must exercise some care when defining recursive modes. For example:

mode bush = **struct** (**int** *v*, **bush** *h,t*)

is incorrect. Suppose that an **int** requires one word of memory, and a **bush** requires k words of memory. Then a declaration like

bush *blueberry*

would require that the variable *blueberry* be allocated enough memory to store one object of mode **int** (one word) and two objects of mode **bush** ($2k$ words) for a total of $2k+1$ words. This contradicts our statement that a **bush** requires only k words. The mode declaration is impossible. A **bush** can hardly contain two **bush**es and then some. In contrast, the mode **tree** presents no such problem since it only claims space for an **int** and two addresses (pointers), not two objects of mode **tree**. As you might expect, ALGOL 68 allows all the modes that are intuitively reasonable and prohibits those that are not (RR 7.4).

Same modes can be "spelled" in more than one way. For example, in

mode m1 = **union** (**int**, **real**);
mode m2 = **union** (**real**, **int**)

m1 and **m2** represent the same mode. On the other hand,

mode m3 = **struct** (**int** *i*, **real** *r*);
mode m4 = **struct** (**int** *j*, **real** *r*);
mode m5 = **struct** (**real** *r*, **int** *i*)

are three different modes because the field selectors are part of the mode. Mode equivalence is dealt with in RR 7.3.

At least one aspect of the orthogonal design of ALGOL 68 may now be clearer. From the 11 primitive modes listed in Section 2.1 and the five simple mode construction rules listed in Sections 2.2 through 2.6, one has the ability to create a large and powerful collection of new data types.

In contrast, PL/I is not orthogonally designed; there are no simple rules telling which combinations of attributes are allowed and which are not. A complete specification of the allowed "modes" in PL/I can only be encoded by giving a large table of compatible and incompatible attributes. This difference is characteristic of other aspects of ALGOL 68 and PL/I as well.

2.8 Using New Modes

Variables of user-created modes are defined in the same way that variables of the primitive modes are: first the mode, then a list of one or more identifiers. Declarations are commands to the compiler to reserve storage for variables. Keep in mind that the compiler needs to know how much storage to reserve. When declaring an array variable, one must specify the actual bounds (evaluated at run time) in order for the compiler to reserve enough space. On the other hand, when declaring a pointer to an array (for example, **ref** [ ] **int**), the bounds are not needed, since the only storage reserved is that required for the pointer, not the array; a pointer to a big array takes up the same space as a pointer to a small array. However, to be used, the pointer must appear on the left-hand side of an assignment, with some array (itself declared with bounds) on the right-hand side.

The rules for when bounds are and are not needed are given in RR 4.6.

When a mode declaration contains a variable or an expression in an array bound, for example, n in mode **vector** above, the question arises whether the value of n at mode declaration time or at variable declaration time is the one that is used. Consider this program:

```
begin
int n;
n := 3;
mode vector = [1:n] int;
n := 25;
vector x;
n := 75;
vector y;
skip ¢ dummy statement ¢
end
```

It is the value of n at variable declaration time that matters; x has 25 elements and y has 75 elements. The value of n at mode declaration time is irrelevant. In a certain sense, variable declarations are "carried out" at run time, providing more flexibility than most languages allow. (Of course, a clever compiler writer will try to do as much as possible at compile time.)

Variables may be declared with initial values by following the identifier with a "becomes" symbol (:=) and the initial value. Structures and arrays may also be initialized, with parenthesized lists of values. It is also possible to partially initialize structures or arrays by using **skip** for some of the fields or elements. The value of **skip** is undefined; these elements or fields must be initialized by explicit assignment before being used.

Some sample variable declarations are shown below.

3. UNITS

Like other programming languages, ALGOL 68 requires that expressions be placed in certain contexts, for example, on the right-hand side of assignments, as actual parameters in procedure calls, and as subscripts. Expressions are called units in ALGOL 68 and are much more general than in many other pro-

```
begin ¢ mentally insert the mode
          declarations of section 2.7 here ¢
int n := 3, size := 2;
char c := "q";
real length := 2.503;
vector v := (14.2,−9.1,3.5678);
matrix a := ((1.0,2.0,3.0), (0.6,−0.9,100.0),
          (1.1,2.1,3.4));
rational rat := (1,2), tar := (3,4);
functionset f := (sin,cos,tan);
book censored := (skip,skip,skip,skip,skip,false);
magazine cs := ("computing surveys", "acm",22000,4);
library mini := (censored,cs);
person tom := ("trj", skip,skip,40,true);
person mary := ("mej", skip,skip,41,false);
family jones := (mary, tom, (skip,skip));
bridgehand south := (
    ("A", "S"), ("K", "S"), ("Q", "S"), ("J", "S"),
    ("A", "H"), ("Q", "H"), ("9", "H"), ("7", "H"),
    ("K", "D"), ("Q", "D"), ("T", "D"),
    ("Q", "C"), ("J", "C"));
word w; memory mem;
flight twa 156 :=
    ("747", "bill", "frankenstein", true, skip);
skip ¢ dummy statement ¢
end
```

gramming languages. In the following sub-sections we discuss 15 kinds of units. The complete list is given in RR 5.1A.

3.1 Denotations

The simplest form of a unit is a **denotation** (usually called a constant in other programming languages). Typical denotations of mode **int, real, bool, char,** and **string** are: 4, 3.6, **true,** "x", and "hi". "Constants" of array and structured modes are also allowed. They are called row displays and structure displays, respectively, and consist of parenthesized lists of values. For example,

$$[1:2,1:3] \textbf{ int } x2 := ((1,2,4),(8,16,32))$$

illustrates the use of a row display. Denotations are described in Chapter 8 of the Revised Report.

3.2 Variables

The next simplest unit is the variable. In this statement,

begin int i,j; $i := 3$; $j := i$ **end**

i, a variable, is used as a unit in the second assignment. (Remember that it is dereferenced to an integer unit.)

3.3 Formulas

A formula (RR 5.4.2) is an operator and its operand or operands. A monadic formula has one operand, for example, **abs** i, $-x$, and **sign** y. Dyadic formulas have two operands, for example, $i-j$, $x<y$, and "abc" + "xyz".

ALGOL 68 has well over 100 "built-in" operators (listed in RR 10.2) and provides a mechanism that allows programmers to define new ones, just as it provides a mechanism to define new modes. Operators are akin to procedures. Each operator expects to have one or two operands of specific modes, and delivers a result of a specific mode. The same symbol may represent two different operators (cf. GENERIC in PL/I).

In the following program:

```
begin
int i := 1, j := 2, k;
real x:= 0.1, y := 0.3, z;
k := i+j;
z := x+y
end
```

the first + represents an operator with integer operands and an integer result, whereas the second + represents a different operator with real operands and a real result. Very likely they will require different hardware instructions.

A formula may be used as an operand. For example, the formula $i+j$ could be used as an operand of $<$, as in $i+j<k$, which is a formula yielding a Boolean result (assuming + has higher precedence than $<$, which it has).

3.4 Slices

Arrays may be subscripted as in other languages. When an object of mode [ ] **m** is subscripted, an object of mode **m** is yielded. ALGOL 68 also permits a generalization of subscripting called trimming, yielding some cross section of the original array. If z has been declared by [1:10] **int** z, then $z[1:7]$, $z[1:10]$, and $z[2:5]$ are examples of units (slices) and can be used in assignments, actual parameters, etc. For example:

```
begin
[1:10] int a,b;
[1:20] real x; [1:20,1:20] real xx;
read((a,b,x,xx));
b[1:4] := a[1:4]; ¢ assigns 4 elements ¢
b[3:9] := a[1:7]; ¢ assigns 7 elements ¢
b[1:10] := a[1:10]; ¢ assigns a to b ¢
b := a; ¢ same as above ¢
xx[4,1:20] := x; ¢ assign to row 4 of xx ¢
xx[8:9,7] := x[1:2] ¢ xx[8,7] := x[1];
                      xx[9,7] := x[2] ¢
end
```

A trimmer, such as 1:4 in the first assignment does not affect the dimensionality of the array, whereas a subscript (just one bound, with no colon) reduces it by one, as in $xx[4,1:20]$.

All combinations of trimming and subscripting are valid. For example, if s is a three-dimensional array, $s[i,j,k]$,$s[i,j,k1:k2]$, $s[i,j1:j2,k1:k2]$, and $s[i1:i2,j1:j2,k1:k2]$ can

be used as a variable, and one-, two-, and three-dimensional arrays, respectively. Furthermore, $s[i, j1:j2, k]$, $s[i1:i2, j, k1:k2]$ and other combinations are also allowed. In an assignment, the bounds must "match," as described in RR 5.3.2. Subscripting and trimming are collectively called slicing.

3.5 Selections

A selection consists of a field selector, the symbol **of**, and a structure to be selected from. The field selector must be an identifier and cannot be computed (because it is not an object): The structure being selected from may, however, be the result of evaluating an expression.

If a mode involves both structures and rows, a unit derived from an object of that mode may involve slicing (subscripting or trimming) and selecting. Slicing binds more tightly than selecting; so *tail* **of** *dog* [k] means *tail* **of** (*dog*[k]) and not (*tail* **of** *dog*)[k]. If *tail* **of** *dog* yields an array, then (*tail* **of** *dog*)[k] is the correct way to extract the kth element of that array. When combining selecting and slicing, keep in mind that any array can be sliced and that any structure can be selected from. Here are some examples:

```
begin int m := 25, n := 40, k := 2;
mode person = struct (string initials,
                              int age);
mode course = struct (person prof,
                              [1:n]person student);
mode dept = [1:m] course;
person smith, jones, brown, davis;
course painting, drawing, etching;
dept art;
¢ begin assigning values ¢
    initials of smith := "rbs";
age of smith := 47;
jones := ("tmj", 32);
prof of painting := ("jed", 47);
prof of drawing := smith;
prof of etching := prof of painting;
art[1:3] := (painting, drawing, etching);
prof of art[2] := jones; ¢ smith quit ¢
age of prof of art[2] := 39;
(student of art[2]) [1] := davis;
age of (student of art[2]) [1] := 18;
(student of art[k+1]) [k−1] := ("tns", 19)
end
```

This may look imposing at first, but it is really quite logical. The key is to keep track of the mode of the objects. When faced with an array, like (*student* **of** *art*[2]), one slices. When confronted with a structure, like *prof* **of** *art*[2], one selects a field from it. If you still think ALGOL 68 is unnecessarily complicated, try to rewrite the preceding program in FORTRAN.

3.6 Procedure Calls

The mode of a procedure is uniquely determined by the modes of its parameters and its result. If a procedure returns mode **m**, then a call of that procedure is a unit of mode **m** and may be used anywhere a unit of mode **m** is needed. If a procedure $p1$ has mode **proc (real, bool) int,** then $a[p1(3.14, \textbf{true})]$ shows a call of $p1$ used as a subscript. Similarly, if a procedure $p2$ has mode **proc (int) bool,** then **if** $p2(6)$ **then** *print*(k) **fi** is legitimate.

A procedure call has two parts: the procedure to be called, and the parameter list. The first part may be the result of a computation, for example,

```
begin int i; real x,y;
[1:3] proc (real) real f := (sin,cos,tan);
to 100 ¢ repeat 100 times ¢
  do read ((i,x));
      ¢ i selects sin, cos, or tan to call ¢
      y := f[i](x);
      print(y)
  od
end
```

A function with no parameters (that is, of mode **proc m**) is not "called". Instead the procedure name is written with no parameter list. For technical reasons this is not regarded as a procedure call, but as a type conversion (coercion) from mode **proc m** to mode **m**. It is called deproceduring (RR 6.3) and is completely analogous to the widening coercion from **int** to **real** in **real** $x := 3$ or the dereferencing coercion in (**int** $i := 1, j; j := i$). If deproceduring did not exist, then **real** $x := random$ would have to be prohibited, since *random* has mode **proc real** and on the right-hand side in the preceding example a **real** is needed.

3.7 Assignments

An assignment (called an assignation in the Revised Report) consists of a destination (the left-hand side), a "becomes" symbol (:=), and a source (the right-hand side). A **ref m** assignment has a **ref m** unit as the destination and an **m** unit, or something coerceable to an **m** unit, as the source (RR 5.2.1.1).

Having detected a **ref m** destination, the compiler will coerce the source by all possible means to **m**. We emphasize that after all coercion the destination is mode **ref m** and the source is mode **m**.

An assignment can stand by itself as a statement, or be used itself as a unit. It may, for example, be used as a source in another assignment (but not as a destination to avoid certain ambiguities). For example, $j := k$ is an assignment and as such may be used as the source in $i := source$, yielding $i := j := k$. Because ALGOL 68 allows assignments as sources, it also gets multiple assignments, as an extra added attraction, for free. Furthermore, $a[i := i+1]$ is a perfectly valid way of subscripting the array a: first the assignment is carried out, and then the newly assigned value of i is used as a subscript.

3.8 Generators

ALGOL 68 provides two storage management strategies: local and heap. Local storage consists of a last-in, first-out stack. Whenever a procedure is called (and perhaps when a **begin end** block is entered, depending on the implementation) a new stack frame is created for all local variables needed in it. When it is exited, the storage is released by resetting the stack pointer to the value it had prior to entry. This leads to a simple and efficient method for allocating storage.

All variables declared in the usual way use the local storage discipline. In addition, the programmer may explicitly request more stack storage to be reserved by using a local generator, **loc**, followed by a specification of the mode desired (the mode is needed because **loc [1:n] compl** may take much more space than **loc bool**). The value of the generator **loc m** is the address of the new object, that is, a pointer to it, and as such has mode **ref m**.

An example may make the use of local generators clearer.

```
begin ¢ calculate something ¢
  begin ¢ demonstrate triangular arrays ¢
  int n; read(n);
  [1:n] ref [ ] real triangle;
  for k from 1 to n
    do triangle[k] := loc[1:k] real;
      ¢ fill in some values ¢
      for j from 1 to k
        do triangle[k][j] := k+j od
  od
  end
  ¢ storage used by triangle is now
  released ¢
end
```

Numerical analysts often deal with symmetric $n \times n$ matrices. Using a representation of n columns of n elements each is wasteful of storage. The preceding program declares *triangle* to be a row of pointers, each pointing to a different real vector. The vectors pointed to are created during execution of the program, each newly created vector being one element larger than its predecessor. When the preceding block is exited, all the storage reserved can be released. That is why these generators are called *local* generators: the effect is local to the block they occur in.

The array *hamlet* in the example at the end of Section 2.2 is allocated by essentially the same mechanism as the array triangle just given. That is why unlabeled statements can be allowed before declarations.

Incidently, the declaration of *triangle* should be carefully noted. Actual bounds are needed in the first brackets, but not in the second because *triangle* is a vector of pointers. The compiler has to know how large the vector is in order to reserve space for it, but for the purposes of allocating space to *triangle*, it does not matter what is being pointed to. In fact, bounds are never needed in a mode following a **ref**.

The other storage management scheme is the heap. The heap is a single homogeneous section of memory from which storage can be acquired by heap generators, of the form **heap m**, where **m** is the specification of the mode of the object needed. Because heap objects are not dependent on the stack discipline, they do not vanish when the block

in which they were created is exited. When the heap is exhausted, a run-time garbage collector has to come in and recycle the garbage. For example,

```
begin ref [ ] real ptr;
to 1 000 000 ¢ repeat a million times ¢
   do ptr := heap[1:1000] real od
end
```

is a lovely little test to see whether your garbage collector is working properly. Passing through the loop the first time, a piece of the heap is allocated for a 1000-element real array and the address of the array is assigned to *ptr*. Passing through the loop the next time, the same thing happens, overwriting the address of the first array, which now becomes garbage because there is no way to access it. On some subsequent pass, all the free space on the heap will be gone, and garbage collection will be automatically invoked to recover unused storage.

Note that if a local instead of a heap generator had been used in the preceding example, the stack frame would have kept growing and growing until all of memory was full. Since stack storage is only released at procedure (or possibly block) exit, the program eventually would have been aborted with a "stack overflow" message.

3.9 Nil

In list processing applications, it is necessary to have some marker to indicate the end of a list. When programming in Assembly Language, zero is often used. In ALGOL 68 a special symbol, **nil** (RR 5.2.4), is provided to end lists.

3.10 Identity Relations

When performing list processing, it is sometimes necessary to compare two pointers to see if they point to the same object. This can be done using identity relations.

Identity relations are also used to compare pointers to **nil**. In practice, it is usually necessary that the programmer specify the

mode required using a cast (see next Section 3.11). For example, consider a variable, *ptr*, declared by: **ref person** *ptr*, that is, *ptr* can point to an object of mode **person**. To see if *ptr* points to **nil**, one uses the construction

$$ptr := : \textbf{ref person (nil)}.$$

The identity relators : = : and : ≠ : are not operators (because they act on an infinite number of modes), but they may be regarded roughly as operators of infinitely low precedence. Thus, for example,

if $i < j \land ptr := :$ **nil then** ...

means

if$(i < j \land ptr) := :$ **nil then** ...

which is probably not what was intended.

To illustrate heap generators, **nil**, and identity relations, we give a simple program that reads in people's bowling scores and stores the information as a singly linked list. In phase two, names are looked up and the scores are retrieved.

```
begin
mode person = struct(string name,
         int score, ref person next);
ref person first := nil, ptr;
string bowler; int bowled;
bool still looking;
      make term (stand in, " ");
while read((bowled,bowler)); bowled > 0
do first := heap person
         := (bowler,bowled,first)
od;

¢ phase 2. look up the scores ¢
while read ((newline,bowler)); bowler ≠ " "
do ptr := first; still looking := true;
   while (ptr := ≠ : ref person(nil)) ∧
            still looking
   do if name of ptr = bowler
         then print((bowler,score of ptr,
                  newline));
            still looking := false
         else ptr := next of ptr
      fi
   od;
   if still looking
      then print((bowler, "not in our league",
            new line))
   fi
od
end
```

Some comments may be helpful. The condition in a **while** statement consists of zero or more statements followed by a unit. In the first **while** statement in the preceding program, two variables are first read, and then the condition (bowled > 0) is evaluated. The data are arranged in such a way that there is one person per card, first a score, and then a name. It is necessary to specify the string delimiter for the name, and this is done by the call to the procedure *make term*, defining space as the string delimiter for the standard input file, *stand in* (see Section 9, Input/Output).

Let us imagine that the first two people are named Adam and Eve, with bowling scores of 105 and 107, respectively. Prior to execution of the initial **while** loop, *first* points to **nil**. After the loop has been executed once, an object of mode **person** has been created, with its three fields initialized to ("Adam", 105, **nil**). The variable *first* then points to this object. Passing through the loop the next time, a second object of mode **person** is created, with its fields initialized to ("Eve", 107, pointer to first object). Now *first* points to Eve, which points to Adam, which points to **nil**.

3.11 Casts

Most of the time it is not necessary to specify the mode of a source, destination, operand, etc., explicitly. It is usually obvious from context. However, to handle those situations that are inherently ambiguous, the required mode may be specified explicitly using a construction called a cast (RR 5.5.1), one form of which consists of a mode followed by a parenthesized unit, as in **ref int**(*i*).

To understand why casts are needed, examine this program:

```
begin int i := 0, k := 1;
ref int ptr := i;
ptr := k;
print (i)
end
```

Consider what *ptr* := *k* does. On one hand, it looks like an innocuous assignment of the address of *k* to a pointer variable (*ptr* has mode **ref ref int**, and *k* has mode **ref int**).

But on the other hand, suppose both *ptr* and *k* were dereferenced, yielding a **ref int** object as destination and an **int** object as source. If that happened, *i* would be assigned the value 1, quite different from assigning *k* to *ptr*. To avoid the occurrence of this ambiguity, the ALGOL 68 grammar was constructed in such a way as to prevent dereferencing destinations. This means that the preceding program prints 0, not 1.

Now comes the 64 dollar question: suppose you actually intended the second interpretation; how can that be achieved? Answer: use a cast; that is, replace the assignment by **ref int** (*ptr*) := *k*. The cast explicitly forces *ptr* to be converted to mode **ref int**. Since *k* cannot be assigned to a **ref int**, *k* is dereferenced. (Dereferencing is allowed for sources.)

When a cast is used, two modes are involved: the starting mode (the mode of the object inside the parentheses), and the goal mode (the mode listed before the open parenthesis). If there is no coercion path between the starting and the goal modes, the cast is invalid. For example, if *ptr* has mode **ref proc ref int**, then **real**(*ptr*) is a valid cast because *ptr* can be dereferenced, deprocedured, dereferenced, again, and widened. However, **bits** (3.14) is invalid because there is no coercion path from **real** to **bits**. Coercion is discussed in more detail in Section 4, Coercions.

3.12 Choice Clauses

ALGOL 68 allows **if** "statements" and **case** "statements" to be used as units if they produce the proper mode. This is illustrated by the following program:

```
begin ¢ examples of choice clauses ¢
int i,j,k;
real x := 0.1, y := 0.2, z := 3.1;
read ((i,j,k));
[1:10] bool a, b;
x := if i<0 then .3/x else z+4.0 fi;
for n from i to if j = 2 then 1 else k fi
   do b[n] := true od;
b[case i in 6,3 out 4 esac] := false;
if i = 0 then j else k fi :=
         if j>0 then j+1 else k−1 fi;
[if i>0 then 1 else k−1 fi : 10] int c;
z := if i>3 then sin else cos fi (3.14);
end
```

Three kinds of choice clauses exist: Boolean, integer, and united.

- The Boolean choice clause is the familiar **if** ... **then** ... **else** ... **fi** construction. If the **else** part is absent and the condition is false, the result is undefined.
- The second choice clause has the form **case** ... **in** clause1, clause2, clause3, ..., clause *n* **out** ... **esac**. The integer expression between **case** and **in** selects one of the clauses by indexing into the clause list. Thus the order of the clauses is critical. If there is no **out** part, and the expression is out of range, the result is undefined.
- The third choice clause takes a united variable (such as *kitchen sink* used in Section 2.5) and selects one of the clauses based upon its current mode. The order of the clauses for this type of choice clause is irrelevant.

Variables may be declared in the condition, or integer parts, initialized, and then used in the succeeding parts; that is, their scope encompasses the entire choice clause. For example:

```
begin ¢ print smaller of 2 numbers ¢
if int i,j; read ((i,j)); i<j
   then print (i)
   else print (j)
fi
end
```

ALGOL 68 (and common sense) requires that all the possible choices in a unit be of the same mode, or be coerceable to the same mode. The unit **if** $i<0$ **then** 4 **else** *j* **fi** can be used anywhere an integer unit is expected, because the **then** part is already an integer and the **else** part can be converted to one by dereferencing it. The unit cannot be used as a destination, however, because the **then** part cannot be converted to a **ref int**; there is no "referencing" coercion.

Now consider the assignment in:

```
begin int i,k; read (k);
   i:= if k<0 then 6 else true fi
end
```

This assignment is incorrect because an integer unit is needed as the source, and it is not possible to coerce all choices to mode **int**; namely, **true** cannot be turned into an integer. The problem of making sure all choices can be converted to the proper mode is called balancing (RR 3.2.1e). Since an assignment may have long **case** units, both as source and destination, just determining the proper mode of the assignment may itself be a substantial task for the compiler. However, the grammar was constructed in such a way as to insure that there is only one possibility.

ALGOL 68 allows **if, then, else,** and **fi** to be written as (, |, |, and), respectively. Thus **if** $k<0$ **then** *i* **else** *j* **fi** can be written $(k<0 \mid i \mid j)$. This is often convenient in constructions like:

$$x := (i<0 \mid y \mid z) + (j<0 \mid 4.0 \mid z+5)$$

3.13 Closed Clauses

ALGOL 68 is an expression language. This means that every executable statement or group of statements can (at least potentially) deliver a value. A serial clause (RR 3.2) is a series of zero or more declarations and/or "statements" followed by a unit. The mode and value of the serial clause consist of the mode and value of the final unit. A closed clause is a serial clause enclosed by **begin end** or by parentheses. A closed clause has the mode and value of the serial clause, that is, of the last unit in the clause.

Some examples of closed clauses follow:

```
begin ¢ closed clauses ¢
begin int i; read(i); i end
begin real x; read(x); sin(x) end;
begin int i,j; read((i,j)); i+j end;
begin [1:10] int a;
   for i from 1 to 10 do a[i] := i*i od; a
end;
(int i; i := 20);
("horse");
((10,20,30,40));
((((((0))))));
(int i; (i := 3))
end
```

Since closed clauses are units, they may be used in the same way any other units are used, even if this seems peculiar at first.

Closed clauses may be used as sources; subscripts; **from, by,** or **to** parts in **for** statements; etc. For example, the following statement is perfectly valid:

$k := ($**int** $i; read(i); i+1)$

3.14 Skip

There is a special unit, **skip**, which is explicitly undefined. It takes on whatever mode is needed. As we have seen earlier, it can be used to omit the initialization of an element or field of a row or structure display, or to serve as a dummy statement. Do not confuse **skip** with **nil**; **nil** is a specific value that can be tested for; **skip** is just "filler" to make a construction syntactically correct, vaguely analogous to CONTINUE statements in FORTRAN.

3.15 Routine Texts

Since ALGOL 68 allows procedure variables, it is only natural that it also allow procedure units, so that there is something to assign to these procedure variables. A routine text is a procedure body, headed by the formal parameter list, if there is one. We discuss routine texts in the context of procedures and operators later. As a preview, we give a few examples of routine texts as sources:

```
begin proc (real) real f;
proc int p; proc void q;
f := (real r) real: 3.14/r;
f := (real s) real: s+4.0;
f := (real t) real: sin(cos(t));
p := int: 3;
p := int: (int k; read(k); k);
q := void: print ("hello")
¢ note: no procedures have been called ¢
end
```

Note that the formal parameters can be used in the body of the routine text, following the colon.

3.16 Other Units

For the sake of completeness, we note that loop clauses (**for** loops), jumps (**goto** statements), formats, parallel clauses, and collateral clauses (for example, row displays) are also units in the technical sense (RR 5.1A).

4. COERCIONS

Coercion is the ALGOL 68 term for automatic mode conversion. Unlike some languages (notably PL/I) that allow practically anything to be converted into practically anything else, ALGOL 68 has very few automatic conversions. Automatic conversions often lead to unexpected and unwanted results, so ALGOL 68 was specifically designed to keep them well in hand.

There are exactly six kinds of coercions, each converting some class of modes into another. The six kinds of coercions are:

coercion	input mode	output mode
dereferencing	**ref m**	**m**
deproceduring	**proc m**	**m**
widening	**int**	**real**
widening	**real**	**compl**
widening	**bits**	**[ ] bool**
widening	**bytes**	**[ ] char**
rowing	**m**	**[ ] m, [,] m** etc.
uniting	**m**	**union (m,ml, ...)**
voiding	**m**	(no mode at all)

We have already discussed dereferencing (Section 2.6, Reference-to Modes), widening (Section 2.6), and deproceduring (Section 3.6, Procedure Calls). Widening also applies to the **long** and **short** forms of **int, real, bits,** and **bytes.**

Rowing can convert a unit into a one-element array where required by the context, such as in [1:1] **int** $a := 3$. Uniting turns a unit into a union where required by the syntax, as in **union(int, real)** $u := 4$. Rowing and uniting happen when needed and are of little interest to the average garden variety programmer.

As is probably apparent by now, constructions called statements (for example, assignments, procedure calls) in most languages are called units in ALGOL 68 and can be used as sources, parameters, etc. Sometimes, however, the value of a unit is not needed. Consider what happens to the value of $i := j$ in the closed clause:

(**int** $i,j := 3; i := j; i+j$)

it is discarded after the assignment is performed. Technically this is called voiding (RR 6.7). ALGOL 68 "statements" are properly called void units. Chapter 6 of the

Revised Report describes the coercions in full.

Note that there is no coercion from **real** to **int**. However, the monadic operators **round** and **entier** operate on reals and deliver integers, rounding and truncating, respectively.

5. CONTEXTS

Not every coercion is allowed in every context (for example, in source, destination, subscript, actual parameter). In Section 3.11 Casts, we saw that ambiguities could result if dereferencing of destinations was allowed. Each context has an intrinsic strength. The strength specifies which coercions are allowed. There are five strengths: strong, firm, meek, weak, and soft. In some contexts no coercions at all are allowed.

Strong contexts are those in which the mode of the unit is uniquely determined by the context. For example, in

(**real** x; x := big hairy mess)

the destination is known to be of mode **ref real**. Any and all coercions may be used (repeatedly) to turn the source into an object of mode **real**. If the source is an **int**, it can be widened; if it is a **ref real**, it can be dereferenced; if it is a **proc real**, it can be deprocedured; if it is a **ref proc ref int**, it can be dereferenced to **proc ref int**, deprocedured to **ref int**, dereferenced again to **int**, and finally widened to **real**. Some examples of strong contexts are: sources in assignments, initial values in declarations, actual parameters, and procedure bodies.

In other contexts some coercions must be prohibited to avoid ambiguities. For example, consider:

```
begin int i := 2, j;
real x := 3.0, y;
j := i+i;
y := x+x
end
```

The + in $i+i$ is an operator that operates on integers and yields an integer. The + in $x+x$ is a different operator acting on reals. The two operators correspond to different hardware instructions. The compiler tells which operator is to be used by looking at the modes of the operands. If operands could be widened, the operands of the first + could be dereferenced and then widened, yielding reals. Then the compiler could not tell which operator was meant. Operands are always in firm context.

If every kind of unit were allowed in every context, certain ambiguities would arise, as can be easily seen by means of an example. Consider what would happen to the integer assignment $i := j+2$ if j, which is an operand of +, were replaced by the assignment $k := 3$. We would have $i := k := 3+2$, which is perfectly legal, but not what was intended. It adds $3+2$ and then assigns the result, 5, to k and i. If we wrote the operand $k := 3$ as a closed clause ($k := 3$), we would get $i := (k := 3)+2$, which first assigns 3 to k, and then 5 to i. This is quite a different result than in the first case! To avoid ambiguities, ALGOL 68 only allows constructions in positions where no confusion can arise.

6. PROCEDURES

In ALGOL 68 procedures are objects and have values, just as any other objects. Procedure variables exist and may be declared, just as other variables. They may also be initialized to some value of the appropriate mode; for example, by using a routine text:

```
proc real p1 := real: 1.0/(1.0+random);
proc int p2 := int: (int k; read(k);k);
proc (int k) int p3 := (int) int:(k+1) div 2
```

Procedures (and all other modes) may also be declared in a slightly different way, by use of what is technically called an identity declaration (RR 4.4.1a). This form consists of **proc**, the identifier, an equals sign, and a routine text. In this form the identifier is no longer a variable and cannot be assigned a new procedure. Some examples of this form are:

```
begin ¢ proc declarations ¢
proc next = (int k) int: k+1;
proc bump = (ref int k) void: k := k+1;
proc less = (int j,k) bool: j<k;
proc readin = int: (int k; read(k);k);
proc eject = void: print(new page);
```

```
proc dot product = (int n,[ ] real a,b) real:
begin real sum := 0;
  for k from 1 to n do sum :=  sum+a[k]*b[k]
  od;
  sum
end;
skip ¢ dummy statement ¢
end
```

Note that the procedure body (the part following the colon) is a unit. In the dot product example, the unit is a closed clause.

6.1 Parameter Mechanism

A procedure may be declared with an arbitrary number of formal parameters, but calls to the procedure must supply precisely the proper number of actual parameters, no more and no less. The nth actual parameter is accessed by using the identifier of the nth formal parameter, just as in FORTRAN, PL/I, ALGOL 60, etc. Thus the order of the formal parameters is very important.

Unlike these other languages, however, the modes of the parameters are specified directly in the formal parameter list. The mode specified before the identifier of each formal parameter is the mode of that parameter. In the declaration:

```
proc recip = (real x) real: 1.0/x
```

the mode of x is **real**, It is not **ref real**. By way of contrast, in the variable declaration **real** x, x is of mode **ref real**. This difference is crucial to the understanding of the ALGOL 68 parameter mechanism.

The parameter passing works as follows. The actual parameters are first coerced to the modes specified by the formal parameters (if necessary). Then each actual parameter is evaluated. (An actual parameter is a unit, and might be a closed clause 10 pages long.) Copies of the values yielded are then passed to the procedure. This may be regarded as a generalization of the call by value used in ALGOL 60, except that in ALGOL 68 a parameter may be of any mode, including **ref** "something," in which case an address is passed.

To shed more light on the parameter mechanism, let us begin with a syntactically incorrect program:

```
begin int n := 4; ¢ incorrect program ¢
proc wrong = (int k) void: k := k+1;
wrong(n);
print(n)
end
```

The problem here is that k has mode **int** and not **ref int**. The destination of an assignment must be of mode **ref** "something;" the assignment $k := k+1$ will be flagged by the compiler as incorrect. Now let us try again.

```
begin int n := 4; ¢ correct program ¢
proc right = (ref int k) void: k := k+1;
right(n);
print(n)
end
```

This program will print 5. When a formal parameter is declared **int** rather than **ref int**, the corresponding actual parameter is protected from being changed. This often helps catch bugs.

To illuminate the more subtle aspects of the parameter mechanism, consider these two programs:

```
begin  int i := 0;
proc jekyll = (int a) void:
  (i := i+1; print (a));
jekyll(i)
end
```

```
begin int i := 0;
proc hyde = (ref int a) void:
  (i := i+1; print (a));
hyde (i)
end
```

The call $jekyll(i)$ is executed in the following steps. Since the formal parameter is of mode **int**, the actual parameter, i, is dereferenced to yield an integer. A copy of this integer value is then passed to $jekyll$ (on the stack, in a register, or some other way). Then $jekyll$ increments i. Finally, $jekyll$ accesses the actual parameter passed to it and prints it. The number 0 is printed.

The call $hyde(i)$ is executed differently. The formal parameter in program 2 is of mode **ref int**; so i is not dereferenced, because it is already in the proper mode. A copy of the address of i is made and put on the stack, in a register, or elsewhere. After incrementing i, $hyde$ picks up the actual parameter, the address of i, dereferences it, getting 1, and then prints the number 1.

An object of mode **int** is passed to *jekyll*, but an object of mode **ref int** is passed to *hyde*. In a sense, *jekyll* uses the ALGOL 60 call-by-value parameter mechanism, whereas *hyde* uses something similar to a call-by-reference mechanism. ALGOL 68 effectively gives the programmer some control over how parameters are passed via the modes of the formal parameters.

In summary, the parameter mechanism has three key features:

1) A formal parameter is written as a mode followed by an identifier. A formal parameter written as **int** k really has mode **int**, not mode **ref int**.
2) An actual parameter may be any unit, and any coercion may be used on it, but the result after coercion must match the mode of the formal parameter. If a formal parameter has mode **ref real**, the actual parameter must yield a real variable; the value 3.14 will not suffice. The calling, and not the called, procedure performs the coercions.
3) A copy is made of the actual parameter (after coercion). This copy is what is passed (conceptually). All references to the formal parameter use this copy. Thus the parameter is only evaluated once (as opposed to the call-by-name mechanism used in ALGOL 60, where the parameter is reevaluated on every access).

6.2 More About Procedures

Unlike PL/I, parameters and results in ALGOL 68 may have any mode; pointers, arrays, structures, unions, and even procedures are all allowed. As an example of using a procedure as a parameter, consider the following procedure for computing the sum:

$$f(1) + f(2) + f(3) + \cdots + f(n).$$

```
proc sum = (int n, proc (real) real f) real:
begin real sum := 0;
for i to n do sum := sum+f(i) od;
sum
end
```

In this example, i is allowed as a parameter to a **proc**(**real**) **real** because parameters are strong units and therefore can be widened. A typical call to *sum* might be *sum*(100,*cos*), which would yield $cos(1) + cos(2) + \cdots + cos(100)$.

In ALGOL 68 a routine text is a unit and as such can be used as an actual parameter. In the previous examples, routine texts were used to the right of the equals sign. Some examples of routine texts as actual parameters of *sum* are:

$$sum(100, (\textbf{real } x) \textbf{ real}: 1/x)$$
$$sum(50, (\textbf{real } x) \textbf{ real}: sin(x))$$
$$sum(k+1, (\textbf{real } x) \textbf{ real}: random)$$

ALGOL 60 fanciers will notice that using a routine text as an actual parameter is essentially equivalent to Jensen's device [5], but a lot less sneaky.

It is sometimes useful to be able to write procedures that accept a variable number of parameters. Although strictly speaking this is not possible in ALGOL 68, something very close is possible. A procedure with one formal parameter, an array, must have one actual parameter, also an array. However, this array may have an arbitrary number of elements, provided it is of the proper mode. Remember that a one-dimensional integer array has mode [ ] **int** no matter how large it is; the bounds are not part of the mode.

When it is expected that a procedure be called with different sized arrays as parameters, there must be some way of determining the bounds of its actual parameters. Two operators are provided for this purpose: **lwb** and **upb**. If *vec* is a one-dimensional array of any mode, **lwb** *vec* and **upb** *vec* have the values of the lower and upper bounds, respectively. For a higher dimensional array, q, n **lwb** q and n **upb** q return the lower and upper bounds of the nth subscript, respectively. The lower bound of a row display is 1.

The following program declares a procedure, *outp*, that accepts an integer array as parameter and prints each of its elements on a new line. Note that calls to *outp* (and also to *read*) have two sets of parentheses. One set is needed to enclose the parameter list and one set is needed to construct the row display;

```
begin int i,j,k;
proc outp = ([ ] int a) void:
  begin for i to upb a
        do print ((new line, a[i])) od
  end;
read ((i,j,k));
outp ((1,2,3,4));
outp ((i,j,7,k,j+1,k−4));
outp ((if i<j then 1 else k fi,
       if j>0 then 4 else 2 fi,
       10,k+6,j,−k,−6,+7,0))
end
```

that is, (1,2,3,4) is a unit, but 1,2,3,4 is nothing. This is why *print((x,y))* and not *print(x,y)* has been used to print two variables.

It is possible to write procedures that accept any one of a prespecified list of modes as a parameter by making the formal parameter a union. The following example is a program that accepts parameters of mode **int**, **real**, or **bool** and returns the mode as a string:

```
begin int k := 0; union(real,bool) u := 4.0;
proc mohd = (union(int,real,bool) a) string:
  case a in
    (int): "int",
    (real): "real",
    (bool): "bool"
  esac;
print((mohd(k), " ", mohd(u)))
end
```

The output of this program consists of
    int **real**.

7. OPERATORS

The following program defines a new mode, **vector**, and a procedure, *vecadd*, to add two vectors:

```
begin int n; read(n);
mode vector = [1:n] real;
vector v1,v2,v3,v4,v5;
proc vecadd = (vector x,y) vector:
  begin vector sum;
    for i to upb x
      do sum[i] := x[i] + y[i] od;
    sum
  end;
```

```
¢ read in 4 vectors ¢
read ((v1,v2,v3,v4));
v5 := vecadd(vecadd(vecadd(v1,v2),v3),v4);
print(v5)
end
```

The statement *v5 := vecadd(vecadd(vecadd(v1,v2),v3),v4)*, although ghastly to look at, is quite correct. Because *vecadd(v1,v2)* is a call, and hence a unit, it may be used as an actual parameter to another call of *vecadd*.

The difficulty with the preceding expression is that although it is perfectly acceptable to the ALGOL 68 compiler, for many applications, infix operators (that is, operators placed between the operands) are much more natural than nested procedure calls. ALGOL 68 solves this problem by allowing programmers to define new infix operators, just as they can define new modes.

Operators are defined very much as procedures are. First comes **op**, followed by the operator symbol (which may also be a **boldface** word), then an equals sign, and a routine text. An operator must have either one or two parameters, no more and no fewer. Like those of a procedure, the parameters and the result of an operator may be of any mode. Let us try the vector addition program again, using an operator this time.

```
begin int n; read(n);
mode vector = [1:n] real;
vector v1,v2,v3,v4,v5;
op + = (vector x,y) vector:
  begin vector sum;
    for i to upb x
      do sum[i] := x[i] + y[i] od;
    sum
  end;
```

```
¢ read in 4 vectors ¢
read ((v1,v2,v3,v4));
v5 := v1 + v2 + v3 + v4;
print (v5)
end
```

Just to prove that any mode can be used as an operand or as a result of an operator, we present an operator that takes an **int** and a **proc void** as operands, does something useful, and delivers nothing.

```
begin
op * = (int n,proc void p) void:
   to n do p od; ¢ deprocedure p n times ¢
proc eject = void: print(new page);
proc skip = void: print(new line);
2 * eject; ¢ skip 2 pages ¢
3 * skip ¢ skip 3 lines ¢
end
```

7.1 Operator Identification

Operators have one complication which procedures lack: the same symbol can be used to represent different routine texts. This property is called GENERIC in PL/I. The + in 1+2 is a completely different + than the + in 8.711+8.72. When the ALGOL 68 compiler sees an operator symbol, it determines which operator definition to use by looking at the modes of the operands. If they have modes **m1** and **m2**, it looks to see if an operator with that symbol and those modes has been defined. If so, it uses it. If not, it begins coercing the operands to see if they can be converted into some other modes for which an operator exists.

The process of determining which operator a symbol corresponds to is called **operator identification** (RR 7.2). It is one of the great achievements of the ALGOL 68 Revised Report that this entire process has been described completely in the grammar; that is, the nonterminal <program> simply does not generate any ambiguous programs. No English text is needed to describe what is and what is not permitted.

After an operator has been identified, the evaluation of its formula is the same as that for procedure calls, including the parameter mechanism. Even Jensen's device will work if you provide a routine text as an operand.

To illustrate how operator identification works, consider the following program:

```
begin
op ? = (int i,j) real: i+j;
op ? = (int i,real x) real: i−x;
op ? = (real x,int i) real: i+x+19;
op ? = (real x,y) real: (x<y | x | y);
print ((2?9, 6?2.0, 3.14?8, 9.2?9.9))
end
```

This program yields: 11.0, 4.0, 30.14, 9.2. Each of the four occurrences of ? in the print procedure invokes a different routine text.

Not only can one define new operators on existing modes (for example, "?" on **int**s) and existing operators on new modes (for example, + on **vectors**) and new operators on new modes (for example, **invert** on **matrix**), but one can even redefine the existing operators on the existing modes. If you really want to redefine + on integers to mean subtract, that is your business; the compiler will not complain.

More realistically, someone writing a simulator for a two's complement computer on a one's complement computer (for example, a PDP-11 simulator running on a CDC Cyber) might be very concerned about the specific bit patterns used to represent integers, rather than just their numerical values. In particular, he might want to redefine integer arithmetic to prevent −0 from ever occurring.

Or a numerical analyst might want to redefine real arithmetic to handle rounding differently, or to print a warning message when too much significance has been lost.

7.2 Operator Priorities

When someone writes $print(6+3*5)$ he expects to get 21, because multiplication has higher precedence (priority) than addition. In ALGOL 68 the priority of an operator symbol can be set by the programmer. For example,

```
begin
   prio + = 3, * = 2;
   print (6+3*5)
end
```

will print 45, that is, (6+3) * 5. Monadic operators all have priority 10 and cannot be changed. Dyadic operators may have priorities 1 to 9. This means that $-1 \uparrow 2$ is + 1, not −1 because it is equivalent to $(-1)^2$.

8. STANDARD PRELUDE

Section 10.2 of the Revised Report consists of several hundred definitions of modes, operators, procedures, and values. Collectively they are called the **standard prelude**. Every ALGOL 68 program is presumed to be declared within the scope of these declarations. The modes, operators, etc., declared in the standard prelude may be used in any ALGOL 68 program. In fact, that is precisely why they are there. The standard prelude is written (almost entirely) in ALGOL 68.

It can now be pointed out that the basic nucleus of ALGOL 68 (the part defined by the grammar) is really much smaller than one might expect. For example, some of the "primitive" modes are not really primitive at all, but are defined in the standard prelude; for example,

mode compl = **struct**(**real** *re,im*)

appears in RR 10.2.2f. Furthermore, none of the operators, trigonometric functions, or input/output procedures are part of the language proper. An implementor who was not concerned at all about compilation or execution efficiency, either in time or in space, could have nearly the whole standard prelude textually substituted in front of every ALGOL 68 program, saving himself a great deal of work.

8.1 Environment Enquiries

The standard prelude begins with the environment enquiries (RR 10.2.1). These enquiries allow a program to learn properties of the implementation it is running under without having to deduce them by experiment. The largest integer is called *max int*, the largest real is called *max real*, the smallest positive real is called *small real*, the number of bits in an object of mode **bits** is called *bits width*, etc. For example, here is a program to determine the largest integer in an implementation: (*print(max int)*).

Since each implementor has the freedom to decide how many long and short integers he wants to provide, environment enquiries are provided to allow the program to find out how many there are. These include *int*

lengths, *real lengths*, *bits lengths*, and *bytes lengths* among others. The purpose of these and the other environment enquiries is to ease the task of exchanging programs between computers. For example, a program needing integers of at least 47 bits could first check the value of *max int*; finding it less than $2^{47}-1$, it could use **long int**s instead of **int**s.

8.2 Standard Prelude Operators

10.2.2 of the Revised Report lists the standard modes. Section 10.2.3.0a of the Revised Report lists the priorities of all the standard operators, followed by the definitions of the standard operators. For example, the operators on Boolean operands are as follows:

$$
\begin{aligned}
\textbf{op} \ \vee \ &= \ (\textbf{bool} \ a,b) \ \textbf{bool} \colon (a \mid \textbf{true} \mid b); \\
\textbf{op} \ \wedge \ &= \ (\textbf{bool} \ a,b) \ \textbf{bool} \colon (a \mid b \mid \textbf{false}); \\
\textbf{op} \ \neg \ &= \ (\textbf{bool} \ a) \ \textbf{bool} \colon (a \mid \textbf{false} \mid \textbf{true}); \\
\textbf{op} \ = \ &= \ (\textbf{bool} \ a,b) \ \textbf{bool} \colon (a \wedge b) \vee (\neg a \wedge \neg b); \\
\textbf{op} \ \neq \ &= \ (\textbf{bool} \ a,b) \ \textbf{bool} \colon \neg (a = b); \\
\textbf{op abs} \ &= \ (\textbf{bool} \ a \ \ ) \ \textbf{int} \colon (a \mid 1 \mid 0)
\end{aligned}
$$

From the standard prelude one can see precisely which operators are defined on which operands, and what they do. For example, to determine if **abs true** has a value of 0 or 1, a glance at the standard prelude will show that it has a value of 1. Few languages offer such precise definitions of their operators as ALGOL 68.

Subsequent sections of the standard prelude define the operators for comparison, arithmetic, string handling, etc. If one wants to see exactly what + on strings (concatenation) means, one can consult RR 10.2.3.10i. A very small number of operators are defined in English, such as − on reals. To provide a full definition one would have in fact had to define how floating point arithmetic works. This would have wreaked havoc with implementations on computers whose floating point hardware worked differently. The implementor would either have had to ignore the standard prelude, or simulate floating point operations in software.

ALGOL 68 allows mixed mode arithmetic. The formula 3.14+6 yields the real 9.14. The mechanism by which this happens can now be safely revealed: The operator + is

defined for parameters of modes (**int, int**), (**int, real**), (**real, int**), and (**real, real**). Four definitions are necessary because operands are firm and because widening is forbidden in firm positions (to avoid ambiguities in operator identification).

An interesting new idea in operators is that of combining arithmetic and assignment. For example, RR 10.2.3.11d states:

op $+ := = ($**ref int** $a,$ **int** $b)$ **ref int**$: a := a+b$

This enables one to write: $n + := 1$ rather than $n := n+1$. The "plus and becomes" operator, $+:=$, may also ease the task of optimizing the object code, especially on computers which can add directly to memory. Similar operators exist for real numbers and the other operations; for example, $-:=$ means "subtract and becomes."

A number of standard mathematical functions are provided in RR 10.2.3.12 including *sqrt, exp, ln, cos, arccos, sin, arcsin, tan,* and *arctan.* Anyone who prefers sines as operators rather than as procedure calls need only write:

op sin $= ($**real** $x)$ **real**$: sin(x)$.

If you don't care what values your functions return, you may enjoy *random* (RR 10.5.1b). And finally, *pi* is defined as a real value close to you-know-what (RR 10.2.3.12a). Standard prelude declarations may be overridden simply by supplying other declarations.

9. INPUT/OUTPUT

ALGOL 60 was widely criticized for not discussing such mundane matters as input/output. That is one problem from which ALGOL 68 will not suffer. An extremely powerful and flexible set of input/output procedures is defined in the standard prelude. A variety of input/output styles is provided, ranging from the lowly *print* procedure to formatted input/output on files with user control over conversion codes, error handling, and the like. The ALGOL 68 term for input/output is transput.

9.1 Books, Channels, and Files

A book is a collection of information in the form of a three-dimensional character array (RR 10.3.1.1a). Books are comparable to what some other languages call data sets. A book consists of a certain number of pages, each page consisting of a certain number of lines, each line consisting of a certain number of characters.

For example, line printer output may consist of many pages of 60 lines, each line having 132 characters. Each position in the output can be described by a triple (page, line, char). Likewise, a multifile magnetic tape can be modeled with page = file number, line = record number, and character = position within a record. A book on a card reader might have only 1 page with many 80-character lines. Books may not be read or written by being subscripted; instead special procedures are provided for reading and writing. We have already seen two of these: *read* and *print*.

A channel (RR 10.3.1.2) corresponds to an input/output device type, for example, a disk, card reader, plotter, holographic store, or on-line experimental rat. A file (RR 10.3.1.3) provides the machinery to use a particular channel.

An object of mode **file** is actually a structure specifying a book, a channel, the current position on the file (page, line, char), the conversion code to use, and a number of procedures of mode **proc(ref file) bool**, as well as a few other details. A typical procedure is: *page mended.* When the program has filled up a page, *page mended* is automatically called. Programmers may supply their own versions of *page mended*: for example, eject to a new page, print a heading, and return **true**, indicating that the difficulty has been corrected. A new version of *page mended*, *p*, can only be associated with a file, *f*, by the call

on page end(f,p)

and not by directly referencing the field selector *page mended.* The other procedures handle end of file, end of line, end of format, and invalid data detected.

To access an existing book via a particular channel, declare a **file** and call the procedure

open to associate the book and channel with it. *Open* has three parameters: the file, an identification string, and the channel. The identification string and channel are installation dependent. To close a file, call *close* with the file as parameter. To create a new book, call *create*, specifying the file and channel.

Three files are declared and opened in the standard prelude (RR 10.5.1c): *stand in*, *stand out*, and *stand back*. These files correspond to the normal input and output files, and the binary scratch files. At some installations the files may be card reader, printer, and magnetic tape; at others they may be an on-line terminal, an on-line terminal and a disk. These files need (must) not be declared by the programmer.

Here is a simple program to copy 1000 lines from file1 to file2:

```
begin file in, out;
string s;
open (in,("file1", stand in channel);
open(out,"file2", stand out channel);
for i from 1 to 1000
   do get(in,(s, new line));
      put(out,(s, new line))
   od;
close(in);
close(out)
end
```

The procedure *open* defines a correspondence between an ALGOL 68 file name and a pre-existing operating system file name. The procedures *get* and *put* are the analogs of *read* and *print*. In fact, *read(x)* is declared (RR 10.5.1e) as *get(stand in,x)* and *print* is declared (RR 10.5.1d) as *put(stand out,x)*. The inclusion of *new line* in the calls to *get* and *put* is needed to advance the current position to the start of the next line.

ALGOL 68 supports random access books as well as sequential books. Each installation must decide which channels are random access, and which are not. Typically, disks and drums will be random access, whereas card readers and paper tape punches will not be. If a book is randomly accessible via a file *f*, the procedure call *set possible(f)* will yield **true**, if not, it will yield **false**. To set the current position of file *f* to (p,l,c) call *set(f,p,l,c)*.

A list of some (but not all) of the file handling procedures declared in the standard prelude follows; *f* represents a file; *p* represents a **proc(ref file) bool**; *c* represents a character, and *x* represents a variable, a constant, or a row display.

get possible (f)	**true** if f is readable
put possible (f)	**true** if f is writeable
bin possible (f)	**true** if binary transput ok
set possible (f)	**true** if f is random access
reset possible (f)	**true** if f is rewindable
chan (f)	yields f's channel
page number (f)	yields the current page
line number (f)	yields the current line
char number (f)	yields the current char
lock (f)	protects f from further access
scratch (f)	detach and burn the book
get (f,x)	read x from file f
put (f,x)	write x to file f
new page (f)	advance to a new page
new line (f)	advance to a new line
space (f)	advance one character
backspace (f)	go back one character
set (f,pg,l,c)	current pos := (pg,l,c)
reset (f)	rewind to (1,1,1)
on logical file end(f,p)	make p the procedure
on page end (f,p)	to be called when the
on line end (f,p)	corresponding event
on format end (f,p)	occurs on file f
make term (f,"c")	make c string terminator on f

It is also possible to perform transput directly to a three-dimensional character array in memory rather than to an external book (cf. ENCODE/DECODE in CDC 6000 FORTRAN). To make an array *buffer* the pseudobook of file *f*, call *associate(f,buffer)*.

9.2 Formatless Transput

The simplest form of transput is formatless transput, of which *read*, *print*, *get*, and *put* are the most important examples. Since *get* works precisely like *read*, except on arbitrary files instead of on *stand in*, and *put* is analogous to *print*, we concentrate on *read* and *print*.

Read and *print* have modes that ordinary programmers cannot construct. Roughly

speaking, the mode of *print* is **proc**([ ] **union**(**int**,**real**,**bool**,**char**,[ ]**int**,[,,]**int**, and everything else that can be printed, and **proc**(**file**)**void**))**void**. *Read* has a similar mode.

The procedure *get* is given in its entirety in RR 10.3.3.2a. For the beginner, the following rules will be enough to get started. The input book is regarded as a continuous stream of values separated by delimiters.

Integers, reals, and complex numbers may be signed. Reals and complex numbers may contain a decimal point and an exponent part, indicated by the letter "*e*". When a character variable is to be read, the next character is taken (even space), except at the end of a line or page, when the line or page will be advanced first. Strings are delimited by end of line or by a special termination character associated with the file.

When reading vectors and matrices, the order in which the elements are read is important. The question of how an array (or structure) is turned into a linear sequence of elements is called **straightening** (RR 10.3.2.3). In short, vectors are read from lowest element to highest element. Matrices are read in row order, beginning with the first row, then the second row, etc.

The procedures *new line, new page, space,* and *backspace* may be passed as parameters to *read*. The first three advance the current position before reading. The last one moves it backwards before reading, but not beyond the beginning of the current line. Using backspace, input data can be reread.

Print works as follows. For each mode of data there is a standard format that is used. The widths of the fields are implementation dependent, depending on *max int* and *max real*. *Print* refrains from splitting numbers across lines or pages; if the number will not fit, the line or page is advanced before printing. The procedures new line, new page, space, and backspace may be included as parameters to print, and both *read* and *print* expect a single parameter. If this is a row display, an extra set of parentheses is required, for example,

print((*new page*, "title",*new line*,*x*,*y*,*z*))

For people who are slightly discriminating about what their output looks like, but who are nevertheless too lazy to use formatted output, the procedures *whole, fixed,* and *float* may be helpful (RR 10.3.2.1). The calls

print(*whole*(*i*,*size*)); ¢ e.g. +3 ¢
print(*fixed*(*x*,*size*,*d*)); ¢ e.g. 6.02 ¢
print(*float*(*x*,*size*,*d*,*e*); ¢ e.g. 1.234e−07 ¢

output the integer *i* or real *x* in a field of width **abs** *size*. If *size* is positive, an explicit sign is printed; if *size* is negative, plus signs are suppressed. The integer *d* specifies the number of places to the right of the decimal point. The integer *e* specifies the number of digits in the exponent field.

9.3 Formatted Transput

The standard prelude declares four procedures for formatted transput: *readf, printf, getf,* and *putf*. Inasmuch as *readf* and *printf* are merely calls to *getf* and *putf* with *stand in* and *stand out*, respectively, used as files, it is not necessary to examine all four of them. For simplicity we discuss only *readf* and *printf*. Note that *readf, printf, getf,* and *putf* are the formatted analogs of *read, print, get,* and *put*.

There is a mode **format** whose values describe how values are to be layed out on the output or are expected to appear on the input. A simple format text (that is, "denotation") and its meaning on output is

$$\text{\$ p "m=" 5d, "n=" 5d \$}$$

This first advances to a new page, then prints the string m=, then the value of a variable as five digits, then the string n=, and finally another value as five more digits. We discuss the construction of format texts in a subsequent paragraph. For now, it is sufficient to say that **format** is a mode (declared in the standard prelude in RR 10.3.4.1.1a) and may be manipulated like any other mode; that is, [ ]**format**, **proc**(**int**)**format**, and **ref format** are all perfectly valid modes. Variables of mode **format** exist and may be assigned values, namely, format texts.

Associated with each file is a format that applies to that file. The format may be changed whenever a new one is needed, but a format remains in effect until explicitly

changed. The four formatted input/output procedures each process their parameters sequentially. If a parameter is a unit, it is transmitted according to the format currently associated with the file. However, if the parameter is a format, it supersedes the current format and is used for transmitting units until it itself is explicitly superseded. Note that a format can remain associated with a file over a time spanning many input/output calls. (Contrast this with FORTRAN, PL/I, and other languages which require exactly one explicit format on each input/output call.)

The procedure *printf* expects a single parameter, roughly [ ]**union**(all transputtable modes, **format**). Here are some examples of calls to the formatted transput procedures:

```
begin real x,y,z;
file f; open (f,"a",disk 1);
readf($ 1 5d, 7d $); ¢ new format for
    stand in ¢
printf($ 1 10x 6d $); ¢ new format for
    stand out ¢
putf(f, $ p "heading", 9d $); ¢ new format
    for f ¢
printf((x,y,z)); ¢ use existing format ¢
printf(($ 1 9d $,x,y,z)); ¢ use this format ¢
close (f)
end
```

A format text can be used directly in a call to one of the formatted transput procedures, as a source in an assignment to a format variable, as the result of a procedure yielding **format**, etc. Format texts are delimited by $ as we have seen. Between the dollar signs are a series of **pictures**, separated by commas. Each value input or output is controled by some picture, although a picture need not input or output a value; for example, it may merely eject to a new page. Pictures may be replicated as in 2(5d 4x, 7d 2x), which means 5d 4x, 7d 2x, 5d 4x, 7d 2x. Replicators need not be constants; the letter "n" followed by a closed clause is also acceptable (among other possibilities).

Pictures can be subdivided into literal strings, alignments, and patterns. Literal strings, such as "x =" or "page heading" are output as is, or are expected to be exactly so on input. Literal strings may be repeated

by putting an integer in front; for example, 7"x" is the same as "xxxxxxx".

Alignments describe changes in the current position of the book, such as "go to the next line before reading or printing." There are six alignments (RR 10.3.4.1.1f):

code	meaning
p	advance to new page
l	advance to new line
x	advance one character
y	backspace one character
q	output/expect one blank
k	move to specific character position

The alignments may also be replicated; for example, p 21 5q on output means go to the next page, skip 2 lines and 5 spaces. The difference between x and q is this: on input x just skips, whereas q expects blanks; on output after backspace, x skips and q overwrites with blanks. The alignments p,l,x,y, and k cause the procedures *new page*, *new line*, *space*, *backspace*, and *set char number* to be called, respectively.

Patterns are used for converting values, for example, integers, reals, Booleans, or strings. They are described in detail in RR 10.3.4. The following is a rough summary of some patterns. Each pattern consists of one or more frames. A frame allows a certain class of character, for example, sign, digit, exponent symbol, or any character. A list of frames and the allowed characters in each follows:

code	meaning
—	blank or minus sign
+	plus or minus sign
z	blank or digit
d	digit
e	letter e (exponent)
.	decimal point
b	Boolean (namely, 0 or 1)
i	letter i (for complex numbers)
a	any character

Rather than attempting to give the precise rules for combining frames into patterns, we give some examples of how the integer 12345 would appear with various patterns. (The letter B is used to indicate a blank space in the output.) Note that z suppresses leading zeros.

pattern	result of printing 12345
8d	00012345
6d	012345
7zd	BBB12345
+7zd	+BBB12345
−7zd	BBBB12345
7z+d	BBB+12345
7z−d	BBBB12345

The following examples show how the real number 123.45 would appear with various patterns:

pattern	result of printing 123.45
5d.2d	00123.45
4d.3d	0123.450
3zd.2d	B123.45
3z+d.2d	B+123.45
+d.4dezd	+1.2345eB2
−d.4dezd	B1.2345eB2

To understand how patterns work, first remove the replicators by writing out the pattern in full. For example, +4zd.2d means +zzzzd.dd. This pattern contains nine frames: one plus, four z's, one d, one point, and two more d's. A number output using this pattern will therefore occupy nine positions. The leftmost position will be a + or − sign. The next four positions will be digits, except that leading zeros will be converted to blanks. The four positions following this will be: one digit (even zero), one point, and two more digits (even 00). For example, 123.45 will be output as +BB123.45.

To allow leading signs to "float rightword" to the immediate left of the first nonzero digit, two special combinations are provided: Nz+d and Nz−d (N is some integer). This does not cause ambiguities, because putting the sign in the middle of the digits is clearly something special. The field width for Nz+d or Nz−d is N+2; for example, 6z+d means zzzzzz+d and gives an eight-position field.

A picture may consist solely of a literal string, an alignment, or a pattern, or a sequence of these. Thus $p 1 8d$ is a format text with one picture, and $p,l,8d$ is an equivalent format text with three pictures.

As a final example of outputting numbers, consider this program:

```
begin int i := 2;
    printf (( $ p "hi" 21 3d, 2z+d, 3q5zd.d,
             z−d.2d $, i, −i, i+999, pi))
end
```

The output begins with "hi" on top of a new page, then a blank line, then

002BB-2BBBBB1001.0BB3.14

Characters and strings are read and written using "a" frames. Booleans are transput using "b" frames, with implementation defined characters flip and flop (as in T and F), corresponding to **true** and **false**, respectively. Values of modes **bits** can be handled in binary, quaternary, octal, or hexadecimal, using 2r, 4r, 8r, or 16r, respectively, as illustrated in the following program:

```
begin bits n;
¢ print the first 100 integers in decimal, binary,
    octal; and hexadecimal, each in an 8 position
    field with 2 spaces between fields. ¢
for i to 100
do ¢ assign bit pattern of i to n (because only
       objects of mode bits can be output in non-
       decimal radices) ¢
    n := bin i;
    printf(( $ l 7zd,2q2r7zd, 2q8r7zd, 2q16r7zd $,
            i, n, n, n))
od
end
```

Pictures may be replicated (as in 71 or 3d), and replicators may be **proc ints**. Furthermore, there is a facility that chooses dynamically among several formats during transput, and a number of other sophisticated techniques.

The procedures *readbin, writebin, getbin,* and *putbin* are the analogs of *readf, printf, getf,* and *putf* for binary transput (cf. PL/I record input/output).

10. SERIAL COLLATERAL, AND PARALLEL PROCESSING

In general, ALGOL 68 statements are executed one after another, in the order written. The semicolon can be regarded as a go-on operator that causes execution to continue.

The void units in a serial clause are executed sequentially, for example. In some situations, however, there is no inherent sequencing. For example, there is no reason for the first unit of a row display to be evaluated before the last one. Nor is there any reason for the left operand of a dyadic operator to be evaluated before the right operand. In some other programming languages operands are evaluated strictly from left to right, but nothing in classical mathematics suggests any precedent for this. Actions that have no specific ordering in time are said to be carried out **collaterally**.

In formulating ALGOL 68, the designers intentionally specified that the order of evaluating certain things, such as the left and right operands of a dyadic operator, be undefined. This was done to help compilers produce an optimized object code and to take advantage of multiprocessor systems.

By not fixing the order of evaluation of operands and certain other constructions, ALGOL 68 provides the compiler writer with the freedom to do the evaluations in the most efficient order. In some situations, evaluating the right operand before the left operand may be more efficient. For example, consider:

```
begin real x,y,z;
proc f = (real x)real: (random < .5 | x | −x);
read(x);
y := (pi+x)/8;
z := f(x) + f(y);
print(z)
end
```

On a computer with a single accumulator used for arithmetic, after evaluating $(pi+x)/8$, y is very likely to be in the accumulator. It is also likely that better object code can be generated if $f(y)$ is evaluated before $f(x)$, because y is already in the accumulator, and x is not. If the ALGOL 68 specifications had required that left operands be evaluated before right operands, the compiler would have no choice but to do the call of $f(x)$ first, even though it is less efficient in that order.

The second reason for having the order of evaluation of certain constructions be explicitly undefined is that some computers have more than one processor and are capable of performing several computations in parallel. As the price of CPU's continues to fall, both in absolute terms and relative to total system cost, multi-CPU systems will become more and more common. Consider the following block, where f is assumed to be a horrendously complicated function declared in an outer block:

```
begin [1:4] real x;
int a,b,c,d;
read((a,b,c,d));
x := (f(a),f(b),f(c),f(d))
end
```

On a computer with four (or more) CPUs, the ALGOL 68 compiler might decide to have $f(a)$, $f(b)$, $f(c)$, and $f(d)$ all evaluated simultaneously, each on its own CPU. If the language required $f(a)$ to be evaluated before $f(b)$, this would be impossible.

Some of the constructions that are evaluated collaterally are: Source and destination in assignments; operands of a dyadic operator; elements of a row display; fields of a structure display; actual parameters in a call; **from, to,** and **by** parts of a **for** statement; subscripts and bounds in a slice; upper and lower bounds in an array declarations; array to be sliced and its subscripts; procedure to be called and its parameters; declarations separated by commas; and units of a collateral clause.

10.1 Collateral Clauses

A collateral clause is a list of units separated by commas and enclosed by **begin** and **end**, or by parentheses. The order in which the units of a collateral clause are evaluated is expressly undefined. An important kind of collateral clause is one composed of statements (technically **void** units). Whereas the statements of a serial clause are executed sequentially, the execution order of the statements in a collateral clause is explicitly undefined. An example of a **void** collateral clause is:

begin $k := 3$, $x := 3.14$, $s := $ "a" **end**

Consider the following two programs; the first contains a closed clause, and the second contains a collateral clause:

```
begin ¢ program 1 ¢
int k := 0;
(k:=k+1; k := k+1);
print(k)
end

begin ¢ program 2 ¢
int k := 0;
(k := k+1, k := k+1);
print(k)
end
```

The only difference between the two programs is the use of a semicolon versus the use of a comma between the assignments. There is only one tiny spot of ink in typography, but a world of difference in meaning, as we shall see.

The first program prints 2, as you would expect; the second program requires closer scrutiny. Since the order of evaluation of the units in a collateral clause is undefined, the first one might be completed before the second one was started, giving 2 as an answer. However, on a computer with two CPUs the compiler might arrange to give each CPU one unit to process with the following sequence of actions occurring.

1) CPU 1 fetches k into its accumulator;
2) CPU 2 fetches k into its accumulator;
3) CPU 1 adds 1 to its accumulator;
4) CPU 2 adds 1 to its accumulator;
5) CPU 1 stores 1 into k;
6) CPU 2 stores 1 into k.

The result is that k becomes 1 instead of 2. Depending upon the order of evaluation, the second program may print 1 or 2. Random numbers are very useful in computer science, but this is not a recommended technique for producing them. On the other hand,

```
begin int m := 0, n := 0;
(m := m+1, n := n+1);
print((m,n))
end
```

operates correctly no matter what the order of evaluation is. The moral of this story is: Collateral clauses are an important programming technique for exploiting parallel processing, but some care is required in their use.

It should be noted, however, that race conditions of this kind are not unique to ALGOL 68; any language or system permitting parallel processes unrestricted access to a common data base can produce the same peculiar effects. To be safe, one should avoid using collateral clauses which have an execution order that matters, or which modify each other's variables.

Collateral clauses may be nested, of course, allowing more complicated mixtures of collateral-serial execution to be described. For example,

$$(a; \qquad (b, (c; d), ((e,f); g)); \qquad h)$$

describes the following situation (the letters are assumed to be **void** units, for example, procedure calls or closed clauses). First a is executed. When a is finished, three actions proceed collaterally:

1) b
2) $(c;d)$
3) $((e,f); g)$

If enough CPUs are available, b, c, e, and f may all begin at once. When c finishes, d may start. When e and f are both finished, g may start. If e finishes before f, then g must be held up until f is also done. When b, c, $,d$, e, f, and g are all completed, h begins.

10.2 Synchronized Parallel Processing

Collateral clauses are primarily useful for allowing independent, noncommunicating processes to run in parallel. For some application,s however, the processes must communicate with each other. Typical examples are producer-consumer problems, where one process fills a shared buffer and the other one empties it. The two processes need to be synchronized to ensure that the producer stops when the buffer is full and that the consumer restarts the producer when it has (partially) emptied it again.

Dijkstra [4] has described a general synchronization method for parallel processing based on semaphores, and operators that increment and decrement them. An attempt to decrement a semaphore which has value 0 causes the decrementing process to be stopped. ALGOL 68 provides a mode **sema** (for semaphore) and two operators, **up** and **down**, to increment and decrement variables of mode **sema**. These are given in RR 10.2.4.

When semaphores are used in a collateral

clause, the symbol **par** must appear directly before the opening **begin** or parenthesis. This is to warn the compiler. Such clauses are then called **parallel clauses** (RR 3.3.1c).

As a simple example of parallel processing using semaphores, consider the problem of two processes running in parallel, each of which needs exclusive access to a certain data base during part of its computation cycle. (Readers unfamiliar with this type of synchronization problem should see Brinch Hansen [2]. A semaphore, mutex, initialized to 1 (using the **level** operator) is used here to achieve mutual exclusion.

```
begin sema mutex := level 1;
bool not finished := true;
¢ declare the data base here ¢
proc producer = void:
   while not finished
      do down mutex;
         ¢ insert item into data base here ¢
         up mutex
      od;
proc consumer = void:
   while not finished
      do down mutex;
         ¢ remove item from data base here ¢
         up mutex
      od;
   ¢ here is the parallel processing ¢
   par (producer, consumer)
end
```

11. Where To From Here?

Readers who want to continue their study of ALGOL 68 may wish to read Lindsey [8], Woodward and Bond [15], Woodward [14], Valentine [11], Branquart *et al.* [1], Cleaveland and Uzgalis [3], Peck [10], and the Revised Report, in roughly that order. For those readers who want a book length exposition, Learner and Powell [6], Peck [9], and Lindsey and van der Meulen [7] are recommended. For those who read German, van der Meulen and Kühling [12] is a good introductory text. In these references, beware of minor differences between the Revised Report, which is described in this article, and the original report, which is described in most of the references.

An even better way to learn ALGOL 68 is to write programs in this language. Compilers for various computers exist, including the IBM 370, CDC Cyber, Burroughs B6700, and ICL 1900. A fairly large subset of the language is even being implemented on a minicomputer (PDP-11).

ACKNOWLEDGMENTS

I wish to express my appreciation to the numerous people who have read and criticized this article, especially Jack Alanen, Willem Paul de Roever, Dick Grune, Ad König, Kees Koster, Efrem Mallach, John Peck, Mitchell Tanenbaum, Robert Uzgalis, Reind van de Riet, A. van Wijngaarden and P. M. Woodward.

REFERENCES

[1] BRANQUART, P.; LEWI, J.; SINTZOFF, M.; AND WODON, P. L. "The composition of semantics in ALGOL 68," *Comm. ACM* **14**, 11 (Nov. 1971), 697–707.

[2] BRINCH HANSEN, PER. "Concurrent programming concepts," *Computing Surveys* **5**, 4 (Dec. 1973), 223–245.

[3] CLEAVELAND, J. C.; AND UZGALIS, R. C. *Grammars for programming languages: What every programmer should know about grammar*, American Elsevier Publ. Co., New York, 1976.

[4] DIJKSTRA, E. W. "Cooperating sequential processes," In *Programming language*, F. Genuys (Ed.), Academic Press, New York, 1968.

[5] JENSEN, J.; AND NAUR, P. "Call by name: An implementation of ALGOL 60 procedures," *BIT* **1**, (1961), 38.

[6] LEARNER, A.; AND POWELL, A. J. *An introduction to ALGOL 68 through problems*, MacMillan, New York, 1974.

[7] LINDSEY, C. H.; AND VAN DER MEULEN, S. G. *An informal introduction to ALGOL 68.* North Holland Publ. Co., Amsterdam, The Netherlands, 1971.

[8] LINDSEY, C. H. "ALGOL 68 with fewer tears," *Computer J.* **15**, (1972), 176–188.

[9] PECK, J. E. L. *An ALGOL 68 companion*, Univ. of British Columbia, 1972.

[10] PECK, J. E. L. "Two-level grammars in action," in *Proc. IFIP Congress 74*, North-Holland Publ. Co., Amsterdam, The Netherlands, 1974, 317–321.

[11] VALENTINE, S. H. "Comparative notes on ALGOL 68 and PL/I," *Computer J.* **17**, (1974), 325–331.

[12] VAN DER MEULEN, S. G.; AND KÜHLING, P. *Programmieren in ALGOL 68.* Walter de Guyter & Co., New York, 1974 (in German).

[13] VAN WIJNGAARDEN, A.; MAILLOUX, B. J.; PECK J. E. L.; KOSTER, C. H. A.; SINTZOFF, M.; LINDSEY, C. H.; MEERTENS, L. G. L. T.; AND FISKER, R. G. "Revised report on the Algorithmic Language Algol 68," *Acta Informatica* **5**, (1975), 1–236.

[14] WOODWARD, P. M. "Practical experience with ALGOL 68" *Software—Practice and Experience*, **2**, (1972), pp. 7–9.

[15] WOODWARD, P. M.; AND BOND, S. G. *ALGOL 68-R users guide*, 2nd Ed. Her Majesty's Stationery Office, London, England, 1974.

[16] PAGAN, F. G., *A practical guide to Algol 68*, John Wiley Inc., New York, 1976.

AMBIGUITIES AND INSECURITIES IN PASCAL*

J. WELSH, W. SNEERINGER AND C. A. R. HOARE

SUMMARY

Ambiguities and insecurities in the programming language Pascal are discussed.

KEY WORDS Pascal Language design Language definition Security

INTRODUCTION

On rare occasions in programming language development there appears a programming language which is widely recognized as superior, and which propagates itself among discerning implementors and users solely by its merits, and without any political or commercial backing. ALGOL 60[1] was such a language. Pascal[2] is another.

One characteristic of such superior languages is that they rapidly give rise to a host of suggested extensions, improvements and imitations. From ALGOL 60 came ALGOL D,[3] ALGOL W,[4] ALGOL 68,[5] PL/I,[6] Simula 67[7] and Pascal itself. Pascal has been followed by the critique by Habermann,[8] Concurrent Pascal,[9] Pasqual,[10] Modula[11] and Euclid.[12] It is one of the symptoms of the superiority of these languages that their original design remains superior to many of their successors, and even the authors themselves can find little to improve in formulating a revised version.[13-15] Thus the very superiority of the language may inhibit for a while the further progress of the art of language design.

One reason for this is that there is no immediate recognition of exactly what constitute the merits of the language. Indeed, the merits of ALGOL 60 have only recently been appreciated under the new name of *structured programming*. Similarly, most criticism of the language is rather superficial, concentrating on critics' favourite 'features' and 'facilities' which have been left out.

If future language designs, and indeed future users, are to benefit fully from the significant advances made by Pascal, it is essential that its defects, as well as its virtues, should be carefully identified and catalogued. The detailed, almost pettifogging nature of the criticisms in this paper may be taken as a testimony to a belief that Pascal is at the present time the best language in the public domain for purposes of systems programming and software implementation. Nevertheless, these criticisms may lead to a better understanding of the definitional problems created in Pascal, and to a better treatment of these problems in the languages which must inevitably follow it.

No consideration is given to changes to Pascal other than those necessary to overcome the ambiguities and insecurities identified.

*Reprinted from *Software Practice and Experience*, 7, 1977, 685–696.

* Present address: IBM Corporation, 11400 Burnet Road, Austin, Texas 78759, U.S.A.
† Address from October 1977: Programming Research Group, Oxford University, 45 Banbury Road, Oxford.

Received 27 May 1977

© 1977 by John Wiley & Sons, Ltd.

Throughout this paper, the abbreviations *User Manual* and *Report* are used to stand for the first and second parts, respectively, of the *Pascal User Manual and Report*.[15] There are several earlier versions of the *Report*.[14] The abbreviation *Axiomatic Definition* is also used for the formal definition of Pascal's semantics given by Hoare and Wirth.[17]

AMBIGUITIES

Ambiguities and omissions in the *Report* or *User Manual* are not mentioned in what follows if they can be easily resolved. The objective is to criticize the language, not the *Report* or the *User Manual*; but insofar as the language's features (or apparent intentions) create problems of definition, the *Report* must be considered as well.

Equivalence of types

Section 9.1.1 of the *Report* states that the two sides of an assignment statement 'must be of identical type', with certain exceptions involving reals and subranges. The phrase *identical type* is not defined and its meaning is not obvious. Much of Habermann's criticism of Pascal hinged on the omission from the *Report* of similar exception rules for other contexts in which subrange or real variables might or might not appear. As the Axiomatic Definition shows, the subrange problem can be resolved by the systematic introduction of implicit subrange–range transfers as context requires. However, the notion of type equivalence creates problems for other Pascal types too.

In the declarations,

```
type T    = array [1..10] of INTEGER;
var A, B:   array [1..10] of INTEGER;
    C:      array [1..10] of INTEGER;
    D:      T;
    E:      T;
```

consider the following two possible definitions of equivalence of types.

Name equivalence

Two variables are considered to be of the same type only if they are declared together (as A and B) or if they are declared using the same type identifier (as D and E). Any type specification other than a type identifier creates a new type which is not equivalent to any other type. Thus A, C and D all have different types. Notice that primitive types are specified using type identifiers, so two variables will have the same type if they are both declared INTEGER. This is called *name equivalence* because two variables that are not declared together can have the same type only if they are declared using the same type name.

Structural equivalence

Two variables are considered to be of the same type whenever they have components of the same type structured in the same way. Using this definition, all of the variables in the example above have the same type.

Name equivalence is quite a nuisance to the programmer, since he or she must often make up extra type names. On the other hand, name equivalence provides extra protection against type errors. Furthermore, structural equivalence causes a logical problem. Consider this example using structural equivalence.

```
var K: (MALE, FEMALE);
    L: (MALE, FEMALE);
```

Clearly the types of K and L are equivalent, since they have the same structure. However,

    var M: (MALE, FEMALE);
           N: (FEMALE, MALE);

is illegal because the identifiers MALE and FEMALE are not unique. Distinguishing between these two cases will be difficult for the compiler. It cannot simply consider the construct (MALE, FEMALE) to be a declaration of the identifiers MALE and FEMALE as it could in the case of name equivalence. If it did, it would reject the legal declaration of identifier L.

Even worse, suppose that the type (MALE, FEMALE) is created and then the identifier MALE is used for an unrelated purpose in an inner block. Then, in a block inside both of these, the construct (MALE, FEMALE) is used again. Is it a reference to the first type? A new type? An error? There seems to be no good answer.

The use of structural equivalence also creates a problem with record types, which is illustrated by the following:

    var F: **record** T, U: REAL **end**;
          G: **record** V, W: REAL **end**;

Do F and G have the same type? Either answer seems reasonable and consistent.

Structural equivalence creates a further dilemma for the implementor in relation to the **packed** prefix for structured types. Section 6.2 of the *Report* states that the prefix 'has no effect on the meaning of the program but is a hint to the compiler that storage should be economized even at the price of some loss in efficiency of access'. Presumably therefore a packed type is equivalent to an otherwise structurally equivalent unpacked one, and the compiler must permit, and generate code for, assignment or, worse still, actual-formal parameter correspondence between them. This problem does not arise with name equivalence since the syntax of ⟨type⟩ excludes the form **packed** ⟨*type identifier*⟩.

Name equivalence is not, however, without its problems. It precludes, for example, the assignment of a string constant to a variable of a corresponding string type. Section 4 of the *Report* states that a string constant of *n* characters has an implicit type

    packed array [1..*n*] **of** *char*

With name equivalence, however, this implied type cannot be equivalent to any other so the string may only appear in certain limited contexts such as calls on the built-in procedure *write*. A similar problem arises with constructed sets, whose type is also implicitly specified; this problem is considered further in a later section of this paper.

Name equivalence also creates a potential confusion for the user of the type definition

    type T1 = T2;

where T2 is the name of a type defined elsewhere. With name equivalence this will not produce a convenient local synonym for type T2 as might be expected, but a new type T1 which is not equivalent to type T2 in any context.

Clearly the current features of Pascal do not permit a simple choice between name or structural equivalence as defined. Some alternative or compromise equivalence definition must be adopted. In practice of course each implementation of Pascal has already made some choice. The ETH compiler (the compiler described by the *User Manual*) uses structural equivalence in most cases.[16] However, a scalar type declaration such as (MALE, FEMALE) is taken to be a declaration of the identifiers MALE and FEMALE, and therefore causes a message about a duplicate declaration if repeated in the same block. (It will create a new type equivalent to the first if used in an inner block.) Record types are equivalent if the corresponding field types are the same, but packed structured types are not equivalent to corresponding unpacked ones.

It is unsatisfactory that implementors should be left to make such decisions, since any divergence in their choice imperils the portability of Pascal programs. The authors of Euclid, Pascal's most recent derivative, were clearly conscious of Pascal's deficiencies in this area. Although the definition of Euclid has been modelled on the Pascal *Report*, it incorporates an explicit definition of type equivalence based on the repeated replacement of type identifiers by the sequence of symbols appearing in their definition. Two types are equivalent if, in the sequences of symbols which they produce,

    (a) corresponding occurrences of free constant identifiers (i.e. those not declared by these types) denote the same value;

    (b) corresponding symbols are otherwise identical.

The resultant definition of type equivalence is close to the structural equivalence suggested above. Whether this particular definition is the best for the language remains an open question, but the provision of *some* such explicit definition is an important requirement, both for Pascal and for any language which imitates its repertoire of data types.

Scope rules and one-pass compilation

One of the design objectives stated for Pascal was to enable efficient compilation of its programs. Although the *Report* does not say so explicitly, the language features appear to favour one-pass compilation as a means to this end, and implementors have assumed this to be the designer's intent. However, this implicit one-pass compilation capability creates some traps for the unwary, into which implementors have duly fallen.

In general, one-pass compilation requires that the declaration of an identifier precede all other references to that identifier. The Pascal *Report* does not specify at any point that an identifier's declaration must precede its use. It does, however, impose a rigid order on the different classes of declaration which are made within a block, thus:

    ⟨*block*⟩ ::= ⟨*label declaration part*⟩
                ⟨*constant definition part*⟩
                ⟨*type definition part*⟩
                ⟨*variable declaration part*⟩
                ⟨*procedure and function declaration part*⟩
                ⟨*statement part*⟩

This has the effect of ensuring that constant identifiers are defined before they can be used in type definitions, that type identifiers are defined before they can be used in variable declarations and that variable identifiers are declared before they can be used in the statement part or as non-locals in nested procedures and function. However, it does not guarantee declaration before use *within* the type definition or procedure declaration parts. For example, the following program segment is unacceptable to a one-pass compiler because the use of the identifier COMPLEX to declare type MATRIX precedes the declaration of COMPLEX.

    type MATRIX = **array** [1..10, 1..10] **of** COMPLEX;
           COMPLEX = **record** REALPART, IMAGPART: REAL **end**;
    var M: MATRIX;
        ⋮
    WRITE(M[2, 2].REALPART);

Now consider the same program segment and assume that this declaration is in the containing block:

    type COMPLEX = **record** RE, IM: REAL **end**;

There are at least two possible interpretations of this program by a one-pass system:

(1) The elements of M each have two real components with names RE and IM, since the outer declaration of COMPLEX was current when the declaration of MATRIX was scanned. (2) The program is in error because the inner declaration of COMPLEX is the one that should apply, and it follows the declaration of MATRIX.

This program is incorrect in either case. Under interpretation (1), the call to WRITE is incorrect because the REALPART is not a valid field name for variable M. We are not just haggling over which statement gets the error message, however. If the field name REAL-PART in the call to WRITE were replaced by RE, the resulting program would be correct according to interpretation (1) and incorrect according to (2).

Notice that (1) is the easier interpretation to implement. Each reference to an identifier is simply bound to the most recent declaration of that identifier. One way to implement (2) might be to bind the element type of MATRIX to the outer definition of COMPLEX, but record this binding so that an error can be declared when the inner definition of COMPLEX is scanned. The recorded binding has to be applied not only in the current scope but also in any enclosing scopes between it and the outer definition.

Unfortunately, interpretation (1) has some problems involving pointer types, and (2) is the better interpretation. Consider the following example:

```
type FLIGHT =
       record
         NUMBER: 0..999;
         FIRSTPAS: ↑PASSENGER;
         ...
       end;

     PASSENGER =
       record
         FLIGHTBOOKED: ↑FLIGHT;
         NEXTPAS: ↑PASSENGER
         ...
       end;
```

Each of the two types in the example refers to the other, so whichever type is declared second in the program will have its identifier referenced before it is declared. This is a case where the rule that identifiers must be declared before they are used is too restrictive to be practical, and Pascal implementations make an exception to accommodate this case. Pointer declarations, such as ↑PASSENGER, are allowed to precede the declaration of the identifier used. Fortunately, the compiler can allocate storage for a pointer without knowing what type of thing it will reference, since the size of a pointer does not depend on what it points at.

The problem with interpretation (1) is illustrated by the example above if there happens to be a type PASSENGER declared in an outer block. In that case, interpretation (1) demands that the name PASSENGER in field FIRSTPAS be bound to the outer definition of type PASSENGER. This is very bad, because the meaning of a valid block can be changed by declaring an identifier in an outer block.

In fact the *Report* does exclude interpretation (1) since Section 4 states that the 'association (of identifiers) must be unique within their scope of validity, i.e. within the procedure or function in which they are declared'. (No explicit definition of scope for main program identifiers is given.) However, the significance of Section 4 is clearly not apparent to its implementors, since the ETH compiler itself follows interpretation (1), even to the extent

of binding the pointer type ↑ PASSENGER to a non-local instance of PASSENGER if one exists.

A similar difficulty arises with mutually recursive procedures and functions. To retain one-pass compilation with checking of parameters the ETH compiler requires a FORWARD declaration, which is not described in the *Report* or included in the syntax diagrams or BNF. It is described only in Section 11.C of the *User Manual*, from which we take the following example.

```
procedure Q(X:T); FORWARD;
procedure P(Y:T);
begin
    Q(A)
end;
procedure Q; (* PARAMETERS NOT REPEATED *)
  begin
    P(B)
  end;
begin
  P(A);
  Q(B)
end.
```

The line

```
procedure Q(X:T); FORWARD;
```

which must precede the procedure P, provides enough information so that the call to Q from within P can be compiled.

These problems arise because the *Report* does not define any precise rules for the relative positions of the declaration and use of identifiers. Implementors of one-pass compilers must impose additional restrictions on the language definition, or create the unsatisfactory implementation effects outlined above. If one-pass compilation is to be a language objective it should be made explicit in the language definition and an explicit declaration-before-use rule should be adopted, with whatever exceptions the language features may require.

With such a rule the rigid order which Pascal imposes on the constant, type, variable and procedure declaration parts could be relaxed, allowing natural groupings of the types, variables and procedures which manipulate them. The inability to make such groupings in structuring large programs is one of Pascal's most frustrating limitations.

Given such groupings, or modules, of course the additional controls on their mutual interaction such as those which Modula and Euclid provide are clearly desirable. The control over the use of identifiers which these languages offer is a clear indication that the current needs of programming have moved well beyond the implicit scope rules of simple block structure, and Pascal.

Set constructors

As was indicated earlier, the implicit types of string constants and constructed sets create problems in defining type equivalence. However, the implicit type definition creates additional problems in the representation of sets.

According to Section 8 of the *Report*, 'Expressions which are members of a set must all be of the same type, which is the base type of the set.' This leads to the conclusion that the type of the set constructor [1, 5, 10..19, 23] is **set of** INTEGER, since Section 4 makes it clear that the types of 1, 5, 10, 19 and 23 are INTEGER. However, Section 14 states that 'The implementer may set a limit to the size of a base type over which a set can be defined.

(Consequently, a bit pattern representation may reasonably be used for sets).' Since the apparent base type in the example is INTEGER and the size of type INTEGER is larger than any reasonable limit, one might conclude that the example is illegal in at least some implementations. The example comes from Section 8 of the *Report*, so it seems fair to say that the *Report* is confusing, if not ambiguous.

In practice the conflict is yet another which is resolved by an implicit range to subrange transfer. Given that a limit on the size of base types exists, the compiler may assume that the intended base type of [1, 5, 10..19, 23] is some subrange of the integers, and apply an implicit range to subrange transfer to its member values. The problem is that the intended subrange is not apparent, which in turn has consequences for the representation of the set.

Using a bit pattern representation for sets, the type

set of 20..29

is represented by a bit pattern very much like the type

packed array [20..29] **of** BOOLEAN

where element N of the array is TRUE if and only if N is in the set. The trouble is that the base type of [1, 5, 10..19, 23] has not been specified, so the compiler does not know what the bounds of its Boolean array should be.

Implementations overcome this problem by imposing an additional limit on the base types of sets. For example, in the ETH compiler the limit on the size of a base type is 59, so the compiler knows that the Boolean array can be no larger than 59. However, the compiler also needs its upper and lower bounds. The ETH compiler therefore adds the restriction that each element of any set of integers must be between 0 and 58. This rule allows any set of integers to be represented by an array with bounds 0 and 58. A similar rule applies to sets of non-integers. In that case, no element E is allowed unless $ORD(E) \leqslant 58$. This solution has the consequence that apparently representable set types such as

DATES = **set of** 1939..1945

are excluded by current implementations.

For implementations which choose, or are forced by short word lengths or byte orientation, to use multilength representations of sets the implicit type of the set constructor presents an additional problem. Either all sets over subranges of a given type must use the same length of representation, or the required length of a constructed set must be deduced from context. The extreme case occurs when the empty set [ ] (which has no implicit base type at all) occurs as an actual parameter of a formal procedure or function (which provides no contextual indication of the representation required).

All these problems can be avoided by requiring an explicit specification of the base type of every set constructor. For example, given a set type

DIGITS = **set of** 0..9

the constructor notation used might be

DIGITS (1, 3, 5)

This makes the programmer write a bit more, but allows the base type of a set to be any scalar type that does not have too many elements. Not only are the restrictions simpler and less constraining, but the language is cleaner because every set constructor has a type which can be determined during compilation without any use of context. A version of Pascal using such a constructor, and a multiword representation of sets, has been implemented[18] and shown to provide a more flexible, and more efficient, set manipulation facility. A similar notation has now been adopted in Euclid.

This notation also reconciles the set constructor with the name equivalence convention for types discussed earlier. A similar solution for string constants might be considered. Given a string type

MESSAGE = **packed array** [1..16] **of** *char*

a constant of the type might be written thus

MESSAGE('ILLEGAL OPERANDS')

In this case the additional burden on the programmer may be unacceptable in contexts where named type specification is unecessary, e.g. in calls to the built-in procedure *write*, and some default for omitting the type name and parentheses may be appropriate.

INSECURITIES

For the purposes of this discussion, an insecurity is a feature that cannot be implemented without either (1) a risk that violations of the language rules will go undetected, or (2) run-time checking that is comparable in cost to the operation being performed.

Pascal has fewer insecurities than most comparable languages. For example, it is not possible to use a pointer to access a dynamic variable of the wrong type. This error is caught during compilation because each pointer can only point at variable or a single type. The remarkable thing about Pascal is that the number of insecurities is small enough to make it worthwhile to prepare a list in the hope that future research will lead to languages with even fewer or perhaps no insecurities.

Variant records

Pascal allows variant records with and without tag fields. An example of a variant record with a tag field is

```
V: record AREA:REAL;
     case S:SHAPE of
       TRIANGLE: (SIDE:REAL;
                  INCLINATION, ANGLE1, ANGLE2:REAL);
       CIRCLE:   (DIAMETER:REAL)
   end
```

The field *AREA* always exists, but whether *DIAMETER* exists or not depends on whether the value of the tag field, *S*, is *CIRCLE* or not. A version of this record without a tag field can be created by omitting 'S' after the symbol *case*.

If there is no tag field, then the variant record is inevitably insecure. Either ANGLE1 or ANGLE2 could be referenced when it is not present, and there is no way to catch the error, even at run-time. This is bad, because such an error is likely to be difficult to find.

The compiler could insert a tag field even when the programmer does not request it, but it would be misleading and pointless to allow the programmer to omit the tag field if the compiler included it anyway. The introduction to Pascal of variant records without tag fields must be regarded as a retrograde step, to be regretted by Pascal users, and avoided by the designers of future languages.

Given that a tag field is present in all variant records, a run-time check is still required to

achieve security. However, the run-time check can be avoided when code like the following is used to reference the variant part

    case V.S **of**
        TRIANGLE: **begin** (references to V.SIDE, etc.) **end**;
        CIRCLE: **begin** (references to V.DIAMETER) **end**
    end

since the value of the tag field when the references occur is known when the program is compiled. This is done in Simula 67 with an **inspect when** statement, which is similar to the **case** statement above. A similar modification to Pascal has been investigated,[19] which showed that direct violations from within the **case** construct were easily detected, but that detection of indirect changes of the variant by reassignment of the entire record variable, possibly during procedure calls from within the case, was impractical. The *Report* does outlaw such changes with a **with** statement (Section 9.2.4) but this restriction is equally impractical to enforce by compile-time or run-time checking.

Euclid incorporates an explicit construct which enables direct variant violations to be detected at compile-time. For more general reasons of program verification Euclid's definition also goes to considerable lengths to enable variable overlaps, such as might cause an implicit change of variant, to be detected. Whether the added complexity of the rules required, and the added restrictions which they impose on the programmer, are an acceptable price to pay for variable access security, may be shown by experience of implementing and using Euclid. The rules and restrictions involved cannot be readily added to current framework of Pascal.

Functions and procedures as parameters

When a Pascal formal parameter is a function or a procedure, the language does not require or even permit the programmer to specify the number and types of any parameters. The following example, which is due to Lecarme and Desjardins,[20] illustrates a program which contains an error that cannot reasonably be detected at compile-time:

    procedure P(**procedure** Q);
      begin Q(2, 'A') **end**;
    procedure R(X:BOOLEAN);
      begin WRITE(X) **end**;
    begin P(R) **end**.

The apparent solution is to allow full specification of parameters in this case, as is done in ALGOL 68. The normal syntax for parameter specification is excessive for this purpose since it includes specification of names of the formal parameters, and these names are not required. Lecarme and Desjardins proposed a syntax for specifying the types without giving names. With their syntax, the first line of the example above is written

    procedure P(**procedure** Q(INTEGER, CHAR));
      begin Q(2, 'A') **end**;

which gives enough information for the error to be detected during compilation.

To enable the correct parameter passing code to be generated for their calls, Pascal currently allows procedures and functions passed as parameters to take value parameters only. Given an adequate notation for expressing the parameter requirements of formal procedures or functions, this restriction can in principle be relaxed. The notation required is more complicated than that of Lecarme and Desjardins, however, since it must distinguish between variable and value parameters. If procedure parameters which themselves

45

take procedure parameters are allowed the notation must also provide a nested, and potentially recursive, specification of parameter requirements.

The Pascal compiler for UNIVAC 1100 computers, developed at DIKU in Copenhagen, incorporates an extension which meets these requirements.[21] Formal parameter lists can be defined and named in a separate parameter declaration part of each block. The parameter requirements of actual procedures may then be specified by reference to a named parameter list, and those of formal procedures must be specified in this way. In the DIKU system formal parameter names are always included in the parameter list specification, so that procedures sharing a parameter specification must use the same formal parameter names as well.

Range violations

As in most compiled languages, accessing an element of a Pascal array is insecure if an index is out of bounds. Since almost all languages have this problem, it is appropriate to try to solve it with hardware. The extra hardware cost is quite small. The descriptor mechanism of the ICL 2900 series computers provides an implicit bound check during array access but, while it works well for the arrays allowed in languages such as FORTRAN or ALGOL 60, it is inadequate for some of the array structures permitted in Pascal.[22]

Array access is just one of a number of contexts in which a value outside a permitted range can arise in Pascal. Others are assignment to a subrange variable, case selection, set membership creation and testing, and indeed overflow in integer and real arithmetic. While it is unreasonable to hope to exclude by language design the possibility of all such violations, designers must aim to reduce the cost of their run-time detection. It should be noted that Pascal's provision of enumerated and subrange types is a significant step in this direction. Each use of a variable of an enumerated type removes a potential insecurity by ensuring that the finite set of values which the variable may take is verified at compile-time. For a subrange variable run-time verification of the values taken may be necessary but, assuming these checks are made, other more frequent and hence more expensive checks may be avoided at each point where the variable value is used. A Pascal compiler which exploits this technique has been constructed[23] for ICL 1900 computers, and has shown that for simple array manipulations run-time subscript checking can be eliminated, or reduced to insignificance.

Uninitialized variables

Uninitialized variables are also difficult to detect, and all hardware detection mechanisms known to us are quite expensive. Possible solutions are to require that every variable be initialized when it is declared or that every variable be assigned in such a way that the compiler can easily verify that there are no references to uninitialized variables. The latter might work very well in a language without jumps, and deserves further investigation.

Dangling references

Accessing of dynamic variables (those found via pointers) is not secure because the storage for the dynamic variable may have been released. This is a very common insecurity for which Pascal allows no obvious solution.

It can be argued that Pascal's pointer is a low-level facility provided for use in those situations for which the high-level data constructs are inadequate, and that it is unreasonable

to expect security from a low-level facility. Whatever the philosophical validity of this argument it is little consolation to a programmer whose pointers go wrong!

Euclid offers an optional security against such errors by enabling reference counts to be maintained for collections of dynamically allocated variables. Storage release is then an implicit operation occurring when a reference count reaches zero, rather than an explicit programmable action. Maintaining reference counts is, of course, a considerable overhead if applied to every pointer variable assignment. The success of the Euclid proposal depends on the degree to which the compiler can detect those program segments which use local pointer variables to trace a dynamically allocated structure without altering the non-local reference pattern in any way. Reference counting code can then be avoided for the pointer manipulation within the segment.

CONCLUSION

At the time that Pascal was first designed and developed, the most fashionable languages in the learned and practical world were ALGOL 68 and PL/I. The discovery that the advantages of a high-level language could be combined with high efficiency in such a simple and elegant manner as in Pascal was a revelation that deserves the title of breakthrough. Because of the very success of Pascal, which greatly exceeded the expectations of its author, the standards by which we judge such languages have also risen. It is grossly unfair to judge an engineering project by standards which have been proved attainable only by the success of the project itself, but in the interests of progress, such criticism must be made.

Of the criticisms made in this paper, some identify shortcomings of Pascal which can readily be made good by minor changes to the language or its definition. Others indicate problems for which there is no easy solution within the current framework. As a language which attempts to overcome most of the problems listed, Euclid deserves special mention, though it should also be pointed out that no implementation of Euclid has yet been reported. Unfortunately, Euclid achieves its goals at the expense of a significant loss of simplicity and elegance in the language definition. Whether this trade-off is inevitable or whether some future breakthrough can restore elegance and simplicity without loss of security is a question which language designers must ponder for some time to come.

ACKNOWLEDGEMENTS

The research on this paper was supported in part by a grant from the Science Research Council of Great Britain.

REFERENCES

1. P. Naur (Ed.), 'Report on the algorithmic language ALGOL 60', *Comm. ACM*, **3**, 299–314 (1960).
2. N. Wirth, 'The programming language Pascal', *Acta Informatica*, **1**, 35–63 (1971).
3. B. A. Galler and A. J. Perlis, 'A proposal for definitions in ALGOL', *Comm. ACM*, **10**, 204–219 (1967).
4. N. Wirth and C. A. R Hoare, 'A contribution to the development of ALGOL', *Comm. ACM*, **9**, 413–432 (1966).
5. A. van Winjngaarden (Ed.), 'Report on the algorithmic language ALGOL 68', *Numerische Mathematik*, **14**, 79–218 (1969).
6. IBM, *PL/I(F) Language Reference Manual, Order Number C28-8201*, IBM, 1969.
7. G. Birtwistle *et al.*, *Simula Begin*, Auerbach, 1975.
8. A. N. Habermann, 'Critical comments on the programming language Pascal', *Acta Informatica*, **3**, 47–57 (1973).

9. P. Brinch Hansen, 'The programming language Concurrent Pascal', *IEEE Trans. Software Engng*, **1**, 2 (1975).

10. R. D. Tennent, 'Pasqual: a proposed generalisation of Pascal', *Technical Report No. 75–32*, Department of Computing and Information Science, Queen's University, Kingston, Ontario, Canada.

11. N. Wirth, 'Modula: a language for modular multiprogramming', *Software—Practice and Experience*, **7**, 3–35 (1977).

12. B. W. Lampson *et al.*, 'Report on the programming language Euclid', *ACM Sigplan Notices*, **12**, 2 (1977).

13. P. Naur, 'Revised report on the algorithmic language ALGOL 60', *Comm. ACM*, **6**, 1 (1963).

14. N. Wirth, 'The programming language Pascal (Revised Report)', *Berichte der Fachgruppe Computer-Wissenschaften Nr. 5*, ETH Zurich (1973).

15. K. Jensen and N. Wirth, 'Pascal—User Manual and Report', *Lecture Notes in Computer Science*, **18**, Springer Verlag, 1974.

16. U. Ammann, 'The Zurich implementation', *Proc. Symp. on Pascal—the language and its implementation, Southampton* (1977).

17. C. A. R. Hoare and N. Wirth, 'An axiomatic definition of the programming language Pascal', *Acta Informatica*, **2**, 335–355 (1973).

18. C. J. Copeland, 'Extensions to Pascal', *MSc. dissertation*, Queen's University, Belfast (1975).

19. P. W. C. Sinte, 'Recursive data structures in Pascal', *MSc. dissertation*, Queen's University, Belfast (1975).

20. O. Lecarme and P. Desjardins, 'More comments on the programming language Pascal', *Acta Informatica*, **4**, 231–243 (1975).

21. J. Steensgaard-Madsen, *Procedures as Monitors in Sequential Programming*, DIKU, Copenhagen, Denmark, 1977.

22. M. Rees, 'Pascal on an advanced architecture', *Proc. Symp. on Pascal—the language and its implementation, Southampton* (1977).

23. J. Welsh, 'Two ICL 1900 Pascal compilers', *Proc. Symp. on Pascal—the language and its implementation, Southampton* (1977).

AN ASSESSMENT OF THE PROGRAMMING LANGUAGE PASCAL*

N. WIRTH

Abstract—The programming language Pascal is assessed in the light of "reliable programming" and with the background of five years of experience with the language. Some features are selected to point out remaining problems, either inherent or specific, from which some guidelines for the design or choice of languages for reliable programming are derived. Among the discussed features are the concept of data type, the sequential file structure, and the type union.

Index Terms—Data types, files and sequences, language evaluation, language and reliable programming, parametrized types, Pascal, program correctness versus reliability, type union.

WHAT IS RELIABLE SOFTWARE?

RELIABLE is the attribute for a person, an organization, or a mechanism that you can trust, that you can depend on, that is worthy of your confidence. For example, a reliable clock is one that indicates accurate time even during an earthquake, a reliable railway system is one where trains run punctually even during a snowstorm, a reliable bridge is a bridge that does not crack even under heavy load, and a reliable transistor is one that operates for years, possibly under extreme temperature and radiation. The common enemy of reliability in these examples are adverse circumstances and influences that may cause a deterioration of the physical properties of material. The accumulation of these influences is called aging. Reliability is achieved by dimensioning the mechanisms properly, taking such adverse conditions into consideration. In a railway system the schedule is arranged such that it leaves room for catching up on lost time, and an ample supply of spare engines is kept on the alert for emergencies. A bridge is built stronger than actually needed most of the time—and a transistor is equipped with cooling devices and radiation shields.

What does this all have to do with software? Well, we all have experienced failures of computer systems; and we all would like them to be reliable too. When a computer fails, the first question among its intimates is usually: is the hardware or the software the culprit? Most customers of a computation center show signs of relief when the latter is announced, for the disruption of service is then quickly ended by a so-called dead start, and life goes on as if (almost) nothing had occurred. Indeed there had been neither an earthquake, nor a snowstorm, nor a weighty load, nor heat or radiation. Instead, merely unpredictable circumstances had led to a state of computa-

tion for which the logical structure of the program had not been designed, which the system's designers did not anticipate. And when pressing the dead start button, the computer operator is reasonably confident that these circumstances would not reoccur too soon.

What must we conclude? We understand by the term software the collection of programs that deterministically prescribe a system's detailed behavior and transitions of state. These programs are constants and are independent of any "adverse conditions" of an environment. Hence, software cannot fail because of unpredictable happenings and age, but only due to defects in its logical design. This leads us to a replacement of the attribute "reliable" by "correct."

We may be accused of nitpicking with words. To this I can only reply that the choice of words often reveals a speaker's *attitude* more profoundly than is dear to him. The attitude through which we content ourselves at producing "reliable" software instead of correct software, bears the danger that we may also consider various *degrees* of reliability. Software may then be termed reliable and "more reliable"; we may also call it correct, but certainly not "more correct."

The difference in these words is also manifested in the techniques to be employed in producing reliability in software versus in clocks, bridges, and transistors. In most technical phenomena, reliability is achieved by over dimensioning the components, by using high-quality material, or by supplying standby equipment that automatically goes into action when a failure occurs. In programs, merely repeating a logical test 18 times instead of performing it once does not help, if the logical structure is correct and the underlying hardware is reliable. In fact, the degree to which a program is unreliable is exactly the probability with which its incorrect parts are executed. But this measure is *not* a property of the program itself.

Reconciling ourselves with the word correct in place of reliable has the advantage that we more readily identify the causes of failures of our products to meet their goal. They are not to be sought in external, unforeseeable, adverse circumstances, but solely in our own inadequate minds, and in our failure to communicate, if several people participate in a program's design. The advantage of this recognition is that we know where to concentrate our efforts; its unpleasant part is the fact that it will be a never-ending crusade, because committing mistakes is a truly human characteristic.

The most sensible targets in our drive at producing correct software are evidently *the programmers themselves*. Nothing whatsoever can replace a sound, systematic

*Reprinted from *IEEE Transactions on Software Engineering*, June 1975, 192–198.

Manuscript received February 1, 1975.
The author is with the Federal Institute of Technology (ETH), Zürich, Switzerland.

FACILITIES AND CONVENTIONS THAT HAMPER THE CLARITY OF PROGRAMS

1) Operator Precedence: In the interest of simplicity and efficient translatability, Pascal aimed at a reasonably small number of operator precedence levels. Algol 60's hierarchy of 9 levels seemed clearly too baroque. An additional incentive for change was the replacement of the equivalence operator for Boolean expressions by the equality operator. Since these two operators reside on different priority levels in Algol 60, some departure from the old rules were mandatory. In retrospect, however, the decision to break with a widely used tradition seems ill-advised, particularly with the growing significance of complicated Boolean expressions in connection with program verification.

Algol 60	Pascal
$\uparrow$	$\neg$
$* / \div$	$* / \textbf{div} \textbf{mod}$ $\wedge$
$+ -$	$+ -$ $\vee$
$= \neq < \leq \geq >$	$= \neq < \leq \geq >$
$\neg$	
$\wedge$	
$\vee$	
$\supset$	
$\equiv$	

Examples of expressions in Algol 60 and Pascal:

$$\neg x < y \qquad\qquad \neg (x < y)$$

$$x < y \wedge y < z \qquad (x < y) \wedge (y < z)$$

$$x < y \equiv y < z \qquad (x < y) = (y < z)$$

2) The GOTO *Statement:* There is hardly any doubt that the use of GOTO statements which disassociate the control structure of a process with the textual structure of its program is a frequent source of mistakes and impairs the verifiability of programs. This was perfectly clear even when the decision to include the GOTO statement in Pascal was taken [2]. Yet even now there is no general agreement on an adequate replacement. Placing further restrictions upon the GOTO statement—for instance, allowing only forward jumps—may be one solution. But clearly, allowing integers only instead of identifiers as labels is no sufficient deterrent to programmers who have previously worked with Fortran! In teaching programming, the use of a subset Pascal system *without* GOTO statement is strongly recommended.

THE EXPLICIT DISTINCTION BETWEEN "TYPES" AND "VARIABLES"

The most widely used technique of program verification is based on the explicit statement of assertions about the state of the computation at different points in the program. Recently, it has been recognized that it would be even more useful to attach assertions to specific variables rather than program points.

Declarations are essentially a statement of invariant properties of the respective variables. In Pascal, every variable is said to be of a certain *type*, and a data type can be defined explicitly by the programmer. It implies essential invariants needed for the verification of programs, and it moreover supplies a compiler with sufficient information to decide on a suitable storage representation. In essence, a compiler translates a type definition into a storage template to be used upon allocation of each variable of this type.

Moreover, the type definition determines the set of operators that are applicable to variables (sometimes called "instances") of that type.

It follows that a type definition should combine all attributes of a variable that are constant and known at the time of compilation (static). In fact, Pascal goes so far as to exclude *all* information from a type definition that cannot be determined from a simple textual scan. This rule has its important merits, but also bears some inconveniences, as shall be explained below. Our experience shows that the advantages of explicit type definitions are enormous and indispensible, if program transparence and efficiency of compiled code are both an issue.

Unfortunately, the Pascal concept of type has also stirred some controversy [3]. It seems to be largely originating from a too strict interpretation of the word *type* based on its use in the world of mathematics. There, the concept of types distinguishes between numbers and truth values, between numbers and sets of numbers, or between sets and sets of sets, but not between integers and natural numbers (a subrange of the former) or between small sets and larger sets. In the world of programming it is both natural and necessary to extend this concept of type, because objects can become different (types) because of far more (detailed) reasons than in abstract mathematics, where problems of representation are immaterial.

Which were, then, the negative consequences of adhering to the rule of strictly static type definitions? They became manifest in the form of two restrictions in the use of arrays, as compared to Algol 60. The first is the exclusion of so-called *dynamic arrays*, because the array type definition includes the specification of its size. There are good reasons for wanting dynamic arrays, but also convincing arguments against them [9]. The fact remains that dynamic arrays in the sense of Algol 60 are sort of a hermaphroditic (hybrid) species: their size can neither be determined at compile time, nor can it be changed during program execution. Instead, it is fixed upon block entry.

The second drawback is in practice much more severe. It originates from the essential requirement that formal procedure parameters specify their types. But in the case of *array parameters*, this once again includes their size. As a consequence, a given procedure can only be applied to arrays of one fixed size. This rule hardly contributes to program security and transparence, but seriously impairs the highly desirable flexibility of procedures.

Both problems can be overcome by allowing type definitions—in particular array types—to be parametrized. The following example shows the use of such a *parametrized type*.

```
type table(m,n) = array[m. . .n] of integer;
var t1: table(1,100);
    t2: table(0,999);
function sum (t: table; u,v: integer): integer;
  var i,s: integer;
begin s := 0;
  for i := u to v do s := t[ i] + s;
  sum := s
end;
begin . . .
  s1 := sum(t1,1,100);
  s2 := sum(t2,0,999);
  . . .
end.
```

From this example we can see both the utility and the dangers of such a generalization, and possibly also the consequences upon a compiler. A most sensible decision is to restrict parametrization to the index bounds of array types, and to allow for constants only as actual parameters (in variable declarations). This already solves the dilemma of array parameters. If dynamic arrays are to be allowed, the latter rule may be relaxed. I would caution, however, against any further generalization: allowing the component type of an array to be a parameter too, for example, would destroy many advantages of the Pascal type concept at once.

AN IMPORTANT CONCEPT AND A PERSISTENT SOURCE OF PROBLEMS: FILES

In Pascal, files are understood to be strictly sequential files, and are defined in terms of the mathematical notion of a *sequence*. Like the array, they are homogeneous structures, but in contrast to the array, their size changes (truly) dynamically. Naturally, we not only aimed at a simple and consistent mathematical definition of files and their operators, but also kept in mind their efficient realization, particularly with a view towards the involvement of secondary storage media. As it turned out, the original file concept was right in terms of implementation, but not in terms of mathematical axiomatization which seemed highly desirable for a tool to construct reliable software. Therefore, the file scheme was slightly modified in a revision of the language made in 1973 that is summarized in [6]. Although the revised file facility proved to be a definite improvement, some inherent difficulties became evident only after extended usage. This may be the reason that the file concept had never been mentioned in any critical commentary about Pascal.

What are these deficiencies, and where do they have their roots? I presume that the main culprit is the attempt to hide from the programmer and the verifier the fact that files must be allocatable on secondary storage media. In this case, an efficient buffering mechanism is involved. Indeed, such technicalities may well be withheld from the programmer who is concerned with correctness only, if the scheme presented to him is rigorously defined and faultless, and if the consequences on efficiency are fully understood and accepted.

Originally, a file f was viewed as a sequence in which at any time only a single element was accessible, if there existed one. Conceptually, one could think of a *window*, through which that element, denoted by $f\uparrow$, could be seen (the arrow denotes the "window position"). But that description is not honest, of course, if $f\uparrow$ actually represents a buffer variable in primary store, via which data are transferred to and from secondary stores (tapes, disks). Therefore the appealing fiction of a sliding window was dropped in favor of a distinct *buffer variable*. But of course, also this is not quite honest, if the true buffer comprises several logical file elements, such that the operation $put(f)$ will actually be effectuated by a mere pointer updating until the buffer is full. For then it is difficult to explain why $f\uparrow$ suddenly changes its value during the operation $put(f)$. In reality we now have a buffer of which a single component is visible through a sliding window; and this situation is slightly too complicated to be neatly expressed by a simple scheme of axioms.

I wish to suggest two possible solutions to this dilemma. Characteristically, the choice depends on the intended application of the language. If Pascal is to serve for system construction purposes, then the file facility might be dropped entirely, because the very purpose would be the description of possible file mechanisms in terms of more primitive concepts. If, however, Pascal is viewed as a general purpose language in which files are an indispensible concept, then the basic operators *get* and *put* might be replaced by *read* and *write* statements defined in terms of the former as follows:

$$read~(f,x) \equiv x := f\uparrow~; get~(f)$$
$$write~(f,x) \equiv f\uparrow~:= x; put~(f)$$

This makes it possible to hide the chosen buffering mechanism entirely, and to ignore the existence of a window or of a buffer variable. (Incidentally, Pascal states exactly these abbreviations, but allows them only for textfiles. The relaxation of this restriction is an obvious step.)

A premise of the axiomatic scheme was that the predicate $eof(f)$ be always defined (true, if the part of the file to the right of the reading position is empty, false otherwise). This implies that a file access must be made before the program actually specifies any reading. The solution lies in combining the rewinding of the file with the initial loading of the buffer. Emptiness can be recognized during this operation. The unpleasant consequence is that a program can never leave a file in a properly rewound state. This may itself not be of any concern, as long as we remain strictly in the world of the Pascal program; but if this program is considered as one action upon a more perma-

nent environment, it must be considered as a deficiency. Indeed, the appropriateness of the primitive *rewrite*(*f*) appears at least questionable. It is, from a theoretical point of view, indispensible, because it is the only operation by which a file variable can be given an initial value, namely the empty sequence (see [6]). In practice, however, rewinding (a tape) is considered as the basic operation, and rewinding does *not* cause the tape to be erased. An obvious "solution" consists in splitting *reset*(*f*) and *rewrite*(*f*) into the "more primitive" operations as follows:

$$reset(f) \equiv rewind(f); openread(f)$$
$$rewrite(f) \equiv rewind(f); openwrite(f)$$

The drawbacks are that the state of the predicate *eof*(*f*) and the buffer *f* ↑ are undetermined in between, and that a programmer is liable to forget to specify the openread or openwrite operation.

The most unsatisfactory consequences of the Pascal file concept lie in the area of substructures, and in particular textfiles. Originally, the idea of substructures could well be ignored. Texts were considered as sequences of characters, separated into lines by control characters. This concept is also embodied by the ISO (and ASCII) conventions, and proved to be most conveniently implementable. On a CDC 6000 computer with 6-bit characters and a set of 63 printing characters, the obvious choice was to introduce a 64th control character **eol** to signal the end of a line.

A program reading a textfile *f*, performing an operation *L* at the beginning of each line and an operation *P* after reading each character, is easily expressed by the following schema:

```
while ¬eof( f) do
  begin L; read( f,ch);
    while ch ≠ eol do
      begin P(ch); read ( f,ch)
      end
  end                                              (1)
```

But then, alas, a new operating system came along with a set of 64 characters. It supposedly incorporates a true miracle: the coding of 64 characters *and* a line separation within 6 bits only! How can reliable software be constructed at all on the basis of such premises?

The new situation left no escape from providing textfiles with an explicit substructure: a textfile was to be considered as a sequence of lines, each line being itself a sequence of characters. In analogy to the predicate *eof*(*f*), a predicate *eoln*(*f*) was introduced to indicate the end of a line. Evidently, also a pair of new operators became necessary, *writeln*(*f*) to terminate the generation of a line, and *readln*(*f*) to initiate the reading of a next line.

Another problem arose simultaneously. At the end of a line, the predicate *eoln*(*f*) becomes true. Should at the end of the last line the predicate *eof*(*f*) also become true simultaneously? Probably so, because evidently the end of the last line is also the end of the text. Once again, we are faced with a dilemma: when reading the end of a line, we either find out whether there exists a next line, and we therefore read on (which may not be the intent of the programmer), or we refrain from looking ahead, and must leave the definition of *eof*(*f*) up to a further explicit *readln* instruction. Neither solution is fully satisfactory.

In the latter case (as in rev. Pascal), the program corresponding to schema (1) is

```
while ¬eof( f) do
begin L;
  while ¬eoln( f) do
    begin read( f,ch); P(ch)
    end;
  readln( f)
end                                                (2)
```

In the former case, the resulting program is slightly but significantly different:

```
while ¬eof( f) do
  begin readln( f); L;
    while ¬eoln( f) do
      begin read( f,ch); P(ch)
      end
  end                                              (3)
```

The difference may appear to be minimal, even negligible. It lies not so much in the form of the program but in the underlying concepts. And frequently such details decide ultimately about the acceptability—the healthiness—of a language. The issue of files is a typical case of the devil persistently and successfully hiding in the details.

SECURITY VERSUS FLEXIBILITY: TYPE UNIONS

It is sometimes desirable that a variable may assume values of different types. Its type is then said to be the *union* of these types. There appear to be three different motivations behind the desire for union types.

1) The need for *heterogeneous structures*. For example, in an interpreter a stack may have to consist of integer, real, and Boolean components. If the stack is represented by an array, its homogeneity is a hindrance. Although each "stack" element assumes only one fixed type during its lifetime, the underlying (static) array element appears to have a varying type.

2) *Storage sharing* (overlays). This implies the use of the same storage area—expressed in the language as "the same actual variable"—for different purposes, i.e., for representing different abstract variables whose lifetimes are disjoint.

3) Realization of implicit *type transfer functions*. For instance, a variable of type real is interpreted as being of type integer for the purpose of printing the internal representation in, say, octal form.

The dangers of the type union facility lie in the possibility to err about the current type of a variable and in the difficulty to identify the mistake. If it occurs in an assignment, the consequences may be disastrous. Efforts must be made to provide automatic checking facilities. We therefore distinguish between *discriminated* and *free unions* [5]. In the former case, the variable carries along a tag which indicates the currently valid type (which is one among the types specified in the definition of the union type). In the latter case, no such direct information is stored. Clearly, the latter provides greater freedom in programming, the former increased security through automatic consistency checks.

In Pascal, the concept of type union is embodied in the form of *variants of record structures*. The discriminated union inherently dictates a record structure, because every value consists of (at least) two components: the actual value and the tag value identifying its current type.

Example:

```
type stackelement =
  record
    case tag: (A,B,C) of
      A: (i: integer);
      B: (r: real);
      C: (b: Boolean)
  end;

var s: array[1..100] of stackelement
```

In a program with these declarations, the occurrence of a variable designator $s[i].r$ is only valid if at this point that variable is of type real. It is so, if and only if $s[i].tag = B$. A compiler may generate this test automatically, provided that it also ensures an appropriate setting of the tag upon assignment. This, however, implies an appreciable, although worthwhile overhead. Suggestions have been made to provide syntactic structures which let the compiler determine the current tag value from context. One such feature is the *inspect when* statement of Simula [1]. But these constructs sometimes turn out to leave insufficient freedom to express a given situation in a natural way.

No such facility was included in Pascal; to the contrary, in its revised version (1973) the tagfield of a variant record definition was declared to be optional. If it is omitted, we obtain the equivalent of a free type union, and a compiler has *no* chance of checking consistency in its application. One may rightly criticize this development which clearly opens the door for a very dangerous sort of programming errors, but there seem to exist applications where the discriminated union is insufficiently flexible. (Even so, my advice is to refrain from using variants without tagfield.)

The issue of type unions is a clear example of a case where a language may offer added security only at the expense of flexibility, or vice versa. The programmer must make his own choice. Yet, we have the impression that a more satisfactory solution must be found. It will not necessarily be found in new language facilities, but may lie in a different approach to data organization.

The truly disconcerting fact is that facilities such as the record variant, provided for a genuine need for flexibility (motivation 1 above), can be (and are!) easily misused. The example for the third motivation (see above) is characteristic for programmers who (habitually) think in terms of machine facilities and assembly code, and (love to) show that their techniques can also be expressed in a higher level language. It is probably the most disheartening experience for a language designer to discover how features provided with honest intentions are "ingeniously" misused to betray the language's very principles.

SUMMARY AND CONCLUSIONS

We have argued that the concept of a *degree of program reliability* is ill conceived and helps to foster a mistaken attitude in software engineering. Instead, a program can be called *correct*, if and only if its operations are fully consistent with static specifications of the expected results of the dynamic process. As programs used in practice are enormously complex and have a tendency to become even more complex in future applications, programming errors will always be with us. Instead of relying too much on either antiquated "debugging tools" or on futuristic automatic program verifiers, we should give more emphasis to the systematic construction of programs with languages that facilitate transparent formulation and automatic consistency checks.

The language Pascal was designed with exactly these aims. Five years of experience in its use have proven its significant merits with respect to ease of programming, suitability for formal program verification [7], [10], efficient implementability, and practical portability. They have also revealed some weaknesses and some remaining difficulties. After analyzing the roots of these problems, we are tempted to list a few conclusions about the design and the choice of languages for "reliable programming."

The language must rest on a foundation of simple, flexible, and neatly axiomatized features, comprising the basic structuring techniques of data and program.

Language rules must not deviate from widely accepted traditions of formal notations, even if these traditions are sometimes inconsistent or inconvenient. More importantly, *new* features must be designed with utmost care to notational regularity and consistency.

The urge to gain flexibility and "power" through generalizations must be restrained. A generalization may easily be carried too far and have revolutionary consequences on implementation (e.g., full parametrization of types).

Every basic feature is to be governed by a consistent set of "obvious" rules (axioms). The rules must be such that efficient implementability does not depend on particular (or even peculiar) properties of a specific computer system (e.g., on the existence of a line-end-character).

In many cases, security and flexibility are antagonistic

properties. Security is obtained through redundancy which is used by the system to perform consistency checks. Often, redundancy is cumbersome to provide, and the programmer must decide whether to choose a straightjacket providing relative security, or a free language where the responsibility is entirely his own (e.g., discriminated versus free type unions).

Every rule of the language must be enforceable by the system. It follows that rules should preferably be checkable by a mere textual scan, but also run-time checks should become widely used.

A rich language may be welcome to the professional program *writer* who's principle delight is his familiarization with all its intricate facets. But the interests of the program *reader* dictate a reasonably frugal language. People who want to understand a program (including their own), compilers, and automatic verification aids all belong to the class of readers.

In the interest of increased quality of software products, we may be well advised to get rid of many facilities of modern, baroque programming languages that are widely advertised in the name of "user-orientation," "scientific sophistication," and "progress."

ACKNOWLEDGMENT

The author wishes to acknowledge the criticism and suggestions of members of the International Federation of Information Processing Working Group 2.3 which helped to clarify this presentation.

REFERENCES

[1] Birtwistle, Dahl, Myhrhaug, Nygaard, "SIMULA Begin," *Studentlitteratur*, Univ. Lund, Lund, Sweden, 1974.
[2] E. W. Dijkstra, "GOTO statements considered harmful," *Commun. Ass. Comput. Mach.*, vol. 11, pp. 147–148, Mar. 1968.
[3] A. N. Habermann, "Critical comments on the programming language PASCAL," *Acta Informatica*, vol. 3, pp. 47–58, 1973.
[4] C. A. R. Hoare, "Set manipulation," *Algol Bulletin*, vol. 27, pp. 29–37, Dec. 1967.
[5] O.-J. Dahl, E. W. Dijkstra, and C. A. R. Hoare, "Notes on data structuring," in *Structured Programming*. New York: Academic, 1972.
[6] C. A. R. Hoare and N. Wirth, "An axiomatic definition of the programming language PASCAL," *Acta Informatica*, vol. 2, pp. 335–355, 1973.
[7] S. Igarashi, R. L. London, and D. C. Luckham, "Automatic program verification: a logical basis and its implementation," Dep. Comput. Sci., Stanford Univ., Stanford, Calif., Comput. Sci. Rep. 73-365, May 1973.
[8] K. Jensen and N. Wirth, "PASCAL—User Manual and Report," in *Lecture Notes in Computer Science*, vol. 18, New York: Springer-Verlag, 1974.
[9] O. Lecarme and P. Desjardins, "Reply to a paper by A. N Habermann on the programming language PASCAL," *SIGPLAN Notices*, vol. 9, pp. 21–27, Oct. 1974.
[10] E. Marmier, "A program verifier for Pascal," in *Proc. Int. Fed. Inform. Processing Congr.*, Inform. Processing 74. Amsterdam, The Netherlands: North-Holland, 1974.
[11] J. Welsh and C. Quinn, "A PASCAL compiler for ICL 1900 series computers," *Software—Practice and Experience*, vol. 2, pp. 73–77, 1972.
[12] N. Wirth, "The design of a Pascal compiler," *Software—Practice and Experience*, vol. 1, pp. 309–333, 1971.
[13] ——, "The programming language PASCAL," *Acta Informatica*, vol. 1, pp. 35–63, 1971.

SECTION 3

APPLICATIVE LANGUAGES

CAN PROGRAMMING BE LIBERATED FROM THE
VON NEUMANN STYLE? A FUNCTIONAL STYLE
AND ITS ALGEBRA OF PROGRAMS
BY J. BACKUS

RECURSIVE FUNCTIONS OF SYMBOLIC
EXPRESSIONS BY J. MCCARTHY

LISP 1.5 PROGRAMMER'S MANUAL BY
J. MCCARTHY, PAUL W. ABRAHAMS,
DANIEL J. EDWARDS, TIMOTHY P. HART,
AND M. LEVIN

THE DESIGN OF APL BY A. D. FALKOFF
AND K. E. IVERSON

INTRODUCTION

APPLICATIVE LANGUAGES

What are applicative languages? The domination of FORTRAN, COBOL, and even Pascal on the computing community have made applicative programming languages an esoteric subject. They are something that is studied in advanced courses of computer science or encountered in the form of the language called LISP. Is the applicative language doomed to remain in this subjugated position? I do not know, but I do know that it is an idea, or rather a model of computation which has merit and therefore it should be studied. But if this were the only reason, then perhaps one paper would be enough. There are other reasons.

The best statement about the weaknesses of existing languages and about the strengths of applicative languages is given in the paper by John Backus, the first in this chapter. It is only right and proper that Backus is making these criticisms, having been a principal developer of both FORTRAN and ALGOL60. In his paper he cogently and eloquently describes the weaknesses of today's languages. They are *both fat and weak in a global sense.* For those people who have gone from FORTRAN to PL/1 to Pascal and now to Ada this thought must seem peculiar if not outright heresy. So read Backus' article and see if you agree or at least if you understand his point of view. If you read through section 10 of Backus' paper and you are still open minded, the remaining sections will present his attempt to define a programming language which is semantically clean, simple and yet fully powerful. Then in section 12, he shows how one can derive theorems about program forms, such that proofs of correctness of programs can be accomplished in a manner similar to the way we prove things in group theory.

The second paper in this chapter is a classic in the programming language field, essentially on a par with the ALGOL60 report. "*Recursive functions of Symbolic Expressions and Their Computation by Machine, Part One*" by John McCarthy is the paper in which the seminal ideas underlying the language LISP were presented. Part II has yet to appear. LISP is a language which has been highly favored by researchers in artificial intelligence since its introduction. Despite the fact that it has not had the backing of a major computer manufacturer it has continued to survive these past twenty or so

years. And the people who favor it are a community of scholars who make high demands on their computing equipment because they build large prototype systems.

This section has two papers on LISP. The first one presents the theoretical basis of the language coupled with many examples and elaborations on the formalism. The second paper is an excerpt from the LISP 1.5 Programmer's Manual. This original manual by McCarthy and Levin embodies a clear and concise description of (pure)-LISP and may still be the best introduction to the language.

One of the most impressive facts about LISP is that its semantics are sufficiently simple that it permits a mathematical model which is relatively tractable. McCarthy used this model as a starting point to develop a theory of computation. He considered many important theoretical issues including proofs of program correctness, proofs of compiler correctness and proofs of program equivalence long before these topics became fashionable. Another important consequence of the simple semantics is the definition of LISP by an interpreter. This interpreter can be found reprinted here in the LISP 1.5 Manual. This interpreter was an early demonstration of the technique of defining a programming language by an interpreter written in the same language. This became the start of the field of operational semantics. In addition to all of the theoretical benefits of LISP, the language has many practical aspects as well. The reliance on the notion of function without side-effects greatly aids modularity. The technique of garbage collection is an important step in freeing the programmer of the responsibility of storage management. This in turn leads to more reliable programs. As prototyping continues to be an important element of large-scale software development, the LISP language and its derivatives continue to offer important advantages not found in the ALGOL-like variety of programming language.

Another important language which has many features in common with LISP is APL. A creation of Iverson, the language was used primarily to describe algorithms until its first implementation appeared about 10 years after its initial development. There are many good primers describing how to use APL. Thus I have included

here a paper which concentrates on the design of the language. But before one can appreciate this paper, one needs to have some experience with the language. APL has a devoted body of followers, most of whom are in industry and using APL to write complicated programs. As with LISP, APL eschews the notion of strong typing and static scoping. It is an interpreted rather than a compiled language. These features appear to make it a better language to use for many applications than the compiled, statically scoped languages. The reader should be aware of these issues in this section.

CAN PROGRAMMING BE LIBERATED FROM THE VON NEUMANN STYLE? A FUNCTIONAL STYLE AND ITS ALGEBRA OF PROGRAMS*

J. BACKUS

General permission to make fair use in teaching or research of all or part of this material is granted to individual readers and to nonprofit libraries acting for them provided that ACM's copyright notice is given and that reference is made to the publication, to its date of issue, and to the fact that reprinting privileges were granted by permission of the Association for Computing Machinery. To otherwise reprint a figure, table, other substantial excerpt, or the entire work requires specific permission as does republication, or systematic or multiple reproduction.

Author's address: 91 Saint Germain Ave., San Francisco, CA 94114.

© 1978 ACM 0001-0782/78/0800-0613 $00.75

*Reprinted from *Comm ACM* 21, 8, August 1978, 613–641, copyright 1978.

grams, and no conventional language even begins to meet that need. In fact, conventional languages create unnecessary confusion in the way we think about programs.

For twenty years programming languages have been steadily progressing toward their present condition of obesity; as a result, the study and invention of programming languages has lost much of its excitement. Instead, it is now the province of those who prefer to work with thick compendia of details rather than wrestle with new ideas. Discussions about programming languages often resemble medieval debates about the number of angels that can dance on the head of a pin instead of exciting contests between fundamentally differing concepts.

Many creative computer scientists have retreated from inventing languages to inventing tools for describing them. Unfortunately, they have been largely content to apply their elegant new tools to studying the warts and moles of existing languages. After examining the appalling type structure of conventional languages, using the elegant tools developed by Dana Scott, it is surprising that so many of us remain passively content with that structure instead of energetically searching for new ones.

The purpose of this article is twofold; first, to suggest that basic defects in the framework of conventional languages make their expressive weakness and their cancerous growth inevitable, and second, to suggest some alternate avenues of exploration toward the design of new kinds of languages.

Introduction

I deeply appreciate the honor of the ACM invitation to give the 1977 Turing Lecture and to publish this account of it with the details promised in the lecture. Readers wishing to see a summary of this paper should turn to Section 16, the last section.

1. Conventional Programming Languages: Fat and Flabby

Programming languages appear to be in trouble. Each successive language incorporates, with a little cleaning up, all the features of its predecessors plus a few more. Some languages have manuals exceeding 500 pages; others cram a complex description into shorter manuals by using dense formalisms. The Department of Defense has current plans for a committee-designed language standard that could require a manual as long as 1,000 pages. Each new language claims new and fashionable features, such as strong typing or structured control statements, but the plain fact is that few languages make programming sufficiently cheaper or more reliable to justify the cost of producing and learning to use them.

Since large increases in size bring only small increases in power, smaller, more elegant languages such as Pascal continue to be popular. But there is a desperate need for a powerful methodology to help us think about pro-

2. Models of Computing Systems

Underlying every programming language is a model of a computing system that its programs control. Some models are pure abstractions, some are represented by hardware, and others by compiling or interpretive programs. Before we examine conventional languages more closely, it is useful to make a brief survey of existing models as an introduction to the current universe of alternatives. Existing models may be crudely classified by the criteria outlined below.

2.1 Criteria for Models
2.1.1 Foundations. Is there an elegant and concise mathematical description of the model? Is it useful in proving helpful facts about the behavior of the model? Or is the model so complex that its description is bulky and of little mathematical use?

2.1.2 History sensitivity. Does the model include a notion of storage, so that one program can save information that can affect the behavior of a later program? That is, is the model history sensitive?

2.1.3 Type of semantics. Does a program successively transform states (which are not programs) until a terminal state is reached (state-transition semantics)? Are states simple or complex? Or can a "program" be successively reduced to simpler "programs" to yield a final

"normal form program," which is the result (reduction semantics)?

2.1.4 Clarity and conceptual usefulness of programs. Are programs of the model clear expressions of a process or computation? Do they embody concepts that help us to formulate and reason about processes?

2.2 Classification of Models

Using the above criteria we can crudely characterize three classes of models for computing systems—simple operational models, applicative models, and von Neumann models.

2.2.1 Simple operational models. Examples: Turing machines, various automata. *Foundations*: concise and useful. *History sensitivity*: have storage, are history sensitive. *Semantics*: state transition with very simple states. *Program clarity*: programs unclear and conceptually not helpful.

2.2.2 Applicative models. Examples: Church's lambda calculus [5], Curry's system of combinators [6], pure Lisp [17], functional programming systems described in this paper. *Foundations*: concise and useful. *History sensitivity*: no storage, not history sensitive. *Semantics*: reduction semantics, no states. *Program clarity*: programs can be clear and conceptually useful.

2.2.3 Von Neumann models. Examples: von Neumann computers, conventional programming languages. *Foundations*: complex, bulky, not useful. *History sensitivity*: have storage, are history sensitive. *Semantics*: state transition with complex states. *Program clarity*: programs can be moderately clear, are not very useful conceptually.

The above classification is admittedly crude and debatable. Some recent models may not fit easily into any of these categories. For example, the data-flow languages developed by Arvind and Gostelow [1], Dennis [7], Kosinski [13], and others partly fit the class of simple operational models, but their programs are clearer than those of earlier models in the class and it is perhaps possible to argue that some have reduction semantics. In any event, this classification will serve as a crude map of the territory to be discussed. We shall be concerned only with applicative and von Neumann models.

3. Von Neumann Computers

In order to understand the problems of conventional programming languages, we must first examine their intellectual parent, the von Neumann computer. What is a von Neumann computer? When von Neumann and others conceived it over thirty years ago, it was an elegant, practical, and unifying idea that simplified a number of engineering and programming problems that existed then. Although the conditions that produced its architecture have changed radically, we nevertheless still identify the notion of "computer" with this thirty year old concept.

In its simplest form a von Neumann computer has three parts: a central processing unit (or CPU), a store, and a connecting tube that can transmit a single word between the CPU and the store (and send an address to the store). I propose to call this tube the *von Neumann bottleneck*. The task of a program is to change the contents of the store in some major way; when one considers that this task must be accomplished entirely by pumping single words back and forth through the von Neumann bottleneck, the reason for its name becomes clear.

Ironically, a large part of the traffic in the bottleneck is not useful data but merely names of data, as well as operations and data used only to compute such names. Before a word can be sent through the tube its address must be in the CPU; hence it must either be sent through the tube from the store or be generated by some CPU operation. If the address is sent from the store, then *its* address must either have been sent from the store or generated in the CPU, and so on. If, on the other hand, the address is generated in the CPU, it must be generated either by a fixed rule (e.g., "add 1 to the program counter") or by an instruction that was sent through the tube, in which case *its* address must have been sent ... and so on.

Surely there must be a less primitive way of making big changes in the store than by pushing vast numbers of words back and forth through the von Neumann bottleneck. Not only is this tube a literal bottleneck for the data traffic of a problem, but, more importantly, it is an intellectual bottleneck that has kept us tied to word-at-a-time thinking instead of encouraging us to think in terms of the larger conceptual units of the task at hand. Thus programming is basically planning and detailing the enormous traffic of words through the von Neumann bottleneck, and much of that traffic concerns not significant data itself but where to find it.

4. Von Neumann Languages

Conventional programming languages are basically high level, complex versions of the von Neumann computer. Our thirty year old belief that there is only one kind of computer is the basis of our belief that there is only one kind of programming language, the conventional—von Neumann—language. The differences between Fortran and Algol 68, although considerable, are less significant than the fact that both are based on the programming style of the von Neumann computer. Although I refer to conventional languages as "von Neumann languages" to take note of their origin and style, I do not, of course, blame the great mathematician for their complexity. In fact, some might say that I bear some responsibility for that problem.

Von Neumann programming languages use variables to imitate the computer's storage cells; control statements elaborate its jump and test instructions; and assignment statements imitate its fetching, storing, and arithmetic.

The assignment statement is the von Neumann bottleneck of programming languages and keeps us thinking in word-at-a-time terms in much the same way the computer's bottleneck does.

Consider a typical program; at its center are a number of assignment statements containing some subscripted variables. Each assignment statement produces a one-word result. The program must cause these statements to be executed many times, while altering subscript values, in order to make the desired overall change in the store, since it must be done one word at a time. The programmer is thus concerned with the flow of words through the assignment bottleneck as he designs the nest of control statements to cause the necessary repetitions.

Moreover, the assignment statement splits programming into two worlds. The first world comprises the right sides of assignment statements. This is an orderly world of expressions, a world that has useful algebraic properties (except that those properties are often destroyed by side effects). It is the world in which most useful computation takes place.

The second world of conventional programming languages is the world of statements. The primary statement in that world is the assignment statement itself. All the other statements of the language exist in order to make it possible to perform a computation that must be based on this primitive construct: the assignment statement.

This world of statements is a disorderly one, with few useful mathematical properties. Structured programming can be seen as a modest effort to introduce some order into this chaotic world, but it accomplishes little in attacking the fundamental problems created by the word-at-a-time von Neumann style of programming, with its primitive use of loops, subscripts, and branching flow of control.

Our fixation on von Neumann languages has continued the primacy of the von Neumann computer, and our dependency on *it* has made non-von Neumann languages uneconomical and has limited their development. The absence of full scale, effective programming styles founded on non-von Neumann principles has deprived designers of an intellectual foundation for new computer architectures. (For a brief discussion of that topic, see Section 15.)

Applicative computing systems' lack of storage and history sensitivity is the basic reason they have not provided a foundation for computer design. Moreover, most applicative systems employ the substitution operation of the lambda calculus as their basic operation. This operation is one of virtually unlimited power, but its complete and efficient realization presents great difficulties to the machine designer. Furthermore, in an effort to introduce storage and to improve their efficiency on von Neumann computers, applicative systems have tended to become engulfed in a large von Neumann system. For example, pure Lisp is often buried in large extensions with many von Neumann features. The resulting complex systems offer little guidance to the machine designer.

5. Comparison of von Neumann and Functional Programs

To get a more detailed picture of some of the defects of von Neumann languages, let us compare a conventional program for inner product with a functional one written in a simple language to be detailed further on.

5.1 A von Neumann Program for Inner Product

```
c := 0
for i := 1 step 1 until n do
    c := c + a[i]×b[i]
```

Several properties of this program are worth noting:

a) Its statements operate on an invisible "state" according to complex rules.

b) It is not hierarchical. Except for the right side of the assignment statement, it does not construct complex entities from simpler ones. (Larger programs, however, often do.)

c) It is dynamic and repetitive. One must mentally execute it to understand it.

d) It computes word-at-a-time by repetition (of the assignment) and by modification (of variable i).

e) Part of the data, n, is in the program; thus it lacks generality and works only for vectors of length n.

f) It names its arguments; it can only be used for vectors a and b. To become general, it requires a procedure declaration. These involve complex issues (e.g., call-by-name versus call-by-value).

g) Its "housekeeping" operations are represented by symbols in scattered places (in the **for** statement and the subscripts in the assignment). This makes it impossible to consolidate housekeeping operations, the most common of all, into single, powerful, widely useful operators. Thus in programming those operations one must always start again at square one, writing "**for** i := ..." and "**for** j := ..." followed by assignment statements sprinkled with i's and j's.

5.2 A Functional Program for Inner Product

Def Innerproduct
$$\equiv (\text{Insert} +)\circ(\text{ApplyToAll} \times)\circ\text{Transpose}$$

Or, in abbreviated form:

Def IP $\equiv (/+)\circ(\alpha\times)\circ\text{Trans}.$

Composition ($\circ$), Insert ($/$), and ApplyToAll (α) are *functional forms* that combine existing functions to form new ones. Thus $f\circ g$ is the function obtained by applying first g and then f, and αf is the function obtained by applying f to every *member* of the argument. If we write $f:x$ for the result of applying f to the object x, then we can explain each step in evaluating Innerproduct applied to the pair of vectors $<<1, 2, 3>, <6, 5, 4>>$ as follows:

IP:$<<1,2,3>, <6,5,4>> =$

Definition of IP	$\Rightarrow (/+)\circ(\alpha\times)\circ\text{Trans}: <<1,2,3>, <6,5,4>>$
Effect of composition, $\circ$	$\Rightarrow (/+):((\alpha\times):(\text{Trans}:$
	$<<1,2,3>, <6,5,4>>))$

Applying Transpose	$\Rightarrow (/+) : ((\alpha\times) : \langle\langle 1,6\rangle, \langle 2,5\rangle, \langle 3,4\rangle\rangle)$
Effect of ApplyToAll, α	$\Rightarrow (/+) : \langle\times : \langle 1,6\rangle, \times : \langle 2,5\rangle, \times : \langle 3,4\rangle\rangle$
Applying $\times$	$\Rightarrow (/+) : \langle 6,10,12\rangle$
Effect of Insert, /	$\Rightarrow + : \langle 6, + : \langle 10,12\rangle\rangle$
Applying +	$\Rightarrow + : \langle 6,22\rangle$
Applying + again	$\Rightarrow 28$

Let us compare the properties of this program with those of the von Neumann program.

a) It operates only on its arguments. There are no hidden states or complex transition rules. There are only two kinds of rules, one for applying a function to its argument, the other for obtaining the function denoted by a functional form such as composition, $f \circ g$, or ApplyToAll, αf, when one knows the functions f and g, the *parameters* of the forms.

b) It is hierarchical, being built from three simpler functions (+, $\times$, Trans) and three functional forms $f \circ g$, αf, and $/f$.

c) It is static and nonrepetitive, in the sense that its structure is helpful in understanding it without mentally executing it. For example, if one understands the action of the forms $f \circ g$ and αf, and of the functions $\times$ and Trans, then one understands the action of $\alpha\times$ and of $(\alpha\times) \circ$ Trans, and so on.

d) It operates on whole conceptual units, not words; it has three steps; no step is repeated.

e) It incorporates no data; it is completely general; it works for any pair of conformable vectors.

f) It does not name its arguments; it can be applied to any pair of vectors without any procedure declaration or complex substitution rules.

g) It employs housekeeping forms and functions that are generally useful in many other programs; in fact, only + and $\times$ are not concerned with housekeeping. These forms and functions can combine with others to create higher level housekeeping operators.

Section 14 sketches a kind of system designed to make the above functional style of programming available in a history-sensitive system with a simple framework, but much work remains to be done before the above applicative style can become the basis for elegant and practical programming languages. For the present, the above comparison exhibits a number of serious flaws in von Neumann programming languages and can serve as a starting point in an effort to account for their present fat and flabby condition.

6. Language Frameworks versus Changeable Parts

Let us distinguish two parts of a programming language. First, its *framework* which gives the overall rules of the system, and second, its *changeable parts,* whose existence is anticipated by the framework but whose particular behavior is not specified by it. For example, the **for** statement, and almost all other statements, are part of Algol's framework but library functions and user-defined procedures are changeable parts. Thus the framework of a language describes its fixed features and provides a general environment for its changeable features.

Now suppose a language had a small framework which could accommodate a great variety of powerful features entirely as changeable parts. Then such a framework could support many different features and styles without being changed itself. In contrast to this pleasant possibility, von Neumann languages always seem to have an immense framework and very limited changeable parts. What causes this to happen? The answer concerns two problems of von Neumann languages.

The first problem results from the von Neumann style of word-at-a-time programming, which requires that words flow back and forth to the state, just like the flow through the von Neumann bottleneck. Thus a von Neumann language must have a semantics closely coupled to the state, in which every detail of a computation changes the state. The consequence of this semantics closely coupled to states is that every detail of every feature must be built into the state and its transition rules.

Thus every feature of a von Neumann language must be spelled out in stupefying detail in its framework. Furthermore, many complex features are needed to prop up the basically weak word-at-a-time style. The result is the inevitable rigid and enormous framework of a von Neumann language.

7. Changeable Parts and Combining Forms

The second problem of von Neumann languages is that their changeable parts have so little expressive power. Their gargantuan size is eloquent proof of this; after all, if the designer knew that all those complicated features, which he now builds into the framework, could be added later on as changeable parts, he would not be so eager to build them into the framework.

Perhaps the most important element in providing powerful changeable parts in a language is the availability of combining forms that can be generally used to build new procedures from old ones. Von Neumann languages provide only primitive combining forms, and the von Neumann framework presents obstacles to their full use.

One obstacle to the use of combining forms is the split between the expression world and the statement world in von Neumann languages. Functional forms naturally belong to the world of expressions; but no matter how powerful they are they can only build expressions that produce a one-word result. And it is in the statement world that these one-word results must be combined into the overall result. Combining single words is not what we really should be thinking about, but it is a large part of programming any task in von Neumann languages. To help assemble the overall result from single words these languages provide some primitive combining forms in the statement world—the **for, while,** and **if-then-else** statements—but the split between the

two worlds prevents the combining forms in either world from attaining the full power they can achieve in an undivided world.

A second obstacle to the use of combining forms in von Neumann languages is their use of elaborate naming conventions, which are further complicated by the substitution rules required in calling procedures. Each of these requires a complex mechanism to be built into the framework so that variables, subscripted variables, pointers, file names, procedure names, call-by-value formal parameters, call-by-name formal parameters, and so on, can all be properly interpreted. All these names, conventions, and rules interfere with the use of simple combining forms.

8. APL versus Word-at-a-Time Programming

Since I have said so much about word-at-a-time programming, I must now say something about APL [12]. We owe a great debt to Kenneth Iverson for showing us that there are programs that are neither word-at-a-time nor dependent on lambda expressions, and for introducing us to the use of new functional forms. And since APL assignment statements can store arrays, the effect of its functional forms is extended beyond a single assignment.

Unfortunately, however, APL still splits programming into a world of expressions and a world of statements. Thus the effort to write one-line programs is partly motivated by the desire to stay in the more orderly world of expressions. APL has exactly three functional forms, called inner product, outer product, and reduction. These are sometimes difficult to use, there are not enough of them, and their use is confined to the world of expressions.

Finally, APL semantics is still too closely coupled to states. Consequently, despite the greater simplicity and power of the language, its framework has the complexity and rigidity characteristic of von Neumann languages.

9. Von Neumann Languages Lack Useful Mathematical Properties

So far we have discussed the gross size and inflexibility of von Neumann languages; another important defect is their lack of useful mathematical properties and the obstacles they present to reasoning about programs. Although a great amount of excellent work has been published on proving facts about programs, von Neumann languages have almost no properties that are helpful in this direction and have many properties that are obstacles (e.g., side effects, aliasing).

Denotational semantics [23] and its foundations [20, 21] provide an extremely helpful mathematical understanding of the domain and function spaces implicit in programs. When applied to an applicative language (such as that of the "recursive programs" of [16]), its

foundations provide powerful tools for describing the language and for proving properties of programs. When applied to a von Neumann language, on the other hand, it provides a precise semantic description and is helpful in identifying trouble spots in the language. But the complexity of the language is mirrored in the complexity of the description, which is a bewildering collection of productions, domains, functions, and equations that is only slightly more helpful in proving facts about programs than the reference manual of the language, since it is less ambiguous.

Axiomatic semantics [11] precisely restates the inelegant properties of von Neumann programs (i.e., transformations on states) as transformations on predicates. The word-at-a-time, repetitive game is not thereby changed, merely the playing field. The complexity of this axiomatic game of proving facts about von Neumann programs makes the successes of its practitioners all the more admirable. Their success rests on two factors in addition to their ingenuity: First, the game is restricted to small, weak subsets of full von Neumann languages that have states vastly simpler than real ones. Second, the new playing field (predicates and their transformations) is richer, more orderly and effective than the old (states and their transformations). But restricting the game and transferring it to a more effective domain does not enable it to handle real programs (with the necessary complexities of procedure calls and aliasing), nor does it eliminate the clumsy properties of the basic von Neumann style. As axiomatic semantics is extended to cover more of a typical von Neumann language, it begins to lose its effectiveness with the increasing complexity that is required.

Thus denotational and axiomatic semantics are descriptive formalisms whose foundations embody elegant and powerful concepts; but using them to describe a von Neumann language can not produce an elegant and powerful language any more than the use of elegant and modern machines to build an Edsel can produce an elegant and modern car.

In any case, proofs about programs use the language of logic, not the language of programming. Proofs talk *about* programs but cannot involve them directly since the axioms of von Neumann languages are so unusable. In contrast, many ordinary proofs are derived by algebraic methods. These methods require a language that has certain algebraic properties. Algebraic laws can then be used in a rather mechanical way to transform a problem into its solution. For example, to solve the equation

$$ax + bx = a + b$$

for x (given that $a+b \neq 0$), we mechanically apply the distributive, identity, and cancellation laws, in succession, to obtain

$$(a + b)x = a + b$$
$$(a + b)x = (a + b)1$$
$$x = 1.$$

Thus we have proved that x = 1 without leaving the "language" of algebra. Von Neumann languages, with their grotesque syntax, offer few such possibilities for transforming programs.

As we shall see later, programs can be expressed in a language that has an associated algebra. This algebra can be used to transform programs and to solve some equations whose "unknowns" are programs, in much the same way one solves equations in high school algebra. Algebraic transformations and proofs use the language of the programs themselves, rather than the language of logic, which talks about programs.

10. What Are the Alternatives to von Neumann Languages?

Before discussing alternatives to von Neumann languages, let me remark that I regret the need for the above negative and not very precise discussion of these languages. But the complacent acceptance most of us give to these enormous, weak languages has puzzled and disturbed me for a long time. I am disturbed because that acceptance has consumed a vast effort toward making von Neumann languages fatter that might have been better spent in looking for new structures. For this reason I have tried to analyze some of the basic defects of conventional languages and show that those defects cannot be resolved unless we discover a new kind of language framework.

In seeking an alternative to conventional languages we must first recognize that a system cannot be history sensitive (permit execution of one program to affect the behavior of a subsequent one) unless the system has some kind of state (which the first program can change and the second can access). Thus a history-sensitive model of a computing system must have a state-transition semantics, at least in this weak sense. But this does *not* mean that every computation must depend heavily on a complex state, with many state changes required for each small part of the computation (as in von Neumann languages).

To illustrate some alternatives to von Neumann languages, I propose to sketch a class of history-sensitive computing systems, where each system: a) has a loosely coupled state-transition semantics in which a state transition occurs only once in a major computation; b) has a simply structured state and simple transition rules; c) depends heavily on an underlying applicative system both to provide the basic programming language of the system and to describe its state transitions.

These systems, which I call applicative state transition (or AST) systems, are described in Section 14. These simple systems avoid many of the complexities and weaknesses of von Neumann languages and provide for a powerful and extensive set of changeable parts. However, they are sketched only as crude examples of a vast area of non-von Neumann systems with various attractive properties. I have been studying this area for the

past three or four years and have not yet found a satisfying solution to the many conflicting requirements that a good language must resolve. But I believe this search has indicated a useful approach to designing non-von Neumann languages.

This approach involves four elements, which can be summarized as follows.

a) *A functional style of programming without variables.* A simple, informal functional programming (FP) system is described. It is based on the use of combining forms for building programs. Several programs are given to illustrate functional programming.

b) *An algebra of functional programs.* An algebra is described whose variables denote FP functional programs and whose "operations" are FP functional forms, the combining forms of FP programs. Some laws of the algebra are given. Theorems and examples are given that show how certain function expressions may be transformed into equivalent infinite expansions that explain the behavior of the function. The FP algebra is compared with algebras associated with the classical applicative systems of Church and Curry.

c) *A formal functional programming system.* A formal (FFP) system is described that extends the capabilities of the above informal FP systems. An FFP system is thus a precisely defined system that provides the ability to use the functional programming style of FP systems and their algebra of programs. FFP systems can be used as the basis for applicative state transition systems.

d) *Applicative state transition systems.* As discussed above. The rest of the paper describes these four elements, gives some brief remarks on computer design, and ends with a summary of the paper.

11. Functional Programming Systems (FP Systems)

11.1 Introduction

In this section we give an informal description of a class of simple applicative programming systems called functional programming (FP) systems, in which "programs" are simply functions without variables. The description is followed by some examples and by a discussion of various properties of FP systems.

An FP system is founded on the use of a fixed set of combining forms called functional forms. These, plus simple definitions, are the only means of building new functions from existing ones; they use no variables or substitution rules, and they become the operations of an associated algebra of programs. All the functions of an FP system are of one type: they map objects into objects and always take a single argument.

In contrast, a lambda-calculus based system is founded on the use of the lambda expression, with an associated set of substitution rules for variables, for building new functions. The lambda expression (with its substitution rules) is capable of defining all possible computable functions of all possible types and of any number of arguments. This freedom and power has its

disadvantages as well as its obvious advantages. It is analogous to the power of unrestricted control statements in conventional languages: with unrestricted freedom comes chaos. If one constantly invents new combining forms to suit the occasion, as one can in the lambda calculus, one will not become familiar with the style or useful properties of the few combining forms that are adequate for all purposes. Just as structured programming eschews many control statements to obtain programs with simpler structure, better properties, and uniform methods for understanding their behavior, so functional programming eschews the lambda expression, substitution, and multiple function types. It thereby achieves programs built with familiar functional forms with known useful properties. These programs are so structured that their behavior can often be understood and proven by mechanical use of algebraic techniques similar to those used in solving high school algebra problems.

Functional forms, unlike most programming constructs, need not be chosen on an ad hoc basis. Since they are the operations of an associated algebra, one chooses only those functional forms that not only provide powerful programming constructs, but that also have attractive algebraic properties: one chooses them to maximize the strength and utility of the algebraic laws that relate them to other functional forms of the system.

In the following description we shall be imprecise in not distinguishing between (a) a function symbol or expression and (b) the function it denotes. We shall indicate the symbols and expressions used to denote functions by example and usage. Section 13 describes a formal extension of FP systems (FFP systems); they can serve to clarify any ambiguities about FP systems.

11.2 Description
An FP system comprises the following:

1) a set O of *objects*;

2) a set F of *functions* f that map objects into objects;

3) an operation, *application*;

4) a set F of *functional forms*; these are used to combine existing functions, or objects, to form new functions in F;

5) a set D of *definitions* that define some functions in F and assign a name to each.

What follows is an informal description of each of the above entities with examples.

11.2.1 Objects, O. An *object* x is either an *atom*, a *sequence* $<x_1, \ldots, x_n>$ whose *elements* x_i are objects, or $\perp$ ("bottom" or "undefined"). Thus the choice of a set A of atoms determines the set of objects. We shall take A to be the set of nonnull strings of capital letters, digits, and special symbols not used by the notation of the FP system. Some of these strings belong to the class of atoms called "numbers." The atom ϕ is used to denote the empty sequence and is the only object which is both an atom and a sequence. The atoms T and F are used to denote "true" and "false."

There is one important constraint in the construction of objects: if x is a sequence with $\perp$ as an element, then $x = \perp$. That is, the "sequence constructor" is "$\perp$-preserving." Thus no proper sequence has $\perp$ as an element.

Examples of objects

$$\perp \quad 1.5 \quad \phi \quad AB3 \quad <AB, 1, 2.3>$$
$$<A, <<B>, C>, D> \quad <A, \perp> = \perp$$

11.2.2 Application. An FP system has a single operation, application. If f is a function and x is an object, then $f:x$ is an *application* and denotes the object which is the result of applying f to x. f is the *operator* of the application and x is the *operand*.

Examples of applications

$$+:<1,2> = 3 \quad tl:<A,B,C> = <B,C>$$
$$1:<A,B,C> = A \quad 2:<A,B,C> = B$$

11.2.3 Functions, F. All functions f in F map objects into objects and are *bottom-preserving*: $f:\perp = \perp$, for all f in F. Every function in F is either *primitive*, that is, supplied with the system, or it is *defined* (see below), or it is a *functional form* (see below).

It is sometimes useful to distinguish between two cases in which $f:x=\perp$. If the computation for $f:x$ terminates and yields the object $\perp$, we say f is *undefined* at x, that is, f terminates but has no meaningful value at x. Otherwise we say f is *nonterminating* at x.

Examples of primitive functions
Our intention is to provide FP systems with widely useful and powerful primitive functions rather than weak ones that could then be used to define useful ones. The following examples define some typical primitive functions, many of which are used in later examples of programs. In the following definitions we use a variant of McCarthy's conditional expressions [17]; thus we write

$$p_1 \rightarrow e_1; \ldots ; p_n \rightarrow e_n; e_{n+1}$$

instead of McCarthy's expression

$$(p_1 \rightarrow e_1, \ldots , p_n \rightarrow e_n, T \rightarrow e_{n+1}).$$

The following definitions are to hold for all objects x, x_i, y, y_i, z, z_i:

Selector functions
$$1:x \equiv x=<x_1, \ldots , x_n> \rightarrow x_1; \perp$$

and for any positive integer s

$$s:x \equiv x = <x_1, \ldots , x_n> \& n \geq s \rightarrow x_s; \perp$$

Thus, for example, $3:<A,B,C> = C$ and $2:<A> = \perp$. Note that the function symbols 1, 2, etc. are distinct from the atoms *1, 2*, etc.

Tail
$$tl:x \equiv x=<x_1> \rightarrow \phi;$$
$$x=<x_1, \ldots , x_n> \& n \geq 2 \rightarrow <x_2, \ldots , x_n>; \perp$$

Identity
$$id:x \equiv x$$

Atom

atom: $x \equiv x$ is an atom $\rightarrow T$; $x \neq \perp \rightarrow F$; $\perp$

Equals

eq: $x \equiv x = \langle y, z \rangle$ & $y = z \rightarrow T$; $x = \langle y, z \rangle$ & $y \neq z \rightarrow F$; $\perp$

Null

null: $x \equiv x = \phi \rightarrow T$; $x \neq \perp \rightarrow F$; $\perp$

Reverse

reverse: $x \equiv x = \phi \rightarrow \phi$;

$\qquad x = \langle x_1, \ldots, x_n \rangle \rightarrow \langle x_n, \ldots, x_1 \rangle$; $\perp$

Distribute from left; distribute from right

distl: $x \equiv x = \langle y, \phi \rangle \rightarrow \phi$;

$\qquad x = \langle y, \langle z_1, \ldots, z_n \rangle \rangle \rightarrow \langle \langle y, z_1 \rangle, \ldots, \langle y, z_n \rangle \rangle$; $\perp$

distr: $x \equiv x = \langle \phi, y \rangle \rightarrow \phi$;

$\qquad x = \langle \langle y_1, \ldots, y_n \rangle, z \rangle \rightarrow \langle \langle y_1, z \rangle, \ldots, \langle y_n, z \rangle \rangle$; $\perp$

Length

length: $x \equiv x = \langle x_1, \ldots, x_n \rangle \rightarrow n$; $x = \phi \rightarrow 0$; $\perp$

Add, subtract, multiply, and divide

$+$: $x \equiv x = \langle y, z \rangle$ & y, z are numbers $\rightarrow y + z$; $\perp$

$-$: $x \equiv x = \langle y, z \rangle$ & y, z are numbers $\rightarrow y - z$; $\perp$

$\times$: $x \equiv x = \langle y, z \rangle$ & y, z are numbers $\rightarrow y \times z$; $\perp$

$\div$: $x \equiv x = \langle y, z \rangle$ & y, z are numbers $\rightarrow y \div z$; $\perp$

$\qquad\qquad\qquad\qquad$ (where $y \div 0 = \perp$)

Transpose

trans: $x \equiv x = \langle \phi, \ldots, \phi \rangle \rightarrow \phi$;

$\qquad x = \langle x_1, \ldots, x_n \rangle \rightarrow \langle y_1, \ldots, y_m \rangle$; $\perp$

where

$\qquad x_i = \langle x_{i1}, \ldots, x_{im} \rangle$ and

$\qquad y_j = \langle x_{1j}, \ldots, x_{nj} \rangle$, $1 \leq i \leq n$, $1 \leq j \leq m$.

And, or, not

and: $x \equiv x = \langle T, T \rangle \rightarrow T$;

$\qquad x = \langle T, F \rangle \vee x = \langle F, T \rangle \vee x = \langle F, F \rangle \rightarrow F$; $\perp$

etc.

Append left; append right

apndl: $x \equiv x = \langle y, \phi \rangle \rightarrow \langle y \rangle$;

$\qquad x = \langle y, \langle z_1, \ldots, z_n \rangle \rangle \rightarrow \langle y, z_1, \ldots, z_n \rangle$; $\perp$

apndr: $x \equiv x = \langle \phi, z \rangle \rightarrow \langle z \rangle$;

$\qquad x = \langle \langle y_1, \ldots, y_n \rangle, z \rangle \rightarrow \langle y_1, \ldots, y_n, z \rangle$; $\perp$

Right selectors; Right tail

1r: $x \equiv x = \langle x_1, \ldots, x_n \rangle \rightarrow x_n$; $\perp$

2r: $x \equiv x = \langle x_1, \ldots, x_n \rangle$ & $n \geq 2 \rightarrow x_{n-1}$; $\perp$

etc.

tlr: $x \equiv x = \langle x_1 \rangle \rightarrow \phi$;

$\qquad x = \langle x_1, \ldots, x_n \rangle$ & $n \geq 2 \rightarrow \langle x_1, \ldots, x_{n-1} \rangle$; $\perp$

Rotate left; rotate right

rotl: $x \equiv x = \phi \rightarrow \phi$; $x = \langle x_1 \rangle \rightarrow \langle x_1 \rangle$;

$\qquad x = \langle x_1, \ldots, x_n \rangle$ & $n \geq 2 \rightarrow \langle x_2, \ldots, x_n, x_1 \rangle$; $\perp$

etc.

11.2.4 Functional forms, F. A functional form is an expression denoting a function; that function depends on the functions or objects which are the *parameters* of the expression. Thus, for example, if f and g are any functions, then $f \circ g$ is a functional form, the *composition* of f

and g, f and g are its parameters, and it denotes the function such that, for any object x,

$$(f \circ g) : x = f : (g : x).$$

Some functional forms may have objects as parameters. For example, for any object x, $\bar{x}$ is a functional form, the *constant* function of x, so that for any object y

$$\bar{x} : y \equiv y = \perp \rightarrow \perp; x.$$

In particular, $\perp$ is the everywhere-$\perp$ function.

Below we give some functional forms, many of which are used later in this paper. We use p, f, and g with and without subscripts to denote arbitrary functions; and x, $x_1, \ldots, x_n$, y as arbitrary objects. Square brackets [...] are used to indicate the functional form for *construction*, which denotes a function, whereas pointed brackets $\langle \ldots \rangle$ denote sequences, which are objects. Parentheses are used both in particular functional forms (e.g., in *condition*) and generally to indicate grouping.

Composition

$(f \circ g) : x \equiv f : (g : x)$

Construction

$[f_1, \ldots, f_n] : x \equiv \langle f_1 : x, \ldots, f_n : x \rangle$ (Recall that since $\langle \ldots, \perp, \ldots \rangle = \perp$ and all functions are $\perp$-preserving, so is $[f_1, \ldots, f_n]$.)

Condition

$(p \rightarrow f; g) : x \equiv (p : x) = T \rightarrow f : x$; $(p : x) = F \rightarrow g : x$; $\perp$

Conditional *expressions* (used outside of FP systems to describe their functions) and the *functional form* condition are both identified by "$\rightarrow$". They are quite different although closely related, as shown in the above definitions. But no confusion should arise, since the elements of a conditional expression all denote values, whereas the elements of the functional form condition all denote functions, never values. When no ambiguity arises we omit right-associated parentheses; we write, for example, $p_1 \rightarrow f_1$; $p_2 \rightarrow f_2$; g for $(p_1 \rightarrow f_1; (p_2 \rightarrow f_2; g))$.

Constant (Here x is an object parameter.)

$\bar{x} : y \equiv y = \perp \rightarrow \perp; x$

Insert

$/f : x \equiv x = \langle x_1 \rangle \rightarrow x_1$; $x = \langle x_1, \ldots, x_n \rangle$ & $n \geq 2$

$\qquad\qquad\qquad \rightarrow f : \langle x_1, /f : \langle x_2, \ldots, x_n \rangle \rangle$; $\perp$

If f has a unique right unit $u_f \neq \perp$, where $f : \langle x, u_f \rangle \in \{x, \perp\}$ for all objects x, then the above definition is extended: $/f : \phi = u_f$. Thus

$/+ : \langle 4, 5, 6 \rangle = + : \langle 4, + : \langle 5, /+ : \langle 6 \rangle \rangle \rangle$

$\qquad\qquad\qquad = + : \langle 4, + : \langle 5, 6 \rangle \rangle = 15$

$/+ : \phi = 0$

Apply to all

$\alpha f : x \equiv x = \phi \rightarrow \phi$;

$\qquad x = \langle x_1, \ldots, x_n \rangle \rightarrow \langle f : x_1, \ldots, f : x_n \rangle$; $\perp$

Binary to unary (x is an object parameter)

(bu f x):$y \equiv f$:$<x,y>$

Thus

(bu $+$ 1):$x = 1+x$

While

(while p f):$x \equiv p$:$x=T \rightarrow$ (while p f):(f:x);

$$p:x=F \rightarrow x; \perp$$

The above functional forms provide an effective method for computing the values of the functions they denote (if they terminate) provided one can effectively apply their function parameters.

11.2.5 Definitions. A *definition* in an FP system is an expression of the form

Def $l \equiv r$

where the left side l is an unused function symbol and the right side r is a functional form (which may depend on l). It expresses the fact that the symbol l is to denote the function given by r. Thus the definition **Def** last1 $\equiv$ 1∘reverse defines the function last1 that produces the last element of a sequence (or $\perp$). Similarly,

Def last $\equiv$ null∘tl $\rightarrow$ 1; last∘tl

defines the function last, which is the same as last1. Here in detail is how the definition would be used to compute last:$<1,2>$:

last:$<1,2>$ =
definition of last $\Rightarrow$ (null∘tl $\rightarrow$ 1; last∘tl):$<1,2>$
action of the form ($p \rightarrow f$; g) $\Rightarrow$ last∘tl:$<1,2>$
     since null∘tl:$<1,2>$ = null:$<2>$
     $= F$
action of the form $f \circ g$ $\Rightarrow$ last:(tl:$<1,2>$)
definition of primitive tail $\Rightarrow$ last:$<2>$
definition of last $\Rightarrow$ (null∘tl $\rightarrow$ 1; last∘tl):$<2>$
action of the form ($p \rightarrow f$; g) $\Rightarrow$ 1:$<2>$
     since null∘tl:$<2>$ = null:$\phi = T$
definition of selector 1 $\Rightarrow$ 2

The above illustrates the simple rule: to apply a defined symbol, replace it by the right side of its definition. Of course, some definitions may define nonterminating functions. A set D of definitions is *well formed* if no two left sides are the same.

11.2.6 Semantics. It can be seen from the above that an FP system is determined by choice of the following sets: (a) The set of atoms A (which determines the set of objects). (b) The set of primitive functions P. (c) The set of functional forms F. (d) A well formed set of definitions D. To understand the semantics of such a system one needs to know how to compute f:x for any function f and any object x of the system. There are exactly four possibilities for f:

(1) f is a primitive function;
(2) f is a functional form;
(3) there is one definition in D, **Def** $f \equiv r$; and
(4) none of the above.

If f is a primitive function, then one has its description

and knows how to apply it. If f is a functional form, then the description of the form tells how to compute f:x in terms of the parameters of the form, which can be done by further use of these rules. If f is defined, **Def** $f \equiv r$, as in (3), then to find f:x one computes r:x, which can be done by further use of these rules. If none of these, then f:$x \equiv \perp$. Of course, the use of these rules may not terminate for some f and some x, in which case we assign the value f:$x \equiv \perp$.

11.3 Examples of Functional Programs

The following examples illustrate the functional programming style. Since this style is unfamiliar to most readers, it may cause confusion at first; the important point to remember is that no part of a function definition is a result itself. Instead, each part is a *function* that must be applied to an argument to obtain a result.

11.3.1 Factorial.

Def ! $\equiv$ eq0 $\rightarrow$ $\bar{1}$; $\times$∘[id, !∘sub1]

where

Def eq0 $\equiv$ eq∘[id, $\bar{0}$]
Def sub1 $\equiv$ $-$∘[id, $\bar{1}$]

Here are some of the intermediate expressions an FP system would obtain in evaluating !:2:

!:2 $\Rightarrow$ (eq0 $\rightarrow$ $\bar{1}$; $\times$∘[id, !∘sub1]):2
     $\Rightarrow$ $\times$∘[id, !∘sub1]:2
$\Rightarrow$ $\times$:$<$id:2, !∘sub1:$2>$ $\Rightarrow$ $\times$:<2, !:$1>$
     $\Rightarrow$ $\times$:<2, $\times$:<1, !:$0>>$
$\Rightarrow$ $\times$:<2, $\times$:$<1,\bar{1}$:$0>>$ $\Rightarrow$ $\times$:<2, $\times$:$<1,1>>$
     $\Rightarrow$ $\times$:$<2,1>$ $\Rightarrow$ 2.

In Section 12 we shall see how theorems of the algebra of FP programs can be used to prove that ! is the factorial function.

11.3.2 Inner product. We have seen earlier how this definition works.

Def   IP $\equiv$ ($/+$)∘($\alpha\times$)∘trans

11.3.3 Matrix multiply. This matrix multiplication program yields the product of any pair $<m,n>$ of conformable matrices, where each matrix m is represented as the sequence of its rows:

$m = <m_1, ... , m_r>$
     where $m_i = <m_{i1}, ... , m_{is}>$ for i = 1, ... , r.
Def MM $\equiv$ ($\alpha\alpha$IP)∘(αdistl)∘distr∘[1, trans∘2]

The program MM has four steps, reading from right to left; each is applied in turn, beginning with [1, trans∘2], to the result of its predecessor. If the argument is $<m,n>$, then the first step yields $<m,n'>$ where n' = trans:n. The second step yields $<<m_1,n'>, ... , <m_r,n'>>$, where the m_i are the rows of m. The third step, αdistl, yields

$$<distl:<m_1,n'>, ... , distl:<m_r,n'>> = <p_1, ... , p_r>$$

where

$p_i = \text{distl}:<m_i,n'> = <<m_i,n_1'>, \dots , <m_i,n_s'>>$
$$\text{for } i = 1, \dots , r$$

and n_j' is the jth column of n (the jth row of n'). Thus p_i, a sequence of row and column pairs, corresponds to the i-th product row. The operator $\alpha\alpha\text{IP}$, or $\alpha(\alpha\text{IP})$, causes αIP to be applied to each p_i, which in turn causes IP to be applied to each row and column pair in each p_i. The result of the last step is therefore the sequence of rows comprising the product matrix. If either matrix is not rectangular, or if the length of a row of m differs from that of a column of n, or if any element of m or n is not a number, the result is $\perp$.

This program MM does not name its arguments or any intermediate results; contains no variables, no loops, no control statements nor procedure declarations; has no initialization instructions; is not word-at-a-time in nature; is hierarchically constructed from simpler components; uses generally applicable housekeeping forms and operators (e.g., αf, distl, distr, trans); is perfectly general; yields $\perp$ whenever its argument is inappropriate in any way; does not constrain the order of evaluation unnecessarily (all applications of IP to row and column pairs can be done in parallel or in any order); and, using algebraic laws (see below), can be transformed into more "efficient" or into more "explanatory" programs (e.g., one that is recursively defined). None of these properties hold for the typical von Neumann matrix multiplication program.

Although it has an unfamiliar and hence puzzling form, the program MM describes the essential operations of matrix multiplication without overdetermining the process or obscuring parts of it, as most programs do; hence many straightforward programs for the operation can be obtained from it by formal transformations. It is an inherently inefficient program for von Neumann computers (with regard to the use of space), but efficient ones can be derived from it and realizations of FP systems can be imagined that could execute MM without the prodigal use of space it implies. Efficiency questions are beyond the scope of this paper; let me suggest only that since the language is so simple and does not dictate any binding of lambda-type variables to data, there may be better opportunities for the system to do some kind of "lazy" evaluation [9, 10] and to control data management more efficiently than is possible in lambda-calculus based systems.

11.4 Remarks About FP Systems

11.4.1 FP systems as programming languages. FP
systems are so minimal that some readers may find it difficult to view them as programming languages. Viewed as such, a function f is a program, an object x is the contents of the store, and $f:x$ is the contents of the store after program f is activated with x in the store. The set of definitions is the program library. The primitive functions and the functional forms provided by the system are the basic statements of a particular programming language. Thus, depending on the choice of prim-

itive functions and functional forms, the FP framework provides for a large class of languages with various styles and capabilities. The algebra of programs associated with each of these depends on its particular set of functional forms. The primitive functions, functional forms, and programs given in this paper comprise an effort to develop just one of these possible styles.

11.4.2 Limitations of FP systems. FP systems have
a number of limitations. For example, a given FP system is a fixed language; it is not history sensitive: no program can alter the library of programs. It can treat input and output only in the sense that x is an input and $f:x$ is the output. If the set of primitive functions and functional forms is weak, it may not be able to express every computable function.

An FP system cannot compute a program since function expressions are not objects. Nor can one define new functional forms within an FP system. (Both of these limitations are removed in formal functional programming (FFP) systems in which objects "represent" functions.) Thus no FP system can have a function, apply, such that

$$\text{apply}:<x,y> \equiv x:y$$

because, on the left, x is an object, and, on the right, x is a function. (Note that we have been careful to keep the set of function symbols and the set of objects distinct: thus 1 is a function symbol, and l is an object.)

The primary limitation of FP systems is that they are not history sensitive. Therefore they must be extended somehow before they can become practically useful. For discussion of such extensions, see the sections on FFP and AST systems (Sections 13 and 14).

11.4.3 Expressive power of FP systems. Suppose two
FP systems, FP_1 and FP_2, both have the same set of objects and the same set of primitive functions, but the set of functional forms of FP_1 properly includes that of FP_2. Suppose also that both systems can express all computable functions on objects. Nevertheless, we can say that FP_1 is more expressive than FP_2, since every function expression in FP_2 can be duplicated in FP_1, but by using a functional form not belonging to FP_2, FP_1 can express some functions more directly and easily than FP_2.

I believe the above observation could be developed into a theory of the expressive power of languages in which a language A would be *more expressive* than language B under the following roughly stated conditions. First, form all possible functions of all types in A by applying all existing functions to objects and to each other in all possible ways until no new function of any type can be formed. (The set of objects is a type; the set of continuous functions $[T \rightarrow U]$ from type T to type U is a type. If $f \in [T \rightarrow U]$ and $t \in T$, then ft in U can be formed by applying f to t.) Do the same in language B. Next, compare each type in A to the corresponding type in B. If, for every type, A's type includes B's corresponding

type, then A is more expressive than B (or equally expressive). If some type of A's functions is incomparable to B's, then A and B are not comparable in expressive power.

11.4.4 Advantages of FP systems. The main reason FP systems are considerably simpler than either conventional languages or lambda-calculus-based languages is that they use only the most elementary fixed naming system (naming a function in a definition) with a simple fixed rule of substituting a function for its name. Thus they avoid the complexities both of the naming systems of conventional languages and of the substitution rules of the lambda calculus. FP systems permit the definition of different naming systems (see Sections 13.3.4 and 14.7) for various purposes. These need not be complex, since many programs can do without them completely. Most importantly, they treat names as functions that can be combined with other functions without special treatment.

FP systems offer an escape from conventional word-at-a-time programming to a degree greater even than APL [12] (the most successful attack on the problem to date within the von Neumann framework) because they provide a more powerful set of functional forms within a unified world of expressions. They offer the opportunity to develop higher level techniques for thinking about, manipulating, and writing programs.

12. The Algebra of Programs for FP Systems

12.1 Introduction

The algebra of the programs described below is the work of an amateur in algebra, and I want to show that it is a game amateurs can profitably play and enjoy, a game that does not require a deep understanding of logic and mathematics. In spite of its simplicity, it can help one to understand and prove things about programs in a systematic, rather mechanical way.

So far, proving a program correct requires knowledge of some moderately heavy topics in mathematics and logic: properties of complete partially ordered sets, continuous functions, least fixed points of functionals, the first-order predicate calculus, predicate transformers, weakest preconditions, to mention a few topics in a few approaches to proving programs correct. These topics have been very useful for professionals who make it their business to devise proof techniques; they have published a lot of beautiful work on this subject, starting with the work of McCarthy and Floyd, and, more recently, that of Burstall, Dijkstra, Manna and his associates, Milner, Morris, Reynolds, and many others. Much of this work is based on the foundations laid down by Dana Scott (denotational semantics) and C. A. R. Hoare (axiomatic semantics). But its theoretical level places it beyond the scope of most amateurs who work outside of this specialized field.

If the average programmer is to prove his programs

correct, he will need much simpler techniques than those the professionals have so far put forward. The algebra of programs below may be one starting point for such a proof discipline and, coupled with current work on algebraic manipulation, it may also help provide a basis for automating some of that discipline.

One advantage of this algebra over other proof techniques is that the programmer can use his programming language as the language for deriving proofs, rather than having to state proofs in a separate logical system that merely talks *about* his programs.

At the heart of the algebra of programs are laws and theorems that state that one function expression is the same as another. Thus the law $[f,g] \circ h \equiv [f \circ h, g \circ h]$ says that the construction of f and g (composed with h) is the same function as the construction of (f composed with h) and (g composed with h) no matter what the functions f, g, and h are. Such laws are easy to understand, easy to justify, and easy and powerful to use. However, we also wish to use such laws to solve equations in which an "unknown" function appears on both sides of the equation. The problem is that if f satisfies some such equation, it will often happen that some extension f' of f will also satisfy the same equation. Thus, to give a unique meaning to solutions of such equations, we shall require a foundation for the algebra of programs (which uses Scott's notion of least fixed points of continuous functionals) to assure us that solutions obtained by algebraic manipulation are indeed least, and hence unique, solutions.

Our goal is to develop a foundation for the algebra of programs that disposes of the theoretical issues, so that a programmer can use simple algebraic laws and one or two theorems from the foundations to solve problems and create proofs in the same mechanical style we use to solve high-school algebra problems, and so that he can do so without knowing anything about least fixed points or predicate transformers.

One particular foundational problem arises: given equations of the form

$$f \equiv p_0 \to q_0; \dots; p_i \to q_i; E_i(f), \qquad (1)$$

where the p_i's and q_i's are functions not involving f and $E_i(f)$ is a function expression involving f, the laws of the algebra will often permit the formal "extension" of this equation by one more "clause" by deriving

$$E_i(f) \equiv p_{i+1} \to q_{i+1}; E_{i+1}(f) \qquad (2)$$

which, by replacing $E_i(f)$ in (1) by the right side of (2), yields

$$f \equiv p_0 \to q_0; \dots; p_{i+1} \to q_{i+1}; E_{i+1}(f). \qquad (3)$$

This formal extension may go on without limit. One question the foundations must then answer is: when can the least f satisfying (1) be represented by the infinite expansion

$$f \equiv p_0 \to q_0; \dots; p_n \to q_n; \dots \qquad (4)$$

in which the final clause involving f has been dropped,

so that we now have a solution whose right side is free of f's? Such solutions are helpful in two ways: first, they give proofs of "termination" in the sense that (4) means that $f:x$ is defined if and only if there is an n such that, for every i less than n, $p_i:x = F$ and $p_n:x = T$ and $q_n:x$ is defined. Second, (4) gives a case-by-case description of f that can often clarify its behavior.

The foundations for the algebra given in a subsequent section are a modest start toward the goal stated above. For a limited class of equations its "linear expansion theorem" gives a useful answer as to when one can go from indefinitely extendable equations like (1) to infinite expansions like (4). For a larger class of equations, a more general "expansion theorem" gives a less helpful answer to similar questions. Hopefully, more powerful theorems covering additional classes of equations can be found. But for the present, one need only know the conclusions of these two simple foundational theorems in order to follow the theorems and examples appearing in this section.

The results of the foundations subsection are summarized in a separate, earlier subsection titled "expansion theorems," without reference to fixed point concepts. The foundations subsection itself is placed later where it can be skipped by readers who do not want to go into that subject.

12.2 Some Laws of the Algebra of Programs

In the algebra of programs for an FP system variables range over the set of functions of the system. The "operations" of the algebra are the functional forms of the system. Thus, for example, $[f,g] \circ h$ is an expression of the algebra for the FP system described above, in which f, g, and h are variables denoting arbitrary functions of that system. And

$$[f,g] \circ h \equiv [f \circ h, g \circ h]$$

is a law of the algebra which says that, whatever functions one chooses for f, g, and h, the function on the left is the same as that on the right. Thus this algebraic law is merely a restatement of the following proposition about any FP system that includes the functional forms $[f,g]$ and $f \circ g$:

PROPOSITION: For all functions f, g, and h and all objects x, $([f,g] \circ h):x \equiv [f \circ h, g \circ h]:x$.
PROOF:
$([f,g] \circ h):x = [f,g]:(h:x)$
　　　　　　　by definition of composition
$= <f:(h:x), g:(h:x)>$
　　　　　　　by definition of construction
$= <(f \circ h):x, (g \circ h):x>$
　　　　　　　by definition of composition
$= [f \circ h, g \circ h]:x$
　　　　　　　by definition of construction　□

Some laws have a domain smaller than the domain of all objects. Thus $1 \circ [f,g] \equiv f$ does not hold for objects x such that $g:x = \bot$. We write

$$\text{defined} \circ g \longrightarrow 1 \circ [f,g] \equiv f$$

to indicate that the law (or theorem) on the right holds within the domain of objects x for which defined $\circ g:x = T$. Where

Def defined $\equiv \bar{T}$

i.e. defined$:x \equiv x = \bot \rightarrow \bot; T$. In general we shall write a *qualified functional equation*:

$$p \longrightarrow f \equiv g$$

to mean that, for any object x, whenever $p:x = T$, then $f:x = g:x$.

Ordinary algebra concerns itself with two operations, addition and multiplication; it needs few laws. The algebra of programs is concerned with more operations (functional forms) and therefore needs more laws.

Each of the following laws requires a corresponding proposition to validate it. The interested reader will find most proofs of such propositions easy (two are given below). We first define the usual ordering on functions and equivalence in terms of this ordering:

DEFINITION $f \leq g$ iff for all objects x, either $f:x = \bot$, or $f:x = g:x$.
DEFINITION $f \equiv g$ iff $f \leq g$ and $g \leq f$.

It is easy to verify that $\leq$ is a partial ordering, that $f \leq g$ means g is an extension of f, and that $f \equiv g$ iff $f:x = g:x$ for all objects x. We now give a list of algebraic laws organized by the two principal functional forms involved.

I　Composition and construction
I.1　　$[f_1, \ldots, f_n] \circ g \equiv [f_1 \circ g, \ldots, f_n \circ g]$
I.2　　$\alpha f \circ [g_1, \ldots, g_n] \equiv [f \circ g_1, \ldots, f \circ g_n]$
I.3　　$/f \circ [g_1, \ldots, g_n]$
　　　　　$\equiv f \circ [g_1, /f \circ [g_2, \ldots, g_n]]$　　when n≥2
　　　　　$\equiv f \circ [g_1, f \circ [g_2, \ldots, f \circ [g_{n-1}, g_n] \ldots]]$
　　　　$/f \circ [g] \equiv g$
I.4　　$f \circ [\bar{x}, g] \equiv (\text{bu } f\ x) \circ g$
I.5　　$1 \circ [f_1, \ldots, f_n] \leq f_1$
　　　　$s \circ [f_1, \ldots, f_s, \ldots, f_n] \leq f_s$ for any selector s, s≤n
　　　　defined$\circ f_i$ (for all i≠s, 1≤i≤n) $\rightarrow \rightarrow$
　　　　　　　　　　　　　　　　　$s \circ [f_1, \ldots, f_n] \equiv f_s$
I.5.1　$[f_1 \circ 1, \ldots, f_n \circ n] \circ [g_1, \ldots, g_n] \equiv [f_1 \circ g_1, \ldots, f_n \circ g_n]$
I.6　　$\text{tl} \circ [f_1] \leq \bar{\phi}$ and
　　　　　　　$\text{tl} \circ [f_1, \ldots, f_n] \leq [f_2, \ldots, f_n]$　for n≥2
　　　　defined$\circ f_1 \rightarrow \rightarrow \text{tl} \circ [f_1] \equiv \bar{\phi}$
　　　　　and $\text{tl} \circ [f_1, \ldots, f_n] \equiv [f_2, \ldots, f_n]$ for n≥2
I.7　　$\text{distl} \circ [f, [g_1, \ldots, g_n]] \equiv [[f,g_1], \ldots, [f,g_n]]$
　　　　defined$\circ f \rightarrow \rightarrow \text{distl} \circ [f,\bar{\phi}] \equiv \bar{\phi}$
　　　　The analogous law holds for distr.
I.8　　$\text{apndl} \circ [f, [g_1, \ldots, g_n]] \equiv [f,g_1, \ldots, g_n]$
　　　　$\text{null} \circ g \rightarrow \rightarrow \text{apndl} \circ [f,g] \equiv [f]$
And so on for apndr, reverse, rotl, etc.
I.9　　$[\ldots, \bot, \ldots] \equiv \bot$
I.10　$\text{apndl} \circ [f \circ g, \alpha f \circ h] \equiv \alpha f \circ \text{apndl} \circ [g,h]$
I.11　$\text{pair \& not} \circ \text{null} \circ 1 \longrightarrow$
　　　　　$\text{apndl} \circ [[1 \circ 1,2], \text{distr} \circ [\text{tl} \circ 1,2]] \equiv \text{distr}$

Where $f \& g \equiv \text{and} \circ [f, g]$;
$$\text{pair} \equiv \text{atom} \rightarrow \bar{F}; \text{eq} \circ [\text{length}, \bar{2}]$$

II   Composition and condition (right associated parentheses omitted) (Law II.2 is noted in Manna et al. [16], p. 493.)

II.1 $(p \rightarrow f; g) \circ h \equiv p \circ h \rightarrow f \circ h; g \circ h$

II.2 $h \circ (p \rightarrow f; g) \equiv p \rightarrow h \circ f; h \circ g$

II.3 $\text{or} \circ [q, \text{not} \circ q] \rightarrow\!\!\!\rightarrow \text{and} \circ [p, q] \rightarrow f;$
   $\text{and} \circ [p, \text{not} \circ q] \rightarrow g; h \equiv p \rightarrow (q \rightarrow f; g); h$

II.3.1 $p \rightarrow (p \rightarrow f; g); h \equiv p \rightarrow f; h$

III   Composition and miscellaneous

III.1 $\bar{x} \circ f \leq \bar{x}$
   $\text{defined} \circ f \rightarrow\!\!\!\rightarrow \bar{x} \circ f \equiv \bar{x}$

III.1.1 $\bar{\perp} \circ f \equiv f \circ \bar{\perp} \equiv \bar{\perp}$

III.2 $f \circ \text{id} \equiv \text{id} \circ f \equiv f$

III.3 $\text{pair} \rightarrow\!\!\!\rightarrow 1 \circ \text{distr} \equiv [1 \circ 1, 2]$ also:
$$\text{pair} \rightarrow\!\!\!\rightarrow 1 \circ \text{tl} \equiv 2 \quad \text{etc.}$$

III.4 $\alpha(f \circ g) \equiv \alpha f \circ \alpha g$

III.5 $\text{null} \circ g \rightarrow\!\!\!\rightarrow \alpha f \circ g \equiv \bar{\phi}$

IV   Condition and construction

IV.1 $[f_1, \ldots, (p \rightarrow g; h), \ldots, f_n]$
   $\equiv p \rightarrow [f_1, \ldots, g, \ldots, f_n]; [f_1, \ldots, h, \ldots, f_n]$

IV.1.1 $[f_1, \ldots, (p_1 \rightarrow g_1; \ldots; p_n \rightarrow g_n; h), \ldots, f_m]$
   $\equiv p_1 \rightarrow [f_1, \ldots, g_1, \ldots, f_m];$
   $\ldots; p_n \rightarrow [f_1, \ldots, g_n, \ldots, f_m]; [f_1, \ldots, h, \ldots, f_m]$

This concludes the present list of algebraic laws; it is by no means exhaustive, there are many others.

Proof of two laws

We give the proofs of validating propositions for laws I.10 and I.11, which are slightly more involved than most of the others.

PROPOSITION 1

$$\text{apndl} \circ [f \circ g, \alpha f \circ h] \equiv \alpha f \circ \text{apndl} \circ [g, h]$$
PROOF. We show that, for every object x, both of the above functions yield the same result.
CASE 1. $h:x$ is neither a sequence nor ϕ.
Then both sides yield $\perp$ when applied to x.
CASE 2. $h:x = \phi$. Then
$\text{apndl} \circ [f \circ g, \alpha f \circ h]: x$
   $= \text{apndl}: <f \circ g:x, \phi> = <f:(g:x)>$
$\alpha f \circ \text{apndl} \circ [g, h]: x$
   $= \alpha f \circ \text{apndl}: <g:x, \phi> = \alpha f: <g:x>$
   $= <f:(g:x)>$
CASE 3. $h:x = <y_1, \ldots, y_n>$. Then
$\text{apndl} \circ [f \circ g, \alpha f \circ h]: x$
   $= \text{apndl}: <f \circ g:x, \alpha f: <y_1, \ldots, y_n>>$
   $= <f:(g:x), f:y_1, \ldots, f:y_n>$
$\alpha f \circ \text{apndl} \circ [g, h]: x$
   $= \alpha f \circ \text{apndl}: <g:x, <y_1, \ldots, y_n>>$
      $= \alpha f: <g:x, y_1, \ldots, y_n>$
   $= <f:(g:x), f:y_1, \ldots, f:y_n>$ □

PROPOSITION 2

Pair & $\text{not} \circ \text{null} \circ 1 \rightarrow\!\!\!\rightarrow$
$$\text{apndl} \circ [[1^2, 2], \text{distr} \circ [t1 \circ 1, 2]] \equiv \text{distr}$$
where $f \& g$ is the function: $\text{and} \circ [f, g]$, and $f^2 \equiv f \circ f$.
PROOF. We show that both sides produce the same result when applied to any pair $<x, y>$, where $x \neq \phi$, as per the stated qualification.
CASE 1. x is an atom or $\perp$. Then distr: $<x, y> = \perp$, since $x \neq \phi$. The left side also yields $\perp$ when applied to $<x, y>$, since $t1 \circ 1: <x, y> = \perp$ and all functions are $\perp$-preserving.
CASE 2. $x = <x_1, \ldots, x_n>$. Then

$\text{apndl} \circ [[1^2, 2], \text{distr} \circ [tl \circ 1, 2]]: <x, y>$
   $= \text{apndl}: <<1:x, y>, \text{distr}: <tl:x, y>>$
   $= \text{apndl}: <<x_1, y>, \phi> = <<x_1, y>>$ if $tl:x = \phi$
   $= \text{apndl}: <<x_1, y>, <<x_2, y>, \ldots, <x_n, y>>>$
      if $tl:x \neq \phi$
   $= <<x_1, y>, \ldots, <x_n, y>>$
$= \text{distr}: <x, y>$ □

12.3 Example: Equivalence of Two Matrix Multiplication Programs

We have seen earlier the matrix multiplication program:

Def $MM \equiv \alpha\alpha IP \circ \alpha\text{distl} \circ \text{distr} \circ [1, \text{trans} \circ 2]$.

We shall now show that its initial segment, MM', where

Def $MM' \equiv \alpha\alpha IP \circ \alpha\text{distl} \circ \text{distr}$,

can be defined recursively. (MM' "multiplies" a pair of matrices after the second matrix has been transposed. Note that MM', unlike MM, gives $\perp$ for all arguments that are not pairs.) That is, we shall show that MM' satisfies the following equation which recursively defines the same function (on pairs):

$$f \equiv \text{null} \circ 1 \rightarrow \bar{\phi}; \text{apndl} \circ [\alpha IP \circ \text{distl} \circ [1 \circ 1, 2], f \circ [tl \circ 1, 2]].$$

Our proof will take the form of showing that the following function, R,

Def $R \equiv \text{null} \circ 1 \rightarrow \bar{\phi};$
   $\text{apndl} \circ [\alpha IP \circ \text{distl} \circ [1 \circ 1, 2], MM' \circ [tl \circ 1, 2]]$

is, for all pairs $<x, y>$, the same function as MM'. R "multiplies" two matrices, when the first has more than zero rows, by computing the first row of the "product" (with $\alpha IP \circ \text{distl} \circ [1 \circ 1, 2]$) and adjoining it to the "product" of the tail of the first matrix and the second matrix. Thus the theorem we want is

$$\text{pair} \rightarrow\!\!\!\rightarrow MM' \equiv R,$$

from which the following is immediate:

$$MM \equiv MM' \circ [1, \text{trans} \circ 2] \equiv R \circ [1, \text{trans} \circ 2];$$

where

Def $\text{pair} \equiv \text{atom} \rightarrow \bar{F}; \text{eq} \circ [\text{length}, \bar{2}]$.

THEOREM: $\text{pair} \rightarrow\!\!\!\rightarrow MM' \equiv R$
where

Def $MM' \equiv \alpha\alpha IP \circ \alpha distl \circ distr$

Def $R \equiv null \circ 1 \rightarrow \bar{\phi};$
$$apndl \circ [\alpha IP \circ distl \circ [1^2, 2], MM' \circ [tl \circ 1, 2]]$$

PROOF.

CASE 1. $pair \& null \circ 1 \rightarrowtail MM' \equiv R.$

$pair \& null \circ 1 \rightarrowtail R \equiv \bar{\phi}$ by def of R
$pair \& null \circ 1 \rightarrowtail MM' \equiv \bar{\phi}$
                    since $distr: <\phi, x> = \phi$ by def of distr
and $\alpha f{:}\phi = \phi$ by def of Apply to all.
And so: $\alpha\alpha IP \circ \alpha distl \circ distr: <\phi, x> = \phi.$
Thus $pair \& null \circ 1 \rightarrowtail MM' \equiv R.$
CASE 2. $pair \& not \circ null \circ 1 \rightarrowtail MM' \equiv R.$

$$pair \& not \circ null \circ 1 \rightarrowtail R \equiv R', \tag{1}$$

by def of R and R', where

Def $R' \equiv apndl \circ [\alpha IP \circ distl \circ [1^2, 2], MM' \circ [tl \circ 1, 2]].$

We note that

$$R' \equiv apndl \circ [f \circ g, \alpha f \circ h]$$

where

$f \equiv \alpha IP \circ distl$
$g \equiv [1^2, 2]$
$h \equiv distr \circ [tl \circ 1, 2]$
$$\alpha f \equiv \alpha(\alpha IP \circ distl) \equiv \alpha\alpha IP \circ \alpha distl \quad \text{(by III.4).} \tag{2}$$

Thus, by I.10,

$$R' \equiv \alpha f \circ apndl \circ [g, h]. \tag{3}$$

Now $apndl \circ [g, h] \equiv apndl \circ [[1^2, 2], distr \circ [tl \circ 1, 2]],$
thus, by I.11,

$$pair \& not \circ null \circ 1 \rightarrowtail apndl \circ [g, h] \equiv distr. \tag{4}$$

And so we have, by (1), (2), (3) and (4),

$pair \& not \circ null \circ 1 \rightarrowtail R \equiv R'$
        $\equiv \alpha f \circ distr \equiv \alpha\alpha IP \circ \alpha distl \circ distr \equiv MM'.$

Case 1 and Case 2 together prove the theorem.   □

12.4 Expansion Theorems

In the following subsections we shall be "solving" some simple equations (where by a "solution" we shall mean the "least" function which satisfies an equation). To do so we shall need the following notions and results drawn from the later subsection on foundations of the algebra, where their proofs appear.

12.4.1 Expansion. Suppose we have an equation of the form

$$f \equiv E(f) \tag{E1}$$

where $E(f)$ is an expression involving f. Suppose further that there is an infinite sequence of functions f_i for $i = 0, 1, 2, \ldots$, each having the following form:

$f_0 \equiv \bar{\bot}$
$f_{i+1} \equiv p_0 \rightarrow q_0; \ldots ; p_i \rightarrow q_i; \bar{\bot} \tag{E2}$

where the p_i's and q_i's are particular functions, so that E has the property:

$$E(f_i) \equiv f_{i+1} \quad \text{for i = 0, 1, 2, \ldots} \tag{E3}$$

Then we say that E is *expansive* and has the f_i's as *approximating functions*.

If E is expansive and has approximating functions as in (E2), and if f is the solution of (E1), then f can be written as the infinite expansion

$$f \equiv p_0 \rightarrow q_0; \ldots ; p_n \rightarrow q_n; \ldots \tag{E4}$$

meaning that, for any x, $f{:}x \neq \bot$ iff there is an $n \geq 0$ such that (a) $p_i{:}x = F$ for all $i < n$, and (b) $p_n{:}x = T$, and (c) $q_n{:}x \neq \bot$. When $f{:}x \neq \bot$, then $f{:}x = q_n{:}x$ for this n. (The foregoing is a consequence of the "expansion theorem".)

12.4.2 Linear expansion. A more helpful tool for solving some equations applies when, for any function h,

$$E(h) \equiv p_0 \rightarrow q_0; E_1(h) \tag{LE1}$$

and there exist p_i and q_i such that

$$E_1(p_i \rightarrow q_i; h) \equiv p_{i+1} \rightarrow q_{i+1}; E_1(h)$$
$$\text{for i = 0, 1, 2, \ldots} \tag{LE2}$$

and

$$E_1(\bar{\bot}) \equiv \bar{\bot}. \tag{LE3}$$

Under the above conditions E is said to be *linearly expansive*. If so, and f is the solution of

$$f \equiv E(f) \tag{LE4}$$

then E is expansive and f can again be written as the infinite expansion

$$f \equiv p_0 \rightarrow q_0; \ldots ; p_n \rightarrow q_n; \ldots \tag{LE5}$$

using the p_i's and q_i's generated by (LE1) and (LE2).

Although the p_i's and q_i's of (E4) or (LE5) are not unique for a given function, it may be possible to find additional constraints which would make them so, in which case the expansion (LE5) would comprise a canonical form for a function. Even without uniqueness these expansions often permit one to prove the equivalence of two different function expressions, and they often clarify a function's behavior.

12.5 A Recursion Theorem

Using three of the above laws and linear expansion, one can prove the following theorem of moderate generality that gives a clarifying expansion for many recursively defined functions.

RECURSION THEOREM: Let f be a solution of

$$f \equiv p \rightarrow g; Q(f) \tag{1}$$

where

$$Q(k) \equiv h \circ [i, k \circ j] \quad \text{for any function } k \tag{2}$$

and p, g, h, i, j are any given functions, then

$$f \equiv p \rightarrow g; p\circ j \rightarrow Q(g); \dots ; p\circ j^n \rightarrow Q^n(g); \dots \quad (3)$$

(where $Q^n(g)$ is $h\circ[i, Q^{n-1}(g)\circ j]$, and j^n is $j\circ j^{n-1}$ for $n \geq 2$) and

$$Q^n(g) \equiv /h \circ [i, i\circ j, \dots , i\circ j^{n-1}, g\circ j^n]. \quad (4)$$

PROOF. We verify that $p \rightarrow g; Q(f)$ is linearly expansive. Let p_n, q_n and k be any functions. Then

$$Q(p_n \rightarrow q_n; k)$$
$$\equiv h\circ[i, (p_n \rightarrow q_n; k)\circ j] \quad \text{by (2)}$$
$$\equiv h\circ[i, (p_n\circ j \rightarrow q_n\circ j; k\circ j)] \quad \text{by II.1}$$
$$\equiv h\circ(p_n\circ j \rightarrow [i, q_n\circ j]; [i, k\circ j]) \quad \text{by IV.1}$$
$$\equiv p_n\circ j \rightarrow h\circ[i, q_n\circ j]; h\circ[i, k\circ j] \quad \text{by II.2}$$
$$\equiv p_n\circ j \rightarrow Q(q_n); Q(k) \quad \text{by (2)} \quad (5)$$

Thus if $p_0 \equiv p$ and $q_0 \equiv g$, then (5) gives $p_1 \equiv p\circ j$ and $q_1 = Q(g)$ and in general gives the following functions satisfying (LE2)

$$p_n \equiv p\circ j^n \quad \text{and} \quad q_n \equiv Q^n(g). \quad (6)$$

Finally,

$$Q(\bar{\perp}) \equiv h\circ[i, \bar{\perp}\circ j]$$
$$\equiv h\circ[i, \bar{\perp}] \quad \text{by III.1.1}$$
$$\equiv h\circ\bar{\perp} \quad \text{by I.9}$$
$$\equiv \bar{\perp} \quad \text{by III.1.1.} \quad (7)$$

Thus (5) and (6) verify (LE2) and (7) verifies (LE3), with $E_1 \equiv Q$. If we let $E(f) \equiv p \rightarrow g; Q(f)$, then we have (LE1); thus E is linearly expansive. Since f is a solution of $f \equiv E(f)$, conclusion (3) follows from (6) and (LE5). Now

$$Q^n(g) \equiv h\circ[i, Q^{n-1}(g)\circ j]$$
$$\equiv h\circ[i, h\circ[i\circ j, \dots , h\circ[i\circ j^{n-1}, g\circ j^n] \dots]]$$
$$\text{by I.1, repeatedly}$$
$$\equiv /h\circ[i, i\circ j, \dots , i\circ j^{n-1}, g\circ j^n] \quad \text{by I.3} \quad (8)$$

Result (8) is the second conclusion (4). □

12.5.1 Example: correctness proof of a recursive factorial function. Let f be a solution of

$$f \equiv eq0 \rightarrow \bar{1}; \times\circ[\text{id}, f\circ s]$$

where

Def $s \equiv -\circ[\text{id}, \bar{1}]$ (subtract 1).

Then f satisfies the hypothesis of the recursion theorem with $p \equiv eq0$, $g \equiv \bar{1}$, $h \equiv \times$, $i \equiv \text{id}$, and $j \equiv s$. Therefore

$$f \equiv eq0 \rightarrow \bar{1}; \dots ; eq0\circ s^n \rightarrow Q^n(\bar{1}); \dots$$

and

$$Q^n(\bar{1}) \equiv /\times \circ [\text{id}, \text{id}\circ s, \dots , \text{id}\circ s^{n-1}, \bar{1}\circ s^n].$$

Now $\text{id}\circ s^k \equiv s^k$ by III.2 and $eq0\circ s^n \longrightarrow \bar{1}\circ s^n \equiv \bar{1}$ by III.1, since $eq0\circ s^n{:}x$ implies defined$\circ s^n{:}x$; and also $eq0\circ s^n{:}x \equiv eq0{:}(x-n) \equiv x{=}n$. Thus if $eq0\circ s^n{:}x = T$, then $x = n$ and

$$Q^n(\bar{1}): n = n \times (n-1) \times \dots \times (n - (n-1))$$
$$\times (\bar{1}: (n-n)) = n!.$$

Using these results for $\bar{1}\circ s^n$, $eq0\circ s^n$, and $Q^n(\bar{1})$ in the previous expansion for f, we obtain

$$f{:}x \equiv x{=}0 \rightarrow \bar{1}; \dots ; x{=}n$$
$$\rightarrow n \times (n-1) \times \dots \times 1 \times 1; \dots$$

Thus we have proved that f terminates on precisely the set of nonnegative integers and that it is the factorial function thereon.

12.6 An Iteration Theorem

This is really a corollary of the recursion theorem. It gives a simple expansion for many iterative programs.

ITERATION THEOREM: Let f be the solution (i.e., the least solution) of

$$f \equiv p \rightarrow g; h\circ f\circ k$$

then

$$f \equiv p \rightarrow g; p\circ k \rightarrow h\circ g\circ k; \dots ; p\circ k^n \rightarrow h^n\circ g\circ k^n; \dots$$

PROOF. Let $h' \equiv h\circ 2$, $i' \equiv \text{id}$, $j' \equiv k$, then

$$f \equiv p \rightarrow g; h'\circ[i', f\circ j']$$

since $h\circ 2\circ[\text{id}, f\circ k] \equiv h\circ f\circ k$ by I.5 (id is defined except for $\perp$, and the equation holds for $\perp$). Thus the recursion theorem gives

$$f \equiv p \rightarrow g; \dots ; p\circ k^n \rightarrow Q^n(g); \dots$$

where

$$Q^n(g) \equiv h\circ 2\circ[\text{id}, Q^{n-1}(g)\circ k]$$
$$\equiv h\circ Q^{n-1}(g)\circ k \equiv h^n\circ g\circ k^n$$
by I.5 □

12.6.1 Example: Correctness proof for an iterative factorial function. Let f be the solution of

$$f \equiv eq0\circ 1 \rightarrow 2; f\circ[s\circ 1, \times]$$

where **Def** $s \equiv -\circ[\text{id}, \bar{1}]$ (substract 1). We want to prove that $f{:}<x,1> = x!$ iff x is a nonnegative integer. Let $p \equiv eq0\circ 1$, $g \equiv 2$, $h \equiv \text{id}$, $k \equiv [s\circ 1, \times]$. Then

$$f \equiv p \rightarrow g; h\circ f\circ k$$

and so

$$f \equiv p \rightarrow g; \dots ; p\circ k^n \rightarrow g\circ k^n; \dots \quad (1)$$

by the iteration theorem, since $h^n \equiv \text{id}$. We want to show that

$$\text{pair} \longrightarrow k^n \equiv [a_n, b_n] \quad (2)$$

holds for every $n \geq 1$, where

$$a_n \equiv s^n\circ 1 \quad (3)$$
$$b_n \equiv /\times \circ [s^{n-1}\circ 1, \dots , s\circ 1, 1, 2] \quad (4)$$

Now (2) holds for $n = 1$ by definition of k. We assume it holds for some $n \geq 1$ and prove it then holds for $n + 1$. Now

$$\text{pair} \longrightarrow k^{n+1} \equiv k\circ k^n \equiv [s\circ 1, \times]\circ[a_n, b_n] \quad (5)$$

since (2) holds for n. And so

pair $\longrightarrow k^{n+1} \equiv [s \circ a_n, \times \circ [a_n, b_n]]$ by I.1 and I.5   (6)

To pass from (5) to (6) we must check that whenever a_n or b_n yield $\bot$ in (5), so will the right side of (6). Now

$$s \circ a_n \equiv s^{n+1} \circ 1 \equiv a_{n+1} \tag{7}$$
$$\times \circ [a_n, b_n] \equiv / \times \circ [s^n \circ 1, s^{n-1} \circ 1, \ldots, s \circ 1, 1, 2]$$
$$\equiv b_{n+1} \text{ by I.3.} \tag{8}$$

Combining (6), (7), and (8) gives

pair $\longrightarrow k^{n+1} \equiv [a_{n+1}, b_{n+1}]$.   (9)

Thus (2) holds for n = 1 and holds for n + 1 whenever it holds for n, therefore, by induction, it holds for every n ≥ 1. Now (2) gives, for pairs:

$$\text{defined} \circ k^n \longrightarrow p \circ k^n \equiv \text{eq} 0 \circ 1 \circ [a_n, b_n]$$
$$\equiv \text{eq} 0 \circ a_n \equiv \text{eq} 0 \circ s^n \circ 1 \tag{10}$$
$$\text{defined} \circ k^n \longrightarrow g \circ k^n$$
$$\equiv 2 \circ [a_n, b_n] \equiv / \times \circ [s^{n-1} \circ 1, \ldots, s \circ 1, 1, 2] \tag{11}$$

(both use I.5). Now (1) tells us that $f:<x,1>$ is defined iff there is an n such that $p \circ k^i:<x,1> = F$ for all i < n, and $p \circ k^n:<x,1> = T$, that is, by (10), $\text{eq} 0 \circ s^n:x = T$, i.e., $x=n$; and $g \circ k^n:<x,1>$ is defined, in which case, by (11),

$$f:<x,1> = / \times:<1, 2, \ldots, x-1, x, 1> = n!,$$

which is what we set out to prove.

12.6.2 Example: proof of equivalence of two iterative programs. In this example we want to prove that two iteratively defined programs, f and g, are the same function. Let f be the solution of

$$f \equiv p \circ 1 \to 2; h \circ f \circ [k \circ 1, 2]. \tag{1}$$

Let g be the solution of

$$g \equiv p \circ 1 \to 2; g \circ [k \circ 1, h \circ 2]. \tag{2}$$

Then, by the iteration theorem:

$$f \equiv p_0 \to q_0; \ldots; p_n \to q_n; \ldots \tag{3}$$
$$g \equiv p_0' \to q_0'; \ldots; p_n' \to q_n'; \ldots \tag{4}$$

where (letting $r^0 \equiv \text{id}$ for any r), for n = 0, 1, ...

$$p_n \equiv p \circ 1 \circ [k \circ 1, 2]^n \equiv p \circ 1 \circ [k^n \circ 1, 2] \quad \text{by I.5.1} \tag{5}$$
$$q_n \equiv h^n \circ 2 \circ [k \circ 1, 2]^n \equiv h^n \circ 2 \circ [k^n \circ 1, 2] \quad \text{by I.5.1} \tag{6}$$
$$p_n' \equiv p \circ 1 \circ [k \circ 1, h \circ 2]^n \equiv p \circ 1 \circ [k^n \circ 1, h^n \circ 2] \quad \text{by I.5.1} \tag{7}$$
$$q_n' \equiv 2 \circ [k \circ 1, h \circ 2]^n \equiv 2 \circ [k^n \circ 1, h^n \circ 2] \quad \text{by I.5.1.} \tag{8}$$

Now, from the above, using I.5,

$$\text{defined} \circ 2 \longrightarrow p_n \equiv p \circ k^n \circ 1 \tag{9}$$
$$\text{defined} \circ h^n \circ 2 \longrightarrow p_n' \equiv p \circ k^n \circ 1 \tag{10}$$
$$\text{defined} \circ k^n \circ 1 \longrightarrow q_n \equiv q_n' \equiv h^n \circ 2 \tag{11}$$

Thus

$$\text{defined} \circ h^n \circ 2 \longrightarrow \text{defined} \circ 2 \equiv \bar{T} \tag{12}$$
$$\text{defined} \circ h^n \circ 2, \longrightarrow p_n \equiv p_n' \tag{13}$$

and

$$f \equiv p_0 \to q_0; \ldots; p_n \to h^n \circ 2; \ldots \tag{14}$$
$$g \equiv p_0' \to q_0'; \ldots; p_n' \to h^n \circ 2; \ldots \tag{15}$$

since p_n and p_n' provide the qualification needed for $q_n \equiv q_n' \equiv h^n \circ 2$.

Now suppose there is an x such that $f:x \neq g:x$. Then there is an n such that $p_i:x = p_i':x = F$ for i < n, and $p_n:x \neq p_n':x$. From (12) and (13) this can only happen when $h^n \circ 2:x = \bot$. But since h is $\bot$-preserving, $h^m \circ 2:x = \bot$ for all m ≥ n. Hence $f:x = g:x = \bot$ by (14) and (15). This contradicts the assumption that there is an x for which $f:x \neq g:x$. Hence $f \equiv g$.

This example (by J. H. Morris, Jr.) is treated more elegantly in [16] on p. 498. However, some may find that the above treatment is more constructive, leads one more mechanically to the key questions, and provides more insight into the behavior of the two functions.

12.7 Nonlinear Equations
The preceding examples have concerned "linear" equations (in which the "unknown" function does not have an argument involving itself). The question of the existence of simple expansions that "solve" "quadratic" and higher order equations remains open.

The earlier examples concerned solutions of $f \equiv E(f)$, where E is linearly expansive. The following example involves an $E(f)$ that is quadratic and expansive (but not linearly expansive).

12.7.1 Example: proof of idempotency ([16] p. 497). Let f be the solution of

$$f \equiv E(f) \equiv p \to \text{id}; f^2 \circ h. \tag{1}$$

We wish to prove that $f \equiv f^2$. We verify that E is expansive (Section 12.4.1) with the following approximating functions:

$$f_0 \equiv \bar{\bot} \tag{2a}$$
$$f_n \equiv p \to \text{id}; \ldots; p \circ h^{n-1} \to h^{n-1}; \bar{\bot} \quad \text{for n > 0} \tag{2b}$$

First we note that $p \longrightarrow f_n \equiv \text{id}$ and so

$$p \circ h^i \longrightarrow f_n \circ h^i \equiv h^i. \tag{3}$$

Now $E(f_0) \equiv p \to \text{id}; \bar{\bot}^2 \circ h \equiv f_1$,   (4)

and

$E(f_n)$
$\equiv p \to \text{id}; f_n \circ (p \to \text{id}; \ldots; p \circ h^{n-1} \to h^{n-1}; \bar{\bot}) \circ h$
$\equiv p \to \text{id}; f_n \circ (p \circ h \to h; \ldots; p \circ h^n \to h^n; \bar{\bot} \circ h)$
$\equiv p \to \text{id}; p \circ h \to f_n \circ h; \ldots; p \circ h^n \to f_n \circ h^n; f_n \circ \bar{\bot}$
$\equiv p \to \text{id}; p \circ h \to h; \ldots; p \circ h^n \to h^n; \bar{\bot} \quad \text{by (3)}$
$\equiv f_{n+1}$.   (5)

Thus E is expansive by (4) and (5); so by (2) and Section 12.4.1 (E4)

$$f \equiv p \to \text{id}; \ldots; p \circ h^n \to h^n; \ldots. \tag{6}$$

But (6), by the iteration theorem, gives

$$f \equiv p \to \text{id}; f \circ h. \tag{7}$$

Now, if $p:x = T$, then $f:x = x = f^2:x$, by (1). If $p:x = F$, then

$$f:x = f^2 \circ h:x \quad \text{by (1)}$$

$$= f:(f{\circ}h{:}x) = f:(f{:}x) \quad \text{by (7)}$$
$$= f^2{:}x.$$

If $p{:}x$ is neither T nor F, then $f{:}x = \bot = f^2{:}x$. Thus $f \equiv f^2$.

12.8 Foundations for the Algebra of Programs

Our purpose in this section is to establish the validity of the results stated in Section 12.4. Subsequent sections do not depend on this one, hence it can be skipped by readers who wish to do so. We use the standard concepts and results from [16], but the notation used for objects and functions, etc., will be that of this paper.

We take as the domain (and range) for all functions the set O of objects (which includes $\bot$) of a given FP system. We take F to be the set of functions, and **F** to be the set of functional forms of that FP system. We write $E(f)$ for any function expression involving functional forms, primitive and defined functions, and the function symbol f; and we regard E as a functional that maps a function f into the corresponding function $E(f)$. We assume that all $f \in$ F are $\bot$-preserving and that all functional forms in **F** correspond to continuous functionals in every variable (e.g., $[f, g]$ is continuous in both f and g). (All primitive functions of the FP system given earlier are $\bot$-preserving, and all its functional forms are continuous.)

DEFINITIONS. Let $E(f)$ be a function expression. Let

$$f_0 \equiv \bot$$
$$f_{i+1} \equiv p_0 \rightarrow q_0; \dots ; p_i \rightarrow q_i; \bot \quad \text{for i = 0, 1, ...}$$

where $p_i, q_i \in$ F. Let E have the property that

$$E(f_i) \equiv f_{i+1} \quad \text{for i = 0, 1, ...}$$

Then E is said to be *expansive* with the *approximating functions* f_i. We write

$$f \equiv p_0 \rightarrow q_0; \dots ; p_n \rightarrow q_n; \dots$$

to mean that $f \equiv \lim_i\{f_i\}$, where the f_i have the form above. We call the right side an *infinite expansion* of f. We take $f{:}x$ to be defined iff there is an $n \geq 0$ such that (a) $p_i{:}x = F$ for all $i < n$, and (b) $p_n{:}x = T$, and (c) $q_n{:}x$ is defined, in which case $f{:}x = q_n{:}x$.

EXPANSION THEOREM: Let $E(f)$ be expansive with approximating functions as above. Let f be the least function satisfying

$$f \equiv E(f).$$

Then

$$f \equiv p_0 \rightarrow q_0; \dots ; p_n \rightarrow q_n; \dots$$

PROOF. Since E is the composition of continuous functionals (from **F**) involving only monotonic functions ($\bot$-preserving functions from F) as constant terms, E is continuous ([16] p. 493). Therefore its least fixed point f is $\lim_i\{E^i(\bot)\} \equiv \lim_i\{f_i\}$ ([16] p. 494), which by definition is the above infinite expansion for f. $\quad\square$

DEFINITION. Let $E(f)$ be a function expression satisfying the following:

$$E(h) \equiv p_0 \rightarrow q_0; E_1(h) \quad \text{for all } h \in \text{F} \quad \text{(LE1)}$$

where $p_i \in$ F and $q_i \in$ F exist such that

$$E_1(p_i \rightarrow q_i; h) \equiv p_{i+1} \rightarrow q_{i+1}; E_1(h)$$
$$\text{for all } h \in \text{F and i = 0, 1, ...} \quad \text{(LE2)}$$

and

$$E_1(\bot) \equiv \bot. \quad \text{(LE3)}$$

Then E is said to be *linearly expansive* with respect to these p_i's and q_i's.

LINEAR EXPANSION THEOREM: Let E be linearly expansive with respect to p_i and q_i, i = 0, 1, ... Then E is expansive with approximating functions

$$f_0 \equiv \bot \quad (1)$$
$$f_{i+1} \equiv p_0 \rightarrow q_0; \dots ; p_i \rightarrow q_i; \bot. \quad (2)$$

PROOF. We want to show that $E(f_i) \equiv f_{i+1}$ for any $i \geq 0$. Now

$$E(f_0) \equiv p_0 \rightarrow q_0; E_1 (\bot) \equiv p_0 \rightarrow q_0; \bot \equiv f_1 \quad (3)$$
$$\text{by (LE1) (LE3) (1).}$$

Let $i > 0$ be fixed and let

$$f_i \equiv p_0 \rightarrow q_0; w_1 \quad (4a)$$
$$w_1 \equiv p_1 \rightarrow q_1; w_2 \quad (4b)$$
etc.
$$w_{i-1} \equiv p_{i-1} \rightarrow q_{i-1}; \bot. \quad (4\text{-})$$

Then, for this $i > 0$

$$E(f_i) \equiv p_0 \rightarrow q_0; E_1(f_i) \quad \text{by (LE1)}$$
$$E_1(f_i) \equiv p_1 \rightarrow q_1; E_1(w_1) \quad \text{by (LE2) and (4a)}$$
$$E_1(w_1) \equiv p_2 \rightarrow q_2; E_1(w_2) \quad \text{by (LE2) and (4b)}$$

etc.

$$E_1(w_{i-1}) \equiv p_i \rightarrow q_i; E_1 (\bot) \quad \text{by (LE2) and (4-)}$$
$$\equiv p_i \rightarrow q_i; \bot \quad \text{by (LE3)}$$

Combining the above gives

$$E(f_i) \equiv f_{i+1} \quad \text{for arbitrary i > 0, by (2).} \quad (5)$$

By (3), (5) also holds for i = 0; thus it holds for all $i \geq 0$. Therefore E is expansive and has the required approximating functions. $\quad\square$

COROLLARY. If E is linearly expansive with respect to p_i and q_i, i = 0, 1, ... , and f is the least function satisfying

$$f \equiv E(f) \quad \text{(LE4)}$$

then

$$f \equiv p_0 \rightarrow q_0; \dots ; p_n \rightarrow q_n; \dots . \quad \text{(LE5)}$$

12.9 The Algebra of Programs for the Lambda Calculus and for Combinators

Because Church's lambda calculus [5] and the system of combinators developed by Schönfinkel and Curry [6]

are the primary mathematical systems for representing the notion of application of functions, and because they are more powerful than FP systems, it is natural to enquire what an algebra of programs based on those systems would look like.

The lambda calculus and combinator equivalents of FP composition, $f \circ g$, are

$$\lambda fgx.(f(gx)) \equiv B$$

where B is a simple combinator defined by Curry. There is no direct equivalent for the FP object $<x,y>$ in the Church or Curry systems proper; however, following Landin [14] and Burge [4], one can use the primitive functions prefix, head, tail, null, and atomic to introduce the notion of list structures that correspond to FP sequences. Then, using FP notation for lists, the lambda calculus equivalent for construction is $\lambda fgx.<fx,gx>$. A combinatory equivalent is an expression involving prefix, the null list, and two or more basic combinators. It is so complex that I shall not attempt to give it.

If one uses the lambda calculus or combinatory expressions for the functional forms $f \circ g$ and $[f,g]$ to express the law I.1 in the FP algebra, $[f,g] \circ h \equiv [f \circ h, g \circ h]$, the result is an expression so complex that the sense of the law is obscured. The only way to make that sense clear in either system is to name the two functionals: composition $\equiv$ B, and construction $\equiv$ A, so that $Bfg \equiv f \circ g$, and $Afg \equiv [f,g]$. Then I.1 becomes

$$B(Afg)h \equiv A(Bfh)(Bgh),$$

which is still not as perspicuous as the FP law.

The point of the above is that if one wishes to state clear laws like those of the FP algebra in either Church's or Curry's system, one finds it necessary to select certain functionals (e.g., composition and construction) as the basic operations of the algebra and to either give them short names or, preferably, represent them by some special notation as in FP. If one does this and provides primitives, objects, lists, etc., the result is an FP-like system in which the usual lambda expressions or combinators do not appear. Even then these Church or Curry versions of FP systems, being less restricted, have some problems that FP systems do not have:

a) The Church and Curry versions accommodate functions of many types and can define functions that do not exist in FP systems. Thus, Bf is a function that has no counterpart in FP systems. This added power carries with it problems of type compatibility. For example, in $f \circ g$, is the range of g included in the domain of f? In FP systems all functions have the same domain and range.

b) The semantics of Church's lambda calculus depends on substitution rules that are simply stated but whose implications are very difficult to fully comprehend. The true complexity of these rules is not widely recognized but is evidenced by the succession of able logicians who have published "proofs" of the Church-Rosser theorem that failed to account for one or another

of these complexities. (The Church-Rosser theorem, or Scott's proof of the existence of a model [22], is required to show that the lambda calculus has a consistent semantics.) The definition of pure Lisp contained a related error for a considerable period (the "funarg" problem). Analogous problems attach to Curry's system as well.

In contrast, the formal (FFP) version of FP systems (described in the next section) has no variables and only an elementary substitution rule (a function for its name), and it can be shown to have a consistent semantics by a relatively simple fixed-point argument along the lines developed by Dana Scott and by Manna et al [16]. For such a proof see McJones [18].

12.10 Remarks

The algebra of programs outlined above needs much work to provide expansions for larger classes of equations and to extend its laws and theorems beyond the elementary ones given here. It would be interesting to explore the algebra for an FP-like system whose sequence constructor is not $\perp$-preserving (law I.5 is strengthened, but IV.1 is lost). Other interesting problems are: (a) Find rules that make expansions unique, giving canonical forms for functions; (b) find algorithms for expanding and analyzing the behavior of functions for various classes of arguments; and (c) explore ways of using the laws and theorems of the algebra as the basic rules either of a formal, preexecution "lazy evaluation" scheme [9, 10], or of one which operates during execution. Such schemes would, for example, make use of the law $1 \circ [f,g] \leq f$ to avoid evaluating $g : x$.

13. Formal Systems for Functional Programming (FFP Systems)

13.1 Introduction

As we have seen, an FP system has a set of functions that depends on its set of primitive functions, its set of functional forms, and its set of definitions. In particular, its set of functional forms is fixed once and for all, and this set determines the power of the system in a major way. For example, if its set of functional forms is empty, then its entire set of functions is just the set of primitive functions. In FFP systems one can create new functional forms. Functional forms are represented by object sequences; the first element of a sequence determines which form it represents, while the remaining elements are the parameters of the form.

The ability to define new functional forms in FFP systems is one consequence of the principal difference between them and FP systems: in FFP systems objects are used to "represent" functions in a systematic way. Otherwise FFP systems mirror FP systems closely. They are similar to, but simpler than, the Reduction (Red) languages of an earlier paper [2].

We shall first give the simple syntax of FFP systems, then discuss their semantics informally, giving examples, and finally give their formal semantics.

13.2 Syntax

We describe the set O of objects and the set E of expressions of an FFP system. These depend on the choice of some set A of *atoms*, which we take as given. We assume that T (true), F (false), ϕ (the empty sequence), and # (default) belong to A, as well as "numbers" of various kinds, etc.

1) Bottom, $\perp$, is an *object* but not an atom.
2) Every atom is an *object*.
3) Every object is an *expression*.
4) If $x_1, \ldots, x_n$ are objects [expressions], then $<x_1, \ldots, x_n>$ is an *object* [resp., *expression*] called a *sequence* (of *length* n) for $n \geq 1$. The object [expression] x_i for $1 \leq i \leq n$, is the ith *element* of the sequence $<x_1, \ldots, x_i, \ldots, x_n>$. ($\phi$ is both a sequence and an atom; its length is 0.)
5) If x and y are expressions, then $(x:y)$ is an *expression* called an *application*. x is its *operator* and y is its *operand*. Both are *elements* of the expression.
6) If $x = <x_1, \ldots, x_n>$ and if one of the elements of x is $\perp$, then $x = \perp$. That is, $<\ldots, \perp, \ldots> = \perp$.
7) All objects and expressions are formed by finite use of the above rules.

A *subexpression* of an expression x is either x itself or a subexpression of an element of x. An FFP object is an expression that has no application as a subexpression. Given the same set of atoms, FFP and FP objects are the same.

13.3 Informal Remarks About FFP Semantics

13.3.1 The meaning of expressions; the semantic function μ.
Every FFP expression e has a *meaning*, μe, which is always an object; μe is found by repeatedly replacing each innermost application in e by its meaning. If this process is nonterminating, the meaning of e is $\perp$. The meaning of an innermost application $(x:y)$ (since it is innermost, x and y must be objects) is the result of applying the function *represented* by x to y, just as in FP systems, except that in FFP systems functions are represented by objects, rather than by function expressions, with atoms (instead of function symbols) representing primitive and defined functions, and with sequences representing the FP functions denoted by functional forms.

The association between objects and the functions they represent is given by the *representation function, ρ,* of the FFP system. (Both ρ and μ belong to the description of the system, not the system itself.) Thus if the atom *NULL* represents the FP function null, then $\rho NULL$ = null and the meaning of $(NULL:A)$ is $\mu(NULL:A) = (\rho NULL):A = \text{null}:A = F$.
From here on, as above, we use the colon in two senses. When it is between two objects, as in $(NULL:A)$, it identifies an FFP application that denotes only itself; when it comes between a *function* and an object, as in $(\rho NULL):A$ or null:A, it identifies an FP-like application that denotes the *result* of applying the function to the object.

The fact that FFP operators are objects makes pos-

sible a function, apply, which is meaningless in FP systems:

$$\text{apply}:<x,y> = (x:y).$$

The result of apply:$<x,y>$, namely $(x:y)$, is meaningless in FP systems on two levels. First, $(x:y)$ is not itself an object; it illustrates another difference between FP and FFP systems: some FFP functions, like apply, map objects into expressions, not directly into objects as FP functions do. However, the *meaning* of apply:$<x,y>$ *is* an object (see below). Second, $(x:y)$ could not be even an intermediate result in an FP system; it is meaningless in FP systems since x is an object, not a function and FP systems do not associate functions with objects. Now if *APPLY* represents apply, then the meaning of $(APPLY:<NULL,A>)$ is

$$
\begin{aligned}
\mu(APPLY&:<NULL,A>) \\
&= \mu((\rho APPLY):<NULL,A>) \\
&= \mu(\text{apply}:<NULL,A>) \\
&= \mu(NULL:A) = \mu((\rho NULL):A) \\
&= \mu(\text{null}:A) = \mu F = F.
\end{aligned}
$$

The last step follows from the fact that every object is its own meaning. Since the meaning function μ eventually evaluates all applications, one can think of apply:$<NULL,A>$ as yielding F even though the actual result is $(NULL:A)$.

13.3.2 How objects represent functions; the representation function ρ.
As we have seen, some atoms (*primitive* atoms) will represent the primitive functions of the system. Other atoms can represent defined functions just as symbols can in FP systems. If an atom is neither primitive nor defined, it represents $\bar{\perp}$, the function which is $\perp$ everywhere.

Sequences also represent functions and are analogous to the functional forms of FP. The function represented by a sequence is given (recursively) by the following rule.

Metacomposition rule

$$(\rho<x_1, \ldots, x_n>):y = (\rho x_1):<<x_1, \ldots, x_n>, y>,$$

where the x_i's and y are objects. Here ρx_1 determines what functional form $<x_1, \ldots, x_n>$ represents, and $x_2, \ldots, x_n$ are the parameters of the form (in FFP, x_1 itself can also serve as a parameter). Thus, for example, let **Def** $\rho CONST \equiv 2 \circ 1$; then $<CONST,x>$ in FFP represents the FP functional form $\bar{x}$, since, by the metacomposition rule, if $y \neq \perp$,

$$
\begin{aligned}
(\rho<CONST,x>):y &= (\rho CONST):<<CONST,x>,y> \\
&= 2 \circ 1:<<CONST,x>,y> = x.
\end{aligned}
$$

Here we can see that the first, controlling, operator of a sequence or form, *CONST* in this case, always has as its operand, after metacomposition, a pair whose first element is the sequence itself and whose second element is the original operand of the sequence, y in this case. The controlling operator can then rearrange and reapply the elements of the sequence and original operand in a great variety of ways. The significant point about metacom-

position is that it permits the definition of new functional forms, in effect, merely by defining new functions. It also permits one to write recursive functions without a definition.

We give one more example of a controlling function for a functional form: **Def** $\rho CONS \equiv \alpha apply \circ tl \circ distr$. This definition results in $<CONS, f_1, \ldots, f_n>$—where the f_i are objects—representing the same function as $[\rho f_1, \ldots, \rho f_n]$. The following shows this.

$$(\rho <CONS, f_1, \ldots, f_n>):x$$
$$= (\rho CONS):<<CONS, f_1, \ldots, f_n >, x>$$
by metacomposition

$$= \alpha apply \circ tl \circ distr:<<CONS, f_1, \ldots, f_n>, x>$$
by def of $\rho CONS$

$$= \alpha apply:<<f_1, x>, \ldots, <f_n, x>>$$
by def of tl and distr and $\circ$

$$= <apply:<f_1, x>, \ldots, apply:<f_n, x>>$$
by def of α

$$= <(f_1:x), \ldots, (f_n:x)> \quad \text{by def of apply.}$$

In evaluating the last expression, the meaning function μ will produce the meaning of each application, giving $\rho f_i:x$ as the ith element.

Usually, in describing the function represented by a sequence, we shall give its overall effect rather than show how its controlling operator achieves that effect. Thus we would simply write

$$(\rho <CONS, f_1, \ldots, f_n>):x = <(f_1:x), \ldots, (f_n:x)>$$

instead of the more detailed account above.

We need a controlling operator, *COMP*, to give us sequences representing the functional form composition. We take $\rho COMP$ to be a primitive function such that, for all objects x,

$$(\rho <COMP, f_1, \ldots, f_n>):x$$
$$= (f_1:(f_2:(\ldots :(f_n:x)\ldots))) \quad \text{for n} \geq 1.$$

(I am indebted to Paul McJones for his observation that ordinary composition could be achieved by this primitive function rather than by using two composition rules in the basic semantics, as was done in an earlier paper [2].)

Although FFP systems permit the definition and investigation of new functional forms, it is to be expected that most programming would use a fixed set of forms (whose controlling operators are primitives), as in FP, so that the algebraic laws for those forms could be employed, and so that a structured programming style could be used based on those forms.

In addition to its use in defining functional forms, metacomposition can be used to create recursive functions directly without the use of recursive definitions of the form **Def** $f \equiv E(f)$. For example, if $\rho MLAST \equiv$ null$\circ$tl$\circ2 \to 1\circ2$; apply$\circ[1, tl\circ2]$, then $\rho <MLAST> \equiv$ last, where last:$x \equiv x = <x_1, \ldots, x_n> \to x_n$; $\perp$. Thus the operator $<MLAST>$ works as follows:

$$\mu(<MLAST>:<A,B>)$$

$$= \mu(\rho MLAST:<<MLAST>,<A,B>>)$$
by metacomposition

$$= \mu(apply \circ [1, tl\circ2]:<<MLAST>,<A,B>>)$$
$$= \mu(apply:<<MLAST>,<B>>)$$
$$= \mu(<MLAST>:<B>)$$
$$= \mu(\rho MLAST:<<MLAST>,<B>>)$$
$$= \mu(1\circ2:<<MLAST>,<B>>)$$
$$= B.$$

13.3.3 Summary of the properties of ρ and μ. So far we have shown how ρ maps atoms and sequences into functions and how those functions map objects into expressions. Actually, ρ and all FFP functions can be extended so that they are defined for all expressions. With such extensions the properties of ρ and μ can be summarized as follows:

1) $\mu \in$ [expressions $\to$ objects].
2) If x is an object, $\mu x = x$.
3) If e is an expression and $e = <e_1, \ldots, e_n>$, then $\mu e = <\mu e_1, \ldots, \mu e_n>$.
4) $\rho \in$ [expressions $\to$ [expressions $\to$ expressions]].
5) For any expression e, $\rho e = \rho(\mu e)$.
6) If x is an object and e an expression, then $\rho x:e = \rho x:(\mu e)$.
7) If x and y are objects, then $\mu(x:y) = \mu(\rho x:y)$. In words: the meaning of an FFP application $(x:y)$ is found by applying ρx, the function represented by x, to y and then finding the meaning of the resulting expression (which is *usually* an object and is then its own meaning).

13.3.4 Cells, fetching, and storing. For a number of reasons it is convenient to create functions which serve as names. In particular, we shall need this facility in describing the semantics of definitions in FFP systems. To introduce naming functions, that is, the ability to *fetch* the contents of a cell with a given name from a store (a sequence of cells) and to *store* a cell with given name and contents in such a sequence, we introduce objects called *cells* and two new functional forms, *fetch* and *store*.

Cells

A *cell* is a triple $<CELL, name, contents>$. We use this form instead of the pair $<name, contents>$ so that cells can be distinguished from ordinary pairs.

Fetch

The functional form *fetch* takes an object n as its parameter (n is customarily an atom serving as a name); it is written $\uparrow n$ (read "fetch n"). Its definition for objects n and x is

$$\uparrow n:x \equiv x = \phi \to \#; \text{atom}:x \to \perp;$$
$$(1:x) = <CELL, n, c> \to c; \uparrow n \circ tl:x,$$

where $\#$ is the atom "default." Thus $\uparrow n$ (fetch n) applied to a sequence gives the contents of the first cell in the sequence whose name is n; If there is no cell named n, the result is default, $\#$. Thus $\uparrow n$ is the name function for the name n. (We assume that $\rho FETCH$ is the primitive function such that $\rho <FETCH, n> \equiv \uparrow n$. Note that $\uparrow n$ simply passes over elements in its operand that are not cells.)

Store and push, pop, purge

Like fetch, *store* takes an object *n* as its parameter; it is written $\downarrow n$ ("store *n*"). When applied to a pair $<x,y>$, where *y* is a sequence, $\downarrow n$ removes the first cell named *n* from *y*, if any, then creates a new cell named *n* with contents *x* and appends it to *y*. Before defining $\downarrow n$ (store *n*) we shall specify four auxiliary functional forms. (These can be used in combination with fetch *n* and store *n* to obtain multiple, named, LIFO stacks within a storage sequence.) Two of these auxiliary forms are specified by recursive functional equations; each takes an object *n* as its parameter.

(cellname *n*) $\equiv$ atom $\rightarrow \bar{F}$;
$\qquad$ eq$\circ$[length, $\bar{3}$] $\rightarrow$ eq$\circ$[[$\overline{CELL}$, $\bar{n}$], [1, 2]]; $\bar{F}$
(push *n*) $\equiv$ pair $\rightarrow$ apndl$\circ$[[$\overline{CELL}$, $\bar{n}$, 1], 2]; $\perp$
(pop *n*) $\equiv$ null $\rightarrow \bar{\phi}$;
$\qquad$ (cellname *n*)$\circ$1 $\rightarrow$ tl; apndl$\circ$[1, (pop *n*)$\circ$tl]
(purge *n*) $\equiv$ null $\rightarrow \bar{\phi}$; (cellname *n*)$\circ$1 $\rightarrow$ (purge *n*)$\circ$tl;
$\qquad$ apndl$\circ$[1, (purge *n*)$\circ$tl]
$\downarrow n \equiv$ pair $\rightarrow$ (push *n*)$\circ$[1, (pop *n*)$\circ$2]; $\perp$

The above functional forms work as follows. For $x \neq \perp$, (cellname *n*):*x* is *T* if *x* is a cell named *n*, otherwise it is *F*. (pop *n*):*y* removes the first cell named *n* from a sequence *y*; (purge *n*):*y* removes all cells named *n* from *y*. (push *n*):$<x,y>$ puts a cell named *n* with contents *x* at the head of sequence *y*; $\downarrow n$:$<x,y>$ is (push *n*):$<x$, (pop *n*):*y*$>$.

(Thus (push *n*):$<x,y>$ = *y'* pushes *x* onto the top of a "stack" named *n* in *y'*; *x* can be read by $\uparrow n$:*y'* = *x* and can be removed by (pop *n*):*y'*; thus $\uparrow n\circ$(pop *n*):*y'* is the element below *x* in the stack *n*, provided there is more than one cell named *n* in *y'*.)

13.3.5 Definitions in FFP systems. The semantics of an FFP system depends on a fixed set of definitions D (a sequence of cells), just as an FP system depends on its informally given set of definitions. Thus the semantic function μ depends on D; altering D gives a new μ' that reflects the altered definitions. We have represented D as an *object* because in AST systems (Section 14) we shall want to transform D by applying functions to it and to fetch data from it—in addition to using it as the source of function definitions in FFP semantics.

If $<CELL,n,c>$ is the first cell named *n* in the sequence D (and *n* is an atom) then it has the same effect as the FP definition **Def** $n \equiv \rho c$, that is, the meaning of (*n*:*x*) will be the same as that of ρc:*x*. Thus for example, if $<CELL,CONST,<COMP,2,1>>$ is the first cell in D named *CONST*, then it has the same effect as **Def** $CONST \equiv 2\circ1$, and the FFP system with that D would find

$$\mu(CONST:<<x,y>,z>) = y$$

and consequently

$$\mu(<CONST,A>:B) = A.$$

In general, in an FFP system with definitions D, the meaning of an application of the form (*atom*:*x*) is de-

pendent on D; if $\uparrow atom$:D $\neq$ # (that is, *atom* is defined in D) then its meaning is $\mu(c$:*x*), where $c = \uparrow atom$:D, the contents of the first cell in D named *atom*. If $\uparrow atom$:D = #, then *atom* is not defined in D and either *atom* is primitive, i.e. the system knows how to compute $\rho atom$:*x*, and $\mu(atom$:*x*$) = \mu(\rho atom$:*x*$)$, otherwise $\mu(atom$:*x*$) = \perp$.

13.4 Formal Semantics for FFP Systems

We assume that a set A of atoms, a set D of definitions, a set P $\subset$ A of primitive atoms and the primitive functions they represent have all been chosen. We assume that ρa is the primitive function represented by *a* if *a* belongs to P, and that $\rho a = \perp$ if *a* belongs to Q, the set of atoms in A-P that are not defined in D. Although ρ is defined for all expressions (see 13.3.3), the formal semantics uses its definition only on P and Q. The functions that ρ assigns to other expressions *x* are implicitly determined and applied in the following semantic rules for evaluating $\mu(x$:*y*$)$. The above choices of A and D, and of P and the associated primitive functions determine the objects, expressions, and the semantic function μ_D for an FFP system. (We regard D as fixed and write μ for μ_D.) We assume D is a sequence and that $\uparrow y$:D can be computed (by the function $\uparrow y$ as given in Section 13.3.4) for any atom *y*. With these assumptions we define μ as the least fixed point of the functional τ, where the function $\tau\mu$ is defined as follows for any function μ (for all expressions *x*, x_i, *y*, y_i, *z*, and *w*):

$$(\tau\mu)x \equiv x \in A \rightarrow x;$$
$$x = <x_1, ..., x_n> \rightarrow <\mu x_1, ..., \mu x_n>;$$
$$x = (y{:}z) \rightarrow$$
$$\quad (y \in A \& (\uparrow y{:}D) = \# \rightarrow \mu((\rho y)(\mu z));$$
$$\quad y \in A \& (\uparrow y{:}D) = w \rightarrow \mu(w{:}z);$$
$$\quad y = <y_1, ..., y_n> \rightarrow \mu(y_1{:}<y,z>); \mu(\mu y{:}z)); \perp$$

The above description of μ expands the operator of an application by definitions and by metacomposition before evaluating the operand. It is assumed that predicates like "$x \in A$" in the above definition of $\tau\mu$ are $\perp$-preserving (e.g., "$\perp \in A$" has the value $\perp$) and that the conditional expression itself is also $\perp$-preserving. Thus $(\tau\mu)\perp \equiv \perp$ and $(\tau\mu)(\perp{:}z) \equiv \perp$. This concludes the semantics of FFP systems.

14. Applicative State Transition Systems (AST Systems)

14.1 Introduction

This section sketches a class of systems mentioned earlier as alternatives to von Neumann systems. It must be emphasized again that these applicative state transition systems are put forward not as practical programming systems in their present form, but as examples of a class in which applicative style programming is made available in a history sensitive, but non-von Neumann system. These systems are loosely coupled to states and depend on an underlying applicative system for both

their programming language and the description of their state transitions. The underlying applicative system of the AST system described below is an FFP system, but other applicative systems could also be used.

To understand the reasons for the structure of AST systems, it is helpful first to review the basic structure of a von Neumann system, Algol, observe its limitations, and compare it with the structure of AST systems. After that review a minimal AST system is described; a small, top-down, self-protecting system program for file maintenance and running user programs is given, with directions for installing it in the AST system and for running an example user program. The system program uses "name functions" instead of conventional names and the user may do so too. The section concludes with subsections discussing variants of AST systems, their general properties, and naming systems.

14.2 The Structure of Algol Compared to That of AST Systems

An Algol program is a sequence of statements, each representing a transformation of the Algol state, which is a complex repository of information about the status of various stacks, pointers, and variable mappings of identifiers onto values, etc. Each statement communicates with this constantly changing state by means of complicated protocols peculiar to itself and even to its different parts (e.g., the protocol associated with the variable x depends on its occurrence on the left or right of an assignment, in a declaration, as a parameter, etc.).

It is as if the Algol state were a complex "store" that communicates with the Algol program through an enormous "cable" of many specialized wires. The complex communications protocols of this cable are fixed and include those for every statement type. The "meaning" of an Algol program must be given in terms of the total effect of a vast number of communications with the state via the cable and its protocols (plus a means for identifying the output and inserting the input into the state). By comparison with this massive cable to the Algol state/store, the cable that is the von Neumann bottleneck of a computer is a simple, elegant concept.

Thus Algol statements are not expressions representing state-to-state functions that are built up by the use of orderly combining forms from simpler state-to-state functions. Instead they are complex *messages* with context-dependent parts that nibble away at the state. Each part transmits information to and from the state over the cable by its own protocols. There is no provision for applying general functions to the *whole* state and thereby making large changes in it. The possibility of large, powerful transformations of the state S by function application, $S \rightarrow f{:}S$, is in fact inconceivable in the von Neumann—cable and protocol—context: there could be no assurance that the new state $f{:}S$ would match the cable and its fixed protocols unless f is restricted to the tiny changes allowed by the cable in the first place.

We want a computing system whose semantics does not depend on a host of baroque protocols for communicating with the state, and we want to be able to make large transformations in the state by the application of general functions. AST systems provide one way of achieving these goals. Their semantics has two protocols for getting information from the state: (1) get from it the definition of a function to be applied, and (2) get the whole state itself. There is one protocol for changing the state: compute the new state by function application. Besides these communications with the state, AST semantics is applicative (i.e. FFP). It does not depend on state changes because the state does not change at all during a computation. Instead, the result of a computation is output *and* a new state. The structure of an AST state is slightly restricted by one of its protocols: It must be possible to identify a definition (i.e. cell) in it. Its structure—it is a sequence—is far simpler than that of the Algol state.

Thus the structure of AST systems avoids the complexity and restrictions of the von Neumann state (with its communications protocols) while achieving greater power and freedom in a radically different and simpler framework.

14.3 Structure of an AST System

An AST system is made up of three elements:

1) An *applicative subsystem* (such as an FFP system).

2) A *state* D that is the set of definitions of the applicative subsystem.

3) A set of *transition rules* that describe how inputs are transformed into outputs and how the state D is changed.

The programming language of an AST system is just that of its applicative subsystem. (From here on we shall assume that the latter is an FFP system.) Thus AST systems can use the FP programming style we have discussed. The applicative subsystem cannot change the state D and it does not change during the evaluation of an expression. A new state is computed along with output and replaces the old state when output is issued. (Recall that a set of definitions D is a sequence of cells; a cell name is the name of a defined function and its contents is the defining expression. Here, however, some cells may name data rather than functions; a data name n will be used in $\uparrow n$ (fetch n) whereas a function name will be used as an operator itself.)

We give below the transition rules for the elementary AST system we shall use for examples of programs. These are perhaps the simplest of many possible transition rules that could determine the behavior of a great variety of AST systems.

14.3.1 Transition rules for an elementary AST system. When the system receives an input x, it forms the application $(SYSTEM{:}x)$ and then proceeds to obtain its meaning in the FFP subsystem, using the current state D as the set of definitions. $SYSTEM$ is the distinguished name of a function defined in D (i.e. it is the "system program"). Normally the result is a pair

$$\mu(SYSTEM:x) = <o,d>$$

where o is the system output that results from input x and d becomes the new state D for the system's next input. Usually d will be a copy or partly changed copy of the old state. If $\mu(SYSTEM:x)$ is not a pair, the output is an error message and the state remains unchanged.

14.3.2 Transition rules: exception conditions and startup. Once an input has been accepted, our system will not accept another (except $<RESET,x>$, see below) until an output has been issued and the new state, if any, installed. The system will accept the input $<RESET,x>$ at any time. There are two cases: (a) If $SYSTEM$ is defined in the current state D, then the system aborts its current computation without altering D and treats x as a new normal input; (b) if $SYSTEM$ is not defined in D, then x is appended to D as its first element. (This ends the complete description of the transition rules for our elementary AST system.)

If $SYSTEM$ is defined in D it can always prevent any change in its own definition. If it is not defined, an ordinary input x will produce $\mu(SYSTEM:x) = \perp$ and the transition rules yield an error message and an unchanged state; on the other hand, the input $<RESET, <CELL,SYSTEM,s>>$ will define $SYSTEM$ to be s.

14.3.3 Program access to the state; the function $\rho DEFS$. Our FFP subsystem is required to have one new primitive function, defs, named $DEFS$ such that for any object $x \neq \perp$,

$$\text{defs}:x = \rho DEFS:x = D$$

where D is the current state and set of definitions of the AST system. This function allows programs access to the whole state for any purpose, including the essential one of computing the successor state.

14.4 An Example of a System Program

The above description of our elementary AST system, plus the FFP subsystem and the FP primitives and functional forms of earlier sections, specify a complete history-sensitive computing system. Its input and output behavior is limited by its simple transition rules, but otherwise it is a powerful system once it is equipped with a suitable set of definitions. As an example of its use we shall describe a small system program, its installation, and operation.

Our example system program will handle queries and updates for a file it maintains, evaluate FFP expressions, run general user programs that do not damage the file or the state, and allow authorized users to change the set of definitions and the system program itself. All inputs it accepts will be of the form $<key,input>$ where key is a code that determines both the input class (*system-change, expression, program, query, update*) and also the identity of the user and his authority to use the system for the given input class. We shall not specify a format for key. *Input* is the input itself, of the class given by key.

14.4.1 General plan of the system program. The state

D of our AST system will contain the definitions of all nonprimitive functions needed for the system program and for users' programs. (Each definition is in a cell of the sequence D.) In addition, there will be a cell in D named $FILE$ with contents *file*, which the system maintains. We shall give FP definitions of functions and later show how to get them into the system in their FFP form. The transition rules make the input the operand of $SYSTEM$, but our plan is to use name-functions to refer to data, so the first thing we shall do with the input is to create two cells named KEY and $INPUT$ with contents *key* and *input* and append these to D. This sequence of cells has one each for *key, input,* and *file*; it will be the operand of our main function called subsystem. Subsystem can then obtain *key* by applying $\uparrow KEY$ to its operand, etc. Thus the definition

Def system $\equiv$ pair $\rightarrow$ subsystem$\circ f$; [$\overline{NONPAIR}$, defs]

where

$$f \equiv \downarrow INPUT\circ[2, \downarrow KEY\circ[1, \text{defs}]]$$

causes the system to output $NONPAIR$ and leave the state unchanged if the input is not a pair. Otherwise, if it is $<key,input>$, then

$$f:<key,input> = <<CELL,INPUT,input>,$$
$$<CELL,KEY,key>, d_1, ... , d_n>$$

where D $= <d_1, ... , d_n>$. (We might have constructed a different operand than the one above, one with just three cells, for *key, input,* and *file*. We did not do so because real programs, unlike subsystem, would contain many name functions referring to data in the state, and this "standard" construction of the operand would suffice then as well.)

14.4.2 The "subsystem" function. We now give the FP definition of the function subsystem, followed by brief explanations of its six cases and auxiliary functions.

```
Def subsystem ≡
    is-system-change∘↑KEY → [report-change, apply]∘[↑INPUT, defs];
    is-expression∘↑KEY → [↑INPUT, defs];
    is-program∘↑KEY → system-check∘apply∘[↑INPUT, defs];
    is-query∘↑KEY → [query-response∘[↑INPUT, ↑FILE], defs];
    is-update∘↑KEY →
            [report-update, ↓FILE∘[update, defs]]
                ∘[↑INPUT, ↑FILE];
            [report-error∘[↑KEY,↑INPUT], defs].
```

This subsystem has five "$p \rightarrow f$;" clauses and a final default function, for a total of six classes of inputs; the treatment of each class is given below. Recall that the *operand* of subsystem is a sequence of cells containing *key, input,* and *file* as well as all the defined functions of D, and that subsystem:*operand* = $<output,newstate>$.

Default inputs. In this case the result is given by the last (default) function of the definition when *key* does not satisfy any of the preceding clauses. The output is report-error: $<key,input>$. The state is unchanged since it is given by defs:*operand* = D. (We leave to the reader's imagination what the function report-error will generate from its operand.)

System-change inputs. When

$$\text{is-system-change} \circ \uparrow KEY{:}operand =$$
$$\text{is-system-change}{:}key = T,$$

key specifies that the user is authorized to make a system change and that *input* = $\uparrow INPUT{:}operand$ represents a function *f* that is to be applied to D to produce the new state *f*:D. (Of course *f*:D can be a useless new state; no constraints are placed on it.) The output is a report, namely report-change:$<input,D>$.

Expression inputs. When is-expression:*key* = *T*, the system understands that the output is to be the meaning of the FFP expression *input*; $\uparrow INPUT{:}operand$ produces it and it is evaluated, as are all expressions. The state is unchanged.

Program inputs and system self-protection. When is-program:*key* = *T*, both the output and new state are given by $(\rho input){:}D = <output,newstate>$. If *newstate* contains *file* in suitable condition and the definitions of system and other protected functions, then
system-check: $<output,newstate> = <output,newstate>$.
Otherwise, system-check:$<output,newstate>$
$$= <error\text{-}report,D>.$$

Although *program* inputs can make major, possibly disastrous changes in the state when it produces *newstate*, system-check can use any criteria to either allow it to become the actual new state or to keep the old. A more sophisticated system-check might correct only prohibited changes in the state. Functions of this sort are possible because they can always access the old state for comparison with the new state-to-be and control what state transition will finally be allowed.

File query inputs. If is-query:*key* = *T*, the function query-response is designed to produce the output = answer to the query *input* from its operand $<input,file>$.

File update inputs. If is-update:*key* = *T*, *input* specifies a file transaction understood by the function update, which computes *updated-file* = update:$<input,file>$. Thus $\downarrow FILE$ has $<updated\text{-}file,D>$ as its operand and thus stores the updated file in the cell *FILE* in the new state. The rest of the state is unchanged. The function report-update generates the output from its operand $<input,file>$.

14.4.3 Installing the system program. We have described the function called system by some FP definitions (using auxiliary functions whose behavior is only indicated). Let us suppose that we have FP definitions for all the nonprimitive functions required. Then each definition can be converted to give the name and contents of a cell in D (of course this conversion itself would be done by a better system). The conversion is accomplished by changing each FP function name to its equivalent atom (e.g., update becomes *UPDATE*) and by replacing functional forms by sequences whose first member is the controlling function for the particular form. Thus $\downarrow FILE \circ [update, defs]$ is converted to

$<COMP,<STORE,FILE>,$
$\qquad\qquad <CONS,UPDATE,DEFS>>,$

and the FP function is the same as that represented by the FFP object, provided that update $\equiv \rho UPDATE$ and *COMP, STORE*, and *CONS* represent the controlling functions for composition, store, and construction.

All FP definitions needed for our system can be converted to cells as indicated above, giving a sequence D_0. We assume that the AST system has an empty state to start with, hence *SYSTEM* is not defined. We want to define *SYSTEM* initially so that it will install its next input as the state; having done so we can then input D_0 and all our definitions will be installed, including our program—system—itself. To accomplish this we enter our first input
$<RESET, <CELL,SYSTEM,loader>>$
where *loader* $\equiv <CONS, <CONST,DONE>,ID>$.
Then, by the transition rule for *RESET* when *SYSTEM* is undefined in D, the cell in our input is put at the head of D = ϕ, thus defining $\rho SYSTEM \equiv \rho loader \equiv [\overline{DONE}, id]$. Our second input is D_0, the set of definitions we wish to become the state. The regular transition rule causes the AST system to evaluate
$\mu(SYSTEM{:}D_0) = [\overline{DONE}, id]{:}D_0 = <DONE,D_0>$. Thus the output from our second input is *DONE*, the new state is D_0, and $\rho SYSTEM$ is now our system program (which only accepts inputs of the form $<key,input>$).

Our next task is to load the file (we are given an initial value *file*). To load it we input a *program* into the newly installed system that contains *file* as a constant and stores it in the state; the input is
$<program\text{-}key, [\overline{DONE},store\text{-}file]>$ where

$$\rho store\text{-}file \equiv \downarrow FILE \circ [\overline{file}, id].$$

Program-key identifies $[\overline{DONE}, store\text{-}file]$ as a program to be applied to the state D_0 to give the output and new state D_1, which is:

$$\rho store\text{-}file{:}D_0 = \downarrow FILE \circ [\overline{file}, id]{:}D_0,$$

or D_0 with a cell containing *file* at its head. The output is $\overline{DONE}{:}D_0 = DONE$. We assume that system-check will pass $<DONE,D_1>$ unchanged. FP expressions have been used in the above in place of the FFP objects they denote, e.g. $\overline{DONE}$ for $<CONST,DONE>$.

14.4.4 Using the system. We have not said how the system's file, queries or updates are structured, so we cannot give a detailed example of file operations. However, the structure of subsystem shows clearly how the system's response to queries and updates depends on the functions query-response, update, and report-update.

Let us suppose that matrices *m, n* named *M*, and *N* are stored in D and that the function MM described earlier is defined in D. Then the input

$$<expression\text{-}key, (MM \circ [\uparrow M, \uparrow N] \circ DEFS{:}\#)>$$

would give the product of the two matrices as output and an unchanged state. *Expression-key* identifies the application as an expression to be evaluated and since defs:$\#$ = D and $[\uparrow M, \uparrow N]{:}D = <m,n>$, the value of the expression is the result MM:$<m,n>$, which is the output.

Our miniature system program has no provision for giving control to a user's program to process many inputs, but it would not be difficult to give it that capability while still monitoring the user's program with the option of taking control back.

14.5 Variants of AST Systems

A major extension of the AST systems suggested above would provide combining forms, "system forms," for building a new AST system from simpler, component AST systems. That is, a system form would take AST systems as parameters and generate a new AST system, just as a functional form takes functions as parameters and generates new functions. These system forms would have properties like those of functional forms and would become the "operations" of a useful "algebra of systems" in much the same way that functional forms are the "operations" of the algebra of programs. However, the problem of finding useful system forms is much more difficult, since they must handle *RESETS*, match inputs and outputs, and combine history-sensitive systems rather than fixed functions.

Moreover, the usefulness or need for system forms is less clear than that for functional forms. The latter are essential for building a great variety of functions from an initial primitive set, whereas, even without system forms, the facilities for building AST systems are already so rich that one could build virtually any system (with the general input and output properties allowed by the given AST scheme). Perhaps system forms would be useful for building systems with complex input and output arrangements.

14.6 Remarks About AST Systems

As I have tried to indicate above, there can be innumerable variations in the ingredients of an AST system—how it operates, how it deals with input and output, how and when it produces new states, and so on. In any case, a number of remarks apply to any reasonable AST system:

a) A state transition occurs once per major computation and can have useful mathematical properties. State transitions are not involved in the tiniest details of a computation as in conventional languages; thus the linguistic von Neumann bottleneck has been eliminated. No complex "cable" or protocols are needed to communicate with the state.

b) Programs are written in an applicative language that can accommodate a great range of changeable parts, parts whose power and flexibility exceed that of any von Neumann language so far. The word-at-a-time style is replaced by an applicative style; there is no division of programming into a world of expressions and a world of statements. Programs can be analyzed and optimized by an algebra of programs.

c) Since the state cannot change during the computation of system:*x*, there are no side effects. Thus independent applications can be evaluated in parallel.

d) By defining appropriate functions one can, I believe, introduce major new features at any time, using the same framework. Such features must be built into the framework of a von Neumann language. I have in mind such features as: "stores" with a great variety of naming systems, types and type checking, communicating parallel processes, nondeterminacy and Dijkstra's "guarded command" constructs [8], and improved methods for structured programming.

e) The framework of an AST system comprises the syntax and semantics of the underlying applicative system plus the system framework sketched above. By current standards, this is a tiny framework for a language and is the only fixed part of the system.

14.7 Naming Systems in AST and von Neumann Models

In an AST system, naming is accomplished by functions as indicated in Section 13.3.3. Many useful functions for altering and accessing a store can be defined (e.g. push, pop, purge, typed fetch, etc.). All these definitions and their associated naming systems can be introduced without altering the AST framework. Different kinds of "stores" (e.g., with "typed cells") with individual naming systems can be used in one program. A cell in one store may contain another entire store.

The important point about AST naming systems is that they utilize the functional nature of names (Reynolds' GEDANKEN [19] also does so to some extent within a von Neumann framework). Thus name functions can be composed and combined with other functions by functional forms. In contrast, functions and names in von Neumann languages are usually disjoint concepts and the function-like nature of names is almost totally concealed and useless, because a) names cannot be applied as functions; b) there are no general means to combine names with other names and functions; c) the objects to which name functions apply (stores) are not accessible as objects.

The failure of von Neumann languages to treat names as functions may be one of their more important weaknesses. In any case, the ability to use names as functions and stores as objects may turn out to be a useful and important programming concept, one which should be thoroughly explored.

15. Remarks About Computer Design

The dominance of von Neumann languages has left designers with few intellectual models for practical computer designs beyond variations of the von Neumann computer. Data flow models [1] [7] [13] are one alternative class of history-sensitive models. The substitution rules of lambda-calculus based languages present serious problems for the machine designer. Berkling [3] has developed a modified lambda calculus that has three kinds of applications and that makes renaming of vari-

ables unnecessary. He has developed a machine to evaluate expressions of this language. Further experience is needed to show how sound a basis this language is for an effective programming style and how efficient his machine can be.

Magó [15] has developed a novel applicative machine built from identical components (of two kinds). It evaluates, directly, FP-like and other applicative expressions from the bottom up. It has no von Neumann store and no address register, hence no bottleneck; it is capable of evaluating many applications in parallel; its built-in operations resemble FP operators more than von Neumann computer operations. It is the farthest departure from the von Neumann computer that I have seen.

There are numerous indications that the applicative style of programming can become more powerful than the von Neumann style. Therefore it is important for programmers to develop a new class of history-sensitive models of computing systems that embody such a style and avoid the inherent efficiency problems that seem to attach to lambda-calculus based systems. Only when these models and their applicative languages have proved their superiority over conventional languages will we have the economic basis to develop the new kind of computer that can best implement them. Only then, perhaps, will we be able to fully utilize large-scale integrated circuits in a computer design not limited by the von Neumann bottleneck.

16. Summary

The fifteen preceding sections of this paper can be summarized as follows.

Section 1. Conventional programming languages are large, complex, and inflexible. Their limited expressive power is inadequate to justify their size and cost.

Section 2. The models of computing systems that underlie programming languages fall roughly into three classes: (a) simple operational models (e.g., Turing machines), (b) applicative models (e.g., the lambda calculus), and (c) von Neumann models (e.g., conventional computers and programming languages). Each class of models has an important difficulty: The programs of class (a) are inscrutable; class (b) models cannot save information from one program to the next; class (c) models have unusable foundations and programs that are conceptually unhelpful.

Section 3. Von Neumann computers are built around a bottleneck: the word-at-a-time tube connecting the CPU and the store. Since a program must make its overall change in the store by pumping vast numbers of words back and forth through the von Neumann bottleneck, we have grown up with a style of programming that concerns itself with this word-at-a-time traffic through the bottleneck rather than with the larger conceptual units of our problems.

Section 4. Conventional languages are based on the programming style of the von Neumann computer. Thus variables = storage cells; assignment statements = fetching, storing, and arithmetic; control statements = jump and test instructions. The symbol ":=" is the linguistic von Neumann bottleneck. Programming in a conventional—von Neumann—language still concerns itself with the word-at-a-time traffic through this slightly more sophisticated bottleneck. Von Neumann languages also split programming into a world of expressions and a world of statements; the first of these is an orderly world, the second is a disorderly one, a world that structured programming has simplified somewhat, but without attacking the basic problems of the split itself and of the word-at-a-time style of conventional languages.

Section 5. This section compares a von Neumann program and a functional program for inner product. It illustrates a number of problems of the former and advantages of the latter: e.g., the von Neumann program is repetitive and word-at-a-time, works only for two vectors named a and b of a given length n, and can only be made general by use of a procedure declaration, which has complex semantics. The functional program is nonrepetitive, deals with vectors as units, is more hierarchically constructed, is completely general, and creates "housekeeping" operations by composing high-level housekeeping operators. It does not name its arguments, hence it requires no procedure declaration.

Section 6. A programming language comprises a framework plus some changeable parts. The framework of a von Neumann language requires that most features must be built into it; it can accommodate only limited changeable parts (e.g., user-defined procedures) because there must be detailed provisions in the "state" and its transition rules for all the needs of the changeable parts, as well as for all the features built into the framework. The reason the von Neumann framework is so inflexible is that its semantics is too closely coupled to the state: every detail of a computation changes the state.

Section 7. The changeable parts of von Neumann languages have little expressive power; this is why most of the language must be built into the framework. The lack of expressive power results from the inability of von Neumann languages to effectively use combining forms for building programs, which in turn results from the split between expressions and statements. Combining forms are at their best in expressions, but in von Neumann languages an expression can only produce a single word; hence expressive power in the world of expressions is mostly lost. A further obstacle to the use of combining forms is the elaborate use of naming conventions.

Section 8. APL is the first language not based on the lambda calculus that is not word-at-a-time and uses functional combining forms. But it still retains many of the problems of von Neumann languages.

Section 9. Von Neumann languages do not have useful properties for reasoning about programs. Axiomatic and denotational semantics are precise tools for describing and understanding conventional programs,

but they only talk about them and cannot alter their ungainly properties. Unlike von Neumann languages, the language of ordinary algebra is suitable both for stating its laws and for transforming an equation into its solution, all within the "language."

Section 10. In a history-sensitive language, a program can affect the behavior of a subsequent one by changing some store which is saved by the system. Any such language requires some kind of state transition semantics. But it does not need semantics closely coupled to states in which the state changes with every detail of the computation. "Applicative state transition" (AST) systems are proposed as history-sensitive alternatives to von Neumann systems. These have: (a) loosely coupled state-transition semantics in which a transition occurs once per major computation; (b) simple states and transition rules; (c) an underlying applicative system with simple "reduction" semantics; and (d) a programming language and state transition rules both based on the underlying applicative system and its semantics. The next four sections describe the elements of this approach to non-von Neumann language and system design.

Section 11. A class of informal functional programming (FP) systems is described which use no variables. Each system is built from objects, functions, functional forms, and definitions. Functions map objects into objects. Functional forms combine existing functions to form new ones. This section lists examples of primitive functions and functional forms and gives sample programs. It discusses the limitations and advantages of FP systems.

Section 12. An "algebra of programs" is described whose variables range over the functions of an FP system and whose "operations" are the functional forms of the system. A list of some twenty-four laws of the algebra is followed by an example proving the equivalence of a nonrepetitive matrix multiplication program and a recursive one. The next subsection states the results of two "expansion theorems" that "solve" two classes of equations. These solutions express the "unknown" function in such equations as an infinite conditional expansion that constitutes a case-by-case description of its behavior and immediately gives the necessary and sufficient conditions for termination. These results are used to derive a "recursion theorem" and an "iteration theorem," which provide ready-made expansions for some moderately general and useful classes of "linear" equations. Examples of the use of these theorems treat: (a) correctness proofs for recursive and iterative factorial functions, and (b) a proof of equivalence of two iterative programs. A final example deals with a "quadratic" equation and proves that its solution is an idempotent function. The next subsection gives the proofs of the two expansion theorems.

The algebra associated with FP systems is compared with the corresponding algebras for the lambda calculus and other applicative systems. The comparison shows some advantages to be drawn from the severely restricted FP systems, as compared with the much more powerful classical systems. Questions are suggested about algorithmic reduction of functions to infinite expansions and about the use of the algebra in various "lazy evaluation" schemes.

Section 13. This section describes formal functional programming (FFP) systems that extend and make precise the behavior of FP systems. Their semantics are simpler than that of classical systems and can be shown to be consistent by a simple fixed-point argument.

Section 14. This section compares the structure of Algol with that of applicative state transition (AST) systems. It describes an AST system using an FFP system as its applicative subsystem. It describes the simple state and the transition rules for the system. A small self-protecting system program for the AST system is described, and how it can be installed and used for file maintenance and for running user programs. The section briefly discusses variants of AST systems and functional naming systems that can be defined and used within an AST system.

Section 15. This section briefly discusses work on applicative computer designs and the need to develop and test more practical models of applicative systems as the future basis for such designs.

Acknowledgments. In earlier work relating to this paper I have received much valuable help and many suggestions from Paul R. McJones and Barry K. Rosen. I have had a great deal of valuable help and feedback in preparing this paper. James N. Gray was exceedingly generous with his time and knowledge in reviewing the first draft. Stephen N. Zilles also gave it a careful reading. Both made many valuable suggestions and criticisms at this difficult stage. It is a pleasure to acknowledge my debt to them. I also had helpful discussions about the first draft with Ronald Fagin, Paul R. McJones, and James H. Morris, Jr. Fagin suggested a number of improvements in the proofs of theorems.

Since a large portion of the paper contains technical material, I asked two distinguished computer scientists to referee the third draft. David J. Gries and John C. Reynolds were kind enough to accept this burdensome task. Both gave me large, detailed sets of corrections and overall comments that resulted in many improvements, large and small, in this final version (which they have not had an opportunity to review). I am truly grateful for the generous time and care they devoted to reviewing this paper.

Finally, I also sent copies of the third draft to Gyula A. Magó, Peter Naur, and John H. Williams. They were kind enough to respond with a number of extremely helpful comments and corrections. Geoffrey A. Frank and Dave Tolle at the University of North Carolina reviewed Magó's copy and pointed out an important error in the definition of the semantic function of FFP systems. My grateful thanks go to all these kind people for their help.

References

1.   Arvind, and Gostelow, K.P. A new interpreter for data flow schemas and its implications for computer architecture. Tech. Rep. No. 72, Dept. Comptr. Sci., U. of California, Irvine, Oct. 1975.

2.   Backus, J. Programming language semantics and closed applicative languages. Conf. Record ACM Symp. on Principles of Programming Languages, Boston, Oct. 1973, 71–86.

3.   Berkling, K.J. Reduction languages for reduction machines. Interner Bericht ISF-76-8, Gesellschaft für Mathematik und Datenverarbeitung MBH, Bonn, Sept. 1976.

4.   Burge, W.H. *Recursive Programming Techniques*. Addison-Wesley, Reading, Mass., 1975.

5.   Church, A. *The Calculi of Lambda-Conversion*. Princeton U. Press, Princeton, N.J., 1941.

6.   Curry, H.B., and Feys, R. *Combinatory Logic, Vol. 1*. North-Holland Pub. Co., Amsterdam, 1958.

7.   Dennis, J.B. First version of a data flow procedure language. Tech. Mem. No. 61, Lab. for Comptr. Sci., M.I.T., Cambridge, Mass., May 1973.

8.   Dijkstra, E.W. *A Discipline of Programming*. Prentice-Hall, Englewood Cliffs, N.J., 1976.

9.   Friedman, D.P., and Wise, D.S. CONS should not evaluate its arguments. In *Automata, Languages and Programming*, S. Michaelson and R. Milner, Eds., Edinburgh U. Press, Edinburgh, 1976, pp. 257–284.

10.   Henderson, P., and Morris, J.H. Jr. A lazy evaluator. Conf. Record Third ACM Symp. on Principles of Programming Languages, Atlanta, Ga., Jan. 1976, pp. 95–103.

11.   Hoare, C.A.R. An axiomatic basis for computer programming. *Comm. ACM 12*, 10 (Oct. 1969), 576–583.

12.   Iverson, K. *A Programming Language*. Wiley, New York, 1962.

13.   Kosinski, P. A data flow programming language. Rep. RC 4264, IBM T.J. Watson Research Ctr., Yorktown Heights, N.Y., March 1973.

14.   Landin, P.J. The mechanical evaluation of expressions. *Computer J. 6*, 4 (1964), 308–320.

15.   Magó, G.A. A network of microprocessors to execute reduction languages. To appear in *Int. J. Comptr. and Inform. Sci.*

16.   Manna, Z., Ness, S., and Vuillemin, J. Inductive methods for proving properties of programs. *Comm. ACM 16*, 8 (Aug. 1973) 491–502.

17.   McCarthy, J. Recursive functions of symbolic expressions and their computation by machine, Pt. 1. *Comm. ACM 3*, 4 (April 1960), 184–195.

18.   McJones, P. A Church-Rosser property of closed applicative languages. Rep. RJ 1589, IBM Res. Lab., San Jose, Calif., May 1975.

19.   Reynolds, J.C. GEDANKEN—a simple typeless language based on the principle of completeness and the reference concept. *Comm. ACM 13*, 5 (May 1970), 308–318.

20.   Reynolds, J.C. Notes on a lattice-theoretic approach to the theory of computation. Dept. Syst. and Inform. Sci., Syracuse U., Syracuse, N.Y., 1972.

21.   Scott, D. Outline of a mathematical theory of computation. Proc. 4th Princeton Conf. on Inform. Sci. and Syst., 1970.

22.   Scott, D. Lattice-theoretic models for various type-free calculi. Proc. Fourth Int. Congress for Logic, Methodology, and the Philosophy of Science, Bucharest, 1972.

23.   Scott, D., and Strachey, C. Towards a mathematical semantics for computer languages. Proc. Symp. on Comptrs. and Automata, Polytechnic Inst. of Brooklyn, 1971.

RECURSIVE FUNCTIONS OF SYMBOLIC EXPRESSIONS*

J. McCARTHY

JOHN McCARTHY, *Massachusetts Institute of Technology, Cambridge, Mass.*

1. Introduction

A programming system called LISP (for LISt Processor) has been developed for the IBM 704 computer by the Artificial Intelligence group at M.I.T. The system was designed to facilitate experiments with a proposed system called the Advice Taker, whereby a machine could be instructed to handle declarative as well as imperative sentences and could exhibit "common sense" in carrying out its instructions. The original proposal [1] for the Advice Taker was made in November 1958. The main requirement was a programming system for manipulating expressions representing formalized declarative and imperative sentences so that the Advice Taker system could make deductions.

In the course of its development the LISP system went through several stages of simplification and eventually came to be based on a scheme for representing the partial recursive functions of a certain class of symbolic expressions. This representation is independent of the IBM 704 computer, or of any other electronic computer, and it now seems expedient to expound the system by starting with the class of expressions called S-expressions and the functions called S-functions.

In this article, we first describe a formalism for defining functions recursively. We believe this formalism has advantages both as a programming language and as vehicle for developing a theory of computation. Next, we describe S-expressions and S-functions, give some examples, and then describe the universal S-function *apply* which plays the theoretical role of a universal Turing machine and the practical role of an interpreter. Then we describe the representation of S-expressions in the memory of the IBM 704 by list structures similar to those used by Newell, Shaw and Simon [2], and the representation of S-functions by program. Then we mention the main features of the LISP programming system for the IBM 704. Next comes another way of describing computations with symbolic expressions, and finally we give a recursive function interpretation of flow charts.

We hope to describe some of the symbolic computations for which LISP has been used in another paper, and also to give elsewhere some applications of our recursive function formalism to mathematical logic and to the problem of mechanical theorem proving.

*Reprinted from *COMM. ACM*, 3, 4, April 1960, 184–195, copyright 1960.

2. Functions and Function Definitions

We shall need a number of mathematical ideas and notations concerning functions in general. Most of the ideas are well known, but the notion of *conditional expression* is believed to be new, and the use of conditional expressions permits functions to be defined recursively in a new and convenient way.

a. *Partial Functions.* A partial function is a function that is defined only on part of its domain. Partial functions necessarily arise when functions are defined by computations because for some values of the arguments the computation defining the value of the function may not terminate. However, some of our elementary functions will be defined as partial functions.

b. *Propositional Expressions and Predicates.* A propositional expression is an expression whose possible values are T (for truth) and F (for falsity). We shall assume that the reader is familiar with the propositional connectives $\wedge$ ("and"), $\vee$ ("or"), and $\sim$ ("not"). Typical propositional expressions are:

$$x < y$$

$$(x < y) \wedge (b = c)$$

$$x \text{ is prime}$$

A predicate is a function whose range consists of the truth values T and F.

c. *Conditional Expressions.* The dependence of truth values on the values of quantities of other kinds is expressed in mathematics by predicates, and the dependence of truth values on other truth values by logical connectives. However, the notations for expressing symbolically the dependence of quantities of other kinds on truth values is inadequate, so that English words and phrases are generally used for expressing these dependences in texts that describe other dependences symbolically. For example, the function $| x |$ is usually defined in words.

Conditional expressions are a device for expressing the dependence of quantities on propositional quantities. A conditional expression has the form

$$(p_1 \rightarrow e_1 , \cdots , p_n \rightarrow e_n)$$

where the p's are propositional expressions and the e's are expressions of any kind. It may be read, "If p_1 then e_1,

otherwise if p_2 then e_2 , $\cdots$, otherwise if p_n then e_n ," or "p_1 yields e_1 , $\cdots$, p_n yields e_n ."

We now give the rules for determining whether the value of $(p_1 \rightarrow e_1, \cdots, p_n \rightarrow e_n)$ is defined, and if so what its value is. Examine the p's from left to right. If a p whose value is T is encountered before any p whose value is undefined is encountered, then the value of the conditional expression is the value of the corresponding e (if this is defined). If any undefined p is encountered before a true p, or if all p's are false, or if the e corresponding to the first true p is undefined, then the value of the conditional expression is undefined. We now give examples.

$$(1 < 2 \rightarrow 4, 1 \geqq 2 \rightarrow 3) = 4$$

$$(2 < 1 \rightarrow 4, 2 > 1 \rightarrow 3, 2 > 1 \rightarrow 2) = 3$$

$$(2 < 1 \rightarrow 4, T \rightarrow 3) = 3$$

$$(2 < 1 \rightarrow \frac{0}{0}, T \rightarrow 3) = 3$$

$$(2 < 1 \rightarrow 3, T \rightarrow \frac{0}{0}) \text{ is undefined}$$

$$(2 < 1 \rightarrow 3, 4 < 1 \rightarrow 4) \text{ is undefined}$$

Some of the simplest applications of conditional expressions are in giving such definitions as

$$| x | = (x < 0 \rightarrow -x, T \rightarrow x)$$

$$\delta_{ij} = (i = j \rightarrow 1, T \rightarrow 0)$$

$$\text{sgn } (x) = (x < 0 \rightarrow -1, x = 0 \rightarrow 0, T \rightarrow 1)$$

d. *Recursive Function Definitions.* By using conditional expressions we can, without circularity, define functions by formulas in which the defined function occurs. For example, we write

$$n! = (n = 0 \rightarrow 1, T \rightarrow n \cdot (n - 1)!)$$

When we use this formula to evaluate 0! we get the answer 1; because of the way in which the value of a conditional expression was defined, the meaningless expression $0 \cdot (0 - 1)!$ does not arise. The evaluation of 2! according to this definition proceeds as follows:

$$2! = (2 = 0 \rightarrow 1, T \rightarrow 2 \cdot (2 - 1)!)$$

$$= 2 \cdot 1!$$

$$= 2 \cdot (1 = 0 \rightarrow 1, T \rightarrow 1 \cdot (1 - 1)!)$$

$$= 2 \cdot 1 \cdot 0!$$

$$= 2 \cdot 1 \cdot (0 = 0 \rightarrow 1, T \rightarrow 0 \cdot (0 - 1)!)$$

$$= 2 \cdot 1 \cdot 1$$

$$= 2$$

We now give two other applications of recursive function definitions. The greatest common divisor, gcd(m,n), of two positive integers m and n is computed by means of the Euclidean algorithm. This algorithm is expressed by the recursive function definition:

$$\gcd(m,n) = (m > n \rightarrow \gcd(n,m), \text{ rem}(n,m)$$

$$= 0 \rightarrow m, T \rightarrow \gcd(\text{rem}(n,m),m))$$

where rem(n, m) denotes the remainder left when n is divided by m.

The Newtonian algorithm for obtaining an approximate square root of a number a, starting with an initial approximation x and requiring that an acceptable approximation y satisfy $| y^2 - a | < \epsilon$, may be written as

$$\text{sqrt}(a, x, \epsilon)$$

$$= (| x^2 - a | < \epsilon \rightarrow x, T \rightarrow \text{sqrt } (a, \frac{1}{2} (x + \frac{a}{x}), \epsilon))$$

The simultaneous recursive definition of several functions is also possible, and we shall use such definitions if they are required.

There is no guarantee that the computation determined by a recursive definition will ever terminate and, for example, an attempt to compute n! from our definition wiil only succeed if n is a non-negative integer. If the computation does not terminate, the function must be regarded as undefined for the given arguments.

The propositional connectives themselves can be defined by conditional expressions. We write

$$p \wedge q = (p \rightarrow q, T \rightarrow F)$$

$$p \vee q = (p \rightarrow T, T \rightarrow q)$$

$$\sim p = (p \rightarrow F, T \rightarrow T)$$

$$p \supset q = (p \rightarrow q, T \rightarrow T)$$

It is readily seen that the right-hand sides of the equations have the correct truth tables. If we consider situations in which p or q may be undefined, the connectives $\wedge$ and $\vee$ are seen to be noncommutative. For example if p is false and q is undefined, we see that according to the definitions given above $p \wedge q$ is false, but $q \wedge p$ is undefined. For our applications this noncommutativity is desirable, since $p \wedge q$ is computed by first computing p, and if p is false q is not computed. If the computation for p does not terminate, we never get around to computing q. We shall use propositional connectives in this sense hereafter.

e. *Functions and Forms.* It is usual in mathematics—outside of mathematical logic—to use the word "function" imprecisely and to apply it to forms such as $y^2 + x$. Because we shall later compute with expressions for functions, we need a distinction between functions and forms and a notation for expressing this distinction. This distinction and a notation for describing it, from which we deviate trivially, is given by Church [3].

Let f be an expression that stands for a function of two integer variables. It should make sense to write $f(3, 4)$ and the value of this expression should be determined. The expression $y^2 + x$ does not meet this requirement;

$y^2 + x(3, 4)$ is not a conventional notation, and if we attempted to define it we would be uncertain whether its value would turn out to be 13 or 19. Church calls an expression like $y^2 + x$ a form. A form can be converted into a function if we can determine the correspondence between the variables occurring in the form and the ordered list of arguments of the desired function. This is accomplished by Church's λ-notation.

If $\mathcal{E}$ is a form in variables $x_1, \cdots, x_n$, then $\lambda((x_1, \cdots, x_n), \mathcal{E})$ will be taken to be the function of n variables whose value is determined by substituting the arguments for the variables $x_1, \cdots, x_n$ in that order in $\mathcal{E}$ and evaluating the resulting expression. For example, $\lambda((x,y), y^2+x)$ is a function of two variables, and $\lambda((x, y), y^2+x)(3,4) = 19$.

The variables occurring in the list of variables of a λ-expression are dummy or bound, like variables of integration in a definite integral. That is, we may change the names of the bound variables in a function expression without changing the value of the expression, provided that we make the same change for each occurrence of the variable and do not make two variables the same that previously were different. Thus $\lambda((x,y), y^2+x), \lambda((u,v), v^2+u)$ and $\lambda((y, x), x^2+y)$ denote the same function.

We shall frequently use expressions in which some of the variables are bound by λ's and others are not. Such an expression may be regarded as defining a function with parameters. The unbound variables are called free variables.

An adequate notation that distinguishes functions from forms allows an unambiguous treatment of functions of functions. It would involve too much of a digression to give examples here, but we shall use functions with functions as arguments later in this report.

Difficulties arise in combining functions described by λ-expressions, or by any other notation involving variables, because different bound variables may be represented by the same symbol. This is called collision of bound variables. There is a notation involving operators that are called combinators for combining functions without the use of variables. Unfortunately, the combinatory expressions for interesting combinations of functions tend to be lengthy and unreadable.

f. *Expressions for Recursive Functions.* The λ-notation is inadequate for naming functions defined recursively. For example, using λ's, we can convert the definition

$$sqrt(a, x, \epsilon)$$

$$= (\,|x^2 - a|\, < \epsilon \to x, T \to sqrt(a, \tfrac{1}{2}(x + \tfrac{a}{x}), \epsilon))$$

into

$$sqrt = \lambda((a, x, \epsilon), (\,|x^2 - a|\, < \epsilon \to x, T \to$$

$$sqrt(a, \tfrac{1}{2}(x + \tfrac{a}{x})\,, \epsilon)))$$

but the right-hand side cannot serve as an expression for the function because there would be nothing to indicate that the reference to sqrt within the expression stood for the expression as a whole.

In order to be able to write expressions for recursive functions, we introduce another notation label($a, \mathcal{E}$) denotes the expression $\mathcal{E}$, provided that occurrences of a within $\mathcal{E}$ are to be interpreted as referring to the expression as a whole. Thus we can write

$$label(sqrt, \lambda((a, x, \epsilon), (\,|x^2 - a|\,$$

$$< \epsilon \to x, T \to sqrt\,(a, \tfrac{1}{2}(x + \tfrac{a}{x}), \epsilon))))$$

as a name for our sqrt function.

The symbol a in label($a, \mathcal{E}$) is also bound, that is, it may be altered systematically without changing the meaning of the expression. It behaves differently from a variable bound by a λ, however.

3. Recursive Functions of Symbolic Expressions

We shall first define a class of symbolic expressions in terms of ordered pairs and lists. Then we shall define five elementary functions and predicates, and build from them by composition, conditional expressions, and recursive definitions an extensive class of functions of which we shall give a number of examples. We shall then show how these functions themselves can be expressed as symbolic expressions, and we shall define a universal function *apply* that allows us to compute from the expression for a given function its value for given arguments. Finally, we shall define some functions with functions as arguments and give some useful examples.

a. *A Class of Symbolic Expressions.* We shall now define the S-expressions (S stands for symbolic). They are formed by using the special characters

.
)
(

and an infinite set of distinguishable atomic symbols. For atomic symbols, we shall use strings of capital Latin letters and digits with single imbedded blanks. Examples of atomic symbols are

A

ABA

APPLE PIE NUMBER 3

There is a twofold reason for departing from the usual mathematical practice of using single letters for atomic symbols. First, computer programs frequently require hundreds of distinguishable symbols that must be formed from the 47 characters that are printable by the IBM 704 computer. Second, it is convenient to allow English words and phrases to stand for atomic entities for mnemonic reasons. The symbols are atomic in the sense that any substructure they may have as sequences of characters is ignored. We assume only that different symbols can be distinguished.

S-expressions are then defined as follows:

1. Atomic symbols are S-expressions.
2. If e_1 and e_2 are S-expressions, so is $(e_1 \cdot e_2)$.

Examples of S-expressions are

$$AB$$
$$(A \cdot B)$$
$$((AB \cdot C) \cdot D)$$

An S-expression is then simply an ordered pair, the terms of which may be atomic symbols or simpler S-expressions. We can represent a list of arbitrary length in terms of S-expressions as follows. The list

$$(m_1, m_2, \cdots, m_n)$$

is represented by the S-expression

$$(m_1 \cdot (m_2 \cdot (\cdots (m_n \cdot NIL) \cdots)))$$

Here NIL is an atomic symbol used to terminate lists.

Since many of the symbolic expressions with which we deal are conveniently expressed as lists, we shall introduce a list notation to abbreviate certain S-expressions. We have

1. (m) stands for $(m \cdot NIL)$.
2. $(m_1, \cdots, m_n)$ stands for $(m_1 \cdot (\cdots (m_n \cdot NIL) \cdots))$.
3. $(m_1, \cdots, m_n \cdot x)$ stands for $(m_1 \cdot (\cdots (m_n \cdot x) \cdots))$.

Subexpressions can be similarly abbreviated. Some examples of these abbreviations are

$$((AB, C), D) \text{ for } ((AB \cdot (C \cdot NIL)) \cdot (D \cdot NIL))$$
$$((A, B), C, D \cdot E) \text{ for } ((A \cdot (B \cdot NIL)) \cdot (C \cdot (D \cdot E)))$$

Since we regard the expressions with commas as abbreviations for those not involving commas, we shall refer to them all as S-expressions.

b. *Functions of S-expressions and the Expressions That Represent Them.* We now define a class of functions of S-expressions. The expressions representing these functions are written in a conventional functional notation. However, in order to clearly distinguish the expressions representing functions from S-expressions, we shall use sequences of lower-case letters for function names and variables ranging over the set of S-expressions. We also use brackets and semicolons, instead of parentheses and commas, for denoting the application of functions to their arguments. Thus we write

$$car [x]$$
$$car [cons [(A \cdot B); x]]$$

In these M-expressions (meta-expressions) any S-expressions that occur stand for themselves.

c. *The Elementary S-functions and Predicates.* We introduce the following functions and predicates:

1. atom.   atom [x] has the value of T or F, accordingly as x is an atomic symbol or not. Thus

$$atom [X] = T$$
$$atom [(X \cdot A)] = F$$

2. eq.   eq [x; y] is defined if and only if both x and y are atomic. eq [x; y] = T if x and y are the same symbol, and eq [x; y] = F otherwise. Thus

$$eq [X; X] = T$$
$$eq [X; A] = F$$
$$eq [X; (X \cdot A)] \text{ is undefined.}$$

3. car.   car [x] is defined if and only if x is not atomic. car $[(e_1 \cdot e_2)] = e_1$. Thus car [X] is undefined.

$$car [(X \cdot A)] = X$$
$$car [((X \cdot A) \cdot Y)] = (X \cdot A)$$

4. cdr.   cdr [x] is also defined when x is not atomic. We have cdr $[(e_1 \cdot e_2)] = e_2$. Thus cdr [X] is undefined.

$$cdr [(X \cdot A)] = A$$
$$cdr [((X \cdot A) \cdot Y)] = Y$$

5. cons.   cons [x; y] is defined for any x and y. We have cons $[e_1; e_2] = (e_1 \cdot e_2)$. Thus

$$cons [X; A] = (X \cdot A)$$
$$cons [(X \cdot A); Y] = ((X \cdot A) \cdot Y)$$

car, cdr, and cons are easily seen to satisfy the relations

$$car [cons [x; y]] = x$$
$$cdr [cons [x; y]] = y$$
$$cons [car [x]; cdr [x]] = x, \quad \text{provided that x is not atomic.}$$

The names "car" and "cons" will come to have mnemonic significance only when we discuss the representation of the system in the computer. Compositions of car and cdr give the subexpressions of a given expression in a given position. Compositions of cons form expressions of a given structure out of parts. The class of functions which can be formed in this way is quite limited and not very interesting.

d. *Recursive S-functions.* We get a much larger class of functions (in fact, all computable functions) when we allow ourselves to form new functions of S-expressions by conditional expressions and recursive definition.

We now give some examples of functions that are definable in this way.

1. ff [x].   The value of ff [x] is the first atomic symbol of the S-expression x with the parentheses ignored. Thus

$$ff [((A \cdot B) \cdot C)] = A$$

We have

$$ff [x] = [atom [x] \rightarrow x; T \rightarrow ff [car [x]]]$$

We now trace in detail the steps in the evaluation of ff $[((A \cdot B) \cdot C)]$:

ff $[((A \cdot B) \cdot C)]$

$$= [atom [((A \cdot B) \cdot C)] \rightarrow ((A \cdot B) \cdot C);$$
$$T \rightarrow ff [car [((A \cdot B) \cdot C)]]]$$

$$= [F \rightarrow ((A \cdot B) \cdot C); T \rightarrow ff [car [((A \cdot B) \cdot C)]]]$$

$$= [T \rightarrow ff [car [((A \cdot B) \cdot C)]]]$$

$= \text{ff} [\text{car} [((A \cdot B) \cdot C)]]$

$= \text{ff} [(A \cdot B)]$

$= [\text{atom} [(A \cdot B)] \rightarrow (A \cdot B); T \rightarrow \text{ff} [\text{car} [(A \cdot B)]]]$

$= [F \rightarrow (A \cdot B); T \rightarrow \text{ff} [\text{car} [(A \cdot B)]]]$

$= [T \rightarrow \text{ff} [\text{car} [(A \cdot B)]]]$

$= \text{ff} [\text{car} [(A \cdot B)]]$

$= \text{ff} [A]$

$= [\text{atom} [A] \rightarrow A; T \rightarrow \text{ff} [\text{car} [A]]]$

$= [T \rightarrow A; T \rightarrow \text{ff} [\text{car} [A]]]$

$= A$

2. subst [x; y; z]. This function gives the result of substituting the S-expression x for all occurrences of the atomic symbol y in the S-expression z. It is defined by

$\text{subst} [x; y; z] = [\text{atom} [z] \rightarrow [\text{eq} [z; y] \rightarrow x; T \rightarrow z];$

$T \rightarrow \text{cons} [\text{subst} [x; y; \text{car} [z]]; \text{subst} [x; y; \text{cdr} [z]]]]$

As an example, we have

$\text{subst} [(X \cdot A); B; ((A \cdot B) \cdot C)] = ((A \cdot (X \cdot A)) \cdot C)$

3. equal [x; y]. This is a predicate that has the value T if x and y are the same S-expression, and has the value F otherwise. We have

$\text{equal} [x; y] = [\text{atom} [x] \wedge \text{atom} [y] \wedge \text{eq} [x; y]]$

$\vee [{\sim}\text{atom} [x] \wedge {\sim}\text{atom} [y] \wedge \text{equal} [\text{car} [x]; \text{car} [y]]$

$\wedge \text{equal} [\text{cdr} [x]; \text{cdr} [y]]]$

It is convenient to see how the elementary functions look in the abbreviated list notation. The reader will easily verify that

(i) $\text{car} [(m_1, m_2, \cdots, m_n)] = m_1$

(ii) $\text{cdr} [(m_1, m_2, \cdots, m_n)] = (m_2, \cdots, m_n)$

(iii) $\text{cdr} [(m)] = \text{NIL}$

(iv) $\text{cons} [m_1; (m_2, \cdots, m_n)] = (m_1, m_2, \cdots, m_n)$

(v) $\text{cons} [m; \text{NIL}] = (m)$

We define

$\text{null} [x] = \text{atom} [x] \wedge \text{eq} [x; \text{NIL}]$

This predicate is useful in dealing with lists.

Compositions of car and cdr arise so frequently that many expressions can be written more concisely if we abbreviate

$\text{cadr} [x] \quad \text{for} \quad \text{car} [\text{cdr} [x]],$

$\text{caddr} [x] \quad \text{for} \quad \text{car} [\text{cdr} [\text{cdr} [x]]], \text{ etc.}$

Another useful abbreviation is to write list $[e_1; e_2; \cdots; e_n]$ for cons $[e_1; \text{cons} [e_2; \cdots; \text{cons} [e_n; \text{NIL}] \cdots]]$. This function gives the list, $(e_1, \cdots, e_n)$, as a function of its elements.

The following functions are useful when S-expressions are regarded as lists.

1. append [x; y].

$\text{append} [x; y] = [\text{null} [x] \rightarrow y; T \rightarrow \text{cons} [\text{car} [x];$

$\text{append} [\text{cdr} [x]; y]]]$

An example is

$\text{append} [(A, B); (C, D, E)] = (A, B, C, D, E)$

2. among [x; y]. This predicate is true if the S-expression x occurs among the elements of the list y. We have

$\text{among} [x; y] = {\sim}\text{null} [y] \wedge [\text{equal} [x; \text{car} [y]]$

$\vee \text{among} [x; \text{cdr} [y]]]$

3. pair [x; y]. This function gives the list of pairs of corresponding elements of the lists x and y. We have

$\text{pair} [x; y] = [\text{null} [x] \wedge \text{null} [y] \rightarrow \text{NIL}; {\sim}\text{atom} [x]$

$\wedge {\sim}\text{atom} [y] \rightarrow \text{cons} [\text{list} [\text{car} [x]; \text{car} [y]];$

$\text{pair} [\text{cdr} [x]; \text{cdr} [y]]]]$

An example is

$\text{pair} [(A, B, C); (X, (Y, Z), U)] = ((A, X),$

$(B, (Y, Z)), (C, U))$

4. assoc [x; y]. If y is a list of the form $((u_1, v_1), \cdots, (u_n, v_n))$ and x is one of the u's, then assoc [x; y] is the corresponding v. We have

$\text{assoc} [x; y] = \text{eq}[\text{caar} [y]; x] \rightarrow \text{cadar} [y];$

$T \rightarrow \text{assoc} [x; \text{cdr} [y]]]$

An example is

$\text{assoc} [X; ((W, (A, B)), (X, (C, D)),$

$(Y, (E, F)))] = (C, D)$

5. sublis [x; y]. Here x is assumed to have the form of a list of pairs $((u_1, v_1), \cdots, (u_n, v_n))$, where the u's are atomic, and y may be any S-expression. The value of sublis [x; y] is the result of substituting each v for the corresponding u in y. In order to define sublis, we first define an auxiliary function. We have

$\text{sub2} [x; z] = [\text{null} [x] \rightarrow z; \text{eq} [\text{caar} [x]; z] \rightarrow \text{cadar} [x];$

$T \rightarrow \text{sub2} [\text{cdr} [x]; z]]$

and

$\text{sublis} [x; y] = [\text{atom} [y] \rightarrow \text{sub2} [x; y];$

$T \rightarrow \text{cons} [\text{sublis} [x; \text{car} [y]]; \text{sublis} [x; \text{cdr} [y]]]]$

We have

$\text{sublis} [((X, (A, B)), (Y, (B, C))); (A, X \cdot Y)]$

$= (A, (A, B), B, C)$

e. *Representation of S-Functions by S-Expressions.* S-functions have been described by M-expressions. We now give a rule for translating M-expressions into S-expressions, in order to be able to use S-functions for making certain computations with S-functions and for answering certain questions about S-functions.

The translation is determined by the following rules in which we denote the translation of an M-expression ε by ε^*.

1. If ε is an S-expression E* is (QUOTE, ε).

2. Variables and function names that were represented by strings of lower-case letters are translated to the corresponding strings of the corresponding upper-case letters. Thus car* is CAR, and subst* is SUBST.

3. A form f[e_1 ; $\cdots$; e_n] is translated to (f*, e_1*, $\cdots$, e_n*). Thus {cons [car [x]; cdr [x]]}* is (CONS, (CAR, X), (CDR, X)).

4. {[$p_1 \rightarrow e_1$; $\cdots$; $p_n \rightarrow e_n$]}* is (COND, (p_1*, e_1*), $\cdots$, (p_n*. e_n*)).

5. {λ[[x_1 ; $\cdots$; x_n]; ε]}* is (LAMBDA, (x_1*, $\cdots$, x_n*), ε*).

6. {label [a; ε]}* is (LABEL, a*, ε*).

With these conventions the substitution function whose M-expression is label [subst; λ[[x; y; z]; [atom [z] $\rightarrow$ [eq [y; z] $\rightarrow$ x; T $\rightarrow$ z]; T $\rightarrow$ cons [subst [x; y; car [z]]; subst [x; y; cdr [z]]]]]] has the S-expression

(LABEL, SUEST, (LAMBDA, (X, Y, Z), (COND

((ATOM, Z), (COND, (EQ, Y, Z), X), ((QUOTE,

T), Z))), ((QUOTE, T), (CONS, (SUBST, X, Y,

(CAR Z)), (SUBST, X, Y, (CDR, Z)))))))))

This notation is writable and somewhat readable. It can be made easier to read and write at the cost of making its structure less regular. If more characters were available on the computer, it could be improved considerably.

f. *The Universal S-Function* apply. There is an S-function *apply* with the property that if f is an S-expression for an S-function f' and args is a list of arguments of the form (argl, $\cdots$, argn), where argl, $\cdots$, argn are arbitrary S-expressions, then apply[f; args] and f'[argl; $\cdots$; argn] are defined for the same values of argl, $\cdots$, argn, and are equal when defined. For example,

λ[[x; y]; cons [car [x]; y]] [(A, B); (C, D)]

= apply [(LAMBDA, (X, Y), (CONS, (CAR, X),

Y)); ((A, B), (C, D))] = (A, C, D)

The S-function *apply* is defined by

apply [f; args] = eval [cons [f; appq [args]]; NIL]

where

appq [m] = [null [m] $\rightarrow$ NIL;

T $\rightarrow$ cons [list [QUOTE; car [m]]; appq [cdr [m]]]]

and

eval [e; a] = [

atom [e] $\rightarrow$ assoc [e; a];

atom [car [e]] $\rightarrow$ [

eq [car [e]; QUOTE] $\rightarrow$ cadr [e];

eq [car [e]; ATOM] $\rightarrow$ atom [eval [cadr [e]; a]];

eq [car [e]; EQ] $\rightarrow$ [eval [cadr [e]; a] = eval [caddr [e]; a]];

eq [car [e]; COND] $\rightarrow$ evcon [cdr [e]; a];

eq [car [e]; CAR] $\rightarrow$ car [eval [cadr [e]; a]];

eq [car [e]; CDR] $\rightarrow$ cdr [eval [cadr [e]; a]];

eq [car [e]; CONS] $\rightarrow$ cons [eval [cadr [e]; a]; eval [caddr [e];

a]]; T $\rightarrow$ eval [cons [assoc [car [e]; a];

evlis [cdr [e]; a]]; a]];

eq [caar [e]; LABEL] $\rightarrow$ eval [cons [caddar [e]; cdr [e]];

cons [list [cadar [e]; car [e]; a]];

eq [caar [e]; LAMBDA] $\rightarrow$ eval [caddar [e];

append [pair [cadar [e]; evlis [cdr [e]; a]; a]]]

and

evcon [c; a] = [eval [caar [c]; a] $\rightarrow$ eval [cadar [c]; a];

T $\rightarrow$ evcon [cdr [c]; a]]

and

evlis [m; a] = [null [m] $\rightarrow$ NIL;

T $\rightarrow$ cons [eval [car [m]; a]; evlis [cdr [m]; a]]]

We now explain a number of points about these definitions.

1. *apply* itself forms an expression representing the value of the function applied to the arguments, and puts the work of evaluating this expression onto a function eval. It uses appq to put quotes around each of the arguments, so that eval will regard them as standing for themselves.

2. eval [e; a] has two arguments, an expression e to be evaluated, and a list of pairs a. The first item of each pair is an atomic symbol, and the second is the expression for which the symbol stands.

3. If the expression to be evaluated is atomic, eval evaluates whatever is paired with it first on the list a.

4. If e is not atomic but car [e] is atomic, then the expression has one of the forms (QUOTE, e) or (ATOM, e) or (EQ, e_1 , e_2) or (COND, (p_1 , e_1) , $\cdots$, (p_n , e_n)), or (CAR, e) or (CDR, e) or (CONS, e_1 , e_2) or (f, e_1 , $\cdots$, e_n) where f is an atomic symbol.

In the case (QUOTE; e) the expression e, itself, is taken. In the case of (ATOM, e) or (CAR, e) or (CDR, e) the expression e is evaluated and the appropriate function taken. In the case of (EQ, e_1 , e_2) or (CONS, e_1 , e_2) two expressions have to be evaluated. In the case of (COND,

$(p_1, e_1), \cdots, (p_n, e_n))$ the p's have to be evaluated in order until a true p is found, and then the corresponding e must be evaluated. This is accomplished by evcon. Finally, in the case of $(f, e_1, \cdots, e_n)$ we evaluate the expression that results from replacing f in this expression by whatever it is paired with in the list a.

5. The evaluation of $((LABEL, f, \varepsilon), e_1, \cdots, e_n)$ is accomplished by evaluating $(\varepsilon, e_1, \cdots, e_n)$ with the pairing $(f, (LABEL, f, \varepsilon))$ put on the front of the previous list a of pairs.

6. Finally, the evaluation of $((LAMBDA, (x_1, \cdots, x_n), \varepsilon), e_1, \cdots, e_n)$ is accomplished by evaluating ε with the list of pairs $((x_1, e_1), \cdots, ((x_n, e_n))$ put on the front of the previous list a.

The list a could be eliminated, and LAMBDA and LABEL expressions evaluated by substituting the arguments for the variables in the expressions ε. Unfortunately, difficulties involving collisions of bound variables arise, but they are avoided by using the list a.

Calculating the values of functions by using *apply* is an activity better suited to electronic computers than to people. As an illustration, however, we now give some of the steps for calculating

apply [(LABEL, FF, (LAMBDA, (X), (COND,

$\qquad$ ((ATOM, X), X), ((QUOTE, T),

$\qquad\qquad$ (FF, (CAR, X)))))); ((A·B))] = A

The first argument is the S-expression that represents the function ff defined in section 3d. We shall abbreviate it by using the letter ϕ. We have

apply $[\phi; ((A·B))]$

$\quad$ = eval [((LABEL, FF, ψ), (QUOTE, (A·B))); NIL]

$\qquad$ where ψ is the part of ϕ beginning (LAMBDA

$\quad$ = eval [((LAMBDA, (X), ω), (QUOTE, (A·B)));
$\qquad$ ((FF, ϕ))]

$\qquad$ where ω is the part of ψ beginning (COND

$\quad$ = eval [(COND, $(\pi_1, \epsilon_1), (\pi_2, \epsilon_2)); ((X, (QUOTE, (A·B))), (FF, \phi))]$

$\qquad$ Denoting $((X, (QUOTE, (A·B))), (FF, \phi))$ by α, we obtain

$\quad$ = evcon $[((\pi_1, \epsilon_1), (\pi_2, \epsilon_2)); \alpha]$

$\qquad$ This involves eval $[\pi_1; \alpha]$

$\quad$ = eval [(ATOM, X); α]

$\quad$ = atom [eval [X; α]]

$\quad$ = atom [eval [assoc [X; ((X, (QUOTE, (A·B))), (FF, ϕ))]; α]]

$\quad$ = atom [eval [(QUOTE, (A·B)); α]]

$\quad$ = atom [(A·B)]

$\quad$ = F

Our main calculation continues with

apply $[\phi; ((A·B))]$

$\quad$ = evcon $[((\pi_2, \epsilon_2)); \alpha],$

which involves eval $[\pi_2; \alpha]$ = eval [(QUOTE, T); α] = T.

Our main calculation again continues with

apply $[\phi; ((A·B))]$

$\quad$ = eval $[\epsilon_2; \alpha]$

$\quad$ = eval [(FF, (CAR, X)); α]

$\quad$ = eval [cons $[\phi;$ evlis [((CAR, X)); α]]; α]

Evaluating evlis [((CAR, X)); α] involves

eval [(CAR, X); α]

$\quad$ = car [eval [X; α]]

$\quad$ = car [(A·B)], where we took steps from the earlier computation of atom [eval [X; α]] = A,

and so evlis [((CAR, X)); α] then becomes

$\qquad$ list [list [QUOTE; A]] = ((QUOTE, A)),

and our main quantity becomes

$\qquad$ = eval [(ϕ, (QUOTE, A)); α]

The subsequent steps are made as in the beginning of the calculation. The LABEL and LAMBDA cause new pairs to be added to α, which gives a new list of pairs α_1. The π_1 term of the conditional eval [(ATOM, X); α_1] has the value T because X is paired with (QUOTE, A) first in α_1, rather than with (QUOTE, (A·B)) as in α.

Therefore we end up with eval [X; α_1] from the *evcon*, and this is just A.

g. Functions with Functions as Arguments. There are a number of useful functions some of whose arguments are functions. They are especially useful in defining other functions. One such function is maplist [x; f] with an S-expression argument x and an argument f that is a function from S-expressions to S-expressions. We define

maplist $[x; f] = [null [x] \rightarrow NIL;$

$\qquad\qquad\qquad T \rightarrow cons [f[x];$ maplist [cdr [x]; f]]]

The usefulness of *maplist* is illustrated by formulas for the partial derivative with respect to x of expressions involving sums and products of x and other variables. The S-expressions that we shall differentiate are formed as follows.

1. An atomic symbol is an allowed expression.

2. If $e_1, e_2, \cdots, e_n$ are allowed expressions, (PLUS, $e_1, \cdots, e_n$) and (TIMES, $e_1, \cdots, e_n$) are also, and represent the sum and product, respectively, of $e_1, \cdots, e_n$.

This is, essentially, the Polish notation for functions, except that the inclusion of parentheses and commas allows functions of variable numbers of arguments. An example of an allowed expression is (TIMES, X, (PLUS, X, A), Y), the conventional algebraic notation for which is X(X + A)Y.

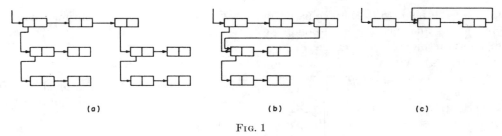

(a)   (b)   (c)

Fig. 1

Our differentiation formula, which gives the derivative of y with respect to x, is

diff [y; x] = [atom [y] → [eq [y; x] → ONE; T → ZERO];
eq [car [y]; PLUS] → cons [PLUS; maplist [cdr [y]; λ[[z];
diff[car [z]; x]]]]; eq[car [y]; TIMES] → cons[PLUS;
maplist[cdr[y]; λ[[z]; cons [TIMES; maplist[cdr [y];
λ[[w]; ∼eq [z; w] → car [w]; T → diff [car [[w]; x]]]]]]]]

The derivative of the allowed expression, as computed by this formula, is

(PLUS, (TIMES, ONE, (PLUS, X, A), Y),

(TIMES, X, (PLUS, ONE, ZERO), Y),

(TIMES, X, (PLUS, X, A), ZERO))

Besides *maplist*, another useful function with functional arguments is *search*, which is defined as

search [x; p; f; u] = [null [x] → u; p[x] → f[x];

T → search [cdr [x]; p; f; u]

The function *search* is used to search a list for an element that has the property p, and if such an element is found, f of that element is taken. If there is no such element, the function u of no argument is computed.

4. The LISP Programming System

The LISP programming system is a system for using the IBM 704 computer to compute with symbolic information in the form of S-expressions. It has been or will be used for the following purposes:

1. Writing a compiler to compile LISP programs into machine language.

2. Writing a program to check proofs in a class of formal logical systems.

3. Writing programs for formal differentiation and integration.

4. Writing programs to realize various algorithms for generating proofs in predicate calculus.

5. Making certain engineering calculations whose results are formulas rather than numbers.

6. Programming the Advice Taker system.

The basis of the system is a way of writing computer programs to evaluate S-functions. This will be described in the following sections.

In addition to the facilities for describing S-functions, there are facilities for using S-functions in programs written as sequences of statements along the lines of Fortran (4) or Algol (5). These features will not be described in this article.

a. Representation of S-Expressions by List Structure. A list structure is a collection of computer words arranged as in figure 1a or 1b. Each word of the list structure is represented by one of the subdivided rectangles in the figure. The *left* box of a rectangle represents the *address* field of the word and the *right* box represents the *decrement* field. An arrow from a box to another rectangle means that the field corresponding to the box contains the location of the word corresponding to the other rectangle.

It is permitted for a substructure to occur in more than one place in a list structure, as in figure 1b, but it is not permitted for a sturcture to have cycles, as in figure 1c.

An atomic symbol is represented in the computer by a list structure of special form called the *association list* of the symbol. The address field of the first word contains a special constant which enables the program to tell that this word represents an atomic symbol. We shall describe association lists in section 4b.

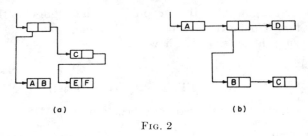

(a)   (b)

Fig. 2

An S-expression x that is not atomic is represented by a word, the address and decrement parts of which contain the locations of the subexpressions car[x] and cdr[x], respectively. If we use the symbols A, B, etc. to denote the locations of the association list of these symbols, then the S-expression ((A·B)·(C·(E·F))) is represented by the list structure *a* of figure 2. Turning to the list form of S-expressions, we see that the S-expression (A, (B, C), D), which is an abbreviation for (A·((B·(C·NIL))·(D·NIL))), is represented by the list structure of figure 2b. When a list structure is regarded as representing a list, we see that each term of the list occupies the address part of a word, the decrement part of which *points* to the word containing the next term, while the last word has NIL in its decrement.

An expression that has a given subexpression occurring more than once can be represented in more than one way. Whether the list structure for the subexpression is or is not repeated depends upon the history of the program. Whether or not a subexpression is repeated will make no

difference in the results of a program as they appear outside the machine, although it will affect the time and storage requirements. For example, the S-expression $((A \cdot B) \cdot (A \cdot B))$ can be represented by either the list structure of figure 3a or 3b.

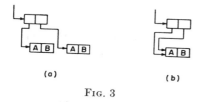

(a)   (b)

Fig. 3

The prohibition against circular list structures is essentially a prohibition against an expression being a subexpression of itself. Such an expression could not exist on paper in a world with our topology. Circular list structures would have some advantages in the machine, for example, for representing recursive functions, but difficulties in printing them, and in certain other operations, make it seem advisable not to use them for the present.

The advantages of list structures for the storage of symbolic expressions are:

1. The size and even the number of expressions with which the program will have to deal cannot be predicted in advance. Therefore, it is difficult to arrange blocks of storage of fixed length to contain them.

2. Registers can be put back on the free-storage list when they are no longer needed. Even one register returned to the list is of value, but if expressions are stored linearly, it is difficult to make use of blocks of registers of odd sizes that may become available.

3. An expression that occurs as a subexpression of several expressions need be represented in storage only once.

b. *Association Lists.* In the Lisp programming system we put more in the association list of a symbol than is required by the mathematical system described in the previous sections. In fact, any information that we desire to associate with the symbol may be put on the association list. This information may include: the *print name,* that is, the string of letters and digits which represents the symbol outside the machine; a numerical value if the symbol represents a number; another S-expression if the symbol, in some way, serves as a name for it; or the location of a routine if the symbol represents a function for which there is a machine-language subroutine. All this implies that in the machine system there are more primitive entities than have been described in the sections on the mathematical system.

For the present, we shall only describe how *print names* are represented on association lists so that in reading or printing the program can establish a correspondence between information on punched cards, magnetic tape or printed page and the list structure inside the machine. The association list of the symbol DIFFERENTIATE has a segment of the form shown in figure 4. Here *pname* is a symbol that indicates that the structure for the print

name of the symbol whose association list this is hangs from the next word on the association list. In the second row of the figure we have a list of three words. The address part of each of these words points to a word containing six 6-bit characters. The last word is filled out with a 6-bit combination that does not represent a character printable by the computer. (Recall that the IBM 704 has a 36-bit word and that printable characters are each represented by 6 bits.) The presence of the words with character information means that the association lists do not themselves represent S-expressions, and that only some of the functions for dealing with S-expressions make sense within as association list.

c. *Free-Storage List.* At any given time only a part of the memory reserved for list structures will actually be in use for storing S-expressions. The remaining registers (in our system the number, initially, is approximately 15,000) are arranged in a single list called the *free-storage list.* A certain register, FREE, in the program contains the location of the first register in this list. When a word is required to form some additional list structure, the first word on the *free-storage list* is taken and the number in register FREE is changed to become the location of the second word on the free-storage list. No provision need be made for the user to program the return of registers to the free-storage list.

This return takes place automatically, approximately as follows (it is necessary to give a simplified description of this process in this report): There is a fixed set of base registers in the program which contains the locations of list structures that are accessible to the program. Of course, because list structures branch, an arbitrary number of registers may be involved. Each register that is accessible to the program is accessible because it can be reached from one or more of the base registers by a chain of car and cdr operations. When the contents of a base register are changed, it may happen that the register to which the base register formerly pointed cannot be reached by a car-cdr chain from any base register. Such a register may be considered abandoned by the program because its contents can no longer be found by any possible program; hence its contents are no longer of interest, and so we would like to have it back on the free-storage list. This comes about in the following way.

Nothing happens until the program runs out of free storage. When a free register is wanted, and there is none left on the free-storage list, a reclamation cycle starts.

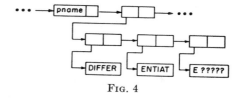

Fig. 4

First, the program finds all registers accessible from the base registers and makes their signs negative. This is accomplished by starting from each of the base registers

and changing the sign of every register that can be reached from it by a car-cdr chain. If the program encounters a register in this process which already has a negative sign, it assumes that this register has already been reached.

After all of the accessible registers have had their signs changed, the program goes through the area of memory reserved for the storage of list structures and puts all the registers whose signs were not changed in the previous step back on the free-storage list, and makes the signs of the accessible registers positive again.

This process, because it is entirely automatic, is more convenient for the programmer than a system in which he has to keep track of and erase unwanted lists. Its efficiency depends upon not coming close to exhausting the available memory with accessible lists. This is because the reclamation process requires several seconds to execute, and therefore must result in the addition of at least several thousand registers to the free-storage list if the program is not to spend most of its time in reclamation.

d. *Elementary S-Functions in the Computer.* We shall now describe the computer representations of atom, =, car, cdr, and cons. An S-expression is communicated to the program that represents a function as the location of the word representing it, and the programs give S-expression answers in the same form.

atom. As stated above, a word representing an atomic symbol has a special constant in its address part: atom is programmed as an open subroutine that tests this part. Unless the M-expression atom[e] occurs as a condition in a conditional expression, the symbol T or F is generated as the result of the test. In case of a conditional expression, a conditional transfer is used and the symbol T or F is not generated.

eq. The program for eq[e; f] involves testing for the numerical equality of the locations of the words. This works because each atomic symbol has only one association list. As with *atom*, the result is either a conditional transfer or one of the symbols T or F.

car. Computing car[x] involves getting the contents of the address part of register x. This is essentially accomplished by the single instruction CLA 0, i, where the argument is in index register i, and the result appears in the address part of the accumulator. (We take the view that the places from which a function takes its arguments and into which it puts its results are prescribed in the definition of the function, and it is the responsibility of the programmer or the compiler to insert the required data-moving instructions to get the results of one calculation in position for the next.) ("car" is a mnemonic for "contents of the address part of register.")

cdr. cdr is handled in the same way as car, except that the result appears in the decrement part of the accumulator. ("cdr" stands for "contents of the decrement part of register.")

cons. The value of cons[x; y] must be the location of a register that has x and y in its address and decrement parts, respectively. There may not be such a register in

the computer and, even if there were, it would be time-consuming to find it. Actually, what we do is to take the first available register from the *free-storage list*, put x and y in the address and decrement parts, respectively, and make the value of the function the location of the register taken. ("cons" is an abbreviation for "construct.")

It is the subroutine for cons that initiates the reclamation when the free-storage list is exhausted. In the version of the system that is used at present cons is represented by a closed subroutine. In the compiled version, cons is open.

e. *Representation of S-Functions by Programs.* The compilation of functions that are compositions of car, cdr, and cons, either by hand or by a compiler program, is straightforward. Conditional expressions give no trouble except that they must be so compiled that only the p's and e's that are required are computed. However, problems arise in the compilation of recursive functions.

In general (we shall discuss an exception), the routine for a recursive function uses itself as a subroutine. For example, the program for subst[x;y;z] uses itself as a subroutine to evaluate the result into the subexpressions car[z] and cdr[z]. While subst[x;y:cdr[z]] is being evaluated, the result of the previous evaluation of subst[x; y; car[z]] must be saved in a temporary storage register. However, subst may need the same register for evaluating subst[x;y;cdr[z]]. This possible conflict is resolved by the SAVE and UNSAVE routines that use the *public push-down list*. The SAVE routine is entered at the beginning of the routine for the recursive function with a request to save a given set of consecutive registers. A block of registers called the *public push-down list* is reserved for this purpose. The SAVE routine has an index that tells it how many registers in the push-down list are already in use. It moves the contents of the registers which are to be saved to the first unused registers in the push-down list, advances the index of the list, and returns to the program from which control came. This program may then freely use these registers for temporary storage. Before the routine exits it uses UNSAVE, which restores the contents of the temporary registers from the push-down list and moves back the index of this list. The result of these conventions is described, in programming terminology, by saying that the recursive subroutine is transparent to the temporary storage registers.

f. *Status of the LISP Programming System* (February 1960). A variant of the function *apply* described in section 5f has been translated into a program APPLY for the IBM 704. Since this routine can compute values of S-functions given their descriptions as S-expressions and their arguments, it serves as an interpreter for the LISP programming language which describes computation processes in this way.

The program APPLY has been imbedded in the LISP programming system which has the following features:

1. The programmer may define any number of S-func-

tions by S-expressions. These functions may refer to each other or to certain S-functions represented by machine language program.

2. The values of defined functions may be computed.

3. S-expressions may be read and printed (directly or via magnetic tape).

4. Some error diagnostic and selective tracing facilities are included.

5. The programmer may have selected S-functions compiled into machine language programs put into the core memory. Values of compiled functions are computed about 60 times as fast as they would if interpreted. Compilation is fast enough so that it is not necessary to punch compiled program for future use.

6. A "program feature" allows programs containing assignment and **go to** statements in the style of ALGOL.

7. Computation with floating point numbers is possible in the system but this is inefficient.

8. A programmer's manual is being prepared.

The LISP programming system is appropriate for computations where the data can conveniently be represented as symbolic expressions allowing expressions of the same kind as subexpressions. A version of the system for the IBM 709 is being prepared.

5. Another Formalism for Functions of Symbolic Expressions

There are a number of ways of defining functions of symbolic expressions which are quite similar to the system we have adopted. Each of them involves three basic functions, conditional expressions, and recursive function definitions, but the class of expressions corresponding to S-expressions is different, and so are the precise definitions of the functions. We shall describe one of these variants called linear LISP.

The L-expressions are defined as follows:

1. A finite list of characters is admitted.

2. Any string of admitted characters ia an L-expression. This includes the null string denoted by Λ.

There are three functions of strings:

1. first[x] is the first character of the string x.

   first[Λ] is undefined.

For example: first[ABC] = A

2. rest[x] is the string of characters which remains when the first character of the string is deleted.

   rest[Λ] is undefined.

For example: rest[ABC] = BC

3. combine[x; y] is the string formed by prefixing the character x to the string y.

For example: combine[A; BC] = ABC

There are three predicates on strings:

1. char[x],   x is a single character.

2. null[x],   x is the null string.

3. x = y, defined for x and y characters.

The advantage of linear LISP is that no characters are given special roles, as are parentheses, dots, and commas in LISP. This permits computations with all expressions

that can be written linearly. The disadvantage of linear LISP is that the extraction of subexpressions is a fairly involved, rather than an elementary, operation. It is not hard to write, in linear LISP, functions that correspond to the basic functions of LISP, so that, mathematically, linear LISP includes LISP. This turns out to be the most convenient way of programming, in linear LISP, the more complicated manipulations. However, if the functions are to be represented by computer routines, LISP is essentially faster.

6. Flowcharts and Recursion

Since both the usual form of computer program and recursive function definitions are universal computationally, it is interesting to display the relation between them. The translation of recursive symbolic functions into computer programs was the subject of the rest of this report. In this section we show how to go the other way, at least in principle.

The state of the machine at any time during a computation is given by the values of a number of variables. Let these variables be combined into a vector ξ. Consider a program block with one entrance and one exit. It defines and is essentially defined by a certain function f that takes one machine configuration into another, that is, f has the form $\xi' = f(\xi)$. Let us call f the associated function of the program block. Now let a number of such blocks be combined into a program by decision elements π that decide after each block is completed which block will be entered next. Nevertheless, let the whole program still have one entrance and one exit.

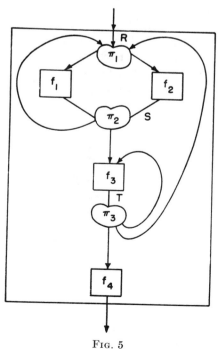

FIG. 5

We give as an example the flowchart of figure 5. Let us describe the function r[ξ] that gives the transformation of the vector ξ between entrance and exit of the whole block.

We shall define it in conjunction with the functions $s[\xi]$ and $t[\xi]$, which give the transformations that ξ undergoes between the points S and T, respectively, and the exit. We have

$$r[\xi] = [\pi_{11}[\xi] \rightarrow s[f_1[\xi]]; T \rightarrow s[f_2[\xi]]]$$

$$s[\xi] = [\pi_{21}[\xi] \rightarrow r[\xi]; T \rightarrow t[f_3[\xi]]]$$

$$t[\xi] = [\pi_{31}[\xi] \rightarrow f_4[\xi]; \pi_{32}[\xi] \rightarrow r[\xi]; T \rightarrow t[f_3[\xi]]]$$

Given a flowchart with a single entrance and a single exit, it is easy to write down the recursive function that gives the transformation of the state vector from entrance to exit in terms of the corresponding functions for the computation blocks and the predicates of the branch points. In general, we proceed as follows.

In figure 6, let β be an n-way branch point, and let $f_1, \cdots, f_n$ be the computations leading to branch points $\beta_1, \beta_2, \cdots, \beta_n$. Let ϕ be the function that transforms ξ between β and the exit of the chart, and let $\phi_1, \cdots, \phi_n$ be the corresponding functions for $\beta_1, \cdots, \beta_n$. We then write

$$\phi[\xi] = [p_1[\xi] \rightarrow \phi_1[f_1[\xi]]; \cdots; p_n[\xi] \rightarrow \phi_n[f_n[\xi]]]$$

Acknowledgments

The inadequacy of the λ-notation for naming recursive functions was noticed by N. Rochester, and he discovered an alternative to the solution involving *label* which has been used here. The form of subroutine for *cons* which permits its composition with other functions was invented, in connection with another programming system, by C. Gerberick and H. L. Gelernter, of IBM Corporation. The LISP programming system was developed by a group including R. Brayton, D. Edwards, P. Fox, L. Hodes, D. Luckham, K. Maling, J. McCarthy, D. Park, S. Russell.

The group was supported by the M.I.T. Computation Center, and by the M.I.T. Research Laboratory of Electronics (which is supported in part by the U.S. Army (Signal Corps), the U.S. Air Force (Office of Scientific Research, Air Research and Development Command), and the U.S. Navy (Office of Naval Research)). The author also wishes to acknowledge the personal financial support of the Alfred P. Sloan Foundation.

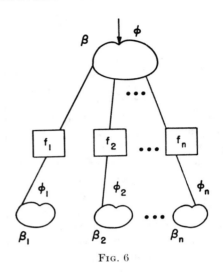

FIG. 6

REFERENCES

1. J. McCarthy, Programs with common sense, Paper presented at the Symposium on the Mechanization of Thought Processes, National Physical Laboratory, Teddington, England, Nov. 24–27, 1958. (Published in Proceedings of the Symposium by H. M. Stationery Office).

2. A. Newell and J. C. Shaw, Programming the logic theory machine, Proc. Western Joint Computer Conference, Feb. 1957.

3. A. Church, *The Calculi of Lambda-Conversion* (Princeton University Press, Princeton, N. J., 1941).

4. FORTRAN Programmer's Reference Manual, IBM Corporation, New York, Oct. 15, 1956.

5. A. J. Perlis and K. Samelson, International algebraic language, Preliminary Report, *Comm. Assoc. Comp. Mach.*, Dec. 1958.

LISP 1.5 PROGRAMMER'S MANUAL*

J. McCARTHY, P. W. ABRAHAMS, D. J. EDWARDS, T. P. HART, AND M. LEVIN

I. THE LISP LANGUAGE

The LISP language is designed primarily for symbolic data processing. It has been used for symbolic calculations in differential and integral calculus, electrical circuit theory, mathematical logic, game playing, and other fields of artificial intelligence.

LISP is a formal mathematical language. It is therefore possible to give a concise yet complete description of it. Such is the purpose of this first section of the manual. Other sections will describe ways of using LISP to advantage and will explain extensions of the language which make it a convenient programming system.

LISP differs from most programming languages in three important ways. The first way is in the nature of the data. In the LISP language, all data are in the form of symbolic expressions usually referred to as S-expressions. S-expressions are of indefinite length and have a branching tree type of structure, so that significant sub-expressions can be readily isolated. In the LISP programming system, the bulk of available memory is used for storing S-expressions in the form of list structures. This type of memory organization frees the programmer from the necessity of allocating storage for the different sections of his program.

The second important part of the LISP language is the source language itself which specifies in what way the S-expressions are to be processed. This consists of recursive functions of S-expressions. Since the notation for the writing of recursive functions of S-expressions is itself outside the S-expression notation, it will be called the meta language. These expressions will therefore be called M-expressions.

Third, LISP can interpret and execute programs written in the form of S-expressions. Thus, like machine language, and unlike most other higher level languages, it can be used to generate programs for further execution.

1.1 Symbolic Expressions

The most elementary type of S-expression is the atomic symbol.

Definition: An atomic symbol is a string of no more than thirty numerals and capital letters; the first character must be a letter.

Examples

```
A
APPLE
PART2
EXTRALONGSTRINGOFLETTERS
A4B66XYZ2
```

These symbols are called atomic because they are taken as a whole and are not capable of being split within LISP into individual characters. Thus A, B, and AB have no relation to each other except in so far as they are three distinct atomic symbols.

All S-expressions are built out of atomic symbols and the punctuation marks "(", ")", and " . ". The basic operation for forming S-expressions is to combine two

*Reprinted from MIT Press, Cambridge, Mass. 1965.

of them to produce a larger one. From the two atomic symbols A1 and A2, one can form the S-expression (A1 . A2).

Definition: An S-expression is either an atomic symbol or it is composed of these elements in the following order: a left parenthesis, an S-expression, a dot, an S-expression, and a right parenthesis.

Notice that this definition is recursive.

Examples

    ATOM
    (A . B)
    (A . (B . C))
    ((A1 . A2) . B)
    ((U . V) . (X . Y))
    ((U . V) . (X . (Y . Z)))

1.2 Elementary Functions

We shall introduce some elementary functions of S-expressions. To distinguish the functions from the S-expressions themselves, we shall write function names in lower case letters, since atomic symbols consist of only upper case letters. Furthermore, the arguments of functions will be grouped in square brackets rather than parentheses. As a separator or punctuation mark we shall use the semicolon.

The first function that we shall introduce is the function cons. It has two arguments and is in fact the function that is used to build S-expressions from smaller S-expressions.

Examples

    cons[A;B]=(A . B)
    cons[(A . B);C]=((A . B) . C)
    cons[cons[A;B];C]=((A . B) . C)

The last example is an instance of composition of functions. It is possible to build any S-expression from its atomic components by compositions of the function cons.

The next pair of functions do just the opposite of cons. They produce the subexpressions of a given expression.

The function car has one argument. Its value is the first part of its composite argument. car of an atomic symbol is undefined.

Examples

    car[(A . B)]=A
    car[(A . (B1 . B2))]=A
    car[((A1 . A2) . B)]=(A1 . A2)
    car[A] is undefined

The function cdr has one argument. Its value is the second part of its composite argument. cdr is also undefined if its argument is atomic.

Examples

    cdr[(A . B)]=B
    cdr[(A . (B1 . B2))]=(B1 . B2)
    cdr[((A1 . A2) . B)]=B
    cdr[A] is undefined
    car[cdr[(A . (B1 . B2))]]=B1
    car[cdr[(A . B)]] is undefined
    car[cons[A;B]]=A

Given any S-expression, it is possible to produce any subexpression of it by a suitable composition of car's and cdr's. If x and y represent any two S-expressions, the following identities are true:

$$car[cons[x;y]]=x$$
$$cdr[cons[x;y]]=y$$

The following identity is also true for any S-expression x such that x is composite (non-atomic):

$$cons[car[x];cdr[x]]=x$$

The symbols x and y used in these identities are called variables. In LISP, variables are used to represent S-expressions. In choosing names for variables and functions, we shall use the same type of character strings that are used in forming atomic symbols, except that we shall use lower case letters.

A function whose value is either true or false is called a predicate. In LISP, the values true and false are represented by the atomic symbols T and F, respectively. A LISP predicate is therefore a function whose value is either T or F.

The predicate eq is a test for equality on atomic symbols. It is undefined for non-atomic arguments.

Examples

$$eq[A;A]=T$$
$$eq[A;B]=F$$
$$eq[A;(A . B)] \text{ is undefined}$$
$$eq[(A . B);(A . B)] \text{ is undefined}$$

The predicate atom is true if its argument is an atomic symbol, and false if its argument is composite.

Examples

$$atom[EXTRALONGSTRINGOFLETTERS]=T$$
$$atom[(U . V)]=F$$
$$atom[car[(U . V)]]=T$$

1.3 List Notation

The S-expressions that have been used heretofore have been written in dot notation. It is usually more convenient to be able to write lists of expressions of indefinite length, such as (A B C D E).

Any S-expression can be expressed in terms of the dot notation. However, LISP has an alternative form of S-expression called the list notation. The list $(m_1 \ m_2 \ldots m_n)$ can be defined in terms of dot notation. It is identical to $(m_1 . (m_2 . (\ldots . (m_n . NIL) \ldots)))$.

The atomic symbol NIL serves as a terminator for lists. The null list ( ) is identical to NIL. Lists may have sublists. The dot notation and the list notation may be used in the same S-expression.

Historically, the separator for elements of lists was the comma (,); however, the blank is now generally used. The two are entirely equivalent in LISP. (A, B, C) is identical to (A B C).

Examples

$$(A\ B\ C)=(A\ .\ (B\ .\ (C\ .\ NIL)))$$
$$((A\ B)\ C)=((A\ .\ (B\ .\ NIL))\ .\ (C\ .\ NIL))$$
$$(A\ B\ (C\ D))=(A\ .\ (B\ .\ ((C\ .\ (D\ .\ NIL))\ .\ NIL)))$$
$$(A)=(A\ .\ NIL)$$
$$((A))=((A\ .\ NIL)\ .\ NIL)$$
$$(A\ (B\ .\ C))=(A\ .\ ((B\ .\ C)\ .\ NIL))$$

It is important to become familiar with the results of elementary functions on S-expressions written in list notation. These can always be determined by translating into dot notation.

Examples

$$car[(A\ B\ C)]=A$$
$$cdr[(A\ B\ C)]=(B\ C)$$
$$cons[A;\ (B\ C)]=(A\ B\ C)$$
$$car[((A\ B)\ C)]=(A\ B)$$
$$cdr[(A)]=NIL$$
$$car[cdr[(A\ B\ C)]]=B$$

It is convenient to abbreviate multiple <u>car</u>'s and <u>cdr</u>'s. This is done by forming function names that begin with c, end with r, and have several a's and d's between them.

Examples

$$cadr[(A\ B\ C)]=car[cdr[(A\ B\ C)]]=B$$
$$caddr[(A\ B\ C)]=C$$
$$cadadr[(A\ (B\ C)\ D)]=C$$

The last a or d in the name actually signifies the first operation in order to be performed, since it is nearest to the argument.

1.4 The LISP Meta-language

We have introduced a type of data called S-expressions, and five elementary functions of S-expressions. We have also discussed the following features of the meta-language.

1. Function names and variable names are like atomic symbols except that they use lower case letters.

2. The arguments of a function are bound by square brackets and separated from each other by semicolons.

3. Compositions of functions may be written by using nested sets of brackets.

These rules allow one to write function definitions such as

$$third[x]=car[cdr[cdr[x]]].$$

This function selects the third item on a list. For example,

$$third[(A\ B\ C\ D)]=C$$

<u>third</u> is actually the same function as <u>caddr</u>.

The class of functions that can be formed in this way is quite limited and not very interesting. A much larger class of functions can be defined by means of the conditional expression, a device for providing branches in function definitions.

A conditional expression has the following form:

$$[p_1 \rightarrow e_1; \ p_2 \rightarrow e_2; \ \ldots; \ p_n \rightarrow e_n],$$

where each p_i is an expression whose value may be truth or falsity, and each e_i is any expression. The meaning of a conditional expression is: if p_1 is true, then the value of e_1 is the value of the entire expression. If p_1 is false, then if p_2 is true the value of e_2 is the value of the entire expression. The p_i are searched from left to right until the first true one is found. Then the corresponding e_i is selected. If none of the p_i are true, then the value of the entire expression is undefined.

Each p_i or e_i can itself be either an S-expression, a function, a composition of functions or may itself be another conditional expression.

Example

$$[eq[car[x];A] \rightarrow cons[B;cdr[x]]; \ T \rightarrow x]$$

The atomic symbol T represents truth. The value of this expression is obtained if one replaces <u>car</u> of x by B if it happens to be A, but leaving x unchanged if <u>car</u> of it is not A.

The main application of conditional expressions is in defining functions recursively.

Example

$$ff[x] = [atom[x] \rightarrow x; \ T \rightarrow ff[car[x]]]$$

This example defines the function <u>ff</u> which selects the first atomic symbol of any given expression. This expression can be read: If x is an atomic symbol, then x itself is the answer. Otherwise the function <u>ff</u> is to be applied to <u>car</u> of x.

If x is atomic, then the first branch which is "x" will be selected. Otherwise, the second branch "ff[car[x]]" will be selected, since T is always true.

The definition of <u>ff</u> is recursive in that <u>ff</u> is actually defined in terms of itself. If one keeps taking <u>car</u> of any S-expression, one will eventually produce an atomic symbol; therefore the process is always well defined.

Some recursive functions may be well defined for certain arguments only, but infinitely recursive for certain other arguments. When such a function is interpreted in the LISP programming system, it will either use up all of the available memory, or loop until the program is halted artificially.

We shall now work out the evaluation of ff[((A . B) . C)]. First, we substitute the arguments in place of the variable x in the definition and obtain

$$ff[((A \ . \ B) \ . \ C)] = [atom[((A \ . \ B) \ . \ C)] \rightarrow ((A \ . \ B) \ . \ C); \ T \rightarrow ff[car[((A \ . \ B) \ . \ C)]]]$$

but ((A . B) . C) is not atomic, and so we have

$$= [T \rightarrow ff[car[((A \ . \ B) \ . \ C)]]]$$
$$= ff[car[((A \ . \ B) \ . \ C)]]$$
$$= ff[(A \ . \ B)]$$

At this point, the definition of ff must be used recursively. Substituting (A . B) for x gives

$$= [\text{atom}[(A . B)] \rightarrow (A . B); T \rightarrow ff[\text{car}[(A . B)]]]$$
$$= [T \rightarrow ff[\text{car}[(A . B)]]]$$
$$= ff[\text{car}[(A . B)]]$$
$$= ff[A]$$
$$= [\text{atom}[A] \rightarrow A; T \rightarrow ff[\text{car}[A]]]$$
$$= A$$

The conditional expression is useful for defining numerical computations, as well as computations with S-expressions. The absolute value of a number can be defined by

$$|x| = [x < 0 \rightarrow -x; T \rightarrow x].$$

The factorial of a non-negative integer can be defined by

$$n! = [n = 0 \rightarrow 1; T \rightarrow n \cdot [n-1]!]$$

This recursive definition does not terminate for negative arguments. A function that is defined only for certain arguments is called a partial function.

The Euclidean algorithm for finding the greatest common divisor of two positive integers can be defined by using conditional expressions as follows:

$$\begin{aligned} gcd[x;y] = [&x > y \rightarrow gcd[y;x]; \\ &rem[y;x] = 0 \rightarrow x; \\ &T \rightarrow gcd[rem[y;x];x]] \end{aligned}$$

$rem[u;v]$ is the remainder when $\underline{u}$ is divided by $\underline{v}$.

A detailed discussion of the theory of functions defined recursively by conditional expressions is found in "A Basis for a Mathematical Theory of Computation" by J. McCarthy, Proceedings of the Western Joint Computer Conference, May 1961 (published by the Institute of Radio Engineers).

It is usual for most mathematicians—exclusive of those devoted to logic—to use the word "function" imprecisely, and to apply it to forms such as $y^2 + x$. Because we shall later compute with expressions that stand for functions, we need a notation that expresses the distinction between functions and forms. The notation that we shall use is the lambda notation of Alonzo Church.[1]

Let $\underline{f}$ be an expression that stands for a function of two integer variables. It should make sense to write $f[3;4]$ and to be able to determine the value of this expression. For example, $\underline{sum[3;4]} = 7$. The expression $y^2 + x$ does not meet this requirement. It is not at all clear whether the value of $y^2 + x[3;4]$ is 13 or 19. An expression such as $y^2 + x$ will be called a form rather than a function. A form can be converted to a function by specifying the correspondence between the variables in the form and the arguments of the desired function.

If ϵ is a form in the variables $x_1; \ldots; x_n$, then the expression $\lambda[[x_1; \ldots; x_n]; \epsilon]$ represents the function of n variables obtained by substituting the n arguments in order for the variables $x_1; \ldots; x_n$, respectively. For example, the function $\lambda[[x;y];$ $y^2 + x]$ is a function of two variables, and $\lambda[[x;y]; y^2 + x][3;4] = 4^2 + 3 = 19$. $\lambda[[y;x]; y^2 + x][3;4]$ $= 3^2 + 4 = 13$.

---

1. A. Church, _The Calculi of Lambda-Conversion_ (Princeton University Press, Princeton, New Jersey, 1941).

The variables in a lambda expression are dummy or bound variables because systematically changing them does not alter the meaning of the expression. Thus $\lambda[[u;v];v^2+u]$ means the same thing as $\lambda[[x;y];y^2+x]$.

We shall sometimes use expressions in which a variable is not bound by a lambda. For example, in the function of two variables $\lambda[[x;y];x^n+y^n]$ the variable n is not bound. This is called a free variable. It may be regarded as a parameter. Unless n has been given a value before trying to compute with this function, the value of the function must be undefined.

The lambda notation alone is inadequate for naming recursive functions. Not only must the variables be bound, but the name of the function must be bound, since it is used inside an expression to stand for the entire expression. The function ff was previously defined by the identity

$$ff[x]=[atom[x]\rightarrow x;\ T\rightarrow ff[car[x]]].$$

Using the lambda notation, we can write

$$ff=\lambda[[x];[atom[x]\rightarrow x;\ T\rightarrow ff[car[x]]]]$$

The equality sign in these identities is actually not part of the LISP meta-language and is only a crutch until we develop the correct notation. The right side of the last equation cannot serve as an expression for the function ff because there is nothing to indicate that the occurrence of ff inside it stands for the function that is being defined.

In order to be able to write expressions that bear their own name, we introduce the label notation. If ϵ is an expression, and a is its name, we write $label[a;\epsilon]$.

The function ff can now be written without an equal sign:

$$label[ff;\lambda[[x];[atom[x]\rightarrow x;\ T\rightarrow ff[car[x]]]]]$$

In this expression, x is a bound variable, and ff is a bound function name.

1.5 Syntactic Summary[1]

All parts of the LISP language have now been explained. That which follows is a complete syntactic definition of the LISP language, together with semantic comments. The definition is given in Backus notation[2] with the addition of three dots(...) to avoid naming unneccessary syntactic types.

In Backus notation the symbols " ::= ", " < ", " > ", and " | " are used. The rule <S-expression>::=<atomic symbol>|(<S-expression> . <S-expression>) means that an S-expression is either an atomic symbol, or it is a left parenthesis followed by an S-expression followed by a dot followed by an S-expression followed by a right parenthesis. The vertical bar means "or", and the angular brackets always enclose elements of the syntax that is being defined.

The Data Language

```
<LETTER>::=A|B|C|...|Z
<number>::=0|1|2|...|9
<atomic-symbol>::=<LETTER><atom part>
<atom part>::=<empty>| <LETTER><atom part>| <number><atom part>
```

Atomic symbols are the smallest entities in LISP. Their decomposition into characters has no significance.

1. This section is for completeness and may be skipped upon first reading.

2. J. W. Backus, The Syntax and Semantics of the Proposed International Algebraic Language of the Zurich ACM-Gamm Conference. ICIP Paris, June 1959.

$$<\text{S-expression}>::=<\text{atomic symbol}>|$$
$$(<\text{S-expression}>.<\text{S-expression}>)|$$
$$(<\text{S-expression}>...<\text{S-expression}>)$$

When three dots are used in this manner, they mean that any number of the given type of symbol may occur, including none at all. According to this rule, ( ) is a valid S-expression. (It is equivalent to NIL.)

The dot notation is the fundamental notation of S-expressions, although the list notation is often more convenient. Any S-expression can be written in dot notation.

The Meta-Language

$$<\text{letter}>::=a|b|c|...|z$$
$$<\text{identifier}>::=<\text{letter}><\text{id part}>$$
$$<\text{id part}>::=<\text{empty}>|<\text{letter}><\text{id part}>|<\text{number}><\text{id part}>$$

The names of functions and variables are formed in the same manner as atomic symbols but with lower-case letters.

$$<\text{form}>::=<\text{constant}>|$$
$$<\text{variable}>|$$
$$<\text{function}>[<\text{argument}>;...;<\text{argument}>]|$$
$$[<\text{form}>\rightarrow<\text{form}>;...;<\text{form}>\rightarrow<\text{form}>]$$
$$<\text{constant}>::=<\text{S-expression}>$$
$$<\text{variable}>::=<\text{identifier}>$$
$$<\text{argument}>::=<\text{form}>$$

A form is an expression that can be evaluated. A form that is merely a constant has that constant as its value. If a form is a variable, then the value of the form is the S-expression that is bound to that variable at the time when we evaluate the form.

The third part of this rule states that we may write a function followed by a list of arguments separated by semicolons and enclosed in square brackets. The expressions for the arguments are themselves forms; this indicates that compositions of functions are permitted.

The last part of this rule gives the format of the conditional expression. This is evaluated by evaluating the forms in the propositional position in order until one is found whose value is T. Then the form after the arrow is evaluated and gives the value of the entire expression.

$$<\text{function}>::=<\text{identifier}>|$$
$$\lambda[<\text{var list}>;<\text{form}>]|$$
$$\text{label}[<\text{identifier}>;<\text{function}>]$$
$$<\text{var list}>::=[<\text{variable}>;...;<\text{variable}>]$$

A function can be simply a name. In this case its meaning must be previously understood. A function may be defined by using the lambda notation and establishing a correspondence between the arguments and the variables used in a form. If the function is recursive, it must be given a name by using a label.

1.6 A Universal LISP Function

An interpreter or universal function is one that can compute the value of any given function applied to its arguments when given a description of that function. (Of course, if the function that is being interpreted has infinite recursion, the interpreter will recur infinitely also.)

We are now in a position to define the universal LISP function evalquote[fn;args]. When evalquote is given a function and a list of arguments for that function, it computes the value of the function applied to the arguments.

LISP functions have S-expressions as arguments. In particular, the argument "fn" of the function evalquote must be an S-expression. Since we have been writing functions as M-expressions, it is necessary to translate them into S-expressions.

The following rules define a method of translating functions written in the meta-language into S-expressions.

1. If the function is represented by its name, it is translated by changing all of the letters to upper case, making it an atomic symbol. Thus car is translated to CAR.

2. If the function uses the lambda notation, then the expression $\lambda[[x_1;\ldots;x_n];\epsilon]$ is translated into (LAMBDA (X1 ... XN) ϵ*), where ϵ* is the translation of ϵ.

3. If the function begins with label, then the translation of label$[a;\epsilon]$ is (LABEL a* ϵ*).

Forms are translated as follows:

1. A variable, like a function name, is translated by using uppercase letters. Thus the translation of var1 is VAR1.

2. The obvious translation of letting a constant translate into itself will not work. Since the translation of x is X, the translation of X must be something else to avoid ambiguity. The solution is to quote it. Thus X is translated into (QUOTE X).

3. The form fn$[arg_1;\ldots;arg_n]$ is translated into (fn* arg_1* ... arg_n*)

4. The conditional expression $[p_1 \rightarrow e_1;\ldots;p_n \rightarrow e_n]$ is translated into (COND (p_1* e_1*) ... (p_n* e_n*)).

Examples

M-expressions	S-expressions
x	X
car	CAR
car[x]	(CAR X)
T	(QUOTE T)
ff[car[x]]	(FF (CAR X))
[atom[x]→x; T→ff[car[x]]]	(COND ((ATOM X) X)
	((QUOTE T) (FF (CAR X))))
label[ff;λ[[x];[atom[x]→x; T→ff[car[x]]]]]	(LABEL FF (LAMBDA (X) (COND
	((ATOM X) X)
	((QUOTE T) (FF (CAR X))))))

Some useful functions for handling S-expressions are given below. Some of them are needed as auxiliary functions for evalquote.

equal[x;y]

This is a predicate that is true if its two arguments are identical S-expressions, and is false if they are different. (The elementary predicate eq is defined only for atomic arguments.) The definition of equal is an example of a conditional expression inside a conditional expression.

$$\text{equal}[x;y]=[\text{atom}[x]\rightarrow[\text{atom}[y]\rightarrow\text{eq}[x;y];\ T\rightarrow F];$$
$$\text{equal}[\text{car}[x];\text{car}[y]]\rightarrow\text{equal}[\text{cdr}[x];\text{cdr}[y]];$$
$$T\rightarrow F]$$

This can be translated into the following S-expression:

```
(LABEL EQUAL (LAMBDA (X Y) (COND
    ((ATOM X) (COND ((ATOM Y) (EQ X Y)) ((QUOTE T) (QUOTE F))))
    ((EQUAL (CAR X) (CAR Y)) (EQUAL (CDR X) (CDR Y)))
    ((QUOTE T) (QUOTE F))     )))
```

subst[x;y;z]

This function gives the result of substituting the S-expression x for all occurrences of the atomic symbol y in the S-expression z. It is defined by

$$subst[x;y;z] = [equal[y;z] \rightarrow x;atom[z] \rightarrow z;T \rightarrow cons[subst$$
$$[x;y;car[z]];subst[x;y;cdr[z]]]]$$

As an example, we have

$$subst[(X \ . \ A);B;((A \ . \ B) \ . \ C)] = ((A \ . \ (X \ . \ A)) \ . \ C)$$

<u>null</u>$[x]$

This predicate is useful for deciding when a list is exhausted. It is true if and only if its argument is NIL.

The following functions are useful when S-expressions are regarded as lists.

1. <u>append</u>$[x;y]$

$$append[x;y] = [null[x] \rightarrow y;T \rightarrow cons[car[x];append[cdr[x];y]]]$$

An example is

$$append[(A \ B);(C \ D \ E)] = (A \ B \ C \ D \ E)$$

2. <u>member</u>$[x;y]$

This predicate is true if the S-expression x occurs among the elements of the list y. We have

$$member[x;y] = [null[y] \rightarrow F;$$
$$equal[x;car[y]] \rightarrow T;$$
$$T \rightarrow member[x;cdr[y]]]$$

3. <u>pairlis</u>$[x;y;a]$

This function gives the list of pairs of corresponding elements of the lists x and y, and appends this to the list a. The resultant list of pairs, which is like a table with two columns, is called an association list. We have

$$pairlis[x;y;a] = [null[x] \rightarrow a;T \rightarrow cons[cons[car[x];car[y]];$$
$$pairlis[cdr[x];cdr[y];a]]]$$

An example is

$$pairlis[(A \ B \ C);(U \ V \ W);((D \ . \ X) (E \ . \ Y))] =$$
$$((A \ . \ U) (B \ . \ V) (C \ . \ W) (D \ . \ X) (E \ . \ Y))$$

4. <u>assoc</u>$[x;a]$

If a is an association list such as the one formed by pairlis in the above example, then assoc will produce the first pair whose first term is x. Thus it is a table searching function. We have

$$assoc[x;a] = [equal[caar[a];x] \rightarrow car[a];T \rightarrow assoc[x;cdr[a]]]$$

An example is

$$assoc[B;((A \ . \ (M \ N)), (B \ . \ (CAR \ X)), (C \ . \ (QUOTE \ M)), (C \ . \ (CDR \ X)))]$$
$$= (B \ . \ (CAR \ X))$$

5. <u>sublis</u>$[a;y]$

Here a is assumed to be an association list of the form $((u_1 \ . \ v_1) \ ... \ (u_n \ . \ v_n))$, where the u's are atomic, and y is any S-expression. What sublis does, is to treat the u's as variables when they occur in y, and to substitute the corresponding v's from the pair list. In order to define sublis, we first define an auxiliary function.

We have

$$sub2[a;z] = [null[a] \rightarrow z; eq[caar[a];z] \rightarrow cdar[a]; T \rightarrow sub2[cdr[a];z]]$$

and

$$sublis[a;y] = [atom[y] \rightarrow sub2[a;y]; T \rightarrow cons[sublis[a;car[y]]; sublis[a;cdr[y]]]]$$

An example is

$$sublis[((X . SHAKESPEARE) (Y . (THE TEMPEST)));(X WROTE Y)] =$$
$$(SHAKESPEARE WROTE (THE TEMPEST))$$

The universal function <u>evalquote</u> that is about to be defined obeys the following identity. Let $\underline{f}$ be a function written as an M-expression, and let $\underline{fn}$ be its translation. ($\underline{fn}$ is an S-expression.) Let $\underline{f}$ be a function of n arguments and let $args=(arg_1 \ldots arg_n)$, a list of the n S-expressions being used as arguments. Then

$$evalquote[fn;args]=f[arg_1; \ldots ;arg_n]$$

if either side of the equation is defined at all.

Example

f:	$\lambda[[x;y];cons[car[x];y]]$
fn:	(LAMBDA (X Y) (CONS (CAR X) Y))
arg_1:	(A B)
arg_2:	(C D)
args:	((A B) (C D))

$$evalquote[(LAMBDA (X Y) (CONS (CAR X) Y)); ((A B) (C D))] =$$
$$\lambda[[x;y];cons[car[x];y]][(A B);(C D)]=$$
$$(A C D)$$

<u>evalquote</u> is defined by using two main functions, called <u>eval</u> and <u>apply</u>. <u>apply</u> handles a function and its arguments, while <u>eval</u> handles forms. Each of these functions also has another argument that is used as an association list for storing the values of bound variables and function names.

$$evalquote[fn;x] = apply[fn;x;NIL]$$

where

$$apply[fn;x;a] =$$
$$[atom[fn] \rightarrow [eq[fn;CAR] \rightarrow caar[x];$$
$$eq[fn;CDR] \rightarrow cdar[x];$$
$$eq[fn;CONS] \rightarrow cons[car[x];cadr[x]];$$
$$eq[fn;ATOM] \rightarrow atom[car[x]];$$
$$eq[fn;EQ] \rightarrow eq[car[x];cadr[x]];$$
$$T \rightarrow apply[eval[fn;a];x;a]];$$
$$eq[car[fn];LAMBDA] \rightarrow eval[caddr[fn];pairlis[cadr[fn];x;a]];$$
$$eq[car[fn];LABEL] \rightarrow apply[caddr[fn];x;cons[cons[cadr[fn];$$
$$caddr[fn]];a]]]$$

$$eval[e;a] = [atom[e] \rightarrow cdr[assoc[e;a]];$$
$$atom[car[e]] \rightarrow$$
$$[eq[car[e],QUOTE] \rightarrow cadr[e];$$
$$eq[car[e];COND] \rightarrow evcon[cdr[e];a];$$
$$T \rightarrow apply[car[e];evlis[cdr[e];a];a]];$$
$$T \rightarrow apply[car[e];evlis[cdr[e];a];a]]$$

pairlis and assoc have been previously defined.

$$evcon[c;a] = [eval[caar[c];a] \rightarrow eval[cadar[c];a];$$
$$T \rightarrow evcon[cdr[c];a]]$$

and
$$evlis[m;a] = [null[m] \rightarrow NIL;$$
$$T \rightarrow cons[eval[car[m];a];evlis[cdr[m];a]]]$$

We shall explain a number of points about these definitions.

The first argument for apply is a function. If it is an atomic symbol, then there are two possibilities. One is that it is an elementary function: car, cdr, cons, eq. or atom. In each case, the appropriate function is applied to the argument(s). If it is not one of these, then its meaning has to be looked up in the association list.

If it begins with LAMBDA, then the arguments are paired with the bound variables, and the form is given to eval to evaluate.

If it begins with LABEL, then the function name and definition are added to the association list, and the inside function is evaluated by apply.

The first argument of eval is a form. If it is atomic, then it must be a variable, and its value is looked up on the association list.

If car of the form is QUOTE, then it is a constant, and the value is cadr of the form itself.

If car of the form is COND, then it is a conditional expression, and evcon evaluates the propositional terms in order, and choses the form following the first true predicate.

In all other cases, the form must be a function followed by its arguments. The arguments are then evaluated, and the function is given to apply.

The LISP Programming System has many added features that have not been described thus far. These will be treated hereafter. At this point, it is worth noting the following points.

1. In the pure theory of LISP, all functions other than the five basic ones need to be defined each time they are to be used. This is unworkable in a practical sense. The LISP programming system has a larger stock of built-in functions known to the interpreter, and provision for adding as many more as the programmer cares to define.

2. The basic functions car, and cdr were said to be undefined for atomic arguments.

In the system, they always have a value, although it may not always be meaningful. Similarly, the basic predicate eq always has a value. The effects of these functions in unusual cases will be understood after reading the chapter on list structures in the computer.

3. Except for very unusual cases, one never writes (QUOTE T) or (QUOTE F), but T, and F respectively.

4. There is provision in LISP for computing with fixed and floating point numbers. These are introduced as psuedo-atomic symbols.

The reader is warned that the definitions of apply and eval given above are pedagogical devices and are not the same functions as those built into the LISP programming system. Appendix B contains the computer implemented version of these functions and should be used to decide questions about how things really work.

II. THE LISP INTERPRETER SYSTEM

The following example is a LISP program that defines three functions union, intersection, and member, and then applies these functions to some test cases. The functions union and intersection are to be applied to "sets," each set being represented by a list of atomic symbols. The functions are defined as follows. Note that they are all recursive, and both union and intersection make use of member.

$$member[a;x] = [null[x] \rightarrow F; eq[a;car[x]] \rightarrow T; T \rightarrow member[a;cdr[x]]]$$

$$union[x;y] = [null[x] \rightarrow y; member[car[x];y] \rightarrow union[cdr[x];y]; T \rightarrow cons[car[x];union[cdr[x];y]]]$$

$$intersection[x;y] = [null[x] \rightarrow NIL; member[car[x];y] \rightarrow cons[car[x];intersection[cdr[x];y]]; T \rightarrow intersection[cdr[x];y]]$$

To define these functions, we use the pseudo-function define. The program looks like this:

```
DEFINE ((
(MEMBER (LAMBDA (A X) (COND ((NULL X) F)
     ( (EQ A (CAR X) ) T) (T (MEMBER A (CDR X))) )))
(UNION (LAMBDA (X Y) (COND ((NULL X) Y) ((MEMBER
     (CAR X) Y) (UNION (CDR X) Y)) (T (CONS (CAR X)
     (UNION (CDR X) Y))) )))
(INTERSECTION (LAMBDA (X Y) (COND ((NULL X) NIL)
     ( (MEMBER (CAR X) Y) (CONS (CAR X) (INTERSECTION
     (CDR X) Y))) (T (INTERSECTION (CDR X) Y)) )))
))
INTERSECTION ((A1 A2 A3) (A1 A3 A5))
UNION ((X Y Z) (U V W X))
```

This program contains three distinct functions for the LISP interpreter. The first function is the pseudo-function define. A pseudo-function is a function that is executed for its effect on the system in core memory, as well as for its value. define causes these functions to be defined and available within the system. Its value is a list of the functions defined, in this case (MEMBER UNION INTERSECTION).

The value of the second function is (A1 A3). The value of the third function is

(Y Z U V W X). An inspection of the way in which the recursion is carried out will show why the "elements" of the "set" appear in just this order.

Following are some elementary rules for writing LISP 1.5 programs.

1. A program for execution in LISP consists of a sequence of doublets. The first list or atomic symbol of each doublet is interpreted as a function. The second is a list of arguments for the function. They are evaluated by <u>evalquote</u>, and the value is printed.

2. There is no particular card format for writing LISP. Columns 1-72 of any number of cards may be used. Card boundaries are ignored. The format of this program, including indentation, was chosen merely for ease of reading.

3. A comma is the equivalent of a blank. Any number of blanks and/or commas can occur at any point in a program except in the middle of an atomic symbol.

4. Do not use the forms (QUOTE T), (QUOTE F), and (QUOTE NIL). Use T, F, and NIL instead.

5. Atomic symbols should begin with alphabetical characters to distinguish them from numbers.

6. Dot notation may be used in LISP 1.5. Any number of blanks before or after the dot will be ignored.

7. Dotted pairs may occur as elements of a list, and lists may occur as elements of dotted pairs. For example,

((A . B) X (C . (E F G)))

is a valid S-expression. It could also be written

((A . B) . (X . ((C . (E . (F . (G . NIL)))) . NIL))) or
((A . B) X (C E F G))

8. A form of the type (A B C . D) is an abbreviation for (A . (B . (C . D))). Any other mixing of commas (spaces) and dots on the same level is an error, e.g. (A . B C).

9. A selection of basic functions is provided with the LISP system. Other functions may be introduced by the programmer. The order in which functions are introduced is not significant. Any function may make use of any other function.

2.1 Variables

A variable is a symbol that is used to represent an argument of a function. Thus one might write "a + b, where a = 341 and b = 216." In this situation no confusion can result and all will agree that the answer is 557. In order to arrive at this result, it is necessary to substitute the actual numbers for the variables, and then add the two number (on an adding machine for instance).

One reason why there is no ambiguity in this case is that "a" and "b" are not acceptable inputs for an adding machine, and it is therefore obvious that they merely represent the actual arguments. In LISP, the situation can be much more complicated. An atomic symbol may be either a variable or an actual argument. To further complicate the situation, a part of an argument may be a variable when a function inside another function is evaluated. The intuitive approach is no longer adequate. An understanding of the formalism in use is necessary to do any effective LISP programming.

Lest the prospective LISP user be discouraged at this point, it should be pointed out that nothing new is going to be introduced here. This section is intended to reinforce the discussion of Section I. Everything in this section can be derived from the rule for translating M-expressions into S-expressions, or alternatively everything in this section can be inferred from the universal function <u>evalquote</u> of Section I.

The formalism for variables in LISP is the Church lambda notation. The part of the interpreter that binds variables is called <u>apply</u>. When <u>apply</u> encounters a function be-

ginning with LAMBDA, the list of variables is paired with the list of arguments and added to the front of the a-list. During the evaluation of the function, variables may be encountered. They are evaluated by looking them up on the a-list. If a variable has been bound several times, the last or most recent value is used. The part of the interpreter that does this is called _eval_. The following example will illustrate this discussion. Suppose the interpreter is given the following doublet:

fn: (LAMBDA (X Y) (CONS X Y))
args: (A B)

evalquote will give these arguments to apply. (Look at the universal function of Section I.)

apply[(LAMBDA (X Y) (CONS X Y)); (A B);NIL]

apply will bind the variables and give the function and a-list to eval.

eval[(CONS X Y); ((X . A) (Y . B))]

eval will evaluate the variables and give it to cons.

cons[A;B] = (A . B)

The actual interpreter skips one step required by the universal function, namely, apply[CONS;(A B);((X . A) (Y . B))].

2.2 Constants

It is sometimes assumed that a constant stands for itself as opposed to a variable which stands for something else. This is not a very workable concept, since the student who is learning calculus is taught to represent constants by a, b, c... and variables by x, y, z... . It seems more reasonable to say that one variable is more nearly constant than another if it is bound at a higher level and changes value less frequently.

In LISP, a variable remains bound within the scope of the LAMBDA that binds it. When a variable always has a certain value regardless of the current a-list, it will be called a constant. This is accomplished by means of the property list[1] (p-list) of the variable symbol. Every atomic symbol has a p-list. When the p-list contains the indicator APVAL, then the symbol is a constant and the next item on the list is the value. _eval_ searches p-lists before a-lists when evaluating variables, thus making it possible to set constants.

Constants can be made by the programmer. To make the variable X always stand for (A B C D), use the pseudo-function _cset_.

---

1. Property lists are discussed in Section VII.

cset[X;(A B C D)]

An interesting type of constant is one that stands for itself. NIL is an example of this. It can be evaluated repeatedly and will still be NIL. T, F, NIL, and other constants cannot be used as variables.

2.3 Functions

When a symbol stands for a function, the situation is similar to that in which a symbol stands for an argument. When a function is recursive, it must be given a name. This is done by means of the form LABEL, which pairs the name with the function definition on the a-list. The name is then bound to the function definition, just as a variable is bound to its value.

In actual practice, LABEL is seldom used. It is usually more convenient to attach

the name to the definition in a uniform manner.   This is done by putting on the property
list of the name, the symbol EXPR followed by the function definition. The pseudo-function
<u>define</u> used at the beginning of this section accomplishes this.   When <u>apply</u> interprets
a function represented by an atomic symbol, it searches the p-list of the atomic symbol
before searching the current a-list.   Thus a <u>define</u> will override a LABEL.

The fact that most functions are constants defined by the programmer, and not variables that are modified by the program, is not due to any weakness of the system.   On the
contrary, it indicates a richness of the system which we do not know how to exploit very
well.

2.4 Machine Language Functions

Some functions instead of being defined by S-expressions are coded as closed machine
language subroutines.   Such a function will have the indicator SUBR on its property list
followed by a pointer that allows the interpreter to link with the subroutine.   There are
three ways in which a subroutine can be present in the system.

1. The subroutine is coded into the LISP system.

2. The function is hand-coded by the user in the assembly type language, LAP.

3. The function is first defined by an S-expression, and then compiled by the LISP
compiler.   Compiled functions run from 10 to 100 times as fast as they do when they
are interpreted.

2.5 Special Forms

Normally, <u>eval</u> evaluates the arguments of a function before applying the function
itself.   Thus if <u>eval</u> is given (CONS X Y), it will evaluate X and Y, and then <u>cons</u> them.
But if <u>eval</u> is given (QUOTE X), X should not be evaluated. QUOTE is a special form
that prevents its argument from being evaluated.

A special form differs from a function in two ways. Its arguments are not evaluated
before the special form sees them. COND, for example, has a very special way of
evaluating its arguments by using <u>evcon</u>. The second way which special forms differ
from functions is that they may have an indefinite number of arguments. Special forms
have indicators on their property lists called FEXPR and FSUBR for LISP-defined forms
and machine language coded forms, respectively.

2.6 Programming for the Interpreter

The purpose of this section is to help the programmer avoid certain common errors.

<u>Example 1</u>

    fn: CAR
    args: ((A B))

The value is A. Note that the interpreter expects a list of arguments. The one argument for <u>car</u> is (A B). The extra pair of parentheses is necessary.

One could write (LAMBDA (X) (CAR X)) instead of just CAR. This is correct but
unnecessary.

<u>Example 2</u>

    fn: CONS
    args: (A (B . C))

The value is cons$[A;(B . C)]$ = (A . (B . C)).
The print program will write this as (A B . C).

Example 3

    fn: CONS
    args: ((CAR (QUOTE (A . B))) (CDR (QUOTE (C . D))))

The value of this computation will be ((CAR (QUOTE (A . B))) . (CDR (QUOTE (C . D)))). This is not what the programmer expected. He expected (CAR (QUOTE (A . B))) to evaluate to A, and expected (A . D) as the value of cons.

The interpreter expects a list of arguments. It does not expect a list of expressions that will evaluate to the arguments. Two correct ways of writing this function are listed below. The first one makes the car and cdr part of a function specified by a LAMBDA. The second one uses quoted arguments and gets them evaluated by eval with a null a-list.

    fn: (LAMBDA (X Y) (CONS (CAR X) (CDR Y)))
    args: ((A . B) (C . D))
    fn: EVAL
    args: ((CONS (CAR (QUOTE (A . B))) (CDR (QUOTE (C . D)))) NIL)

The value of both of these is (A . D).

III. EXTENSION OF THE LISP LANGUAGE

Section I of this manual presented a purely formal mathematical system that we shall call pure LISP. The elements of this formal system are the following.
1. A set of symbols called S-expressions.
2. A functional notation called M-expressions.
3. A formal mapping of M-expressions into S-expressions.
4. A universal function (written as an M-expression) for interpreting the application of any function written as an S-expression to its arguments.

Section II introduced the LISP Programming System. The basis of the LISP Programming System is the interpreter, or evalquote and its components. A LISP program in fact consists of pairs of arguments for evalquote which are interpreted in sequence.

In this section we shall introduce a number of extensions of elementary LISP. These extensions of elementary LISP are of two sorts. The first includes propositional connectives and functions with functions as arguments, and they are also of a mathematical nature; the second is peculiar to the LISP Programming System on the IBM 7090 computer.

In all cases, additions to the LISP Programming System are made to conform to the functional syntax of LISP even though they are not functions. For example, the command to print an S-expression on the output tape is called print. Syntactically, print is a function of one argument. It may be used in composition with other functions, and will be evaluated in the usual manner, with the inside of the composition being evaluated first. Its effect is to print its argument on the output tape (or on-line). It is a function only in the trivial sense that its value happens to be its argument, thus making it an identity function.

Commands to effect an action such as the operation of input-output, or the defining functions define and cset discussed in Chapter II, will be called pseudo-functions. It is characteristic of the LISP system that all functions including psuedo-functions must have values. In some cases the value is trivial and may be ignored.

This Chapter is concerned with several extensions of the LISP language that are in the system.

3.1 Functional Arguments

Mathematically, it is possible to have functions as arguments of other functions. For example, in arithmetic one could define a function operate [op;a;b], where op is a functional argument that specifies which arithmetic operation is to be performed on a and b. Thus

operate[+;3;4]=7   and

operate[x;3;4]=12

In LISP, functional arguments are extremely useful. A very important function w a functional argument is maplist. Its M-expression definition is

maplist[x;fn]=[null[x]→NIL;

$\qquad$ T→cons[fn[x];maplist[cdr[x];fn]]]

An examination of the universal function evalquote will show that the interpreter can handle maplist and other functions written in this manner without any further addition. The functional argument is, of course, a function translated into an S-expression. It is bound to the variable fn and is then used whenever fn is mentioned as a function. The S-expression for maplist itself is as follows:

(MAPLIST (LAMBDA (X FN) (COND ((NULL X) NIL)
$\qquad$ (T (CONS (FN X) (MAPLIST (CDR X) FN))))))

Now suppose we wish to define a function that takes a list and changes it by cons-ing an X onto every item of the list so that, for example,

change[(A B (C D))]=((A . X) (B . X) ((C . D) . X))

Using maplist, we define change by

change[a]=maplist[a;λ[[j];cons[car[j];X]]]

This is not a valid M-expression as defined syntactically in section 1.5 because a function appears where a form is expected. This can be corrected by modifying the rule defining an argument so as to include functional arguments:

< argument >:: = < form >|< function >

We also need a special rule to translate functional arguments into S-expression. If fn is a function used as an argument, then it is translated into (FUNCTION fn*).

Example

$\qquad$ (CHANGE (LAMBDA (A) (MAPLIST A (FUNCTION
$\qquad\qquad$ (LAMBDA (J) (CONS (CAR J) (QUOTE X))))))

An examination of evalquote shows that QUOTE will work instead of FUNCTION, provided that there are no free variables present. An explanation of how the interpreter processes the atomic symbol FUNCTION is given in the Appendix B.

3.2 Logical Connectives

The logical or Boolian connectives are usually considered as primitive operators. However, in LISP, they can be defined by using conditional expressions:

p∧q=[p→q;T→F]

p∨q=[p→T;T→q]

~q=[q→F;T→T]

In the System, <u>not</u> is a predicate of one argument. However, <u>and</u> and <u>or</u> are predicates of an indefinite number of arguments, and therefore are special forms. In writing M-expressions it is often convenient to use infix notation and write expressions such as a$\vee$b$\vee$c for or[a;b;c]. In S-expressions, one must, of course, use prefix notation and write (OR A B C).

The order in which the arguments of <u>and</u> and <u>or</u> are given may be of some significance in the case in which some of the arguments may not be well defined. The definitions of these predicated given above show that the value may be defined even if all of the arguments are not.

<u>and</u> evaluates its arguments from left to right. If one of them is found that is false, then the value of the <u>and</u> is false and no further arguments are evaluated. If the arguments are all evaluated and found to be true, then the value is true.

<u>or</u> evaluates its arguments from left to right. If one of them is true, then the value of the <u>or</u> is true and no further arguments are evaluated. If the arguments are all evaluated and found to be false, then the value is false.

3.3 Predicates and Truth in LISP

Although the rule for translating M-expressions into S-expressions states that T is (QUOTE T), it was stated that in the system one must always write T instead. Similarly, one must write F rather than (QUOTE F). The programmer may either accept this rule blindly or understand the following Humpty-Dumpty semantics.

In the LISP programming system there are two atomic symbols that represent truth and falsity respectively. These two atomic symbols are *T* and NIL. It is these symbols rather than T and F that are the actual value of all predicates in the system. This is mainly a coding convenience.

The atomic symbols T and F have APVAL's whose values are *T* and NIL, respectively. The symbols T and F for constant predicates will work because:

eval[T;NIL]=*T*
eval[F;NIL]=NIL

The forms (QUOTE *T*) and (QUOTE NIL) will also work because

eval[(QUOTE *T*);NIL]=*T*
eval[(QUOTE NIL);NIL]=NIL

T and NIL both have APVAL's that point to themselves. Thus *T* and NIL are also acceptable because

eval[*T*;NIL]=*T*
eval[NIL;NIL]=NIL

But

eval[(QUOTE F);NIL]=F

which is wrong and this is why (QUOTE F) will not work. Note that

eval[(QUOTE T);alist]=T

which is wrong but will work for a different reason that will be explained in the paragraph after next.

There is no formal distinction between a function and a predicate in LISP. A predicate can be defined as a function whose value is either *T* or NIL. This is true of all predicates in the System.

One may use a form that is not a predicate in a location in which a predicate is called for, such as in the p position of a conditional expression, or as an argument of a logical predicate. Semantically, any S-expression that is not NIL will be regarded as truth in such a case. One consequence of this is that the predicates null and not are identical. Another consequence is that (QUOTE T) or (QUOTE X) is equivalent to T as a constant predicate.

The predicate eq has the following behavior.

1. If its arguments are different, the value of eq is NIL.

2. If its arguments are both the same atomic symbol, its value is *T*.

3. If its arguments are both the same, but are not atomic, then the value is *T* or NIL depending upon whether the arguments are identical in their representation in core memory.

4. The value of eq is always *T* or NIL. It is never undefined even if its arguments are bad.

IV. ARITHMETIC IN LISP

Lisp 1.5 has provision for handling fixed-point and floating-point numbers and logical words. There are functions and predicates in the system for performing arithmetic and logical operations and making basic tests.

4.1 Reading and Printing Numbers

Numbers are stored in the computer as though they were a special type of atomic symbol. This is discussed more thoroughly in section 7.3. The following points should be noted :

1. Numbers may occur in S-expressions as though they were atomic symbols.

2. Numbers are constants that evaluate to themselves. They do not need to be quoted.

3. Numbers should not be used as variables or function names.

a. Floating-Point Numbers

The rules for punching these for the read program are:

1. A decimal point must be included but not as the first or last character.

2. A plus sign or minus sign may precede the number. The plus sign is not required.

3. Exponent indication is optional. The letter E followed by the exponent to the base 10 is written directly after the number. The exponent consists of one or two digits that may be preceded by a plus or minus sign.

4. Absolute values must lie between 2^{128} and 2^{-128} (10^{38} and 10^{-38}).

5. Significance is limited to 8 decimal digits.

6. Any possible ambiguity between the decimal point and the point used in dot notation may be eliminated by putting spaces before and after the LISP dot. This is not required when there is no ambiguity.

Following are examples of correct floating-point numbers. These are all different forms for the same number, and will have the same effect when read in.

$$60.0$$
$$6.E1$$
$$600.00E-1$$
$$0.6E+2$$

The forms .6E+2 and 60. are incorrect because the decimal point is the first or last character respectively.

b. Fixed-Point Numbers

These are written as integers with an optional sign.

<u>Examples</u>

          -17

          32719

c. Octal Numbers or Logical Words

The correct form consists of

1. A sign (optional).
2. Up to 12 digits (0 through 7).
3. The letter Q.
4. An optional scale factor. The scale factor is a decimal integer, no sign allowed.

<u>Example</u>

    a. 777Q
    b. 777Q4
    c. -3Q11
    d. -7Q11
    e. +7Q11

The effect of the read program on octal numbers is as follows.

1. The number is placed in the accumulator three bits per octal digit with zeros added to the left-hand side to make twelve digits. The rightmost digit is placed in bits 33-35; the twelfth digit is placed in bits P, 1, and 2.

2. The accumulator is shifted left three bits (one octal digit) times the scale factor. Thus the scale factor is an exponent to the base 8.

3. If there is a negative sign, it is OR-ed into the P bit. The number is then stored as a logical word.

The examples a through e above will be converted to the following octal words. Note that because the sign is OR-ed with the 36th numerical bit c, d, and e are equivalent.

    a. 000000000777
    b. 000007770000
    c. 700000000000
    d. 700000000000
    e. 700000000000

4.2 Arithmetic Functions and Predicates

We shall now list all of the arithmetic functions in the System. They must be given numbers as arguments; otherwise an error condition will result. The arguments may be any type of number. A function may be given some fixed-point arguments and some floating-point arguments at the same time.

If all of the arguments for a function are fixed-point numbers, then the value will be a fixed-point number. If at least one argument is a floating-point number, then the value of the function will be a floating-point number.

<u>plus</u>$[x_1; \ldots; x_n]$ is a function of any number of arguments whose value is the algebraic sum of the arguments.

difference[x;y] has for its value the algebraic difference of its arguments.

minus[x] has for its value −x.

times[x₁;...;xₙ] is a function of any number of arguments, whose value is the product (with correct sign) of its arguments.

add1[x] has x+1 for its value. The value is fixed-point or floating-point, depending on the argument.

sub1[x] has x−1 for its value. The value is fixed-point or floating-point, depending on the argument.

max[x₁;...;xₙ] chooses the largest of its arguments for its value. Note that max[3;2.0] = 3.0.

min[x₁;...;xₙ] chooses the smallest of its arguments for its value.

recip[x] computes 1/x. The reciprocal of any fixed point number is defined as zero.

quotient[x;y] computes the quotient of its arguments. For fixed-point arguments, the value is the number theoretic quotient. A divide check or floating-point trap will result in a LISP error.

remainder[x;y] computes the number theoretic remainder for fixed-point numbers, and the floating-point residue for floating-point arguments.

divide[x;y] = cons[quotient[x;y]; cons[remainder[x;y];NIL]]

expt[x;y] = x^y. If both x and y are fixed-point numbers, this is computed by iterative multiplication. Otherwise the power is computed by using logarithms. The first argument cannot be negative.

We shall now list all of the arithmetic predicates in the System. They may have fixed-point and floating-point arguments mixed freely. The value of a predicate is *T* or NIL.

lessp[x;y] is true if x < y, and false otherwise.

greaterp[x;y] is true if x > y.

zerop[x] is true if x=0, or if $|x| \leq 3 \times 10^{-6}$.

onep[x] is true if $|x-1| \leq 3 \times 10^{-6}$.

minusp[x] is true if x is negative.

"−0" is negative.

numberp[x] is true if x is a number (fixed-point or floating-point).

fixp[x] is true only if x is a fixed-point number. If x is not a number at all, an error will result.

floatp[x] is similar to fixp[x] but for floating-point numbers.

equal[x;y] works on any arguments including S-expressions incorporating numbers inside them. Its value is true if the arguments are identical. Floating-point numbers must satisfy $|x-y| < 3 \times 10^{-6}$.

The logical functions operate on 36−bit words. The only acceptable arguments are fixed-point numbers. These may be read in as octal or decimal integers, or they may be the result of a previous computation.

logor[x₁;...;xₙ] performs a logical OR on its arguments.

logand[x₁;...;xₙ] performs a logical AND on its arguments.

logxor[x₁;...;xₙ] performs an exclusive OR
(0 v 0 = 0, 1 v 0 = 0 v 1 = 1, 1 v 1 = 0).

leftshift[x;n] = $x \times 2^n$. The first argument is shifted left by the number of bits specified by the second argument. If the second argument is negative, the first argument will be shifted right.

4.3 Programming with Arithmetic

The arithmetic functions may be used recursively, just as other functions available to the interpreter. As an example, we define _factorial_ as it was given in Section I.

$$n! = [\ n = 0 \rightarrow 1;\ T \rightarrow n.(n-1)\ !\ ]$$

```
DEFINE ((
(FACTORIAL (LAMBDA (N) (COND
    ((ZEROP N) 1)
    (T (TIMES N (FACTORIAL (SUB1 N)))) )))
))
```

4.4 The Array Feature

Provision is made in LISP 1.5 for allocating blocks of storage for data. The data may consist of numbers, atomic symbols or other S-expressions.

The pseudo-function array reserves space for arrays, and turns the name of an array into a function that can be used to fill the array or locate any element of it.

Arrays may have up to three indices. Each element (uniquely specified by its co-ordinates) contains a pointer to an S-expression (see Section VII).

array is a function of one argument which is a list of arrays to be declared. Each item is a list containing the name of an array, its dimensions, and the word LIST. (Non-list arrays are reserved for future developments of the LISP system.)

For example, to make an array called alpha of size 7×10, and one called beta of size $3 \times 4 \times 5$ one should execute:

array[((ALPHA (7 10) LIST) (BETA (3 4 5) LIST))]

After this has been executed, both arrays exist and their elements are all set to NIL. Indices range from 0 to n-1.

alpha and beta are now functions that can be used to set or locate elements of these respective arrays.

To set $\text{alpha}_{i,j}$ to x, execute —

alpha[SET;x;i;j]

To set $\text{alpha}_{3,4}$ to (A B C) execute —

alpha[SET;(A B C);3;4]

Inside a function or program X might be bound to (A B C), I bound to 3, and J bound to 4, in which case the setting can be done by evaluating —

(ALPHA (QUOTE SET) X I J)

To locate an element of an array, use the array name as a function with the coordinates as axes. Thus any time after executing the previous example —

alpha[3;4] = (A B C)

Arrays use marginal indexing for maximum speed. For most efficient results, specify dimensions in increasing order. Beta[3;4;5] is better than beta[5;3;4].

Storage for arrays is located in an area of memory called binary program space.

V. THE PROGRAM FEATURE

The LISP 1.5 program feature allows the user to write an Algol-like program containing LISP statements to be executed.

An example of the program feature is the function length, which examines a list and decides how many elements there are in the top level of the list. The value of length is an integer.

Length is a function of one argument ℓ. The program uses two program variables u and v, which can be regarded as storage locations whose contents are to be changed by the program. In English the program is written:

This is a function of one argument ℓ.

It is a program with two program variables u and v.

Store 0 in v.

Store the argument ℓ in u.

A   If u contains NIL, then the program is finished,

and the value is whatever is now in v.

Store in u, cdr of what is now in u.

Store in v, one more than what is now in v.

Go to A.

We now write this program as an M-expression, with a few new notations. This corresponds line for line with the program written above.

$$length[\ell] = prog[[u;v];$$

$$v := 0;$$

$$u := \ell;$$

A $[null[u] \rightarrow return[v]];$

$$u := cdr[u];$$

$$v := v+1;$$

$$go[A]]$$

Rewriting this as an S-expression, we get the following program.

```
DEFINE ((
(LENGTH (LAMBDA (L)
(PROG (U V)
        (SETQ V 0)
        (SETQ U L)
A       (COND ((NULL U) (RETURN V)))
        (SETQ U (CDR U))
        (SETQ V (ADD1 V))
        (GO A) )))        ))
LENGTH ((A  B  C  D))

        LENGTH (((X · Y) A CAR (N B) (X Y Z)))
```

The last two lines are test cases. Their values are four and five, respectively.

The program form has the structure —

(PROG, list of program variables, sequence of statements and atomic symbols...) An atomic symbol in the list is the location marker for the statement that follows. In the above example, A is a location marker for the statement beginning with COND.

The first list after the symbol PROG is a list of program variables. If there are none, then this should be written NIL or (). Program variables are treated much like bound variables, but they are not bound by LAMBDA. The value of each program variable is NIL until it has been set to something else.

To set a program variable, use the form SET. To set variable PI to 3.14 write (SET (QUOTE PI) 3.14). SETQ is like SET except that it quotes its first argument. Thus (SETQ PI 3.14). SETQ is usually more convenient. SET and SETQ can change variables that are on the a-list from higher level functions. The value of SET or SETQ is the value of its second argument.

Statements are normally executed in sequence. Executing a statement means evaluating it with the current a-list and ignoring its value. Program statements are often executed for their effect rather than their value.

GO is a form used to cause a transfer. (GO A) will cause the program to continue at statement A. The form GO can be used only as a statement on the top level of a PROG or immediately inside a COND which is on the top level of a PROG.

Conditional expressions as program statements have a useful peculiarity. If none of the propositions are true, instead of an error indication which would otherwise occur, the program continues with the next statement. This is true only for conditional expressions that are on the top level of a PROG.

RETURN is the normal end of a program. The argument of RETURN is evaluated, and this is the value of the program. No further statements are executed.

If a program runs out of statements, it returns with the value NIL.

The program feature, like other LISP functions, can be used recursively. The function $\underline{rev}$, which reverses a list and all its sublists is an example of this.

$$rev[x] = prog[[y;z];$$
$$A \quad [null[x] \rightarrow return[y]];$$
$$z := car[x];$$
$$[atom[z] \rightarrow go[B]];$$
$$z := rev[z];$$
$$B \quad y := cons[z;y];$$
$$x := cdr[x];$$
$$go[A]]$$

The function $\underline{rev}$ will reverse a list on all levels so that

$$rev[(A ((B C) D))] = ((D (C B)) A)$$

THE DESIGN OF APL*

A. D. FALKOFF AND K. E. IVERSON

Abstract: This paper discusses the development of APL, emphasizing and illustrating the principles underlying its design. The principle of simplicity appears most strongly in the minimization of rules governing the behavior of APL objects, while the principle of practicality is served by the design process itself, which relies heavily on experimentation. The paper gives the rationale for many specific design choices, including the necessary adjuncts for system management.

Introduction

This paper attempts to identify the general principles that guided the development of APL and its computer realizations, and to show the role these principles played in the evolution of the language. The reader will be assumed to be familiar with the current definition of APL [1]. A brief chronology of the development of APL is presented in an appendix.

Different people claiming to follow the same broad principles may well arrive at radically different designs; an appreciation of the actual role of the principles in design can therefore be communicated only by illustrating their application in a variety of specific instances. It must be remembered, of course, that in the heat of battle principles are not applied as consciously or systematically as may appear in the telling. Some notion of the evolution of the ideas may be gained from consulting earlier discussions, particularly Refs. 2–4.

The actual operative principles guiding the design of any complex system must be few and broad. In the present instance we believe these principles to be simplicity and practicality. Simplicity enters in four guises: *uniformity* (rules are few and simple), *generality* (a small number of general functions provide as special cases a host of more specialized functions), *familiarity* (familiar symbols and usages are adopted whenever possible), and *brevity* (economy of expression is sought). Practicality is manifested in two respects: concern with actual application of the language, and concern with the practical limitations imposed by existing equipment.

We believe that the design of APL was also affected in important respects by a number of procedures and circumstances. Firstly, from its inception APL has been developed by *using* it in a succession of areas. This emphasis on application clearly favors practicality and simplicity. The treatment of many different areas fostered generalization; for example, the general inner product was developed in attempting to obtain the advantages of ordinary matrix algebra in the treatment of symbolic logic.

Secondly, the lack of any machine realization of the language during the first seven or eight years of its development allowed the designers the freedom to make radical changes, a freedom not normally enjoyed by designers who must observe the needs of a large working population dependent on the language for their daily computing needs. This circumstance was due more to the dearth of interest in the language than to foresight.

Thirdly, at every stage the design of the language was controlled by a small group of not more than five people. In particular, the men who designed (and coded) the implementation were part of the language design group, and all members of the design group were involved in broad decisions affecting the implementation. On the other hand, many ideas were received and accepted from people outside the design group, particularly from active users of some implementation of APL.

Finally, design decisions were made by Quaker consensus; controversial innovations were deferred until they could be revised or reevaluated so as to obtain unanimous agreement. Unanimity was not achieved without cost in time and effort, and many divergent paths were explored and assessed. For example, many different notations for the circular and hyperbolic functions were entertained over a period of more than a year

*Reprinted from *IBM Journal of Research and Development*, July 1973, 324–334, copyright 1973.

before the present scheme was proposed, whereupon it was quickly adopted. As the language grows, more effort is needed to explore the ramifications of any major innovation. Moreover, greater care is needed in introducing new facilities, to avoid the possibility of later retraction that would inconvenience thousands of users. An example of the degree of preliminary exploration that may be involved is furnished by the depth and diversity of the investigations reported in the papers by Ghandour and Mezei [5] and by More [6].

The character set

The typography of a language to be entered at a simple keyboard is subject to two major practical restrictions: it must be linear, rather than two-dimensional, and it must be printable by a limited number of distinct symbols.

When one is not concerned with an immediate machine realization of a language, there is no strong reason to so limit the typography and for this reason the language may develop in a freer *publication form*. Before the design of a machine realization of APL, the restrictions appropriate to a keyboard form were not observed. In particular, different fonts were used to indicate the rank of a variable. In the keyboard form, such distinctions can be made, if desired, by adopting classes of names for certain classes of things.

The practical objective of linearizing the typography also led to increased uniformity and generality. It led to the present bracketed form of indexing, which removes the rank limitation on arrays imposed by use of superscripts and subscripts. It also led to the regularization of the form of dyadic functions such as $N\alpha J$ and $N\omega J$ (later eliminated from the language). Finally, it led to writing inner and outer products in the linear form $+.\times$ and $\circ.\times$ and eventually to the recognition of such expressions as instances of the use of *operators*.

The use of arrays and of operators greatly reduced the demand for distinct characters in APL, but the limitations imposed by the normal 88-symbol typewriter keyboard fostered two innovations which greatly increased the utility of the 88 symbols: the systematic use of most function symbols to represent both a dyadic and a monadic function, as suggested in conventional notation by the double use of the minus sign to represent both subtraction (a *dyadic* function) and negation (a *monadic* function); and the use of composite characters formed by typing one symbol over another (through the use of a backspace), as in ϕ and ! and $\circledast$.

It was necessary to restrict the alphabetic characters to a single font and capitals were chosen for readability. Italics were initially favored because of their common use for denoting variables in mathematics, but were finally chosen primarily because they distinguished the letter O from the digit 0 and letters like L and T from the graphic symbols $\llcorner$ and $\top$.

To allow the possibility of adding complete alphabetic fonts by overstriking, the underscore (_), diaeresis ($\ddot{}$), overbar ($\bar{}$), and quad ($\square$) were provided. In the APL\360 realization, only the underscore is used in this way. The inclusion of the overbar on the typeball fortunately filled a need we had not anticipated—a symbol for negative constants, distinct from the symbol for the negation function. The quad proved a useful symbol alone and in combination (as in $\boxplus$), and the diaeresis still remains unassigned.

The SELECTRIC® typewriter imposed certain practical limitations on the placement of symbols on the keyboard, e.g., only narrow characters can appear in the upper row of the typing element. Within these limitations we attempted to make the keyboard easy to learn by grouping related symbols (such as the relations) in a rational order and by making mnemonic associations between letters and the functions associated with them in the shifted case (such as the *magnitude* function $|$ with M, and the membership symbol ϵ with E).

Valence and order of execution

The *valence* of a function is the number of arguments it takes; APL primitives have valences of 1 (monadic functions) and 2 (dyadic functions), and user-defined functions may have a valence of 0 as well. The form for all APL primitives follows the familiar model of arithmetic, that is, the symbol for a dyadic function occurs between its arguments (as in 3+4) and the symbol for a monadic function occurs before its argument (as in -4).

A function f of valence greater than two is conventionally written in the form $f(a,b,c,d)$. This can be construed as a monadic function F applied to the vector argument a,b,c,d, and this interpretation is used in APL. In the APL\360 realization, the arguments a,b,c, and d must share a common structure. The definition and implementation of generalized arrays, whose elements include *enclosed* arrays, will, of course, remove this restriction.

The result of any primitive APL function depends only on its immediate arguments, and the interpretation of each part of an APL statement is therefore localized. Likewise, the interpretation of each statement is independent of other statements in a program. This independence of context contributes significantly to the readability and ease of implementation of the language.

The order of execution of an APL expression is controlled by parentheses in the familiar way, and parentheses are used for no other purpose. The order is otherwise determined by one simple rule: the right argument of any function is the value of the entire expression following it. In particular, there is no precedence among

functions; all functions, user-defined as well as primitive, are treated alike.

This simple rule has several consequences of practical advantage to the user:

a) An unparenthesized expression is easy to read from left to right because the first function encountered is the major function, the next is the major function in its right argument, etc.

b) An unparenthesized expression is also easy to read from right to left because this is the order in which it is executed.

c) If T is any vector of numerical terms, then the present rule makes the expressions $-/T$ and $\div/T$ very useful: the former is the alternating sum of T and the latter is the alternating product. Moreover, a continued fraction may be written without parentheses in the form $3+\div 4+\div 5+\div 6$, and the efficient evaluation of a polynomial can be written without parentheses in the form $3+X\times 4+X\times 5+X\times 6$.

The rule that multiplication is executed before addition and that the power function is executed before multiplication has been long accepted in mathematics. In discarding any established rule it is wise to speculate on the reasons for its adoption and on whether they still apply. This rule makes parentheses unnecessary in the writing of polynomials, and this alone appears to be a sufficient reason for its original adoption. However, in APL a polynomial can be written more perspicuously in the form $+/C\times X\ast E$, which also requires no parentheses. The question of the order of execution has been discussed in several places: Falkoff et al. [2,3], Berry [7], and Appendix A of Iverson [8].

The order in which isolated parts of a statement, such as the parts $(X+4)$ and $(Y-2)$ in the statement $(Y+4)\times(Y-2)$, are executed is normally immaterial, but does matter when repeated specifications are permitted in a statement as in $(A\leftarrow 2)+A$. Although the use of such expressions is poor practice, it is desirable to make the interpretation unequivocal: the rule adopted (as given in Lathwell and Mezei [9]) is that the rightmost function or specification which can be performed is performed first.

It is interesting to note that the use of embedded assignment was first suggested during the course of the implementation when it was realized that special steps were needed to prevent it. The order of executing isolated parts of a statement was at first left unspecified (as stated in Falkoff and Iverson [1]) to allow freedom in implementation, since isolated parts could then be executed in parallel on any machine offering parallel processing. However, embedded assignment found such wide use that an unambiguous definition became essential to fix the behavior of programs moving from system to system.

Another aspect of the order of execution is the order among statements, which is normally taken as the order of appearance, except as modified by explicit *branches*. In the publication form of the language branches were denoted by arrows drawn from a branch point to the set of possible destinations, and the drawing of branch arrows is still to be recommended as an adjunct for clarifying the structure of a program (Iverson [10], page 3).

In formalizing branching it was necessary to introduce only one new concept (denoted by $\rightarrow$) and three simple conventions: 1) continuing with the statement indicated by the first element of a vector argument of $\rightarrow$, or with the next statement in sequence if the argument is an empty vector, 2) terminating the function if the indicated continuation is not the index of a statement in the program, and 3) the use of *labels*, local names defined by the indices of juxtaposed statements. At first labels were treated as local variables, but it was found to be more convenient in both use and implementation to treat them as local constants.

Since the branch arrow can be followed by any valid expression it provides convenient multi-way conditional branches. For example, if L is a Boolean vector and S is a corresponding set of statement numbers (often formed as the catenation of a set of labels), then $\rightarrow L/S$ provides a $(1+\rho L)$-way branch (to one of the elements of S or falling through if every element of L is zero); if I is an empty vector or an index to the vector S, then $\rightarrow S[I]$ provides a similar $(1+\rho L)$-way branch.

Programming languages commonly incorporate special forms of sequence control, typified by the DO statement of FORTRAN. These forms are excluded from APL because their cost in complication of the language outweighs their utility. The array operations in APL obviate many instances of iteration, and those which remain can be represented in a variety of ways. For example, grouping the initialization, modification, and testing of the control variable at the head of the iterated segment provides a particularly perspicuous arrangement. Moreover, specialized sequence control statements are usually context dependent and necessarily introduce new rules.

Conditional statements of the IF THEN ELSE type are not only context dependent, but their inherent limitation to a sequence of binary choices often leads to awkward constructions. These, and other, special sequence control forms can usually be modeled readily in APL and provided as application packages if desired.

Scalar functions

The emphasis on generality is illustrated in the definitions of many of the scalar functions. For example, the definition of the factorial is not limited to non-negative integers but is extended in the manner of the gamma function. Similarly, the residue is extended to all num-

bers in a simple and useful way: $M|N$ is defined as the smallest (in magnitude) among the quantities $N-M\times I$ (where I is an integer) which lie in the range from 0 to M. If no such quantity exists (as in the case where M is zero) then the restriction to the range 0 to M is discarded, that is, $0|X$ is X. As another example, $0*0$ is defined as 1 because that is the limiting value of $X*Y$ when the point 0 0 is approached along any path other than the X axis, and because this definition is needed to make the common general form of writing a polynomial (in which the constant term C is written as $C\times X*0$) applicable when the value of the argument X is zero.

The urge to generality must be tempered to avoid setting traps for the unwary, and compromise is sometimes necessary. For example, $X\div 0$ could be defined as infinity (i.e., the largest representable number in an implementation) so as to obviate special treatment of the case $Y=0$ when computing the arc tangent of $X\div Y$, but is instead defined to yield a domain error. Nevertheless, $0\div 0$ is given the value 1, in spite of the fact that the mathematical argument for it is much weaker than that for $0*0$, because it was deemed desirable to avoid an error stop in this case.

Eventually it will be desirable to be able to set separate limits on domains to suit various classes of users. For example, an implementation that incorporates complex numbers must yield a result for the expression $1*.5$ but should admit of being set to yield a domain error for a user studying elementary arithmetic. The experienced user should be permitted to use an implementation in a mode that gives him complete control of domain and other errors, i.e., an error should not stop execution but should give necessary information about the error in a form which can be used by the program in which it occurs. Such a facility has not yet been incorporated in APL implementations.

A very general and useful set of functions was introduced by adopting the relation symbols $< \leq = \geq > \neq$ to represent functions (i.e., propositions) rather than assertions. The result of any proposition was defined to be 0 or 1 (rather than, say, *true* or *false*) so that it would lie in the domain of other arithmetic functions. Thus $X=Y$ and $X\neq Y$ represent general comparisons, but if X and Y are integers then $X=Y$ is the Kronecker delta and $X\neq Y$ is its inverse; if X and Y are Boolean variables, then $X\neq Y$ is the *exclusive-or* and $X\leq Y$ is material implication. This definition also allows expressions that incorporate both relational and arithmetic functions (such as $(2=+/[1]0=S\circ.|S)/S\leftarrow\iota N$, which yields the primes up to integer N). Moreover, identities among Boolean functions are more evident when expressed in these terms than when expressed in more conventional symbols.

The adoption of the relation symbols as functions does not preclude their use as *assertions* in informal sentences. For example, although one might feel compelled to substitute "$X\leq Y$ is true" for "$X\leq Y$" in the sentence "If $X\leq Y$ then $(X<Y)\vee(X=Y)$", there is no more reason to do so than to substitute "Bob is there is true" for "Bob is there" in the sentence which begins "If Bob is there then . . ."

Although we strove to adopt familiar symbols and usage, any clash with the principle of uniformity was invariably resolved in favor of uniformity. For example, familiar symbols (such as $+ - \times \div$) are used where possible, but anomalies such as $|X|$ for magnitude and $N!$ for factorial are regularized to $|X$ and $!N$. Notation such as X^N for power and $\binom{M}{N}$ for the binomial coefficient are replaced by regular dyadic forms $X*N$ and $M!N$. Elision of the times sign is not permitted; this allows the use of multiple-character names and avoids confusion between multiplication, as in $X(X+3)$, and the application of a function, as in $F(X+3)$.

Moreover, each of the primitive scalar functions in APL is extended to arrays in exactly the same way. In particular, if V and W are vectors the expressions $V\times W$ and $3+V$ are permitted as well as the expressions $V+W$ and $3\times V$, although only the latter pair would be permitted (in the sense used in APL) in conventional vector algebra.

One view of simplicity might exclude as redundant those functions which are easily expressed in terms of others. For example, $\lceil X$ may be written as $-\lfloor -X$, and $\lceil/X$ may be written as $-\lfloor/-X$, and $\wedge/L$ may be written as $\sim\vee/\sim L$. From another viewpoint it is simpler to use a more complete or symmetric set of primitives, since one need not remember which of a pair is provided and how to express the other in terms of it. In APL, completeness has been favored. For example, symbols are provided for all of the nontrivial logical functions although all are easily expressed in terms of a small subset of them.

The use of the circle to denote the whole family of functions related to the circular functions is a practical technique for conserving symbols as well as a useful generalization. It leads to many convenient expressions involving reduction and inner and outer products (such as $1\ 2\ 3\circ.OX$ for a table of sines, cosines and tangents). Moreover, anyone wishing to use the symbol SIN for the sine function can define the function SIN as either $1OX$ (for radian arguments) or $1OX\times 180\div O1$ (for degree arguments). The notational scheme employed for the circular functions must clearly be used with discretion; it could be used to replace all monadic functions by a single dyadic function with an integer left argument to encode each monadic function.

Operators

The dot in the expression $M+.\times N$ is an example of an *operator*; it takes functions (in this case + and ×) as

arguments and produces a new function called an *inner product*. (In elementary mathematics the term *operator* is also used as a synonym for *function*, but in APL we eschew this usage.) The evolution of operators in APL furnishes an example of growing generality which has as yet been neither fully exploited nor fully regularized.

The operators now in APL were introduced one by one (reduction, then inner product, then outer product, then axis operators such as $\phi[I]$) without being recognized as members of a class. When this class property was recognized it was apparent that the operators had not been given a consistent syntax and that the notation should eventually be regularized to give operators the same syntax as functions, i.e., an operator taking two arguments occurs between its (function) arguments (as in $+.\times$) and an operator taking one argument appears in front of it. It also became evident that our treatment of operators had introduced a useful heirarchy into the order of execution, operators being executed before functions.

The recognition of operators as such has also made clear the much broader role they might be expected to play—derivative and integral operators are only two of many useful operators that must be added to the language.

The use of the outer product operator furnishes a clear example of a significant process in the evolution of the language: when a new facility is introduced it takes considerable time to recognize the many ways in which it can be used and therefore to appreciate its role in the further development of the language. The notation $\alpha^j(n)$ (later regularized to $N\alpha J$) had been introduced early to represent a *prefix* vector, i.e., a Boolean vector of N elements with J leading 1's. Some thought had been given to extending the definition to a *vector* J (perhaps to yield an N=column matrix whose rows were prefix vectors determined by the elements of J) but no decision had been taken. When considering such an extension we normally communicate by defining any proposed notation in terms of existing primitives. After the outer product was introduced the proposed extension was written simply as $J\circ.\geq\iota N$, and it became clear that the function α was now redundant.

One should not conclude from this example that every function or set of functions easily expressed in terms of another is discarded as redundant; judgment must be exercised. In the present instance the α was discarded partly because it was too restrictive, i.e., the outer product form could be applied to yield a host of related functions (such as $J\circ.<\iota N$ and $J\circ.<\phi\iota N$) not all of which were expressible in terms of the prefix and suffix functions α and ω. As mentioned in the discussion of scalar functions, the completeness of an obvious family of functions is also a factor to be considered.

Operators are attractive from several points of view. Because they provide a scheme for denoting whole classes of related functions, they offer uniformity of expression and great economy of symbols. The conciseness of expression that they allow can also be directly related to efficiency of implementation. Moreover, they introduce a new level of generality which plays an important role in the formal manipulability of the language.

Formal manipulation

APL is rich in identities and is therefore amenable to a great deal of fruitful formal manipulation. For example, many of the familiar identities of ordinary matrix algebra extend to inner products other than $+.\times$, and de Morgan's law and other dualities extend to inner and outer products on arrays. The emphasis on generality, uniformity, and simplicity is likely to lead to a language rich in identities, but our emphasis on identities has been such that it should perhaps be enunciated as a separate and important guiding principle. Indeed, the preface to Iverson [10] cites one chapter (on the logical calculus) as illustration of "the formal manipulability of the language and its utility in theoretical work". A variety of identities is treated in [10] and [11], and a schema for proofs in APL is presented in [12].

Two examples will be used to illustrate the role of identities in the development of the language. The identity

$$(+/X)=(+/U/X)++/(\sim U)/X$$

applies for any numerical vector X and logical vector U. Maintaining this identity for the case where U is a vector of zeros forces one to define the sum over an empty vector as zero. A similar identity holds for reduction by any associative and commutative function and leads one to define the reduction of an empty array by any function as the identity element of that function.

The dyadic transpose $I\mathbb{Q}A$ performs a general permutation on the coordinates of A as specified by the argument I. The monadic transpose is a special case which, in order to yield ordinary matrix transpose for an array of rank two, was initially defined to interchange the last two coordinates. It was later realized that the identity

$$\wedge/,(M+.\times N)=\mathbb{Q}(\mathbb{Q}N)+.\times\mathbb{Q}M$$

expected to hold for matrices would not hold for higher rank arrays. To make the identity true in general, the monadic transpose was defined to reverse the order of the coordinates as follows:

$$\wedge/,(\mathbb{Q}A)=(\phi\iota\rho\rho A)\mathbb{Q}A.$$

Moreover, the form chosen for the left argument of the dyadic transpose led to the following important identity:

$$\wedge/,(I\mathbb{Q}J\mathbb{Q}A)=I[J]\mathbb{Q}A.$$

Execute and format

In designing an executable language there is a fundamental choice to be made: Is the statement of an expression to be taken as an order to evaluate it, or must the evaluation be indicated by an explicit function in the language? This decision was made very early in the development of APL, albeit with little deliberation. Nevertheless, once the choice became manifest, early in the development of the implementation, it was applied uniformly in all situations.

There were some arguments against this, of course, particularly in the application of a function to its arguments, where it is often useful to be able to "call by name," which requires that the evaluation of the argument be deferred. But if implemented literally (i.e., if functions could be defined with this as an option) then names per se would have to be known to the language and would constitute an additional object type with its own rules of behavior and specialized primitive functions. A deliberate effort had been made to eliminate unnecessary type distinctions, as in the uniform language treatment of numbers regardless of their internal representation, and this point of view prevailed. In the interest of keeping the semantic rules simple, the idea of "call by name" was rejected as a primitive concept in APL.

Nevertheless, there are important cases where the formal argument of a function should not be evaluated at the time of invocation—as in the application of a generalized root finder to an arbitrary function. There are also situations where it is useful to inhibit evaluation of an expression, as in certain conditional forms, and the need for some treatment of the problem was clear. The basis for a solution was at hand in the form of character arrays, which were already objects of the language. Effectively, putting quotes around a statement inhibits its execution by making it a data item, a character array subject to the normal language functions. To get the effect of working with names, or with expressions to be conditionally evaluated, it was only necessary to introduce the notion of "unquote," or more properly "execute," as a function that would cause a character array to be evaluated as if it were the same expression without the inhibition.

The actual introduction of the execute function did not come for some time after its recognition as the likely solution. The development that preceded its final acceptance into APL illustrates several design principles.

The concept of an execute function is a very powerful one. In a sense, it makes the language "self-conscious," and introduces endless possibilities for obscurity in programs. This might have been a reason for not allowing it, but we had long since realized that a general-purpose language cannot be made foolproof and remain effective. Furthermore, APL is easily partitioned, and beginning users, or users of application packages, need not know about more sophisticated aspects of the language. The real issues were whether the function was of sufficiently broad utility, whether it could be defined simply, and whether it was perhaps a special case of a more general capability that should be implemented instead. There was also the need to establish a symbol for it.

The case for general utility was easily made. The execute function does allow names to be used as arguments to functions without the need for a new data type; it provides the means for generating variables under program control, which can be useful, for example, in managing data that do not conveniently fit into rectangular arrays; it allows the construction and execution of statements under program control; and in interpretive implementations it provides conversion from characters to numbers at machine speeds.

The behavior of the execute function is simply described: it treats a character array argument as a representation of an APL statement and attempts to evaluate or execute the statement so represented. System commands and attempts to enter function definition mode are not valid APL statements and are excluded from the domain of execute. It can be said that, except for these exclusions, execute acts upon a character array as if the elements of the array were entered at a terminal in the immediate execution mode.

Incidentally, there was pressure to arbitrarily include system commands in the domain of execute as a means of providing access to other workspaces under program control in order to facilitate work with large collections of data. This was resisted on the basis that the execute function should not allow by subterfuge what was otherwise disallowed. Indeed, consideration of this aspect of the behavior of execute led to the removal of certain anomalies in function definition and a clarification of the role of the escape characters) and ∇.

The question of generality has not been finally settled. Certainly, the execute function could be considered a member of a class that includes constructs like those of the lambda calculus. But it is not necessary to have the ultimate answer in order to proceed, and the simplicity of the definition adopted gives some assurance that generalizations are not being foreclosed.

For some time during its experimental implementation the symbol for execute was the epsilon. This was chosen for obvious mnemonic reasons and because no other monadic use was made of this symbol. As thought was being given to another new function—format—it was observed that over some part of each of their domains format and execute were inverses. Furthermore, over these parts of their domains they were strongly related to the functions encode and decode, and we therefore adopted their symbols overstruck by the symbol ∘.

The format function furnishes another example of a primitive whose behavior was first defined and long experimented with by means of APL defined functions. These defined functions were the *DFT* (Decimal Format) and *EFT* (Exponential Format) familiar to most users of the APL system. The main advantage of the primitive format function over these definitions is its much more efficient use of computer time.

The format function has both a dyadic and a monadic definition, but the execute function is monadic only. This leaves the way open for a related dyadic function, for which there has been no dearth of suggestions, but none will be adopted until more experience has been gained in the use of what we already have.

System commands and other environmental facilities

The definition of APL is purely abstract: the objects of the language, arrays of numbers and characters, are acted upon by the primitive functions in a manner independent of their representation and independent of any practical interpretation placed upon them. The advantages of such an abstract definition are that it makes the language truly machine independent, and avoids bias in favor of particular application areas. But not everything in a computing system is abstract, and provision must be made to manage system resources and otherwise communicate with the environment in which the language functions operate.

Maintaining the abstract nature of the language in a real computing system therefore seemed to imply a need for language-like facilities in some sense outside of APL. The need was first met by the use of system commands, which are syntactically not part of APL, and are also excluded from dynamic use within APL programs. They provided a simple and, in some ways, convenient answer to the problem of system management, but proved insufficient because the actions and information provided by them are often required dynamically.

The exclusion of system commands from programs was based more strongly on engineering considerations than on a theoretic compulsion, since the syntactic distinction alone sets them apart from the language, but there remained a reluctance to allow such syntactic anomalies in a program. The real issue, which was whether the functions provided by the system commands were properly the province of APL, was tabled for the time being, and defined functions that mimic the actions of certain of them were introduced to allow dynamic execution. The functions so provided were those affecting only the environment within a workspace, such as width and origin, while those that would have affected major physical resources of the system were still excluded for engineering reasons.

These environmental defined functions were based on the use of still another class of functions—called "I-beams" because of the shape of the symbol used for them—which provide a more general facility for communication between APL programs and the less abstract parts of the system. The I-beam functions were first introduced by the system programmers to allow them to execute System/360 instructions from within APL programs, and thus use APL as a direct aid in their programming activity. The obvious convenience of functions of this kind, which appeared to be part of the language, led to the introduction of the monadic I-beam function for direct use by anyone. Various arguments to this function yielded information about the environment such as available space and time of day.

Though clearly an ad hoc facility, the I-beam functions appear to be part of the language because they obey APL syntax and can be executed from within an APL program. They were too useful to do without in the absence of a more rational solution to the problem, and so were graced with the designation "system-dependent functions," while we continued to use the system and think about the general problem of communication among the subsystems composing it.

Shared variables

The logical basis for a generalized communication facility in APL\360 was laid in 1964 with the publication of the formal description of System/360 [2]. It was then observed that the interaction between concurrent "asynchronous" processes (programs) could be completely comprehended by an interface comprising variables that were shared by the cooperating processes. (Another facility was also used, where one program forced a branch in another, but this can be regarded as a derivative representation based on variables shared between one program and a processor that drives the other.) It was not until six or seven years later, however, that the full force of this observation was brought to bear on the practical problem of controlling in an organic way the environment in which APL programs run.

Three processors can be identified during the execution of an APL program: APL, or the processor that actually executes the program; the *system*, or host that manages libraries and other environmental factors, which in APL\360 is the System/360 processor; and the user, who may be observing and processing output or providing input to the program. The link between APL and system is the set of I-beam functions, that between user and system is the set of system commands, and between user and APL, the quad and quote-quad. With the exception of the quote-quad, which is a true variable, all these links are constructs on the interfaces rather than the interfaces themselves.

It can be seen that the quote-quad is shared by the user and APL. Characteristically, a value assigned to it in a program is presented to the user at the terminal, who utilizes this information as he sees fit. If later read by the program, the value of the quote-quad then has no fixed relationship to what was earlier specified by the program. The values written and read by the program are *a fortiori* APL objects—abstract arrays—but they may have practical significance to the user-processor, suggesting, for example, that an experimental observation be made and the results entered at the keyboard.

Using the quote-quad as the paradigm for their behavior, a general facility for shared variables was designed and implemented starting in late 1969 (see Lathwell [13]). The underlying concept was to provide communication across the boundary between independent processors by explicitly establishing certain variables as being shared between them. A shared variable is syntactically indistinguishable from others and may be used normally either on the right or left of an assignment arrow.

Although motivated most strongly at the time by a need to provide a "file and I/O" capability for APL\360, the shared variable facility satisfied other needs as well, a significant criterion for the inclusion of a new feature in the language. It provides for general communication, not only between APL and the host system, but also between APL programs running concurrently at different terminals, which is in a sense a more fundamental use of the idea.

Perhaps as important as the practical use of the facility is the potency that an implementation lends to the concept of shared variables as a basis for understanding communication in any system. With respect to APL\360, for example, we had long used the term "distinguished variable" in discussing the interface between APL and system, meaning thereby variables, like trace and stop vectors, which hold control or state information. It is now clear that "distinguished variables" are shared variables, distinguished from ordinary variables by the fact of their being shared, and further qualified by their membership in a particular interface. In principle, the environment and resources of APL\360 could be completely controlled through the use of an appropriate set of such distinguished variables.

System functions

In a given application area it is usually easier to work with APL augmented by defined functions, designed to embody the significant concepts of the area, than with the primitive functions of the language alone. Such defined functions, together with the relevant variables or data objects, constitute an application language, or application extension. Managing the resources or environment of an APL computing system is a particular application, in which the data objects are the distinguished variables that define the interface between APL and system.

For convenience, the defined functions constituting an application extension for system management should behave differently from other defined functions, at least to the extent of being available at all times, like the primitives, without having to be copied from workspace to workspace. Such ubiquity requires that the names of these functions be distinguished from those a user might invent. This distinction can only be made, if APL is to remain essentially context independent, by the establishment of a class of reserved names. This class has been defined as names starting with the quad character, and functions having such names are called *system functions*. A similar naming convention applies to distinguished variables, or *system variables*, as they are now called.

In principle, system functions work with system variables that are independently identifiable. In practice, the system variables in a particular situation may not be available explicitly, and the system functions may be locked. This can come about because direct access to the interface by the user is deemed undesirable for technical reasons, or because of economic considerations such as efficiency or protection of proprietary rights. In such situations system functions are superficially distinguishable from primitive functions only by virtue of the naming convention.

The present I-beam functions behave like system functions. Fortunately, there are only two of them: the monadic function that is familiar to all users of APL, and the dyadic function that is still known mostly to system programmers. Despite their usefulness, these functions are hardly to be taken as examples of good application language design, depending as they do on arbitrary numerical arguments to give them meaning, and having no meaningful relationships with each other. The monadic I-beams are more like read-only variables—changeable constants, as it were—than functions. Indeed, except for their syntax, they behave precisely like shared variables where the processor on the other side replaces the value between each reference on the APL side.

The shared variable facility itself requires communication between APL and system in order to establish a desired interface between APL and cooperating processors. The prospect of inventing new system commands for this, or otherwise providing an ad hoc facility, was most distasteful, and consideration of this problem was a major factor in leading toward the system function concept. It was taken as an indication of the validity of the shared variable approach to communication when the solution to the problem it engendered was found within the conceptual framework it provided, and this solution also proved to be a basis for clarifying the role of facilities already present.

In due course a set of system functions must be designed to parallel the facilities now provided by system commands and go beyond them. Aside from the obvious advantage of being dynamically executable, such a set of system functions will have other advantages and some disadvantages. The major operational advantage is that the system functions will be able to use the full power of APL to generate their arguments and exploit their results. Countering this, there is the fact that this power has a price: the automatic name isolation provided by the extralingual system commands will not be available to the system functions. Names used as arguments will have to be presented as character arrays, which is not a disadvantage in programs, although it is less convenient for casual keyboard entry than is the use of unadorned names in system commands.

A more profound advantage of system functions over system commands lies in the possibility of designing the former to work together constructively. System commands are foreclosed from this by the rudimentary nature of their syntax; they do constitute a language, but one having no constructive potential.

Workspaces, files, and input-output

The workspace organization of APL\360 libraries serves to group together functions and variables intended to work together, and to render them active or inactive as a group, preserving the state of the computation during periods of inactivity. Workspaces also implicitly qualify the names of objects within them, so that the same name may be used independently in a multiplicity of workspaces in a given system. These are useful attributes; the grouping feature, for example, contributes strongly to the convenience of using APL by obviating the linkage problems found in other library systems.

On the other hand, engineering decisions made early in the development of APL\360 determined that the workspaces be of fixed size. This limits the size of objects that can be managed within them and often becomes an inconvenience. Consequently, as usage of APL\360 developed, a demand arose for a "file" facility, at first to work with large volumes of data under program control, and later to utilize data generated by other systems. There was also a demand to make use of high-speed input and output equipment. As noted in an earlier section, these demands led in time to the development of the shared variable facility. Three considerations were paramount in arriving at this solution.

One consideration was the determination to maintain the abstract nature of APL. In particular, the use of primitive functions whose definitions depend on the representation of their arguments was to be avoided. This alone was sufficient to rule out the notion of a file as a formal concept in the language. APL has primitive array structures that either encompass the logical structure of files or can be extended to do so by relatively simple functions defined on them. The user of APL may regard any array or collection of arrays as a file, and in principle should be able to use the data so organized without regard to the medium on which these arrays may be stored.

The second consideration was the not uncommon observation that files are used in two ways, as a medium for exchange of information and as a dynamic extension of working storage during computation (see Falkoff [14]). In keeping with the principle just noted, the proper solution to the second problem must ultimately be the removal of workspace size limitations, and this will probably be achieved in the course of general developments in the industry. We saw no prospect of a satisfactory direct solution being achieved locally in a reasonable time, so attention was concentrated on the first problem in the expectation that, with a good general communication facility, on-line storage devices could be used for workspace extension at least as effectively as they are so used in other systems.

The third consideration was one of generality. One possible approach to the communication problem would have been to increase the roster of system commands and make them dynamically executable, or add variations to the I-beam functions to manage specific storage media and I/O equipment or access methods. But in addition to being unpleasant because of its ad hoc nature, this approach did not promise to be general enough. In working interactively with large collections of data, for example, the possible functional variations are almost limitless. Various classes of users may be allowed access for different purposes under a variety of controls, and unless it is intended to impose restrictive constraints ahead of time, it is futile to try to anticipate the solutions to particular problems. Thus, to provide a communication facility by accretion appeared to be an endless task.

The shared variable approach is general enough because, by making the interface explicitly available with primitive controls on the behavior of the shared variable, it provides only the basic communication mechanism. It then remains for the specific problem to be managed by bringing to bear on it the full power of APL on one side, and that of the host system on the other. The only remaining question is one of performance: does the shared variable concept provide the basis for an effective implementation? This question has been answered affirmatively as a result of direct experimentation.

The net effect of this approach has been to provide for APL an application extension comprising the few system functions necessary to manage shared variables. Actual file or I/O applications are managed, as required, by

user-defined functions. The system functions are used only to establish sharing, and the shared variables are then used for the actual transfer of information between APL workspaces and file or I/O processors.

Appendix. Chronology of APL development

The development of APL was begun in 1957 as a necessary tool for writing clearly about various topics of interest in data processing. The early development is described in the preface of Iverson [10] and Brooks and Iverson [15]. Falkoff became interested in the work shortly after Iverson joined IBM in 1960, and used the language in his work on parallel search memories [16]. In early 1963 Falkoff began work on a formal description of System/360 in APL and was later joined in this work by Iverson and Sussenguth [2].

Throughout this early period the language was used by both Falkoff and Iverson in the teaching of various topics at various universities and at the IBM Systems Research Institute. Early in 1964 Iverson began using it in a course in elementary functions at the Fox Lane High School in Bedford, New York, and in 1966 published a text that grew out of this work [8]. John L. Lawrence (who, as editor of the *IBM Systems Journal*, procured and assisted in the publication of the formal description of System/360) became interested in the use of APL at high school and college level and invited the authors to consult with him in the development of curriculum material based on the use of computers. This work led to the preparation of curriculum material in a number of areas and to the publication of an APL\360 Reference Manual by Sandra Pakin [17].

Although our work through 1964 had been focused on the language as a tool for communication among *people*, we never doubted that the same characteristics which make the language good for this purpose would make it good for communication with a machine. In 1963 Herbert Hellerman implemented a portion of the language on an IBM/1620 as reported in [18]. Hellerman's system was used by students in the high school course with encouraging results. This, together with our earlier work in education, heightened our interest in a full-scale implementation.

When the work on the formal description of System/360 was finished in 1964 we turned our attention to the problem of implementation. This work was brought to rapid fruition in 1965 when Lawrence M. Breed joined the project and, together with Philip S. Abrams, produced an implementation on the 7090 by the end of 1965. Influenced by Hellerman's interest in time-sharing we had already developed an APL typing element for the IBM 1050 computer terminal. This was used in early 1966 when Breed adapted the 7090 system to an experimental time-sharing system developed under Andrew Kinslow, allowing us the first use of APL in the manner familiar today. By November 1966, the system had been reprogrammed for System/360 and APL service has been available within IBM since that date. The system became available outside IBM in 1968.

A paper by Falkoff and Iverson [3] provided the first published description of the APL\360 system, and a companion paper by Breed and Lathwell [19] treated the implementation. R. H. Lathwell joined the design group in 1966 and has since been concerned primarily with the implementations of APL and with the use of APL itself in the design process. In 1971 he published, together with Jorge Mezei, a formal definition of APL in APL [9].

The APL\360 System benefited from the contributions of many outside of the central design group. The preface to the User's Manual [1] acknowledges many of these contributions.

References

1. A. D. Falkoff and K. E. Iverson, *APL\360 User's Manual*, IBM Corporation, (GH20-0683-1) 1970.
2. A. D. Falkoff, K. E. Iverson, and E. H. Sussenguth, "A Formal Description of System/360," *IBM Systems Journal*, **3**, 198 (1964).
3. A. D. Falkoff and K. E. Iverson, "The APL\360 Terminal System", *Symposium on Interactive Systems for Experimental Applied Mathematics*, eds., M. Klerer and J. Reinfelds, Academic Press, New York, 1968.
4. A. D. Falkoff, "Criteria for a System Design Language," *Report on NATO Science Committee Conference on Software Engineering Techniques*, April 1970.
5. Z. Ghandour and J. Mezei, "General Arrays, Operators and Functions," *IBM J. Res. Develop.* **17**, 335 (1973, this issue).
6. T. More, "Axioms and Theorems for a Theory of Arrays—Part I," *IBM J. Res. Develop.* **17**, 135 (1973).
7. P. C. Berry, *APL\360 Primer*, IBM Corporation, (GH-20-0689-2) 1971.
8. K. E. Iverson, *Elementary Functions: An Algorithmic Treatment*, Science Research Associates, Chicago, 1966.
9. R. H. Lathwell and J. E. Mezei, "A Formal Description of APL," *Colloque APL*, Institut de Recherche d'Informatique et d'Automatique, Rocquencourt, France, 1971.
10. K. E. Iverson, *A Programming Language*, Wiley, New York, 1962.
11. K. E. Iverson, "Formalism in Programming Languages," *Communications of the ACM*, **7**, 80 (February, 1964).
12. K. E. Iverson, *Algebra: an algorithmic treatment*, Addison-Wesley Publishing Co., Reading, Mass., 1972.
13. R. H. Lathwell, "System Formulation and APL Shared Variables," *IBM J. Res. Develop.* **17**, 353 (1973, this issue).
14. A. D. Falkoff, "A Survey of Experimental APL File and I/O Systems in IBM", *Colloque APL*, Institut de Recherche d'Informatique et D'Automatique, Rocquencourt, France, 1971.
15. F. P. Brooks and K. E. Iverson, *Automatic Data Processing*, Wiley, New York, 1963.
16. A. D. Falkoff, "Algorithms for Parallel Search Memories," *Journal of the ACM*, 488 (1962).
17. S., Pakin, *APL\360 Reference Manual*, Science Research Associates, Inc., Chicago, 1968.

18. H. Hellerman, "Experimental Personalized Array Translator System," *Communications of the ACM* **7**, 433 (July, 1964).

19. L. M. Breed and R. H. Lathwell, "Implementation of APL/360," *Symposium on Interactive Systems for Experimental Applied Mathematics*, eds., M. Klerer and J. Reinfelds, Academic Press, New York, 1968.

Received May 16, 1972

The authors are located at the IBM Data Processing Division Scientific Center, 3401 Market Street, Philadelphia, Pennsylvania 19104.

SECTION 4

PROGRAMMING LANGUAGES AND DATA ABSTRACTION

ABSTRACTION MECHANISMS IN CLU BY
B. LISKOV, A. SNYDER, R. ATKINSON
AND C. SCHAFFERT

EXCEPTION HANDLING IN CLU BY
B. LISKOV AND A. SNYDER

NOTES ON THE DESIGN OF EUCLID BY
G. J. POPEK, J. J. HORNING, B. W.
LAMPSON, J. G. MITCHELL AND
R. L. LONDON

INTRODUCTION

PROGRAMMING LANGUAGES AND DATA ABSTRACTION

All of us who have programmed computers appreciate the importance of the procedure as a mechanism for structuring programs. In fact, the procedure was the main structuring feature provided by all of the early higher level programming languages such as FORTRAN, ALGOL60, PL/1, and ALGOL68. The 1970's have seen an important step forward in language design in the form of another basic structuring mechanism, the so-called *abstract data type*. A data type is a set of objects and an associated set of operations. The operations are designed to create instances of the data type, to build up and take apart these instances. For example a stack is a last-in-first-out list (these are the objects) which has the operations: *push, pop* and *isempty*. Or, the integers are a data type with the operations being the usual *addition, subtraction, multiplication* and *division*.

So what is new about abstract data types? As we see above some data types are already built into the language, like the integers, while others must be created by the programmer. The notion of abstract data types in a programming language is concerned with those types that are created by the programmer. But languages such as Pascal introduced the idea of user defined data types and provided the enumerated data type feature, the array and the record to form new types of data from the basic set. This concept is not what we mean by the term abstract data type.

The idea of an abstract data type in a programming language is to provide a mechanism whereby a new type definition is *isolated* and *protected* from the rest of the program. Access to the data type may be made only in a very restricted manner, thus guaranteeing greater program reliability. The representation of the data type will be hidden from the rest of the program so that outside the definition of the type the programmer cannot rely on its representation. These ideas of good program structuring were espoused by many including David Parnas in his concept called information hiding. Therefore we conclude that an abstract data type as seen in a modern programming language is a means whereby the programmer defines and protects new data types he creates. Thus its scoping elements are one of its most important characteristics.

The first two papers in this section present the language CLU which was developed at MIT by B. Liskov and her team. The language is now flourishing there and is being distributed around the world. Though CLU has many interesting aspects, the one we are most concerned with here is the manner in which abstract data types are implemented and the way exceptions are handled. In CLU an abstract data type is referred to as a *cluster*. As one reads this paper one should keep in mind how the design is done incorporating the idea of an abstract data type. This concept is used at the design stage, but then one should have a language which offers support for abstract data types. The authors show how CLU supports such a design with special language features.

As an example of a cluster in CLU, consider from their paper the abstract data type tree. This is an abstract data type which represents a tree. First we observe that the cluster is parameterized and has one argument called T. T is a type which permits the operations: *equal* and *lt*. The data items contained in the tree will be of type T. The operations on the tree include: *create, insert* and *increasing*. Following the heading there appears the definition of the structure in terms of a record called node. The keyword **rep** stands for representation and it encloses the representation of trees. This representation will be shielded from outside use. Following the representation is the implementation of the three operations on this data type. Note how in the definition of *insert* the CLU **case**-statement appears. Also one observes the use of the **if-then-elseif** statement. The CLU cluster is similar in form to several other abstract data type facilities found in modern programming languages. Therefore I have tried to point out some of its key features. It will be instructive to compare the cluster in CLU with the package in Ada.

It should be noted that CLU provides not only a means for data abstraction, but means for procedural and control abstraction as well. These three concepts are described in the paper. Together they imply that CLU supports a software development methodology which is based upon these three concepts.

The next paper addresses itself to the exception handling facility in CLU. A regular mechanism for treating this common situation in programming has been lacking, even in more recent languages such

as Pascal. The facility as offered in PL/1 gives us a glimpse as to how useful the feature is and also into the problems of defining the feature adequately. The paper by Liskov and Snyder discusses the problem of exception handling design in a general way. Then they discuss the implementation in CLU. The CLU solution was so well thought out that it became the basis for exception handling in Ada.

While you are reading this paper please consider the following points which are important for assessing the quality of exception handling:

- can the normal system interrupt action be overridden;
- are user defined exceptions possible and how are they raised;
- what are the scope rules for an enabled exception;
- can exceptions be attached to statements, blocks, procedures or expressions;
- what are the scope rules of the exception handler;
- is the procedure where an exception arose resumed after the handler is executed or not;
- can signaled exceptions have parameters;
- is there a mechanism for catching unexpected exceptions;
- can exceptions be raised within an exception handler?

By keeping these points in mind one will see that the CLU solution works fairly well, and adequately addresses many of these points.

The next paper describes a language which was created using Pascal as a base. Therefore we must not expect that it will be radically different from its predecessor. We should read this article in the spirit of "given a good language what can you do to improve it for writing systems programs?" Actually Euclid does not have an abstract data type facility as well worked out as that of CLU. But the scoping rules have been radically altered and these new rules coupled with records provide a form of the concept which is well worth studying. Another reason why this paper is included here is because it covers a broad range of programming language topics and discusses why things were deemed to be insufficient in Pascal. Therefore it can be used as a further support of the papers in section 2 on Pascal.

There are 11 major differences between Pascal and Euclid. First, is the different rules pertaining to scope. In Pascal, as in all ALGOL-like languages, variables are automatically inherited in an inner block. These variables are called global. In Euclid this automatic inheritance was changed, requiring the programmer to list the names of all variables desired for import into the inner block. The second difference has to do with the idea of aliasing. Two variables which point to the same area of storage are said to be aliases. Aliases are normally allowed in programming languages, and in fact FORTRAN provides the EQUIVALENCE statement to help the programmer define two variables as equivalent. In Euclid aliasing is viewed as a dangerous programming practice and its use has been outlawed. The third difference is the treatment of pointers. In an effort to forbid aliasing, pointers are not permitted to point to the same object unless they are in the same *collection*. The fourth major distinction has to do with storage allocation. In Pascal there is provision for dynamic allocation of records, but no provision for the return of storage, either automatically or via the programmer. In Euclid storage is reference-counted and is automatically returned to the free-list when the count goes to zero. The fifth difference has to do with types, allowing them to be parameterized. This permits arrays with dynamic bounds within a program. Also corrected are the use of variant records. The sixth factor is the addition to the language of the module type. This is a form of abstract data type which collects together variables, constants, routines and types. There are both initialization and finalization code segments. No finalization segment is contained in CLU. Another rather novel feature contained in Euclid is the use of assertions. These can be placed at various points in the program and used by the compiler as run-time checks or to assist in program verification. Besides adding features, the Euclid designers have taken some things out including the go-to statement, real numbers, multi-dimensional arrays and labels.

In summary the paper by Popek, Horning, Lampson, Mitchell, and London describes what might be done by building upon Pascal as a base, but by limiting oneself to minor surgery. Nevertheless even small changes can have substantial effects on how the language is used. There are now compilers for Euclid under development and I expect to see some experience with the language reported soon.

ABSTRACTION MECHANISMS IN CLU*

B. LISKOV, A. SNYDER, R. ATKINSON AND C. SCHAFFERT

CLU is a new programming language designed to support the use of abstractions in program construction. Work in programming methodology has led to the realization that three kinds of abstractions — procedural, control, and especially data abstractions — are useful in the programming process. Of these, only the procedural abstraction is supported well by conventional languages, through the procedure or subroutine. CLU provides, in addition to procedures, novel linguistic mechanisms that support the use of data and control abstractions. This paper provides an introduction to the abstraction mechanisms in CLU. By means of programming examples, the utility of the three kinds of abstractions in program construction is illustrated, and it is shown how CLU programs may be written to use and implement abstractions. The CLU library, which permits incremental program development with complete type checking performed at compile time, is also discussed.

Key Words and Phrases: programming languages, data types, data abstractions, control abstractions, programming methodology, separate compilation

CR Categories: 4.0, 4.12, 4.20, 4.22

*Reprinted from *Comm ACM*, 20, 8, August 1977, 564–576, copyright 1977.

1. Introduction

The motivation for the design of the CLU programing language was to provide programmers with a tool that would enhance their effectiveness in constructing programs of high quality—programs that are reliable and reasonably easy to understand, modify, and maintain. CLU aids programmers by providing constructs that support the use of abstractions in program design and implementation.

The quality of software depends primarily on the programming methodology in use. The choice of programming language, however, can have a major impact on the effectiveness of a methodology. A methodology can be easy or difficult to apply in a given language, depending on how well the language constructs match the structures that the methodology deems desirable. The presence of constructs that give a concrete form for the desired structures makes the methodology more understandable. In addition, a programming language influences the way that its users think about programming; matching a language to a methodology increases the likelihood that the methodology will be used.

CLU has been designed to support a methodology (similar to [6, 22]) in which programs are developed by means of problem decomposition based on the recognition of abstractions. A program is constructed in many stages. At each stage, the problem to be solved is how to implement some abstraction (the initial problem is to implement the abstract behavior required of the entire program). The implementation is developed by envisioning a number of subsidiary abstractions (abstract objects and operations) that are useful in the problem domain. Once the behavior of the abstract objects and operations has been defined, a program can be written to solve the original problem; in this program, the abstract objects and operations are used as primitives. Now the original problem has been solved, but new problems have arisen, namely, how to implement the subsidiary abstractions. Each of these abstractions is considered in turn as a new problem; its implementation may introduce further abstractions. This process terminates when all the abstractions introduced at various stages have been implemented or are present in the programming language in use.

In this methodology, programs are developed incrementally, one abstraction at a time. Further, a distinction is made between an abstraction, which is a kind of behavior, and a program, or *module*, which implements that behavior. An abstraction isolates use from implementation: an abstraction can be used without knowledge of its implementation and implemented without knowledge of its use. These aspects of the methodology are supported by the CLU *library*, which maintains information about abstractions and the CLU modules that implement them. The library permits separate compilation of modules with complete type checking at compile time.

To make effective use of the methodology, it is necessary to understand the kinds of abstractions that are useful in constructing programs. In studying this question, we identified an important kind of abstraction, the data abstraction, that had been largely neglected in discussions of programming methodology.

A data abstraction [8, 12, 20] is used to introduce a new type of data object that is deemed useful in the domain of the problem being solved. At the level of use, the programmer is concerned with the *behavior* of these data objects, what kinds of information can be stored in them and obtained from them. The programmer is *not* concerned with how the data objects are represented in storage nor with the algorithms used to store and access information in them. In fact, a data abstraction is often introduced to delay such implementation decisions until a later stage of design.

The behavior of the data objects is expressed most naturally in terms of a set of operations that are meaningful for those objects. This set includes operations to create objects, to obtain information from them, and possibly to modify them. For example, push and pop are among the meaningful operations for stacks, while meaningful operations for integers include the usual arithmetic operations. Thus a data abstraction consists of a set of objects and a set of operations characterizing the behavior of the objects.

If a data abstraction is to be understandable at an abstract level, the behavior of the data objects must be *completely* characterized by the set of operations. This property is ensured by making the operations the *only direct means* of creating and manipulating the objects. One effect of this restriction is that, when defining an abstraction, the programmer must be careful to include a sufficient set of operations, since every action he wishes to perform on the objects must be realized in terms of this set.

We have identified the following requirements that must be satisfied by a language supporting data abstractions:

1. A linguistic construct is needed that permits a data abstraction to be implemented as a unit. The implementation involves selecting a representation for the data objects and defining an algorithm for each operation in terms of that representation.

2. The language must limit access to the representation to just the operations. This limitation is necessary to ensure that the operations completely characterize the behavior of the objects.

CLU satisfies these requirements by providing a linguistic construct called a *cluster* for implementing data abstractions. Data abstractions are integrated into the language through the data type mechanism. Access to the representation is controlled by type checking, which is done at compile time.

In addition to data abstractions, CLU supports two other kinds of abstractions: procedural abstractions and control abstractions. A procedural abstraction per-

forms a computation on a set of input objects and produces a set of output objects; examples of procedural abstractions are sorting an array and computing a square root. CLU supports procedural abstractions by means of procedures, which are similar to procedures in other programming languages.

A control abstraction defines a method for sequencing arbitrary actions. All languages provide built-in control abstractions; examples are the **if** statement and the **while** statement. In addition, however, CLU allows user definitions of a simple kind of control abstraction. The method provided is a generalization of the repetition methods available in many programming languages. Frequently the programmer desires to perform the same action for all the objects in a collection, such as all characters in a string or all items in a set. CLU provides a linguistic construct called an *iterator* for defining how the objects in the collection are obtained. The iterator is used in conjunction with the **for** statement; the body of the **for** statement describes the action to be taken.

The purpose of this paper is to illustrate the utility of the three kinds of abstractions in program construction and to provide an informal introduction to CLU. We do not attempt a complete description of the language; rather, we concentrate on the constructs that support abstractions. The presence of these constructs constitutes the most important way in which CLU differs from other languages. The language closest to CLU is Alphard [24], which represents a concurrent design effort with goals similar to our own. The design of CLU has been influenced by Simula 67 [4] and to a lesser extent by Pascal [23] and Lisp [15].

In the next section we introduce CLU and, by means of a programming example, illustrate the use and implementation of data abstractions. Section 3 describes the basic semantics of CLU. In Section 4, we discuss control abstractions and more powerful kinds of data abstractions. We present the CLU library in Section 5. Section 6 briefly describes the current implementation of CLU and discusses efficiency considerations. Finally, we conclude by discussing the quality of CLU programs.

2. An Example of Data Abstraction

This section introduces the basic data abstraction mechanism of CLU, the cluster. By means of an example, we intend to show how abstractions occur naturally in program design and how they are used and implemented in CLU. In particular, we show how a data abstraction can be used as structured intermediate storage.

Consider the following problem: given some document, we wish to compute, for each distinct word in the document, the number of times the word occurs and its frequency of occurrence as a percentage of the total

number of words. The document will be represented as a sequence of characters. A word is any nonempty sequence of alphabetic characters. Adjacent words are separated by one or more nonalphabetic characters such as spaces, punctuation, or newline characters. In recognizing distinct words, the difference between upper and lower case letters should be ignored.

The output is also to be a sequence of characters, divided into lines. Successive lines should contain an alphabetical list of all the distinct words in the document, one word per line. Accompanying each word should be the total number of occurrences and the frequency of occurrence. For example:

a	2	3.509%
access	1	1.754%
and	2	3.509%

Specifically, we are required to write the procedure *count_words*, which takes two arguments: an *instream* and an *outstream*. The former is the source of the document to be processed, and the latter is the destination of the required output. The form of this procedure will be

count_words = **proc** (i: instream, o: outstream);

. . .

    end count_words;

Note that *count_words* does not return any results; its only effects are modifications of *i* (reading the entire document) and of *o* (printing the required statistics).

Instream and *outstream* are data abstractions. An *instream i* contains a sequence of characters. Of the primitive operations on *instreams*, only two will be of interest to us. *Empty* (*i*) returns **true** if there are no characters available in *i* and returns **false** otherwise. *Next* (*i*) removes the first character from the sequence and returns it. Invoking the *next* operation on an empty *instream* is an error.[1] An *outstream* also contains a sequence of characters. The interesting operation on *outstreams* is *put_string* (*s*, *o*), which appends the string *s* to the existing sequence of characters in *o*.

Now consider how we might implement *count_words*. We begin by deciding how to handle words. We could define a new abstract data type *word*. However, we choose instead to use strings (a primitive CLU type), with the restriction that only strings of lower case alphabetic characters will be used.[2]

Next we investigate how to scan the document. Reading a word requires knowledge of the exact way in which words occur in the input stream. We choose to isolate this information in a procedural abstraction, called *next_word*, which takes in the *instream i* and returns the next word (converted to lower case charac-

---

[1] The CLU error handling mechanism is discussed in [10].

[2] Sometimes it is difficult to decide whether to introduce a new data abstraction or to use an existing abstraction. Our decision to use strings to represent words was made partly to shorten the presentation.

ters) in the document. If there are no more words, *next_word* must communicate this fact to *count_words*. A simple way to indicate that there are no more words is by returning an "end of document" word, one that is distinct from any other word. A reasonable choice for the "end of document" word is the empty string.

It is clear that in *count_words* we must scan the entire document before we can print our results, and therefore we need some receptacle to retain information about words between these two actions (scanning and printing). Recording the information gained in the scan and organizing it for easy printing will probably be fairly complex. Therefore we defer such considerations until later by introducing a data abstraction *wordbag* with the appropriate properties. In particular, *wordbag* provides three operations: *create*, which creates an empty *wordbag*; *insert*, which adds a word to the *wordbag*; and *print*, which prints the desired statistical information about the words in the *wordbag*.[3]

The implementation of *count_words* is shown in Figure 1. The "%" character starts a comment, which continues to the end of the line. The "~" character stands for boolean negation. The notation *variable*: *type* is used in formal argument lists and declarations to specify the types of variables; a declaration may be combined with an assignment specifying the initial value of the variable. Boldface is used for reserved words, including the names of primitive CLU types.

The *count_words* procedure declares four variables: *i*, *o*, *wb*, and *w*. The first two denote the *instream* and *outstream* that are passed as arguments to *count_words*. The third, *wb*, denotes the *wordbag* used to hold the words read so far, and the fourth, *w*, the word currently being processed.

Operations of a data abstraction are named by a compound form that specifies both the type and the operation name. Three examples of operation calls appear in *count_words*: *wordbag*$*create*( ), *wordbag*$*insert* (*wb*, *w*) and *wordbag*$*print* (*wb*, *o*). The CLU system provides a mechanism that avoids conflicts between names of abstractions; this mechanism is discussed in Section 5. However, operations of two different data abstractions may have the same name; the compound form serves to resolve this ambiguity. Although the ambiguity could in most cases be resolved by context, we have found in using CLU that the compound form enhances the readability of programs.

The implementation of *next_word* is shown in Figure 2. The *string*$*append* operation creates a new string by appending a character to the characters in the string argument (it does *not* modify the string argument). Note the use of the *instream* operations *next* and *empty*. Note also that two additional procedures have been used: *alpha* (*c*), which tests whether a character is alphabetic or not, and *lower_case* (*c*), which returns the lower case version of a character. The implementations

---
[3] The *print* operation is not the ideal choice, but a better solution requires the use of control abstractions. This solution is presented in Section 4.

Fig. 1. The *count_words* procedure.

```
count_words = proc (i: instream, o: outstream);
  % create an empty wordbag
  wb: wordbag := wordbag$create ( );
  % scan document, adding each word found to wb
  w: string := next_word (i);
  while w ~= " " do
    wordbag$insert (wb, w);
    w := next_word (i);
    end;
  % print the wordbag
  wordbag$print (wb, o);
  end count_words;
```

Fig. 2. The *next_word* procedure.

```
next_word = proc (i: instream) returns (string);
  c: char := '';
  % scan for first alphabetic character
  while ~alpha (c) do
    if instream$empty (i)
      then return " ";
      end;
    c := instream$next (i);
    end;
  % accumulate characters in word
  w: string := " ";
  while alpha (c) do
    w := string$append (w, c);
    if instream$empty (i)
      then return (w);
      end;
    c := instream$next (i);
    end;
  return (w);      % the nonalphabetic character c is lost
  end next_word;
```

of these procedures are not shown in the paper.

Now we must implement the type *wordbag*. The cluster will have the form

wordbag = **cluster is** create, insert, print;

. . .

    end wordbag;

This form expresses the idea that the data abstraction is a set of operations as well as a set of objects. The cluster must provide a representation for objects of the type *wordbag* and an implementation for each of the operations. We are free to choose from the possible representations the one best suited to our use of the *wordbag* cluster.

The representation that we choose should allow reasonably efficient storage of words and easy printing, in alphabetic order, of the words and associated statistics. For efficiency in computing the statistics, maintaining a count of the total number of words in the document would be helpful. Since the total number of words in the document is probably much larger than the number of distinct words, the representation of a *wordbag* should contain only one "item" for each distinct word (along with a multiplicity count), rather than one "item" for each occurrence. This choice of representation requires that, at each insertion, we check whether

the new word is already present in the *wordbag*. We would like a representation that allows the search for a matching "item" and the insertion of a not previously present "item" to be efficient. A binary tree representation [9] fits our requirements nicely.

Thus the main part of the *wordbag* representation consists of a binary tree. The binary tree is another data abstraction, *wordtree*. The data abstraction *wordtree* provides operations very similar to those of *wordbag*: *create* ( ) returns an empty *wordtree*; *insert* (*tr*, *w*) returns a *wordtree* containing all the words in the *wordtree tr* plus the additional word *w* (the *wordtree tr* may be modified in the process); and *print* (*tr*, *n*, *o*) prints the contents of the *wordtree tr* in alphabetic order on *outstream o* along with the number of occurrences and the frequency (based on a total of *n* words).

The implementation of *wordbag* is given in Figure 3. Following the header, we find the definition of the representation selected for *wordbag* objects:

rep = **record** [contents: wordtree, total: **int**];

The reserved type identifier **rep** indicates that the type specification to the right of the equal sign is the representing type for the cluster. We have defined the representation of a *wordbag* object to consist of two pieces: a *wordtree*, as explained above, and an integer, which records the total number of words in the *wordbag*.

A CLU record is an object with one or more named components. For each component name, there is an operation to select and an operation to set the corresponding component. The operation *get_n* (*r*) returns the *n* component of the record *r* (this operation is usually abbreviated *r.n*). The operation *put_n* (*r*, *x*) makes *x* the *n* component of the record *r* (this operation is usually abbreviated *r.n* := *x*, by analogy with the assignment statement). A new record is created by an expression of the form type${name_1: value_1, ...}$.

There are two different types associated with any cluster: the abstract type being defined (*wordbag* in this case) and the representation type (the record). Outside of the cluster, type checking ensures that a *wordbag* object will always be treated as such. In particular, the ability to convert a *wordbag* object into its representation is not provided (unless one of the *wordbag* operations does so explicitly).

Inside the cluster, however, it is necessary to view a *wordbag* object as being of the representation type, because the implementations of the operations are defined in terms of the representation. This change of viewpoint is signalled by having the reserved word **cvt** appear as the type of an argument (as in the *insert* and *print* operations). **Cvt** may also appear as a return type (as in the *create* operation); here it indicates that a returned object will be changed into an object of abstract type. Whether **cvt** appears as the type of an argument or as a return type, it stipulates a "conversion" of viewpoint between the external abstract type

Fig. 3. The *wordbag* cluster.

```
wordbag = cluster is
  create,      % create an empty bag
  insert,      % insert an element
  print;       % print contents of bag
  rep = record [contents: wordtree, total: int];
create = proc ( ) returns (cvt);
          return (rep${contents: wordtree$create ( ), total: 0});
          end create;
insert = proc (x: cvt, v: string);
          x.contents := wordtree$insert (x.contents, v);
          x.total := x.total + 1;
          end insert;
print = proc (x: cvt, o: outstream);
          wordtree$print (x.contents, x.total, o);
          end print;
end wordbag;
```

and the internal representation type. **Cvt** can be used only within a cluster, and conversion can be done only between the single abstract type being defined and the (single) representation type.[4]

The procedures in *wordbag* are very simple. *Create* builds a new instance of the **rep** by use of the record constructor

rep${contents: wordtree$create ( ), total: 0}$

Here *total* is initialized to 0 and *contents* to the empty *wordtree* (by calling the *create* operation of *wordtree*). This **rep** object is converted into a *wordbag* object as it is being returned. *Insert* and *print* are implemented directly in terms of *wordtree* operations.

The implementation of *wordtree* is shown in Figure 4. In the *wordtree* representation, each node contains a word and the number of times that word has been inserted into the *wordbag*, as well as two subtrees. For any particular node, the words in the "lesser" subtree must alphabetically precede the word in the node, and the words in the "greater" subtree must follow the word in the node. This information is described by

node = **record** [value: **string**, count: **int**,
                  lesser: wordtree, greater: wordtree];

which defines "node" to be an abbreviation for the information following the equal sign. (The reserved word **rep** is used similarly as an abbreviation for the representation type.)

Now consider the representation of *wordtrees*. A nonempty *wordtree* can be represented by its top node. An empty *wordtree*, however, contains no information. The ideal type to represent an empty *wordtree* is the CLU type **null**, which has a single data object **nil**. So the representation of a *wordtree* should be either a node or **nil**. This representation is expressed by

rep = **oneof** [empty: **null**, non_empty: node];

Just as the record is the basic CLU mechanism to

_____
[4] **Cvt** corresponds to Morris' seal and unseal [16] except that **cvt** represents a change in viewpoint only; no computation is required.

form an object that is a collection of other objects, the oneof is the basic CLU mechanism to form an object that is "one of" a set of alternatives. Oneof is CLU's method of forming a discriminated union, and is somewhat similar to a variant component of a record in Pascal [23].

An object of the type **oneof** $[s_1: T_1 \ldots s_n: T_n]$ can be thought of as a pair. The "tag" component is an identifier from the set $\{s_1 \ldots s_n\}$. The "value" component is an object of the type corresponding to the tag. That is, if the tag component is s_i, then the value is some object of type T_i.

Objects of type **oneof** $[s_1: T_1 \ldots s_n: T_n]$ are created by the operations $make\_s_i(x)$, each of which takes an object x of type T_i and returns the pair $\langle s_i, x \rangle$. Because the type of the value component of a oneof object is not known at compile time, allowing direct access to the value component could result in a run-time type error (e.g. assigning an object to a variable of the wrong type). To eliminate this possibility, we require the use of a special **tagcase** statement to decompose a oneof object:

tagcase e

    tag s_1 (id$_1$: T_1):   statements . . .

       . . .

    tag s_n (id$_n$: T_n):   statements . . .
    end;

This statement evaluates the expression e to obtain an object of type **oneof** $[s_1: T_1 \ldots s_n: T_n]$. If the tag is s_i, then the value is assigned to the new variable id$_i$ and the statements following the ith alternative are executed. The variable id$_i$ is local to those statements. If, for some reason, we do not need the value, we can omit the parenthesized variable declaration.

The reader should now know enough to understand Figure 4. Note, in the *create* operation, the use of the construction operation *make_empty* of the representation type of *wordtree* (the discriminated union **oneof** [empty: **null**, nonempty: node]) to create the empty *wordtree*. The **tagcase** statement is used in both *insert* and *print*. Note that if *insert* is given an empty *wordtree*, it creates a new top node for the returned value, but if *insert* is given a nonempty *wordtree*, it modifies the given *wordtree* and returns it.[5] The *insert* operation depends on the dynamic allocation of space for newly created records (see Section 3).

The *print* operation uses the obvious recursive descent. It makes use of procedure *print_word* (w, c, t, o), which generates a single line of output on o consisting of the word w, the count c, and the frequency of occurrence derived from c and t. The implementation of *print_word* has been omitted.

We have now completed our first discussion of the

---

[5] It is necessary for *insert* to return a value in addition having a side effect because in the case of an empty *wordtree* argument side effects are not possible. Side effects are not possible because of the representation chosen for the empty *wordtree* and because of the CLU parameter passing mechanism (see Section 3).

Fig. 4. The *wordtree* cluster.

```
wordtree = cluster is
   create,       % create empty contents
   insert,       % add item to contents
   print;        % print contents
   node = record [value: string, count: int,
                  lesser: wordtree, greater: wordtree];
   rep = oneof [empty: null, non_empty: node];
create = proc ( ) returns (cvt);
   return (rep$make_empty (nil));
   end create;
insert = proc (x: cvt, v: string) returns (cvt);
   tagcase x
      tag empty:
            n: node := node${value: v, count: 1,
                         lesser: wordtree$create ( ),
                         greater: wordtree$create ( )};
            return (rep$make_non_empty (n));
      tag non_empty (n: node):
            if v = n.value
                  then n.count := n.count + 1;
               elseif v < n.value
                  then n.lesser := wordtree$insert (n.lesser, v);
               else n.greater := wordtree$insert (n.greater, v);
               end;
            return (x);
      end;
   end insert;
print = proc (x: cvt, total: int, o: outstream);
   tagcase x
      tag empty: ;
      tag non_empty (n: node):
         wordtree$print (n.lesser, total, o);
         print_word (n.value, n. count, total, o);
         wordtree$print (n.greater, total, o);
      end;
   end print;
end wordtree;
```

court_words procedure. We return to this problem in Section 4, where we present a superior solution.

3. Semantics

All languages present their users with some model of computation. This section describes those aspects of CLU semantics that differ from the common Algol-like model. In particular, we discuss CLU's notions of objects and variables and the definitions of assignment and argument passing that follow from these notions. We also discuss type correctness.

3.1 Objects and Variables

The basic elements of CLU semantics are *objects* and *variables*. Objects are the data entities that are created and manipulated by CLU programs. Variables are just the names used in a program to refer to objects.

In CLU, each object has a particular *type*, which characterizes its behavior. A type defines a set of operations that create and manipulate objects of that type. An object may be created and manipulated only via the operations of its type.

An object may *refer* to objects. For example, a

record object refers to the objects that are the components of the record. This notion is one of logical, not physical, containment. In particular, it is possible for two distinct record objects to refer to (or *share*) the same component object. In the case of a cyclic structure, it is even possible for an object to "contain" itself. Thus it is possible to have recursive data structure definitions and shared data objects without explicit reference types. The *wordtree* type described in the previous section is an example of a recursively defined data structure. (This notion of object is similar to that in Lisp.)

CLU objects exist independently of procedure activations. Space for objects is allocated from a dynamic storage area as the result of invoking constructor operations of certain primitive CLU types. For example, the record constructor is used in the implementation of *wordbag* (Figure 3) to acquire space for new *wordbag* objects. In theory, all objects continue to exist forever. In practice, the space used by an object may be reclaimed when the object is no longer accessible to any CLU program.[6]

An object may exhibit time-varying behavior. Such an object, called a *mutable* object, has a state which may be modified by certain operations without changing the identity of the object. Records are examples of mutable objects. The record update operations (*put_s* (r, v), written as $r.s := v$ in the examples), change the state of record objects and therefore affect the behavior of subsequent applications of the select operations (*get_s* (r), written as $r.s$). The *wordbag* and *wordtree* types are additional examples of types with mutable objects.

If a mutable object m is shared by two other objects x and y, then a modification to m made via x will be visible when m is examined via y. Communication through shared mutable objects is most beneficial in the context of procedure invocation, described below.

Objects that do not exhibit time-varying behavior are called *immutable* objects, or *constants*. Examples of constants are integers, booleans, characters, and strings. The value of a constant object can not be modified. For example, new strings may be computed from old ones, but existing strings do not change. Similarly, none of the integer operations modify the integers passed to them as arguments.

Variables are names used in CLU programs to *denote* particular objects at execution time. Unlike variables in many common programming languages, which *are* objects that *contain* values, CLU variables are simply names that the programmer uses to refer to objects. As such, it is possible for two variables to denote (or *share*) the same object. CLU variables are much like those in Lisp and are similar to pointer variables in other languages. However, CLU variables are *not* objects; they cannot be denoted by other variables or

referred to by objects. Thus variables are completely private to the procedure in which they are declared and cannot be accessed or modified by any other procedure.

3.2 Assignment and Procedure Invocation

The basic actions in CLU are *assignment* and *procedure invocation*. The assignment primitive $x := E$, where x is a variable and E is an expression, causes x to denote the object resulting from the evaluation of E. For example, if E is a simple variable y, then the assignment $x := y$ causes x to denote the object denoted by y. The object is *not* copied; after the assignment is performed, it will be *shared* by x and y. Assignment does not affect the state of any object. (Recall that $r.s := v$ is not a true assignment, but an abbreviation for $put\_s (r, v)$.)

Procedure invocation involves passing argument objects from the caller to the called procedure and returning result objects from the procedure to the caller. The formal arguments of a procedure are considered to be local variables of the procedure and are initialized, by assignment, to the objects resulting from the evaluation of the argument expressions. Thus argument objects are shared between the caller and the called procedure. A procedure may modify mutable argument objects (e.g. records), but of course it cannot modify immutable ones (e.g. integers). A procedure has no access to the variables of its caller.

Procedure invocations may be used directly as statements; those that return objects may also be used as expressions. Arbitrary recursive procedures are permitted.

3.3 Type Correctness

Every variable in a CLU module must be declared; the declaration specifies the type of object that the variable may denote. All assignments to a variable must satisfy the variable's declaration. Because argument passing is defined in terms of assignment, the types of actual argument objects must be consistent with the declarations of the corresponding formal arguments.

These restrictions, plus the restriction that only the code in a cluster may use **cvt** to convert between the abstract and representation types, ensure that the behavior of an object is indeed characterized completely by the operations of its type. For example, the type restrictions ensure that the only modification possible to a record object that represents a *wordbag* (Figure 3) is the modification performed by the *insert* operation.

Type checking is performed on a module by module basis at compile time (it could also be done at run time). This checking can catch all type errors—even those involving intermodule references—because the CLU library maintains the necessary type information for all modules (see Section 5).

---

[6] An object is accessible if it is denoted by a variable of an active procedure or is a component of an accessible object.

4. More Abstraction Mechanisms

In this section we continue our discussion of abstraction mechanisms in CLU. A generalization of the *wordbag* abstraction, called *sorted_bag*, is presented as an illustration of parameterized clusters, which are a means for implementing more generally applicable data abstractions. The presentation of *sorted_bag* is also used to motivate the introduction of a control abstraction called an *iterator*, which is a mechanism for incrementally generating the elements of a collection of objects. Finally, we show an implementation of the *sorted_bag* abstraction and illustrate how *sorted_bag* can be used in implementing *count_words*.

4.1 Properties of the Sorted_bag Abstraction

In the *count_words* procedure given earlier, a data abstraction called *wordbag* was used. A *wordbag* object is a collection of strings, each with an associated count. Strings are inserted into a *wordbag* object one at a time. Strings in a *wordbag* object may be printed in alphabetical order, each with a count of the number of times it was inserted.

Although *wordbag* has properties that are specific to the usage in *count_words*, it also has properties in common with a more general abstraction, *sorted_bag*. A bag is similar to a set (it is sometimes called a multiset) except that an item can appear in a bag many times. For example, if the integer 1 is inserted in the set {1, 2}, the result is the set {1, 2}, but if 1 is inserted in the bag {1, 2}, the result is the bag {1, 1, 2}. A *sorted_bag* is a bag that affords access to the items it contains according to an ordering relation on the items.

The concept of a *sorted_bag* is meaningful not only for strings but for many types of items. Therefore we would like to parameterize the *sorted_bag* abstraction, the parameter being the type of item to be collected in the *sorted_bag* objects.

Most programming languages provide built-in parameterized data abstractions. For example, the concept of an array is a parameterized data abstraction. An example of a use of arrays in Pascal is

array 1..n **of integer**

These arrays have two parameters, one specifying the array bounds (1..n) and one specifying the type of element in the array (integer). In CLU we provide mechanisms allowing user-defined data abstractions (like *sorted_bag*) to be parameterized.

In the *sorted_bag* abstraction, not all types of items make sense. Only types that define a total ordering on their objects are meaningful since the *sorted_bag* abstraction depends on the presence of this ordering. In addition, information about the ordering must be expressed in a way that is useful for programming. A natural way to express this information is by means of operations of the item type. Therefore we require that the item type provide less than and equal operations

(called *lt* and *equal*). This constraint is expressed in the header for *sorted_bag*:

sorted_bag = **cluster** [t: **type**] **is** create, insert, . . .
   where t **has**
      lt, equal: **proctype** (t, t) **returns** (**bool**);

The item type *t* is a *formal parameter* of the *sorted_bag* cluster; whenever the *sorted_bag* abstraction is used, the item type must be specified as an *actual parameter*, e.g.

sorted_bag[**string**]

The information about required operations informs the programmer about legitimate uses of *sorted_bag*. The compiler will check each use of *sorted_bag* to ensure that the item type provides the required operations. The **where** clause specifies exactly the information that the compiler can check. Of course, more is assumed about the item type *t* than the presence of operations with appropriate names and functionalities: these operations must also define a total ordering on the items. Although we expect formal and complete specifications for data abstractions to be included in the CLU library eventually, we do not include in the CLU language declarations that the compiler cannot check. This point is discussed further in Section 7.

Now that we have decided to define a *sorted_bag* abstraction that works for many item types, we must decide what operations this abstraction provides. When an abstraction (like *wordbag*) is written for a very specific purpose, it is reasonable to have some specialized operations. For a more general abstraction, the operations should be more generally useful.

The *print* operation is a case in point. Printing is only one possible use of the information contained in a *sorted_bag*. It was the only use in the case of *wordbag*, so it was reasonable to have a *print* operation. However, if *sorted_bags* are to be generally useful, there should be some way for the user to obtain the elements of the *sorted_bag*; the user can then perform some action on the elements (for example, print them).

What we would like is an operation on *sorted_bags* that makes all of the elements available to the caller in increasing order. One possible approach is to map the elements of a *sorted_bag* into a sequence object, a solution potentially requiring a large amount of space. A more efficient method is provided by CLU and is discussed below. This solution computes the sequence one element at a time, thus saving space. If only part of the sequence is used (as in a search for some element), then execution time can be saved as well.

4.2 Control Abstractions

The purpose of many loops is to perform an action on some or all of the objects in a collection. For such loops, it is often useful to separate the selection of the next object from the action performed on that object.

Fig. 5. Use and definition of a simple iterator.

```
count_numeric = proc (s: string) returns (int);
    count: int := 0;
    for c: char in string_chars (s) do
        if char_is_numeric (c)
            then count := count + 1;
            end;
        end;
    return (count);
    end count_numeric;
string_chars = iter (s: string) yields (char);
    index: int := 1;
    limit: int := string$size (s);
    while index < limit do
        yield (string$fetch (s, index));
        index := index + 1;
        end;
    end string_chars;
```

CLU provides a control abstraction that permits a complete decomposition of the two activities. The **for** statement available in many programming languages provides a limited ability in this direction: it iterates over ranges of integers. The CLU **for** statement can iterate over collections of any type of object. The selection of the next object in the collection is done by a user-defined *iterator*. The iterator produces the objects in the collection one at a time (the entire collection need not physically exist); each object is consumed by the **for** statement in turn.

Figure 5 gives an example of a simple iterator called *string_chars*, which produces the characters in a string in the order in which they appear. This iterator uses string operations *size(s)*, which tells how many characters are in the string *s*, and *fetch* (*s*, *n*), which returns the *n*th character in the string *s* (provided the integer *n* is greater than zero and does not exceed the size of the string).[7]

The general form of the CLU **for** statement is

for declarations **in** iterator_invocation **do**
    body
    end;

An example of the use of the **for** statement occurs in the *count_numeric* procedure (see Figure 5), which contains a loop that counts the number of numeric characters in a string. Note that the details of how the characters are obtained from the string are entirely contained in the definition of the iterator.

Iterators work as follows: A **for** statement initially invokes an iterator, passing it some arguments. Each time a **yield** statement is executed in the iterator, the objects yielded[8] are assigned to the variables declared in the **for** statement (following the reserved word **for**)

in corresponding order, and the body of the **for** statement is executed. Then the iterator is resumed at the statement following the **yield** statement, in the same environment as when the objects were yielded. When the iterator terminates, by either an implicit or explicit **return**, the invoking **for** statement terminates. The iteration may also be prematurely terminated by a **return** in the body of the **for** statement.

For example, suppose that *string_chars* is invoked with the string "a3". The first character yielded is 'a'. At this point, within *string_chars*, *index* = 1 and *limit* = 2. Next the body of the **for** statement is performed. Since the character 'a' is not numeric, *count* remains at 0. Next *string_chars* is resumed at the statement after the **yield** statement, and when resumed, *index* = 1 and *limit* = 2. Then *index* is assigned 2, and the character '3' is selected from the string and yielded. Since '3' is numeric, *count* becomes 1. Then *string_chars* is resumed, with *index* = 2 and *limit* = 2, and *index* is incremented, which causes the **while** loop to terminate. The implicit **return** terminates both the iterator and the **for** statement, with control resuming at the statement after the **for** statement, and *count* = 1.

While iterators are useful in general, they are especially valuable in conjunction with data abstractions that are collections of objects (such as sets, arrays, and *sorted_bags*). Iterators afford users of such abstractions access to all objects in the collection without exposing irrelevant details. Several iterators may be included in a data abstraction. When the order of obtaining the objects is important, different iterators may provide different orders.

4.3 Implementation and Use of Sorted_bag

Now we can describe a minimal set of operations for *sorted_bag*. The operations are *create*, *insert*, *size*, and *increasing*. *Create*, *insert*, and *size* are procedural abstractions that, respectively, create a *sorted_bag*, insert an item into a *sorted_bag*, and give the number of items in a *sorted_bag*. *Increasing* is a control abstraction that produces the items in a *sorted_bag* in increasing order; each item produced is accompanied by an integer representing the number of times the item appears in the *sorted_bag*. Note that other operations might also be useful for *sorted_bag*, for example, an iterator yielding the items in decreasing order. In general, the definer of a data abstraction can provide as many operations as seems reasonable.

In Figure 6, we give an implementation of the *sorted_bag* abstraction. It is implemented by using a sorted binary tree, just as *wordbag* was implemented. Thus a subsidiary abstraction is necessary. This abstraction, called *tree*, is a generalization of the *wordtree* abstraction (used in Section 2), which has been parameterized to work for all ordered types. An implementation of *tree* is given in Figure 7. Notice that both the *tree* abstraction and the *sorted_bag* abstraction place the same constraints on their type parameters.

---

[7] A **while** loop is used in the implementation of *string_chars* so that the example will be based on familiar concepts. In actual practice, such a loop would be written by using a **for** statement invoking a primitive iterator.

[8] Zero or more objects may be yielded, but the number and types of objects yielded each time by an iterator must agree with the number and types of variables in a **for** statement using the iterator.

Fig. 6. The *sorted_bag* cluster.

```
sorted_bag = cluster [t: type] is create, insert, size, increasing
    where t has equal, lt: proctype (t, t) returns (bool);
  rep = record [contents: tree[t], total: int];
create = proc ( ) returns (cvt);
  return (rep${contents: tree[t]$create ( ), total: 0});
  end create;
insert = proc (sb: cvt, v: t);
  sb.contents := tree[t]$insert (sb.contents, v);
  sb.total := sb.total + 1;
  end insert;
size = proc (sb: cvt) returns (int);
  return (sb.total);
  end size;
increasing = iter (sb: cvt) yields (t, int);
  for item: t, count: int
    in tree[t]$increasing (sb.contents) do
      yield (item, count);
      end;
  end increasing;
end sorted_bag;
```

Fig. 7. The *tree* cluster.

```
tree = cluster [t: type] is create, insert, increasing
    where t has equal, lt: proctype (t, t) returns (bool);
  node = record [value: t, count: int,
                 lesser: tree[t], greater: tree[t]];
  rep = oneof [empty: null, non_empty: node];
create = proc ( ) returns (cvt);
  return (rep$make_empty (nil));
  end create;
insert = proc (x: cvt, v: t) returns (cvt);
  tagcase x
    tag empty:
      n: node := node${value: v, count: 1,
                       lesser: tree[t]$create ( ),
                       greater: tree[t]$create ( )};
      return (rep$make_non_empty (n));
    tag non_empty (n: node):
      if t$equal (v, n.value)
              then n.count := n.count + 1;
        elseif t$lt (v, n.value)
              then n.lesser := tree[t]$insert (n.lesser, v);
        else n.greater := tree[t]$insert (n.greater, v);
        end;
      return (x);
    end;
  end insert;
increasing = iter (x: cvt) yields (t, int);
  tagcase x
    tag empty: ;
    tag non_empty (n: node):
      for item: t, count: int
        in tree[t]$increasing (n.lesser) do
          yield (item, count);
          end;
      yield (n.value, n.count);
      for item: t, count: int
        in tree[t]$increasing (n.greater) do
          yield (item, count);
          end;
    end;
  end increasing;
end tree;
```

An important feature of the *sorted_bag* and *tree* clusters is the way that the cluster parameter is used in places where the type **string** was used in *wordbag* and *wordtree*. This usage is especially evident in the implementation of *tree*. For example, *tree* has a representation that stores values of type *t*: the *value* component of a *node* must be an object of type *t*.

In the *insert* operation of *tree*, the *lt* and *equal* operations of type *t* are used. We have used the compound form, e.g. $t\$equal(v, n.value)$, to emphasize that the *equal* operation of *t* is being used. The short form, $v = n.value$, could have been used instead.

The *increasing* iterator of *tree* works as follows: first it yields all items in the current tree that are less than the item at the top node; the items are obtained by a recursive use of itself, passing the *lesser* subtree as an argument. Next it yields the contents of the top node, and then it yields all items in the current tree that are greater than the item at the top node (again by a recursive use of itself). In this way it performs a complete walk over the tree, yielding the values at all nodes, in increasing order.

Finally, we show in Figure 8 how the original procedure *count_words* can be implemented in terms of *sorted_bag*. Note that the *count_words* procedure now uses *sorted_bag*[**string**] instead of *wordbag*. *Sorted_bag*[**string**] is legitimate since the type **string** provides both *lt* and *equal* operations. Note that two **for** statements are used in *count_words*. The second **for** statement prints the words in alphabetic order, using the *increasing* iterator of *sorted_bag*. The first **for** statement inserts the words into the *sorted_bag*; it uses an iterator

words = **iter** (i: instream) **yields** (**string**);

. . .

    end words;

The definition of *words* is left as an exercise for the reader.

5. The CLU Library

So far, we have shown CLU modules as separate pieces of text, without explaining how they are bound together to form a program. This section describes the CLU library, which plays a central role in supporting intermodule references.

The CLU library contains information about abstractions. The library supports incremental program development, one abstraction at a time, and, in addition, makes abstractions that are defined during the construction of one program available as a basis for subsequent program development. The information in the library permits the separate compilation of single modules with complete type checking of all external references (such as procedure invocations).

The structure of the library derives from the funda-

mental distinction between abstractions and implementations. For each abstraction, there is a *description unit* which contains all system-maintained information about that abstraction. Included in the description unit are zero or more modules that implement the abstraction.[9]

The most important information contained in a description unit is the abstraction's *interface specification*, which is that information needed to type-check uses of the abstraction. For procedural and control abstractions, this information consists of the number and types of parameters, arguments, and output values, plus any constraints on type parameters (i.e. required operations, as described in Section 4). For data abstractions, it includes the number and types of parameters, constraints on type parameters, and the name and interface specification of each operation.

An abstraction is entered in the library by submitting the interface specification; no implementations are required. In fact, a module can be compiled before any implementations have been provided for the abstractions that it uses; it is necessary only that interface specifications have been given for those abstractions. Ultimately, there can be many implementations of an abstraction; each implementation is required to satisfy the interface specification of the abstraction. Because all uses and implementations of an abstraction are checked against the interface specification, the actual selection of an implementation can be delayed until just before (or perhaps during) execution. We imagine a process of binding together modules into programs, prior to execution, at which time this selection would be made.

An important detail of the CLU system is the method by which CLU modules refer to abstractions. To avoid problems of name conflicts that can arise in large systems, the names used by a module to refer to abstractions can be chosen to suit the programmer's convenience. When a module is submitted for compilation, its external references must be bound to description units so that type checking can be performed. The binding is accomplished by constructing an *association list*, mapping names to description units, which is passed to the compiler along with the source code when compiling the module. The mapping in the association list is stored by the compiler in the library as part of the module. A similar process is involved in entering interface specifications of abstractions, as these will include references to other (data) abstractions.

When the compiler type-checks a module, it uses the association list to map the external names in the module to description units and then uses the interface specifications in those description units to check that the abstractions are used correctly. The type correctness of the module thus depends upon the binding of

Fig. 8. The *count_words* procedure using iterators.

```
count_words = proc (i: instream, o: outstream);
  wordbag = sorted_bag[string];
  % create an empty wordbag
  wb: wordbag := wordbag$create ( );
  % scan document, adding each word found to wb
  for word: string in words (i) do
    wordbag$insert (wb, word);
    end;
  % print the wordbag
  total: int := wordbag$size (wb);
  for w: string, count: int in wordbag$increasing (wb) do
    print_word (w, count, total, o);
    end;
  end count_words;
```

names to description units and the interface specifications in those description units, and could be invalidated if changes to the binding or the interface specifications were subsequently made. For this reason, the process of compilation permanently binds a module to the abstractions it uses, and the interface description of an abstraction, once defined, is not allowed to change. (Of course, a new description unit can be created to describe a modified abstraction.)

6. Implementation

This section briefly describes the current implementation of CLU and discusses its efficiency.

The implementation is based on a decision to represent all CLU objects by *object descriptors*, which are fixed-size values containing a type code and some type-dependent information.[10] In the case of mutable types, the type-dependent information is a pointer to a separately allocated area containing the state information. For constant types, the information either directly contains the value (if the value can be encoded in the information field, as for integers, characters, and booleans) or contains a pointer to separately allocated space (as for strings). The type codes are used by the garbage collector to determine the physical representation of objects so that the accessible objects can be traced; they are also useful for supporting program debugging.

The use of fixed-size object descriptors allows variables to be fixed-size cells. Assignment is efficient: the object descriptor resulting from the evaluation of the expression is simply copied into the variable. In addition, a single size for variables facilitates the separate compilation of modules and allows most of the code of a parameterized module to be shared among all instantiations of the module. The actual parameters are made available to this code by means of a small parameter-dependent section, which is initialized prior to execution.

---

[9] Other information that may be stored in the library includes information about relationships among abstractions, as might be expressed in a module interconnection language [5, 21].

[10] Object descriptors are similar to capabilities [11].

Procedure invocation is relatively efficient. A single program stack is used, and argument passing is as efficient as assignment. Iterators are a form of coroutine; however, their use is sufficiently constrained that they are implemented using just the program stack. Using an iterator is therefore only slightly more expensive than using a procedure.

The data abstraction mechanism is not inherently expensive. No execution-time type checking is necessary. Furthermore, the type conversion implied by **cvt** is merely a change in the view taken of an object's type and does not require any computation.

A number of optimization techniques can be applied to a collection of modules if one is willing to give up the flexibility of separate compilation. The most effective such optimization is the inline substitution of procedure (and iterator) bodies for invocations [18]. The use of data abstractions tends to introduce extra levels of procedure invocations that perform little or no computation. As an example, consider the *wordbag$insert* operation (Figure 3), which merely invokes the *wordtree$insert* operation and increments a counter. If data abstractions had not been used, these actions would most likely have been performed directly by the *count_words* procedure. The *wordbag$insert* operation is thus a good candidate for being compiled inline. Once inline substitution has been performed, the increase in context will enhance the effectiveness of conventional optimization techniques [1–3].

7. Discussion

Our intent in this paper has been to provide an informal introduction to the abstraction mechanisms in CLU. By means of programming examples, we have illustrated the use of data, procedural, and control abstractions and have shown how CLU modules are used to implement these abstractions. We have not attempted to provide a complete description of CLU, but, in the course of explaining the examples, most features of the language have appeared. One important omission is the CLU exception handling mechanism (which does support abstractions); this mechanism is described in [10].

In addition to describing constructs that support abstraction, previous sections have covered a number of other topics. We have discussed the semantics of CLU. We have described the organization of the CLU library and discussed how it supports incremental program development and separate compilation and type checking of modules. Also we have described our current implementation and discussed its efficiency.

In designing CLU, our goal was to simplify the task of constructing reliable software that is reasonably easy to understand, modify, and maintain. It seems appropriate, therefore, to conclude this paper with a discussion of how CLU contributes to this goal.

The quality of any program depends upon the skill of the designer. In CLU programs, this skill is reflected in the choice of abstractions. In a good design, abstractions will be used to simplify the connections between modules and to encapsulate decisions that are likely to change [17]. Data abstractions are particularly valuable for these purposes. For example, through the use of a data abstraction, modules that share a system database rely only on its abstract behavior as defined by the database operations. The connections among these modules are much simpler than would be possible if they shared knowledge of the format of the database and the relationship among its parts. In addition, the database abstraction can be reimplemented without affecting the code of the modules that use it. CLU encourages the use of data abstractions and thus aids the programmer during program design.

The benefits arising from the use of data abstractions are based on the constraint, inherent in CLU and enforced by the CLU compiler, that only the operations of the abstraction may access the representations of the objects. This constraint ensures that the distinction made in CLU between abstractions and implementations applies to data abstractions as well as to procedural and control abstractions.

The distinction between abstractions and implementations eases program modification and maintenance. Once it has been determined that an abstraction must be reimplemented, CLU guarantees that the code of all modules using that abstraction will be unaffected by the change. The modules need not be reprogrammed or even recompiled; only the process of selecting the implementation of the abstraction must be redone. The problem of determining what modules must be changed is also simplified because each module has a well-defined purpose – to implement an abstraction – and no other module can interfere with that purpose.

Understanding and verification of CLU programs is made easier because the distinction between abstractions and implementations permits this task to be decomposed. One module at a time is studied to determine that it implements its abstraction. This study requires understanding the behavior of the abstractions it uses, but it is not necessary to understand the modules implementing those abstractions. Those modules can be studied separately.

A promising way to establish the correctness of a program is by means of a mathematical proof. For practical reasons, proofs should be performed (or at least checked) by a verification system, since the process of constructing a proof is tedious and error-prone. Decomposition of the proof is essential for program proving, which is practical only for small programs (like CLU modules). Note that when the CLU compiler does type checking, it is, in addition to enforcing the constraint that permits the proof to be decomposed, also performing a small part of the actual proof.

We have included as declarations in CLU just the information that the compiler can check with reasonable efficiency. We believe that the other information required for proofs (specifications and assertions) should be expressed in a separate "specification" language. The properties of such a language are being studied [7, 13, 14, 19]. We intend eventually to add formal specifications to the CLU system; the library is already organized to accommodate this addition. At that time various specification language processors could be added to the system.

We believe that the constraints imposed by CLU are essential for practical as well as theoretical reasons. It is true that data abstractions can be used in any language by establishing programming conventions to protect the representations of objects. However, conventions are no substitute for enforced constraints. It is inevitable that the conventions will be violated — and are likely to be violated just when they are needed most, in implementing, maintaining, and modifying large programs. It is precisely at this time, when the programming task becomes very difficult, that a language like CLU will be most valuable and appreciated.

Acknowledgments. The authors gratefully acknowledge the contributions made by members of the CLU design group over the last three years. Several people have made helpful comments about this paper, including Toby Bloom, Dorothy Curtis, Mike Hammer, Eliot Moss, Jerry Saltzer, Bob Scheifler, and the referees.

References
1. Allen, F.E., and Cocke, J. A catalogue of optimizing transformations. Rep. RC 3548. IBM Thomas J. Watson Res. Ctr., Yorktown Heights, N.Y., 1971.
2. Allen, F.E. A program data flow analysis procedure. Rep. RC 5278, IBM Thomas J. Watson Res. Ctr., Yorktown Heights, N.Y., 1975.
3. Atkinson, R.R. Optimization techniques for a structured programming language. S.M. Th., Dept. of Electr. Eng. and Comptr. Sci., M.I.T., Cambridge, Mass., June 1976.
4. Dahl, O.J., Myhrhaug, B., and Nygaard, K. The SIMULA 67 common base language. Pub. S-22, Norwegian Comptng. Ctr., Oslo, 1970.
5. DeRemer, F., and Kron, H. Programming-in-the-large versus programming-in-the-small. Proc. Int. Conf. on Reliable Software, SIGPLAN Notices 10, 6 (June 1975), 114–121.
6. Dijkstra, E.W. Notes on structured programming. *Structured Programming, A.P.I.C. Studies in Data Processing No. 8*, Academic Press, New York, 1972, pp. 1–81.
7. Guttag, J.V., Horowitz, E., and Musser, D.R. Abstract data types and software validation. Rep ISI/RR-76-48, Inform. Sci. Inst., U. of Southern California, Marina del Rey, Calif., Aug. 1976.
8. Hoare, C.A.R. Proof of correctness of data representations. *Acta Informatica 4* (1972), 271–281.
9. Knuth, D. *The Art of Computer Programming, Vol. 3: Sorting and Searching.* Addison Wesley, Reading, Mass., 1973.
10. Laboratory for Computer Science Progress Report 1974–1975. Comput. Structures Group. Rep. PR-XII, Lab. for Comptr. Sci., M.I.T. To be published.
11. Lampson, B.W. Protection. Proc. Fifth Annual Princeton Conf. on Inform. Sci. and Syst., Princeton U., Princeton, N.J., 1971, pp. 437–443.
12. Liskov, B.H., and Zilles, S.N. Programming with abstract data types. Proc. ACM SIGPLAN Conf. on Very High Level Languages, SIGPLAN Notices 9, 4 (April 1974), 50–59.
13. Liskov, B.H., and Zilles, S.N. Specification techniques for data abstractions. *IEEE Trans. Software Eng., SE-1* (1975), 7–19.
14. Liskov, B.H., and Berzins, V. An appraisal of program specifications. Comput. Structures Group Memo 141, Lab. for Comptr. Sci., M.I.T., Cambridge, Mass., July 1976.
15. McCarthy, J., et al. *LISP 1.5 Programmer's Manual.* M.I.T. Press, Cambridge, Mass., 1962.
16. Morris, J.H. Protection in programming languages. *Comm. ACM 16*, 1 (Jan. 1973), 15–21.
17. Parnas, D.L. Information distribution aspects of design methodology. Information Processing 71, Vol. 1, North-Holland Pub. Co., Amsterdam, 1972, pp. 339–344.
18. Scheifler, R.W. An analysis of inline substitution for the CLU programming language. Comput. Structures Group Memo 139, Lab. for Comptr. Sci., M.I.T., Cambridge, Mass., June 1976.
19. Spitzen, J., and Wegbreit, B. The verification and synthesis of data structures. *Acta Informatica 4* (1975), 127–144.
20. Standish, T.A. Data structures: an axiomatic approach. Rep. 2639, Bolt, Beranek and Newman, Cambridge, Mass., 1973.
21. Thomas, J.W. Module interconnection in programming systems supporting abstraction. Rep. CS-16, Comptr. Sci. Prog., Brown U., Providence, R.I., 1976.
22. Wirth, N. Program development by stepwise refinement. *Comm. ACM 14*, 4 (1971), 221–227.
23. Wirth, N. The programming language PASCAL. *Acta Informatica 1* (1971), 35–63.
24. Wulf, W.A., London, R., and Shaw, M. An introduction to the construction and verification of Alphard programs. *IEEE Trans. Software Eng. SE-2* (1976), 253–264.

EXCEPTION HANDLING IN CLU*

B. LISKOV AND A. SNYDER

Abstract—For programs to be reliable and fault tolerant, each program module must be defined to behave reasonably under a wide variety of circumstances. An exception handling mechanism supports the construction of such modules. This paper describes an exception handling mechanism developed as part of the CLU programming language. The CLU mechanism is based on a simple model of exception handling that leads to well-structured programs. It is engineered for ease of use and enhanced program readability. This paper discusses the various models of exception handling, the syntax and semantics of the CLU mechanism, and methods of implementing the mechanism and integrating it in debugging and production environments.

Index Terms—Exception handling, exit mechanisms, procedural abstractions, programming languages, structured programming.

I. Introduction

RECENTLY, there has been considerable emphasis on the development of programming language features that enhance the verifiability of programs [5]. While it is desirable that the task of developing correct programs be simplified as

Manuscript received March 8, 1979; revised June 25, 1979. This work was supported in part by the Advance Research Projects Agency of the Department of Defense, monitored by the Office of Naval Research under Contract N00014-75-C-0661, and in part by the National Science Foundation under Grants DCR74-21892 and MCS 74-21892.

B. H. Liskov is with the Laboratory for Computer Science, Massachusetts Institute of Technology, Cambridge, MA 02139.

A. Snyder is with the Hewlett-Packard Corporation, Palo Alto, CA 94304.

*Reprinted from *IEEE Transactions on Software Engineering*, Nov. 1979, 546–558.

much as possible, another important goal of program construction is that programs behave "reasonably" under a wide range of circumstances. Such programs have been variously termed as reliable, robust, or fault tolerant.

In a reliable program, each procedure must be designed to behave as generally as possible. Its specifications should require a well-defined response to all possible combinations of legal inputs (inputs satisfying the type constraints), even when lower level modules on which this procedure is depending fail. Of course, different responses will be appropriate in the different cases. Note that even if the software has been verified, the possibility of hardware failure implies that software modules may fail, as does the presence of resource constraints.

This paper describes a linguistic mechanism that supports the construction of reliable software. The mechanism, called an *exception handling mechanism*, facilitates communication of certain information among procedures at different levels. The mechanism supports the view that different responses are appropriate in different situations. We assume that for each procedure there is a set of circumstances in which it will terminate "normally"; in general, this happens when the input arguments satisfy certain constraints and the lower level modules (implemented in both hardware and software) on which the procedure depends are all working properly. In other circumstances, the procedure is unable to perform any action that would lead to normal termination, but instead must notify some other procedure (for example, the invoking

procedure) that an *exceptional condition* (or *exception*) has occurred.

For example, suppose *search* is a procedure that retrieves information associated with a given identifier in a symbol table. *Search* can return this information only if the identifier is present in the symbol table. The absence of the identifier constitutes an exceptional condition. Other exceptional conditions might also occur, for example, if the symbol table is implemented using a stack and the module implementing stacks is not working properly.

In referring to the condition as exceptions rather than errors we are following Goodenough [2]. The term "exception" is chosen because, unlike the term "error," it does not imply that anything is wrong; this connotation is appropriate because an event that is viewed as an error by one procedure may not be viewed that way by another. In fact, the term "exception" indicates that something unusual has occurred, and even this may be misleading: if the exception handling mechanism were efficient enough, exceptions might be used to convey information about normal and usual situations. For example, the *search* procedure might terminate normally only if the identifier were a local variable of the current block and use the exception handling mechanism to convey extra information about nonlocal variables.

Exception handling mechanisms have been largerly ignored in programming languages. For a discussion of existing mechanisms, the reader is referred to [2] and [3]. In our opinion, the existing mechanisms are overly powerful and ill-structured. For example, in the on-condition mechanism of PL/I, on-units are associated with invocations dynamically rather than statically, and global variables must be used to communicate data between the procedure performing the **signal** and the on-unit. Goodenough [2] proposes a new mechanism that is more constrained and better structured. The mechanism presented in this paper is still more constrained. We also believe it to be more conducive to the development of well-structured programs.

The mechanism we describe facilitates communication of information that can be used to recover from faults such as erroneous data and failures of lower level modules. We do not discuss the methods, e.g., redundancy, that are used for fault detection and recovery. Mechanisms that are designed to facilitate fault detection and recovery, e.g., recovery blocks [8], are complementary to ours, as was noted in [7].

The mechanism we describe has been defined as part of the CLU programming language [4]. The mechanism is of general interest because it is constrained and simple. Its design was based on a tradeoff between simplicity and expressive power; major design goals were ease of use and program readability. The mechanism was designed for a sequential language (without coroutines or parallel processes). Otherwise, however, the mechanism is not dependent on CLU semantics, and could be incorporated in any procedure oriented language.

In the next section we discuss the main decisions that must be made in designing an exception handling mechanism and the exception handling models that result from these decisions; we also discuss our decisions and our reasons for making them. In Section III we describe the syntax and semantics of the CLU exception handling mechanism. In Section IV we discuss some methods of implementing the mechanism and also how the mechanism can enhance programmer effectiveness in a debugging and a production environment. In Section V, we discuss the expressive power of our mechanism and compare it with some other mechanisms of greater power. Finally, in Section VI we summarize and evaluate what we have done.

II. The Model

To discuss exception handling we must first introduce some terminology about programs. The term *procedure* will be used to mean program text, either in a higher level language or in machine language. A procedure implements a *procedural abstraction*, which is a mapping from a set of argument objects to a set of result objects, possibly modifying some of the argument objects. A procedure may be *invoked* (or called) by an *invocation*, which is textually part of some procedure; that procedure is referred to as the *caller*. Invocation results in *activation* of the invoked procedure. An activation may **signal** an exception; the invocation that caused the activation *raises* that exception. The program text intended to be executed when an exception is raised is called the *handler*.

Our model of exception handling involves the communication of information from the procedure activation that detects an exceptional condition (the *signaler*) to some other procedure activation that is prepared to handle an occurrence of that condition (the *catcher*). In designing this model, we faced two major questions: 1) which procedure activations may catch an exception signaled by a procedure activation and 2) does the signaler continue to exist after signaling. These two questions are independent and may be addressed separately.

A. Single Versus Multilevel Mechanisms

The obvious candidates[1] for handling an exception signaled by some procedure activation are the activations in existence at the time the signal occurs. We can rule out the signaler itself, as exceptions are, by definition, conditions that the signaling procedure is unable to handle. The remaining question is whether to allow activations other than the immediate caller of the signaler to handle the exception.

Our answer to this question is based on the hierarchical program design methodology that CLU is intended to support [4]. As was explained above, each procedure implements a mapping. The caller of a procedure invokes the procedure to have the mapping performed; the caller need know only what the mapping is, and not how the procedure implements the mapping. Thus, while it is appropriate for the caller to know about the exceptions signaled by the procedure (and these are part of the abstraction implemented by that procedure), the caller should know nothing about the exceptions signaled by procedures used in the implementation of the invoked procedure.

The above considerations lead us to allow only the immediate caller of a procedure to handle exceptions signaled

---

[1] Levin [3] proposes an additional set of candidates. We will discuss Levin's work in Section V.

by that procedure. Of course, the handler in the caller can itself signal an exception, but that exception will then be part of the caller's abstraction.

We believe that the decision to limit handling of exceptions to the immediate caller is necessary for any well-structured exception handling mechanism. To maintain intellectual manageability of software, program structures that support understanding and verification through local code examination are needed. In particular, to understand how a procedure is implemented, one should not have to examine implementations of any other procedures. An understanding of the mappings performed by invoked procedures is needed, but this understanding should be obtained by reading specifications of those procedures and not their code. This requirement implies that specifications must describe all exceptions arising from invoking a procedure, including information about exceptions arising from procedures called at a lower level if the mechanism does not limit the handling of these exceptions. The point is that all exceptions that may be raised by a procedure, whether explicitly or implicitly, must be considered part of that procedural abstraction. Limiting the handling of exceptions to just the caller simply ensures that the linguistic constructs match the proper conceptual view. Note, however, that this constraint does *not* prevent the language designer from providing simplified ways of passing exceptions from one level to the next where appropriate.

The exception handling mechanism proposed by Goodenough [2] does impose our constraint on handling exceptions. The PL/I mechanism does not, nor does the mechanism in Mesa [6].

B. Resumption Versus Termination Model

The second question, whether the signaler should continue to exist after the exception is signaled, involves a tradeoff between expressive power and the complexity of the semantics. If the signaler can continue to exist after signaling, then it is possible that a catcher may fix up the exceptional condition so that processing of the signaler may be resumed. For this reason, we refer to this model as the *resumption model*. The model in which the signaling activation ceases to exist we refer to as the *termination model*. In this section we assume that the decision to support a one-level mechanism has been made, and we therefore limit our analysis to this case.

A one-level resumption model works as follows. Suppose that there are three procedures P, Q, and R, and that P invokes Q and Q invokes R. If R signals an exception r, then Q must handle it. Let H_r denote the statements in Q that handle r (H_r is the handler for r). In the course of handling r, H_r may signal an exception q, which must be handled by P (since P is the caller of Q).[2] Let H_q denote the statements in P that handle q (H_q is the handler for q). When H_q terminates, then

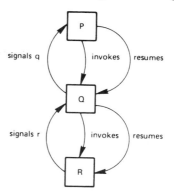

Fig. 1. Flow of control in the resumption model.

Q is resumed in the middle of H_r; only when H_r terminates is the execution of R continued. This situation is illustrated in Fig. 1. Note that information about signals flows upward one level at a time, while resumption flows downward one level at a time; multilevel flow is not permitted in either direction.

The resumption model is most easily understood by viewing the handler as an implicit procedure parameter of the signaler. The handler is called by the signaler when the exception it handles is signaled. The handler procedure is declared in the calling procedure, and its free variables get their meaning in the caller's environment, as do any exceptions it signals.[3]

In the termination model, occurrence of an exception causes the signaler to terminate. However, different kinds of behavior are expected of the called procedure under different conditions. The view taken is that a procedure may terminate in one of a number of conditions. One of these is the *normal condition*, while others are *exception conditions*. In each condition, it may be convenient to return a number of result objects; these will differ in number and type in the different conditions.

The resumption model is more complex than the termination model. This can be appreciated by considering how resumption affects the interrelationships among procedures, specifications of procedures, and linguistic mechanisms for exception handling.

The ordinary view of procedures is that, in the absence of recursion, the calling procedure is dependent on the called procedure but not vice versa. This view is upheld in the termination model. However, in the resumption model, the signaler and caller are mutually dependent: the caller invokes the signaler to perform some mapping, or satisfy some input/output relation, but the signaler depends on (the handler in) the caller to satisfy a similar relation when an exception is signaled.

Specifications of procedural abstractions in the termination model consist of a number of clauses, one specifying the behavior for the normal case and one for each exception case. Such clauses also exist in the resumption model, since it is still possible that the signaler is unable to terminate normally, for example, because a handler is unable to clear up the prob-

---

[2] If dynamic binding for exception names is used (as in PL/I), then R would be required to handle q. Making this assumption leads to a model at least as complex as the one we are considering. Furthermore, it is impossible under this assumption for H_r to raise exception in P without resorting to a multilevel mechanism.

[3] That is, exception names have static scope.

lem that led to the exception. In general, specifications have a termination model form (several termination states are defined) even when the resumption model is in use.

The interdependence between procedures in the resumption model show up in specifications as extra information. In addition to the clauses describing different termination states, it is also necessary to include descriptions of the behavior expected from the handlers when exceptions are signaled. Such descriptions are analogous to what must be given for a procedure taking procedure parameters, since handlers are implicit procedure parameters, as was discussed earlier.

The complexity of a linguistic mechanism supporting resumption is illustrated by Goodenough's proposal [2], which is a carefully considered design of a complete mechanism. Goodenough's design recognizes that to be really useful, termination must be supported as well as resumption. Three types of signals are recognized, corresponding to cases where the signaler may not be resumed, must be resumed, or where resumption is optional. In case the caller does not resume a signaler that must or could be resumed, a special ability is provided to permit the signaler to clean up (i.e., restore some nonlocal variables to a consistent state) before its activation is terminated. In addition, a default mechanism is provided to permit the signaler to handle its own exception in case the caller does not.

The termination model requires a simpler linguistic mechanism for its support than does the resumption model. Since a signal terminates the signaler, there is no need for multiple kinds of signals. Also, special mechanisms for cleaning up are not needed (the signaler must always clean up before signaling).

Since the termination model is simpler, it is preferable to the resumption model, provided it supplies adequate expressive power. We conjecture that the expressive power is adequate: that situations handled awkwardly by the termination model and simply by the resumption model are not frequent. We will discuss this conjecture further in Section V. In the next section we discuss the design of an exception handling mechanism based on the termination model.

III. Syntax and Semantics of the CLU Exception Mechanism

In Section II we explained the rationale for our major decisions.

1) The exceptions signaled by a procedure must be caught by the immediate caller.

2) Signaling an exception terminates the signaling procedure.

These two decisions lead to a single-level termination model of computation in which a procedure may terminate in one of a number of conditions. Thus, instead of a single return path, each procedure has several return paths. One of these is considered the normal path, while others are considered exceptional. In each case, result objects may be returned; the result objects may differ in number and type in the different cases.

An exception handling semantics that terminates execution of the signaling procedure could be incorporated in a programming language with no additional mechanism. The signaling procedure could simply return, passing back in addition to the real result objects a tag that identifies the reason for termination. Indeed, such a convention is often adopted as a way of dealing with exceptions in a language that has no exception handling mechanism. However, this approach has a major defect: every invocation must be followed by a conditional test to determine what the outcome was. This requirement leads to programs that are difficult to read, and probably inefficient as well, thus discouraging programmers from signaling and handling exceptions.

To aid programmers in building reliable software, an exception handling mechanism must be devised that can be implemented efficiently and that enhances program readability. In the remainder of this section we describe the CLU exception handling mechanism, which was developed to satisfy these goals. The discussion identifies some problems that arise in designing any such mechanism; the CLU mechanism provides a possible set of solutions to these problems.

A. Signaling

To provide a convenient method of signaling information about exceptions, we included directly in CLU the model of a procedure having many kinds of returns. A CLU procedure, therefore, can terminate in the normal way by returning and can terminate in an exceptional condition by signaling. In each case, result objects, differing in number and type, can be returned.

The information about the ways in which a procedure may terminate must be included in its heading. For example, the procedure performing integer division has the following heading:

div = **proc** (x, y: int) **returns** (int) **signals** (zero_divide)

which indicates that *div* may terminate by returning a single integer (the quotient of the two input arguments) or by signaling *zero_divide* (which indicates that the second argument was zero) and returning no results.

A CLU procedure terminates its execution by performing a *return statement* or a *signal statement*. The return statement terminates execution normally, while the signal statement terminates execution in the named exceptional condition. For example, the following (fairly useless) procedure determines the sign of an integer:

```
sign = proc(x: int) returns (int) signals (zero, neg (int))
       if x < 0 then signal neg (x)
           elseif x = 0 then signal zero
           else return (x)
           end
       end sign
```

The information in the procedure heading is used to check that the exception names actually signaled are the correct ones and that the correct number and types of result objects are returned in both the normal and exceptional cases. This information is also used to determine that the exceptions handled by a calling procedure are named in the heading of the called procedure, and that, again, the number and types of result objects are correct in both the normal and exceptional cases.

B. Handling Exceptions

In CLU, exceptions arise only from invocations.[4] In particular, all uses of infix and prefix operators in CLU are considered to be "syntactic sugar" for invocations. For example, the expression

x + y

is syntactic sugar for the invocation

t$add (x, y)

where t is the type of x. Thus, if x is an integer, $x + y$ is an invocation of the integer addition operation. This viewpoint permits exceptions arising from built-in operations and user-defined procedures to be treated uniformly.[5]

In this section we discuss how handlers are associated with invocations. For usability and program readability, it is necessary to permit considerable flexibility in the placement of handlers. For example, requiring that the text of a handler be attached to the invocation that raises the exception would lead to unreadable programs in which expressions were broken up with handlers. Furthermore, the control flow of a program is often affected by the occurrence of an exception (for example, an *end_of_file* exception will terminate a loop). Therefore, our mechanism was designed to permit placement of a handler where the programmer deemed convenient, out of the main flow when possible to enhance readability, and altering the control flow when this was desired.

Two major decisions determined the form of CLU exception handling statements.

1) Handlers are statically associated with invocations.

2) Handlers may be attached only to statements, not to expressions.

Static association means that the handler associated with a particular exception condition that may be raised by a particular invocation can be determined by static analysis of the program text. This decision not only enhances program readability, but makes possible a more efficient implementation of the exception handling mechanism.

The decision to attach handlers only to statements and not expressions was made to simplify the mechanism. When a handler attached to an expression terminates, unless an explicit return, signal, or exit (see Section III-C) is performed, it must provide a value to be used as the value of the expression. By allowing handlers to be attached only to statements, we avoid providing a mechanism for substituting new values for expressions. We believe that the need to substitute a value for an expression is not great. In any case, the effect of attaching handlers to expressions can be obtained by breaking up complex expressions into sequences of assignment statements.

Handlers are placed in CLU programs by means of the *except statement*, which has the form

statement **except** *handler list* **end**

This statement has the following interpretation: the *statement* raises all the exceptions raised by the invocations it textually contains, excluding those handled by embedded except statements. The *handler list* will handle some subset (possibly all) of these exceptions. The except statement as a whole raises all the exceptions of the *statement* that are not handled by the *handler list* plus any exceptions raised by the *handler list*. Thus, when an exception is raised by an invocation, control goes to the innermost handler that handles that exception and is part of an except statement containing the invocation in its *statement* part.

Each handler in the *handler list* names one or more exceptions to be handled, followed by a list of statements (called the *handler body*) describing what to do. Permitting several exceptions to be named in the same handler avoids code duplication when the exceptions are all handled in the same way.

Several different forms are available for handlers depending on whether the named exceptions have associated result objects and whether those objects are used in the handler body. To handle one or more exceptions with no associated objects, the exception names are simply listed. For example,

when underflow, zero_divide: *body*

will handle exceptions named *underflow* and *zero_divide*, neither of which has any associated result objects.

To handle exceptions with result objects that are to be used in the handler body, names must be associated with the objects. Again a list of exception names is given, but it is followed by declarations of local variables to name the result objects, for example,

when e1, e2 (s: string, i: int): *body*

The scope of the declarations is the handler body. All of the named exceptions must return objects of the types listed in the declaration, in the order stated. When the handler is executed, these objects are bound to the declared variables and the body is executed. (This binding is similar to the binding of actual arguments to formal arguments that occurs when procedures are invoked. However, a return or signal in the handler body, rather than terminating just the handler, will instead terminate the entire enclosing procedure.)

To handle exceptions with result objects when the objects are not used in the handler body, the list of exception names is followed by (∗) as shown below:

when neg, underflow (∗): *body*

There need be no agreement between the number and types of result objects associated with the exceptions in this form; for example, the *neg* exception had a single argument, while *underflow* had none. This form encourages a programming style in which a procedure returns all possibly useful information when signaling; if this information is not needed in the calling procedure, it can easily be ignored.

If the programmer wishes to handle all remaining exceptions without listing their names, one of the following two forms

---

[4]Except for the special exception *failure* (described in Section III-D), which may be signaled at any point by the underlying implementation of CLU.

[5]The viewpoint does *not* require that a built-in operation be implemented by a closed routine; in-line code is perfectly permissible and consistent.

can be used as the last handler in an except statement. The form

others: *body*

is used when information about exception names and result objects is not important. If information about the exception name is desired, the form

others (e_name: string): *body*

may be used. Here the name of the exception is given to the handler body as a string.

The handler body may contain any legal CLU statement. If the handler body returns or signals, then the containing procedure will be terminated as discussed in Section III-A. The handler body may also be terminated by an exit (see next section) or because an invocation within it raises an exception that is not handled within the handler body. Otherwise, when the handler body is finished, the next statement following the except statement in the normal flow will be executed.

The example below illustrates the association of handlers with exceptions:

```
begin % start of inner block
    S1 except
        when zero: S2
        end
    . . .
    end % end of inner block
    except
        when zero: S3
        others: S4
        end
```

If *zero* is raised by an invocation in *S1*, it will be handled by *S2*, not *S3*. However, if *zero* is raised by an invocation in *S2*, it will be handled by *S3*. All other exceptions raised in *S1* and *S2* will be handled by *S4*.

C. Exits and the Placement of Handlers

Our intention in defining the except statement is to permit the programmer to position handlers as is convenient. There are two constraints on the placement of handlers.

1) The handler must be placed on the statement whose execution is to be terminated if the handler body terminates without returning or signaling.

2) Suppose that an exception named *e* is raised by two invocations, and we wish to handle the occurrences of *e* differently. We do not permit multiple handlers to be provided for *e* in a single except statement. (This rule holds even if the invocations raising *e* provide different numbers or types of result objects; we do not allow such information to be used in selecting a handler.) Therefore, the two handlers must be in two except statements, each situated such that only one of the invocations raising *e* is in its scope.

These two constraints may conflict. For example, suppose that within a statement, *S*, the procedure *sign*, mentioned earlier, is invoked at two different points. Suppose also that the programmer wishes to handle the *neg* exception signaled

```
begin   % beginning of S
    a := sign(x)
        except when neg(i: int):
            S1
            exit done
        end
    b := sign(y)
        except when neg(i: int):
            S2
            exit done
        end
    ...
    end   % end of S
        except when done:
            ...
        end
```

Fig. 2. Example illustrating use of the exit mechanism.

by *sign* in a different manner for each of the two invocations, but in each case wishes execution to then continue with the statement following *S*. The first constraint would require that both handlers be placed on *S*, so that the execution of *S* would be terminated when the exceptions are raised. However, the second constraint requires that at least one handler be placed within *S* to resolve the ambiguous association between the invocations and the handlers.

We resolve this conflict in CLU by the addition of an exit mechanism, similar to those proposed by Zahn [9] and Bochmann [1]. The handlers are placed near the invocations. They terminate by exiting to a handler attached to the statement *S*. For example, one could handle the *neg* exceptions as shown in Fig. 2.

The exit statement can be used anywhere within a CLU procedure; its use is not restricted to handler bodies. The exit statement is similar to the signal statement, except that while the signal statement signals the condition to the calling procedure activation, the exit statement directly raises the condition so that it can be handled in the same procedure activation. The exit statement can specify a number of result objects to be passed to the handler.

We chose to have separate mechanisms for exits and exceptions (rather than using the signal statement for both exits and exceptions) because the two mechanisms capture different programmer intentions and thus naturally have different restrictions on their use. The intent of an exit is a local transfer of control. Thus, we require that exits be handled in the same procedure activation where they are raised. Furthermore, we require that exits be handled by a when arm (not an others arm), and if there are result objects, these must be accepted as arguments by the handler. The justification for these requirements is that exit names and result objects (unlike exception names and result objects) are under the control of the programmer of the procedure, and therefore should be chosen to mean something within that procedure.

The exit mechanism meshes nicely with the exception handling mechanism. In fact, the signal statement can be viewed simply as terminating a procedure invocation and exiting to the appropriate handler in the caller.

D. Uncaught Exceptions

Now we address the question of what happens if a procedure provides no handler for an exception raised by some contained invocation. One possibility is to consider the procedure to be illegal; checking for unhandled exceptions can be performed at compile-time. This approach is taken by Goodenough [2].

We have taken another approach. We felt it was unrealistic to require the programmer to provide handlers in situations where no meaningful action can be taken. Such situations will occur when a used abstraction is not working properly. For example, consider the statement

```
if ~ stack$empty (s) then
    · · ·
    x := stack$pop (s)
    · · ·
    end
```

Here the programmer invokes the *pop* operation for stacks only when the stack is nonempty. Now suppose that nevertheless stack underflow occurs. This situation is unlikely to arise in a debugged or verified program (but see Section IV). If it does arise, it indicates that the stack abstraction is not behaving correctly. Often there is no appropriate action for this procedure to take other than to report the fact to its caller. Since almost every abstraction can potentially behave incorrectly or in a way not expected by its caller, procedures must always be prepared to handle such cases. However, the action taken is almost always the same, and to require explicit handling of such cases would load every procedure with uninteresting code.

To facilitate reporting of failures and to relieve the programmer of the burden of handling such errors, CLU has one language-defined exception, named *failure*. *Failure* has one associated result object, a string that may contain some information about the cause of the failure. Every procedure can potentially signal *failure*; therefore *failure* is implicitly an exception of every procedure and may not be listed in the procedure heading explicitly. *Failure* may be signaled explicitly, however, in the usual way:

signal failure ("reason is . . . ")

The most common way that *failure* is signaled, however, is by an uncaught exception being automatically turned into a *failure* exception. For example, procedure *nonzero*

```
nonzero = proc (x: int) returns (int)
        return (sign (x))
            except
                when neg (y: int): return (y)
                end
        end nonzero
```

does not catch exception *zero* signaled by *sign*. If this exception is signaled, the invocation of *nonzero* will be terminated with the exception

failure ("unhandled exception: zero")

The effect is equivalent to attaching a handler to the procedure body, e.g.,

```
nonzero = · · ·
        · · ·
        except
            others (s: string): signal failure (
                        "unhandled exception: "|| s)
            end
        end nonzero
```

Here the symbol || is string concatenation.

A common case in which an exception will not be handled is when the unhandled exception is *failure*. Note that in this case it is the string argument of *failure* (rather than the string "failure") that is of interest. Therefore, this string is retained when *failure* is passed up to the next level. This effect is equivalent to attaching to the procedure body the handler

```
except
        when failure (s:  string): signal failure (s)
        end
```

Sometimes before signaling *failure* some cleaning up is needed. In this case, the others or when form is used explicitly, and after cleaning up, *failure* is signaled explicitly.

E. Example

We now present an example demonstrating the use of exception handlers. We will write a procedure, *sum_stream*, which reads in a sequence of signed decimal integers from a character stream and returns the sum of those integers. The input stream is viewed as containing a sequence of fields separated by spaces and newlines; each field must consist of a nonempty sequence of digits, optionally preceded by a single minus sign. *Sum_stream* has the form

```
sum_stream = proc (s: stream) returns (int)
            signals (overflow,
                    unrepresentable_integer (string),
                    bad_format (string))
        · · ·
        end sum_stream
```

Sum_stream will signal *overflow* if the sum of the numbers or an intermediate sum is outside the implemented range of integers. *Unrepresentable_integer* will be signaled if the stream contains an individual number that is outside the implemented range of integers. *Bad_format* will be signaled if the stream contains a field that is not an integer.

An implementation of *sum_stream* is presented in Fig. 3. It consists of a simple loop that accumulates the sum, using a procedure *get_number* to remove the next integer from the stream. *Get_number* will signal *end_of_file* if the stream contains no more fields, in which case *sum_stream* will return the accumulated sum. *Get_number* will also signal *bad_format* or *unrepresentable_integer* if an invalid field is encountered; these exceptions are passed upward by *sum_stream*. The *overflow* handler in *sum_stream* catches exceptions signaled by the *int$add* procedure, which is invoked using the infix + notation. We have placed the exception handlers on

```
sum_stream = proc (s: stream) returns (int)
                    signals (overflow,
                             unrepresentable_integer (string),
                             bad_format (string))
         sum: int := 0
         while true do
                 sum := sum + get_number (s)
                 end
           except
             when end_of_file:
                   return (sum)
             when unrepresentable_integer (f: string):
                   signal unrepresentable_integer (f)
             when bad_format (f: string):
                   signal bad_format (f)
             when overflow:
                   signal overflow
             end
         end sum_stream
```

Fig. 3. The sum_stream procedure.

```
get_number = proc (s: stream) returns (int)
                    signals (end_of_file,
                             unrepresentable_integer (string),
                             bad_format (string))
         field: string := get_field (s)
           except when end_of_file:
                   signal end_of_file
                   end
         return (s2i (field))
           except
             when unrepresentable_integer:
                   signal unrepresentable_integer (field)
             when bad_format, invalid_character (*):
                   signal bad_format (field)
             end
         end get_number
```

Fig. 4. The get_number procedure.

the while statement for readability; they could also have been placed directly on the assignment statement.

The procedure *get_number* is presented in Fig. 4. It calls a procedure *get_field* to obtain the next field in the stream and then uses *s2i* to convert the returned string to an integer. *S2i* has the following form:

```
s2i = proc (s: string) returns (int)
         signals (invalid_character (char),
                  bad_format,
                  unrepresentable_integer)
         . . .
         end s2i
```

S2i will signal *invalid_character* if the string *s* contains a character other than a digit or a minus sign. *Bad_format* will be signaled if *s* contains a minus sign following a digit, more than one minus sign, or no digits. *Unrepresentable_integer* will be signaled if *s* represents an integer that is outside the implemented range of integers. *Get_number* handles the excep-

tions signaled by *get_field* and *s2i* and signals them upward in terms that are meaningful to its callers. Although some of the names may be unchanged, the meanings of the exceptions (and even the number of arguments) are different in the two levels. Note the use of the (*) form in the handler for the *bad_format* and *invalid_character* exceptions since the signal arguments are not used.

The *get_field* procedure is presented in Fig. 5. It uses the following operation of the *stream* data type:

```
getc = proc (s: stream) returns (char) signals (end_of_file)
         . . .
         end getc
```

The *stream$getc* operation returns the next character from the stream and signals *end_of_file* if the stream is empty. Note that if *end_of_file* is signaled when a field is being accumulated, then that field is returned. Otherwise, *get_field* signals *end_of_file*.

Programming of the procedures in Figs. 3-5 would be

```
get_field = proc (s: stream) returns (string) signals (end_of_file)
        field: string := ""
    begin   % delimits scope of outermost end_of_file handler
            c: char := stream$getc (s)
            % search for field
            while c = ' ' cor c = '\n' do
                    c := stream$getc (s)
                    end
            % accumulate field
            while c ~= ' ' cand c ~= '\n' do
                    field := string$append (field, c)
                    c := stream$getc (s)
                        except when end_of_file:
                            return (field)
                            end
                    end
            end
        except when end_of_file:
            signal end_of_file
            end
    return (field)
    end get_field
```

Fig. 5. The get_ field procedure.

simplified if the mechanism permitted implicit upward propagation of exceptions. This would permit arms of the form

```
when unrepresentable_ integer (f: string):
        signal unrepresentable_ integer (f)
```

to be omitted from the program text. As we gain experience in using the mechanism, we will learn how to modify it to enhance its convenience.

F. On Disabling Exceptions

One question that naturally arises about an exception handling mechanism is whether exceptions can be disabled. By disabling exceptions two kinds of savings can (potentially) be realized: the time spent detecting the occurrence of the exception can be saved, and the space used for the handlers and the information used to find the handlers can be saved. However, it is unacceptable if the result of disabling exceptions is that errors still occur, but are simply not recognized. Therefore, we do not believe that providing a means for programmer disabling of exceptions is consistent with encouraging good programming practice, and no such mechanism has been provided in CLU.

The situation still arises, however, in which it is possible to *guarantee* that the exception cannot occur, and it is desirable to take advantage of that guarantee to generate more efficient code. Looked at in this way, disabling of exceptions is seen as a kind of program optimization technique, since program optimization makes use of properties detected from program analysis to control the generation of code. There are two ways in which such properties can be detected. First, the combination of in-line substitution followed by analysis across module boundaries can result in more efficient code. For example, consider

```
if ~stack$empty (s) then x := stack$pop (s) · · ·
```

where *s* is a *stack*. If both *empty* and *pop* are expanded in-line, the result will be code roughly like

```
if s.size > 0 % body of empty
    then % body of pop
        if s.size > 0 then · · ·
```

Conventional techniques like redundant expression elimination and dead code removal can then be used to improve the code.

Alternatively, it would be fruitful to integrate the activities of a program verification system with the compiler. Then, for example, a verifier might prove of the user of *s* that *pop* is never called if *s* is empty. This assertion could then be used later to control the compilation of both the program using *s*, and the program implementing the *stack* module.

IV. IMPLEMENTATION, DEBUGGING, AND DIAGNOSTICS

In this section we discuss some implementation issues. First we sketch some methods for implementing the exception handling mechanism. Then we discuss how the mechanism can be incorporated in a debugging environment and in a production environment.

A. Implementation

There are several possible methods of implementing the exception handling mechanism. As usual, tradeoffs must be made between efficiency of space and time. We believe the following are appropriate criteria for an implementation:

1) normal case execution efficiency should not be impaired at all;

2) exceptions should be handled reasonably quickly, but not necessarily as fast as possible;

3) use of space should be reasonably efficient.

The tradeoff to be made is the speed with which exceptions are handled versus the space required for code or data used to locate handlers.

The implementation of signaling an exception involves the following actions:

1) discarding the activation record of the signaling activation (but saving the result objects associated with the exception),

2) locating the appropriate handler in the calling procedure,

3) adjusting the caller's activation record to reflect the possible termination of execution of expressions and statements,

4) copying the result objects into the caller's activation record,

5) transferring control to the handler.

Actions 3) and 5) are equivalent to a **goto** from the invocation to the handler. Actions 1) and 4) are similar to those occurring in normal procedure returns. Because the association between invocations and handlers is static, the compiler can provide the information needed to perform actions 2) and 3). Below we sketch two methods of providing this information; these methods differ considerably in their performance characteristics.

The first method, called the *branch table method*, is to follow each invocation with a branch table containing one entry for each exception that can be raised by the invocation. The

Code for invocation p( ) of p = **proc** ( ) **returns** ( ) **signals** (el, e2):

```
        call   p
        el_handler          ; branch table
        e2_handler
        failure_handler
        ...                 ; normal return here
- - - - - - - - - - - - - - - - - - - - - - - - - - - - - - - - - - - - - -
        sizel               ; new activation record size
        ...                 ; other information about the handler
el_handler:  ...            ; code for el handler
```

Fig. 6. Sketch of code generated by the branch table method.

invocation of a procedure whose heading lists n exceptions will have a branch table of $n + 1$ entries; the first n entries correspond to the exceptions listed in the heading, while the last entry is for *failure*. Each entry contains the location of a handler for the corresponding exception.

Using this method, return and signal are easy to implement: return transfers control to the location following the branch table, while signal transfers control to the location stored in the branch table entry for the exception being signaled. The information needed to adjust the caller's activation record could be stored with the handler, as could information about whether to discard the returned objects and whether this is an others handler; for example, this information could be stored in a table placed just before the first instruction of the handler. An example is given in Fig. 6 of the code generated by this method.

The branch table method provides for efficient signaling of exceptions, but at a considerable cost in space, since every invocation must be followed by a branch table (all invocations may at least signal *failure*). A second method, the *handler table method*, is the one used by the current CLU implementation. This method trades off some speed for space, and was designed under the assumption that there are many fewer handlers than invocations, which is consistent with our experience in using the mechanism.

The handler table method works as follows. Rather than build a branch table per invocation, the compiler builds a single table for each procedure. This table contains an entry for each handler in the procedure. An entry contains the following information: 1) a list of the exceptions handled by the handler (a null list can be used to indicate an **others** handler), 2) a pair of values defining the scope of the handler, that is, the object code corresponding to the statement to which the handler is attached, 3) the location of the code of the handler, 4) the new activation record size, and 5) an indicator of whether the returned objects are used in the handler. The scope and exceptions list together permit candidate handlers to be located: only an invocation occurring within the scope and raising an exception named in the exception list can possibly be handled by the handler (for an others handler, only the scope matters).

In this method, a return statement is implemented just as it would be in a language without exception handling. A signal statement requires searching the handler table to find entries for candidate handlers; if several candidates exist, the one with the smallest scope is selected. Placing the entries in the table in the (linear) order in which the corresponding handlers appear in the source text guarantees that the first candidate found is the handler to use. Unhandled exceptions can be recognized either by the absence of candidates or by storing one additional entry at the end of the handler table for this case.

B. Debugging and Diagnostics

Our exception handling mechanism is designed explicitly to provide information that programs, not programmers, can use to recover from exceptional conditions. However, the mechanism can also mesh smoothly with mechanisms intended to collect information of interest to programmers. The kind of behavior desired will differ, however, from a debugging environment to a production environment.

In an interactive debugging environment it is likely that a programmer would wish to be informed about the occurrence of some or all exceptions as they are signaled and be given a chance to handle them himself or take some other corrective action. Two possible modes might be useful here. The programmer may be interested only in signals of *failure* (especially those resulting from unhandled exceptions), or he may in addition name some particular exceptions of interest.

An exception handling mechanism running in such an environment, before locating a handler, would consult some debugging system information to determine if the current exception is one that the programmer wishes to know about. If the exception is of interest to the programmer, then system routines can be invoked to initiate a dialogue with the programmer. This dialogue may result in the program being continued or terminated.

It is worth noting that one argument in favor of the resumption model has been that it integrates debugging with program execution. The programmer (or actually the system as his representative) is thought of as the highest level activation, which will handle all exceptions not otherwise handled and which may later resume execution of some lower level activation. Note that this viewpoint allows the programmer to examine only unhandled exceptions. At any rate, we believe that it is not productive to try to merge debugging with ordinary processing, since the requirements in the two cases are quite different.

In a production environment, there is no programmer

available to interact with the program. Of course, there may be an operator present, and a program may attempt to recover by requesting some operator action (e.g., mounting a tape). This action can be accomplished by ordinary program structures (e.g., invoking a procedure to print a message on the operator's console).

When *failure* occurs in a production environment, there is still a good chance that program error is responsible. Therefore, it would be helpful if information about the failing program were collected for later examination by a programmer. This capability can easily be provided. Whenever *failure* is signaled, the exception handling mechanism can output information about each activation before terminating it. In the case of the first implicit signal of the "unhandled exception" failure, the mechanism should also provide information about the activation that signaled the unhandled exception. The information collected as *failure* propagates upwards will provide a trace of the failing program, which should be helpful for the programmer who determines later what the problem was. Debugging in a batch environment can be facilitated similarly, except that information about more exceptions than just *failure* may be of interest. Note that in either case the information being collected is *not* useful to programs (since it describes the states of implementations of other procedures) and therefore need not be made available to them.

V. Expressive Power

As we stated earlier, the decision to choose a termination model instead of a resumption model involves a tradeoff between the expressive power of the exception handling mechanism and its complexity. In our opinion, a more complex mechanism can be justified only if the additional expressive power it provides is frequently needed. In this section we explore this issue by considering examples of problems often put forth as justifying a resumption model.

The first problem concerns exceptions such as *underflow* that are generated by numeric operations. Often when an operation like *multiply* signals *underflow*, the desired action is to substitute a particular value (e.g., zero) for the result of the operation and continue the computation. In a resumption model, this behavior can be obtained by resuming the operation and passing it the value to be returned.

This behavior is equally easily obtained using a termination model. Because the *multiply* operation is not performing any computation after being resumed (it is merely returning the value provided), it is acceptable to terminate its activation. The only problem is for the handler to somehow substitute the new value for the result of the operation. For simple examples like

z := x * y

"substituting" for the result of the invocation of *multiply* can be done simply by assigning to z. For more complicated examples, e.g.,

z := x * y + z

using our mechanism it is necessary to introduce additional statements and temporary variables. However, such awkward-

ness is not a defect of the termination model but rather a result of our decision not to allow handlers to be attached to expressions. If such examples turned out to be frequent, our mechanism could be changed to accommodate them.

In fact, resumption is truly useful only in the following situation: when the exception is signaled, the signaler is in the middle of a computation that can be completed by performing additional computation upon receipt of a value from the handler. Resumption permits completion of the computation in this situation without redoing work already performed.

We can imagine that such a situation could arise during a numeric computation. If it did, and resumption were not available, then a default value (or, in the most general case, a procedure to compute a default value) could be passed as an extra input of the numeric routine.

This method is clearly not as convenient as using resumption; it becomes unacceptable if there are many default values or if there is deep nesting of procedures within the numeric routine, so that even a single default value must be passed down through many invocations. In our experience, neither of these characteristics hold for the routines in numeric libraries; on the contrary, default values are almost never of use, and the nesting is shallow.

The other example often used to support the choice of a resumption model is that of a storage pool that performs storage allocation for a number of objects in a program. If the amount of free storage in the storage pool becomes too low to satisfy a particular allocation request, it may still be possible to satisfy the request if some of the objects stored in the pool can be reorganized to use less storage. Many objects can be implemented in a number of ways, some that permit fast execution but use a lot of space and others that are slower but use less space. The idea would be to start out using fast representations but switch to more compact representations if free storage became too low. Note that this example is an instance of the general situation, described above, in which resumption is truly useful.

Levin [3] has designed an exception handling mechanism that directly supports the desired behavior. In Levin's mechanism, an exception can be associated with an object (the mechanisms discussed previously associate exceptions only with invocations). Thus, if the storage pool were unable to satisfy a request, it could signal an exception associated with the storage pool object. The mechanism would then allow all users of the object (in this case, modules that have objects allocated in the storage pool) to handle the exception. The handlers would attempt to free storage by reorganizing their associated objects.

Note that Levin's mechanism is strictly more powerful (in terms of expressive power) than the resumption models we discussed in Section II, since the users of the storage pool do not necessarily have any outstanding procedure activations at the time the exception is signaled. Furthermore, those objects that are in the middle of being operated upon are likely to be in an inconsistent state and thus not prepared for reorganization. Levin's mechanism makes it easy to inhibit the handling of an exception for objects in an inconsistent state.

In CLU, this recovery algorithm could be programmed by

having the storage pool explicitly maintain a collection of handler procedures to be invoked whenever free storage became too low.[6] The storage pool abstraction provides operations *alloc*, to add an object to a pool, and *delete*, to remove an object from a pool. *Alloc* would have an additional argument: the handler procedure to invoke if it becomes necessary to shrink the object being added to the pool. *Alloc* would add this procedure to the collection, while *delete* would remove from the collection the handler procedure associated with the object being deleted from the pool.

There is no doubt that the method sketched above is more complicated and more error prone than what could be done using Levin's mechanism. However, we believe that the storage pool example is both unusual and a special case. We doubt the existence of a large number of cases where the amount of storage freed would make the difference between successful and unsuccessful execution of a program.

In selecting examples for discussion, we examined those presented in papers favoring the resumption model [2], [3], and chose the ones that made the strongest case for resumption. In both examples, the solutions achieved using resumption were more natural than those possible without resumption. However, unless it is shown that such cases arise frequently, they do not justify the more complex mechanism.

VI. Discussion

In this paper we have discussed exception handling and described an exception handling mechanism. An exception handling mechanism is a tool for enhancing program reliability and fault tolerance. To enhance reliability procedures should be defined as generally as possible, that is, they should respond "reasonably" in as many situations as possible. An exception handling mechanism simplifies the writing of such procedures; it is primarily a mechanism for generalizing the behavior of procedures.

In Section II we discussed major decisions that must be made in designing an exception handling mechanism and the exception handling models that result from these decisions. We argued that any well-structured mechanism should be one-level: only the caller should handle exceptions raised by the invoked procedure. We further argued that the termination model, in which the signaling activation terminates, is better than the resumption model, in which the signaling activation continues to exist. The termination model is clearly simpler than the resumption model; we also believe that it has sufficient expressive power. Note that in our termination model, a procedure may terminate in one of a number of conditions (one of which is the so-called "normal" condition) and may return result objects differing in number and type for each condition. The ability to return objects provides a kind of expressive power not found in most other exception handling mechanisms.

Section III described the syntax and semantics of the CLU exception handling mechanism, which supports the termina-

tion model. While in Section II we were concerned primarily with interprocedure control and data flow, in Section III, we were concerned primarily with intraprocedure control and data flow. Our goal was to permit the programmer to place handlers where they are needed, without constraints due to conflict of exception names. This goal led to the introduction of an exit mechanism similar to those described by Zahn [9] and Bochmann [1]. Our design also acknowledged that many exceptions cannot be handled. These exceptions may not occur often, but they can potentially occur almost anywhere. The special exception named *failure*, which is signaled implicitly for all uncaught exceptions, was introduced to accommodate this situation. We also discussed why disabling exceptions is not a good idea, and suggested that research in program optimization techniques may be fruitful in avoiding the cost of checking for errors that are known not to occur.

In Section IV, we discussed two methods of implementing the exception handling mechanism, the branch table method and the handler table method. Both methods process normal returns as fast as possible; the branch table method also processes exceptions as fast as possible, while the handler table method is somewhat slower, but more space efficient. We also discussed the integration of the mechanism in debugging and production environments. The mechanism is defined to communicate information that can be used by *programs*, but this does not preclude an implementation that produces additional information for use by *programmers*.

In Section V, we discussed the expressive power of our exception handling model. We described two examples commonly put forward to justify the resumption model and discussed how they could be programmed in the termination model. The termination model solutions were inferior to the resumption model solutions. However, we believe that the examples under discussion occur very rarely, so a mechanism like the resumption model, which eases their programming at the cost of extra complexity, is not justified.

The CLU exception handling mechanism has been implemented by the handler table method. We have used the mechanism in writing many CLU programs (for example, most of the CLU compiler is written in CLU). We are convinced that our programs are better structured than they would be in the absence of the mechanism. Furthermore, we have not encountered any situations where a more powerful exception handling mechanism (e.g., resumption) was desired. Thus, our experience so far supports our belief that the mechanism is a good compromise between expressive power and simplicity. However, we have not written programs that attempt to handle the problem of resource constraints, a situation where resumption is most likely to be needed. Further experimentation is needed to reach a final conclusion on the wisdom of our choices.

Acknowledgment

The design of our exception handling mechanism was the work of the CLU design team, including R. Atkinson, T. Bloom, E. Moss, C. Schaffert, and R. Scheifler. This paper was improved by the comments of the referees and many others.

---

[6]Each procedure would have to be bound to the environment in which reorganization should be done. Since CLU procedures do not have free variables, the storage pool would have to maintain these environment objects also.

REFERENCES

[1] G. V. Bochmann, "Multiple exits from a loop without the GOTO," *Commun. Ass. Comput. Mach.*, vol. 16, pp. 443–444, July 1973.

[2] J. B. Goodenough, "Exception handling: Issues and a proposed notation," *Commun. Ass. Comput. Mach.*, vol. 18, pp. 683–696, Dec. 1975.

[3] R. Levin, "Program structures for exceptional condition handling," Ph.D. dissertation, Dep. Comput. Sci., Carnegie-Mellon Univ., Pittsburgh, PA, June 1977.

[4] B. Liskov, A. Snyder, R. Atkinson, and C. Schaffert, "Abstraction mechanisms in CLU," *Commun. Ass. Comput. Mach.*, vol. 20, pp. 564–576, Aug. 1977.

[5] *Proc. ACM Conf. on Language Design for Reliable Software, SIGPLAN Notices*, vol. 12, Mar. 1977.

[6] J. G. Mitchell, W. Maybury, and R. Sweet, "Mesa language manual," Xerox Res. Cent., Palo Alto, CA, Rep. CSL-78-1, Feb. 1978.

[7] P. M. Melliar-Smith and B. Randell, "Software reliability: The role of programmed exception handling," in *Proc. ACM Conf. on Language Design for Reliable Software, SIGPLAN Notices*, vol. 12, pp. 95–100, Mar. 1977.

[8] B. Randell, "System structure for software fault tolerance," *IEEE Trans. Software Eng.*, vol. SE-1, pp. 220–232, June 1975.

[9] C. T. Zahn, Jr., "A control statement for natural top-down structured programming," *Programming Symposium, Lecture Notes in Computer Science*, vol. 19, B. Robinet, Ed. New York: Springer-Verlag, 1974, pp. 170–180.

Barbara H. Liskov received the B.A. degree in mathematics from the University of California, Berkeley, and the M.S. and Ph.D. degrees in computer science from Stanford University, Stanford, CA.

From 1968 to 1972, she was associated with the Mitre Corporation, Bedford, MA, where she participated in the design and implementation of the Venus Machine and the Venus Operating System. She is presently Associate Professor of Electrical Engineering and Computer Science at the Massachusetts Institute of Technology, Cambridge. Her research interests include programming methodology, distributed systems, and the design of languages and systems to support structured programming.

Alan Snyder received the S.B., S.M., and Ph.D. degrees in computer science from the Massachusetts Institute of Technology, Cambridge.

He is currently a member of the Technical Staff in the Computer Research Laboratory at Hewlett-Packard Laboratories, Palo Alto, CA, working primarily in the area of integrated circuit design automation. His other interests include programming languages and machine architecture.

Dr. Snyder is a member of the Association for Computing Machinery.

NOTES ON THE DESIGN OF EUCLID*

G. J. POPEK, J. J. HORNING, B. W. LAMPSON, J. G. MITCHELL AND R. L. LONDON

Euclid is a language for writing system programs that are to be verified. We believe that verification and reliability are closely related, because if it is hard to reason about programs using a language feature, it will be difficult to write programs that use it properly. This paper discusses a number of issues in the design of Euclid, including such topics as the scope of names, aliasing, modules, type-checking, and the confinement of machine dependencies; it gives some of the reasons for our expectation that programming in Euclid will be more reliable (and will produce more reliable programs) than programming in Pascal, on which Euclid is based.

Key Words and Phrases: Euclid, verification, systems programming language, reliability, Pascal, aliasing, data encapsulation, parameterized types, visibility of names, machine dependencies, legality assertions, storage allocation.

CR Categories: 4.12, 4.2, 4.34, 5.24

Introduction

Euclid is a programming language evolved from Pascal [Wirth 1971] by a series of changes intended to make it more suitable for verification and for system programming. We expect many of these changes to improve the reliability of the programming process, firstly by enlarging the class of errors that can be detected by the compiler, and secondly by making explicit in the program text more of the information needed for understanding and maintenance. In addition, we expect that effort expended in program verification will directly improve program reliability. Although Euclid is intended for a rather restricted class of applications, much of what we have done could surely be extended to languages designed for more general purposes.

Like all designs, Euclid represents a compromise among conflicting goals, reflecting the skills, knowledge, and tastes (i.e., prejudices) of its designers. Euclid was conceived as an attempt to integrate into a practical language the results of several recent developments in programming methodology and program verification. As Hoare [1973] has pointed out, it is considerably more difficult to design a good language than it is to select one's favorite set of good language features or to propose new ones. A language is more than the sum of its parts, and the interactions among its features are often more important than any feature considered separately. Thus this paper does not present many new language features. Rather, it discusses several aspects of our design that, taken together, should improve the reliability of programming in Euclid.

We believe that the goals of reliability, understandability, and verifiability are mutually reinforcing. We never consciously sacrificed one of these in Euclid to achieve another. We had a tangible measure only for the third (namely, our ability to write reasonable proof rules [London et al. 1977]), so we frequently used it as the touchstone for all three. Much of this paper is devoted to decisions motivated by the problems of verification.

Another important goal of Euclid, the construction of acceptably efficient system programs, did not seem attainable without some sacrifices in the preceeding three goals. Much of the language design effort was expended in finding ways to allow the precise control of machine resources that seemed to be necessary, while narrowly confining the attendant losses of reliability, understandability, and verifiability. These aspects of the language are discussed in more detail by [Barnard and Elliott 1977]. The focus here is on features that *contribute* to reliability.

Goals, History, And Relation To Pascal

The chairman originally charged the committee as follows: "Let me outline our charter as I understand it. We are being asked to make *minimal* changes and extensions to Pascal in order to make the resulting language one that would be suitable for systems programming while retaining those characteristics of the language that are attractive for good programming style and verification. Because it is highly desirable that the language and appropriate compilers be available in a short time, the language definition effort is to be quite limited: only a month or two in duration. Therefore, we should not attempt to design a significantly different language, for that, while highly desirable, is a research project in itself. Instead, we should aim at a 'good' result, rather than the superb." [Popek 1976] We defer to the Conclusions a discussion of our current feelings about these goals and how well we have met them.

The design of Euclid took place at four two-day meetings of the authors in 1976, supplemented by a great deal of individual effort and uncounted Arpanet messages. Almost all of the basic changes to Pascal were agreed upon during the first meeting; most of the effort since then has been devoted to smoothing out unanticipated interactions among the changes and to developing a suitable exposition of the language. Three versions of the Euclid Report have been widely circulated for comment and criticism; the most recent appeared in the February 1977 *Sigplan Notices* [Lampson et al. 1977]. Proof rules are currently being prepared for publication [London et al. 1977].

*Reprinted from *ACM Sigplan Notices*, 12, 3, 1977, 11-19, copyright 1977.

The System Development Corporation is currently implementing Euclid [Lauer 1977]. Since the implementation is incomplete and no sizable Euclid programs have been written, our expectations are still untested. Further experience may dictate changes in the language.

We developed Euclid by modifying Pascal only where we saw "sufficient reason." We see it as a (perhaps eccentric) step along one of the main lines of current programming language development: transferring more and more of the work of producing a correct program, and verifying that it is consistent with its specification, from the programmer and the verifier (human or mechanical) to the language and its compiler.

Our changes to Pascal generally took the form of restrictions, which allow stronger statements about the properties of programs to be based on the rather superficial, but quite reliable, analysis that the compiler can perform. In some cases, we introduced new constructions whose meaning could be explained by expanding them in terms of existing Pascal constructions. These were not merely "syntactic sugaring": we had to introduce them, rather than leaving the expansion to the programmer, because the expansion would have been forbidden by our restrictions. Because the new constructions were sufficiently restrictive in some other way, breaking our own restrictions in these controlled ways did not break the protections they offered.

The main differences between Euclid and Pascal are

Visibility of names. Euclid provides explicit control over the visibility of names by requiring the program to list all the names imported into a routine (i.e., procedure or function) or module body, or exported from a module. The imported names must be accessible in every scope in which the routine or module name is used.

Variables. Euclid guarantees that two names in the same scope can never refer to the same or overlapping variables. There is a single, uniform mechanism for binding a name to a variable in a procedure call, on block entry (replacing the Pascal *with* statement), or in a variant record discrimination.

Pointers. The avoidance of overlapping is extended to pointers by allowing dynamic variables to be partitioned into *collections*, and guaranteeing that two pointers into different collections can never point to overlapping variables.

Storage allocation. The program can control the allocation of storage for dynamic variables explicitly, in a way that narrowly confines knowledge about the allocation scheme used and opportunities for making type errors. It is also possible to declare that the dynamic variables in a collection should be reference-counted and automatically deallocated when no pointers to them remain.

Types. Type declarations are generalized to allow formal parameters, so that arrays can have bounds that are fixed only when they are allocated, and variant records can be handled in a type-safe manner. Records are generalized to include constant components.

Modules. A new type-constructor, *module*, provides a mechanism for packaging a collection of logically related declarations (including variables, constants, routines, and types) together with initialization and finalization components that are executed whenever instances of the type are created or destroyed. This provides some of the advantages of abstract data types.

Constants. Euclid defines a *constant* to be a literal or a name whose value is fixed throughout the scope in which it is declared, but not necessarily at compile time. A constant whose value is fixed at compile time (as in Pascal) is called a *manifest* constant.

For statements. The parameter of the for statement is a controlled constant in Euclid. A module can be used as a *generator* to enumerate a sequence of values for the controlled constant.

Loopholes. Features of the underlying machine can be accessed, and the type-checking can be overridden, in a controlled way. Except for these explicit loopholes, Euclid is designed to be type-safe.

Assertions. The syntax allows assertions to be supplied at convenient points to assist in verification and to provide useful documentation. Some assertions can be compiled into run-time checks to assist in the debugging of programs whose verification is incomplete.

Deletions. Several Pascal features have been omitted from Euclid: input-output, real numbers, multi-dimensional arrays, labels and go to's, and functions and procedures as parameters.

The only new features which can make it hard to convert a Euclid program into a valid Pascal program by straightforward rewriting are parameterized type declarations, storage allocation, finalization, and some of the loopholes.

The balance of this paper presents the motivations and consequences of several of the changes.

Verification And Legality

One of our fundamental assumptions is that (in principle) all Euclid programs are to be verified before use. That is, we expect formal proofs of the consistency between programs and their specifications. These proofs may be either manual or automatic; we expect similar considerations to apply in either case. We used the axiomatic method of [Hoare and Wirth 1973] for guidance.

Perhaps the most obvious consequence of this assumption is the provision within the language of syntactic means for including specifications and intermediate assertions. Routines are specified by pre- and post-assertions; modules, by a pre-assertion, an invariant, an abstraction function, and specifications for exported routines and types. In addition, assertions may be placed at any point in the flow of control. (Most verifiers require at least one such assertion to "cut" each loop.) Effort invested in writing such assertions should pay off in more understandable, better-structured programs, even before the verification process is begun.

The basic assertion language consists of the Boolean expressions of Euclid. Most verifiers will require somewhat richer languages, containing, for example, quantifiers, ghost variables, and specification routines. Rather than picking a particular form for this extended language, we decided that extended assertions would be bracketed as comments; each verifier may choose a private syntax, without affecting Euclid compilers. (Indeed, a program might be augmented with two distinct sets of assertions, intended for different verifiers.)

Most programs presented to verifiers are actually wrong; considerable time can be wasted looking for proofs of incorrect programs before discovering that debugging is still needed. This problem can be reduced (although not eliminated) by judicious testing, which is generally the most efficient way to demonstrate the presence of bugs. To assist in the testing process, any scope in Euclid can be prefixed by *checked*, which will cause the compilation of run-time checks for all *basic assertions* (Boolean expressions not enclosed in comment brackets) within the scope; this includes all *legality assertions*, which will be discussed later. If any assertion

evaluates to False when it is reached in the program, execution will be aborted with a suitable message.

Because we expect all Euclid programs to be verified, we have not made special provisions for exception handling [Melliar-Smith and Randell 1977][McClaren 1977]. Run-time software errors should not occur in verified programs (correctness is a compile-time property), and we know of no efficient general mechanisms by which software can recover from unanticipated failures of current hardware. *Anticipated* conditions can be dealt with using the normal constructs of the language; most proposals for providing special mechanisms for exception handling would add considerable complexity to the language [Goodenough 1975].

We have also been led to a somewhat unorthodox position on uninitialized variables and dangling pointers. We do not forbid these syntactically (cf. [Dijkstra 1976] for a rather elaborate proposal), nor, for reasons of efficiency, do we supply a default initialization (e.g., to "undefined"). Our reasoning is as follows: verification generally places stronger constraints on variables (pointers) than that they merely have valid values when they are used--they must have *suitable* values. However, if a program can be verified without reference to the initial value of a variable (current variable to which a pointer points), then *any* value (variable) is acceptable.

Relying so heavily on verification has an obvious pitfall: suppose that the formal language definition and the implementation don't agree. (Indeed, for Pascal, they do not.) We could then be in the embarrassing situation of having failures in programs that have formally been proved "correct" [Gerhart and Yelowitz 1976]. Aside from some omissions and known technical difficulties (e.g., [Ashcroft 1976]), the major discrepancies between the Pascal definition and implementation take the form of restrictions imposed by the definition, but not enforced by the implementation. For example, "The axioms and rules of inference...explicitly forbid the presence of certain 'side-effects' in the evaluation of functions and execution of statements. Thus programs which invoke such side-effects are, from a formal point of view, undefined. The absence of such side-effects can in principle be checked by a textual (compile-time) scan of the program. However, it is not obligatory for a Pascal implementation to make such checks." [Hoare and Wirth 1973, p.337]

In the design of Euclid, we have made a major effort to ensure that there are no gaps between what is required by the definition and what must be enforced by any implementation (and that such enforcement is a reasonable task). Gaps have been eliminated by a variety of means: removing features from the language, extending the formal definition, placing more definite requirements on the implementation, and finally, introducing *legality assertions* as messages from the compiler to the verifier about necessary checking.

There are many language-imposed restrictions that must be satisfied by every legal Euclid program. In addition to syntactic constraints, many of them (e.g., declaration of identifiers before use) are easily checked by the compiler, and it would be silly to ask the verifier to duplicate this effort. Others (e.g., type constraints) can usually be checked rather easily by the compiler, but may occasionally depend on dynamically generated values. Still others (e.g., array indices within bounds, arithmetic overflow) will usually depend on dynamic information, although the compiler can often use declared ranges or flow analysis to do partial checking. (For example, $i := i + 1$ will obviously never assign a value that is too small if i was previously in range.) Our philosophy is that the verifier should rely as much as possible on the checking done by the compiler. In fact, unless the compiler indicates differently, the verifier is entitled to assume that the program is completely legal. The compiler is to augment the program with a *legality assertion* (which the verifier is to prove) whenever it has not fully checked that some constraint is satisfied. Any program whose legality assertions can all be verified is a legal program, with well-defined semantics.

The compiler may produce legality assertions only for certain conditions specifically indicated in the Euclid Report. They always take the form of Boolean expressions, and are usually quite simple (e.g., $i < 10$, $i = j$, p **not**= C.nil). Note that legality is a more fundamental property than correctness, since (a) it is defined as consistency with the language specification, rather than consistency with a particular program specification (a program could be consistent with one specification, and inconsistent with another), and (b) a program that is illegal has no defined meaning, and hence cannot be said to be consistent with any specification. Also note that a particular program is not sometimes legal and sometimes illegal (e.g., depending on whether $i = j$ on some run): the verifier must show that the legality assertions are *valid* (always true).

Later sections of this paper discuss some of the non-obvious legality conditions of Euclid.

Names And Scopes

In "Algol-like" languages the rules connecting names (identifiers) to what they denote (e.g., variables) give rise to some subtle, but troublesome, problems for both programmers and verifiers. Some variables, for example those passed as variable parameters, may be accessible by more than one name. Thus, assignment to x may change y: we will call this *aliasing*. Access to a global variable can accidentally be lost in a scope by the interposition of a new declaration involving the same name (the "hole in scope" problem). Conversely, failure to declare a variable locally may result in a more global access than was intended. (Such problems are generally not detected by compilers.) The intimate connection between a variable's lifetime and its scope frequently forces variables to be declared outside the local scopes in which they are intended to be used. Finally, the automatic importation of all names in outer scopes into contained scopes, unless redeclared, tends to create large name spaces with correspondingly large opportunities for error. For more complete discussions of these problems, and some suggested solutions, see [Wulf and Shaw 1973] and [Gannon and Horning 1975].

Several Euclid features are intended to remove these problems; they are discussed here and in the following two sections. Unlike the designers of Gypsy [Ambler et al. 1977], we did not discard the Algol notion of nested scopes, which seems to us to be a natural representation of hierarchy, and a good first approximation to the necessary name control. Rather, we have chosen to strengthen it by a number of restrictions.

The first restriction requires the programmer to control the "flow" of names between levels of abstraction by means of an *import list*. Every *closed scope* (routine or module body) must be accompanied by such a list specifying those names accessible in the containing scope that are to be accessible within the closed scope, and, in the case of variables, whether the access is to be read-only or read-write. Other names are simply inaccessible. An *open scope* (e.g., an Algol-like block) may access any name accessible within the scope that contains it.

The control supplied by import lists allows us to place a further restriction: no name accessible in a scope may be redeclared in that scope. Such a restriction would probably be intolerable in Pascal, where a scope has no "protection" against unwanted names from the outside, but it seems sensible in Euclid. In fact, it is generally a programming error to redeclare an imported name. Undiagnosed holes in scopes would certainly cause problems for the reader and maintainer, and for the human verifier.

In practice, we found it desirable to relax slightly the requirement of explicit importation. We do not wish every routine that uses built-in types, such as **integer**, or routines, such as abs(x), to import them explicitly. Many programs will have user-defined types and routines that are almost as widely used. Therefore, we have provided an overriding mechanism: constant, routine, and type names may be declared *pervasive* in a scope, which means that they will be implicitly imported into all contained scopes (and hence may not be redeclared). The standard Euclid types are all pervasive: therefore, a program cannot override them.

Euclid prohibits "sneak access" to variables by means of procedure calls. The name of a closed scope may not be imported (or used) if the names that are imported into its body are not also imported (accessible) at the point of use. It is this restriction that simplifies the enforcement of a complete ban on side-effects in functions (and hence in expressions). Functions cannot have variable parameters or import variables. Although they may import and call procedures, they cannot change any nonlocal variables by doing so: thus, they behave like mathematical functions. The possibility of side-effects in functions and expressions complicates the verifier's task, and we believe that their use is rather error-prone. We are willing to sacrifice a few well-known programming tricks that rely on "benign" side-effects in order to simplify life for the readers, maintainers, and verifiers of programs, and to open up new optimization possibilities for the implementors of the language. Programs involving functions with side-effects can be rewritten to use procedures instead.

Import lists are intended to make the interface to each closed scope explicit. However, the list supplied by the programmer is incomplete (for the reader) in two respects: 1) only names are given, not complete declarations, and 2) pervasive names do not appear. The compiler is expected to complete the interface description from its symbol table. It must augment the listing with information from the declarations of the imported names, and the user-defined pervasive declarations for that scope. Requiring the programmer to supply this information (which is mere duplication) would invite error, for no identifiable gain.

Aliasing And Collections

The disadvantages of aliasing (for programmers, readers, verifiers and implementors) have been well-documented [Hoare 1973, 1975] [Fischer and LeBlanc 1977]. If assignment to x has the "side-effect" of changing the value of y, it is likely to cause surprise and difficulty all around. However, programmers and language designers have been reluctant to eliminate all features that can give rise to aliasing, e.g., passing parameters by reference, and pointer variables. In designing Euclid, we took a slightly different approach: we kept the language features, but banned aliasing. Essentially, we examined each feature that could give rise to aliases, and imposed the minimum restrictions necessary to prevent them. Every variable starts with a single name: if no aliases can be created, then, by induction, aliasing will not occur.

The case of variable parameters to procedures is typical, and easily generalized to import lists and binding lists. All of the actual **var** parameters in a call must be *nonoverlapping*. If the actual parameters are simple names ("entire variables"), this requirement merely means that they must all be distinct. However, we must also prohibit passing a structured variable and one of its components (e.g., A and $A(1)$). What about two components of the same variable? This is allowed if they are distinct (e.g., $A(1)$ and $A(2)$), and disallowed if they are the same (e.g., $A(1)$ and $A(1)$). Since subscripts may be expressions, it may be necessary to generate a legality assertion (e.g., I **not**= J in the case of $A(I)$ and $A(J)$) to guarantee their distinctness.

It may appear that arrays already violate our rule that assignment to one entire variable can never change another. After all, assignment to $A(I)$ may change $A(J)$. However, these are not entire variables. We adopt the view of [Hoare and Wirth 1973, p.345] that an "assignment to an array component" is actually an assignment to the containing array. Thus $A(1) := 1$ is an assignment to A, and can be expected to change $A(J)$ if $J = 1$.

Pointers appeared to pose a more difficult problem. Assignment to $p\uparrow$ (i.e., to the variable to which p refers) may change the value of $q\uparrow$ (if p and q happen to point to the same variable, i.e., if $p = q$), or may even change the value of x (if pointer variables are allowed to point at program variables). We avoided the latter problem by retaining Pascal's restriction that pointers may only point to dynamically generated (anonymous) variables. (This is enforced by not providing an "address of" operator or coercion.) The usual treatment of the former problem is to consider pointers as indices into "implicit arrays" (one for each type of dynamic variable), and dereferencing as subscripting [Luckham and Suzuki 1976, Wegbreit and Spitzen 1976]. Thus $p\uparrow$ is merely a shorthand for $C(p)$, where C denotes p's implicit array, and the proof rules for arrays can be carried over directly. In particular, assignment via a dereferenced pointer is considered to be an assignment to its implicit array. From the verifier's standpoint, the situation is slightly better than that for arrays, since the decision of whether two subscripts are equal may involve arbitrary arithmetic expressions, while the decision of whether two pointers are equal reduces to the question of whether they resulted from the same dynamic variable generation ("New" invocation).

We have not yet discussed dereferenced pointers as variable parameters. If $p\uparrow$ and $q\uparrow$ (really $C(p)$ and $C(q)$) are both passed, the nonoverlapping requirement demands p **not**= q. Passing both p and $p\uparrow$ (really p and $C(p)$) is not a problem unless the formal parameter corresponding to p is dereferenced, which can only happen if C is accessible (i.e., imported). But then there would be an overlap between $C(p)$ and C, which makes the call clearly illegal. Passing pointers themselves as parameters (like passing array indices) does not create aliasing problems, since dereferenced pointers (like subscripted arrays) are not entire variables; assignment to one of them is considered as assignment to its implicit array.

Although the solution in the previous paragraph is formally complete, it is unsatisfactory in practice. The minor difficulty is that Euclid provides no way of naming implicit arrays for purposes of importation. The major problem is that it is too restrictive. It prohibits passing a dereferenced pointer as a variable parameter to any procedure that is allowed to dereference pointers to variables of the same type (i.e., that imports the implicit array for that type). We have solved both these problems by introducing the notion of *collections*, which are explicit program variables that act like the "implicit arrays" indexed by pointers. Each pointer is limited to a single collection, and $p\uparrow$ is still an acceptable shorthand for $C(p)$, where C is now the collection name. $p\uparrow$ is only allowed where C is accessible. Note that this makes it possible to pass pointers as parameters to procedures that are not allowed to dereference them, although they can copy them.

We allow any number of collections to have elements of the same type, with no more difficulty than arises from multiple arrays of the same type. Thus, the programmer can partition his dynamic variables and pointers into separate collections to indicate some of his knowledge about how they will be used; the verifier is assured that pointers in different collections can never point to overlapping variables. The astute reader will have noted that we have returned to the "class variables" that were in the original Pascal, but dropped in the revised version.

Collections also provide convenient units for storage management. We have chosen to associate with each

collection both the decision of whether to reference-count, and the selection of the (system- or user-supplied) storage management module (called a *zone*) to provide the space.

One consequence of our complete elimination of aliasing is that "value-result" and "reference" are completely equivalent implementation mechanisms for variable parameters, and a compiler is free to choose between them strictly on the basis of efficiency.

Modules

Since the introduction of "classes" by Simula 67 [Dahl et al. 1968], several programming languages have introduced mechanisms for "data encapsulation" or "information hiding" [Parnas 1971]. A survey of desirable properties of such mechanisms is given in [Horning 1976]. For Euclid, we chose something less powerful than "classes," "forms" [Shaw et al. 1977], or "clusters" [Liskov et al. 1977]. Our *modules* are closely akin to, but somewhat more complex than, the "modules" of Modula [Wirth 1977]. Adjusting the details of modules satisfactorily has been more difficult than expected. Perhaps this is because we still have an imperfect understanding, but it may also be because we violated our usual practice, and started from implementation considerations, rather than from verification issues.

The basic idea is that a module should "package up" a data structure and a related set of routines for its manipulation, and should hide its internal details from the outside world. We originally viewed it as a sort of glorified record, with some extra components (routines, types, initialization, finalization) and some control over the external visibility of its names (an export list). Like *record*, *module* is a type constructor, and a module type can be used to create many instances; this is the major source of differences between Euclid and Modula "modules."

Modules provide natural units for program construction. In fact, Euclid programs take the form of modules, rather than procedures; this is particularly appropriate when the program is to provide a number of entry points sharing a common data base that is to survive the various invocations (e.g., an operating system kernel). The "protection" provided by control over exported names serves as a useful first step towards abstract data types [Sigplan 1976]. In addition, they are used within the language in two places where it seemed important to effect a separation of concerns. The first is in iteration, where the knowledge of *how* to enumerate the elements of some data type should generally be associated with the type (module), rather than with each loop that needs such an enumeration. The problem, and its solution using *generators* is discussed in more detail in [Shaw et al. 1977]. We have chosen to use a simplification of the Alphard solution that seems powerful enough for the most common cases.

Similarly, the issues of *how* to allocate storage are quite separable from the uses to which that storage is put. We have chosen to isolate that knowledge in *zones*, which are (system- or user-defined) modules solely concerned with allocating and deallocating storage and ensuring that storage allocations never overlap. A zone deals with blocks of "raw storage"; it is the compiler's responsibility to ensure that its procedures are invoked at proper times, with correct parameters, and that the storage it allocates is properly initialized for its intended use, and that there is no type confusion or variable overlap outside the zone.

Types

One of the principal contributions of Pascal was its development of the notion of data types. Despite certain deficiencies [Habermann 1973], we find it more satisfactory than competitive approaches (e.g., the *modes* of Algol 68 [van

Wijngaarden et al. 1976]). Pascal's types provide a flexible and convenient set of efficient data structuring mechanisms, and are useful conceptual tools for partitioning and organizing data within programs. In a type-rich language, such as Pascal, type-checking serves as a very effective compile-time error screen [Gannon and Horning 1975] [Gannon 1977].

It is a major undertaking to develop a new approach to data types that is both consistent and useful, and we did not attempt to do so within Euclid. Nevertheless, we felt compelled to try some small changes in the directions of safety and flexibility. Even these were difficult to get right.

Almost all type-checking in Pascal can be done at compile-time; the major exceptions are due to variant records and to the incomplete specification of formal parameters that are functions and procedures [Fischer and LeBlanc 1977]. The former are not a problem in Euclid, since such parameters are disallowed, but Euclid retains variant records. The problems in Pascal arise from aliasing (which we have already dealt with), from the treatment of the *tag* (which selects the current variant) as an ordinary, assignable field of a variant record, and from the accessibility of variant field selectors even when they do not apply to the current variant.

In Pascal, uncontrolled assignment to the tag field can change the current variant without ensuring that the corresponding fields contain values of appropriate types. We have eliminated this possibility in Euclid by making the tag a constant component of a variant record, and hence not assignable. If a variable is of variant record type, its current variant can only be changed by assignment of a record of one of the other variant record types; this assignment supplies a complete set of fields appropriate to that variant.

Variant field selectors are only accessible within the alternatives of a *discriminating case* statement, where the alternative is selected by the current tag. In the case statement, a local name is provided for the variant record (either as a constant or a variable); within any alternative, that name has the (nonvariant) type selected by the corresponding tag value, and all field selectors of that type are accessible. If the local name is bound to a variant record variable, the nonaliasing rule makes its more global name unusable in the scope; hence, there is no danger that its type may be changed within the scope (e.g., by calling a procedure that does so surreptitiously). If the local name is a constant, the variable may still be changed, but this will not affect the (discriminated) constant in any way, so access to its fields remains safe. Thus, variant records cannot be used to circumvent Euclid's type-checking. As a minor benefit, we avoid the need for the Pascal restriction that the same field names may not be used in separate variants.

Pascal treats (sub)ranges as types, and requires that all bounds be known at compile-time (i.e., be manifest constants). This is somewhat irksome for array bounds, and almost intolerable for routines that take array parameters. However, it allows a number of simplifications throughout the language, compiler, and verification system. We have allowed only a minor relaxation: bounds must still be constants, but they need not be manifest. In particular, a constant formal parameter of a routine may be used to specify a bound of another formal parameter. This will require verification that the bounds for the latter parameter are correct in all calls to the procedure since they are not fixed at compile time. We expect this usage to be common, and have supplied a shorthand; if a bound is specified as *parameter*, an additional (implicit) actual parameter containing the actual bound will be supplied automatically for each call.

A type declaration in Pascal provides a shorthand for a single type. In Euclid, a type declaration may have formal parameters. A parameterized declaration represents a set of

types, one of which is specified (by supplying actual parameters for all the formals) each time the type is referenced (e.g., to declare a variable). This allows the relationships among similar types to be made explicit in the program, and makes it easier for the program to exploit such relationships. Variant record definitions will usually appear within parameterized type declarations, with the tag being one of the formal parameters. Each particular value supplied as the corresponding actual parameter in a reference to such a type will select a particular alternative, i.e., will yield a nonvariant record. This is a useful feature (not available in Pascal), but it is often desirable to defer the choice of a variant. This can be done by using the special actual parameter *any*, which specifies that the type contains all values of the types corresponding to any choice for the tag, i.e., that the variant may be changed dynamically, by assignment.

Collections of variant records allow another degree of freedom. It is possible to select a variant at the time a dynamic variable is allocated, and to disallow any changes of variant by assignment. This is done by using the special actual parameter *unknown* in defining the object type of a collection. For each such *unknown* parameter, every call of New must supply an additional actual parameter that specifies the variant of the new dynamic variable. Both *any* and *unknown* specifications will lead to the use of discriminating case statements for access to the variant parts of records.

The *Pascal Report* is not very explicit about when two types are "the same," and it is not always clear what type-checking is allowed (required). E.g., 1..10 and 2..11 define subrange types that (in some sense) are clearly different. But what is the type of 2, which could be assigned to a variable of either type? Are we to assume that there are some subtle "coercions" going on (as is hinted in [Hoare and Wirth 1973])? Another problem: If **type** *Miles* = 1..10, and **type** *Hours* = 1..10, are *Miles* and *Hours* "the same" type or not? If the answer is "yes," the programmer has not gotten any protection by using different type names for conceptually different types; if it is "no," how do we justify using the same addition operator for both, and how can we write a routine that would accept either as a parameter? Should we go to the Algol 68 extreme of treating as "the same" all types that have the same representation, completely ignoring programmer-supplied type names? (See [Habermann 1973] for further examples of the difficulty of reasoning strictly from the hints given in [Wirth 1971] and [Hoare and Wirth 1973].)

We decided that the rules for type-checking must be quite explicit in Euclid (i.e., we would rather be wrong than vague in our answers to these questions). We have devoted considerable effort to spelling them out clearly. Firstly, we separately specified two kinds of checking: in a binding (e.g., formal/actual correspondence for a variable parameter) the two types must be *the same* (defined below); in other contexts (e.g., assignment, constant definition, constant parameter, operands of operators) a value of one type must be *compatible* with another type (e.g., within the proper subrange). Secondly, we never associate a subrange type with a value, rather the value gets the containing type (e.g., integer). Thirdly (after toying with having *synonym* and *nonsynonym* type declarations), we decided not to treat type declarations as creating new types; a type name is *the same* as its definition. Fourthly, every module definition creates an *opaque* type (i.e., one whose internal structure is not visible); types exported from modules are also opaque. Opaque types are only *the same* if they are defined by the same piece of text (i.e., even identical definitions define distinct types); exported types are *the same* only if exported (with the same name) from the same instance of the module type. Finally, two references to a parameterized type are *the same* only if their actual parameters are equal (this may cause the generation of legality assertions).

Containment Of Machine Dependencies

Euclid contains most of the "escape hatches" (providing direct access to machine features) typical of system implementation languages [Mohll 1975]. There is provision for machine-code routine bodies, for placing variables at fixed addresses, for specifying the internal representation of a record, and for explicitly overriding type-checking. Many of these features are difficult to define formally, and all of them pose problems for verification. We have not solved most of these problems; we have merely provided a mechanism for containing their effects.

Some modules may be explicitly declared to be machine-dependent; these are the only modules that are allowed to contain the various machine-dependencies mentioned above, or to contain machine-dependent modules. Machine-dependent modules serve to textually isolate these features, and to encapsulate their use; they may be imported into modules that are not machine-dependent (and rely only on the specifications, not the implementations of the imported modules). This does not simplify the process of verifying that machine-dependent modules actually do meet their specifications; it merely means that the verification of all other modules can proceed in a machine-independent manner.

We expect machine-dependent modules to be used for two different purposes: to provide efficient machine-dependent implementations for packages whose specification is machine-independent (e.g., string manipulation, high-level I/O), and to provide controlled access to machine features (e.g., channels, clocks, page tables). Programs using only the former should be quite portable, requiring changes to (and reverification of) only the bodies of the machine-dependent modules. However, in the latter case, machine-dependencies in the module specifications themselves will work against portability (which is not required for many of Euclid's intended applications, such as operating system kernels).

Conclusions

Even though Euclid does not represent a dramatic advance in the state of the art, we have accomplished several things relevant to reliability. Firstly, we have designed a useful language (Euclid minus machine-dependent modules), all of whose features are (in principle) verifiable in their full generality by existing techniques. Secondly, we have demonstrated that it is possible to completely eliminate aliasing in a practical programming language. Thirdly, we have made variant records completely type-safe.

By and large, the changes that we made to Pascal could be justified without reference to verification, and would be useful even in situations where verification is not a formal requirement. However, it is unlikely that many of them would have been made had verification not been one of our primary concerns. Furthermore, we seem to have been somewhat more successful at "getting it right the first time" when we started from a verification issue (e.g., nonaliasing, collections) than when we "worked back" from the implementation (e.g., modules, zones). Perhaps this is because the construction of proof rules is a useful discipline that makes it necessary to be very explicit about the interactions of language features.

This paper has not been able to convey the extent to which various design decisions were interdependent. None of them was made in isolation, and some of them caused ripples throughout the language. We feel good about the decision to make the control of visibility explicit, for example, because it supported so many of the other changes we made. The decisions to totally ban side effects in functions was triggered by an observation concerning legality assertions. It was the introduction of generators that reconciled some of us to the elimination of functions and procedures as parameters.

We are all reasonably happy with the way that Euclid has turned out. However, it is appropriate to ask how well it meets our original goals. Among other things, we were asked to "make *minimal* changes and extensions to Pascal," and our effort was to be "quite limited: only a month or two in duration." Even though we did not satisfy either goal, in retrospect it seems that both were quite necessary for whatever success we have had. It has taken us a year to carefully work through and document the interactions of the small set of changes to Pascal that we agreed to in the first two days; had we been more ambitious at the start, we would still be discovering surprising implications of "innocuous" changes.

It is hard to feel guilty about making more than minimal changes to the form of Pascal. As we have stressed in this paper, the conceptual changes have been relatively small; however, we expect them to lead to significantly different programming styles. Euclid is a language with its own "flavor" and style. It would be as wrong to try to cast it as "pidgin Pascal" as it would have been to cast Pascal as "pidgin Algol."

Finally, a few comments on language design by committee: It is not easy, under the best of circumstances. It is clear that any one of us could have designed a new language by himself with less effort than he expended on Euclid; it is equally clear that each of those languages would have contained hidden problems or limitations that we managed to expose and eliminate in the process of designing Euclid. The substantial variety in our backgrounds was very helpful in the design process, although it could have been a major stumbling block had we not started with a highly compatible set of views on what needed to be done. Surprisingly, our geographical distribution, which could have been expected to be an obstacle to close cooperation, was turned into an asset by the Arpanet. It made rapid communication convenient, and encouraged both five-way interaction on all issues and the maintenance of a complete record of all "discussions."

We surprised ourselves by spending much more time on "exposition" (writing the defining report and proof rules) than we spent on "language design." The latter would have been useless without the former, and it could be argued that the design will not be complete until we are satisfied with the exposition, but we somehow hadn't planned to spend so much time explaining. Conceptual unity in a report cannot be obtained by having everyone write a few sections; we found no substitute for having a single person (Butler Lampson) write and edit the entire defining document, with the advice and consent of the rest.

Acknowledgements

Obviously, we are greatly indebted to Wirth, whose Pascal language formed the principal basis of our work. We have also relied heavily on Hoare's work in the areas of programming language design, axiomatic methods, and program verification. We have consciously borrowed ideas from most of the languages represented at this conference, and have probably been influenced by many other languages and suggestions for language features. We have benefitted from comments and criticisms on the various drafts of the *Euclid Report* that have been provided by colleagues too numerous to mention here. Lauer and the other implementors have been particularly helpful in pointing out inadequacies of our design and exposition. Guttag, as an author of the proof rules, has similarly helped us. Our work has been significantly aided by the Arpanet, which allowed us to maintain effective and rapid communication in stating and resolving problems (and in maintaining a permanent record of such "discussions"), despite the wide geographical distribution of the authors. Lastly, both the *Euclid Report* and this paper owe much to Gail Pilkington's expert use of a computer editing and formatting system; the visual quality of both documents compelled us to work hard on their contents

so that the beauty would be more than ink deep.

References

[Ambler et al. 1977] A. L. Ambler et al., "Gypsy: A Language for Specification and Implementation of Verifiable Programs," in [LDRS 1977].

[Ashcroft 1976] E. A. Ashcroft, M. Clint, and C. A. R. Hoare, "Remarks on 'Program Proving: Jumps and Functions' by M. Clint and C. A. R. Hoare," *Acta Informatica* 6, pp. 317-318.

[Barnard and Elliott 1977] D. Barnard and D. Elliott (eds.), "Notes on Euclid," University of Toronto, Computer Systems Research Group Technical Report.

[Dahl et al. 1968] O.-J. Dahl et al., *The Simula 67 Common Base Language*, Norwegian Computer Center, Oslo.

[Dijkstra 1976] E. W. Dijkstra, *A Discipline of Programming*, Prentice-Hall.

[Fischer and LeBlanc 1977] C. N. Fischer and R. J. LeBlanc, "Efficient Implementation and Optimization of Run-Time Checking in Pascal," in [LDRS 1977].

[Gannon and Horning 1975] J. D. Gannon and J. J. Horning, "Language Design for Programming Reliability," *IEEE Transactions on Software Engineering* SE-1, 2, pp. 179-191.

[Gannon 1977] J. D. Gannon, "An Experimental Evaluation of the Effect of Data Types on Programming Reliability," in [LDRS 1977].

[Gerhart and Yelowitz 1976] S. L. Gerhart and L. Yelowitz, "Observations of Fallibility in Applications of Modern Programming Methodologies," *IEEE Transactions on Software Engineering* SE-2, 3, pp. 195-207.

[Goodenough 1975] J. B. Goodenough, "Exception Handling: Issues and a Proposed Notation," *Communications of the ACM*, 18, 12, pp. 683-696.

[Habermann 1973] A. N. Habermann, "Critical Comments on the Programming Language Pascal," *Acta Informatica* 3, pp. 47-57.

[Hoare 1973] C. A. R. Hoare, "Hints on Programming Language Design," *ACM Symposium on the Principles of Programming Languages*, Boston, pp. 1-30. (Also published as Stanford Computer Science Technical Report STAN-CS-73-403.)

[Hoare and Wirth 1973] C. A. R. Hoare and N. Wirth, "An Axiomatic Definition of the Programming Language PASCAL," *Acta Informatica* 2, pp. 335-355.

[Hoare 1975] C. A. R. Hoare, "Data Reliability," 1975 International Conference on Reliable Software, Los Angeles, pp. 528-533. (*SIGPLAN Notices* 10, 6)

[Horning 1976] J. J. Horning, "Some Desirable Properties of Data Abstraction Facilities," *SIGPLAN Notices* 11, 2.

[Lampson et al. 1977] B. W. Lampson et al., "Report on the Programming Language Euclid," *SIGPLAN Notices* 12, 2.

[Lauer 1977] Further information may be obtained from H. C. Lauer, System Development Corporation, 2500 Colorado Avenue, Santa Monica, California.

[LDRS 1977] "Proceedings of a Conference on Language Design for Reliable Software," *SIGPLAN Notices* 12, 3.

[Liskov et al. 1977] B. Liskov, et al., "Abstraction Mechanisms in CLU," in [LDRS 1977].

[London et al. 1977] R. L. London et al., "Proof Rules for the Programming Language Euclid," in preparation.

[Luckham and Suzuki 1976] D. Luckham and N. Suzuki, "Automatic Program Verification V: Verification-Oriented Proof Rules for Arrays, Records and Pointers," Stanford AI Lab Memo AIM-278, Stanford Computer Science Technical Report STAN-CS-76-549.

[McLaren 1977] M. D. McLaren, "Exception Handling in PL/I," in [LDRS 1977].

[Melliar-Smith and Randell 1977] P. M. Melliar-Smith and B. Randell, "Software Reliability: The Role of Programmed Exception Handling," in [LDRS 1977].

[Mohll 1975] W. L. van der Poel and L. Maarssen (eds.), *Machine Oriented Higher Level Languages*, North-Holland/American Elsevier.

[Parnas 1971] D. L. Parnas, "Information Distribution Aspects of Design Methodology," *Proceedings of IFIP Congress 71*, North-Holland, pp. 339-344.

[Popek 1976] G. J. Popek, Arpanet message, 6 Jan. 1976.

[Shaw et al. 1977] M. Shaw et al., "Abstraction and Verification in Alphard: Defining and Specifying Iteration and Generators," in [LDRS 1977].

[Sigplan 1976] "Proceedings of Conference on Data: Abstraction, Definition, and Structure," *SIGPLAN Notices*, 11, 2.

[Wegbreit and Spitzen 1976] B. Wegbreit and J. Spitzen, Proving Properties of Complex Data Structures, *Journal of the ACM*, 23, 2 pp. 389-396.

[van Wijngaarden et al. 1976] A. van Wijngaarden (ed.) et al., *Revised Report on the Algorithmic Language ALGOL 68*, Springer-Verlag, Berlin, New York.

[Wirth 1971] N. Wirth, "The Programming Language Pascal," *Acta Informatica* 1, pp. 35-63.

[Wirth 1977] N. Wirth, "Towards a Discipline of Real-Time Programming," in [LDRS 1977].

[Wulf et al. 1977] W. A. Wulf, M. Shaw, and R. L. London, "An Introduction to the Construction and Verification of Alphard Programs," *IEEE Transactions on Software Engineering* SE-2, 4, pp. 253-265.

[Wulf and Shaw 1973] W. A. Wulf and M. Shaw, "Global Variables Considered Harmful," *SIGPLAN Notices* 8, 2, pp. 28-34.

SECTION 5

PROGRAMMING LANGUAGES AND CONCURRENCY

THE PROGRAMMING LANGUAGE
CONCURRENT PASCAL BY P. BRINCH-HANSEN

MODULA: A LANGUAGE FOR MODULAR
MULTIPROGRAMMING BY N. WIRTH

COMMUNICATING SEQUENTIAL PROCESSES
BY C. A. R. HOARE

INTRODUCTION

PROGRAMMING LANGUAGES AND CONCURRENCY

Concurrent execution of processes is a problem that has been with us for as long as people have been writing operating systems. It also appears naturally with applications such as process control or discrete event simulation. But despite these rather important applications not many languages have provided explicitly for describing concurrent execution. Perhaps PL/1 was the first with multitasking followed by ALGOL 68's parallel and collateral clauses. This chapter is devoted to newer languages which have been designed with concurrency in mind.

Concurrent Pascal is an effort to adjoin to an already successful language the features necessary to achieve the description of concurrency. Three new kinds of entities, processes, monitors and classes, have been added to the language. Classes are a form of data abstraction first introduced in SIMULA and therefore serves to augment the material in the previous section as well as in this section. The essential contribution of Concurrent Pascal is that it shows how to exploit the monitor concept for the description of parallel programs. A *monitor* defines a shared data structure and all the operations which can be performed on it. These operations are synchronized by the monitor, so that only one person has access at any given time. If this person requests a resource which is busy, the request is suspended and another person is granted access rights. For example in this paper a disk buffer is defined as a monitor type. There are two operations called *send* and *receive* and an initialization segment which sets the disk to empty. The Concurrent Pascal system has been running on a PDP-11 for several years and is available from the author, Per Brinch-Hansen at USC.

The second language is MODULA, developed by Niklaus Wirth. Apparently even he felt that an entirely new language would be preferable to Pascal, though many of Pascal's features can be found there. The basic structuring unit in MODULA is the module. The module is used both as a form of abstract data type and for concurrent execution of processes. Both MODULA and Concurrent Pascal rely upon the monitor concept to provide mutual exclusion and synchronization of processes. One important distinction between Concurrent Pascal and MODULA is the extent to which the module supports data abstraction. As with the CLU cluster,

the MODULA module represents a closed scope. It shields the data representation. However, contrary to clusters, the module is not a type constructor. It uses a define-list for exporting names and a use-list for importing names. Exported variables are read-only, though this has been changed in subsequent implementations of the language. The facilities which are added for multiprogramming include processes, interface modules and signals. A process is a procedure which may be executed concurrently with other procedures. Signals are used for synchronization. They are declared like variables and sent to processes which are waiting. The signals in MODULA correspond to the queue in Concurrent Pascal. Since processes can cooperate via common variables there is a need for mutual exclusion of critical sections. This is handled by the interface modules which correspond to Brinch-Hansen's use of monitors. However in contrast to a monitor an interface module allows more than one process to be in its critical section as long as all but one are either waiting or sending a signal.

The last paper does not actually present an implemented language, but instead concentrates on some language features for describing concurrency. In contrast to the previous languages, the concurrency in Communicating Sequential Processes (CSP), is based upon the concept of message passing. Message passing as a paradigm for concurrency makes sense in the context of a distributed computer system where many processors are connected via communication links. Hoare introduces a generalized form of input and output as a means for communicating between concurrent processes. He also adapts the so-called guarded commands, first introduced by E. Dijkstra, for determining which of several alternatives will be executed. This mechanism is a means for controlling nondeterminancy in the language. A guarded command is executed if and only if the execution of the guard condition is true. If more than one guard is simultaneously true, then the decision as to which one is selected is made at random. As an example of a CSP program consider the following rather simple routine:

$$*[\, n : integer;\ X\ ?\ insert(n) \rightarrow INSERT\, |$$

$$n{:}integer;\ X\ ?\ has(n) \rightarrow SEARCH;\ X\ !\ (\, i < size)]$$

We see this program is enclosed in square brackets and the left bracket is preceded by an asterisk. The brackets are scope delimiters and the asterisk stands for repetition. It means that the program contained within will be successively repeated until no conditions (or guards) are true. There are two alternatives contained within the brackets, separated by the vertical bar. Consider the first alternative. The variable *n* is declared. The question mark denotes that an input operation is expected from the process named X. If the input message is *insert(n)* then the first alternative can be chosen, whereas if the message is *has(n)* the second can be selected. If *insert* is selected then the program segment INSERT is invoked, which is not visible here but is contained within the article. If the request is *has*, then a call to SEARCH is made. SEARCH will look for an *i* such that $A(i) = n$. If i is less than size then the answer is true and this is output to X by virtue of the exclamation point. Otherwise the result of the comparison is false and that is output.

This paper is a carefully developed tutorial on the use of these primitives to express concurrency. Note that in this paper the author discusses the famous *dining philosophers* problem. This problem has become a standard one for testing the expressibility of any concurrency primitives.

THE PROGRAMMING LANGUAGE CONCURRENT PASCAL*

P. BRINCH-HANSEN

Abstract—The paper describes a new programming language for structured programming of computer operating systems. It extends the sequential programming language Pascal with concurrent programming tools called processes and monitors. Section I explains these concepts informally by means of pictures illustrating a hierarchical design of a simple spooling system. Section II uses the same example to introduce the language notation. The main contribution of Concurrent Pascal is to extend the monitor concept with an explicit hierarchy of access rights to shared data structures that can be stated in the program text and checked by a compiler.

Index Terms—Abstract data types, access rights, classes, concurrent processes, concurrent programming languages, hierarchical operating systems, monitors, scheduling, structured multiprogramming.

I. THE PURPOSE OF CONCURRENT PASCAL

A. Background

SINCE 1972 I have been working on a new programming language for structured programming of computer operating systems. This language is called Concurrent Pascal. It extends the sequential programming language Pascal with concurrent programming tools called processes and monitors [1]–[3].

This is an informal description of Concurrent Pascal. It uses examples, pictures, and words to bring out the creative aspects of new programming concepts without getting into their finer details. I plan to define these concepts precisely and introduce a notation for them in later papers. This form of presentation may be imprecise from a formal point of view, but is perhaps more effective from a human point of view.

B. Processes

We will study concurrent processes inside an operating system and look at one small problem only: how can large amounts of data be transmitted from one process to another by means of a buffer stored on a disk?

Fig. 1 shows this little system and its three components: a process that produces data, a process that consumes data, and a disk buffer that connects them.

The circles are *system components* and the arrows are the *access rights* of these components. They show that both processes can use the buffer (but they do not show that data flows from the producer to the consumer). This kind of picture is an *access graph*.

Manuscript received February 1, 1975. This project is supported by the National Science Foundation under Grant DCR74-17331.

The author is with the Department of Information Science, California Institute of Technology, Pasadena, Calif. 91125.

*Reprinted from *IEEE Transactions on Software Engineering*, June 1975, 199–207.

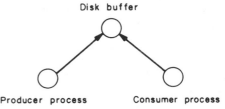

Fig. 1.   Process communication.

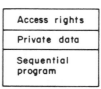

Fig. 2.   Process.

The next picture shows a process component in more detail (Fig. 2).

A *process* consists of a *private data* structure and a *sequential program* that can operate on the data. One process cannot operate on the private data of another process. But concurrent processes can share certain data structures (such as a disk buffer). The *access rights* of a process mention the shared data it can operate on.

C. Monitors

A disk buffer is a data structure shared by two concurrent processes. The details of how such a buffer is constructed are irrelevant to its users. All the processes need to know is that they can *send* and *receive* data through it. If they try to operate on the buffer in any other way it is probably either a programming mistake or an example of tricky programming. In both cases, one would like a compiler to detect such misuse of a shared data structure.

To make this possible, we must introduce a language construct that will enable a programmer to tell a compiler how a shared data structure can be used by processes. This kind of system component is called a monitor. A monitor can synchronize concurrent processes and transmit data between them. It can also control the order in which competing processes use shared, physical resources. Fig. 3 shows a monitor in detail.

A *monitor* defines a *shared data* structure and all the operations processes can perform on it. These synchronizing operations are called *monitor procedures*. A monitor also defines an *initial operation* that will be executed when its data structure is created.

Fig. 3. Monitor.

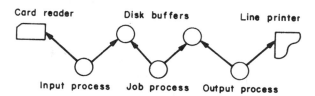

Fig. 4. Spooling system.

We can define a *disk buffer* as a monitor. Within this monitor there will be shared variables that define the location and length of the buffer on the disk. There will also be two monitor procedures, *send* and *receive*. The initial operation will make sure that the buffer starts as an empty one.

Processes cannot operate directly on shared data. They can only call monitor procedures that have access to shared data. A monitor procedure is executed as part of a calling process (just like any other procedure).

If concurrent processes simultaneously call monitor procedures that operate on the same shared data these procedures must be executed strictly one at a time. Otherwise, the results of monitor calls will be unpredictable. This means that the machine must be able to delay processes for short periods of time until it is their turn to execute monitor procedures. We will not be concerned about how this is done, but will just notice that a monitor procedure has *exclusive access* to shared data while it is being executed.

So the (virtual) machine on which concurrent programs run will handle *short-term scheduling* of simultaneous monitor calls. But the programmer must also be able to delay processes for longer periods of time if their requests for data and other resources cannot be satisfied immediately. If, for example, a process tries to receive data from an empty disk buffer it must be delayed until another process sends more data.

Concurrent Pascal includes a simple data type, called a *queue*, that can be used by monitor procedures to control *medium-term scheduling* of processes. A monitor can either *delay* a calling process in a queue or *continue* another process that is waiting in a queue. It is not important here to understand how these queues work except for the following essential rule: a process only has exclusive access to shared data as long as it continues to execute statements within a monitor procedure. As soon as a process is delayed in a queue it loses its exclusive access until another process calls the same monitor and wakes it up again. (Without this rule, it would be impossible for other processes to enter a monitor and let waiting processes continue their execution.)

Although the disk buffer example does not show this yet, monitor procedures should also be able to call procedures defined within other monitors. Otherwise, the language will not be very useful for hierarchical design. In the case of a disk buffer, one of these other monitors could perhaps define simple input/output operations on

the disk. So a monitor can also have *access rights* to other system components (see Fig. 3).

D. System Design

A process executes a sequential program—it is an active component. A monitor is just a collection of procedures that do nothing until they are called by processes—it is a passive component. But there are strong similarities between a process and a monitor: both define a data structure (private or shared) and the meaningful operations on it. The main difference between processes and monitors is the way they are scheduled for execution.

It seems natural therefore to regard processes and monitors as *abstract data types* defined in terms of the operations one can perform on them. If a compiler can check that these operations are the only ones carried out on the data structures, then we may be able to build very reliable, concurrent programs in which *controlled access* to data and physical resources is guaranteed before these programs are put into operation. We have then to some extent solved the *resource protection* problem in the cheapest possible manner (without hardware mechanisms and run time overhead).

So we will define processes and monitors as data types and make it possible to use several instances of the same component type in a system. We can, for example, use two disk buffers to build a *spooling system* with an input process, a job process, and an output process (Fig. 4). I will distinguish between definitions and instances of components by calling them *system types* and *system components*. Access graphs (such as Fig. 4) will always show system components (not system types).

Peripheral devices are considered to be monitors implemented in hardware. They can only be accessed by a single procedure *io* that delays the calling process until an input/output operation is completed. Interrupts are handled by the virtual machine on which processes run.

To make the programming language useful for stepwise system design it should permit the division of a system type, such as a disk buffer, into smaller system types. One of these other system types should give a disk buffer access to the disk. We will call this system type a *virtual disk*. It gives a disk buffer the illusion that it has its own private disk. A virtual disk hides the details of disk input/output from the rest of the system and makes the disk look like a data structure (an array of disk pages). The only operations on this data structure are *read* and *write* a page.

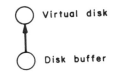

Virtual disk

Disk buffer

Fig. 5.   Buffer refinement.

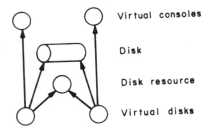

Virtual consoles

Disk

Disk resource

Virtual disks

Fig. 6.   Decomposition of virtual disks.

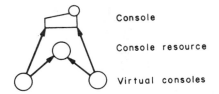

Console

Console resource

Virtual consoles

Fig. 7.   Decomposition of virtual consoles.

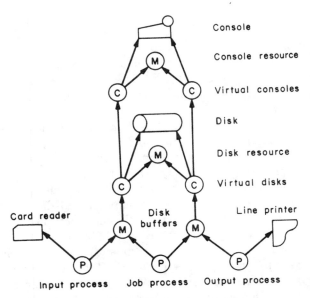

Console

Console resource

Virtual consoles

Disk

Disk resource

Virtual disks

Card reader   Disk buffers   Line printer

Input process   Job process   Output process

Fig. 8.   Hierarchical system structure.

Each virtual disk is only used by a single disk buffer (Fig. 5). A system component that cannot be called simultaneously by several other components will be called a *class*. A class defines a data structure and the possible operations on it (just like a monitor). The exclusive access of class procedures to class variables can be guaranteed completely at compile time. The virtual machine does not have to schedule simultaneous calls of class procedures at run time, because such calls cannot occur. This makes class calls considerably faster than monitor calls.

The spooling system includes two virtual disks but only one real disk. So we need a single *disk resource* monitor to control the order in which competing processes use the disk (Fig. 6). This monitor defines two procedures, *request* and *release* access, to be called by a virtual disk before and after each disk transfer.

It would seem simpler to replace the virtual disks and the disk resource by a single monitor that has exclusive access to the disk and does the input/output. This would certainly guarantee that processes use the disk one at a time. But this would be done according to the built-in short-term scheduling policy of monitor calls.

Now to make a virtual machine efficient, one must use a very simple short-term scheduling rule (such as first come, first served) [2]. If the disk has a moving access head this is about the worst possible algorithm one can use for disk transfers. It is vital that the language make it possible for the programmer to write a medium-term scheduling algorithm that will minimize disk head movements [3]. The data type *queue* mentioned earlier makes it possible to implement arbitrary scheduling rules within a monitor.

The difficulty is that while a monitor is performing an input/output operation it is impossible for other processes to enter the same monitor and join the disk queue. They will automatically be delayed by the short-term scheduler and only allowed to enter the monitor one at a time after each disk transfer. This will, of course, make the attempt

to control disk scheduling within the monitor illusory. To give the programmer complete control of disk scheduling, processes should be able to enter the disk queue during disk transfers. Since *arrival* and *service* in the disk queueing system potentially are simultaneous operations they must be handled by different system components, as shown in Fig. 6.

If the disk fails persistently during input/output this should be reported on an operator's console. Fig. 6 shows two instances of a class type, called a *virtual console*. They give the virtual disks the illusion that they have their own private consoles.

The virtual consoles get exclusive access to a single, real console by calling a *console resource* monitor (Fig. 7). Notice that we now have a standard technique for dealing with virtual devices.

If we put all these system components together, we get a complete picture of a simple spooling system (Fig. 8). Classes, monitors, and processes are marked C, M, and P.

E. Scope Rules

Some years ago I was part of a team that built a multi-programming system in which processes can appear and disappear dynamically [4]. In practice, this system was used mostly to set up a fixed configuration of processes. Dynamic process deletion will certainly complicate the semantics and implementation of a programming language considerably. And since it appears to be unnecessary for

a large class of real-time applications, it seems wise to exclude it altogether. So an operating system written in Concurrent Pascal will consist of a fixed number of processes, monitors, and classes. These components and their data structures will exist forever after system initialization. An operating system can, however, be extended by recompilation. It remains to be seen whether this restriction will simplify or complicate operating system design. But the poor quality of most existing operating systems clearly demonstrates an urgent need for simpler approaches.

In existing programming languages the data structures of processes, monitors, and classes would be called "global data." This term would be misleading in Concurrent Pascal where each data structure can be accessed by a single component only. It seems more appropriate to call them *permanent data structures*.

I have argued elsewhere that the most dangerous aspect of concurrent programming is the possibility of *time-dependent programming errors* that are impossible to locate by program testing ("lurking bugs") [2], [5], [6]. If we are going to depend on real-time programming systems in our daily lives, we must be able to find such obscure errors before the systems are put into operation.

Fortunately, a compiler can detect many of these errors if processes and monitors are represented by a structured notation in a high-level programming language. In addition, we must exclude low-level machine features (registers, addresses, and interrupts) from the language and let a virtual machine control them. If we want real-time systems to be highly reliable, we must stop programming them in assembly language. (The use of hardware protection mechanisms is merely an expensive, inadequate way of making arbitrary machine language programs behave almost as predictably as compiled programs.)

A Concurrent Pascal compiler will check that the private data of a process only are accessed by that process. It will also check that the data structure of a class or monitor only is accessed by its procedures.

Fig. 8 shows that *access rights* within an operating system normally are not tree structured. Instead they form a directed graph. This partly explains why the traditional scope rules of block-structured languages are inconvenient for concurrent programming (and for sequential programming as well). In Concurrent Pascal one can state the access rights of components in the program text and have them checked by a compiler.

Since the execution of a monitor procedure will delay the execution of further calls of the same monitor, we must prevent a monitor from calling itself recursively. Otherwise, processes can become *deadlocked*. So the compiler will check that the access rights of system components are hierarchically ordered (or, if you like, that there are no cycles in the access graph).

The *hierarchical ordering* of system components has vital consequences for system design and testing [7].

A hierarchical operating system will be tested component by component, bottom up (but could, of course, be conceived top down or by iteration). When an incomplete operating system has been shown to work correctly (by proof or testing), a compiler can ensure that this part of the system will continue to work correctly when new untested program components are added on top of it. Programming errors within new components cannot cause old components to fail because old components do not call new components, and new components only call old components through well-defined procedures that have already been tested.

(Strictly speaking, a compiler can only check that single monitor calls are made correctly; it cannot check sequences of monitor calls, for example whether a resource is always reserved before it is released. So one can only hope for compile time assurance of *partial correctness*.)

Several other reasons besides program correctness make a hierarchical structure attractive:

1) a hierarchical operating system can be studied in a stepwise manner as a sequence of *abstract machines* simulated by programs [8];

2) a partial ordering of process interactions permits one to use *mathematical induction* to prove certain overall properties of the system (such as the absence of deadlocks) [2];

3) *efficient resource utilization* can be achieved by ordering the program components according to the speed of the physical resources they control (with the fastest resources being controlled at the bottom of the system) [8];

4) a hierarchical system designed according to the previous criteria is often *nearly decomposable* from an analytical point of view. This means that one can develop stochastic models of its dynamic behavior in a stepwise manner [9].

F. Final Remarks

It seems most natural to represent a hierarchical system structure, such as Fig. 8, by a two-dimensional picture. But when we write a concurrent program we must somehow represent these access rules by linear text. This limitation of written language tends to obscure the simplicity of the original structure. That is why I have tried to explain the purpose of Concurrent Pascal by means of pictures instead of language notation.

The class concept is a restricted form of the class concept of Simula 67 [10]. Dijkstra suggested the idea of monitors [8]. The first structured language notation for monitors was proposed in [2], and illustrated by examples in [3]. The queue variables needed by monitors for process scheduling were suggested in [5] and modified in [3].

The main contribution of Concurrent Pascal is to extend monitors with explicit access rights that can be checked at compile time. Concurrent Pascal has been implemented at Caltech for the PDP 11/45 computer. Our system uses sequential Pascal as a job control and user programming language.

II. THE USE OF CONCURRENT PASCAL

A. Introduction

In Section I the concepts of Concurrent Pascal were explained informally by means of pictures of a hierarchical spooling system. I will now use the same example to introduce the language notation of Concurrent Pascal. The presentation is still informal. I am neither trying to define the language precisely nor to develop a working system. This will be done in other papers. I am just trying to show the flavor of the language.

B. Processes

We will now program the system components in Fig. 8 one at a time from top to bottom (but we could just as well do it bottom up).

Although we only need one *input process*, we may as well define it as a general system type of which several copies may exist:

```
type inputprocess =
process(buffer: diskbuffer);
var block: page;
cycle
  readcards(block);
  buffer.send(block);
end
```

An input process has access to a *buffer* of type diskbuffer (to be defined later). The process has a private variable *block* of type page. The data type page is declared elsewhere as an array of characters:

$$\text{type page} = \text{array } (.1..512.) \text{ of char}$$

A process type defines a *sequential program*—in this case, an endless cycle that inputs a block from a card reader and sends it through the buffer to another process. We will ignore the details of card reader input.

The *send* operation on the buffer is called as follows (using the block as a parameter):

$$\text{buffer.send(block)}$$

The next component type we will define is a *job process*:

```
type jobprocess =
process(input, output: diskbuffer);
var block: page;
cycle
  input.receive(block);
  update(block);
  output.send(block);
end
```

A job process has access to two disk buffers called *input* and *output*. It receives blocks from one buffer, updates them, and sends them through the other buffer. The details of updating can be ignored here.

Finally, we need an *output process* that can receive data from a disk buffer and output them on a line printer:

```
type outputprocess =
process(buffer: diskbuffer);
var block: page;
cycle
  buffer.receive(block);
  printlines(block);
end
```

The following shows a declaration of the main system components:

```
var buffer1, buffer2: diskbuffer;
  reader: inputprocess;
  master: jobprocess;
  writer: outputprocess;
```

There is an input process, called the *reader*, a job process, called the *master*, and an output process, called the *writer*. Then there are two disk buffers, *buffer1* and *buffer2*, that connect them.

Later I will explain how a disk buffer is defined and initialized. If we assume that the disk buffers already have been initialized, we can initialize the input process as follows:

$$\text{init reader(buffer1)}$$

The *init* statement allocates space for the *private variables* of the reader process and starts its execution as a sequential process with access to buffer1.

The *access rights* of a process to other system components, such as buffer1, are also called its *parameters*. A process can only be initialized once. After initialization, the parameters and private variables of a process exist forever. They are called *permanent variables*.

The init statement can be used to start concurrent execution of several processes and define their access rights. As an example, the statement

```
init reader(buffer1), master(buffer1, buffer2),
  writer(buffer2)
```

starts concurrent execution of the reader process (with access to buffer1), the master process (with access to both buffers), and the writer process (with access to buffer2).

A process can only access its own parameters and private variables. The latter are not accessible to other system components. Compare this with the more liberal scope rules of block-structured languages in which a program block can access not only its own parameters and local variables, but also those declared in outer blocks. In Concurrent Pascal, all variables accessible to a system component are declared within its type definition. This access rule and the init statement make it possible for a programmer to state access rights explicitly and have them checked by a compiler. They also make it possible to study a system type as a self-contained program unit.

Although the programming examples do not show this, one can also define constants, data types, and procedures within a process. These objects can only be used within the process type.

C. Monitors

The *disk buffer* is a monitor type:

```
type diskbuffer =
monitor(consoleaccess, diskaccess: resource;
  base, limit: integer);

var disk: virtualdisk; sender, receiver: queue;
  head, tail, length: integer;

procedure entry send(block: page);
begin
  if length = limit then delay(sender);
  disk.write(base + tail, block);
  tail:= (tail + 1) mod limit;
  length:= length + 1;
  continue(receiver);
end;

procedure entry receive(var block: page);
begin
  if length = 0 then delay(receiver);
  disk.read(base + head, block);
  head:= (head + 1) mod limit;
  length:= length - 1;
  continue(sender);
end;

begin "initial statement"
  init disk(consoleaccess, diskaccess);
  head:= 0; tail:= 0; length:= 0;
end
```

A disk buffer has access to two other components, *consoleaccess* and *diskaccess*, of type resource (to be defined later). It also has access to two integer constants defining the *base* address and *limit* of the buffer on the disk.

The monitor declares a set of *shared variables*: the *disk* is declared as a variable of type virtualdisk. Two variables of type queue are used to delay the *sender* and *receiver* processes until the buffer becomes nonfull and nonempty. Three integers define the relative addresses of the *head* and *tail* elements of the buffer and its current *length*.

The monitor defines two *monitor procedures*, send and receive. They are marked with the word *entry* to distinguish them from local procedures used within the monitor (there are none of these in this example).

Receive returns a page to the calling process. If the buffer is empty, the calling process is *delayed* in the receiver queue until another process sends a page through the buffer. The receive procedure will then read and remove a page from the head of the disk buffer by calling a *read* operation defined within the virtual disk type:

$$\text{disk.read(base + head, block)}$$

Finally, the receive procedure will *continue* the execution of a sending process (if the latter is waiting in the sender queue).

Send is similar to receive.

The queuing mechanism will be explained in detail in the next section.

The *initial statement* of a disk buffer initializes its virtual disk with access to the console and disk resources. It also sets the buffer length to zero. (Notice, that a disk buffer does not use its access rights to the console and disk, but only passes them on to a virtual disk declared within it.)

The following shows a declaration of two system components of type resource and two integers defining the base and limit of a disk buffer:

```
var consoleaccess, diskaccess: resource;
    base, limit: integer;
    buffer: diskbuffer;
```

If we assume that these variables already have been initialized, we can initialize a disk buffer as follows:

```
init buffer(consoleaccess, diskaccess, base, limit)
```

The *init* statement allocates storage for the parameters and shared variables of the disk buffer and executes its initial statement.

A monitor can only be initialized once. After initialization, the parameters and shared variables of a monitor exist forever. They are called *permanent variables*. The parameters and local variables of a monitor procedure, however, exist only while it is being executed. They are called *temporary variables*.

A monitor procedure can only access its own temporary and permanent variables. These variables are not accessible to other system components. Other components can, however, call procedure entries within a monitor. While a monitor procedure is being executed, it has *exclusive access* to the permanent variables of the monitor. If concurrent processes try to call procedures within the same monitor simultaneously, these procedures will be executed strictly one at a time.

Only monitors and constants can be permanent parameters of processes and monitors. This rule ensures that processes only communicate by means of monitors.

It is possible to define constants, data types, and local procedures within monitors (and processes). The local procedures of a system type can only be called within the system type. To prevent *deadlock* of monitor calls and ensure that access rights are hierarchical the following rules are enforced: a procedure must be declared before it can be called; procedure definitions cannot be nested and cannot call themselves; a system type cannot call its own procedure entries.

The absence of recursion makes it possible for a compiler to determine the store requirements of all system components. This and the use of permanent components make it possible to use *fixed store allocation* on a computer that does not support paging.

Since system components are permanent they must be declared as permanent variables of other components.

D. Queues

A monitor procedure can delay a calling process for any length of time by executing a *delay* operation on a queue variable. Only one process at a time can wait in a queue. When a calling process is delayed by a monitor procedure it loses its exclusive access to the monitor variables until another process calls the same monitor and executes a continue operation on the queue in which the process is waiting.

The *continue* operation makes the calling process return from its monitor call. If any process is waiting in the selected queue, it will immediately resume the execution of the monitor procedure that delayed it. After being resumed, the process again has exclusive access to the permanent variables of the monitor.

Other variants of process queues (called "events" and "conditions") are proposed in [3], [5]. They are multi-process queues that use different (but fixed) scheduling rules. We do not yet know from experience which kind of queue will be the most convenient one for operating system design. A single-process queue is the simplest tool that gives the programmer complete control of the scheduling of individual processes. Later, I will show how multi-process queues can be built from single-process queues.

A queue must be declared as a permanent variable within a monitor type.

E. Classes

Every disk buffer has its own virtual disk. A virtual disk is defined as a class type:

```
type virtualdisk =
class(consoleaccess, diskaccess: resource);

var terminal: virtualconsole; peripheral: disk;

procedure entry read(pageno: integer; var block: page);
var error: boolean;
begin
  repeat
    diskaccess.request;
    peripheral.read(pageno, block, error);
    diskaccess.release;
    if error then terminal.write('disk failure');
  until not error;
end;

procedure entry write(pageno: integer; block: page);
begin "similar to read" end;

begin "initial statement"
  init terminal(consoleaccess), peripheral;
end
```

A virtual disk has access to a console resource and a disk resource. Its permanent variables define a virtual console and a disk. A process can access its virtual disk by means of *read* and *write* procedures. These procedure entries *request* and *release* exclusive access to the real disk before and after each block transfer. If the real disk fails, the virtual disk calls its virtual console to report the error.

The *initial statement* of a virtual disk initializes its virtual console and the real disk.

Section II-C shows an example of how a virtual disk is declared and initialized (within a disk buffer).

A class can only be initialized once. After initialization, its parameters and private variables exist forever. A class procedure can only access its own temporary and permanent variables. These cannot be accessed by other components.

A class is a system component that cannot be called simultaneously by several other components. This is guaranteed by the following rule: a class must be declared as a permanent variable within a system type; a class can be passed as a permanent parameter to another class (but not to a process or monitor). So a chain of nested class calls can only be started by a single process or monitor. Consequently, it is not necessary to schedule simultaneous class calls at run time—they cannot occur.

F. Input/Output

The real *disk* is controlled by a class

$$\text{type disk} = \text{class}$$

with two procedure entries

```
read(pageno, block, error)
write(pageno, block, error)
```

The class uses a standard procedure

$$\text{io(block, param, device)}$$

to transfer a block to or from the disk device. The io parameter is a record

```
var param: record
        operation: iooperation;
        result: ioresult;
        pageno: integer
      end
```

that defines an input/output operation, its result, and a page number on the disk. The calling process is delayed until an io operation has been completed.

A *virtual console* is also defined as a class

```
type virtualconsole =
class(access: resource);
var terminal: console;
```

It can be accessed by read and write operations that are similar to each other:

```
procedure entry read(var text: line);
begin
  access.request;
  terminal.read(text);
  access.release;
end
```

The real *console* is controlled by a class that is similar to the disk class.

G. Multiprocess Scheduling

Access to the console and disk is controlled by two monitors of type *resource*. To simplify the presentation, I will assume that competing processes are served in first-come, first-served order. (A much better disk scheduling algorithm is defined in [3]. It can be programmed in Concurrent Pascal as well, but involves more details than the present one.)

We will define a multiprocess queue as an array of single-process queues

type multiqueue = array (.0..qlength-1.) of queue

where qlength is an upper bound on the number of concurrent processes in the system.

A first-come, first-served scheduler is now straight-forward to program:

```
type resource =
monitor

var free: Boolean; q: multiqueue;
  head, tail, length: integer;

procedure entry request;
var arrival: integer;
begin
  if free then free:= false else
  begin
    arrival:= tail;
    tail:= (tail + 1) mod qlength;
    length:= length + 1;
    delay(q(.arrival.));
  end;
end;

procedure entry release;
var departure: integer;
begin
  if length = 0 then free:= true else
  begin
    departure:= head;
    head:= (head + 1) mod qlength;
    length:= length − 1;
    continue(q(.departure.));
  end;
end;

begin "initial statement"
  free:= true; length:= 0;
  head:= 0; tail:= 0;
end
```

H. Initial Process

Finally, we will put all these components together into a concurrent program. A Concurrent Pascal program consists of nested definitions of system types. The outermost system type is an anonymous process, called the initial process. An instance of this process is created during system loading. It initializes the other system components.

The initial process defines system types and instances of them. It executes statements that initialize these system components. In our example, the initial process can be sketched as follows (ignoring the problem of how base addresses and limits of disk buffers are defined):

```
type
  resource = monitor···end;
  console = class···end;
  virtualconsole =
    class(access: resource);···end;
  disk = class···end;
  virtualdisk =
    class(consoleaccess, diskaccess: resource);···end;
  diskbuffer =
    monitor(consoleaccess, diskaccess: resource;
      base, limit: integer);···end;
  inputprocess =
    process(buffer: diskbuffer);···end;
  jobprocess =
    process(input, output: diskbuffer);···end;
  outputprocess =
    process(buffer: diskbuffer);···end;
var
  consoleaccess, diskaccess: resource;
  buffer1, buffer2: diskbuffer;
  reader: inputprocess;
  master: jobprocess;
  writer: outputprocess;
begin
  init consoleaccess, diskaccess,
    buffer1(consoleaccess, diskaccess, base1, limit1),
    buffer2(consoleaccess, diskaccess, base2, limit2),
    reader(buffer1),
    master(buffer1, buffer2),
    writer(buffer2);
end.
```

When the execution of a process (such as the initial process) terminates, its private variables continue to exist. This is necessary because these variables may have been passed as permanent parameters to other system components.

ACKNOWLEDGMENT

It is a pleasure to acknowledge the immense value of a continuous exchange of ideas with C. A. R. Hoare on structured multiprogramming. I also thank my students L. Medina and R. Varela for their helpful comments on this paper.

REFERENCES

[1] N. Wirth, "The programming language Pascal," *Acta Informatica*, vol. 1, no. 1, pp. 35–63, 1971.
[2] P. Brinch Hansen, *Operation System Principles*. Englewood Cliffs, N. J.: Prentice-Hall, July 1973.
[3] C. A. R. Hoare, "Monitors: An operating system structuring concept," *Commun. Ass. Comput. Mach.*, vol. 17, pp. 549–557, Oct. 1974.
[4] P. Brinch Hansen, "The nucleus of a multiprogramming

system," *Commun. Ass. Comput. Mach.*, vol. 13, pp. 238–250, Apr. 1970.

[5] ——, "Structured multiprogramming," *Commun. Ass. Comput. Mach.*, vol. 15, pp. 574–578, July 1972.

[6] ——, "Concurrent programming concepts," *Ass. Comput. Mach. Comput. Rev.*, vol. 5, pp. 223–245, Dec. 1974.

[7] ——, "A programming methodology for operating system design," in *1974 Proc. IFIP Congr.* Stockholm, Sweden: North-Holland, Aug. 1974, pp. 394–397.

[8] E. W. Dijkstra, "Hierarchical ordering of sequential processes," *Acta Informatica*, vol. 1, no. 2, pp. 115–138, 1971.

[9] H. A. Simon, "The architecture of complexity," in *Proc. Amer. Philosophical Society*, vol. 106, no. 6, 1962, pp. 468–482.

[10] O.-J. Dahl and C. A. R. Hoare, "Hierarchical program structures," in *Structured Programming*, O.-J. Dahl, E. W. Dijkstra, and C. A. R. Hoare. New York: Academic, 1972.

Per Brinch Hansen was born in Copenhagen, Denmark, on November 13, 1938. He received the M.S. degree in electronic engineering from the Technical University of Denmark, Copenhagen, in 1963.

Afterwards he joined the Danish computer manufacturer, Regnecentralen, as a systems programmer and designer. In 1967 he became head of the department at Regnecentralen which developed the architecture of the RC 4000 computer and its multiprogramming system. From 1970 to 1972 he visited Carnegie-Mellon University, Pittsburgh, Pa., where he wrote the book *Operating System Principles* (Englewood Cliffs, N. J., Prentice-Hall, July 1973). This book contains the first proposal of the *monitor concept* on which the programming language Concurrent Pascal is based. In 1972 he became Associate Professor of Computer Science at the California Institute of Technology, Pasadena. He has been a consultant to Burroughs Corporation, Control Data Corporation, Jet Propulsion Laboratory, Philips, and Varian Data Machines. His main research interests are computer architecture and programming methodology.

Dr. Brinch Hansen is a member of the Working Group 2.3 on Programming Methodology sponsored by the International Federation for Information Processing.

MODULA: A LANGUAGE FOR MODULAR MULTIPROGRAMMING*

N. WIRTH

Institut für Informatik, Eidgenössische Technische Hochschule, Zürich, Switzerland

SUMMARY

This paper defines a language called Modula, which is intended primarily for programming dedicated computer systems, including process control systems on smaller machines. The language is largely based on Pascal, but in addition to conventional block structure it introduces a so-called module structure. A module is a set of procedures, data types and variables, where the programmer has precise control over the names that are imported from and exported to the environment. Modula includes general multiprocessing facilities, namely processes, interface modules and signals. It also allows the specification of facilities that represent a computer's specific peripheral devices. Those given in this paper pertain to the PDP-11.

KEY WORDS   Multiprogramming   Module   Interface   Synchronization   Device handling
Programming language

INTRODUCTION

The advantages of high-level programming languages over assembly code in the design of complex systems have been widely recognized and commented upon.[3] The primary benefit of the use of a suitable high-level language lies in the possibility of defining abstract machines in a precise manner that is reasonably independent of characteristics of particular hardware. Assembly code is still used virtually exclusively in those applications whose predominant purpose is not to design a new system based on abstract specifications, but to operate an existing machine with all its particular devices. Good examples are process control systems, computerized laboratory equipment and input/output device drivers.

A major aim of the research on Modula is to conquer that stronghold of assembly coding, or at least to attack it vigorously. There is strong evidence that the influence of high-level languages may become equally significant for process control programming as it is now for compiler and operating system design. It may become even more important, considering the availability of microprocessors at very low cost.

There are two requirements of such languages that are characteristic of this area of application, and that have not existed for general-purpose languages in the past. They must offer facilities for *multiprogramming*, i.e. they must allow expression of the concurrent execution of several activities, and they must offer facilities for operation of a computer's *peripheral devices*. The principal obstacle is that such facilities are inherently machine- and even configuration-dependent, and as such elude a comprehensive abstract definition. A practical solution lies in accepting this situation and introducing a language construction that encapsulates such machine-dependent items, i.e. restricts their validity or existence to a specific, usually very small, section of a program. We call this construction a *module*. Its usefulness is quite general and by no means restricted to the domain of device-dependent

Received 30 July 1976

*Reprinted from *Software Practice and Experience*, 7, 1977, 3–35, copyright 1977.

operations. It is indeed of central importance, and has given the language its name (*modular programming language*).

Modula relies very strongly on Pascal.[6,10] Some of Pascal's features, however, have been omitted. The reason is not their inadequacy, but rather the necessity and the desire to keep the language reasonably small. This seemed particularly advisable for a language intended primarily for small computers.

The second section of this paper gives a brief overview of the language, and concentrates on its 'novel' features for modular design, multiprogramming and device operation. The third and fourth sections define the formalism for the syntactic definition of Modula and of the actual representation of programs. The fifth section defines the core of the language in detail. It constitutes the conventional part restricted to sequential programming. Most of these features have been adopted from Pascal. The sixth section describes the facilities added to express concurrency. The typical Modula program consists of several processes that are themselves sequential algorithms and which are loosely coupled through synchronization operations. Its multiprogramming facilities are designed accordingly.

The language described in the fifth and sixth sections is defined in an abstract way which does not refer to any specific computer. It is well suited to implementation on any existing computer. However, the purpose of a system programming language is not only to aid in constructing and specifying abstract systems, but also to operate existing hardware. For this purpose, additional features must be provided that serve to operate particular facilities of a given computer, in particular its peripheral devices. The seventh section describes a set of such features that were added to operate the PDP-11. Such machine-dependent objects can only be declared in specially designated device modules.

In this connection the total lack of any kind of input/output facilities must be explained. Even the file structure of Pascal is missing. The reason is that the typical application of Modula is regarded as the design of systems that implement rather than use such a file facility. It should be possible to run Modula programs on a bare machine with a minimal run-time support. Hence, Modula cannot contain 'high-level' features such as file operations. Instead, they may be programmed in terms of device operations, neatly encapsulated within modules.

Another concept that is conspicuously absent is the interrupt. The explanation is that the interrupt is a processor-oriented concept. The purpose of interrupts is to let a processor take part in the execution of several processes (tasks). Hence, in a language that focuses on sequential processes as principal constituents of its programs, the interrupt is a *technique* to implement a multiprocess program on a single-processor computer, rather than a language *concept*.

A most important consideration in the design of Modula was its efficient implementability. In particular, the presented solution allows processor management and 'interrupt handling' to be implemented equally efficiently as in assembly coding. Guarantee of efficiency and absence of additional overhead in the use of a high-level language is an absolute prerequisite for a successful campaign to promote the use of such languages in this traditional stronghold of assembly coding.

The current implementation of Modula is experimental. The presence or absence of certain facilities is still subject to controversy. The usefulness of their presence or the effects of their absence will only be known after a considerable amount of actual experience in the use of Modula for the development of many different systems.

So far, a cross-compiler has been completed. It relies on a very small run-time support package to handle the switching of the processor from one process to another. In modern

systems, this nucleus could well be incorporated as a microprogram or, perhaps, even directly in the hardware. (The current compiler is not available for distribution.)

OVERVIEW

By far the largest part of Modula consists of facilities typical of any sequential programming language. This is not surprising, because even large operating and control systems consist of processes that are themselves purely sequential. Brinch Hansen, in describing the design of an entire operating system, reports that only 4 per cent were coded in a language with multiprogramming facilities.[2]

Most of the sequential programming facilities of Modula have been adopted from Pascal, notably the concepts of *data types* and structures. Modula offers the basic types integer, Boolean and char. In addition, scalar types can be defined by the programmer by enumerations. In the realm of structures, only the *array* and the *record*—the latter without variants—have been adopted. The role of sets is partially taken over by a standard type called bits, which constitutes a short Boolean array. The language does not include any pointers.

Modula provides a rich set of program *control structures*, including *if, case, while,* and *repeat* statements. Their syntax slightly differs from that of Pascal, because the principle was followed that every structured statement not only begins but also ends with an explicit bracketing symbol. The for statement has been replaced by a more general *loop* statement that allows specification of one or several termination points.

Procedures can be used recursively and can have two kinds of parameters, namely constant and variable parameters. In the former case, assignments to the formal parameter are prohibited, and the corresponding actual parameter is an expression. In the latter case, the actual parameter must be a variable, and assignments to the formal parameter are assignments to that actual variable. (In both cases, parameters may—but do not have to—be implemented by passing an address.)

Procedures form a *block* in the sense of Algol and Pascal. Hence, constants, types, variables and other procedures can be declared local to a procedure. This implies that their existence is not known outside the procedure, which thereby constitutes the scope of these local objects. Block structure has proved to be a most valuable facility in systematic program design. However, block structure alone does not provide the possibility of retaining local objects after termination of the procedure, nor of letting several procedures share retained (hidden) objects. For this purpose, the *module* has been introduced as an essential supplement to the block concept.

A module is a collection of constant-, type-, variable- and procedure declarations. They are called *objects* of the module and come into existence when control enters the procedure to which the module is local. The module should be thought of as a fence around its objects. The essential property of the module construction is that it allows the precise determination of this fence's transparency. In its heading, a module contains two lists of identifiers: The *define-list* mentions all module objects that are to be accessible (visible) outside the module. The *use-list* mentions all objects declared outside the module that are to be visible inside. This facility provides an effective means of making available selectively those objects that represent an intended abstraction, and of hiding those objects that are considered as details of implementation. A module encapsulates those parts that are non-essential to the remainder of a program, or that are even to be protected from inadvertent access.[7] Modules may be nested.

Example: Suppose that an object a is declared in the environment of M1. Then *a, b,* and *c* are accessible in this environment:

```
module M1;
  define b, c;
  use a;
  {declare d}

  module M2;
    define c, e;
    use d;
    {declare c, e, f}
    {c, d, e, f are accessible here}
  end M2;

  procedure b;
    {declare f}
    {a, b, c, d, e, f are accessible here}
  end b;

  {a, b, c, d, e are accessible here}
end M1
```

Identifiers in the define-list are said to be *exported*, those in the use-list are *imported*. If a type is exported, then only its identity is exported, but not its structural details. This means that outside the module from which a type is exported we do not know whether a type is a scalar, an array or a record.

Therefore, variables of this type can be operated by procedures only that are exported from the same module. The module[8] therefore assumes a similar role as the class construction of Concurrent Pascal[1] which was developed from the class structure of Simula.[4]

Exported variables cannot be changed except in the module to which they are local, i.e. they appear as read-only variables. It must be emphasized that the module does not determine the 'life-time' of its local objects. It merely establishes a new scope. Objects declared within a module are considered local to the procedure in which the module itself is local, i.e. they come into existence when that procedure is called, and they vanish when it is completed.

Only a minimal number of facilities for multiprogramming are added to the language described so far, which we may call *sequential Modula*. The additional facilities are processes, interface modules and signals. A *process* looks like a procedure. But unlike the procedure it is executed concurrently with the program that called, i.e. initiated, it. When control reaches the end of a process, the process goes out of existence. Processes cannot create other processes. Process creation is possible in the main program only, which should be regarded as a system initialization phase. However, it is possible to activate several instances of the same process declaration.

Synchronization is achieved by the use of *signals*. They are declared similar to variables (syntactically, the signal appears as a data type). Signals can be sent, and a process can wait for a signal. Signals correspond to conditions of Hoare[5] and to queues of Brinch Hansen.[1] A central aspect of this concept is that processes, once started, are anonymous. They can be influenced by signals (and shared variables) only. But the environment cannot force a process to notice these signals (or changes of variables), and there is no way to disrupt or terminate a process by outside intervention.

Processes co-operate *via* common variables. This requires a facility to guarantee mutual exclusion of processes from critical sections of a program. In Modula, such sections are

declared as procedures and these procedures are gathered within a specially designated, so-called *interface module*, which corresponds to Brinch Hansen's[11] and Hoare's monitor.[5] The monitor is a set of corresponding critical sections, where simultaneous execution by several processes is excluded. In contrast to the critical section, however, the interface module allows more than one process to be in a critical section, provided that all but one are either waiting for a signal or sending a signal. This relaxation of the mutual exclusion condition not only simplifies implementation of the signalling and processor switching mechanism, but also corresponds to many practical patterns of usage. A typical program pattern with two co-operating processes P and Q is shown below, where v stands for the common variables, for instance data buffers in a producer–consumer constellation, s stands for the signals by which P and Q synchronize their activities, and p and q are their critical sections formulated as interface procedures (see Figure 1).

```
interface module M;
    define p, q;
    {declare v, s}
    procedure p(x);
        {uses v, s, x}
    end p;
    procedure q(y);
        {uses v, s, y}
    end q;
begin {initialize v}
end M;

process P;
    {uses p}
end P;

process Q;
    {uses q}
end Q
```

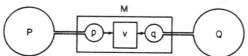

Figure 1. Processes P and Q interfacing via module M

These general multiprogramming facilities are supplemented by a few computer-dependent features. They are necessary, for instance, to operate a computer's peripheral devices. We describe as an example those which were designed and implemented for the PDP-11. The underlying intention was to keep the number of such facilities minimal, and to express them in strong analogy with machine-independent concepts wherever feasible and economical.

A necessary condition is that the computer's *device registers* and operators on them are made available. They appear in Modula as variables with a specification of their (hardware-defined) address and (programmer-defined) type. Status registers are usually declared of type *bits*, which allows the convenient setting and resetting of individual status and function bits.

Moreover, a system implementation language should allow the effective utilization of a computer's interrupt facility, including its interrupt priority system, if one exists. Traditionally, an input/output device is regarded as a process by itself, communicating with a master process by starting signals and completion interrupts. In Modula, the operations performed by the device and those executed by its associated interrupt routine are considered as a single process, the former part being represented by the statement *doio*[9] (see Figure 2). This statement is allowed within so-called *device processes* (or *drivers*) only which are declared within a so-called *device module*. In contrast to regular processes drivers are declared entirely within the device interface module. This is possible, because the doio statement—representing the actions performed by the device—also constitutes a singular point within the interface in the sense that during its execution the mutual exclusion constraint is lifted.

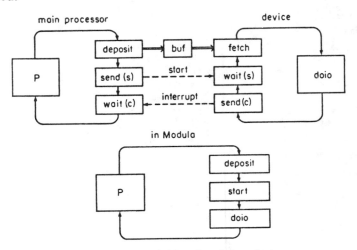

Figure 2. I/O practivities viewed as a device ocess

The explicit designation of device interface modules and drivers facilitates for an implementation of the efficient utilization of a given computer system, but also exhibits the close relationship or even identity of these machine-oriented parts of a program with the machine-independent concepts of the language.

NOTATION FOR SYNTACTIC DESCRIPTION

To describe the syntax an extended Backus–Naur formalism is used. It allows use of syntax expressions as right-hand parts in a production. Syntactic entities are denoted by English words expressing their intuitive meaning. Symbols of the language are enclosed by quote marks ('') and appear as so-called literals in the right-hand parts of productions. Each production has the form

   $S = E.$

where S is a syntactic entity and E a syntax expression denoting the set of sentential forms (sequences of symbols) for which S stands. An expression E has the form

   $T_1 | T_2 | ... | T_n \quad (n > 0)$

where the T_i's are the terms of E. Each T_i stands for a set of sentential forms, and E denotes their union. Each term T has the form

   $F_1 \, F_2 \, ... \, F_n \quad (n > 0)$

where the F_i's are the factors of T. Each F_i stands for a set of sentential forms, and T denotes their product. The product of two sets of sentences is the set of sentences consisting of all possible concatenations of a sentence from the first factor followed by a sentence from the second factor. Each factor F has either the form

   "x"

(x is a literal, and "x" denotes the singleton set consisting of this single symbol), or

   (E)

(denoting the expression E), or

   [E]

(denoting the union of the set denoted by E and the empty sentence), or

   {E}

(denoting the set consisting of the union of the empty sequence and the sets E, EE, EEE, etc.).

Examples:

The syntax expressions

   ("a"|"b") ("b"|"c"),   "a" {"bc"},   "a" ["b"|"c"] "d"

denote the following sets of sentences respectively:

ab	a	ad
ac	abc	abd
bb	abcbc	acd
bc	abcbcbc	
	...	

LANGUAGE VOCABULARY AND REPRESENTATION

The language is an infinite set of sentences (programs), namely the sentences well formed according to the syntax. Each sentence (program) is a finite sequence of symbols from a finite vocabulary. The vocabulary consists of identifiers, (unsigned) numbers, literals, operators and delimiters. They are called lexical *symbols* or tokens, and in turn are composed of sequences of *characters*. Their representation therefore depends on the underlying character set. The ASCII set is used in this paper, but the following rules must be observed for any set:

1. Identifiers are sequences of letters and digits. The first character must be a letter.
     ident = letter {letter|digit}.

2. Numbers (integers) are sequences of digits, possibly followed by the letter B signifying 'octal'.
     number = integer.
     integer = digit {digit}|octaldigit {octaldigit} "B".

3. Strings are sequences of characters enclosed in quote marks. If a quote mark itself is to occur within that sequence, then it is denoted by two consecutive quote marks. A single character string may also be denoted by its ordinal number (in octal) followed by the letter C. (The ordinal refers to the character set used.)
     string = """ {character} """|octaldigit {octaldigit} "C".

4. Operators and delimiters are special characters, character pairs, or (reserved) words listed in Table I below. In this report, they are printed in bold face for clear distinction from identifiers. These (reserved) words must not be used in the role of identifiers.

Table I. Operators and delimiters

+	(	**div**	**until**	**const**
−	)	**mod**	**while**	**var**
*	[	**or**	**do**	**type**
/	]	**and**	**loop**	**array**
=	.	**not**	**when**	**record**
<>	,	**if**	**exit**	**procedure**
<	;	**then**	**begin**	**process**
<=	:	**elsif**	**end**	**module**
>	'	**else**	**with**	**interface**
>=		**case**	**value**	**device**
	(*	**of**	**xor**	**use**
:=	*)	**repeat**		**define**

5. Blank spaces (and line separation) are ignored unless they are essential to separate two consecutive symbols. Hence, blanks cannot occur within symbols, including identifiers, and numbers.

6. Comments may be inserted between any two symbols in a program. They are opened by the bracket (* and closed by *). Comments may be nested, and they do not affect the meaning of a program.

FACILITIES FOR SEQUENTIAL PROGRAMMING

Every program contains two essential components: parts where objects of the computation are defined and associated with identifiers, and parts where the algorithmic actions to be performed on (and with) these objects are defined. The former parts are called *declarations*, the latter *statements*. A *block* is a textual unit (usually) consisting of elements of both kinds in a well-defined order.

Objects to be declared are constants, data types and structures, variables, procedures, modules and processes. Procedures and modules consist themselves of a block. Hence blocks are defined recursively and can be nested (see also *Procedures*).

Constant declarations

A constant declaration associates an identifier with a constant value.

    constantdeclaration = ident ''='' constant.
    constant = unsignedconstant|(''+''|''−'') number.
    unsignedconstant = ident|number|string|bitconstant.
    bitconstant = ''[''[bitlist]'']''.
    bitlist = bitlistelement {'','' bitlistelement}.
    bitlistelement = constant ['' : '' constant].

Numbers are constants of type integer. A constant denoted by a single-character string (or by an ordinal) is of type char (see *Basic types*), a string consisting of n characters is of type (see *Array structures*)

array 1 : n **of** char

A bit constant is a constant of type bits (see *Basic types*). The elements of the bitlist are the indices of those bits that are *true*. An element of the form m : n specifies that all bits with indices m through n are *true*. All other bits have the value *false*.

Type declarations

Every constant, variable and expression is of a certain type. In the case of numbers and literals their type is implicitly defined, for variables it is specified by their declaration, and

for expressions it is derivable from the types of their constituent operands and operators. A data type determines the set of values that a variable of that type may assume; it also defines the structure of a variable. There are four standard types, namely integer, Boolean, char and bits. Enumeration types (enumerations) and the types integer, Boolean and char are unstructured, i.e. their values are atomic. *Structured types* (structures) can be declared in terms of these elementary types and of structures.

> typedeclaration = ident " = " type.
> type = ident | enumeration | arraystructure | recordstructure.

Basic types

integer	The values of type integer are the whole numbers in the range *min* to *max*, where *min* and *max* are constants dependent on available implementations. (For the PDP-11: *min* = − 32768, *max* = 32767.)
Boolean	The values are the truth values denoted by the predefined identifiers *true* and *false*.
char	The values are the characters belonging to the character set determined by each implementation. (For the PDP-11: the ASCII set.)
bits	Its values are arrays of w Boolean elements. This type is predeclared as (see *Array structures*)

> **array** $0 : w$ **of** Boolean.

The constant w is the wordlength minus 1 of the computer on which Modula is implemented. (For the PDP-11: $w = 15$.)

Enumerations

An enumeration is a list of identifiers that denote the values which constitute a data type. These identifiers are used as constants in a program. They, and no other values, belong to this type. An ordering relation is defined on these values by their sequence in the enumeration.

> enumeration = "("identlist")".
> identlist = ident {"," ident}.

Array structures

An array structure consists of a number of components which are all of the same *component type*. Each component is identified by a number of *indices*. This number is called the dimensionality of the array. The range of index values of each dimension is specified in the declaration of the array structure. The types of the indices must not be structured.

> arraystructure = "**array**" indexrangelist "**of**" type.
> indexrangelist = indexrange {"," indexrange}.
> indexrange = constant ":" constant.

Record structures

A record structure consists of a number of components, called *record fields*. Each component is identified by a unique field identifier. Field identifiers are known only within the record structure definition and within field designators, i.e. when they are preceded by a qualifying record variable identifier. The data type of each component is specified in the field list.

> recordstructure = "**record**" fieldlist {";" fieldlist} "**end**".
> fieldlist = [identlist ":" type].

Examples of type declarations:
     colour = (red, yellow, green, blue)
     vector = **array** 1 : 100 **of** colour
     matrix = **array** 1 : 20, 0 : 10 **of** integer
     account = **record** x: integer;
                          y: Boolean;
                          z: **array** 0 : 9 **of** char
              end

Variables

Variable declarations serve to introduce variables and associate them with a unique identifier and a fixed data type or structure. Variables whose identifiers appear in the same list all obtain the same type.
     variabledeclaration = identlist '':'' type.

Examples of variable declarations:
     i, j, k: integer
     p, q: Boolean
     ch: char
     u: **record** s: bits;
                   a: vector
        end
     s, t: bits
     r: account
     a: vector
     m: matrix
     w: **array** 1 : 10 **of** account

The syntactic construction of a designation of a variable is simply called 'variable'. It either refers to a variable as a whole, namely when it consists of the identifier of the variable, or to one of its components, when the identifier is followed by a selector. If a variable, say v, has a record structure with a field f, this component variable is designated by $v.f$. If v has an array structure, its component with index i is designated by $v[i]$.

     variable = ident | variable ''.'' ident |
                     variable ''['' indices '']''.
     indices = expression {'','' expression}.

Examples of variables (see declarations above):
     i   r.x   a[i]   m[i + 1, j − 1]   w[i].x   u.a[k]

Expressions

Expressions are composed of operands (constants, variables and functions), operators and parentheses. They specify rules of computing values; evaluation of an expression yields a value of the type of the expression.

There are four classes of *operators* with different precedence (binding strength). Relational operators have the least precedence, then follow the so-called adding operators, the multiplying operators and the negation operator **not** with highest precedence. Sequences of operators with equal precedence are executed from left to right.

Denotations of a *variable* in an expression refer to the current value of the variable. *Function calls* denote activation of a function procedure declaration (i.e. execution of the

statements which constitute its body). The result acts as an operand in the expression. The same rules about parameter evaluation and substitution hold as in the case of a procedure call (see *Procedure calls*).

    expression = simpleexpression [relation simpleexpression].
    relation = ''=''|''<>''|''<=''|''<''|''>''|''>=''.
    simpleexpression = [''+''|''−''] term {addoperator term}.
    addoperator = ''+''|''−''|''**or**''|''**xor**''.
    term = factor {muloperator factor}.
    muloperator = ''*''|''/''|''**div**''|''**mod**''|''**and**''.
    factor = unsignedconstant|variable|functioncall|''('' expression '')''|''**not**'' factor.
    functioncall = ident parameterlist.

Arithmetic operators (+ − * / **div mod**) apply to operands of type integer and yield a result of this type. The operators + − * and / denote addition, subtraction, multiplication, and division with truncated fraction. The monadic operators + and − denote identity and sign inversion. The operators **div** and **mod** yield a quotient $q = x$ **div** y and a remainder $r = x$ **mod** y such that $x = q*y+r$, $0 \leqslant r < y$. The divisor (or modulus) y must be strictly positive.
Example:

$$x = -15, \quad y = 4$$
$$x/y = -3, \quad x \text{ \bf div } y = -4, \quad x \text{ \bf mod } y = 1.$$

Boolean operators (**or xor and not**) apply to Boolean operands and yield a result of type Boolean. The term a **and** b is evaluated as '**if** a **then** b **else** false', and the expression a **or** b is evaluated as '**if** a **then** true **else** b.' Boolean operators can also be applied to operands of type bits. The specified operation is then performed on all corresponding elements of the operands.

Relations yield a result of type Boolean. (< > <= >= stand for $\neq$ $\leqslant$ $\geqslant$ respectively). They apply to operands of the standard types integer, char, Boolean and bits (to the latter only = and < >), and of enumeration types.

Examples of factors:

    27   i   (i+j+k)   **not** p   [2, 3, 5, 7, 11]

Examples of terms:

    i*k   i/(i−1)   i **div** 2   (i<j) **and** (j<k)   s **and** t

Examples of simple expressions:

    i+j   i+5*k   −i   p **or** q   s **or** t

Examples of expressions:

    (i+j)*(j+k)   i   k+5   i = j   t **xor** [0 : 7]

(Given the variables declared in *Variables*, the first three examples in each line are of type integer, the fourth is of type Boolean and the fifth of type bits.)

Statements

Statements denote actions. Elementary statements are the assignment statement and the procedure call. Composite statements may be constructed out of elementary statements and other composite statements.

    statement = assignment|procedurecall|processstatement|ifstatement|casestatement|
       whilestatement|repeatstatement|loopstatement|withstatement|.

Assignments

An assignment denotes the action of evaluating an expression and of assigning the resulting value to a variable. The symbol := is called assignment operator (pronounced 'becomes').

assignment = variable ":=" expression.

After an assignment is executed, the variable has the value obtained by evaluating the expression. The old value is lost ('overwritten'). The variable must be of the same type as (the value of) the expression.

Examples of assignments:
```
i := 100
p := true
m[i, j] := 10*i + j
```

Procedure calls

A procedure call denotes the execution of the specified procedure, i.e. of the statement part of its body. The procedure call must contain the same number of parameters as the corresponding procedure declaration. Those of the call are called *actual parameters*. An actual parameter corresponding (by its position in the parameter list) to a *const-parameter* must be an expression. The types of the actual and the formal parameters must be the same, and the formal parameter appears as a read-only parameter, i.e. assignments to this parameter are prohibited. If the actual parameter corresponds to a *var-parameter*, it must be a variable. That variable is substituted for the formal parameter throughout the procedure body. Types must be identical, and if the actual parameter is an indexed variable, the index expressions are evaluated upon procedure call.

```
procedurecall = ident [parameterlist].
parameterlist = "(" parameter {"," parameter} ")".
parameter = expression | variable.
```

Examples of procedure calls:
```
inc (i, 10)
sort (a, 100)
```

Statement sequences

A sequence of statements separated by semicolons is called a statement sequence and specifies the sequential execution of the statements in the order of their occurrence.

```
statementsequence = statement {";" statement}.
```

If statements

If statements specify conditional execution of actions depending on the value of Boolean expressions.

```
ifstatement = "if" expression "then" statementsequence
    {"elsif" expression "then" statementsequence}
    ["else" statementsequence] "end".
```

Case statements

Case statements specify the selective execution of a statement sequence depending on the value of an expression. First the case expression is evaluated, then the statement sequence

with label equal to the resulting value is executed. The type of the case expression must not be structured.

casestatement = "**case**" expression "**of**" case {"**;**" case} "**end**".
case = [caselabels "**:**" "**begin**" statementsequence "**end**"].
caselabels = constant {"**,**" constant}.

While statements

While statements specify the repeated execution of a statement sequence depending on the value of a Boolean expression. The expression is evaluated before the first and after each execution of the statement sequence. The repetition stops as soon as this evaluation yields the value false.

whilestatement = "**while**" expression "**do**" statementsequence "**end**".

Repeat statements

Repeat statements specify the repeated execution of a statement sequence depending on the value of a Boolean expression. The expression is evaluated after each execution of the statement sequence, and the repetition stops as soon as it yields the value true. Hence, the statement sequence is executed at least once.

repeatstatement = "**repeat**" statementsequence "**until**" expression.

Loop statements

Loop statements specify the repeated execution of statement sequences. The repetition can be terminated depending on the values of possibly several Boolean expressions, called *exit conditions*.

loopstatement = "**loop**" statementsequence
    {"**when**" expression ["**do**" statementsequence] "**exit**"
    statementsequence} "**end**".

Hence, the general form is
loop S1 **when** B1 **do** X1 **exit**
        S2 **when** B2 **do** X2 **exit**
            ...
        Sn **when** Bn **do** Xn **exit**
        S
    end

First, S1 is executed, then B1 is evaluated. If it yields the value true, X1 is executed and thereupon execution of the loop statement is terminated. Otherwise it continues with S2, etc. After S, execution continues unconditionally with S1.

Note: all repetitions can be expressed by loop statements alone, the while and repeat statement merely express simple and frequently occurring cases.

With statements

The with statement specifies a record variable and a statement sequence to be executed. In these statements field identifiers of that record variable may occur without preceding qualification, and refer to the fields of the variable specified.

withstatement = "**with**" variable "**do**" statementsequence "**end**".

Procedures

Procedure declarations consist of a *procedure heading* and a *block* which is said to be the procedure body. The heading specifies the procedure identifier by which the procedure is called, and its formal parameters. The block contains declarations and statements.

There are two kinds of procedures, namely *proper procedures* and *function procedures*. The latter are activated by a function call as a constituent of an expression, and yield a result that acts as operand in the expression. The former are activated by a procedure call. The function procedure is distinguished in the declaration by the fact that the type of its result is indicated following the parameter list. Its body must contain an assignment to the procedure identifier which defines the value of the function procedure. There are two kinds of formal parameters, namely constant and variable parameters. The kind is indicated in the formal parameter list. Constant parameters stand for a value obtained through evaluation of the corresponding actual parameter when the procedure is called. Assignments cannot be made to a constant parameter. Variable parameters correspond to actual variables, and assignments to them are permitted (see *Procedure calls*). Formal parameters are local to the procedure, i.e. their *scope* is the program text which constitutes the procedure declaration.

All constants, variables, types, modules and procedures declared within the block that constitutes the procedure body are local to the procedure. The values of local variables, including those defined within a local module, are not defined upon entry to the procedure. Since procedures may be declared as local objects too, procedure declarations may be nested. Every object is said to be declared at a certain *level of nesting*. If it is declared local to a procedure (or process) at level k, it has itself level $k + 1$. Objects declared in the block that constitutes the main program are defined to be at level 0.

In addition to its formal parameters and local objects, also the objects declared in the environment of the procedure are known and accessible in the procedure, unless the procedure declaration contains a so-called *use-list*. In this case, only formal parameters, local objects and the identifiers occurring in the use-list are known inside the procedure (see *Modules*). Standard objects are accessible in any case.

```
proceduredeclaration = "procedure" ident
    ["(" formalparameters ")"] [":" ident] ";" [uselist] block ident.
formalparameters = section {";" section}.
section = ["const"|"var"] ident {"," ident} ":" formaltype.
formaltype = ["array" indextypes "of"] ident.
indextypes = identlist.
uselist = "use" [identlist] ";".
block = {declarationpart} [initializationpart] [statementpart] "end".
declarationpart = "const" {constantdeclaration ";"}|
    "type" {typedeclaration ";"}|
    "var" {variabledeclaration ";"}|module ";"|
    proceduredeclaration ";"|processdeclaration ";".
initializationpart = "value" {ident "=" initialvalue}.
initialvalue = constant|"[" repetition "]" initialvalue|
    "(" initialvalue {"," initialvalue} ")".
repetition = integer|ident.
statementpart = "begin" statementsequence.
```

The identifier ending the procedure declaration must be the same as the one following the symbol **procedure**, i.e. the procedure identifier. If the specifier **const** or **var** is missing in

a section of formal parameters, then its elements are assumed to be constant (read-only) parameters.

An initialization part serves to assign initial values to variables declared in the same block. Parentheses indicate the structure of the assigned value, which must correspond to that of the initialized variable. Initialization parts can only occur in blocks at level 0, i.e. in the main program and in modules declared in the main program.

The use of the procedure identifier in a call within its declaration implies recursive activation of the procedure. If a formal type indicates an array structure, then only the types but not the bounds of the indices are specified.

Examples of procedure declarations:

```
procedure readinteger (var x: integer);
    var i: integer; ch: char;
begin i: = 0;
    repeat readcharacter (ch)
    until ('0' <= ch) and (ch <= '9');
    repeat i: = 10*i + (integer(ch) − integer('0'));
        readcharacter(ch)
    until (ch < '0') or ('9' < ch);
end readinteger

procedure writeinteger(x: integer);
    var i, q: integer;   (*assume x > =0*)
    buf: array 1: 10 of integer;
begin i: = 0;   q: = x;   writecharacter(' ');
    repeat i: = i + 1;   buf[i]: = q mod 10;   q: = q div 10
    until q = 0;
    repeat writecharacter(buf[i]);   i: = i − 1
    until i = 0
end writeinteger

procedure gcd(x, y: integer): integer;
    var a, b: integer;   (*assume x, y > 0*)
begin a: = x;   b: = y;
    while a < > b do
        if a < b then b: = b − a else a: = a − b
        end
    end
    gcd: = a
end gcd
```

Standard procedures.   Standard procedures are predeclared and available throughout every program.

Proper procedures

inc(x, n)	=	x: = x + n
dec(x, n)	=	x: = x − n
inc(x)	=	x: = x + 1
dec(x)	=	x: = x − 1
halt	=	terminates the entire program

2

Function procedures

off (b1, b2)	=	b1 **and** b2 = [ ]	(b1, b2 of type bits)
off (b)	=	b = [ ]	
among (i, b)	=	b[i] (b is a bit expression)	
low (a)	=	low index bound of array a	
high (a)	=	high index bound of array a	
adr (v)	=	address of variable v	
size (v)	=	size of variable v	

Type transfer functions

integer (x)	=	ordinal of x in the set of values defined by the type of x.
char (x)	=	character with ordinal x.

(*adr* and *size* are of type integer, and are implementation-dependent.)

Modules

A module constitutes a collection of declarations and a sequence of statements. They are enclosed in the brackets **module** and **end**. The module heading contains the module identifier, and possibly a so-called *use-list* and a so-called *define-list*. The former specifies all identifiers of objects that are used within the module and declared outside it. The latter specifies all identifiers of objects declared within the module that are to be used outside it. Hence, a module constitutes a wall around its local objects whose transparency is strictly under control of the programmer. Objects local to a module are said to be at the same level as the module.

> module = moduleheading [definelist] [uselist] block ident.
> moduleheading = ["**interface**"] "**module**" ident ";" |
>   "**device**" "**module**" ident priority ";".
> definelist = "**define**" identlist ";".

The identifier at the end of the module must be the same as the one following the symbol **module**, i.e. the module identifier. (For an explanation of the prefixes **interface** and **device** see the sections *Interface modules* and *Device modules and processes*.) Identifiers which occur in the module's use-list are said to be *imported*, and those in the define-list are said to be *exported*.

If a type is defined local to a module and its identifier occurs in the define-list of the module, then only the type's identity, but none of its structural details becomes known outside the module. If it is a record type, the field names remain unknown, if it is an array type, index range and elements type remain unknown outside. Hence, variables declared of a type that was exported in this way from a module can be used only by procedures declared within and exported from that same module. This implies that if a module defines a type, it also has to include the definition of all operators belonging to this type.

If a local variable occurs in the define-list of a module, it cannot be changed outside the module, i.e. it appears as a read-only variable.

The statement sequence that constitutes the module body (block) is executed when the procedure to which the module is local is called. If several modules are declared, then these bodies are executed in the sequence in which the modules occur. The bodies serve to initialize local variables. Example:

```
      procedure P;
        module M1;
          define F1, n1;
          var n1: integer;
          procedure F1(x: integer): integer;
            begin ... inc (n1) ... F1: = ...
            end F1;
        begin n1: = 0
        end M1;

        module M2;
          define F2, n2;
          var n2: integer;
          procedure F2(x: integer): integer;
            begin ... inc (n2) ... F2: = ...
            end F2;
        begin n2: = 0
        end M2;

      begin (* use procedures F1 and F2; n1 and n2 are counters of their calls and cannot
              be changed at this place *)
      end P
```

In this example, the two statements n1: = 0 and n2: = 0 can be considered as being prefixed to the body of procedure P. Within this body, assignments to these variables are prohibited.

Examples:

The following sample module serves to scan a text and to copy it onto an output character sequence. Input is obtained characterwise by a procedure inchr and delivered by a procedure outchr. The characters are given in the ASCII code; control characters are ignored, with the exception of *lf* (linefeed) and *fs* (file separator). They are both translated into a blank, and cause the Boolean variables *eoln* (end of line) and *eof* (end of file) to be set respectively. *fs* is assumed to follow *lf* immediately.

```
    module lineinput;
      define read, newline, newfile, eoln, eof, lno;
      use inchr, outchr;
      const lf = 12C; cr = 15C; fs = 34C;
      var lno: integer; (*line number*)
        ch: char; (*last character read*)
          eof, eoln: Boolean;

    procedure newfile;
    begin
        if not eof then
            repeat inchr(ch) until ch = fs;
        end;
        eof: = false; lno: = 0
    end newfile;
    procedure newline;
    begin
        if not eoln then
            repeat inchr(ch) until ch = lf;
```

```
            outchr(cr); outchr(lf)
        end;
        eoln: = false; inc(lno)
    end newline;

    procedure read (var x: char);
    begin (*assume not eoln and not eof*)
        loop inchr(ch); outchr(ch);
            when ch > = ' ' do x: = ch exit
            when ch =  lf do x: = ' '; eoln: = true exit
            when ch = fs do x: = ' '; eoln: = true; eof: = true exit
        end
    end read;
begin eof: = true; eoln: = true
end lineinput
```

The next example is a module which operates a disk track reservation table, and protects it from unauthorized access. A function procedure *newtrack* yields the number of a free track which is becoming reserved. Tracks can be released by calling procedure *returntrack*.

```
module trackreservation;
    define newtrack, returntrack;
    const m = 64; w = 16;   (*there are m*w tracks*)
    var i: integer;
        reserved: array 0 : 63 of bits;

    procedure newtrack: integer;
        (*reserves a new track, yields its index as function
            result, if a free track is found, and −1 otherwise*)
        var i, j: integer; found: Boolean;
    begin found: = false; i: = m;
        repeat dec(i); j: = w;
            repeat dec(j);
                    if not reserved[i, j] then found: = true end
            until found or (j = 0)
        until found or (i = 0);
        if found then newtrack: = i*w + j; reserved[i, j]: = true
                else newtrack: = −1 end
    end newtrack;

    procedure returntrack (k: integer);
    begin (*assume 0 <= k < m*w *)
        reserved[k div w, k mod w]: = false
    end returntrack;

begin i: = m;   (*mark all tracks free*)
    repeat dec(i); reserved[i]: = [ ]
    until i = 0
end trackreservation
```

Programs

A Modula program is formulated as a module.

```
program =  module ".".
```

FACILITIES FOR MULTIPROGRAMMING

This section defines those facilities that are needed to express the concurrent execution of several program parts. They are already referenced in the syntax of the preceding section, and comprise three essential facilities: processes, interface modules and synchronization primitives.

Processes

A process declaration describes a sequential algorithm—including its local objects—that is intended to be executed concurrently with other processes. No assumption is made about the speed of execution of processes, except that this speed is greater than zero.

A process declaration has the form of a procedure declaration, and the same rules about locality and accessibility of objects hold.

> processdeclaration =
>   "**process**" ident ["(" formalparameters ")"] [intvector] ";" uselist block ident.

The identifier at the end of the declaration must be the same as the one following the symbol **process**, namely the process identifier. (For an explanation of intvector see *Device modules and processes*.)

Restriction:

Processes must be declared at level 0, i.e. they cannot be nested or be local to procedures. Objects local to a process are said to be at level 1.

Process control statements

A process statement expresses the starting of a new process. Syntactically it corresponds to the procedure call. However, in the case of a procedure call, the calling program can be thought to be suspended until the procedure execution has been completed, whereas a program starting a new process is not suspended. Rather the execution of the started process may proceed concurrently with the continuation of the starting program.

> processstatement = ident [parameterlist].

Whereas a process declaration defines a pattern of behaviour, a process statement initiates the execution of actions according to this pattern. This implies that reference to the same process declaration in several process statements initiates the concurrent execution of several processes according to the same pattern (usually according to different parameters).

Restriction:

Process statements are confined to the body of the main program, i.e. they can neither occur within procedures nor processes.

Interface modules

The interface module is the facility which provides exclusion of simultaneous access from several processes to common objects. Variables that are to establish communication or data transfers between processes are declared local to an interface module. They are accessed *via* procedures also declared local (so-called interface procedures) and which are exported from the module. If a process has called any such procedure, another process calling the same or another one of these procedures is delayed, until the first process has completed its procedure or starts waiting for a signal (see *Signals*).

An interface module is syntactically distinguished from regular modules by the prefix symbol **interface**. Interface procedures must not call on procedures declared outside the interface module (except standard procedures). Examples of interface modules are given below.

Signals

In general, processes communicate *via* common variables, usually declared within interface modules. However, it is not recommended that synchronization be achieved by means of such common, shared variables. A delay of a process could in this way be realized only by a 'busy waiting' statement, i.e. by polling. Instead, a facility called a *signal* should be used.

Signals are introduced in a program (usually within interface modules) like other objects. In particular, the syntactic form of their declaration is like that of variables, although the signal is not a variable in the sense of having a value and being assignable. There are only two operations and a test that can be applied to signals. They are represented by three standard procedures.

1. The procedure call *wait*(s, r) delays the process until it receives the signal s. The process is given delay rank r, where r must be a positive valued integer expression. *wait*(s) is a short form for wait(s, 1).

2. The procedure call *send*(s) sends the signal s to that process which had been waiting for s with least delay rank. If several processes are waiting for s with same delay rank, that process receives s which had been waiting longest. If no process is waiting for s, the statement send(s) has no effect.

3. The Boolean function procedure *awaited*(s) yields the value *true*, if there is at least one process waiting for signal s, *false* otherwise.

If a process executes a wait statement within an interface procedure, then other processes are allowed to execute other such procedures, although the waiting process has not completed its interface procedure. If a send statement is executed within an interface procedure, and if the signal is sent to a process waiting within the same interface module, then the receiving process obtains control over the module and the sending process is delayed until the other process has completed its interface procedure. Hence, both the wait and send operations must be considered as 'singular points' or enclaves in the interface module, which are exempted from the mutual exclusion rule.

If a signal variable is exported from a module, then no send operations can be applied to it outside the module.

Examples of interface modules with signal operations[5]:

```
interface module resourcereservation;
    define semaphore, P, V, init;
    type semaphore = record taken: Boolean;
                                    free: signal
                          end;
    procedure P (var s: semaphore);
        begin if s.taken then wait (s.free) end;
               s.taken:= true
        end P;
```

```
        procedure V (var s: semaphore);
          begin s.taken:=false;
                send (s.free)
          end V;

        procedure init (var s: semaphore);
          begin s.taken:=false
          end init;

    end resourcereservation


    interface module bufferhandling;
      define get, put, empty;
      const nmax = 256;
      var n, in, out: integer;
          nonempty, nonfull: signal;
          buf: array 1: nmax of char;

        procedure empty: Boolean;
          begin empty:=n = 0
          end empty;

        procedure put (ch: char);
          begin if n = nmax then wait (nonfull) end;
                inc(n);
                buf[in]:=ch; in:=(in mod nmax)+1;
                send(nonempty)
          end put;

        procedure get(var ch: char);
          begin if n = 0 then wait(nonempty) end;
                dec(n);
                ch:=buf[out]; out:=(out mod nmax)+1;
                send(nonfull)
          end get;

      begin n:=0; in:=1; out:=1
      end bufferhandling


    interface module diskheadscheduler;
      define request, release;
      use cylmax;   (*no. of cylinders*)
      var headpos: integer;
          up, busy: Boolean;
          upsweep, downsweep: signal;

      procedure request(dest: integer);
      begin
        if busy then
          if headpos < dest then wait(upsweep, dest)
            else wait(downsweep, cylmax-dest) end
        end;
        busy:=true; headpos:=dest
      end request;
```

```
    procedure release;
    begin busy: = false;
      if up then
        if awaited(upsweep) then send(upsweep)
          else up: = false; send(downsweep)
        end else
        if awaited(downsweep) then send(downsweep)
          else up: = true; send(upsweep)
        end
      end
    end release;

begin headpos: = 0; up: = true; busy: = false
end diskheadscheduler
```

PDP-11 SPECIFIC FACILITIES

All language facilities described in the two previous sections are defined without reference to a specific computer, i.e. they are defined by this report alone. This is not the case for the additional facilities introduced in this section, for they refer to features particular to the PDP-11 computer family, and can only be fully understood by referring to a PDP-11 description. They represent that computer's features for *communicating with peripheral devices*. These language facilities are available to the programmer only within modules specially designed as device modules.

Device modules and processes

A device module is an interface module that interfaces one or more so-called *device processes*—also called *drivers*—with other processes—also called 'regular' processes. A device process is a process that contains operations that activate (drive) a peripheral device, and its heading is marked by the prefix symbol **device**. Whereas regular processes are declared outside interface modules and interact *via* procedures declared within the interface module, device processes are entirely declared within the interface module (and hence need not be especially distinguished by a mark or symbol). They, and only they, may contain a statement denoted by the identifier *doio*. While executing this statement, the process relinquishes exclusive access to the module's variables (as in the case of *wait* and *send*). The doio statement represents that part of the device process that is executed by the peripheral device. Usually it is preceded by some statement initiating the device operation by accessing a device register.

The PDP-11 processor operates at a certain priority level. According to this level, interrupts from devices at lower levels are disabled and saved until the processor drops its level and 'returns to duties of lower priority'. The integer in the module heading specifies that level ($4 \leqslant L \leqslant 6$), and signifies that all procedures and processes defined in this module are executed with this processor priority. The programmer is advised to include in a device module only operations on devices that have exactly that interrupt priority.

priority = "[" integer "]".

If a device process sends a signal to a process of lower priority, then the signalling process continues until it encounters a wait or a doio statement. This is an exception of the rule given in *Signals*, which specifies that the signalled process continues. Regular processes have priority 0.

All processes defined within a device module are device processes, and each such process is associated with a so-called interrupt vector, i.e. with all devices that are interrupting to one and the same store location. The address of that location (interrupt vector) is to be specified in the device process heading (also enclosed in brackets). Interrupts must be disabled during the execution of wait statements. Two examples of device modules are given in *Device register declarations*.

intvector = ''['' integer '']''.

Restrictions:

1. Device processes must not send signals to other device processes.
2. Device processes must not call any non-local procedures.
3. Only a single instance of a device process can be activated. Device processes are not 're-entrant'.
4. Wait statements within device processes must not specify a rank.

Device register declarations

Register declarations serve to introduce interface registers that are needed to communicate with peripheral devices. In the PDP-11 each device is associated with one or several registers. These registers have fixed store addresses which are to be specified in register declarations.

A register appears in a Modula program as a variable of the basic type specified in its declaration. Hence registers are also declared like variables by a variable declaration. Status registers are usually declared to be of type bits, whereas buffer registers are usually of type integer or char.

The address of a register is prescribed by the hardware and it is specified immediately following the identifier and is enclosed in brackets. Hence, the syntax of variable declarations within a device module is slightly extended as follows:

variabledeclaration = ident [address] {'','' ident [address]} '':'' type.
address = ''['' integer '']''.

Examples:

The following module defines two procedures, *readch* and *writech*, which input a character from the typewriter keyboard and output a character to its printer. Both routines communicate with the devices *via* device processes and data buffers.

```
device module typewriter [4];
    define readch, writech;
  const n = 64;   (*buffer size*)
  var KBS [177560B]: bits;   (*keyboard status*)
      KBB [177562B]: char;   (*keyboard buffer*)
      PRS [177564B]: bits;   (*printer status*)
      PRB [177566B]: char;   (*printer buffer*)
      in1, in2, out1, out2: integer;
      n1, n2: integer;
      nonfull1, nonfull2, nonempty1, nonempty2: signal;
      buf1, buf2: array 1: n of char;
```

```
procedure readch(var ch: char);
begin
    if n1 =  0 then wait(nonempty1) end;
    ch:= buf1[out1]; out1:=(out1 mod n)+1;
    dec(n1); send(nonfull1)
end readch;

procedure writech(ch: char);
begin
    if n2 = n then wait(nonfull2) end;
    buf2[in2]:=ch; in2:=(in2 mod n)+1;
    inc(n2); send(nonempty2)
end writech;

process keyboarddriver [60B];
begin
    loop
        if n1 = n then wait(nonfull1) end;
        KBS[6]:=true; doio; KBS[6]:=false;
        buf1[in1]:=KBB; in1:=(in1 mod n)+1;
        inc(n1); send(nonempty1)
    end
end keyboarddriver;

process printerdriver [64B];
begin
    loop
        if n2 = 0 then wait(nonempty2) end;
        PRB:=buf2[out2]; out2:=(out2 mod n)+1;
        PRS[6]:=true; doio; PRS[6]:=false;
        dec(n2); send(nonfull2)
    end
end printerdriver;

begin in1:=1; in2:=1; out1:=1; out2:=1;
    n1:=0; n2:=0;
    keyboarddriver; printerdriver
end typewriter
```

The following module defines a variable *time* that is incremented every 20 msec, a signal *tick* that is sent every 20 msec and a procedure *pause(n)* which delays the calling process by n*20 msec.

```
device module realtime [6];
    define time, tick, pause;
    var time: integer; tick: signal;
        LCS [177546B]: bits;   (*Line Clock Status*)

    procedure pause(n: integer);
        var delay: integer;
```

```
begin delay:=n;
  while delay>0 do
    wait(tick); dec(delay)
  end
end pause;

process clock [100B];
begin LCS[6]:=true;
    loop doio; inc(time);
        while awaited(tick) do send(tick) end
    end
end clock;

begin time:=0; clock
end realtime
```

According to Restriction 1 (*Device modules and processes*), other device processes can neither wait for the signal *tick* nor can they call the procedure *pause*.

ACKNOWLEDGEMENTS

I wish to thank U. Ammann, J. Hoppe, V. K. Le and R. Schoenberger for their contributions to the experimental Modula implementation. Thanks are due to H. Sandmayr for many valuable suggestions, and to J. Spillmann for the preparation of the program to draw syntax diagrams automatically.

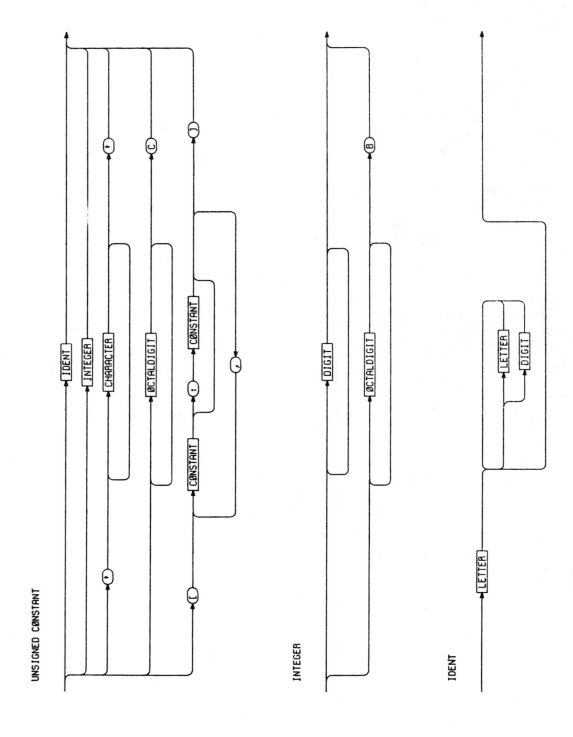

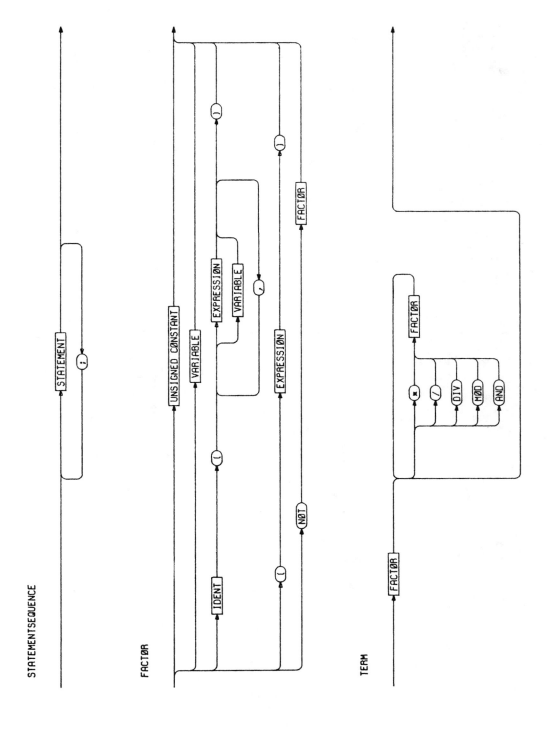

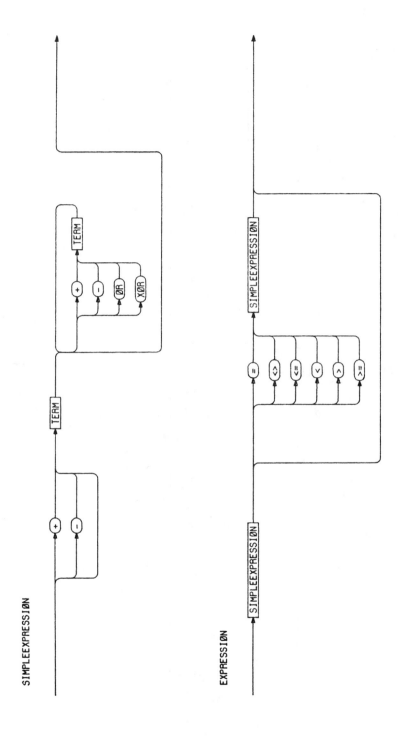

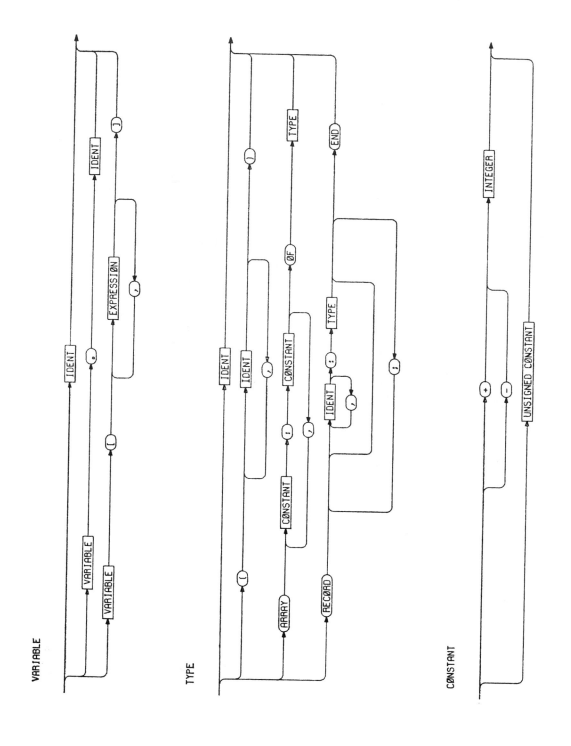

PHILLIPS MEMORIAL
LIBRARY
PROVIDENCE COLLEGE

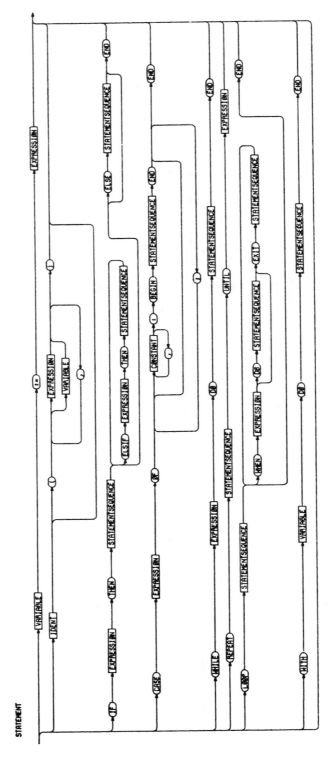

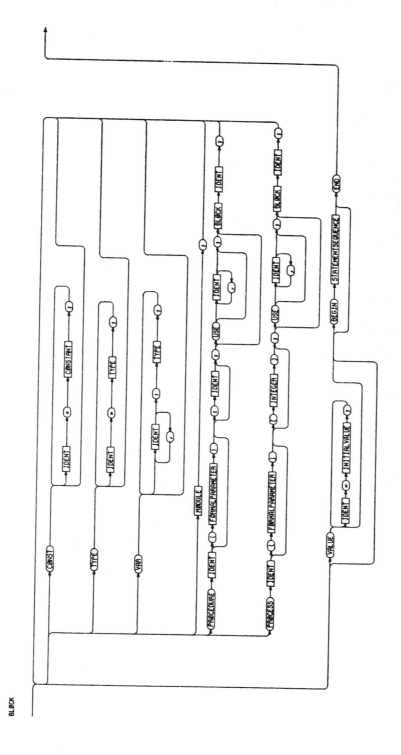

3

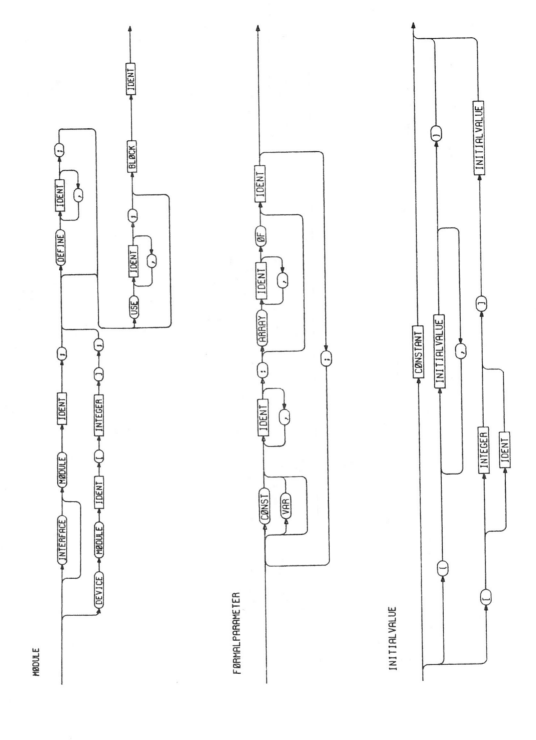

MODULE

FORMAL PARAMETER

INITIAL VALUE

REFERENCES

1. P. Brinch Hansen, *Concurrent Pascal Report*, Calif. Inst. of Technology, June 1975.
2. P. Brinch Hansen, *The Solo Operating System*, Calif. Inst. of Technology, July 1975.
3. F. P. Brooks, Jr., *The Mythical Man Month*, Addison-Wesley, Reading, Mass., 1975.
4. O.-J. Dahl, B. Myhrhaug and K. Nygaard, *The SIMULA 67 Common Base Language*, Norwegian Comp. Center, Oslo, 1968.
5. C. A. R. Hoare, 'Monitors: An operating system structuring concept', *Comm. ACM*, **17**, 10, 549–557 (1974).
6. K. Jensen and N. Wirth, *PASCAL—User Manual and Report*, Springer-Verlag, New York, 1974/5.
7. D. L. Parnas, 'Information distribution aspects of design methodology', *IFIP Congress* 71, Booklet TA-3, 26–30.
8. H. Sandmayr, 'Strukturen und Konzepte zur Multiprogrammierung und ihre Anwendung auf ein System für Datenstationen (Hexapus)', *ETH-Dissertation* 5537, 1975.
9. N. Wirth, 'On multiprogramming, machine coding, and computer organization', *Comm. ACM*, **12**, 9, 489–498 (1969).
10. N. Wirth, 'The programming language Pascal', *Acta Informatica*, **1**, 35–63 (1971).
11. P. Brinch Hansen, *Operating System Principles*, Prentice-Hall, Englewood Cliffs, N.J., 1973.

COMMUNICATING SEQUENTIAL PROCESSES*

C. A. R. HOARE

This paper suggests that input and output are basic primitives of programming and that parallel composition of communicating sequential processes is a fundamental program structuring method. When combined with a development of Dijkstra's guarded command, these concepts are surprisingly versatile. Their use is illustrated by sample solutions of a variety of familiar programming exercises.

Key Words and Phrases: programming, programming languages, programming primitives, program structures, parallel programming, concurrency, input, output, guarded commands, nondeterminacy, coroutines, procedures, multiple entries, multiple exits, classes, data representations, recursion, conditional critical regions, monitors, iterative arrays

CR Categories: 4.20, 4.22, 4.32

1. Introduction

Among the primitive concepts of computer programming, and of the high level languages in which programs are expressed, the action of assignment is familiar and well understood. In fact, any change of the internal state of a machine executing a program can be modeled as an assignment of a new value to some variable part of that machine. However, the operations of input and output, which affect the external environment of a machine, are not nearly so well understood. They are often added to a programming language only as an afterthought.

Among the structuring methods for computer pro-

General permission to make fair use in teaching or research of all or part of this material is granted to individual readers and to nonprofit libraries acting for them provided that ACM's copyright notice is given and that reference is made to the publication, to its date of issue, and to the fact that reprinting privileges were granted by permission of the Association for Computing Machinery. To otherwise reprint a figure, table, other substantial excerpt, or the entire work requires specific permission as does republication, or systematic or multiple reproduction.

This research was supported by a Senior Fellowship of the Science Research Council.

Author's present address: Programming Research Group, 45, Banbury Road, Oxford, England.

© 1978 ACM 0001-0782/78/0800-0666 $00.75

*Reprinted from *Comm ACM*, 21, 8, August 1978, 666–677, copyright 1978.

grams, three basic constructs have received widespread recognition and use: A repetitive construct (e.g. the **while** loop), an alternative construct (e.g. the conditional **if..then..else**), and normal sequential program composition (often denoted by a semicolon). Less agreement has been reached about the design of other important program structures, and many suggestions have been made: Subroutines (Fortran), procedures (Algol 60 [15]), entries (PL/I), coroutines (UNIX [17]), classes (SIMULA 67 [5]), processes and monitors (Concurrent Pascal [2]), clusters (CLU [13]), forms (ALPHARD [19]), actors (Hewitt [1]).

The traditional stored program digital computer has been designed primarily for deterministic execution of a single sequential program. Where the desire for greater speed has led to the introduction of parallelism, every attempt has been made to disguise this fact from the programmer, either by hardware itself (as in the multiple function units of the CDC 6600) or by the software (as in an I/O control package, or a multiprogrammed operating system). However, developments of processor technology suggest that a multiprocessor machine, constructed from a number of similar self-contained processors (each with its own store), may become more powerful, capacious, reliable, and economical than a machine which is disguised as a monoprocessor.

In order to use such a machine effectively on a single task, the component processors must be able to communicate and to synchronize with each other. Many methods of achieving this have been proposed. A widely adopted method of communication is by inspection and updating of a common store (as in Algol 68 [18], PL/I, and many machine codes). However, this can create severe problems in the construction of correct programs and it may lead to expense (e.g. crossbar switches) and unreliability (e.g. glitches) in some technologies of hardware implementation. A greater variety of methods has been proposed for synchronization: semaphores [6], events (PL/I), conditional critical regions [10], monitors and queues (Concurrent Pascal [2]), and path expressions [3]. Most of these are demonstrably adequate for their purpose, but there is no widely recognized criterion for choosing between them.

This paper makes an ambitious attempt to find a single simple solution to all these problems. The essential proposals are:

(1) Dijkstra's guarded commands [8] are adopted (with a slight change of notation) as sequential control structures, and as the sole means of introducing and controlling nondeterminism.

(2) A parallel command, based on Dijkstra's *parbegin* [6], specifies concurrent execution of its constituent sequential commands (processes). All the processes start simultaneously, and the parallel command ends only when they are all finished. They may not communicate with each other by updating global variables.

(3) Simple forms of input and output command are introduced. They are used for communication between concurrent processes.

(4) Such communication occurs when one process names another as destination for output *and* the second process names the first as source for input. In this case, the value to be output is copied from the first process to the second. There is *no* automatic buffering: In general, an input or output command is delayed until the other process is ready with the corresponding output or input. Such delay is invisible to the delayed process.

(5) Input commands may appear in guards. A guarded command with an input guard is selected for execution only if and when the source named in the input command is ready to execute the corresponding output command. If several input guards of a set of alternatives have ready destinations, only one is selected and the others have *no* effect; but the choice between them is arbitrary. In an efficient implementation, an output command which has been ready for a long time should be favored; but the definition of a language cannot specify this since the relative speed of execution of the processes is undefined.

(6) A repetitive command may have input guards. If all the sources named by them have terminated, then the repetitive command also terminates.

(7) A simple pattern-matching feature, similar to that of [16], is used to discriminate the structure of an input message, and to access its components in a secure fashion. This feature is used to inhibit input of messages that do not match the specified pattern.

The programs expressed in the proposed language are intended to be implementable both by a conventional machine with a single main store, and by a fixed network of processors connected by input/output channels (although very different optimizations are appropriate in the different cases). It is consequently a rather static language: The text of a program determines a fixed upper bound on the number of processes operating concurrently; there is no recursion and no facility for process-valued variables. In other respects also, the language has been stripped to the barest minimum necessary for explanation of its more novel features.

The concept of a communicating sequential process is shown in Sections 3–5 to provide a method of expressing solutions to many simple programming exercises which have previously been employed to illustrate the use of various proposed programming language features. This suggests that the process may constitute a synthesis of a number of familiar and new programming ideas. The reader is invited to skip the examples which do not interest him.

However, this paper also ignores many serious problems. The most serious is that it fails to suggest any proof method to assist in the development and verification of correct programs. Secondly, it pays no attention to the problems of efficient implementation, which may be particularly serious on a traditional sequential computer. It is probable that a solution to these problems will require (1) imposition of restrictions in the use of the proposed features; (2) reintroduction of distinctive no-

tations for the most common and useful special cases; (3) development of automatic optimization techniques; and (4) the design of appropriate hardware.

Thus the concepts and notations introduced in this paper (although described in the next section in the form of a programming language fragment) should not be regarded as suitable for use as a programming language, either for abstract or for concrete programming. They are at best only a partial solution to the problems tackled. Further discussion of these and other points will be found in Section 7.

2. Concepts and Notations

The style of the following description is borrowed from Algol 60 [15]. Types, declarations, and expressions have not been treated; in the examples, a Pascal-like notation [20] has usually been adopted. The curly braces { } have been introduced into BNF to denote none or more repetitions of the enclosed material. (Sentences in parentheses refer to an implementation: they are not strictly part of a language definition.)

```
<command> := <simple command>|<structured command>
<simple command> := <null command>|<assignment command>
       |<input command>|<output command>
<structured command> := <alternative command>
       |<repetitive command>|<parallel command>
<null command> := skip
<command list> := {<declaration>; |<command>;} <command>
```

A command specifies the behavior of a device executing the command. It may succeed or fail. Execution of a simple command, if successful, may have an effect on the internal state of the executing device (in the case of assignment), or on its external environment (in the case of output), or on both (in the case of input). Execution of a structured command involves execution of some or all of its constituent commands, and if any of these fail, so does the structured command. (In this case, whenever possible, an implementation should provide some kind of comprehensible error diagnostic message.)

A null command has no effect and never fails.

A command list specifies sequential execution of its constituent commands in the order written. Each declaration introduces a fresh variable with a scope which extends from its declaration to the end of the command list.

2.1 Parallel Commands

```
<parallel command> := [<process>{||<process>}]
<process> := <process label> <command list>
<process label> := <empty>|<identifier> ::
       |<identifier>(<label subscript>{,<label subscript>}) ::
<label subscript> := <integer constant>|<range>
<integer constant> := <numeral>|<bound variable>
<bound variable> := <identifier>
<range> := <bound variable>:<lower bound>..<upper bound>
<lower bound> := <integer constant>
<upper bound> := <integer constant>
```

Each process of a parallel command must be *disjoint* from every other process of the command, in the sense that it does not mention any variable which occurs as a target variable (see Sections 2.2 and 2.3) in any other process.

A process label without subscripts, or one whose label subscripts are all integer constants, serves as a name for the command list to which it is prefixed; its scope extends over the whole of the parallel command. A process whose label subscripts include one or more ranges stands for a series of processes, each with the same label and command list, except that each has a different combination of values substituted for the bound variables. These values range between the lower bound and the upper bound inclusive. For example, $X(i:1..n)$ :: CL stands for

$$X(1) :: CL_1 || X(2) :: CL_2 ||...|| X(n) :: CL_n$$

where each CL_j is formed from CL by replacing every occurrence of the bound variable i by the numeral j. After all such expansions, each process label in a parallel command must occur only once and the processes must be well formed and disjoint.

A parallel command specifies concurrent execution of its constituent processes. They all start simultaneously and the parallel command terminates successfully only if and when they have all successfully terminated. The relative speed with which they are executed is arbitrary.

Examples:

(1) [cardreader?cardimage||lineprinter!lineimage]

Performs the two constituent commands in parallel, and terminates only when both operations are complete. The time taken may be as low as the longer of the times taken by each constituent process, i.e. the sum of its computing, waiting, and transfer times.

(2) [west :: DISASSEMBLE||X :: SQUASH||east :: ASSEMBLE]

The three processes have the names "west," "X," and "east." The capitalized words stand for command lists which will be defined in later examples.

(3) [room :: ROOM||fork(i:0..4) :: FORK||phil(i:0..4) :: PHIL]

There are eleven processes. The behavior of "room" is specified by the command list ROOM. The behavior of the five processes fork(0), fork(1), fork(2), fork(3), fork(4), is specified by the command list FORK, within which the bound variable i indicates the identity of the particular fork. Similar remarks apply to the five processes PHIL.

2.2 Assignment Commands

<assignment command> ::= <target variable> := <expression>
<expression> ::= <simple expression>|<structured expression>
<structured expression> ::= <constructor>(<expression list>)
<constructor> ::= <identifier>|<empty>
<expression list> ::= <empty>|<expression>{,<expression>}
<target variable> ::= <simple variable>|<structured target>
<structured target> ::= <constructor>(<target variable list>)
<target variable list> ::= <empty>|<target variable>
    {,<target variable>}

An expression denotes a value which is computed by an executing device by application of its constituent operators to the specified operands. The value of an expression is undefined if any of these operations are undefined. The value denoted by a simple expression may be simple or structured. The value denoted by a structured expression is structured; its constructor is that of the expression, and its components are the list of values denoted by the constituent expressions of the expression list.

An assignment command specifies evaluation of its expression, and assignment of the denoted value to the target variable. A simple target variable may have assigned to it a simple or a structured value. A structured target variable may have assigned to it a structured value, with the same constructor. The effect of such assignment is to assign to each constituent simpler variable of the structured target the value of the corresponding component of the structured value. Consequently, the value denoted by the target variable, if evaluated *after* a successful assignment, is the same as the value denoted by the expression, as evaluated *before* the assignment.

An assignment fails if the value of its expression is undefined, or if that value does not *match* the target variable, in the following sense: A *simple* target variable matches any value of its type. A *structured* target variable matches a structured value, provided that: (1) they have the same constructor, (2) the target variable list is the same length as the list of components of the value, (3) each target variable of the list matches the corresponding component of the value list. A structured value with no components is known as a "signal."

Examples:

(1) $x := x + 1$	the value of x after the assignment is the same as the value of $x + 1$ before.
(2) $(x, y) := (y, x)$	exchanges the values of x and y.
(3) $x := cons(left, right)$	constructs a structured value and assigns it to x.
(4) $cons(left, right) := x$	fails if x does not have the form $cons(y, z)$; but if it does, then y is assigned to left, and z is assigned to right.
(5) $insert(n) := insert(2*x + 1)$	equivalent to $n := 2*x + 1$.
(6) $c := P()$	assigns to c a "signal" with constructor P, and no components.
(7) $P() := c$	fails if the value of c is not P(); otherwise has no effect.
(8) $insert(n) := has(n)$	fails, due to mismatch.

Note: Successful execution of both (3) and (4) ensures the truth of the postcondition $x = cons(left, right)$; but (3) does so by changing x and (4) does so by changing left and right. Example (4) will fail if there is *no* value of left and right which satisfies the postcondition.

2.3 Input and Output Commands

<input command> ::= <source>?<target variable>
<output command> ::= <destination>!<expression>
<source> ::= <process name>

```
<destination> := <process name>
<process name> := <identifier>|<identifier>(<subscripts>)
<subscripts> := <integer expression>{,<integer expression>}
```

Input and output commands specify communication between two concurrently operating sequential processes. Such a process may be implemented in hardware as a special-purpose device (e.g. cardreader or lineprinter), or its behavior may be specified by one of the constituent processes of a parallel command. Communication occurs between two processes of a parallel command whenever (1) an input command in one process specifies as its source the process name of the other process; (2) an output command in the other process specifies as its destination the process name of the first process; and (3) the target variable of the input command matches the value denoted by the expression of the output command. On these conditions, the input and output commands are said to *correspond*. Commands which correspond are executed simultaneously, and their combined effect is to assign the value of the expression of the output command to the target variable of the input command.

An input command fails if its source is terminated. An output command fails if its destination is terminated or if its expression is undefined.

(The requirement of synchronization of input and output commands means that an implementation will have to delay whichever of the two commands happens to be ready first. The delay is ended when the corresponding command in the other process is also ready, or when the other process terminates. In the latter case the first command fails. It is also possible that the delay will never be ended, for example, if a group of processes are attempting communication but none of their input and output commands correspond with each other. This form of failure is known as a deadlock.)

Examples:

(1) cardreader?cardimage	from cardreader, read a card and assign its value (an array of characters) to the variable cardimage
(2) lineprinter!lineimage	to lineprinter, send the value of lineimage for printing
(3) $X?(x, y)$	from process named X, input a pair of values and assign them to x and y
(4) DIV!$(3*a + b, 13)$	to process DIV, output the two specified values.

Note: If a process named DIV issues command (3), and a process named X issues command (4), these are executed simultaneously, and have the same effect as the assignment: $(x, y) := (3*a + b, 13)$ $(\equiv x := 3*a + b; y := 13)$.

(5) console$(i)?c$	from the ith element of an array of consoles, input a value and assign it to c
(6) console$(j - 1)!$"A"	to the $(j - 1)$th console, output character "A"
(7) $X(i)?V( )$	from the ith of an array of processes X, input a signal V( ); refuse to input any other signal
(8) sem!P( )	to sem output a signal P( )

2.4 Alternative and Repetitive Commands

```
<repetitive command> :=*<alternative command>
<alternative command> := [ <guarded command>
     {□<guarded command>}]
<guarded command> := <guard> → <command list>
     |(<range>{,<range>})<guard> → <command list>
<guard> := <guard list>|<guard list>;<input command>
     |<input command>
     <guard list> := <guard element>{;<guard element>}
<guard element> := <boolean expression>|<declaration>
```

A guarded command with one or more ranges stands for a series of guarded commands, each with the same guard and command list, except that each has a different combination of values substituted for the bound variables. The values range between the lower bound and upper bound inclusive. For example, $(i:1..n)G \to CL$ stands for

$$G_1 \to CL_1 \llbracket G_2 \to CL_2 \rrbracket ... \llbracket G_n \to CL_n$$

where each $G_j \to CL_j$ is formed from $G \to CL$ by replacing every occurrence of the bound variable i by the numeral j.

A guarded command is executed only if and when the execution of its guard does not fail. First its guard is executed and then its command list. A guard is executed by execution of its constituent elements from left to right. A Boolean expression is evaluated: If it denotes false, the guard fails; but an expression that denotes true has no effect. A declaration introduces a fresh variable with a scope that extends from the declaration to the end of the guarded command. An input command at the end of a guard is executed only if and when a corresponding output command is executed. (An implementation may test whether a guard fails simply by trying to execute it, and discontinuing execution if and when it fails. This is valid because such a discontinued execution has no effect on the state of the executing device.)

An alternative command specifies execution of exactly one of its constituent guarded commands. Consequently, if all guards fail, the alternative command fails. Otherwise an arbitrary one with successfully executable guard is selected and executed. (An implementation should take advantage of its freedom of selection to ensure efficient execution and good response. For example, when input commands appear as guards, the command which corresponds to the earliest ready and matching output command should in general be preferred; and certainly, no executable and ready output command should be passed over unreasonably often.)

A repetitive command specifies as many iterations as possible of its constituent alternative command. Consequently, when all guards fail, the repetitive command terminates with no effect. Otherwise, the alternative command is executed once and then the whole repetitive command is executed again. (Consider a repetitive command when all its true guard lists end in an input guard. Such a command may have to be delayed until either (1) an output command corresponding to one of the input

guards becomes ready, or (2) all the sources named by the input guards have terminated. In case (2), the repetitive command terminates. If neither event ever occurs, the process fails (in deadlock.)

Examples:

(1) $[x \geq y \rightarrow m := x \,[\!]\, y \geq x \rightarrow m := y]$

If $x \geq y$, assign x to m; if $y \geq x$ assign y to m; if both $x \geq y$ and $y \geq x$, either assignment can be executed.

(2) $i := 0; *[i < size; content(i) \neq n \rightarrow i := i + 1]$

The repetitive command scans the elements content(i), for $i = 0, 1, \ldots$, until either $i \geq$ size, or a value equal to n is found.

(3) $*[c:character; west?c \rightarrow east!c]$

This reads all the characters output by west, and outputs them one by one to east. The repetition terminates when the process west terminates.

(4) $*[(i:1..10)continue(i); console(i)?c \rightarrow X!(i, c); console(i)!ack(\,);$
    $continue(i) := (c \neq sign\ off)]$

This command inputs repeatedly from any of ten consoles, provided that the corresponding element of the Boolean array continue is true. The bound variable i identifies the originating console. Its value, together with the character just input, is output to X, and an acknowledgment signal is sent back to the originating console. If the character indicated "sign off," continue(i) is set false, to prevent further input from that console. The repetitive command terminates when all ten elements of continue are false. (An implementation should ensure that no console which is ready to provide input will be ignored unreasonably often.)

(5) $*[n:integer; X?insert(n) \rightarrow INSERT$
    $[\!]n:integer; X?has(n) \rightarrow SEARCH; X!(i < size)$
    $]$

(Here, and elsewhere, capitalized words INSERT and SEARCH stand as abbreviations for program text defined separately.)

On each iteration this command accepts from X either (a) a request to "insert(n)," (followed by INSERT) or (b) a question "has(n)," to which it outputs an answer back to X. The choice between (a) and (b) is made by the next output command in X. The repetitive command terminates when X does. If X sends a nonmatching message, deadlock will result.

(6) $*[X?V(\,) \rightarrow val := val + 1$
    $[\!]val > 0; Y?P(\,) \rightarrow val := val - 1$
    $]$

On each iteration, accept *either* a V( ) signal from X and increment val, *or* a P( ) signal from Y, and decrement val. But the second alternative cannot be selected unless val is positive (after which val will remain invariantly nonnegative). (When val > 0, the choice depends on the relative speeds of X and Y, and is not determined.) The repetitive command will terminate when both X and Y are terminated, or when X is terminated and val ≤ 0.

3. Coroutines

In parallel programming coroutines appear as a more fundamental program structure than subroutines, which can be regarded as a special case (treated in the next section).

3.1 COPY
Problem: Write a process X to copy characters output by process west to process east.
Solution:

$X :: *[c:character; west?c \rightarrow east!c]$

Notes: (1) When west terminates, the input "west?c" will fail, causing termination of the repetitive command, and of process X. Any subsequent input command from east will fail. (2) Process X acts as a single-character buffer between west and east. It permits west to work on production of the next character, before east is ready to input the previous one.

3.2 SQUASH
Problem: Adapt the previous program to replace every pair of consecutive asterisks "$**$" by an upward arrow "$\uparrow$". Assume that the final character input is not an asterisk.
Solution:

$X :: *[c:character; west?c \rightarrow$
    $[c \neq asterisk \rightarrow east!c$
    $[\!]c = asterisk \rightarrow west?c;$
        $[c \neq asterisk \rightarrow east!asterisk; east!c$
        $[\!]c = asterisk \rightarrow east!upward\ arrow$
    $]\,]\quad]$

Notes: (1) Since west does not end with asterisk, the second "west?c" will not fail. (2) As an exercise, adapt this process to deal sensibly with input which ends with an odd number of asterisks.

3.3 DISASSEMBLE
Problem: to read cards from a cardfile and output to process X the stream of characters they contain. An extra space should be inserted at the end of each card.
Solution:

$*[cardimage:(1..80)character; cardfile?cardimage \rightarrow$
    $i:integer; i := 1;$
    $*[i \leq 80 \rightarrow X!cardimage(i); i := i + 1]$
    $X!space$
$]$

Notes: (1) "$(1..80)$character" declares an array of 80 characters, with subscripts ranging between 1 and 80. (2) The repetitive command terminates when the cardfile process terminates.

3.4 ASSEMBLE
Problem: To read a stream of characters from process X and print them in lines of 125 characters on a lineprinter. The last line should be completed with spaces if necessary.

Solution:

```
lineimage:(1..125)character;
i:integer; i := 1;
*[c:character; X?c →
    lineimage(i) := c;
    [i ≤ 124 → i := i + 1
    []i = 125 → lineprinter!lineimage; i := 1
    ]     ];
[i = 1 → skip
[]i > 1 → *[i ≤ 125 → lineimage(i) := space; i := i + 1];
    lineprinter!lineimage
]
```

Note: (1) When X terminates, so will the first repetitive command of this process. The last line will then be printed, if it has any characters.

3.5 Reformat
Problem: Read a sequence of cards of 80 characters each, and print the characters on a lineprinter at 125 characters per line. Every card should be followed by an extra space, and the last line should be completed with spaces if necessary.
Solution:

```
[west::DISASSEMBLE||X::COPY||east::ASSEMBLE]
```

Notes: (1) The capitalized names stand for program text defined in previous sections. (2) The parallel command is designed to terminate after the cardfile has terminated. (3) This elementary problem is difficult to solve elegantly without coroutines.

3.6 Conway's Problem [4]
Problem: Adapt the above program to replace every pair of consecutive asterisks by an upward arrow.
Solution:

```
[west::DISASSEMBLE||X::SQUASH||east::ASSEMBLE]
```

4. Subroutines and Data Representations

A conventional nonrecursive subroutine can be readily implemented as a coroutine, provided that (1) its parameters are called "by value" and "by result," and (2) it is disjoint from its calling program. Like a Fortran subroutine, a coroutine may retain the values of local variables (*own* variables, in Algol terms) and it may use input commands to achieve the effect of "multiple entry points" in a safer way than PL/I. Thus a coroutine can be used like a SIMULA class instance as a concrete representation for abstract data.

A coroutine acting as a subroutine is a process operating concurrently with its user process in a parallel command: [subr::SUBROUTINE||X::USER]. The SUBROUTINE will contain (or consist of) a repetitive command: *[X?(value params) → ... ; X!(result params)], where ... computes the results from the values input. The subroutine will terminate when its user does. The USER will call the subroutine by a pair of commands: subr!(arguments);

... ; subr?(results). Any commands between these two will be executed concurrently with the subroutine.

A multiple-entry subroutine, acting as a representation for data [11], will also contain a repetitive command which represents each entry by an alternative input to a structured target with the entry name as constructor. For example,

```
*[X?entry1(value params) → ...
[]X?entry2(value params) → ...
]
```

The calling process X will determine which of the alternatives is activated on each repetition. When X terminates, so does this repetitive command. A similar technique in the user program can achieve the effect of multiple exits.

A recursive subroutine can be simulated by an array of processes, one for each level of recursion. The user process is level zero. Each activation communicates its parameters and results with its predecessor and calls its successor if necessary:

```
[recsub(0)::USER||recsub(i:1..reclimit)::RECSUB].
```

The user will call the first element of

```
recsub: recsub(1)!(arguments); ... ; recsub(1)?(results);.
```

The imposition of a fixed upper bound on recursion depth is necessitated by the "static" design of the language.

This clumsy simulation of recursion would be even more clumsy for a mutually recursive algorithm. It would not be recommended for conventional programming; it may be more suitable for an array of microprocessors for which the fixed upper bound is also realistic.

In this section, we assume each subroutine is used only by a *single* user process (which may, of course, itself contain parallel commands).

4.1 Function: Division With Remainder
Problem: Construct a process to represent a function-type subroutine, which accepts a positive dividend and divisor, and returns their integer quotient and remainder. Efficiency is of no concern.
Solution:

```
[DIV::*[x,y:integer; X?(x,y) →
    quot,rem:integer;quot := 0; rem := x;
    *[rem ≥ y → rem := rem − y; quot := quot + 1];
    X!(quot,rem)
    ]
||X::USER
]
```

4.2 Recursion: Factorial
Problem: Compute a factorial by the recursive method, to a given limit.
Solution:

```
[fac(i:1..limit)::
*[n:integer;fac(i − 1)?n →
    [n = 0 → fac(i − 1)!1
```

```
 [n > 0 → fac(i + 1)!n − 1;
    r:integer;fac(i + 1)?r;fac(i − 1)!(n ∗ r)
 ]]
||fac(0)::USER
]
```

Note: This unrealistic example introduces the technique of the "iterative array" which will be used to a better effect in later examples.

4.3 Data Representation: Small Set of Integers [11]

Problem: To represent a set of not more than 100 integers as a process, S, which accepts two kinds of instruction from its calling process X: (1) S!insert(n), insert the integer n in the set, and (2) S!has(n); ... ; S?b, b is set true if n is in the set, and false otherwise. The initial value of the set is empty.

Solution:

```
S::
content:(0..99)integer; size:integer; size := 0;
*[n:integer; X?has(n) → SEARCH; X!(i < size)
 [n:integer; X?insert(n) → SEARCH;
   [i < size → skip
   [i = size; size < 100 →
      content (size) := n; size := size + 1
 ]    ]
```

where SEARCH is an abbreviation for:

```
i:integer; i := 0;
*[i < size; content(i) ≠ n → i := i + 1]
```

Notes: (1) The alternative command with guard "size < 100" will fail if an attempt is made to insert more than 100 elements. (2) The activity of insertion will in general take place concurrently with the calling process. However, any subsequent instruction to S will be delayed until the previous insertion is complete.

4.4 Scanning a Set

Problem: Extend the solution to 4.3 by providing a fast method for scanning all members of the set without changing the value of the set. The user program will contain a repetitive command of the form:

```
  S!scan( ); more:boolean; more := true;
*[more;x:integer; S?next(x) → ... deal with x ....
 [more; S?noneleft( ) → more := false
 ]
```

where S!scan( ) sets the representation into a scanning mode. The repetitive command serves as a **for** statement, inputting the successive members of x from the set and inspecting them until finally the representation sends a signal that there are no members left. The body of the repetitive command is *not* permitted to communicate with S in any way.

Solution: Add a third guarded command to the outer repetitive command of S:

```
... [X?scan( ) → i:integer; i := 0;
           *[i < size → X!next(content(i)); i := i + 1];
           X!noneleft( )
```

4.5 Recursive Data Representation: Small Set of Integers

Problem: Same as above, but an array of processes is to be used to achieve a high degree of parallelism. Each process should contain at most one number. When it contains no number, it should answer "false" to all inquiries about membership. On the first insertion, it changes to a second phase of behavior, in which it deals with instructions from its predecessor, passing some of them on to its successor. The calling process will be named S(0). For efficiency, the set should be sorted, i.e. the ith process should contain the ith largest number.

Solution:

```
S(i:1..100)::
*[n:integer; S(i − 1)?has(n) → S(0)!false
 [n:integer; S(i − 1)?insert(n) →
   *[m:integer; S(i − 1)?has(m) →
     [m ≤ n → S(0)!(m = n)
     [m > n → S(i + 1)!has(m)
     ]
    [m:integer; S(i − 1)?insert(m) →
      [m < n → S(i + 1)!insert(n); n := m
      [m = n → skip
      [m > n → S(i + 1)!insert(m)
 ]]]
```

Notes: (1) The user process S(0) inquires whether n is a member by the commands S(1)!has(n); ... ; [(i:1..100)S(i)? b → skip]. The appropriate process will respond to the input command by the output command in line 2 or line 5. This trick avoids passing the answer back "up the chain." (2) Many insertion operations can proceed in parallel, yet any subsequent "has" operation will be performed correctly. (3) All repetitive commands and all processes of the array will terminate after the user process S(0) terminates.

4.6 Multiple Exits: Remove the Least Member

Exercise: Extend the above solution to respond to a command to yield the least member of the set and to remove it from the set. The user program will invoke the facility by a pair of commands:

```
S(1)!least( ); [x:integer;S(1)?x → ... deal with x ...
              [S(1)?noneleft( ) → ...
              ]
```

or, if he wishes to scan and empty the set, he may write:

```
S(1)!least( );more:boolean; more := true;
    *[more; x:integer; S(1)?x → ... deal with x ... ; S(1)!least( )
     [more; S(1)?noneleft( ) → more := false
     ]
```

Hint: Introduce a Boolean variable, b, initialized to true, and prefix this to all the guards of the inner loop. After responding to a !least( ) command from its predecessor, each process returns its contained value n, asks its successor for its least, and stores the response in n. But if the successor returns "noneleft( )," b is set false and the inner loop terminates. The process therefore returns to its initial state (solution due to David Gries).

5. Monitors and Scheduling

This section shows how a monitor can be regarded as a single process which communicates with more than one user process. However, each user process must have a different name (e.g. producer, consumer) or a different subscript (e.g. $X(i)$) and each communication with a user must identify its source or destination uniquely.

Consequently, when a monitor is prepared to communicate with *any* of its user processes (i.e. whichever of them calls first) it will use a guarded command with a range. For example: $*[(i{:}1..100)X(i)?(\text{value parameters}) \rightarrow ... ; X(i)!(\text{results})]$. Here, the bound variable i is used to send the results back to the calling process. If the monitor is not prepared to accept input from some particular user (e.g. $X(j)$) on a given occasion, the input command may be preceded by a Boolean guard. For example, two successive inputs from the same process are inhibited by $j = 0$; $*[(i{:}1..100)i \neq j; X(i)?(\text{values}) \rightarrow ... ; j := i]$. Any attempted output from $X(j)$ will be delayed until a subsequent iteration, after the output of some other process $X(i)$ has been accepted and dealt with.

Similarly, conditions can be used to delay acceptance of inputs which would violate scheduling constraints—postponing them until some later occasion when some other process has brought the monitor into a state in which the input can validly be accepted. This technique is similar to a conditional critical region [10] and it obviates the need for special synchronizing variables such as events, queues, or conditions. However, the absence of these special facilities certainly makes it more difficult or less efficient to solve problems involving priorities—for example, the scheduling of head movement on a disk.

5.1 Bounded Buffer

Problem: Construct a buffering process X to smooth variations in the speed of output of portions by a producer process and input by a consumer process. The consumer contains pairs of commands $X!more( )$; $X?p$, and the producer contains commands of the form $X!p$. The buffer should contain up to ten portions.
Solution:

```
X::
buffer:(0..9) portion;
in,out:integer; in := 0; out := 0;
comment 0 ≤ out ≤ in ≤ out + 10;
  *[in < out + 10; producer?buffer(in mod 10) → in := in + 1
  []out < in; consumer?more( ) → consumer!buffer(out mod 10);
    out := out + 1
  ]
```

Notes: (1) When $out < in < out + 10$, the selection of the alternative in the repetitive command will depend on whether the producer produces before the consumer consumes, or vice versa. (2) When $out = in$, the buffer is empty and the second alternative cannot be selected even if the consumer is ready with its command $X!more( )$.

However, after the producer has produced its next portion, the consumer's request can be granted on the next iteration. (3) Similar remarks apply to the producer, when $in = out + 10$. (4) X is designed to terminate when $out = in$ and the producer has terminated.

5.2 Integer Semaphore
Problem: To implement an integer semaphore, S, shared among an array $X(i{:}1..100)$ of client processes. Each process may increment the semaphore by $S!V( )$ or decrement it by $S!P( )$, but the latter command must be delayed if the value of the semaphore is not positive.
Solution:

```
S::val:integer; val := 0;
  *[(i:1..100)X(i)?V( ) → val := val + 1
  [](i:1..100)val > 0; X(i)?P( ) → val := val − 1
  ]
```

Notes: (1) In this process, no use is made of knowledge of the subscript i of the calling process. (2) The semaphore terminates only when all hundred processes of the process array X have terminated.

5.3 Dining Philosophers (Problem due to E.W. Dijkstra)
Problem: Five philosophers spend their lives thinking and eating. The philosophers share a common dining room where there is a circular table surrounded by five chairs, each belonging to one philosopher. In the center of the table there is a large bowl of spaghetti, and the table is laid with five forks (see Figure 1). On feeling hungry, a philosopher enters the dining room, sits in his own chair, and picks up the fork on the left of his place. Unfortunately, the spaghetti is so tangled that he needs to pick up and use the fork on his right as well. When he has finished, he puts down both forks, and leaves the room. The room should keep a count of the number of philosophers in it.

Fig. 1.

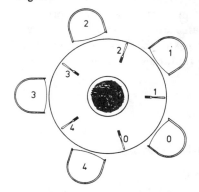

Solution: The behavior of the ith philosopher may be described as follows:

```
PHIL = *[... during ith lifetime ... →
    THINK;
    room!enter( );
    fork(i)!pickup( ); fork((i + 1) mod 5)!pickup( );
    EAT;
    fork(i)!putdown( ); fork((i + 1) mod 5)!putdown( );
    room!exit( )
    ]
```

The fate of the *i*th fork is to be picked up and put down by a philosopher sitting on either side of it

```
FORK =
    *[phil(i)?pickup( ) → phil(i)?putdown( )
    []phil((i − 1)mod 5)?pickup( ) → phil((i − 1) mod 5)?putdown( )
    ]
```

The story of the room may be simply told:

```
ROOM = occupancy:integer; occupancy := 0;
    *[(i:0..4)phil(i)?enter( ) → occupancy := occupancy + 1
    [](i:0..4)phil(i)?exit( ) → occupancy := occupancy − 1
    ]
```

All these components operate in parallel:

```
[room::ROOM||fork(i:0..4)::FORK||phil(i:0..4)::PHIL].
```

Notes: (1) The solution given above does not prevent all five philosophers from entering the room, each picking up his left fork, and starving to death because he cannot pick up his right fork. (2) Exercise: Adapt the above program to avert this sad possibility. Hint: Prevent more than four philosophers from entering the room. (Solution due to E. W. Dijkstra).

6. Miscellaneous

This section contains further examples of the use of communicating sequential processes for the solution of some less familiar problems; a parallel version of the sieve of Eratosthenes, and the design of an iterative array. The proposed solutions are even more speculative than those of the previous sections, and in the second example, even the question of termination is ignored.

6.1 Prime Numbers: The Sieve of Eratosthenes [14]

Problem: To print in ascending order all primes less than 10000. Use an array of processes, SIEVE, in which each process inputs a prime from its predecessor and prints it. The process then inputs an ascending stream of numbers from its predecessor and passes them on to its successor, suppressing any that are multiples of the original prime. Solution:

```
[SIEVE(i:1..100)::
    p,mp:integer;
    SIEVE(i − 1)?p;
    print!p;
    mp := p; comment mp is a multiple of p;
    *[m:integer; SIEVE(i − 1)?m →
        *[m > mp → mp := mp + p];
        [m = mp → skip
        []m < mp → SIEVE(i + 1)!m
    ]   ]
||SIEVE(0)::print!2; n:integer; n := 3;
        *[n < 10000 → SIEVE(1)!n; n := n + 2]
||SIEVE(101)::*[n:integer;SIEVE(100)?n → print!n]
||print::*[(i:0..101) n:integer; SIEVE(i)?n → ...]
]
```

Note: (1) This beautiful solution was contributed by David Gries. (2) It is algorithmically similar to the program developed in [7, pp. 27–32].

6.2 An Iterative Array: Matrix Multiplication

Problem: A square matrix A of order 3 is given. Three streams are to be input, each stream representing a column of an array IN. Three streams are to be output, each representing a column of the product matrix IN × A. After an initial delay, the results are to be produced at the same rate as the input is consumed. Consequently, a high degree of parallelism is required. The solution should take the form shown in Figure 2. Each of the nine nonborder nodes inputs a vector component from the west and a partial sum from the north. Each node outputs the vector component to its east, and an updated partial sum to the south. The input data is produced by the west border nodes, and the desired results are consumed by south border nodes. The north border is a constant source of zeros and the east border is just a sink. No provision need be made for termination nor for changing the values of the array A.

Fig. 2.

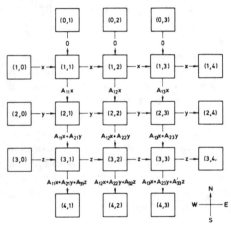

Solution: There are twenty-one nodes, in five groups, comprising the central square and the four borders:

```
[M(i:1..3,0)::WEST
||M(0,j:1..3)::NORTH
||M(i:1..3,4)::EAST
||M(4,j:1..3)::SOUTH
||M(i:1..3,j:1..3)::CENTER
]
```

The WEST and SOUTH borders are processes of the user program; the remaining processes are:

```
NORTH = *[true → M(1,j)!0]
EAST = *[x:real; M(i,3)?x → skip]
CENTER = *[x:real; M(i,j − 1)?x →
        M(i, j + 1)!x; sum:real;
        M(i − 1, j)?sum; M(i + 1,j)!(A(i, j)*x + sum)
    ]
```

7. Discussion

A design for a programming language must necessarily involve a number of decisions which seem to be

fairly arbitrary. The discussion of this section is intended to explain some of the underlying motivation and to mention some unresolved questions.

7.1 Notations

I have chosen single-character notations (e.g. !,?) to express the primitive concepts, rather than the more traditional boldface or underlined English words. As a result, the examples have an APL-like brevity, which some readers find distasteful. My excuse is that (in contrast to APL) there are only a very few primitive concepts and that it is standard practice of mathematics (and also good coding practice) to denote common primitive concepts by brief notations (e.g. $+, \times$). When read aloud, these are replaced by words (e.g. plus, times).

Some readers have suggested the use of assignment notation for input and output:

<target variable> := <source>
<destination> := <expression>

I find this suggestion misleading: it is better to regard input and output as distinct primitives, justifying distinct notations.

I have used the same pair of brackets ([...]) to bracket all program structures, instead of the more familiar variety of brackets (if..fi, begin..end, case...esac, etc.). In this I follow normal mathematical practice, but I must also confess to a distaste for the pronunciation of words like fi, od, or esac.

I am dissatisfied with the fact that my notation gives the same syntax for a structured expression and a subscripted variable. Perhaps tags should be distinguished from other identifiers by a special symbol (say #).

I was tempted to introduce an abbreviation for combined declaration and input, e.g. $X?(n:integer)$ for n:integer; $X?n$.

7.2 Explicit Naming

My design insists that every input or output command must name its source or destination explicitly. This makes it inconvenient to write a library of processes which can be included in subsequent programs, independent of the process names used in that program. A partial solution to this problem is to allow one process (the *main* process) of a parallel command to have an empty label, and to allow the other processes in the command to use the empty process name as source or destination of input or output.

For construction of large programs, some more general technique will also be necessary. This should at least permit substitution of program text for names defined elsewhere—a technique which has been used informally throughout this paper. The Cobol COPY verb also permits a substitution for formal parameters within the copied text. But whatever facility is introduced, I would recommend the following principle: Every program, after assembly with its library routines, should be printable as a text expressed wholly in the language, and it is this

printed text which should describe the execution of the program, independent of which parts were drawn from a library.

Since I did not intend to design a complete language, I have ignored the problem of libraries in order to concentrate on the essential semantic concepts of the program which is actually executed.

7.3 Port Names

An alternative to explicit naming of source and destination would be to name a *port* through which communication is to take place. The port names would be local to the processes, and the manner in which pairs of ports are to be connected by channels could be declared in the head of a parallel command.

This is an attractive alternative which could be designed to introduce a useful degree of syntactically checkable redundancy. But it is semantically equivalent to the present proposal, provided that each port is connected to exactly one other port in another process. In this case each channel can be identified with a tag, together with the name of the process at the other end. Since I wish to concentrate on semantics, I preferred in this paper to use the simplest and most direct notation, and to avoid raising questions about the possibility of connecting more than two ports by a single channel.

7.4 Automatic Buffering

As an alternative to synchronization of input and output, it is often proposed that an outputting process should be allowed to proceed even when the inputting process is not yet ready to accept the output. An implementation would be expected automatically to interpose a chain of buffers to hold output messages that have not yet been input.

I have deliberately rejected this alternative, for two reasons: (1) It is less realistic to implement in multiple disjoint processors, and (2) when buffering is required on a particular channel, it can readily be specified using the given primitives. Of course, it could be argued equally well that synchronization can be specified when required by using a pair of buffered input and output commands.

7.5 Unbounded Process Activation

The notation for an array of processes permits the same program text (like an Algol recursive procedure) to have many simultaneous "activations"; however, the exact number must be specified in advance. In a conventional single-processor implementation, this can lead to inconvenience and wastefulness, similar to the fixed-length array of Fortran. It would therefore be attractive to allow a process array with no a priori bound on the number of elements; and to specify that the exact number of elements required for a particular execution of the program should be determined dynamically, like the maximum depth of recursion of an Algol procedure or the number of iterations of a repetitive command.

However, it is a good principle that every actual run of a program with unbounded arrays should be identical to the run of some program with all its arrays bounded in advance. Thus the unbounded program should be defined as the "limit" (in some sense) of a series of bounded programs with increasing bounds. I have chosen to concentrate on the semantics of the bounded case—which is necessary anyway and which is more realistic for implementation on multiple microprocessors.

7.6 Fairness

Consider the parallel command:

$[X:: Y!\text{stop}(\ )|| Y::\text{continue:boolean; continue} := \text{true};$
$*[\text{continue}; X?\text{stop}(\ ) \rightarrow \text{continue} := \text{false}$
$[\text{continue} \rightarrow n := n + 1$
$]$
$].$

If the implementation always prefers the second alternative in the repetitive command of Y, it is said to be *unfair*, because although the output command in X could have been executed on an infinite number of occasions, it is in fact always passed over.

The question arises: Should a programming language definition specify that an implementation must be *fair*? Here, I am fairly sure that the answer is NO. Otherwise, the implementation would be obliged to successfully complete the example program shown above, in spite of the fact that its nondeterminism is unbounded. I would therefore suggest that it is the programmer's responsibility to prove that his program terminates correctly—without relying on the assumption of fairness in the implementation. Thus the program shown above is incorrect, since its termination cannot be proved.

Nevertheless, I suggest that an efficient implementation should try to be reasonably fair and should ensure that an output command is not delayed unreasonably often after it first becomes executable. But a proof of correctness must not rely on this property of an efficient implementation. Consider the following analogy with a sequential program: An efficient implementation of an alternative command will tend to favor the alternative which can be most efficiently executed, but the programmer must ensure that the logical correctness of his program does not depend on this property of his implementation.

This method of avoiding the problem of fairness does not apply to programs such as operating systems which are intended to run forever because in this case termination proofs are not relevant. But I wonder whether it is ever advisable to write or to execute such programs. Even an operating system should be designed to bring itself to an orderly conclusion reasonably soon after it inputs a message instructing it to do so. Otherwise, the *only* way to stop it is to "crash" it.

7.7 Functional Coroutines

It is interesting to compare the processes described here with those proposed in [12]; the differences are most striking. There, coroutines are strictly deterministic: No choice is given between alternative sources of input. The output commands are automatically buffered to any required degree. The output of one process can be automatically fanned out to any number of processes (including itself!) which can consume it at differing rates. Finally, the processes there are designed to run forever, whereas my proposed parallel command is normally intended to terminate. The design in [12] is based on an elegant theory which permits proof of the properties of programs. These differences are not accidental—they seem to be natural consequences of the difference between the more abstract applicative (or functional) approach to programming and the more machine-oriented imperative (or procedural) approach, which is taken by communicating sequential processes.

7.8 Output Guards

Since input commands may appear in guards, it seems more symmetric to permit output commands as well. This would allow an obvious and useful simplification in some of the example programs, for example, in the bounded buffer (5.1). Perhaps a more convincing reason would be to ensure that the externally visible effect and behavior of every parallel command can be modeled by some sequential command. In order to model the parallel command

$Z :: [X!2 || Y!3]$

we need to be able to write the sequential alternative command:

$Z :: [X!2 \rightarrow Y!3 [] Y!3 \rightarrow X!2]$

Note that this *cannot* be done by the command

$Z :: [\text{true} \rightarrow X!2; Y!3 [] \text{true} \rightarrow Y!3; X!2]$

which can fail if the process Z happens to choose the first alternative, but the processes Y and X are synchronized with each other in such a way that Y must input from Z before X does, e.g.

$Y :: Z?y; X!\text{go}(\ )$
$|| X :: Y?\text{go}(\ ); Z?x$

7.9 Restriction: Repetitive Command With Input Guard

In proposing an unfamiliar programming language feature, it seems wiser at first to specify a highly restrictive version rather than to propose extensions—especially when the language feature claims to be primitive. For example, it is clear that the multidimensional process array is not primitive, since it can readily be constructed in a language which permits only single-dimensional arrays. But I have a rather more serious misgiving about the repetitive command with input guards.

The automatic termination of a repetitive command on termination of the sources of all its input guards is an extremely powerful and convenient feature but it also involves some subtlety of specification to ensure that it

is implementable; and it is certainly not primitive, since the required effect can be achieved (with considerable inconvenience) by explicit exchange of "end()" signals. For example, the subroutine DIV(4.1) could be rewritten:

```
[DIV :: continue:boolean; continue := true;
*[continue; X?end() → continue := false
[]continue; x,y:integer; X?(x,y) → ... ; X!(quot,rem)
||X :: USER PROG; DIV!end()
  ]
```

Other examples would be even more inconvenient.

But the dangers of convenient facilities are notorious. For example, the repetitive commands with input guards may tempt the programmer to write them without making adequate plans for their termination; and if it turns out that the automatic termination is unsatisfactory, reprogramming for explicit termination will involve severe changes, affecting even the interfaces between the processes.

8. Conclusion

This paper has suggested that input, output, and concurrency should be regarded as primitives of programming, which underlie many familiar and less familiar programming concepts. However, it would be unjustified to conclude that these primitives can wholly replace the other concepts in a programming language. Where a more elaborate construction (such as a procedure or a monitor) is frequently useful, has properties which are more simply provable, and can also be implemented more efficiently than the general case, there is a strong reason for including in a programming language a special notation for that construction. The fact that the construction can be defined in terms of simpler underlying primitives is a useful guarantee that its inclusion is logically consistent with the remainder of the language.

Acknowledgments. The research reported in this paper has been encouraged and supported by a Senior Fellowship of the Science Research Council of Great Britain. The technical inspiration was due to Edsger W. Dijkstra [9], and the paper has been improved in presentation and content by valuable and painstaking advice from D. Gries, D. Q. M. Fay, Edsger W. Dijkstra, N. Wirth, Robert Milne, M. K. Harper, and its referees. The role of IFIP W.G.2.3 as a forum for presentation and discussion is acknowledged with pleasure and gratitude.

Received March 1977; revised August 1977

References
1. Atkinson, R., and Hewitt, C. Synchronisation in actor systems. Working Paper 83, M.I.T., Cambridge, Mass., Nov. 1976.
2. Brinch Hansen, P. The programming language Concurrent Pascal. *IEEE Trans. Software Eng. 1*, 2 (June 1975), 199–207.
3. Campbell, R.H., and Habermann, A.N. The specification of process synchronisation by path expressions. *Lecture Notes in Computer Science 16*, Springer, 1974, pp. 89–102.
4. Conway, M.E. Design of a separable transition-diagram compiler. *Comm. ACM 6*, 7 (July 1963), 396–408.
5. Dahl, O-J., et al. SIMULA 67, common base language. Norwegian Computing Centre, Forskningveien, Oslo, 1967.
6. Dijkstra, E.W. Co-operating sequential processes. In *Programming Languages*, F. Genuys, Ed., Academic Press, New York, 1968, pp. 43–112.
7. Dijkstra, E.W. Notes on structured programming. In *Structured Programming*, Academic Press, New York 1972, pp. 1–82.
8. Dijkstra, E.W. Guarded commands, nondeterminacy, and formal derivation of programs. *Comm. ACM 18*, 8 (Aug. 1975), 453–457.
9. Dijkstra, E.W. Verbal communication, Marktoberdorf, Aug. 1975.
10. Hoare, C.A.R. Towards a theory of parallel programming. In *Operating Systems Techniques*, Academic Press, New York, 1972, pp. 61–71.
11. Hoare, C.A.R. Proof of correctness of data representations. *Acta Informatica 1*, 4 (1972), 271–281.
12. Kahn, G. The semantics of a simple language for parallel programming. In *Proc. IFIP Congress 74*, North Holland, 1974.
13. Liskov, B.H. A note on CLU. Computation Structures Group Memo. 112, M.I.T., Cambridge, Mass, 1974.
14. McIlroy, M.D. Coroutines. Bell Laboratories, Murray Hill, N.J., 1968.
15. Naur, P., Ed. Report on the algorithmic language ALGOL 60. *Comm. ACM 3*, 5 (May 1960), 299–314.
16. Reynolds, J.C. COGENT. ANL-7022, Argonne Nat. Lab., Argonne, Ill., 1965.
17. Thompson, K. The UNIX command language. In *Structured Programming*, Infotech, Nicholson House, Maidenhead, England, 1976, pp. 375–384.
18. van Wijngaarden, A. Ed. Report on the algorithmic language ALGOL 68. *Numer. Math. 14* (1969), 79–218.
19. Wulf, W.A., London, R.L., and Shaw, M. Abstraction and verification in ALPHARD. Dept. of Comptr. Sci., Carnegie-Mellon U., Pittsburgh, Pa., June 1976.
20. Wirth, N. The programming language PASCAL. *Acta Informatica 1*, 1 (1971), 35–63.

SECTION 6

MORE LANGUAGES FOR THE 1980s

AN OVERVIEW OF ADA BY J. G. P. BARNES

FORTRANNER'S LAMENT BY S. I. FELDMAN

THE C PROGRAMMING LANGUAGE BY
D. M. RITCHIE, S. C. JOHNSON,
M. E. LESK AND B. W. KERNIGHAN

C REFERENCE MANUAL BY D. M. RITCHIE

ADA PROGRAMMING LANGUAGE REFERENCE
MANUAL BY J. ICHBIAH ET AL.

INTRODUCTION

MORE LANGUAGES FOR THE 1980s

By the time this anthology appears, it is hard for me to believe that a reader may not have heard of Ada, the new programming language sponsored by the U.S. Department of Defense. The Ada design effort was initiated several years ago and culminated in a competition between the Yellow, Green, Red and Blue teams. The winning group was from Honeywell Bull, a French firm, with the team leader being Jean Ichbiah. The resultant language was renamed to Ada, after the collaborator of Charles Babbage, Ada Augusta, Countess of Lovelace.

The first paper in this section presents an overview of the Ada language. Ada is especially interesting as it has tried to incorporate all that is known about good programming language features. This paper by Barnes gives one a solid introduction to almost all of these features and thus covers the very broad scope of the language.

Ada was designed for so-called embedded computer systems, systems which must reside in aircraft or ships. Thus it must fit into a machine which usually has severe constraints on size and speed. Nevertheless the language which was developed is very broad in scope and will likely find itself most suited for large-scale software development on a large computer. It will be a while until the complete language can be fitted onto a microprocessor. At the time of this writing no production compiler for the complete language has appeared.

Ada is so vast in scope that it is impossible to succinctly summarize its most interesting features in the limited space here. The reader is advised to peruse the Barnes paper first. Nevertheless I will try to list some of the essential traits to look for:

- ☐ Pascal is a subset, but truly a small subset of Ada. However all of the data typing facilities of Pascal are contained therein.
- ☐ Character strings are a predefined type.
- ☐ The priority of operators has been altered to have six levels.
- ☐ Boolean expressions allow short-circuit as well as complete evaluation.
- ☐ Comments are started by double hyphens and terminated at end-of-line.
- ☐ Statements for selection and looping are mostly traditional.

- ☐ The go-to statement is included.
- ☐ Besides the usual typing convention there exist two additional facilities called subtypes and derived types. Type equivalence is determined by the name rule.
- ☐ A feature called a package exists and permits the definition and use of an abstract data type. A package defines a type which can be used to instantiate variables, protect the representation, and to simply collect together related objects. Tasks are packages which can be executed concurrently. The mechanism used to communicate between processes is in the form of the remote procedure call. Nondeterministic statements are used as in CSP.
- ☐ Separate compilation is provided for including the testing of interfaces at load time via a library which was created during compilation.
- ☐ Exception handling is an included feature and follows closely the lines laid down by Liskov in CLU.
- ☐ Procedures and packages may be made generic, thus providing an additional means of abstraction.
- ☐ Overloading of operators and functions is permitted.
- ☐ Various forms of input and output are predefined parts of the language.

In addition to the Barnes paper I have decided to reprint the entire Ada Language Reference Manual. One reason for doing so is that the complete manual has not, up to this time received wide distribution. The version contained here is the one which was reprinted in April, 1982. This contains the standardized language as it was defined in the July, 1980 report and also removes many typographical errors which were present in earlier reports.

The paper by Feldman deals with an old friend, FORTRAN. The FORTRAN77 language represents the new standard FORTRAN as developed by the American National Standards Institute. Despite the rise of Ada and the success of many newer languages, we will continue to see a

great deal of programming done in FORTRAN. As FORTRAN is supported by all of the major manufacturers, they have all supplied FORTRAN77 compilers for their machines. Of course the real reason for including a discussion of FORTRAN77 in this anthology is as an aid to those people who wish to consider this question: can a programming language which has been standardized be continually updated so that it remains upwardly compatible yet successfully incorporates new programming language concepts? The article by Feldman may help to answer this question. The paper was originally composed by Feldman as an attack on an earlier draft than the one which was finally adopted. In fact several of his suggestions were eventually incorporated into the new standard. The paper is a careful and intelligent discussion of the limitations of the language and will be enjoyed by all those who believe they know FORTRAN well.

The next pair of papers present a language which has become very popular with the success of the operating system called UNIX[2]. C is the main programming language which was used to develop systems on the PDP-11 running under UNIX. Its history traces back to the systems programming language BCPL developed by Martin Richards at Cambridge University in England. Some people do not like C because of its reliance on special symbols and the tendency to use one or two letter identifiers. But C is truly a systems programming language designed for experienced programmers and for this group it seems most suitable.

---

[2]UNIX is a trademark of Bell Laboratories

AN OVERVIEW OF ADA*

J. G. P. BARNES

SPL International Research Centre, The Charter, Abingdon, Oxfordshire OX14 3UE, U.K.

SUMMARY

This paper commences with an outline description of the development of the Ada programming language and its position in the overall language scene. The body of the paper is an informal description of the main features of the final language as revised after the Test and Evaluation phase of the DoD project. Comparison with the preliminary version is made where appropriate.

KEY WORDS   Ada   Languages

INTRODUCTION

The final form of the Ada programming language procured by the U.S. Department of Defense has just been made publicly available.[1] This paper contains an informal description of the main features of Ada with some notes on the parts of the language which have changed since the preliminary version.[2]

Before describing Ada we will first outline its historical development and its place in the overall language scene.

HISTORICAL BACKGROUND

In the early 1970s the United States Department of Defense perceived that it needed to take action to stem the tide of rising software costs. In 1973 for instance it is reputed that software cost the DoD some $3000M of which 56 per cent was incurred by the embedded systems sector. By comparison, data processing took 19 per cent and scientific programming 5 per cent with indirect costs accounting for the remainder.

Big savings were clearly possible by concentrating on the embedded systems sector which embraces applications such as tactical weapon systems, communications, command and control and so on. A survey of programming languages in use revealed that whereas data processing and scientific programming were catered for by the standard languages COBOL and FORTRAN respectively, the scene for embedded systems was confused. Languages in use included several variants of JOVIAL, CMS-2, TACPOL, SPL/1 plus many many more.

It was therefore concluded that it would be of major benefit if some degree of standardization could be brought into the embedded systems area. This led to the setting up of the U.S. DoD High Order Language project with two goals. The first, short term, goal was to introduce a list of approved interim languages. The second, long term, goal was to identify or procure a single language for embedded systems.

The short term goal was quickly achieved and resulted in a list of five approved languages: TACPOL, CMS-2, SPL/1, JOVIAL J3 AND JOVIAL J73.

---

*Reprinted from *Software Practice and Experience* vol. 10, 851–887, 1980, copyright 1980.

The first step in proceeding to the long term goal was to develop a set of requirements and to evaluate existing languages against the requirements to see if an existing language was suitable. The requirements were developed in progressively more refined documents entitled STRAWMAN, WOODENMAN, TINMAN, IRONMAN and finally STEELMAN.[3] These documents were refined as a result of wide and public consultation.

The evaluation of existing languages occurred in 1976 against TINMAN. Evaulation of FORTRAN, COBOL, PL/I, HAL/S, TACPOL, CMS-2, CS-4, SPL/1, J3B, J73, Algol 60, Algol 68, CORAL 66, Pascal, SIMULA 67, LIS, LTR, RTL/2, Euclid, PDL2, PEARL, MORAL and EL-1 have been made public. These evaluations resulted in four major conclusions:

1. No language was suitable as it was.
2. A single language was a desirable goal.
3. The state-of-the-art can meet the requirements.
4. Development should start from a suitable base.

The languages evaluated fell into three classes:

'not appropriate'. These were languages which were obsolete or addressed the wrong problem area. Little could be learnt from these. This category included FORTRAN and CORAL 66.

'appropriate'. These were languages which although not directly suitable nevertheless contained interesting features which should be drawn upon. This category included RTL/2 and LIS.

'recommended bases'. These were the three languages Pascal, PL/I and Algol 68 which were perceived as starting points for design of a final language.

At this point in time TINMAN was revised to give IRONMAN and proposals were invited from potential contractors to design a new language starting from one of the recommended bases. Seventeen proposals were received and of these four were chosen to go ahead and design languages in parallel and in competition. The four contractors with their colour codings were:

CII Honeywell Bull — Green
Intermetrics — Red
Softech — Blue
SRI International — Yellow

(The colour codings were introduced to allow comparisons on an unbiased basis.) All four chose Pascal as the base.

At the end of the first phase, the Blue and Yellow designs were eliminated leaving Green and Red to fight on. The final choice was made in May 1979 and the Green design was the winner.

The choice between Green and Red was probably not an easy one for the DoD. It has been said that the Red language contained the embryo of a better language. However the Red language had changed dramatically during the second phase and there had not been time for the full development of all the consequences. The Green language had changed much less and the definition was essentially complete. Clearly Green was the choice with the lower risk. Green could and would work whereas there was significant doubt about the implementability of some basic concepts in Red.

At this time the DoD announced that the new language would be known as Ada. Ada was the Countess of Lovelace, daughter of Lord Byron and the assistant of Babbage. She was the world's first programmer.

The HOL project then entered its third and final phase. The objective of this was to refine the definition of Ada and a large component was the Test and Evaluation exercise. This exercise consisted of various groups writing programs in Ada in order to probe its applicability. Some 82 reports were written and conclusions presented at a conference in Boston in October 1979. The general conclusion was that Ada was good

but a few areas needed correcting.

The Test and Evaluation exercise was not without its problems. The time available had not really been long enough to design programs in the Ada style—it had usually been necessary to more or less take an existing program in another language and rewrite it at the procedural level. Some of the newer, 'programming in the large', features of Ada were therefore not always used as intended. Another problem was the difficulty of using the interpretive Test Translator on sizeable programs. The Test Translator had been developed as part of the phase 2 effort in order to show the feasibility of executing the language. A third problem was the terse nature of the Ada manual. Although the manual attempted to fully define the language, it had not been designed as a tutorial document. The need for thorough and extensive training was therefore underlined by the Test and Evaluation exercise.

Using material from the evaluation exercise the language was then refined and the result is the language outlined in this paper.

TECHNICAL BACKGROUND

We will now briefly describe the position of Ada in the overall language scene. We first note the emergence of two programming language cultures which we can refer to as the professional culture and the amateur culture although these terms are not completely satisfactory.

The professional culture is concerned with writing programs of a fairly permanent nature. These programs are usually fairly large and written by teams of programmers whose profession is primarily the design and writing of programs. The programs will or should be adequately documented and will need maintenance throughout a lifetime which may be several years long. Such maintenance will often arise as the environment in which they work changes throughout their lifetime. Because of this maintenance need it is essential that the language used is standard and stable. Any language changes should occur in a controlled way at infrequent intervals. Important characteristics of such a language are the need for separate compilation, readability and compile time error detection. Interactive use is not required. Examples of existing languages aimed at this culture are COBOL, PL/I, CORAL 66, RTL/2 and CHILL.

The amateur culture is concerned with writing programs of a less permanent nature. These programs are usually small and often written by individuals who are amateur programmers; that is to say that their profession is in a different field such as accountancy, medicine or chemical engineering and they use the computer merely as a tool in the furtherance of their main goals. The programs are often very short lived—perhaps used only once—and consequently need little or no maintenance and hence do not deserve or get significant documentation. Because of the short-lived nature of the program it is not vital that the language used is standard or stable. Indeed, languages in this area are under rapid development and standardization could be counter product-ive. Important characteristics of such languages are the need for ease of writing and general 'user friendliness'; interactive use is inevitable. Examples of such languages are BASIC and APL.

Ada is a language for the professional culture.

A great milestone in the development of programming languages was the publication of the Algol report in 1960. The step forward taken by Algol 60 was truly remarkable; no language since then has made such an impact on later developments. In fact, 1960 can be taken as the beginning of the awakening out of the dark ages. At that time there were just three languages FORTRAN, COBOL and Algol 60. Since then all new languages can be traced back to Algol 60. FORTRAN and COBOL have developed and COBOL in particular has borne dialects but these developments are not of the same degree as those emanating from Algol 60.

An early and ambitious development from Algol 60 was PL/I. Of course, it included much from FORTRAN and COBOL but it could not have existed without the Algol framework. PL/I has, of course, been an expensive failure. It contains too much of the

same sort of thing and not enough in real power to justify its size.

Algol 60 itself never really caught on. It was a little academic and unfortunately neglected the need for separate compilation and input–output. (Pascal made similar mistakes a decade later).

A practical early language was JOVIAL, in fact derived from Algol 58, a little known prototype of Algol 60. Descendents of JOVIAL are currently widely used in USAF systems. CORAL 64 and then CORAL 66 sprang from JOVIAL and Algol 60.

CORAL 66 is well-known as a language for embedded systems. It was designed as a permissive language framework to woo programmers away from assembly languages. Unfortunately it was too permissive and the variation between the different implementations of CORAL 66 means that program portability is rarely achieved.

A big step (although with hindsight not wholly in the right direction) was the development of Algol 68. Algol 68 developed the concepts of reference and expression to an extreme degree. Unfortunately Algol 68 took an academic approach towards publicity; the definition was couched in terms quite inaccessible to the normal programmer and this was one reason for the very slow take up of the language. Another reason was the sheer complexity of the language and the large compilers needed. The task of writing an Algol 68 compiler was really too large for an academic group and too obscure for a commercial group.

A very practical language derived from Algol 68 is RTL/2. RTL/2 is small, contains the best of Algol 68 and does not neglect the important concepts of separate compilation and input–output.

An underlying common feature that makes the Algol 60-based languages successful is the ability to write programs with a clearly discernible flow of control. This 'control abstraction' is a key feature of the so called 'structured programming' revolution. It distinguishes these languages from FORTRAN which despite attempts at cosmetic improvement does not encourage the writing of legible programs.

However, it remains a fact that these languages take a very simple view of data types. In all cases the data is directly described in numerical terms. Thus if the data to be manipulated is not really numerical (it could be traffic light colours) then some mapping of the abstract type must be made by the programmer into a numerical type (usually integer). This mapping is purely in the mind of the programmer and does not appear in the written program except perhaps as a comment. It is probably a consequence of this fact that software libraries have not emerged except in numerical analysis. Numerical algorithms, such as those for finding eigenvalues of a matrix, are directly concerned with manipulating numbers and so these languages, whose data items are numbers have proved appropriate. The point is that the languages provide the correct abstract values in this case only. In other cases, libraries are not successful because there is unlikely to be agreement on the required mappings. Indeed different situations may best be served by different mappings and these mappings pervade the whole program. A change in mapping usually requires a complete rewrite of the program.

Pascal took the first significant step towards providing data abstraction in programming languages. A good example is the enumeration type. Enumeration types allow us to talk about the traffic light colours in their own terms without our having to know how they are represented in the computer. Moreover, they prevent us from making an important class of programming errors—accidently mixing traffic lights with some other abstract type such as the names of fish. When all such types are described in the program as numerical types such errors can occur.

But the success of Pascal cannot be attributed to the introduction of enumeration types alone since they are but a small step along the road to data abstraction. Pascal was designed as a reaction against the enormity of Algol 68. It derives from Algol 60 and Algol W. Unfortunately the good ideas of Algol 68 were thrown away with the bad ones and Pascal inherits many of the poor syntactic features of Algol 60. Other problems with Pascal are its stringent view of types which leads to its inability to handle arrays in as flexible a manner as Algol 60 and the absence of a facility for separate compilation. Input–output, although included in Pascal is handled in an *ad hoc* and inextensible

manner. Pascal has found favour in the academic environment. Its small size makes it a useful teaching tool and easy to implement. It is also finding increasing favour among users of small machines although most implementations contain extensions to overcome the difficulties mentioned above. Unfortunately these extensions are rarely compatible and as a consequence investment in Pascal needs care.

Another later language from the same source as Pascal is MODULA. This puts right some of the syntactic errors of Pascal but more importantly introduces the concept of a module as a scope wall. It has long been recognized that the traditional block structure of Algol 60 does not allow enough control of visibility. For example it is not possible in Algol 60 to write two procedures to operate on some common data and make the procedures accessible without also making the data directly accessible. Many languages have provided such control through the medium of separate compilation. Examples are PL/I and RTL/2. This technique is adequate for medium sized systems but since the separate compilation facility usually leans on some external system, total control of visibility is not gained. The module of MODULA separates scope control from separate compilation. Indeed, MODULA ignores the separate compilation issue.

The concept of type introduced by Pascal and module introduced by MODULA sowed the seed for the second great software revolution which one can see on the horizon. Other experimental languages too numerous to mention have also made detailed contributions.

Data abstraction is the message of the second revolution whereas control abstraction was the message of the first.

Data abstraction means separating the details of the representation of the data from the abstract operations defined upon it. Data abstraction offers the possibility of writing significant reusable software libraries for areas other than numerical analysis. It should therefore greatly increase the possibilities for the sale of software packages.

Ada is the first practical language of the second revolution and embodies the fruits of research of the last decade. It could not have been brought about without the tenacity of purpose and funding available from a large user organization such as the U.S. DoD.

KEY TECHNICAL FEATURES

The remainder of this paper is a technical overview of Ada. Key modern features which the reader should note are:

- Strong typing—how this makes more errors detectable at compilation.
- Programming in the large—the mechanisms for encapsulation and separate compilation.
- Exception handling—giving the user appropriate control of error recovery.
- Tasking—Ada is the first language likely to be widely used which has contained embedded facilities for tasking.
- Data abstraction—private data types and representation specifications which separate the abstract properties of data from its physical realization.
- Generic units—the ability to parameterize units over appropriate data types; of particular value for libraries.

OVERALL STYLE

Ada identifiers are a sequence of letters, digits and medial underscores of which the first is a letter. The case of letters is not significant but underscores are. Ada follows modern practice of reserving those words which introduce syntactic forms thereby avoiding the necessity for a special notation. Sixty-two such words are reserved (e.g. **array**, **case**, **with** etc.) and cannot be redefined. Words associated with built in types are merely predefined (INTEGER, TRUE, STRING etc.) and can be redefined. In this paper we follow the usual Ada style of using lower case bold face for the reserved words and uppercase for all others.

Ada has the same number of reserved words as the preliminary version (**rem**, **with** and **terminate** have been added; **assert**, **initiate** and **packing** deleted; **restricted** has been replaced by **limited**).

Comments start with a double minus (hyphen) and are terminted by the end of line. (There is no facility for embedded comments such as in RTL/2).

    - - this is a comment.

Character strings are enclosed in double quotes, must be on one line and treat spaces as significant. The concatenation operator & caters for control characters and strings which will not fit on one line.

    "THIS IS A STRING"

Ada distinguishes a string of length one (an array of one item) from a single literal character (a scalar).

    "A"   - - string of length one
    'A'   - - the literal A

Numeric literals take two forms, those denoting integers and those denoting approximate numbers used for both fixed point and floating point. In both cases the notation allows for any base from 2 to 16 as well as conventional decimal notation. Medial underscores are allowed in order to break up long numbers but are, of course, not significant.

    123_456_789   - - decimal integer
    1E6   - - exponent form of integer
    2#1011#   - - binary integer
    5#1234#   - - base 5 integer
    3.14159   - - decimal approximate
    16#FF.FF#   - - hexadecimal approximate
    16#FF.FF#e1   - - with exponent

TYPES

A type introduces a set of values and a set of operations on those values. In addition a subtype introduces a shorthand for a base type with possible constraints. Type equivalence in Ada is by name. Two type definitions always introduce two distinct types. Structural equivalence as in Algol 68 introduces both complexity and risk.

Ada contains a limited form of type parameterization for use with records, especially variant records and private types.

ENUMERATION TYPES

As a simple example of the benefits of strong typing consider the following fragment:

```
declare
    type COLOUR is (RED, AMBER, GREEN);
    type FISH is (COD, HAKE, PLAICE);
    X, Y: COLOUR;
    A, B: FISH:= COD;
begin
    X:= Y;        - - ok
    A:= HAKE;     - - ok
    X:= COD;      - - no
end;
```

First note the general style. This fragment is a block which introduces declarations in a declarative part between **declare** and **begin** and a sequence of statements between

begin and **end.** All declarations and statements are terminated by a semicolon ; it is a terminator and not a separator as in Pascal.

> **type** COLOUR **is** (RED, AMBER, GREEN);

declares COLOUR as an enumeration type with literal values RED, AMBER and GREEN.

> X, Y: COLOUR;

declares X and Y as variables which can take values of the type COLOUR.

> A, B: FISH := COD;

similarly declares A and B as variables which can take values of the type FISH but also gives them both the initial value COD.

> X := Y;   and   A := HAKE;

are legal assignment statements which place values of the respective types in X and A.

> X := COD;

is however not legal since it attempts to assign a fish to a colour. This is a consequence of the rules of strong typing which protect the user by preventing him from accidentally mixing objects of different types.

It T is an enumeration type and V a value of the type then

> T'SUCC(V) and T'PRED(V)

give the successor and predecessor while T'FIRST and T'LAST are the first and last values of the type.

Observe that the BOOLEAN type is predefined as

> **type** BOOLEAN **is** (FALSE, TRUE);

NUMERIC TYPES

Although Ada was not designed specifically for numerical analysis nevertheless it solves the numerical accuracy problems far better than FORTRAN. It will be interesting to see whether Ada can overcome the inertia behind FORTRAN and replace it for numerical analysis.

The basic objective is to be able to write a program in as portable a way as possible despite differing word lengths on target computers.

Ada contains predefined types INTEGER and FLOAT and a given implementation may have additional types LONG_INTEGER, LONG_FLOAT etc. as appropriate. It is not intended that the programmer use these predefined types directly if he wishes to write portable programs. Instead we use the concept of a derived type.

A derived type is introduced by a definition of the form

> **type** T **is new** S;

In such a case T inherits the literals and predefined operations of S but is nevertheless a distinct type. Thus if we write

> **type** LIGHT **is new** COLOUR;

then LIGHT is an enumeration type with literals RED, AMBER and GREEN. However values of the two types cannot be arbitrarily mixed since they are different although they can be converted using the type name.

```
declare
   C : COLOUR;
   L : LIGHT;
begin
   C := L;            -- no
```

```
        C := COLOUR(L);   -- ok
     end;
```

(It should be noted that derived types are simpler than those of preliminary Ada and in the case of a user defined type, the only operations inherited are those defined in the same package specification as the type. This simplification has been necessary because of the inconsistencies which seemed inherent in the previous formulation).

Returning now to our numeric types, consider

type REAL **is new** FLOAT;

REAL will have all the literals (0.0 etc.) and operations ($+$, $-$ etc.) of FLOAT and in general can be considered as equivalent. Now suppose we transfer our program to a different computer on which the built in FLOAT type is not so accurate and that LONG_FLOAT is necessary. The only change needed is to replace our definition by

type REAL **is new** LONG_FLOAT;

However Ada enables the choice of FLOAT or LONG_FLOAT to be made automatically.

type REAL **is digits** 10;

indicates the REAL is to be derived from a built in type with at least 10 digits of accuracy. The implementation will choose FLOAT or LONG_FLOAT as required without any change to the program. Thus provided all the variable declarations are in terms of the derived type REAL rather than the built in types then the desired portability will be achieved.

Additionally there is the so-called mathematical library problem. We assume that there exist functions SQRT etc. for each of the built in types FLOAT, LONG_FLOAT. The problem is to ensure that one can write SQRT(X) where X is of type REAL and for the compiler to then call the appropriate version of SQRT according to the predefined type from which REAL is derived. This is solved by the use of the generic facility and writing

package REAL_MATHLIB **is new** MATHLIB(REAL);
use REAL_MATHLIB;

It should be observed that in preliminary Ada there was no need for action on behalf of the user—but unfortunately the mechanism did not work!

We now see that the source text is entirely portable; Ada therefore has more power than FORTRAN since there is no need to systematically change E to D in literals or change SQRT to DSQRT for the mathematical functions.

Observe of course that the user can define several types such as

type REAL **is digits** 10;
type LONG_REAL **is digits** 14;

and then use the more accurate type in the sensitive part of the program; conversion between types again uses the type name

```
     declare
        X : REAL;
        XX : LONG_REAL;
     begin
        X := REAL(XX);
     end;
```

In some implementations both types will map onto the same predefined type and the conversion will be null. In other cases a genuine conversion will be necessary but this need not concern the user.

A similar approach is taken with integers. A declaration

type INT **is range** $-10000 .. +10000$;

will result in the introduction of an integer type equivalent to

type INT **is new** integer_type **range** $-10000 .. +10000$;

where integer_type will be INTEGER, SHORT_INTEGER etc as appropriate. Note that the expressed range constraint still applies.

The above discussion has been simplified somewhat but the general principles should be clear. Ada also contains fixed point types but the author has a personal aversion to fixed point arithmetic and so does not intend to discuss them.

The attributes FIRST and LAST also apply to all numeric types while SUCC and PRED also apply to integer types.

The following subtype will be useful for a later discussion on strings

subtype NATURAL **is** INTEGER **range** $1 ..$ INTEGER'LAST;

Note that NATURAL'FIRST is 1.

ARRAY TYPES

Ada overcomes one of the major problems with Pascal. It allows formal array parameters to have arbitrary bounds.

Array types take two forms

type TABLE **is array** (INTEGER **range** $1 .. 6$) **of** INTEGER;
type MATRIX **is array** (INTEGER **range** $<>$, INTEGER **range** $<>$) **of** REAL;

In the case TABLE the bounds are explicitly given. In the case MATRIX they are not. The type MATRIX may be used as a formal parameter in which case the bounds will be obtained from the actual parameter. Otherwise the bounds must be given when an object (or subtype) is declared for type MATRIX either by an index constraint or by deduction from the initial value if the object is a constant. Possible declarations are

A : TABLE;
M : MATRIX$(1 .. 2, 1 .. 3)$;
z2 : **constant** MATRIX $: = ((0.0, 0.0), (0.0, 0.0))$;

or we could introduce

subtype MATRIX_2 **is** MATRIX$(1 .. 2, 1 .. 2)$;
V : MATRIX_2;

Of course index ranges do not have to be of type INTEGER, they can be any discrete type, for example

type COLOURS **is array** (COLOUR) **of** BOOLEAN;

This is an array of 3 elements indexed by RED, AMBER and GREEN. In this case we give no range qualification and so the range is that of the whole type. There is a difference here

A : TABLE $: = (2,4,4,4,0,0)$;

gives initial values for the 6 elements of A in order. This is the positional form. The following named forms are equivalent.

$(1 => 2, 2 | 3 | 4 => 4,$ **others** $= > 0)$;
$(1 => 2, 2 .. 4 => 4,$ **others** $= > 0)$;
$(1 => 2, 5 .. 6 => 0,$ **others** $= > 4)$;

In the named form the order is immaterial but **others**, if used, must be last. Moreover, **others** may not be used if the aggregate is expected to provide bounds information. Named and positional notation may not be mixed in array aggregates although **others** may be used with either form; this restriction eliminates some problems of preliminary Ada.

Note the form for multidimensional arrays. Mixed forms such as

$$(1 => (0.0, 0.0), 2 => (0.0, 0.0));$$
$$((0.0, 0.0), (1 => 0.0, 2 => 0.0));$$

are allowed since there is no mixing within one level. Note also possibilities such as

$$(1 .. 2 => (1 .. 2 => 0.0));$$

Access to array elements uses the conventional parentheses as in M(I,J).

CHARACTERS AND STRINGS

A character type is an enumeration type that contains character literals and possibly identifiers. A special case is the predefined type CHARACTER denoting the full ASCII set of 128 characters. It is rather as if the declaration took the form

type CHARACTER **is**
    (NUL, SOH, .. 'A', 'B', .., DEL);

The printable characters are denoted by literals in single quotes and control characters such as CR and LF by identifiers.

There is also the predefined type STRING—

type STRING **is array** (NATURAL **range** < >) **of** CHARACTER;

Note that the bounds of STRING are not explicit and any string object must therefore derive its bounds from a constraint or initial value. In the case of arrays of character types the lexical string is an alternative form of aggregate for those elements denoted by character literals. Thus we may write

S : **constant** STRING := ''GIN'';

and S is then an array whose bounds are 1 and 3. The lower bound is NATURAL'FIRST since the index is of subtype NATURAL.

Alternatively we could write

S : **constant** STRING := ('G', 'I', 'N');

If we wished to use control characters then we would write

CRLF : **constant** STRING := (CR, LF);

It should be noted that the lexical string can be used for an aggregate of any character type and not just the built in type. The following is permissible

type ROMAN_DIGIT **is** ('I','V','X','L','C','D','M');
type ROMAN_NUMBER **is array** (NATURAL **range** < >) **of** ROMAN_DIGIT;
NINETY_SIX : **constant** ROMAN_NUMBER := ''XCVI'';

RECORD TYPES

Record types without discriminants are illustrated by the following.

declare
    type MONTH_NAME **is** (JAN, FEB, ..., DEC);
    type DATE **is**
      record
        DAY : INTEGER **range** 1 .. 31;
        MONTH : MONTH_NAME;
        YEAR : INTEGER;
      end record;
    type COMPLEX **is**
      record
        RE, IM : FLOAT := 0.0;
      end record;

```
D : DATE := (4, JUL, 1776);
c1 : COMPLEX;
c2 : COMPLEX := (1.0, 2.0);
```

If initial values are given for components (as in COMPLEX) then any variable declared of that type without an explicit initial value (such as c1) takes the values by default.

Again there is the possibility of named aggregates

```
D : DATE : = (MONTH => JUL, DAY => 4, YEAR => 1776);
```

This is perhaps of particular relevance in this example because of lack of international agreement on the ordering of components of dates.

Access to record components uses the conventional dot notation as in D.YEAR.

DISCRIMINATED TYPES

Discriminated record types provide a limited form of type parameterization. This gives more power to private types as discussed later. Variant record types are a form of discriminated type.

Consider

```
JOHN: PERSON := (M, (19, AUG, 1937), FALSE);
BARBARA : PERSON := (F, (13, MAY, 1943), 2);
```

A person is a record containing a variant part discriminated by SEX which is a component. Thus one can write JOHN . SEX giving M. The discriminant can only be changed by a whole record assignment. The usual subtype and object constraints can be applied.

```
subtype MALE is PERSON(M);
JOHN : MALE := (M, (19, AUG, 1937), FALSE);
```

Note that the discriminants must occur first in an aggregate and the aggregate must be complete even when the discriminant has already been constrained as in the above example.

A discriminant can be given a default initial value; thus

```
type PERSON(SEX : GENDER := F) is ...
```

All declarations must ensure that the discriminant is set either from an initial value or from the default value. Thus

```
P : PERSON;
```

is only allowed if the discriminant has a default value.

A discriminant can also be used as the bound of an array component of the record as in

```
type TEXT(MAX : NATURAL) is
  record
    LENGTH : INTEGER := 0;
    VALUE : STRING(1 .. MAX);
  end record;
```

An object of type TEXT can be thought of as a varying string whose maximum is MAX and current size is LENGTH. One could then write

```
DAY : TEXT(9);
```

with the intention of storing strings such as "MONDAY" in DAY. Direct manipulation is tedious

```
DAY := (9, 6, "MONDAY      ");
```

but one can introduce functions which provide a more convenient notation.

ACCESS TYPES

Ada introduces the concept of an access type for manipulating references or pointers. The term reference has been brought into disrepute because of dangling references in Algol 68 and pointer has been brought into disrepute because of anonymous pointers in PL/I. Thus the new term access should therefore be thought of as a polite term for reference. However, as we shall see there are no dangling reference problems in Ada.

Consider

```
type LINK;
type CELL is
  record
    VALUE : INTEGER
    PRED, SUCC : LINK;
  end record;
type LINK is access CELL;
HEAD : LINE : = null;
```

These declarations introduce type LINK which accesses CELL. The object HEAD can be thought of as a reference variable which can point at objects of type CELL containing three components, a VALUE of type INTEGER and SUCC and PRED which are also references to objects of type CELL. The records can therefore be formed into a doubly linked list. Initially there are no record objects, only the single pointer HEAD which is initialized to **null** which points nowhere.

The accessed objects are created by calls of an allocator thus

```
HEAD := new CELL(0, null, null);
```

The keyword **new** is followed by the type of the object and an aggregate giving values for the components of the new object. The new object has zero as its VALUE component and the two other components are **null**. The access variable HEAD now points to this new object.

Suppose we introduce a further variable

```
NEXT : LINK;
```

and then consider the sequence of statements

```
NEXT := new CELL(0, null, HEAD);
HEAD . PRED := NEXT;
HEAD := NEXT;
```

This sequence acquires a further object and links it onto the front of the chain accessed by HEAD. Note how HEAD . PRED gives access to the component of the object. Unlike Pascal, dereferencing is automatic. The notation

```
HEAD . all
```

is used to refer to the whole object accessed by HEAD. Thus

```
HEAD := NEXT;            - - copies the pointer
HEAD . all := NEXT . all;   - - copies the object
```

Access types need not only refer to records although they often will. Thus one could have

```
type REF_INT is access INTEGER;
R : REF_INT := new INTEGER(46);
```

However the objects to which R refers must all be acquired through the allocator and not be directly declared as in

```
I : INTEGER;
R : REF_INT := I;   - - is illegal
```

The accessed objects are conceptually all at the scope level of the declaration of the access type. In general they will cease to exist only when that scope is left but of course by then all the access variables will also have ceased to exist. Thus no dangling reference problems can arise.

An inconvenience with Ada access types is that all the objects have to be created using the allocator. One cannot as say in RTL/2 declare some records and cross linkages between them in the form of initial values.

EXPRESSIONS

The predefined operators in Ada are shown in the following tables

Table I. Unary operators

OPERATOR	OPERAND	RESULT
+	numeric	same
−	numeric	same
not	boolean [array]	same

Table II. Binary operators

OPERATOR	OPERANDS		RESULT
and or xor **and then**	boolean [array]		same
or else	boolean		same
= / =	any		boolean
< <= > >=	scalar, discrete array		boolean
in not in	value	range, subtype, constraint	boolean
+ −	numeric		same
&	one dim array		same
*	integer	integer	same
	fixed	integer	same fixed
	integer	fixed	same fixed
	fixed	fixed	univ fixed
	floating	floating	same
/	integer	integer	same
	fixed	integer	same fixed
	fixed	fixed	univ fixed
	floating	floating	same
mod rem	integer	integer	same
**	integer	nonneg integer	same integer
	floating	integer	same floating

These operators are grouped into classes given in the following order of increasing precedence

and or xor and then or else
$=$ /$=$ $<$ $<=$ $>$ $>=$ **in not in**
$+$ $-$ $\&$ (binary $+$, $-$)
$+$ $-$ **not** (unary $+$, $-$)
*** / mod rem**
******

Curiously the unary operators are not the most binding but have intermediate precedence. the precedence rules are otherwise as expected and far preferable to those of Pascal.

Some additional rules protect the user from himself. For example **and**, **or** and **xor** cannot be mixed without using parentheses.

In general the operators are much as expected but the following points are notable.

Not equals is represented by / $=$ rather than the unpronouncable $<>$ of Pascal which in Ada does good service in array ranges and generic formals. The real objection to $<>$ is that $<$ and $>$ areot defined for all types and therefore the conceptual pun of combining them misfires.

Ada contains **rem** as well as **mod**. Division truncates towards zero and **rem** is the remainder of division whereas **mod** is the mathematical modulus operator.

A **rem** B has the sign of A whereas A **mod** B has the sign of B.

Note also that Ada has upgraded the short circuit forms **and then** and **or else** as operators. These forms indicate that the second operand is only to be evaluated if the result of the opration cannot be determined from the value of the first operand.

It will be noticed that some operators apply to many different types. The operators may be thought of as being defined by several functions distinguished by different formal parameters. This multiple definition is known as overloading. The particular definition to be used is decided by, for example, the types of the actual parameters.

CONTROL STATEMENTS

Ada contains the normal conditional, case and loop statements of modern languages. In all cases bracketed syntactic forms are used (as in Algol 68) rather than the archaic notation which Pascal inherited from Algol 60.

The closing bracket is consistently **end** followed by the main opening keyword thus

```
if HEAD /= null then
   HEAD . PRED := NEXT;
end if;
```

The normal **else** alternative is provided and the contracted form **elsif** saves an **end if.** Thus

```
if I = 1 then
  s1;
else
  if I = 2 then
    s2;
  end if;
end if;
```

and

```
if I = 1 then
  s1;
elsif I = 2 then
  s2;
end if;
```

are equivalent.

The case statement allows a sequence of statements after each choice and as in aggregates a choice may be composed of several individual values or ranges thus

```
case TODAY is
   when MON => INITIAL_BALANCE;
   when FRI => CLOSING BALANCE;
   when TUE .. THU => REPORT(TODAY);
   when SAT | SUN => null;
end case;
```

Note the explicit null statement which emphasises the fact that no action is to be performed. The null statement is mandatory in this context although it was not in preliminary Ada. Note also **is** rather than **of**.

Three forms of loop statement are provided. The traditional iteration in which a control variable takes successive values in a range; thus

```
for I in A'RANGE loop
   A(I) := 0;
end loop;
```

sets all elements of A to zero.

Unlike Pascal the control variable is implicitly declared. The iteration proceeds backwards if **in** is followed by **reverse**. Of course the range can also take a form such as 1 .. N.

There is also a while loop; thus

```
while NEXT /= null loop;
   SUM := SUM + NEXT . VALUE;
   NEXT := NEXT . SUCC;
end loop;
```

adds together the value components of our chain of access objects.

The third form is the infinite loop

```
loop
   :
end loop;
```

The statement **exit**; transfers control out of the immediately embracing loop. There are also forms for conditional exit and exit from a named outer loop.

There is also the maligned label and goto statement:

```
<<L>>
goto L;
```

Note the interesting notation for a label. The goto statement is necessary for the easy creation of automatically generated programs.

SUBPROGRAMS

Subprograms in Ada are classified into procedures and functions. Procedures are called as separate statements whereas functions are components of expressions and return values. (The value returning procedures of preliminary Ada have been eliminated; a satisfactory distinction between them and functions in the face of aliasing and side effects seemed unattainable.)

Consider

```
type VECTOR is array (INTEGER range < >) of REAL
function INNER(A, B : VECTOR) return REAL is
   SUM : REAL := 0.0;
begin
```

```
for I in A'RANGE loop
    SUM := SUM + A(I)*B(I);
end loop;
return SUM;
end INNER;
```

The function INNER computes the element by element inner product of the two vectors A and B. It is assumed that A and B have similar bounds—a better formulation would check this. The local variable SUM is declared in the declarative part between **is** and **begin** and the statements of the body are between **begin** and **end**. Note the occurrence of INNER after **end**—this is optional but if present must match the designator of the function. Return from a function occurs via a return statement which contains an expression of the appropriate mode and is the result of calling the function. There could be several return statements.

The function INNER could be used in a sequence such as

```
declare
    P, Q : VECTOR(1 .. 100);
    R : REAL;
begin
    ⋮
    R : = INNER(P, Q);
    ⋮
end;
```

A function can be designated by an identifier such as INNER or by a character string denoting a language operator such as "*". A function so designated provides an additional overloading of the language operator and is called with the same syntax. So if we write

```
function "*"(A, B : VECTOR) return REAL is
    ⋮
end "*";
```

then we could write

```
R : = P*Q;
```

The compiler determines that it is the newly declared function that is to be called rather than one of the predefined multiplication operations because of the types of P and Q. In cases of ambiguity, an expression can always be qualified by a type mark thus

```
R : = VECTOR'(P)*VECTOR'(Q);
```

The parameters of a subprogram may be of three modes.

in   The formal parameter acts as a local constant whose value is provided by the corresponding actual parameter.

out   the formal parameter acts as a local variable whose value is assigned to the corresponding actual parameter as a result of the execution of the subprogram.

in out   the formal parameter acts as a local variable and permits access and assignment to the corresponding actual parameter.

In the case of a function only **in** parameters are permitted. If no mode is given (as in the example of INNER) then it is **in** by default.

Ada specifies that scaler and access types are passed by copy but that composite types may be passed by copy or reference.

As an example of a procedure we consider the following which performs the action of linking an extra record onto the chain referenced by HEAD in an earlier example and takes account of the possibility of the chain initially being empty.

```
procedure ADD_TO_LIST (L : in out LINK; V : INTEGER) is
```

```
    NEXT : LINK;
begin
    NEXT := new CELL(V, null, L);
    if L /= null then
        L . PRED := NEXT;
    end if;
    L := NEXT;
end ADD_TO_LIST;
```

This can be called by a statement such as

```
ADD_TO_LIST(HEAD, 3);
```

As well as the conventional calling notation in which the parameters are given in order, there is also a named form similar to aggregates

```
ADD_TO_LIST(L => HEAD, V => 3);
```

Like record aggregates, named and positional forms can be mixed and the order of named parameters is immaterial. (The notation for named parameters is different from the preliminary version.)

In some cases it may be necessary to specify a subprogram without giving its body. This will occur with mutually recursive procedures since in Ada one cannot use something until after its declaration. It also occurs with packages. In such cases we write for example

```
function INNER(A, B : VECTOR) return REAL;
```

and give the body later but when the body is given the specification is repeated in full.

An interesting facility in Ada is the ability to provide default parameters—this applies only to those of mode **in**. The subprogram heading contains initial values which are used if no corresponding actual parameters are provided.

Consider the problem of ordering a dry martini in the USA. One is faced with choices described by the following enumeration types

```
type SPIRIT is (GIN, VODKA);
type STYLE is (ON_THE_ROCKS, STRAIGHT_UP);
type TRIMMING is (OLIVE, TWIST);
```

Standard default values are indicated by the following specification of a suitable procedure

```
procedure DRY MARTINI
    (BASE : SPIRIT : = GIN;
    HOW : STYLE : = ON_THE_ROCKS;
    WITH : TRIMMING : = OLIVE);
```

Typical calls might be

```
DRY_MARTINI(VODKA, WITH => TWIST);
DRY_MARTINI(HOW => STRAIGHT_UP);
DRY_MARTINI;
```

The first call shows mixed positional and named parameters. The last call produces the standard gin-based drink on the rocks with an olive.

PACKAGES

The package is the main structuring unit of Ada. It typically encapsulates data and subprograms providing access to that data. Normally a package occurs in two parts, a specification describing the facilities it provides and a body which is the implementation of the facilities.

As an example consider the following

```
package STACK is                        -- specification
  procedure PUSH(X : REAL);
  function POP return REAL;
end;

package body STACK is                   -- body
  MAX : constant := 100;
  S : array (1 .. MAX) of REAL;
  PTR : INTEGER range 0 .. MAX;

  procedure PUSH(X : REAL) is
  begin
    PTR := PTR + 1;
    S(PTR) := X;
  end PUSH;

  function POP return REAL is
  begin
    PTR := PTR - 1;
    return S(PTR + 1);
  end POP;
begin
  PTR := 0;
end STACK;
```

This declares a package STACK which provides access to subprograms PUSH and POP which manipulate a stack of up to 100 REAL values. The stack is implemented as the array S and PTR indexes the top element. MAX is a constant giving the size of the stack. The statements between the begin and end of the body are obeyed when the package is declared and may be used to initialize the package. The items MAX, S and PTR are not accessible outside the package.

The items in the specification may be accessed from outside the package by dotted notation.

```
begin
  STACK . PUSH(X);
  ...
  X : = STACK . POP( );
end;
```

or alternatively by a use clause

```
declare
  use STACK;
begin
  PUSH(X);
  ...
  X := POP( );
end;
```

The use clause indicates that the identifiers in the specification may be used without naming the package explicitiy; in cases of ambiguity the dotted notation can still be used.

A further possibility is to use renames

```
declare
  procedure SPUSH(X : REAL) renames STACK . PUSH;
  function SPOP return REAL renames STACK . POP;
begin
```

```
        SPUSH(X);
        ...
        X := SPOP( );
    end;
```

Note that the signatures of SPUSH and SPOP are given in full.

A parameterless function call takes mandatory empty parentheses whereas they are not required or allowed for a parameterless procedure call.

Renaming is both a shorthand and a partial evaluation; one can write

```
    AI : REAL renames A(I);
```

and then

```
    AI := AI + 1;
```

in order to avoid repeated evaluation of the subscript I. If I changes subsequently then AI continues to refer to the previous location. Renaming does not hide the old name.

Note that a package need not have a body in the degenerate case where the specification merely acts as a common pool of items such as variables. If, on the other hand, the specification contains the specification of a subprogram then the subprogram body must occur in the corresponding package body. Similarly a specification may contain the specification of an internal package and again the internal body must be in the main body.

PRIVATE TYPES

An important form of package is one with a private part. This enables a type to be made visible without revealing its internal structure.

As an example suppose we wish to provide a package for the manipulation of complex numbers but do not wish the user to know how they are represented. We wish to retain the freedom to change their representation from say cartesian form to perhaps polar form and to know that the user's program will not need altering (although it will need recompiling).

The specification of such a package might be

```
    package COMPLEX_NUMBERS is
      type COMPLEX is private;
      function "+"(X, Y : COMPLEX) return COMPLEX;
      function "-"(X, Y : COMPLEX) return COMPLEX;
      function "*"(X, Y : COMPLEX) return COMPLEX;
      function "/"(X, Y : COMPLEX) return COMPLEX;
      function CONS(R, I : REAL) return COMPLEX;
      function RL_PART(X : COMPLEX) return REAL;
      function IM_PART(X : COMPLEX) return REAL;
    private
      type COMPLEX is
        record
          RL : REAL;
          IM : REAL;
        end record;
    end;
```

In this the specification has a private part after the normal visible part. The private part gives in full the definition of any types declared as private in the visible part.

It is also possible to have a private constant in the visible part

```
    I : constant COMPLEX;
```

and then in the private part

I : **constant** COMPLEX := (0.0, 1.0);

The package body might be

```
package body COMPLEX_NUMBERS is

  function "+"(X, Y : COMPLEX) return COMPLEX is
  begin
    return (X.RL + Y.RL, X.IM + Y.IM);
  end;
      .
      .
  function "−"(X, Y : COMPLEX) return COMPLEX is
  begin
    return (X.RL*Y.RL − X.IM*Y.IM, X.RL*Y.IM + X.IM*Y.RL);
  end;
      .
      .
  function CONS(R, I : REAL) return COMPLEX is
  begin
    return (R, I);
  end;
      .
      .
  function RL PART(X : COMPLEX) return REAL is
  begin
    return X.RL;
  end;
      .
      .
end COMPLEX_NUMBERS;
```

The package can then be used in a fragment such as

```
declare
  use COMPLEX_NUMBERS;
  I : constant COMPLEX := CONS(0.0, 1.0);
  C, D  COMPLEX;
  R, S : REAL;
begin
  C := CONS(1.5, −6.0);
  D := C + I;                -- complex +
  R := RL_PART(D) + 6.0;     -- real +
end;
```

In practise further overloadings of the operators could be introduced in order to allow convenient mixed operations between types REAL and COMPLEX.

Now if we change the definition of COMPLEX to

```
type COMPLEX is
  record
    R : REAL;            --polars
    THETA : REAL;
  end record;
```

then the package body will need rewriting but the user program will not. The functions CONS, RL_PART and IM_PART must still present a cartesian appearance of course. The constant I (if in the package) would now be

I : **constant** COMPLEX := (1.0, 0.5*PI);

Thus the private type enables the abstract properties to be separated from their implementation.

A private type may have discriminants. Our earlier example of TEXT could be made private thus

type TEXT(MAX : NATURAL) **is private**;

The implementing type in the private part must have the same discriminants.

Assignment and the operators = and / = are normally available to private types but if the definition is prefixed **limited** then this is not so. Furthermore, = and / = may not be redefined, although they may be explicitly defined for limited private types.

TASKS

A task declaration introduces a separate 'thread of control' which executes conceptually in parallel with other tasks. A single task may be declared with a similar lexical form to a package

```
declare
    task T is              - - specification
    .
    .
    end;
    task body T is         - - body
    .
    .
    end T;
begin                      - - active here
```

The task automatically becomes active (i.e. its body is executed) when the task elaborating its declaration reaches the following **begin**. (The initiate statement of preliminary Ada has been deleted.)

Consider the following example which illustrates the problem of a family arriving at an airport and faced with three tasks, booking a hotel, claiming their baggage and renting a car.

```
procedure ARRIVE_AT_AIRPORT is
    task CLAIM_BAGGAGE is
    :
    end;
    task body CLAIM_BAGGAGE is
    :
    end;
    task RENT_A_CAR is
    :
    end;
    task body RENT_A_CAR is
    :
    end;
```

```
begin
  BOOK_HOTEL;
end ARRIVE_AT_AIRPORT;
```

On reaching the **begin** of the **procedure** ARRIVE_AT_AIRPORT, the subtasks CLAIM_BAGGAGE and RENT_A_CAR are automatically set active (we can imagine the children and mother being dispatched to do these tasks) while the main task (the father) calls the procedure BOOK_HOTEL. The three tasks meet again at the **end** of the procedure ARRIVE_AT_AIRPORT. A task terminates normally by reaching its final end. The main procedure cannot be left until both the subtasks have terminated and will wait at its end until they have done so. Thus the family is reunited.

An alternative formulation would be to treat the three activities as equal and to have three subtasks and a null body.

The primary means of communication between tasks is through entries. An entry declaration is similar to a procedure specification and can only appear in a task specification. The only declarations allowed in a task specification are entries—this restriction solves several problems with tasking in preliminary Ada and emphasizes the concept that the package is the main structuring tool.

One or more bodies for the entry are provided by accept statements; these must appear in the corresponding task body. An entry is called by another task in the same way as a procedure call. The mechanism is that of the extended rendezvous.

Consider a task T containing

```
entry PUT(X : INTEGER);
```

in its specification and

```
accept PUT(X : INTEGER) do
  ⋮
end;
```

in its body and another task with a call

```
T . PUT(V);
```

Whichever task reaches its statement (call or accept) first waits for the other. When they rendezvous the parameters are transferred in the usual manner and the body of the accept statement executed. The calling task is held up while this happens and is only allowed to continue when the accept statement is completed. The two tasks then continue on their separate ways.

As an example consider the following task which represents a box which can contain a single integer value. A value can only be placed into the box when it is empty and taken out when it is full.

```
task BOX is
  entry PUT(X : in INTEGER);
begin
  loop
    accept PUT(X : in INTEGER) do
      V := X;
    end;
    accept GET(X : out INTEGER) do
      X := V;
    end;
  end loop;
end BOX;
```

Calls of PUT and GET take the form

```
BOX . PUT(57);
BOX . GET(Y);
```

A use clause cannot refer to a task and so entry calls from outside a task always refer to the task explicitly. But an entry could be renamed as a procedure thus

```
procedure PUT(X : INTEGER) renames BOX . PUT;
```

The rendezvous mechanism in Ada is asymmetric. The called task is named by the caller but not vice versa. Associated with each entry there is a (possibly empty) queue of waiting tasks—these are processed on a first in first out basis. Note that a task can only be on one queue since it can only call one entry at a time.

In some cases the purpose of a rendezvous is only to synchronize the tasks and not to transfer data. In such cases a degenerate form applies. The entry declaration and accept statement become

```
entry SIGNAL;
accept SIGNAL;
```

and the call is then

```
T . SIGNAL;
```

Non-determinism is introduced by the select statement as illustrated by the following task which provides access to the variable v of the previous example in a slightly different manner. In this case the ordering requirement that calls of GET and PUT must alternate is deleted and the only intent is that multiple access is prevented.

```
task PROTECTED_VARIABLE is
  entry READ(X : out ELEM);
  entry WRITE(X : in ELEM);
end;

task body PROTECTED_VARIABLE is
  V : ELEM := ...;
begin
  loop
    select
      accept READ(X : out ELEM) do
        X := V;
      end;
    or
      accept WRITE(X : in ELEM) do
        V := X;
      end;
    end select;
  end loop;
end PROTECTED_VARIABLE;
```

This shows a simple form of select statement. It contains branches separated by **or** and each branch commences with an accept statement. When the select statement is obeyed various possibilities arise. If neither READ nor WRITE has been called then the task waits until one is called; if one of READ or WRITE has been called then the appropriate branch is taken; if both have been called then one branch is selected in an unspecified but fair manner. Of course on each execution of the select statement only one branch is obeyed.

The next example introduces guards. It shows the classical bounded buffer example. The task BUFFERING contains an internal buffer which is used cyclicly and can hold N values. The problem is to ensure that the buffer cannot be over filled or under emptied.

```
task BUFFERING is
  entry READ(X : out ELEM);
  entry WRITE(X : in ELEM);
end;

task body BUFFERING is
  BUFFER : array (1 . . N) of ELEM;
  I, J : INTEGER range 1 . . N := 1;
  COUNT : INTEGER range 0 . . N := 0;
```

```
begin
  loop
    select
      when COUNT > 0 =>
      accept READ(X : out ELEM) do
        X := BUFFER(J);
      end;
      J := J mod N + 1; COUNT := COUNT - 1;
    or
      when COUNT < N =>
      accept WRITE(X : in ELEM) do
        BUFFER(I) := X;
      end;
      I := I mod N + 1; COUNT := COUNT + 1;
    end select;
  end loop;
end BUFFERING;
```

The integers I and J index the next free and last used elements of BUFFER. The integer COUNT indicates how many elements of the buffer are in use.

In this case the branches of the select statement commence with

```
when condition =>
```

Each time the select statement is obeyed these guarding conditions are evaluated and only those branches for which the guard is TRUE are eligible for consideration on that execution. In the example, COUNT is initialized to zero since the buffer is initially empty and so on the first execution of the select statement the guard on the READ branch is FALSE. Hence the first time round only the WRITE branch can be taken. When the rendezvous occurs the value is copied into the buffer. Note how the subsequent updating of I and COUNT take place outside the rendezvous but within the select statement. The select statement is then repeated and the guards reevaluated. This time both are TRUE (assuming N > 1) and so either another item can be added to the buffer or the first one removed.

The final classical example considered is that of the readers and writers. The intent is to allow several readers at a time but only one writer. A solution is as follows

```
package READER_WRITER is
  procedure READ(X : out ELEM);
  procedure WRITE(X : in ELEM);
end;

package body READER_WRITER is
  V : ELEM := ...;

  task CONTROL is
    entry START;
    entry STOP;
    entry WRITE(X : in ELEM);
  end;

  task body CONTROL is
    RDRS : INTEGER := 0;
  begin
    loop
      select
        accept START; RDRS := RDRS + 1;
      or
        accept STOP; RDRS := RDRS - 1;
      or
        when RDRS = 0 =>
        accept WRITE(X : in ELEM) do
          V := X;
        end;
      end select;
    end loop;
  end CONTROL;

  procedure READ(X : out ELEM) is
  begin
```

```
        CONTROL . START; X := V; CONTROL . STOP;
    end READ;
    procedure WRITE(X : in ELEM) is
    begin
        CONTROL . WRITE(X);
    end WRITE;
  end READER_WRITER;
```

The solution above involves a package containing an internal task whereas in preliminary Ada it was a task containing a procedure in its visible part but as observed above the only declarations now allowed in the visible part of a task are entries.

The task CONTROL is automatically made active when the package body is elaborated—a notional **begin** and null initialization part to the package are assumed.

The procedure READ imposes a protocol on internal rendezvous with the control task. The current number of readers is RDRS and calls of START and STOP act as logging on and off signals. Writing is only allowed when there are no readers by the guarding condition RDRS = 0.

A problem with this simple solution is that a steady stream of readers will block out any writers. The following alternative formulation of the body of the task CONTROL overcomes this by only allowing a new reader if there are no writers waiting. This change alone could swing the balance too far in favour of the writers and so additionally after a writer any waiting readers are immediately dealt with.

```
    task body CONTROL is
        RDRS : INTEGER := 0;
    begin
      loop
        select
          when WRITE'COUNT = 0 =>
          accept START; RDRS := RDRS + 1;
        or
          accept STOP; RDRS := RDRS - 1;
        or
          when RDRS = 0 =>
          accept WRITE(X : in ELEM) do
            V := X;
          end;
          loop
            select
          end loop;
        end select;
      end loop;
    end CONTROL;
```

This formulation uses the COUNT attribute of an entry and a form of select statement with an else part.

WRITE COUNT is the number of tasks on the queue of the entry WRITE and so the guard prevents new readers from being accepted if writers are waiting.

If a select statement has an else part and if no rendezvous is immediately possible then the else part is obeyed. Thus after the rendezvous with a writer we loop accepting calls of START so long as there are calls to be processed. When the queue is exhausted the else part is taken and this causes the loop to be terminated. The reader will note that this revised formulation is not perfect since it allows readers to block out further activity provided they arrive more rapidly than they can be dealt with. But in such a case the system is grossly overloaded anyway.

TIMING

The delay statement allows a task to suspend itself for a given interval. The statement takes an argument of a predefined fixed point type DURATION given in seconds. Thus

> **delay** 3.5;   -- delay 3.5 seconds

The user may provide constants such as

> SECONDS : **constant** DURATION := 1.0;
> MINUTES : **constant** DURATION := 60.0;
> HOURS : **constant** DURATION := 3600.0;

and then write

> **delay** 2.0*HOURS + 45.0*MINUTES;

There is also a library package CALENDAR with specification

```
package CALENDAR is
  type TIME is
    record
      YEAR : INTEGER range 1901 .. 2099;
      MONTH : INTEGER range 1 .. 12;
      DAY : INTEGER range 1 .. 31;
      SECOND : DURATION;
    end record;
  function CLOCK return TIME;
  function "+"(A : TIME; B : DURATION) return TIME;
  function "+"(A : DURATION; B : TIME) return TIME;
  function "-"(A : TIME; B : DURATION) return TIME;
  function "-"(A,B : TIME) return DURATION;
end;
```

The range of YEAR in the type TIME simplifies the leap year calculation. The function CLOCK returns the current TIME.

Repetitive action without cumulative drift can be achieved as in the following

```
declare
  use CALENDAR;
  INTERVAL : DURATION := ...;
  NEXT_TIME : TIME := ...;          -- first time
begin
  loop
    delay NEXT_TIME - CLOCK( );
    ACTION;
    NEXT_TIME : = NEXT_TIME + INTERVAL;
  end loop;
end;
```

The operators − and + in the above are overloadings from the package CALENDAR.

A delay statement may occur as a branch in a select statement in order to give a time out facility. Thus

```
select
   accept READ ...
or
   delay 1.0;
                          -- time out action
end select;
```

If a call of READ has not been accepted within one second, the time out action is taken instead.

Ada also allows timed out and conditional entry calls, thus

```
select                      select
   T . READ(...);              T. READ(...);
or                          else
   delay 1.0;
      ...                       ...
end select;                 end select;
```

TASK TYPES

A task type is specified by the form

```
task type T is
   entry E;
      ...
end;
```

The body is as before. A task type acts as a template and individual tasks are declared using the task name in the usual way. Thus

```
A : T;
```

introduces a new task referred to as A. All task types act as limited types. The entry E can then be called as A . E;. The simple tasks introduced earlier can be considered as single instances of anonymous task types.

Task types are useful for creating synchronization objects. Consider

```
task type SEMAPHORE is
   entry P;
   entry V;
end;
task body SEMAPHORE is
   ACQUIRED : BOOLEAN := FALSE;
begin
   loop
      select
         when not ACQUIRED =>
         accept P;
         ACQUIRED := TRUE;
      or
         accept V;
         ACQUIRED := FALSE;
      end select;
   end loop;
end SEMAPHORE;
```

It would then be possible to declare semaphores as if they were normal data objects. Indeed one could declare records containing a semaphore and the data it is to protect.

```
type R is
   record
      S : SEMAPHORE;
```

```
    D : DATA;
  end record;
```

One problem with synchronization objects is leaving the scope in which they are declared. There is a general rule that one cannot leave a scope unless all locally declared tasks have terminated. To have to explicitly terminate such tasks would be tedious and so Ada contains a feature whereby a task can indicate that it is willing to be terminated when its declaring scope is left. This is done through a further alternative in a select statement. In the above case we would write

```
select
  when not ACQUIRED =>
  accept P;
    ACQUIRED := TRUE;
or
  accept V;
    ACQUIRED := FALSE;
or
  terminate;
end select;
```

Each time around the loop the task is then willing to accept a call of P or a call of V or to be terminated if the scope declaring it is left.

EXCEPTIONS

Ada provides a means for dealing with errors or other exceptional situations. The language contains several predefined exceptions such as NUMERIC ERROR. The user can provide a handler on units such as blocks and subprograms thus

```
begin
  -- sequence of statements
exception
  when NUMERIC_ERROR =>
  -- emergency action
end;
```

If the NUMERIC_ERROR exception is raised during the sequence of statements, control is immediately transferred to the handler which in a similar form to a case statement specifies the emergency action to be performed. It is important to notice that the block is then left and control is not returned to where the exception was raised.

Exception handling is a dynamic mechanism. If a handler is not provided for a particular exception at one level then the level is terminated and the exception propagated to the dynamically calling level. It is possible to provide an **others** alternative to catch all exceptions.

It is also possible to declare user exceptions. Our earlier example of the package STACK did not check for stack overflow or underflow. This could conveniently be done by introducing an exception thus

```
package STACK is
  ERROR : exception;
  procedure PUSH(X : REAL);
  function POP return REAL;
end;

package body STACK is
  MAX : constant := 100;
  S : array (1 .. MAX) of REAL;
  PTR : INTEGER range 0 .. MAX;

  procedure PUSH(X : REAL) is
  begin
    if PTR = MAX then
```

```
        raise ERROR;
      end if;
      PTR := PTR + 1;
      S(PTR) := X;
    end PUSH;
    function POP return REAL is
    begin
      if PTR = 0 then
        raise ERROR;
      end if;
      PTR := PTR - 1;
      return S(PTR + 1);
    end POP;
  begin
    PTR := 0;
  end STACK;
```

The user could then write

```
  begin
    STACK . PUSH(X);
    ...
    X := STACK . POP( );
  exception
    when STACK . ERROR =>
      ...
  end;
```

The statement

```
  raise;
```

within a handler reraises the current exception at the next level. This is convenient for recovery on a layered basis.

A minor change from preliminary Ada is that a handler applies only to the statements in a block. An exception occurring in the declarations is raised at the next higher level. This overcomes a problem in preliminary Ada whereby a handler could attempt to access objects whose declaration had not been elaborated.

The interaction between exceptions and tasking is somewhat complex and will not be described here. However one of the more irritating interactions of preliminary Ada has been removed: if a caller is aborted during a rendezvous the called task is no longer disrupted the caller is essentially 'propped up' until the rendezvous is complete and only then allowed to die.

The number of exceptions has been reduced: NO_VALUE_ERROR, OVERLAP_ERROR, INITIATE_ERROR and UNDERFLOW are removed and some other exceptions have been grouped on the grounds that their distinction is rarely helpful for recovery purposes: thus OVERFLOW and DIVIDE_ERROR have both become NUMERIC_ERROR.

GENERICS

The generic mechanism allows a subprogram or package to be parameterized by types and subprograms as well as normal **in** parameters. The generic mechanism allows a more precise categorization of type parameters than in preliminary Ada; this reduces the need for additional parameters.

As a simple example consider the package STACK introduced earlier. This only declared a single stack of length 100 and operating on elements of type REAL. The following formulation gives a generic package with the length and type of element as parameters.

```
  generic
    MAX : INTEGER;
    type ELEM is private;
  package STACK is
```

```
        ERROR : exception;
        procedure PUSH(X : ELEM);
        function POP return ELEM;
    end;

    package body STACK is
      S : array (1 .. MAX) of ELEM;
        :
    end STACK;
```

A particular stack is then declared by a generic instantiation which includes appropriate actual parameters.

```
    declare
      package MY_STACK is new STACK(100, REAL);
      use MY_STACK;
    begin
      PUSH(X);
        ...
      X := POP( );
    exception
      when ERROR =>
        ...
    end;
```

Note that a use clause can now appear anywhere in a declarative part thereby avoiding the necessity for two blocks for this example as in preliminary Ada.

The next example illustrates dependencies between generic formal parameters.

```
    generic
      type ITEM is private;
      type VECTOR is array (INTEGER range < >) of ITEM;
      with function SUM(X, Y : ITEM) return ITEM;
    package ON_VECTORS is
      function SIGMA(A : VECTOR) return ITEM;
    end;

    package body ON_VECTORS is

      function SIGMA(A : VECTOR) return ITEM is
        TOTAL : ITEM : = A(A'FIRST);
      begin
        for I in A'FIRST + 1 .. A'LAST loop
          TOTAL := SUM(TOTAL, A(I));
        end loop;
        return TOTAL;
      end;

    end ON_VECTORS;
```

Since we know that VECTOR is an array we are assured of the existence of attributes such as A'FIRST. In preliminary Ada such attributes would have been passed as separate parameters. Note however that no constraint is placed on the type ITEM and therefore no attributes can be assumed.

Other forms of formal generic parameters enable distinctions to be made between enumeration types, integer, fixed and floating types and access types.

SEPARATE COMPILATION

Ada recognizes the need to be able to compile a program in distinct pieces and provides

facilities for both bottom up and top down approaches.

In the bottom up approach, packages and subprograms may be separately compiled and placed in a program library. Another unit may then be compiled later and refer to the units in the library. The dependency is indicated by a with clause.

Thus the package COMPLEX NUMBERS could be separately compiled and placed in the library. A procedure to solve quadratic equations could then take the form

```
with (COMPLEX_NUMBERS, REAL_MATHLIB)
procedure SOLVE(A, B, C : REAL; R1, R2 : out COMPLEX) is
  use COMPLEX_NUMBERS, REAL_MATHLIB;
begin
  ...
end;
```

The with clause allows the packages and subprograms mentioned to be used in the unit in the usual way.

The library system ensures that separately compiled units have conforming interfaces. If a unit is recompiled then all dependent units must be recompiled.

It should be noted that a package specification and package body are treated as distinct units for library purposes and that the body must be compiled after the specification. Moreover any unit using the package is dependent only on the specification and not the body. Therefore if the body is changed in a manner consistent with not changing the specification then any unit using the package will not need recompiling. It is because of the desire to obtain this independence that the private part is in the specification and not the body.

The top down approach introduces the notion of a subunit. In this case a unit body nested inside a parent unit is replaced by a stub in the parent and the body is compiled separately.

As an example the body of the package STACK could be written as

```
package body STACK is
  MAX : constant := 100;
  s : array (1 .. MAX) of REAL;
  PTR : INTEGER range 0 .. MAX;
  procedure PUSH(X : REAL) is separate;
  function POP return REAL is separate;
begin
  PTR : = 0;
end STACK;
```

The two subunits are then separately compiled and take the form

```
separate (STACK)
procedure PUSH(X : REAL) is
begin
  PTR := PTR + 1;
  s(PTR) := X;
end PUSH;
```

and similarly for POP.

The general philosophy is similar to preliminary Ada although there are minor changes. Perhaps the most significant change is the replacement of the restricted clause by the with clause. Note that the with clause is only used at the outermost level. The complexity of the internal restricted clause has been abandoned.

INPUT–OUTPUT

Input–output is provided by a generic package INPUT OUTPUT for the manipulation of files of a single type and a standard package TEXT_IO for handling text. These packages are not part of the language but notionally written in it. Ada contains adequate functionality (overloading, default parameters etc.) to enable convenient facilities to be provided for the user without having to embed them in the language as in Pascal. The problem with embedding such things into a language is that extension and functional composition are not possible. On the other hand the risk with leaving them out is that different implementations will produce different standards as occurred with Algol 60. In the case of Ada this latter risk should be overcome by the adoption of the currently defined packages.

A full description is not possible here but as an example consider calls of PUT for the output of text. This is an overloaded procedure with different versions for different types. Moreover, default parameters allow a standard field to be used if none is given.

```
PUT(I);              -- integer in standard field
PUT(I,6);            -- integer in field of width 6
PUT("MESSAGE");      -- string
```

CONCLUSION

It is hoped that this paper will have given the reader some idea of the power of Ada. The discussion has not been complete and no doubt contains some inaccuracies for which the author is solely to blame; this paper is no substitute for the language reference manual which should be consulted for a full and accurate description. Indeed, important aspects such as representation specifications and the name identification rules have not been discussed.

However, Ada should not be looked upon as just another programming language. A very important complementary activity has been the development of a parallel series of documents intitled SANDMAN, PEBBLEMAN and finally STONEMAN[4] relating to the concept of an Ada Programming Support Environment (APSE). It is recognized that for program and programmer portability it is not enough to have a portable language. The environment must also be portable. The development of one or more APSE's will be an important factor in the acceptance and success of Ada.

Another important factor is the recognition that strictly enforced standards are important. The U.S. DoD is developing a validation suite which will be a key factor in ensuring that compilers conform to the standard. It should be noted that this suite will be available before the first compilers.

Whether Ada will be successful or not remains to be seen. However, it is clearly a significant step forward both technically and politically. If the willingness and needs of large organizations such as the U.S. DoD cannot produce the climate for the introduction of a good general purpose modern language then we will have to continue to use out-of-date and/or non-standard languages such as FORTRAN and Pascal for ever.

ACKNOWLEDGEMENTS

The author would like to acknowledge all those engaged in the design of Ada with whom he has had the privilege to be associated but especially Jean Ichbiah who as the team leader is the prime designer of Ada.

REFERENCES

1. *Reference Manual for the Ada Programming Language*, United States Department of Defense, July 1980.
2. 'Preliminary Ada reference manual', *SIGPLAN Notices*, **14**, 6, Part A, (June 1979).
3. *STEELMAN*, Defense Advanced Research Projects Agency, Arlington, Virginia, 1978.
4. *STONEMAN*, Defense Advanced Research Projects Agency, Arlington, Virginia, 1980.

TECHNICAL BACKGROUND

We will now briefly describe the position of Ada in the overall language scene. We first note the emergence of two programming language cultures which we can refer to as the professional culture and the amateur culture although these terms are not completely satisfactory.

The professional culture is concerned with writing programs of a fairly permanent nature. These programs are usually fairly large and written by teams of programmers whose profession is primarily the design and writing of programs. The programs will or should be adequately documented and will need maintenance throughout a lifetime which may be several years long. Such maintenance will often arise as the environment in which they work changes throughout their lifetime. Because of this maintenance need it is essential that the language used is standard and stable. Any language changes should occur in a controlled way at infrequent intervals. Important characteristics of such a language are the need for separate compilation, readability and compile time error detection. Interactive use is not required. Examples of existing languages aimed at this culture are COBOL, PL/I, CORAL 66, RTL/2 and CHILL.

The amateur culture is concerned with writing programs of a less permanent nature. These programs are usually small and often written by individuals who are amateur programmers; that is to say that their profession is in a different field such as accountancy, medicine or chemical engineering and they use the computer merely as a tool in the furtherance of their main goals. The programs are often very short lived—perhaps used only once—and consequently need little or no maintenance and hence do not deserve or get significant documentation. Because of the short-lived nature of the program it is not vital that the language used is standard or stable. Indeed, languages in this area are under rapid development and standardization could be counter productive. Important characteristics of such languages are the need for ease of writing and general 'user friendliness'; interactive use is inevitable. Examples of such languages are BASIC and APL.

Ada is a language for the professional culture.

A great milestone in the development of programming languages was the publication of the Algol report in 1960. The step forward taken by Algol 60 was truly remarkable; no language since then has made such an impact on later developments. In fact, 1960 can be taken as the beginning of the awakening out of the dark ages. At that time there were just three languages FORTRAN, COBOL and Algol 60. Since then all new languages can be traced back to Algol 60. FORTRAN and COBOL have developed and COBOL in particular has borne dialects but these developments are not of the same degree as those emanating from Algol 60.

An early and ambitious development from Algol 60 was PL/I. Of course, it included much from FORTRAN and COBOL but it could not have existed without the Algol framework. PL/I has, of course, been an expensive failure. It contains too much of the

FORTRANNER'S LAMENT*

S. I. FELDMAN

Bell Laboratories,
Murray Hill, New Jersey 07974

The Fortran Standard is now ten years old, and the X3J3 Committee has recently published a proposal for a new one. Much has been learned about programming during this period. Many Fortran extensions have been implemented in various compilers. We must agree that a new standard is timely. The Committee undertook a Herculean task, for which they deserve great credit. Changing Fortran must be like fighting the Hydra—repairing one problem must introduce two new ones in its place. (We wish they had adopted the Augean Stables approach instead.)

The Draft includes some new, good, and long-needed features. The description is far easier to understand than the old one. Unfortunately, many of the confusions in the language persist, though frequently in an attenuated form. Some new features are not added as neatly as one might have wished. The following are one reader's opinions of the proposed language definition.

Definitions

In the following, "the Committee" refers to American National Standards Committee X3J3, "the Draft" refers to the *draft proposed ANS FORTRAN* published as the March 1976 issue of *SIGPLAN Notices*. "The Standard" refers to *USA Standard FORTRAN* as approved March 7, 1966, and explained in "Clarification I" (*Comm. ACM* **12,** 289 [1969]) and "Clarification II" (*Comm. ACM* **14,** 628 [1971]),

Introduction

In the past, the "Fortran standard" has codified existing practice by specifying a set of rules that were satisfied by most of the major available compilers and programs. The standards made no pretense of leading the design of the language, they only cleaned up and made explicit the accepted rules. The Draft, however, defines a new language that is not currently available: no major compiler provides anything like the full facilities of this language. Despite their both being called "Fortran", the Standard and Draft languages are quite different. Not all legal Standard programs are also legal Draft programs. The additions to the language (primarily the character data type and file-oriented input/output) are sufficiently sweeping that it will require a major effort to provide good compilers. It is our opinion that this job should not be undertaken until the language is improved.

It appears to an outsider that the Committee could have taken two reasonable approaches to writing a new Standard for the Fortran language:

They could have updated the 1966 Standard somewhat. Some constructs might have been generalized, a few small extensions might have been recognized, the exposition of the Standard might have been improved, but the language and the compilers would have remained basically as we have known them.

or, They could have devised a seriously augmented language, basically upward compatible with the old Fortran. The new language might have been extended considerably and compatibly in a number of directions to meet the needs of programmers, as shown both in practice and in theory. The new characteristics might have been few, understandable, yet far-reaching in their impact.

Instead, the Committee added a few major features and a large number of small and unrelated changes to the Standard language. The Draft describes an unpleasant language in which it is hard to write good programs.

This discussion is, alas, not purely academic. Fortran has become the *de facto* standard scientific computer language. Many non-scientific programs are written in Fortran simply because it is so widely available. Fortran is the closest approximation we have to a universal intermediate language, and a number of pre-processors and compilers (including one being written by this author) generate Fortran rather than an artificial intermediate language or a specific assembly language. Accordingly, it is vital that the new standard Fortran retain the desirable characteristic of universal availability while improving the areas in which the language is deficient.

We will discuss a number of aspects of the Draft.

(1)   Exposition.
Not bad for a standard, especially given the design of the language. The Draft could be much shorter and more lucid if the language were simpler.

(2)   Compatibility with previous Fortran Standards.
Good marks. Only a few major incompatibilities have been introduced, usually with good reason and relative ease of conversion.

(3)   Consistency and generality of the language.
Poor. All previous versions of Fortran have suffered from a welter of rules and restrictions intended to make particular implementations easy or efficient. The Draft continues this grand tradition. Yet it is now well known that a simple and complete language is far easier to teach, use, and generate than one with a large number of special cases. A programmer is more likely to write a good, algorithmically efficient program in a clean language than in a messy one. Uniformity of structure permits the compiler writer to include good general optimizations rather than a melange of tricks.

Consistency ought to have been the overriding design principle for a new Fortran; the Committee does not seem to have considered this criterion at all.

After discussing these general topics, we will comment on a few particular areas in the language:

(4)   Program Form.
Statement ordering restrictions are slightly less onerous than before, but the rules for the form of a program have been tightened unnecessarily.

(5)   Data Types.
The Draft adds the long-needed CHARACTER data type to the language — badly. This extension, as proposed, greatly complicates the description and implementation of the language. At the same time, the Draft does not include a double precision complex data type, which would have been trivial both linguistically and practically.

(6)   Control Flow.
It is now generally recognized that good control structures make programming both easier and more reliable. That the fundamental structures (grouping, selection, and repetition) can be added to Fortran without causing compatibility problems has been proved by a number of extensions to Fortran which have been defined to provide these facilities. Almost any plausible way of writing these constructs would be better than leaving them out entirely, as does the Draft. It is definitely time to introduce decent control structures into the language; their lack is probably the largest single failure of the Draft.

(7)   Procedures.
Intrinsic and generic procedures have been added to the language in a generally successful way. We feel that a few more functions should be added, and that the definitions of a few others should be modified.

(8)   Input/Output.
Input and output are now based on files, and there are new formats, new modes of file access, and new commands. Welcome though these additions be, there are too many assumptions about files and their structure, and the specific choices for syntax and semantics are much poorer than they could be.

(9)   Portability.
The Draft discusses portability, but fails to take steps that would have made it a more easily achieved goal. In particular, a number of modes of argument transmission are permitted; this diversity is covered by a general rule about association of arguments. It is very difficult to verify the portable behavior of a given program mechanically.

Because of this assessment, we do not feel it would be worthwhile to accept the Draft as a new standard for the Fortran language. The recommendations are too sweeping to be acted on easily, too timid to be worth a major effort.

Exposition

The Draft is fairly readable for a proposed standard. Most of the complaints have more to do with the substance than the style of presentation. The draft is a long document; it would be much shorter and easier to read if the language were more regular. The reader frequently gets annoyed when faced with a typical rule that states that some construct may be any of a long list of things; the authors really meant to say that any meaningful form in the language could have been used, with certain glaring exceptions.

Providing the full and subset versions in parallel columns is a good idea, but the column breaks and line numbers should have been lined up exactly.

An additional appendix outlining the assumptions made about hardware and software architecture would have been useful and enlightening. Many of the restrictions can be 'understood' by assuming that a particular implementation is intended. The act of making these assumptions explicit might have persuaded the Committee to retract some of the restrictions.

Compatibility

The Committee is to be congratulated on achieving such a high degree of compatibility with the Standard and previous practice. Though I/O facilities were considerably revamped, character data were added to the language, and numerous smaller changes were made, it is probably true that most old Fortran programs conform to the Draft. The major incompatible change is the removal of the Hollerith data type. Since this was always an awkward construct, we cannot mourn its loss, and the Draft does have an appendix guiding implementors to an extension that interprets old programs correctly. It might have been worthwhile to retain Hollerith initializations to increase the fraction of existing programs that need no changes. (We presume that H editing was retained in formats for this reason).

DO loops work differently than they usually did. (Most compilers went through the range at least once, even though the Standard carefully fails to define the meaning of the statement "DO 10 I=2,1".) We are fairly happy with the new definition of the actions of DO loops.

BLOCK DATA subprograms may now be named, but there may be no more than one unnamed BLOCK DATA in an executable program. Any program that conforms with the Standard and has more than one BLOCK DATA subprogram cannot conform with the Draft.

An example of a niggling change: columns $1-5$ of a continuation card must now be blank, a restriction specifically not in the Standard (see Clarification I).

Consistency and Generality

The Draft makes a laudable attempt in places to remove some of the old restrictions of the language. For example, subscripts need not be in the form $c*v \pm c'$. There are still many remnants of the bad old days, however, and a large number of picky new rules have been added to accommodate new data types and statements. Most of these restrictions seem to have some particular implementation in mind; others appear purely random. One of the steepest barriers to learning the Fortran language has always been the need to assimilate a welter of seemingly unrelated rules. In this section we will discuss a few of these; others appear later under other headings. It is our belief that a fundamental design rule ought to have been that the use of every construct be permitted anywhere it makes sense. If a compiler can recognize a particular form in one context, it can probably recognize it elsewhere as well. Regularity in a language is worth considerable implementation effort.

New notations and commands have been added to extract a substring of a character string (" : "), to concatenate two strings (" // "), and to inquire about input/output status. Adding builtin procedures would have been a better solution; we will discuss the individual cases later.

No relational operators are defined for LOGICAL operands. It seems perfectly sensible to define .EQ. and .NE. for them, though purists might prefer new names for logical equivalence and nonequivalence. (The Draft defines order relations for characters; certainly logicals are less trouble.)

A new construct has been defined for use in I/O lists, the "array block": the expression $A(7,1):A(3,3)$ represents the set of elements in the storage sequence starting at $A(7,1)$ and ending at $A(3,3)$. It is not clear why array blocks are really needed, and they do clutter up the language. If they are to be added, however, their use should be general. Since an array block really defines a sub-array, an array block could sensibly be permitted in DATA statements, and as an internal file, format, or procedure argument. These uses are all trivial to implement. (The notation would probably be more useful in DATA statements than in I/O statements.)

There are a number of small and unnecessary distinctions between functions and subroutines. It is now possible to invoke a function without arguments, so one may say RANDOM( ) instead of RANDOM(JUNK). This is an obvious and welcome improvement. But to invoke a subroutine without arguments, one must say CALL S and may not say CALL S( ). The parentheses are clearly necessary to signal the function invocation; they can do no harm in the CALL. Alternate returns are permitted in subroutines but not in functions. Describing the result of an expression from which an alternate return is possible may be tricky, but it is no harder than explaining the result of an input error during an input list. The language and the Draft would both be simpler if these rules were dropped.

Statement functions may be an abomination, but they are in the language, so they might as well be regular. It would probably be neater to define them as macro substitutions followed by a type coercion. In the Draft, there are arithmetic and logical statement functions, but no character statement functions. Statement functions may not redefine their arguments. Dummy arguments to statement functions may not be procedures or arrays.

DO variables may not be array elements. It would be reasonable to permit an array element, but to freeze the subscript upon entrance to the loop. (The values of the iteration parameters are frozen upon entrance.)

A notation for substrings of variables and array elements has been introduced: $V(3:6)$ is the string containing the third through sixth characters of V. We would have preferred the introduction of a construct akin to the PL/I pseudo-variable SUBSTR, since that is a more general and natural type of notation. In any case, it is not legal to extract a substring of an expression, or even of a constant, though there is no syntactic ambiguity about expressions like $F(X)(I:J)$ or ´ABC´(K:K).

The rules about which forms are permitted in which contexts are thoroughly confusing. There are a number of places in the language where an integer value is required for one purpose or another, but the permitted forms are multifarious. Subscripts, substring expressions, computed GOTO variables, alternate return numbers, external unit specifiers, RECL, MAXREC, and REC input/output specifiers, may be arbitrary integer, real, or double precision expressions. Dimension bound expressions must be integer expressions without references to functions or array elements. Character lengths have the same form as dimension bounds, except that the exponentiation operator is also forbidden.

How is any ordinary user supposed to keep track of this mess? It would be simple to permit arbitrary arithmetic expressions wherever one of these values is needed. The use of a floating point value in most of these control contexts is both silly and dangerous. If double precision, why not complex? We do not see why $a_{\sqrt{2}}$ should be allowed but $a_{\sqrt{-2}}$ should be forbidden. (Note that the INT function is applied when a real or double precision expression is permitted; INT is also defined for a complex argument.)

We would prefer allowing all of the quantities listed above to be general integer expressions. A programmer who really wants to use a floating point value can invoke INT explicitly. It is not hard to invoke a procedure during the prologue, and recursion is forbidden in Fortran anyway. It may be necessary to add rules about order of evaluation to prevent impossible declarations like

INTEGER   A(B(2,2),B(2,3)), B(A(2,2),A(2,3))

but these are no more complicated than the existing rules about what is permitted. (By the way, can anyone explain why powers are easy to compute for dimension bounds but hard for lengths?)

The use of concatenation is hedged in by many restrictions. To avoid dynamic storage allocation, concatenations involving strings of nonconstant length are permitted only in character assignment statements. Concatenation causes so many problems in describing the language,

and has such limited value when applied to fixed-length strings, that it might be provided by a procedure such as

```
        SUBROUTINE CONCAT(A,B,C)
C       A = B // C
        CHARACTER(*) A, B, C
        A( :LEN(B) ) = B
        A( LEN(B)+1 : ) = C
        END
```

If this procedure were built in, it could take a variable number of arguments, as the MAX and MIN functions do.

The PARAMETER statement can be a great convenience, but it really is not as general as it ought to be. A general string substitution mechanism would be much more useful, and would be simple to implement. As rules now stand, parameters may not even be constant expressions. Symbolic constants may not be used as statement numbers nor may they appear in subsequent PARAMETER statements. A PARAMETER statement is really a statement function without arguments.

Program Form

There is a new requirement that continuation lines be blank in columns 1−5. Clarification I of the Standard specifically permits nonblank characters in those columns. What is the purpose of the rule?

Most computers have a larger character set than the Draft assumes. It would certainly aid the readability of programs if symbols like $<$, $> =$, and & were permitted. The old forms could be retained for compatibility.

Restricting identifiers to be six characters or less seems senseless — surely the art of compiler writing has advanced sufficiently to lift the rule.

Many ordering restrictions have been relaxed, but DATA statements must still follow all specification statements. It would be a great convenience if they only had to follow their declaration, or could come anywhere at all. Relaxing these restrictions would permit all declarations relevant to a variable to appear together in the text and would make understanding a program easier. (It would make automatic generation of Fortran code much easier.)

Data Types

The Draft adds the character data type and deletes the old Hollerith. Character strings are of fixed length; character dummies carry their lengths with them. Character data have been included in such a way that there is almost no mingling with noncharacter data. A character datum and a noncharacter datum may not share storage (no EQUIVALENCE), nor may they live in the same common block. The only context in which they may be mingled is in an unformatted record.

We assume these restrictions were included to avoid discussing alignment and byte size. However, there are already problems involving alignment of double precision data (see below). Note that the Draft "does not specify a relationship between a noncharacter storage unit and a character storage unit" (page 2-6) but on page 12-1 a formula is introduced using a constant (a) equal, in effect, to the number of characters per integer word. These decisions have significant effects on the proposed language.

The rule against mixing the types in a common block rules out one of the best uses of common blocks: structuring one's data by combining related quantities in one accessible place. The restrictions on common blocks would force the symbol table of a compiler to be split into two pieces, one containing the names, the other containing the flags, pointers, etc.

There is no way to convert a character to an integer value, even though the set of characters is totally ordered and the operation is perfectly meaningful. Without this facility, there is no clean way to compute a hashing function or to index into a character table in Fortran. There should be a pair of intrinsic functions between integer and character types.

We are not sure that ignoring trailing blanks during string comparison is a good idea. According to the Draft,

```
    ′ABC′ .EQ. ′ABC
```

is true. There are no zero-length character strings although they are an obvious generalization and have been found useful in other languages.

There are a number of peculiar rules involving character functions. There are no character function actual arguments or character statement functions. If a function has multiple entries, either they must all be character strings of the same length, or they may be any mixture of noncharacter data — a thoroughly confusing rule. (The Draft seems to contemplate an implementation in which noncharacter return values are stored in the function, but character return values are stored in the caller.)

The left and right sides of a character assignment may not share storage elements, so the statement

    S = T // S

is illegal. Since concatenation is a truly associative operation, there is no need to define the order of evaluation. If concatenation were provided through explicit procedure call as suggested above, the rules about associativity and storage association would follow directly from the rules about dummy association.

Single precision arithmetic on many computers is simply too imprecise to do serious calculations. We feel quite strongly that the Draft should have included a double precision complex data type. Adding the type would be compatible, and would cause no implementation difficulties; any compiler smart enough to handle double precision real and single precision complex numbers can handle double precision complex easily. The only significant effort would be in providing the extra mathematical functions.

In the Draft, complex and double precision data may not be mixed in an expression. If a double precision complex data type were added, this rule could be removed, since those expressions would have a natural meaning. The Draft does not permit raising numbers to complex powers, or raising complex numbers to noninteger powers. Except for 0^0, these quantities have definite principal values. The failure to add this type is a real blow.

The Draft has no rules about alignment of double precision quantities. The following fragment appears to conform to the Draft:

    DOUBLE PRECISION X, Y
    REAL A(3)
    EQUIVALENCE (A(1),X), (A(2),Y)

Unfortunately, it cannot be implemented directly on any computer that has a doubleword alignment rule (IBM System/360, Honeywell 6000 Series, etc.)

Control Flow

It is hardly necessary to recapitulate the "Structured Programming Controversy" here, but it seems fair to note that many programmers feel that their work is made easier and more reliable when certain types of constructs are available. The ideas are hardly new; many of the basic facilities were available in Algol in 1960. We view the lack of a standard set of control facilities as the most important lacuna in the Draft.

Three types of facilities have been found sufficient:

    Statement grouping
    Selection (IF-THEN-ELSE; CASE)
    Repetition (WHILE, FOR, UNTIL, DO, . . .)

Each of these facilities can be added to Fortran in a number of ways that do not affect Standard-conforming programs. Indeed, these constructs are so simple that many preprocessors generate Fortran from augmented languages. A Standards Committee ought to choose one of the better forms and foster its use. We feel that the exact spelling of these constructs is less important than having a single accepted form. This *is* the time to make a decision.

Of course, we do have definite opinions on the structures that ought to be added. The absolute essentials are IF-THEN-ELSE, WHILE, and some sensible statement bracketing convention. We are strongly in favor of a uniform convention for grouping statements anywhere in a program; selection and repetition constructs are then fairly obvious and there is no need for extra keywords like **fi** and **od**, or ENDIF and ENDWHILE. Personally, we like the Ratfor notation. (See B. W. Kernighan, "RATFOR — A Preprocessor for a Rational FORTRAN", *Software Practice and Experience* **3**, 395 [October 1975]).

We would also like to comment on some of the control flow forms already in the language. The committee is to be congratulated on finally defining the actions of the DO statement and the DO variable. A fair number of existing programs assume that every DO range is performed at least once per DO statement, but we feel the gain in having a cleaner language outweighs this danger.

On the other hand, allowing the DO variable to be real or double precision seems extremely dangerous, so dangerous it ought to be forbidden. This 'generalization' grants little convenience or power since mixed mode arithmetic is now permitted. However, the unwary programmer is certain to be led down the garden path; the number of times the loop

DO 10 X = 0.0, 1.0, 0.1

is executed depends critically on the roundoff error of floating point arithmetic. It is safer and not much more costly to force the programmer to use a transformed variable.

The Draft still includes extended DO ranges; we recommend they be expunged. This construction has been botched in a number of compilers, violates reasonable assumptions about loops, and a programmer can usually accomplish the same result by adding procedure references.

Causing a computed GOTO to 'fall through' if the variable is out of range seems dangerous. A programmer can achieve the same result by using the computed GOTO as the consequent of a logical IF. It would probably be better to leave the result undefined, so that a compiler could generate an error message. These comments also apply to alternate return numbers. (In the Draft, if the alternate return number is out of range, an ordinary RETURN is taken).

The whole area of statement label variables is very murky. Though their use violates most of the structuring tenets, it might be better to generalize them than to have to explain all of the weird rules evolved for them. Failing that, the reader deserves an appendix explaining these peculiar rules: a statement label may not be stored in an array element, may not be moved using a normal assignment statement, and its value evaporates upon return from a procedure despite the presence of a SAVE statement. The Standard does not force the compiler to store an absolute machine address in an associated variable; it would cost little more to store an index into a label array or to store a floatable machine address. Statement label variables could be used sensibly as alternate return specifiers and in END= and ERR= clauses.

Procedures

A number of issues relating to procedures have already been discussed above under "Consistency and Generality". Other issues relating to this topic are:

The ranges of the mathematical functions have finally been specified. The imaginary part of CLOG should have a semi-open range; the Draft defines the range to be the closed interval $[-\pi, \pi]$.

"Arguments for which the result is not mathematically defined . . . cause the result of the function to become undefined." Does this mean that invoking LOG(0.0) must result in a number rather than an error message?

Even though these functions are unlikely to be heavily used, we would prefer that complex versions be defined for all the trigonometric and hyperbolic functions, so that the programmer need not consult Table 5 of the Draft every time he wants to write a program.

The "floor" and "ceil" functions ($\lfloor \cdot \rfloor$ and $\lceil \cdot \rceil$) ought to be intrinsics; they are at least as important as the nearest integer function NINT (normally called "round").

Having intrinsic and generic functions is certainly a convenience, but the typing rules are baroque. The three fragments

```
COMPLEX Z           COMPLEX Z           COMPLEX Z
INTEGER COS         REAL COS
Z = COS(Z)          Z = COS(Z)          Z = COS(Z)
```

do quite different things: The first invokes an external integer function, the second invokes the intrinsic single precision cosine function with an argument of the wrong type, and the third invokes the intrinsic complex cosine function.

BLOCK DATA subprograms may now have names, though the purpose of these names is not specified. More mysterious, these names may be mentioned in EXTERNAL statements. Unfortunately, a new rule has been added: only one unnamed block data subprogram may appear in an executable program. Many executable Standard-conforming programs will violate this rule. Mechanical generation of programs is now made more difficult, since globally unique names will have to be created for BLOCK DATA subprograms; this task is impossible if pieces of programs are produced separately. We guess that these rules are to make it easier to load block data subprograms from libraries; if true, the loaders ought to be fixed, not the language.

Input/Output

The Draft describes a much richer set of I/O facilities than does the Standard. Internal and direct access files are both excellent additions to the language. However, the Draft makes too many assumptions about operating system conventions. As described, the ACCESS= and FORM= clauses of the INQUIRE statement require that the file system keep track of whether a file contains formatted or unformatted records, and whether Fortran may access it as a direct, sequential, or stream file. In some systems these questions do not make sense: a file can be accessed in any way that is convenient. These options are attributes of the particular connection, not of the associated file.

The new rule that formatted and unformatted records may not be mixed on the same file is incompatible with the Standard (see Clarification II) and with standard practice on most systems.

Internal files seem a very good idea, but the Draft-writers have too limited an idea of their usefulness. As proposed, internal files must be sequential and formatted. In other words, they are only useful for implementing the encode and decode operations common in many compilers. A more significant prospective use of an internal file is for testing programs; it is easier to initialize and examine values in memory than on a physical device. Permitting general internal files would be trivial. What could be easier to implement than unformatted I/O into an integer array? What is easier to access randomly than an array in memory? What has fewer record boundaries than a character string? It would be especially nice if an internal file could be OPENed (perhaps using a new STATUS= value) and be INQUIREd about.

The need for stream I/O is not clear, though the feature may be convenient. Instead, we would have preferred a true stream-oriented facility that would permit us to read and write one or more characters (possibly including an end-of-file signal) at a time, possibly under format control. It is not always desirable to build or swallow a whole line at a time.

Several new formats have been added. This may cause some difficulty, since the format cracker is one of the most delicate parts of a Fortran system. The colon format (halt processing if the I/O list is exhausted) is a fine idea. The BN, BZ, S, SS, SP, and Iw.m formats seem less important, but *someone* may want them.

The INQUIRE statement is startlingly ugly — values are returned into the quantities on the right side of an equal sign. A set of intrinsic functions, one for each parameter, would have provided the same functions in a far cleaner and more useful way. A statement like

        IF(FILENAME(10) .EQ. 'GORP') . . .

reads better than does

        INQUIRE(10, NAME=F)
        IF(F .EQ. 'GORP') . . .

The STATUS= specifiers take on different sets of values in the OPEN and CLOSE statement; different keywords should probably be used for these different uses. The FORM= specifier can only take on two values ('FORMATTED' and 'UNFORMATTED') in the OPEN and INQUIRE statements, so it should probably have logical rather than character string value. One ought to be able to INQUIRE about any characteristic of a connection, yet there is no way to find out the STATUS or BLANK value of a connection.

The use of statement labels to detect input/output errors (the END= and ERR= clauses), though now common in practice, tempts one to write confused code. It would have been better to define an error function whose value could have been interrogated; the Draft does not define a way to find out what went wrong.

It is not at all clear that printing a field of asterisks is the right response to a value out of range. Instead, we propose printing out the number with a sufficient number of columns instead. The visual effect of this default in the middle of a table is as striking as the stars would be, and gives a useful answer to boot.

Portability

Because of the near universal availability of Fortran compilers, program portability is a crucial issue. There is one area in which the Draft falls down badly: in order to accommodate a number of schemes for argument transmission, if two dummies are associated, or if a dummy and a common entry are associated, that dummy may not be defined by a procedure. Problems of unsafe references can result in insidious bugs, but there is no mechanical way to find the exact set of nonportable references. It would have been better to define the argument transmission process exactly.

Compilers are allowed to reorder expressions, subject to the rules of mathematics, precedence, and parentheses. The indeterminacy of the order of evaluation of expressions with side effects is carefully described; life would be easier, and programs little slower, if left-to-right evaluation were required.

Conclusion

The objectives of the new standard should have been stated explicitly in the introduction to the proposed draft. We feel that they ought to have been:

(1) Cleanness of design (regularity and completeness)

(2) Compatibility with existing practice

(3) Inclusion of needed data types (character and double precision complex)

(4) Provision of good control structures

The current Draft does not satisfy these requirements. We hope the Committee will agree on an overall approach (perhaps one of those suggested in the introduction) and propose a standard that fits it.

THE C PROGRAMMING LANGUAGE*

D. M. RITCHIE, S. C. JOHNSON, M. E. LESK AND B. W. KERNIGHAN

C is a general-purpose programming language that has proven useful for a wide variety of applications. It is the primary language of the UNIX* system, and is also available in several other environments. This paper provides an overview of the syntax and semantics of C and a discussion of its strengths and weaknesses.

C is a general-purpose programming language featuring economy of expression, modern control flow and data structure capabilities, and a rich set of operators and data types.

C is not a "very high-level" language nor a big one and is not specialized to any particular area of application. Its generality and an absence of restrictions make it more convenient and effective for many tasks than supposedly more powerful languages. C has been used for a wide variety of programs, including the UNIX operating system, the C compiler itself, and essentially all UNIX applications software. The language is sufficiently expressive and efficient to have completely displaced assembly language programming on UNIX.

C was originally written for the PDP-11 under UNIX, but the language is not tied to any particular hardware or operating system. C compilers run on a wide variety of machines, including the Honeywell 6000, the IBM System/370, and the Interdata 8/32.

I. THE LINGUISTIC HISTORY OF C

The C language in use today[1] is the product of several years of evolution. Many of its most important ideas stem from the considerably older, but still quite vital, language BCPL[2] developed by Martin Richards. The influence of BCPL on C proceeded indirectly through the language B,[3] which was written by Ken Thompson in 1970 for the first UNIX system on the PDP-11.

Although neither B nor C could really be considered dialects of BCPL, both share several characteristic features with it:

(*i*) All are able to express the fundamental flow-control constructions required for well-structured programs: statement grouping, decision-making (if), looping (while) with the termination test either at the top or the bottom of the loop, and branching out to a sequence of possible cases (switch). It is interesting that BCPL provided these constructions in 1967, well before the current vogue for "structured programming."

(*ii*) All three languages include the concept of "pointer" and provide the ability to do address arithmetic.

(*iii*) In all three languages, the arguments to functions are passed by copying the value of the argument, and it is impossible for

---

* UNIX is a trademark of Bell Laboratories.

the function to change the actual argument. When it is desired to achieve "call by reference," a pointer may be passed explicitly, and the function may change the object to which the pointer points. Any function is allowed to be recursive, and its local variables are typically "automatic" or specific to each invocation.

(*iv*) All three languages are rather low-level, in that they deal with the same sorts of objects that most computers do. BCPL and B restrict their attention almost completely to machine words, while C widens its horizons somewhat to characters and (possibly multi-word) integers and floating-point numbers. None deals directly with composite objects such as character strings, sets, lists, or arrays considered as a whole. The languages themselves do not define any storage allocation facility beside static definition and the stack discipline provided by the local variables of functions; likewise, I/O is not part of any of these languages. All these higher mechanisms must be provided by explicitly called routines from libraries.

B and BCPL differ mainly in their syntax, and many differences stemmed from the very small size of the first B compiler (fewer than 4K 18-bit words on the PDP-7). Several constructions in BCPL encourage a compiler to maintain a representation of the entire program in memory. In BCPL, for example,

```
valof $(
```

```
    resultis expression
```

```
$)
```

is syntactically an expression. It provides a way of packaging a block of many statements into a sort of unnamed internal procedure yielding a single result (delivered by the **resultis** statement). The **valof** construction can occur in the middle of any expression, and can be arbitrarily large. The B language avoided the difficulties caused by this and some other constructions by rigorously simplifying (and in some cases adjusting to personal taste) the syntax of BCPL.

In spite of many syntactic changes, B remained very close to BCPL semantically. The most characteristic feature of both languages is their nearly identical treatment of addresses (pointers). They support a model of the storage of the machine consisting of a sequence of equal-sized cells, into which values can be placed; in typical implementations, these cells will be machine words. Each identifier in a program corresponds to a cell, and a cell may contain a variety of values. Most often the value is an integer, or perhaps a representation of a character. All the cells, however, are numbered; the address of a cell is just the integer giving its ordinal position. BCPL has a unary operator **lv** (in some versions, and also in B and C, shortened to **&**) that, when applied to a name, yields the address of the cell corresponding to the name. The inverse operator **rv** (later *****) yields the value in the cell pointed to its argument. Thus the statement

```
        px  =  &x;
```

of B assigns to **px** the number that can be interpreted as the address of **x**; the statements

$$y = *px + 2;$$
$$*px = 5;$$

first use the value in the cell pointed to by px (which is the same cell as x) and then assign 5 to this cell.

Arrays in BCPL and B are intimately tied up with pointers. An array declaration, which might in BCPL be written

$$\text{let Array} = \text{vec } 10$$

and in B

$$\text{auto Array}[10];$$

creates a single cell named Array and initializes it with the address of the first of a sequence of 10 unnamed cells containing the array itself. Since the quantity stored in Array is just the address of the cell of the first element of the array, the expression

$$\text{Array} + i$$

is the address of the ith element, counting from zero. Likewise, applying the indirection operator,

$$* (\text{Array} + i)$$

refers to the value of the ith member of the array. This operation is so frequent that special syntax was invented to express it:

$$\text{Array}[i]$$

Thus, despite its asymmetric appearance, subscripting is a commutative operation; the above example could equally well be written

$$i[\text{Array}]$$

In BCPL and B there is only one type of object, the machine word, so when the same language operator is applied to two operands, the calculation actually carried out must always be the same. Thus, for example, if one wishes to provide the ability to do floating-point arithmetic, the "+" operator notation cannot be used, since it implies an integer addition. Instead (in a version of BCPL for the GE 635), a "." was placed in front of each operator that had floating-point operands. As may be appreciated, this was a frequent source of errors.

The machine model implied by the definitions of BCPL and B is simple and self-consistent. It is, however, inadequate for many purposes, and on many machines it causes inefficiencies when implemented. The problems became evident to us after B began to be used heavily on the first PDP-11 version of UNIX. The first followed from the fact that the PDP-11, like a number of machines (including, for example, the IBM System/370), is byte addressed; a machine address refers to any of several bytes (characters) in a word, not the word alone. Most obviously, the word orientation of B cut us off from any convenient ability to access individual bytes. Equally important was the fact that before any address could be used, it had to be shifted left by one place. The reason for this is simple: there are two bytes per PDP-11 word. On the one hand, the language guaranteed that if 1 was added to an address quantity, it would point to the next word; on the other, the machine architecture required that word addresses be even and equal to the byte number of the

first byte in the word. Since, finally, there was no way to distinguish cells containing ordinary integers from those containing pointers, the only solution visible was to represent pointers as word numbers and then, at the point of use, convert to the byte representation by multiplication by 2.

Yet another problem was introduced by the desire to provide for floating-point arithmetic. The PDP-11 supports two floating-point formats, one of which requires two words, the other four. In neither case was it satisfactory to use the trick used on the GE 635 (operators like ".+") because there was no way to represent the requirement for a single data item occupying four or eight bytes. This problem did not arise on the 635 because integers and single-precision floating-point both require only one word.

Thus the problems evidenced by B led us to design a new language that (after a brief period under the name NB) was dubbed C. The major advance provided by C is its typing structure, which completely solved the difficulties mentioned above. Each declaration in a C program specifies (sometimes implicitly) a *type*, which determines how much storage the object requires and how it is to be interpreted. The original fundamental types provided were single character (byte), integer, single-precision floating-point, and double-precision floating-point. (Others discussed below were added later.) Thus in the program

```
double a, b;
    . . .
a  =  b  +  3;
```

the compiler is able to determine from the declarations of a and b the fact that they require four words of storage each, that the "+" means a double-precision floating add, and that "3" must be converted to floating.

Of course, the idea of typing variables is in no way original with C; in fact, it was the general rule among the most widely used and influential languages, including Algol, Fortran, and PL/I. Nevertheless, the introduction of types marked an important change in our own thinking. The typeless nature of BCPL and B had seemed to promise a great simplification in the implementation, understanding, and use of these languages. By the time that C was created (circa 1972), advocates of languages like Algol 68 and Pascal recommended a strongly enforced type structure on psychological grounds; but even disregarding their arguments, the typeless nature of BCPL and B seemed inappropriate, for purely technological reasons, to the available hardware.

II. THE TYPE STRUCTURE OF C

The introduction of types in C, although a major departure from the tradition of BCPL and B, was done in such a way that many of the characteristic usages of the earlier languages survived. To some extent, this continuity was an attempt to preserve as much as possible of the considerable corpus of existing software written in B, but even more important, especially in retrospect, was the desire to minimize the intellectual distance between the past and the future ways of expression.

2.1 Pointers, arrays and address arithmetic

One clear example of the similarity of C to the earlier languages is its treatment of pointers and arrays. In C an array of 10 integers might be declared

int Array[10];

which is identical to the corresponding declaration in B. (Arrays begin at zero; the elements of Array are Array[0], ..., Array[9].) As discussed above, the B implementation caused a cell named Array to be allocated and initialized with a pointer to 10 otherwise unnamed cells to hold the array. In C, the effect is a bit different; 10 integers are allocated, and the first is associated with the name Array. But C also includes a general rule that, whenever the name of an array appears in an expression, it is converted to a pointer to the first member of the array. Strictly speaking, we should say, for this example, it is converted to an *integer pointer* since all C pointers are associated with a particular type to which they point. In most usages, the actual effects of the slightly different meanings of Array are indistinguishable. Thus in the C expression

Array + i

the identifier Array is converted to a pointer to the first element of the array; i is scaled (if required) before it is added to the pointer. For a byte-addressed machine, the scale factor is the number of bytes in an integer; for a word-addressed machine the scale factor is unity. In any event, the result is a pointer to the ith member of the array. Likewise identical in effect to the interpretation of B,

* (Array + i)

is the ith member itself, and

Array[i]

is another notation for the same thing. In all these cases, of course, should **Array** be an array of, or pointer to, some objects other than integers, the scale factor is adjusted appropriately. The pointer arithmetic, as written, is independent of the type of object to which the pointer points and indeed of the internal representation of the pointer.

2.2 Derived types

As mentioned above, the basic types in C were originally int, which represents an integer in the basic size provided by the machine architecture; char, which represents a single byte; float, a single-precision floating-point number; and double, double-precision floating-point. Over the years, long, short, and unsigned integers have been added. In current C implementations, long is at least 32 bits; short is usually 16 bits; and int remains the "natural" size for the machine at hand. Unsigned integers exist mainly to squeeze an extra bit out of the machine, since the sign bit need not be represented.

In addition to these basic types, C provides a conceptually infinite hierarchy of derived types, which are formed by composition of the basic types with pointers, arrays, structures, unions, and functions. Examples of pointer and array declarations have already been exhibited; another is

```
double *vecp, vector[100];
```

which declares a pointer **vecp** to double-precision floating numbers, and an array **vector** of the same kind of objects. The size of an array, when specified, must always be a constant.

A *structure* is an aggregate of one or more objects, usually of various types, which can be treated as a unit. C structures are essentially the same as records in languages like Pascal, and semantically, though not syntactically, like PL/I and Cobol structures. Thus,

```
struct tag {
        int    i;
        float  f;
        char   c[3];
};
```

defines a template, called **tag**, for a structure containing three *members*: an integer **i**, a floating point number **f**, and a three-character array **c**. The declaration

```
struct tag x, y[10], *p;
```

declares a structure **x** of this type, an array **y** of 10 such structures, and a pointer **p** to this kind of structure. The hierarchical nature of derived types is clearly evident here: **y** is an array of structures whose members include an array of characters. References to individual members of structures use the . operator:

```
x.i
x.f
y[i].c[0]
(*p).c[1]
```

Parentheses in the last line are necessary because the . binds more tightly than *. It turns out that pointers to structures are so common that special syntax is called for to express structure access through a pointer.

```
p->c[1]
p->i
```

This soon becomes more natural than the equivalent

```
(*p).c[1]
(*p).i
```

A union is capable of holding, at different times, objects of different types, with the compiler keeping track of size and alignment requirements. Unions provide a way to manipulate different kinds of data in a single part of storage, without embedding machine-dependent information (like the relative sizes of **int** and **float**) in a program. For example, the union **u**, declared

```
union {
        int    i;
        float  f;
} u;
```

can hold either an int (written u.i) or a float (written u.f). Regardless of the machine it is compiled on, it will be large enough to hold either one of these quantities. A union is syntactically identical to a structure; it may be considered as a structure in which all the members begin at the same offset. Unions in C are more analogous to PL/I's CELL than to the unions of Algol 68 or the variant records of Pascal, because it is the responsibility of the programmer to avoid referring to a union that does not currently contain an object of the implied type.

A *function* is a subprogram that returns an object of a given type:

$$\text{unsigned unsf();}$$

declares a function that returns unsigned. The type of a function ignores the number and types of its arguments, although in general the call and the definition must agree.

2.3 Type composition

The syntax of declarations borrows from that of expressions. The key idea is that a declaration, say

$$\text{int   ... ;}$$

contains a part "..." that, if it appeared in an expression, would be of type int. The constructions seen so far, for example,

```
int    *iptr;
int    ifunc();
int    iarr[10];
```

exhibit this approach, but more complicated declarations are common. For example,

```
int    *funcptr();
int    (*ptrfunc)();
```

declare respectively a function that returns a pointer to an integer, and a pointer to a function that returns an integer. The extra parentheses in the second are needed to make the * apply directly to ptrfunc, since the implicit function-call operator () binds more tightly than *. Functions are not variables, so arrays or structures of functions are not permitted. However, a pointer to a function, like ptrfunc, may be stored, copied, passed as an argument, returned by a function, and so on, just as any other pointer.

Arrays of pointers are frequently used instead of multi-dimensional arrays. The usage of a and b when declared

```
int a[10][10];
int *b[10];
```

may be similar, in that a[5][5] and b[5][5] are both legal references to a single int, but a is a true array: all 100 storage cells have been allocated, and the conventional rectangular subscript calculation is done. For b, however, the declaration has only allocated 10 pointers; each must be set to point to an array of integers. Assuming each does point to a 10-element array, then there will be 100 storage cells set aside, plus the 10 cells for the pointers. Thus the array of pointers uses slightly more space and may require an extra initialization step, but has two advantages: it trades an indirection

for a subscript multiplication, and it permits the rows of the array to be of different lengths. (That is, each element of **b** need not point to a 10-element vector; some may point to 2 elements, some to 20). Particularly with strings whose length is not known in advance, an array of pointers is often used instead of a multidimensional array. Every C main program gets access to its invoking command line in this form, for example.

The idea of specifying types by appropriating some of the syntax of expressions seems to be original with C, and for the simpler cases, it works well. Occasionally some rather ornate types are needed, and the declaration may be a bit hard to interpret. For example, a pointer to an array of pointers to functions, each returning an int, would be written

```
int (*(*funnyarray)[])();
```

which is certainly opaque, although understandable enough if read from the inside out. In an expression, funnyarray might appear as

```
i = (*(*funnyarray)[j])(k);
```

The corresponding Algol 68 declaration is

ref [] ref proc int *funnyarray*

which reads from left to right in correspondence with the informal description of the type if **ref** is taken to be the equivalent of C's "pointer to." The Algol may be clearer, but both are hard to grasp.

III. STATEMENTS AND CONTROL FLOW

Control flow in C differs from other languages primarily in details of syntax. As in PL/I, semicolons are used to terminate statements, not to separate them. Most statements are just expressions followed by a semicolon; since assignments are expressions, there is no need for a special assignment statement.

Statements are grouped with braces { and }, rather than with words like **begin-end** or **do-od**, because the more concise form seems much easier to read and is certainly easier to type. A sequence of statements enclosed in { } is syntactically a single statement.

The **if-else** statement has the form

if (*expression*)
    statement
else
    statement

The *expression* is evaluated; if it is "true" (that is, if *expression* has a non-zero value), the first statement is done. If it is "false" (*expression* is zero) and if there is an **else** part, the second *statement* is executed instead. The **else** part is optional; if it is omitted in a sequence of nested if's, the resulting ambiguity is resolved in the usual way by associating the **else** with the nearest previous **else**-less if.

The **switch** statement provides a multi-way branch depending on the value of an integer expression:

```
switch (expression) {
    case const:
            code
    case const:
            code

    ...

    default:
            code
}
```

The *expression* is evaluated and compared against the various **cases**, which are labeled with distinct integer constant values. If any case matches, execution begins at that point. If no case matches but there is a default statement, execution begins there; otherwise, no part of the **switch** is executed.

The **cases** are just labels, and so control may flow through one case to the next. Although this permits multiple labels on cases, it also means that in general most cases must be terminated with an explicit exit from the **switch** (the break statement below).

The **switch** construction is part of C's legacy from BCPL; it is so useful and so easy to provide that the lack of a corresponding facility of acceptable generality in languages ranging from Fortran through Algol 68, and even to Pascal (which does not provide for a **default**), must be considered a real failure of imagination in language designers.

C provides three kinds of loops. The **while** is simply

```
while (expression)
    statement
```

The *expression* is evaluated; if it is true (non-zero), the *statement* is executed, and then the process repeats. When *expression* becomes false (zero), execution terminates.

The do statement is a test-at-the-bottom loop:

```
do
    statement
while (expression);
```

statement is performed once, then *expression* is evaluated. If it is true, the loop is repeated; otherwise it is terminated.

The for loop is reminiscent of similarly named loops in other languages, but rather more general. The for statement

```
for (expr1; expr2; expr3)
    statement
```

is equivalent to

```
expr1;
while (expr2) {
    statement
    expr3;
}
```

Grammatically, the three components of a for loop are expressions. Any of the three parts can be omitted, although the semicolons must remain. If *expr1* or *expr3* is left out, it is simply dropped from

the expansion. If the test, *expr2*, is not present, it is taken as permanently true, so

```
for (;;) {
    ...
}
```

is an "infinite" loop, to be broken by other means, for example by **break**, below.

The **for** statement keeps the loop control components together and visible at the top of the loop, as in the idiomatic

```
for (i = 0; i < N; i = i+1)
```

which processes the first N elements of an array, the analogue of the Fortran or PL/I DO loop. The **for** is more general, however. The test is re-evaluated on each pass through the loop, and there is no restriction on changing the variables involved in any of the expressions in the **for** statement. The controlling variable i retains its value regardless of how the loop terminates. And since the components of a **for** are arbitrary expressions, **for** loops are not restricted to arithmetic progressions. For example, the classic walk along a linked list is

```
for (p = top; p != NULL; p = p->next)
    ...
```

There are two statements for controlling loops. The **break** statement, as mentioned, causes an immediate exit from the immediately enclosing **while, for, do** or **switch**. The **continue** statement causes the next iteration of the immediately enclosing loop to begin. **break** and **continue** are asymmetric, since **continue** does not apply to **switch**.

Finally, C provides the oft-maligned **goto** statement. Empirically, **goto**'s are not much used, at least on our system. The operating system itself, for example, contains 98 in some 8300 lines. The PDP-11 C compiler, in 9660 lines, has 147. Essentially all of these implement some form of branch to the top or bottom of a loop, or to error recovery code.

IV. OPERATORS AND EXPRESSIONS

C has been characterized as having a relatively rich set of operators. Some of these are quite conventional. For example, the basic binary arithmetic operators are $+$, $-$, $*$ and $/$. To these, C adds the modulus operator %; m%n is the remainder when m is divided by n.

Besides the basic logical or bitwise operators & (bitwise AND), and | (bitwise OR), there are also the binary operators ^ (bitwise exclusive OR), $>>$ (right shift), and $<<$ (left shift), and the unary operator ~ (ones complement). These operators apply to all integers; C provides no special bit-string type.

The relational operators are the usual $>$, $>=$, $<$, $<=$, $==$ (equality test), and $!=$ (inequality test). They have the value 1 if the stated relation is true, 0 if not.

The unary pointer operators * (for indirection) and & (for taking the address) were described in Section I. When y is such as to make the expressions &*y or &*y legal, either is just equal to y.

Note that & and * are used as both binary and unary operators (with different meanings).

The simplest assignment is written =, and is used conventionally: the value of the expression on the right is stored in the object whose address is on the left. In addition, most binary operators can be combined with assignment by writing

$$\text{a } op= \text{ b}$$

which has the effect of

$$\text{a } = \text{ a } op \text{ b}$$

except that a is only evaluated once. For example,

$$\text{x } += \text{ 3}$$

is the same as

$$\text{x } = \text{ x } + \text{ 3}$$

if x is just a variable, but

$$\text{p[i}+\text{j}+1] \ += \ 3$$

adds 3 to the element selected from the array p, calculating the subscript only once, and, more importantly, requiring it to be written out only once. Compound assignment operators also seem to correspond well to the way we think; "add 3 to x" is said, if not written, much more commonly than "assign x+3 to x."

Assignment expressions have a value, just like other expressions, and may be used in larger expressions. For example, the multiple assignment

$$\text{i } = \text{ j } = \text{ k } = \text{ 0;}$$

is a byproduct of this fact, not a special case. Another very common instance is the nesting of an assignment in the condition part of an if or a loop, as in

$$\text{while ((c } = \text{ getchar()) != EOF) ...}$$

which fetches a character with the function **getchar**, assigns it to c, then tests whether the result is an end of file marker. (Parentheses are needed because the precedence of the assignment = is lower than that of the relational !=.)

C provides two novel operators for incrementing and decrementing variables. The increment operator $++$ adds 1 to its operand; the decrement operator $--$ subtracts 1. Thus the statement

$$++\text{i;}$$

increments i. The unusual aspect is that $++$ and $--$ may be used either as prefix operators (before the variable, as in $++$i), or postfix (after the variable: i$++$). In both cases, the effect is to increment i. But the expression $++$i increments i *before* using its value, while i$++$ increments i *after* its value has been used. If i is 5, then

$$\text{x } = \text{ i}++;$$

sets x to 5, but

$$x = ++i;$$

sets x to 6. In both cases, i becomes 6.

For example,

$$stack[i++] = \ldots ;$$

pushes a value on a stack stored in an array **stack** indexed by i, while

$$\ldots = stack[--i];$$

retrieves the value and pops the stack. Of course, when the quantity incremented or decremented is a pointer, appropriate scaling is done, just as if the "1" were added explicitly:

$$*stackp++ = \ldots ;$$
$$\ldots = *--stackp;$$

are analogous to the previous example, this time using a stack pointer instead of an index.

Tests may be combined with the logical connectives **&&** (AND), **||** (OR), and **!** (truth value negation). The **&&** and **||** operators guarantee left-to-right evaluation, with termination as soon as the truth value is known. For example, in the test

$$if (i <= N \&\& array[i] > 0) \ldots$$

if i is greater than N, then array[i] (presumably at that point an out-of-bounds reference) will not be accessed. This predictable behavior is especially convenient, and much preferable to the explicitly random order of evaluation promised by most other languages. Most C programs rely heavily on the properties of **&&** and **||**.

Finally, the *conditional expression*, written with the ternary operator **? :**, provides an analogue of if-else in expressions. In the expression

$$e1 \; ? \; e2 \; : \; e3$$

the expression *e1* is evaluated first. If it is non-zero (true), then the expression *e2* is evaluated, and that is the value of the conditional expression. Otherwise, *e3* is evaluated, and that is the value. Only one of *e2* and *e3* is evaluated. Thus to set z to the maximum of a and b,

$$z = (a > b) \; ? \; a \; : \; b; \quad /* z = max(a, b) */$$

We have already discussed how integers are scaled appropriately in pointer arithmetic. C does a number of other automatic conversions between data types, more freely than Pascal, for example, but without the wild abandon of PL/I. In all contexts, **char** variables and constants are promoted to int. This is particularly handy in code like

$$n = c - '0';$$

which assigns to n the integer value of the character stored in c, by subtracting the value of the character '0'. Generally, in fact, the basic types fall into only two classes, integral and floating-point; **char** variables, and the various lengths of int's, are taken to be

representations of the same kind of thing. They occupy different amounts of storage but are essentially compatible. Boolean values as such do not exist; relational or truth-value expressions have value 1 if true, and 0 if false.

Variables of type int are converted to floating-point when combined with floats or doubles and in fact all floating arithmetic is carried out in double precision, so floats are widened to double in expressions.

Conversions that involve "narrowing" an expression (for example, when a longer value is assigned to a shorter) are also well behaved. Floating point values are converted to integer by truncation; integers convert to shorter integers or characters by dropping high-order bits.

When a conversion is desired, but is not implicit in the context, it is possible to force a conversion by an explicit operator called a *cast*. The expression

$$(\textit{type}) \; \textit{expression}$$

is a new expression whose type is that specified in *type*. For example, the sin routine expects an argument of type double; in the statement

$$x \; = \; sin((double) \; n);$$

the value of n is converted to double before being passed to sin.

V. THE STRUCTURE OF C PROGRAMS

Complete programs consist of one or more files containing function and data declarations. Thus, syntactically, a program is made up of a sequence of declarations; executable code appears only inside functions. Conventionally, the run-time system arranges to call a function named main to start execution.

The language distinguishes the notions of *declaration* and *definition*. A declaration merely announces the properties of a variable (like its type); a definition declares a variable and also allocates storage for it or, in the case of a function, supplies the code.

5.1 Functions

The notion of *function* in C includes the subroutines and functions of Fortran and the procedures of most other languages. A function call is written

$$\textit{name} \, (\textit{arglist})$$

where the parentheses are required even if the argument list is empty. All functions may be used recursively.

Arguments are passed by value, so the called function cannot in any way affect the actual argument with which it was called. This permits the called program to use its formal arguments as conveniently initialized local variables. Call by value also eliminates the class of errors, familiar to Fortran programmers, in which a constant is passed to a subroutine that tries to alter the corresponding argument. An array name as an actual argument, however, is converted to a pointer to the first array element (as it always is), so the effect is as if arrays were called by reference; given the pointer, the called function can work its will on the individual elements of the array.

When a function must return a value through its argument list, an explicit pointer may be passed, and the function references the ultimate target through this pointer. For example, the function swap(pa, pb) interchanges two integers pointed to by its arguments:

```
swap(px, py)          /* flip int's pointed to by px and py */
int *px, *py;
{
        int temp;

        temp = *px;
        *px = *py;
        *py = temp;
}
```

This also demonstrates the form of a function definition: the name is followed by an argument list; the arguments are declared, and the body of the function is a block, or compound statement, enclosed in braces. Declarations of local variables may follow the opening brace.

A function returns a value by

```
return expression;
```

The *expression* is automatically coerced to the type that the function returns. By default, functions are assumed to return int; if this is not the case, the function must be declared both in the calling routine and when it is defined. For example, a function definition is

```
double sqrt(x)        /* returns square root of x */
double x;
{
        ...
}
```

In the caller, the declaration is

```
double y, sqrt();

y = sqrt(y);
```

A function argument may be any of the basic types or a pointer, but not an array, structure, union, or function. The same is true of the value returned by a function. (The most recent versions of the language, still not standard everywhere, permit structures and unions as arguments and values of functions and allow them to be assigned.)

5.2 Data

Data declared at the top level (that is, outside the body of any function definition) are static in lifetime, and exist throughout the execution of the program. Variables declared within a function body are by default *automatic*: they come into existence when the function is entered and vanish when it is exited. Automatic variables may be declared to be **register** variables; when possible they will be placed in machine registers, which may result in smaller, faster code. The **register** declaration is only considered a hint to the com-

piler; no hardware register names are mentioned, and the hint may be ignored if the compiler wishes.

Static variables exist throughout the execution of a program, and retain their values across function calls. Static variables may be local to a function or (if defined at the top level) common to several functions.

External variables have the same lifetime as static, but they are also accessible to programs from other source files. That is, all references to an identically named external variable are references to the same thing.

The "storage class" of a variable can be explicitly announced in its declaration:

```
static int x;
extern double y[10];
```

More often the defaults for the context are sufficient. Inside a function, the default is **auto** (for automatic). Outside a function, at the top level, the default is **extern**. Since automatic and register variables are specific to a particular call of a particular function, they cannot be declared at the top level. Neither top-level variables nor functions explicitly declared **static** are visible to functions outside the file in which they appear.

5.3 Scope

Declarations may appear either at the top level or at the head of a block (compound statement). Declarations in an inner block temporarily override those of identically named variables outside. The scope of a declaration persists until the end of its block, or until the end of the file, if it was at the top level.

Since function definitions may be given only at the top level (that is, they may not be nested), there are no internal procedures. They have been forbidden not for any philosophical reason, but only to simplify the implementation. It has turned out that the ability to make certain functions and data invisible to programs in other files (by explicitly declaring them **static**) is sufficient to provide one of their most important uses, namely hiding their names from other functions. (However, it is not possible for one function to access the internal variables of another, as internal procedures could do.) Similarly, the ability to conceal functions and data in one file from access by another satisfies some of the most crucial requirements of modular programming (as in languages like Alphard, CLU, and Euclid), even though it does not satisfy them all.

VI. C PREPROCESSOR

It is well recognized that "magic numbers" in a program are a sign of bad programming. Most languages, therefore, provide a way to define symbolic names for constants, so that the value of a magic number need be specified in only one place, and the rest of the code can refer to the value by some mnemonic name. In C such a mechanism is available, but it is not part of the syntax of the language; instead, symbolic naming is provided by a macro preprocessor automatically invoked as part of every C compilation. For example, given the definitions

```
#define    PI    3.14159
#define    E     2.71284
```

the preprocessor replaces all occurrences of a defined name by the corresponding defining string. (Upper-case names are normally chosen to emphasize that these are not variables.) Thus, when the programmer recognizes that he has written an incorrect value for *e*, only the definition line has to be changed to

```
#define    E     2.71828
```

instead of each instance of the constant in the program.

Providing this service by a macro processor instead of by syntax has some significant advantages. The replacement text is not restricted to being numbers; any string of characters is permitted. Furthermore, the token being replaced need not be a variable, although it must have the form of a name. For example, one can define

```
#define    forever         for (;;)
```

and then write infinite loops as

```
forever {
        ...
}
```

The macro processor also permits macros to have arguments; this capability is heavily used by some I/O packages.

A second service of the C preprocessor is library file inclusion: a source line of the form

```
#include    "name"
```

causes the contents of the file name to be interpolated into the source at that point. (includes may be nested.) This feature is much used, especially in larger programs, for making sure that all the source files of the program are supplied with identical #defines, global data declarations, and the like.

VII. ENVIRONMENTAL CONSIDERATIONS

By intent, the C language confines itself to facilities that can be mapped relatively efficiently and directly into machine instructions. For example, writing matrix operations that look exactly like scalar operations is possible in some programming languages and occasionally misleads programmers into believing that matrix operations are as cheap as scalar operations. More important, restricting the domain of the C compiler to those areas where it knows how to do a relatively effective job provides the freedom to design subroutine libraries for the remaining tasks without constraining them to fit into some language specification. When the compiler cannot implement some facility without heavy costs in nonportability, complexity, or efficiency, there are many benefits to leaving out such a facility: it simplifies the language and the compiler, frequently without inconveniencing the user (who often rejects a high-cost built-in operation and does it himself anyway).

At present, C is restricted to simple operations on simple data types. As a result, although the C area of operation is comparatively clean and pleasant, the user must know something about the pollut-

ing effects of the environment to get most jobs done. A program can always access the raw system calls on each system if very close interaction with the operating system is needed, but standard library routines have been implemented in each C environment that try to encourage portability while retaining speed and flexibility. The basic areas covered by the standard library at present are storage allocation, string handling, and I/O. Additional libraries and utilities are available for such areas as graphics, coroutine sequencing, execution time monitoring, and parsing.

The only automatic storage management service provided by C itself is the stack discipline for automatic variables. Two subroutines exist for more flexible storage handling. The function calloc (n, s) returns a pointer to a properly aligned storage block that will hold n items each of which is s bytes long. Normally s is obtained from the sizeof pseudo-function, a compile-time function that yields the size in bytes of a variable or data type. To return a block obtained from calloc to the free storage pool, cfree (p) may be called, where p is a value returned by a previous call to calloc.

Another set of routines deals with string handling. There is no "string" data type, but an array of characters, with a convention that the end of a string is indicated by a null byte, can be used for the same purpose. The most commonly used string routines perform the functions of copying one string to another, comparing two strings, and computing a string length. More sophisticated string operations can often be performed using the I/O routines, which are described next.

Most of the routines in the standard library deal with input and output. Most C programmers use stream I/O, although there is no reason why record I/O could not be used with the language. There are three default streams: the standard input, the standard output, and the error output. The most elementary routines for dealing with these streams are getchar() which reads a character from the standard input, and putchar(c), which writes the character c on the standard output. In the environments in which C programs run, it is generally possibly to redirect these streams to files or other programs; the program itself does not change and is unaware of the redirection.

The most common output function is printf (format, data1, data2, ...), which performs data conversion for formatted output. The string format is copied to the standard output, except that when a conversion specification introduced by a % character is found in format it is replaced by the value of the next data argument, converted according to the specification. For example,

$$printf("n = \%d, x = \%f", n, x);$$

prints n as a decimal integer and x as a floating point number, as in

$$n = 17, x = 12.34$$

A similar function scanf performs formatted input conversion.

All the routines mentioned have versions that operate on streams other than the standard input or output, and printf and scanf variants may also process a string, to allow for in-memory format conversion. Other routines in the I/O library transmit whole lines between memory and files, and check for error or end-of-file status.

Many other routines and utilities are used with C, somewhat more on UNIX than on other systems. As an example, it is possible to compile and load a C program so that when the program is run, data are collected on the number of times each function is called and how long it executes. This profile pinpoints the parts of a program that dominate the run-time.

VIII. EXPERIENCE WITH C

C compilers exist for the most widely used machines at Bell Laboratories (the IBM S/370, Honeywell 6000, PDP-11) and perhaps 10 others. Several hundred programmers within Bell Laboratories and many outside use C as their primary programming language.

8.1 Favorable experiences

C has completely displaced assembly language in UNIX programs. All applications code, the C compiler itself, and the operating system (except for about 1000 lines of initial bootstrap, etc.) are written in C. Although compilers or interpreters are available under UNIX for Fortran, Pascal, Algol 68, Snobol, APL, and other languages, most programmers make little use of them. Since C is a relatively low-level language, it is adequately efficient to prevent people from resorting to assembler, and yet sufficienctly terse and expressive that its users prefer it to PL/I or other very large languages.

A language that doesn't have everything is actually easier to program in than some that do. The limitations of C often imply shorter manuals and easier training and adaptation. Language design, especially when done by a committee, often tends toward including all doubtful features, since there is no quick answer to the advocate who insists that the new feature will be useful to some and can be ignored by others. But this results in long manuals and hierarchies of "experts" who know progressively larger subsets of the language. In practice, if a feature is not used often enough to be familiar and does not complete some structure of syntax or semantics, it should probably be left out. Otherwise, the manual and compiler get bulky, the users get surprises, and it becomes harder and harder to maintain and use the language. It is also desirable to avoid language features that cannot be compiled efficiently; programmers like to feel that the cost of a statement is comparable to the difficulty in writing it. C has thus avoided implementing operations in the language that would have to be performed by subroutine call. As compiler technology improves, some extensions (e.g., structure assignment) are being made to C, but always with the same principles in mind.

One direction for possible expansion of the language has been explicitly avoided. Although C is much used for writing operating systems and associated software, there are no facilities for multiprogramming, parallel operations, synchronization, or process control. We believe that making these operations primitives of the language is inappropriate, mostly because language design is hard enough in itself without incorporating into it the design of operating systems. Language facilities of this sort tend to make strong assumptions about the underlying operating system that may match very poorly what it actually does.

8.2 Unfavorable experiences

The design and implementation of C can (or could) be criticized on a number of points. Here we discuss some of the more vulnerable aspects of the language.

8.2.1 Language level

Some users complain that C is an insufficiently high-level language; for example, they want string data types and operations, or variable-size multi-dimensional arrays, or generic functions. Sometimes a suggested extension merely involves lifting some restriction. For example, allowing variable-size arrays would actually simplify the language specification, since it would only involve allowing general expressions in place of constants in certain contexts.

Many other extensions are plausible; since the low level of C was praised in the previous section as an advantage of the language, most will not be further discussed. One is worthy of mention, however. The C language provides no facility for I/O, leaving this job to library routines. The following fragment illustrates one difficulty with this approach:

```
printf("%d\n", x);
```

The problem arises because on machines on which int is not the same as long, x may not be long; if it were, the program must be written

```
printf("%D\n", x);
```

so as to tell printf the length of x. Thus, changing the type of x involves changing not only its declaration, but also other parts of the program. If I/O were built into the language, the association between the type of an expression and the format in which it is printed could be reconciled by the compiler.

8.2.2 Type safety

C has traditionally been permissive in checking whether an expression is used in a context appropriate to its type. A complete list of examples would be long, but two of the most important should illustrate sufficiently. The types of formal arguments of functions are in general not known, and in any case are not checked by the compiler against the actual arguments at each call. Thus in the statement

```
s = sin(1);
```

the fact that the sin routine takes a floating-point argument is not noticed until the erroneous result is detected by the programmer.

In the structure reference

```
p->memb
```

p is simply assumed to point to a structure of which memb is a member; p might even be an integer and not a pointer at all.

Much of the explanation, if not justification, for such laxity is the typeless nature of C's predecessor languages. Fortunately, a justification need no longer be attempted, since a program is now

available that detects all common type mismatches. This utility, called lint because it picks bits of fluff from programs, examines a set of files and complains about a great many dubious constructions, ranging from unused or uninitialized variables through the type errors mentioned. Programs that pass unscathed through lint enjoy about as complete freedom from type errors as do Algol 68 programs, with a few exceptions: unions are not checked dynamically, and explicit escapes are available that in effect turn off checking.

Some languages, such as Pascal and Euclid, allow the writer to specify that the value of a given variable may assume only a given subrange of the integers. This facility is often connected with the usage of arrays, in that any array index must be a variable or expression whose type specifies a subset of the set given by the bounds of the array. This approach is not without theoretical difficulties, as suggested by Habermann.[4] In itself it does not solve the problems of variables assuming unexpected values or of accessing outside array bounds; such things must (in general) be detected dynamically. Still, the extra information provided by specifying the permissible range for each variable provides valuable information for the compiler and any verifier program. C has no corresponding facility.

One of the characteristic features of C is its rather complete integration of the notion of pointer and of address arithmetic. Some writers, notably Hoare,[5] have argued against the very notion of pointer. We feel, however, that the facilities offered by pointers are too valuable to give up lightly.

8.2.3 Syntax peculiarities

Some people are annoyed by the terseness of expression that is one of the characteristics of the language. We view C's short operators and general lack of noise as a benefit. For example, the use of braces { } for grouping instead of begin and end seems appropriate in view of the frequency of the operation. The use of braces even fits well into ordinary mathematical notation.

Terseness can lead to code that is hard to read, however. For example,

$$*++*argv$$

where argv has been declared char **argv (pointer into an array of character pointers) means: select the character pointer pointed at by argv (*argv), increment it by one (++*argv), then fetch the character that *that* pointer points at (*++*argv). This is concise and efficient but reminiscent of APL.

An example of a minor problem is the comment convention, which is PL/I's /* ... */. Comments do not nest, so an effort to "comment out" a section of code will fail if that section contains a comment. And a number of us can testify that it is surprisingly hard to recognize when an "end comment" delimiter has been botched, so that the comment silently continues until the next comment is reached, deleting a line or two of code. It would be more convenient if a single unique character were reserved to introduce a comment, and if comments always terminated at an end of line.

8.2.4 Semantic peculiarities

There are some occasionally surprising operator precedences. For example,

$$a >> 4 + 5$$

shifts right by 9. Perhaps worse,

$$(x \text{ \& } MASK) == 0$$

must be parenthesized to associate the proper way. Users learn quickly to parenthesize such doubtful cases; and when feasible lint warns of suspicious expressions (including both of these).

We have already mentioned the fact that the **case** actions in a switch flow through unless explicitly broken. In practice, users write so many **switch** statements that they become familiar with this behavior and some even prefer it.

Some problems arise from machine differences that are reflected, perhaps unnecessarily, into the semantics of C. For example, the PDP-11 does sign extension on byte fetches, so that a character (viewed arithmetically) can have a value ranging from -128 to $+127$, rather than 0 to $+255$. Although the reference manual makes it quite clear that the precise range of a **char** variable is machine dependent, programmers occasionally succumb to the temptation of using the full range that their local machine can represent, forgetting that their programs may not work on another machine. The fundamental problem, of course, is that C permits small numbers, as well as genuine characters, to be stored in **char** variables. This might not be necessary if, for example, the notion of subranges (mentioned above) were introduced into the language.

8.2.5 Miscellaneous

C was developed and is generally used in a highly responsive interactive environment, and accordingly the compiler provides few of the services usually associated with batch compilers. For example, it prepares no listing of the source program, no cross reference table, and no indication of the nature of the generated code. Such facilities are available, but they are separate programs, not parts of the compiler. Programmers used to batch environments may find it hard to live without giant listings; we would find it hard to use them.

IX. CONCLUSIONS AND FUTURE DIRECTIONS

C has continued to develop in recent years, mostly by upwardly compatible extensions, occasionally by restrictions against manifestly nonportable or illegal programs that happened to be compiled into something useful. The most recent major changes were motivated by the extension of C to other machines, and the resulting emphasis on portability. The advent of **union** and of casts reflects a desire to be more precise about types when moving to other machines is in prospect. These changes have had relatively little effect on programmers who remained entirely on the UNIX system. Of more importance was a new library, which changed the use of a "portable" library from an option into an effective standard, while simultane-

ously increasing the efficiency of the library so that users would not object.

It is more difficult, of course, to speculate about the future. C is now encountering more and more foreign environments, and this is producing many demands for C to adapt itself to the hardware, and particularly to the operating systems, of other machines. Bit fields, for example, are a response to a request to describe externally imposed data layouts. Similarly, the procedures for external storage allocation and referencing have been made tighter to conform to requirements on other systems. Portability of the basic language seems well handled, but interactions with operating systems grow ever more complex. These lead to requests for more sophisticated data descriptions and initializations, and even for assembler windows. Further changes of this sort are likely.

What is not likely is a fundamental change in the level of the language. Realistically, the very acceptance of C has compelled changes to be made only most cautiously and compatibly. Should the pressure for improvements become too strong for the language to accommodate, C would probably have to be left as is, and a totally new language developed. We leave it to the reader to speculate on whether it should be called D or P.

REFERENCES

1. B. W. Kernighan and D. M. Ritchie, *The C Programming Language,* Englewood Cliffs, N.J.: Prentice-Hall, 1978.
2. M. Richards, "BCPL: A Tool for Compiler Writing and Systems Programming," Proc. AFIPS SJCC, *34* (1969), pp. 557-566.
3. S. C. Johnson and B. W. Kernighan, "The Programming Language B," Comp. Sci. Tech. Rep. No. 8, Bell Laboratories (January 1973).
4. A. N. Habermann, "Critical Comments on the Programming Language PASCAL," Acta Informatica, *3* (1973), pp. 47-58.
5. C. A. R. Hoare, "Data Reliability," ACM SIGPLAN Notices, *10* (June 1975), pp. 528-533.

C REFERENCE MANUAL*

D. M. RITCHIE

1. Introduction

This manual describes the C language on the DEC PDP-11, the Honeywell 6000, the IBM System/370, and the Interdata 8/32. Where differences exist, it concentrates on the PDP-11, but tries to point out implementation-dependent details. With few exceptions, these dependencies follow directly from the underlying properties of the hardware; the various compilers are generally quite compatible.

2. Lexical conventions

There are six classes of tokens: identifiers, keywords, constants, strings, operators, and other separators. Blanks, tabs, newlines, and comments (collectively, "white space") as described below are ignored except as they serve to separate tokens. Some white space is required to separate otherwise adjacent identifiers, keywords, and constants.

If the input stream has been parsed into tokens up to a given character, the next token is taken to include the longest string of characters which could possibly constitute a token.

2.1 Comments

The characters /* introduce a comment, which terminates with the characters */. Comments do not nest.

2.2 Identifiers (Names)

An identifier is a sequence of letters and digits; the first character must be a letter. The underscore _ counts as a letter. Upper and lower case letters are different. No more than the first eight characters are significant, although more may be used. External identifiers, which are used by various assemblers and loaders, are more restricted:

DEC PDP-11	7 characters, 2 cases
Honeywell 6000	6 characters, 1 case
IBM 360/370	7 characters, 1 case
Interdata 8/32	8 characters, 2 cases

2.3 Keywords

The following identifiers are reserved for use as keywords, and may not be used otherwise:

int	extern	else
char	register	for
float	typedef	do
double	static	while
struct	goto	switch
union	return	case
long	sizeof	default
short	break	entry
unsigned	continue	
auto	if	

The entry keyword is not currently implemented by any compiler but is reserved for future use. Some implementations also reserve the words fortran and asm.

2.4 Constants

There are several kinds of constants, as listed below. Hardware characteristics which affect sizes are summarized in §2.6.

2.4.1 Integer constants

An integer constant consisting of a sequence of digits is taken to be octal if it begins with 0 (digit zero), decimal otherwise. The digits 8 and 9 have octal value 10 and 11 respectively. A sequence of digits preceded by 0x or 0X (digit zero) is taken to be a hexadecimal integer. The hexadecimal digits include a or A through f or F with values 10 through 15. A decimal constant whose value exceeds the largest signed machine integer is taken to be long; an octal or hex constant which exceeds the largest unsigned machine integer is likewise taken to be long.

2.4.2 Explicit long constants

A decimal, octal, or hexadecimal integer constant immediately followed by l (letter ell) or L is a long constant. As discussed below, on some machines integer and long values may be considered identical.

2.4.3 Character constants

A character constant is a character enclosed in single quotes, as in 'x'. The value of a character constant is the numerical value of the character in the machine's character set.

Certain non-graphic characters, the single quote ' and the backslash \, may be represented according to the following table of escape sequences:

newline	NL (LF)	\n
horizontal tab	HT	\t
backspace	BS	\b
carriage return	CR	\r
form feed	FF	\f
backslash	\	\\
single quote	'	\'
bit pattern	*ddd*	*ddd*

The escape *ddd* consists of the backslash followed by 1, 2, or 3 octal digits which are taken to specify the value of the desired character. A special case of this construction is \0 (not followed by a digit), which indicates the character NUL. If the character following a backslash is not one of those specified, the backslash is ignored.

2.4.4 Floating constants

A floating constant consists of an integer part, a decimal point, a fraction part, an e or E, and an optionally signed integer exponent. The integer and fraction parts both consist of a sequence of digits. Either the integer part or the fraction part (not both) may be missing; either the decimal point or the e and the exponent (not both) may be missing. Every floating constant is taken to be double-precision.

2.5 Strings

A string is a sequence of characters surrounded by double quotes, as in "...". A string has type "array of characters" and storage class static (see §4 below) and is initialized with the given characters. All strings, even when written identically, are distinct. The compiler places a null byte \0 at the end of each string so that programs which scan the string can find its end. In a string, the double quote character " must be preceded by a \; in addition, the same escapes as described for character constants may be used. Finally, a \ and an immediately following newline are ignored.

2.6 Hardware characteristics

The following table summarizes certain hardware properties which vary from machine to machine. Although these affect program portability, in practice they are less of a problem than might be thought *a priori*.

	DEC PDP-11	Honeywell 6000	IBM 370	Interdata 8/32
	ASCII	ASCII	EBCDIC	ASCII
char	8 bits	9 bits	8 bits	8 bits
int	16	36	32	32
short	16	36	16	16
long	32	36	32	32
float	32	36	32	32
double	64	72	64	64
range	$\pm 10^{\pm 38}$	$\pm 10^{\pm 38}$	$\pm 10^{\pm 76}$	$\pm 10^{\pm 76}$

For these four machines, floating point numbers have 8 bit exponents.

3. Syntax notation

In the syntax notation used in this manual, syntactic categories are indicated by *italic* type, and literal words and characters in **bold** type. Alternative categories are listed on separate lines. An optional terminal or non-terminal symbol is indicated by the subscript "opt," so that

$$\{ \ expression_{opt} \ \}$$

indicates an optional expression enclosed in braces. The syntax is summarized in §18.

4. What's in a name?

C bases the interpretation of an identifier upon two attributes of the identifier: its *storage class* and its *type*. The storage class determines the location and lifetime of the storage associated with an identifier; the type determines the meaning of the values found in the identifier's storage.

There are four declarable storage classes: automatic, static, external, and register. Automatic variables are local to each invocation of a block (§9.2), and are discarded upon exit from the block; static variables are local to a block, but retain their values upon reentry to a block even after control has left the block; external variables exist and retain their values throughout the execution of the entire program, and may be used for communication between functions, even separately compiled functions. Register variables are (if possible) stored in the fast registers of the machine; like automatic variables they are local to each block and disappear on exit from the block.

C supports several fundamental types of objects:

Objects declared as characters (**char**) are large enough to store any member of the implementation's character set, and if a genuine character from that character set is stored in a character variable, its value is equivalent to the integer code for that character. Other quantities may be stored into character variables, but the implementation is machine-dependent.

Up to three sizes of integer, declared **short int**, **int**, and **long int**, are available. Longer integers provide no less storage than shorter ones, but the implementation may make either short integers, or long integers, or both, equivalent to plain integers. "Plain" integers have the natural size suggested by the host machine architecture; the other sizes are provided to meet special needs.

Unsigned integers, declared **unsigned,** obey the laws of arithmetic modulo 2^n where n is the number of bits in the representation. (On the PDP-11, unsigned long quantities are not supported.)

Single-precision floating point (**float**) and double-precision floating point (**double**) may be synonymous in some implementations.

Because objects of the foregoing types can usefully be interpreted as numbers, they will be referred to as *arithmetic* types. Types **char** and **int** of all sizes will collectively be called *integral* types. **float** and **double** will collectively be called *floating* types.

Besides the fundamental arithmetic types there is a conceptually infinite class of derived types constructed from the fundamental types in the following ways:

arrays of objects of most types;

functions which return objects of a given type;

pointers to objects of a given type;

structures containing a sequence of objects of various types;

unions capable of containing any one of several objects of various types.

In general these methods of constructing objects can be applied recursively.

5. Objects and lvalues

An *object* is a manipulatable region of storage; an *lvalue* is an expression referring to an object. An obvious example of an lvalue expression is an identifier. There are operators which yield lvalues: for example, if E is an expression of pointer type, then *E is an lvalue expression referring to the object to which E points. The name "lvalue" comes from the assignment expression E1 = E2 in which the left operand E1 must be an lvalue expression. The discussion of each operator below indicates whether it expects lvalue operands and whether it yields an lvalue.

6. Conversions

A number of operators may, depending on their operands, cause conversion of the value of an operand from one type to another. This section explains the result to be expected from such conversions. §6.6 summarizes the conversions demanded by most ordinary operators; it will be supplemented as required by the discussion of each operator.

6.1 Characters and integers

A character or a short integer may be used wherever an integer may be used. In all cases the value is converted to an integer. Conversion of a shorter integer to a longer always involves sign extension; integers are signed quantities. Whether or not sign-extension occurs for characters is machine dependent, but it is guaranteed that a member of the standard character set is non-negative. Of the machines treated by this manual, only the PDP-11 sign-extends. On the PDP-11, character variables range in value from −128 to 127; the characters of the ASCII alphabet are all positive. A character constant specified with an octal escape suffers sign extension and may appear negative; for example, '\377' has the value −1.

When a longer integer is converted to a shorter or to a char, it is truncated on the left; excess bits are simply discarded.

6.2 Float and double

All floating arithmetic in C is carried out in double-precision; whenever a float appears in an expression it is lengthened to double by zero-padding its fraction. When a double must be converted to float, for example by an assignment, the double is rounded before truncation to float length.

6.3 Floating and integral

Conversions of floating values to integral type tend to be rather machine-dependent; in particular the direction of truncation of negative numbers varies from machine to machine. The result is undefined if the value will not fit in the space provided.

Conversions of integral values to floating type are well behaved. Some loss of precision occurs if the destination lacks sufficient bits.

6.4 Pointers and integers

An integer or long integer may be added to or subtracted from a pointer; in such a case the first is converted as specified in the discussion of the addition operator.

Two pointers to objects of the same type may be subtracted; in this case the result is converted to an integer as specified in the discussion of the subtraction operator.

6.5 Unsigned

Whenever an unsigned integer and a plain integer are combined, the plain integer is converted to unsigned and the result is unsigned. The value is the least

unsigned integer congruent to the signed integer (modulo $2^{wordsize}$). In a 2's complement representation, this conversion is conceptual and there is no actual change in the bit pattern.

When an unsigned integer is converted to `long`, the value of the result is the same numerically as that of the unsigned integer. Thus the conversion amounts to padding with zeros on the left.

6.6 Arithmetic conversions

A great many operators cause conversions and yield result types in a similar way. This pattern will be called the "usual arithmetic conversions."

First, any operands of type `char` or `short` are converted to `int`, and any of type `float` are converted to `double`.

Then, if either operand is `double`, the other is converted to `double` and that is the type of the result.

Otherwise, if either operand is `long`, the other is converted to `long` and that is the type of the result.

Otherwise, if either operand is `unsigned`, the other is converted to `unsigned` and that is the type of the result.

Otherwise, both operands must be `int`, and that is the type of the result.

7. Expressions

The precedence of expression operators is the same as the order of the major subsections of this section, highest precedence first. Thus, for example, the expressions referred to as the operands of + (§7.4) are those expressions defined in §§7.1-7.3. Within each subsection, the operators have the same precedence. Left- or right-associativity is specified in each subsection for the operators discussed therein. The precedence and associativity of all the expression operators is summarized in the grammar of §18.

Otherwise the order of evaluation of expressions is undefined. In particular the compiler considers itself free to compute subexpressions in the order it believes most efficient, even if the subexpressions involve side effects. The order in which side effects take place is unspecified. Expressions involving a commutative and associative operator (`*`, `+`, `&`, `|`, `^`) may be rearranged arbitrarily, even in the presence of parentheses; to force a particular order of evaluation an explicit temporary must be used.

The handling of overflow and divide check in expression evaluation is machine-dependent. All existing implementations of C ignore integer overflows; treatment of division by 0, and all floating-point exceptions, varies between machines, and is usually adjustable by a library function.

7.1 Primary expressions

Primary expressions involving `.`, `->`, subscripting, and function calls group left to right.

> *primary-expression:*
> *identifier*
> *constant*
> *string*
> (*expression*)
> *primary-expression* [*expression*]
> *primary-expression* (*expression-list$_{opt}$*)
> *primary-lvalue* . *identifier*
> *primary-expression* $->$ *identifier*

> *expression-list:*
> *expression*
> *expression-list* , *expression*

An identifier is a primary expression, provided it has been suitably declared as discussed below. Its type is specified by its declaration. If the type of the identifier is

"array of ...", however, then the value of the identifier-expression is a pointer to the first object in the array, and the type of the expression is "pointer to ...". Moreover, an array identifier is not an lvalue expression. Likewise, an identifier which is declared "function returning ...", when used except in the function-name position of a call, is converted to "pointer to function returning ...".

A constant is a primary expression. Its type may be `int`, `long`, or `double` depending on its form. Character constants have type `int`; floating constants are `double`.

A string is a primary expression. Its type is originally "array of `char`"; but following the same rule given above for identifiers, this is modified to "pointer to `char`" and the result is a pointer to the first character in the string. (There is an exception in certain initializers; see §8.6.)

A parenthesized expression is a primary expression whose type and value are identical to those of the unadorned expression. The presence of parentheses does not affect whether the expression is an lvalue.

A primary expression followed by an expression in square brackets is a primary expression. The intuitive meaning is that of a subscript. Usually, the primary expression has type "pointer to ...", the subscript expression is `int`, and the type of the result is "...". The expression `E1[E2]` is identical (by definition) to `*((E1)+(E2))`. All the clues needed to understand this notation are contained in this section together with the discussions in §§ 7.1, 7.2, and 7.4 on identifiers, `*`, and + respectively; §14.3 below summarizes the implications.

A function call is a primary expression followed by parentheses containing a possibly empty, comma-separated list of expressions which constitute the actual arguments to the function. The primary expression must be of type "function returning ...", and the result of the function call is of type "...". As indicated below, a hitherto unseen identifier followed immediately by a left parenthesis is contextually declared to represent a function returning an integer; thus in the most common case, integer-valued functions need not be declared.

Any actual arguments of type `float` are converted to `double` before the call; any of type `char` or `short` are converted to `int`; and as usual, array names are converted to pointers. No other conversions are performed automatically; in particular, the compiler does not compare the types of actual arguments with those of formal arguments. If conversion is needed, use a cast; see §7.2, 8.7.

In preparing for the call to a function, a copy is made of each actual parameter; thus, all argument-passing in C is strictly by value. A function may change the values of its formal parameters, but these changes cannot affect the values of the actual parameters. On the other hand, it is possible to pass a pointer on the understanding that the function may change the value of the object to which the pointer points. An array name is a pointer expression. The order of evaluation of arguments is undefined by the language; take note that the various compilers differ.

Recursive calls to any function are permitted.

A primary expression followed by a dot followed by an identifier is an expression. The first expression must be an lvalue naming a structure or a union, and the identifier must name a member of the structure or union. The result is an lvalue referring to the named member of the structure or union.

A primary expression followed by an arrow (built from a – and a >) followed by an identifier is an expression. The first expression must be a pointer to a structure or a union and the identifier must name a member of that structure or union. The result is an lvalue referring to the named member of the structure or union to which the pointer expression points.

Thus the expression `E1->MOS` is the same as `(*E1).MOS`. Structures and unions are discussed in §8.5. The rules given here for the use of structures and unions are not enforced strictly, in order to allow an escape from the typing mechanism. See §14.1.

7.2 Unary operators

Expressions with unary operators group right-to-left.

unary-expression:
    * *expression*
    & *lvalue*
    − *expression*
    ! *expression*
    ~ *expression*
    ++ *lvalue*
    −− *lvalue*
    lvalue ++
    lvalue −−
    (*type-name*) *expression*
    `sizeof` *expression*
    `sizeof` (*type-name*)

The unary * operator means *indirection*: the expression must be a pointer, and the result is an lvalue referring to the object to which the expression points. If the type of the expression is "pointer to ...", the type of the result is "...".

The result of the unary & operator is a pointer to the object referred to by the lvalue. If the type of the lvalue is "...", the type of the result is "pointer to ...".

The result of the unary − operator is the negative of its operand. The usual arithmetic conversions are performed. The negative of an unsigned quantity is computed by subtracting its value from 2^n, where n is the number of bits in an `int`. There is no unary + operator.

The result of the logical negation operator ! is 1 if the value of its operand is 0, 0 if the value of its operand is non-zero. The type of the result is `int`. It is applicable to any arithmetic type or to pointers.

The ~ operator yields the one's complement of its operand. The usual arithmetic conversions are performed. The type of the operand must be integral.

The object referred to by the lvalue operand of prefix ++ is incremented. The value is the new value of the operand, but is not an lvalue. The expression ++x is equivalent to x+=1. See the discussions of addition (§7.4) and assignment operators (§7.14) for information on conversions.

The lvalue operand of prefix −− is decremented analogously to the prefix ++ operator.

When postfix ++ is applied to an lvalue the result is the value of the object referred to by the lvalue. After the result is noted, the object is incremented in the same manner as for the prefix ++ operator. The type of the result is the same as the type of the lvalue expression.

When postfix −− is applied to an lvalue the result is the value of the object referred to by the lvalue. After the result is noted, the object is decremented in the manner as for the prefix −− operator. The type of the result is the same as the type of the lvalue expression.

An expression preceded by the parenthesized name of a data type causes conversion of the value of the expression to the named type. This construction is called a *cast*. Type names are described in §8.7.

The `sizeof` operator yields the size, in bytes, of its operand. (A *byte* is undefined by the language except in terms of the value of `sizeof`. However, in all existing implementations a byte is the space required to hold a `char`.) When applied to an array, the result is the total number of bytes in the array. The size is determined from the declarations of the objects in the expression. This expression is semantically an integer constant and may be used anywhere a constant is required. Its major use is in communication with routines like storage allocators and I/O systems.

The `sizeof` operator may also be applied to a parenthesized type name. In that case it yields the size, in bytes, of an object of the indicated type.

The construction `sizeof(`*type*`)` is taken to be a unit, so the expression `sizeof(`*type*`)`−2 is the same as `(sizeof(`*type*`))`−2.

7.3 Multiplicative operators

The multiplicative operators *, /, and % group left-to-right. The usual arithmetic conversions are performed.

> *multiplicative-expression:*
> expression * expression
> expression / expression
> expression % expression

The binary * operator indicates multiplication. The * operator is associative and expressions with several multiplications at the same level may be rearranged by the compiler.

The binary / operator indicates division. When positive integers are divided truncation is toward 0, but the form of truncation is machine-dependent if either operand is negative. On all machines covered by this manual, the remainder has the same sign as the dividend. It is always true that (a/b)*b + a%b is equal to a (if b is not 0).

The binary % operator yields the remainder from the division of the first expression by the second. The usual arithmetic conversions are performed. The operands must not be float.

7.4 Additive operators

The additive operators + and − group left-to-right. The usual arithmetic conversions are performed. There are some additional type possibilities for each operator.

> *additive-expression:*
> expression + expression
> expression − expression

The result of the + operator is the sum of the operands. A pointer to an object in an array and a value of any integral type may be added. The latter is in all cases converted to an address offset by multiplying it by the length of the object to which the pointer points. The result is a pointer of the same type as the original pointer, and which points to another object in the same array, appropriately offset from the original object. Thus if P is a pointer to an object in an array, the expression P+1 is a pointer to the next object in the array.

No further type combinations are allowed for pointers.

The + operator is associative and expressions with several additions at the same level may be rearranged by the compiler.

The result of the − operator is the difference of the operands. The usual arithmetic conversions are performed. Additionally, a value of any integral type may be subtracted from a pointer, and then the same conversions as for addition apply.

If two pointers to objects of the same type are subtracted, the result is converted (by division by the length of the object) to an int representing the number of objects separating the pointed-to objects. This conversion will in general give unexpected results unless the pointers point to objects in the same array, since pointers, even to objects of the same type, do not necessarily differ by a multiple of the object-length.

7.5 Shift operators

The shift operators << and >> group left-to-right. Both perform the usual arithmetic conversions on their operands, each of which must be integral. Then the right operand is converted to int; the type of the result is that of the left operand. The result is undefined if the right operand is negative, or greater than or equal to the length of the object in bits.

> *shift-expression:*
> expression << expression
> expression >> expression

The value of E1<<E2 is E1 (interpreted as a bit pattern) left-shifted E2 bits; vacated bits are 0-filled. The value of E1>>E2 is E1 right-shifted E2 bit positions. The right

shift is guaranteed to be logical (0-fill) if E1 is unsigned; otherwise it may be (and is, on the PDP-11) arithmetic (fill by a copy of the sign bit).

7.6 Relational operators

The relational operators group left-to-right, but this fact is not very useful; a<b<c does not mean what it seems to.

> *relational-expression:*
>> *expression < expression*
>> *expression > expression*
>> *expression <= expression*
>> *expression >= expression*

The operators < (less than), > (greater than), <= (less than or equal to) and >= (greater than or equal to) all yield 0 if the specified relation is false and 1 if it is true. The type of the result is int. The usual arithmetic conversions are performed. Two pointers may be compared; the result depends on the relative locations in the address space of the pointed-to objects. Pointer comparison is portable only when the pointers point to objects in the same array.

7.7 Equality operators

> *equality-expression:*
>> *expression == expression*
>> *expression != expression*

The == (equal to) and the != (not equal to) operators are exactly analogous to the relational operators except for their lower precedence. (Thus a<b == c<d is 1 whenever a<b and c<d have the same truth-value).

A pointer may be compared to an integer, but the result is machine dependent unless the integer is the constant 0. A pointer to which 0 has been assigned is guaranteed not to point to any object, and will appear to be equal to 0; in conventional usage, such a pointer is considered to be null.

7.8 Bitwise AND operator

> *and-expression:*
>> *expression & expression*

The & operator is associative and expressions involving & may be rearranged. The usual arithmetic conversions are performed; the result is the bitwise AND function of the operands. The operator applies only to integral operands.

7.9 Bitwise exclusive OR operator

> *exclusive-or-expression:*
>> *expression ^ expression*

The ^ operator is associative and expressions involving ^ may be rearranged. The usual arithmetic conversions are performed; the result is the bitwise exclusive OR function of the operands. The operator applies only to integral operands.

7.10 Bitwise inclusive OR operator

> *inclusive-or-expression:*
>> *expression | expression*

The | operator is associative and expressions involving | may be rearranged. The usual arithmetic conversions are performed; the result is the bitwise inclusive OR function of its operands. The operator applies only to integral operands.

7.11 Logical AND operator

> *logical-and-expression:*
>> *expression && expression*

The && operator groups left-to-right. It returns 1 if both its operands are non-zero, 0 otherwise. Unlike &, && guarantees left-to-right evaluation; moreover the second operand is not evaluated if the first operand is 0.

The operands need not have the same type, but each must have one of the fundamental types or be a pointer. The result is always int.

7.12 Logical OR operator

> *logical-or-expression:*
>> *expression* | | *expression*

The | | operator groups left-to-right. It returns 1 if either of its operands is non-zero, and 0 otherwise. Unlike |, | | guarantees left-to-right evaluation; moreover, the second operand is not evaluated if the value of the first operand is non-zero.

The operands need not have the same type, but each must have one of the fundamental types or be a pointer. The result is always int.

7.13 Conditional operator

> *conditional-expression:*
>> *expression* ? *expression* : *expression*

Conditional expressions group right-to-left. The first expression is evaluated and if it is non-zero, the result is the value of the second expression, otherwise that of third expression. If possible, the usual arithmetic conversions are performed to bring the second and third expressions to a common type; otherwise, if both are pointers of the same type, the result has the common type; otherwise, one must be a pointer and the other the constant 0, and the result has the type of the pointer. Only one of the second and third expressions is evaluated.

7.14 Assignment operators

There are a number of assignment operators, all of which group right-to-left. All require an lvalue as their left operand, and the type of an assignment expression is that of its left operand. The value is the value stored in the left operand after the assignment has taken place. The two parts of a compound assignment operator are separate tokens.

> *assignment-expression:*
>> *lvalue* = *expression*
>> *lvalue* += *expression*
>> *lvalue* -= *expression*
>> *lvalue* *= *expression*
>> *lvalue* /= *expression*
>> *lvalue* %= *expression*
>> *lvalue* >>= *expression*
>> *lvalue* <<= *expression*
>> *lvalue* &= *expression*
>> *lvalue* ^= *expression*
>> *lvalue* |= *expression*

In the simple assignment with =, the value of the expression replaces that of the object referred to by the lvalue. If both operands have arithmetic type, the right operand is converted to the type of the left preparatory to the assignment.

The behavior of an expression of the form E1 *op*= E2 may be inferred by taking it as equivalent to E1 = E1 *op* (E2); however, E1 is evaluated only once. In += and -=, the left operand may be a pointer, in which case the (integral) right operand is converted as explained in §7.4; all right operands and all non-pointer left operands must have arithmetic type.

The compilers currently allow a pointer to be assigned to an integer, an integer to a pointer, and a pointer to a pointer of another type. The assignment is a pure copy operation, with no conversion. This usage is nonportable, and may produce pointers which cause addressing exceptions when used. However, it is guaranteed that assignment of the constant 0 to a pointer will produce a null pointer distinguishable from a pointer to any object.

7.15 Comma operator

> *comma-expression:*
>   *expression , expression*

A pair of expressions separated by a comma is evaluated left-to-right and the value of the left expression is discarded. The type and value of the result are the type and value of the right operand. This operator groups left-to-right. In contexts where comma is given a special meaning, for example in a list of actual arguments to functions (§7.1) and lists of initializers (§8.6), the comma operator as described in this section can only appear in parentheses; for example,

        f(a, (t=3, t+2), c)

has three arguments, the second of which has the value 5.

8. Declarations

Declarations are used to specify the interpretation which C gives to each identifier; they do not necessarily reserve storage associated with the identifier. Declarations have the form

> *declaration:*
>   *decl-specifiers declarator-list$_{opt}$;*

The declarators in the declarator-list contain the identifiers being declared. The decl-specifiers consist of a sequence of type and storage class specifiers.

> *decl-specifiers:*
>   *type-specifier decl-specifiers$_{opt}$*
>   *sc-specifier decl-specifiers$_{opt}$*

The list must be self-consistent in a way described below.

8.1 Storage class specifiers

The sc-specifiers are:

> *sc-specifier:*
>   auto
>   static
>   extern
>   register
>   typedef

The `typedef` specifier does not reserve storage and is called a "storage class specifier" only for syntactic convenience; it is discussed in §8.8. The meanings of the various storage classes were discussed in §4.

The `auto`, `static`, and `register` declarations also serve as definitions in that they cause an appropriate amount of storage to be reserved. In the `extern` case there must be an external definition (§10) for the given identifiers somewhere outside the function in which they are declared.

A `register` declaration is best thought of as an `auto` declaration, together with a hint to the compiler that the variables declared will be heavily used. Only the first few such declarations are effective. Moreover, only variables of certain types will be stored in registers; on the PDP-11, they are `int`, `char`, or pointer. One other restriction applies to register variables: the address-of operator & cannot be applied to them. Smaller, faster programs can be expected if register declarations are used appropriately, but future improvements in code generation may render them unnecessary.

At most one sc-specifier may be given in a declaration. If the sc-specifier is missing from a declaration, it is taken to be `auto` inside a function, `extern` outside. Exception: functions are never automatic.

8.2 Type specifiers

The type-specifiers are

> *type-specifier:*
>   `char`
>   `short`
>   `int`
>   `long`
>   `unsigned`
>   `float`
>   `double`
>   *struct-or-union-specifier*
>   *typedef-name*

The words `long`, `short`, and `unsigned` may be thought of as adjectives; the following combinations are acceptable.

> `short int`
> `long int`
> `unsigned int`
> `long float`

The meaning of the last is the same as `double`. Otherwise, at most one type-specifier may be given in a declaration. If the type-specifier is missing from a declaration, it is taken to be `int`.

Specifiers for structures and unions are discussed in §8.5; declarations with `typedef` names are discussed in §8.8.

8.3 Declarators

The declarator-list appearing in a declaration is a comma-separated sequence of declarators, each of which may have an initializer.

> *declarator-list:*
>   *init-declarator*
>   *init-declarator , declarator-list*

> *init-declarator:*
>   *declarator initializer$_{opt}$*

Initializers are discussed in §8.6. The specifiers in the declaration indicate the type and storage class of the objects to which the declarators refer. Declarators have the syntax:

> *declarator:*
>   *identifier*
>   (*declarator*)
>   * *declarator*
>   *declarator* ( )
>   *declarator* [*constant-expression$_{opt}$*]

The grouping is the same as in expressions.

8.4 Meaning of declarators

Each declarator is taken to be an assertion that when a construction of the same form as the declarator appears in an expression, it yields an object of the indicated type and storage class. Each declarator contains exactly one identifier; it is this identifier that is declared.

If an unadorned identifier appears as a declarator, then it has the type indicated by the specifier heading the declaration.

A declarator in parentheses is identical to the unadorned declarator, but the binding of complex declarators may be altered by parentheses. See the examples below.

Now imagine a declaration

T D1

where T is a type-specifier (like int, etc.) and D1 is a declarator. Suppose this declaration makes the identifier have type "... T," where the "..." is empty if D1 is just a plain identifier (so that the type of x in "int x" is just int). Then if D1 has the form

> *D

the type of the contained identifier is "... pointer to T."

If D1 has the form

> D()

then the contained identifier has the type "... function returning T."

If D1 has the form

> D[*constant-expression*]

or

> D[]

then the contained identifier has type "... array of T." In the first case the constant expression is an expression whose value is determinable at compile time, and whose type is int. (Constant expressions are defined precisely in §15.) When several "array of" specifications are adjacent, a multi-dimensional array is created; the constant expressions which specify the bounds of the arrays may be missing only for the first member of the sequence. This elision is useful when the array is external and the actual definition, which allocates storage, is given elsewhere. The first constant-expression may also be omitted when the declarator is followed by initialization. In this case the size is calculated from the number of initial elements supplied.

An array may be constructed from one of the basic types, from a pointer, from a structure or union, or from another array (to generate a multi-dimensional array).

Not all the possibilities allowed by the syntax above are actually permitted. The restrictions are as follows: functions may not return arrays, structures, unions or functions, although they may return pointers to such things; there are no arrays of functions, although there may be arrays of pointers to functions. Likewise a structure or union may not contain a function, but it may contain a pointer to a function.

As an example, the declaration

> int i, *ip, f(), *fip(), (*pfi)();

declares an integer i, a pointer ip to an integer, a function f returning an integer, a function fip returning a pointer to an integer, and a pointer pfi to a function which returns an integer. It is especially useful to compare the last two. The binding of *fip() is *(fip()), so that the declaration suggests, and the same construction in an expression requires, the calling of a function fip, and then using indirection through the (pointer) result to yield an integer. In the declarator (*pfi)(), the extra parentheses are necessary, as they are also in an expression, to indicate that indirection through a pointer to a function yields a function, which is then called; it returns an integer.

As another example,

> float fa[17], *afp[17];

declares an array of float numbers and an array of pointers to float numbers. Finally,

> static int x3d[3][5][7];

declares a static three-dimensional array of integers, with rank 3×5×7. In complete detail, x3d is an array of three items; each item is an array of five arrays; each of the latter arrays is an array of seven integers. Any of the expressions x3d, x3d[i], x3d[i][j], x3d[i][j][k] may reasonably appear in an expression. The first three have type "array," the last has type int.

8.5 Structure and union declarations

A structure is an object consisting of a sequence of named members. Each member may have any type. A union is an object which may, at a given time, contain any one of several members. Structure and union specifiers have the same form.

> *struct-or-union-specifier:*
> > *struct-or-union* { *struct-decl-list* }
> > *struct-or-union identifier* { *struct-decl-list* }
> > *struct-or-union identifier*
>
> *struct-or-union:*
> > `struct`
> > `union`

The struct-decl-list is a sequence of declarations for the members of the structure or union:

> *struct-decl-list:*
> > *struct-declaration*
> > *struct-declaration struct-decl-list*
>
> *struct-declaration:*
> > *type-specifier struct-declarator-list ;*
>
> *struct-declarator-list:*
> > *struct-declarator*
> > *struct-declarator , struct-declarator-list*

In the usual case, a struct-declarator is just a declarator for a member of a structure or union. A structure member may also consist of a specified number of bits. Such a member is also called a *field*; its length is set off from the field name by a colon.

> *struct-declarator:*
> > *declarator*
> > *declarator : constant-expression*
> > *: constant-expression*

Within a structure, the objects declared have addresses which increase as their declarations are read left-to-right. Each non-field member of a structure begins on an addressing boundary appropriate to its type; therefore, there may be unnamed holes in a structure. Field members are packed into machine integers; they do not straddle words. A field which does not fit into the space remaining in a word is put into the next word. No field may be wider than a word. Fields are assigned right-to-left on the PDP-11, left-to-right on other machines.

A struct-declarator with no declarator, only a colon and a width, indicates an unnamed field useful for padding to conform to externally-imposed layouts. As a special case, an unnamed field with a width of 0 specifies alignment of the next field at a word boundary. The "next field" presumably is a field, not an ordinary structure member, because in the latter case the alignment would have been automatic.

The language does not restrict the types of things that are declared as fields, but implementations are not required to support any but integer fields. Moreover, even `int` fields may be considered to be unsigned. On the PDP-11, fields are not signed and have only integer values. In all implementations, there are no arrays of fields, and the address-of operator & may not be applied to them, so that there are no pointers to fields.

A union may be thought of as a structure all of whose members begin at offset 0 and whose size is sufficient to contain any of its members. At most one of the members can be stored in a union at any time.

A structure or union specifier of the second form, that is, one of

> `struct` *identifier* { *struct-decl-list* }
> `union` *identifier* { *struct-decl-list* }

declares the identifier to be the *structure tag* (or union **tag**) of the structure specified by the list. A subsequent declaration may then use the third form of specifier, one of

```
struct identifier
union identifier
```

Structure tags allow definition of self-referential structures; they also permit the long part of the declaration to be given once and used several times. It is illegal to declare a structure or union which contains an instance of itself, but a structure or union may contain a pointer to an instance of itself.

The names of members and tags may be the same as ordinary variables. However, names of tags and members must be mutually distinct.

Two structures may share a common initial sequence of members; that is, the same member may appear in two different structures if it has the same type in both and if all previous members are the same in both. (Actually, the compiler checks only that a name in two different structures has the same type and offset in both, but if preceding members differ the construction is nonportable.)

A simple example of a structure declaration is

```
struct tnode {
        char tword[20];
        int count;
        struct tnode *left;
        struct tnode *right;
};
```

which contains an array of 20 characters, an integer, and two pointers to similar structures. Once this declaration has been given, the declaration

```
struct tnode s, *sp;
```

declares s to be a structure of the given sort and sp to be a pointer to a structure of the given sort. With these declarations, the expression

```
sp->count
```

refers to the count field of the structure to which sp points;

```
s.left
```

refers to the left subtree pointer of the structure s; and

```
s.right->tword[0]
```

refers to the first character of the tword member of the right subtree of s.

8.6 Initialization

A declarator may specify an initial value for the identifier being declared. The initializer is preceded by =, and consists of an expression or a list of values nested in braces.

> *initializer:*
>   = *expression*
>   = { *initializer-list* }
>   = { *initializer-list ,* }
>
> *initializer-list:*
>   *expression*
>   *initializer-list , initializer-list*
>   { *initializer-list* }

All the expressions in an initializer for a static or external variable must be constant expressions, which are described in §15, or expressions which reduce to the address of a previously declared variable, possibly offset by a constant expression. Automatic or register variables may be initialized by arbitrary expressions involving constants, and previously declared variables and functions.

Static and external variables which are not initialized are guaranteed to start off as 0; automatic and register variables which are not initialized are guaranteed to start off as garbage.

When an initializer applies to a *scalar* (a pointer or an object of arithmetic type), it consists of a single expression, perhaps in braces. The initial value of the object is taken from the expression; the same conversions as for assignment are performed.

When the declared variable is an *aggregate* (a structure or array) then the initializer consists of a brace-enclosed, comma-separated list of initializers for the members of the aggregate, written in increasing subscript or member order. If the aggregate contains subaggregates, this rule applies recursively to the members of the aggregate. If there are fewer initializers in the list than there are members of the aggregate, then the aggregate is padded with 0's. It is not permitted to initialize unions or automatic aggregates.

Braces may be elided as follows. If the initializer begins with a left brace, then the succeeding comma-separated list of initializers initializes the members of the aggregate; it is erroneous for there to be more initializers than members. If, however, the initializer does not begin with a left brace, then only enough elements from the list are taken to account for the members of the aggregate; any remaining members are left to initialize the next member of the aggregate of which the current aggregate is a part.

A final abbreviation allows a `char` array to be initialized by a string. In this case successive characters of the string initialize the members of the array.

For example,

```
int x[] = { 1, 3, 5 };
```

declares and initializes `x` as a 1-dimensional array which has three members, since no size was specified and there are three initializers.

```
float y[4][3] = {
    { 1, 3, 5 },
    { 2, 4, 6 },
    { 3, 5, 7 },
};
```

is a completely-bracketed initialization: 1, 3, and 5 initialize the first row of the array `y[0]`, namely `y[0][0]`, `y[0][1]`, and `y[0][2]`. Likewise the next two lines initialize `y[1]` and `y[2]`. The initializer ends early and therefore `y[3]` is initialized with 0. Precisely the same effect could have been achieved by

```
float y[4][3] = {
    1, 3, 5, 2, 4, 6, 3, 5, 7
};
```

The initializer for `y` begins with a left brace, but that for `y[0]` does not, therefore 3 elements from the list are used. Likewise the next three are taken successively for `y[1]` and `y[2]`. Also,

```
float y[4][3] = {
    { 1 }, { 2 }, { 3 }, { 4 }
};
```

initializes the first column of `y` (regarded as a two-dimensional array) and leaves the rest 0.

Finally,

```
char msg[] = "Syntax error on line %s\n";
```

shows a character array whose members are initialized with a string.

8.7 Type names

In two contexts (to specify type conversions explicitly by means of a cast, and as an argument of `sizeof`) it is desired to supply the name of a data type. This is

accomplished using a "type name," which in essence is a declaration for an object of that type which omits the name of the object.

> *type-name:*
> > *type-specifier abstract-declarator*
>
> *abstract-declarator:*
> > *empty*
> > (*abstract-declarator*)
> > * *abstract-declarator*
> > *abstract-declarator* ( )
> > *abstract-declarator* [*constant-expression*_{opt}]

To avoid ambiguity, in the construction

> (*abstract-declarator*)

the abstract-declarator is required to be non-empty. Under this restriction, it is possible to identify uniquely the location in the abstract-declarator where the identifier would appear if the construction were a declarator in a declaration. The named type is then the same as the type of the hypothetical identifier. For example,

```
int
int *
int *[3]
int (*)[3]
int *()
int (*)()
```

name respectively the types "integer," "pointer to integer," "array of 3 pointers to integers," "pointer to an array of 3 integers," "function returning pointer to integer," and "pointer to function returning an integer."

8.8 Typedef

Declarations whose "storage class" is `typedef` do not define storage, but instead define identifiers which can be used later as if they were type keywords naming fundamental or derived types.

> *typedef-name:*
> > *identifier*

Within the scope of a declaration involving `typedef`, each identifier appearing as part of any declarator therein become syntactically equivalent to the type keyword naming the type associated with the identifier in the way described in §8.4. For example, after

```
typedef int MILES, *KLICKSP;
typedef struct ( double re, im;) complex;
```

the constructions

```
MILES distance;
extern KLICKSP metricp;
complex z, *zp;
```

are all legal declarations; the type of `distance` is `int`, that of `metricp` is "pointer to `int`," and that of `z` is the specified structure. `zp` is a pointer to such a structure.

`typedef` does not introduce brand new types, only synonyms for types which could be specified in another way. Thus in the example above `distance` is considered to have exactly the same type as any other `int` object.

9. Statements

Except as indicated, statements are executed in sequence.

9.1 Expression statement

Most statements are expression statements, which have the form

> *expression* ;

Usually expression statements are assignments or function calls.

9.2 Compound statement, or block

So that several statements can be used where one is expected, the compound statement (also, and equivalently, called "block") is provided:

> *compound-statement:*
>   { *declaration-list$_{opt}$ statement-list$_{opt}$* }
>
> *declaration-list:*
>   *declaration*
>   *declaration declaration-list*
>
> *statement-list:*
>   *statement*
>   *statement statement-list*

If any of the identifiers in the declaration-list were previously declared, the outer declaration is pushed down for the duration of the block, after which it resumes its force.

Any initializations of `auto` or `register` variables are performed each time the block is entered at the top. It is currently possible (but a bad practice) to transfer into a block; in that case the initializations are not performed. Initializations of `static` variables are performed only once when the program begins execution. Inside a block, `extern` declarations do not reserve storage so initialization is not permitted.

9.3 Conditional statement

The two forms of the conditional statement are

> `if` (*expression*) *statement*
> `if` (*expression*) *statement* `else` *statement*

In both cases the expression is evaluated and if it is non-zero, the first substatement is executed. In the second case the second substatement is executed if the expression is 0. As usual the "else" ambiguity is resolved by connecting an `else` with the last encountered `else`-less `if`.

9.4 While statement

The `while` statement has the form

> `while` (*expression*) *statement*

The substatement is executed repeatedly so long as the value of the expression remains non-zero. The test takes place before each execution of the statement.

9.5 Do statement

The do statement has the form

> `do` *statement* `while` (*expression*) ;

The substatement is executed repeatedly until the value of the expression becomes zero. The test takes place after each execution of the statement.

9.6 For statement

The `for` statement has the form

> `for` (*expression-1$_{opt}$* ; *expression-2$_{opt}$* ; *expression-3$_{opt}$*) *statement*

This statement is equivalent to

> *expression-1* ;
> `while` (*expression-2*) {
>   *statement*
>   *expression-3* ;
> }

Thus the first expression specifies initialization for the loop; the second specifies a test, made before each iteration, such that the loop is exited when the expression becomes 0; the third expression often specifies an incrementation which is performed after each iteration.

Any or all of the expressions may be dropped. A missing *expression-2* makes the implied `while` clause equivalent to `while(1)`; other missing expressions are simply dropped from the expansion above.

9.7 Switch statement

The `switch` statement causes control to be transferred to one of several statements depending on the value of an expression. It has the form

switch (*expression*) *statement*

The usual arithmetic conversion is performed on the expression, but the result must be `int`. The statement is typically compound. Any statement within the statement may be labeled with one or more case prefixes as follows:

case *constant-expression* :

where the constant expression must be `int`. No two of the case constants in the same switch may have the same value. Constant expressions are precisely defined in §15.

There may also be at most one statement prefix of the form

default :

When the `switch` statement is executed, its expression is evaluated and compared with each case constant. If one of the case constants is equal to the value of the expression, control is passed to the statement following the matched case prefix. If no case constant matches the expression, and if there is a `default` prefix, control passes to the prefixed statement. If no case matches and if there is no `default` then none of the statements in the switch is executed.

`case` and `default` prefixes in themselves do not alter the flow of control, which continues unimpeded across such prefixes. To exit from a switch, see `break`, §9.8.

Usually the statement that is the subject of a switch is compound. Declarations may appear at the head of this statement, but initializations of automatic or register variables are ineffective.

9.8 Break statement

The statement

break ;

causes termination of the smallest enclosing `while`, `do`, `for`, or `switch` statement; control passes to the statement following the terminated statement.

9.9 Continue statement

The statement

continue ;

causes control to pass to the loop-continuation portion of the smallest enclosing `while`, `do`, or `for` statement; that is to the end of the loop. More precisely, in each of the statements

```
while (...) {        do {              for (...) {
    ...                  ...               ...
contin: ;            contin: ;         contin: ;
}                    } while (...);    }
```

a `continue` is equivalent to `goto contin`. (Following the `contin:` is a null statement, §9.13.)

9.10 Return statement

A function returns to its caller by means of the `return` statement, which has one of the forms

```
return ;
return expression ;
```

In the first case the returned value is undefined. In the second case, the value of the expression is returned to the caller of the function. If required, the expression is converted, as if by assignment, to the type of the function in which it appears. Flowing off the end of a function is equivalent to a return with no returned value.

9.11 Goto statement

Control may be transferred unconditionally by means of the statement

```
goto identifier ;
```

The identifier must be a label (§9.12) located in the current function.

9.12 Labeled statement

Any statement may be preceded by label prefixes of the form

```
identifier :
```

which serve to declare the identifier as a label. The only use of a label is as a target of a `goto`. The scope of a label is the current function, excluding any sub-blocks in which the same identifier has been redeclared. See §11.

9.13 Null statement

The null statement has the form

A null statement is useful to carry a label just before the) of a compound statement or to supply a null body to a looping statement such as `while`.

10. External definitions

A C program consists of a sequence of external definitions. An external definition declares an identifier to have storage class `extern` (by default) or perhaps `static`, and a specified type. The type-specifier (§8.2) may also be empty, in which case the type is taken to be `int`. The scope of external definitions persists to the end of the file in which they are declared just as the effect of declarations persists to the end of a block. The syntax of external definitions is the same as that of all declarations, except that only at this level may the code for functions be given.

10.1 External function definitions

Function definitions have the form

> *function-definition:*
>   *decl-specifiers*$_{opt}$ *function-declarator function-body*

The only sc-specifiers allowed among the decl-specifiers are `extern` or `static`; see §11.2 for the distinction between them. A function declarator is similar to a declarator for a "function returning ..." except that it lists the formal parameters of the function being defined.

> *function-declarator:*
>   *declarator (parameter-list*$_{opt}$ *)*

> *parameter-list:*
>   *identifier*
>   *identifier , parameter-list*

The function-body has the form

function-body:
    declaration-list compound-statement

The identifiers in the parameter list, and only those identifiers, may be declared in the declaration list. Any identifiers whose type is not given are taken to be `int`. The only storage class which may be specified is `register`; if it is specified, the corresponding actual parameter will be copied, if possible, into a register at the outset of the function.

A simple example of a complete function definition is

```
int max(a, b, c)
int a, b, c;
{
        int m;

        m = (a > b) ? a : b;
        return((m > c) ? m : c);
}
```

Here `int` is the type-specifier; `max(a, b, c)` is the function-declarator; `int a, b, c;` is the declaration-list for the formal parameters; `{ ... }` is the block giving the code for the statement.

C converts all `float` actual parameters to `double`, so formal parameters declared `float` have their declaration adjusted to read `double`. Also, since a reference to an array in any context (in particular as an actual parameter) is taken to mean a pointer to the first element of the array, declarations of formal parameters declared "array of ..." are adjusted to read "pointer to ...". Finally, because structures, unions and functions cannot be passed to a function, it is useless to declare a formal parameter to be a structure, union or function (pointers to such objects are of course permitted).

10.2 External data definitions

An external data definition has the form

data-definition:
    declaration

The storage class of such data may be `extern` (which is the default) or `static`, but not `auto` or `register`.

11. Scope rules

A C program need not all be compiled at the same time: the source text of the program may be kept in several files, and precompiled routines may be loaded from libraries. Communication among the functions of a program may be carried out both through explicit calls and through manipulation of external data.

Therefore, there are two kinds of scope to consider: first, what may be called the *lexical scope* of an identifier, which is essentially the region of a program during which it may be used without drawing "undefined identifier" diagnostics; and second, the scope associated with external identifiers, which is characterized by the rule that references to the same external identifier are references to the same object.

11.1 Lexical scope

The lexical scope of identifiers declared in external definitions persists from the definition through the end of the source file in which they appear. The lexical scope of identifiers which are formal parameters persists through the function with which they are associated. The lexical scope of identifiers declared at the head of blocks persists until the end of the block. The lexical scope of labels is the whole of the function in which they appear.

Because all references to the same external identifier refer to the same object (see §11.2) the compiler checks all declarations of the same external identifier for compatibility; in effect their scope is increased to the whole file in which they appear.

In all cases, however, if an identifier is explicitly declared at the head of a block,

including the block constituting a function, any declaration of that identifier outside the block is suspended until the end of the block.

Remember also (§8.5) that identifiers associated with ordinary variables on the one hand and those associated with structure and union members and tags on the other form two disjoint classes which do not conflict. Members and tags follow the same scope rules as other identifiers. `typedef` names are in the same class as ordinary identifiers. They may be redeclared in inner blocks, but an explicit type must be given in the inner declaration:

```
typedef float distance;
...
(
        auto int distance;
...
```

The `int` must be present in the second declaration, or it would be taken to be a declaration with no declarators and type `distance`†.

11.2 Scope of externals

If a function refers to an identifier declared to be `extern`, then somewhere among the files or libraries constituting the complete program there must be an external definition for the identifier. All functions in a given program which refer to the same external identifier refer to the same object, so care must be taken that the type and size specified in the definition are compatible with those specified by each function which references the data.

The appearance of the `extern` keyword in an external definition indicates that storage for the identifiers being declared will be allocated in another file. Thus in a multi-file program, an external data definition without the `extern` specifier must appear in exactly one of the files. Any other files which wish to give an external definition for the identifier must include the `extern` in the definition. The identifier can be initialized only in the declaration where storage is allocated.

Identifiers declared `static` at the top level in external definitions are not visible in other files. Functions may be declared `static`.

12. Compiler control lines

The C compiler contains a preprocessor capable of macro substitution, conditional compilation, and inclusion of named files. Lines beginning with # communicate with this preprocessor. These lines have syntax independent of the rest of the language; they may appear anywhere and have effect which lasts (independent of scope) until the end of the source program file.

12.1 Token replacement

A compiler-control line of the form

> #define *identifier token-string*

(note: no trailing semicolon) causes the preprocessor to replace subsequent instances of the identifier with the given string of tokens. A line of the form

> #define *identifier*(*identifier* , ... , *identifier*) *token-string*

where there is no space between the first identifier and the (, is a macro definition with arguments. Subsequent instances of the first identifier followed by a (, a sequence of tokens delimited by commas, and a) are replaced by the token string in the definition. Each occurrence of an identifier mentioned in the formal parameter list of the definition is replaced by the corresponding token string from the call. The actual arguments in the call are token strings separated by commas; however commas in quoted strings or protected by parentheses do not separate arguments. The number of formal and actual parameters must be the same. Text inside a string or a character constant is not subject to replacement.

---

†It is agreed that the ice is thin here.

In both forms the replacement string is rescanned for more defined identifiers. In both forms a long definition may be continued on another line by writing \ at the end of the line to be continued.

This facility is most valuable for definition of "manifest constants," as in

```
#define TABSIZE 100

int table[TABSIZE];
```

A control line of the form

#undef *identifier*

causes the identifier's preprocessor definition to be forgotten.

12.2 File inclusion

A compiler control line of the form

#include *"filename"*

causes the replacement of that line by the entire contents of the file *filename*. The named file is searched for first in the directory of the original source file, and then in a sequence of standard places. Alternatively, a control line of the form

#include *<filename>*

searches only the standard places, and not the directory of the source file.

#include's may be nested.

12.3 Conditional compilation

A compiler control line of the form

#if *constant-expression*

checks whether the constant expression (see §15) evaluates to non-zero. A control line of the form

#ifdef *identifier*

checks whether the identifier is currently defined in the preprocessor; that is, whether it has been the subject of a #define control line. A control line of the form

#ifndef *identifier*

checks whether the identifier is currently undefined in the preprocessor.

All three forms are followed by an arbitrary number of lines, possibly containing a control line

#else

and then by a control line

#endif

If the checked condition is true then any lines between #else and #endif are ignored. If the checked condition is false then any lines between the test and an #else or, lacking an #else, the #endif, are ignored.

These constructions may be nested.

12.4 Line control

For the benefit of other preprocessors which generate C programs, a line of the form

#line *constant identifier*

causes the compiler to believe, for purposes of error diagnostics, that the line number of the next source line is given by the constant and the current input file is named by the identifier. If the identifier is absent the remembered file name does not change.

13. Implicit declarations

It is not always necessary to specify both the storage class and the type of identifiers in a declaration. The storage class is supplied by the context in external definitions and in declarations of formal parameters and structure members. In a declaration inside a function, if a storage class but no type is given, the identifier is assumed to be `int`; if a type but no storage class is indicated, the identifier is assumed to be `auto`. An exception to the latter rule is made for functions, since `auto` functions are meaningless (C being incapable of compiling code into the stack); if the type of an identifier is "function returning ...", it is implicitly declared to be `extern`.

In an expression, an identifier followed by (and not already declared is contextually declared to be "function returning `int`".

14. Types revisited

This section summarizes the operations which can be performed on objects of certain types.

14.1 Structures and unions

There are only two things that can be done with a structure or union: name one of its members (by means of the `.` operator); or take its address (by unary `&`). Other operations, such as assigning from or to it or passing it as a parameter, draw an error message. In the future, it is expected that these operations, but not necessarily others, will be allowed.

§7.1 says that in a direct or indirect structure reference (with `.` or `->`) the name on the right must be a member of the structure named or pointed to by the expression on the left. To allow an escape from the typing rules, this restriction is not firmly enforced by the compiler. In fact, any lvalue is allowed before `.`, and that lvalue is then assumed to have the form of the structure of which the name on the right is a member. Also, the expression before a `->` is required only to be a pointer or an integer. If a pointer, it is assumed to point to a structure of which the name on the right is a member. If an integer, it is taken to be the absolute address, in machine storage units, of the appropriate structure.

Such constructions are non-portable.

14.2 Functions

There are only two things that can be done with a function: call it, or take its address. If the name of a function appears in an expression not in the function-name position of a call, a pointer to the function is generated. Thus, to pass one function to another, one might say

```
int f();
...
g(f);
```

Then the definition of g might read

```
g(funcp)
int (*funcp)();
{
    ...
    (*funcp)();
    ...
}
```

Notice that f must be declared explicitly in the calling routine since its appearance in g(f) was not followed by (.

14.3 Arrays, pointers, and subscripting

Every time an identifier of array type appears in an expression, it is converted into a pointer to the first member of the array. Because of this conversion, arrays are not lvalues. By definition, the subscript operator [] is interpreted in such a way that E1[E2] is identical to *((E1)+(E2)). Because of the conversion rules which

apply to +, if E1 is an array and E2 an integer, then E1 [E2] refers to the E2-th member of E1. Therefore, despite its asymmetric appearance, subscripting is a commutative operation.

A consistent rule is followed in the case of multi-dimensional arrays. If E is an n-dimensional array of rank $i \times j \times \cdots \times k$, then E appearing in an expression is converted to a pointer to an $(n-1)$-dimensional array with rank $j \times \cdots \times k$. If the $\star$ operator, either explicitly or implicitly as a result of subscripting, is applied to this pointer, the result is the pointed-to $(n-1)$-dimensional array, which itself is immediately converted into a pointer.

For example, consider

```
int x[3] [5];
```

Here x is a 3×5 array of integers. When x appears in an expression, it is converted to a pointer to (the first of three) 5-membered arrays of integers. In the expression x[i], which is equivalent to $\star$ (x+i), x is first converted to a pointer as described; then i is converted to the type of x, which involves multiplying i by the length the object to which the pointer points, namely 5 integer objects. The results are added and indirection applied to yield an array (of 5 integers) which in turn is converted to a pointer to the first of the integers. If there is another subscript the same argument applies again; this time the result is an integer.

It follows from all this that arrays in C are stored row-wise (last subscript varies fastest) and that the first subscript in the declaration helps determine the amount of storage consumed by an array but plays no other part in subscript calculations.

14.4 Explicit pointer conversions

Certain conversions involving pointers are permitted but have implementation-dependent aspects. They are all specified by means of an explicit type-conversion operator, §§7.2 and 8.7.

A pointer may be converted to any of the integral types large enough to hold it. Whether an int or long is required is machine dependent. The mapping function is also machine dependent, but is intended to be unsurprising to those who know the addressing structure of the machine. Details for some particular machines are given below.

An object of integral type may be explicitly converted to a pointer. The mapping always carries an integer converted from a pointer back to the same pointer, but is otherwise machine dependent.

A pointer to one type may be converted to a pointer to another type. The resulting pointer may cause addressing exceptions upon use if the subject pointer does not refer to an object suitably aligned in storage. It is guaranteed that a pointer to an object of a given size may be converted to a pointer to an object of a smaller size and back again without change.

For example, a storage-allocation routine might accept a size (in bytes) of an object to allocate, and return a char pointer; it might be used in this way.

```
extern char *alloc();
double *dp;

dp = (double *) alloc(sizeof(double));
*dp = 22.0 / 7.0;
```

alloc must ensure (in a machine-dependent way) that its return value is suitable for conversion to a pointer to double; then the *use* of the function is portable.

The pointer representation on the PDP-11 corresponds to a 16-bit integer and is measured in bytes. chars have no alignment requirements; everything else must have an even address.

On the Honeywell 6000, a pointer corresponds to a 36-bit integer; the word part is in the left 18 bits, and the two bits that select the character in a word just to their right. Thus char pointers are measured in units of 2^{16} bytes; everything else is measured in units of 2^{18} machine words. double quantities and aggregates containing them must lie on an even word address (0 mod 2^{19}).

The IBM 370 and the Interdata 8/32 are similar. On both, addresses are meas-

ured in bytes; elementary objects must be aligned on a boundary equal to their length, so pointers to short must be 0 mod 2, to int and float 0 mod 4, and to double 0 mod 8. Aggregates are aligned on the strictest boundary required by any of their constituents.

15. Constant expressions

In several places C requires expressions which evaluate to a constant: after case, as array bounds, and in initializers. In the first two cases, the expression can involve only integer constants, character constants, and sizeof expressions, possibly connected by the binary operators

$$+ \quad - \quad * \quad / \quad \% \quad \& \quad | \quad \wedge \quad << \quad >> \quad == \quad != \quad < \quad > \quad <= \quad >=$$

or by the unary operators

$$- \quad \sim$$

or by the ternary operator

$$? :$$

Parentheses can be used for grouping, but not for function calls.

More latitude is permitted for initializers; besides constant expressions as discussed above, one can also apply the unary & operator to external or static objects, and to external or static arrays subscripted with a constant expression. The unary & can also be applied implicitly by appearance of unsubscripted arrays and functions. The basic rule is that initializers must evaluate either to a constant or to the address of a previously declared external or static object plus or minus a constant.

16. Portability considerations

Certain parts of C are inherently machine dependent. The following list of potential trouble spots is not meant to be all-inclusive, but to point out the main ones.

Purely hardware issues like word size and the properties of floating point arithmetic and integer division have proven in practice to be not much of a problem. Other facets of the hardware are reflected in differing implementations. Some of these, particularly sign extension (converting a negative character into a negative integer) and the order in which bytes are placed in a word, are a nuisance that must be carefully watched. Most of the others are only minor problems.

The number of register variables that can actually be placed in registers varies from machine to machine, as does the set of valid types. Nonetheless, the compilers all do things properly for their own machine; excess or invalid register declarations are ignored.

Some difficulties arise only when dubious coding practices are used. It is exceedingly unwise to write programs that depend on any of these properties.

The order of evaluation of function arguments is not specified by the language. It is right to left on the PDP-11, left to right on the others. The order in which side effects take place is also unspecified.

Since character constants are really objects of type int, multi-character character constants are permitted. The specific implementation is very machine dependent, however, because the order in which characters are assigned to a word varies from one machine to another.

Fields are assigned to words and characters to integers right-to-left on the PDP-11 and left-to-right on other machines. These differences are invisible to isolated programs which do not indulge in type punning (for example, by converting an int pointer to a char pointer and inspecting the pointed-to storage), but must be accounted for when conforming to externally-imposed storage layouts.

The language accepted by the various compilers differs in minor details. Most notably, the current PDP-11 compiler will not initialize structures containing bitfields, and does not accept a few assignment operators in certain contexts where the value of the assignment is used.

17. Anachronisms

Since C is an evolving language, certain obsolete constructions may be found in older programs. Although most versions of the compiler support such anachronisms, ultimately they will disappear, leaving only a portability problem behind.

Earlier versions of C used the form =*op* instead of *op*= for assignment operators. This leads to ambiguities, typified by

    x=-1

which actually decrements x since the = and the − are adjacent, but which might easily be intended to assign −1 to **x**.

The syntax of initializers has changed: previously, the equals sign that introduces an initializer was not present, so instead of

    int   x   = 1;

one used

    int   x   1;

The change was made because the initialization

    int   f   (1+2)

resembles a function declaration closely enough to confuse the compilers.

18. Syntax Summary

This summary of C syntax is intended more for aiding comprehension than as an exact statement of the language.

18.1 Expressions

The basic expressions are:

> *expression:*
> > *primary*
> > ⋆ *expression*
> > & *expression*
> > − *expression*
> > ! *expression*
> > ˜ *expression*
> > ++ *lvalue*
> > −− *lvalue*
> > *lvalue* ++
> > *lvalue* −−
> > sizeof *expression*
> > (*type-name*) *expression*
> > *expression binop expression*
> > *expression* ? *expression* : *expression*
> > *lvalue asgnop expression*
> > *expression* , *expression*

> *primary:*
> > *identifier*
> > *constant*
> > *string*
> > (*expression*)
> > *primary* (*expression-list$_{opt}$*)
> > *primary* [*expression*]
> > *lvalue* . *identifier*
> > *primary* −> *identifier*

lvalue:
>   *identifier*
>   *primary* [*expression*]
>   *lvalue* . *identifier*
>   *primary* -> *identifier*
>   ⋆ *expression*
>   (*lvalue*)

The primary-expression operators

>   ()   []   .   ->

have highest priority and group left-to-right. The unary operators

>   ⋆   &   -   !   ~   ++   --   sizeof   (*type-name*)

have priority below the primary operators but higher than any binary operator, and group right-to-left. Binary operators and the conditional operator all group left-to-right, and have priority decreasing as indicated:

binop:
>   ⋆   /   %
>   +   -
>   >>   <<
>   <   >   <=   >=
>   ==   !=
>   &
>   ^
> |
>   &&
> ||
>   ?:

Assignment operators all have the same priority, and all group right-to-left.

asgnop:
>   =   +=   -=   ⋆=   /=   %=   >>=   <<=   &=   ^= |=

The comma operator has the lowest priority, and groups left-to-right.

18.2 Declarations

declaration:
>   decl-specifiers init-declarator-list*opt* ;

decl-specifiers:
>   *type-specifier decl-specifiers*_{*opt*}
>   *sc-specifier decl-specifiers*_{*opt*}

sc-specifier:
>   auto
>   static
>   extern
>   register
>   typedef

type-specifier:
>   char
>   short
>   int
>   long
>   unsigned
>   float
>   double
>   *struct-or-union-specifier*
>   *typedef-name*

init-declarator-list:
      init-declarator
      init-declarator , init-declarator-list

init-declarator:
      declarator initializer$_{opt}$

declarator:
      identifier
      (declarator)
      ★ declarator
      declarator ()
      declarator [constant-expression$_{opt}$ *]*

struct-or-union-specifier:
      struct *{ struct-decl-list }*
      struct *identifier { struct-decl-list }*
      struct *identifier*
      union *{ struct-decl-list }*
      union *identifier { struct-decl-list }*
      union *identifier*

struct-decl-list:
      struct-declaration
      struct-declaration struct-decl-list

struct-declaration:
      type-specifier struct-declarator-list ;

struct-declarator-list:
      struct-declarator
      struct-declarator , struct-declarator-list

struct-declarator:
      declarator
      declarator : constant-expression
      : constant-expression

initializer:
      = expression
      = { initializer-list }
      = { initializer-list , }

initializer-list:
      expression
      initializer-list , initializer-list
      { initializer-list }

type-name:
      type-specifier abstract-declarator

abstract-declarator:
      empty
      (abstract-declarator)
      ★ abstract-declarator
      abstract-declarator ()
      abstract-declarator [constant-expression$_{opt}$ *]*

typedef-name:
      identifier

18.3 Statements

compound-statement:
    { *declaration-list*$_{opt}$ *statement-list*$_{opt}$ }

declaration-list:
    declaration
    declaration declaration-list

statement-list:
    statement
    statement statement-list

statement:
    compound-statement
    expression ;
    `if` (*expression*) *statement*
    `if` (*expression*) *statement* `else` *statement*
    `while` (*expression*) *statement*
    `do` *statement* `while` (*expression*) ;
    `for` (*expression-1*$_{opt}$; *expression-2*$_{opt}$; *expression-3*$_{opt}$) *statement*
    `switch` (*expression*) *statement*
    `case` *constant-expression* :   *statement*
    `default` : *statement*
    `break` ;
    `continue` ;
    `return` ;
    `return` *expression* ;
    `goto` *identifier* ;
    identifier : *statement*
    ;

18.4 External definitions

program:
    external-definition
    external-definition program

external-definition:
    function-definition
    data-definition

function-definition:
    type-specifier$_{opt}$ *function-declarator function-body*

function-declarator:
    declarator (*parameter-list*$_{opt}$)

parameter-list:
    identifier
    identifier , *parameter-list*

function-body:
    type-decl-list function-statement

function-statement:
    { *declaration-list*$_{opt}$ *statement-list* }

data-definition:
    `extern`$_{opt}$ *type-specifier*$_{opt}$ *init-declarator-list*$_{opt}$;
    `static`$_{opt}$ *type-specifier*$_{opt}$ *init-declarator-list*$_{opt}$;

18.5 Preprocessor

```
#define identifier token-string
#define identifier( identifier ,  ...  , identifier ) token-string
#undef identifier
#include "filename"
#include <filename>
#if constant-expression
#ifdef identifier
#ifndef identifier
#else
#endif
#line constant identifier
```

MILITARY STANDARD

ADA PROGRAMMING LANGUAGE

DEPARTMENT OF DEFENSE

Washington, D. C. 20301

1. This Military Standard is approved for use by all Departments and Agencies of the Department of Defense. Only compilers which have been certified by the Ada Compiler Validation Facility (ACVF), shall be used in DoD systems.

2. Recommended corrections, additions or deletions should be addressed to: Ada Joint Program Office (AJPO),OUSD (R&E), Washington, D.C. 20301.

FOREWORD

This Military Standard describes the real-time programming language Ada, designed in accordance with the United States Department of Defense requirements for use in embedded systems. Such applications typically involve real-time constraints, fail-safe execution, control of non-standard input-output devices and management of concurrent activities. Ada is intended as a common high order programming language and has the mechanisms for distributing large libraries of application programs, packages, utilities and software development and maintenance tools. Machine and operating system independence is therefore emphasized throughout its design.

The Ada Language is the result of a multinational industry, academic and government effort to design a common high order language for programming embedded computer and real-time defense systems. This standard was developed, coordinated and approved under the authority of DoDD 5000.29, Management of Computer Resources in Major Defense Systems, and the DoD Management Steering Committee for Embedded Computer Resources. It is the intent of this document, although not in MIL-STD format, to serve DoD's immediate needs until a voluntary standard has been adopted by consensus.

Ada is the result of a collective effort to design a common language for programming large scale and real-time systems.

The common high order language program began in 1974. The DoD requirements were formalized in a series of documents which were extensively reviewed by the Services, industrial organizations, universities, and foreign military department. The culmination of that process was the Steelman Report to which the Ada language has been designed.

The Ada design team was led by Jean D. Ichbiah and has included Bernd Krieg-Brueckner, Brian A. Wichmann, Henry F. Ledgard, Jean-Claude Heliard, Jean-Raymond Abrial, John G. P. Barnes, Mike Woodger, Olivier Roubine, Paul N. Hilfinger and Robert Firth.

At various stages of the project, several people closely associated with the design team made major contributions. They include J.B. Goodenough, M.W. Davis, G. Ferran, L. MacLaren, E. Morel, I.R. Nassi, I.C. Pyle, S.A. Schuman, and S.C. Vestal.

Two parallel efforts that were started in the second phase of this design has a deep influence on the language. One is the development of a formal definition using denotational semantics, with the participation of V. Donzeau-Gouge, G. Kahn and B. Lang. The other is the design of a test translator with the participation of K. Ripken, P. Boullier, P. Cadiou, J. Holden, J. F. Hureras, R. G. Lange, and D. T. Cornhill. The entire effort benefitted from the dedicated assistance of Lyn Churchill and Marion Myers, and the effective technical support of B. Gravem and W. L. Heimerdinger. H. G. Schmitz served as program manager.

Over the three years spent on this project, five intense one-week design reviews were conducted with the participation of H. Harte, A. L. Hisgen, P. Knueven, M. Kronental, G. Seegmueller, V. Stehning, F. Belz, P. Cohen, R. Converse, K. Correll, R. Dewar, A. Evans, N. Habermann, J. Sammet, S. Squires, J. Teller, P. Wegner, and P. R. Wetherall.

Several persons has a constructive influence with their comments, criticisms, and suggestions. They include P. Brinch Hansen, G. Goos, C. A. R. Hoare, Mark Rain, W. A. Wulf, P. Belmont, E. Boebert, P. Bonnard, R. Brender, B. Brosgol, H. Clausen, M. Cox, T. Froggatt, H. Ganzinger, C. Hewitt, S. Kamin, J. L. Mansion, F. Minel, T. Phinney, J. Roehrich, V. Schneider, A. Singer, D. Slosberg, I. C. Wand, the reviewers of the group Ada-Europe, and the reviewers of the Tokyo study group assembled by N. Yoneda and K. Kakehi.

These reviews and comments, the numerous evaluation reports received at the end of the first and second phases, the more than nine hundred language issue reports, comments, and test and evaluation reports received from fifteen different countries during the third phase of the project, and the on-going work of the IFIP Working Group 2.4 on system implementation languages and that of LTPL-E of Purdue Europe all had a substantial influence on the final definition of Ada.

The Military Departments and Agencies have provided a broad base of support including funding, extensive reviews, and countless individual contributions by the members of the High Order Language Working Group and other interested personnel. In particular, William A. Whitaker provided leadership for the program during the formative stages. David A. Fisher was responsible for the successful development and iteration of language requirements documents, leading to the Steelman specification.

This language definition was developed by Cii Honeywell Bull and Honeywell Systems and Research Center under contract to the United States Department of Defense. William E. Carlson served as the technical representative of the Government and effectively coordinated the efforts of all participants in the Ada program.

This standard was originally published as "Reference Manual for the Ada Programming Language, July 1980."

Between July 1980 and October 1980 approximately 80 minor typographical errors were identified. Correction of these errors was authorized by the Interim Ada Configuration Control Board and the standard was reprinted with corrections as "Reference Manual for the Ada Programming Language, July 1980 (Reprinted November 1980)."

The photo composition process which produced the masters for the November 1980 reprinting introduced errors on seven pages (i, 3-12, 3-24, 4-2, 10-10, 14-6, C-3).

This MIL-STD has been prepared from the November 1980 masters with corrections made on the above seven pages.

MILITARY STANDARD

Copies of this standard required by contractors in connection with specific procurement functions should be obtained from the procuring activity or as directed by the contracting officer, from the DoD Single Stock Point, Commanding Officer, Naval Publications and Forms Center, 5801 Tabor Avenue, Philadelphia, PA 19120.

Military Coordinating Activity:

OUSD-SD

Preparing Activity:

Air Force - 02

(Project MISC-OD64)

Custodians:

Army - CR

Navy - NM

Air Force - 01

DCA-DC

NSA-NS

Table of Contents

Appendices

Index

1. Introduction

This report describes the programming language Ada, designed in accordance with the Steelman requirements of the United States Department of Defense. Overall, the Steelman requirements call for a language with considerable expressive power covering a wide application domain. As a result the language includes facilities offered by classical languages such as Pascal as well as facilities often found only in specialized languages. Thus the language is a modern algorithmic language with the usual control structures, and the ability to define types and subprograms. It also serves the need for modularity, whereby data, types, and subprograms can be packaged. It treats modularity in the physical sense as well, with a facility to support separate compilation.

In addition to these aspects, the language covers real time programming, with facilities to model parallel tasks and to handle exceptions. It also covers systems program applications. This requires access to system dependent parameters and precise control over the representation of data. Finally, both application level and machine level input-output are defined.

1.1 Design Goals

Ada was designed with three overriding concerns: a recognition of the importance of program reliability and maintenance, a concern for programming as a human activity, and efficiency.

The need for languages that promote reliability and simplify maintenance is well established. Hence emphasis was placed on program readability over ease of writing. For example, the rules of the language require that program variables be explicitly declared and that their type be specified. Since the type of a variable is invariant, compilers can ensure that operations on variables are compatible with the properties intended for objects of the type. Furthermore, error prone notations have been avoided, and the syntax of the language avoids the use of encoded forms in favor of more English-like constructs. Finally, the language offers support for separate compilation of program units in a way that facilitates program development and maintenance, and which provides the same degree of checking as within a unit.

Concern for the human programmer was also stressed during the design. Above all, an attempt was made to keep the language as small as possible, given the ambitious nature of the application domain. We have attempted to cover this domain with a small number of underlying concepts integrated in a consistent and systematic way. Nevertheless we have tried to avoid the pitfalls of excessive involution, and in the constant search for simpler designs we have tried to provide language constructs with an intuitive mapping on what the user will normally expect.

Like many other human activities, the development of programs is becoming more and more decentralized and distributed. Consequently the ability to assemble a program from independently produced software components has been a central idea in this design. The concepts of packages, of private types, and of generic program units are directly related to this idea, which has ramifications in many other aspects of the language.

No language can avoid the problem of efficiency. Languages that require overly elaborate compilers or that lead to the inefficient use of storage or execution time force these inefficiencies on all machines and on all programs. Every construct of the language was examined in the light of present implementation techniques. Any proposed construct whose implementation was unclear or required excessive machine resources was rejected.

Perhaps most importantly, none of the above goals was considered something that could be achieved after the fact. The design goals drove the entire design process from the beginning.

1.2 Language Summary

An Ada program is composed of one or more program units, which can be compiled separately. Program units may be subprograms (which define executable algorithms), packages (which define collections of entities), or tasks (which define concurrent computations). Each unit normally consists of two parts: a specification, containing the information that must be visible to other units, and a body, containing the implementation details, which need not be visible to other units.

This distinction of the specification and body, and the ability to compile units separately allow a program to be designed, written, and tested as a set of largely independent software components.

An Ada program will normally make use of a library of program units of general utility. The language provides means whereby individual organizations can construct their own libraries. To allow accurate control of program maintenance, the text of a separately compiled program unit must name the library units it requires.

Program units.

A subprogram is the basic unit for expressing an algorithm. There are two kinds of subprograms: procedures and functions. A procedure is the logical counterpart to a series of actions. For example, it may read in data, update variables, or produce some output. It may have parameters, to provide a controlled means of passing information between the procedure and the point of call. A function is the logical counterpart to the computation of a value. It is similar to a procedure, but in addition will return a result.

A package is the basic unit for defining a collection of logically related entities. For example, a package can be used to define a common pool of data and types, a collection of related subprograms, or a set of type declarations and associated operations. Portions of a package can be hidden from the user, thus allowing access only to the logical properties expressed by the package specification.

A task is the basic unit for defining a sequence of actions that may be executed in parallel with other similar units. Parallel tasks may be implemented on multicomputers, multiprocessors, or with interleaved execution on a single processor. A task unit may define either a single executing task object or a task type defining similar task objects.

Declarations and Statements

The body of a program unit generally contains two parts: a declarative part, which defines the logical entities to be used in the program unit, and a sequence of statements, which defines the execution of the program unit.

The declarative part associates names with declared entities. For example, a name may denote a type, a constant, a variable, or an exception. A declarative part also introduces the names and parameters of other nested subprograms, packages, and tasks to be used in the program unit.

The sequence of statements describes a sequence of actions that are to be performed. The statements are executed in succession (unless an exit, return, or goto statement, or the raising of an exception causes execution to continue from another place).

An assignment statement changes the value of a variable. A procedure call invokes execution of a procedure after associating any arguments provided at the call with the corresponding formal parameters of the subprogram.

Case statements and if statements allow the selection of an enclosed sequence of statements based on the value of an expression or on the value of a condition.

The basic iterative mechanism in the language is the loop statement. A loop statement specifies that a sequence of statements is to be executed repeatedly until an iteration clause is completed or an exit statement is encountered.

A block comprises a sequence of statements preceded by the declaration of local entities used by the statements.

Certain statements are only applicable to tasks. A delay statement delays the execution of a task for a specified duration. An entry call is written as a procedure call; it specifies that the task issuing the call is ready for a rendezvous with another task that has this entry. The called task is ready to accept the entry call when its execution reaches a corresponding accept statement, which specifies the actions then to be performed. After completion of the rendezvous, both the calling task and the task having the entry may continue their execution in parallel. A select statement allows a selective wait for one of several alternative rendezvous. Other forms of the select statement allow conditional or timed entry calls.

Execution of a program unit may lead to exceptional situations in which normal program execution cannot continue. For example, an arithmetic computation may exceed the maximum allowed value of a number, or an attempt may be made to access an array component by using an incorrect index value. To deal with these situations, the statements of a program unit can be textually followed by exception handlers describing the actions to be taken when the exceptional situation arises. Exceptions can be raised explicitly by a raise statement.

Data Types

Every object in the language has a type which characterizes a set of values and a set of applicable operations. There are four classes of types: scalar types (comprising enumeration and numeric types), composite types, access types, and private types.

An enumeration type defines an ordered set of distinct enumeration literals, for example a list of states or an alphabet of characters. The enumeration types BOOLEAN and CHARACTER are predefined.

Numeric types provide a means of performing exact or approximate computations. Exact computations use integer types, which denote sets of consecutive integers. Approximate computations use either fixed point types, with absolute bound on the error, or floating point types, with relative bound on the error. The numeric types INTEGER and DURATION are predefined.

Composite types allow definitions of structured objects with related components. The composite types in the language provide for arrays and records. An array is an object with indexed components of the same type. A record is an object with named components of possibly different types.

A record may have distinguished components called discriminants. Alternative record structures that depend on the values of discriminants can be defined within a record type.

Access types allow the construction of linked data structures created by the execution of allocators. They allow several variables of an access type to designate the same object, and components of one object to designate the same or other objects. Both the elements in such a linked data structure and their relation to other elements can be altered during program execution.

Private types can be defined in a package that conceals irrelevant structural details. Only the logically necessary properties (including any discriminants) are made visible to the users of such types.

The concept of a type is refined by the concept of a subtype, whereby a user can constrain the set of allowed values in a type. Subtypes can be used to define subranges of scalar types, arrays with a limited set of index values, and records and private types with particular discriminant values.

Other Facilities

Representation specifications can be used to specify the mapping between data types and features of an underlying machine. For example, the user can specify that objects of a given type must be represented with a specified number of bits, or that the components of a record are to be represented in a specified storage layout. Other features allow the controlled use of low level, non portable, or implementation dependent aspects, including the direct insertion of machine code.

Input-output is defined in the language by means of predefined library packages. Facilities are provided for input-output of values of user-defined as well as of predefined types. Standard means of representing values in display form are also provided.

Finally the language provides a powerful means of parameterization of program units, called generic program units. The generic parameters can be types and subprograms (as well as objects) and so allow general algorithms to be applied to all types of a given class.

1.3 Sources

A continual difficulty in language design is that one must both identify the capabilities required by the application domain and design language features that provide these capabilities.

The difficulty existed in this design, although to a much lesser degree than usual because of the Steelman requirements. These requirements often simplified the design process by permitting us to concentrate on the design of a given system satisfying a well defined set of capabilities, rather than on the definition of the capabilities themselves.

Another significant simplification of our design work resulted from earlier experience acquired by several successful Pascal derivatives developed with similar goals. These are the languages Euclid, Lis, Mesa, Modula, and Sue. Many of the key ideas and syntactic forms developed in these languages have a counterpart in Ada. We may say that whereas these previous designs could be considered as genuine research efforts, the language Ada is the result of a project in language design engineering, in an attempt to develop a product that represents the current state of the art.

Several existing languages such as Algol 68 and Simula and also recent research languages such as Alphard and Clu, influenced this language in several respects, although to a lesser degree than the Pascal family.

Finally, the evaluation reports received on the initial formulation of the Green language, the Red, Blue and Yellow language proposals, the language reviews that took place at different stages of this project, and the more than nine hundred reports received from fifteen different countries on the preliminary definition of Ada, all had a significant impact on the final definition of the language.

1.4 Syntax Notation

The context-free syntax of the language is described using a simple variant of Backus-Naur Form. In particular,

(a) Lower case words, some containing embedded underscores, denote syntactic categories, for example

    adding_operator

(b) Boldface words denote reserved words, for example

    array

(c) Square brackets enclose optional items, for example

    end [identifier];

(d) Braces enclose a repeated item. The item may appear zero or more times. Thus an identifier list is defined by

    identifier_list ::= identifier {, identifier}

(e) A vertical bar separates alternative items, unless it occurs immediately after an opening brace, in which case it stands for itself:

    letter_or_digit ::= letter | digit
    component_association ::= [choice {| choice} =>] expression

(f) Any syntactic category prefixed by an italicized word and an underscore is equivalent to the unprefixed corresponding category name. The prefix is intended to convey some semantic information. For example *type*_name and *task*_name are both equivalent to the category name.

In addition, the syntax rules describing structured constructs are presented in a form that corresponds to the recommended paragraphing. For example, an if statement is defined as

```
if_statement ::=
    if condition then
        sequence_of_statements
    | elsif condition then
        sequence_of_statements}
    [ else
        sequence_of_statements]
    end if;
```

1.5 Structure of the Reference Manual

This reference manual contains fourteen chapters, six appendices and an index. Each chapter is divided into sections that have a common structure. Each section introduces its subject, gives any necessary syntax equations, and describes the semantics of the corresponding language constructs. Examples, notes, and references, when present, follow in this order.

Examples are meant to illustrate the possible forms of the constructs described. Notes are to emphasize consequences of the rules described in the section or elsewhere. References refer to related sections. Neither examples, nor notes, nor references are part of the standard definition of the Ada language. In addition the appendices D (glossary), F (Implementation dependent characteristics), and any section whose title starts by "example" do not form part of the standard definition.

1.6 Classification of Errors

The language recognizes three categories of errors.

(1) Errors that must be detected at compilation time by every Ada compiler. These errors correspond to any violation of a rule of the language, other than those corresponding to (2) or (3) below. Any rule that uses the terms *legal, allowed, must*, or *may only* belongs to this category.

(2) Errors that must be detected at run time. These are called exceptions. In certain situations compilers may give warning during compilation that an exception is certain to occur in every execution of the program.

(3) Finally the language specifies certain rules that must be obeyed by Ada programs, although Ada compilers are not required to check that such rules are not violated. For any error belonging to this category, the reference manual uses the word *erroneous* to qualify the corresponding programs. If an erroneous program is executed, its effect is unpredictable.

2. Lexical Elements

This chapter defines the lexical elements of the language.

2.1 Character Set

All language constructs may be represented with a basic graphic character set, which is subdivided as follows:

(a) upper case letters
A B C D E F G H I J K L M N O P Q R S T U V W X Y Z

(b) digits
0 1 2 3 4 5 6 7 8 9

(c) special characters
" # % & ' ( ) * + , - . / : ; < = > _ |

(d) the space character

The character set may be extended to include further characters from the 95 character *ASCII* graphics set. These are:

(e) lower case letters
a b c d e f g h i j k l m n o p q r s t u v w x y z

(f) other special characters
! $? @ [\ ] ^ ` { } ~

Every program may be converted into an equivalent program which uses only the basic character set. Any lower case letter is equivalent to the corresponding upper case letter, except within character strings and character literals; rules for the transliteration of strings into the basic character set appear in section 2.10.

References:

ascii package C, character literal 2.5, character string 2.6, transliteration 2.10.

2.2 Lexical Units and Spacing Conventions

A program is a sequence of lexical units; the partitioning of the sequence into lines and the spacing between lexical units does not affect the meaning of the program. The lexical units are identifiers (including reserved words), numeric literals, character literals, strings, delimiters and comments. A delimiter is either one of the following special characters in the basic character set

     & ' ( ) * + , - . / : ; < = > |

or one of the following compound symbols

     =>   ..   **   :=   /=   >=   <=   <<   >>   <>

Adjacent lexical units may be separated by spaces or by passage to a new line. An identifier or numeric literal must be separated in this way from an adjacent identifier or numeric literal. Spaces must not occur within lexical units, excepting strings, comments, and the space character literal. Each lexical unit must fit on one line.

Control characters of the *ASCII* set are used to effect this layout.

Any of carriage return, line feed, vertical tabulate, form feed, and only these, causes passage to a new line. Horizontal tabulate is allowed in comments. Otherwise no control character may occur within a lexical unit. Between lexical units horizontal tabulate is equivalent to a space, backspace is not allowed, and delete and null characters are ignored.

Note:

The number of lines produced by combinations of control characters is not prescribed. Thus carriage return terminates a lexical unit, whether or not a line feed follows it. Note that the double quote, double hyphen, and sharp sign are not delimiters; they are part of other lexical units.

References:

ascii package C, character literal 2.5, comment 2.7, identifier 2.3, numeric literal 2.4, reserved word 2.9, string 2.6

2.3 Identifiers

Identifiers are used as names (also as reserved words). Isolated underscore characters may be included. All characters, including underscores, are significant.

```
identifier ::=
    letter {[underscore] letter_or_digit}

letter_or_digit ::= letter | digit

letter ::= upper_case_letter | lower_case_letter
```

Note that identifiers differing only in the use of corresponding upper and lower case letters are considered as the same.

Examples:

COUNT	X	get_symbol	Ethelyn	Marion
SNOBOL_4	X1	PageCount	STORE_NEXT_ITEM	

References:

lower case letter 2.1, name 4.1, upper case letter 2.1

2.4 Numeric Literals

There are two classes of numeric literals: integer literals and real literals. Integer literals are the literals of the type *universal_integer*. Real literals are the literals of the type *universal_real*.

```
numeric_literal    ::= decimal_number | based_number

decimal_number ::= integer [.integer] [exponent]

integer      ::= digit {[underscore] digit}

exponent ::= E [+] integer | E - integer
```

Isolated underscore characters may be inserted between adjacent digits of a decimal number, but are not significant.

The conventional decimal notation is used. Real literals are distinguished by the presence of a decimal point. An exponent indicates the power of ten by which the preceding number is to be multiplied to obtain the value represented. An integer literal can have an exponent; the exponent must be positive or zero.

Examples:

12	0	123_456	1E6		--	integer literals
12.0	0.0	0.456	3.14159_26		--	real literals
1.34E-12	1.0E+6	--	real literals with exponent			

Note:

The exponent may be indicated by either an upper case E or a lower case e (see 2.1).

References:

universal_integer type 3.5.4, universal_real type 3.5.6

2.4.1 Based Numbers

Numbers may be represented with a base other than ten. Based numbers can have any base from 2 to 16.

    based_number ::=
       base # based_integer [.based_integer] # [exponent]

    base ::= integer

    based_integer ::=
       extended_digit {[underscore] extended_digit}

    extended_digit ::= digit | letter

Isolated underscore characters may be inserted between adjacent extended digits of a based number, but are not significant. An exponent indicates the power of the base by which the preceding number is to be multiplied to obtain the value represented. The base and the exponent are in decimal notation. For bases above ten, the extended digits include the letters A through F, with the conventional significance 10 through 15.

Examples:

    2#1111_1111#   16#FF#   -- integer literals of value 255
    16#E#E1   2#1110_0000#   -- integer literals of value 224
    16#F.FF#E+2   2#1.1111_1111_111#E11   -- real literals of value 4095.0

Note:

An extended digit that is a letter can be written either in lower case or in upper case.

2.5 Character Literals

A character literal is formed by enclosing one of the 95 *ASCII* graphic characters (including the space) between single quote characters.

Examples:

    'A'   '*'   '''   ' '

References:

ascii package C, character 2.1

2.6 Character Strings

A character string is a sequence of zero or more characters prefixed and terminated by the string bracket character.

> character_string ::= "{character}"

In order that arbitrary strings of characters may be represented, any included string bracket character must be written twice. The length of a string is the length of the sequence represented. Catenation must be used to represent strings longer than one line, and strings containing control characters.

Examples:

```
""                       -- an empty string
" "      "A"     """"     -- three strings of length 1

"characters such as $, % and } may appear in strings"

"FIRST PART OF A STRING THAT " &
"CONTINUES ON THE NEXT LINE"

"String containing" & ASCII.CR &   ASCII.LF & "Control characters"
```

References:

catenation 3.6.3 4.5.3, character 2.1

2.7 Comments

A comment starts with two hyphens and is terminated by the end of the line. It may only appear following a lexical unit or at the beginning or end of a program unit. Comments have no effect on the meaning of a program; their sole purpose is the enlightenment of the human reader.

Examples:

```
--   the last sentence above echoes the Algol 68 report

end;  --   processing of LINE is complete

--   a long comment may be split onto
--   two or more consecutive lines

----------------   the first two hyphens start the comment
```

References:

lexical unit 2.2, program unit 6 7 9

2.8 Pragmas

Pragmas are used to convey information to the compiler. A pragma begins with the reserved word
pragma followed by the name of the pragma, which distinguishes it from other pragmas.

```
pragma ::=
    pragma identifier [(argument {, argument})];

argument ::=
      [identifier =>] name
   |  [identifier =>] static_expression
```

Pragmas may appear before a program unit, or wherever a declaration or a statement may appear,
depending on the pragma. Some pragmas have arguments, which may involve identifiers visible at
the place of the pragma. The extent of the effect of a pragma depends on the pragma.

A pragma may be language defined or implementation defined. All language defined pragmas are
described in Appendix B. All implementation defined pragmas must be described in Appendix F. A
pragma whose identifier is not recognized by the compiler has no effect.

Examples:

```
pragma LIST(OFF);
pragma OPTIMIZE(TIME);
pragma INCLUDE("COMMONTEXT");
pragma INLINE(SETMASK);
pragma SUPPRESS(RANGE_CHECK, ON => INDEX);
```

References:

declaration 3.1, implementation defined pragma F, language defined pragma B, program unit 6 7 9,
reserved word 2.9, statement 5, static expression 4.9, visibility rules 8

2.9 Reserved Words

The identifiers listed below are called *reserved words* and are reserved for special significance in
the language. Declared identifiers may not be reserved words.   For readability of this manual, the
reserved words appear in lower case boldface.

abort	declare	generic	of	select
accept	delay	goto	or	separate
access	delta		others	subtype
all	digits	if	out	
and	do	in		task
array		is	package	terminate
at			pragma	then
	else		private	type
	elsif	limited	procedure	
	end	loop		
begin	entry		raise	use
body	exception		range	
	exit	mod	record	when
		rem		while
		new	renames	with
case	for	not	return	
constant	function	null	reverse	xor

2.10 Transliteration

A character string may contain characters not in the basic character set. A string containing such characters can be converted to a string written with the basic character set by using identifiers denoting these characters in catenated strings. Such identifiers are defined in the predefined package ASCII. Thus the string "AB$CD" could be written as "AB" & ASCII.DOLLAR & "CD". Similarly, the string "ABcd" with lower case letters could be written as "AB" & ASCII.LC_C & ASCII.LC_D.

The following replacements are allowed for characters that may not be available:

* the vertical bar character |, which appears on some terminals as a broken bar, may be replaced by the exclamation mark ! as a delimiter.

* the sharp character # may be replaced by the colon : throughout any based number.

* the double quote character " used as string bracket may be replaced by a percent character % at both ends of a string, provided that the string contains no double quote character. Any percent character within the string must then be written twice. A string which contains a double quote character can be represented using catenation and a name for that character.

Note:

The preferred character set is the one employed in the rest of this manual. It is recommended that use of these replacements be restricted to cases where the characters replaced are not available.

References:

ascii package C, based number 2.4.1, basic character set 2.1, character string 2.6, choice 3.7.3, identifier 2.3

3. Declarations and Types

This chapter describes the types in the language and the rules for declaring constants, variables, and named numbers.

3.1 Declarations

The language defines several forms of named entities. A named entity can be either a number, an enumeration literal, an object, a discriminant, a record component, a loop parameter, a type, a subtype, an attribute, a subprogram, a package, a task, an entry, a named block, a named loop, a labeled statement, an exception, or finally, a parameter of a subprogram, of an entry, or of a generic subprogram or package.

A declaration associates an identifier with a declared entity. Each identifier must be explicitly declared before it is used, excepting only labels, block identifiers, and loop identifiers; these are declared implicitly. There are several forms of declarations.

```
declaration  ::=
     object_declaration        | number_declaration
   | type_declaration          | subtype_declaration
   | subprogram_declaration    | package_declaration
   | task_declaration          | exception_declaration
   | renaming_declaration
```

A declaration may declare one or more entities. Discriminant declarations, component declarations, entry declarations, and parameter declarations occur as part of one of the above forms of declarations. Enumeration literals are declared by an enumeration type definition. A loop parameter is declared by an iteration clause. Attributes are predefined and cannot be declared.

The process by which a declaration achieves its effect is called the *elaboration* of the declaration. This process generally involves several successive actions:

- First, the identifier of a declared entity is *introduced* at the point of its first occurrence; it may *hide* other previously declared identifiers from then on (the rules defining visibility and hiding of identifiers are given in section 8.3).

- The second action is the elaboration of the declared entity. For all forms of declarations, except those of subprograms, packages, and tasks, an identifier can only be used as a *name* of a declared entity once the elaboration of the entity is completed. A subprogram, package, or task identifier can be used as a name of the corresponding entity as soon as the identifier is introduced, hence even within the declaration of the entity.

- The last action performed by the elaboration of an object declaration may be the initialization of the declared object (or objects).

Section 8
Programming Language Design Experience

One of the best ways to gain insight into the process of language design is to examine features of some recently designed languages in papers that include discussion of the design process, especially as to why certain features were incorporated into the respective languages. All of the languages described in this section have been designed and implemented within the past five years, each with somewhat different goals in mind.

CLU was the first language to incorporate the notion of data abstractions. In addition to that feature, CLU included numerous other design advances, among them the exception-handling facility described in the previous section and an abstraction mechanism for iteration. The paper by Liskov and colleagues describes the abstraction mechanisms of CLU, along with their design rationale.

Gypsy was designed by Don Good and colleagues to support the simultaneous specification and implementation of programs as a means to achieve verifiable software. Gypsy is intended primarily for realtime applications, such as communications systems. One of the interesting features of Gypsy is that it has no global variables and requires that all data be passed explicitly. Experience in the use of Gypsy has shown that the number of parameters passed between program units can be minimized through judicious use of structured variables.

Brinch Hansen's Concurrent Pascal is an extension of Pascal that incorporates data abstractions and monitors. It has been used to implement a well-structured operating system (Solo) for the PDP-11 operating system. The paper by Brinch Hansen describes those features of Concurrent Pascal that are extensions of Pascal.

PLAIN, designed by Wasserman and colleagues, is intended to support the systematic construction of interactive information systems, including string handling, data abstraction, and relational data base management facilities. Although based on Pascal, PLAIN addresses some of the trouble spots in Pascal, as Wasserman's paper explains.

Mesa, designed at Xerox Palo Alto Research Center, was intended as a system implementation language. Mesa has seen extensive use by the Xerox programmers to implement a variety of sophisticated systems. The paper by Geschke, Morris, and Satterthwaite describes some of that experience. It is particularly interesting to note those places where the Mesa programmers found it necessary to escape from the type checking requirements of the language and take advantage of loopholes.

The elaboration of an object declaration consists of the elaboration of the declared objects, followed by their explicit initialization, if any:

(a) For the elaboration of the declared objects, the identifiers of the list are first introduced; the type is then established by elaborating the corresponding array type definition or by evaluating any constraint in the subtype indication; objects of this type and named by the identifiers are then created; these objects are subject to any constraint resulting from either the subtype indication or the constrained array type definition. Finally, in the absence of an explicit initialization, if a default initial value exists for objects of the type or for some of their components, the corresponding default initializations are performed. In particular, for objects of types with discriminants, the default discriminant values are assigned to the corresponding discriminants unless the objects are constrained, in which case the discriminant values specified by the constraints are assigned.

(b) If an explicit initialization is specified in an object declaration, the corresponding expression is then evaluated and its value is assigned to each of the declared objects. This value must satisfy any constraint on the objects as for assignment statements. An explicit initialization overrides a default initialization (but of course an explicit initialization cannot modify a discriminant value of an object with a discriminant constraint).

An object is a constant if the reserved word **constant** appears in the object declaration or if it is a component of a constant array or of a constant record. The initial value of a constant cannot be modified; this value must be given in the constant declaration except in the case of a *deferred* constant (that is, a constant declared in the visible part of a package and whose type is a private type declared in the same visible part, as explained in section 7.4).

Objects that are not constant are called *variables*. The value of a variable is undefined after elaboration of the corresponding object declaration unless either the latter contains an explicit initialization, or a default initial value exists for objects of the type. A program whose result depends upon an undefined value is erroneous.

A number declaration introduces one or more identifiers naming a number defined by a *literal expression*, which involves only numeric literals, names of numeric literals, calls of the predefined function ABS, parenthesized literal expressions, and the predefined arithmetic operators (see section 4.10 for literal expression). A named number is of the type *universal_integer* if every numeric literal (or name of a numeric literal) contained in the literal expression is of this type; otherwise it is of the type *universal_real*.

Elaboration of an object declaration with either an explicit or a default initialization raises the exception CONSTRAINT_ERROR if the initial value fails to satisfy some constraint on the object.

Examples of variable declarations:

```
COUNT SUM      :  INTEGER;
SORTED         :  BOOLEAN := FALSE;
COLOR_TABLE    :  array (1 .. N) of COLOR;
OPTION         :  BIT_VECTOR(1 .. 10) := (OPTION'RANGE => TRUE);
```

Examples of constant declarations:

```
LIMIT          :  constant INTEGER := 10_000;
LOW_LIMIT      :  constant INTEGER := LIMIT / 10;
TOLERANCE      :  constant COEFFICIENT := DISPERSION(1.15);
NULL_KEY       :  constant KEY;  -- deferred initialization
```

Examples of number declarations:

```
PI                 :  constant := 3.14159_26536;   -- a real number
TWO_PI             :  constant := 2.0 * PI;        -- a real number
POWER_16           :  constant := 2**16;           -- the integer 65_536
ONE, UN, EINS      :  constant := 1;               -- three different names for 1
```

Notes:

Once an object is elaborated, its name can be used. In particular it can serve to form the names of attributes of the object. Such attributes can even appear in the expression defining the initial value of the object. In the above examples, the attribute OPTION'RANGE, denoting the range 1 .. 10, is used as a choice in the aggregate initializing the array OPTION.

The expression initializing a constant object may (but need not) be a static expression (see 4.9). In the above examples, LIMIT and LOW_LIMIT are initialized with static expressions, but TOLERANCE is not since it is initialized with the result of the call of a user defined function.

References:

arithmetic operator 4.5, assignment statement 5.2, component 3.6 3.7, constraint 3.3, default initial value 3.7 3.8, deferred constant 7.1, discriminant 3.7.1 7.1, discriminant constraint 3.7.2, elaboration 3.1 3.9, expression 4.4, formal parameter 6.2, generic program unit 12, literal expression 4.10, name 4.1, numeric literal 2.4, package visible part 7.2, private type definition 7.4 static expression 4.9, type definition definition 3.3, type definition mark 3.3, universal integer type 2.4 3.5.4, universal real type 2.4 3.5.6.

3.3 Type and Subtype Declarations

A type characterizes a set of values and a set of operations applicable to those values. The values are denoted either by literals or by aggregates of the type, and can be obtained as the result of operations.

There exist several classes of types. *Scalar* types are types whose values have no components; they comprise types defined by enumeration of their values, integer types, and real types. *Array* and *record* types are composite; their values consist of several component values. An *access* type is a type whose values provide access to other objects. Finally, there are *private* types where the set of possible values is well defined, but not known to the users of such types.

Record and private types may have special components called *discriminants* whose values distinguish alternative forms of values of one of these types. Discriminants are defined by a *discriminant part*. The possible discriminants of a private type are known to its users. Hence a private type is only known by its name, its discriminants if any, and the set of operations applicable to its values.

The set of possible values for an object of a given type can be restricted without changing the set of applicable operations. Such a restriction is called a *constraint* (the case of no restriction is also included). A value is said to belong to a *subtype* of a given type if it obeys such a constraint; the given type is called the *base type* of the subtype. A type is a subtype of itself; the base type of a type is the type itself.

Certain types may have *default initial values* defined for objects of the type or for some of their components.

Certain characteristics of types and subtypes, such as certain specific values and operations, are called *attributes* of the types and subtypes. Attributes are denoted by the form of names described in section 4.1.4.

```
type_declaration ::=
       type identifier [discriminant_part] is type_definition;
   | incomplete_type_declaration

type_definition ::=
       enumeration_type_definition  | integer_type_definition
   | real_type_definition          | array_type_definition
   | record_type_definition        | access_type_definition
   | derived_type_definition        | private_type_definition

subtype_declaration ::=
       subtype identifier is subtype_indication;

subtype_indication ::= type_mark [constraint]

type_mark ::= type_name | subtype_name

constraint ::=
       range_constraint   | accuracy_constraint
   | index_constraint     | discriminant_constraint
```

The elaboration of a type definition always produces a distinct type. For the elaboration of a type declaration, the type identifier is first introduced; elaboration of any discriminant part and of the type definition follow in this order. The type identifier can then serve as a name of the type resulting from the elaboration of the type definition and of the optional discriminant part.

The elaboration of certain forms of the type definitions for derived types, numeric types, and array types has the effect of specifying a constraint for a type defined by an underlying unconstrained type definition. The identifier introduced by a type declaration containing such a type definition is the name of a subtype of the (anonymous) unconstrained type.

For the elaboration of a subtype declaration the subtype identifier is first introduced; if there is a constraint in the subtype indication it is then evaluated, that is, any contained expression is evaluated. The subtype identifier can then serve as a name of the declared subtype. In the absence of a constraint in the subtype declaration, the subtype name is an alternative name to the type mark. If the subtype declaration includes a constraint, the subtype name is an abbreviation for the name of the base type of the type mark together with the constraint, with the meanings that they both have at the subtype declaration.

Whenever a constraint appears after a type mark in a subtype indication, the constraint imposed on the type mark must be compatible with any constraint already imposed by the type mark; the exception CONSTRAINT_ERROR is raised if this condition is not satisfied. Compatibility is defined for each form of constraint in the corresponding section (see 3.5, 3.5.7, 3.5.9, 3.6.1, 3.7.2, 3.8). An index constraint (or a discriminant constraint) may only be imposed on a type mark that does not already impose an index constraint (or a discriminant constraint).

Incomplete type declarations are used for the definition of recursive and mutually dependent access types. Recursion in type definitions is not allowed unless an intermediate access type is used (see 3.8).

Attribute:

For any type or subtype T, the following attribute is defined

T'BASE   The base type of T. This attribute can only be used to form the names of other attributes, for example T'BASE'FIRST.

Examples of type declarations:

```
type COLOR      is (WHITE, RED, YELLOW, GREEN, BLUE, BROWN, BLACK);
type COL_NUM is range 1 .. 72;
type TABLE      is array (1 .. 10) of INTEGER;
```

Examples of subtype declarations:

```
subtype RAINBOW    is COLOR range RED .. BLUE;
subtype RED_BLUE   is RAINBOW;
subtype SMALL_INT  is INTEGER range -10 .. 10;
subtype ZONE       is COL_NUM range 1 .. 6;
subtype SQUARE     is MATRIX(1 .. 10, 1 .. 10);
subtype MALE       is PERSON(SEX => M);
```

Notes:

Two type definitions always introduce two distinct types, even if they are textually identical. For example, the array type definitions given in the declarations of A and B below define distinct types.

```
A  : array(1 .. 10) of BOOLEAN;
B  : array(1 .. 10) of BOOLEAN;
```

On the other hand, C and D in the following declaration are of the same type, since only one type definition is given.

```
C, D : array(1 .. 10) of BOOLEAN;
```

A subtype declaration does not introduce a new type.

References:

access type 3.8, array type definition 3.6, constraint_error exception 11.1, derived type 3.4, discriminant 3.7.1, elaboration 3.1 3.9, enumeration type 3.5.1, identifier 2.3, incomplete type declaration 3.8, name 4.1, numeric type 3.5, private type definition 7.4, record type 3.7, scalar type 3.5

3.4 Derived Type Definitions

The elaboration of a derived type definition defines an unconstrained type deriving its characteristics from those of a *parent* type; it may further define a subtype obtained by imposing a constraint upon the unconstrained derived type. A derived type definition is only allowed in a type declaration. The identifier introduced by such a type declaration can be either the name of the derived type if unconstrained, or it can be the name of a subtype of the (anonymous) derived type.

```
derived_type_definition ::= new subtype_indication
```

The parent type is the base type of the subtype indicated after the reserved word **new**. If the subtype indication includes an explicit constraint, it is evaluated as part of the elaboration of the derived type definition. Such an explicit constraint, or in its absence any constraint already imposed by the type mark of the parent subtype, becomes associated with the type mark introduced by the derived type declaration (subject to the same rules of compatibility as described in section 3.3).

The characteristics of a derived type are as follows:

- The derived type belongs to the same class of types as the parent type (for example, the derived type is a record type if the parent type is).

- The set of possible values for the derived type is a copy of the set of possible values for the parent type. Explicit conversion of a value of the parent type into the corresponding value of the derived type is possible and vice versa (see 4.6). If a default initial value exists for the parent type, a corresponding initial value exists for the derived type.

- The notation for any literals or aggregates of the derived type is the same as for the parent type. Such literals and aggregates are said to be *overloaded*. The notation used to denote any component of objects of the derived type is the same as for the parent type.

- The same attributes are defined for the derived type as for the parent type. If the parent type is an access type, the parent and the derived type share the same collection. Any representation specification already elaborated for the parent type (consequently, not in the same declarative part) also applies to the derived type (see 13.1).

- Certain subprograms *applicable* to the parent type, that is, subprograms that have a parameter or result of the parent type (or of one of its subtypes) are derived by the derived type. These derived subprograms are implicitly declared at the place of the derived type definition but may be redefined in the same declaration list.

For a predefined type, the subprograms that are derived are the corresponding predefined operations. The subprograms derived by a derived type can be further derived if this type is used as parent type in another derived type definition. If a type is declared in a package specification, the subprograms applicable to the type and declared in the package specification are derived by any derived type definition given after the end of the package specification.

The specification of a derived subprogram is obtained by systematic replacement of the parent type by the unconstrained derived type in the specification of the subprogram applicable to the parent type; a type conversion to the derived type is applied to the bounds of any range constraint for a parameter of the parent type and to any default value of the parent type. Prior to this transformation any subtype of the parent type is first expanded into the corresponding base type (that is, the parent type) and any associated constraint.

The effect of a call of a derived subprogram is achieved by a call of the parent subprogram preceded by (implicit) conversion of any **in** and **in out** parameters to the parent type, and followed by (implicit) conversion of any **in out** parameters, **out** parameters, or function result to the derived type.

Example:

```
type MIDWEEK is new DAY range TUE .. THU;
```

Notes:

The above rules mean that a type declaration of the form

  type NEW_TYPE **is new** OLD_TYPE *constraint*;

where the *constraint* is compatible with those of OLD_TYPE, is equivalent to the succession of declarations:

  type *new_type* **is new** *base_type_of_*OLD_TYPE;
  subtype NEW_TYPE **is** *new_type constraint*;

where *new_type* is an identifier distinct from those of the program. Hence, the values and operations of the old type are derived by the new type, but objects of the new type must satisfy the added constraint. For example, the name MIDWEEK is the name of a subtype of an anonymous type derived from the type DAY.

The rule given in section 3.3, concerning the compatibility of a constraint imposed on a type mark with any constraint already imposed by the type mark, applies to the subtype indication given in a derived type definition. Note however that the constraint imposed on a parameter of a subprogram applicable to the parent type may be incompatible with the constraint of the derived type. In such a case all calls of the derived subprogram will raise the exception CONSTRAINT_ERROR.

References:

access type 3.8, aggregate 4.3, attribute 4.1.4, base type 3.3, constraint 3.3, declaration 3.1, elaboration 3.1 3.9, in parameter 6.2, in out parameter 6.2, literal 4.2, package specification 7.2, predefined operation C, predefined type C, representation specification 13.1, subprogram specification 6.1, subtype 3.3, subtype indication 3.3, type conversion 4.6, type mark 3.3

3.5 Scalar Types

Scalar types comprise discrete types and real types. All scalar types are ordered. A range constraint specifies a subset of values of a scalar type or subtype. Discrete types are the enumeration types and integer types; they may be used for indexing and iteration over loops. Each discrete value has a *position number* which is an integer number. Integer and real types are called *numeric* types.

  range_constraint ::= **range** range

  range ::= simple_expression .. simple_expression

The range L .. R describes the values from L to R inclusive. The values L and R are called, respectively, the *lower bound* and *upper bound* of the range. A value is said to *satisfy* a range constraint if it is a value of the range. A *null range* is a range for which the upper bound is less than the lower bound. For a range constraint appearing after a type mark in a subtype indication, the type of the simple expressions is given by the type mark. A range constraint is said to be *compatible* with an earlier range constraint when both bounds of the later constraint lie within the range of the earlier constraint, or when the range of the later constraint is null.

Attributes:

For any scalar type or subtype T the attributes FIRST and LAST are defined (see also Apppendix A for the definition of the attributes IMAGE and VALUE).

T'FIRST   The minimum value of the type T or the lower bound of the subtype T

T'LAST   The maximum value of the type T or the upper bound of the subtype T

References:

constraint 3.3, discrete range 3.6.1, loop statement 5.6, simple expression 4.4, subtype 3.3

3.5.1 Enumeration Types

An enumeration type definition defines an ordered set of distinct values that are denoted by enumeration literals.

```
enumeration_type_definition ::=
    (enumeration_literal {, enumeration_literal})

enumeration_literal ::= identifier | character_literal
```

An enumeration value is denoted by an identifier or a character literal. Order relations between enumeration values follow the order of listing, the first being less than the last (when more than one). The position number of the first listed literal is zero; the position number of each other literal is one more than that of its predecessor in the list.

For the elaboration of an enumeration type definition, each enumeration literal is introduced at the point of its occurrence in the enumeration type definition; this elaboration declares the enumeration literals.

The same identifier or character literal can appear in different enumeration types whose scopes overlap. Such enumeration literals are said to be *overloaded*. An overloaded enumeration literal may only appear at points of the program text where its type can be determined from the context (see 6.6). A qualified expression can be used to resolve the type ambiguity where the context does not otherwise suffice (see 4.7).

Examples:

```
type DAY    is (MON, TUE, WED, THU, FRI, SAT, SUN);
type SUIT   is (CLUBS, DIAMONDS, HEARTS, SPADES);
type LEVEL  is (LOW, MEDIUM, URGENT);
type COLOR  is (WHITE, RED, YELLOW, GREEN, BLUE, BROWN, BLACK);
type LIGHT  is (RED, AMBER, GREEN);   --   RED and GREEN are overloaded

type HEXA   is ('A', 'B', 'C', 'D', 'E', 'F');
type MIXED  is ('A', 'B', '*', B, NONE);

subtype WEEKDAY is DAY    range MON .. FRI;
subtype MAJOR   is SUIT   range HEARTS .. SPADES;
subtype RAINBOW is COLOR  range RED .. BLUE;   --   the color RED,   not the light
```

References:

character literal 2.5, elaboration 3.1 3.9, identifier 2.3, position number 3.5, qualified expression 4.7, scope rules 8.1 8.2

3.5.2 Character Types

A character type is an enumeration type that contains character literals and possibly identifiers. The values of the predefined type CHARACTER are the 128 characters of the *ASCII* character set. Each of the 95 graphic characters of the *ASCII* character set can be denoted by a character literal. The predefined package ASCII includes the declaration of constants denoting control characters and of constants denoting graphic characters that are not in the basic character set.

Example:

```
type ROMAN_DIGIT is ('I', 'V', 'X', 'L', 'C', 'D', 'M');
```

Note:

Character literals of character types can be used in character strings.

References:

ascii package C, character literal 2.5, character string 2.6 3.6.3, identifier 2.3

3.5.3 Boolean Type

There is a predefined enumeration type named BOOLEAN. It contains the two literals FALSE and TRUE ordered with the relation FALSE < TRUE. The evaluation of a condition must deliver a result of this predefined type.

References:

condition 5.3 5.5 5.7

3.5.4 Integer Types

The elaboration of an integer type definition introduces a set of consecutive integers as values of the type.

```
integer_type_definition ::= range_constraint
```

Each bound of a range used for an integer type definition must be an integer value defined by a static expression of some integer type. The range must not be a null range; it may include negative values.

A type declaration of the form

    type T **is range** L .. R;

is equivalent to the declaration of a type derived from one of the predefined integer types

    type T **is new** *integer_type* **range** L .. R;

where the predefined *integer_type* is implicitly chosen so as to contain the values L through R inclusive.

The predefined integer types include the type INTEGER. An implementation may also have predefined types such as SHORT_INTEGER and LONG_INTEGER, which have respectively significantly shorter and longer ranges than INTEGER. The range of each of these types must be symmetric about zero (excepting an extra negative value for two's complement machines). The base type of each of these types is the type itself.

The same arithmetic operators are defined for all predefined integer types and consequently for all integer types (see 4.5 and appendix C). The position number of an integer number is the number itself.

Integer literals are the literals of the type *universal_integer*; there are no bounds on values of this type. Implicit conversions exist from this type to any predefined or user defined integer type, so that integer literals can appear in expressions of these types. The exception CONSTRAINT_ERROR is raised by such an implicit conversion if the value is not within the range of the required type.

Examples:

```
type PAGE_NUM   is range 1 .. 2_000;
type LINE_SIZE  is new INTEGER range 1 .. MAX_LINE_SIZE;

subtype SMALL_INT   is INTEGER range -10 .. 10;
subtype COLUMN_PTR  is LINE_SIZE range 1 .. 10;
```

Notes:

The name introduced by an integer type declaration is the name of a subtype of an anonymous type derived from one of the predefined integer types (see 3.4). The value contained by an object of an integer type must satisfy the constraint given in the corresponding integer type definition (an attempt to violate this constraint will raise the exception CONSTRAINT_ERROR). On the other hand, the operations of an integer type deliver results whose range is defined by the parent predefined type; such a result need not therefore lie within the range defined by the constraint (the exception NUMERIC_ERROR may be raised by an operation whose result is not within the predefined range).

The smallest (most negative) integer value supported by the predefined integer types of an implementation is the integer number SYSTEM.MIN_INT and the largest (most positive) value SYSTEM.MAX_INT (see 13.7).

References:

arithmetic operator 4.5 C, constraint_error exception 11.1, derived type 3.4, elaboration 3.1 3.9, integer literal 2.4, name 4.1, numeric_error exception 11.1, parent type 3.3, position number 3.5, static expression 4.9, subtype 3.3, universal integer type 2.4 3.2

3.5.5 Attributes of Discrete Types and Subtypes

For every discrete type T the attributes T'POS, T'SUCC, T'PRED, and T'VAL are functions defined as follows:

T'POS(X)   The parameter X must be a value of type T; the result of the function is the position number of X; the type of the result of this overloaded function is of an integer type determined by the context (see 6.6).

T'SUCC(X)   The parameter X must be a value of type T; the result of the function is the value of type T whose position number is one greater than that of X. The exception CONSTRAINT_ERROR is raised if X = T'LAST.

T'PRED(X)   The parameter X must be a value of type T; the result of the function is the value of type T whose position number is one less than that of X. The exception CONSTRAINT_ERROR is raised if X = T'FIRST.

T'VAL(N)   The parameter N must be a value of an integer type; the result of the function is the value of type T whose position number is N. The exception CONSTRAINT_ERROR is raised if N is not in the range T'POS(T'FIRST) .. T'POS(T'LAST).

For a subtype S of a discrete type, each of these four attributes denotes the corresponding attribute of the base type. Consequently, the results delivered by S'SUCC, S'PRED, and S'VAL need not be in the range of S; similarly, the actual parameters of S'POS, S'SUCC, and S'PRED need not be in the range of S.

Examples:

```
--  For  the  types  and  subtypes  declared  in  section  3.5.1  we  have

--  COLOR'FIRST    = WHITE,     COLOR'LAST     = BLACK
--  RAINBOW'FIRST  = RED,       RAINBOW'LAST   = BLUE

--  COLOR'SUCC(BLUE)  = RAINBOW'SUCC(BLUE)  = BROWN
--  COLOR'POS(BLUE)   = RAINBOW'POS(BLUE)   = 4
--  COLOR'VAL(0)      = RAINBOW'VAL(0) ·     = WHITE
```

Note:

The following relations are satisfied (in the absence of an exception) by these four attributes of discrete types

```
T'POS(T'SUCC(X))   = T'POS(X)  +  1
T'POS(T'PRED(X))   = T'POS(X)  -  1

T'VAL(T'POS(X))    = X
T'POS(T'VAL(N))    = N
```

References:

attribute 4.1.4, base type 3.3, constraint_error exception 11.1, discrete type 3.5, first attribute 3.5, function 6.5, last attribute 3.5, position number 3.5, subtype 3.3, type 3.3

3.5.6 Real Types

Real types provide approximations to the real numbers, with relative bounds on errors for floating point types, and with absolute bounds for fixed point types.

    real_type_definition ::=   accuracy_constraint

    accuracy_constraint ::=
        floating_point_constraint | fixed_point_constraint

The elaboration of a real type definition defines a set of numbers called *model numbers*. Error bounds on the predefined operations are defined in terms of the model numbers. An implementation of the type must include at least these model numbers and represent them exactly.

Real literals are the literals of the type *universal_real*; there are no bounds on values of this type. Implicit conversions exist from this type to any predefined or user defined real type, so that real literals can appear in expressions of these types. If the universal real value is a model number, the conversion delivers the corresponding value. Otherwise, the converted value can be any value within the range defined by the model numbers next above and below the universal real value. The exception CONSTRAINT_ERROR is raised by such an implicit conversion if the value is not within the range of the required type.

Note:

An algorithm written to rely only upon the minimum numerical properties guaranteed by the type definition will be portable without further precautions.

References:

accuracy of operations 4.5.8, elaboration 3.1 3.9, fixed point constraint 3.5.9, fixed point type 3.5.9, floating point constraint 3.5.7, floating point type 3.5.7, model fixed point number 3.5.9, model floating point number 3.5.7, universal real type 2.4 3.2

3.5.7 Floating Point Types

For floating point types, the error bound is specified as a relative precision by giving the minimum required number of decimal digits for the decimal mantissa (that is, for the decimal value when the power of ten and leading zeros are ignored).

    floating_point_constraint ::=
        digits *static*_simple_expression [range_constraint]

The required number D of decimal digits is specified by the value of the static expression following the reserved word **digits**; it must be positive and of some integer type. This value determines a corresponding minimum number B of binary digits for the binary mantissa, such that the relative precision of the binary form is no less than that specified for the decimal form. (B is the integer next above $D*\ln(10)/\ln(2)$).

The model numbers of the type comprise zero and all numbers of the form

> *sign* ∗ *binary_mantissa* ∗ (2.0 ∗∗ *exponent*)

such that

- *sign* is +1 or -1

- 0.5 $<=$ *binary_mantissa* $<$ 1.0

- *binary_mantissa* has exactly B digits after the point when expressed in base two

- *exponent* is an integer in the range -4∗B .. 4∗B

A floating point type declaration of one of the two forms (that is, with or without a range):

> **type** NEW_TYPE **is digits** D [**range** L .. R];

where L and R if present must be static expressions of some real types, is equivalent to the declaration of a type derived from one of the predefined floating point types

> **type** NEW_TYPE **is new** *floating_point_type* **digits** D [**range** L .. R];

where the predefined *floating_point_type* is chosen appropriately such that its model numbers include the model numbers defined by D. The predefined floating point types include the type FLOAT. An implementation may also have predefined types such as SHORT_FLOAT and LONG_FLOAT, which have respectively substantially less and more precision than FLOAT.

Where the range constraint is present the same model numbers are used, but objects of type NEW_TYPE must satisfy the range constraint. Thus the value of D in the type definition guarantees specific minimal properties for the type.

For a subtype or object declaration, the constraint can either be a range constraint or a floating point constraint. In either case, the expressions giving the upper and lower bounds must be of the type or subtype specified and within the range of the type or subtype. The expression following **digits** in the floating point constraint must be a static expression of an integer type and its value must not be greater than the corresponding number D for the floating point type or subtype.

A subtype declaration defines a set of model numbers which is a subset of the model numbers of the base type. If the subtype indication includes a floating point constraint specifying fewer decimal digits than the base type, then the mantissa length B of the model numbers is correspondingly reduced; otherwise the model numbers for the subtype are the same as for the base type.

The *compatibility* of a floating point constraint with an earlier one is defined as follows. The number of digits of the later one must not exceed that of the earlier one; if both floating point constraints have range constraints, the later range constraint must be compatible with the earlier range constraint (within the accuracy of the corresponding real operations, see 4.5.8). A value of a floating point type satisfies a floating point constraint if it satisfies any included range constraint.

Examples:

```
type COEFFICIENT is digits 10 range -1.0 .. 1.0;

type REAL   is digits 8;
type MASS is new REAL digits 7 range 0.0 .. 1.0E10;

subtype SHORT_COEFF is COEFFICIENT digits 5;
```

Notes on the examples:

The implemented range for REAL is derived from a predefined type having at least 8 digits of precision. The definition for MASS is valid because REAL has more than 7 digits precision and because

```
MASS'LAST  <  REAL'LARGE  <=  REAL'LAST
```

References:

accuracy constraint 3.5.6, base type 3.3, bounds 3.5, integer type 3.5.4, model number 3.5.6, range constraint 3.3, static expression 4.9, subtype 3.3, subtype indication 3.3

3.5.8 Attributes of Floating Point Types

For every floating point type or subtype F the following attributes are defined:

F'DIGITS	For a predefined type F, the equivalent number of decimal digits precision for model numbers of the type. For other types or subtypes, the number of decimal digits specified by the accuracy constraint. Of type *universal_integer*.
F'MANTISSA	The length of the binary mantissa of model numbers of F. Of type *universal_integer*. (The number B of section 3.5.7).
F'EMAX	The number such that the binary exponent range of model numbers of F is -F'EMAX .. F'EMAX. Of type *universal_integer*.
F'SMALL	The smallest positive model number of F. Of type *universal_real*.
F'LARGE	The largest positive model number of F. Of type *universal_real*.
F'EPSILON	The absolute value of the difference between 1.0 and the next model number above 1.0. Of type *universal_real*.

In addition, the usual attributes of scalar types FIRST and LAST are defined. (They need not be model numbers).

Notes:

The attributes EMAX, SMALL, LARGE and EPSILON are provided for convenience. They are all related to MANTISSA, the parameter which defines the model numbers and is in turn related to DIGITS, by the following formulas:

```
F'EMAX      = 4*F'MANTISSA
F'SMALL     = 2.0**(-F'EMAX - 1)
F'LARGE     = 2.0**F'EMAX  * (1.0 - 2.0**(-F'MANTISSA))
F'EPSILON   = 2.0**(-F'MANTISSA + 1)
```

Since F'FIRST and F'LAST need not be model numbers, they may have machine dependent properties.

Certain attributes of floating point types are machine dependent. They are described in section 13.7.1.

References:

accuracy constraint 3.5.6, binary mantissa 3.5.7, boolean type 3.5.3, digits 3.5.7, exponent 3.5.7, first attribute 3.5, floating point type 3.5.7, integer type 3.5.4, last attribute 3.5, model number 3.5.6, numeric_error exception 11.1, universal_integer type 2.4 3.2, universal real type 2.4 3.2

3.5.9 Fixed Point Types

For fixed point types, the error bound is specified as an absolute value, called the *delta* of the fixed point type.

```
fixed_point_constraint ::=
    delta static_simple_expression [range_constraint]
```

The delta is specified by the value of the static expression following the reserved word **delta**; it must be positive and of some real type. The range constraint is required in a fixed point type definition; it is optional in a subtype indication.

The model numbers of a fixed point type comprise consecutive integer multiples of a certain number called *actual_delta*. The multipliers comprise all integers in the range

```
-(2**N) + 1 .. (2**N) - 1
```

for some positive integer N. This implemented error bound *actual_delta* must be positive and not greater than the specified delta. For a fixed point type definition with a range constraint of the form

```
range L .. R
```

L and R must be static expressions of some real types; the integer N must be chosen so that model numbers of the type lie at most delta distant from each of L and R, although neither L nor R need be model numbers. Thus the values of L and R and the delta in the type definition guarantee specific minimal properties for the type.

For a subtype or object declaration, the constraint can be either a range constraint or a fixed point constraint. In either case, the expressions giving the lower and upper bounds must be of the type specified and within the range of the type or subtype. The expression in the fixed point constraint must be a static expression of a real type and its value must not be less than the corresponding value delta for the type or subtype.

A subtype declaration defines a set of model numbers which is a subset of the model numbers of the base type. The actual delta of the subtype is a non negative power of two, times the actual delta of the base type, and must not be greater than the specified delta.

Multiplication and division of fixed point values deliver results of a fixed point type with an arbitrarily fine accuracy, whose name cannot be used in programs and which is referred to in this text for explanatory purposes as *universal_fixed*. The values of this type must be converted explicitly to some numeric type.

The compatibility of a fixed point constraint with an earlier one is defined as follows. The delta of the later one must not be less than that of the earlier one; if both fixed point constraints have range constraints, the later constraint must be compatible with the earlier range constraint (within the accuracy of the corresponding real operations; see 4.5.8). A value of a fixed point type satisfies a fixed point constraint if it satisfies any included range constraint.

Examples:

```
    --   A pure fraction which requires all the available space in a word
    --   on a two's complement machine can be declared as type FRAC:

DEL : constant := 1.0/2**(WORD_LENGTH - 1);
type FRAC is delta DEL range -1.0 .. 1.0 - DEL;

type LONG_FRAC is delta DEL/1000 range -1.0 .. 1.0 - DEL;
    --   a pure fraction requiring more bits

type VOLT is delta 0.125 range 0.0 .. 255.0;

subtype S_VOLT is VOLT delta 0.5;   --   same range as VOLT
```

Note:

The actual delta is ordinarily a power of two, in order to make conversions fast. The actual delta may be specified explicitly by a representation specification (see 13.2).

References:

accuracy constraint 3.5.6, bounds 3.5, integer type 3.5.4, model number 3.5.6, range constraint 3.3, real type 3.5.6, simple expression 4.4, static expression 4.9, subtype indication 3.3,

3.5.10 Attributes of Fixed Point Types

For every fixed point type or subtype F the following attributes are defined:

F'DELTA
If F is a type, or a subtype without a fixed point constraint, this is the delta of the base type. Otherwise it is the delta specified by the fixed point constraint. Of type *universal_real*.

F'ACTUAL_DELTA
The actual delta of F. Of type *universal_real*.

F'BITS
When positive values of model numbers of F are expressed as K∗F'ACTUAL_DELTA, the attribute F'BITS is the number of binary digits used to represent the unsigned integer K. Of type *universal_integer*. The attribute F'BITS is the number N of section 3.5.9.

F'LARGE
The largest model number of F.

Notes:

Machine dependent attributes of real types are described in section 13.7. The following relation is satisfied by the attributes LARGE, BITS, and ACTUAL_DELTA:

$$F'LARGE = (2**F'BITS - 1) * F'ACTUAL\_DELTA$$

References:

accuracy constraint 3.5.6, base type 3.3, boolean type 3.5.3, delta 3.5.9, model number 3.5.6

3.6 Array Types

An array object is a composite object consisting of components of the same component type. A component of an array is designated using one or more index values belonging to specified discrete types. The value of an array object is a composite value consisting of the values of its components.

```
array_type_definition ::=
    array (index (, index)) of component_subtype_indication
  | array index_constraint of component_subtype_indication

index ::= type_mark range <>

index_constraint ::=   (discrete_range (, discrete_range))

discrete_range   ::=   type_mark [range_constraint] | range
```

An array object is characterized by the number of indices (the *dimensionality* of the array), the type and position of each index, the lower and upper bounds for each index, and the type and possible constraints of the components. The order of the indices is significant.

A one-dimensional array has a distinct component for each possible index value. A multi-dimensional array has a distinct component for each possible sequence of index values that can be formed by selecting one value for each index position. The possible values for an index are all values between the lower and upper bounds, inclusive.

There are unconstrained and constrained forms of array type definitions:

(1) *Unconstrained array type definitions*

These are array type definitions of the form

array (index {, index}) **of** *component*_subtype_indication

The elaboration of such a type definition includes the evaluation of any constraint in the component subtype indication; it defines an array type. For all objects of this array type, the number of indices, the type and position of each index, and the subtype of the components are as in the type definition. (The compound symbol <> is called a *box*; it stands here for an undefined range).

For each index, the actual values of the lower and upper bounds can be different for different objects of the array type but they must satisfy any range constraint imposed by the type mark.

(2) *Constrained array type definitions*

These are array type definitions of the form

array index_constraint **of** *component*_subtype_indication

The elaboration of such a type definition includes the evaluation of the index constraint and of any constraint in the component subtype indication. It defines an unconstrained array type in which each index has the base type of the corresponding discrete range, and with the same component subtype; it further defines the subtype obtained by imposing the index constraint upon the unconstrained array type. Consequently all arrays of a type declared with a constrained array type definition have the same bounds.

Unconstrained array type definitions are only allowed for type definitions used in type declarations.

Examples of unconstrained array type declarations:

```
type MATRIX     is array(INTEGER   range <>, INTEGER range <>) of REAL;
type BIT_VECTOR is array(INTEGER   range <>) of BOOLEAN;
type ROMAN      is array(NATURAL   range <>) of ROMAN_DIGIT;
```

Examples of constrained array type declarations:

```
type TABLE     is array(1 .. 10) of INTEGER;
type SCHEDULE  is array(DAY) of BOOLEAN;
type LINE      is array(1 .. MAX_LINE_SIZE) of CHARACTER;
```

Examples of array declarations including a constrained type definition:

```
GRID  : array(1 .. 80, 1 .. 100) of BOOLEAN;
MIX   : array(COLOR range RED .. GREEN) of BOOLEAN;
PAGE  : array(1 .. 50) of LINE;   --  an array of arrays
```

Note:

For a one-dimensional array, the rule given means that a type declaration with a constrained array type definition such as

```
type T is array (INDEX) of COMPONENT;
```

is equivalent to the succession of declarations

```
type unconstrained is array (INDEX range <>) of COMPONENT;
subtype T is unconstrained (INDEX);
```

where *unconstrained* is an identifier distinct from those of the program. Similar transformations apply to multi-dimensional arrays.

References:

boolean type 3.5.3, character 3.5.2, discrete type 3.5, elaboration 3.1 3.9, index value 3.6.1, integer type 3.5.4, real type 3.5.6, subtype indication 3.3, type mark 3.3

3.6.1 Index Constraints and Discrete Ranges

An index constraint specifies the possible range of each index of an array type, and thereby the corresponding array bounds.

An index constraint can be imposed on an array type mark in a subtype indication, if and only if the type mark designates an unconstrained array type. To be compatible with the type mark, the index constraint must provide a discrete range for each index; the type of each discrete range must be the same as that of the corresponding index; the range defined by each discrete range, if not a null index range (see below), must be compatible with any range constraint already imposed by the type mark given in the corresponding index.

If the bounds of a discrete range given by a range without a type mark are integer numbers or integer literal expressions, the bounds are assumed to be of the predefined type INTEGER. This rule also applies to discrete ranges used in for loops (see 5.5) and entry declarations (see 9.5).

The discrete range supplied for a given index defines a *null index range* if its upper bound is the predecessor of its lower bound. If an index constraint contains a null index range, any array thus constrained is a null array having no component. The lower bound of a null index range must satisfy any range constraint imposed by the type mark of the index. The upper bound of a null index range must also be a value of the base type of the index but this value need not satisfy the range constraint (if any). The exception CONSTRAINT_ERROR is raised for any incompatible discrete range or if the upper bound of a discrete range is less than the predecessor of the lower bound.

The bounds of an array object defined by an object declaration, or as component of another object, must be known when the corresponding declaration is elaborated. These bounds are necessarily known if the array subtype is given in this declaration by the type mark of a constrained array type; the corresponding index constraint defines the bounds. If the array subtype contains the type mark of an unconstrained array type, index bounds must be specified by an explicit index constraint in variable declarations and in the subtype of components; the index constraint can be omitted from the declaration of a constant, in which case the bounds are those of the initial value. The bounds of an array value satisfy an index constraint if they are equal to the bounds of the index constraint.

For an array formal parameter whose parameter declaration specifies an unconstrained array type, the bounds are obtained from the actual parameter. Within the body of the corresponding subprogram, or generic unit, the formal parameter is constrained by the values of these bounds.

The bounds of any array object created by an allocator must be known upon allocation.

The expressions defining the discrete range allowed for an index need not be static, but can depend on computed results. Arrays, one or more of whose bounds are not static, are called *dynamic arrays*. In records, dynamic arrays may only appear when the dynamic bounds are discriminants of the record type.

Examples of array declarations including an index constraint:

```
BOARD       : MATRIX(1 .. 8,   1 .. 8);
RECTANGLE   : MATRIX(1 .. 20, 1 .. 30);
INVERSE     : MATRIX(1 .. N,   1 .. N);   --  N need not be static

FILTER      : BIT_VECTOR(0 .. 31);
```

Example of array declaration with a constrained array type:

```
MY_TABLE  : TABLE;  --   all arrays of type TABLE have the same bounds
```

Example of record type with a dynamic array as component:

```
type VAR_LINE(LENGTH : INTEGER) is
  record
    IMAGE : STRING(1 .. LENGTH);
  end record;

NULL_LINE : VAR_LINE(0);   --   NULL_LINE.IMAGE is a null array
```

References:

actual parameter 6.4, allocator 4.8, base type 3.3, compatible range constraint 3.5, constant declaration 3.2, bounds 3.5, discriminant 3.7.1, elaboration 3.1 3.9, entry declaration 9.5, for loop 5.5, formal parameter 6.2 6.4 12.1, generic program unit 12, integer type 3.5.4, initial value 3.2, parameter declaration 6.1, range constraint 3.5, record type 3.7, subprogram body 6.3, subtype 3.3, type mark 3.3, unconstrained array type 3.6, variable declaration 3.2

3.6.2 Array Attributes

For an array object A (or for the type mark A of a constrained array type), the following attributes are defined (N is an integer value given by a static expression):

A'FIRST	The lower bound of the first index.
A'LAST	The upper bound of the first index.
A'LENGTH	The number of values of the first index (zero for a null range). This attribute is overloaded and produces a result of an integer type determined by the context (see 6.6).
A'RANGE	The subtype defined by the range A'FIRST .. A'LAST.
A'FIRST(N)	The lower bound of the N-th index.
A'LAST(N)	The upper bound of the N-th index.
A'LENGTH(N)	The number of values of the N-th index (zero for a null range). This attribute is overloaded and produces a result of an integer type determined by the context (see 6.6).
A'RANGE(N)	The subtype defined by the range A'FIRST(N) .. A'LAST(N).

Examples (using arrays declared in the examples of section 3.6.1):

```
--    FILTER'FIRST       =    0
--    FILTER'LAST        =    31
--    FILTER'LENGTH      =    32
--    BOARD'LAST(1)      =    8
--    RECTANGLE'LAST(2)  =    30
```

Note:

The above attributes are not defined for unconstrained array types. The following relations are satisfied by the above attributes if the index type is an integer type:

```
A'LENGTH    = A'LAST    - A'FIRST    + 1
A'LENGTH(N) = A'LAST(N) - A'FIRST(N) + 1
```

References:

attribute A, bounds 3.6, constrained array type 3.6, index 3.6, integer type 3.5.4, range 3.5, static expression 4.9 10.6, subtype 3.3, type mark 3.3

3.6.3 Strings

The predefined type STRING denotes one-dimensional arrays of the predefined type CHARACTER, indexed by values of the predefined subtype NATURAL:

```
subtype NATURAL is INTEGER range 1 .. INTEGER'LAST;
type STRING is array (NATURAL range <>) of CHARACTER;
```

Character strings (see 2.6) are a special form of positional aggregate applicable to the type STRING and other one-dimensional arrays of characters. Catenation is a predefined operator for the type STRING and for one-dimensional array types; it is represented as &. The relational operators <, <=, >, and >= are defined for strings, and correspond to lexicographic order (see 4.5.2).

Examples:

```
STARS       : STRING(1 .. 120)  := (1 .. 120 => '*' );
QUESTION    : constant STRING    := "HOW MANY CHARACTERS?";
--  QUESTION'FIRST = 1, QUESTION'LAST = 20 (the number of characters)

ASK_TWICE   : constant STRING    := QUESTION & QUESTION;
NINETY_SIX  : constant ROMAN     := "XCVI";
```

References:

aggregate 4.3, character type 3.5.2, character string 2.6, catenation 3.6.3 4.5.3, subtype 3.3

3.7 Record Types

A record object is a composite object consisting of named components, which may be of different types. The value of a record object is a composite value consisting of the values of its components.

```
record_type_definition ::=
    record
      component_list
    end record

component_list ::=
    { component_declaration} [variant_part]   | null;

component_declaration ::=
      identifier_list : subtype_indication [:= expression];
    | identifier_list : array_type_definition [:= expression];
```

The elaboration of a record type definition defines a record type; it consists of the elaboration of any included component declarations, in the order in which they appear (including any component declaration in a variant part).

A component declaration defines one or more components of a type given either by a subtype indication or by a constrained array type definition.

For the elaboration of a component declaration, the identifiers of the list are first introduced; the component type is then established by elaborating the corresponding array type definition or by evaluating any constraint in the subtype indication; the identifiers can then be used to name the corresponding components. Finally, if a component declaration indicates an explicit initialization, the corresponding expression is evaluated; this initial value must satisfy any constraint imposed by the subtype indication (or by the array type definition), otherwise the exception CONSTRAINT_ERROR is raised.

If a component declaration indicates an explicit initialization, the value thus specified is the default initial value for the corresponding components. In the absence of an explicit initialization in a component declaration, a default initial value exists for the corresponding components if and only if there is one for their type. An explicit initialization may only be given if assignment is available for the component type (see 7.4).

All objects of a record type that has neither a discriminant nor a variant part have the same components. If the component list is defined by the reserved word **null**, the record type has no component; all records of the type are *null records*.

Examples:

```
type  DATE is
  record
    DAY    : INTEGER range 1 .. 31;
    MONTH : MONTH_NAME;
    YEAR   : INTEGER range 0 .. 4000;
  end record;

type  COMPLEX is
  record
    RE  : REAL := 0.0;
    IM  : REAL := 0.0;
  end record;

  -- both components of every complex record are initialized to zero (if no explicit initialization).
```

Note:

If a default initial value exists for a component of a record type without a discriminant, it is the same for all objects of the type since it is the value obtained during the elaboration of the record type definition.

References:

array type definition 3.6, constraint 3.3, constraint_error exception 11.1, discriminant 3.7.1, elaboration 3.1, enumeration type 3.5.1, expression 4.4, identifier 2.3, object 3.2, subtype indication 3.3, variant part 3.7.3

3.7.1 Discriminants

A discriminant part can be given in the type declaration for a record type; it defines the discriminants of the type. A discriminant is a named component of any object of such a record type (appearing before any of the components in the type definition).

```
discriminant_part ::=
    (discriminant_declaration {; discriminant_declaration})

discriminant_declaration ::=
    identifier_list : subtype_indication [:= expression]
```

Each discriminant must belong to a discrete type. The elaboration of a discriminant declaration proceeds in the same way as that of a component declaration. Default initial values must be provided either for all or for none of the discriminants of a discriminant part.

Within a record type definition the name of a discriminant may be used either as a bound in an index constraint, or as the discriminant name of a variant part, or to specify a discriminant value in a discriminant specification. In each of these three cases, the discriminant name must appear by itself, that is, not as part of a larger expression. No other dependence between record components is allowed.

Each record value includes a value for each discriminant declared for the record type; it also includes a value for each record component that does not depend on a discriminant. The values of the discriminants determine which other component values must appear in the record value.

The discriminants of a record object can only be changed by assigning a complete record value to the object.

Record types and private types implemented as record types are the only types that may have discriminants.

Examples:

```
type BUFFER(SIZE : INTEGER range 0 .. MAX := 100) is
    record
        POS    : INTEGER range 0 .. MAX := 0;
        VALUE  : STRING(1 .. SIZE);
    end record;

type SQUARE(SIDE : INTEGER) is
    record
        MAT : array(1 .. SIDE, 1 .. SIDE) of REAL;
    end record;
```

```
type DOUBLE(NUMBER : INTEGER) is
  record
    LEFT  : BUFFER (NUMBER);
    RIGHT : SQUARE (NUMBER);
  end record;

type CUBE(SIDE : INTEGER) is
  record
    VALUE : array(1 .. SIDE) of SQUARE(SIDE);   --   double dependency
  end record;
```

Notes:

A discriminant need not be referred to by any record component, as shown in the example below

```
type ITEM(NUMBER : NATURAL) is
  record
    CONTENT : INTEGER;
  end record;
```

References:

array type definition 3.6, bound 3.6, component 3.7, component declaration 3.7, constraint 3.3, discrete type 3.5, dynamic array 3.6.1, elaboration 3.1, private types 7.4.1, object 3.2, record component 3.7, record type 3.7

3.7.2 Discriminant Constraints

The allowable discriminant values for a record object can be fixed by a discriminant constraint. A record value satisfies a discriminant constraint if each discriminant of the record value has the value imposed by the corresponding discriminant specification.

```
discriminant_constraint ::=
    (discriminant_specification {, discriminant_specification})

discriminant_specification ::=
    [discriminant_name {| discriminant_name} =>] expression
```

Each expression specifies the value of a discriminant. The expressions can be given by position (in the order of discriminant declarations) or by naming the chosen discriminant. Named discriminant specifications can be given in any order, but if both notations are used in one discriminant constraint, the positional discriminant specifications must be given first. A discriminant constraint must provide a value for every discriminant of the type.

A discriminant constraint can be imposed on a type mark in a subtype indication if and only if the type mark does not already impose a discriminant constraint. The discriminant constraint is compatible with the type mark if and only if each specified discriminant value satisfies any range constraint imposed on the corresponding discriminant.

In the absence of default initial values for the discriminants of a type, a discriminant constraint must be supplied for every object declaration declaring an object of the type. Similarly a discriminant constraint must be imposed on such a type if this type is used in a record component declaration or as the component type in an array type definition. The constraint can be imposed either explicitly or by supplying the name of a subtype that incorporates such a constraint.

If a discriminant constraint is imposed on an object declaration, a record component, or an array component, each discriminant is initialized with the value specified in the constraint. This value overrides any discriminant default initialization and cannot later be changed.

For a formal parameter whose parameter declaration indicates a type with discriminants, these are initialized with the discriminants of the actual parameter (subject to any discriminant constraint on the formal parameter). Within the body of the corresponding subprogram, or generic unit, the value of a discriminant of the formal parameter cannot be changed if the corresponding actual parameter is constrained.

Attribute:

For any object A of a type with discriminants, the following boolean attribute is defined.

A'CONSTRAINED   True if and only if a discriminant constraint applies to the object A; if A is a formal parameter, the value of this attribute is obtained from that of the actual parameter. Of type BOOLEAN.

Examples:

```
LARGE    : BUFFER(200);    --  always 200 characters:  LARGE'CONSTRAINED = TRUE
MESSAGE  : BUFFER;         --  initially 100 characters:  MESSAGE'CONSTRAINED = FALSE

BASIS    : SQUARE(5);      --  constrained, always 5 by 5
ILLEGAL  : SQUARE;         --  illegal, a SQUARE must be constrained
```

Notes:

The above rules ensure that discriminants always have a value, either because they must be constrained, or because of the existence of a default initial value.

If a subtype declaration includes a discriminant constraint, all objects of this subtype are constrained and their discriminants are initialized accordingly.

References:

actual parameter 6.4, array type definition 3.6, component subtype 3.6, constraint_error exception 11.1, default initial value 3.7, discriminant 3.7.1, expression 4.4, formal parameter 6.2 6.4, generic program unit 12, record component 3.7, record object 3.7, subtype declaration 3.3, type mark 3.3

3.7.3 Variant Parts

A record type with a variant part specifies alternative lists of components. Each variant defines the components for the corresponding value (or values) of the discriminant. A variant can have an empty component list, which must be specified by **null**.

```
variant_part ::=
  case discriminant name is
    {when choice {| choice} =>
      component_list}
  end case;
```

```
choice ::= simple_expression | discrete_range | others
```

A record value must contain the component values of a given variant if the discriminant value is equal to one of the values specified by the choices prefixing the corresponding component list. This rule applies in turn to any further variants which may be included in the component list of the given variant.

A choice given as a discrete range stands for all values in the corresponding range. The choice **others** stands for all values of the discriminant type (possibly none) that are not specified in previous choices; it can only appear alone and for the last component list. Each value of the discriminant subtype if this subtype is static, otherwise each value of the discriminant type, must be represented once and only once in the set of choices of a variant part. The value of a choice given in a variant part must be determinable statically (see 4.9).

Example of record type with a variant part:

```
type DEVICE is (PRINTER, DISK, DRUM);
type STATE  is (OPEN, CLOSED);

type PERIPHERAL(UNIT : DEVICE := DISK) is
  record
    STATUS : STATE;
    case UNIT is
      when PRINTER =>
        LINE_COUNT : INTEGER range 1 .. PAGE_SIZE;
      when others =>
        CYLINDER    : CYLINDER_INDEX;
        TRACK       : TRACK_NUMBER;
    end case;
  end record;
```

Examples of record subtypes:

```
subtype DRUM_UNIT is PERIPHERAL(DRUM);
subtype DISK_UNIT  is PERIPHERAL(DISK);
```

Examples of constrained record variables:

```
WRITER  : PERIPHERAL(UNIT => PRINTER);
ARCHIVE : DISK_UNIT;
```

Choices with discrete values are also used in case statements and in aggregates.

References:

aggregate 4.3, case statement 5.4, discrete range 3.6.1, discriminant 3.7.1, discrete type 3.5, simple expression 4.4, subtype 3.3

3.8 Access Types

Objects declared in a program are accessible by their name. They exist during the lifetime of the declarative part to which they are local. In contrast, objects may also be created by the execution of *allocators* (see 4.8). Since they do not occur in an explicit object declaration, they cannot be denoted by their name. Instead, access to such an object is achieved by an *access value* returned by an allocator; the access value is said to *designate* the object.

```
access_type_definition ::= access subtype_indication

incomplete_type_declaration ::= type identifier [discriminant_part];
```

The elaboration of an access type definition causes the evaluation of any constraint given in the subtype indication. The access type resulting from this elaboration is the type of a set of access values. This set includes the value **null** designating no object at all. Other access values of the type can be obtained by execution of an allocator associated with the type. Each such access value designates an object of the subtype indicated after the reserved word **access**. The objects created by an allocator and designated by the values of an access type form a *collection* implicitly associated with the type.

The **null** value of an access type is the default initial value of the type. An access value obtained by an allocator can be assigned to several access variables. Hence an object created by an allocator may be designated by more than one variable or constant of the access type. If an access object is constant, the contained access value always designates the same object but the value of the designated object can be modified.

If the subtype indication in the access type definition denotes either an unconstrained array type or a type with discriminants but without a discriminant constraint, the corresponding index bounds or discriminant values must be supplied for each allocator. The allocated object is constrained by these values.

Components of an object designated by a value of an access type may have values of the same or of another access type. This permits recursive and mutually dependent access types. Their declaration requires a prior incomplete type declaration for one or more types. Whenever an incomplete type declaration appears in a list of declarative items, the full type declaration must appear later in the same list of declarative items. Both the incomplete type declaration and the corresponding full type declaration must have the same discriminant part (if any) which is elaborated only once, at the earlier occurrence. The correspondence between the incomplete and the full type declaration follows the same rules as for private types (see 7.4.1). The name of a yet incompletely defined type can be used only as the type mark of the subtype indication of an access type definition.

The only constraint that can appear after the name of an access type in a subtype indication (for example one used in the declaration of an access variable) is either a discriminant constraint or an index constraint. Such a constraint is imposed on any object designated by a value of the access type (hence by any value other than **null**); the type of the designated objects must be a type with the corresponding discriminants or indexes.

Examples:

```
type FRAME is access MATRIX;

type BUFFER_NAME is access BUFFER;

type CELL;  --  incomplete type declaration
type LINK is access CELL;

type CELL is
  record
    VALUE  : INTEGER;
    SUCC   : LINK;
    PRED   : LINK;
  end record;


HEAD : LINK := new CELL(0, null, null);
```

Examples of mutually dependent access types:

```
type PERSON(SEX : GENDER);    --  incomplete type declaration
type CAR;                     --  incomplete type declaration

type PERSON_NAME  is access PERSON;
type CAR_NAME     is access CAR;

type PERSON(SEX : GENDER) is
  record
    NAME    : STRING(1 .. 20);
    AGE     : INTEGER range 0 .. 130;
    VEHICLE : CAR_NAME;
    case SEX is
      when M  => WIFE     : PERSON_NAME(SEX => F);
      when F  => HUSBAND  : PERSON_NAME(SEX => M);
    end case;
  end record;

type CAR is
  record
    NUMBER  : INTEGER;
    OWNER   : PERSON_NAME;
  end record;


MY_CAR, YOUR_CAR, NEXT_CAR : CAR_NAME;  --  initialized with null
```

References:

allocator 4.8, array type definition 3.6, collection size 13.2, discriminant constraint 3.7.2, discriminant part 3.7, index bound 3.6, index constraint 3.7.1, subtype indication 3.3

3.9   Declarative Parts

A declarative part contains declarations and related information that apply over a region of program text. Declarative parts may appear in blocks, subprograms and packages.

```
declarative_part ::=
    {declarative_item} {representation_specification} {program_component}

declarative_item ::= declaration | use_clause

program_component ::= body
    | package_declaration | task_declaration | body_stub

body ::= subprogram_body | package_body | task_body
```

For the elaboration of a declarative part, its constituents (possibly none) are successively elaborated in the order in which they appear in the program text.

The body of a subprogram, package, or task declared in a declarative part must be provided in the same declarative part; but if the body of one of these program units is a separately compiled sub-unit (see 10.2), it must be represented by a body stub at the place where it would otherwise appear.

Access to any entity before its elaboration is not allowed. In particular, a subprogram must not be called during the elaboration of a declarative part if its subprogram body appears later than the place of the call.

The exception STORAGE_ERROR may be raised by the elaboration of a declarative part if storage does not suffice for the declared entities.

References:

Elaboration of declarations 3.1, discriminant d. 3.7.1, entry d. 9.5, generic d. 12.1, loop parameter d. 5.5, number d. 3.2, object d. 3.2, package d. 7.2, parameter d. 6.1, renaming d. 8.5, subprogram d. 6.1, subtype d. 3.3, type d. 3.3

Elaboration of type definitions 3.3, access t.d. 3.8, array t.d. 3.6, derived t.d. 3.4, enumeration t.d. 3.5.1, integer t.d. 3.5.4, private t.d. 7.4, real t.d. 3.5.6, record t.d. 3.7

Elaboration of context 10.1, compilation unit 10.1 10.5, declarative part 3.9, discriminant part 3.3, generic body 12.2, generic formal parameter 12.1, library unit 10.5, package body 7.3, representation specification 13.1, subprogram body 6.3, subunit 10.2, task body 9.1, task object 9.2, task specification 9.1, use clause 8.4, with clause 10.1.1

exception during elaboration 11.4.2, order of elaboration 10.5

4. Names and Expressions

4.1 Names

Names can denote declared entities. These are objects, numbers, types and subtypes, sub-programs, packages, tasks and their entries, and exceptions. Names can also be labels, block names, or loop names. Particular forms of names denote attributes, operators, and components of objects. Finally, a name can denote the result returned by a function call.

```
name ::= identifier
    | indexed_component  | slice
    | selected_component | attribute
    | function_call      | operator_symbol
```

The simplest form for the name of an entity is the identifier given in its declaration. Function calls and operator symbols are described in Chapter 6. The remaining forms of names are described here.

Examples of simple names:

```
PI       --  the name of a number
LIMIT    --  the name of a constant
COUNT    --  the name of a scalar variable
BOARD    --  the name of an array variable
MATRIX   --  the name of a type
SQRT     --  the name of a function
ERROR    --  the name of an exception
```

References:

array type definition 3.6, boolean type 3.5.3, bound 3.6, component 3.2, identifier 2.3, index value 3.6.1, function call 6.4, numeric type 3.5, numeric_error exception 4.5.8 11.1, operator symbol 6.1, range 3.5, type declaration 3.3

4.1.1 Indexed Components

An indexed component denotes either a component of an array or an entry in a family of entries.

```
indexed_component ::= name(expression {, expression})
```

In the case of a component of an array, the name denotes an array object (or an access object whose value designates an array object). Alternatively, the name can be a function call delivering an array (or delivering an access value that designates an array). The expressions specify the index values for the component; there must be one such expression for each index position of the array type.

In the case of an entry in a family of entries, the name denotes an entry family and the expression (only one can be given) specifies the index value for the individual entry.

Each expression must be of the type of the corresponding index. If evaluation of an expression gives an index value that is outside the range specified for the index, the exception CONSTRAINT_ERROR is raised. This exception is also raised if the name denotes an access object whose value is **null**.

Examples of indexed components:

```
MY_TABLE(5)          -- a component of a one dimensional array
PAGE(10)             -- a component of a one dimensional array
BOARD(M, J + 1)      -- a component of a two dimensional array
PAGE(10)(20)         -- a component of a component
REQUEST(MEDIUM)      -- an entry of the family REQUEST
NEXT_FRAME(F)(M, N)  -- an indexed component of the function call NEXT_FRAME(F)
```

Notes on the examples:

Distinct notations are used for components of multidimensional arrays (such as BOARD) and arrays of arrays (such as PAGE). The components of an array of arrays are arrays and can therefore be indexed. Thus PAGE(10)(20) denotes the 20th component of PAGE(10).

Note:

The language does not define the order of evaluation of the different expressions of an indexed component of a multi-dimensional array. Hence programs that rely on a particular order are erroneous.

References:

access value 3.8, array type definition 3.6, array component 3.6, constraint_error exception 11.1, entry 9.5, entry family 9.5, expression 4.4, function 6.5, function call 6.4, index value 3.6.1, name 4.1 range 3.5

4.1.2 Slices

A slice is a one dimensional array denoting a sequence of consecutive components of a one dimensional array.

```
slice ::= name (discrete_range)
```

The name given in a slice denotes an array object (or an access object whose value designates an array object). The name can be a function call delivering an array (or delivering an access value that designates an array).

The type of a slice is the base type of the named array. The bounds of the slice are given by the discrete range; the slice is a *null slice* denoting a null array if the discrete range is a null index range (see 3.6.1).

If a slice is not null, the index values of its discrete range must be possible index values for the named array; otherwise the exception CONSTRAINT_ERROR is raised. This exception is also raised if the name denotes an access object whose value is **null**.

Examples of slices:

```
STARS(1 .. 15)              -- a slice of 15 characters
PAGE(10 .. 10 + SIZE)       -- a slice of 1 + SIZE components
PAGE(L)(A .. B)             -- a slice of the array PAGE(L)
STARS(1 .. 0)               -- a null slice
MY_SCHEDULE(WEEKDAY)        -- bounds given by subtype
STARS(5 .. 15)(9)           -- same as STARS(9)
```

Note:

For a one dimensional array A, the name A(N .. N) is a slice of one component; its type is the base type of A. On the other hand A(N) is a component of the array A and has the corresponding component type.

References:

access object 3.8, access value ·3.8, array type definition 3.6, base type 3.3, bound 3.6, 3.6.1, constraint_error exception 11.1, discrete range 3.6.1, function 6.5, function call 6.4, index 3.6, name 4.1, null array 3.6.1, null range 3.6.1, type definition 3.3

4.1.3 Selected Components

Selected components are used to denote record components. They are also used for objects designated by access values. Finally, selected components are used to form names of declared entities.

```
selected_component ::=
    name.identifier | name.all | name.operator_symbol
```

A selected component can denote either

(a) A component of a record:

The name denotes a record (or an access object whose value designates a record) and the identifier specifies the record component. The name can be a function call delivering a record (or delivering an access value that designates a record).

(b) An object designated by an access value:

The name denotes an access object and is followed by a dot and the reserved word **all**. The name can be a function call delivering an access value.

(c) An entity declared in the visible part of a package:

The name denotes a package and the identifier specifies the declared entity. For an operator, the corresponding operator symbol (that is, the operator enclosed by double quotes) follows the name of the package and the dot.

(d) An entry (or entry family) of a task:

The name denotes a task object (or if the selected component occurs in a task body, this program unit) and the identifier specifies one of its entries (one of its entry families).

(e) An entity declared in an enclosing subprogram body, package body, task body, block, or loop:

The name denotes this (immediately) enclosing unit and the identifier (or the operator symbol) specifies the declared entity. This notation is only allowed within the named enclosing unit. If there is more than one visible enclosing overloaded subprogram of the given name, the selected component is ambiguous, independently of the identifier (see section 8.3 on visibility rules).

For variant records, a component identifier can denote a component in a variant part. In such a case, the component must be one of those that must be present for the existing discriminant value (or values), otherwise the exception CONSTRAINT_ERROR is raised. This exception is also raised if the name has the access value **null** in the above cases (a) and (b).

Examples of selected components:

```
APPOINTMENT.DAY          --  a record component
NEXT_CAR.OWNER           --  a record component
NEXT_CAR.OWNER.AGE       --  a record component
WRITER.UNIT              --  a record component (a discriminant)
MIN_CELL(H).VALUE        --  a selected component of the function call MIN_CELL(H)

NEXT_CAR.all             --  the object designated by the access variable NEXT_CAR

TABLE_MANAGER.INSERT     --  a procedure in the package TABLE_MANAGER
APPLICATION."*"          --  an operator in the package APPLICATION
CONTROL.SEIZE            --  an entry of the task CONTROL
POOL(K).WRITE            --  an entry of the task POOL(K)

MAIN.ITEM_COUNT          --  a variable declared in the procedure MAIN
```

Notes:

Every parameterless function call must use empty parentheses (see 6.4). Hence F().C can only be a selected component of the function result and, within the body of F, F.L can only be used to denote a locally declared entity L. For a record with components that are other records, the identifier of each level must be given to name a nested component.

References:

access object 3.8, access value 3.8, constraint_error exception 11.1, discriminant value 3.7.1, entity 3.1, function call 6.4, identifier 2.3, name 4.1, operator 4.5, operator symbol 6.1, overloading a subprogram 6.6, package 7, package body 7.3, record type 3.7, record component 3.7, subprogram body 6.3, task 9, task body 9.1, variant part 3.7.3, visible part 7.2

4.1.4 Attributes

Attributes denote certain predefined characteristics of named entities.

    attribute ::= name'identifier

An attribute identifier is always prefixed by an apostrophe; such an identifier is not reserved (unless it is already reserved for another reason). An attribute can be a value, a function, or a type or subtype. Specific attributes are described with the language constructs associated with their use.

Appendix A gives a list of all the language defined attributes. Additional attributes may exist for an implementation.

Examples of attributes:

```
COLOR'FIRST              —  minimum value of the enumeration type COLOR
RAINBOW'BASE'FIRST       —  same as COLOR'FIRST
REAL'DIGITS              —  precision of the type REAL
BOARD'LAST(2)            —  upper bound of the second dimension of BOARD
BOARD'RANGE(1)           —  subtype of index range of the first dimension of BOARD
POOL(K)'TERMINATED       —  TRUE if task POOL(K) is terminated
DATE'SIZE                —  number of bits for records of type DATE
CARD'ADDRESS             —  address of the record variable CARD
```

References:

enumeration type 3.5.1, function 6.5, identifier 2.3, real type 3.5.6, record variable 3.7, subtype declaration 3.3, task 9, type declaration 3.3, upper bound 3.6 3.6.1, value 3.2 3.3

4.2 Literals

A literal denotes an explicit value of a given type.

    literal ::=
        numeric_literal | enumeration_literal | character_string | **null**

Numeric literals are the literals of the types *universal_integer* and *universal_real*. Enumeration literals include character literals and denote values of the corresponding enumeration types. A character string denotes a one dimensional array of characters. The literal **null** stands for the null access value which designates no object at all.

Examples:

```
3.14159_26536    --  a real literal
1_345            --  an integer literal
CLUBS            --  an enumeration literal
'A'              --  an enumeration literal that is a character literal
"SOME TEXT"      --  a character string
```

References:

array type definition 3.6, character literal 2.5, character string 2.6, enumeration literal 3.5.1, null access value 3.8, numeric literal 2.4 3.2 4.10, universal_integer type 2.4 3.2 3.5.4 4.10, universal_real type 2.4 3.2 3.5.6 4.10

4.3 Aggregates

An aggregate denotes a record or an array value constructed from component values.

```
aggregate ::=
    (component_association  {, component_association})

component_association ::=
    [choice {| choice} => ] expression
```

The expressions define the values to be associated with components. An aggregate must be complete, that is, a value must be provided for each component of the composite value. Component associations can be given by position (in textual order for record components) or by naming the chosen components. Choices have the same syntax as in variant parts (see 3.7.3); they are component identifiers in the case of record aggregates, index values or ranges of index values in the case of array aggregates. Each value, or each component identifier must be represented once and only once in the set of choices of an aggregate. The choice **others** can only appear alone and in the last component association; it stands for all remaining components, if any.

For named components, the component associations can be given in any order (except for the choice **others**), but if both notations are used in one aggregate, all positional component associations must be given first. Aggregates containing a single component association must always be given in named notation. Specific rules concerning component associations exist for record aggregates and array aggregates.

An expression given in a component association must satisfy any constraint associated with a corresponding component, otherwise the exception CONSTRAINT_ERROR is raised.

Note:

The language does not define the order of evaluation of the expressions of the different component associations. Hence programs relying on a particular order are erroneous.

Aggregates may be *overloaded*, that is, a given aggregate may be an aggregate for more than one array or record type, its interpretation depending on the context.

References:

array type definition 3.6, array aggregate 4.3.2, composite value 3.3, constraint 3.3, constraint_error exception 11.1, expression 4.4, index value 3.6, others 3.7.3, record 3.7, record aggregate 4.3.1, value 3.3, variant 3.7.3

4.3.1 Record Aggregates

A record aggregate denotes a record value and must specify an explicit value for each component (including discriminants) of the record value, whether or not a default initial value exists for the component. A component association with more than one choice is only allowed if the denoted components are of the same type. The same rule applies for the choice **others** representing all other components.

The value specified for a discriminant governing a variant part must be given by a static expression.

Examples of positional record aggregate:

    (4, JULY, 1776)

Examples of record aggregates with named components:

    (DAY => 4, MONTH => JULY, YEAR => 1776)
    (MONTH => JULY, DAY => 4, YEAR => 1776)
    (UNIT => DISK, STATUS => CLOSED, CYLINDER => 9, TRACK => 1)
    (DISK, CLOSED, TRACK => 5, CYLINDER => 12)

Note:

For positional aggregates, discriminant values appear first since the discriminant part is given first; they must be in the same order as in the discriminant part.

References:

component association 4.3, default initial value 3.3 3.7, discriminant 3.7.1, discriminant part 3.7.1, discriminant value 3.7.1, record value 3.3 3.7, static expression 4.9, variant part 3.7.3

4.3.2 Array Aggregates

An array aggregate denotes an array value.

For aggregates in named notation, a choice given by a simple expression stands for the corresponding index value; a choice given by a discrete range stands for all possible index values in the range. The value of each choice (excepting **others**) must be determinable statically unless the aggregate consists of a single component association, including a single choice.

The bounds of a named aggregate that does not contain the choice **others** are determined by the smallest and largest choices given.

The bounds of any aggregate containing the choice **others** are defined by the context. The only allowable contexts for such an aggregate are as follows:

(a) The aggregate is an actual parameter corresponding to a formal parameter of a constrained array subtype.

(b) The aggregate appears in a return statement as the expression specifying the value returned by a function whose result is of a constrained array subtype.

(c) The aggregate is either qualified by a constrained array subtype, or used in an allocator for a constrained array subtype.

(d) The aggregate is used to specify the value of a component of an enclosing aggregate, and the enclosing aggregate is itself in one of these four contexts.

In each of these four cases the bounds are defined by the applicable index constraint.

The bounds of a positional aggregate not containing the choice **others** are similarly defined by the applicable index constraint, if the aggregate appears in one of the above four contexts. Otherwise, the lower bound is given by S'FIRST, where S is the index subtype; the upper bound is determined by the number of components.

An aggregate for an n-dimensional array is written as a one-dimensional aggregate of components that are (n-1)-dimensional array values. If an array aggregate contains positional component associations, the only named association it may contain is a component association with the choice **others**.

The exception CONSTRAINT_ERROR is raised if the number of components of the aggregate is incompatible with the context.

Examples of positional array aggregates:

```
(7, 9, 5, 1, 3, 2, 4, 8, 6, 0)
TABLE'(5, 8, 4, 1, others => 0)
```

Examples of array aggregates in named notation:

```
(1 .. 5 => (1 .. 8 => 0.0))

TABLE'(2 | 4 | 10 => 1, others => 0)  -- qualified by TABLE, see 4.7
SCHEDULE'(MON .. FRI => TRUE,   others => FALSE)
SCHEDULE'(WED | SUN => FALSE,  others => TRUE )
```

Examples of aggregates as initial values:

```
A : TABLE := (7, 9, 5, 1, 3, 2, 4, 8, 6, 0);        -- A(1) = 7, A(10) = 0
B : TABLE := TABLE'(2 | 4 | 10 => 1,others => 0);   -- B(1) = 0, B(10) = 1
C : constant MATRIX := (1 .. 5 => (1 .. 8 => 0.0)); -- C'FIRST(1) = 1, C'LAST(2) = 8

D : BIT_VECTOR(M .. N) := (M .. N    => TRUE);
E : BIT_VECTOR(M .. N) := (E'RANGE => TRUE);
F : STRING(1 .. 1) := (1 => 'F');  -- a one component aggregate:  same as "F"
```

References:

actual parameter 6.4, bound 3.6 3.6.1, component association 4.3, constrained array 3.6, discrete range 3.6.1, first attribute 3.6.2, formal parameter 6.2, function 6.5, index constraint 3.7.1, index value 3.6, others 3.7.3, qualified expression 4.7, simple expression 4.4

4.4 Expressions

An expression is a formula that defines the computation of a value.

```
expression ::=
     relation {and relation}
   | relation {or relation}
   | relation {xor relation}
   | relation {and then relation}
   | relation {or else relation}

relation ::=
     simple_expression [relational_operator simple_expression]
   | simple_expression [not] in range
   | simple_expression [not] in subtype_indication

simple_expression ::= [unary_operator] term {adding_operator term}

term ::= factor {multiplying_operator factor}

factor ::= primary [** primary]

primary ::=
     literal | aggregate | name | allocator | function_call
   | type_conversion | qualified_expression | (expression)
```

Each primary has a value and a type. The only names allowed as primaries are attributes (those which have a value) and names denoting objects (the value of such a primary is the value of the object). The type of an expression depends only on the type of its constituents and on the operators applied; for an overloaded constituent or operator, the determination of the constituent type, or the identification of the appropriate operator, may depend on the context. The rules defining the allowed operand types and the corresponding result types for all predefined operators are given in section 4.5 below.

Examples of primaries:

```
4.0                   -- real literal
(1 .. 10 => 0)        -- aggregate array value
VOLUME                -- value of a variable
DATE'SIZE             -- attribute
SINE(X)               -- function call
COLOR'(BLUE)          -- qualified expression
REAL(M*N)             -- conversion
(LINE_COUNT + 10)     -- parenthesized expression
```

Examples of expressions:

```
VOLUME                          --  primary
B**2                            --  factor
LINE_COUNT mod PAGE_SIZE        --  term

-4.0                            --  simple expression
not DESTROYED                   --  simple expression
B**2 - 4.0*A*C                  --  simple expression

PASSWORD(1 .. 5) = "JAMES"      --  relation
N not in 1 .. 10                --  relation

INDEX = 0 or ITEM_HIT           --  expression
(COLD and SUNNY) or WARM        --  expression, the parentheses are required
A**(B**C)                       --  expression, the parentheses are required
```

References:

adding operator 4.5.3, aggregate 4.3, allocator 4.8, array aggregate 4.3.2, attribute 4.1.4, function call 6.4, literal 2.5 4.2, multiplying operator 4.5.5, name 4.1, object 3.2, overloading 3.5.1 6.6 6.7, qualified expression 4.7, range 3.5, subtype indication 3.3, type 3, type conversion 4.6, unary operator 4.5.4, value 3.3, variable 3.2 4.1

4.5 Operators and Expression Evaluation

The following operators, divided into six classes, have a predefined meaning in the language. These operators, and only these, may be overloaded for user defined types and, excepting equality and inequality, may be redefined (see 6.7). They are given in the order of increasing precedence.

```
logical_operator        ::=  and | or | xor

relational_operator     ::=  =  | /= | <   | <= | > | >=

adding_operator         ::=  +  | -  | &

unary_operator          ::=  +  | -  | not

multiplying_operator    ::=  *  | /  | mod | rem

exponentiating_operator ::=  **
```

The short circuit control forms **and then** and **or else** have the same precedence as logical operators. The membership tests **in** and **not in** have the same precedence as relational operators.

All operands of a factor, term, simple expression, or relation, and the operands of an expression that does not contain a short circuit control form, are evaluated (in an undefined order) before application of the corresponding operator. The right operand of a short circuit control form is evaluated if and only if the left operand has a certain value (see 4.5.1).

For a term, simple expression, relation, or expression, operators of higher precedence are applied first. In this case, for a sequence of operators of the same precedence level, the operators are applied in textual order from left to right (or in any order giving the same result); parentheses can be used to impose a specific order.

The execution of some operations may raise an exception for certain values of the operands. Real expressions are not necessarily evaluated with exactly the specified accuracy (precision or delta), but the accuracy will be at least as good as that specified.

Examples of precedence:

```
not SUNNY or WARM          -- same as (not SUNNY) or WARM
X > 4.0 and Y > 0.0        -- same as (X > 4.0) and (Y > 0.0)

-4.0*A**2                  -- same as -(4.0 * (A**2))
Y**(-3)                    -- parentheses are necessary
A / B * C                  -- same as (A/B)*C
A + (B + C)                -- evaluate B + C before adding it to A
```

Note:

The language does not define the order of evaluation of the two operands of an operator (excepting short circuit control forms). A program that relies on a specific order (for example because of mutual side effects) is therefore erroneous.

References:

accuracy of operations with real operands 4.5.8, adding operator 4.5.3, delta 3.5.9, exception 11, expression 4.4, factor 4.4, logical operator 4.5.1, membership operator 4.5.2, name 4.1, overloading an operator 6.7, precision 3.5.6, real type definition 3.5.6, relation 4.4, relational operator 4.5.2, short circuit control form 4.5.1, simple expression 4.4, term 4.4, type 3

4.5.1 Logical Operators and Short Circuit Control Forms

The predefined logical operators are applicable to BOOLEAN values and to one dimensional arrays of BOOLEAN values having the same number of components.

Operator	Operation	Operand Type	Result Type
and	conjunction	BOOLEAN array of BOOLEAN components	BOOLEAN same array type
or	inclusive disjunction	BOOLEAN array of BOOLEAN components	BOOLEAN same array type
xor	exclusive disjunction	BOOLEAN array of BOOLEAN components	BOOLEAN same array type

The operations on (non null) arrays are performed on a component by component basis on matching components (as for equality, see 4.5.2). The lower bound of the index of the resulting array is the lower bound of the index subtype of the array type.

The operands need not have the same bounds, but must have the same number of components, otherwise the exception CONSTRAINT_ERROR is raised.

The short circuit control forms **and then** and **or else** are applied to operands of the predefined type BOOLEAN and deliver a value of this type. If the left operand of an expression with the control form **and then** evaluates to FALSE, the right operand is not evaluated and the value of the expression is FALSE. If the left operand of an expression with the control form **or else** evaluates to TRUE, the right operand is not evaluated and the value of the expression is TRUE. If both operands are evaluated, **and then** delivers the same result as **and**, and **or else** delivers the same result as **or**.

Examples of logical operators:

```
SUNNY or WARM
FILTER(1 .. 10) and FILTER(15 .. 24)
```

Examples of short circuit control forms:

```
NEXT_CAR.OWNER /= null and then NEXT_CAR.OWNER.AGE > 25
N = 0 or else A(N) = HIT_VALUE
```

References:

array type definition 3.6, boolean type 3.5.3, boolean value 3.5.3, bound 3.6.1, component 3.6, constraint_error exception 11.1, equality 4.5.2, expression 4.4, false 3.5.3, index 3.6, true 3.5.3

4.5.2 Relational and Membership Operators

The predefined relational operators have operands of the same type and return values of the predefined type BOOLEAN. Equality and inequality are predefined for any two objects of the same type, excepting limited private types and composite types having components of limited private types.

Operator	Operation	Operand Type	Result Type
= /=	equality and inequality	any type	BOOLEAN
< <= > >=	test for ordering	any scalar type discrete array type	BOOLEAN BOOLEAN

Equality for the discrete types is equality of the values. For real operands whose values are *nearly* equal, the results of the predefined relational operators are given in section 4.5.8. Two access values are equal either if they designate the same object, or if both are equal to **null**.

The values of two non null arrays or two non null records, of the same type, are equal if and only if their matching components are equal, as given by the predefined equality operator for the component type. Two null arrays of the same type are always equal; two null records of the same type are always equal. If equality is explicitly defined for a limited private type, it does not extend to composite types having components of the limited private type. Equality can be defined explicitly for such composite types.

For comparing two non null records of the same type, matching components are those which have the same component identifier.

For comparing two non null one dimensional arrays of the same type, matching components are those whose index values match in the following sense: the lower bounds of the index ranges are defined to match, and the successors of matching indices are defined to match. For multidimensional arrays, matching components are those whose index values match in successive index positions. If any component of an array has no matching component in the other array, the two arrays are not equal.

The inequality operator gives the complementary result to the equality operator.

The ordering operators <, <=, >, and >= are defined for one dimensional arrays of an array type whose components are of a discrete type. These operators correspond to lexicographic order using the order relation of the component type for corresponding components. A null array is less than any array having at least one component.

The membership tests **in** and **not in** test whether a value is within a corresponding range, or whether it satisfies any constraint imposed by a subtype indication. The value must be of the same type as the bounds of the range or as the base type of the subtype. These operators return a value of the predefined type BOOLEAN. A test for an accuracy constraint always yields the result TRUE.

Examples:

```
X /= Y                         --  with real X and Y, is implementation dependent

"" < "A" and "A" < "AA"        --  TRUE
"AA" < "B"                     --  TRUE

MY_CAR = null                  --  true if MY_CAR has been set to null
MY_CAR = YOUR_CAR              --  true if we both share the same car
MY_CAR.all = YOUR_CAR.all      --  true if the two cars are identical

N not in 1 .. 10               --  range check
TODAY in WEEKDAY               --  subtype check
TODAY in DAY range MON .. FRI  --  same subtype check
ARCHIVE in DISK_UNIT           --  subtype check
```

References:

access value 3.8, accuracy constraint 3.5.6, accuracy of operations with real operands 4.5.8, array type definition 3.6, boolean type 3.5.3, bounds 3.6, component 3.3, composite type 3.6 3.7, constraint 3.3, delta attribute 3.5.10, discrete type 3.5, fixed point type 3.5.9, floating point type 3.5.7, index range 3.6, index value 3.6, limited private type 7.4.2, range 3.5, real type 3.5.6, record value 3.7, scalar type 3.5, subtype declaration 3.3, small attribute 3.5.8, type declaration 3

4.5.3 Adding Operators

The predefined adding operators + and - return a result of the same type as the operands.

Operator	Operation	Operand Type	Result Type
+	addition	numeric type	same numeric type
-	subtraction	numeric type	same numeric type
&	catenation	one dimensional array type	same array type

For real types, the accuracy of the result is determined by the operand type. For all numeric types the exception NUMERIC_ERROR is raised if the result of addition or subtraction does not lie within the implemented range of the type (for real operands see 4.5.8).

The adding operator & (catenation) is applied to two operands of a one dimensional array type. Catenation is also defined for a left operand of a one dimensional array type and a right operand of the corresponding component type and vice versa. The result is an array of the same type. For any one-dimensional array type T whose component type is C and whose index is specified as

```
INDEX range <>
```

the effect of catenation is defined by the three following functions

```
LOW : constant INDEX := INDEX'FIRST;

function "&" (X, Y : T) return T is
   RESULT : T(LOW .. INDEX'VAL(INDEX'POS(LOW) + (X'LENGTH + Y'LENGTH - 1)));
begin
   RESULT(LOW .. INDEX'VAL(INDEX'POS(LOW) + (X'LENGTH - 1))) := X;
   RESULT(INDEX'VAL(INDEX'POS(LOW) + X'LENGTH) .. RESULT'LAST) := Y;
   return RESULT;
end;

function "&" (X : C; Y : T) return T is
begin
   return (LOW => X) & Y;
end;

function "&" (X : T; Y : C) return T is
begin
   return X & (LOW => Y);
end;
```

The exception CONSTRAINT_ERROR is raised if the upper bound of the result exceeds the range of the index subtype.

Examples:

```
Z + 0.1       --  Z must be of a real type
"A" & "BCD"   --  catenation of two strings
```

References:

accuracy of operations 4.5.8, array type 3.6, catenation 3.6.3, numeric type 3.5, numeric_error exception 11.1, real type 3.5.6, string 2.6 3.6.3, type declaration 3

4.5.4 Unary Operators

The predefined unary operators are applied to a single operand and return a result of the same type.

Operator	Operation	Operand Type	Result Type
+	identity	numeric type	same numeric type
-	negation	numeric type	same numeric type
not	logical negation	BOOLEAN array of BOOLEAN components	BOOLEAN same array type

The operator **not** may be applied to a one dimensional array of BOOLEAN components. The result is a one dimensional boolean array with the same bounds; each component of the result is obtained by logical negation of the corresponding component of the operand (that is, the component which has the same index value).

For a numeric operand, the exception NUMERIC_ERROR is raised if the result does not lie within the implemented range of the type (for real operands see 4.5.8).

References:

accuracy of operations with real operands 4.5.8, array type 3.6, numeric type 3.5, numeric_error exception 11.1

4.5.5 Multiplying Operators

The predefined operators ∗ and / for integer and floating point values and the predefined operators **mod** and **rem** for integer values return a result of the same type as the operands.

Operator	Operation	Operand Type	Result Type
∗	multiplication	integer floating	same integer type same floating point type
/	integer division floating division	integer floating	same integer type same floating point type
mod	modulus	integer	same integer type
rem	remainder	integer	same integer type

Integer division and remainder are defined by the relation

$$A = (A/B)*B + (A \text{ rem } B)$$

where (A **rem** B) has the sign of A and an absolute value less than the absolute value of B. Integer division satisfies the identity

$$(-A)/B = -(A/B) = A/(-B)$$

The result of the modulus operation is such that (A **mod** B) has the sign of B and an absolute value less than the absolute value of B; in addition this result must satisfy the relation

$$A = B*N + (A \text{ mod } B)$$

for some integer value of N.

For fixed point values, the following multiplication and division operations are provided. The types of the left and right operands are denoted by L and R.

Operator	Operation	Operand Type L	R	Result Type
*	multiplication	fixed	integer	same as L
		integer	fixed	same as R
		fixed	fixed	*universal_fixed*
/	division	fixed	integer	same as L
		fixed	fixed	*universal_fixed*

Integer multiplication of fixed point values is equivalent to repeated addition and hence is an accurate operation. Division of a fixed point value by an integer does not involve a change in type but is approximate.

Multiplication of operands of the same or of different fixed point types is exact and delivers a result of the type *universal_fixed* whose delta is arbitrarily small. The result of any such multiplication must always be explicitly converted to some numeric type. This ensures explicit control of the accuracy of the computation. The same considerations apply to division of a fixed point value by another fixed point value.

The exception NUMERIC_ERROR is raised by any multiplying operator if the result does not lie within the implemented range of the type (for real operands see 4.5.8). In particular it is raised by integer division, **rem**, and **mod** if the second operand is zero.

Examples:

```
I  : INTEGER := 1;
J  : INTEGER := 2;
K  : INTEGER := 3;

X  : MY_FLOAT digits 6 := 1.0;
Y  : MY_FLOAT digits 6 := 2.0;

F  : FRAC delta 0.0001 := 0.1;
G  : FRAC delta 0.0001 := 0.1;
```

Expression	Value	Result Type
I*J	2	same as I and J, that is, INTEGER
K/J	1	same as K and J, that is, INTEGER
K **mod** J	1	same as K and J, that is, INTEGER
X/Y	0.5	same as X and Y, that is, MY_FLOAT
F/2	0.05	same as F, that is, FRAC
3*F	0.3	same as F, that is, FRAC
F*G	0.01	*universal_fixed*, conversion needed
FRAC(F*G)	0.01	FRAC, as stated by the conversion
MY_FLOAT(J)*Y	4.0	MY_FLOAT, the type of both operands after conversion of J

Notes:

For positive A and B, A/B is the quotient and A **rem** B is the remainder when A is divided by B. The following relations are satisfied by the **rem** operator:

$$A \ \textbf{rem} \ (-B) \ = \ A \ \textbf{rem} \ B$$
$$(-A) \ \textbf{rem} \ B \ = \ -(A \ \textbf{rem} \ B)$$

For any integer K the following identity holds

$$A \quad \textbf{mod} \quad B \ = \ (A + K*B) \ \textbf{mod} \ B$$

The relations between integer division, remainder and modulus are illustrated by the following table

A	B	A/B	A **rem** B	A **mod** B	A	B	A/B	A **rem** B	A **mod** B
10	5	2	0	0	-10	5	-2	0	0
11	5	2	1	1	-11	5	-2	-1	4
12	5	2	2	2	-12	5	-2	-2	3
13	5	2	3	3	-13	5	-2	-3	2
14	5	2	4	4	-14	5	-2	-4	1
10	-5	-2	0	0	-10	-5	2	0	0
11	-5	-2	1	-4	-11	-5	2	-1	-1
12	-5	-2	2	-3	-12	-5	2	-2	-2
13	-5	-2	3	-2	-13	-5	2	-3	-3
14	-5	-2	4	-1	-14	-5	2	-4	-4

References:

accuracy of operations 4.5.8, addition 4.5.3, fixed point type 3.5.9, floating point type 3.5.7, integer type 3.5.4, numeric type 3.5, numeric_error exception 4.5.8 11.1, relation 4.4, type definition 3.3

4.5.6 Exponentiating Operator

The predefined exponentiating operator ** is used for exponentiation.

Operator	Operation	Operand Type		Result Type
		L	R	
**	exponentiation	integer	non-negative integer	same as L
		floating	integer	same as L

Exponentiation of an operand by a positive exponent is equivalent to repeated multiplication (as indicated by the exponent) of the operand by itself. For a floating operand, the exponent can be negative, in which case the value is the reciprocal of the value with the positive exponent. Exponentiation by a zero exponent delivers the value one.

Exponentiation of an integer raises the exception CONSTRAINT_ERROR for a negative exponent. Exponentation raises the exception NUMERIC_ERROR if the result does not lie within the implemented range of the type (for real operands see 4.5.8).

References:

constraint_error exception 11.1, floating point type 3.5.7, multiplication 4.5.5, numeric type 3.5, numeric_error exception 11.1

4.5.7 The Function Abs

The predefined function ABS returns the absolute value of its operand.

Function	Operation	Operand type	Result type
ABS	absolute value	numeric type	same numeric type

The exception NUMERIC_ERROR is raised if the result does not lie within the implemented range of the type (for a real argument see 4.5.8).

Examples:

    ABS(J - K)

References:

accuracy of operations with real operands 4.5.8, numeric_error exception 11.1

4.5.8 Accuracy of Operations with Real Operands

A real type or subtype specifies a set of model numbers. Both the accuracy to be expected from any operation giving a real result, and the result of any relation between real operands are defined in terms of these model numbers.

Given a real value of a type or subtype T there (normally) exists a smallest interval whose bounds are model numbers and which encloses the given real value. This interval is called the *model interval* associated with the real value. This model interval is not defined where the absolute value of the given value exceeds the largest model number, that is, T'LARGE; the model interval is then said to *overflow*.

The model interval associated with a model number is an interval consisting of the number alone. The model interval associated with a real interval (that is, a range of real values) is the smallest interval whose bounds are model numbers and which encloses the values of the real interval.

The bounds on a real value resulting from a predefined operation are defined by the three following steps:

(1) A model interval of the appropriate type or subtype is associated with the value of each operand.

(2) A new interval is formed by applying the (exact) mathematical operation to operands from the model intervals produced in step (1); for one operand the new interval consists of the range of results produced for all operands in the model interval; for two operands the new interval consists of the range of results produced for all pairs of operands selected from the corresponding model intervals.

(3) A model interval of the type of the result of the operation is associated with the interval produced in step (2).

Step (3) gives the required bounds on the result of the machine operation, except when one of the model intervals in step (1) or (3) overflows. The exception NUMERIC_ERROR can only (but need not) be raised in the case of interval overflow.

The result of a relation between two real operands (which need not be of the same subtype) is defined by associating a model interval of the appropriate type or subtype with each operand, and then according to the cases which follow:

(a) The intervals are disjoint (no real value is in both): the result is the (exact) mathematical result.

(b) Each interval is a single model number, and they are equal; the result is the (exact) mathematical result.

(c) The intervals have only a single number in common (this number can only be a model number): the result is the (exact) mathematical result either of comparing the given operands or of comparing the first operand with itself.

(d) Either the intervals have more than one value in common, or one of the intervals (at least) overflows: the result is implementation defined.

The exception NUMERIC_ERROR can only (but need not) be raised in the case of interval overflow.

Notes:

Given X/Y where X = 15.0 and Y = 3.0 which are both model numbers, then the result is exactly 5.0 provided this is a model number of the resulting type. In the general case, division does not yield model numbers and in consequence one cannot assume that (1.0/3.0)∗3.0 = 1.0

References:

bound 3.5, large attribute 3.5.8, model number 3.5.6, numeric_error exception 11.1, predefined operator 4.5, range 3.5, real type 3.5.6, relational operator 4.5.2, subtype declaration 3.3

4.6 Type Conversions

Explicit type conversions are allowed between closely related types as defined below:

    type_conversion ::= type_mark (expression)

The only allowed type conversions correspond to the following three cases:

(a) Numeric types

The expression can be of any numeric type; the value of the expression is converted to the base type of the type mark; this base type must also be a numeric type. For conversions involving real types, the result is within the accuracy of the specified type. Conversion of a real value into an integer type involves rounding.

(b) Array types

The conversion is allowed when for both array types (the operand type, and the base type of the type mark) the index types for each dimension are the same or one is derived from the other, and the component types are the same or one is derived from the other. If the type mark denotes an unconstrained array type, the bounds of the result are the same as those of the operand. If the type mark denotes a constrained array (sub)type, for each component of either array there must be a matching component of the other array; the bounds of the result are then those imposed by the type mark. In either case the value of each component of the result is the same as that of the matching component of the operand (see 4.5.2 for the definition of matching components).

(c) Derived types

The conversion is allowed when the type of the operand is (directly) derived from the type denoted by the type mark, or vice versa. The conversion may result in a change of representation (see 13.6).

The exception CONSTRAINT_ERROR is raised by a type conversion if the value of the operand fails to satisfy a constraint imposed by the type mark. For array type conversions this includes any index constraint.

If a conversion is allowed from one type to another, the reverse conversion is also allowed. This reverse conversion is used where an actual parameter of mode **in out** or **out** is a type conversion of a (variable) name. For a parameter of mode **in out** the value of the named object is converted before the call and the converted value is passed as actual parameter; for parameters of modes **in out** or **out**, the value of the formal parameter is converted back to the operand type upon return from the subprogram.

Examples of numeric type conversion:

```
REAL(2*J)        --   value is converted to floating point
INTEGER(1.6)     --   value is 2
INTEGER(-0.4)    --   value is 0
```

Examples of conversions between array types:

```
type SEQUENCE is array (INTEGER range <>) of INTEGER;
subtype DOZEN is SEQUENCE(1 .. 12);
LEDGER : array(1 .. 100) of INTEGER;

SEQUENCE(LEDGER)              --   bounds are those of LEDGER
SEQUENCE(LEDGER(31 .. 42))    --   bounds are 31 and 42
DOZEN(LEDGER(31 .. 42))       --   bounds are those of DOZEN
```

Example of conversion between derived types:

```
type A_FORM is new B_FORM;

X   : A_FORM;
Y   : B_FORM;

X   := A_FORM(Y);
Y   := B_FORM(X);   --   the reverse conversion
```

References:

actual parameter 6.4, array type definition 3.6, base type 3.3, bounds 3.6.1, component 3.2, constrained array 3.6, constraint 3.3, constraint_error exception 11.1, derived type 3.4, expression 4.4, floating point type 3.5.7, formal parameter 6.2, in out parameter 6.2, index constraint 3.6.1, integer type 3.5.4, name 3.1 4.1, numeric type 3.5, out parameter 6.2, real type 3.5.6, type definition 3.3, type mark 3.3, unconstrained array type 3.6, variable 3.2 4.1

4.7 Qualified Expressions

A qualified expression is used to state explicitly the type, and possibly the subtype, of an expression or aggregate.

```
qualified_expression ::=
    type_mark'(expression)  |  type_mark'aggregate
```

The expression (or the aggregate) must have the same type as the base type of the type mark. In addition it must satisfy any constraint imposed by the type mark, otherwise the exception CONSTRAINT_ERROR is raised.

Examples:

```
type MASK is (FIX, DEC, EXP, SIGNIF);
type CODE is (FIX, CLA, DEC, TNZ, SUB);

PRINT (MASK'(DEC));      -- DEC is of type MASK
PRINT (CODE'(DEC));      -- DEC is of type CODE

for I in CODE'(FIX) .. CODE'(DEC) loop ...    -- qualification needed for either FIX or DEC
for I in CODE range FIX .. DEC loop ...       -- qualification unnecessary
for I in CODE'(FIX) .. DEC loop ...           -- qualification unnecessary for DEC

DOZEN'(1 | 3 | 5 | 7 => 2, others => 0)
```

Notes:

The same enumeration literal may appear in several types; it is then said to be overloaded. In these cases and whenever the type of an enumeration literal or aggregate is not known from the context, a qualified expression may be used to state the type explicitly. In particular, an overloaded enumeration literal must be qualified in a subprogram call to an overloaded subprogram that cannot be identified when given as a parameter on the basis of remaining parameter or result types, in a relational expression where both operands are overloaded enumeration literals, or in an array or loop parameter range where both bounds are overloaded enumeration literals. Explicit qualification is also used to specify which one of a set of overloaded parameterless functions is meant, or to constrain a value to a given subtype.

References:

aggregate 4.3, base type 3.3, constraint 3.3, constraint_error exception 11.1, enumeration literal 3.5.1, expression 4.4, literal 4.2, loop parameter 5.5, overloaded literal 3.4 3.5.1, overloaded subprogram 6.6, parameter 6.2, relational expression 4.4, subprogram call 6.4, subtype declaration 3.3, type declaration 3.3, type mark 3.3

4.8 Allocators

The execution of an allocator creates an object and delivers as result an access value that designates the object.

```
allocator ::=
      new type_mark [(expression)]
    | new type_mark aggregate
    | new type_mark discriminant_constraint
    | new type_mark index_constraint
```

The type mark given in an allocator denotes the type of the object created; the type of the access value returned by the allocator is defined by the context.

For the execution of an allocator, any expression, aggregate, discriminant constraint or index constraint is first evaluated; a new object of the type given by the type mark is then created. If the type mark denotes an unconstrained array type or an unconstrained type with discriminants, the allocator must contain either an explicit initial value (an expression or an aggregate), or an index or discriminant constraint; this is the only case in which an index or discriminant constraint is permitted. The created object is constrained by such an explicit constraint, or by the bounds or discriminants of the initial value.

If a default initial value exists for objects of the type or for some of their components, excepting discriminants, then the corresponding default initializations are performed. Finally any explicitly given initial value is assigned to the object, subject to the constraint of the type mark, and an access value designating the created object is returned.

The exception CONSTRAINT_ERROR is raised if either the initial value, or the discriminant or bound values imposed by the constraint, fail to satisfy any constraint imposed by the type mark.

An object created by the execution of an allocator remains allocated for as long as this object is accessible directly or indirectly, that is, as long as it can be designated by some name. When such an object becomes inaccessible, the storage it occupies can be reclaimed (but need not be), depending on the implementation.

When an application needs closer control over storage allocation for objects of an access type, such control may be achieved by one or more of the following means.

(a)   The total amount of storage available for the collection of objects of an access type can be set by means of a length specification (see 13.2).

(b)   The pragma CONTROLLED informs the implementation that automatic storage reclamation should not be performed except upon leaving the scope of the access type definition. The form of this pragma is as follows

   pragma CONTROLLED (*access_type_*name);

   The position of a CONTROLLED pragma is governed by the same rules as for a representation specification (see 13.1). This pragma cannot be used for a derived type.

(c)   Explicit deallocation of individual access objects may be done by calling a procedure obtained by instantiation of the predefined generic library procedure UNCHECKED_DEALLOCATION (see 13.10.1).

The exception STORAGE_ERROR is raised by an allocator if there is not enough storage.

Examples:

```
new  CELL(0, null, null)
new  CELL(VALUE => 0, SUCC => null, PRED => null)
new  MATRIX(1 .. 10, 1 .. 20)              --   not initialized
new  MATRIX(1 .. 10 => (1 .. 20 => 0.0))   --   initialized
new  BUFFER(100)                           --   constrained
new  BUFFER(SIZE => 100, POS => 0, VALUE => (1 .. 100 => 'A'))
```

References:

access value 3.8, aggregate 4.3, bounds 3.6.1, component 3.2, discriminant constraint 3.7.2, expression 4.4, index constraint 3.7.1, type declaration 3.3, type mark 3.3, unconstrained array type 3.6

4.9 Static Expressions

Static expressions are defined in terms of their possible constituents. Every constituent of a static expression must be one of the following:

(a) a literal or a literal expression

(b) an aggregate whose components and choices are static expressions; if the choice **others** occurs it must correspond to a static range

(c) a constant initialized by a static expression

(d) a predefined operator, a membership test, the predefined function ABS, or a short circuit control form

(e) an attribute whose value is static; for attributes that are function names, the arguments must also be static expressions

(f) a qualified static expression or the result of a type conversion applied to a static expression, provided that any constraint imposed by the type mark is static

(g) a selected component of a record constant initialized by a static expression

(h) an indexed component of an array constant initialized by a static expression, where the indices are static expressions

Static expressions must be evaluated at compilation time when they appear in a construct in which a static expression is required by the rules of the language. If compile time analysis of such a static expression shows that its evaluation will raise an exception then the static expression must be replaced by code that raises the exception.

References:

aggregate 4.3, attribute 3.3, component 3.2, constant 3.2, constraint 3.3, exception 11, function 6.1 6.4 6.5, indexed component 4.1.1, literal 2.4 3.2 4.2, operator 4.5, qualified expression 4.7, type conversion 4.6

4.10 Literal Expressions

Literal expressions are defined in terms of their possible primary constituents and operators. A primary in a literal expression must be either a numeric literal, a name of a numeric literal, a call of the predefined function ABS, or a literal expression enclosed in parentheses. The value of a literal expression is of the type *universal_integer* if all its primaries are of this type, otherwise it is of the type *universal_real*.

The only operators allowed in a universal integer literal expression are the predefined operators which take operands of integer type.

The only operators allowed in a universal real literal expression are as follows:

- The unary operators +, and -, the function ABS, and the binary operators +, -, *, and /, for universal real operands

- Multiplication of a universal real value by a universal integer value and vice versa.

- Division and exponentiation with a universal real first operand and universal integer second operand

The relational operators are also available with universal real operands and deliver a BOOLEAN result.

The evaluation of a literal expression must deliver a result that is at least as accurate as the most accurate numeric type supported by the implementation.

Examples:

```
1 + 1          -- 2
ABS(-10)*3     -- 30

KILO   : constant := 1000;
MEGA   : constant := KILO*KILO;
LONG   : constant := FLOAT'DIGITS*2;

HALF_PI     : constant := PI/2;
DEG_TO_RAD  : constant := HALF_PI/180;
RAD_TO_DEG  : constant := 1.0/DEG_TO_RAD;   --   equivalent to (1.0/(((3.14159_26536)/2)/180))
```

References:

abs function 4.5.7, expression 4.4, integer type 3.5.4, name of numeric literal 3.2, numeric literal 2.4, operator 4.5, primary 4.4, relational operator 4.5.2, universal integer type 2.4 3.2 3.5.4, universal real type 2.4 3.2 3.5.6

5. Statements

The execution of statements causes actions to be performed.

This section describes the general rules applicable to all statements. Some specific statements are discussed in later chapters: Procedure calls are described in Chapter 6 on subprograms. Entry calls, delay, accept, select, and abort statements are described in Chapter 9 on tasks. Raise statements are described in Chapter 11 on exceptions and code statements in Chapter 13. The remaining forms of statements are presented here.

References:

abort statement 9.10, accept statement 9.5, code statement 13.8, delay statement 9.6, entry call 9.5, procedure call 6.4, raise statement 11.3

5.1 Simple and Compound Statements - Sequences of Statements

A statement may be simple or compound. A simple statement contains no other statement. A compound statement may contain simple statements and other compound statements.

```
sequence_of_statements ::= statement {statement}

statement ::=
    {label} simple_statement | {label} compound_statement

simple_statement ::= null_statement
    | assignment_statement    | exit_statement
    | return_statement        | goto_statement
    | procedure_call          | entry_call
    | delay_statement         | abort_statement
    | raise_statement         | code_statement

compound_statement ::=
      if_statement            | case_statement
    | loop_statement          | block
    | accept_statement        | select_statement

label ::= <<identifier>>

null_statement ::= null;
```

A statement may be labeled with an identifier enclosed by double angle brackets. Labels are implicitly declared at the end of the declarative part of the innermost enclosing subprogram body, package body, or task body. Consequently, within the sequence of statements of a subprogram, package, or task body, any two labels given for the same statement or for different statements must have different identifiers.

The implicit declarations for different labels, loop identifiers and block identifiers are assumed to occur in the same order as the beginnings of the labeled statements, loop statements and blocks themselves.

Execution of a null statement has no other effect than to pass to the next action.

The statements in a sequence of statements are executed in succession unless an exception is raised or an exit, return, or goto statement is executed.

Examples of labeled statements:

    <<AFTER>> null;
    <<THERE>> <<LA>> <<DORT>> null;

References:

abort statement 9.10, accept statement 9.5, assignment statement 5.2, block 5.6, case statement 5.4, code statement 13.8, delay statement 9.6, exception 11, exit statement 5.7, goto statement 5.9, if statement 5.3, loop statement 5.5, package body 7.1 7.3, procedure 6, raise statement 11.3, return statement 5.8, select statement 9.7, subprogram body 6.3, task body 9.1

5.2 Assignment Statement

An assignment statement replaces the current value of a variable with a new value specified by an expression. The named variable and the right hand side expression must be of the same type.

    assignment_statement ::=
        *variable*_name := expression;

For the execution of an assignment statement, the expression of the right hand side, and any expression used in the specification of the variable name are first evaluated. The value of the expression must satisfy any range, index, or discriminant constraint applicable to the variable; then the value of the expression is assigned to the variable. Otherwise the exception CONSTRAINT_ERROR is raised.

Examples:

    VALUE   := MAX_VALUE - 1;
    SHADE   := BLUE;

    NEXT_FRAME(F)(M, N) := 2.5;
    U := DOT_PRODUCT(V, W);

    WRITER   := (STATUS => OPEN, UNIT => PRINTER, LINE_COUNT => 60);
    NEXT_CAR.all := (72074, null);

Examples of constraint checks:

```
I, J : INTEGER range 1 .. 10;
K    : INTEGER range 1 .. 20;

I := J;    --   identical ranges
K := J;    --   compatible ranges
J := K;    --   will raise the exception CONSTRAINT_ERROR if K > 10
```

Notes:

The language does not define whether evaluation of the expression on the right hand side precedes, follows, or is concurrent with that of any expression used in the specification of the variable name. A program that relies on a specific order is therefore erroneous.

The discriminants of an object designated by an access value cannot be altered (even by a complete object assignment) since such objects, created by allocators, are always constrained (see 4.8).

References:

access value 3.8, allocator 4.8, constraint_error exception 11.1, discriminant 3.7.1, discriminant constraint 3.7.2, expression 4.4, index constraint 3.6, name 4.1, range constraint 3.5, variable 3.2

5.2.1 Array Assignments

For an assignment to an array variable (including assignment to a slice), each component of the array value is assigned to the matching component of the array variable. For each component of either the array value or the array variable, there must be a matching component in the other array. Otherwise, no assignment is performed and the exception CONSTRAINT_ERROR is raised.

Examples:

```
A  : STRING(1 .. 31);
B  : STRING(3 .. 33);

A := B;    --   same number of components

A(1 .. 9)  := "tar sauce";
A(4 .. 12) := A(1 .. 9);   --   A(1 .. 12) = "tartar sauce"
```

Notes:

Array assignment is defined even in the case of overlapping slices, because the expression on the right hand side is evaluated before performing any component assignment. In the above example, an implementation yielding A(1 .. 12) = "tartartartar" would be incorrect.

References:

array component 3.6, array value 3.6, array variable 3.2 3.6, assignment statement 5.2, constraint_error exception 11.1, expression 4.4, matching components 4.5.2, slice 4.1.2

5.3 If Statements

An if statement selects for execution one or none of a number of sequences of statements, depending on the truth value of one or more corresponding conditions. The expressions specifying conditions must be of the predefined type BOOLEAN.

```
if_statement ::=
    if condition then
        sequence_of_statements
  { elsif condition then
        sequence_of_statements}
  [ else
        sequence_of_statements]
    end if;

condition ::= boolean_expression
```

For the execution of an if statement the condition specified after **if** and any conditions specified after **elsif** are evaluated in succession (treating a final **else** as **elsif** TRUE **then**), until one evaluates to TRUE; then the corresponding sequence of statements is executed. If none of the conditions evaluates to TRUE, none of the sequences of statements is executed.

Examples:

```
if MONTH = DECEMBER and DAY = 31 then
    MONTH := JANUARY;
    DAY   := 1;
    YEAR  := YEAR + 1;
end if;

if INDENT then
    CHECK_LEFT_MARGIN;
    LEFT_SHIFT;
elsif OUTDENT then
    RIGHT_SHIFT;
else
    CARRIAGE_RETURN;
    CONTINUE_SCAN;
end if;

if MY_CAR.OWNER.VEHICLE /= MY_CAR then
    FAIL ("INCORRECT RECORD");
end if;
```

References:

boolean type 3.5.3, boolean expression 3.5.3 4.4, sequence of statements 5.1, true 3.5.3, truth value 3.5.3

5.4 Case Statements

A case statement selects for execution one of a number of alternative sequences of statements, depending on the value of an expression. The expression must be of a discrete type.

```
case_statement ::=
   case expression is
      {when choice {| choice} => sequence_of_statements}
   end case;
```

Each alternative sequence of statements is preceded by a list of choices (see 3.7.3) specifying the values for which the alternative is selected. The type of the expression must be known independently of the context (for example, it cannot be an overloaded literal). Each value of the subtype of the expression, if this subtype is static, otherwise each value of the type of the expression, must be represented once and only once in the set of choices of a case statement. The choice **others** may only be given as the choice for the last alternative, to cover all values (possibly none) not given in previous choices. The values specified by choices given in a case statement must be determinable statically.

Examples:

```
case SENSOR is
   when ELEVATION   => RECORD_ELEVATION (SENSOR_VALUE);
   when AZIMUTH     => RECORD_AZIMUTH  (SENSOR_VALUE);
   when DISTANCE    => RECORD_DISTANCE (SENSOR_VALUE);
   when others      => null;
end case;

case TODAY is
   when MON         => COMPUTE_INITIAL_BALANCE;
   when FRI         => COMPUTE_CLOSING_BALANCE;
   when TUE .. THU  => GENERATE_REPORT(TODAY);
   when SAT .. SUN  => null;
end case;

case BIN_NUMBER(COUNT) is
   when 1       => UPDATE_BIN(1);
   when 2       => UPDATE_BIN(2);
   when 3 | 4   =>
      EMPTY_BIN(1);
      EMPTY_BIN(2);
   when others => raise ERROR;
end case;
```

Notes:

The execution of a case statement will choose one and only one alternative, since the choices are exhaustive and mutually exclusive. It is always possible to use a qualified expression for the expression of the case statement to limit the number of choices that need be given explicitly.

References:

discrete type 3.5, expression 4.4, literal 2.5 3.2.5.2, overloading a subprogram 6.6, sequence of statements 5.1, static determination 4.9

5.5 Loop Statements

A loop statement specifies that a sequence of statements in a basic loop is to be executed repeatedly zero or more times.

```
loop_statement  ::=
    [ loop_identifier:] [ iteration_clause] basic_loop [ loop_identifier];

basic_loop  ::=
    loop
        sequence_of_statements
    end loop

iteration_clause  ::=
        for loop_parameter in [reverse] discrete_range
    |   while condition

loop_parameter  ::=  identifier
```

If a loop identifier appears in a loop statement, the identifier must be given both at the beginning and at the end. A loop identifier is implicitly declared at the end of the declarative part of the inner-most enclosing block, subprogram body, package body, or task body; where this block has no declarative part, an implicit declarative part (and preceding **declare**) is assumed.

A loop statement without an iteration clause specifies repeated execution of the basic loop. The basic loop may be left as the result of an exit or return statement; as the result of selecting a terminate alternative of a select statement; or also as the result of a goto statement, or as the result of an exception.

In a loop statement with a while iteration clause, the condition is evaluated and tested before each execution of the basic loop. If the while condition is TRUE the sequence of statements of the basic loop is executed, if FALSE the execution of the loop statement is terminated.

The execution of a loop statement with a for iteration clause starts with the elaboration of this clause, which acts as the declaration of the loop parameter. The identifier of the loop parameter is first introduced and the discrete range is then evaluated; the loop parameter is declared as a variable, local to the loop statement, whose type is that of the elements in the discrete range and whose range constraint is given by the discrete range. If the discrete range is a range whose bounds are integer literals or integer literal expressions, the type is assumed to be the predefined type INTEGER.

If the discrete range of a for loop is null, the basic loop is not executed. Otherwise, the sequence of statements of the basic loop is executed once for each value of the discrete range (subject to the basic loop not being left as described above). Prior to each such iteration, the corresponding value of the discrete range is assigned to the loop parameter. These values are assigned in increasing order unless the reserved word **reverse** is present, in which case the values are assigned in decreasing order.

Within the basic loop, the loop parameter acts as a constant. Hence the loop parameter may not be changed by an assignment statement, nor may the loop parameter be given as an **out** or **in out** parameter of a procedure or entry call.

Examples:

```
while  BID(N).PRICE  <  CUT_OFF.PRICE loop
   RECORD_BID(BID(N).PRICE);
   N := N + 1;
end loop;

SUMMATION:
   while  NEXT /= HEAD loop
      SUM    := SUM + NEXT.VALUE;
      NEXT   := NEXT.SUCC;
   end loop SUMMATION;

for J in BUFFER'RANGE loop   --   valid even with empty range
   if BUFFER(J) /= SPACE then
      PUT(BUFFER(J));
   end if;
end loop;
```

Notes:

The discrete range of a for loop is evaluated just once. Loop names can be referred to by exit statements.

References:

assignment statement 5.2, block 5.6, bounds 3.6, condition 5.3, discrete range 3.6, elaboration 3.1 3.9, entry call 9.5, exception 11, exit statement 5.7, false 3.5.3, goto statement 5.9, identifier 2.3, in out parameter 6.2, integer literal 2.4, integer type 3.5.4, name 4.1, null range 3.6.1, out parameter 6.2, package body 7.1 7.3, procedure 6.1, range attribute 3.6.2, return statement 5.8, sequence of statements 5.1, subprogram body 6.3, task body 9.1, terminate alternative 9.7.1, true 3.5.3, variable 4.1

5.6 Blocks

A block introduces a sequence of statements optionally preceded by a governing declarative part.

```
block ::=.
   [block_identifier:]
   [declare
       declarative_part]
    begin
       sequence_of_statements
   [exception
      {exception_handler}]
    end [block_identifier];
```

If a block identifier is given for a block, it must be given both at the beginning and at the end.   A block identifier is implicitly declared at the end of the declarative part of the innermost enclosing block, subprogram body, package body, or task body; where this enclosing block has no declarative part, an implicit declarative part (and preceding **declare**) is assumed.

The execution of a block results in the elaboration of its declarative part followed by the execution of the sequence of statements. A block may also contain exception handlers to service exceptions occurring during the execution of the sequence of statements (see 11.2).

Example:

```
SWAP:
  declare
    TEMP : INTEGER;
  begin
    TEMP := V; V := U; U := TEMP;
  end SWAP;
```

Notes:

Within a block, the block name can be used in selected components denoting local entities such as SWAP.TEMP in the above example (see 4.1.3 (e)).

References:

declarative part 3.9, elaboration 3.1 3.9, exception 11, exception handler 11.2, name 4.1, package body 7.1 7.3, sequence of statements 5.1, subprogram body 6.3, task body 9.1

5.7 Exit Statements

An exit statement may cause the termination of an enclosing loop, depending on the truth value of a condition.

```
exit_statement ::=
    exit [loop_name] [when condition];
```

The loop exited is the innermost loop unless the exit statement specifies the name of an enclosing loop, in which case the named loop is exited (together with any enclosing loop inner to the named loop). If an exit statement contains a condition, this condition is evaluated and loop termination occurs if and only if its value is TRUE.

An exit statement may only appear within a loop (a named exit statement only within the named loop). An exit statement must not transfer control out of a subprogram body, package body, task body, or accept statement.

Examples:

```
for I in 1 .. MAX_NUM_ITEMS loop
  GET_NEW_ITEM(NEW_ITEM);
  MERGE_ITEM(NEW_ITEM, STORAGE_FILE);
  exit when NEW_ITEM = TERMINAL_ITEM;
end loop;

MAIN_CYCLE:
  loop
    --   initial statements
    exit MAIN_CYCLE when FOUND;
    --   final statements
  end loop MAIN_CYCLE;
```

References:

condition 5.3, loop statement 5.5, name 4.1, true 3.5.3, truth value 3.5.3

5.8 Return Statements

A return statement terminates the execution of a function, procedure, or accept statement.

    return_statement ::= **return** [expression];

A return statement may only appear within a function body, procedure body, or accept statement. A return statement for a procedure body or for an accept statement must not include an expression.

A return statement for a function must include an expression whose value is the result returned by the function. The expression must be of the type specified in the return clause of the function specification, and must satisfy any constraint imposed by the return clause. Otherwise, the execution of the function is not terminated and the exception CONSTRAINT_ERROR is raised at the place of the return statement.

A return statement must not transfer control out of a package body or task body.

Examples:

    return;
    return KEY_VALUE(LAST_INDEX);

References:

accept statement 9.5, constraint 3.3, constraint_error exception 11.1, expression 4.4, function 6.1, function body 6.3, function specification 6.1, package body 7.1 7.3, procedure 6.1, procedure body 6.3, sequence of statements 5.1, task body 9.1

5.9 Goto Statements

The execution of a goto statement results in an explicit transfer of control to another statement specified by a label.

    goto_statement ::= **goto** *label*_name;

A goto statement must not transfer control from outside into a compound statement or exception handler, nor from one of the sequences of statements of an if statement, case statement, or select statement to another. A goto statement must not transfer control from one exception handler to another, nor from an exception handler back to the statements of the corresponding block, subprogram body, package body, or task body.

A goto statement must not transfer control out of a subprogram body, package body, task body, or accept statement.

Example:

```
<<COMPARE>>
  if A(I) < ELEMENT then
    if LEFT(I) /= 0 then
      I := LEFT(I);
      goto COMPARE;
    end if;
    --   some statements
  end if;
```

Notes:

It follows from the scope rules that a goto statement cannot transfer control from outside into the body of a subprogram, package, or task (see 5.1 and 8.1).

References:

accept statement 9.5, block 5.6, case statement 5.4, compound statement 5.1, exception handler 11.2, if statement 5.3, label 5.1, package body 7.1 7.3, scope rules 8, select statement 9.7, sequence of statements 5.1, subprogram body 6.3, task body 9.1

6. Subprograms

A subprogram is an executable program unit that is invoked by a subprogram call. Its definition can be given in two parts: a subprogram declaration defining its calling convention, and a subprogram body defining its execution. There are two forms of subprograms: procedures and functions. A procedure call is a statement; a function call returns a value.

Subprograms are one of the three forms of program units of which programs can be composed. The other forms are packages and tasks.

References:

function 6.1 6.5, function call 6.4, procedure 6.1 procedure call 6.4, subprogram body 6.3, subprogram call 6.4, subprogram declaration 6.1

6.1 Subprogram Declarations

A subprogram declaration declares a procedure or a function.

```
subprogram_declaration ::= subprogram_specification;
    | generic_subprogram_declaration
    | generic_subprogram_instantiation

subprogram_specification ::=
    procedure identifier [formal_part]
    | function designator [formal_part] return subtype_indication

designator ::= identifier | operator_symbol

operator_symbol ::= character_string

formal_part ::= (parameter_declaration {; parameter_declaration})

parameter_declaration ::=
    identifier_list : mode subtype_indication [:= expression]

mode ::= [in] | out | in out
```

The specification of a procedure specifies its identifier and its formal parameters (if any). The specification of a function specifies its designator, its formal parameters (if any) and the subtype of the returned value. A designator that is an operator symbol is used for overloading operators of the language. The sequence of characters represented by an operator symbol must be an operator belonging to one of the six classes of overloadable operators defined in section 4.5.

For the elaboration of a subprogram declaration (other than a generic subprogram declaration or a generic subprogram instantiation), the subprogram identifier (or operator symbol) is first introduced and can from then on be used as a name of the corresponding subprogram. Elaboration of parameter declarations and result subtype follow in the order in which they are written.

For the elaboration of a parameter declaration, the identifiers of the list are first introduced; then the mode and parameter subtype are established; the identifiers then name the corresponding parameters. If the parameter declaration has the mode **in**, and only then, it may include an initialization. In that case, the corresponding expression is next evaluated. Its value is the default initial value of the parameter; it must satisfy any constraint imposed by the subtype indication, otherwise the exception CONSTRAINT_ERROR is raised.

Neither the name of a variable, nor a call to a user-defined operator, function, or allocator, may appear in any expression occurring in a formal part. A parameter declaration, or a constraint on the result of a function, may not mention the name of a parameter declared in another parameter declaration of the same formal part.

A generic subprogram declaration defines a template for several subprograms obtained by generic subprogram instantiation (see 12.1 and 12.3).

Examples of subprogram declarations:

```
procedure  TRAVERSE_TREE;
procedure  RIGHT_INDENT(MARGIN : out LINE_POSITION);
procedure  INCREMENT(X : in out INTEGER);

function  RANDOM return REAL range -1.0 .. 1.0;
function  COMMON_PRIME (M,N  : INTEGER) return INTEGER;
function  DOT_PRODUCT   (X,Y  : VECTOR)  return REAL;
function  "*" (X,Y : MATRIX) return MATRIX;
```

Examples of in parameters with default values:

```
procedure PRINT_HEADER(PAGES    : in  INTEGER;
                       HEADER   : in  LINE       := BLANK_LINE;
                       CENTER   : in  BOOLEAN  := TRUE);
```

Note:

All subprograms can be called recursively and are reentrant.

References:

constraint 3.3, constraint_error exception 11.1, expression 4.4, formal parameter 6.2, function 6.5, function call 6.4, generic part 12.1, operator 4.5, overloading an operator 6.7, procedure call 6.4, subtype declaration 3.3, variable name 3.2 4.1

6.2 Formal Parameters

The formal parameters of a subprogram are considered local to the subprogram. A parameter has one of three modes:

in   The parameter acts as a local constant whose value is provided by the corresponding actual parameter.

out   The parameter acts as a local variable whose value is assigned to the corresponding actual parameter as a result of the execution of the subprogram.

in out The parameter acts as a local variable and permits access and assignment to the corresponding actual parameter.

If no mode is explicitly given, the mode **in** is assumed. If a parameter of mode **in** is an array or a record, none of its components may be changed by the subprogram. For parameters of a scalar or access type, at the start of each call, the value of each actual parameter which corresponds to a formal parameter of mode **in** or **in out** is copied into the corresponding formal parameter; upon return from the subprogram, the value of each formal parameter of mode **in out** or **out** is copied back into the corresponding actual parameter.

For parameters of an array, record, or private type, the values may be copied as in the above case; alternatively, the formal parameter may provide access to the corresponding actual throughout the execution of the subprogram. The language does not define which of these two mechanisms is used for parameter passing. A program that relies on one particular mechanism is therefore erroneous.

Within the body of a subprogram, a formal parameter is subject to any constraint given in its parameter declaration. For a formal parameter of an unconstrained array type, the bounds are obtained from the actual parameter. For a formal parameter whose declaration specifies an unconstrained (private or record) type with discriminants, the discriminants of the formal parameter are initialized with the values of the corresponding discriminants of the actual parameter; if the actual parameter is constrained by these discriminant values then so also is the formal.

Notes:

For parameters of array, record, or private types, the parameter passing rules have these consequences:

- If the execution of a subprogram is abnormally terminated by an exception, the final value of an actual parameter of such a type can be either its value before the call or a value assigned to the formal parameter during the execution of the subprogram.

- If no actual parameter of such a type is accessible by more than one path, then the effect of a (normally terminating) subprogram call is the same whether or not the implementation uses copying for parameter passing. If however there are multiple access paths to such a parameter (for example, if a global variable, or another formal parameter, refers to the same actual parameter), then after an assignment to the actual other than via the formal, the value of the formal is undefined. A program using such an undefined value is erroneous.

References:

access type 3.8, actual parameter association 6.4.1, array type definition 3.6, bounds 3.6.1, component 3.2, constant 3.2, constraint 3.3, discriminant 3.7.1, discriminant constraint 3.7.2, exception 11, global variable 8.3, private type 7.4, record type 3.7, scalar type 3.5, subprogram body 6.3, subprogram call 6.4, unconstrained array type 3.6

6.3 Subprogram Bodies

A subprogram body specifies the execution of a subprogram.

```
subprogram_body ::=
    subprogram_specification is
      declarative_part
    begin
      sequence_of_statements
  [ exception
      {exception_handler}]
    end [designator];
```

If both a subprogram declaration and a subprogram body are given, the subprogram specification provided in the body must be the same as that given in the corresponding subprogram declaration: the parameter names, the subtype indications, and the expressions specifying any default values must be the same and in the same order. The only variation allowed is that names can be written differently, provided that they denote the same entity.

A subprogram declaration must be given if the subprogram is declared in the visible part of a package, or if it is called by other subprogram, package, or task bodies that appear before its own body. Otherwise, the declaration can be omitted and the specification appearing in the subprogram body acts as the declaration. The elaboration of a subprogram body consists of the elaboration of its specification if that has not already been done; the effect is to establish the subprogram body as defining the execution of the corresponding subprogram.

The execution of a subprogram body is invoked by a subprogram call (see 6.4). For this execution, (after establishing the association between formal parameters and actual parameters) the declarative part of the body is elaborated, and the sequence of statements of the body is then executed. Upon completion of the body, return is made to the caller (and any necessary copying back of formal to actual parameters occurs (see 6.2)). A subprogram body may contain exception handlers to service any exceptions that occur during the execution of its sequence of statements (see 11).

The optional designator at the end of a subprogram body must repeat the designator of the subprogram specification.

A subprogram body may be expanded in line at each call if this is requested by the pragma INLINE:

```
pragma INLINE(subprogram_name{,subprogram_name});
```

This pragma (if given) must appear in the same declarative part as the named subprograms (a single subprogram name may stand for several overloaded subprograms); for subprograms declared in a package specification the pragma must also be in this package specification. The meaning of a subprogram is not changed by the pragma INLINE.

Example of subprogram body:

```
procedure PUSH(E : in ELEMENT_TYPE; S : in out STACK) is
begin
  if  S.INDEX  =  S.SIZE  then
      raise  STACK_OVERFLOW;
  else
      S.INDEX  :=  S.INDEX  +  1;
      S.SPACE(S.INDEX)  :=  E;
  end  if;
end  PUSH;
```

Note:

As stated above, where a subprogram specification is repeated, the second occurrence is never elaborated. Therefore there is no question of expressions in the second occurrence delivering a different value.

References:

actual parameter association 6.4.1, declarative part 3.9, default parameter value 6.1, designator 6.1, exception 11, formal parameter 6.2, mode 6.2, package body 7.1 7.3, package specification 7.2, package visible part 7.2, parameter association 6.4.1, parameter name 6.2, pragma 2.8, statement 5, subprogram declaration 6.1, subprogram specification 6.1, subtype indication 3.3, task body 9.1

6.4 Subprogram Calls

A subprogram call is either a procedure call or a function call.   It invokes the execution of the corresponding subprogram body. The call specifies the association of any actual parameters with formal parameters of the subprogram. An actual parameter is either a variable or the value of an expression.

```
procedure_call  ::=
    procedure_name  [actual_parameter_part];

function_call  ::=
    function_name  actual_parameter_part | function_name  ()

actual_parameter_part  ::=
    (parameter_association  {,  parameter_association})

parameter_association  ::=
    [ formal_parameter  =>]  actual_parameter

formal_parameter  ::=  identifier

actual_parameter  ::=  expression
```

Actual parameters may be passed in positional order (positional parameters) or by explicitly naming the corresponding formal parameters (named parameters). For positional parameters, the actual parameter corresponds to the formal parameter with the same position in the formal parameter list. For named parameters, the corresponding formal parameter is explicitly given in the call. Named parameters may be given in any order.

Positional parameters and named parameters may be used in the same call provided that positional parameters occur first at their normal position, that is, once a named parameter is used, the rest of the call must use only named parameters.

The call of a parameterless function is written as the function name followed by empty parentheses. This is also done for a function call in which default initial values are used for all parameters. The call of a parameterless procedure is written as the procedure name followed by a semicolon.

Examples of procedure calls:

```
RIGHT_SHIFT;
TABLE_MANAGER.INSERT(E);
SEARCH_STRING(STRING, CURRENT_POSITION, NEW_POSITION);

PRINT_HEADER(PAGES => 128, HEADER => TITLE, CENTER => TRUE);
SWITCH(FROM => X, TO => NEXT);
REORDER_KEYS(NUMBER_OF_ITEMS, KEY_ARRAY => RESULT_TABLE);
```

Examples of function calls:

```
DOT_PRODUCT(U, V)
CLOCK()
```

References:

default parameter value 6.1, expression 4.4, function 6.1 6.5, identifier 2.3, name 4.1, procedure 6.1, subprogram body 6.3, variable 3.2 4.1

6.4.1   Actual Parameter Associations

An expression used as an actual parameter of mode **in out** or **out** must be a variable name or a type conversion of a variable name (see 4.6). An expression used as an actual parameter of mode **in** is evaluated before the call. If a variable given as an actual parameter of mode **in out** or **out** is a selected component or an indexed component, its identity is established before the call.

For a parameter of a scalar type, if the mode is **in** or **in out**, any range constraint on the formal parameter must be satisfied by the value of the actual parameter before each call. If the mode is **in out** or **out**, any range constraint on the actual parameter must be satisfied by the value of the formal parameter upon return from the subprogram.

For a parameter of an access type the only possible constraints are index and discriminant constraints applying to the objects designated by the access values. These constraints must be satisfied (that is, are checked) before the call (for the modes **in** and **in out**) and upon return (for the modes **in out** and **out**).

For a parameter of an array type, or of a record or private type with discriminants, any constraint specified for the formal parameter must be satisfied by the corresponding actual parameter before the call for all parameter modes.

The exception CONSTRAINT_ERROR is raised at the place of the subprogram call if any of the above-mentioned constraints is not satisfied.

Notes:

For array types, and for record and private types with discriminants, the language rules guarantee that if the actual parameter satisfies the constraint of the formal parameter before the call, then the formal parameter satisfies the constraint of the actual parameter upon return. Hence no constraint check is needed upon return.

The language does not define in which order different parameter associations are evaluated. A program relying on some specific order is therefore erroneous.

References:

access type 3.8, access value 3.8, array type definition 3.6, constraint_error exception 11.1, discriminant 3.7.1, discriminant constraint 3.7.2, expression 4.4, indexed component 4.1.1, mode 6.2, object 3.2, private type definition 7.4, range constraint 3.5, record type 3.7, scalar type 3.5, selected component 4.1.3, variable name 3.2 4.1

6.4.2 Default Actual Parameters

If a subprogram declaration specifies a default value for an **in** parameter, then the corresponding parameter may be omitted from a call. In such a case the rest of the call, following any initial positional parameters, must use only named parameters.

Example of procedure with default values:

```
procedure ACTIVATE( PROCESS  : in PROCESS_NAME;
                    AFTER    : in PROCESS_NAME := NO_PROCESS;
                    WAIT     : in DURATION := 0.0;
                    PRIOR    : in BOOLEAN := FALSE);
```

Examples of its call:

```
ACTIVATE(X);
ACTIVATE(X, AFTER => Y);
ACTIVATE(X, WAIT => 60.0, PRIOR => TRUE);
ACTIVATE(X, Y, 10.0, FALSE);
```

Note:

The default value for an **in** parameter is evaluated when the subprogram specification is elaborated and is thus not reevaluated at each call. Hence the same default value is used for all calls.

References:

default parameter value 6.1, named parameter 6.4, subprogram specification 6.1

6.5 Function Subprograms

A function is a subprogram that returns a value. The specification of a function starts with the reserved word **function**. A function may only have parameters of the mode **in**. The sequence of statements in the function body (excluding statements in nested bodies) must include one or more return statements specifying the returned value. If the body of a function is left by reaching the end, the value returned by the function call is undefined. A program that relies upon such an undefined value is erroneous.

Example:

```
function DOT_PRODUCT(X, Y : VECTOR) return REAL is
   SUM : REAL := 0.0;
begin
   CHECK(X'FIRST = Y'FIRST and X'LAST = Y'LAST);
   for J in X'RANGE loop
      SUM := SUM + X(J)*Y(J);
   end loop;
   return SUM;
end DOT_PRODUCT;
```

References:

exception 11, function body 6.3, function call 6.4, function specification 6.1, mode 6.2, parameter 6.2, return statement 5.8

6.6 Overloading of Subprograms

The same subprogram identifier can be used in several otherwise different subprogram specifications; it is then said to be *overloaded*. The declaration of an overloaded subprogram identifier does not hide another subprogram declaration made in an outer declarative part unless, in the two declarations, the order, the names, and the types of the parameters are the same, the same parameters have default values, and (for functions) the result type is the same. When this condition for hiding is satisfied, the two subprogram specifications are said to be *equivalent*. On the other hand the default values themselves, the constraints, and the parameter modes are not taken into account to determine if one subprogram hides another.

Overloaded subprogram declarations may occur in the same declarative part, but they must then differ by more than just the parameter names.

A call to an overloaded subprogram is ambiguous (and therefore illegal) if the types and the order of the actual parameters, the names of the formal parameters (if named associations are used), and the result type (for functions) are not sufficient to identify exactly one (overloaded) subprogram specification.

Examples of overloaded subprograms:

```
procedure PUT(X : INTEGER);
procedure PUT(X : STRING);

procedure SET(TINT    : COLOR);
procedure SET(SIGNAL  : LIGHT);
```

Example of calls;

```
PUT(28);
PUT("no possible ambiguity here");

SET(TINT    => RED);
SET(SIGNAL  => RED);
SET(COLOR'(RED));

--   SET(RED) would be ambiguous since RED may
--   denote a value of type either COLOR or LIGHT
```

Notes:

Ambiguities may (but need not) arise when actual parameters of the call of an overloaded sub-program are themselves overloaded function calls, literals or aggregates. Ambiguities may also arise when several overloaded subprograms belonging to different packages are applicable. These ambiguities can usually be resolved in several ways: qualified expressions can be used for some or all actual parameters and for any result; the name of the subprogram can be expressed more explicitly as a selected component (prefixing the subprogram identifier by the package name); finally the subprogram can be renamed.

References:

actual parameter 6.4, constraints on parameters 6.4.1, declarative part 3.9, default parameter value 6.1, function 6.5, hide 8.3, named parameter association 6.4, overloaded aggregate 4.3, overloaded literal 3.5.1 4.7, package 7, parameter type 6.1, qualified expression 4.7, renaming declaration 8.5, result type 6.1, selected component 4.1.3, subprogram call 6.4, subprogram declaration 6.1, subprogram identifier 6.1, subprogram specification 6.1

6.7 Overloading of Operators

A function declaration whose designator is an operator symbol is used to define an additional overloading for an operator. The sequence of characters of the operator symbol must be either a logical, a relational, an adding, a unary, a multiplying, or an exponentiating operator (see 4.5). Neither membership operators nor the short circuit control forms are allowed.

The declaration of an overloaded operator hides the declaration of another operator, with the same designator, made in an outer declarative part, if for both declarations the types of the parameters are the same, and the result type is the same; the names of the parameters are not taken into account.

The declaration of a unary operator must be a function declaration with a single parameter. The declaration of any other operator must be a function declaration with two parameters; for each use of this operator, the first parameter takes the left operand as actual parameter, the second parameter takes the right operand. Default values for parameters are not allowed in operator declarations. The operators "+" and "-" may be overloaded both as unary and as binary operators.

The equality operator "=" can only be overloaded for two parameters of the same limited private type or of a composite type that has one or more components (or components of components, and so on) of a limited private type. An overloading of equality must deliver a result of the predefined type BOOLEAN; it also implicitly overloads the inequality operator "/=" so that this still gives the complementary result to the equality operator. Explicit overloading of the inequality operator is not allowed.

Examples:

```
function "*" (X, Y : MATRIX)  return MATRIX;
function "*" (X, Y : VECTOR)  return VECTOR;
```

Note:

Overloading of relational operators does not affect basic comparisons in the language such as testing for membership in a range or the choices in a case statement.

References:

actual parameter 6.4, adding operator 4.5.3, boolean type 3.5.3, case statement 5.4, composite type 3.3, declarative part 3.9, default parameter value 6.1, designator 6.1, equality operator 4.5.2, function declaration 6.1, hide 8.3, limited private type 7.4.2, mode 6.2, operator symbol 6.1, parameter type 6.1, range 3.5, relational operator 4.5.2, result type 6.1, unary operator 4.5.4

7. Packages

Packages allow the specification of groups of logically related entities. In their simplest form packages can represent pools of common data and type declarations. More generally, packages can be used to describe groups of related entities such as types, objects, and subprograms, whose inner workings are concealed and protected from their users.

Packages are one of the three forms of *program units*, of which programs can be composed. The other forms are subprograms and tasks.

References:

object 3.2, subprogram 6, task 9, type declaration 3.3

7.1 Package Structure

A package is generally provided in two parts: a package specification and a package body. The simplest form of package, that representing a pool of data and types, does not require a package body.

```
package_declaration ::= package_specification;
    |  generic_package_declaration
    |  generic_package_instantiation

package_specification ::=
    package identifier is
      {declarative_item}
    [ private
      {declarative_item}
      {representation_specification}]
    end [identifier]

package_body ::=
    package body identifier is
      declarative_part
    [ begin
      sequence_of_statements
    [ exception
      {exception_handler}]]
    end [identifier];
```

A package specification and the corresponding package body have the same identifier; only this identifier may appear as the optional identifier at the end of the package specification or body (or both).

With respect to visibility and redeclaration rules (see 8.1), the declarative items and representation specifications in a package specification and the declarative part of the corresponding package body (if any) are considered as forming a single declarative part. A package declaration may be separately compiled (see 10.1) or it may appear within a declarative part. In the latter case the corresponding body (if any) must appear later in the same declarative part.

Package specifications and package bodies may contain further package declarations. The body of any program unit (that is, any subprogram, package, or task) declared in a package specification must appear in the corresponding package body (unless the unit declared is obtained by generic instantiation or is a subprogram for which an INTERFACE pragma is given, see 13.9).

A generic package declaration defines a template for several packages obtained by generic package instantiation (see 12.1 and 12.3).

References:

declarative item 3.9, declarative part 3.9, generic instantiation 12.3, generic part 12.1, identifier 2.3, program unit 6 7 9, redeclaration rules 8.2, representation specification 13.1, subprogram 6, task 9, visibility 8.1

7.2 Package Specifications and Declarations

The first list of declarative items of a package specification is called the *visible part* of the package. The entities declared in the visible part can be referred to from other program units by means of selected components; they can be made directly visible to other program units by means of use clauses (see 4.1.3 and 8.4). The visible part contains all the information that another program unit is able to know about the package. The optional lists of declarative items and representation specifications after the reserved word **private** form the *private part* of the package.

For the elaboration of a package declaration (other than a generic package declaration or a generic package instantiation), the package identifier is first introduced and can from then on be used as a name of the corresponding package; elaboration of the visible part, and of any declarative items and representation specifications appearing after the reserved word **private** follow in this order.

A package consisting of only a package specification (that is, without a package body) can be used to represent a group of common constants or variables, or a common pool of data and types.

Example of a group of common variables:

```
package PLOTTING_DATA is
   PEN_UP : BOOLEAN;

   CONVERSION_FACTOR,
   X_OFFSET, Y_OFFSET,
   X_MIN, X_MAX,
   Y_MIN, Y_MAX : REAL;

   X_VALUE, Y_VALUE : array (1 .. 500) of REAL;
end PLOTTING_DATA;
```

Example of a common pool of data and types:

```
package WORK_DATA is
    type DAY is (MON, TUE, WED, THU, FRI, SAT, SUN);
    type HOURS_SPENT is delta 0.01 range 0.0 .. 24.0;
    type TIME_TABLE    is array (DAY) of HOURS_SPENT;

    WORK_HOURS    : TIME_TABLE;
    NORMAL_HOURS  : constant TIME_TABLE :=
                        (MON .. THU => 8.25, FRI => 7.0, SAT | SUN => 0.0);
end WORK_DATA;
```

References:

constant 3.2, declarative item 3.9, elaboration 3.1, generic package instantiation 12.3, generic part 12.1, package specification 7.1, program unit 6 7 9, representation specification 13.1, selected component 4.1.3, separate compilation 10.1, type declaration 3.3, use clause 8.4, variable 3.2

7.3 Package Bodies

The specification of a package, in particular the visible part, may contain the specifications of subprograms, tasks and other packages. In such cases, the bodies of the specified program units must appear within the declarative part of the package body (unless a pragma INTERFACE is given, see 13.9). This declarative part may also include local declarations and local program units needed to implement the visible items.

In contrast to the entities declared in the visible part, the entities declared in the package body are not accessible outside the package. As a consequence, a package with a package body can be used for the construction of a group of related subprograms (a *package* in the usual sense), where the logical operations accessible to the users are clearly isolated from the internal entities.

For the elaboration of a package body, its declarative part is elaborated first, and its sequence of statements (if any) is then executed. Any entity declared in this declarative part remains in existence for as long as the package itself.

The optional exception handlers at the end of a package body handle exceptions raised during the execution of its sequence of statements.

Example of a package:

```
package RATIONAL_NUMBERS is
    type RATIONAL is
        record
            NUMERATOR      : INTEGER;
            DENOMINATOR    : INTEGER range 1 .. INTEGER'LAST;
        end record;

    function EQUAL (X,Y : RATIONAL) return BOOLEAN;
    function "+"    (X,Y : RATIONAL) return RATIONAL;
    function "*"    (X,Y : RATIONAL) return RATIONAL;
end;
```

```
package body RATIONAL_NUMBERS is

    procedure SAME_DENOMINATOR (X,Y : in out RATIONAL) is
    begin
        --    reduces X and Y to the same denominator
    end;

    function EQUAL(X,Y : RATIONAL) return BOOLEAN is
        U,V : RATIONAL;
    begin
        U := X;
        V := Y;
        SAME_DENOMINATOR (U,V);
        return U.NUMERATOR = V.NUMERATOR;
    end EQUAL;

    function "+"  (X,Y : RATIONAL) return RATIONAL is    ...   end "+";
    function "*"  (X,Y : RATIONAL) return RATIONAL is    ...   end "*";

end RATIONAL_NUMBERS;
```

Notes:

A variable declared in a package specification or body retains its value between calls to subprograms declared in the visible part. Such a variable is said to be an *own* variable of the package.

If a package body contains the declarations of subprograms specified in the visible part then it is only after the elaboration of the package body that these subprograms can be called from outside the package (see 3.9 and 10.5).

References:

declarative part 3.9, elaboration 3.1, exception handler 11.2, exception 11, package specification 7.1, sequence of statements 5.1, subprogram 6, task 9, variable 3.2, visible part 7.2

7.4 Private Type Definitions

The structural details of some declared type may be irrelevant to the use of its logical properties outside a package, and one may wish to protect them from external influence. This can be accomplished by declaring such a type with a private type definition in the visible part of a package specification.

```
private_type_definition ::= [limited] private
```

A private type definition may only occur in a type declaration given in the visible part of a package or in a generic part (see 12.1.2). The corresponding types are called (limited) private types. The only effect of the elaboration of a private type declaration is to introduce the name of a (limited) private type, and to elaborate its discriminant part, if any.

If a package specification includes a private type declaration it must also include a full declaration of the type in the private part of the package (that is, in the list of declarative items following the reserved word **private**).

A constant of a private type can be declared in the visible part as a *deferred* constant, that is, as a constant whose initial value is not specified in its declaration. The initial value must be specified in the private part by redeclaring the constant in full.

References:

constant 3.2, declarative item 3.9, discriminant part 3.3 3.7.1, elaboration 3.1, generic part 12.1, limited private type 7.4.2, name 4.1, package specification 7.1, private part 7.2, type declaration 3.3, visible part 7.2

7.4.1 Private Types

For a private type not designated as limited, the only information available to other external program units is that given in the visible part of the defining package. Thus the name of the type is available. In addition, any subprogram specified within the visible part with a parameter or result of the private type defines an available operation for objects of the private type. Finally, assignment and the predefined comparison for equality or inequality are available.

These are the only externally available operations on objects of a private type. External units can declare objects of the private type and apply available operations to the objects; in contrast, they cannot directly access the structural details of objects of private types.

For each private type declaration given in the visible part of a package specification, a corresponding type declaration (with the same name) must be given in full in the private part, that is, with a type definition other than a private type definition. Assignment and equality must be available for this type.

If the private type declaration has discriminants, the full declaration must have the same discriminants: the discriminant names, the subtype indications, and any default values must be the same and in the same order. The only variation allowed is that names may be written differently, provided that they denote the same entity. The elaboration of the full type declaration consists only of the elaboration of the corresponding type definition (since the type name has already been introduced and any discriminant part has already been elaborated). The full type declaration cannot include a discriminant part if the private type declaration does not have one; it cannot declare an unconstrained array type.

Within the private part and the body of a package, the operations available on objects of the private type are those defined in both the visible part and the private part. If the full declaration is in terms of a derived type definition, an inherited operation may be redefined (and thereby hidden) by an operation declared in the visible part.

Example:

```
package KEY_MANAGER is
   type KEY is private;
   NULL_KEY : constant KEY;
   procedure GET_KEY(K : out KEY);
   function "<" (X, Y : KEY) return BOOLEAN;
private
   type KEY is new INTEGER range 0 .. INTEGER'LAST;
   NULL_KEY : constant KEY := 0;
end;
```

```
--    the only externally available operations of the private type KEY are assignment,
--    equality, inequality, "<", and the procedure GET_KEY returning a KEY value

package body KEY_MANAGER is
  LAST_KEY : KEY := 0;
  procedure GET_KEY(K : out KEY) is
  begin
    LAST_KEY := LAST_KEY + 1;
    K := LAST_KEY;
  end GET_KEY;

  function "<" (X, Y : KEY) return BOOLEAN is
  begin
    return INTEGER(X) < INTEGER(Y);
  end "<";
  --    this definition of "<" hides the definition inherited from INTEGER;   hence X<Y would
  --    be a recursive call and conversion is necessary to invoke the "<" of INTEGER
end KEY_MANAGER;
```

Note:

Outside its defining package a private type is just a private type. The fact that it may be *implemented* as a particular type class (for example, as an array type) is irrelevant. Consequently any language rule which applies specifically to that class does not apply to that private type outside its defining package.

References:

array type definition 3.6, assignment statement 5.2, derived type definition 3.4, discriminant 3.7.1, elaboration 3.1, equality 4.5.2, inherited 3.4, limited private type 7.4.2, name 4.1, parameter 6.2, private part 7.2, subprogram 6, subtype indication 3.3, type class 3.3, type declaration 3.3, unconstrained array type 3.6, visible part 7.2

7.4.2 Limited Private Types

Outside the package defining a limited private type, assignment and the comparisons for equality or inequality are not available for objects of the type. Moreover if a composite type has components of a limited private type, assignment, equality and inequality are not available for objects of the composite type, outside the package defining the limited private type. The only externally available operations on objects of a limited private type are those defined by the subprograms declared in the visible part of the defining package.

The following are consequences of the non-availability of assignment:

- A declaration of a variable of a limited private type cannot include an initialization.

- Parameters of a limited private type may not have default values.

- No constant of a limited private type can be declared outside the defining package.

- An allocator for an access type designating objects of a limited private type is not allowed to specify an initial value for the allocated object.

Outside the defining package, subprograms having parameters of any mode can be defined for objects of a limited private type, provided that the above rules are satisfied.

The type definition given in the full declaration of a limited private type need not (but may) define a type for which assignment and equality are available; the full type declaration may be the declaration of a task type.

Example:

In the example below, an external subprogram making use of I_O_PACKAGE may obtain a file name by calling OPEN and later use it in calls to READ and WRITE. Thus, outside the package, a file name obtained from OPEN acts as a kind of password; its internal properties (such as containing a numeric value) are not known and no other operations (such as addition or comparison of internal names) can be performed on a file name.

```
package I_O_PACKAGE is
   type FILE_NAME is limited private;

   procedure OPEN  (F : in out FILE_NAME);
   procedure CLOSE (F : in out FILE_NAME);
   procedure READ  (F : in FILE_NAME; ITEM : out INTEGER);
   procedure WRITE (F : in FILE_NAME; ITEM : in  INTEGER);
private
   type FILE_NAME is
      record
         INTERNAL_NAME : INTEGER := 0;
      end record;
end I_O_PACKAGE;

package body I_O_PACKAGE is
   LIMIT : constant := 200;
   type FILE_DESCRIPTOR is record   ...   end record;
   DIRECTORY : array (1 .. LIMIT) of FILE_DESCRIPTOR;
   ...
   procedure OPEN  (F : in out FILE_NAME) is   ...   end;
   procedure CLOSE (F : in out FILE_NAME) is   ...   end;
   procedure READ  (F : in FILE_NAME; ITEM : out  INTEGER) is ... end;
   procedure WRITE (F : in FILE_NAME; ITEM : in   INTEGER) is ... end;
begin
   ...
end I_O_PACKAGE;
```

This example is characteristic of any case where complete control over the operations of a type is desired. Such packages serve a dual purpose. They prevent a user from making use of the internal structure of the type. They also implement the notion of an *encapsulated* data type where the only operations on the type are those given in the package specification.

References:

access type 3.8, allocator 4.8, assignment statement 5.2, composite type 3.6 3.7, constant 3.2, equality 4.5.2, initialization 3.2, inequality 4.5.2, mode 6.2, name 4.1, package specification 7.1, subprogram 6, task type 9, type definition 3.3, variable 3.2, visible part 7.2

7.5 Example of a Table Management Package

The following example illustrates the use of packages in providing high level procedures with a simple interface to the user.

The problem is to define a table management package for inserting and retrieving items. The items are inserted into the table as they are supplied. Each inserted item has an order number. The items are retrieved according to their order number, where the item with the lowest order number is retrieved first.

From the user's point of view, the package is quite simple. There is a type called ITEM designating table items, a procedure INSERT for inserting items, and a procedure RETRIEVE for obtaining the item with the lowest order number. There is a special item NULL_ITEM that is returned when the table is empty, and an exception TABLE_FULL that may be raised by INSERT.

A sketch of such a package is given below. Only the specification of the package is exposed to the user.

```
package TABLE_MANAGER is

    type ITEM is
      record
         ORDER_NUM   : INTEGER;
         ITEM_CODE   : INTEGER;
         QUANTITY    : INTEGER;
         ITEM_TYPE   : CHARACTER;
      end record;

    NULL_ITEM : constant ITEM :=
      (ORDER_NUM | ITEM_CODE | QUANTITY => 0, ITEM_TYPE => ' ');

    procedure INSERT   (NEW_ITEM   : in   ITEM);
    procedure RETRIEVE (FIRST_ITEM : out  ITEM);

    TABLE_FULL : exception;   --   may be raised by INSERT
end;
```

The details of implementing such packages can be quite complex; in this case they involve a two way linked table of internal items. A local housekeeping procedure EXCHANGE is used to move an internal item between the busy and the free lists. The initial table linkages are established by the initialization part. The package body need not be shown to the users of the package.

```
package body TABLE_MANAGER is
   SIZE : constant := 2000;
   subtype INDEX is INTEGER range 0 .. SIZE;

   type INTERNAL_ITEM is
      record
         CONTENT : ITEM;
         SUCC    : INDEX;
         PRED    : INDEX;
      end record;

   TABLE : array (INDEX) of INTERNAL_ITEM;
   FIRST_BUSY_ITEM  : INDEX := 0;
   FIRST_FREE_ITEM  : INDEX := 1;

   function FREE_LIST_EMPTY  return BOOLEAN is ... end;
   function BUSY_LIST_EMPTY  return BOOLEAN is ... end;
   procedure EXCHANGE (FROM : in INDEX; TO : in INDEX) is ... end;

   procedure INSERT (NEW_ITEM : in ITEM) is
   begin
      if FREE_LIST_EMPTY() then
         raise TABLE_FULL;
      end if;
      --  remaining code for INSERT
   end INSERT;

   procedure RETRIEVE (FIRST_ITEM : out ITEM) is ... end;

begin
   --  initialization of the table linkages
end TABLE_MANAGER;
```

References:

exception 11, procedure 6, package body 7.3, visible part 7.2

7.6 Example of a Text Handling Package

This example illustrates a simple text-handling package. The user only has access to the visible part; the implementation is hidden from him in the private part and the package body (not shown).

From the user's point of view, a TEXT is a variable length string. Each text object has a maximum length, which must be given when the object is declared, and a current value, which is a string of some length between zero and the maximum. The maximum possible length of a text object is an implementation-defined constant.

The package defines first the necessary types, then functions that return some characteristics of objects of the type, then the conversion functions between texts and the predefined CHARACTER and STRING types, and finally some of the standard operations on varying strings. Most operations are overloaded on strings and characters as well as on texts, in order to minimize the number of explicit conversions the user has to write.

```
package TEXT_HANDLER is
    MAXIMUM : constant INTEGER := SOME_VALUE;   --   implementation defined
    subtype INDEX is INTEGER range 0 .. MAXIMUM;

    type TEXT(MAXIMUM_LENGTH : INDEX) is limited private;

    function LENGTH (T : TEXT) return INDEX;
    function VALUE  (T : TEXT) return STRING;
    function EMPTY  (T : TEXT) return BOOLEAN;

    function TO_TEXT (S : STRING;    MAX : INDEX) return TEXT;    --   maximum length MAX
    function TO_TEXT (C : CHARACTER; MAX : INDEX) return TEXT;
    function TO_TEXT (S : STRING)    return TEXT;   --   maximum length S'LENGTH
    function TO_TEXT (C : CHARACTER) return TEXT;

    function "&" (LEFT : TEXT;      RIGHT : TEXT)      return TEXT;
    function "&" (LEFT : TEXT;      RIGHT : STRING)    return TEXT;
    function "&" (LEFT : STRING;    RIGHT : TEXT)      return TEXT;
    function "&" (LEFT : TEXT;      RIGHT : CHARACTER) return TEXT;
    function "&" (LEFT : CHARACTER; RIGHT : TEXT)      return TEXT;

    procedure SET(OBJECT : in out TEXT; VALUE : in TEXT);
    procedure SET(OBJECT : in out TEXT; VALUE : in STRING);
    procedure SET(OBJECT : in out TEXT; VALUE : in CHARACTER);

    procedure APPEND(TAIL : in TEXT;      TO : in out TEXT);
    procedure APPEND(TAIL : in STRING;    TO : in out TEXT);
    procedure APPEND(TAIL : in CHARACTER; TO : in out TEXT);

    procedure AMEND(OBJECT : in out TEXT; BY : in TEXT;      POSITION : in INDEX);
    procedure AMEND(OBJECT : in out TEXT; BY : in STRING;    POSITION : in INDEX);
    procedure AMEND(OBJECT : in out TEXT; BY : in CHARACTER; POSITION : in INDEX);

    --   amend replaces part of the object by the given text, string, or character
    --   starting at the given position in the object

    function LOCATE(FRAGMENT : TEXT;      WITHIN : TEXT) return INDEX;
    function LOCATE(FRAGMENT : STRING;    WITHIN : TEXT) return INDEX;
    function LOCATE(FRAGMENT : CHARACTER; WITHIN : TEXT) return INDEX;

    --   all return 0 if the fragment is not located

private
    type TEXT(MAXIMUM_LENGTH : INDEX) is
      record
        POS    : INDEX := 0;
        VALUE  : STRING(1 .. MAXIMUM_LENGTH);
      end record;
end TEXT_HANDLER;
```

Example of use of the text handling package:

A program opens an output file, whose name is supplied by the string NAME. This string has the form

    [DEVICE :] [FILENAME [.EXTENSION]]

There are standard defaults for device, filename, and extension. The user-supplied name is passed to EXPAND_FILE_NAME as a parameter, and the result is the expanded version, with any necessary defaults added.

```
function EXPAND_FILE_NAME(NAME : STRING) return STRING is
  use TEXT_HANDLER;

  DEFAULT_DEVICE     : constant STRING := "SY:";
  DEFAULT_FILE_NAME  : constant STRING := "RESULTS";
  DEFAULT_EXTENSION  : constant STRING := ".DAT";

  MAXIMUM_FILE_NAME_LENGTH : constant INDEX := SOME_APPROPRIATE_VALUE;
  FILE_NAME : TEXT(MAXIMUM_FILE_NAME_LENGTH);

begin

  SET(FILE_NAME, NAME);

  if EMPTY(FILE_NAME) then
    SET(FILE_NAME, DEFAULT_FILE_NAME);
  end if;

  if LOCATE(':', FILE_NAME) = 0 then
    SET(FILE_NAME, DEFAULT_DEVICE & FILE_NAME);
  end if;

  if LOCATE('.', FILE_NAME) = 0 then
    APPEND(DEFAULT_EXTENSION, TO => FILE_NAME);
  end if;

  return VALUE(FILE_NAME);

end EXPAND_FILE_NAME;
```

8. Visibility Rules

The rules defining the scope of declarations and the rules defining which identifiers are visible at various points in the text of the program are described in this chapter. These rules are stated here as applying to identifiers. They apply equally to character strings used as function designators and to character literals used as enumeration literals.

References:

character literal 2.5, character string 2.6, enumeration literal 3.5.1, function designator 6.1, identifier 2.3

8.1 Definitions of Terms

Scope of a declaration:

A declaration associates an identifier with a program entity (see 3.1) such as a variable, a type, a subprogram, a formal parameter, a record component. The region of text over which a declaration has an effect is called the *scope* of the declaration. This region starts at the point where the declared identifier is introduced (within a compilation unit).

The same identifier may be introduced by different declarations in the text of a program and may thus be associated with different entities. The scopes of several declarations with the same identifier may even overlap.

Overlapping scopes of declarations with the same identifier can result from overloading of subprograms and of enumeration literals (see 6.6 and 3.5.1). They can also occur for record components, entities declared in package visible parts, and for formal parameters, where there is overlap of the scopes of the enclosing record type definitions, packages, subprograms, entries, or generic program units. Finally, overlapping scopes can result from nesting. In particular, subprograms, packages, tasks, and blocks can be nested within each other, and can contain record type definitions or (possibly nested) loop statements.

Visibility of a declaration - visibility of an identifier:

The declaration of an entity with a certain identifier is said to be *visible* at (or from) a given point in the text when an occurrence of the identifier at this point can refer to the entity, that is, when the entity is an acceptable meaning for this occurrence. Some suitable context may be required to realize this visibility, as explained in section 8.3.

For overloaded identifiers, there may be *several* meanings acceptable at a given point, and the ambiguity must be resolved by the rules of overloading (see 4.6 and 6.6). For identifiers that are not overloaded (the usual case) there can be *at most one* acceptable meaning.

Whenever the declaration of an entity with a certain identifier is visible from a given point, the identifier and the entity are also said to be visible from that point. The *visibility rules* are the rules defining which identifiers are visible from various points of the text.

References:

block 5.6, compilation unit 10.1, declaration 3.1, enumeration literal 3.5.1, formal parameter 6.2, identifier 2.3, loop statement 5.5, overloaded literal 3.4 3.5.1 4.7, overloading a subprogram 6.6, package 7, record component 3.7, record type 3.7, subprogram 6, task 9, type 3.3, variable 3.2

8.2 Scope of Declarations

Entities can be declared in various ways. An entity can be declared in the declarative part of a block or in the declarative part of the body of a subprogram, package, or task; alternatively, an entity can be declared in the specification of a package or task. A separately compiled subprogram or package, other than a subunit, is effectively declared by its presence in a compilation.

An entity can be declared, alternatively, as a record component, as a discriminant, or as a formal parameter of a subprogram, entry or generic program unit. A loop parameter is declared by its occurrence in an iteration clause, an enumeration literal by its occurrence in an enumeration type definition. Finally, the declaration of a label, block identifier, or loop identifier is implicit.

The scope of each form of declaration (that is, the region of text over which the declaration has an effect) is defined below. Whenever the scope of an entity is said to extend *from its declaration*, this means that the scope extends from the point where the declared identifier is introduced.

(a) The scope of a declaration given in the declarative part of a block or in the declarative part of the body of a subprogram, package, or task extends from the declaration to the end of the block, subprogram, package, or task.

(b) The scope of a declaration given in the visible part of a package extends from the declaration to the end of the scope of the package declaration itself. It therefore includes the corresponding package body.

(c) The scope of a declaration given in the private part of a package extends from the declaration to the end of the package specification; it also extends over the corresponding package body.

(d) The scope of an entry declaration given in a task specification extends from the declaration to the end of the scope of the task declaration. It therefore includes the corresponding task body.

(e) The scope of a separately compiled subprogram or package, other than a subunit, comprises that compilation unit, its subunits (if any), any other compilation unit that mentions the name of the subprogram or package in a with clause, and the body of this subprogram or package. (See Chapter 10 for compilation units, subunits and with clauses).

The scope of record components, discriminants, formal parameters, loop parameters, and enumeration literals is defined by the following rules:

(f) The scope of a record component extends from the component declaration to the end of the scope of the record type declaration itself.

(g) The scope of a discriminant extends from the discriminant declaration to the end of the scope of the corresponding type declaration.

(h) The scope of a formal parameter of a subprogram, entry, or generic program unit extends from the parameter declaration to the end of the scope of the declaration of the subprogram, entry, or generic program unit itself. It therefore includes the body of the corresponding subprogram or generic program unit, and, for an entry, the corresponding accept statements.

(i) The scope of a loop parameter extends from its occurrence in an iteration clause to the end of the corresponding loop.

(j) The scope of an enumeration literal extends from its occurrence in the corresponding enumeration type declaration to the end of the scope of the enumeration type declaration itself.

Note:

The usual rules (a), (b), and (c) apply to subunits since they are declared in the declarative part of another compilation unit (see 10.2). Rule (a) also applies to the implicit declaration of a label, block identifier, or loop identifier, inserted at the end of a declarative part (see 5.1, 5.5, 5.6). For rule (e), note that the subprogram specification given only in the subprogram body acts as the subprogram declaration (see 6.3).

References:

accept statement 9.5, block 5.6, block identifier 5.6, compilation unit 10.1, component declaration 3.7, declarative part 3.9, discriminant 3.7.1, entry 9.5, entry declaration 9.5, enumeration literal 3.5.1, enumeration type definition 3.5.1, enumeration type declaration 3.5.1, formal parameter 6.2, generic program unit 12, iteration clause 5.5, label declaration 5.1, loop 5.5, loop identifier 5.5, loop parameter 5.5, package 7, package body 7.1, package specification 7.1, parameter declaration 6.1, private part 7.4, record component 3.7, scope 8.1, separate compilation 10, subprogram 6, subprogram body 6, subunit 10.2, task 9, task body 9.1, task specification 9.1, type declaration 3, with clause 10.1.1

8.3 Visibility of Identifiers and Declarations

The scope of the declaration of an identifier, as defined in the previous section, is the region of text over which the declaration has an effect. For each declaration, there exists a subset of this region where the declared entity can be named simply by its identifier; the entity, its declaration, and its identifier are then said to be *directly visible* from this subset. Where it is not directly visible (but within its scope), some suitable context may be required to make the entity visible. This context can be the prefix of a selected component, the place of a choice in a named record aggregate, the place of a discriminant name in a named discriminant constraint, or the place of a formal parameter name in a named parameter association.

An entity for which overloading is not possible and that is declared within a given construct is said to be *hidden* within an inner construct when the inner construct contains another declaration with the same identifier. Within the inner construct the hidden outer entity is not directly visible.

A subprogram declaration hides another subprogram declaration only if their specifications are equivalent with respect to the rules of subprogram overloading (see 6.6). Otherwise a subprogram identifier (also an enumeration literal) overloads, but does not hide, another subprogram (or enumeration literal) with the same identifier. A character literal may overload but cannot hide another character literal. The inner declaration of a subprogram or enumeration literal hides the declaration of any other non overloadable outer entity with the same identifier.

The name of an entity declared immediately within a subprogram, package, or task, or immediately within a named block or loop can always be written as a selected component within this unit, whether the entity is directly visible or hidden (a declaration is said to be immediately within a construct if it is within that construct but not within an inner one). The name of the unit is used as a prefix (possibly also using component selection); the unit must be visible and the name unambiguous (even for an overloaded subprogram). Component selection thus provides the necessary context for realizing visibility of the selected entity from the point where the identifier occurs (after the dot).

This form of selected component is available for an identifier denoting an enumeration literal but is not available for record components or discriminants (since they are not declared immediately within one of the above units). For formal parameters of subprograms and generic program units, this notation is only available within the unit of which they are parameters (since the parameters are declared for that unit and not immediately within the unit in which the subprogram or generic program unit is itself declared). For formal parameters of an entry this notation is only available within an accept statement for the entry.

An entity declared immediately within a unit is said to be *local* to the unit; an entity visible within but declared outside the unit is said to be *global* to the unit.

For each form of declaration (within its scope), the region of text in which a declared identifier is visible (and directly visible unless hidden by an inner declaration) is defined as follows:

(a) An identifier declared in the declarative part of a block or in that of the body of a subprogram, package, or task is directly visible within this block or body.

(b) An identifier declared in the visible part of a package is directly visible within the package specification and body.

Outside the package, but within its scope, such an identifier is made visible by a selected component whose prefix names the package. The identifier can also be made directly visible by means of a use clause (see section 8.4).

(c) An identifier declared in the private part of a package is directly visible within the package private part and body.

(d) An (entry) identifier declared in a task specification is directly visible within the task specification and body.

Outside the task, but within its scope, the identifier is made visible by a selected component whose prefix names the task or a task object of the task type.

(e) The identifier of a separately compiled subprogram or package is directly visible within the compilation unit itself and its subunits, and within any other compilation unit that has a with clause which mentions the identifier.

(f) The identifier of a record component is directly visible within the record type definition that declares the component, and within a record type representation specification for the record type.

Outside the record type definition, but within the scope of that definition, a record component is made visible by a selected component whose prefix names a record of the type of which it is a component. It is also visible as a choice in a component association of an aggregate of the record type.

(g) The identifier of a discriminant is directly visible within the discriminant part that declares the discriminant and within the associated record type definition.

Where it is not directly visible, but within the scope of the type, a discriminant is made visible by being in a selected component or in an aggregate, as for any other record component. It is also visible at the place of a discriminant name in a named discriminant specification of a discriminant constraint.

(h) The identifier of a formal parameter of a subprogram is directly visible within the formal part where the parameter is declared and within the subprogram body. The identifier of a formal parameter of an entry is directly visible within the formal part where the parameter is declared and within any accept statement for the entry. The identifier of a generic formal parameter is directly visible within the generic part where the parameter is declared and within the specification and body of the generic subprogram or package.

Where it is not directly visible, but within its scope, a formal parameter of a subprogram, entry, or generic program unit is visible at the place of a formal parameter name in a named parameter association of a corresponding subprogram call, entry call, or generic instantiation.

(i) The identifier of a loop parameter is directly visible within the loop where it is declared.

(j) An enumeration literal is directly visible within the scope of the enumeration type that declares the literal.

A declaration must not hide another declaration in the same declarative part (that is, at the same level, not in a nested declarative part). For this rule a generic part, a formal part of a subprogram, and the declarative part of the subprogram body are considered as comprising one declarative part. Similarly, a generic part, a package specification, and the declarative part of a package body are considered as comprising a single declarative part.

Example:

```
procedure P is
   A   : BOOLEAN;
   B   : BOOLEAN;

   procedure Q is
      C   : BOOLEAN;
      B   : BOOLEAN;   --   an inner redeclaration of B
   begin
      ...
      B   := A;    --   means Q.B  := P.A;
      C   := P.B;  --   means Q.C  := P.B;
   end;
begin
   ...
   A  := B;   --   means P.A  := P.B;
end;
```

Note:

An enumeration literal may overload but cannot hide another enumeration literal since enumeration literals are declared by their occurrence in an enumeration type declaration, and since two type declarations introduce distinct types.

References:

accept statement 9.5, aggregate 4.3, block 5.6, character literal 2.5, compilation unit 10.1, declaration 3.1, declarative part 3.9, discriminant 3.7.1, discriminant constraint 3.7.2, entry 9.5, entry call 9.5, enumeration literal 3.5.1, enumeration type 3.5.1, formal parameter 6.2, formal part 6.1, generic formal parameter 12.1, generic instantiation 12.3, generic package 12.1, generic part 12.1, generic program unit 12, generic subprogram 12.1, identifier 2.3, loop 5.5, loop parameter 5.5, name 4.1, overloading 3.4 3.5.1 4.6 6.6, package 7, package body 7.1, package specification 7.1, private part 7.4, record component 3.7, record type definition 3.7, record type representation 13.4, scope 8.1, selected component 4.1.3, subprogram 6, subprogram body 6, subprogram call 6.4, subprogram declaration 6, subprogram overloading 6.6, subprogram specification 6.1, subunit 10.2, task 9, task body 9.1, task object 9.2, task specification 9.1, task type 9.2, use clause 8.4, visible 8.1, visible part 7.2, with clause 10.1.1

8.4 Use Clauses

If the name of a package is visible at a given point of the text, the entities declared within the visible part of the package can be denoted by selected components. In addition, direct visibility of such entities can be achieved by means of use clauses.

```
use_clause ::= use package_name {, package_name};
```

A use clause is a declarative item. The effect of the elaboration of a use clause is to cause certain identifiers of the visible parts of the named packages to become directly visible from the text subject to the use clause. This effect takes place only on completion of this elaboration.

In order to define the set of identifiers (and entities) that are made directly visible by use clauses at a given point of the text, consider the set of package names appearing in the use clauses of all (nested) units enclosing this point, up to the compilation unit itself.

- An identifier is made directly visible by a use clause if it is declared in the visible part of one and only one package of the set and if the same identifier declared elsewhere is not already directly visible otherwise (that is in the absence of any use clause).

- An enumeration literal declared in the visible part of a package of the set is made directly visible if and only if the corresponding identifier is not otherwise directly visible, and in any case if it is a character literal.

- A subprogram declared in the visible part of a package of the set is made directly visible if and only if the two following conditions are satisfied. First, the specification of the subprogram must not be equivalent (see 6.6) to that of another subprogram in the set or to that of a subprogram that is otherwise directly visible. Second, an entity other than a subprogram or an enumeration literal and with the same identifier must not be declared in the visible part of any of the packages of the set, nor may such an entity be otherwise directly visible.

Thus an identifier made directly visible by a use clause can never hide another identifier although it may overload it. If an entity declared in the visible part of a package cannot be made visible by a use clause (because of one of the above conflicts), the name of the entity must take the form of a selected component.

For overloading resolution within an expression, identifiers made visible by a use clause are only considered if an interpretation of the complete expression cannot otherwise be found (that is, if the expression would be undefined without the use clause). Similarly, for overloading resolution of a procedure or entry call, identifiers made visible by a use clause are only considered if an interpretation of the complete procedure or entry call cannot otherwise be found. An ambiguity exists if there is more than one interpretation without the use clauses or if there is no interpretation without the use clauses but more than one can be given in their presence.

Example of conflicting names in two packages:

```
procedure R is
    use TRAFFIC, WATER_COLORS;
    --   subtypes used to resolve the conflicting type name COLOR
    subtype T_COLOR  is TRAFFIC.COLOR;
    subtype W_COLOR  is WATER_COLORS.COLOR;

    SIGNAL : T_COLOR;
    PAINT  : W_COLOR;
begin
    SIGNAL := GREEN;   --   that of TRAFFIC
    PAINT  := GREEN;   --   that of WATER_COLORS
end R;
```

Example of name identification with a use clause:

```
package D is
  T, U, V : BOOLEAN;
end D;

procedure P is

  package E is
    B, W, V : INTEGER;
  end E;

  procedure Q is
    T, X : REAL;
  begin
    declare
      use D, E;
    begin
      --  the name T    means Q.T, not D.T
      --  the name U    means D.U
      --  the name B    means E.B
      --  the name W    means E.W
      --  the name X    means Q.X
      --  the name V    is illegal : either D.V or E.V must be used
    end;
  end Q;
begin
  ...
end P;
```

Example of overloading resolution with a use clause:

```
procedure MAIN is
  ...
  package P is
    function F (X : REAL)      return TARGET;      --  P.F
    function G (X : SOURCE)    return REAL;        --  P.G
    function K (X : SOURCE)    return BOOLEAN;     --  P.K
  end P;

  function F (X : BOOLEAN)  return TARGET;     --  MAIN.F
  function G (X : SOURCE)   return BOOLEAN;    --  MAIN.G
  function H (X : SOURCE)   return REAL;       --  MAIN.H
  function K (X : SOURCE)   return REAL;       --  MAIN.K
  S  : SOURCE;
  T  : TARGET;
  use P;
  ...
begin
  T := F(G(S));   --  MAIN.F(MAIN.G(S)), interpreted without considering use clause
  T := F(H(S));   --  P.F(MAIN.H(S))

  --  T := F(K(S)) would be ambiguous
  --  it could mean either MAIN.F(P.K(S)) or P.F(MAIN.K(S))
end;
```

Note:

Renaming declarations and subtype declarations may help to avoid excessive use of selected components.

References:

character literal 2.5, compilation unit 10.1, declarative item 3.9, direct visibility 8.3, elaboration 3.1, entry call 9.5, enumeration literal 3.5.1, expression 4.4, identifier 2.3, hidden 8.3, name 4.1, overloading 3.4 3.5.1 4.6 6.6, package 7, procedure call 6.4, renaming declaration 8.5, selected component 4.1.3, subprogram 6, subprogram specification 6.1, subtype declaration 3.3, type 3.3, visible 8.1, visible part 7.2

8.5 Renaming Declarations

A renaming declaration declares another name for an entity.

```
renaming_declaration ::=
      identifier : type_mark  renames name;
    | identifier : exception  renames name;
    | package identifier renames name;
    | task     identifier renames name;
    | subprogram_specification renames name;
```

For the elaboration of a renaming declaration, the identifier is first introduced, or the subprogram specification is elaborated, and then the identity of the entity following the reserved word **renames** is established. The identifier can be used as the name of this entity from then on.

The first form is used for renaming objects. The newly declared identifier is constant if the renamed entity is.

The type mark given in the renaming declaration must express the same constraints as those of the renamed entity. A component of an unconstrained object of a type with discriminants cannot be renamed if the existence of the component depends on the value of a discriminant.

The last form is used for renaming a subprogram (or entry) whose specification matches the one given in the renaming declaration in the following sense. The renamed subprogram and this specification must have parameters in the same order, of the same mode and with the same types and constraints. For functions the result type and constraints must be the same. Parameter names, the presence or absence of defaults, and the values of any defaults, are ignored for this matching; hence a renaming declaration can introduce different default parameters.

A function can be renamed as an operator and vice versa (renaming cannot, of course, declare an operator with default parameters, see 6.7). An entry can only be renamed as a procedure.

A renaming declaration is ambiguous, and therefore illegal, if more than one visible subprogram (or entry) matches the subprogram specification. The exception CONSTRAINT_ERROR is raised if the constraints of the parameters or results of the two subprograms (or entries) are not the same.

Examples:

```
procedure TMR (ELEM : out ITEM) renames TABLE_MANAGER.RETRIEVE;
procedure SORT (X : in out LIST)    renames QUICKSORT2;
task T renames POOL(6);
FULL : exception renames TABLE_MANAGER.TABLE_FULL;

declare
   L : PERSON renames LEFTMOST_PERSON;
begin
   L.AGE := L.AGE + 1;
end;

function REAL_PLUS(X,Y : REAL    ) return REAL      renames "+";
function INT_PLUS (X,Y : INTEGER ) return INTEGER renames "+";
function "*" (X,Y : VECTOR) return REAL renames DOT_PRODUCT;
```

Notes:

Renaming may be used to resolve name conflicts, to achieve partial evaluation and to act as a shorthand. Renaming does not hide the old name. Neither a label, nor a block or loop identifier may be renamed. A subtype can effectively be used to rename a type as in

```
subtype INPUT is TEXT_IO.IN_FILE;
```

References:

block identifier 5.6, constant 3.2, constraint 3.3, constraint on parameters 6.4.1, constraint_error exception 11.1, declaration 3, elaboration 3.1, entry 9.5, function 6.1 6.5, identifier 2.3, label 5.1, loop identifier 5.5, mode 6.2, name 4.1, operator 4.5, parameter 6.1, parameter name 6.2, parameter type 6.1, subprogram 6, subprogram specification 6.1, subtype 3.3, type 3.3, type mark 3.3, unconstrained record type 3.7, variant record 3.7.1

8.6 Predefined Environment

All predefined identifiers, for example those of built in types such as INTEGER, BOOLEAN, and CHARACTER, operators and the predefined function ABS, are assumed to be declared in the predefined package STANDARD given in Appendix C. All identifiers declared in the visible part of the package STANDARD are assumed to be declared at the outermost level of every program. In addition, the separately compiled subprograms and packages named in a with clause are assumed to be implicitly declared in STANDARD.

Note:

If all blocks of a program are named, the name of any program unit can always be written as a selected component starting with STANDARD (unless this name is itself hidden by a redeclaration). Apart from the local package SYSTEM and the definitions of predefined numeric types and subtypes, the package STANDARD must be the same for all implementations of the language.

References:

abs function C, block 5.6, boolean type 3.5.3, character type 3.5.2, identifier 2.3, integer type 3.5.4, name 4.1, operator 4.5, package 7, program unit 7, selected component 4.1.3, standard package C, subprogram 6, type 3.3, visible part 7.2, with clause 10.1.1

9. Tasks

Tasks are entities that may operate in parallel. Parallel tasks may be implemented on multicomputers, multiprocessors, or with interleaved execution on a single processor. Tasks may have entries which may be called by other tasks. Synchronization is achieved by rendezvous between a task issuing an entry call and a task accepting the call. Entries are also the principal means of communication between tasks.

Tasks are one of the three forms of *program units*, of which programs can be composed. The other forms are subprograms and packages. The properties of tasks and entries, and the statements specific to tasking (that is, accept statements and selective waits) are described in this chapter.

9.1 Task Specifications and Task Bodies

A task specification which starts with the reserved words **task type** defines a task type. An object of a task type denotes a task having the entries, if any, that are declared in the task specification. The task specification therefore specifies the interface between tasks of the type and other tasks of the same or of different types.

The execution of a task is defined by a task body. A task specification and the corresponding task body have the same identifier and must occur in the same declarative part, the specification first.

```
task_declaration ::= task_specification

task_specification ::=
    task [type] identifier [is
        {entry_declaration}
        {representation_specification}
    end [identifier]];

task_body ::=
    task body identifier is
        [declarative_part]
    begin
        sequence_of_statements
  [ exception
        {exception_handler}]
    end [identifier];
```

A task specification without the reserved word **type** defines a single task. A task declaration of this form introduces a task name (rather than the name of a task type) and is equivalent to the declaration of an anonymous task type immediately followed by the declaration of an object of the type. In the remainder of this chapter, explanations are given in terms of task type specifications; the corresponding explanations for single task declarations follow from the stated equivalence.

For the elaboration of a task specification the task type (or task) identifier is first introduced and can from then on be used as the name of the corresponding task type (or task). Entry declarations and representation specifications, if any, are then elaborated in the given order. Such representation specifications only apply to the entries declared in the task specification, or to the task type (or task) itself (see 13.2 and 13.5).

The elaboration of a task body has no other effect than to establish the body as defining the execution of tasks of the corresponding type.

Examples of specifications of task types:

```
task type RESOURCE is
  entry SEIZE;
  entry RELEASE;
end RESOURCE;

task type KEYBOARD_DRIVER is
  entry READ (C : out  CHARACTER);
  entry WRITE (C : in    CHARACTER);
end KEYBOARD_DRIVER;
```

Examples of specifications of single tasks:

```
task PRODUCER_CONSUMER is
  entry READ (V : out ELEM);
  entry WRITE (E : in   ELEM);
end;

task CONTROLLER is
  entry REQUEST(LEVEL)(D : DATA);    --  a family of entries
end CONTROLLER;

task USER;  --  has no entry
```

Example of task specification and corresponding body:

```
task PROTECTED_ARRAY is
  --   INDEX and ELEM are global types
  entry READ (N : in INDEX; V : out ELEM);
  entry WRITE (N : in INDEX; E : in   ELEM);
end;

task body PROTECTED_ARRAY is
  TABLE : array(INDEX) of ELEM := (INDEX => 0);
begin
  loop
    select
      accept READ (N : in INDEX; V : out ELEM) do
        V := TABLE(N);
      end READ;
    or
      accept WRITE (N : in INDEX; E : in   ELEM) do
        TABLE(N) := E;
      end WRITE;
    end select;
  end loop;
end PROTECTED_ARRAY;
```

References:

accept statement 9.5, declarative part 3.9, elaboration 3.1, entry 9.5, entry representation specification 13.1, length specification 13.2, selective wait 9.7.1

9.2 Task Objects and Task Types

Objects of a task type are defined by object declarations where the type indicated is the task type. Task objects can also be components of records and arrays. Finally, objects of a task type can be the objects (or components of the objects) designated by the values of an access type.

The value of an object of a task type denotes a task of the type (this task has the corresponding entries). This value is defined either by the elaboration of the corresponding object or by its creation by an allocator. Entries of the corresponding task can be called once this value is defined.

Neither assignment nor comparison for equality or inequality are defined for objects of task types. In this respect, a task type has the properties of a limited private type; it can appear as the definition of a limited private type given in a private part, and as a generic actual parameter associated with a formal parameter that is a limited private type.

In subprogram calls and generic instantiations, a task object can be passed as an actual parameter associated with a formal **in** parameter of the same task type. Since the value of a task object denotes a task, both the formal parameter and the actual parameter denote the same task. The **in out** and **out** parameter modes are not allowed for parameters of a task type.

Examples:

```
CONTROL  : RESOURCE;
TELETYPE : KEYBOARD_DRIVER;
POOL     : array(1 .. 10) of KEYBOARD_DRIVER;
--   see also examples of declarations of single tasks in 9.1
```

Example of access type designating task objects:

```
type KEYBOARD is access KEYBOARD_DRIVER;

TERMINAL : KEYBOARD := new KEYBOARD_DRIVER;
```

Notes:

Task objects behave as constants since their values are implicitly defined and no assignment is available. If an application needs to store and exchange task identities, it can do so by defining an access type designating the corresponding task objects and by using access values for identification purposes (see above example). Assignment is available for such an access type as for any access type.

There are no constraints applicable to task types.

References:

access type 3.8, allocator 4.8, entry 9.5, generic parameter 12.1, limited private type 7.4.2, object declaration 3.2

9.3 Task Execution

A task body defines the execution of the tasks of the corresponding type. The *activation* of a task object consists of the elaboration of the declarative part, if any, of the corresponding task body. After activation the statements of the task body are executed.

Task objects declared immediately within a declarative part (that is, not within a nested declarative part), and task objects that are components of other objects declared immediately within a declarative part, are all activated before execution of the first statement following the declarative part. Each task can continue its execution as a parallel entity once its activation is completed.

Should an exception occur during the activation of one of these tasks, that task and any other of these tasks that are not yet activated become *terminated* tasks (see 9.4); already activated tasks are unaffected. Such an exception is treated as if raised within the statements following the declarative part in question. Should an exception occur within the declarative part itself, all of the declared tasks so far elaborated become terminated tasks.

For the above rules, in a package body without statements, a null statement is assumed; in the absence of a package body, one containing a single null statement is assumed to occur not earlier than the task body.

The creation of a task object by an allocator is followed by its activation and execution. Execution of the allocator is complete when all created task objects have been activated. Each task can continue its execution as a parallel entity as soon as its activation is completed. Should an exception occur during the activation of one of these tasks, that task and any other of these tasks that are not yet activated become terminated tasks.

A task must not be activated before the elaboration of the corresponding task body is complete. An entry of a task can be called before the task has been activated. If the called task terminates before accepting an entry call, the exception TASKING_ERROR is raised in the calling task (see 11.5).

Example:

```
procedure P is
    A, B : RESOURCE;      --  elaborate A, B
    ...
    C : RESOURCE;          --  elaborate C
begin
    --  A, B, C are activated in any order
    ...
end;
```

Notes:

The language does not specify the order in which tasks declared within a declarative part are activated.

References:

allocator 4.8, declarative part 3.9, elaboration 3.1, entry 9.5, exception 11, handling an exception 11, package body 7.3, statement 5, task body 9.1, task termination 9.4, task object 9.2, task type 9.2, tasking_error exception 11.5

9.4 Normal Termination of Tasks

Each task *depends* either on a block, a subprogram body, a task body, or on a library package (no task depends on a package declared within another unit). For each of these units a *dependent* task is one of:

(a) A task object that is an object (or a component of an object) declared within the unit considered, including within an inner package, but excluding within any inner block, subprogram body, or task body.

(b) A task object that is the object (or a component of the object) designated by the value of an access type, if this access type is declared within the unit considered, including within an inner package, but excluding within any inner block, subprogram body, or package body.

A block, subprogram body, or task body is not left until all dependent tasks have terminated their execution (including the case where the end of this block or body is reached as the result of an unhandled exception).

Normal termination of a task occurs when its execution reaches the end of its task body and all dependent tasks, if any, have terminated. Normal termination also occurs on selection of a terminate alternative in a selective wait statement (see 9.7.1). After its termination, a task is said to be *terminated*.

Example:

```
declare
   type GLOBAL is access RESOURCE;
   A, B : RESOURCE;
   G    : GLOBAL;
begin
   --  activation of A and B
   declare
      type LOCAL is access RESOURCE;
      X : GLOBAL := new RESOURCE;   --  activation of X.all
      L : LOCAL  := new RESOURCE;   --  activation of L.all
      C : RESOURCE;
   begin
      --  activation of C
      ...
   end;   --  await termination of C and L.all but not X.all
   ...
end;   --  await termination of A, B, G.all and X.all
```

Notes:

The usual rules apply to the main program. Consequently, termination of the main program awaits termination of any dependent task even if the corresponding task type is declared in a library package. On the other hand, termination of the main program does not await termination of tasks denoted by task objects declared in library packages; the language does not define whether such tasks are required to terminate.

References:

access type 3.8, block 5.6, component 3.2 3 3.6 3.7 4.1, library package 10.1, main program 10.1, object 3.2, selective wait 9.7.1, task type 9.2, terminate alternative 9.7

9.5 Entries and Accept Statements

An entry declaration is similar to a subprogram declaration and can be given only in a task specification. An entry of a task can be called by another task. The actions to be performed when an entry is called are specified by corresponding accept statements. Entry call and accept statements are the primary means of communication between tasks and of synchronization of tasks.

```
entry_declaration ::=
    entry identifier [(discrete_range)] [formal_part];

entry_call ::= entry_name [actual_parameter_part];

accept_statement ::=
    accept entry_name [formal_part] [do
        sequence_of_statements
    end [identifier]];
```

For the elaboration of an entry declaration the entry identifier is first introduced; any discrete range is then evaluated; finally, any formal part is elaborated as for a subprogram declaration. From then on, the entry identifier can be used as a name of the corresponding entry (or entry family). An entry declaration including a discrete range declares a family of distinct entries having the same formal part (if any); that is, one such entry for each value of the discrete range.

Each task of a task type has the entries declared in the specification of the task type. Within the body of a task, each of its entries (or entry families) can be named by the corresponding identifier; the name of an entry of a family takes the form of an indexed component, the family name being followed by the index in parentheses. Outside the body of a task an entry name has the form of a selected component, with the name of the task object prefixing the identifier of one of its entries. Selected component notation may also be used within a task body, with the name of the task or task type as the prefix.

The syntax of an entry call is similar to that of a procedure call. The semantics is as follows.

An accept statement specifies the actions to be performed at a call of a named entry (it can be an entry of a family). The formal part given in the accept statement must match that given in the corresponding entry declaration; the matching rules are the same as for the match between the formal part of a subprogram body and the formal part of the corresponding subprogram declaration.

An accept statement for an entry of a given task may only appear within the sequence of statements of the corresponding task body. The consequence of this rule is that a task can execute accept statements only for its own entries. A task body may contain more than one accept statement for the same entry.

Execution of an accept statement starts with the evaluation of any entry index (in the case of an entry of a family). Execution of an entry call also starts with the evaluation of any entry index, followed by the evaluation of any expression in the actual parameter list. Further execution of the accept statement and of a corresponding entry call are synchronized. There are two possibilities:

- If a calling task issues an entry call before a corresponding accept statement is reached by the task owning the entry, the execution of the calling task is suspended.

- If a task reaches an accept statement prior to any call of that entry, the execution of the task is suspended until such a call occurs.

When an entry has been called and a corresponding accept statement is reached, the sequence of statements, if any, of the accept statement is executed by the called task (while the calling task remains suspended). This interaction is called a *rendezvous*. Thereafter, the calling task and the task owning the entry can continue their execution in parallel.

If several tasks call the same entry before a corresponding accept statement is reached, the calls are queued; there is one queue associated with each entry. Each execution of an accept statement removes one call from the queue. The calls are processed in order of arrival.

Entries may be overloaded both with each other and with procedures with the same identifier. An entry may be renamed as a procedure.

An attempt to call an entry of a terminated task raises the exception TASKING_ERROR. The exception CONSTRAINT_ERROR is raised by the evaluation of the name of an entry of a family if the index is not within the specified discrete range.

Examples of entry declarations:

```
entry READ(V : out ELEM);
entry SEIZE;
entry REQUEST(RANK)(D : DATA);   --   a family of entries
```

Example of entry calls:

```
CONTROL.RELEASE;
PRODUCER_CONSUMER.WRITE(E);
POOL(5).READ(NEXT_CHAR);
CONTROLLER.REQUEST(LOW)(SOME_DATA);
```

Example of accept statements:

```
accept SEIZE;

accept READ(V : out ELEM) do
  V := LOCAL_ELEM;
end READ;

accept REQUEST(LOW)(D : DATA) do ... end REQUEST;
```

Notes:

An accept statement may contain other accept statements (possibly for the same entry) and may call subprograms issuing entry calls. An accept statement need not have a sequence of statements even if the corresponding entry has parameters. Equally, it may have a sequence of statements even if the corresponding entry has no parameters. A task may call its own entries but it will, of course, deadlock. The language permits conditional and timed entry calls (see 9.7.2 and 9.7.3). The language rules ensure that a task can only be in one queue at a given time.

If the bounds of the discrete range of an entry family are integer numbers, the indexes must be of the predefined type INTEGER (see 3.6.1).

References:

actual parameter 6.4, conditional entry call 9.7.2, constraint_error exception 11.1, discrete range 3.6.1, elaboration 3.1 3.9, formal part 6.2, indexed component 4.1.1, name 4.1, overloading a subprogram 6.6, procedure call 6.4, renaming 8.5, selected component 4.1.3, sequence of statements 5.1, subprogram call 6.4, subprogram declaration 6.1, subprogram body 6.3, task body 9.1, task specification 9.1, task type 9.2, tasking_error exception 11.5, timed entry call 9.7.3

9.6 Delay Statements, Duration and Time

A delay statement suspends further execution of the task that executes it for at least the given time interval.

```
delay_statement ::= delay simple_expression;
```

The argument of the delay statement is of the predefined fixed point type DURATION and is given in seconds. A delay statement with a non-positive argument has no effect.

The type DURATION allows representation of durations (both positive and negative) up to at least 86400 seconds (one day). The definition of the type TIME is provided in the predefined library package CALENDAR. The function CLOCK returns the current value of TIME at the time it is called. The operators "+" and "-" for addition and subtraction of times and durations have a conventional meaning.

```
package CALENDAR is
   type TIME is
     record
        YEAR    : INTEGER range 1901 .. 2099;
        MONTH   : INTEGER range 1 .. 12;
        DAY     : INTEGER range 1 .. 31;
        SECOND  : DURATION;
     end record;

   function CLOCK return TIME;

   function "+" (A : TIME;     B : DURATION) return TIME;
   function "+" (A : DURATION; B : TIME)     return TIME;
   function "-" (A : TIME;     B : DURATION) return TIME;
   function "-" (A : TIME;     B : TIME)     return DURATION;
end CALENDAR;
```

Examples:

```
delay  3.0;  --   delay  3.0 seconds

declare
   INTERVAL   : constant DURATION := 60.0;
   NEXT_TIME : CALENDAR.TIME := CALENDAR.CLOCK() + INTERVAL;
begin
   loop
      delay NEXT_TIME - CALENDAR.CLOCK();
      --   some actions
      NEXT_TIME := NEXT_TIME + INTERVAL;
   end loop;
end;
```

Notes:

The second example causes the loop to be repeated every 60 seconds on the average. This interval between two successive iterations is only approximate. However there will be no cumulative drift as long as the duration of each iteration is (sufficiently) less than INTERVAL.

References:

fixed point type 3.5.9, library package 10.1

9.7 Select Statements

There are three forms of select statements. One form provides a selective wait for one or more alternatives. The other two provide conditional and timed entry calls

```
select_statement ::= selective_wait
   |conditional_entry_call | timed_entry_call
```

9.7.1 Selective Wait Statements

This form of the select statement allows a combination of waiting for, and selection of, one or more alternatives. The selection may depend on conditions associated with each alternative of the selective wait statement.

```
selective_wait ::=
   select
      [when condition =>]
         select_alternative
   { or [when condition =>]
         select_alternative}
   [ else
      sequence_of_statements]
   end select;
```

```
select_alternative ::=
    accept_statement  [sequence_of_statements]
  | delay_statement   [sequence_of_statements]
  | terminate;
```

A select alternative is said to be open if there is no preceding when clause or if the corresponding condition is true. It is said to be closed otherwise.

A selective wait can contain at most one terminate alternative; it cannot contain both a terminate alternative and an alternative starting with a delay statement. Each of these possibilities excludes the presence of an else part. A selective wait must contain at least one alternative commencing with an accept statement.

Execution of a selective wait statement proceeds as follows:

(a) All conditions are evaluated to determine which alternatives are open. For an open alternative starting with a delay statement, the delay expression is evaluated immediately after the evaluation of the corresponding condition. Similarly, if an open alternative starts with an accept statement for an entry of a family, the entry index is evaluated immediately after the evaluation of the condition.

(b) An open alternative starting with an accept statement may be selected if a corresponding rendezvous is possible (that is, when a corresponding entry call has been issued by another task). When such an alternative is selected, the corresponding accept statement and possible subsequent statements are executed.

(c) An open alternative starting with a delay statement will be selected if no other alternative has been selected before the specified duration has elapsed. Any subsequent statements of the alternative are then executed.

(d) An open alternative with the reserved word terminate may be selected only if the task containing the selective wait belongs to the set of dependent tasks of a block, subprogram, or task, and either the end of this block, subprogram body or task body has been reached (see 9.4), or in the case of a task body, a terminate alternative has been reached. This (first mentioned) alternative will be selected if and only if all other tasks of the set, also any task depending on a task of the set, and so on, are either terminated or waiting at a selective wait with a terminate alternative. Selection of a terminate alternative causes normal termination of the task. A terminate alternative may not appear in an inner block that declares task objects.

(e) If no alternative can be immediately selected, and there is an else part, the else part is executed. If there is no else part, the task waits until an open alternative can be selected.

(f) If all alternatives are closed and there is an else part, the else part is executed. If all alternatives are closed and there is no else part, the exception SELECT_ERROR is raised.

In general, several entries of a task may have been called before a selective wait is encountered. As a result, several alternative rendezvous are possible. Similarly, several open alternatives may start with an accept statement for the same entry. In such cases one of these alternatives is selected arbitrarily.

Example:

```
task body RESOURCE is
  BUSY : BOOLEAN := FALSE;
begin
  loop
    select
      when not BUSY =>
        accept SEIZE do
          BUSY := TRUE;
        end;
    or
      accept RELEASE do
        BUSY := FALSE;
      end;
    or
      when not BUSY => terminate;
    end select;
  end loop;
end RESOURCE;
```

Notes:

Selection among open alternatives starting with accept statements is performed *arbitrarily*. This means that the selection algorithm is not defined by the language and that any program relying on a particular selection algorithm is therefore erroneous. Several open alternatives may start with a delay statement. A consequence of the above rules is that only the alternative with the shortest duration can be selected (a negative duration being shorter than a positive one).

The language does not define in which order to evaluate the conditions of a select statement. A program that relies on a specific order is therefore erroneous.

References:

accept statement 9.5, condition 5.3, delay statement 9.6, dependent task 9.4, duration 9.6, entry call 9.5, entry family 9.5, rendezvous 9.5, sequence of statements 5.1, task 9.2 task termination 9.4

9.7.2 Conditional Entry Calls

A conditional entry call issues an entry call if and only if a rendezvous is immediately possible.

```
conditional_entry_call ::=
  select
    entry_call [sequence_of_statements]
  else
    sequence_of_statements
  end select;
```

For the execution of a conditional entry call an entry index (in the case of an entry of a family) is first evaluated. This is followed by the evaluation of any expression occurring in the actual parameters. If a rendezvous with the called task is immediately possible, it is performed and the optional sequence of statements after the entry call is then executed. Otherwise the else part is executed.

Example:

```
procedure SPIN(R : RESOURCE) is
begin
  loop
    select
      R.SEIZE;
      return;
    else
      null;  --  busy  waiting
    end  select;
  end  loop;
end;
```

References:

accept 9.5, actual parameter 6.4, entry call 9.5, entry family 9.5, rendezvous 9.5, sequence of statements 5.1

9.7.3 Timed Entry Calls

A timed entry call issues an entry call if and only if this entry call can be accepted within a given delay.

```
timed_entry_call ::=
  select
    entry_call [sequence_of_statements]
  or
    delay_statement [sequence_of_statements]
  end select;
```

For the execution of a timed entry call an entry index (in the case of an entry of a family) is first evaluated. This is followed by the evaluation of any expression occurring in the actual parameters and by the evaluation of the expression stating the delay.

If a rendezvous can be started within the specified duration, it is performed and the optional sequence of statements after the entry call is then executed. Otherwise the optional sequence of statements of the delay alternative is executed.

Example:

```
select
   CONTROLLER.REQUEST(URGENT)(SOME_DATA);
or
   delay 45.0;
   --  controller too busy, try something else
end select;
```

References:

actual parameter 6.4, accept statement 9.5, delay statement 9.6, duration 9.6, entry call 9.5, entry family 9.5, expression 4.4, rendezvous 9.5, sequence of statements 5.1,

9.8 Priorities

Each task may (but need not) have a priority, which is an integer value of the predefined subtype PRIORITY. A lower value indicates a lower degree of urgency; the range of priorities is implementation defined. A priority is associated with a task if a pragma

   pragma PRIORITY (*static*_expression);

appears in the corresponding task specification; the priority is given by the value of the expression. A priority is associated with the main program if such a pragma appears in its outermost declarative part. At most one such pragma can appear within a given task specification (or for the main program).

The specification of a priority is an indication given to the compiler, to assist in the allocation of processing resources to parallel tasks when there are more tasks eligible for execution than can be supported simultaneously by the available processing resources. The effect of priorities on scheduling is defined by the following rule:

> If two tasks with different priorities are both eligible for execution and could sensibly be executed using the same processing resources then it cannot be the case that the task with the lower priority is executing while the task with the higher priority is not.

For tasks of the same priority, the scheduling order is not defined by the language. For tasks without explicit priority, the scheduling rules are not defined, except when such tasks are engaged in rendezvous. If the priorities of both tasks engaged in a rendezvous are defined, the rendezvous is executed with the higher of the two priorities. If only one of the two priorities is defined, the rendezvous is executed with at least that priority. If neither is defined, the priority of the rendezvous is undefined.

Notes:

The priority of a task is static and therefore fixed. Priorities should be used only to indicate relative degrees of urgency; they should not be used for task synchronization.

References:

declarative part 3.9, main program 10.1, pragma 2.8, rendezvous 9.5, static expression 4.9, synchronization 9.5, task 9.2, task specification 9.1

9.9 Task and Entry Attributes

For a task object or for a task type T the following attributes are defined:

T'TERMINATED   Of type BOOLEAN. This attribute is initially equal to FALSE when the task T is declared (or allocated) and becomes TRUE when the task is terminated.

T'PRIORITY   Of the subtype PRIORITY. The value of this attribute is the priority of the task T if one is defined; use of this attribute is otherwise not allowed.

T'STORAGE_SIZE   This attribute indicates the number of storage units allocated for the task T. Of type *universal_integer*.

For an entry E of a task T the following attribute may be used within the body of the task T:

E'COUNT   The number of entry calls presently on the queue associated with the entry E. Of type INTEGER.

Note:

Algorithms interrogating the attribute E'COUNT should take precautions to allow for the increase of the value of this attribute for incoming entry calls, and its decrease, for example with timed entry calls. Within an accept statement for an entry, the count does not include the calling task.

References:

attribute 4.1.4, entry call 9.5, entry queue 9.5, integer number 2.4, integer type 3.5.4, priority 9.8, storage unit 13.2, task body 9.1, task termination 9.4

9.10 Abort Statements

Abnormal termination of one or several tasks is achieved by an abort statement.

    abort_statement ::= **abort** *task*_name {, *task*_name};

An abort statement causes the unconditional asynchronous termination of the named tasks. If a task is already terminated there is no effect; if a task has not yet been activated it is terminated and there is no other effect.

Abnormal termination of a task causes the abnormal termination of any task dependent on it. It further causes the abnormal termination of any task dependent on any subprogram (or block) being called directly or indirectly by the task. On completion of the abort statement each of these tasks is terminated.

If a task calling an entry is abnormally terminated it is removed from the entry queue; if the rendezvous is already in progress the calling task is terminated but the task executing the accept statement is allowed to complete the rendezvous normally. If there are pending entry calls (possibly timed) for the entries of a task that is abnormally terminated, an exception TASKING_ERROR is raised for each calling task at the point where it calls the entry (including for the task presently engaged in a rendezvous, if any); for a timed entry call, such an exception cancels the delay.

Example:

```
abort USER, TERMINAL.all, POOL(3);
```

Notes:

An abort statement should be used only in extremely severe situations requiring unconditional termination. In less extreme cases (where the task to be terminated can be given the possibility of executing some cleanup actions before termination), the exception FAILURE could be raised for the task (see 11.5). A task may abort any task, including itself.

References:

accept statement 9.5, block 5.6, dependent task 9.4, entry call 9.5, entry queue 9.5, name 4.1, rendezvous 9.5, subprogram 6, task 9.2, task activation 9.3, task elaboration 9.1, task termination 9.4, tasking_error exception 11.4, timed entry call 9.7.3

9.11 Shared Variables

The normal means of communication between tasks is via entry calls.

If two tasks operate on common global variables, then neither of them may assume anything about the order in which the other performs its operations except at the points where they synchronize. Two tasks are synchronized at the start and at the end of their rendezvous. At the time of its activation a task is synchronized with the task that causes this activation.

If shared variables are used, it is the programmer's responsibility to ensure that two tasks do not simultaneously modify the same shared variable.

Compilers will normally assume all variables not to be shared and may consequently maintain some of them in local registers. Whenever one must ensure that a shared variable has been updated with its latest value, this can be achieved by calling a procedure obtained by instantiation of the predefined generic library procedure SHARED_VARIABLE_UPDATE, for the type of the shared variable.

```
generic
   type SHARED is limited private;
procedure SHARED_VARIABLE_UPDATE(X : in out SHARED);
```

A call to such a procedure will generate no code, other than any code needed to update the shared variable with its latest value (for example, if this value is in a register).

References:

entry call 9.5, generic procedure 12.1, rendezvous 9.5, task 9.2, task activation 9.3

9.12 Example of Tasking

The following example defines a buffering task to smooth variations between the speed of output of a producing task and the speed of input of some consuming task. For instance, the producing task may contain the statements

```
loop
   --   produce the next character CHAR
   BUFFER.WRITE(CHAR);
   exit when CHAR = END_OF_TRANSMISSION;
end loop;
```

and the consuming task may contain the statements

```
loop
   BUFFER.READ(CHAR);
   --  consume the character CHAR
   exit when CHAR = END_OF_TRANSMISSION;
end loop;
```

The buffering task contains an internal pool of characters processed in a round-robin fashion. The pool has two indices, an IN_INDEX denoting the space for the next input character and an OUT_INDEX denoting the space for the next output character.

```
task BUFFER is
   entry READ (C : out  CHARACTER);
   entry WRITE(C : in    CHARACTER);
end;

task body BUFFER is
   POOL_SIZE  : constant INTEGER := 100;
   POOL        : array(1 .. POOL_SIZE) of CHARACTER;
   COUNT       : INTEGER range 0 .. POOL_SIZE := 0;
   IN_INDEX, OUT_INDEX : INTEGER range 1 .. POOL_SIZE := 1;
begin
   loop
     select
       when COUNT < POOL_SIZE =>
         accept WRITE(C : in CHARACTER) do
           POOL(IN_INDEX) := C;
         end;
         IN_INDEX  := IN_INDEX mod POOL_SIZE + 1;
         COUNT     := COUNT + 1;
     or when COUNT > 0 =>
         accept READ(C : out CHARACTER) do
           C := POOL(OUT_INDEX);
         end;
         OUT_INDEX  := OUT_INDEX mod POOL_SIZE + 1;
         COUNT      := COUNT - 1;
     or
         terminate
       end select;
     end loop;
   end BUFFER;
```

The overall structure of programs and the facilities for separate compilation are described in this chapter. A program is a collection of one or more compilation units submitted to a compiler in one or more compilations. A compilation unit can be a subprogram declaration or body, a package declaration or body, a generic declaration, or a subunit, that is, the body of a subprogram, package, or task declared within another compilation unit.

References:

package body 7.1, package declaration 7.1, subprogram body 6.3, subprogram declaration 6.1, subunit 10.2, task body 9.1

10.1 Compilation Units - Library Units

The text of a program can be submitted to the compiler in one or more compilations. Each compilation is a succession of one or more compilation units. A simple program may consist of a single compilation units.

```
compilation ::= {compilation_unit}

compilation_unit ::=
      context_specification  subprogram_declaration
    | context_specification  subprogram_body
    | context_specification  package_declaration
    | context_specification  package_body
    | context_specification  subunit

context_specification ::= {with_clause [use_clause]}

with_clause ::= with unit_name {, unit_name};
```

The compilation units of a program are said to belong to a *program library*. A compilation unit that is not a subunit of another unit is called a *library unit*. Within a program library the names of all library units must be distinct (except, of course, that a body has the same name as the corresponding declaration).

The compilation units of a compilation are compiled in the given order. The effect of compiling a subprogram or package declaration is to define (or redefine) the corresponding unit as one of the library units. The effect of compiling a subunit, or the body of a subprogram or package, is to define that body. The declaration of a subprogram that is not generic need not be supplied in a compilation, in which case compilation of the body serves as both the declaration and the body.

A compilation unit is effectively declared by its presence in a compilation. For the elaboration of a compilation unit, its context specification is first elaborated; the following subprogram declaration or body, package declaration or body, or subunit is then elaborated. The order of elaboration of compilation units need not be the order in which they appear in a compilation; this order of elaboration is defined in section 10.5.

The elaboration of a context specification consists of the elaboration of its constituent with clauses and use clauses. The only identifiers that are visible within a with clause are names of library units. The only package names that can be listed in the use clause of a context specification are those declared in the package STANDARD and those made visible by previous with clauses and previous use clauses. Any with clause and any use clause given in the context specification of a subprogram, package, or generic declaration applies also to the corresponding subprogram or package body (whether repeated or not). Any with clause and any use clause given for a compilation unit also applies to its subunits (if any).

The designator of a separately compiled subprogram must be an identifier (not an operator symbol). However, a separately compiled function may be renamed as an operator.

A library unit that is a subprogram can be a *main* program in the usual sense. The means by which the execution of a main program is initiated are not prescribed within the language definition.

Example 1 : *A main program*:

The following is an example of a program consisting of a single compilation unit, a procedure printing the real roots of a quadratic equation. The predefined package TEXT_IO and the package REAL_OPERATIONS (containing the definition of the type REAL and of the packages REAL_IO and REAL_FUNCTIONS) are assumed to be already present in the program library. Such packages may be used by different main programs.

```
with TEXT_IO, REAL_OPERATIONS; use REAL_OPERATIONS;
procedure QUADRATIC_EQUATION is
   A, B, C, D : REAL;
   use  REAL_IO,            --  defines GET and PUT for REAL
        TEXT_IO,            --  defines PUT for strings and NEW_LINE
        REAL_FUNCTIONS;     --  defines SQRT
begin
   GET(A); GET(B); GET(C);
   D := B**2 - 4.0*A*C;
   if D < 0.0 then
      PUT("Imaginary Roots.");
   else
      PUT("Real Roots : X1 = ");
      PUT((-B - SQRT(D))/(2.0*A)); PUT(" X2 = ");
      PUT((-B + SQRT(D))/(2.0*A));
   end if;
   NEW_LINE;
end QUADRATIC_EQUATION;
```

Notes:

A compilation unit may be a generic package or a generic subprogram; alternatively, it may be an instantiation of a generic subprogram or package.

References:

elaboration 3.1, function 6.1, generic package 12.1, generic instantiation 12.3, generic subprogram 12.1, identifier 2.3, operator 4.5, operator symbol 6.1, package body 7.1, package declaration 7.1, real type 3.5.6, subprogram body 6.3, subprogram declaration 6.1, subunit 10.2, use clause 8.4

10.1.1 With Clauses

The names that appear in a with clause must be the names of library units. The effect of the elaboration of a with clause is to create an implicit declaration of the named library units at the end of the package STANDARD; the order of these implicit declarations does not necessarily correspond to the order in which the units are named in a with clause (see 10.3 and 10.5). If the name of a library unit occurs in more than one with clause of a given context specification, only the first occurrence is considered.

The names of library units mentioned in with clauses are directly visible (except where hidden) within the corresponding compilation unit. In particular, the names of these library units can be used as follows:

- If the name of a generic subprogram or package is mentioned in a with clause of a compilation unit, instances of this generic program unit can be declared within the compilation unit.

- If the name of a (non generic) subprogram is mentioned in a with clause of a compilation unit, this subprogram can be called within the compilation unit.

- If the name of a (non generic) package is mentioned in a with clause of a compilation unit, this name can be used to form the names of selected components and may appear in use clauses.

With clauses define dependences among compilation units; that is, a compilation unit that mentions other library units in its with clauses depends on those library units. These dependences between units have an influence on the order of compilation (and recompilation) of compilation units, as explained in section 10.3.

Notes:

The with clauses of a compilation unit need only mention the names of those library subprograms and packages whose visibility is actually necessary within the unit. They need not (and should not) mention other library units that are used in turn by some of the units named in the with clause unless these other library units are also used directly by the compilation unit prefixed by the with clauses. For example, the implementation of the package REAL_OPERATIONS may need the operations provided by other more basic packages. The latter should not appear in the with clause of QUADRATIC_EQUATION since these basic operations are not directly called within its body.

The name of a library unit C can be written as the selected component STANDARD.C (unless the name STANDARD is hidden) since library units are implicitly declared in the package STANDARD.

References:

declaration 3, directly visible 8.3, elaboration 3.1, generic package 12.1, generic subprogram 12.1, hidden 8.3, name 3.1 4.1, package 7, package standard, program unit 7, selected component 4.1.3, subprogram 6, use clause 8.4, visibility 8

10.1.2 Examples of Compilation Units.

A compilation unit can be split into a number of compilation units. For example consider the following program.

```
procedure PROCESSOR is
   package D is
      LIMIT  : constant := 1000;
      TABLE : array (1 .. LIMIT) of INTEGER;
      procedure RESTART;
   end D;

   package body D is
      procedure RESTART is
      begin
         for N in 1 .. LIMIT loop
            TABLE(N) := N;
         end loop;
      end;
   begin
      RESTART;
   end D;

   procedure Q(X : INTEGER) is
      use D;
   begin
      ...
      TABLE(X) := TABLE(X) + 1;
      ...
   end Q;

begin
   ...
   D.RESTART;  -- reinitializes TABLE
   ...
end PROCESSOR;
```

The following three compilation units define a program with an equivalent effect (the broken lines between compilation units serve to remind the reader that these units need not be contiguous texts).

Example 2 : *Several compilation units*:

```
package D is
   LIMIT  : constant := 1000;
   TABLE : array (1 .. LIMIT) of INTEGER;
   procedure RESTART;
end D;
```

```
--------------------------------------------------

package body D is
   procedure RESTART is
   begin
      for N in 1 .. LIMIT loop
         TABLE(N) := N;
      end loop;
   end;
begin
   RESTART;
end D;


--------------------------------------------------

with D;
procedure PROCESSOR is
   procedure Q(X : INTEGER) is
      use D;
   begin
      ...
      TABLE(X) := TABLE(X) + 1;
      ...
   end Q;
begin
   ...
   D.RESTART;   --   reinitializes TABLE
   ...
end PROCESSOR;
```

Note that in the latter version, the package D has no visibility of outer identifiers other than the predefined identifiers (of the package STANDARD). In particular, D does not depend on any identifier declared in PROCESSOR; otherwise D could not have been extracted from PROCESSOR in the above manner. The procedure PROCESSOR, on the other hand, depends on D and mentions this package in a with clause. This permits the inner occurrences of D in a use clause and in a selected component.

These three compilation units can be submitted in one or more compilations. For example, it is possible to submit the package specification and the package body together in a single compilation.

References:

identifier 2.3, package 7, package body 7.1, package specification 7.1, procedure 6, selected component 4.1.3, standard package C, use clause 8.4, visibility 8, with clause 10.1.1

10.2 Subunits of Compilation Units

The body of a subprogram, package, or task declared in the outermost declarative part of another compilation unit (either a library unit or a subunit) can be separately compiled and is then said to be a subunit of that compilation unit. Within the subprogram, package, or task where a subunit is declared, its body is represented by a body stub at the place where the body would otherwise appear. This method of splitting a program permits hierarchical program development.

```
subunit ::=
    separate (unit_name) body

body_stub ::=
        subprogram_specification  is separate;
    |   package body identifier   is separate;
    |   task body identifier       is separate;
```

Each subunit mentions the name of its *parent* unit, that is, the compilation unit where the corresponding stub is given. If the parent unit is itself a subunit, this name must be given in full as a selected component, starting with the ancestor library unit. The names of all subunits of a given library unit and the names of all subunits of these subunits, and so on, must all be distinct. A generic subprogram or package can be a subunit.

Visibility within a subunit is as at the corresponding body stub; hence the name of a library unit that is named in a with clause of a parent unit is also directly visible within a subunit (except if it is hidden). The context specification of the subunit may mention additional library units; these names are directly visible within the subunit (except where they are hidden). For the elaboration of a subunit, this visibility is first established, then the subunit body is elaborated.

Elaboration of a body stub has no other effect than to establish that the corresponding body is separately compiled as a subunit and to elaborate the body of the subunit.

Note:

The name of a library unit mentioned in the with clause of a subunit may be hidden if the same identifier is declared within the subunit, or even within one of its parents (since library units are implicitly declared in STANDARD). In such cases this does not affect the interpretation of the with clauses themselves, since only names of library units can appear in with clauses.

Two subunits of different library units in the same program library need not have distinct identifiers. Their full names are distinct, in any case, since the names of library units are distinct and since the names of all subunits of a given library unit are also distinct. By means of renaming declarations, overloaded subprogram names that rename (distinct) subunits can be introduced.

References:

compilation unit 10.1, declarative part 3.9, elaboration 3.1, generic package 12.1, generic subprogram 12.1, identifier 2.3, library unit 10.1, overloading a subprogram 6.6, package body 7.1, program library 10.1 10.4, renaming declaration 8.5, selected component 4.1.3, standard package C, subprogram body 6.3, task body 9.1, visibility 8, with clause 10.1.1

10.2.1 Examples of Subunits

The procedure TOP is first written as a compilation unit without subunits.

```
with INPUT_OUTPUT;
procedure TOP is
   type REAL is digits 10;
   R, S : REAL := 1.0;

   package D is
      PI : constant := 3.14159_26536;
      function    F (X : REAL) return REAL;
      procedure   G (Y, Z : REAL);
   end D;

   package body D is
      --   some local declarations followed by
      function F(X : REAL) return REAL is
      begin
         --   sequence of statements of F
      end F;

      procedure G(Y, Z : REAL) is
         --   use of INPUT_OUTPUT
      begin
         --   sequence of statements of G
      end G;
   end D;

   procedure Q(U : in out REAL) is
      use D;
   begin
      U := F(U);
      ...
   end Q;
begin -- TOP
   Q(R);
   ...
   D.G(R, S);
end TOP;
```

The body of the package D and that of the procedure Q can be made into separate subunits of TOP. Similarly the body of the procedure G can be made into a subunit of D as follows.

Example 3:

```
procedure TOP is
   type REAL is digits 10;
   R, S : REAL := 1.0;

   package D is
      PI : constant := 3.14159_26536;
      function   F (X : REAL) return REAL;
      procedure  G (Y, Z : REAL);
   end D;

   package body D is separate;                -- stub of D
   procedure Q(U : in out REAL) is separate;  -- stub of Q
begin  -- TOP
   Q(R);

   ...
   D.G(R, S);
end TOP;
```

```
separate (TOP)
procedure Q(U : in out REAL) is
   use D;
begin
   U := F(U);

   ...
end Q;
```

```
separate (TOP)
package body D is
   --  some local declarations followed by
   function F(X : REAL) return REAL is
   begin
      --  sequence of statements of F
   end F;

   procedure G(Y, Z : REAL) is separate;     -- stub of G
end D;
```

```
with INPUT_OUTPUT;
separate (TOP.D)                             -- full name of D
procedure G(Y, Z : REAL) is
   --  use of INPUT_OUTPUT
begin
   --  sequence of statements of G
end;
```

In the above example Q and D are subunits of TOP, and G is a subunit of D. The visibility in the split version is the same as in the initial version except for one change: since INPUT_OUTPUT is only used in G, the corresponding with clause appears for G instead of for TOP. Apart from this change, the same identifiers are visible at corresponding program points in the two versions. For example, the procedure TOP, the type REAL, the variables R and S, the package D and the contained constant PI and subprograms F and G are visible within the subunit body of G.

References:

constant 3.2, identifier 2.3, package 7, procedure 6, real type 3.5.6, subprogram 6, visibility 8, with clause 10.1.1

10.3 Order of Compilation

The rules defining the order in which units can be compiled are direct consequences of the visibility rules and, in particular, of the need for a given unit to see the identifiers listed in its with clauses. A unit must be compiled after all units whose names appear in one of its with clauses. A subprogram or package body must be compiled after the corresponding subprogram or package declaration. The subunits of a unit must be compiled after the unit.

The compilation units of a program can be compiled in any order that is consistent with the partial ordering defined by the above rules.

Similar rules apply for recompilations. Any change in a compilation unit may affect its subunits. In addition, any change in a library unit that is a subprogram declaration or package declaration may affect other compilation units that mention its name in their with clauses. The potentially affected units must be recompiled. An implementation may be able to reduce the compilation costs if it can deduce that some of the potentially affected units are not actually affected by the change.

The subunits of a unit can be recompiled without affecting the unit itself. Similarly, changes in a subprogram or package body do not affect other compilation units (apart from the subunits of the body) since these compilation units only have access to the subprogram or package specification. Deviations from this rule are only permitted for inline inclusions, for certain compiler optimizations, and for certain implementations of generic program units, as described below.

If a pragma INLINE is applied to the declaration of a subprogram declared in a package specification, inline inclusion will only be achieved if the package body is compiled before units calling the subprogram. In such a case, inline inclusion creates a dependence of the calling unit on the package body and the compiler must recognize this dependence when deciding on the need for recompilation. If a calling unit is compiled before the package body, the pragma may be ignored by the compiler for such calls (a warning that inline inclusion was not achieved may be issued). Similar considerations apply to a separately compiled subprogram for which an INLINE pragma is specified.

For optimization purposes, an implementation may compile several units of a given compilation in a way that creates further dependences among these compilation units. The compiler must then take these dependences into account when deciding on the need for recompilations. Finally an implementation may also introduce a dependence on the body of a separately compiled generic program unit.

Examples of Compilation Order:

(a) In example 2, the package body D must be compiled after the corresponding package specification.

(b) The specification of the package D must be compiled before the procedure PROCESSOR; on the other hand, the procedure PROCESSOR can be compiled either before or after the package body D.

(c) In example 1, the procedure QUADRATIC_EQUATION must be compiled after the library packages TEXT_IO and REAL_OPERATIONS since they appear in its with clause. Similarly, in example 3, the procedure G must be compiled after the package INPUT_OUTPUT, which appears in its with clause. On the other hand INPUT_OUTPUT can be compiled either before or after TOP.

(d) In example 3, the subunits Q and D must be compiled after the main program TOP. Similarly the subunit G must be compiled after its parent unit D.

References:

compilation unit 10.1, generic program unit 12, inline pragma B, library unit 10.1, name 4.1, package body 7.1, package declaration 7.1, package specification 7.1, pragma 2.8, procedure 6, subprogram body 6.3, subprogram declaration 6.1, subprogram specification 6.1, subunit 10.2, visibility rules 8, with clause 10.1.1

10.4 Program Library

Compilers must preserve the same degree of type safety, for a program consisting of several compilation units and subunits, as for a program submitted as a single compilation unit. Consequently a library file containing information on the compilation units of the program library must be maintained by the compiler. This information may include symbol tables and other information pertaining to the order of previous compilations.

A normal submission to the compiler consists of the compilation unit(s) and the library file. The latter is used for checks and is updated as a consequence of the current compilation.

There should be compiler commands for creating the program library of a given program or of a given family of programs. These commands may permit the reuse of units of other program libraries. Finally, there should be commands for interrogating the status of the units of a program library. The form of these commands is not specified by the language definition.

References:

compilation unit 10.1, library unit 10.1, subunit 10.2

10.5 Elaboration of Library Units

Before the execution of a main program, all library units used by the main program are elaborated. These library units are those which are mentioned in the with clauses of the main program and its subunits, and in the with clauses of these library units themselves, and so on, in a transitive manner.

The elaboration of these units is performed consistently with the partial ordering defined by the dependence relations imposed by with clauses (see 10.3).

The order of elaboration of library units that are package bodies must also be consistent with any dependence relations resulting from the actions performed during the elaboration of these bodies. Thus if a subprogram defined in a given package is called during the elaboration of the body of another package (that is, either during the elaboration of its declarative part or during the execution of its sequence of statements), the body of the given package must be elaborated first.

The program is illegal if no consistent order can be found (that is, if a circularity exists in the dependence relations). If there are several possible orders, the program is erroneous if it relies on a specific order (among the possible orders).

References:

compilation unit 10.1, declarative part 3.9, dependence relation 10.1.1, elaboration 3.1, library unit 10.1, main program 10.1, package 7, package body 7.1, statement 5, subprogram 6, subunit 10.2, with clause 10.1

10.6 Program Optimization

Optimization of the elaboration of declarations and the execution of statements may be performed by compilers. In particular, a compiler may be able to optimize a program by evaluating certain expressions, in addition to those that are static expressions. Should one of these expressions (whether static or not) be such that an exception would be raised by its evaluation, then the code in that path of the program can be replaced by code to raise the exception.

A compiler may find that some statements or subprograms will never be executed, for example, if their execution depends on a condition known to be false. The corresponding code can then be omitted. This rule permits the effect of *conditional compilation* within the language.

Note:

An expression whose evaluation is known to raise an exception need not represent an error if it occurs in a statement or subprogram that is never executed. The compiler may warn the programmer of a potential error.

References:

condition 5.3, declaration 3, elaboration 3.1, exception 11, expression 4.4, raise an exception 11.3, statement 5, static expression 4.9, subprogram 6

11. Exceptions

This chapter defines the facilities for dealing with errors or other exceptional situations that arise during program execution. An *exception* is an event that causes suspension of normal program execution. Drawing attention to the event is called *raising* the exception. Executing some actions, in response to the occurrence of an exception, is called *handling* the exception.

Exception names are introduced by exception declarations. Exceptions can be raised by raise statements, or they can be raised by subprograms, blocks, or language defined operations that *propagate* the exceptions. When an exception occurs, control can be passed to a user-provided exception handler at the end of a block or at the end of the body of a subprogram, package, or task.

References:

block 5.6, propagation of exception 11.4, raise statement 11.3, subprogram 6

11.1 Exception Declarations

An exception declaration defines one or more exceptions whose names can appear in raise statements and in exception handlers within the scope of the declaration.

    exception_declaration ::= identifier_list : **exception**;

The identity of the exception introduced by an exception declaration is established at compilation time (an exception can be viewed as a constant of some predefined enumeration type, the constant being initialized with a static expression). Hence the declaration of an exception introduces only one exception, even if the declaration occurs in a recursive subprogram.

The following exceptions are predefined in the language and are raised in the following situations:

CONSTRAINT_ERROR When a range constraint, an index constraint, or a discriminant constraint is violated. This can occur in object, type, subtype, component, subprogram, and renaming declarations; in initializations; in assignment and return statements; in component associations of aggregates; in qualified expressions, type conversions, subprogram and entry calls, and generic instantiations. This exception is also raised when an attempt is made to designate a component that cannot exist under the applicable constraint, in an indexed component, a selected component, a slice, or an aggregate. Finally, this exception is raised on an attempt to select from or index an object designated by an access value, if the access value is equal to **null**.

NUMERIC_ERROR   When the result of a predefined numeric operation does not lie within the implemented range of the numeric type; division by zero is one such situation. This exception need not be raised by an implementation.

SELECT_ERROR   When all alternatives of a select statement that has no else part are closed.

STORAGE_ERROR   When the dynamic storage allocated to a task is exceeded, or during the execution of an allocator, if the available space for the collection of allocated objects is exhausted.

TASKING_ERROR   When exceptions arise during intertask communication.

Examples of user-defined exception declarations:

```
SINGULAR  : exception;
ERROR     : exception;
OVERFLOW, UNDERFLOW : exception;
```

References:

access value 3.8, aggregate 4.3, allocator 4.8, assignment statement 5.2, component declaration 3.7, constraint 3.3, constraint_error exception 3.3 3.5.4 3.5.5 3.5.6 3.6.1 3.7 3.7.2 4.1.1 4.1.2 4.1.3 4.3 4.5.1 4.5.6 4.6 4.7 5.2 5.2.1 5.8 6.1 6.4.1 8.5 9.5 12.3.1 12.3.2 12.3.4 12.3.5 12.3.6 14.3.5, declaration 3.1, discriminant constraint 3.7.2, entry call 9.5, enumeration type 3.5.3, generic instantiation 12.3, index constraint 3.6.1, indexed component 4.1.1, initialization 3.2 3.7 6.1, name 4.1, numeric_error exception 3.5.8 4.5.3 4.5.4 4.5.5 4.5.6 4.5.7 4.5.8, numeric operation 4.5, numeric type 3.5, object declaration 3.2, qualified expression 4.7, raise statement 11.3, range constraint 3.5, recursive procedure 6.1, renaming declaration 8.5, return statement 5.8, scope of a declaration 8.2, select_error exception 9.7.1, select statement 9.7, selected component 4.1.3, slice 4.1.2, static expression 4.9, storage_error exception 3.9 4.8 13.2, subprogram call 6.4, subprogram declaration 6.1, subtype declaration 3.3, tasking_error exception 9.3 9.5 9.10 11.4, task 9.1, type conversion 4.6, type declaration 3.3

11.2 Exception Handlers

The response to one or more exceptions is specified by an exception handler. A handler may appear at the end of a unit, which must be a block or the body of a subprogram, package, or task. The word *unit* will have this meaning in this section.

```
exception_handler ::=
    when exception_choice {| exception_choice} =>
        sequence_of_statements

exception_choice ::= exception_name | others
```

An exception handler of a unit handles the named exceptions when they are raised within the sequence of statements of this unit; an exception name may only occur once in the exception choices of the unit. A handler containing the choice others can only appear last and can only contain this exception choice; it handles all exceptions not listed in previous handlers, including exceptions whose names are not visible within the unit.

When an exception is raised during the execution of the sequence of statements of a unit, the execution of the corresponding handler (if any) replaces the execution of the remainder of the unit: the actions following the point where the exception is raised are skipped and the execution of the handler terminates the execution of the unit. If no handler is provided for the exception (either explicitly or by others), the execution of the unit is abandoned and the exception is propagated according to the rules stated in 11.4.1.

Since a handler acts as a substitute for (the remainder of) the corresponding unit, the handler has the same capabilities as the unit it replaces. For example, a handler within a function body has access to the parameters of the function and may execute a return statement on its behalf.

Example:

```
begin
   --   sequence of statements
exception
   when SINGULAR | NUMERIC_ERROR =>
      PUT(" MATRIX IS SINGULAR ");
   when others =>
      PUT(" FATAL ERROR ");
      raise ERROR;
end;
```

References:

block 5.6, function 6.1, package body 7.1, parameter declaration 6.1, program unit 7, return statement 5.8, statement 5.1, subprogram body 6.3, task body 9.1, visible 8.1

11.3 Raise Statements

An exception can be raised explicitly by a raise statement.

      raise_statement ::= **raise** [*exception*_name];

For the execution of a raise statement with an exception name, the identity of the exception is established, and then the exception is raised. A raise statement without an exception name can only appear in an exception handler (but not in a nested subprogram, package or task). It raises again the exception that caused transfer to the handler.

Examples:

```
raise SINGULAR;
raise NUMERIC_ERROR;   --   explicitly raising a predefined exception
raise;
raise POOL(K)'FAILURE;   --   see section 11.5
```

References:

name 4.1

11.4 Dynamic Association of Handlers with Exceptions

When an exception is raised, normal program execution is suspended and control is transferred to an exception handler. The selection of this handler depends on whether the exception is raised during the execution of statements or during the elaboration of declarations.

11.4.1 Exceptions Raised During the Execution of Statements

The handling of an exception raised during the execution of a sequence of statements depends on the innermost block or body that encloses the statement.

(a) If an exception is raised in the sequence of statements of a subprogram body that does not contain a handler for the exception, execution of the subprogram is abandoned and the same exception is raised again at the point of call of the subprogram. In such a case the exception is said to be *propagated*. The predefined exceptions are exceptions that can be propagated by the language defined constructs. If the subprogram is itself the main program, the execution of the main program is abandoned.

(b) If an exception is raised in the sequence of statements of a block that does not contain a handler for the exception, execution of the block is abandoned and the same exception is raised again in the unit whose sequence of statements includes the block. In such a case, also, the exception is said to be *propagated*.

(c) If an exception is raised in the sequence of statements of a package body that does not contain a handler for the exception, the elaboration of the package body is abandoned. If the package appears in a declarative part (or is a subunit) the exception is raised again in the unit enclosing the package body (or enclosing the body stub that corresponds to the subunit). If the package is a library unit, the execution of the main program is abandoned.

(d) If an exception is raised in the sequence of statements of a task body that does not contain a handler for the exception, the execution of the task is abandoned; the task is terminated. The exception is not further propagated.

(e) If a local handler has been provided, execution of the handler replaces the execution of the remainder of the unit (see 11.2).

(f) A further exception raised in the sequence of statements of a handler (but not in a nested block) causes execution of the current unit to be abandoned; this further exception is propagated if the current unit is a subprogram body, a block, or a package body as in cases (a), (b), and (c).

Example:

```
procedure P is
   ERROR : exception;
   procedure R;

   procedure Q is
   begin
     R;
     ...                     --  exception situation (2)
   exception
     ...
     when ERROR =>    --  handler E2
     ...
   end Q;

   procedure R is
   begin
     ...              --  exception situation (3)
   end R;

begin
   ...                --  exception situation (1)
   Q;
   ...
exception
   ...
   when ERROR =>      --  handler E1
   ...
end P;
```

The following situations can arise:

(1) If the exception ERROR is raised in the sequence of statements of the outer procedure P, the handler E1 provided within P is used to complete the execution of P.

(2) If the exception ERROR is raised in the sequence of statements of Q, the handler E2 provided within Q is used to complete the execution of Q. Control will be returned to the point of call of Q upon completion of the handler.

(3) If the exception ERROR is raised in the body of R, called by Q, the execution of R is abandoned and the same exception is raised in the body of Q. The handler E2 is then used to complete the execution of Q, as in situation (2).

Note that in the third situation, the exception raised in R results in (indirectly) passing control to a handler that is local to Q and hence not enclosed by R. Note also that if a handler were provided within R for the choice **others**, situation (3) would cause execution of this alternative, rather than direct termination of R.

Lastly, if ERROR had been declared in R, rather than in P, the handlers E1 and E2 could not provide an explicit handler for ERROR since this identifier would not be visible within the bodies of P and Q. In situation (3), the exception could however be handled in Q by providing a handler for the choice **others**.

Example:

```
function FACTORIAL (N : NATURAL) return FLOAT is
begin
  if N = 1 then
    return 1.0;
  else
    return FLOAT(N) * FACTORIAL(N-1);
  end if;
exception
  when NUMERIC_ERROR => return FLOAT'LARGE;
end FACTORIAL;
```

If the multiplication raises NUMERIC_ERROR then FLOAT'LARGE is returned by the handler. This value will cause further NUMERIC_ERROR exceptions to be raised in the remaining activations of the function, so that for large values of N the function will ultimately return the value FLOAT'LARGE.

References:

block 5.6, body 6.3 7.1, body stub 10.2, declarative part 3.9, elaboration 3.1, identifier 2.3, library unit 10.1 10.1.1, local 8.3, main program 10.1, multiplication operation 4.5.5, overflow 4.5.8, package body 7.1, procedure 6, statement 5.1, subprogram body 6.3, subprogram call 6.4, subunit 10.2, task body 9.1, visible 8.1

11.4.2 Exceptions Raised During the Elaboration of Declarations

If an exception occurs during the elaboration of the declarative part of a block or body, or during the elaboration of a subprogram, package, or task declaration, this elaboration is abandoned. The exception is propagated to the unit causing the elaboration, if there is one:

(a) An exception raised in the declarative part of a subprogram is propagated to the unit calling the subprogram, unless the subprogram is the main program itself, in which case execution of the program is abandoned.

(b) An exception raised in the declarative part of a block is propagated to the unit whose statements include the block.

(c) An exception raised in the declarative part of a package body is propagated to the unit enclosing the body (or body stub, for a subunit) unless the package is a library unit, in which case execution of the program is abandoned.

(d) An exception raised in the declarative part of a task body is propagated to the unit that caused the task activation.

(e) An exception raised during the elaboration of a subprogram, package, or task declaration is propagated to the unit enclosing this declaration, unless the subprogram or package declaration is the declaration of a library unit, in which case execution of the program is abandoned.

Example:

```
declare
   ...
begin
   declare
      N : INTEGER := F();     --  F may raise ERROR
   begin
      ...
   exception
      when ERROR =>           --  handler E1
   end;
   ...
exception
   when ERROR =>              --  handler E2
end;
```

-- if the exception ERROR is raised in the declaration of N, it is handled by E2

References:

body 6.3 7.1, body stub 10.2, declaration 3.1, declarative part of block 5.6, elaboration of declaration 3.1 3.9, library unit 10.1.1, main program 10.1, package body 7.1, package declaration 7.1, program unit 7, statement 5, subprogram declaration 6.1, subunit 10.2, task activation 9.3, task declaration 9.1

11.5 Exceptions Raised During Task Communication

An exception can be propagated to a task communicating, or attempting to communicate, with another task.

When a task calls an entry of another task, the exception TASKING_ERROR is raised in the calling task, at the place of the call, if the called task terminates before accepting the entry call or is already terminated at the time of the call.

A rendezvous can be terminated abnormally in two cases:

(a) When an exception is raised inside an accept statement and not handled locally. In this case, the exception is propagated both to the unit containing the accept statement, and to the calling task at the point of the entry call.

A different treatment is used for the special exception attribute FAILURE as explained in section 11.6 below.

(b) When the task containing the accept statement is terminated abnormally (for example, as the result of an abort statement). In this case, the exception TASKING_ERROR is raised in the calling task at the point of the entry call.

On the other hand, abnormal termination of a task issuing an entry call does not raise an exception in the called task. If the rendezvous has not yet started, the entry call is cancelled. If the rendezvous is in progress, it is allowed to complete, and the called task is unaffected.

References:

accept statement 9.5, entry 9.5, entry call 9.5, rendezvous 9.5, task 9.1, task termination 9.3 9.4

11.6   Raising the Exception Failure in Another Task

Each task has an attribute named FAILURE which is an exception. Any task can raise the FAILURE exception of another task (say T) by the statement

   raise T'FAILURE;

The execution of this statement has no direct effect on the task issuing the statement (unless, of course, it raises FAILURE for itself). This exception is the only exception that can be raised explicitly by one task in another task.

For the task receiving the FAILURE exception, this exception is raised at the current point of execution, whether the task is actually executing or suspended. If the task is suspended on a delay statement, the corresponding wait is cancelled. If the task has issued an entry call (or a timed entry call) the call is cancelled if the rendezvous has not yet started; alternatively the rendezvous is allowed to complete if it has already started; in both cases the called task is unaffected. If the task is suspended by an accept or select statement, execution of the task is scheduled (according to the usual priority rules, see 9.8) in order to allow the exception to be handled. Finally, if the exception FAILURE is received within an accept statement and not handled locally, the rendezvous is terminated and the exception TASKING_ERROR is raised in the calling task at the place of the entry call.

Within the body of a task or task type T (and only there) there may be handlers for the exception name T'FAILURE.

Note:

The name FAILURE is not reserved. Hence it could be declared as any entity, including an exception, No conflict can arise with the attribute FAILURE because of the distinct notation for attributes.

References:

accept statement 9.5, attribute 4.1.4, delay statement 9.6, entry call 9.5, rendezvous 9.5, select statement 9.7, statement 5, suspended task 9.5 9.6 9.7, task 9.1, task scheduling 9.8, wait 9.7.1

11.7   Suppressing Checks

The detection of the conditions under which some predefined exceptions are raised (as a preliminary to raising them) may be suppressed within a block or within the body of a subprogram, package, or task. This suppression may be achieved by the insertion of a SUPPRESS pragma in the declarative part of such a unit. The form of this pragma is as follows:

   pragma SUPPRESS (*check*_name [, [ON =>] name]);

The first name designates the check to be suppressed; the second name is optional and may be either an object name or a type name. In the absence of the optional name, the pragma applies to all operations within the unit considered. Otherwise its effect is restricted to operations on the named object or to operations on objects of the named type.

The following checks correspond to situations in which the exception CONSTRAINT_ERROR may be raised:

ACCESS_CHECK — Check that an access value is not **null** when attempting to select from or index the object designated by the access value.

DISCRIMINANT_CHECK — When accessing a record component, check that it exists for the current discriminant value. Check that a value specified for a discriminant satisfies or is compatible with a discriminant constraint.

INDEX_CHECK — Check that a specified index value or range of index values satisfies an index constraint or is compatible with an index type.

LENGTH_CHECK — Check that the number of components for an index is equal to a required number.

RANGE_CHECK — Check that a value satisfies a range constraint or that an index constraint, discriminant constraint, or range constraint is compatible with a type mark.

The following checks correspond to situations under which the exception NUMERIC_ERROR is raised:

DIVISION_CHECK — Check that the second operand is not zero for the operations /, **rem** and **mod**.

OVERFLOW_CHECK — Check that the result of a numeric operation does not overflow.

The following check corresponds to situations under which the exception STORAGE_ERROR is raised:

STORAGE_CHECK — Check that execution of an allocator does not require more space than is available for a collection. Check that the space available for a task or program unit has not been exceeded.

The SUPPRESS pragma indicates that the corresponding run time check need not be provided. The occurrence of such a pragma within a given unit does not guarantee that the corresponding exceptions will not arise, since the pragma is merely a recommendation to the compiler, and since the exceptions may be propagated by called units. Should an exception situation occur when the corresponding run time checks are suppressed, the program would be erroneous (the results would be unpredictable).

Examples:

```
pragma SUPPRESS(RANGE_CHECK);
pragma SUPPRESS(INDEX_CHECK, ON => TABLE);
```

Note:

For certain implementations, it may be impossible, or too costly to suppress certain checks. The corresponding SUPPRESS pragmas can be ignored.

References:

access value 3.8, array component 3.6, assignment statement 5.2, block 5.6, declarative part 3.9, division operation 4.5.5, index range 3.6, mod operator 4.5,5, name 4.1, object name 3.2, overflow 3.5.8 4.5.8, package body 7.1, pragma 2.8, record component 3.7, record discriminant 3.7.1, rem operator 4.5.6, subprogram body 6.3, task body 9.1, type declaration 3, type name 3.3

11.8 Exceptions and Optimization

The purpose of this section is to specify the conditions under which certain operations can be invoked either earlier or later than indicated by the exact place in which their invocation occurs in the program text. The operations concerned comprise any function (including operators) whose value depends only on the values of its arguments (the actual parameters) but which raises an exception for certain argument values (this exception depending only on the value of the arguments). Other operations also included are the basic operations involved in array indexing, slicing, and component selection, including the case of objects designated by access values.

If it were not for the fact that these operations may propagate exceptions, they could be invoked as soon as the values of their arguments were known, since the value returned depends only on the argument values. However the possible occurrence of exceptions imposes stricter limits upon the allowable displacements of the points where such operations are invoked as explained below:

- Consider the statements and expressions contained in the sequence of statements of a block, body, or accept statement (but excluding any nested inner block, body, or accept statement). For a given operation, choose a subset of these statements and expressions such that if any statement (or expression) in the subset is executed (or evaluated), one or more invocations of the given operation is required (according to rules stated elsewhere than in this section). Then, within the chosen subset the operation can be invoked as soon as the values of its arguments are known, even if this invocation may cause an exception to be propagated. The operation need not be invoked at all if its value is not needed, even if the invocation would raise an exception. If the operation may raise an exception and if the value is needed, the invocation must occur no later than the end of the sequence of statements of the enclosing, block, body or accept statement.

- The rules given in section 4.5 for operators and expression evaluation leave the order of evaluation of the arguments of such operations undefined except for short circuit control forms. Also, in the case of a sequence of operators of the same precedence level (and in the absence of parentheses imposing a specific order), these rules allow any order of evaluation that yields the same result as the textual (left to right) order. Any reordering of evaluation allowed by these rules is permitted even if some of the operations may propagate exceptions, as long as no further exception can be introduced.

Notes:

The above rules guarantee that an operation is not moved across a return, an exit, a goto, a raise, or an abort statement. Moreover, an optimization cannot move an operation in such a way that an exception would be handled by a different handler.

Whenever the evaluation of an expression may raise an exception for an allowed order of evaluation, it is the programmer's responsibility to impose a specific order by explicit parentheses. In their absence, a compiler is allowed to choose any order satisfying the above rules, even if this order removes the risk of an exception being raised. In addition, the code produced by different compilers may raise different exceptions for a given expression since the order of evaluation of arguments is not defined.

References:

accept statement 9.5, access value 3.8, actual parameter 6.4, array indexing 4.1.1, block 5.6, body 6.3 7.1, expression 4.4, expression evaluation 4.5, function 6.1, operator 4.5, propagation of exception 11.4.1, selected component 4.1.3, slice 4.1.2, statement 5

12. Generic Program Units

Subprograms and packages can be generic. Generic program units are *templates* of program units and are often parameterized. Being templates, they cannot be used directly as ordinary subprograms or packages; for example a generic subprogram cannot be called. *Instances* (that is, copies) of the template are obtained by generic instantiation. The resulting subprograms and packages are ordinary program units, which can be used directly.

A generic subprogram or package is defined by a generic declaration. This form of declaration has a generic part, which may include the definition of generic formal parameters. An instance of a generic unit, with appropriate actual parameters for the generic formal parameters, is obtained as the result of a generic subprogram instantiation or a generic package instantiation.

References:

declaration 3.1, generic actual parameter 12.3, generic declaration 12.1, generic formal parameter 12.1, generic part 12.1, package 7, program unit 6 7 9, subprogram 6

12.1 Generic Declarations

A generic declaration includes a generic part and declares a generic subprogram or a generic package. The generic part may include the definition of generic parameters.

For the elaboration of a generic declaration the subprogram designator or package identifier is first introduced and can from then on be used as the name of the corresponding generic program unit. The generic part is next elaborated. Finally, the subprogram or package specification is established as the template for the specification of the corresponding generic program unit.

```
generic_subprogram_declaration ::=
    generic_part   subprogram_specification;

generic_package_declaration ::=
    generic_part   package_specification;

generic_part ::= generic {generic_formal_parameter}

generic_formal_parameter ::=
      parameter_declaration;
    | type identifier [discriminant_part] is generic_type_definition;
    | with subprogram_specification [is name];
    | with subprogram_specification is <>;

generic_type_definition ::=
      (<>) | range <> | delta <> | digits <>
    | array_type_definition | access_type_definition
    | private_type_definition
```

12 - 1

For the elaboration of a generic part, the generic formal parameters (if any) are elaborated one by one in the given order. A generic parameter may only be referred to by another generic parameter of the same generic part if it (the former parameter) is a type and appears first.

Expressions appearing in a generic part are evaluated during the elaboration of the generic part, excepting any primary referring to a type that is a generic parameter (for example, an attribute of such a type); such primaries are evaluated during the elaboration of generic instantiations.

References to generic parameters of any form (not only types) may occur in the specification and body of a generic subprogram or package. However neither a choice, nor an integer type definition, nor an accuracy constraint, may depend on a generic formal parameter.

Examples of generic parts:

```
generic        --  parameterless

generic
   SIZE : NATURAL;

generic
   LENGTH : INTEGER := 200;  --  default value

generic
   type ENUM is (<>);
   with function IMAGE (E : ENUM)  return STRING  is ENUM'IMAGE;
   with function VALUE (S : STRING) return ENUM    is ENUM'VALUE;
```

Examples of generic subprogram declarations:

```
generic
   type ELEM is private;
procedure EXCHANGE(U, V : in out ELEM);

generic
   type ITEM is private;
   with function "*"(U, V : ITEM) return ITEM is <>;
function SQUARING(X : ITEM) return ITEM;
```

Example of generic package declaration:

```
generic
   type ITEM       is private;
   type VECTOR  is array (INTEGER range <>) of ITEM;
   with function SUM(X, Y : ITEM) return ITEM;
package ON_VECTORS is
   function SUM    (A, B  : VECTOR) return VECTOR;
   function SIGMA (A       : VECTOR) return ITEM;
end;
```

Note:

A subprogram or package specification given in a generic declaration is the template for the specifications of the corresponding subprograms or packages obtained by generic instantiation. Hence the template specification is not elaborated during elaboration of the generic declaration (this specification is merely *established* as being the template specification). The subprogram or package specification obtained by instantiation of the generic program unit is elaborated as part of this instantiation.

When a template is established all names occurring within it must be identified in the context of the generic declaration.

References:

accuracy constraint 3.5.6, attribute 4.1.4, designator 6.1, elaboration 3.1, expression 4.4, identifier 2.3, integer type definition 3.5.4, name 4.1, object 3.2, package 7, package identifier 7.1, package specification 7.1, primary 4.4, program unit 7, subprogram 6.1, subprogram specification 6.1, type 3.3

12.1.1 Parameter Declarations in Generic Parts

The usual forms of parameter declarations available for subprogram specifications can also appear in generic parts. Only the modes **in** and **in out** are allowed (the mode **out** is not allowed for generic parameters). If no mode is explicitly given, the mode **in** is assumed.

A generic parameter of mode **in** acts as a constant; its value is a copy of the value provided by the corresponding generic actual parameter in a generic instantiation.

A generic parameter of mode **in out** acts as an object name renaming the corresponding generic actual parameter supplied in a generic instantiation. This actual parameter must be a variable of a type for which assignment is available (in particular, it cannot be a limited private type). The actual parameter cannot be a component of an unconstrained object with discriminants, if the existence of the component depends on the value of a discriminant.

References:

assignment 5.2, constant 3.2, generic actual parameter 12.3, in mode 6.1, in out mode 6.1, object name 3.2, out mode 6.1, parameter declaration 6.1, subprogram specification 6, type 3.3

12.1.2 Generic Type Definitions

The elaboration of a generic formal parameter containing a generic type definition proceeds according to the same rules as that of a type declaration (see 3.3). Generic type definitions may be array, access, or private type definitions, or one of the forms including a *box* (that is, the compound symbol <>).

Within the specification and body of a generic program unit, the operations available on values of a generic formal type are those associated with the corresponding generic type definition, together with any given by generic formal subprograms.

For an array type definition, the usual operations on arrays (such as indexing, slicing, assignment, equality, and so on), and the notation for aggregates, are available. For an access type definition, the usual operations on access types are available; for example allocators can be used.

For a limited private type no operation is available; for a private type, assignment, equality and inequality are available. Additional operations can be supplied as generic formal subprograms. The only form of constraint applicable to a generic formal type that is a (limited) private type is a discriminant constraint in the case where the generic formal parameter includes a discriminant part.

The generic type definitions including a box correspond to the major forms of scalar types:

Syntactic Form	Meaning
(<>)	any discrete type
range <>	any integer type
digits <>	any floating point type
delta <>	any fixed point type

For each generic formal type declared with one of these forms, the predefined operators and the function ABS of the corresponding scalar type are available (see 4.5). The attributes defined for the corresponding scalar types (see 3.5) are also available, excepting the attributes IMAGE and VALUE (see appendix A).

Examples of generic formal types:

```
type ITEM is private;
type BUFFER(LENGTH : NATURAL) is limited private;

type ENUM    is (<>);
type INT     is range <>;
type ANGLE   is delta <>;
type MASS    is digits <>;

type TABLE is array (ENUM) of ITEM;
```

Notes:

Since the attributes IMAGE and VALUE are not already available for the generic type definitions including a box, extra generic formal subprograms must be supplied for these attributes where they are needed.

References:

abs function 4.5.7, access type definition 3.8, aggregate notation 4.3, allocator 4.8, array type definition 3.6, array operations 4.5, assignment 5.2, attribute 4.1.4, constraint 3.3, discriminant constraint 3.7.2, discriminant part 3.7.1, elaboration 3.1, equality 4.5.2, formal parameter 6.4, image attribute A, incomplete access type predeclaration 3.8, indexing 3.6.1, inequality 4.5.2, limited private type 7.4.2, predefined operators C, private type definition 7.4, scalar type 3.5, slicing 4.1.2, subprogram 6.1, type declaration 3.3, value attribute A

12.1.3 Generic Formal Subprograms

A generic formal parameter that includes a subprogram specification defines a generic formal subprogram. Such subprograms may have (non generic) parameters and results of any visible type, including types that are previously declared generic formal types.

If the subprogram specification is followed by the reserved word **is** and by either a name or a box, an actual parameter is optional for this generic formal subprogram. If a name is used, the named subprogram is used by default in any generic instantiation that does not contain an explicit actual parameter for this generic formal subprogram. If a box is used, a default actual subprogram that matches the specification of the generic formal subprogram may be selected at the point of generic instantiation (see 12.3.6).

For the elaboration of a generic formal parameter that includes a subprogram specification, the subprogram specification is first elaborated; this elaboration introduces the names of any parameters and identifies the corresponding types (which may be generic types). The identity of any name that follows the reserved word **is** is then established (it may be an attribute of a generic type). This subprogram name must match the subprogram specification according to the rules given in section 12.3.6.

Examples of generic formal subprograms:

```
with function INCREASE(X : INTEGER) return INTEGER;
with function SUM(X, Y : ITEM) return ITEM;

with function "+"(X, Y : ITEM) return ITEM is <>;
with function IMAGE(X : ENUM) return STRING is ENUM'IMAGE;

with procedure UPDATE is DEFAULT_UPDATE;
```

References:

generic actual parameter 12.3, name 4.1, parameter 6.1, subprogram declaration 6.1, subprogram specification 6.1, type 3.3, visible 8.1

12.2 Generic Bodies

The body of a generic subprogram or package is a template for the bodies of the corresponding program units obtained by generic instantiation. The only effect of the elaboration of a generic body is to establish this body as the template to be used for the corresponding instantiations.

Examples of generic subprogram bodies:

```
procedure EXCHANGE(U, V : in out ELEM) is
   T : ELEM;   --   the generic formal type
begin
   T := U; U := V; V := T;
end EXCHANGE;

function SQUARING(X : ITEM) return ITEM is
begin
   return X*X;   --   the formal operator "*"
end;
```

Example of a generic package body:

```
package body ON_VECTORS is
  function SUM(A, B : VECTOR) return VECTOR is
    RESULT : VECTOR(A'RANGE);          --  the formal type VECTOR
  begin
    for N in A'RANGE loop
      RESULT(N) := SUM(A(N), B(N));    --  the formal function SUM
    end loop;
    return RESULT;
  end;

  function SIGMA(A : VECTOR) return ITEM is
    TOTAL : ITEM := A(A'FIRST);        --  the formal type ITEM
  begin
    for N in A'FIRST + 1 .. A'LAST loop
      TOTAL := SUM(TOTAL, A(N));       --  the formal function SUM
    end loop;
    return TOTAL;
  end;
end;
```

References:

elaboration 3.1 3.9, package 7, program unit 7, subprogram 6

12.3 Generic Instantiation

An instance of a generic program unit is obtained as the result of the elaboration of a generic sub-program instantiation or package instantiation.

```
generic_subprogram_instantiation ::=
      procedure identifier is generic_instantiation;
    | function designator is generic_instantiation;

generic_package_instantiation ::=
    package identifier is generic_instantiation;

generic_instantiation ::=
    new name [(generic_association {, generic_association })]

generic_association ::=
    [ formal_parameter =>] generic_actual_parameter

generic_actual_parameter ::=
    expression | subprogram_name | subtype_indication
```

A generic actual parameter must be supplied for each generic formal parameter unless the cor-responding generic part allows a default to be used. Generic associations can be given in positional form or in named form as for subprogram calls (see 6.4). Each generic actual parameter must *match* the corresponding generic formal parameter. An object matches an object; a subprogram or an entry matches a subprogram; a type matches a type. The detailed matching rules are given in subsections below.

For the elaboration of a generic subprogram instantiation or package instantiation, the designator of the procedure or function, or the identifier of the package is first introduced, and the generic instantiation is then elaborated. The designator or identifier can be used as the name of the instantiated unit from then on.

The elaboration of a generic instantiation first creates an instance of the template defined by the generic program unit, by replacing every occurrence of a generic formal parameter in both the specification and body of the unit by the corresponding generic actual parameter. This instance is a subprogram or package whose specification and body are then elaborated in this order according to the usual elaboration rules applicable to such entities (see 6.1 and 6.3 for subprograms, 7.2 and 7.3 for packages). Note however, that any identifier other than a generic parameter and which occurs within the generic declaration or body names an entity which is visible at the point where it occurs with the generic declaration or body (not at the point of instantiation).

Examples of generic instantiations:

```
procedure   SWAP  is new  EXCHANGE(ELEM =>  INTEGER);
procedure   SWAP  is new  EXCHANGE(CHARACTER);   --   SWAP is overloaded

function SQUARE  is new  SQUARING (INTEGER);   --   "*" of INTEGER used by default
function SQUARE  is new  SQUARING (MATRIX,  MATRIX_PRODUCT);

package INT_VECTORS is new  ON_VECTORS(INTEGER, TABLE, "+");
```

Examples of uses of instantiated units:

```
SWAP(A, B);
A  :=  SQUARE(A);

T   : TABLE(1 .. 5) := (10, 20, 30, 40, 50);
N   : INTEGER := INT_VECTORS.SIGMA(T);   --   150

use INT_VECTORS;
```

References:

elaboration 3.1 3.9, entry 9.5, function 6, generic actual parameter 12.3, generic formal parameter 12.1, identifier 2.3, name 4.1, named parameter association 6.4, object 3.2, package 7, package body 7.1, package specification 7.1, parameter 6.1, positional parameter association 6.4, subprogram 6, subprogram body 6.1, subprogram call 6.4, subprogram specification 6.1, type 3.3

12.3.1 Matching Rules for Formal Objects

An expression of a given type matches a generic formal parameter of the same type; it must satisfy any constraint imposed on the generic formal parameter otherwise the exception CONSTRAINT_ERROR is raised by the generic instantiation.

An expression used as a generic actual parameter of mode **in out** must be a variable name (an expression that is a type conversion is not allowed as a generic actual parameter if the mode is **in out**).

References:

constraint 3.3, constraint_error exception 11.1, expression 4.4, in out mode 6.1, type 3.3, type conversion 4.6, variable name 4

12.3.2 Matching Rules for Formal Private Types

A generic formal private type is matched by any type other than an unconstrained array type, in the following conditions:

- If the formal type is limited, the actual type can be any type (including a task type); if the formal type is not limited, assignment and the comparison for equality or inequality must be available for the actual type.

- If the formal type has a discriminant part, the actual type must have the same discriminants: the discriminant names, subtypes, and any default values must be the same and in the same order. The exception CONSTRAINT_ERROR is raised at the place of the generic instantiation if the constraint or default values differ.

References:

assignment 5.2, constraint 3.3, constraint_error exception 11.1, discriminant part 3.7.1, equality 4.5.2, inequality 4.5.2, limited generic formal type 12.1.2, subtype 3.3, task type 9.1, type 3.3, unconstrained array type 3.6

12.3.3 Matching Rules for Formal Scalar Types

A generic formal type defined by (<>) is matched by any discrete type (that is, any enumeration or integer type). A generic formal type defined by **range** <> is matched by any integer type. A generic formal type defined by **digits** <> is matched by any floating point type. A generic formal type defined by **delta** <> is matched by any fixed point type. No other matches are possible for these generic formal types.

References:

delta 3.5.9, digits 3.5.7, discrete type 3.5 3.5.5, enumeration type 3.5.1, fixed point type 3.5.9, floating point type 3.5.7, integer type 3.5.4

12.3.4 Matching Rules for Formal Array Types

A formal array type is matched by an actual array type with the same number of indices.

If any of the index and component types of the formal array type is itself a formal type, its name is replaced by the name of the corresponding actual type. All such substitutions having been achieved, a formal array type is matched by an actual array type if the following conditions are satisfied:

- The component type and constraint must be the same for the formal array type as for the actual array type.

- For each index position, the index subtype must be the same for the formal array type as for the actual array type.

- Either both array types must be unconstrained or, for each index position, the index constraint must be the same for the formal array type as for the actual array type.

The exception CONSTRAINT_ERROR is raised during the elaboration of a generic instantiation if the constraints on the component type are not the same, or if the index subtype, or the index constraint for any given index position are not the same for the formal array type as for the actual array type.

Example:

```
    --   given the generic package

    generic
       type ELEM     is private;
       type INDEX    is (<>);
       type VECTOR   is array (INDEX range <>) of ELEM;
       type TABLE    is array (INDEX) of ELEM;
    package P is
       ...
    end;

    --   and the types

    type MIX     is array (COLOR range <>) of BOOLEAN;
    type OPTION  is array (COLOR) of BOOLEAN;

    --   then MIX  can match VECTOR and OPTION can match TABLE
    --   but not the other way round:

    package Q is new P(ELEM => BOOLEAN, INDEX => COLOR,
                       VECTOR => MIX, TABLE => OPTION);
```

References:

array 3.6, array index 3.6, component type 3.6, constraint 3.3, constraint_error exception 11.1, unconstrained array type 3.6

12.3.5 Matching Rules for Formal Access Types

If the type of the objects designated by values of the formal access type is itself a formal type, its name is replaced by the name of the corresponding actual type. Any such substitution having been achieved, a formal access type is matched by an actual access type if the type of the designated objects is the same in both the formal and the actual access types.

If a constraint is specified in the generic type definition for the type of the objects designated by the access type, the same constraint must exist for the actual access type, otherwise the exception CONSTRAINT_ERROR is raised at the place of the generic instantiation.

Example:

```
    --   the formal types

    generic
       type NODE  is private;
       type LINK   is access NODE;
    package P is
       ...
    end;

    --   can be matched by the actual types

    type CAR;
    type CAR_NAME is access CAR;

    type CAR is
       record
          PRED, SUCC  : CAR_NAME;
          NUMBER       : LICENSE_NUMBER;
          OWNER        : PERSON;
       end record;


    --   in the generic instantiation

    package R is new P(NODE => CAR, LINK => CAR_NAME);
```

References:

access type 3.8, constraint 3.3, constraint_error exception 11.1, object 3.2, type 3.3

12.3.6 Matching Rules for Formal Subprograms

Any occurrence of the name of a formal type in the formal subprogram specification is replaced by the name of the corresponding actual type or subtype. Any such substitution having been achieved, a formal subprogram is matched by an actual subprogram that has parameters in the same order, of the same mode and type, and with the same constraints. For functions, the result type and constraints must be the same. Parameter names and the presence or absence of default values are ignored for this matching. Should any constraint not match, the exception CONSTRAINT_ERROR is raised at the place of the generic instantiation.

If a box appears after the reserved word **is** in the definition of the generic formal subprogram, the corresponding actual subprogram can be omitted if a subprogram with the same designator and with a matching specification is visible at the place of the generic instantiation; this subprogram (there must only be one) is then used by default.

Example:

```
--  given the generic function specification

generic
   type ITEM is private;
   with function "*" (U, V : ITEM) return ITEM is <>;
function SQUARING(X : ITEM) return ITEM;

--  and the function

function MATRIX_PRODUCT(A, B : MATRIX) return MATRIX;

--  the following instantiations are possible

function SQUARE is new SQUARING(MATRIX, MATRIX_PRODUCT);
function SQUARE is new SQUARING(INTEGER, "*");
function SQUARE is new SQUARING(INTEGER);

--  the last two instantiations are equivalent
```

Note:

The matching rule for formal subprograms is the same as the matching rule given for subprogram renaming declarations (see 8.5).

References:

constraint 3.3, constraint_error exception 11.1, function 6, name 4.1, parameter 6.2, parameter mode 6.1, renaming declaration 8.5, subprogram 6, subprogram specification 6.1, subtype 3.3, type 3.3, visibility 8.1 8

12.3.7 Matching Rules for Actual Derived Types

A formal generic type cannot be a derived type. On the other hand, an actual type may be a derived type, in which case the matching rules are the same as if its parent type were the actual type, subject to any constraints imposed on the derived type.

References:

constraint 3.3, derived type 3.4, parent type 3.4

12.4 Example of a Generic Package

The following example provides a possible formulation of stacks by means of a generic package. The size of each stack and the type of the stack elements are provided as generic parameters.

```
generic
   SIZE : NATURAL;
   type ELEM is private;
package STACK is
   procedure PUSH (E : in    ELEM);
   procedure POP  (E : out   ELEM);
   OVERFLOW, UNDERFLOW : exception;
end STACK;

package body STACK is

   SPACE   : array (1 .. SIZE) of ELEM;
   INDEX   : INTEGER range 0 .. SIZE := 0;

   procedure PUSH(E : in ELEM) is
   begin
     if INDEX = SIZE then
        raise OVERFLOW;
     end if;
     INDEX := INDEX + 1;
     SPACE(INDEX) := E;
   end PUSH;

   procedure POP(E : out ELEM) is
   begin
     if INDEX = 0 then
        raise UNDERFLOW;
     end if;
     E := SPACE(INDEX);
     INDEX := INDEX - 1;
   end POP;

end STACK;
```

Instances of this generic package can be obtained as follows:

```
package STACK_INT    is new STACK(SIZE => 200, ELEM => INTEGER);
package STACK_BOOL   is new STACK(100, BOOLEAN);
```

Thereafter, the procedures of the instantiated packages can be called as follows:

```
STACK_INT.PUSH(N);
STACK_BOOL.PUSH(TRUE);
```

Alternatively, a generic formulation of the type STACK can be given as follows (package body omitted):

```
generic
   type ELEM is private;
package ON_STACKS is
   type STACK(SIZE : NATURAL) is limited private;
   procedure PUSH (S : in out STACK; E : in    ELEM);
   procedure POP  (S : in out STACK; E : out   ELEM);
   OVERFLOW, UNDERFLOW : exception
private
   type STACK(SIZE : NATURAL) is
      record
         SPACE  : array(1 .. SIZE) of ELEM;
         INDEX  : INTEGER range 0 .. INTEGER'LAST := 0;
      end record;
end;
```

In order to use such a package an instantiation must be created and thereafter stacks of the corresponding type can be declared:

```
declare
   package STACK_INT is new ON_STACKS(INTEGER); use STACK_INT;
   S : STACK(100);
begin
   ...
   PUSH(S, 20);
   ...
end;
```

13. Representation Specifications and Implementation Dependent Features

13.1 Representation Specifications

Representation specifications specify how the types of the language are to be mapped onto the underlying machine. Mappings acceptable to an implementation do not alter the net effect of a program. They can be provided to give more efficient representation or to interface with features that are outside the domain of the language (for example, peripheral hardware).

```
representation_specification ::=
      length_specification          | enumeration_type_representation
    | record_type_representation     | address_specification
```

Representation specifications may appear in a declarative part, after the list of declarative items, and can only apply to items declared in the same declarative part. A representation specification given for a type applies to all objects of the type. For a given type, more than one representation specification can be given if and only if they specify different aspects of the representation. Thus for an enumeration type, both a length specification and an enumeration type representation can be given (but of course, at most one of each kind).

Representation specifications may also appear in package specifications and task specifications. A representation specification given in the private part of a package specification may only apply to an item declared in either the visible part or the private part of the package. A representation specification given in a task specification may only apply to an entry of the task (type) or to the task (type) itself.

In the absence of explicit representation specifications for a particular item, its representation is determined by the compiler.

The representation specifications in a declarative part, package specification, or task specification are elaborated in the order in which they appear. The effect of the elaboration of a representation specification is to define the corresponding representation and any consequent representation attribute (see 13.7). Any reference to such an attribute assumes that the choice of a representation has already been made, either explicitly by a specification, or by default by the compiler. Consequently a representation specification for a given entity must not appear after an occurrence of a representation attribute of this entity, nor may the specification mention such an attribute.

No representation specification may be given for a type derived from an access type. The only allowable representation specification for a type (other than an access type) that has derived user defined subprograms from its parent type is a length specification.

The interpretation of some of the expressions appearing in representation specifications may be implementation dependent, for example, expressions specifying addresses. An implementation may limit representation specifications to those that can be handled simply by the underlying hardware. For each implementation, the corresponding implementation dependences must be documented in Appendix F of the reference manual.

Whereas representation specifications are used to specify a mapping completely, pragmas can be used to provide criteria for choosing a mapping. The pragma PACK specifies that storage minimization should be the main criterion when selecting the representation of a record or array type. Its form is as follows:

> **pragma** PACK(*type*_name);

Packing means that gaps between the storage areas allocated to consecutive components should be minimized. It does not, however, affect the mapping of each component onto storage. This mapping can only be influenced (or controlled) by a pragma (or representation specification) for the component or component type. The position of a PACK pragma is governed by the same rules as for a representation specification; in particular, it must appear before any use of a representation attribute of the packed entity.

Additional representation pragmas may be provided by an implementation; these must be documented in Appendix F.

References:

access type 3.8, array type 3.6, declarative item 3.9, declarative part 3.9, derived type 3.4, elaboration 3.1, entry 9.5, enumeration type 3.5.1, expression 4.4, object 3.2, package 7, package specification 7.1, parent type 3.4, pragma 2.8, private part 7.2, record type 3.7, subprogram 6, task specification 9.1, type 3, visible part 7.2

13.2 Length Specifications

A length specification controls the amount of storage associated with an entity.

> length_specification ::= **for** attribute **use** expression;

The expression must be of some numeric type; it is evaluated during the elaboration of the length specification, unless it is a static expression. The effect of the length specification depends on the attribute given. This must be an attribute of a type (task types included), or of a task, denoted here by T:

(a) Size specification: T'SIZE

> The type T can be any type, other than a task type. The expression must be a static expression of some integer type; its value specifies the maximum number of bits to be allocated to objects of the type T. This number must be at least equal to the minimum number needed for the representation of objects of this type.

A size specification for a composite type may affect the size of the gaps between the storage areas allocated to consecutive components. On the other hand, it does not affect the size of the storage area allocated to each component.

Size specifications are not allowed for types whose constraints are not static.

(b) Specification of collection size: T'STORAGE_SIZE

The type T must be an access type. The expression must be of some integer type (but need not be static); its value specifies the number of storage units to be reserved for the collection, that is, the storage space needed to contain all objects designated by values of the access type.

(c) Specification of task storage: T'STORAGE_SIZE

The name T must be the name of a task type or task, introduced by a task specification. The expression must be of some integer type (but need not be static); its value specifies the number of storage units to be reserved for an activation of a task of the type (or for the single task). This length specification has, of course, no effect on the size of the storage occupied by the code of the task type.

(d) Specification of an actual delta: T'ACTUAL_DELTA

The type T must be a fixed point type. The expression must be a literal expression expressing a real value. This value specified as actual delta must not be greater than the delta of the type. The effect of the length specification is to use this value of actual delta for the representation of values of the fixed point type.

The exception STORAGE_ERROR may be raised by an allocator, or by the execution of a task, if the space reserved is exceeded.

Examples:

```
--  assumed declarations

type MEDIUM is range  0 .. 65000;
type SHORT  is delta  0.01  range -100.0  .. 100.0;
type DEGREE is delta  0.1   range -360.0  .. 360.0;

BYTE : constant := 8;
PAGE : constant := 2000;

--  length specifications

for COLOR'SIZE    use 1*BYTE;
for MEDIUM'SIZE   use 2*BYTE;
for SHORT'SIZE    use 15;

for CAR_NAME'STORAGE_SIZE use  --  approximately 2000 cars
        2000*((CAR'SIZE/SYSTEM.STORAGE_UNIT) + 1);

for KEYBOARD_DRIVER'STORAGE_SIZE use 1*PAGE;

for DEGREE'ACTUAL_DELTA use 360.0/2**(SYSTEM.STORAGE_UNIT - 2);
```

Notes:

In the length specification for SHORT, fifteen bits is the minimum necessary, since the type definition requires at least 20001 model numbers (((2∗100)∗100) + 1).

Objects allocated in a collection need not occupy the same amount of storage if they are records with variants or dynamic arrays. Note also that the allocator itself may require some space for internal tables and links. Hence a length specification for the collection of an access type does not always give precise control over the maximum number of allocated objects.

The method of allocation for objects denoted by an access type or for tasks is not defined by a length specification. For example, the space allocated could be on a stack; alternatively, a general allocator or fixed storage could be used.

References:

access type 3.8, actual delta 3.5.9, allocator 4.8, collection 3.8, delta 3.5.9, composite type 3.7, dynamic array 3.6.1, elaboration 3.1, expression 4.4, fixed point type 3.5.9, integer type 3.5.4, literal expression 4.10, object 3.2, real value 3.5.6, record 3.7, static expression 4.9, storage_error exception 11.1, task 9, task type 9, type 3, variant 3.7.1

13.3 Enumeration Type Representations

An enumeration type representation specifies the internal codes for the literals of an enumeration type.

        enumeration_type_representation ::= **for** *type*_name **use** aggregate;

The aggregate used to specify this mapping is an array aggregate of type

        array (*type*_name) **of** *universal_integer*

All enumeration literals must be provided with distinct integer codes, and the aggregate must be a static expression. The integer codes specified for the enumeration type must satisfy the ordering relation of the type.

Example:

        type MIX_CODE **is** (ADD, SUB, MUL, LDA, STA, STZ);

        for MIX_CODE **use**
            (ADD => 1, SUB => 2, MUL => 3, LDA => 8, STA => 24, STZ => 33);

Notes:

The attributes SUCC, PRED, and POS are defined even for enumeration types with a non-contiguous representation; their definition corresponds to the (logical) type declaration and is not affected by the enumeration type representation. In the example, because of the need to avoid the omitted values, the functions are less efficiently implemented than they could be in the absence of representation specification. Similar considerations apply when such types are used for indexing.

References:

aggregate 4.3, enumeration literal 3.5.1, enumeration type 3.5.1, function 6, index 3.6, static expression 4.9, type 3, type declaration 3.1

13.4 Record Type Representations

A record type representation specifies the storage representation of records, that is, the order, position, and size of record components (including discriminants, if any). Any expression contained in a record type representation must be a static expression of some integer type.

```
record_type_representation ::=
    for type_name use
        record [alignment_clause;]
            {component_name location;}
        end record;

location ::= at static_simple_expression range range

alignment_clause ::= at mod static_simple_expression
```

The position of a component is specified as a location relative to the start of the record. The integer defined by the static expression of the **at** clause of a location is a relative address expressed in storage units. The range defines the bit positions of the component, relative to the storage unit. The first storage unit of a record is numbered 0. The first bit of a storage unit is numbered 0. The ordering of bits in a storage unit is machine dependent and may extend to adjacent storage units. For a specific machine, the size in bits of a storage unit is given by the configuration dependent constant SYSTEM.STORAGE_UNIT.

Locations may be specified for some or for all components of a record, including discriminants. If no location is specified for a component, freedom is left to the compiler to define the location of the component. If locations are specified for all components, the record type representation completely specifies the representation of the record type and must be obeyed exactly. Locations within a record variant must not overlap, but the storage for distinct variants may overlap. Each location must allow for enough storage space to accommodate every allowable value of the component. Locations can only be specified for components whose constraints are static.

An alignment clause forces each record of the given type to be allocated at a starting address which is a multiple of the value of the given expression (that is, the address modulo the expression must be zero). An implementation may place restrictions on the allowable alignments. Components may overlap storage boundaries, but an implementation may place restrictions on how components may overlap storage boundaries.

An implementation may generate names that denote certain system dependent components (for example, one containing the offset of another component that is a dynamic array). Such names can be used in record type representations. The conventions to be followed for such names must be documented in Appendix F.

Example:

```
WORD : constant := 4;   --   storage unit is byte, 4 bytes per word

type STATE is (A, M, W, P);
type MODE is (FIX, DEC, EXP, SIGNIF);

type PROGRAM_STATUS_WORD is
   record
      SYSTEM_MASK          : array(0 .. 7) of BOOLEAN;
      PROTECTION_KEY       : INTEGER range 0 .. 3;
      MACHINE_STATE        : array(STATE) of BOOLEAN;
      INTERRUPT_CAUSE      : INTERRUPTION_CODE;
      ILC                  : INTEGER range 0 .. 3;
      CC                   : INTEGER range 0 .. 3;
      PROGRAM_MASK         : array(MODE) of BOOLEAN;
      INST_ADDRESS         : ADDRESS;
   end record;

for PROGRAM_STATUS_WORD use
   record at mod 8;
      SYSTEM_MASK        at 0*WORD   range 0    .. 7;
      PROTECTION_KEY     at 0*WORD   range 10   .. 11;    --  bits 8, 9 unused
      MACHINE_STATE      at 0*WORD   range 12   .. 15;
      INTERRUPT_CAUSE    at 0*WORD   range 16   .. 31;
      ILC                at 1*WORD   range 0    .. 1;     --  second word
      CC                 at 1*WORD   range 2    .. 3;
      PROGRAM_MASK       at 1*WORD   range 4    .. 7;
      INST_ADDRESS       at 1*WORD   range 8    .. 31;
   end record;

for PROGRAM_STATUS_WORD'SIZE use 8*SYSTEM.STORAGE_UNIT;
```

Note on the example:

The record type representation defines the record layout; the length specification guarantees that exactly eight storage units are used.

References:

component 3.7, constraint 3.3, discriminant 3.7.1, expression 4.4, integer type 3.5.4, name 4.1, range 3.5, record component 3.7, record type 3.7, static expression 4.9, type 3, value 3.7.1, variant 3.7.1 3.7.3

13.5 Address Specifications

An address specification defines the location of an object in storage or the starting address of a program unit. An address specification given for an entry links the entry to a hardware interrupt.

    address_specification ::= for name use at *static*_simple_expression;

The static expression given after the reserved word **at** must be of some integer type. The conventions that define the interpretation of this integer value as an address, as an interrupt level, or whatever it may be, are implementation dependent. They must be documented in Appendix F.

The name must be one of the following:

(a) Name of an object: the address is the address assigned to the object (variable or constant).

(b) Name of a subprogram, package, or task: the address is that of the machine code associated with the body of the program unit.

(c) Name of an entry: the address specifies a hardware interrupt to which the entry is linked. This form of address specification cannot be used for an entry of a family.

Address specifications should not be used to achieve overlays of objects or overlays of program units. Nor should a given interrupt be linked to more than one entry. Any program using address specifications to that effect is erroneous.

Example:

> **for** CONTROL **use at** 16#0020#;

Notes:

For address specifications an implementation may allow static expressions containing terms that are only known when *linking* the program. Such terms may be written as representation attributes. An implementation may provide pragmas for the specification of program overlays.

References:

constant 3.2, entry 9.5, family of entries 9.5, integer type 3.5.4, name 4.1, object 3.2, package 7, pragma 2.8, program unit 7, static expression 4.9, subprogram 6, task 9, value 3.3, variable 3.2 4.1

13.5.1 Interrupts

An address specification given for an entry associates the entry with an interrupt; such an entry is referred to in this section as an *interrupt entry*. If control information is supplied by an interrupt, it is passed to an associated interrupt entry as one or more **in** parameters.

The occurrence of an interrupt acts as an entry call issued by a task whose priority is higher than that of any user-defined task. The entry call may be an ordinary entry call, a timed entry call, or a conditional entry call, depending on the type of interrupt and on the implementation.

Example:

```
task INTERRUPT_HANDLER is
  entry DONE;
  for DONE use at 16#40#;
end;
```

Notes:

Interrupt entry calls need only have the semantics described above; they may be implemented by having the hardware directly execute the appropriate accept statements.

Queued interrupts correspond to ordinary entry calls. Interrupts that are lost if not immediately processed correspond to conditional entry calls. It is a consequence of the priority rules that an accept statement executed in response to an interrupt takes precedence over ordinary, user-defined tasks, and can be executed without first invoking a scheduling action.

One of the possible effects of an address specification for an interrupt entry is to specify the priority of the interrupt (directly or indirectly). Direct calls to an interrupt entry are allowed.

References:

accept statement 9.5, alternative 9.7.1, conditional entry call 9.7.2, entry 9.5, in parameter 6.2, select statement 9.7, task 9

13.6 Change of Representation

Only one representation can be defined for a given type. If therefore an alternative representation is desired, it is necessary to declare a second type derived from the first and to specify a different representation for the second type.

Example:

```
--   PACKED_DESCRIPTOR and DESCRIPTOR are two different types
--   with identical characteristics, apart from their representation

type DESCRIPTOR is
   record
      --   components of a descriptor
   end;

type PACKED_DESCRIPTOR is new DESCRIPTOR;

for PACKED_DESCRIPTOR use
   record
      --   locations of all components
   end record;
```

Change of representation can now be accomplished by assignment with explicit type conversions:

```
D  : DESCRIPTOR;
P  : PACKED_DESCRIPTOR;

P  := PACKED_DESCRIPTOR(D);    --  pack D
D  := DESCRIPTOR(P);           --  unpack P
```

References:

assignment 5.2, derived type 3.4, type 3, type conversion 4.6

13.7 Configuration and Machine Dependent Constants

For a given implementation the package SYSTEM (declared in STANDARD) will contain the definitions of certain constants designating configuration dependent characteristics. The exact definition of the package SYSTEM is implementation dependent and must be given in Appendix F. The specification of this package must contain at least the following declarations.

```
package SYSTEM is
    type SYSTEM_NAME is   --   implementation defined enumeration type

    NAME : constant SYSTEM_NAME :=   --   the name of the system

    STORAGE_UNIT  : constant :=  --   the number of bits per storage unit
    MEMORY_SIZE   : constant :=  --   the number of available storage units in memory
    MIN_INT       : constant :=  --   the smallest integer value supported by a predefined type
    MAX_INT       : constant :=  --   the largest integer value supported by a predefined type
    ...
end SYSTEM;
```

The corresponding characteristics of the configuration can be specified in the program by supplying appropriate pragmas:

```
pragma SYSTEM(name);              --  to establish the name of the object machine
pragma STORAGE_UNIT(number);      --  to establish the number of bits per storage unit
pragma MEMORY_SIZE(number);       --  to establish the required number of storage units
```

The values corresponding to other implementation dependent characteristics of specific program constructs, including the characteristics established by representation specifications, can be obtained by the use of appropriate *representation attributes*. These include the attributes ADDRESS, SIZE, POSITION, FIRST_BIT, LAST_BIT, and so on. The list of language defined attributes is given in Appendix A.

An implementation may provide additional pragmas that influence representation, and it may also provide corresponding representation attributes. These implementation specific pragmas and attributes must be documented in Appendix F.

Examples:

```
INTEGER'SIZE      --  number of bits actually used for implementing INTEGER
TABLE'ADDRESS     --  address of TABLE

X.COMPONENT'POSITION    --  position of COMPONENT in storage units
X.COMPONENT'FIRST_BIT   --  first bit of bit range
X.COMPONENT'LAST_BIT    --  last bit of bit range
```

References:

attribute A, constant 3.2, declaration 3.1, package 7, package specification 7.2, pragma 2.8

13.7.1 Representation Attributes of Real Types

For every floating point type or subtype F, the following machine dependent attributes are defined which are not related to the model numbers. Programs using these attributes may thereby exploit properties that go beyond the minimal properties associated with the numeric type. Precautions must consequently be taken when using these machine dependent attributes if portability is to be ensured.

F'MACHINE_ROUNDS	True if and only if all machine operations using type F perform rounding. Of type BOOLEAN.
F'MACHINE_RADIX	The machine radix of numerical representation. Of type *universal_integer*.
F'MACHINE_MANTISSA	The number of machine radix places in the mantissa. Of type *universal_integer*.
F'MACHINE_EMAX	The maximum exponent of numerical representation (to the base of the radix). Of type *universal_integer*.
F'MACHINE_EMIN	The smallest exponent of numerical representation. Of type *universal_integer*.
F'MACHINE_OVERFLOWS	True if and only if the exception NUMERIC_ERROR is raised for computations which exceed the range of real arithmetic. Of type BOOLEAN.

For every fixed point type or subtype F, the following machine dependent attribute is defined.

F'MACHINE_ROUNDS	True if and only if all machine operations using type F perform rounding. Of type BOOLEAN.

Note:

The largest machine representable number is almost

$$(F'MACHINE\_RADIX)**(F'MACHINE\_EMAX),$$

and the smallest is

$$F'MACHINE\_RADIX ** (F'MACHINE\_EMIN - 1)$$

References:

accuracy of operations with real operands 4.5.8, boolean type 3.5.3, exponent 3.5.7, fixed point type 3.5.9, floating point type 3.5.7, mantissa 3.5.7, model number 3.5.7, numeric_error exception 11.1, universal integer type 2.4 3.2

13.8 Machine Code Insertions

A machine code insertion can be achieved by a call to an inline procedure whose sequence of statements contains only code statements. Only use clauses and pragmas may appear in the declarative part of such a procedure. No exception handler may appear in such a procedure.

```
code_statement ::= qualified_expression;
```

Each machine instruction appears as a record aggregate of a record type that defines the corresponding instruction.   Declarations of such record types will generally be available in a predefined package for each machine. A procedure that contains a code statement must contain only code statements.

An implementation may provide machine dependent pragmas specifying register conventions and calling conventions. Such pragmas must be documented in Appendix F.

Example:

```
M  : MASK;
procedure SET_MASK; pragma INLINE(SET_MASK);

procedure SET_MASK is
   use INSTRUCTION_360;
begin
   SI_FORMAT'(CODE => SSM, B => M'BASE, D => M'DISP);
   --   M'BASE and M'DISP are implementation specific predefined attributes
end;
```

References:

declarative part 3.9, exception handler 11.2, inline pragma 6.3, inline procedure 6.3, package 7, pragma 2.8, procedure 6, qualified expression 4.7, record aggregate 4.3.1, record type definition 3.7, statement 5.1, use clause 8.4

13.9 Interface to Other Languages

A subprogram written in another language can be called from an Ada program provided that all communication is achieved via parameters and function results. A pragma of the form

```
pragma INTERFACE (language_name, subprogram_name);
```

must be given for each such subprogram (a subprogram name may stand for several overloaded subprograms). This pragma must appear after the subprogram specification, either in the same declarative part or in the same package specification. The pragma specifies the calling conventions and informs the compiler that an object module will be supplied for the corresponding subprogram. Neither a body nor a body stub may be given for such a subprogram.

This capability need not be provided by all compilers. An implementation may place restrictions on the allowable forms and places of parameters and calls.

Example:

```
package FORT_LIB is
   function SQRT (X : FLOAT) return FLOAT;
   function EXP   (X : FLOAT) return FLOAT;
private
   pragma INTERFACE(FORTRAN, SQRT);
   pragma INTERFACE(FORTRAN, EXP);
end FORT_LIB;
```

Note:

The conventions used by other language processors that call Ada programs are not part of the Ada language definition. These conventions must be defined by these other language processors.

References:

body 6.3 7.3, body stub 10.2, declarative part 3.9, package specification 7.2, parameter 6.1, pragma 2.8, subprogram 6, subprogram specification 6.1

13.10 Unchecked Programming

The predefined generic library subprograms UNCHECKED_DEALLOCATION and UNCHECKED_-CONVERSION are used for unchecked storage deallocation and for unchecked type conversions.

```
generic
   type OBJECT  is limited private;
   type NAME    is access OBJECT;
procedure UNCHECKED_DEALLOCATION(X : in out NAME);

generic
   type SOURCE is limited private;
   type TARGET is limited private;
function UNCHECKED_CONVERSION(S : SOURCE) return TARGET;
```

13.10.1 Unchecked Storage Deallocation

Unchecked storage deallocation of an object designated by a value of an access type is achieved by a call of a procedure obtained by instantiation of the generic procedure UNCHECKED_DEAL-LOCATION. For example.

```
procedure FREE is new UNCHECKED_DEALLOCATION(object_type_name, access_type_name);
```

Such a FREE procedure has the following effect:

(a)   after executing FREE(X), the value of X is **null**

(b)   FREE(X), when X is already equal to **null**, has no effect

(c)   FREE(X), when X is not equal to **null**, is an indication that the object denoted by X is no longer required, and that the storage it occupies is to be reclaimed.

If two access variables X and Y designate the same object, then any reference to this object using Y is erroneous after the call FREE(X);   the effect of a program containing such a reference is unpredictable.

It is a consequence of the visibility rules of the language that any compilation unit using unchecked storage deallocations must include UNCHECKED_DEALLOCATION in one of its with clauses.

References:

access type 3.8, generic function 12.1, generic instantiation 12.3, library unit 10.1, type 3.3, visibility rules 8, with clause 10.1.1

13.10.2   Unchecked Type Conversions

Unchecked type conversions can be achieved by instantiating the generic function UNCHECKED_-CONVERSION.

The effect of an unchecked conversion is to return the (uninterpreted) parameter value as a value of the target type, that is, the bit pattern defining the source value is returned unchanged as the bit pattern defining a value of the target type. An implementation may place restrictions on unchecked conversions, for example restrictions depending on the respective sizes of objects of the source and target type.

Whenever unchecked conversions are used, it is the programmer's responsibility to ensure that these conversions maintain the properties to be expected from objects of the target type. Programs that violate these properties by means of unchecked conversions are erroneous.

It is a consequence of the visibility rules of the language that any compilation unit using unchecked conversions must include UNCHECKED_CONVERSION in one of its with clauses.

References:

constraint 3.3, constraint_error exception 11.1, generic procedure 12.1, generic instantiation 12.3, library unit 10.1, type 3.3, type conversion 4.6, visibility rules 8, with clause 10.1.1

14. Input-Output

Input-output facilities are predefined in the language by means of two packages. The generic package INPUT_OUTPUT defines a set of input-output primitives applicable to files containing elements of a single type. Additional primitives for text input-output are supplied in the package TEXT_IO. These facilities are described here, together with the conventions to be used for dealing with low level input-output operations.

References:

generic package 12.1, input-output package 14.2, package 7, type 3

14.1 General User Level Input-Output

The high level input-output facilities are defined in the language. A suitable package is described here and is given explicitly in section 14.2; it defines file types and the procedures and functions that operate on files.

Files are declared, and subsequently associated with appropriate sources and destinations (called *external files*) such as peripheral devices or data sets. Distinct file types are defined to provide either read-only access, write-only access or read-and-write access to external files. The corresponding file types are called IN_FILE, OUT_FILE, and INOUT_FILE.

External files are named by a character string, which is interpreted by individual implementations to distinguish peripherals, access rights, physical organization, and so on.

The package defining these facilities is generic and is called INPUT_OUTPUT. Any program which requires these facilities must instantiate the package for the appropriate element type.

A file can be read or written, and it can be set to a required position; the current position for access and the number of elements in the file may be obtained.

When the term *file* is used in this chapter, it refers to a declared object of a file type; the term *external file* is used otherwise. Whenever there is a possible ambiguity, the term *internal file* is used to denote a declared file object.

References:

character string 2.6, declaration 3.1, function 6.1, generic instantiation 12.3, generic package 12.1, package 7, procedure 6, type 3

14.1.1 Files

A file is associated with an unbounded sequence of elements, all of the same type. With each element of the file is associated a positive integer number that is its (ordinal) position number in this sequence. Some of the elements may be undefined, in which case they cannot be read.

The file types for a given element type, and the appropriate subprograms for dealing with it, are produced by instantiating a generic package. For example:

```
package INT_IO is new INPUT_OUTPUT(ELEMENT_TYPE => INTEGER);
```

establishes types and procedures for files of integers, so that

```
RESULTS_FILE : INT_IO.OUT_FILE;
```

declares RESULTS_FILE as a write-only file of integers.

Before any file processing can be carried out, the internal file must first be associated with an external file. When such an association is in effect, the file is said to be open. This operation is performed by one of the CREATE or OPEN procedures which operate on a file and a character string used to name an external file:

```
procedure CREATE(FILE : in out OUT_FILE;   NAME : in STRING);
procedure CREATE(FILE : in out INOUT_FILE; NAME : in STRING);
```

> Establishes a new external file with the given name and associates with it the given file. A new external file established by a CREATE operation corresponds to a sequence of elements all of which are initially undefined. If the given internal file is already open, the exception STATUS_ERROR is raised. If creation is prohibited for the external file (for example, because an external file with that name already exists), the exception NAME_ERROR is raised.

```
procedure OPEN(FILE : in out IN_FILE;    NAME : in STRING);
procedure OPEN(FILE : in out OUT_FILE;   NAME : in STRING);
procedure OPEN(FILE : in out INOUT_FILE; NAME : in STRING);
```

> Associates the given internal file with an existing external file having the given name. If the given internal file is already open, the exception STATUS_ERROR is raised. If no such external file exists, or if this access is prohibited, the exception NAME_ERROR is raised.

After processing has been completed on a file, the association may be severed by the CLOSE procedure:

```
procedure CLOSE(FILE : in out IN_FILE);
procedure CLOSE(FILE : in out OUT_FILE);
procedure CLOSE(FILE : in out INOUT_FILE);
```

> Severs the association between the internal file and its associated external file. The exception STATUS_ERROR is raised if the internal file is not open.

The functions IS_OPEN and NAME take a file as argument:

```
function IS_OPEN(FILE : in IN_FILE)     return BOOLEAN;
function IS_OPEN(FILE : in OUT_FILE)    return BOOLEAN;
function IS_OPEN(FILE : in INOUT_FILE)  return BOOLEAN;
```

Returns TRUE if the internal file is associated with an external file, FALSE otherwise.

```
function NAME(FILE : in IN_FILE)     return STRING;
function NAME(FILE : in OUT_FILE)    return STRING;
function NAME(FILE : in INOUT_FILE)  return STRING;
```

Returns a string representing the name of the external file currently associated with the given internal file. If there is no external file currently associated, the exception STATUS_ERROR is raised. The string returned is implementation dependent, but must be sufficient to identify uniquely the corresponding external file if used subsequently, for example, in an OPEN operation.

The following procedure operates on external files:

```
procedure DELETE(NAME : in STRING);
```

Deletes the named external file; no OPEN operation can thereafter be performed on the external file, and the external file can cease to exist as soon as it is no longer associated with any internal file. Raises the NAME_ERROR exception if no such external file exists, or if this operation is otherwise prohibited.

Example: *create a new external file on backing store*:

```
CREATE(FILE => RESULTS_FILE, NAME => "<ADA>COUNTS.1;P77000");
--   write the file
CLOSE(RESULTS_FILE);
```

Example: *read a paper tape*:

```
declare
    package CHAR_IO is new INPUT_OUTPUT(CHARACTER);
    PT : CHAR_IO.IN_FILE;
begin
    CHAR_IO.OPEN(PT, "ttyg");
    --   input the data from device ttyg
    CHAR_IO.CLOSE(PT);
end;
```

References:

exception 11, false 3.5.3, function 6, generic parameter 12.1, name 4.1, package declaration 7.1, procedure 6, raise an exception 11.3, string 3.6.3, true 3.5.3, type 3

14.1.2 File Processing

An open IN_FILE or INOUT_FILE can be read; an open OUT_FILE or INOUT_FILE can be written. A file that can be read has a *current read position*, which is the position number of the element available to the next read operation. A file that can be written has a *current write position*, which is the position number of the element available to be modified by the next write operation. The current read or write positions can be changed. Positions in a file are expressed in the implementation defined integer type FILE_INDEX.

A file has a *current size*, which is the number of defined elements in the file, and an *end position*, which is the position number of the last defined element if any, and is otherwise zero.

When a file is opened or created, the current write position is set to 1, and the current read position is set to the position number of the first defined element, or to 1 if no element is defined.

The operations available for file processing are described below; they apply only to open files. The exception STATUS_ERROR is raised if one of these operations is applied to a file that is not open. The exception DEVICE_ERROR is raised if an input-output operation cannot be completed because of a malfunction of the underlying system. The exception USE_ERROR is raised if an operation is incompatible with the properties of the external file.

```
procedure READ(FILE : in IN_FILE;    ITEM : out ELEMENT_TYPE);
procedure READ(FILE : in INOUT_FILE; ITEM : out ELEMENT_TYPE);
```

> Returns, in the ITEM parameter, the value of the element at the current read position of the given file. Advances the current read position to the next defined element in the sequence, if any, and otherwise increments it by one. The exception DATA_ERROR is raised if the value is not defined and may (but need not) be raised if it is not of the required element type. The exception END_ERROR is raised if the current read position is higher than the end position. Any previous WRITE on the same external file must have been completed before this READ. Note that READ is not defined for an OUT_FILE.

```
procedure WRITE(FILE : in OUT_FILE;   ITEM : in ELEMENT_TYPE);
procedure WRITE(FILE : in INOUT_FILE; ITEM : in ELEMENT_TYPE);
```

> Gives the specified value to the element in the current write position of the given file, and adds 1 to the current write position. Adds 1 to the current size if the element in the current write position was not defined, and sets the end position to the written position if the written position exceeds the end position. Note that WRITE is not defined for an IN_FILE.

```
function NEXT_READ(FILE : in IN_FILE)    return FILE_INDEX;
function NEXT_READ(FILE : in INOUT_FILE) return FILE_INDEX;
```

> Returns the current read position of the given file.

```
procedure SET_READ(FILE : in IN_FILE;    TO : in FILE_INDEX);
procedure SET_READ(FILE : in INOUT_FILE; TO : in FILE_INDEX);
```

> Sets the current read position of the given file to the specified index value. (The specified value may exceed the end position).

procedure RESET_READ(FILE : **in** IN_FILE);
procedure RESET_READ(FILE : **in** INOUT_FILE);

> Sets the current read position of the given file to the position number of the first defined element, or to 1 if no element is defined.

function NEXT_WRITE(FILE : **in** OUT_FILE)   **return** FILE_INDEX;
function NEXT_WRITE(FILE : **in** INOUT_FILE) **return** FILE_INDEX;

> Returns the current write position of the given file.

procedure SET_WRITE(FILE : **in** OUT_FILE;   TO : **in** FILE_INDEX);
procedure SET_WRITE(FILE : **in** INOUT_FILE; TO : **in** FILE_INDEX);

> Sets the current write position of the given file to the value specified by TO. (The specified value may exceed the end position).

procedure RESET_WRITE(FILE : **in** OUT_FILE);
procedure RESET_WRITE(FILE : **in** INOUT_FILE);

> Sets the current write position of the given file to 1.

function SIZE(FILE : **in** IN_FILE)   **return** FILE_INDEX;
function SIZE(FILE : **in** OUT_FILE)   **return** FILE_INDEX;
function SIZE(FILE : **in** INOUT_FILE) **return** FILE_INDEX;

> Returns the current size of the file.

function LAST(FILE : **in** IN_FILE)   **return** FILE_INDEX;
function LAST(FILE : **in** OUT_FILE)   **return** FILE_INDEX;
function LAST(FILE : **in** INOUT_FILE) **return** FILE_INDEX;

> Returns the end position of the file.

function END_OF_FILE(FILE : **in** IN_FILE)   **return** BOOLEAN;
function END_OF_FILE(FILE : **in** INOUT_FILE) **return** BOOLEAN;

> Returns TRUE if the current read position of the given file exceeds the end position, otherwise FALSE.

procedure TRUNCATE(FILE: **in** OUT_FILE;   TO: **in** FILE_INDEX);
procedure TRUNCATE(FILE: **in** INOUT_FILE; TO: **in** FILE_INDEX);

> Sets the end position of the given file to the specified index value, if it is not larger than the current end position, and changes the current size accordingly. Any element after the given position becomes undefined. Raises the USE_ERROR exception if the specified index value exceeds the current end position.

The predefined package does not restrict the physical representation of an external file, providing only that this representation implements a sequence of elements, indexed by position. An external file can thus be a collection of records stored on disks, tapes or other media, or a keyboard, a terminal, a line-printer, a communication link or other device. The interpretation of the character string used to name an external file depends on the implementation: this external file name can be used to specify devices, system addresses, file organization, access rights and so on.

A file may be implemented using various access methods. In a sequential organization, all the elements up to the size of the file are always defined (although their value may be arbitrary), and a successful READ operation will always increment the current read position by 1. In an indexed organization however, the only defined elements are those whose position numbers are given by existing key values.

Certain accesses to particular external files may be prohibited; attempts at such accesses will raise the exception USE_ERROR. Examples are the attempt to backspace on a paper tape, to write a protected file, to extend a file whose size is fixed, to manipulate the current read to write position on a communication link, or to ask for the SIZE or the LAST of an interactive device.

Example of file processing:

```
    --   Accumulate the values of a sequential external file and append the total

    declare
       use INT_IO;
       COUNTS : INOUT_FILE;
       VALUE   : INTEGER;
       TOTAL   : INTEGER := 0;
    begin
       OPEN(COUNTS, ">udd>ada>counts");
       while not END_OF_FILE(COUNTS) loop
          READ(COUNTS, VALUE);
          TOTAL := TOTAL + VALUE;
       end loop;
       SET_WRITE(COUNTS, LAST(COUNTS) + 1);
       WRITE(COUNTS, TOTAL);
       CLOSE(COUNTS);
    end;
```

Example of file positioning:

```
    RESET_READ(COUNTS);                                        --  could mean rewind
    SET_WRITE(RESULTS_FILE, NEXT_WRITE(RESULTS_FILE) - 1 );    --  backspace
    SET_WRITE(RESULTS_FILE, LAST(RESULTS_FILE) + 1 );          --  advance to end of file
```

References:

character string 2.6, false 3.5.3, name 4.1, out parameter 6.2, package 7, record 3.7, true 3.5.3, type 3

14.2 Specification of the Package Input_Output

The specification of the generic package INPUT_OUTPUT is given below. It provides the calling conventions for the operations described in section 14.1.

```
generic
    type ELEMENT_TYPE is limited private;
package INPUT_OUTPUT is
    type IN_FILE      is limited private;
    type OUT_FILE     is limited private;
    type INOUT_FILE   is limited private;

    type FILE_INDEX   is range 0 .. implementation_defined;

    --  general operations for file manipulation

    procedure  CREATE (FILE : in out OUT_FILE;    NAME : in STRING);
    procedure  CREATE (FILE : in out INOUT_FILE;  NAME : in STRING);

    procedure  OPEN   (FILE : in out IN_FILE;     NAME : in STRING);
    procedure  OPEN   (FILE : in out OUT_FILE;    NAME : in STRING);
    procedure  OPEN   (FILE : in out INOUT_FILE;  NAME : in STRING);

    procedure  CLOSE  (FILE : in out IN_FILE);
    procedure  CLOSE  (FILE : in out OUT_FILE);
    procedure  CLOSE  (FILE : in out INOUT_FILE);

    function   IS_OPEN(FILE : in IN_FILE)     return BOOLEAN;
    function   IS_OPEN(FILE : in OUT_FILE)    return BOOLEAN;
    function   IS_OPEN(FILE : in INOUT_FILE)  return BOOLEAN;

    function   NAME   (FILE : in IN_FILE)     return STRING;
    function   NAME   (FILE : in OUT_FILE)    return STRING;
    function   NAME   (FILE : in INOUT_FILE)  return STRING;

    procedure  DELETE (NAME : in STRING);


    function   SIZE   (FILE : in IN_FILE)     return FILE_INDEX;
    function   SIZE   (FILE : in OUT_FILE)    return FILE_INDEX;
    function   SIZE   (FILE : in INOUT_FILE)  return FILE_INDEX;

    function   LAST   (FILE : in IN_FILE)     return FILE_INDEX;
    function   LAST   (FILE : in OUT_FILE)    return FILE_INDEX;
    function   LAST   (FILE : in INOUT_FILE)  return FILE_INDEX;

    procedure TRUNCATE(FILE: in OUT_FILE;    TO: in FILE_INDEX);
    procedure TRUNCATE(FILE: in INOUT_FILE; TO: in FILE_INDEX);
```

```
--    input and output operations

procedure   READ         (FILE : in IN_FILE;       ITEM : out ELEMENT_TYPE);
procedure   READ         (FILE : in INOUT_FILE;    ITEM : out ELEMENT_TYPE);

function    NEXT_READ    (FILE : in IN_FILE)       return FILE_INDEX;
function    NEXT_READ    (FILE : in INOUT_FILE)    return FILE_INDEX;

procedure   SET_READ     (FILE : in IN_FILE;       TO : in FILE_INDEX);
procedure   SET_READ     (FILE : in INOUT_FILE;    TO : in FILE_INDEX);

procedure   RESET_READ   (FILE : in IN_FILE);
procedure   RESET_READ   (FILE : in INOUT_FILE);

procedure   WRITE        (FILE : in OUT_FILE;      ITEM : in ELEMENT_TYPE);
procedure   WRITE        (FILE : in INOUT_FILE;    ITEM : in ELEMENT_TYPE);

function    NEXT_WRITE   (FILE : in OUT_FILE)      return FILE_INDEX;
function    NEXT_WRITE   (FILE : in INOUT_FILE)    return FILE_INDEX;

procedure   SET_WRITE    (FILE : in OUT_FILE;      TO : in FILE_INDEX);
procedure   SET_WRITE    (FILE : in INOUT_FILE;    TO : in FILE_INDEX);

procedure   RESET_WRITE(FILE : in OUT_FILE);
procedure   RESET_WRITE(FILE : in INOUT_FILE);

function    END_OF_FILE (FILE : in IN_FILE)        return BOOLEAN;
function    END_OF_FILE (FILE : in INOUT_FILE)     return BOOLEAN;

--    exceptions that can be raised

NAME_ERROR      : exception;
USE_ERROR       : exception;
STATUS_ERROR    : exception;
DATA_ERROR      : exception;
DEVICE_ERROR    : exception;
END_ERROR       : exception;

private
    --    declarations of the file private types
end INPUT_OUTPUT;
```

14.3 Text Input-Output

Facilities are available for input and output in human readable form, with the external file consisting of characters. The package defining these facilities is called TEXT_IO; it is described here and is given explicitly in section 14.4. It uses the general INPUT_OUTPUT package for files of type CHARACTER, so all the facilities described in section 14.1 are available. In addition to these general facilities, procedures are provided to GET values of suitable types from external files of characters, and PUT values to them, carrying out conversions between the internal values and appropriate character strings.

All the GET and PUT procedures have an ITEM parameter, whose type determines the details of the action and determines the appropriate character string in the external file. Note that the ITEM parameter is an **out** parameter for GET and an **in** parameter for PUT. The general principle is that the characters in the external file are composed and analyzed as lexical elements, as described in Chapter 2. The conversions are based on the IMAGE and VALUE attributes described in Appendix A.

For all GET and PUT procedures, there are forms with and without a file specified. If a file is specified, it must be of the correct type (IN_FILE for GET, OUT_FILE for PUT). If no file is specified, a *default input file* or a *default output file* is used. At the beginning of program execution, the default input and output files are the so-called *standard input file* and *standard output file*, which are open and associated with two implementation defined external files.

Although the package TEXT_IO is defined in terms of the package INPUT_OUTPUT, the execution of an operation of one of these packages need not have a well defined effect on the execution of subsequent operations of the other package. For example, if the function LAST (of the package INPUT_OUTPUT) is called immediately before and after a call of the function NEWLINE (of the package TEXT_IO) for a given file and with spacing one, the difference between the two values of LAST is undefined; it could be any non negative value. The effect of the package TEXT_IO is defined only if the characters written by a PUT operation or read by a GET operation belong to the 95 graphic *ASCII* characters. The effect of a program that reads or writes any other character is implementation dependent.

Note:

Text input output is not defined for files of type INOUT_FILE.

References:

character 2.6, character string 2.6, character type 3.5.2, external file 14.1, image attribute A, in parameter 6.1, out parameter 6.1, package 7, procedure 6, type 3, value attribute A

14.3.1 Default Input and Output Files

Control of the particular default files used with the short forms of GET and PUT can be achieved by means of the following functions and procedures:

```
function STANDARD_INPUT    return IN_FILE;   --  returns INITIAL default input file
function STANDARD_OUTPUT   return OUT_FILE;  --  returns INITIAL default output file
function CURRENT_INPUT     return IN_FILE;   --  returns CURRENT default input file
function CURRENT_OUTPUT    return OUT_FILE;  --  returns CURRENT default output file

procedure SET_INPUT  (FILE : in IN_FILE);   --  sets the default input file to FILE
procedure SET_OUTPUT (FILE : in OUT_FILE);  --  sets the default output file to FILE
```

The exception STATUS_ERROR is raised by the functions CURRENT_INPUT and CURRENT_OUTPUT if there is no corresponding default file, and by the procedure SET_INPUT and SET_OUTPUT if the parameter is not an open file.

14.3.2 Layout

A text file consists of a sequence of lines, numbered from 1. The characters in each line are considered to occupy consecutive character positions called *columns*, counting from 1. Each character occupies exactly one column. A file may have a particular *line length* that is explicitly set by the user. If no line length has been specified, lines can be of any length up to the size of the file. The line length can be set or reset during execution of a program, so that the same file can be written using both fixed line length (for instance for the production of tables), and variable line length (for instance during interactive dialogues). A file which is open (or simply created) has a *current line* number and a *current column* number. These determine the starting position available for the next GET or PUT operation.

The following subprograms provide for control of the line structure of the file given as first parameter, or of the corresponding default file if no file parameter is supplied. Unless otherwise stated, this default file is the current output file. As in the general case, these subprograms may raise the USE_ERROR exception if the request is incompatible with the associated external file.

```
function COL(FILE : in IN_FILE)   return NATURAL;
function COL(FILE : in OUT_FILE)  return NATURAL;
function COL return NATURAL;
```

Returns the current column number.

```
procedure SET_COL(FILE : in IN_FILE;   TO : in NATURAL);
procedure SET_COL(FILE : in OUT_FILE;  TO : in NATURAL);
procedure SET_COL(TO : in NATURAL);
```

Sets the current column number to the value specified by TO. The current line number is unaffected. The exception LAYOUT_ERROR is raised if the line length has been specified and is less than the specified column number.

```
function LINE(FILE : in IN_FILE)   return NATURAL;
function LINE(FILE : in OUT_FILE)  return NATURAL;
function LINE return NATURAL;
```

Returns the current line number.

```
procedure NEW_LINE(FILE : in OUT_FILE; SPACING : in NATURAL := 1);
procedure NEW_LINE(SPACING : in NATURAL := 1);
```

Resets the current column number to 1 and increments the current line number by SPACING. Thus a SPACING of 1 corresponds to single spacing, a SPACING of 2 to double spacing. This terminates the current line and adds SPACING - 1 empty lines. If the line length is fixed, extra space characters are inserted when needed to fill the current line and add empty lines.

procedure SKIP_LINE(FILE : **in** IN_FILE; SPACING : **in** NATURAL := 1);
procedure SKIP_LINE(SPACING : **in** NATURAL := 1);

Resets the current column number to 1 and increments the current line number by SPACING (A value of SPACING greater than 1 causes SPACING - 1 lines to be skipped as well as the remainder of the current line). The default file is the current input file.

function END_OF_LINE(FILE : **in** IN_FILE) **return** BOOLEAN;
function END_OF_LINE **return** BOOLEAN;

Returns TRUE if the line length of the specified input file is not set, and the current column number exceeds the length of the current line (that is, if there are no more characters to be read on the current line), otherwise FALSE. The default file is the current input file. (END_OF_LINE is meant to be used primarily for files containing lines of different lengths).

procedure SET_LINE_LENGTH(FILE : **in** IN_FILE; N : **in** INTEGER);
procedure SET_LINE_LENGTH(FILE : **in** OUT_FILE; N : **in** INTEGER);
procedure SET_LINE_LENGTH(N : **in** INTEGER);

Sets the line length of the specified file to the value specified by N. The value zero indicates that line length is not set; it is the initial value for any file. The exception LAYOUT_ERROR is raised by a GET operation if a line mark does not correspond to the specified line length.

function LINE_LENGTH(FILE : **in** IN_FILE) **return** INTEGER;
function LINE_LENGTH(FILE : **in** OUT_FILE) **return** INTEGER;
function LINE_LENGTH **return** INTEGER;

Returns the current line length of the specified file if it is set, otherwise zero.

Examples:

SET_COL(((COL() - 1)/10 + 1)*10 + 1); -- advance to next multiple of 10
                                        -- plus 1 on current output-file

if END_OF_LINE(F) **then**   -- advance to next line at end of current line
   SKIP_LINE(F);   -- (the line length of F is not set)
end if;

SET_LINE_LENGTH(F, 132);

References:

character 2.1, exception 11, false 3.5.3, number 2.4, parameter 6, subprogram 6, true 3.5.3

14.3.3 Input-Output of Characters and Strings

The GET and PUT procedures for these types work with individual characters. The current line and column number are affected as explained below. Special *line marks* are used to implement the line structure, in addition to the individual characters.

For an ITEM of type CHARACTER

```
procedure  GET(FILE  : in   IN_FILE; ITEM : out CHARACTER);
procedure  GET(ITEM  : out  CHARACTER);
```

> Returns, in the **out** parameter ITEM, the value of the character from the specified input file at the position given by the current line number and the current column number. Adds 1 to the current column number, unless the line length is fixed and the current column number equals the line length, in which case the current column number is set to 1 and the current line number is increased by 1. (This case corresponds to a line mark following the character that was read; thus line marks are always skipped when the line length is fixed). The default file is the current input file.

```
procedure  PUT(FILE  : in OUT_FILE; ITEM : in CHARACTER);
procedure  PUT(ITEM  : in CHARACTER);
```

> Outputs the specified character to the specified output file on the current column of the current line. Adds 1 to the current column number, unless the line length is fixed and the current column number equals the line length, in which case a line mark is output and the current column number is set to 1 and the current line number is increased by 1. The default file is the current output file.

When the ITEM type is a string, the length of the string is determined and that exact number of GET or PUT operations for individual characters is carried out.

```
procedure GET (FILE  : in IN_FILE;   ITEM : OUT STRING);
procedure GET (ITEM  : out STRING);
procedure PUT (FILE  : in OUT_FILE; ITEM : in STRING);
procedure PUT (ITEM  : in STRING);
```

In addition, the following functions and procedures are provided:

```
function GET_STRING(FILE : in IN_FILE) return STRING;
function GET_STRING return STRING;
```

> Performs GET operations on the specified **in** file, skipping any leading blanks (that is, spaces, tabulation characters or line marks) and returns as result the next sequence of characters up to (and not including) a blank. The default file is the current input file.

```
function GET_LINE(FILE : in IN_FILE) return STRING;
function GET_LINE return STRING;
```

> Returns the next sequence of characters up to, but not including, a line mark. If the input line is already at the end of a line, a null string is returned. The input file is advanced just past the line mark, so successive calls of GET_LINE return successive lines. The default file is the current input file.

```
procedure PUT_LINE(FILE    : in OUT_FILE; ITEM : in STRING),
procedure PUT_LINE(ITEM    : in STRING);
```

Calls PUT to write the given STRING to the specified file, and appends a line mark. The default file is the current output file.

Example : variable line length

```
PUT(F, "01234567");
NEW_LINE(F);
PUT(F, "89012345");
```

will output

```
01234567
89012345
```

The string can subsequently be input by

```
GET_STRING(G) & GET_STRING(G)
```

Alternatively, it can be obtained by

```
X : STRING(1 .. 16);
    ...
GET(G, X(1 .. 8));
SKIP_LINE(G);
GET(G, X(9 .. 16));
```

Example : fixed line length

```
SET_LINE_LENGTH(F, 8);
    ...
PUT(F, "0123456789012345");
```

will output

```
01234567
89012345
```

The string can subsequently be input by

```
X : STRING(1 .. 16);
SET_LINE_LENGTH(G, 8);
GET(G, X);
```

Note that the double-quote marks enclosing an actual parameter of PUT are not output, but the string inside is output with any doubled double-quote marks written once, thus matching the rule for character strings (see 2.6).

References:

actual parameter 6.4, character 2.1, character string 2.6, character type 3.5.2, double-quote marks 2.6, function 6, out parameter 6.2, space character 2.1, string 3.6.3, type 3

14.3.4 Input-Output for Other Types

All ITEM types other than CHARACTER or STRING are treated in a uniform way, in terms of lexical units (see 2.2, 2.3, 2.4). The output is a character string having the syntax described for the appropriate unit and the input is taken as the longest possible character string having the required syntax. For input, any leading spaces, leading tabulation characters, and leading line marks are ignored. A consequence is that no such units can cross a line boundary.

If the character string read is not consistent with the syntax of the required lexical unit, the exception DATA_ERROR is raised.

The PUT procedures for numeric and enumeration types include an optional WIDTH parameter, which specifies a minimum number of characters to be generated. If the width given is larger than the string representation of the value, the value will be preceded (for numeric types) or followed (for enumeration types) by the appropriate number of spaces. If the field width is smaller than the string representation of the value, the field width is ignored. A default width of 0 is provided, thus giving the minimum number of characters.

In each PUT operation, if the line can accommodate all the characters generated, then the characters are placed on that line from the current column. If the line cannot accommodate all the characters, then a new line is started and the characters are placed on the new line starting from column 1. If however the line length is fixed and smaller than the length of the string to be output, then the exception LAYOUT_ERROR is raised instead, and a new line is not started.

For each GET operation an IN file may be specified, and the default file is the current input file. For each PUT operation an OUT file may be specified, and the default file is the current output file.

References:

character string 2.6, character type 3.5.2, enumeration type 3.5.1, exception 11, in_file 14.1, lexical unit 2.2, numeric type 3.5, out_file 14.1, space character 2.1, string type 3.6.3, tabulation character 2.2

14.3.5 Input-Output for Numeric Types

Input for numeric types is defined by means of three generic packages; these packages must be instantiated for the corresponding numeric types (indicated by NUM in the specifications given here).

Integer types:

The following procedures are defined in the generic package INTEGER_IO:

    procedure GET(FILE   : **in**   IN_FILE; ITEM : **out** NUM);
    procedure GET(ITEM : **out** NUM);

> Reads an optional plus or minus sign, then according to the syntax of an integer literal (which may be a based number). The value obtained is implicitly converted to the type of the **out** parameter ITEM (see 3.5.4), and returned in ITEM if the converted value is within the range of this type; otherwise the exception CONSTRAINT_ERROR is raised and ITEM is unaffected.

    procedure PUT(FILE   : **in** OUT_FILE;
                ITEM   : **in** NUM;
                WIDTH : **in** INTEGER := 0;
                BASE   : **in** INTEGER **range** 2 .. 16 := 10);
    procedure PUT(ITEM   : **in** NUM;
                WIDTH : **in** INTEGER := 0;
                BASE   : **in** INTEGER **range** 2 .. 16 := 10);

> Expresses the value of the parameter ITEM as an integer literal, with no underscores and no leading zeros (but a single 0 for the value zero), and a preceding minus sign for a negative value. Uses the syntax of based number if the parameter BASE is given with a value different from 10 (the default value), otherwise the syntax of decimal number.

Examples:

In the examples for numeric types the string quotes are shown only to reveal the layout; they are not output. Similarly leading spaces are indicated by the lower letter b.

    PUT(126);   --   "126"
    PUT(-126, 7);   --   "bbb-126"
    PUT(126, WIDTH => 13, BASE => 2); --   "bbb2#1111110#"

Floating point numbers:

The following procedures are defined in the generic package FLOAT_IO:

    procedure GET(FILE   : **in** IN_FILE ; ITEM: **out** NUM);
    procedure GET(ITEM : **out** NUM);

> Reads an optional plus or minus sign, then according to the syntax of a real literal (which may be a based number). The value obtained is implicitly converted to the type of the **out** parameter ITEM (see 3.5.7), and returned in ITEM if the converted value is within the range of this type; otherwise the exception CONSTRAINT_ERROR is raised and ITEM is unaffected.

```
procedure PUT(FILE      : in  OUT_FILE;
              ITEM      : in  NUM;
              WIDTH     : in  INTEGER := 0;
              MANTISSA  : in  INTEGER := NUM'DIGITS;
              EXPONENT  : in  INTEGER := 2);
procedure PUT(ITEM      : in  NUM;
              WIDTH     : in  INTEGER := 0;
              MANTISSA  : in  INTEGER := NUM'DIGITS;
              EXPONENT  : in  INTEGER := 2);
```

Expresses the value of the parameter ITEM as a decimal number, with no under-scores, a preceding minus sign for a negative value, a mantissa with the decimal point immediately following the first non-zero digit and no leading zeros (but 0.0 for the value zero), and a signed exponent part. A minimum number of digits in the mantissa (excluding sign and point characters) can be specified (leading zeros being supplied as necessary); the default value is given by the type of ITEM; rounding is performed if fewer digits are specified than the implemented precision. A minimum number of digits in the exponent part (excluding sign and E) can be specified (leading zeros being supplied as necessary); the default value is 2; if the value of ITEM needs more digits than specified for the exponent part, the exact number of significant digits is used.

Examples:

```
package REAL_IO is new FLOAT_IO(REAL); use REAL_IO;
X : REAL := 0.001266;  --   digits 8

PUT(X);                                              --  "1.2660000E-03"
PUT(X, WIDTH => 14, MANTISSA => 4, EXPONENT => 1);   --  "bbbbbb1.266E-3"
```

Fixed point numbers:

The following procedures are defined in the generic package FIXED_IO:

```
procedure GET(FILE  : in   IN_FILE; ITEM : out NUM);
procedure GET(ITEM  : out  NUM);
```

Reads an optional plus or minus sign, then according to the syntax of a real literal (which may be a based number). The value obtained is implicitly converted to the type of the **out** parameter ITEM (see 3.5.9), rounded to the implemented delta for the type, and returned in ITEM if the resulting value is within the range of the type; otherwise the exception CONSTRAINT_ERROR is raised and ITEM is unaffected.

```
procedure PUT(FILE   : in  OUT_FILE;
              ITEM   : in  NUM;
              WIDTH  : in  INTEGER := 0;
              FRACT  : in  INTEGER := DEFAULT_DECIMALS);
procedure PUT(ITEM   : in  NUM;
              WIDTH  : in  INTEGER := 0;
              FRACT  : in  INTEGER := DEFAULT_DECIMALS);
```

Expresses the value of the parameter ITEM as a decimal number, with no under-scores, a preceding minus sign for a negative value, and a mantissa but no exponent part. At least one digit precedes the decimal point; if this requires leading zeros, just the number needed are inserted. The number of digits after the point can be specified; the default value is given by the type of ITEM; rounding is performed if fewer digits are specified than are needed to represent the delta of the type.

14 - 16

Example:

```
type FIX is delta 0.05 range -10 .. 10;
package FIX_IO is new FIXED_IO(FIX);
use FIX_IO;
X : FIX := 1.25;

PUT(X);                             --  "1.25"
PUT(X, WIDTH => 8, FRACT => 3);     --  "bbb1.250"
PUT(X-1.3);                         --  "-0.05"
```

References:

based number 2.4.1, constraint_error exception 11.1, decimal number 2.4, digit 2.1, exception 11, exponent part 2.4, fixed point number 3.5.9, floating point number 3.5.7, generic package 12.1, generic package instantiation 12.3, integer literal 2.4, integer type 3.5.4, layout_error exception 14.3.2, mantissa 3.5.7, minus sign 2.4 4.5.4, numeric type 3.5, out parameter 6.2, plus sign 2.4 4.5.9, point character 2.4, precision 3.5.6, range 3.5, real literal 2.4, sign character 4.5.4, underscore 2.3 2.4.1

14.3.6 Input-Output for Boolean Type

```
procedure GET(FILE    : in IN_FILE ; ITEM : out BOOLEAN);
procedure GET(ITEM    : out BOOLEAN);
```

Reads an identifier according to the syntax given in 2.3, with no distinction between corresponding upper and lower case letters. If the identifier is TRUE or FALSE, then the boolean value is given; otherwise the exception DATA_ERROR is raised.

```
procedure PUT(FILE       : in OUT_FILE ;
              ITEM       : in BOOLEAN;
              WIDTH      : in INTEGER := 0;
              LOWER_CASE : in BOOLEAN := FALSE);
procedure PUT(ITEM       : in BOOLEAN;
              WIDTH      : in INTEGER := 0;
              LOWER_CASE : in BOOLEAN := FALSE);
```

Expresses the value of the parameter ITEM as the words TRUE or FALSE. An optional parameter is used to specify upper or lower case (default is upper case). If a value of WIDTH is given, exceeding the number of letters produced, then spaces follow to fill a field of this width.

Note:

The procedures defined in this section are directly available (that is, not by generic instantiation).

References:

boolean type 3.5.3, boolean value 3.5.3, data_error exception 14.3.4, exception 11, false 3.5.3, identifier 2.3, space character 2.1, true 3.5.3

14.3.7 Input-Output for Enumeration Types

Because each enumeration type has its own set of literals, these procedures are contained in the generic package ENUMERATION_IO. An instantiation must specify the type, indicated here by ENUM.

```
procedure GET(FILE  : in IN_FILE; ITEM : out ENUM);
procedure GET(ITEM  : out ENUM);
```

> Reads an identifier (according to the syntax given in 2.3, with no distinction between corresponding upper and lower case letters) or a character literal (according to the syntax of 2.5, a character enclosed by single quotes). If this is one of the enumeration literals of the type, then the enumeration value is given; otherwise the exception DATA_ERROR is raised.

```
procedure PUT(FILE        : in OUT_FILE;
              ITEM        : in ENUM;
              WIDTH       : in INTEGER := 0;
              LOWER_CASE  : in BOOLEAN := FALSE);
procedure PUT(ITEM        : in ENUM;
              WIDTH       : in INTEGER := 0;
              LOWER_CASE  : in BOOLEAN := FALSE);
```

> Outputs the value of the parameter ITEM as an identifier or as a character literal. An optional parameter indicates upper or lower case for identifiers (default is upper case); it has no effect for character literals. If a field width is given, exceeding the number of characters produced, then spaces follow to fill a field of this width.

Note:

There is a difference between PUT defined for characters, and for enumeration values. Thus

```
TEXT_IO.PUT('A');  --   the character A

package CHAR_IO is new TEXT_IO.ENUMERATION_IO(CHARACTER);
CHAR_IO.PUT('A');  --   the character 'A' between single quotes
```

References:

character literal 2.5, data_error exception 14.3.4, enumeration literal 3.5.1, enumeration type 3.5.1, generic package 12.1, generic instantiation 12.3, literal 2.4 3.2 4.2, procedure 6, type 3

14.4 Specification of the Package Text_IO

The package TEXT_IO contains the definition of all the text input-output primitives.

```
package TEXT_IO is
   package CHARACTER_IO is new INPUT_OUTPUT(CHARACTER);

   type IN_FILE    is new CHARACTER_IO.IN_FILE;
   type OUT_FILE   is new CHARACTER_IO.OUT_FILE;

   -- Character Input-Output

   procedure GET ( FILE  : in   IN_FILE; ITEM : out CHARACTER);
   procedure GET ( ITEM  : out  CHARACTER);
   procedure PUT ( FILE  : in   OUT_FILE; ITEM : in CHARACTER);
   procedure PUT ( ITEM  : in   CHARACTER);

   -- String Input-Output

   procedure  GET ( FILE  : in   IN_FILE; ITEM : out STRING);
   procedure  GET ( ITEM  : out  STRING);
   procedure  PUT ( FILE  : in   OUT_FILE; ITEM : in STRING);
   procedure  PUT ( ITEM  : in   STRING);

   function   GET_STRING(FILE : in IN_FILE) return STRING;
   function   GET_STRING return STRING;

   function   GET_LINE (FILE   : in IN_FILE) return STRING;
   function   GET_LINE return STRING;
   procedure  PUT_LINE (FILE   : in OUT_FILE, ITEM : in STRING);
   procedure  PUT_LINE (ITEM   : in STRING);

   -- Generic package for Integer Input-Output

   generic
      type NUM is range <>;
      with function IMAGE(X : NUM)    return STRING is NUM'IMAGE;
      with function VALUE(X : STRING) return NUM is NUM'VALUE;
   package INTEGER_IO is
      procedure GET ( FILE     : in   IN_FILE; ITEM : out NUM);
      procedure GET ( ITEM     : out  NUM);
      procedure PUT ( FILE     : in   OUT_FILE;
                      ITEM     : in   NUM;
                      WIDTH    : in   INTEGER := 0;
                      BASE     : in   INTEGER range 2 .. 16 := 10);
      procedure PUT ( ITEM     : in   NUM;
                      WIDTH    : in   INTEGER := 0;
                      BASE     : in   INTEGER range 2 .. 16 := 10);
   end INTEGER_IO;
```

```
-- Generic package for Floating Point Input-Output

generic
   type NUM is digits <>;
   with function IMAGE (X : NUM)     return STRING is NUM'IMAGE;
   with function VALUE (X : STRING)  return NUM is NUM'VALUE;
package FLOAT_IO is
   procedure GET(FILE  : in IN_FILE ; ITEM: out NUM);
   procedure GET(ITEM  : out NUM);

   procedure PUT(FILE        : in OUT_FILE;
                 ITEM        : in NUM;
                 WIDTH       : in INTEGER := 0;
                 MANTISSA    : in INTEGER := NUM'DIGITS;
                 EXPONENT    : in INTEGER := 2);

   procedure PUT(ITEM        : in NUM;
                 WIDTH       : in INTEGER := 0;
                 MANTISSA    : in INTEGER := NUM'DIGITS;
                 EXPONENT    : in INTEGER := 2);
end FLOAT_IO;
```

```
-- Generic package for Fixed Point Input-Output

generic
   type NUM is delta <>;
   with function IMAGE (X : NUM)     return STRING is NUM'IMAGE;
   with function VALUE (X : STRING)  return NUM is NUM'VALUE;
package FIXED_IO is
   DELTA_IMAGE        : constant STRING   := IMAGE(NUM'DELTA - INTEGER(NUM'DELTA));
   DEFAULT_DECIMALS   : constant INTEGER  := DELTA_IMAGE'LENGTH - 2;

   procedure GET ( FILE   : in   IN_FILE; ITEM : out NUM);
   procedure GET ( ITEM   : out  NUM);

   procedure PUT ( FILE   : in   OUT_FILE;
                   ITEM   : in   NUM;
                   WIDTH  : in   INTEGER := 0;
                   FRACT  : in   INTEGER := DEFAULT_DECIMALS);

   procedure PUT ( ITEM   : in   NUM;
                   WIDTH  : in   INTEGER := 0;
                   FRACT  : in   INTEGER := DEFAULT_DECIMALS);
end FIXED_IO;
```

-- Input-Output for Boolean

```
procedure GET ( FILE          : in IN_FILE   ; ITEM : out BOOLE AN);
procedure GET ( ITEM          : out BOOLEAN);

procedure PUT ( FILE          : in OUT_FILE ;
                ITEM          : in BOOLEAN;
                WIDTH         : in INTEGER := 0;
                LOWER_CASE : in BOOLEAN := FALSE);

procedure PUT ( ITEM          : in BOOLEAN;
                WIDTH         : in INTEGER := 0;
                LOWER_CASE : in BOOLEAN := FALSE);
```

-- Generic package for Enumeration Types

```
generic
   type ENUM is (<>);
   with function IMAGE (X : ENUM)    return STRING is ENUM'IMAGE;
   with function VALUE (X : STRING)  return ENUM is ENUM'VALUE;
package ENUMERATION_IO is
   procedure GET ( FILE          : in IN_FILE; ITEM : out ENUM);
   procedure GET ( ITEM          : out ENUM);

   procedure PUT ( FILE          : in OUT_FILE ;
                   ITEM          : in ENUM;
                   WIDTH         : in INTEGER := 0;
                   LOWER_CASE : in BOOLEAN := FALSE);

   procedure PUT ( ITEM          : in ENUM;
                   WIDTH         : in INTEGER := 0;
                   LOWER_CASE : in BOOLEAN := FALSE);
end ENUMERATION_IO;
```

-- Layout control

```
function LINE(FILE : in IN_FILE)   return NATURAL;
function LINE(FILE : in OUT_FILE)  return NATURAL;
function LINE return NATURAL;        --   for default output file

function COL(FILE : in IN_FILE)    return NATURAL;
function COL(FILE : in OUT_FILE)   return NATURAL;
function COL return NATURAL;         --   for default output file

procedure SET_COL(FILE : in IN_FILE;   TO : in NATURAL);
procedure SET_COL(FILE : in OUT_FILE;  TO : in NATURAL);
procedure SET_COL(TO : in NATURAL);    --   for default output file
```

```
      procedure NEW_LINE(FILE : in OUT_FILE; N : in NATURAL := 1);
      procedure NEW_LINE(N : in NATURAL := 1);

      procedure SKIP_LINE(FILE : in IN_FILE; N : in NATURAL := 1);
      procedure SKIP_LINE(N : in NATURAL := 1);

      function END_OF_LINE(FILE : in IN_FILE) return BOOLEAN;
      function END_OF_LINE return BOOLEAN;

      procedure SET_LINE_LENGTH(FILE : in IN_FILE; N   : in INTEGER);
      procedure SET_LINE_LENGTH(FILE : in OUT_FILE; N : in INTEGER);
      procedure SET_LINE_LENGTH(N : in INTEGER);  --  for default output file

      function LINE_LENGTH(FILE : in IN_FILE)  return INTEGER;
      function LINE_LENGTH(FILE : in OUT_FILE) return INTEGER;
      function LINE_LENGTH return INTEGER;        --   for default output file


      -- Default input and output manipulation

      function STANDARD_INPUT    return IN_FILE;
      function STANDARD_OUTPUT return OUT_FILE;

      function CURRENT_INPUT    return IN_FILE;
      function CURRENT_OUTPUT return OUT_FILE;

      procedure SET_INPUT  (FILE : in IN_FILE   );
      procedure SET_OUTPUT (FILE : in OUT_FILE );


      -- Exceptions

      NAME_ERROR    : exception renames CHARACTER_IO.NAME_ERROR;
      USE_ERROR     : exception renames CHARACTER_IO.USE_ERROR;
      STATUS_ERROR  : exception renames CHARACTER_IO.STATUS_ERROR;
      DATA_ERROR    : exception renames CHARACTER_IO.DATA_ERROR;
      DEVICE_ERROR  : exception renames CHARACTER_IO.DEVICE_ERROR;
      END_ERROR     : exception renames CHARACTER_IO.END_ERROR;
      LAYOUT_ERROR  : exception;
   end TEXT_IO;
```

References:

boolean type input-output 14.3.6, character input-output 14.3.3, default input-output 14.3.1, enumeration
type input-output 14.3.7, exceptions for input-output 14.1.1 14.1.2 14.3.2 14.3.4, fixed point input-output
14.3.5, floating point input-output 14.3.5, generic package 12.1, integer input-output 14.3.5, item
parameter 14.3, layout for input-output 14.3.2, package 7, string input-output 14.3.3

14.5 Example of Text Input-Output

The following example shows the use of the text input-output primitives in a dialogue with a user at a terminal. The user is asked to select a color, and the program output in response is the number of items of the color available in stock. The default input and output files are used.

```
procedure DIALOGUE is
  use TEXT_IO;
  type COLOR is (WHITE, RED, ORANGE, YELLOW, GREEN, BLUE, BROWN);
  INVENTORY : array (COLOR) of INTEGER := (20, 17, 43, 10, 28, 173, 87);
  CHOICE : COLOR;
  package COLOR_IO is new ENUMERATION_IO(COLOR); use COLOR_IO;

  function ENTER_COLOR return COLOR is
    SELECTION : COLOR;
  begin
    loop
      begin
        PUT("Color selected: ");
        GET(SELECTION);
        return SELECTION;
      exception
        when DATA_ERROR =>
          PUT("Invalid color, try again. ");
      end;
    end loop;
  end;
begin    --   body of DIALOGUE;
  CHOICE := ENTER_COLOR();
  NEW_LINE;
  PUT(CHOICE, LOWER_CASE => TRUE);
  PUT(" items available: ");
  SET_COL(25);
  PUT(INVENTORY(CHOICE), WIDTH => 5);
  PUT(";");
  NEW_LINE;
end DIALOGUE;
```

Example of an interaction (characters typed by the user are italicized):

    Color selected: *black*
    Invalid color, try again. Color selected: *blue*
    blue items available: 173;

References:

default input file 14.3, default output file 14.3, text input-output primitives 14.4

14.6 Low Level Input-Output

A low level input-output operation is an operation acting on a physical device. Such an operation is handled by using one of the (overloaded) predefined procedures SEND_CONTROL and RECEIVE_CONTROL.

A procedure SEND_CONTROL may be used to send control information to a physical device. A procedure RECEIVE_CONTROL may be used to monitor the execution of an input-output operation by requesting information from the physical device.

Such procedures are declared in the standard package LOW_LEVEL_IO and have two parameters identifying the device and the data. However, the kinds and formats of the control information will depend on the physical characteristics of the machine and the device. Hence the types of the parameters are implementation defined. Overloaded definitions of these procedures should be provided for the supported devices.

The visible part of the package defining these procedures is outlined as follows:

```
package LOW_LEVEL_IO is
    --   declarations of the possible types for DEVICE and DATA;
    --   declarations of overloaded procedures for these types:
    procedure SEND_CONTROL      (DEVICE : device_type; DATA : in out data_type);
    procedure RECEIVE_CONTROL   (DEVICE : device_type; DATA : in out data_type);
end;
```

The bodies of the procedures SEND_CONTROL and RECEIVE_CONTROL for various devices can be supplied in the body of the package LOW_LEVEL_IO. These procedure bodies may be written with code statements.

References:

actual parameter 6.4, code statement 13.8, overloaded definition 3.4, overloaded predefined procedure 6.6, package 7, package body 7.1 7.3, procedure 6.1, procedure body 6.1, type 3, visible part 7.2

A. Predefined Language Attributes

The following attributes are predefined in the language. They are denoted in the manner described in 4.1.4: the name of an entity is followed by a prime, and then by the identifier of an attribute appropriate to the entity.

Attribute of any object or subprogram X

ADDRESS   A number corresponding to the first storage unit occupied by X (see 13.7). Overloaded on all predefined integer types.

Attribute of any type or subtype T (except a task type)

BASE   Applied to a subtype, yields the base type; applied to a type, yields the type itself. This attribute may be used only to obtain further attributes of a type, e.g. T'BASE'-FIRST (see 3.3).

SIZE   The maximum number of bits required to hold an object of that type (see 13.3). Of type INTEGER.

Attributes of any scalar type or subtype T

FIRST   The minimum value of T (see 3.5).

LAST   The maximum value of T (see 3.5).

IMAGE   If X is a value of type T, T'IMAGE(X) is a string representing the value in a standard display form.

For an enumeration type, the values are represented, in minimum width, as either the corresponding enumeration literal, in upper case, or as the corresponding character literal, within quotes.

For an integer type, the values are represented as decimal numbers of minimum width.   For a fixed point type, the values are represented as decimal fractions of minimum width, with sufficient decimal places just to accommodate the declared accuracy.   For a floating point type, the values are represented in exponential notation with one significant characteristic digit, sufficient mantissa digits just to accommodate the declared accuracy, and a signed three-digit exponent. The exponent letter is in upper case. For all numeric types, negative values are prefixed with a minus sign and positive values have no prefix.

| VALUE | If S is a string, T'VALUE(S) is the value in T that can be represented in display form by the string S. If the string does not denote any possible value, the exception DATA_ERROR is raised; if the value lies outside the range of T, the exception CONSTRAINT_ERROR is raised. All legal lexical forms are legal display forms (see 2.3, 2.4). |

Attributes of any discrete type or subtype T

| POS | If X is a value of type T, T'POS(X) is the integer position of X in the ordered sequence of values T'FIRST .. T'LAST, the position of T'FIRST being itself for integer types and zero for enumeration types (see 3.5.5). |

| VAL | If J is an integer, T'VAL(J) is the value of enumeration type T whose POS is J. If no such value exists, the exception CONSTRAINT_ERROR is raised (see 3.5.5). |

| PRED | If X is a value of type T, T'PRED(X) is the preceding value. The exception CONSTRAINT_ERROR is raised if X = T'FIRST (see 3.5.5). |

| SUCC | If X is a value of type T, T'SUCC(X) is the succeeding value. The exception CONSTRAINT_ERROR is raised if X = T'LAST (see 3.5.5). |

Attributes of any fixed point type or subtype T

| DELTA | The delta specified in the declaration of T (see 3.5.10). Of type *universal real*. |

| ACTUAL_DELTA | The delta of the model numbers used to represent T (see 3.5.10). Of type *universal real*. |

| BITS | The number of bits required to represent the model numbers of T (see 3.5.10). Of type *universal integer*. |

| LARGE | The largest model number of T (see 3.5.10). Of type *universal real*. |

| MACHINE_ROUNDS | True if the machine performs true rounding (to nearest even) when computing values of type T (see 13.7.1). Of type BOOLEAN. |

Attributes of any floating point type or subtype T

| DIGITS | The number of digits specified in the declaration of T (see 3.5.8). Of type *universal integer*. |

| MANTISSA | The number of bits in the mantissa of the representation of model numbers of T (see 3.5.8). Of type *universal integer*. |

| EMAX | The largest exponent value of the representation of model numbers of T (see 3.5.8). The smallest exponent value is -EMAX. Of type *universal integer*. |

| SMALL | The smallest positive model number of T (see 3.5.8). Of type *universal real*. |

LARGE	The largest model number of T (see 3.5.8). Of type *universal real*.
EPSILON	The difference between unity and the smallest model number of T greater than unity (see 3.5.8). Both unity and T'EPSILON are model numbers of T. Of type *universal real*.
MACHINE_RADIX	The radix of the exponent of the underlying machine representation of T (see 13.7.1). Of type *universal integer*.
MACHINE_MANTISSA	The number of bits in the mantissa of the underlying machine representation of T (see 13.7.1). Of type *universal integer*.
MACHINE_EMAX	The largest exponent value of the underlying machine representation of T (see 13.7.1). Of type *universal integer*.
MACHINE_EMIN	The smallest exponent value of the underlying machine representation of T (see 13.7.1). Of type *universal integer*.
MACHINE_ROUNDS	True if the machine performs true rounding (to nearest even) when computing values of type T (see 13.7.1). Of type BOOLEAN.
MACHINE_OVERFLOWS	True if, when a computed value is too large to be represented correctly by the underlying machine representation of T, the exception NUMERIC_ERROR is raised (see 13.7.1). Of type BOOLEAN.

Attributes of any array type or subtype, or object thereof

FIRST	If A is a constrained array type or subtype, or an array object, A'FIRST is the lower bound of the first index (see 3.6.2).
FIRST(J)	Similarly, the lower bound of the J'th index, where J must be a static integer expression (see 3.6.2).
LAST	If A is a constrained array type or subtype, or an array object, A'LAST is the upper bound of the first index (see 3.6.2).
LAST(J)	Similarly, the upper bound of the J'th index, where J must be a static integer expression (see 3.6.2).
LENGTH	If A is a constrained array type or subtype, or an array object, A'LENGTH is the number of elements in the first dimension of A (see 3.6.2).
LENGTH(J)	Similarly, the number of elements in the J'th dimension, where J must be a static expression (see 3.6.2).
RANGE	If A is a constrained array type or subtype, or an array object, A'RANGE is the subtype A'FIRST .. A'LAST, whose base type is the first index type of A (see 3.6.2).

RANGE(J)   Similarly, the subtype A'FIRST(J) .. A'LAST(J), whose base type is the J'th index type of A, and where J must be a static integer expression (see 3.6.2).

Attribute of any record type with discriminants

CONSTRAINED   If R is an object of any record type with discriminants, or of any subtype thereof, R'CONSTRAINED is true if and only if the discriminant values of R cannot be modified (see 3.7.2). Of type BOOLEAN.

Attributes of any record component C

POSITION   The offset within the record, in storage units, of the first unit of storage occupied by C (see 13.7). Of type INTEGER.

FIRST_BIT   The offset, from the start of C'POSITION, of the first bit used to hold the value of C (see 13.7). Of type INTEGER.

LAST_BIT   The offset, from the start of C'POSITION, of the last bit used to hold the value of C. C'LAST_BIT need not lie within the same storage unit as C'FIRST_BIT (see 13.7). Of type INTEGER.

Attribute of any access type P

STORAGE_SIZE   The total number of storage units reserved for allocation for all objects of type P (see 13.2). Overloaded on all predefined integer types.

Attributes of any task, or object of a task type, T

TERMINATED   True when T is terminated (see 9.9). Of type BOOLEAN.

PRIORITY   The (static) priority of T (see 9.9). Of type *universal integer*.

FAILURE   The exception that, if raised, causes FAILURE within T (see 9.9).

STORAGE_SIZE   The number of storage units allocated for the execution of T (see 9.9). Overloaded on all predefined integer types.

Attribute of any entry E

COUNT   Momentarily, the number of calling tasks waiting on E (see 9.9). Of type INTEGER.

B. Predefined Language Pragmas

Pragma	Meaning

Pragma   *Meaning*

CONTROLLED

Takes an access type name as argument. It must appear in the same declarative part as the access type definition (see 4.8). It specifies that automatic storage reclamation should not be performed for objects of the access type except upon leaving the scope of the access type definition (see 4.8).

INCLUDE

Takes a string as argument, which is the name of a text file. This pragma can appear anywhere a pragma is allowed. It specifies that the text file is to be included where the pragma is given.

INLINE

Takes a list of subprogram names as arguments. It must appear in the same declarative part as the named subprograms. It specifies that the subprogram bodies should be expanded inline at each call (see 6.3).

INTERFACE

Takes a language name and subprogram name as arguments. It must appear after the subprogram specification in the same declarative part or in the same package specification. It specifies that the body of the subprogram is written in the given other language, whose calling conventions are to be observed (see 13.9).

LIST

Takes ON or OFF as argument. This pragma can appear anywhere. It specifies that listing of the program unit is to be continued or suspended until a LIST pragma is given with the opposite argument.

MEMORY_SIZE

Takes an integer number as argument. This pragma can only appear before a library unit. It establishes the required number of storage units in memory (see 13.7).

OPTIMIZE

Takes TIME or SPACE as argument. This pragma can only appear in a declarative part and it applies to the block or body enclosing the declarative part. It specifies whether time or space is the primary optimization criterion.

PACK

Takes a record or array type name as argument. The position of the pragma is governed by the same rules as for a representation specification. It specifies that storage minimization should be the main criterion when selecting the representation of the given type (see 13.1).

PRIORITY

Takes a static expression as argument. It must appear in a task (type) specification or the outermost declarative part of a main program. It specifies the priority of the task (or tasks of the task type) or the main program (see 9.8).

STORAGE_UNIT

Takes an integer number as argument. This pragma can only appear before a library unit. It establishes the number of bits per storage unit (see 13.7).

SUPPRESS   Takes a check name and optionally also either an object name or a type
                   name as arguments. It must appear in the declarative part of a unit (block
                   or body). It specifies that the designated check is to be suppressed in the
                   unit. In the absence of the optional name, the pragma applies to all opera-
                   tions within the unit. Otherwise its effect is restricted to operations on the
                   named object or to operations on objects of the named type (see 11.7).

SYSTEM   Takes a name as argument. This pragma can only appear before a library
                   unit. It establishes the name of the object machine (see 13.7).

C. Predefined Language Environment

This appendix outlines the specification of the package STANDARD containing all predefined identifiers in the language. The corresponding package body is implementation defined and is not shown.

```
package STANDARD is

    type BOOLEAN is (FALSE, TRUE);

    function "not" (X : BOOLEAN) return BOOLEAN;

    function "and" (X,Y : BOOLEAN) return BOOLEAN;
    function "or"  (X,Y : BOOLEAN) return BOOLEAN;
    function "xor" (X,Y : BOOLEAN) return BOOLEAN;

    type SHORT_INTEGER  is range implementation_defined;
    type INTEGER        is range implementation_defined;
    type LONG_INTEGER   is range implementation_defined;

    function "+"  (X : INTEGER) return INTEGER;
    function "-"  (X : INTEGER) return INTEGER;
    function ABS  (X : INTEGER) return INTEGER;

    function "+"   (X,Y : INTEGER) return INTEGER;
    function "-"   (X,Y : INTEGER) return INTEGER;
    function "*"   (X,Y : INTEGER) return INTEGER;
    function "/"   (X,Y : INTEGER) return INTEGER;
    function "rem" (X,Y : INTEGER) return INTEGER;
    function "mod" (X,Y : INTEGER) return INTEGER;
    function "**"  (X : INTEGER; Y : INTEGER range 0 .. INTEGER'LAST) return INTEGER;

    -- Similarly for SHORT_INTEGER and LONG_INTEGER

    type SHORT_FLOAT  is digits implementation_defined range implementation_defined;
    type FLOAT        is digits implementation_defined range implementation_defined;
    type LONG_FLOAT   is digits implementation_defined range implementation_defined;

    function "+"  (X : FLOAT) return FLOAT;
    function "-"  (X : FLOAT) return FLOAT;
    function ABS  (X : FLOAT) return FLOAT;

    function "+"  (X,Y : FLOAT) return FLOAT;
    function "-"  (X,Y : FLOAT) return FLOAT;
    function "*"  (X,Y : FLOAT) return FLOAT;
    function "/"  (X,Y : FLOAT) return FLOAT;
    function "**" (X : FLOAT; Y : INTEGER) return FLOAT;

    -- Similarly for SHORT_FLOAT and LONG_FLOAT
```

-- The following characters comprise the standard ASCII character set.
-- Character literals corresponding to control characters are not identifiers;
-- They are indicated in italics in this definition:

type CHARACTER **is**

```
( nul,    soh,   stx,   etx,      eot,    enq,   ack,   bel,
  bs,     ht,    lf,    vt,       ff,     cr,    so,    si,
  dle,    dc1,   dc2,   dc3,      dc4,    nak,   syn,   etb,
  can,    em,    sub,   esc,      fs,     gs,    rs,    us,

  ' ',    '!',   '"',   '#',      '$',    '%',   '&',   ''',
  '(',    ')',   '*',   '+',      ',',    '-',   '.',   '/',
  '0',    '1',   '2',   '3',      '4',    '5',   '6',   '7',
  '8',    '9',   ':',   ';',      '<',    '=',   '>',   '?',

  '@',    'A',   'B',   'C',      'D',    'E',   'F',   'G',
  'H',    'I',   'J',   'K',      'L',    'M',   'N',   'O',
  'P',    'Q',   'R',   'S',      'T',    'U',   'V',   'W',
  'X',    'Y',   'Z',   '[',      '\',    ']',   '^',   '_',

  '`',    'a',   'b',   'c',      'd',    'e',   'f',   'g',
  'h',    'i',   'j',   'k',      'l',    'm',   'n',   'o',
  'p',    'q',   'r',   's',      't',    'u',   'v',   'w',
  'x',    'y',   'z',   '{',      '|',    '}',   '~',   del);
```

package ASCII **is**

-- Control characters:

```
NUL : constant CHARACTER := nul;
SOH : constant CHARACTER := soh;
STX : constant CHARACTER := stx;
ETX : constant CHARACTER := etx;
EOT : constant CHARACTER := eot;
ENQ : constant CHARACTER := enq;
ACK : constant CHARACTER := ack;
BEL : constant CHARACTER := bel;
BS  : constant CHARACTER := bs;
HT  : constant CHARACTER := ht;
LF  : constant CHARACTER := lf;
VT  : constant CHARACTER := vt;
FF  : constant CHARACTER := ff;
CR  : constant CHARACTER := cr;
SO  : constant CHARACTER := so;
SI  : constant CHARACTER := si;
DLE : constant CHARACTER := dle;
DC1 : constant CHARACTER := dc1;
DC2 : constant CHARACTER := dc2;
DC3 : constant CHARACTER := dc3;
DC4 : constant CHARACTER := dc4;
```

```
NAK  : constant CHARACTER := nak;
SYN  : constant CHARACTER := syn;
ETB  : constant CHARACTER := etb;
CAN  : constant CHARACTER := can;
EM   : constant CHARACTER := em;
SUB  : constant CHARACTER := sub;
ESC  : constant CHARACTER := esc;
FS   : constant CHARACTER := fs;
GS   : constant CHARACTER := gs;
RS   : constant CHARACTER := rs;
US   : constant CHARACTER := us;
DEL  : constant CHARACTER := del;

-- Other characters

EXCLAM      : constant CHARACTER := '!';
SHARP       : constant CHARACTER := '#';
DOLLAR      : constant CHARACTER := '$';
QUERY       : constant CHARACTER := '?';
AT_SIGN     : constant CHARACTER := '@';
L_BRACKET   : constant CHARACTER := '[';
BACK_SLASH  : constant CHARACTER := '\';
R_BRACKET   : constant CHARACTER := ']';
CIRCUMFLEX  : constant CHARACTER := '~';
GRAVE       : constant CHARACTER := '`';
L_BRACE     : constant CHARACTER := '{';
BAR         : constant CHARACTER := '|';
R_BRACE     : constant CHARACTER := '}';
TILDE       : constant CHARACTER := '~';

-- Lower case letters

LC_A : constant CHARACTER := 'a';
...
LC_Z : constant CHARACTER := 'z';

end ASCII;

-- Predefined types and subtypes

subtype NATURAL  is INTEGER range 1 .. INTEGER'LAST;
subtype PRIORITY is INTEGER range implementation_defined;

type STRING   is array(NATURAL range <>) of CHARACTER;

type DURATION is delta implementation_defined range implementation_defined;

-- The predefined exceptions

CONSTRAINT_ERROR  : exception;
NUMERIC_ERROR     : exception;
SELECT_ERROR      : exception;
STORAGE_ERROR     : exception;
TASKING_ERROR     : exception;
```

```
-- The machine dependent package SYSTEM

package SYSTEM is
    type SYSTEM_NAME is implementation_defined_enumeration_type;

    NAME: constant  SYSTEM_NAME  := implementation_defined;
    STORAGE_UNIT  : constant      := implementation_defined;
    MEMORY_SIZE   : constant      := implementation_defined;
    MIN_INT       : constant      := implementation_defined;
    MAX_INT       : constant      := implementation_defined;
    ...
end SYSTEM;

private
    for CHARACTER use  --  128 ASCII character set without holes
        (0, 1, 2, 3, 4, 5, ..., 125, 126, 127);

    pragma PACK(STRING);

end STANDARD;
```

Certain aspects of the predefined entities cannot be completely described in the language itself. For example, although the enumeration type BOOLEAN can be written showing the two enumeration literals FALSE and TRUE, the relationship of BOOLEAN to conditions cannot be expressed in the language.

The language definition predefines certain library units (other than the package STANDARD). These library units are

-   The package CALENDAR   (see 9.6)
-   The generic procedure SHARED_VARIABLE_UPDATE   (see 9.11)
-   The generic procedure UNCHECKED_DEALLOCATION   (see 13.10.1)
-   The generic function UNCHECKED_CONVERSION   (see 13.10.2)
-   The generic package INPUT_OUTPUT   (see 14.2)
-   The package TEXT_IO   (see 14.4)
-   The package LOW_LEVEL_IO   (see 14.6)

D. Glossary

Access type An access type is a type whose objects are created by execution of an *allocator*. An *access value* designates such an object.

Aggregate An aggregate is a written form denoting a *composite value*. An *array aggregate* denotes a value of an array type; a *record aggregate* denotes a value of a record type. The components of an aggregate may be specified using either *positional* or *named* association.

Allocator An allocator creates a new object of an *access type*, and returns an *access value* designating the created object.

Attribute An attribute is a predefined characteristic of a named entity.

Body A body is a program unit defining the execution of a subprogram, package, or task. A *body stub* is a replacement for a body that is compiled separately.

Collection A collection is the entire set of allocated objects of an *access type*.

Compilation Unit A compilation unit is a *program unit* presented for compilation as an independent text. It is preceded by a *context specification*, naming the other compilation units on which it depends. A compilation unit may be the specification or body of a subprogram or package.

Component A component denotes a part of a composite object. An *indexed component* is a name containing expressions denoting indices, and names a component in an array or an entry in an entry family. A *selected component* is the identifier of the component, prefixed by the name of the entity of which it is a component.

Composite type An object of a composite type comprises several components. An *array type* is a composite type, all of whose components are of the same type and subtype; the individual components are selected by their *indices*. A *record type* is a composite type whose components may be of different types; the individual components are selected by their identifiers.

Constraint A constraint is a restriction on the set of possible values of a type. A *range constraint* specifies lower and upper bounds of the values of a scalar type. An *accuracy constraint* specifies the relative or absolute error bound of values of a real type. An *index constraint* specifies lower and upper bounds of an array index. A *discriminant constraint* specifies particular values of the discriminants of a record or private type.

Context specification A context specification, prefixed to a compilation unit, defines the other compilation units upon which it depends.

Declarative Part A declarative part is a sequence of declarations and related information such as subprogram bodies and representation specifications that apply over a region of a program text.

Derived Type A derived type is a type whose operations and values are taken from those of an existing type.

Discrete Type A discrete type has an ordered set of distinct values. The discrete types are the enumeration and integer types. Discrete types may be used for indexing and iteration, and for choices in case statements and record variants.

Discriminant A discriminant is a syntactically distinguished component of a record. The presence of some record components (other than discriminants) may depend on the value of a discriminant.

Elaboration Elaboration is the process by which a declaration achieves its effect. For example it can associate a name with a program entity or initialize a newly declared variable.

Entity An entity is anything that can be named or denoted in a program. Objects, types, values, program units, are all entities.

Entry An entry is used for communication between tasks. Externally an entry is called just as a subprogram is called; its internal behavior is specified by one or more accept statements specifying the actions to be performed when the entry is called.

Enumeration type An enumeration type is a discrete type whose values are given explicitly in the type declaration. These values may be either identifiers or character literals.

Exception An exception is an event that causes suspension of normal program execution. Bringing an exception to attention is called *raising* the exception. An *exception handler* is a piece of program text specifying a response to the exception. Execution of such a program text is called *handling* the exception.

Expression An expression is a part of a program that computes a value.

Generic program unit A generic program unit is a subprogram or package specified with a generic clause. A *generic clause* contains the declaration of generic parameters. A generic program unit may be thought of as a possibly parameterized model of program units. Instances (that is, filled-in copies) of the model can be obtained by *generic instantiation*. Such instantiated program units define subprograms and packages that can be used directly in a program.

Introduce An identifier is introduced by its declaration at the point of its first occurrence.

Lexical unit A lexical unit is one of the basic syntactic elements making up a program. A lexical unit is an identifier, a number, a character literal, a string, a delimiter, or a comment.

Literal A literal denotes an explicit value of a given type, for example a number, an enumeration value, a character, or a string.

Model number A model number is an exactly representable value of a real numeric type. Operations of a real type are defined in terms of operations on the model numbers of the type. The properties of the model numbers and of the operations are the minimal properties preserved by all implementations of the real type.

Object An object is a variable or a constant. An object can denote any kind of data element, whether a scalar value, a composite value, or a value in an access type.

Overloading Overloading is the property of literals, identifiers, and operators that can have several alternative meanings within the same scope. For example an overloaded enumeration literal is a literal appearing in two or more enumeration types; an overloaded subprogram is a subprogram whose designator can denote one of several subprograms, depending upon the kind of its parameters and returned value.

Package A package is a program unit specifying a collection of related entities such as constants, variables, types and subprograms. The *visible part* of a package contains the entities that may be used from outside the package. The *private part* of a package contains structural details that are irrelevant to the user of the package but that complete the specification of the visible entities. The *body* of a package contains implementations of subprograms or tasks (possibly other packages) specified in the visible part.

Parameter A parameter is one of the named entities associated with a subprogram, entry, or generic program unit. A *formal parameter* is an identifier used to denote the named entity in the unit body. An *actual* parameter is the particular entity associated with the corresponding formal parameter in a subprogram call, entry call, or generic instantiation. A *parameter mode* specifies whether the parameter is used for input, output or input-output of data. A *positional parameter* is an actual parameter passed in positional order. A *named parameter* is an actual parameter passed by naming the corresponding formal parameter.

Pragma A pragma is an instruction to the compiler, and may be language defined or implementation defined.

Private type A private type is a type whose structure and set of values are clearly defined, but not known to the user of the type. A private type is known only by its discriminants and by the set of operations defined for it. A private type and its applicable operations are defined in the visible part of a package. Assignment and comparison for equality or inequality are also defined for private types, unless the private type is marked as *limited*.

Qualified expression A qualified expression is an expression qualified by the name of a type or subtype. It can be used to state the type or subtype of an expression, for example for an overloaded literal.

Range A range is a contiguous set of values of a scalar type. A range is specified by giving the lower and upper bounds for the values.

Rendezvous A rendezvous is the interaction that occurs between two parallel tasks when one task has called an entry of the other task, and a corresponding accept statement is being executed by the other task on behalf of the calling task.

Representation specification Representation specifications specify the mapping between data types and features of the underlying machine that execute a program. In some cases, they completely specify the mapping, in other cases they provide criteria for choosing a mapping.

Scalar types A scalar type is a type whose values have no components. Scalar types comprise discrete types (that is, enumeration and integer types) and real types.

Scope The scope of a declaration is the region of text over which the declaration has an effect.

Static expression A static expression is one whose value does not depend on any dynamically computed values of variables.

Subprograms A subprogram is an executable program unit, possibly with parameters for communication between the subprogram and its point of call. A *subprogram declaration* specifies the name of the subprogram and its parameters; a *subprogram body* specifies its execution. A subprogram may be a *procedure*, which performs an action, or a *function*, which returns a result.

Subtype A subtype of a type is obtained from the type by constraining the set of possible values of the type. The operations over a subtype are the same as those of the type from which the subtype is obtained.

Task A task is a program unit that may operate in parallel with other program units. A *task specification* establishes the name of the task and the names and parameters of its entries; a *task body* defines its execution. A *task type* is a specification that permits the subsequent declaration of any number of similar tasks.

Type A type characterizes a set of values and a set of operations applicable to those values and a set of operations applicable to those values. A *type definition* is a language construct introducing a type. A *type declaration* associates a name with a type introduced by a type definition.

Use clause A use clause opens the visibility to declarations given in the visible part of a package.

Variant A variant part of a record specifies alternative record components, depending on a discriminant of the record. Each value of the discriminant establishes a particular alternative of the variant part.

Visibility At a given point in a program text, the declaration of an entity with a certain identifier is said to be *visible* if the entity is an acceptable meaning for an occurrence at that point of the identifier.

E. Syntax Summary

2.3

```
identifier ::=
    letter {[underscore] letter_or_digit}

letter_or_digit ::= letter | digit

letter ::= upper_case_letter | lower_case_letter
```

2.4

```
numeric_literal ::= decimal_number | based_number

decimal_number ::= integer [.integer] [exponent]

integer ::= digit {[underscore] digit}

exponent ::= E [+] integer | E - integer
```

2.4.1

```
based_number ::=
    base # based_integer [.based_integer] # [exponent]

base ::= integer

based_integer ::=
    extended_digit {[underscore] extended_digit}

extended_digit ::= digit | letter
```

2.6

```
character_string ::= "{character}"
```

2.8

```
pragma ::=
    pragma identifier [(argument {, argument})];

argument ::=
    [identifier =>] name
  | [identifier =>] static_expression
```

3.1

```
declaration ::=
    object_declaration      | number_declaration
  | type_declaration        | subtype_declaration
  | subprogram_declaration  | package_declaration
  | task_declaration        | exception_declaration
  | renaming_declaration
```

3.2

```
object_declaration ::=
    identifier_list : [constant] subtype_indication [:= expression];
  | identifier_list : [constant] array_type_definition [:= expression];

number_declaration ::=
    identifier_list : constant := literal_expression;

identifier_list ::= identifier {, identifier}
```

3.3

```
type_declaration ::=
    type identifier [discriminant_part] is type_definition;
  | incomplete_type_declaration

type_definition ::=
    enumeration_type_definition | integer_type_definition
  | real_type_definition        | array_type_definition
  | record_type_definition      | access_type_definition
  | derived_type_definition      | private_type_definition

subtype_declaration ::=
    subtype identifier is subtype_indication;

subtype_indication ::= type_mark [constraint]

type_mark ::= type_name | subtype_name

constraint ::=
    range_constraint   | accuracy_constraint
  | index_constraint   | discriminant_constraint
```

3.4

```
derived_type_definition ::= new subtype_indication
```

3.5

```
range_constraint ::= range range

range ::= simple_expression .. simple_expression
```

3.5.1

```
enumeration_type_definition ::=
    (enumeration_literal {, enumeration_literal})

enumeration_literal ::= identifier | character_literal
```

3.5.4

```
integer_type_definition ::= range_constraint
```

3.5.6

```
real_type_definition ::= accuracy_constraint

accuracy_constraint ::=
    floating_point_constraint | fixed_point_constraint
```

3.5.7

```
floating_point_constraint ::=
    digits static_simple_expression [range_constraint]
```

3.5.9

```
fixed_point_constraint ::=
    delta static_simple_expression [range_constraint]
```

3.6

```
array_type_definition ::=
    array (index {, index}) of component_subtype_indication
  | array index_constraint of component_subtype_indication

index ::= type_mark range <>

index_constraint ::= (discrete_range {, discrete_range})

discrete_range ::= type_mark [range_constraint] | range
```

3.7

```
record_type_definition ::=
  record
      component_list
  end record

component_list ::=
  | component_declaration} [variant_part] | null;

component_declaration ::=
      identifier_list : subtype_indication [:= expression];
  | identifier_list : array_type_definition [:= expression];
```

3.7.1

```
discriminant_part ::=
  (discriminant_declaration {; discriminant_declaration})

discriminant_declaration ::=
  identifier_list : subtype_indication [:= expression]
```

3.7.2

```
discriminant_constraint ::=
  (discriminant_specification {, discriminant_specification})

discriminant_specification ::=
  [discriminant_name {| discriminant_name} =>] expression
```

3.7.3

```
variant_part ::=
  `case discriminant_name is
      {when choice {| choice} =>
          component_list}
  end case;

choice ::= simple_expression | discrete_range | others
```

3.8

```
access_type_definition ::= access subtype_indication

incomplete_type_declaration ::= type identifier [discriminant_part];
```

3.9

```
declarative_part ::=
  {declarative_item} {representation_specification} {program_component}

declarative_item ::= declaration | use_clause

program_component ::= body
  | package_declaration | task_declaration | body_stub

body ::= subprogram_body | package_body | task_body
```

4.1

```
name ::= identifier
  | indexed_component   | slice
  | selected_component  | attribute
  | function_call       | operator_symbol
```

4.1.1

```
indexed_component ::= name(expression {, expression})
```

4.1.2

```
slice ::= name (discrete_range)
```

4.1.3

```
selected_component ::=
  name.identifier | name.all | name.operator_symbol
```

4.1.4

```
attribute ::= name'identifier
```

4.2

```
literal ::=
  numeric_literal | enumeration_literal | character_string | null
```

4.3

```
aggregate ::=
  (component_association {, component_association})

component_association ::=
  [choice {| choice} => ] expression
```

4.4

```
expression ::=
      relation {and relation}
  |   relation {or relation}
  |   relation {xor relation}
  |   relation {and then relation}
  |   relation {or else relation}

relation ::=
      simple_expression [relational_operator simple_expression]
  |   simple_expression [not] in range
  |   simple_expression [not] in subtype_indication

simple_expression ::= [unary_operator] term {adding_operator term}

term ::= factor {multiplying_operator factor}

factor ::= primary [** primary]

primary ::=
      literal | aggregate | name | allocator | function_call
  |   type_conversion | qualified_expression | (expression)
```

4.5

```
logical_operator        ::= and | or | xor
relational_operator     ::= =   | /= | <   | <= | > | >=

adding_operator         ::= +   | -  | &

unary_operator          ::= +   | -  | not

multiplying_operator    ::= *   | /  | mod | rem

exponentiating_operator ::= **
```

4.6

type_conversion ::= type_mark (expression)

4.7

qualified_expression ::=
    type_mark'(expression) | type_mark'aggregate

4.8

allocator ::=
    new type_mark [(expression)]
    | **new** type_mark aggregate
    | **new** type_mark discriminant_constraint
    | **new** type_mark index_constraint

5.1

sequence_of_statements ::= statement {statement}

statement ::=
    {label} simple_statement | {label} compound_statement

simple_statement ::= null_statement
    | assignment_statement | exit_statement
    | return_statement | goto_statement
    | procedure_call | entry_call
    | delay_statement | abort_statement
    | raise_statement | code_statement

compound_statement ::=
        if_statement | case_statement
    | loop_statement | block
    | accept_statement | select_statement

label ::= <<identifier>>

null_statement ::= **null**;

5.2

assignment_statement ::=
    *variable*_name := expression;

5.3

if_statement ::=
    if condition **then**
        sequence_of_statements
    {**elsif** condition **then**
        sequence_of_statements}
    [**else**
        sequence_of_statements]
    end if;

condition ::= *boolean*_expression

5.4

case_statement ::=
    case expression **is**
        {**when** choice {| choice} => sequence_of_statements}
    end case;

5.5

loop_statement ::=
    [*loop*_identifier:] [iteration_clause] basic_loop [*loop*_identifier];

basic_loop ::=
    loop
        sequence_of_statements
    end loop

iteration_clause ::=
    for loop_parameter **in** [**reverse**] discrete_range
    | **while** condition

loop_parameter ::= identifier

5.6

block ::=
    [*block*_identifier:]
    [**declare**
        declarative_part]
    begin
        sequence_of_statements
    [**exception**
        {exception_handler}]
    end [*block*_identifier];

5.7

exit_statement ::=
    exit [*loop*_name] [**when** condition];

5.8

return_statement ::= **return** [expression];

5.9

goto_statement ::= **goto** *label*_name;

6.1

subprogram_declaration ::= subprogram_specification;
    | generic_subprogram_declaration
    | generic_subprogram_instantiation

subprogram_specification ::=
        procedure identifier [formal_part]
    | **function** designator [formal_part] **return** subtype_indication

designator ::= identifier | operator_symbol

operator_symbol ::= character_string

formal_part ::=
    (parameter_declaration {; parameter_declaration})

parameter_declaration ::=
    identifier_list : mode subtype_indication [:= expression]

mode ::= [**in**] | **out** | **in out**

6.3

subprogram_body ::=
    subprogram_specification **is**
        declarative_part
    begin
        sequence_of_statements
    [**exception**
        {exception_handler}]
    end [designator];

6.4

procedure_call ::=
    *procedure*_name [actual_parameter_part];

function_call ::=
    *function*_name actual_parameter_part | *function*_name ()

actual_parameter_part ::=
    (parameter_association {, parameter_association})

```
parameter_association ::=
   [formal_parameter =>] actual_parameter

formal_parameter ::= identifier

actual_parameter ::= expression
```

7.1

```
package_declaration ::= package_specification;
   | generic_package_declaration
   | generic_package_instantiation

package_specification ::=
     package identifier is
       {declarative_item}
   [ private
       {declarative_item}
       {representation_specification}]
     end [identifier]

package_body ::=
     package body identifier is
       declarative_part
   [ begin
       sequence_of_statements
   [ exception
       {exception_handler}]]
     end [identifier];
```

7.4

```
private_type_definition ::= [limited] private
```

8.4

```
use_clause ::= use package_name {, package_name};
```

8.5

```
renaming_declaration ::=
      identifier : type_mark   renames name;
   |  identifier : exception   renames name;
   |  package   identifier renames name;
   |  task      identifier renames name;
   |  subprogram_specification renames name;
```

9.1

```
task_declaration ::= task_specification

task_specification ::=
   task [type] identifier [is
      {entry_declaration}
      {representation_specification}
   end [identifier]];

task_body ::=
     task body identifier is
       [declarative_part]
     begin
       sequence_of_statements
   [ exception
       {exception_handler}]
     end [identifier];
```

9.5

```
entry_declaration ::=
   entry identifier [(discrete_range)] [formal_part];

entry_call ::= entry_name [actual_parameter_part];

accept_statement ::=
   accept entry_name [formal_part] [do
      sequence_of_statements
   end [identifier]];
```

9.6

```
delay_statement ::= delay simple_expression;
```

9.7

```
select_statement ::= selective_wait
   |conditional_entry_call | timed_entry_call
```

9.7.1

```
selective_wait ::=
     select
       [when condition =>]
          select_alternative
   { or [when condition =>]
          select_alternative}
   [ else
       sequence_of_statements]
     end select;

select_alternative ::=
      accept_statement  [sequence_of_statements]
   |  delay_statement   [sequence_of_statements]
   |  terminate;
```

9.7.2

```
conditional_entry_call ::=
   select
      entry_call [sequence_of_statements]
   else
      sequence_of_statements
   end select;
```

9.7.3

```
timed_entry_call ::=
   select
      entry_call [sequence_of_statements]
   or
      delay_statement [sequence_of_statements]
   end select;
```

9.10

```
abort_statement ::= abort task_name {, task_name};
```

10.1

```
compilation ::= {compilation_unit}

compilation_unit ::=
      context_specification subprogram_declaration
   |  context_specification subprogram_body
   |  context_specification package_declaration
   |  context_specification package_body
   |  context_specification subunit

context_specification ::= {with_clause [use_clause]}

with_clause ::= with unit_name {, unit_name};
```

10.2

```
subunit ::=
    separate (unit_name) body

body_stub ::=
        subprogram_specification   is separate;
    |   package body identifier    is separate;
    |   task body identifier        is separate;
```

11.1

```
exception_declaration ::= identifier_list : exception;
```

11.2

```
exception_handler ::=
    when exception_choice {| exception_choice} =>
        sequence_of_statements

exception_choice ::= exception_name | others
```

11.3

```
raise_statement ::= raise [exception_name];
```

12.1

```
generic_subprogram_declaration ::=
        generic_part subprogram_specification;

generic_package_declaration ::=
        generic_part package_specification;

generic_part ::= generic {generic_formal_parameter}

generic_formal_parameter ::=
        parameter_declaration;
    |   type identifier [discriminant_part] is generic_type_definition;
    |   with subprogram_specification [is name];
    |   with subprogram_specification is <>;

generic_type_definition ::=
        (<>) | range <> | delta <> | digits <>
    |   array_type_definition | access_type_definition
    |   private_type_definition
```

12.3

```
generic_subprogram_instantiation ::=
        procedure identifier is generic_instantiation;
    |   function designator is generic_instantiation;

generic_package_instantiation ::=
    package identifier is generic_instantiation;

generic_instantiation ::=
    new name [(generic_association {, generic_association })]

generic_association ::=
    [ formal_parameter =>] generic_actual_parameter

generic_actual_parameter ::=
    expression | subprogram_name | subtype_indication
```

13.1

```
representation_specification ::=
        length_specification          | enumeration_type_representation
    |   record_type_representation  | address_specification
```

13.2

```
length_specification ::= for attribute use expression;
```

13.3

```
enumeration_type_representation ::= for type_name use aggregate;
```

13.4

```
record_type_representation ::=
    for type_name use
        record [alignment_clause;]
            {component_name location;}
        end record;

location ::= at static_simple_expression range range

alignment_clause ::= at mod static_simple_expression
```

13.5

```
address_specification ::= for name use at static_simple_expression;
```

13.8

```
code_statement ::= qualified_expression;
```

Syntax Cross Reference

In the list given below each syntactic category is followed by the section and page numbers where it is defined. For example:

adding_operator   4.5   4_10

In addition, each syntactic category is followed by the names of other categories in whose definition it appears. For example, adding_operator appears in the definition of simple_expression:

adding_operator   4.5   4-10
simple_expression   4.4   4-9

An ellipsis (...) is used when the syntactic category is not defined by a syntax rule. For example:

lower_case_letter   ...   ...

All uses of parentheses are combined in the term "( )". The italicized prefixes used with some terms have been deleted here.

F. Implementation Dependent Characteristics

This appendix is to be supplied in the reference manual of each Ada implementation. The Ada language definition allows for certain machine dependences in a controlled manner. No machine dependent syntax or semantic extensions or restrictions are allowed. The only allowed implementation dependences correspond to implementation dependent pragmas and attributes, certain machine dependent values and conventions as mentioned in chapter 13, and certain allowed restrictions on representation specifications.

The appendix F for a given implementation must list in particular:

(1) The form, allowed places, and effect of every implementation dependent pragma.

(2) The name and the type of every implementation dependent attribute.

(3) The specification of the package SYSTEM.

(4) the list of all restrictions on representation specifications (see 13.1)

(5) The conventions used for any system generated name denoting system dependent components (see 13.4).

(6) The interpretation of expressions that appear in address specifications, including those for interrupts, (see 13.5).

(7) Any restriction on unchecked conversions (see 13.10.2).

Index

☆ U.S. GOVERNMENT PRINTING OFFICE: 1981 — 706-575:506

BIBLIOGRAPHY

FURTHER READINGS

The following bibliography contains a list of references on the general subject of programming languages. No attempt has been made to be inclusive. I wish merely to supply to the reader a wide set of references on a variety of programming language topics. The section is divided into the following subject areas: Programming Languages (Ada, ALGOL60, COBOL, FORTRAN, LISP, Pascal, SNOBOL, Other Languages), Semantics, Programming Language Comparisons, Concurrency and other Topics of Interest. By following these references, the reader can determine where to look for any particular article or subject they desire to read about. However, as these lists invariably go out of date, the reader should be aware that more recent topics subsequent to this printing are likely to be covered less adequately than I would have hoped, or not at all.

PROGRAMMING LANGUAGES

Ada

"Rationale for the Design of the Ada Programming Language" *ACM Sigplan Notices*, 14, 6, June 1979.

Wegner, P. *Ada: A Graduated Introduction* Prentice-Hall, revised edition, Englewood Cliffs, N.J., 1981.

Welsh, J., Lister, A. "A Comparative Study of Task Communication in Ada" *Software Practice and Experience*, vol. 11, 1981, 257 - 290.

ALGOL60

Extended ALGOL Reference Manual Burroughs Corp., Detroit, Mich., Form no. 5000128, 1971.

"Suggestions on ALGOL 60 (Rome) Issues" *Comm ACM*, 6, 1, 20-23.

Knuth, D.E. et al. "A Proposal for Input/Output

Conventions in ALGOL60" *Comm. ACM*, 7,5, 1964, 273-283.

de Morgan, R.M.; Hill, I.D.; and Wichmann, B.A. "A Supplement to the ALGOL60 Revised Report" *Computer Journal*, 19,3 1976, 276-288.

de Morgan, R.M.; Hill, I.D.; and Wichmann, B.A. "Modified Report on the Algorithmic Language ALGOL60" *Computer Journal*, 19,4, 1976, 364-379.

Randell, B., and Russell, L. *ALGOL 60 Implementation* Academic Press, New York, 1964.

COBOL

American National Standard COBOL (ANS X3.23-1968) American National Standards Institute, New York, 1968.

FORTRAN

American National Standard FORTRAN (ANS X3.9-1966) American National Standards Institute, New York, 1966.

American National Standard FORTRAN (ANS X3.9-1977) American National Standards Institute, N.Y., 1977.

Backus, J.W.; Beeber, R.J.; Best, S.; Goldberg, R.; Haibt, L.M.; Herrick, H.L.; Nelson, R.A.; Sayre, D.; Sheridan, P.B.; Stern, H.; Ziller, I.; Hughes, R.A.; and Nutt, R. "The FORTRAN Automatic Coding System" *Proc. Western Jt. Comp. Conf.*, AIEE (now IEEE), Los Angeles.

Backus, J. "The history of FORTRAN I, II, and III" *ACM Sigplan Notices*, 13, 8, August, 1978, 165-180.

LISP

Allen, J. *The Anatomy of LISP* McGraw-Hill, New York, 1979.

Friedman, D. *The Little Lisper* Science Research Associates, Chicago, 1974.

McCarthy, J. "Towards a Mathematical Theory of

Computation" *Proc. IFIP Congress 62.* 21-28, North-Holland, Amsterdam, 1962.

Moses, J. "The Function of FUNCTION in LISP" *SIGSAM Bull.* July, 1970, 13-27.

Weissman, C. *LISP 1.5 Primer* Dickenson Publishing Company, Inc., Encino, Calif.

Pascal

Brinch-Hansen, P. "The Programming Language Concurrent-Pascal" *IEEE Trans. on Soft. Eng.*, 1,2, June 1975, 199-207.

Fischer, Charles N., and LeBlanc, R.J., "Efficient Implementation and Optimization of Run-Time Checking in Pascal" *ACM Sigplan Notices 12,* 3, March 1977, 19-24.

Habermann, A.N. "Critical Comments on the Programming Language Pascal" *Acta Informatica* 3, 1973,47-57.

Hoare, C.A.R. and Wirth, N. "An Axiomatic Definition of the Programming Language Pascal" *Acta Informatica,* 2, 1973, 335-355.

Jensen, K. and Wirth, N. *Pascal Users Manual and Report* Springer-Verlag Berlin, 1974.

Strait, J.P.; Mickel, A.B.; and Easton, J.T. "Pascal 6000 Release 3 Manual" University of Minnesota, January 1979.

Sale, A.H.J. "Strings and the Sequence Abstraction in Pascal" *Software Practice and Experience* 9, 8, 1979, 671-683.

Sale, A.H.J. "Implementing Strings in Pascal - Again" *Software Practice and Experience,* 9, 1979, 839-841.

Wirth, N. "The Programming Language Pascal" *Acta Informatica,* 1, 1, 1971, 35-63.

SNOBOL

Gimpel, J. "A Theory of Discrete Patterns and Their Implementation in SNOBOL4." *Comm. ACM,* 16, 2, 1973, 91-100.

Griswold, R.; Poage, J.; and Polonsky, I. *The SNOBOL4 Programming Language* 2nd ed., Prentice-Hall, Englewood Clifs, N.J., 1971.

Griswold, R., and Griswold, M. *A SNOBOL4 Primer* Prentice-Hall, Englewood Cliffs, N.J., 1973.

Griswold, R. *The Macro Implementation of SNOBOL4* W. H. Freeman, San Francisco, 1971.

Farber, D.J.; Griswold, R.E.; Polonsky, F.P. "SNOBOL, a String Manipulation Language" *JACM,* 11, 1, 1964, 21-30.

Griswold, R.; Poage, J.; and Polonsky, I. *The SNOBOL4 Programming Language* 2nd ed. Prentice-Hall, Englewood Cliffs, N.J. 1971.

Tennent, R. "Mathematical Semantics of SNOBOL4" *Acm Symp. Principles Prog. Langs.,* ACM, Boston, 1973, 95-108.

Other Languages

Backus, J. "Can Programming be Liberated from the von Neumann Style? A Functional Style and its Algebra of Programs" *Comm. ACM,* 21, 8, August 1978, 613-641.

Birtwistle, G.M.; Dahl, O-J.; Myhrhaug, B.; Nygaard, K. *SIMULA Begin* Petrocelli/Charter, New York, 1973.

Brinch-Hansen, P. "Edison" *Software Practice and Experience* 11, 4, April 1981.

Dahl, O., and Nygaard, K. "SIMULA-An ALGOL-Based Simulation Language" *Comm. ACM* 9, 9, 1966, 671-678.

Dennis, J.B. and Ackermann, W.B. "VAL-a Value Oriented Algorithmic Language: Preliminary Reference Manual", Laboratory for Computer Science, MIT, Cambridge, Mass. 1979.

Geschke, C.M., Morris Jr., J.H., and Satterthwaite, E.H. "Early Experience with MESA" *Comm. ACM,* 20,8, 1977.

Horning, J.J. "A Case Study in Language Design: Euclid" *Lecture notes in computer science (compiler construction)* Springer-Verlag, 1979.

Iverson, K. *A Programming Language* Wiley, New York, 1962.

"JOVIAL J73/1 Specifications" Rome Air Development Center, Air Force Systems Command, Griffis Air Force Base, New York, 13441, 1976.

Kiviat, P.; Villanueva, R.; and Markowitz, H. *The SIMSCRIPT II Programming Language* Prentice-Hall, Englewood Cliffs, N.J., 1969.

Lampson, B.W., Horning, J.J.; London, R.L.; Mitchell, J.G.; and Popek, G.J, "Report on the Programming Language Euclid" *ACM Sigplan Notices,* 12,2,1977.

Lawson, H. "PL/1 List Processing" *Comm. ACM,* 10, 6, 1967, 358-367.

Liskov, B. et al. "CLU Reference Manual" Laboratory for Computer Science, MIT, TR-225, October, 1979.

Mitchell, James G., Maybury, William; and Sweet, Richard, "Mesa Language Manual." Technical Report CSL-78-1, Xerox Palo Alto Research Center, 1979.

Pakin, S. *APL/360 Reference Manual* 2nd ed., Science Research Associates, Chicago, 1972.

Richards, M., Whitby-Strevens, C. *BCPL - The Language and its Compiler* Cambridge University Press, 1980.

Shaw, Mary "Abstraction and Verification in ALPHARD: Design and Verification of a Tree Handler" *Proc. Fifth Texas Conf. Computing Systems.*, 1976, 86-94.

Shaw, M.; Wulf, W.; and London, R., "Abstraction and Verification in ALPHARD: Defining and Specifying Iteration and Generators" *Comm. ACM*, 20, 1977, 553.

Teitelman, W. *INTERLISP Reference Manual* Xerox Palo Alto Res. Center, Palo Alto, Ca. 1975.

Van Wijngaarden, A., ed.; Mailloux, B.; Peck, J.; and Koster C., "Report on the Algorithmic Language ALGOL 68" *Numerische Mathematik,* 14, 2, 1969, 79-218.

Van Wijngaarden et al., "Revised Report on the Algorithmic Language ALGOL68" *Acta Informatica* 5, 1975, 1-236.

Wegbreit, B. "The ECL Programming System" *Proc. Fall Joint Computer Conference*, vol 39, 1971.

Wirth, N. "Design and Implementation of MODULA" *Software Practice and Experience* 7, 1977, 67-84.

Wirth, N. "The Use of MODULA" *Software Practice and Experience* 7, 1977, 37-65.

Wulf, W.; Russell, D.B.; and Habermann, A.N. "BLISS: A Language for Systems Programming" *Comm. ACM*, 14, 12, December 1971, 780-790.

SEMANTICS

Floyd, R.W. "Assigning Meanings to Programs." In *Mathematical Aspects of Computers Science,* ed. J. T. Schwartz, American Mathematical Society, Providence, 1967.

Gordon, M. "The Denotational Description of Programming Languages" Springer-Verlag, 1979.

Hoare, C.A.R. "An Axiomatic Basis for Computer Programming" *Comm. ACM,* 12, 10, 1969, 576-583.

Hoare, C.A.R. "Proofs of Correctness of Data Representation." *Acta Informatica* 1, 1972, 271-281.

Johnston, J. "The Contour Model of Block Structured Processes." *ACM Sigplan Notices*, 6, 2, 1971, 55-82.

Lee, J. *Computer Semantics* Van Nostrand Reinhold, New York, 1972.

Scott D. "Outline of a Mathematical Theory of Computation" *Proc. 4th Princeton Conf. on Info. Sci. and Sys.* 1970.

Scott, D. and Strachey, C., "Towards a Mathematical Semantics for Computer Languages" *Proc. Symp. on Computers and Automata* Polytechnic Inst. of Brooklyn, 1971.

Scott D. "Mathematical Concepts in Programming Language Semantics" *AFIPS conf. proc. SJCC*, vol. 40, 1972, 225-234.

Scott, D. "Data Types as Lattices" *SIAM J. on Computing*, 5, September, 1976, 522-587.

Stoy, J.E. *Denotational Semantics - The Scott-Strachey Approach to Programming Language Theory* M.I.T. Press, 1977.

Wegner, P. "The Vienna Definition Language" *ACM Computing Surveys*, 4, 1, March 1972, 5-63.

PROGRAMMING LANGUAGE COMPARISONS

Boom, H.J., DeJong, E. "A Critical Comparison of Several Programming Language Implementations" *Software Practice and Experience*, 10, 1980, 435-473.

Cheatham, T. "The Recent Evolution of Programming Languages" *Proc. IFIP Cong. 1971,* C. V. Freiman, (ed.), North-Holland, Amsterdam, 118-134.

Horning, J.J. "Programming Languages" *Computing Systems Reliability*, T. Anderson and B. Randell eds., Cambridge University Press, 1979.

Leavenworth, B. (ed.) "Control Structures in Programming Languages" *ACM Sigplan Notices* 7, 11, 1972.

Ledgard, H. "Ten Mini-Languages: A Study of Topical Issues in Programming Languages" *Computing Surveys*, 3, 3, 1971, 115-146.

Sammet, J. *Programming Languages: History and Fundamentals* Prentice-Hall, Englewood Cliffs N.J., 1969.

Shaw, M.; Almes, G.T.; Newcomer, J.M.; Reid, B.K.; Wulf, W.A. "A Comparison of Programming Languages for Software Engineering" *Software Practice and Experience*, 11, 1-52, 1981.

Wegner, P. "Programming Languages - Concepts and Research Directions" *Research Directions in Software Technology*, MIT Press, Cambridge, 1979, 425-489.

CONCURRENCY

Brinch-Hansen, P. "Structured Multiprogramming" *Comm. ACM*, 15, 7, July 1972, 574-578.

Brinch-Hansen, P. "Distributed Processes: A Concurrent Programming Concept" *Comm. ACM*, 21, 11, November, 1978, 934-941.

Dijkstra, E. "Cooperating Sequential Processes" In *Programming Languages*, ed. Genuys, Academic Press, 1968.

Dijkstra, E. "Guarded Commands, Nondeterminacy and Formal Derivation of Programs" *Comm. ACM*, 18, 8, August 1975, 453-457.

Dijkstra, E. *A Discipline of Programming.* Prentice-Hall, Englewood Cliffs.

Floyd, R. "Nondeterministic Algorithms" *J. ACM,* 14, 4, 1967, 636-644.

Hoare, C.A.R. "Monitors: An Operating System Structuring Concept" *Comm. ACM*, 17,10, October 1974, 549-557.

Holt, R.C.; Lazowska, E.D.; Graham, G.S.; Scott, M.A. *Structured Concurrent Programming with Operating Systems Applications* Addison-Wesley, 1978.

Wirth, N. "Toward a Discipline of Real-Time Programming" *Comm ACM*, 20, 8, August 1977.

OTHER SUBJECTS OF INTEREST

Aho, A., and Ullman, J., *The Theory of Parsing, Translation and Compiling* Prentice-Hall, Englewood Cliffs, N.J.

Burge, W.H. *Recursive Programming Techniques* Addison-Wesley, Reading, Mass. 1975.

Dahl, O. J.; Dijkstra, E.W.; and Hoare, C.A.R., *Structured Programming* Academic Press, London and New York, 1972.

Dijkstra, E. "GoTo Statement Considered Harmful" *Comm. ACM,* 11, 3, 1968,147-148.

Dijkstra, E. "The Humble Programmer" *Comm. ACM,* 15, 10, 1972, 859-866.

Freiburghouse, R. "The Multics PL/1 Compiler" *Proc. AFIPS Fall Jt. Comp. Conf.* 35, 1969, 1870-199.

Friedman, D.P. and Wise, D.S., "CONS Should not Evaluate its Arguments" *Automata, Languages and Programming*, S. Michaelson and R. Milner eds., Edinburgh Univ. Press, Edinburgh, England, 1976.

Friedman, D.P. and Wise, D.S., "The Impact of Applicative Programming on Multiprocessing" *Proc. 1976 Intl. Conf. on Parallel Processing*, August 1976, 263-272.

Friedman, D.P. and Wise, D.S., "A Note on Conditional Expressions" *Comm ACM*, 21, 11, November 1978.

Gannon, J.D., and Horning, J.J., "Language Design for Programming Reliability." *IEEE Trans. Software Engineering SE-1* 2, 179-191, 1975.

Gannon, J. "An Experimental Evaluation of Data Type Conventions." *Comm. ACM 20,* 8, 1977, 584-595.

Goodenough, J.B. "Exception Handling: Issues and a Proposed Notation." *Comm. ACM 18,* 12, December 1975, 683-696.

Guttag, J. "Abstract Data Types and the Development of Data Structures" *Comm. ACM,* 20,6, June 1977, 396-404.

Guttag, J.; Horowitz, E.; and Musser, D., "The Design of Data Type Specifications" *Current Trends in Programming Methodology*, ed. R. Yeh, vol IV, Prentice Hall, 1978.

Guttag, J.; Horowitz, E.; and Musser, D., "Abstract Data Types and Software Validation" *Comm. ACM,* 21,12, December 1978, 1048-1064.

Henderson, P. *Functional Programming: Application and Implementation* Prentice-Hall, Englewood Cliffs, New Jersey, 1980.

Hoare, C.A.R. "A Note on the FOR Statement" *BIT,* 12, 1972, 334-341.

Hoare, C.A.R. "Recursive Data Structures." *Int. J. Comp. Inf. Sci.* 4, 1975.

Horning, J.J. and Wortman, D.B. "Software Hut: a Computer Program Engineering Program in the Form of a Game." *IEEE Trans. Software Engineering* SE-3, 4, 325-330, 1978.

Knuth, D. and Floyd, R. "Notes on Avoiding GoTo Statements" *Info. Proc. Letters,* 1, 1, 1971, 23-32

Knuth, D. "Structured Programming with **GoTo** Statements" *Comp. Surveys,* 6, 4, 1974, 261-301.

Landin, P.J. "The Mechanical Evaluation of Expressions" *Computer Journal*, 6, 1964, 308-320.

Landin, P.J. "The Next 700 Programming Languages" *Comm. ACM,* 9,3, March 1966, 157-164.

McKeeman, W.M. "On Preventing Programming Languages from Interfering with Programming." *IEEE Trans. Software Engineering,* SE-1, 1, 1975, 19-26.

Morgan, H.L. "Spelling Correction in System Programs." *Comm. ACM,* 13, 2, 90-94.

Morris, J.H. Jr. "Protection in Programming Languages" *Comm ACM*, 16, 1, January 1973.

Morris, J.H. Jr. "Types are not Sets" *ACM Symposium on the Principles of Programming Languages*, October 1973.

Parnas, D.L. "Information Distribution Aspects of Design Methodology." *Proc. IFIP Congress 71* 339-344, North-Holland, Amsterdam.

Ripley, G.D. and Druseikis, F.C. "A Statistical Analysis of Syntax Errors" *Computer Languages*, vol. 3, 1978, 227-240.

Sammet, J. "Programming Languages: History and Future" *Comm. ACM,* 15, 7, 1972, 601-610.

Satterthwaite, E. "Debugging Tools for High-Level Languages." *Software-Practice and Experience* 2, 1972, 197-217.

Teitelman, W. "Toward a Programming Laboratory" *Proc. Inter. Jt. Conf. Artif. Intel.,* Washington, D.C., 1969.

Wegbreit, B., "The Treatment of Data Types in EL1" *Comm. ACM,* 17,5, May 1974, 251-264.

Winograd, T. "Beyond Programming Languages" *Comm ACM*, 22, 7, July 1979.

Wirth, N. "Program Development by Stepwise Refinement" *Comm. ACM,* 14 4, 1971, 221-227.

INDEX